C0-APL-857

32.50

32.50

WORLD REGIONS
CHANGING INTERACTIONS

CHARLES A. STANSFIELD, JR.
CHESTER E. ZIMOLZAK

Glassboro State College

CHARLES E. MERRILL PUBLISHING COMPANY
A Bell & Howell Company
COLUMBUS   TORONTO   LONDON   SYDNEY

Cover: *Nova Totius Terrarum Orbis Tabula* by
Louis Renard, ca. 1834
from the collection of W. Graham Arader III

Published by Charles E. Merrill Publishing Co.
A Bell & Howell Company
Columbus, Ohio 43216

This book was set in Korinna.
Production Editor: Mary Pound
Text Design: Ann Mirels
Cartography: Alice Thiede
          Chesha Zimolzak

Copyright © 1982, by Bell & Howell Company. All
rights reserved.
No part of this book may be reproduced in any form,
electronic, or mechanical, or mechanical, including
photocopy, recording, or any information storage and
retrieval system, without permission in writing from the
publisher.

Library of Congress Catalog Card Number: 81-85718
International Standard Book Number: 0-675-09855-6
Printed in the United States of America
1 2 3 4 5 6 7 8 9 10—86 85 84 83 82

To Lisa, Wayne, and Paul
and
to Matt, Joanne, and Tom

May the world they come to know
be one of justice and peace.

PREFACE

In the age of the information explosion, the essential problem is not that of acquiring data on any topic for any part of the globe, but that of selecting and organizing these data in some meaningful way. In studying the total complex of physical and cultural geographic factors throughout the world, geographers utilize the region as an organizational frame. To present a world pattern that is comprehensible within a semester, we have devised twelve regions within a traditional frame plus a chapter on the last frontiers—the world's oceans and polar regions, areas not always included in a survey of world regional geography but of increasing economic and political significance. An introductory chapter reviews the nature of geography and the regional concept, together with a brief overview of geographic tools used for data acquisition and analysis.

There is considerable agreement apparent among various textbook regionalizations of the world; the major regions are identified and bounded in fundamentally similar form because they make sense in the context of an introductory survey. We have modified the conventional regionalization specifically in recognition of the profound differences in political-economic philosophy and strategic alignment between East and West Europe. Further, we have divided Latin America into Middle and South America on the basis of these areas' respective differences in economic orientations, cultural backgrounds, and prospects. While many smaller national territories are classed as subregions or even several states grouped as a subregion, the larger nations (Australia, Brazil, Canada, China, India, Mexico, the United States, and the Soviet Union are subdivided into subregions in recognition of their vast areas and internal diversity.

The organization of each regional chapter features a prologue that keynotes some major characteristics of the region, especially as they commonly have been perceived by U.S. citizens. Past interactions of each region with the U.S. and Canada region are explored briefly, with a note on significant changes in these interactions. Following a brief survey of salient physical, cultural, economic, and political characteristics of the region, there is a more detailed examination of its physical frame. The structure and rationale of subregions is presented, followed by a consideration of each one's population characteristics, ratio of population to resource base, type of economic development, relevant political factors, and developmental strategies. The detail of development of each topic within each subregion varies with the topic's significance and relevance to comprehending major trends in that region. In a summary section, the relationships, both positive and negative, with other world regions are surveyed, and the region's prevalent "world views" explored. Each chapter includes a list of key terms identifying major geographic concepts and terms that are of particular importance to understanding that region. Because users of the book may choose to devise their own order of consideration of regional chapters, some key terms are highlighted in more than one chapter to avoid a sequential list tied to the chapter order. A list of review questions is provided at the end of each chapter to help students evaluate their comprehension of material and to organize their study. A compact bibliography of the more interesting general survey materials (in English and generally available in undergraduate libraries) is included for the convenience of students who wish to explore a region in somewhat more detail.

Foremost among the perceptive and thorough reviewers who commented on the manuscript are Jane Ehemann, Shippensburg State College; Steven Kimbrel, University of New Orleans; Jerry McDonald, Radford College; and Joseph G. Spinelli, Bowling Green State University. Needless to say, any faults that may have persisted are not their responsibility. The book is much better for their comments and criticisms.

In addition, the following friends and colleagues kindly reviewed early partial manuscripts, for which we extend our deepest thanks: Walter Bates, Toowoomba, Australia; William Top, Hove, England; and Dr. Takashi Yamaguchi of Tokyo University.

The maps in the text were designed by both authors and skillfully executed by Alice Thiede and Chesha Zimolzak, who have our sincere thanks and appreciation.

Our friends and colleagues at Glassboro State graciously allowed us to ransack their private libraries, borrow their photographs, pick their brains, and generally involve them in our project. These tolerant, congenial, and stimulating intellectual companions include: Edward F. Behm, Marvin C. Creamer, Wade Currier, Robert H. Edwards, Robert Hewsen, David Kasserman, Sidney Kessler, Jerry Lint, and Dick Scott.

Janice Bittle typed the manuscript; her organizational skills and friendship helped the book to become a reality. We owe her our deepest thanks. She was ably assisted by Colleen McElroy.

We gratefully acknowledge the professional guidance and cheerful persistance of our administrative editor, Pam Cooper. We undertook this particular project at the friendly urging of Greg Spatz, executive editor at Charles E. Merrill Publishing Company; his counsel continued through completion and we appreciate his judgement as well as his friendship.

Others of Merrill's professional staff who provided continuing assistance, encouragement, and timely advice were Meg Malde, developmental editor; Mary Pound, production editor; Ann Mirels, text designer; Pat Welch, art production coordinator; and Jim Hubbard, staff artist.

Finally, we appreciate our families' tolerance of our absence those many evenings and weekends; we know they share the pleasure of completion of this book.

CONTENTS

KEY MAPS

Some geographic phenomena—the distribution of population and growth rates of populations; such basic physical geographic information as climate, landforms, vegetation and soils; such basic economic indicators as petroleum production, raw steel production, and Gross National Product (GNP) per capita; and such fundamental cultural-historical data as colonial empires, religion and language—are best presented in a worldwide context. Rather than scatter these essential world-scale maps through various regional chapters, they are grouped at the beginning of this survey of world regions for convenience of reference. It will be useful to refer to these maps repeatedly as each region is studied, preferably at the beginning of each region. Because these world maps bear the same relationship to the entire book that "key terms" do to each chapter, they are the "key maps" to comprehending every region.

Within each chapter are more-detailed maps for the particular region being discussed; most of these specialized maps present distribution patterns and dynamic relationships within the region and between regions. A few regional maps portray some key-map topics in more detail for that specific region.

A.   WORLD LANDFORMS

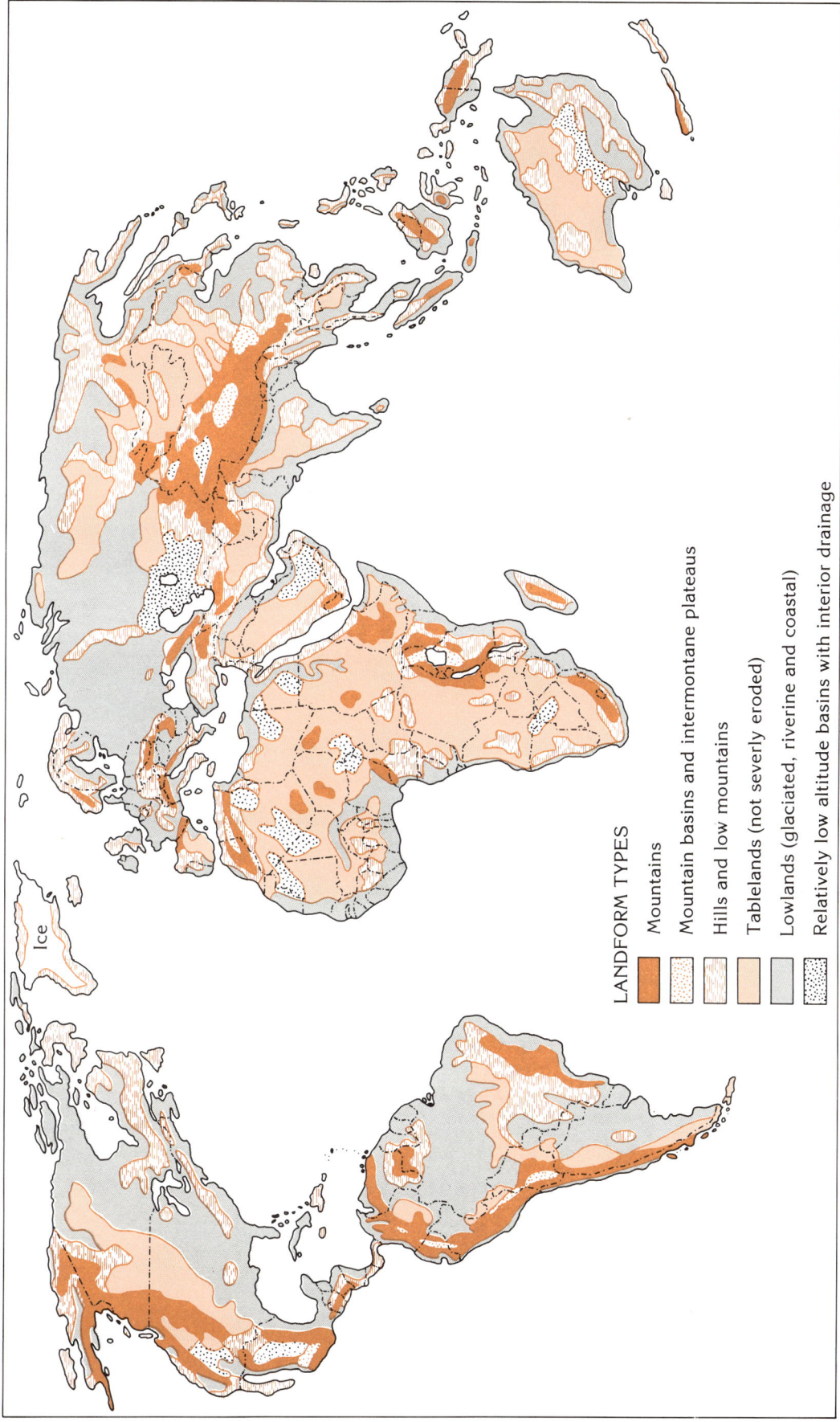

LANDFORM TYPES

Mountains

Mountain basins and intermontane plateaus

Hills and low mountains

Tablelands (not severly eroded)

Lowlands (glaciated, riverine and coastal)

Relatively low altitude basins with interior drainage

Ice

B.   KÖPPEN'S CLIMATIC CLASSIFICATION

A. Tropical Rainy
    tropical rainforest (Af, Am)
    tropical savanna (Aw)
B. Dry
    steppe (BS)
    desert (BW)
C. Humid Mesothermal
    dry summer (Cs)
    humid temperate (Ca)
    marine (Cb)

D. Humid Microthermal
    warm summer (Da)
    cool summer (Db)
    subarctic (Dc)
E. Polar
    tundra (ET)
    ice cap (EF)
    highlands (H)

(Adapted from Albert Miller and Jack C. Thompson. *Elements of Meteorology*. 3rd ed. [Columbus, Ohio: Charles E. Merrill Publishing Company, 1979], p. 199.)

C. WORLD SOIL DISTRIBUTION

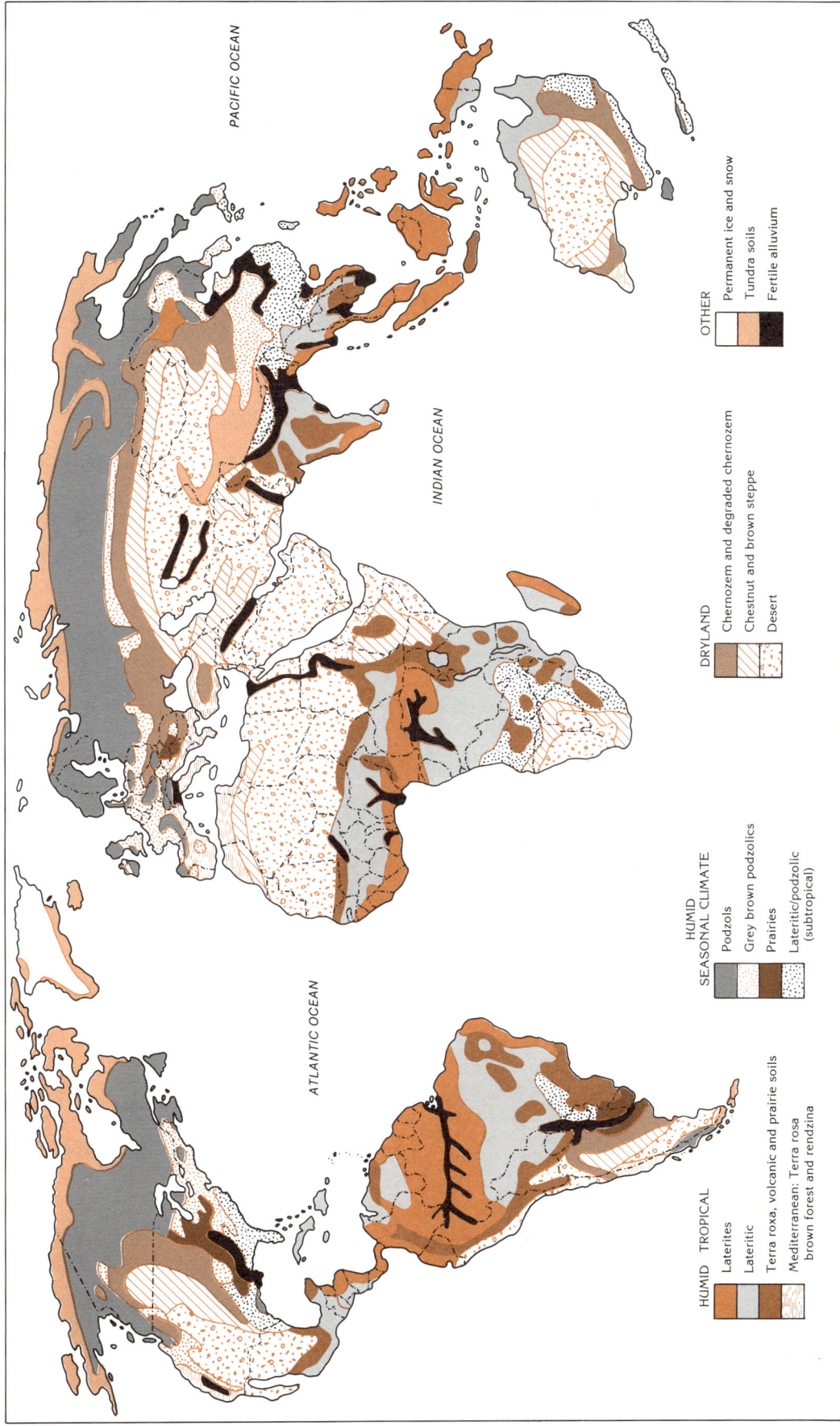

PACIFIC OCEAN

INDIAN OCEAN

ATLANTIC OCEAN

HUMID TROPICAL
- Laterites
- Lateritic
- Terra roxa, volcanic and prairie soils
- Mediterranean: Terra rosa brown forest and rendzina

HUMID SEASONAL CLIMATE
- Podzols
- Grey brown podzolics
- Prairies
- Lateritic/podzolic (subtropical)

DRYLAND
- Chernozem and degraded chernozem
- Chestnut and brown steppe
- Desert

OTHER
- Permanent ice and snow
- Tundra soils
- Fertile alluvium

D. WORLD VEGETATION DISTRIBUTION

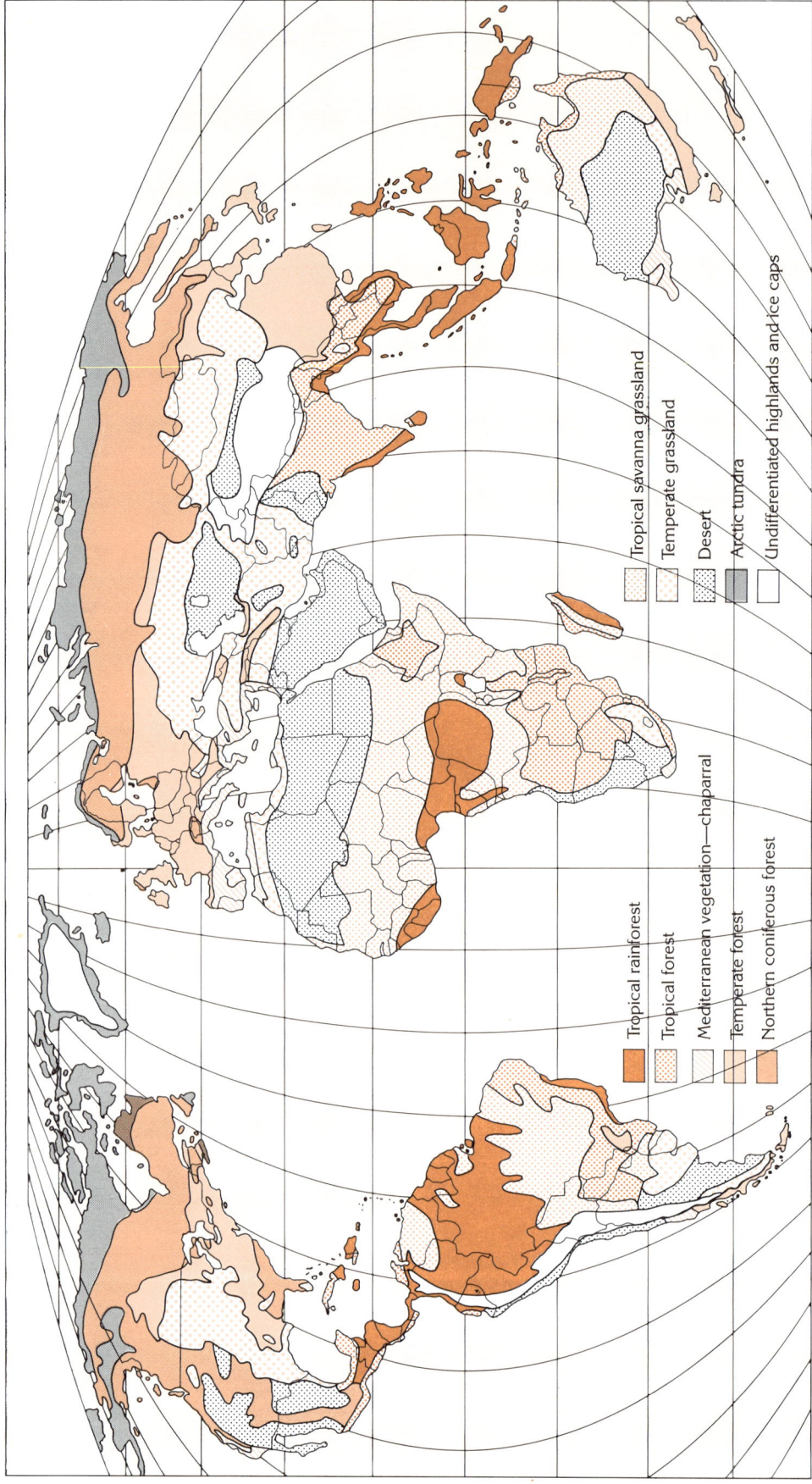

Tropical rainforest

Tropical forest

Mediterranean vegetation—chaparral

Temperate forest

Northern coniferous forest

Tropical savanna grassland

Temperate grassland

Desert

Arctic tundra

Undifferentiated highlands and ice caps

(Adapted from P. Walton Purdom and Stanley H. Anderson, *Environmental Science* [Columbus, Ohio: Charles E. Merrill Publishing Company, 1980], p. 179.

E.   WORLD POPULATION DENSITY

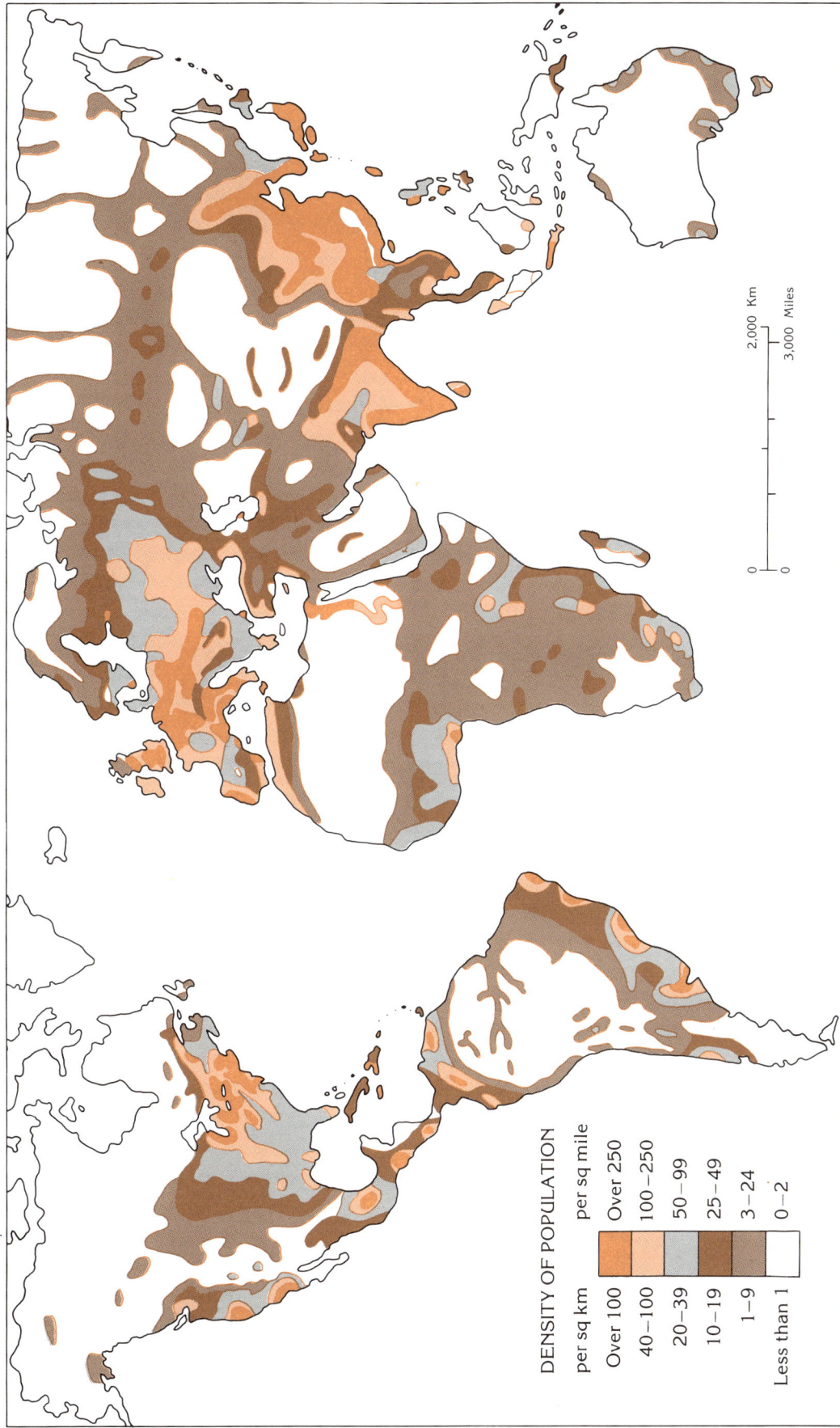

DENSITY OF POPULATION

per sq km	per sq mile
Over 100	Over 250
40–100	100–250
20–39	50–99
10–19	25–49
1–9	3–24
Less than 1	0–2

2,000 Km

3,000 Miles

0

0

F.   WORLD POPULATION GROWTH RATES

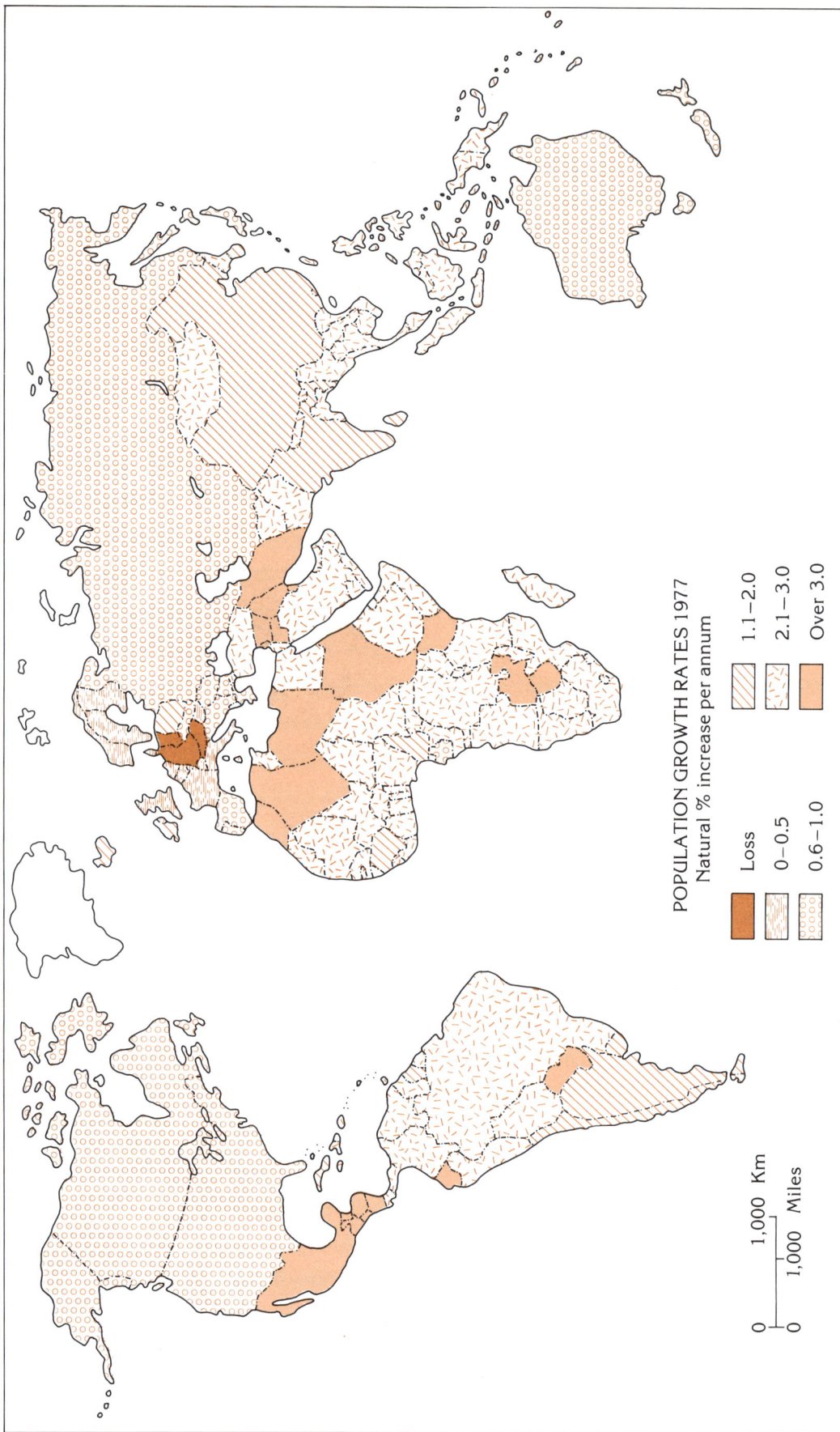

POPULATION GROWTH RATES 1977
Natural % increase per annum

Loss		1.1–2.0
0–0.5		2.1–3.0
0.6–1.0		Over 3.0

0   1,000 Km

0   1,000 Miles

G. WORLD LANGUAGE PATTERNS

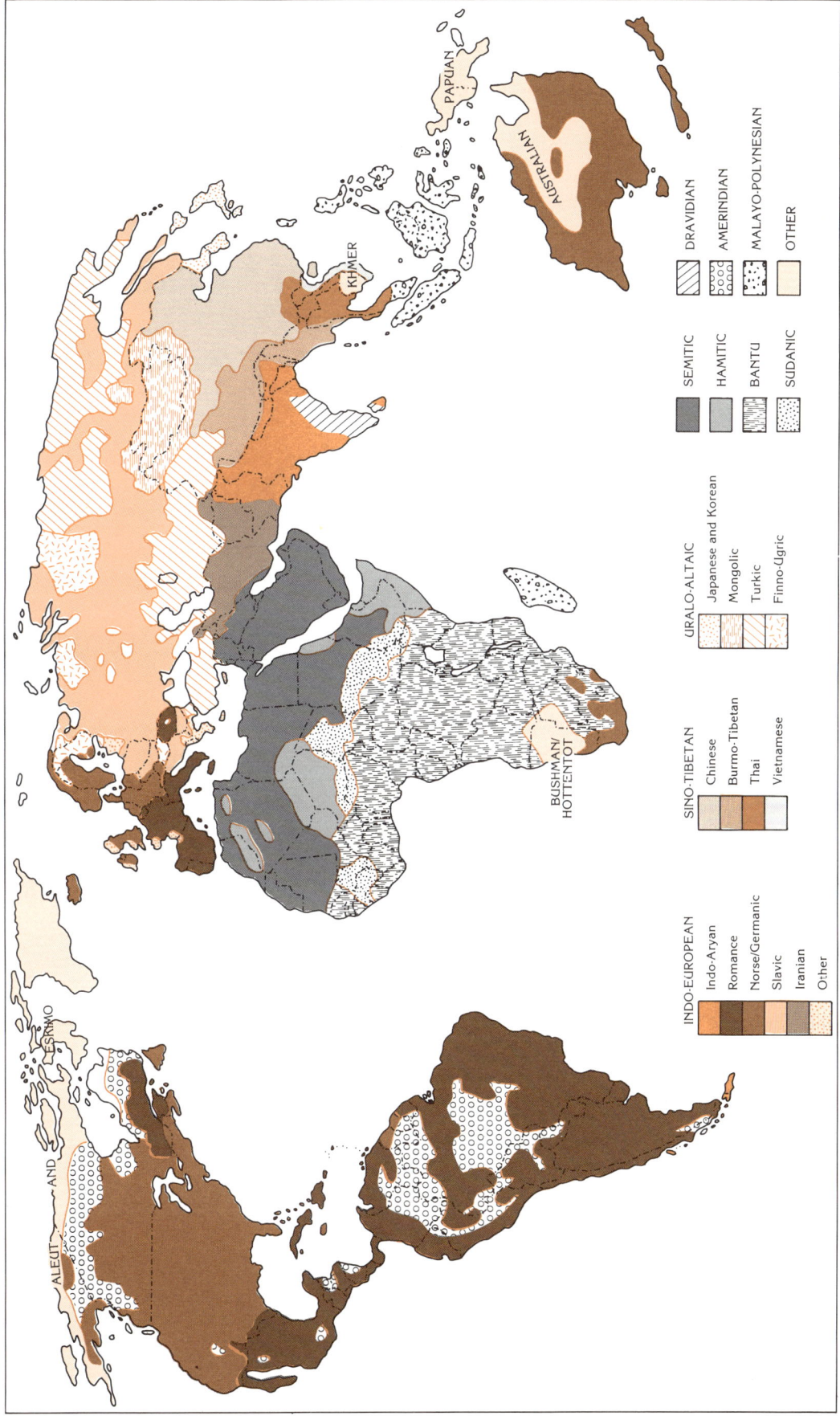

INDO-EUROPEAN
- Indo-Aryan
- Romance
- Norse/Germanic
- Slavic
- Iranian
- Other

SINO-TIBETAN
- Chinese
- Burmo-Tibetan
- Thai
- Vietnamese

URALO-ALTAIC
- Japanese and Korean
- Mongolic
- Turkic
- Finno-Ugric

SEMITIC

HAMITIC

BANTU

SUDANIC

DRAVIDIAN

AMERINDIAN

MALAYO-POLYNESIAN

OTHER

ESKIMO

ALEUT

PAPUAN

AUSTRALIAN

KHMER

BUSHMAN/HOTTENTOT

H.   WORLD RELIGION

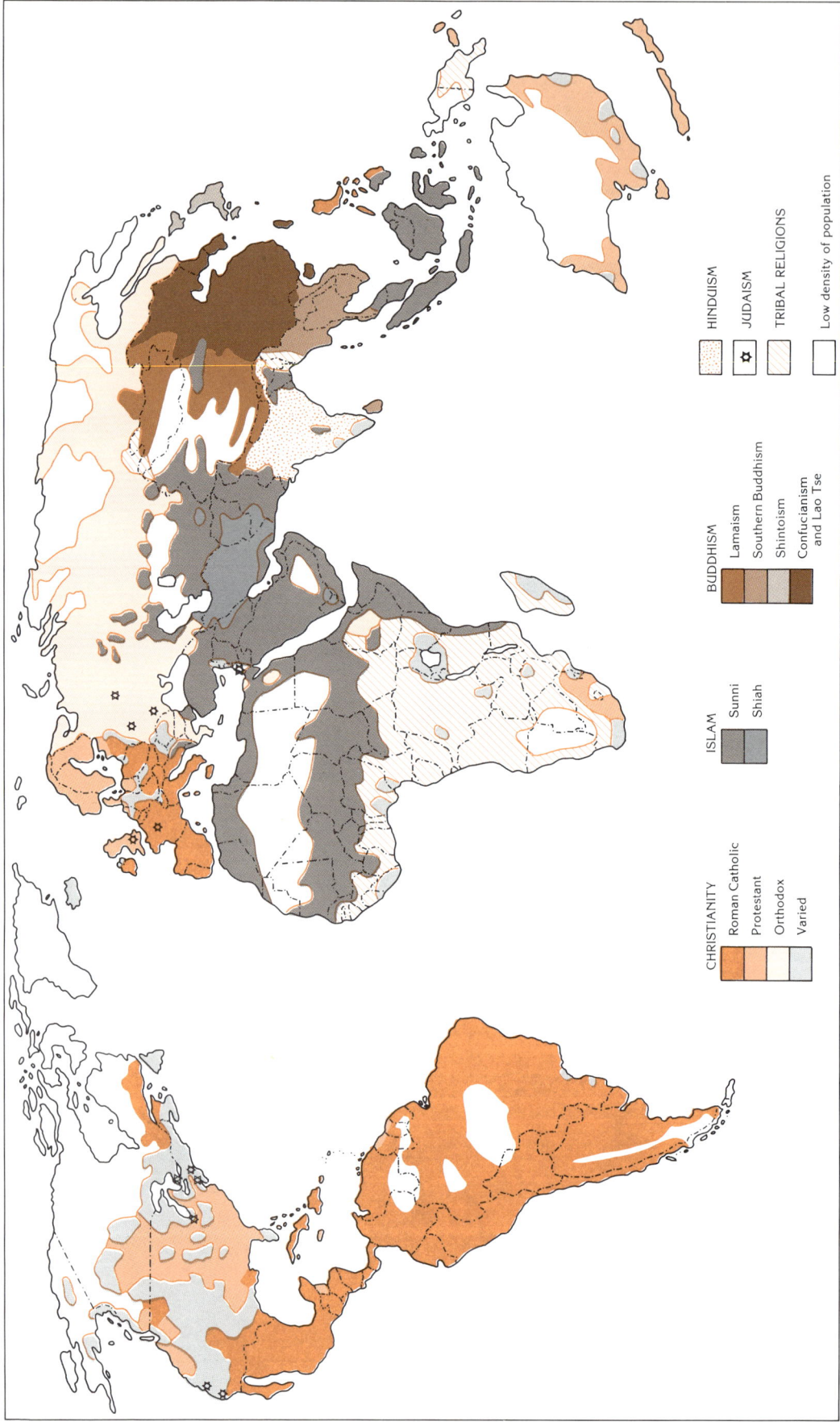

CHRISTIANITY

Roman Catholic
Protestant
Orthodox
Varied

ISLAM

Sunni
Shiah

BUDDHISM

Lamaism
Southern Buddhism
Shintoism
Confucianism
and Lao Tse

HINDUISM

JUDAISM

TRIBAL RELIGIONS

Low density of population

I.   HUMAN CALORIC INTAKE

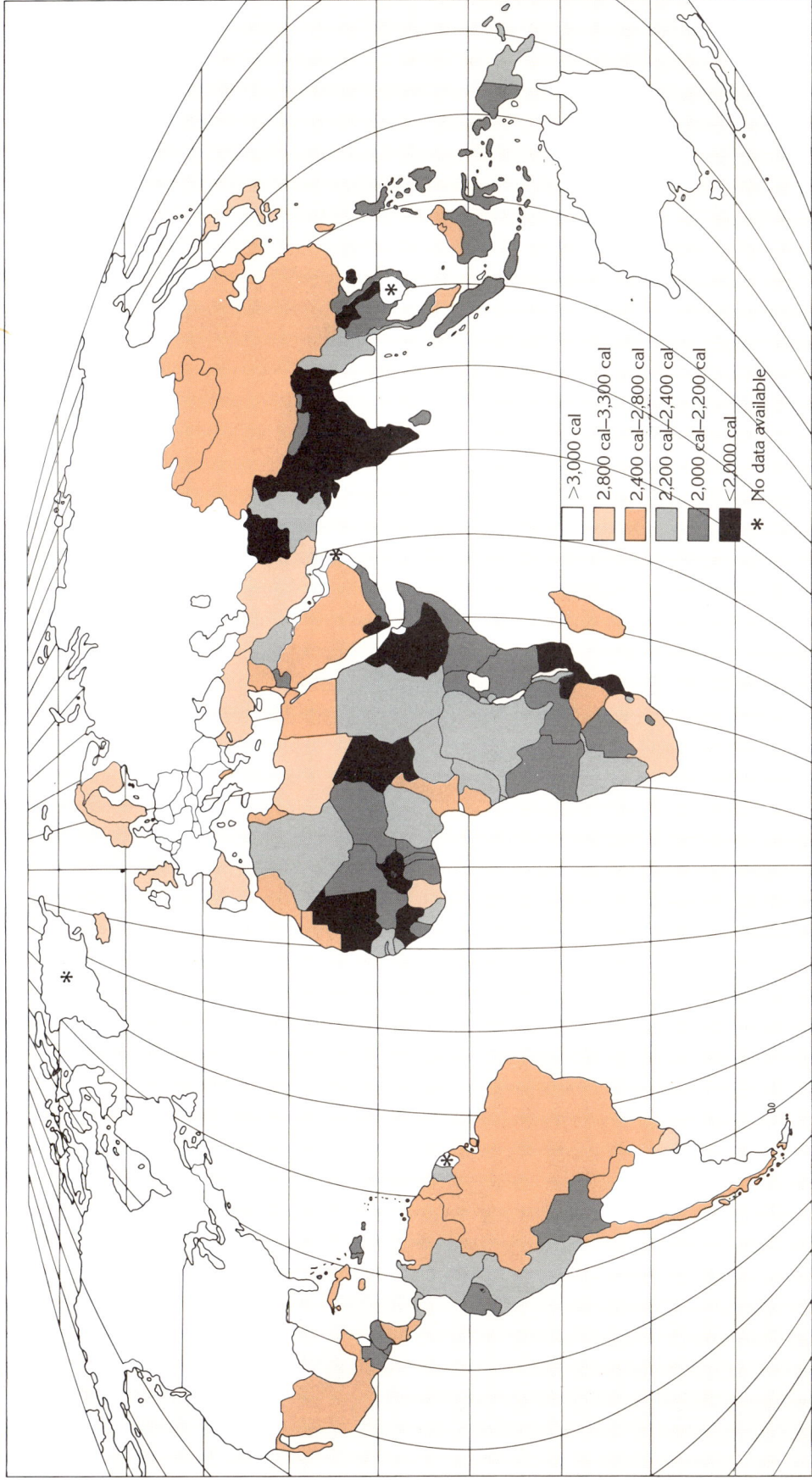

>3,000 cal

2,800 cal–3,300 cal

2,400 cal–2,800 cal

2,200 cal–2,400 cal

2,000 cal–2,200 cal

<2,000 cal

* No data available

(Data from FAO Production Yearbook for 1979. United Nations, Rome, 1980.)

J. **WORLD OIL RESERVES**

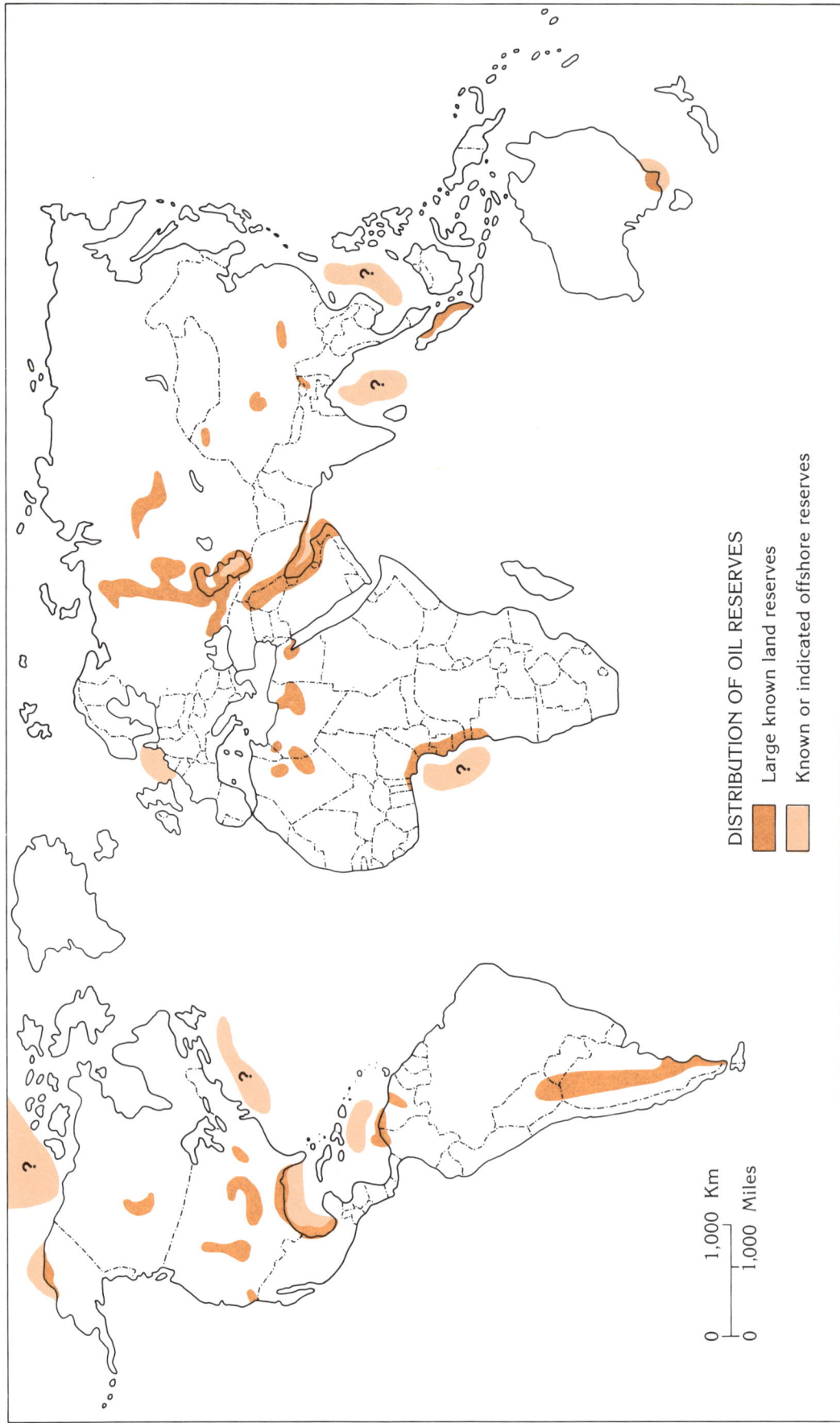

DISTRIBUTION OF OIL RESERVES

Large known land reserves

Known or indicated offshore reserves

1,000 Km

1,000 Miles

0
0

K.   PER CAPITA GROSS NATIONAL PRODUCT, 1980 (IN U.S. DOLLARS)

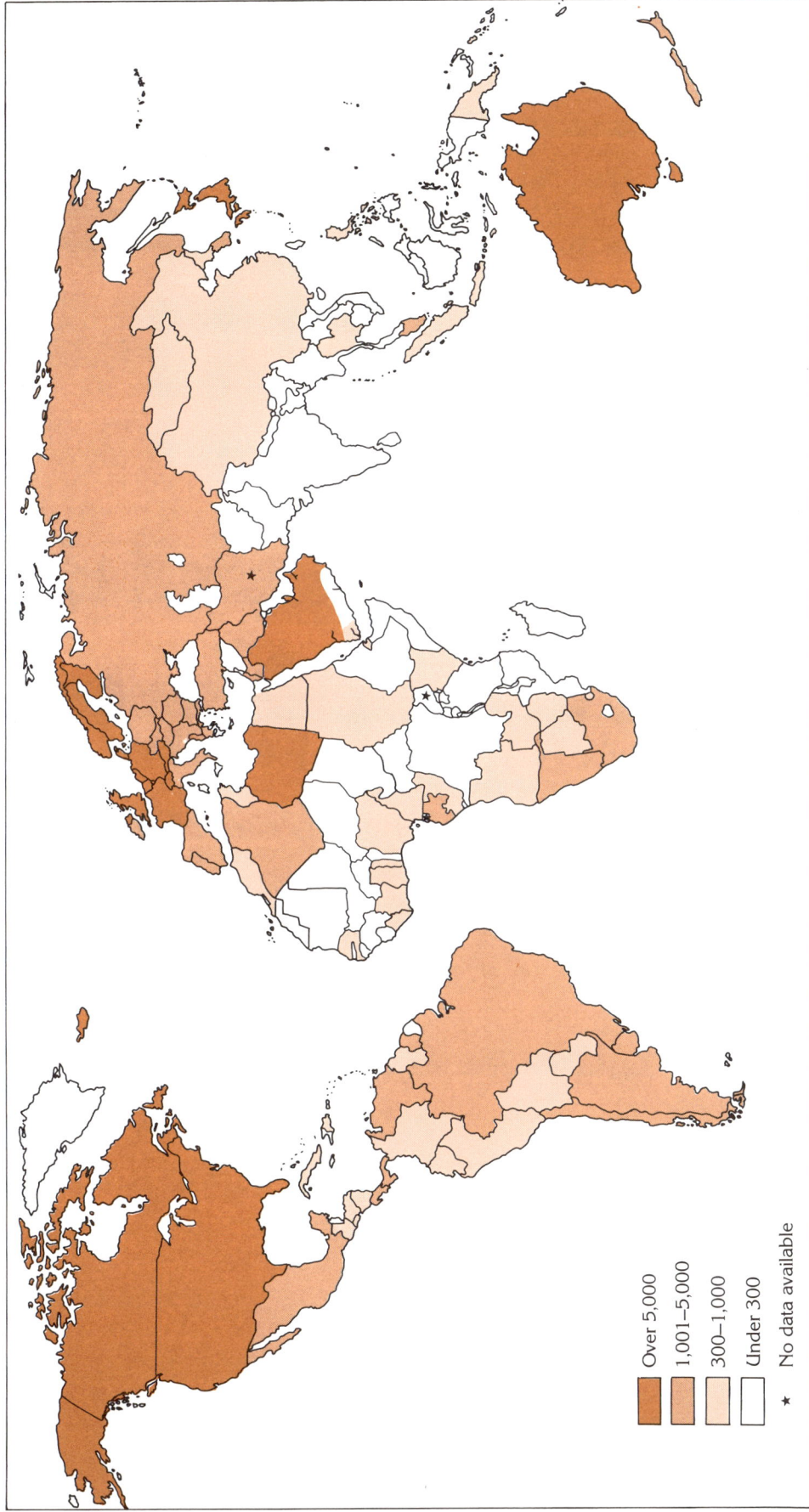

Over 5,000

1,001–5,000

300–1,000

Under 300

★   No data available

(Data from the 1980 World Population Data Sheet. Courtesy of the Population Reference Bureau, Inc., Washington, D.C.)

L.   WORLD COLONIAL POWERS

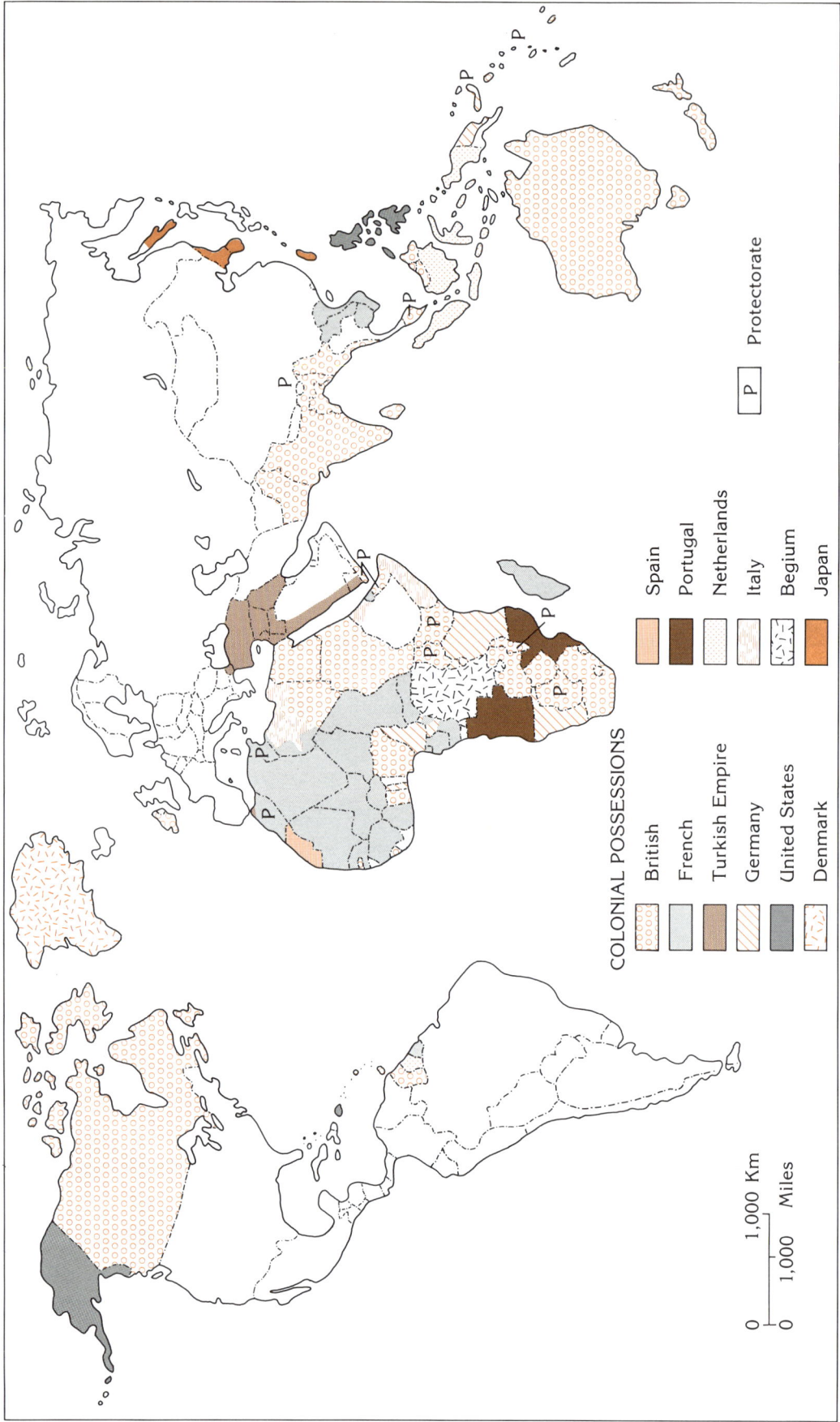

COLONIAL POSSESSIONS

British
French
Turkish Empire
Germany
United States
Denmark

Spain
Portugal
Netherlands
Italy
Begium
Japan

P   Protectorate

1,000 Km
0
1,000
0   Miles

M.   REGIONS OF THE WORLD

KEY TERMS

- spatial interaction
- global interaction
- environmental degradation
- geographic context
- changing interactions
- geographic perspective
- distributional pattern
- environmental determinist
- spatial correlation
- causal relationship
- environmentalism
- remote sensing
- correlation
- site
- situation
- geographic explanation
- regional approach
- systematic approach
- core
- functional region (nodal region)
- formal region
- tectonic plate
- diffusion
- innovation
- demographic transition
- takeoff
- population explosion
- central place
- regional interdependence

1

INTRODUCTION
to
GEOGRAPHIC
and
REGIONAL CONCEPTS

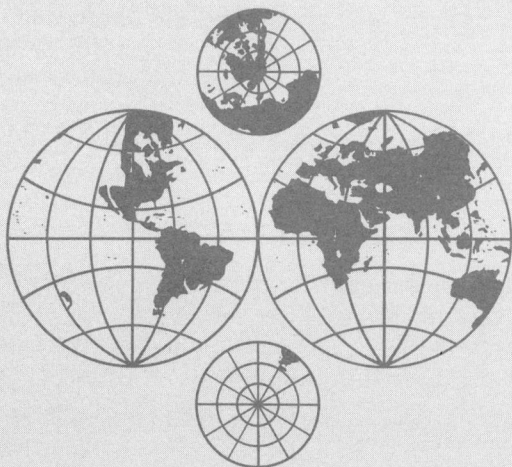

PROLOGUE: A WORLD OF CRISES, A WORLD OF CHANGE

According to current projections, the world's population in 1990 will be about 5.3 billion, nearly 1 billion people more than inhabited the earth in 1980. Ninety percent of this increase will occur in developing countries, many of which cannot provide a decent life for all of the people they now have. Coping with another billion or so people is not a problem isolated to developing countries, though. The developed, industrialized countries, too, will have to cope with various aspects of the worldwide problems associated with mounting population pressures because they are part of two broad sets of worldwide systems of **spatial interactions.** The first general category of **global interaction** is both physical and ecological. The time span required to add another billion people has steadily decreased. It took all of the history of the human species on the planet to reach one billion people in approximately 1820. It took little more than a century to add the second billion (around 1930), then thirty years to add a third billion (1960), then sixteen years for the fourth billion (1976); the fifth billion is projected to take about twelve years. In other words, there are many people still living who were born when the earth had 2 billion people fewer; 2 billion fewer people relative to the physical resource base of the planet, including food, clean water, living space, and at least some metals and fuels. Of course, there were 2 billion fewer *producers,* too. These are two aspects of the population "problem."

The living requirements of these added billions on the self-contained support system shared, however unevenly, by us all, will demand more cultivated land. Deforestation will result. Forests are being eliminated now at a worldwide annual rate of 50 million acres (20 million hectares)—an area about one third the size of France. Inevitably, some of this formerly forested land will be subject to increased floods and soil erosion. This **environmental degradation** could lead to *decreases* rather than *increases* of some local food supplies and destruction of lifeforms. These are but a few of the serious consequences of human population growth for other forms of life and for the physical environment.

The second general category of global interaction is in economic and political interrelationships. Truly isolated populations now exist only due to political decisions. Given permission to land and the price of the ticket, there is almost no place on earth that any of us could *not* visit within one or, at the most, two, days. The same highly advanced technologies that make this possible also tie together distant places in global markets and resource exchanges. Jet aircraft would not be possible without intercontinental flows of a wide variety of metals, metallic ores, fossil fuels, and technology. The continuing upward surge in human numbers means vast increases in demand for food, fuels, metals—even living space itself. Between 1983 and 1990, a quarter of a billion jobs must be added to provide paid employment for these new people. By the year 2000, a further three quarters of a billion jobs must be available within the world economy. Food imports by many developing countries will rise sharply—they must be paid for by increasing industrialization and increasing exports of raw materials as well. This will increase worldwide demands on the natural resource base and undoubtedly increase pollution levels.

Increased population growth will accelerate urbanization—cities in the *developing* world are expanding at faster rates now. *If* present trends were to continue to 2000 A.D., there would be ten cities of the developing world each exceeding 15 million people, led by Mexico City at 30 million. This increased congestion, combined with the poverty apparent in the slums of developing world cities, could lead to political unrest. The world already has several million international refugees; their number can only

A Poor District in Cairo. People are central in this study of regional geography. As consumers of food and some resources, their numbers can pose problems for nations and regions, but people are also producers and developers of new resources. Human energies and talents are the one irreplaceable and vital resource for any state. (Courtesy of United Nations/B. P. Wolff)

increase as a result of political chaos and severe economic pressures.

The picture is not totally bleak. The rate of population increase has been falling slowly in most of the developing world. There are underused, mismanaged, and even empty lands that could easily produce more food for the world; a UN projection asserts that a 4 percent annual increase in food production over the next decade is a realistic goal (the world average population increase rate is 1.7 percent). Large new water projects around the world should increase cultivated land area and generate electrical power to take some of the pressure off world oil markets, one of the most obvious arenas of resource competition.

All of these problems of population growth, food supply, industrialization and urbanization, environmental degradation and pollution, and scarcities of metals and fuels are interrelated in a spatial sense. Many of these global problems are better understood within a **geographic context,** that is, in their spatial relationships with each other. We do not live in the same world now as last year, and the world our grandparents grew up in is almost unrecognizeable in many respects, both for the better and for the worse. Not only is our immediate environment changing, economically, culturally, and even physically, in both obvious and subtle ways, but the rest of the world is changing too. The changes are more than localized, more than internal. Critical relationships among regions and states continue to evolve as well; both these levels of **changing interactions** will be placed in **geographic perspective** throughout this book.

THE GOALS OF GEOGRAPHY

The literal meaning of the word *geography* is "description of the earth." However, explanation and interpretation are just as important a part of modern geography as is description. Geography begins with location, but it does not end with mere knowledge of place location.

DEFINITIONS OF GEOGRAPHY

Definitions of geography include statements that it is the "science of distribution" and the "study of distributional patterns." For example, a study of the world's population should start, obviously, with a map of the distribution of humans across the planet. *Where* are people concentrated, and where are they scarce or even absent? Students of geography sense an immediate second question, beyond *where,* and it is usually both more demanding and more satisfying of intellectual curiosity. Just as historians are not satisfied with just knowing *when* an event occurred, but want to understand *why* it happened then, there, and to whom, geographers do not stop with place knowledge. The second key question is *why there?*; that is, what accounts for that observed location or **distributional pattern?** How can it be explained, especially in its possible relationships with other distributional or geographic patterns?

THE PHILOSOPHY OF GEOGRAPHY

Geography seeks to explain locational patterns and explores spatial associations, along with possible cause-and-effect relationships. Having first determined the distributional pattern of any phenomenon (physical *or* cultural) geographers try to develop an accurate, comprehensive, logical answer to questions of *why there?* Periodically through the over two-thosand-year history of the discipline, a misdirected passion for precise and uncomplicated answers has resulted in a deterministic view of the exceedingly complex relationships among physical and cultural geographic phenomena. **Environmental determinists** claimed that the physical environment, particularly climate, exerted a controlling influence on people and culture. The search for cause and effect sometimes detours through oversimplification; contemporary geographers stress the complex nature of cultural distribution patterns and try to avoid the lure of easy answers. When people make a decision on the use of, and modification of, the physical environment, they consider also many aspects of the cultural environment—economic, political, and technological. The environmental determinists failed the test of scientific laws—they could not predict what would happen under given circumstances. For example, an environmental determinist in 1840 might have asserted that the North American Great Plains would never become a grain producing region, based on observations of low precipitation. In 1840, the plains indeed were not cultivated. But changes in the cultural environment—the inventions of farm machinery, barbed wire, deep-well drilling, and the introduction of hybrid, drought-adapted seed—resulted in a land-use revolution. The physical environment did not change perceptively, but the cultural environment did.

GEOGRAPHY AS AN INTEGRATIVE DISCIPLINE

By its nature, geography seeks to comprehend whole regions and types of worldwide distributional patterns.

Commonly, this search for explanation requires geographers to search out data from a wide range of physical, biological, and social sciences and humanities. For example, a good, adequately detailed and up-to-date map of population distribution would answer the initial *where* question concerning world population patterns.

In attempting an *explanation* of this geographic pattern, however, information compiled by or interpreted by scholars of many diverse fields of study would be necessary. Many aspects of the physical world—climate, natural vegetation, soils, terrain, geology—*could* have a relationship with the distribution of people. The presence or absence of fresh water, economic minerals, productive soils, mountain passes, plains, seacoasts, swamps, valuable timber, or fisheries resources *could* all be related to population density. When two geographic variables show a tendency to be concentrated or sparsely represented or absent together in roughly the same pattern, this represents a **spatial correlation.** Spatial correlations do not necessarily imply a **causal relationship,** however.

People are responsive to and consider many other aspects of the total environment in making a decision to migrate, for example. While such migration motivations may involve a physical geographic factor, such as the discovery of gold or oil or the availability of cheap, good-quality farmland, cultural, economic, and political factors are also involved. An oil discovery would be meaningless unless that society had access to the technology to exploit it, and had a market for it; likewise, the very availability of potential farmland for settlement would be based on economic decisions concerning accessibility and cost of transport, and, probably, on the general level of technology. Thus, in addition to considering the probable effects of physical geographic factors, geographers must be prepared to locate, evaluate, and apply information from various social sciences and the humanities. Geography integrates data from any relevant source as it seeks to explain complex spatial patterns. A tendency to become encyclopedic in geographic studies, particularly regional studies, can be counteracted by developing the ability to recognize important concepts and changing spatial relationships among these myriad facts.

GEOGRAPHY IN RELATION TO THE SOCIAL SCIENCES

The first university-level American geographers in the early 1900's tended to be geologists who were interested in the interrelationships of human activities with subsurface and landform geology. This early emphasis on physical "causes" of cultural "effects" may have encouraged a deterministic viewpoint. There was an eventual reaction against determinism. Contemporary geographers recognize that the physical world does not determine the nature of human cultures; however, a sharp dichotomy of "physical" and "cultural" geographic factors does not exist. There *is* a relationship between the two, but it is not as simple or direct as the determinists believed. People occupy a central position in any geographic study, and for this reason, geography is as much a social science as a physical science. Human societies are always changing; very little is constant. Accurate measurement of quantitative changes occurring under controlled conditions such as in a laboratory is not possible with human groups under normal social, economic, and political conditions. Social scientists must consider qualitative and subjective variables not capable of precise measurement or prediction. Geography, functioning as a bridge between physical-biological and social sciences, thus experiences the handicaps and opportunities of the other social sciences. Among the many definitions of geography, some describe it as "human ecology," implying that it "seeks to describe and interpret the variable character of the earth as the home of people."

GEOGRAPHY AND CONTEMPORARY ENVIRONMENTALISM

Geographers study the interactions of people and environment, using a wide range of scholarly approaches. The discipline's past experience with the philosophy of environmental determinism, which has helped make geographers cautious about accepting simplistic explanations, is also good training for dealing with the often vastly complicated interactions of environmental problems. A common theme of geographic studies is the environmental impact of people and cultures and the complex interrelationships of the physical and cultural environments. To a considerable extent, the interaction is two-way, a fact not recognized by the environmental determinists. It was the growing appreciation of mankind's impacts on the physical environment, often negative, which spurred the most recent rise of environmentalism, a concern for minimizing negative effects on the environment but not related to determinism.

THE TOOLS OF GEOGRAPHY

Each field of study is characterized by the research methods and techniques with which its students gather, organize, and interpret data. The tools of geography are as varied as the discipline itself.

MEANS OF OBTAINING GEOGRAPHIC DATA

An important, almost characteristically geographic, means of obtaining data is through field observation and study. Field observation is more than just gazing at a landscape; it implies trained observation of phenomena and patterns that the researcher believes to be important.

Maps   Maps have been such an inseparable tool of geographers that their use is often regarded as an identifying characteristic of the field. Maps and geographers deserve this popular association, although of course students of other disciplines find use for maps also. Because spatial patterns and spatial associations are basic data for geographers, the use of maps is second only to the use of language itself as a universal in any geographic study. Maps are intended to represent selected portions of reality at a convenient scale. Just as a scale model of a ship is a smaller, proportionately accurate representation of the real thing, a map is a proportionally accurate model of one or more sets of phenomena in the real world. The scale of a map shows the *ratio* of distance and area on the earth to distance and area on the map itself. Scale is commonly expressed as a fractional proportion or ratio (1:1,000,000 would mean that one unit of measure on the map represents 1 million units on the earth; as long as the same unit is used on both sides of the ratio, any linear unit can be used), a verbal statement (1 inch equals 1 mile), or a linear scale, in which a line is marked on the map showing the actual distance represented on the map. (Most of the maps used in this book use a linear scale.)

In map scales, as in fractions, a very high ratio of actual area to map area, say 1 to 1 million, would be known as a small-scale map, just as one millionth of something would be a very small fraction. A large-scale map is capable of showing a large amount of detail; it would be one on which one unit of map distance or area represented relatively few such units on the earth. Thus, a 1 to 100 scale would be a much larger scale than the 1 to 1 million mentioned above. Whereas a larger-scale map can be used to show far greater detail than a smaller-scale map, smaller-scale maps of large states or regions would have practical advantages of compactness. (See Figure 1–1.)

Unfortunately, it is not possible to transfer an accurate model of the round surface of the earth (the planet is actually not a perfect sphere but is slightly flattened at the poles and very slightly pear-shaped as well) to a flat-surfaced map without tearing or stretching it. It *is* possible to choose *which* type of accuracy is most desirable (accurate representations of area, direction, or shape) for a particular purpose. All three cannot be achieved with the

FIGURE 1–1

The Meaning of Scale. These three maps illustrate the concept of scale in maps. Scale, the ratio of map size to earth size, the actual area on the Earth's surface represented on the map, must be chosen to suit the level of local detail versus regional or world geographic relationships desired.

same *map projection* (a systematic way of constructing a map to control for the amount, type, and location of distortion that occurs when representing a curved earth surface on a flat map).

Many maps have a grid composed of lines of *latitude* and *longitude,* a system devised for locational reference. Lines of *latitude* run east-west, but are used to measure distance north and south of the equator. *Longitude* mea-

sures distance east or west of a *prime* or central *meridian,* which is a line designated as zero longitude. Lines of longitude thus run north-south across a map and meet at the poles. Lines of latitude are portions of parallel, concentric circles; thus they cannot cross or converge.

A variety of map symbols are used to show locations and patterns on maps. These symbols must be explained on the map with captions. Many symbols are so generally used that they hardly need explanation, such as a circled star for capitals.

Aerial Photography and Remote Sensing   Perhaps the most famous photograph of the past few decades is an Apollo Moon Program view of the earth taken by the U.S. astronauts. Only a handful of astronauts have actually seen the planet from deep space as a small, greenish blue sphere; the rest of us have seen the photograph and thus have viewed it through **remote sensing.** Remote sensing, literally any technique of "seeing" objects without being in personal contact with or close proximity to the object, is a rapidly expanding source of information for geographers and other scientists. The most common remote sensing device is the camera. Photographs, taken of the earth's surface from a tall building, airplane, or orbiting satellite, are but one of a growing array of remote sensing data acquisition and display systems now available. Aerial photography is the oldest truly *remote* sensing tool and remains the one most familiar to and useful to geographers.

The vast potentials of aerial photography have been expanded in three general ways: (a) the platform on which the camera is mounted has gone from balloons, kites, and primitive low-flying planes to orbiting satellites, rockets, and unmanned deep space probes; (b) the art and science of interpretation of aerial photography has advanced enormously; and (c) the qualities and capabilities of both cameras and types of film (including electronic transmission of images from vehicles incapable of physically returning film) has resulted in a broadening spectrum of types of photography. False color, or infrared photography, for example, can be helpful in identifying patterns not discernible with ordinary photography. Aerial photos, particularly those high-level views obtained from satellites, can provide new information or make it possible to more readily interpret existing information.

MEANS OF ANALYZING AND COLLATING GEOGRAPHIC DATA

The speed and accuracy with which computers can perform mathematical exercises has enabled geographers to develop complex statistical analyses of many different, spatially related factors to investigate **correlations.** The validity of these correlations can be estimated with the aid of computers. Beyond analysis of data, and analysis of geographer's inferences about those data, is the rapidly expanding field of computer simulation. For example, historical trend data and information on relationships among different factors can be entered into a computer along with a program to depict current spatial relationships, to project future spatial relationships, or to recreate historical development of these relationships. Using a program involving locational references, computers can be instructed to design and produce maps of many spatial variables and correlations entered into its data banks. The computer-generated map, Figure 1–2, was photographed directly from the display screen of a computer.

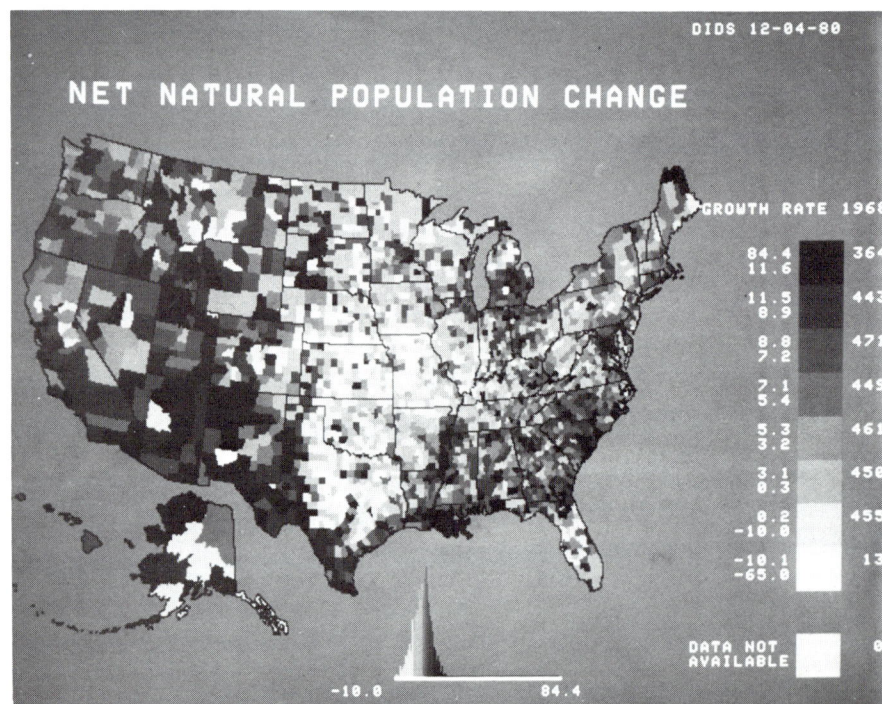

FIGURE 1–2
Computer-Generated Map. As in other computer functions, the programming of computers to arrange data according to spatial coordinates and to present the data as a map represents an almost unbelievable compression of work time. Once geographically identified data is stored in the computer and the appropriate program entered, maps such as this, which was photographed directly from a video display screen, can be generated very quickly.

APPLYING GEOGRAPHIC KNOWLEDGE AND INSIGHTS

What do geographers do with this potentially enormous mass of data after they have gathered it and organized it in some meaningful way? The two key questions of geography, *where* and *why there,* provide some guidance. Location is a deceptively simple concept; it must be divided into *location-description* (what is it, where is it in terms of a location grid—north/south and east/west of fixed points or lines) and *relative location* (location *in relation* to other geographic phenomena and to the larger region and the world).

Location can be studied at either, or both, of two levels or scales. **Site** is the most local and immediate scale of location; it refers to the immediate surroundings. **Situation** is a broader definition of location, and at a larger scale; situation is *relative* location with reference to a larger region, country, or the world.

After determining location, the questions of spatial associations and possible correlations come up. Does the observed phenomenon have a pattern that seems to be associated with the spatial pattern of another phenome-non? An apparently consistent spatial association may reflect a correlation—a definite relationship that *may* be a causal one between two different phenomena. Possible correlations are often suggested by comparing two maps of the same area but showing different variables. If, for example, two maps of the same metropolitan area were compared, one showing average income, another showing average number of years of education completed by adults, an apparent correlation is noted (see Figure 1–3). Where educational levels are high, income levels generally are high also. This would indicate a positive correlation, as two factors vary together. A negative correlation is reflected in a situation where one factor, say income, varied inversely with another, such as deaths related to malnutrition. Where income was highest, it is likely that deaths related to malnutrition would be lowest, showing a negative correlation. Of course, such spatial correlations as income and education, shown in our sample, do *not* prove any specific cause-and-effect relationship, nor can they be isolated from many other social and economic factors. Wealth may just as easily, in some instances, *produce* a higher education, as *result* from it. In individual instances, wealth may not be related to educational attainments at

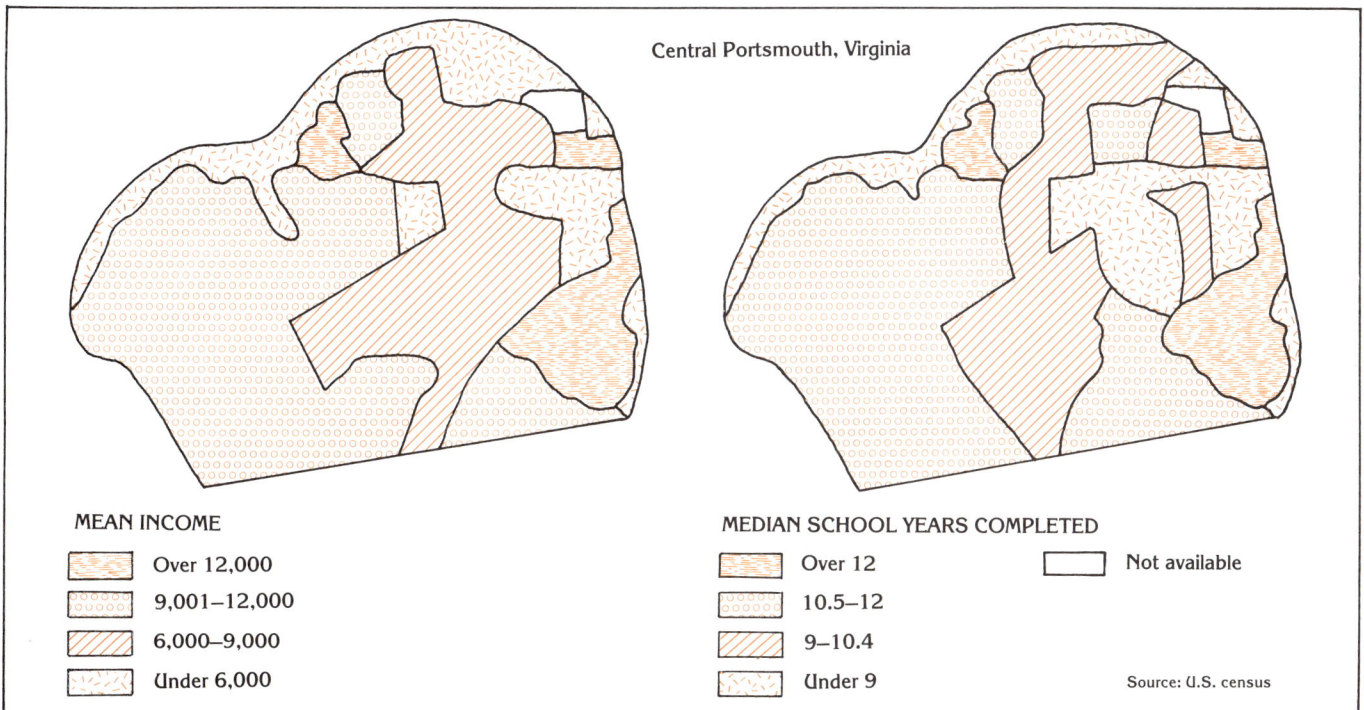

Central Portsmouth, Virginia

MEAN INCOME
- Over 12,000
- 9,001–12,000
- 6,000–9,000
- Under 6,000

MEDIAN SCHOOL YEARS COMPLETED
- Over 12
- 10.5–12
- 9–10.4
- Under 9
- Not available

Source: U.S. census

FIGURE 1–3
Spatial Correlation Example: Education and Income. When two or more distinct phenomena show a spatial correlation (they vary in intensity or degree of distribution in an apparent relationship with one another), geographers consider possible cause-and-effect relationships. Spatial correlations as such do not indicate which is cause and which the effect, nor necessarily indicate any such relationship. Education level and income have some relationship, but which is the cause and which the effect?

all. Perhaps the real value of this spatial correlation, like the models of statisticians, is that it suggests a general relationship. When researchers find a case that does not "fit" or reflect the general situation, then they *recognize* it as an exception, study it in more detail, and look for alternative explanations.

Geographic explanation, an objective of studying location, relative location, and spatial associations, will seldom be satisfactorily complete without some sense of time dimension as well as spatial dimensions. Any map, just as any photograph, "freezes" a moment; any spatial pattern must be regarded as portraying a distribution at a particular time, a static time. An understanding of any part of the earth requires some knowledge of how the present patterns came to be. Geographers need to place most observed geographic patterns into a historical context to fully understand them. Present patterns do not, and cannot, supply all the answers. In a sense, they represent one frame, perhaps the latest frame, of a motion picture. A geographical study lacking a time-change dimension could result in a limited level of comprehension, one lacking a sense of context.

TWO BASIC ORGANIZATIONAL APPROACHES TO THE STUDY OF GEOGRAPHY

The two fundamental frameworks for studying any geographic phenomena are to focus either on a particular area or a specific topic. The framework that concentrates on a particular area is the **regional approach;** the one that stresses a specific topic is the **systematic approach.** The regional approach to geography emphasizes the area itself. A subsection of the earth is identified through some degree of internal homogeneity or an interaction system. All physical and cultural phenomena within that region are then studied, with the objective of understanding the region as a whole and perhaps its relationships with other regions. Regional geography must first concern itself with identifying and then bounding the region. While certain types of regions, such as political regions, will be easily recognized and generate little discussion, others are much more commonly debated. Most likely, there would be agreement concerning a central *core* but divergence on determining boundaries.

The fact that some researcher has considered an area to be a region for purposes of study is often of little or no consequence to the people of that region. Living in a region identified as the Corn Belt or a desert vegetational zone would have little relevance or significance to the inhabitants of that area, even though such physical elements as climate and soil type (used to delimit the region) do affect the area's economy and do indirectly influence the lives and livelihoods of all dwellers within the region. The designation of a region as Illinois or Israel is, of course, of much greater significance.

There are two types of regions, formal and functional. A formal region is relatively uniform throughout in terms of its identifying criteria. A **functional region,** sometimes called a **nodal region,** has a definite center or node. It is from this center that an interaction system or network implies movement to all parts of the region, or vice versa. For purposes of legal jurisdiction or voting in state or government elections, anywhere within the state's boundaries would have the same significance as any other part. Thus, a state or other political region would be a **formal region**. Likewise, taxi fare zones or railroad freight zones are uniform and formal; *any* location within a $2.00 taxi fare zone is the same as *any other* in that zone in terms of fares. Functional regions would include such regions as the trade hinterlands of cities. As these could be measured or inferred by the use of several sets of criteria, and because the economic and cultural relationships involved are dynamic, the precise boundary may be drawn differently (based on somewhat different criteria) by different geographers (see Figure 1–4).

The systematic approach to geography concentrates on things rather more than place, on phenomena rather than the area per se. Usually the focus is on only one thing or phenomenon at a time. For instance, if population were studied within a specific areal unit, a region would not necessarily be delineated, and any topic other than population would be involved only peripherally in explaining population patterns. Systematic geography retains the spatial perspective of geography in interpreting the distribution and pattern of a phenomenon. Systematic geography is subdivided into a series of topics that correspond with the disciplines and specializations of the physical-biological and social sciences. For example, political geography studies the spatial aspects and geographic relationships of a set of concepts related to political science.

The guiding philosophy of geography, the questions it seeks to answer and its methodology, remains intact whether the researcher is trying to develop a full understanding of a region or a complete explanation of a pattern of distribution. While a thorough regional study requires some familiarity with all the systematic fields (see Figure 1–5), the researcher has the advantage of becoming very familiar with one particular region and the unique interrelationships present therein. The student of systematic ge-

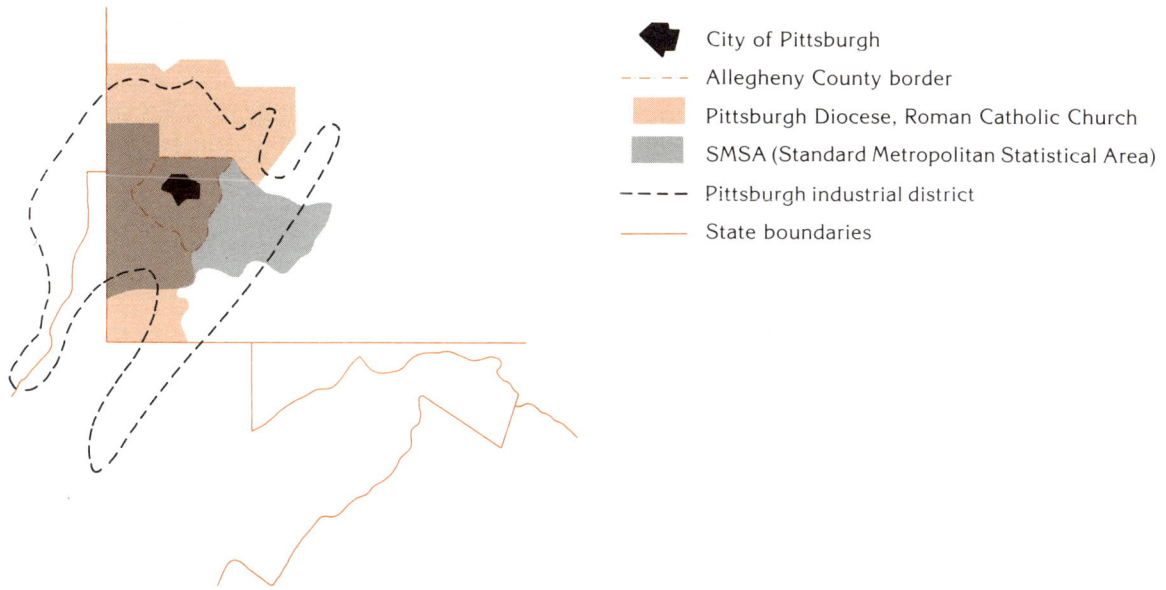

	City of Pittsburgh
	Allegheny County border
	Pittsburgh Diocese, Roman Catholic Church
	SMSA (Standard Metropolitan Statistical Area)
	Pittsburgh industrial district
	State boundaries

FIGURE 1–4

Functional Regions: An Example. In functional regions, there is some degree of functional interaction, as in the relationship of a port to its hinterland, or a metropolitan center to its commuting area.

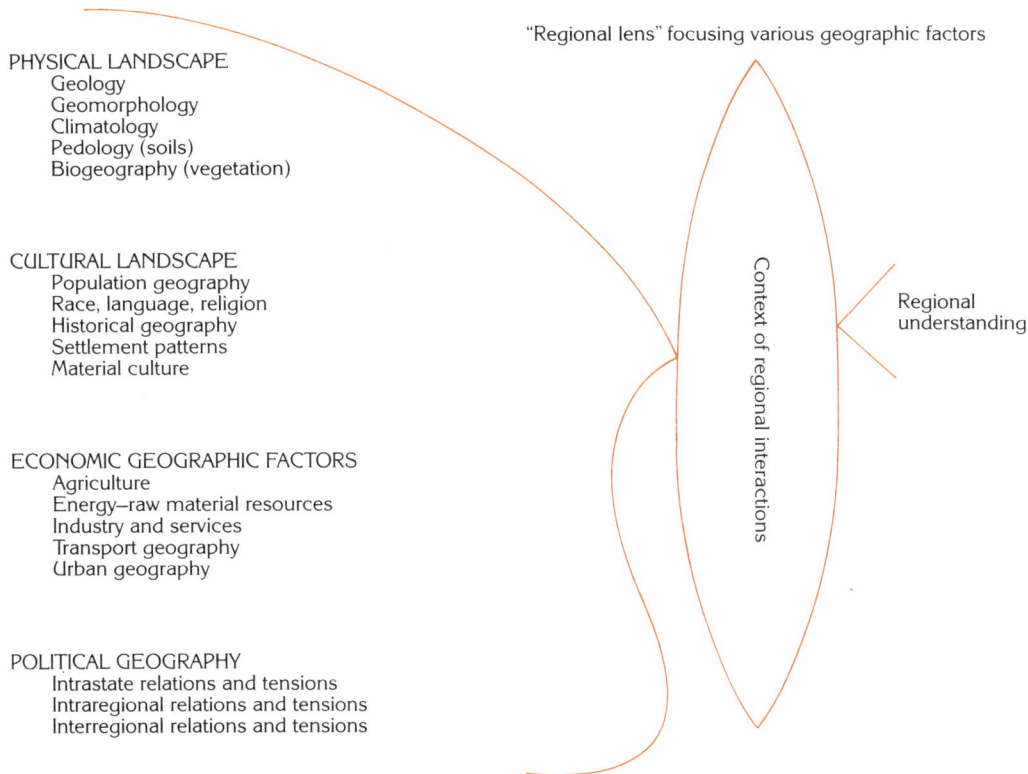

"Regional lens" focusing various geographic factors

PHYSICAL LANDSCAPE
   Geology
   Geomorphology
   Climatology
   Pedology (soils)
   Biogeography (vegetation)

CULTURAL LANDSCAPE
   Population geography
   Race, language, religion
   Historical geography
   Settlement patterns
   Material culture

ECONOMIC GEOGRAPHIC FACTORS
   Agriculture
   Energy–raw material resources
   Industry and services
   Transport geography
   Urban geography

POLITICAL GEOGRAPHY
   Intrastate relations and tensions
   Intraregional relations and tensions
   Interregional relations and tensions

Context of regional interactions

Regional understanding

FIGURE 1–5

Systematic Fields of Geography. In seeking an understanding of the complex nature of world regions, especially in terms of causal relationships, geographers must be concerned with the full range of physical, economic, cultural, and political geographic factors. The regional concept provides an organizational focus for these many inputs.

ography can master that topic but may then apply that set of research techniques and informational body across many different cultures, whose complex web of physical-cultural interactions must be well understood to facilitate the systematic study within each special milieu. A study of world regional geography thus involves a general appreciation of the entire systematic-regional matrix (see Figure 1–6).

REGIONS AS A COMMON AND NECESSARY TOOL OF ORGANIZING SPACE

Regions are a form or structure for organizing and presenting geographic generalizations. Generalization is abstraction; it tries to go beyond a single phenomenon to identify broader patterns and relationships. Generalization can be misleading because there *are* exceptions. The existence of exceptional, contradictory facts must be recognized as probable in the generalization process, and users of generalizations learn to be wary of cause-and-effect assumptions based on generalizations. Nevertheless, generalizations are an obvious necessity in describing and interpreting the variable character of the whole planet as

the home of the human race. Too much emphasis on noting exceptions can obscure the fundamental spatial distribution patterns and underlying interactions that help people to comprehend the predominant geographic patterns of the world. Since world regional geography seeks to explain the spatial variation of all physical and cultural, or human-created, phenomena, geographers need a system for ordering and classifying information and relationships.

JUSTIFICATION FOR REGIONS

It is not possible to comprehend the geography of everything for everywhere without deliberately fragmenting this mass of data into understandable units. Geographers identify and study regions for purposes of rational organization.

One can study the cultural, physical, economic, and political patterns of a subunit of the earth and comprehend those interrelationships much more readily than tackling the whole world as a unit.

Except for gross physical regions such as continents, regions are seldom defined by purely physical circumstances. Almost all regions are defined by some specific aspect of the physical environment considered critical or useful, or by some cultural phenomenon, or a combina-

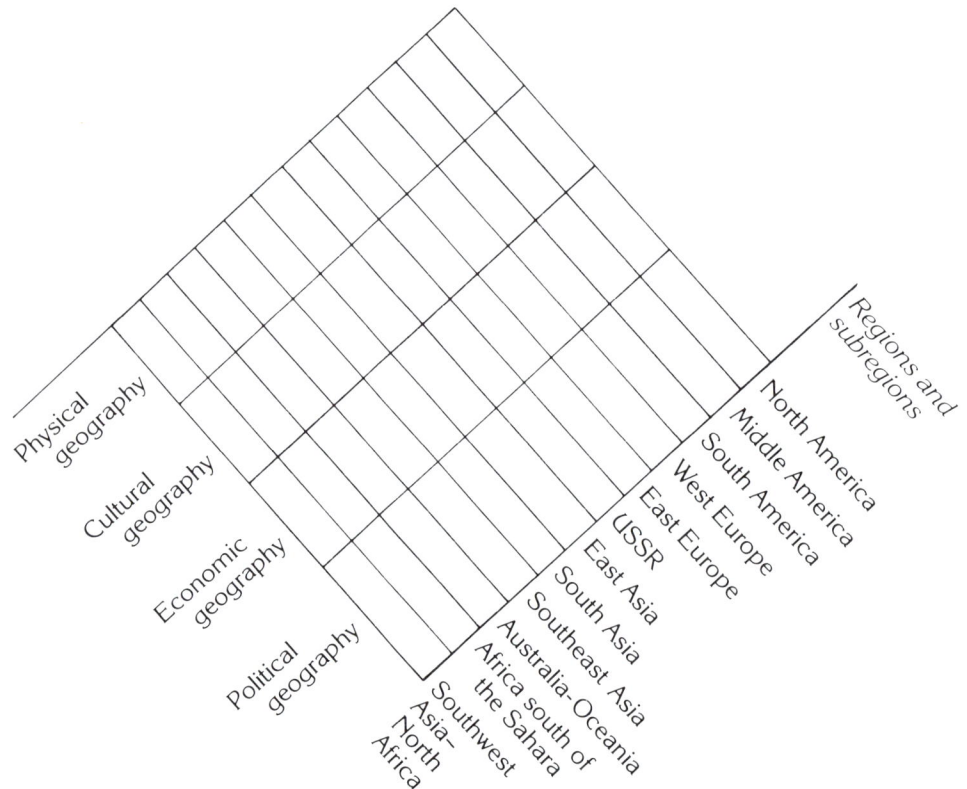

FIGURE 1–6
Systematic Regional Matrix. The challenge of a world regional geography is to organize a potentially encyclopedic breadth of information into comprehensible regional relationships. Each major set of systematic topics is considered within each world region.

tion of these. People choose identifying (and bounding) criteria from an almost infinite number of possibilities. Regions can be defined at virtually any scale of territory or space, from a city neighborhood to a continent. To identify a region it is only necessary to select some overall characteristic or function that can be used to establish a regional boundary, differentiating that region from others and from the rest of the world.

The intellectual challenge is to bring some rational order to a mass of geographic data. The concept of a region or system of regions forms an areal framework for arranging information in a rational way.

DIFFERENT REGIONS, DIFFERENT PERSPECTIVES

Because regions are really identified by people for their own purposes, they are "intellectual constructs"—products of human imagination, values, and perceptions. Regions can be envisioned as a hierarchy of regions, with macro-regions comprised of a number of subregions or micro-regions. The smaller the area of the region, the more precisely it might be bounded or identified, and the more homogeneous it might be. With larger regions, one would expect a larger level of generalization. The critical decision that is made concerning most regions is the choice of *significant* criteria from among an abundance of facts. Too much detail would obscure the facts, not convey them in all their completeness. Facts do not speak for themselves—they must be selectively used to illustrate reality without smothering it.

Urban Neighborhoods as Examples of Regions An urban neighborhood or district may be defined as a small region on the basis of physical, cultural, social, or political boundaries or degree of homogeneity or interaction. Part of the boundary might be a ravine, a rail yard, a freeway, or a park. The definition may relate to political voting precincts, fire districts, or an elementary school service area. The approximate area served by a church or temple in an ethnic neighborhood may define it, as could the residences of particular racial or ethnic group. It could be the area served by a specific shopping center or the housing for a particular factory.

The point is that there is some *reason* for saying that this side of the freeway is a different neighborhood than that on the other side. Distinctive graffiti or other deliberate markings may delineate gang territory within cities; children may be acutely aware of social boundaries in urban areas. Again, these regions are defined by criteria accepted or recognized by the researcher.

Recreation Areas Another type of commonly understood region is the recreation area that serves mainly the population of a specific metropolitan area. In many metropolitan areas, references to "the mountains," "the lake," or "the (sea) shore" need not be further identified. Everyone in the urban area will recognize which geographic area is implied. Nearly everyone recognizes the concept of regions as places with special identities, special functions, and special relationships with other regions.

Common Regional Concepts There are as many different types, scales, and concepts of regions as there are human motivations and needs for their creation. Regions are not fixed forever. Their conceptualization, identification, and bounding reflect changing concerns and changing perceptions of people.

Continental Landmasses Continental landmasses have, traditionally, been the largest subdivisions and most generalized regions of the earth. In any organized study of geography, or even history, the continents are common subdivisions, such as course units at the college level.

Physical Regions Most commonly these are based on rainfall, climate, landform, vegetation, soil or all of these. Although the data are measures of physical variables, the choice of significant or bounding data is a human decision.

Economic Regions Economic regions concern human activities, systems, and structures. Economic regions may focus on any economic activity with spatial distribution. Thus we could devise regions such as corn belts or manufacturing regions. On a world scale, the level of development, industrialization, or technological level could be used to identify gross regions. Many besides geographers, as an example, discuss the developed world and the developing world.

Cultural-Historical Regions The "New World" is a good example of a cultural-historical region that is accepted by scholars of the social sciences and humanities. Other cultural and historical regions would include the Roman Empire and the Islamic world.

Political Regions Political regions are sharply defined as they almost invariably correspond to international boundaries. Political regions at the most generalized world scale would include such concepts as the Communist world and the non-Communist world, although this book will emphasize the internal varieties and tensions of the supposedly monolithic "Communist world."

Development Regions Development regions may be more useful than gross political regions such as the Communist world. These development regions may focus on population density, income levels, energy consumption per capita, or proportions of the population urbanized, in addition to the economic-technological measures mentioned above.

The Significance of National Boundaries in a Scheme of Regionalization There was a time when school children's first, and perhaps only, experience with geography focused on a world map showing national boundaries, rivers, major cities, capitals, and little else. Mastery of geography was accepted as memorization of states and their capitals, perhaps augmented by lists of longest rivers and highest mountains. Clearly this very limited definition of geography has long since been surpassed. However, the overly simplistic earlier emphasis on national states and boundaries should not be allowed to taint contemporary recognition of their importance. Naitonal boundaries are a vitally important factor throughout the world, primarily in economic development, standard of living, equality of opportunities, and, frequently, cultural factors such as race, language, and religion. Political boundaries can be far more significant than physical factors in resulting cultural landscape and development levels. Anyone who has crossed the U.S.-Mexican border, Dominican-Haitian border, or Soviet-Chinese border would agree. Whether one lives in Corpus Christi, Texas, or Monterrey, Mexico, can have a far greater significance than whether one lives in Anchorage or Boston, or Mexico City or Vera Cruz. Because national states *are* regions, in the economic and cultural senses as well as the political sense, national boundaries will be used as portions of interregional boundaries even though political factors are not the sole criterion for establishing the regions themselves.

Ethnocentrism in Regional Designations The cultural background, experiences, and values of people enter into their regionalization schemes. A kind of "cultural lens," described by cultural geographer George Carter[1] tints one's view of the world. Different people, from different cultures or even different time periods in the same culture, would perceive the landscape differently and establish regionalizations on different criteria. Their available technologies would have resulted in widely varying identifications of what was important. Even the names given to regions reflect both the "cultural lens" and *ethnocentrism,* the tendency to view the world from one's personal viewpoint and geographic location.

[1] George Carter, *Man and the Land,* 3rd ed. (New York: Holt, Rinehart & Winston, 1975).

PHYSICAL LANDSCAPE DYNAMICS

Changes in the cultural landscape are the more obvious because they commonly happen within brief time periods, well within a single human's lifetime, even within days or weeks. Yet, change is universal and ongoing in the physical landscape, too, if sometimes on a much slower timetable. Details of the physical world change quickly enough to be casually noticed by people—sandbars in rivers appear and disappear, coastal erosion destroys houses, and earthquakes may be accompanied by sudden shifts in the land itself. Less immediately obvious to nonspecialists is that even very large-scale changes are occurring, if at imperceptible rates of speed in the context of a lifespan. The "eternal hills" are anything but, and the mightiest mountains will be worn down. The continents themselves move, changing their relationships with one another and even their shapes and masses, however slowly. The great Sahara once had a humid climate; tropical forests flourished, eons ago, in Antarctica and Alaska. While the tempo of these enormous changes is so slow that we cannot witness significant changes in a lifetime, the changes are none the less measurable. More important, the *results* of drifting continents, erosion and deposition, and temperature and precipitation variables across the planet are an important part of the total environment, physical and cultural, in which we live. The familiar assumption that the physical landscape is inert, changing only in superficial details is simply untrue when viewed in long-term perspective.

TECTONIC PLATE THEORY

The complexity of the earth's topography results from the contact of large, rigid rock plates. The crust of the earth (the brittle, outermost layer) and the upper mantle that underlies it form a zone called the lithosphere or zone of rock. It is composed of a series of plates about 60 miles (100 kilometers) thick. These plates move over the surface of the earth. Some are ocean bottom, while others carry continents above them. Where these plates collide, there is much deformation of the crust through folding and faulting, as one plate tends to buckle and slide under the other. Earthquakes and volcanic eruptions accompany these collisions and the splitting apart of some plates. (See Figure 1–7.)

The plates are set in motion by convection cells within the earth. Enormously hot molten material rises towards the surface much as hot water rises in a boiling pot. As it rises, cooling takes place; and when the temperature ap-

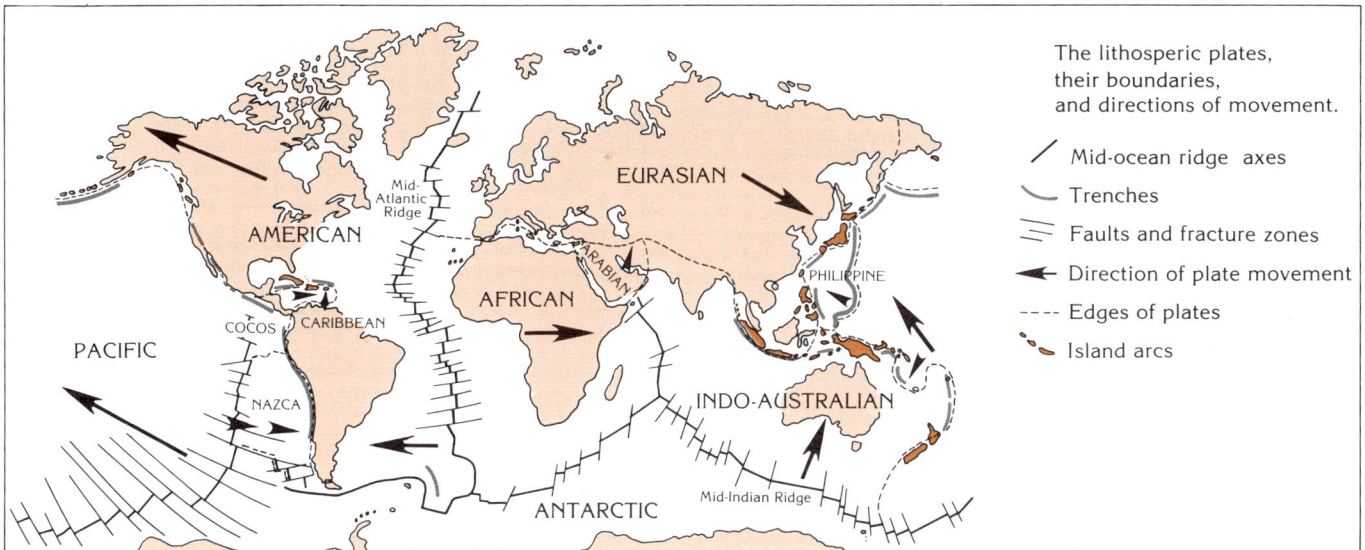

FIGURE 1–7

Tectonic Plate Theory. The earth's solid crust and upper mantle are not a uniform shell but rather a series of rigid plates that are in measurable, if imperceptibly slow, motion. These plates, perhaps originating in great fissures in ocean beds, collide with one another, with one tending to ride over a foundering one. The deformation of crustal materials results in mountain-building, accompanied by earthquakes and volcanoes as molten material moves surface-ward along cracks or zones of weakness.

proximates that of surrounding material, the cooling mass moves laterally and then sinks (much as colder water sinks). The movement of these giant convection cells carries plates with it.

Tectonic processes (mountain-building, elevation-causing), it is theorized, are all caused by such plate movement. Most agree that one large continent once existed and has since broken up. Vulcanism is associated with the movements of, and stresses within, **tectonic plates** as volcanoes occur most likely where rifts and cracks in the crust allow molten material to break through to the surface. We can theorize the number and location of plates by mapping activity like earthquakes and vulcanism.

EROSION AND DEPOSITION

Opposed to tectonic processes, which are constructional forces creating relief differences on the surface, are a set of abrading and smoothing forces, which are attempting to gradually level and obliterate relief differences. These forces of reduction and transport of materials are weathering and erosion. *Weathering* refers to the in-place disintegration of earth materials, while *erosion* means the movement of these disintegrated materials through the agencies of gravity, running water, moving ice, wind, or ocean currents. Erosion eventually results in *deposition,* the creation of new physical features through the (gener-

Soil Sampling, Jamaica. A necessary early step in planning economic development is a scientific inventory of resources available. These Jamaican government workers are making a soil survey. (Courtesy of United Nations)

ally selective) deposit of erosion-transported materials. Landforms associated with weathering, erosion, and deposition are seldom as spectacular as the grand-scale forms that can result from vulcanism (movement of molten material into the crust and to the surface) and diastrophism (crustal movement of solid materials). However, depositional landforms such as river deltas and barrier beaches can be of great size and the residual (left behind after erosion) landforms of erosion, such as the ice-sharpened peaks of the Rockies, can be quite dramatic.

The importance of these concepts to a study of world regional geography is that virtually any sizeable area of the world will include representative landforms of the varied and continuing interactions of tectonic and weathering-erosional-depositional forces. People and societies are sensitive to, and make careful evaluations of, the problems and potentials of the physical landscape. Individually and collectively, people are also modifiers and shapers of the physical landscape, frequently accelerating erosion and otherwise participating in, at least on a minor scale, natural physical processes.

CONTINENTAL GLACIATION

By far the most dramatic agent of erosion and deposition—capable of literally stripping a land surface to bare bedrock and gouging out huge chunks of that as well—is a glacier or moving sheet of ice. Glaciers are capable of transporting a wide range of particle sizes, from finely ground "rock flour" to boulders the size of a small house. Since we can observe the actions and effects of many relatively small glaciers in high mountains, it is possible to interpret evidence in the landscapes of North America, Europe, and Siberia of mammoth, continental-scale glaciers that operated in the recent geological past (within the past 2 to 3 million years). The positive and negative consequences of continental glaciation for the areas directly affected are significant and are discussed in the appropriate regions. (See Figure 1–8.)

CLIMATES

People's favorite climates (the long-term annual averages and seasonality of temperature and precipitation) are reflected in travel posters of palm-tree-lined beaches—we have a strong preference for tropical, moist climates such as those of the South Pacific or the Caribbean. It is not

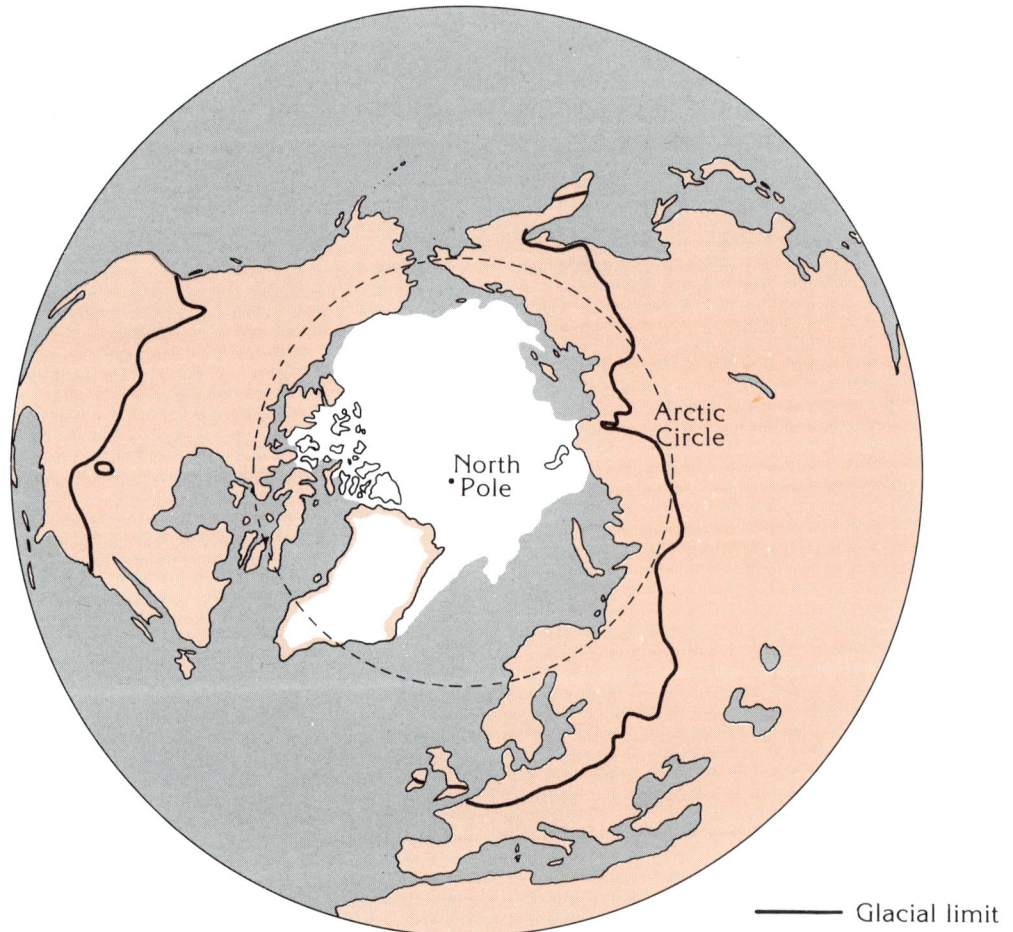

FIGURE 1–8
Northern Hemisphere Pleistocene Glaciers (Generalized). While the cultural factors in the landscape are obviously dynamic, the physical world is not unchanging. Within the most recent geologic era, the Pleistocene, the last 1 to 2 million years, climatic changes produced immense ice sheets in the area around the Arctic basin; the erosional and depositional features left by the glaciers are still prominent in the lands directly and indirectly affected.

——— Glacial limit

coincidence that the human race probably originated in the tropics. People have long since spread into a wide variety of combinations of temperature and precipitation *regimes* (the characteristic annual rhythms of distribution of these two climatic variables) by using cultural adaptations to minimize the discomforts and problems to human survival present in less ideal climates. As climate is one of the most important variables in the physical environment and is best understood in the context of broad, general patterns across the planet, these generalized patterns are presented here, with a more detailed discussion in each regional chapter.

Earth-Sun Relations and Temperature Variations   The nature of the relationship of the earth to the sun is the fundamental control on climate. Temperature variations at the surface are strongly related, as both cause and effect, to the atmospheric pressure and wind systems and, through them, to precipitation patterns. The more concentrated, more directly overhead rays of the sun (see Figure 1–9) deliver more incoming solar energy per areal unit in the tropics than the more oblique rays delivering energy to the higher latitudes, both north and south of the tropics. This produces an equator-straddling belt of "heat-surplus," where the heating effects of the incoming solar rays outweigh outgoing heat radiation. Flanking this central heat energy surplus belt are two areas of net heat loss, the high latitude polar and subpolar zones. If the earth's atmosphere and oceans did not function as temperature equalizers by continuously transferring heat poleward and cold equatorward, the tropics would be even hotter, and the

polar-subpolar regions even colder than they are now. Just as heat energy can be moved vertically and horizontally within the world ocean (the interconnected oceans and seas), heat energy is transferred vertically and horizontally through the earth's envelope of relatively dense atmosphere, the troposphere. Air near the relatively hot surface of the equatorial region has a strong tendency to rise vertically, while air near the cold surfaces of the polar regions has the *least* tendency to be heated, to expand, and to rise. In general, there are huge convection cells developed within the troposphere associated with temperature variations on the surface. (See Figure 1–10.) The equatorial low pressure, or intertropical convergence, is an updraft of cooling, rising air that recycles down to the surface in the vicinity of 30 degrees N and S, where it produces subtropical high pressures. Air moving parallel to the surface either heads equatorward to complete the convection cell or moves toward the poles, where this relatively warm air collides with the cooler air of the subpolar regions, forming a subpolar low pressure. This contact zone of air masses of sharply different temperature characteristics produces low-pressure cells or cyclonic storms.

Precipitation Variations and the Hydrologic Cycle   Low atmospheric pressures, with their rising, cooling air currents, commonly produce precipitation, as moisture condenses into clouds when an air mass is cooled. High pressures, with their tendency to descending, stagnant or warming air seldom induce condensation and thus produce dry surface conditions. (See Figure 1–10.) There are two general areas of heavier precipitation in each (north-

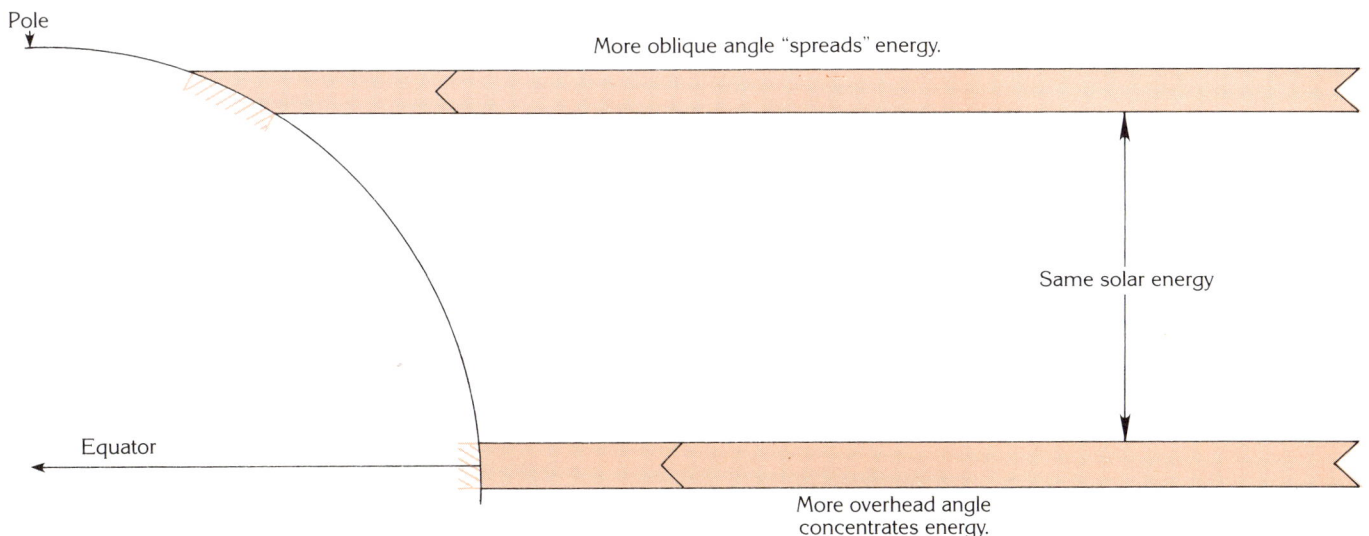

FIGURE 1–9
Concentration of Solar Energy. A fundamental climate control is the variable concentration of incoming solar energy at the Earth's surface. The higher the angle (the more nearly perpendicular or directly overhead), the more concentrated the incoming light energy.

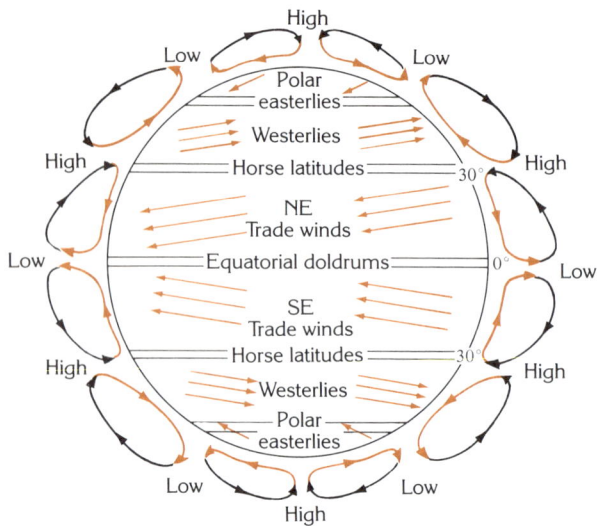

FIGURE 1–10
World Atmospheric Circulation, Generalized. Although the differential heating and cooling rates of land and water surfaces can interrupt or reinforce these generalized circulation patterns, there is a predictable sequence of pressure and wind systems related to variations in sun angle and to temperature-induced high and low pressures and subsequent air circulation.

ern and southern) hemisphere: the equatorial zone and the subpolar zone. There are also two general areas of lower precipitation in each hemisphere, at the subtropical highs and polar highs.

Water, the absolute essential to humans (and every other form of life), is in motion from atmosphere to surface (land or water) and back to the atmosphere in an endless cycle called the hydrologic cycle (see Figure 1–11). The condensation of water vapor into tiny droplets of water or crystals of ice, their precipitation as liquid or solid to the surface, and the eventual evaporation of water

(or sublimation of ice) back into gas form in the atmosphere is one of the great energy recyclers or systems on the planet as heat energy is absorbed in evaporation or sublimation and released in condensation. The hydrologic cycle also powers agents of erosion and deposition and provides a major source of potential energy through hydro power development.

Generalized World Climate Patterns Latitude and associated atmospheric circulation patterns are basic climate controls, but certainly not the only ones. The different heating and cooling rates of land and water surfaces, the blocking and channelling effects of mountain ranges, ocean currents, onshore and offshore winds, and the seasonal shifts in latitudinal pressure and wind systems, following the migration of the overhead rays of the sun as they oscillate between the Tropics of Cancer and Capricorn, all have significant impact as well. The emphasis in a world regional geography, however, must be more on the results than the physical processes themselves. The world climates map, Figure B, shows the highly generalized results of temperature and precipitation regimes.

CULTURAL LANDSCAPE DYNAMICS

A world regional geography is, at least in part, also a geography of world crises. The world energy crisis, world food crisis, and population time bomb are a few of the alarming phrases with which all are familiar. Each of these crises has a spatial or geographic aspect, and each is

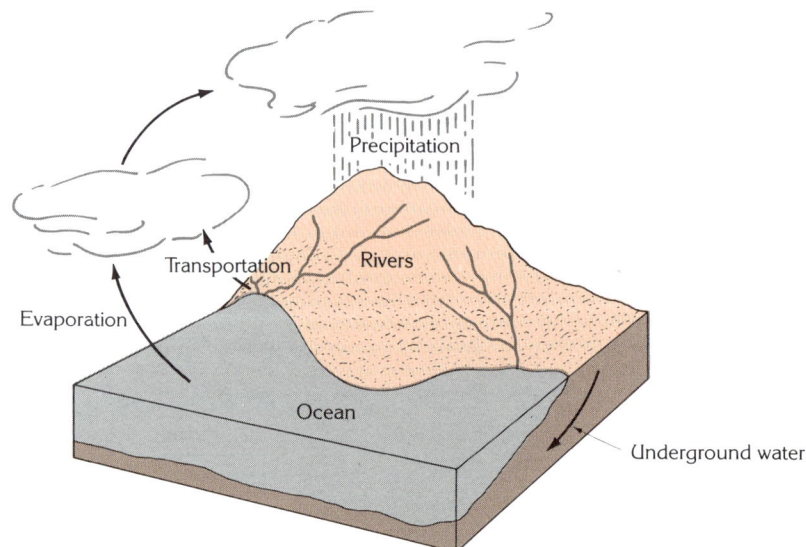

FIGURE 1–11
Hydrologic Cycle. The hydrologic cycle describes the constant movement of water as vapor or as liquid or solid, through the atmosphere, precipitated to the surface, entering drainage networks or ground water, eventually being evaporated into the atmosphere and recycling again.

related to population and the relationships of population to resources, technology, and economic systems. How well people live on various parts of this planet is closely related to the current *ratio* of population to resource base, the *rate of growth* of population (and thus the changing ratio of people and resources), and the *available technology level* for making use of the range of resources. Also, it must be remembered that systems of government, education, and family organization can be "resources" too. The basic resource of any nation is its people—their energies, talents, and motivation are absolutely essential to take full advantage of any other resources. A nation able to devise political and social systems that liberate and enhance its citizens' talents will achieve the one absolutely vital resource.

Progress toward a modern industrial society depends on the technological level and the economic system. In addition, some fundamental relationships among land value, accessibility to market, and spacing of urban services settlements have cross-cultural applications and are also factors that must be examined.

Most of these factors are dynamic, that is, change is not only possible, but probable and ongoing. For example, the quantity and variety of the known natural resource base changes over time. Technological advances continually redefine "resources" as these are just naturally available materials for which people have use and which can be extracted, processed, and marketed economically. The oil and gas under northwest Europe's North Sea was *not* a resource until undersea drilling technology and high prices for these products combined to make exploitation possible and profitable. More efficient mining techniques and machinery have combined with higher prices to redefine what is considered a copper ore. "Ore" now includes rock materials with as little as 1 percent copper content; a generation ago, this would not have qualified as an "ore." The natural resource "inventory" of any state or region is thus not fixed, but variable and expandable through technological advances. Also, it is most probable that new mineral resources will continue to be found, especially in remote and developing areas such as the Arctic, the Amazon Basin, and tropical Africa. The level of technology available is another variable as nations or even subregions of nations can be categorized as technology innovators (and thus exchangers) or technology deficient (and thus recipients).

INNOVATION AND DIFFUSION

The geographic aspect of the processes by which ideas and technology spread across space and time is called **diffusion.** It is possible, of course, and it has happened, that the same idea or invention occurs more or less simultaneously at two or more separate locations. The basic principles of photography, for example, seem to have been conceived at about the same time in France, England, and the United States. In most cases, however, an invention or **innovation** (the development of a new concept, process, technology, or a significant modification or elaboration of an older idea or piece of technology) occurs *once,* at a particular time and place. Its outward spread, or diffusion, to other people in other places may be mapped; it is a geographic phenomenon. Thus, we can follow the outward flows of innovations from their sources to their

Hand Tractor, Los Banos, Philippines. These Filipine farmers are attaching tillers to a hand tractor. Modernization of agriculture and improvement of yields can upgrade diets in developing countries while reducing expenditures of scarce foreign exchange on food imports. (Courtesy of United Nations)

recipients and adapters. Characteristically, however, the innovation does not necessarily spread outward or diffuse *evenly* from its center in relation to distance alone. Rarely would a pattern of diffusion resemble a series of expanding concentric circles as with dropping a rock in a pool of water (see Figure 1–13). The barriers to diffusion can be physical or cultural (or both). A great desert, a vast ocean, or some other physical feature that serves to eliminate or minimize contacts, as between peoples with primitive transport and communications technology, would be a physical barrier to diffusion, if only temporary. A people neighboring the *hearth* or center of innovation may simply refuse to accept and/or transmit the innovation. In that case they may also deny its availability, again at least temporarily, to other peoples on the distant side of them from the source. This rejecting group would function as a cultural barrier to diffusion. The study of innovation and diffusion is an important part of the study of *changing interactions* among (and within) the world's regions.

POPULATION DENSITY AND CHARACTERISTICS

The variable that is changing fastest in large areas of the earth is population. The world maps of populations distri-

bution and growth rates (see Figures E and F) portray this dynamic nature of the world's human population.

The Prevalence of People The popular term, "population explosion" refers to the recent spectacular change in the rate of growth of the human population. A chart of world population (Figure 1–13) shows a long period of relatively slow growth up until about 1500 A.D. The change in human numbers for the whole world is of course the result of the relationship of two vital rates—birth and deaths, usually expressed per 1,000 population per year. Net migration must also be considered in any one part of the world. Growth depends on a surplus of births (additions) over deaths (subtractions). If, within a population in a year, a million people were born (added), and a million people died (were subtracted), and net migration was zero, the net difference, or growth, would be zero. Historically, births have barely "replaced" deaths for the world as a whole, with a resulting low increase rate. As will be noted below in the **demographic transition,** low rates of growth reflect only the relationship between birth, death, and net migration rates, not any particular vital rate. Humans have proven highly adaptable to the range of climates, soils, vegetation types, and landforms over the earth. While population density varies from very heavy urban concentrations of up to 100,000 per square mile (39,000 per square kilometer) to less than 1 per square mile (less than 0.4 per

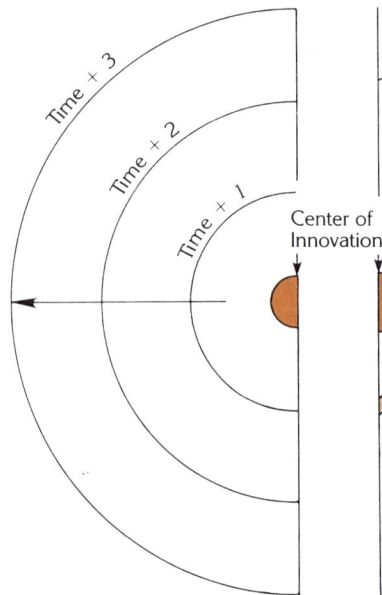
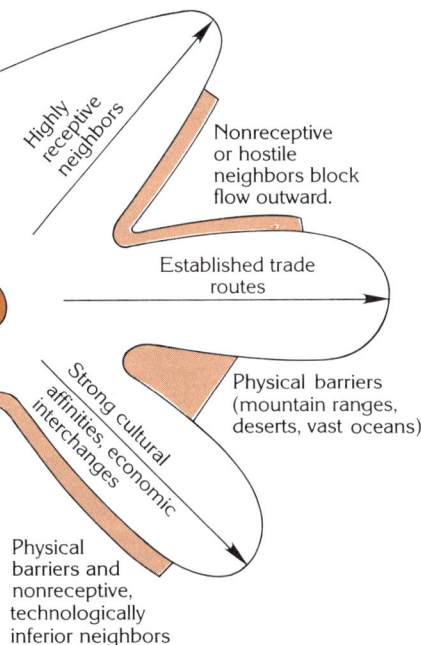

FIGURE 1–12

Diffusion. The spread of a new idea, technique, or piece of technology seldom occurs in a simple relationship of distance and time. Diffusion may be retarded, or prevented, by cultural as well as physical barriers.

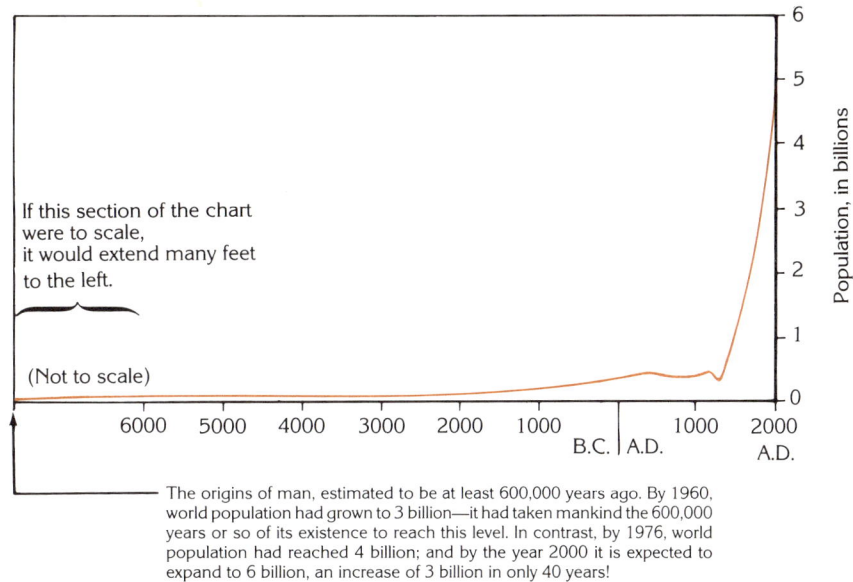

If this section of the chart were to scale, it would extend many feet to the left.

(Not to scale)

The origins of man, estimated to be at least 600,000 years ago. By 1960, world population had grown to 3 billion—it had taken mankind the 600,000 years or so of its existence to reach this level. In contrast, by 1976, world population had reached 4 billion; and by the year 2000 it is expected to expand to 6 billion, an increase of 3 billion in only 40 years!

Life Expectancy at Birth over the Ages

Prehistoric Times	18 years
Roman Empire	25 years
Medieval England	35 years
New England, 1789	38 years
U.S.A., 1900	49 years
U.S.A., 1950	74 years
U.S.A., 1977	77 years

FIGURE 1–13
Population Growth Over Time.
The human population has grown, for most of its existence, erratically slowly; only in the past few centuries has the growth rate accellerated, creating the phenomenon popularly termed the *Population Explosion.*

square kilometer) in parts of the Arctic and desert "frontiers," some people are found as permanent residents everywhere except Antarctica, most of Greenland, and the Arctic archipelagoes. Population, its *relative density* and growth rates, and reasons for those growth rates, form one basis for analyzing regional differences.

Characteristics of Population Characteristics of populations, in addition to density and growth rates, include their age and sex compositions. A commonly used chart showing age and sex components of a population is called a "population pyramid" (see Figure 1–14) because it typically resembles a pyramid. In a typical population as shown, approximately equal numbers of males and females are born each year (slightly more males than females). Attrition in the form of disease and accident gradually reduces the number of people in older age groupings or *cohorts;* males generally have a higher death rate, especially in late maturity, so that the female side of each cohort surviving becomes larger than the male. Significant variations from this average "pyramid" can present special problems to a population. The high birthrates and

falling death rates of most developing nation's populations can produce a broader based age-sex profile with very large numbers of young and dependent people and relatively few elderly. Such a population will have to spend a disproportionate share of national income on education and on creating jobs fast enough to absorb large numbers of new arrivals in job markets. On the other hand, a mature industrial state will have an almost rectangularly-shaped chart, reflecting low birthrates and low death rates. A birthrate lower than the death rate, unless balanced by in-migration, could threaten the future of a nation. In-migration of a different ethnic or national group would of course result in sweeping cultural changes in a very low birthrate situation. Some states such as West Germany and Poland are actively trying to *increase* their birthrates in order to maintain stable numbers of their own nationals. There are many types of "population problems," just as the concept of "overpopulation" is a highly subjective one, not limited to the developing world.

A high proportion of dependent elderly will result from long life expectancies, with a smaller proportion of economically active population to support the retired cohorts.

Medical costs will be disproportionately high. Normal age and sex ratios can be affected by war, high migration rates due to economic problems or opportunities, or inadequate medical care. For example, East Germany has a distorted "pyramid" because females greatly outnumber males in the age cohorts that were of military service age during World War II. Because males tend to migrate out in search of jobs from such countries as Greece and Portugal, young adult cohorts there show a predominance of females left at home. In societies where primitive sanitation and health care result in high numbers of deaths in childbirth, young adult males may outnumber young adult females. These various characteristics of population can be just as significant as total numbers or density in geographic studies.

Population and Resource Pressures   Population and resource pressures have been major topics of study for centuries. The almost infinite capacity of populations to expand, compared with the much slower "expansion" of the resource base through technological-economic redefinition of resources, has attracted pessimistic attention at least since 1798. In that year, the publication of Thomas Malthus's *Essay on Population* labeled as *Malthusian* the view that populations tend to increase faster than the means of supporting those populations, leading to disaster. Malthus predicted such disasters based on his estimate that a population could double in approximately twenty-five years. Unchecked population growth would lead to famine, which would reduce the population, which would then begin to grow again until the next famine. The Marxist counterview will be examined in Chapter 7. Malthus's dire predictions for Britain never materialized; as agricultural productivity increased, industrialization provided more jobs (which produced products for export to pay for imported food), and heavy out-migration commenced to North America and Oceania. Neo-Malthusians contend that his point was valid, and assert that his timetable for disaster luckily has been delayed, unfortunately not cancelled.

Many countries of the developing world are in a vital race between expanding population and expanding food supply and general resource base. The demographic transition, to be described in this chapter, depicts the relationship between industrialization-modernization and population increase. It offers some hope, based on historical trends, that world average population growth rates will continue to gradually drop.

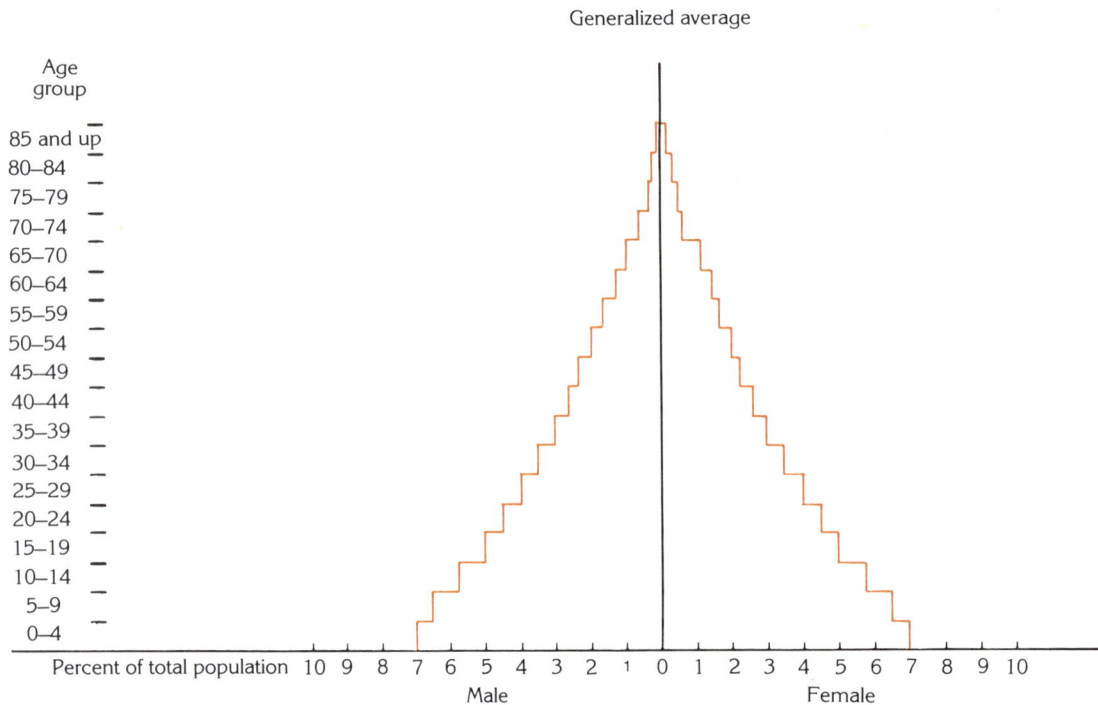

FIGURE 1–14

Population Pyramid. The characteristic "pyramid" shape of a chart showing the age and sex character of a population reflects the normal, or average sex balance and attrition of successively older population cohorts or age groups. Many developing countries have a broad base, indicating a high proportion of youth, while industrialized nations tend toward more nearly vertical sides.

Population as a Resource Without unduly minimizing the unfortunate, even catastrophic implications of unchecked population expansion, it must be remembered that human population is the ultimate resource to any society or area. While the threats of overpopulation are a clear and imminent danger in some areas, any other resource is useless without human enterprise, effort, and consumption. While many developing nations, particularly those of Latin America, Southeast Asia, and Africa south of the Sahara, are deeply concerned about the future implications of rapid population growth, others, including the Germanies and the Norden states (Scandinavia, Finland, and Iceland) are just as concerned about birthrates *below* "zero population growth" (in zero population growth, births just "replace" deaths).

The vigor, innovation and productivity of its human population is the most valuable resource of any state. People, not minerals, are the key to economic development. Resource-rich Zaire has a per capita income of $210, whereas resource-poor Japan has one of the highest average incomes in the world, $7,330.

QUESTIONS OF DEVELOPMENT

The importance and worldwide significance of regional variations in development levels is so great that some aspects of economic development must be considered in advance of progressing through the world's regions. Once the general structure of industrialization and related changes in the human populations characteristics are understood, each region and subregion can be comprehended in developmental terms.

People generally perceive rising standards of living and quality of life as the end products of economic development. Certainly, everyone has a personal interest in income levels, longevity, and less measurable aspects of quality of life. A critical and dominant aspect of development is the stage of industrialization that a region is in currently. There is not an absolute relationship between level of industrialization and standard of living. Some preindustrial but resource-rich areas enjoy high living standards; individual poverty in wealthy industrial nations unfortunately is common. But in general terms, highly industrialized countries have higher average standards of living than do preindustrial ones. There seems to be a close relationship between growth characteristics of the population and the stage or level of industrialization within a particular part of the world. In the early phases of industrialization, for example, the death rate of the population begins to decrease. In the later phases of industrial development, the birthrate declines. Two fundamental geo-

graphic patterns—the level of economic development or industrialization and the growth rates of the human population—are thus considered before the determination of world regions.

Resources, Technology, and Industrialization Industrialization of any area is a process. It is not instantaneous, but rather happens over a varying time span. Industrialization appears to have an internal sequence of development that persists independently of regional, cultural, political, or other variables. The best-known, succinct statement of the sequence of industrialization is that of American economic historian Walt Rostow.[2] The geographical relationships among industrial development and natural resources, population characteristics, or any other geographic variables are best understood with references to Rostow's discussion.

In Rostow's interpretation of the history of industrial states, there is no significant difference from one culture to another. Even capitalism and communism appear to make little difference in either the sequence or its outcome. Once industrialization is under way cultural variables seem to be of limited importance; equally important is the fact that physical geographic variables (like natural resource base) have no clear relationship to industrialization, at least in a cause-and-effect sense.

Social, economic, and political conditions *are* critical to the beginning phase of industrialization. The right economic-political-social "climate" must precede industrial development. In traditional societies, political power and wealth are concentrated in the hands of a landed aristocracy. Land is the source of food and of the raw materials for clothes and crafts; land is thus the key to wealth and power. Land ownership confers prestige as well as income. The predominantly farming economy produces very little surplus; what surplus exists is concentrated in the hands of the few at the top. They tend to spend this wealth on luxuries and palaces rather than investing it in expanding the economy. Beyond a point, there is little interest in maximizing income; few aristocrats apply much effort to increasing productivity. Such concerns are not proper to their social rank. Should the work force work harder and produce more, the results will be another palace, not reinvestment in expansion of new enterprises. Rostow emphasized that a high rate of savings, of reinvestment in the economy, is an absolute necessity for an economy to **takeoff** towards a modern industrial state. Clearly, if the aristocracy does not reinvest in expansion and new economic activity, its power must be destroyed or severely

---

[2]Walt Rostow, *Stages of Economic Growth* (Cambridge: Cambridge University Press, 1960).

restricted if the economy is to move forward. Not all industrial states have first had an upheaval on the scale of the Russian Revolution, but all have limited the power of feudal aristrocracies. Following this revolution or evolutionary change in society, the country must have political stability. A high rate of reinvestment is likely only when the decision to postpone consumption, or enjoyment, of the surplus in favor of reinvestment is a logical one. Reinvestment postpones enjoyment and consumption, but its *attraction* is that an expanding enterprise will eventually generate still larger surpluses for enjoyment in the future. If one cannot reasonably expect to eventually collect the fruits of reinvestment, there is little incentive to make that reinvestment.

During the preconditions for the takeoff, government policy must favor the expansion of the economy through tax, tariff, labor, and regulatory policies. The critical stage, the take-off, follows establishment of the preconditions. The sluggishly expanding agricultural economy is replaced by a rapid growth of industrial and transportation facilities and output. Economic growth is not only desirable; it is accepted as normal. Reinvestment takes place at a high rate, fueling this rapid growth. The takeoff may be at first limited to one or two industries. Textiles factories are a common beginning. Later, all sectors of the economy—agriculture, mining, construction, transportation, and communications along with manufacturing—expand and modernize. Practical science and technology are thus applied, with inanimate power and machines, throughout the entire economy in the "drive-to-maturity" stage.

The concluding stage of the sequence is that of "high mass consumption." The mature industrial plant of the country no longer requires the very high rates of reinvestment that characterized the drive to maturity. A smaller portion of a larger gross product is sufficient reinvestment. A large consumable surplus can now be used to raise standards of living. Some nations may choose to spend some of this new surplus in building military forces. This military machine is then used to redress old grievances, seek international prestige, or acquire territories or economic spheres of influence. Some societies will choose to spend some surplus in funding social welfare programs—socialized education, housing, and medicine. Geographers can better understand a country's economic position, domestic policies, and also its international objectives if that country is seen in the context of the stages of development.

Industrialization and the Demographic Transition During industrialization the vital characteristics of the human population also go through a sequence of change known as the demographic transition. The demographic transition

chart (see Figure 1–15) shows the generalized relationship of birth- and death rates over time, as a population progresses from a preindustrial society through industrialization to a high technology society. Migration has *not* been included in the chart in order to simplify it. Both birth- and death rates together produce the population increase rate, again ignoring migration. If the birth- and death rates were matching, then the national increase rate would be zero. Births would exactly replace deaths. Only if the birthrate is *higher* than the death rates will our sample population increase. Obviously, there are two ways in which the surplus of births over deaths needed for a gain in population can be achieved. Either the birthrate can go up higher, *or* the death rate can drop lower. In the first stage of the demographic transition on the chart, the growth rate is relatively low because there is only a small "surplus" of births over deaths. However, in this preindustrial stage, both birth- *and* death rates are high by industrial nation standards. High death rates at this time reflect a lack of modern sanitation and medicine, a local food supply highly vulnerable to local drought or other natural hazard, and a probability of less stable government, leading to many petty wars and banditry. The smooth trend lines as generalized on the chart would be, in reality, continually fluctuating from year to year but the long-time trend would be as shown. Only high birthrates could counterbalance high death rates and ensure the continuity of the population.

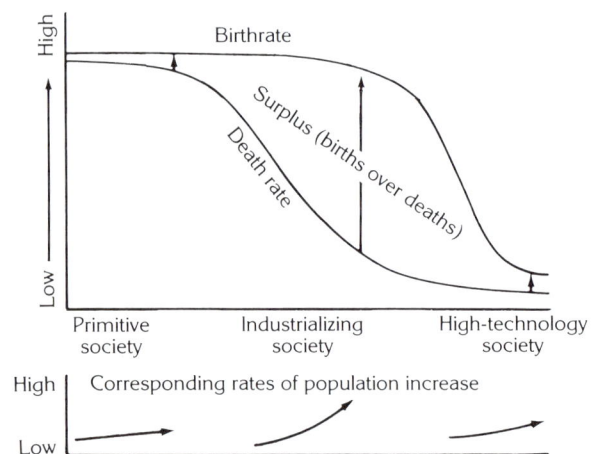

Rate of increase is the surplus of birthrate over death rate. If birthrate and death rates were exactly the same, deaths would be "replaced" by births and populations would be stable, with no rate of increase (rate of increase = 0). If death rate is reduced without a corresponding reduction of birthrate, rate of increase goes up even though birthrate does not increase.

FIGURE 1–15
The Demographic Transition. As a society moves through the process of industrialization-urbanization, both birthrates and death rates are affected by changing economic and social conditions. The demographic transition is a model of the relationships among industrialization and vital rates.

During industrialization, the death rate will begin to fall. Although the early industrial cities were notoriously unhealthy environments, their poor sanitation, poor food and housing, and inadequate medical care were slowly improved. Cheap, efficient long-distance transport of food and development of food preservation technologies improve both the quantity and quality of diet. Because industrialization, as we have seen, is most likely in a stable political situation, deaths from warfare and banditry decrease also. Medical and sanitation technology advance. The result of all of these changes is a falling death rate (see Figure 1–15). As the birthrate at first remains high, a much larger surplus of births over deaths develops. This is the critical stage in an industrializing society; the explosive growth rate is sometimes termed the **population explosion.** The western European states, which industrialized mostly during the nineteenth century, were able to send out large members of migrants to the New World, Oceania, and even Africa. The United States could absorb a high birthrate during industrialization together with many immigrants because it had sparsely settled frontier lands to be developed. Contemporary countries now in this first phase of industrialization do not have the option of large-scale out-migration to relieve population pressures—their plight can be serious.

During the maturation phase or "drive to industrial maturity," the birthrate begins to drop. Precisely why is open to discussion, but it *does* drop; it happens in societies of different religious beliefs, different races, and in different parts of the world. It seems to be related to the urbanization of the population. Children may be viewed as economic assets in a farming society, but in an urban-industrial one, they do not become economically productive until much later. In a high-technology society like the United States, children may be economically dependent for several decades after birth. Education stretches out over more years and is correspondingly expensive. Also, there is a greater likelihood that each child born *will* survive to maturity; there is no longer such a grim race between high birthrate and high death rate so that a family survives into the next generation. Then too, many children used to guarantee support for aged parents; now this "social security" is institutionalized rather than dependent on children. Also, as more and more women join the labor force, their changing role favors later marriage and fewer children.

Thus the motivation shifts from having lots of children to having fewer. Demographers have concluded that motivation to limit the number of children is far more important than any official policies or the availability of any specific technology of birth control.

The Fruits of Industrialization   These are alluring. Those parts of the world yet to industrialize, the "developing" nations, are eager to enjoy the cornucopia of goods they see associated with industrialization. Indeed, the very word "developing" implies positive change, a dynamic process that will result in achieving a desired goal. Some of the positive benefits of industrialization are apparent in its relationship to the demographic transition—people live longer, have more and better quality food and medical care, and have more discretionary income (income on which they can make value judgments on spending, beyond taxes and basic necessities).

Family Planning Education, Aurangabad, India. This course on family planning is being presented free under the sponsorship of trade unions. Many feel that real economic progress will not occur until population growth rates are slowed in already densely populated countries. (Courtesy of United Nations/ILO)

Power and Power Politics Power was an outcome, if not always a goal, of industrialization. With industrial maturation comes the capacity to build a military machine. Different societies have different goals; a dictatorship of right or left might assign highest priority to military spending of its newly found surplus, and thus industrial maturation of any one country can rejuggle international relations and create new tensions.

The Threat to the Environment The conservation movement of the 1880's in America is a direct ancestor of the "earth day" movements of the late 1960's, and there are ample examples, both historical and contemporary, of preindustrial societies experiencing the negative effects of their impact on the environment. The ancient Greeks poetically observed that "the bare bones (bedrock) of Attica's hills show through as the rains wash away the flesh (soil)," and contemporary Haiti exemplifies the power of a preindustrial, dense farming population to degrade the environment.

Obviously, a society equipped with bulldozers, power shovels, diesel tractors, petrochemical plants, and nuclear-generating facilities can effect drastic change faster than a comparable number of hunters and gatherers, but environmental degradation essentially is a worldwide problem.

LAND-USE DYNAMICS

Some items of the cultural landscape, such as agricultural land-use patterns and the spacing of urban places functioning as service centers for farm population, may be examined in terms of theoretical assumptions about location, transport cost, land value, and land use. Such basic factors as the need for convenient service centers, the higher value of the most accessible land, and perishability of some items may be considered universals or cross-cultural factors. They will be considered in Brazil as well as in Nigeria; they are important in communist and capitalist societies alike, and value, competition, and profit are human concerns in any language.

The von Thünen Theory More than 150 years ago, J. H. von Thünen studied the interactions of transport cost, land value, and land use by theorizing an "isolated state" featuring a large town in the center of a uniformly productive plain. Only horse and wagon transportation was then available; more modern modes of transport would have an effect similar to that of adding a navigable river in von Thünen's modification of his "featureless plain" (see Figure 1–16). In his featureless plain concept, von Thünen held constant the normal variables of land fertility and transport mode so that distance from the market town became the simple determinant of land value. Assuming that all of the town's hinterland population would like to locate as conveniently close to market as possible, the successful bidders for close-in locations will be either those with high profit potentials or those who cannot function further away (whose products were highly perishable or had a very high transport cost). (See Figure 1–16.) In

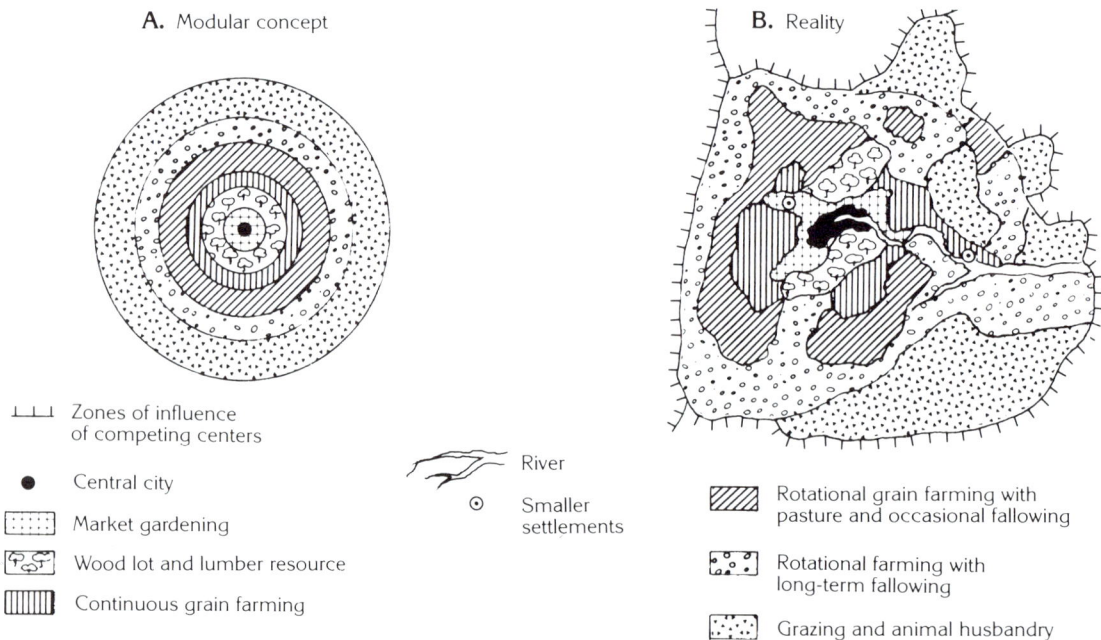

A. Modular concept

B. Reality

⊔⊔⊔ Zones of influence of competing centers

● Central city

Market gardening

Wood lot and lumber resource

Continuous grain farming

River

⊙ Smaller settlements

Rotational grain farming with pasture and occasional fallowing

Rotational farming with long-term fallowing

Grazing and animal husbandry

FIGURE 1–16
The von Thünen Theory. Nineteenth century German economist J. H. von Thünen devised this model of the theoretical relationships among accessibility to market, land value, and land use. His basic assumptions on resulting land use still have validity, if details of his model have been altered by technology.

its details of relative distance outward from the market, von Thünen's theory becomes less appropriate when applied to regions with modern food-preservation technology and efficient transport, but his basic idea is useful to understanding agricultural land use and to comprehending various urban functional zone theories.

The Christaller Hypothesis   Half a century ago, German geographer Walter Christaller advanced the Central Place Theory to establish the theoretical spacing of service centers in a "featureless agricultural plain" much like von Thünen's. Christaller reasoned that, while every farm family might wish for the conveniences of an adjacent service center, not all could enjoy such convenience. There would be a minimum of customers necessary to support such a center, and a maximum distance that people would be willing to travel to patronize these services. In his initial study area in southern Germany, Christaller discovered that the smallest service centers, ("lowest order centers" in Figure 1–17), were about two hours travel time, in walking or horse travel speed, apart. (In southern Germany, as in any part of the world densely settled before modern transport modes were available, the spacing of towns will reflect the slower transport of the past). These smallest centers thus had a roughly circular hinterland with a radius of about 2.2 miles (3.5 kilometers), the distance one could walk in one hour. The trade center itself was termed a **central place.** Because circular hinterlands would overlap

or leave unserved gaps, Christaller further theorized hexagonal hinterlands. Not all central places are small, limited-function "lowest order centers" offering only a limited range of basic goods and services. Larger towns, spaced further apart from other comparably large centers in a hierarchy of central places, perform a wider range of service functions, from more specialized through to the range offered by the lowest order centers. The trade hinterlands of these larger centers occupy several spatial levels. For the most common services or merchandise, customers will travel only as far as they have to, to the nearest center of any level in the hierarchy. For more specialized goods and services, purchased less frequently, people are willing to travel further and thus the hinterland for those more specialized offerings is larger, and the higher order centers correspondingly further apart.

Advocates of both von Thünen's and Christaller's theories do not pretend, of course, that the earth really has evenly distributed farm populations on uniformly productive featureless plains served by an intricate network of a hierarchy of central places at precise geometric relationships to one another. When reality does *not* match the theoretical prediction (it almost never matches precisely), then we recognize that it *is* different, and we can then investigate the geographical reasons for this discrepancy. When the real world approaches the theoretical "featureless plain," as in portions of the American Midwest, then the theoretical pattern of the spacing of urban settlements comes close to reality also. Most large urban centers have multiple functions; thus, mining towns, resorts, naval bases, and other towns also have central place service functions and distort the regular pattern theorized by Christaller. Again, the value of these theories lies in their assistance in interpreting reality, not in predicting rigid, ideal patterns.

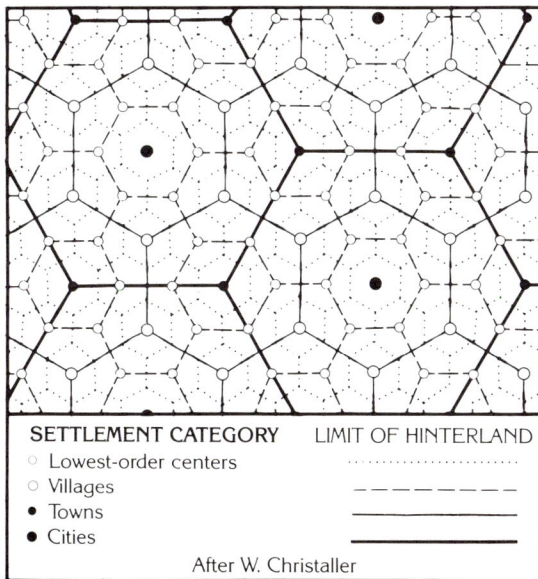

SETTLEMENT CATEGORY	LIMIT OF HINTERLAND
○ Lowest-order centers	··················
○ Villages	– – – – – –
● Towns	————
● Cities	————

After W. Christaller

FIGURE 1–17
The Christaller Hypothesis. Christaller's study of the development of urban hierarchies envisioned a series of central places, each with a distinctive set of service functions. Higher-order places perform a greater range of functions as part of an interrelated settlement network.

REGIONAL INTERDEPENDENCE

A major theme of this book will be the importance and changing nature of **regional interdependence.** Just as the regions and their subregions are experiencing more or less continual internal change, the economic, cultural, and political nature of their relationships with each other changes and, for the most part, become more important. One would have to go far back in history in most world regions to find a society or region that was truly isolated and noninterdependent for any significant time period. Certainly since the age of European exploration and colonialism, very few parts of the earth have escaped becoming part of or associated with some global system of trade, political expansion, migration, or technological inter-

Lagos, Nigeria. Rising incomes and even faster-rising expectations constitute a social revolution of sorts in those third world nations with high-value exports such as Nigeria, a major oil supplier. (Courtesy of United Nations)

change. However, regional interdependence, as opposed to interregional *contacts,* is mainly a product of modern transportation of bulk goods and rapid communications systems.

For thousands of years, there has been a diffusion of ideas without a development of true interdependence. Ancient trade patterns, related to diffusion, linked far-distant cultures. The Roman Empire had some indirect trade contacts with China, for example, and Roman coins found their way to such outposts as Iceland and Ethiopia. These limited trade contacts, specializing in luxury goods, were highly significant for diffusion of ideas but did not represent general interdependence. The societies involved would have experienced little economic dislocation if these early trade patterns had suddenly altered. As the efficiency of transport and communication developed, accompanied by proliferating specializations of regions and rapid advances of technology in general, true interdependence began to develop. Now instead of virtually every region producing all basic necessities by and for its own people, global systems of interchange provide interdependence on a grand and vital scale.

NO ONE REGION CAN BE TRULY ISOLATED AND INDEPENDENT

For countries like Belgium, Switzerland, or Japan, the connections with raw material sources around the world are so obvious and so vital that isolation would be the worst possible catastrophe; internal chaos and starvation would result from even a relatively brief period of "independence"

from their highly developed intra- and interregional contacts. If not as quickly and dramatically obvious, underdeveloped states and subregions are sensitive also to their interdependence relationships. Impoverished, preindustrial Haiti, for example, would be even poorer without access to industrial world markets for its bauxite, agricultural exports, and products of its light manufacturing plants set up largely by foreign capital. If tourism from North America were to be shut off, an important, growing source of income would be gone. Capital flows in the form of government-to-government loans and subsidies are important to Haiti's hopes of further industrialization, as are private investments and loans from the wealthier nations. Perhaps most important would be the loss of a continuing flow of technology to all sectors of the Haitian economy—pesticides; deep-well drilling machinery; satellite scans to detect plant diseases, erosion problems, and potential mineralized areas; and equipment for local hydroelectric projects, public health, and sanitation technology. The transfer of "know-how," of technology and systems, techniques and specialized knowledge, often developed at high cost in a developed country, is one of the most important interchanges among states and continents.

LONG-TERM RESOURCE SELF-SUFFICIENCY AND ITS PROBABLE UNATTAINABILITY

The complexity of high-technology societies with their elaborate varieties of goods and services, their sophisticated machines, and their elevated living standards requires an increasing quantity and variety of raw materials. In metallurgy alone, a long list of alloy "additives" alters the qualities of steel for special purposes. Modern industrial societies are unthinkable without access to chromite, tungsten, molybdenum, nickel, manganese, tin, copper, aluminum, industrial diamonds—the list of absolute necessities goes on and on. Even a highly innovative, research-oriented industrial society would be hard-pressed to maintain its industrial strength (and military power) without self-sufficiency in all the above, not to mention food and fuels. The larger, the more geologically, topographically, and climatically varied a national territory, the generally lower the degree of strategic dependence on international trade. No modern nation, though, has attained self-sufficiency in all raw materials and manufactures. Such a state of self-sufficiency, theoretically immune to interruptions in trade, is known as *autarky*. Some states such as Nazi Germany, anticipating war, which would disrupt normal trade relationships, have set autarky as an official goal, but never attained it. Contemporary South Africa, fearful of trade embargoes from nations critical of its racial policies, is trying to minimize the negative impact of such potential embargoes but recognizes that true autarky is as impossible for it as it is for its major trading partners. South African minerals are absolutely vital to other countries, diminishing the probability of a total cutoff of trade in the items South Africa must import.

REGIONAL INTERACTIONS

Even if raw-material, food, and fuel autarky could be achieved, national isolation from the interchange of ideas

and technology would shortly become counterproductive. Throughout history, the most influential, wealthiest cities and states have been those that were able to "cross fertilize" the cultures and ideas of different areas. The power and splendor of Venice from the thirteenth through sixteenth centuries were related to both its international trade and its function as a meeting ground and interchange of people, ideas, and technology from Asian, African, and European cultures. Postwar Japan exploded with new vitality after the American occupation led to large-scale adaptation of Western ideas, techniques, and industrial strategies into a receptive and innovative Japanese culture. Earlier, the Arab world had led in most spheres of learning, the arts, and technology as it absorbed ideas from Mediterranean Europe, the eastern Roman Empire, India, and Africa. The most brilliant cultures have been built as amalgams of many different cultures, ideas, and peoples. Isolation has usually meant stagnation. China is both a good historical and contemporary example of a major world culture commanding a large, varied territory and a large, industrious population falling into a period of technological stagnation. The first example of stagnation, from the mid-seventeenth to nineteenth centuries, came as a result of a chauvanistic belief that China was superior to all other cultures and should therefore stay aloof. As a result, Chinese technology, which indeed had been unsurpassed by any other in the mid-seventeenth century, had fallen so far behind that of Europe by the nineteenth century that China's existence as a state was seriously threatened. In the 1950's to 1960's period, Chinese isolation was again largely self-imposed (and reinforced by U.S. policy aimed at isolation of China) by a resurgent cultural nationalism. Once humiliated by European colonial powers, led

Oil Refinery on the Persian Gulf, Saudi Arabia. The "oil shocks," which rocked the industrial economies of the West and Japan, also had severe effects on those third world states without significant energy resources of their own. The complex interrelationships among the world's regions are dramatically illustrated by the world's oil industry. (Courtesy of United Nations/Aramco)

by Russia, Britain, and Germany in the late nineteenth century, China had once again established a strong central government in full control of most of its historic, national territory (excluding Taiwan). A rejection of any "reliance" on foreign ideas or technology was in partial reaction to the abrupt withdrawal of Soviet technicians and advisors and the isolation policies of the United States. By the late 1960's, a major internal policy dispute focused on the failure of the rigidly doctrinaire policies to modernize agriculture, industry, and natural resource exploitation. The "Nixon initiative" of 1972 was welcomed by a Chinese government in the process of turning again in favor of a mutually beneficial interaction on a larger scale.

THE REGIONAL ORGANIZATION OF THIS BOOK

Because the regional boundaries follow international boundaries and never subdivide a country into two or more regions, the world regions developed here may be considered formal regions. The *uniformity* of these world regions is almost entirely in terms of their political status as states and groups of states; their physical, economic, and cultural geographic characteristics are usually anything but homogenous. Uniformity, indeed similarity, is a *relative* status rather than an absolute one in the world regions utilized here. Many, but not all, of those subregions composed of one or more national political units are also essentially formal regions. Those subregions identified *within* some larger political units (such as Brazil, India, or Canada) that do not conform necessarily to any provincial or internal boundaries are generally functional rather than formal regions. Thus, the book's overall organization emphasizes formal regions at the most generalized level and includes both formal and functional types of regions at the subregion level.

The sequence of regions begins with the United States and Canada. This is one of the most advanced and geopolitically important cores in the world, and it contains a major population core. Middle America, that transition area economically tied to the North American core, is next, followed by South America; all these regions bear the strong historical-cultural imprint of another core, that of West Europe, the next region. East Europe, with a somewhat different cultural history and orientation to the Soviet superpower rather than western Europe's U.S. orientation, is next, followed by the major geopolitical core of the Soviet Union. The East Asian culture realm, including the only non-Western fully mature industrial economy (Japan) and the world's largest nation and a future superpower

(China), is next, followed by the densely populated, contrasting Asian culture realm of South Asia. Four less populated peripheral areas are then examined: the Southeast Asian "land between," the Western culture offshoot of Australia dominating the Oceania region, Africa south of the Sahara, and the sprawling, diverse Southwest Asia–North African region. A final chapter considers the lightly settled or nonpopulated resource frontiers—Antarctica, the Arctic, and the oceans.

The bases for regionalization has been a composite of many various possibilities. The reasons for identifying each region are almost entirely internal—that is, the unifying factors apparent in their cultural, economic, and physical, or even political, geography. The precise boundaries of regions may include both internal and external factors in their rationale. Boundaries reflect not only a degree of homogeneity within the region, but a distinctive difference outside the designated boundary. A list of major world regions and a brief explanation of their distinctive characteristics follows.

UNITED STATES AND CANADA

Most of North America is composed of only two states, the United States and Canada. These two countries share a British heritage of political and economic philosophy. In each, English is the predominant but not universal language. Each produces huge surpluses for the world grain markets with heavily mechanized agriculture. There is emphasis on high individual income, although social welfare programs are of increasing importance in both. Each country has grown through heavy migration from Europe with numerically less significant inflows from Africa and Asia. Both have highly developed, heavily urbanized economies, which feature large amounts of leisure time for its citizens when compared to the average for the world.

MIDDLE AMERICA

Middle America consists of Mexico, the Central American republics of Guatemala, Honduras, Belize, El Salvador, Nicaragua, Costa Rica, Panama, and the Caribbean islands. This region shares locational access to the North American markets, is dominated in large part by tourism economics, and includes in Mexico one of the largest, most rapidly industrializing Latin American states with a large and varied resource base. It shares a common focus on the Caribbean and Gulf of Mexico.

SOUTH AMERICA

South America includes Brazil, Argentina, Chile, Uruguay, Paraguay, Bolivia, Peru, Colombia, Venezuela, Suriname, French Guiana, Guyana, and Ecuador. This region's characteristics include Spanish-Portuguese culture and language, an early overthrow of colonial control, and, to some extent, a regionalization based on river basins. With rare exceptions, the countries of the region have modified and adapted Iberian culture to some degree.

WEST EUROPE

West Europe includes all those European countries that, while containing economies with a varying mix of capitalism and socialism, are not controlled by a Communist government: the United Kingdom, Ireland, Iceland, Norway, Sweden, Finland, Denmark, Netherlands, Belgium, Luxembourg, West Germany (Federal Republic of Germany), France, Switzerland, Austria, Spain, Portugal, Italy, and Greece. The highly industrialized areas of most of West Europe remain innovators of technology and are very active in world trade. Indo-European languages, the Greco-Roman cultural heritage, heavy reliance on trade, a past imperialism, and continuing strong aspirations to international leadership in culture and technology are common characteristics.

EAST EUROPE

East Europe, a very compact region physically, is characterized by Communist control and political and economic philosophy. East Europe is comprised of East Germany (German Democratic Republic), Poland, Czechoslovakia, Hungary, Romania, Bulgaria, Yugoslavia, and Albania. The region is dominated by the USSR in economic, political, and military affairs (although several states, notably Yugoslavia, have shown a considerable degree of independence from this Soviet domination), and was somewhat later industrialized than West Europe. This region has been described as a *shatterbelt,* a politically fragmented zone of contact between two expansionist powers or cultures. Slavic peoples predominate in the majority of states.

USSR

The Soviet Union is of continental scale and sufficiently important to make it the only world region that consists of a single country. The first and largest Communist state, it regards itself as the modern source of true Communist philosophy. The Soviets are striving to meld a unit from an area of great physical and ethnic diversity, to create "Soviet Man" from an assembly of European and Asiatic cultures. The Russians constitute slightly less than a majority among Soviet citizens in this "last of the great empires."

EAST ASIA

As in all of the regions, no country is split between different regions. Very large states may be divided into several subregions; subregions may group together several countries as do all major regions except the USSR. East Asia includes China, Japan, North and South Korea, Taiwan (Republic of China), Hong Kong, and Mongolia. The People's Republic of China (PRC) has been subdivided into three subregions. The characteristic factors are primarily cultural, reflecting the dominant role of Chinese culture and the transnational use of adaptations of the Chinese system of written communication.

Rice culture feeds much of the population, and the mountain rim of China provides a physical boundary, which coincides fairly closely with the political boundaries and the ethnic boundaries. Varieties of Buddhism and the industrial asset of plentiful, willing labor are other common factors.

SOUTH ASIA

South Asia is comprised of India, Pakistan, Bangladesh, Sri Lanka (Ceylon), and the Himalayan countries of Nepal and Bhutan. The common experience of British colonialism and the struggle for independence, a history of Moslem invasion (except Ceylon), and continuing Moslem-Hindu tensions help make this a distinctive area. The political and cultural domination of India and a tendency to political instability also mark the region.

SOUTHEAST ASIA

Southeast Asia includes the mainland states of Burma, Thailand, Laos, Kampuchea (Cambodia), Vietnam, Singapore, and the Malay confederation, which includes both mainland and islands. Island archipelagoes are Indonesia and the Philippines. Southeast Asia is in large part a shatter belt or politically fragmented region where different cultural and political influences have expanded and clashed. There is a marked climatic unity and a tendency for the mainland nations to focus on a few valley or floodplain areas surrounded by highland barriers.

AUSTRALIA-OCEANIA

Australia-Oceania consists of Australia, Papua New Guinea, New Zealand, and the far-scattered small islands of the Pacific basin. The relative isolation of this region has been a factor in its development. English and French prevail, with native Polynesian culture languages spoken throughout the majority of the small islands. English language and culture prevail in Australia and New Zealand, although aboriginal cultures are present in relatively minor populations. A perceptible shift in military and security relationships from reliance on Britain to a firmer alliance with the United States has occurred since World War II.

AFRICA SOUTH OF THE SAHARA

Countries in this region include Senegal, Gambia, Guinea, Guinea-Bissau, Sierra Leone, Liberia, Ivory Coast, Upper Volta, Ghana, Togo, Benin, Nigeria, Camaroon, Central African Republic, Gabon, Congo, Zaire, Ruwanda, Burundi, Kenya, Ethiopia, Somalia, Djibouti, Tanzania, Angola, Mozambique, Zambia, Malawi, Malagasy (Madagascar) Zimbabwe (Rhodesia), Southwest Africa (Namibia), Botswana, Swaziland, Lesotho, and South Africa. Negroid people predominate, and, for much of the region, there are tropical forest and savanna climates. Except in the southern part of the continent, most areas are preindustrial, with mining and plantations earning foreign exchange for incipient industrialization.

SOUTHWEST ASIA—NORTH AFRICA

The Southwest Asia–North Africa region includes North Africa, the Near East, and Middle East with the Arabian peninsula and the zone of Islamic culture eastward to Iran and Afghanistan. It is predominately an arid and semiarid zone, with some better watered areas on the margins and some important oases. The largest cultural-religious group is Islam, but Jewish and Christian groups are prominent within particular countries. This region includes Morocco, Mauretania, Western Sahara, Algeria, Mali, Niger, Chad, Tunisia, Libya, Egypt, Sudan, Turkey, Cyprus, Syria, Lebanon, Israel, Jordan, Saudi Arabia, Yemen (North and South), Oman, the United Arab Emirates, Iraq, Iran, and Afghanistan. Portions of this region were the "cultural hearths," or origin areas, of much of Western civilization, and the region gave birth to the three great monotheistic religions that now dominate Europe, the Americas, Africa, Oceania, and, historically, the USSR, as well as large parts of Asia.

THE "LAST FRONTIERS"

Greenland, newly independent but with very small population, and Antarctica, of uncertain future political control and only scientific exploration teams as its "population," are considered in the concluding chapter, which also studies the world oceans. These "last frontiers" are of significance primarily as vulnerable ecosystems that may become far more important sources of raw materials in the near future.

REVIEW QUESTIONS

1 Briefly describe the positive and negative aspects of the decreasing "doubling time" of the world's population.

2 Identify the unique perspective of geography in examining the changing world patterns of production, technology, innovation, consumption, and standards of living.

3 Why were the environmental determinists incomplete, at best, in their interpretation of physical-cultural interactions?

4 Why do some spatial correlations *not* necessarily imply a cause-and-effect relationship?

5 Briefly describe recent technological innovations that greatly increase the detail of information available to geographers and that facilitate the search for spatial correlations.

6 What are the fundamental differences between a regional approach and a systematic one?

7 Why is some system of regionalization a necessary tool in organizing a geographic study of the world?

8   How would you identify a neighborhood and determine its boundaries? Is there a similarity to identifying and bounding major world regions?

9   Why are national boundaries still an important consideration in regionalization, despite increasing international flows of raw materials, manufactured goods, technology, and people?

10   Identify and describe, briefly, physical landscape dynamics.

11   Identify and describe, briefly, cultural landscape dynamics.

12   Why is the definition of *natural resources* changing, usually expanding, over time?

13   Why does diffusion from a center of innovation virtually never occur at an even pace related to distance?

14   Briefly describe the demographic transition.

15   Why does the death rate of a society decline earlier than the birthrate?

16   Give both historical and contemporary examples of nations within each of Rostow's stages of economic growth.

17   Does the von Thünen Theory of the relationships among accessibility, land value, and land use retain any validity in understanding intraregional and even interregional land-use patterns?

18   Why is it almost impossible for any state or region to become independent of international flows of materials and technologies?

19   Why do higher technology societies become progressively more dependent on international raw material flows rather than more self-sufficient?

20   Choose any world region as defined here and speculate on revising its boundaries, providing logical geographic reasons for the revisions.

GENERAL BIBLIOGRAPHICAL NOTE

The end-of-chapter bibliographies are intended to guide students to books whose quality, relevance, and general availability all rank high. All sources listed are in English. While many of the books listed have been read in preparation for writing this book, they are *not* a comprehensive bibliography in that sense. Students interested in more detailed, up-to-date studies on specific topics are advised to become familiar with these standard geographical journals: *Annals of the Association of American Geographers; Economic Geography; Geographical Review; Journal of Cultural Geography; Journal of Geography*, and *Professional Geographer.*

Depending on the nature of your interest, your geography instructor may recommend geography-related journals such as *Annals of Tourism Research, Landscape,* or *Land Economics.*

Good quality, general sources not separately listed in the end-of-chapter bibliographies but generally available in college libraries are the U.S. Government series publications; the *Area Handbooks* series features good reviews of geographical, historical, political, and economic data on most countries of the world, including information on culture and present political conditions. The State Department's *Background Notes* series are capsule summaries of much the same range of data. Generally four to eight pages in length, they include a suggested reading list, and the address and telephone number of each country's embassy in the United States.

A serious student of any region or topic in this text can develop an extensive bibliography from the references listed in the Suggested Readings for each chapter and in the *Background Notes.*

SUGGESTED READINGS

1   BRIAN BERRY, EDGAR CONKLING, and MICHAEL RAY, *The Geography of Economic Systems*. Englewood Cliffs, N.J.: Prentice Hall, 1976.

2   GERALD BREESE, ed., *The City in Newly Developing Countries*. Englewood Cliffs, N.J.: Prentice Hall, 1969.

3   SAUL COHEN, *Geography and Politics in a World Divided*. New York: Oxford University Press, 1973.

4   ANTHONY DeSOUZA and PHILIP PORTER, *The Underdevelopment and Modernization of the Third World*. Washington, D.C.: Association of American Geographers, 1974.

5   PAUL ENGLISH and ROBERT MAYFIELD, eds., *Man, Space and Environment*. New York: Oxford University Press, 1972.

6   PETER HALL, *The World Cities*. New York: McGraw Hill, World University Library, 1966.

7   MARVIN HARRIS, *Culture, Man and Nature*. New York: Crowell, 1971.

8   DON HOY, ed., *Essentials of Geography and Development*. New York: MacMillan, 1980.

9   SIDNEY JUMPER, THOMAS BELL, and BRUCE RALSON, *Economic Growth and Disparities: A World View*. Englewood Cliffs, N.J.: Prentice Hall, 1980.

10   ALAN MOUNTJOY, *Industrialization and Under-Developed Countries*. Chicago: Aldine, 1966.

11   LEWIS MUMFORD, *The City in History*. New York: Harcourt Brace and World, 1961.

12   GUNNAR NYRDAL, *The Challenge of World Poverty*. New York: Vintage Books, 1970.

13   WALT ROSTOW, *The Stages of Economic Growth*. Cambridge, Mass.: Cambridge University Press, 1960.

14   CARL SAUER, *Agricultural Origins and Dispersals*. New York: American Geographical Society, 1952.

15   GLENN TREWARTHA, *A Geography of Population: World Patterns*. New York: Wiley, 1969.

16   GLENN TREWARTHA, *The Less Developed Realm: A Geography of Its Population*. New York: Wiley, 1972.

17   UNITED STATES COUNCIL ON ENVIRONMENTAL QUALITY, *The Global 2000 Report to the President of the U.S.: Entering the 21st Century, Volume I: The Summary Report*. New York: Pergamon Press, 1980.

18   ERICH ZIMMERMAN, *Introduction to World Resources,* ed. Henry L. Hunker. New York: Harper & Row, 1964.

KEY TERMS

- primate city
- complementarity
- core
- fall line
- permafrost
- caliche
- Megalopolis
- hinge function
- von Thünen model
- general farming
- agribusiness
- Industrial Revolution
- value added
- machine tool
- hinterland
- leisureopolis
- world city
- infrastructure
- push-pull factors
- regional capital
- environmental degradation
- barrier and channel effect
- intervening opportunity
- perception
- forward port
- national minority

2

UNITED STATES and CANADA

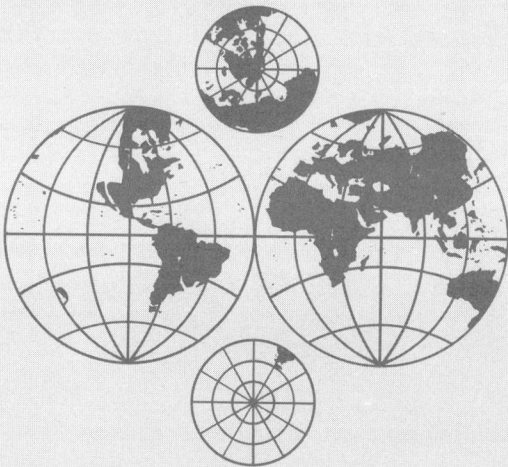

PROLOGUE: TWO NATIONS IN TRANSITION

The United States and Canada form a logical region for many reasons—economic, cultural, and even political. Both are democracies with a strong emphasis on individual freedoms. Both are essentially capitalist economies, but with extensive social welfare programs and strong regulatory controls over private business. They plan to function militarily as a single unit in the event of any attack on North America, and their foreign policies, although certainly not copies of one another, tend to agree on basic issues. They are each other's best customer in trade and exchange large numbers of tourists. Each is predominantly English-speaking, but with varying degrees of recognition of another language. Yet with these many similarities and close economic relations, the United States and Canada are distinctive nations with their own cultures, problems, and solutions.

TRANS-ATLANTIC AND TRANS-PACIFIC: THE EVOLUTION TOWARD ORIENTATIONAL EQUALITY

Both Canada and the United States have historically had an Atlantic focus. Although the original inhabitants of the Americas came from Asia, the predominant streams of later migrants, who came to form the majority, have crossed the Atlantic. The dominant cultures, languages, and political philosophies and systems are of European origin. With notable but few exceptions, the continuing stream of immigrants to both have been overwhelmingly European until quite recently. The involuntary immigration of Africans to the United States is a major exception to this generalization, and that too is a trans-Atlantic event.

Both the United States and Canada historically have experienced a westward-moving frontier starting from the east coast. This westward expansion has meant that, psychologically, the West was "new" and the East "old." The great cities of the East have long functioned as financial and cultural "capitals" of both nations. For centuries following colonization, trans-Atlantic trade far overshadowed that of trans-Pacific, even though yankee ships were early participants in the "China trade." The trans-Atlantic connection functioned as a psychological umbilical cord to the "mother" countries of western Europe.

It would be absurd to assert, of course, that the Pacific formerly held no interest to Americans or Canadians. Intellectual, political, and economic interests have always existed. What has happened is a gradual expansion of these interests, expecially since the early part of this century.

The trans-Atlantic focus is not so much replaced as it is supplemented by the rising importance of trans-Pacific relationships. America's last two wars have been fought to resist perceived threats to the security of American interests in the Asian rim of the Pacific. The second most important trading partner of the United States, after Canada, is Japan. The most dramatic, and potentially most important, shift in U.S. foreign policy in the last thirty years was the 1971 "China Initiative" seeking to restore normal diplomatic relations and to greatly expand trade. The rising significance of trans-Pacific relations is nicely illustrated by the challenge of West Coast cities to the primacy of eastern cities.

THE CONCEPT OF MULTI-PRIMACY

The concept of the **primate city** was advanced by geographer Mark Jefferson in 1939. He observed that among urban centers in most developed countries, one would clearly dominate. Its metropolitan population would far surpass the "second city," and it would unquestionably dominate the economic, cultural, and political life of the country (such primate cities most often have been national capitals).

Paris is the archetypical primate city. Because of the centralized government, compact shape, and relatively small territory of France, Paris is the central headquarters for any agency or enterprise whose interests or clients are nationwide. The great size of its market and labor force, together with its position in the center of transport and communications webs, has continually attracted still more economic functions, strengthening its role as trendsetter and cultural innovator.

In much larger countries of more varied cultural and economic landscapes, the primate city may be considerably less dominant. Some of the traditional primate functions may be dispersed among several cities. Neither Canada nor the United States has primate cities on the clear-cut model of Paris. Canada, like the United States, has deliberately created a federal capital on a cultural divide; neither of the two federal capitals is the largest city nor even among the top three. Canada has two great rivals for the title of largest metropolitan area, Montreal having been recently surpassed by Toronto. This rivalry has more to do with the French Canadian–British Canadian cultural rivalry than a westward reorientation. By contrast, the two largest U.S. cities, New York and Los Angeles, do accurately reflect the rapid expansion of population and economic-political power on the U.S. west coast. In the United States, Chicago remains the predominant midwestern center, while Vancouver is becoming a western "primate" city for Canada.

New York remains America's largest metropolitan area, sprawling over parts of three states and exercising leadership in finance, corporate headquarters, and many of the arts. It is of major international significance; indeed, by being the location of the United Nations headquarters, New York comes closer than any other city to being an international capital in addition to an economic-cultural leader. Its hinterland is richly productive and thickly settled. There is little general agreement on the precise boundaries of the functional metropolitan area, so that any count of metropolitan population varies with the boundary accepted. It may be the biggest metropolitan area in the world if uniform boundary criteria could be applied to its major rivals, Tokyo and London. Its leadership in communications, entertainment, and style setting has been seriously rivaled by Los Angeles and Chicago, and its proportionate dominance of many other typical primate city functions has diminished. While still a leader, its superiority is in doubt.

Penn Center, Philadelphia. Despite the relative decline of the older, industrial subregions of the Aging Core, its central cities retain an obvious vitality. The core's problems are serious, and its overall growth relatively stagnant in comparison with the South and West, but its economic power is still impressive. (Photo by Stansfield)

In contrast to New York, already the largest city in the United States by 1810, Los Angeles' growth has occurred explosively in the past eighty years. Founded in 1781 by the Spanish, Los Angeles was long overshadowed by San Francisco. In 1860, for example, Los Angeles had a mere 4,400 people in contrast to San Francisco's 57,000. While San Francisco (Oakland) became the Pacific terminal of a transcontinental railroad in 1869, Los Angeles later became a "double" terminus, linked with the eastern United States, first by the Southern Pacific and then the Santa Fe railroads. The competition between these two rail systems led to rate wars that greatly benefited Los Angeles.

In addition, sizable local supplies of oil, that essential twentieth century energy source, were soon discovered in the Los Angeles area. In 1892, the first oil well in Los Angeles began production; six years later there were more than three thousand wells within the city. Los Angeles quickly exhibited its trendsetting, life-style leadership in the auto age. By 1928, Los Angeles already had one car for every 2.25 people. Los Angeles County has more cars registered than all but six states. The metropolitan area consumes more than an estimated $2 billion worth of gasoline per year.

Los Angeles has helped pioneer many of the now-common forms of the age of individual mobility. Los Angeles opened its first freeway in 1940; it was 8.2 miles long. (The first freeway traffic jam follwed three days later.) The metro area now has more land in freeways than the total area of the land in Miami.

In cultural leadership, Los Angeles has mounted a very powerful challenge to both New York and Chicago. The production of films and television programs shown around the world makes Los Angeles an international factor in popular culture.

The sheer size and diversity of the United States, coupled with the size and influence of Los Angeles and Chicago, argue for the concept of "multi-primacy." The "westward tilt" of the United States in domestic and international economics doubtless will favor a continuous enlargement of Los Angeles' role, while the vast productive "heartland" of the Midwest will support a robust third contender for primacy. The analagous size and diversity of Canada will likely result in a similar situation.

THE UNIQUE CHARACTER OF THE REGION

Like Middle and South America, or Australia, this region was a product of European colonial ventures; unlike the other Americas, however, there was a very low density resident native population. Too, the source areas of migrants were more diverse, even more so than in similarly "empty" Australia. Migration has been a sustained and continuing phenomenon, consisting not only of waves of colonizing rural migrants, but also those moving into an urban industrial millieu at a later date. North America may be the most poly-cultural of the late-settled major regions of the world.

Despite the existence, at differing times, of Russian, English, Spanish, Mexican, French, Dutch, and Swedish control over portions of the region, only two political units

Los Angeles Freeways. Southern California has long been recognized as an innovator of American popular culture and lifestyles. Los Angeles, one of the first big cities to be redesigned for the automobile age, challenges New York for primacy in mass media, helping to spread its cultural concepts across the continent. (Photo by Stansfield)

evolved. Regardless of differences in origin and history, they are startlingly similar in attitudes, development, and certain elements of culture. Their economies produce similar surpluses, yet there is a **complementarity** (a situation in which two units produce different goods and develop an exchange) of production in certain areas, which results in a brisk trade between the two. Though there are occasional differences of opinion between the two states, the border remains unarmed and the relationships cordial.

There is a dynamism associated with the development of both states. Droves of immigrants came from overseas to colonize the new farmlands, but generations of their descendants and other, newer immigrants continued the process until most of the arable land was cleared, plowed, cultivated, and integrated into the economy and political jurisdiction of the **core** (the densely settled, productive, economic and political "heart"). This emphasis on expansion, growth, and development came to be a hallmark of the thought and action patterns of the region's inhabitants; it carried over beyond agriculture and territorial conquest into the industrial and mercantile societies that evolved. Progress, change, and material betterment are seemingly synonymous in the minds of the region's inhabitants, who have evolved societies not tightly bound by tradition, land, or even regional ties.

POLYCULTURAL AMALGAMS OF IMMIGRANTS

There are only informed guesses concerning the number of Native Americans present at the time of the "European invasion of North America"; average estimates place the total within the present United States and Canada at about 1 million. Of these, perhaps 200,000 lived in what became Canada. Today, there are about 900,000 Amerindians and Inuit (Eskimo) in the United States, representing 0.4 percent of the total population, and 300,000 "registered" (officially recognized) Amerindians and 19,000 Inuit in Canada, representing about 0.9 percent of the Canadian population. Thus, 99 percent of the population of both countries is composed of relatively recent migrants and their descendants.

In each country, both the volume and sources of these inflows of migrants have changed over time. The respective sizes of ethnic groups today are directly related to the length of time that has elapsed since they first arrived. For example, the original French migration to Canada, before the British victory at Quebec in 1759, is estimated to have involved no more than 15,000 people. Despite very few French immigrants since 1759, the French Canadian population is now 27 percent of the total, or about 6.3 million. Similarly, although it is believed

that fewer than 500,000 Africans were imported as slaves into the United States, Afro-Americans now number about 12 percent of the United States' population, or about 27.5 million.

In 1800 there were only about 5.5 million people living in the area now included in the United States and Canada. The preceding two centuries had seen small inflows of Europeans. In the century between the end of the Napoleonic wars and World War I (1815 to 1914), 30 million immigrants came to the United States, reaching an average tempo of over half a million per year just prior to World War I (1.25 million in 1907 alone). At first primarily from the British Isles, Germany, and Scandinavia, the most important source areas had shifted to southern and eastern Europe by 1900. The predominant source areas for the most recent arrivals has shifted radically from Europe to Middle America (especially Mexico) and Asia. (See Table 2–1.) As indicated in the table, Africa has provided the smallest proportion of immigrants of any major region after 1820.

TABLE 2–1
Percentage of total immigration to the United States from world regions

	Overall Immigration to the United States 1820–1977 (percent of total)	Pre–World War II Sample 1935–1939 (percent of total)	Modern Sample 1971–1977 (percent of total)
Northwest Europe	43.4	39.5	6.7
East and South Europe	31.9	28.6	13.7
Africa	0.3	0.2	1.5
Asia	5.4	2.5	31.7
Middle America	7.5	7.6	34.6
South America	2.2	1.2	6.9
Canada	8.5	19.5	3.9

SOURCE: Immigration & Naturalization Service

Canada's major immigrations occurred between 1900 and World War I, in the 1920's, and after 1945. The first period was a result of the opening up of the prairies to settlement, an opportunity that attracted many Germans, Ukrainians, and Russians. Although a full third of Canada's total immigrants over time have come from Britain, the later waves of immigrants have been primarily from Italy, Germany, eastern Europe, and then Asia. Canada has not had the sharp rise in immigrants from Middle America experienced in the United States, but otherwise it has shared the general United States trend toward shifting sources of immigrants.

COMPLEMENTARITY AND INTERDEPENDENCE OF THE U.S. AND CANADIAN ECONOMIES

Canada purchases about 20 percent of the exports of the United States, and the United States buys almost two-thirds of Canada's exports (which make up about 23 percent of the United States' total imports). The long common border, which cuts across some major transport arteries and divides some relatively dense population clusters, has been a very busy one. Not only commodities and manufactured goods flow across it; more than 30 million U.S. tourists visit Canada in an average year, more than fifteen times the total of foreign tourists from other countries. In recent years the net balance of receipts and expenditures has shifted to a surplus in the United States' favor, as Canadians spend over $700 million more in the United States than vice versa.

The massive trade between the United States and Canada was once based on an exchange of Canadian raw materials for American manufactured goods. Now, Canada's major sources of foreign exchange are autos and auto parts, lumber, newsprint, wood pulp, natural gas, and tourism. Although wheat exports earn almost $2 billion a year for Canada, autos and auto parts earn more than $10 billion. Industry is now the leading segment of the Canadian economy, producing a greater value of goods than agriculture, forestry, mines, and fisheries combined. Furthermore, the industrial structure is changing; service industries are expanding employment faster than is manufacturing. The rapid maturation of the Canadian economy is intimately related to its relationships with the United States.

The tremendous expansion of the automotive industry is an excellent example of United States–Canadian economic cooperation. The major U.S. automakers established assembly plants in Canada because high taxes were placed on assembled cars, while low taxes were levied on parts. However, the technological nature of auto assembly and the character of the auto market combined to make totally separate car production inefficient. Since the Canadian car market was a little over one tenth that of the United States, a typical Canadian plant repeatedly had to change over to making different sized cars in order to produce a full range of cars just for the Canadian market. Then, in 1965, the United States and Canada agreed to joint free trade in autos and auto parts. The result was a huge increase in the two-way trade in automotive products, from $715 million in 1964 to over $13 billion by 1975. Now, for example, a decision may be made that all full-sized cars for the United States and Canadian markets will be manufactured at the Canadian plant, and all other

models for both markets made in the United States. The free trade agreement has been very successful for Canada; Canada produces more than its proportional market share of autos (but less than its market share of trucks).

The very close economic ties between the United States and Canada, together with their evident close cooperation and friendship, should not mislead Americans into regarding Canada merely as a branch office. Canadians are highly conscious of both the advantages and disadvantages of living next to the United States. While there is no doubt that American markets and American capital investments have sped the remarkable growth of the Canadian economy since World War II, Canadians see some potential problems in their economy being so closely linked with that of the United States. Canadians are wary; too many vital economic decisions affecting them are made in New York, Washington, Detroit, Pittsburgh, or Chicago rather than Ottawa, Montreal, Toronto, or Vancouver. Canadian Prime Minister Pierre Trudeau once likened living next to the United States to sleeping next to an elephant: no matter how friendly and well intentioned the beast, one must remain very sensitive to its every move!

THE FRONTIER AND THE CONQUEST OF NATURE AS A DEVELOPMENTAL FRAMEWORK

The United States and Canada both are today undergoing a reassessment of what has long been accepted as a positive value—the conquest of the frontier (and its corollary, the conquest of nature). As in the settlement of Brazil, the supply of land appeared limitless, and careless farming practices resulted in the degradation of soil and massive erosion. Similarly, the forests were treated as an endless resource to be cut in an unplanned and often destructive fashion. Each new mineral find was instantly followed by mining techniques that gave no thought to conservation or future needs. Even the expansion of suburban settlement and highway building have been cited in recent times as a flagrant waste of the land resource.

The impetus to the recent reconsideration of values has been the energy crisis of the 1970's. It has become apparent to the public of both countries that there are limits to their resources.

There is still dichotomy of thought. Neither of these populations wishes to relinquish their respective high standards of living. Canada, with cheap gasoline, has chosen to conserve its oil by limiting exports, while the United States has emphasized the reduction of oil consumption and a switch to other sources of energy. Both countries have come to limit immigration, though Canada's policies are somewhat more liberal. Canada encourages the development of its sparsely populated areas, especially its frontier areas in the Northland; yet it is hard to induce settlers to go to the difficult northern areas, and many return after short stays. The United States is in a different situation regarding its sparsely populated western states, still popularly considered an unspoiled, almost frontier area; so many internal migrants are attracted to this area that pressures on the slim regional water resources now present severe limitations to the expansion of dense populations.

People now accept the need to conserve; that aspect of the frontier mentality advocating the conquest of nature has been modified in a positive way. The other aspects—mobility, hope, a fresh start, new opportunity—are the very things that give dynamism to both societies, and there is extreme reluctance to relinquish these patterns of thought. Indeed, there is a real question as to whether these particular aspects of a frontier mentality are undesirable or destructive. Both societies have traditionally felt that the status quo is equal to stagnation; this is a region and population noted for its fluidity of attitude and adaptability to change.

THE PHYSICAL FRAME

At the grossest level of generalization, the North American region has a simple arrangement of physical patterns. Two mountain systems parallel the east and west coasts with a large interior lowland in between and an exceptionally broad coastal plain along its southern and southeastern edges. Climatically, three quarters of the region is well watered; only the southwestern portion of the United States is classified as truly arid. In the more humid area, climatic zones run east-west with progressively longer and colder winters from south to north. In the drier quarter, the climatic zonation is more strikingly oriented north-south. Vegetational patterns correspond to climatic patterns in detail except for the extension of grasslands eastward into quite humid areas.

Four huge river systems drain the interior lowland, whereas four less major river systems drain most of the mountain complex of the west. A series of short streams drain the fringing lowlands of the region.

The soils of the wetter three quarters are fairly heavily leached, while those of the drier quarter are characterized by the opposite—mineral accumulation. Vast areas of wind-blown loess and accumulations of alluvium occur in coastal and interior lowlands. A great diversity of soil types results. The southern two thirds of the region has a high degree of agricultural utility. Glaciation has played a major role in the formation of some of North America's soils.

Essentially, much of the northern one third of the continent has been almost scraped bare of soil by the continental glaciers. The Great Lakes of both the United States and Canada form the approximate divide between the areas dominated by glacial erosion or deposition. The northern Rockies and the Missouri and Ohio rivers essentially separate the area of glacial deposition from nonglaciated areas. (See Figure 1–8.)

THE TOPOGRAPHY

The continent has a prevalent north-south grain of topographic features. (See Figure 2–1.) This is frequently interpreted as disadvantageous since the orientation of transportation is generally east-west, and the two political units of the region are east-west—oriented entities.

The Gulf-Atlantic Coastal Plain   In the United States, a low, relatively flat coastal plain stretches from the Mexican border, narrowing to the Maritimes of Canada. This level to rolling area originally made penetration into the interior a great deal easier than was the case in much of South America or Africa. For most of its extent it is drained by short rivers that originate in the Appalachians, (such as the Potomac and Delaware) or in the case of the western Gulf coast, streams that originate in the Rockies or the lower Mississippi Basin. It is generally divided into two portions designated as inner and outer. The Outer Coastal Plain is a flat sandy expanse that is often poorly drained. For much of its length it is fringed by sandy beaches and offshore sand bars enclosing backwater lagoons, as at Cape Hatteras and the New Jersey Shore. The Inner Coastal Plain is composed of older material, some of it cemented into rock. Subject to a longer period of erosion, the landscape has a gently rolling nature.

There are three exceptions to this general pattern. The Mississippi River has created a giant inland delta that reaches up to southern Illinois. This delta is a landscape of meandering streams, temporary lakes, and back swamp that extends for over 100 miles (160 kilometers) in either direction from the streambed in a huge delta plain. The surrounding countryside has been eroded or filled to the point where the coastal lowland includes the eastern third of Texas and virtually all of Mississippi and Louisiana.

The second exception is the Florida arch, where gently folded limestone material has risen above the sea to form a long peninsular extension of the plain. The third exception is the glaciated coastal area extending from New York northward to Cape Cod. Here the plain is of variable width, eventually disappearing, and everywhere greatly modified by the deposits of sand and gravel laid

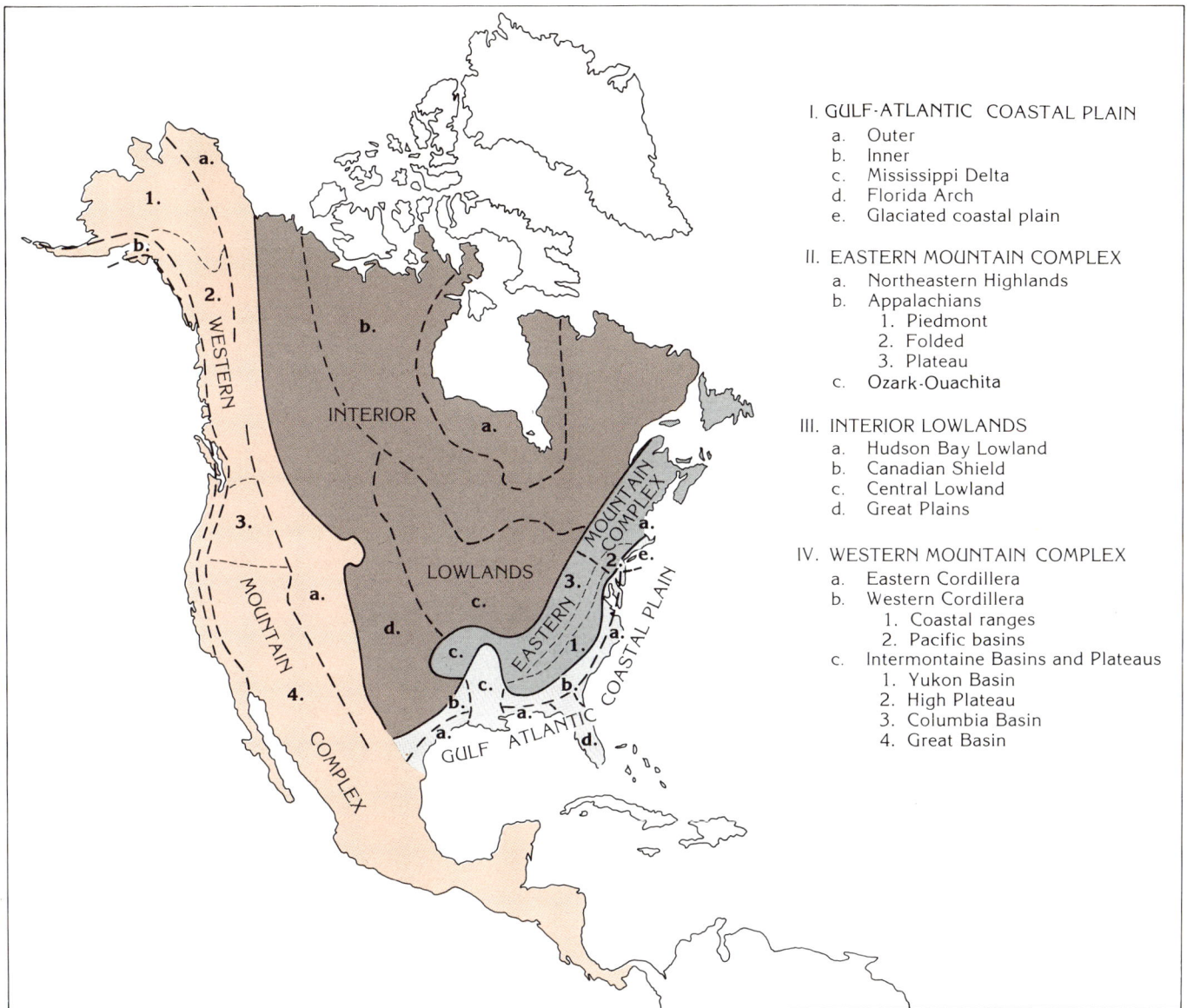

I. GULF-ATLANTIC COASTAL PLAIN
  a. Outer
  b. Inner
  c. Mississippi Delta
  d. Florida Arch
  e. Glaciated coastal plain

II. EASTERN MOUNTAIN COMPLEX
  a. Northeastern Highlands
  b. Appalachians
      1. Piedmont
      2. Folded
      3. Plateau
  c. Ozark-Ouachita

III. INTERIOR LOWLANDS
  a. Hudson Bay Lowland
  b. Canadian Shield
  c. Central Lowland
  d. Great Plains

IV. WESTERN MOUNTAIN COMPLEX
  a. Eastern Cordillera
  b. Western Cordillera
      1. Coastal ranges
      2. Pacific basins
  c. Intermontaine Basins and Plateaus
      1. Yukon Basin
      2. High Plateau
      3. Columbia Basin
      4. Great Basin

FIGURE 2–1
Major Landform Regions and Drainage Patterns. The predominantly north-south "grain" of the region's landforms is apparent in this generalized map of landform regions and major drainage patterns. The relationship of landforms to climate in the western part of the region becomes obvious when this map is compared with one of climate.

down during continental glaciation. This area has a very irregular coastline, with islands and peninsulas along the continental margin.

The whole surface is fringed by a broad continental shelf (shallow water over a surface that is, geologically, part of the continent), which contains offshore deposits of oil and gas as well as rich fishing grounds. Just as the plain widens southward, the shelf tends to widen northward except along the western edge of Florida where the continental shelf is also extremely wide. The landward transition of the Coastal Plain to the Eastern Mountain

Complex is rather gentle, with a line of small falls marking the boundary between softer sediments of the Coastal Plain with the more resistant rock that is the eroded base of ancient mountains. These falls or rapids offered water-power potential as well as blocked upstream shipping; both factors supported urban growth at the **fall line,** as exemplified by Philadelphia, Baltimore, and Richmond.

The Eastern Mountain Complex   The Eastern Mountain Complex consists of three principle segments, the Northeastern Highlands, the Appalachians, and the outlying

Ozark-Ouachita group of highlands detached from the main body of these eastern mountains. Relatively low, geologically old, and much eroded, this chain of eastern mountains extends in a crescent from Newfoundland almost to the Great Plains, changing directional orientation from northeast-southwest to due east-west (after interruption by the Mississippi embayment) in the Ozark-Ouachitas.

The Northeastern Highlands The Northeastern Highlands consist primarily of variably metamorphosed rocks interspersed with volcanics. North-south flowing rivers have cut across the diagonal grain of the topography, cutting the mountains and hill lands into blocky segments, each given a local name. The Adirondacks of New York represent a detached segment of the Canadian Shield, an ancient surface of resistant material. They are connected to the shield by an axis that underlies and forms the Thousand Islands of the St. Lawrence. The Adirondacks are separated from both the Appalachians and the mountains of New England by lowland troughs that extend to Lake Ontario and the St. Lawrence at Montreal.

The mountains of New England and the Atlantic Provinces are folded Paleozoic sediments and volcanics. As in the Appalachians, this folded portion occupies the center, but the folding, and accompanying metamorphosis, has been more intense. A plateaulike segment is found in the east, and has been reduced to low hills in New Brunswick and Nova Scotia. Some small coalfields indicate its presence. Newfoundland, still further east, is a rough surface of folded and metamorphosed material.

The Appalachians The Appalachian segment, largest of the three, consists of three distinct zones. The easternmost, the Piedmont, consists of an intensely eroded surface of ancient rocks that have been eroded to a countryside of low hills and small valleys, in places covered by more recent sediments. At its lower eastern edge the contact zone with the coastal plain is marked by a line of falls. The softer coastal plain sediments erode more easily than the piedmont rock, leaving a precipice of varying height in the river bed. As noted, this so-called fall line gave rise to early industrial centers in the United States. Along its western edge, the Piedmont is higher and a residual line of relatively high mountains, the Blue Ridge, marks the transition to the Ridge and Valley Country, the second subportion of the Appalachians.

The Ridge and Valley Country consists of layers of sedimentary rock that have been folded into a series of parallel ridges and valleys many miles long. At times the work of erosion has reversed nature, creating valleys from ancient mountains and the ridges of crests from former valleys.

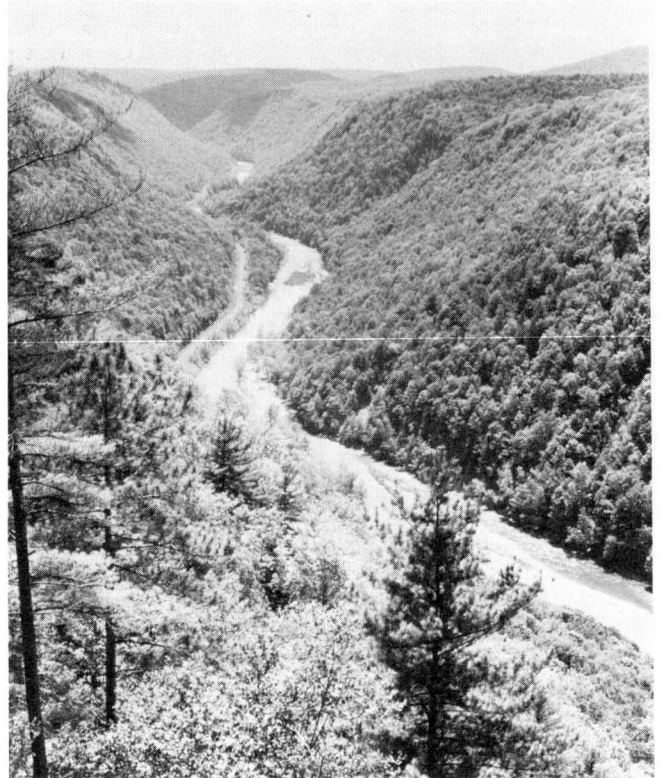

The Appalachians. The stream-erosion of the Appalachian Plateaus, seen here in Pennsylvania, has created a mountainous terrain that, if lacking the grandeur of the Rockies, served to channel and impede early westward movements. Today, the Appalachians are important for their minerals, forest products and tourism industry. (Photo by Stansfield)

The western edge of the folded Appalachians is marked by a steep ridge, the Allegheny front, the gently upturned edge of the Allegheny-Cumberland Plateau. Most of the plateau is underlain by rich coal deposits and gas and oil, particularly in western Pennsylvania, West Virginia, eastern Ohio, southwestern Virginia, and eastern Kentucky.

This threefold pattern characterizes the Appalachians throughout their length from upstate New York to Alabama. Generally, the Piedmont is widest and the plateau narrowest in the southern section. The northernmost portion has been mantled with glacial debris.

The Ozark-Ouachita Highlands Though separated from the Appalachians by the Mississippi Delta, the Ozark-Ouachita Mountains are of essentially the same age and structure. The Ozarks are a lower, much eroded plateau surface while the Ouachitas and other ranges of Oklahoma and western Arkansas are folded mountains or associated fault block mountains. This mountain complex provides welcome relief from summer heat to midwestern and southern residents alike; it has developed tourist functions on a considerable scale. Coal reserves are of lower quality and lesser scale than those of the Appalachians proper, but they form a valuable regional resource.

The Interior Lowland   The vast level-to-rolling stretches of interior plains, low plateaus, and denuded rock surfaces that cover the bulk of the region are generally referred to as the interior lowlands despite the fact that the Great Plains are at a considerable elevation above sea level and parts of the Canadian Shield might better be described as hills or even low mountains. Whatever structural or erosion-induced relief that once existed there has been planed down or filled in by the work of continental glaciation. A rather diverse topographic picture, it is wise to divide the region into four parts: the Hudson Bay lowland, the Canadian Shield, the Central Lowland, and the Great Plains.

The Hudson Bay Lowland   This lightly populated plain surrounds Hudson Bay, the huge water embayment that penetrates the continent from the north. It was the center of expanding continental ice sheets during Pleistocene times. Later, as the ice melted, the continent rebounded, exposing progressively more land. Much of it is swampy, poorly drained lowland. There are marine terraces that rise to surprising heights encircling the bay and marking former sea levels. There is immense hydroelectric potential in the district, but the land supports only poor forest or scrubland where the climate warms up beyond tundra.

The Canadian Shield   The Canadian Shield is composed of ancient crystalline rocks that have been heavily eroded by continental glaciation, exposing a bare rock surface that has since developed little in the way of a soil covering. Its southern edge is marked by the Great Lakes of the United States and Canada. There are another five mammoth lakes totally within Canada (Winnipeg, Manitoba, Athabaska, Great Slave, and Great Bear) that round out the semicircular edge of the shield. Dotted with lakes and bare rock hills, the shield's surface supports a cover of coniferous trees mixed with birch and aspen. The Canadian Shield is rich in metallic minerals, such as the famed deposits at Sudbury, and possesses enormous hydroelectric potential. A few areas of former lake plain have a thicker clay soil capable of supporting farming.

The Central Lowland   South of the shield, the land surface is covered with glacial till of varying richness and texture. Gravelly morainal hills mark varying stages of glacial retreat. Most of the surface, however, consists of broad plains formed under temporary meltwater lakes (which formed at the edge of the ice sheet), or a rolling, pockmarked surface deposited under the ice. Poorly drained areas are quite common.

South of the Ohio and Missouri rivers, the surface remained unglaciated. Eroded by streams, it is rather more hill country at its southern margins. In places a covering of loess (wind-blown earth materials) has covered the surface, both glaciated and unglaciated, with layers of mineral-rich soil material of varying depth.

In the lowland area of Canada's Northwest Territories, a series of unusual glacial features developed where underlain with **permafrost,** permanently frozen subsoil. Underneath the Central Lowland are a series of basins and arches or domes: broad-scale, gently folded structures, such as the Michigan Basin. In some of the basins there are coal, gas, and oil resources hidden deep beneath the surface.

The Great Plains   The Great Plains are almost a plateau surface, reaching elevations of up to 5,000 or 6,000 feet (1,500 to 1,800 meters). Sediments arranged in horizontal sheets stretch eastward from the Rockies. Streams such as the Platte and Missouri have incised deep valleys, but most of the high lying surface remains intact as a broad, level surface. The heavily eroded badlands of the Dakotas are among a few stark exceptions.

The Western Mountain Complex   Younger by far than the Appalachians, the western mountains widen from north to south. There are essentially two main mountain chains, the Eastern and Western Cordilleras, separated by rough plateau country north of the Columbia River in Washington State and a vast disrupted basin to its south. The westernmost range is flanked by a series of depressions paralleling it, including Puget Sound and the Central Valley of California. These are in turn paralleled by low coastal hills. There is little in the way of coastal plain development except in Alaska. The basin portion, largely a desert, contains dryland topographic features on a grand scale.

The Eastern Cordillera   Broader, on average, than its western counterpart, the Eastern Cordillera consists of three portions: the Brooks Range in Alaska, the Mackenzie Mountains in the Yukon, and the Rockies from there on southward. The little-known Brooks Range faces northward and is noteworthy more for the adjacent lowland, which contains the North Slope oilfield of Alaska. The Mackenzies, astride the border between the Yukon and the Northwest Territories of Canada, are composed of steeply folded sedimentary rocks whose geology is little known. They are offset to the east of the main ranges of the Rockies; the Laird River flows through this giant breech in the system. It is here that the Alaska Highway penetrates the Rockies on its route to Alaska.

The Rocky Mountains   The Rockies were developed when a tremendous, mountain-building uplift occurred in

The Great Plains: Pivot (Circular) Irrigation in Western Nebraska. The flat-to-gently-rolling Great Plains were a more effective barrier to advancing waves of settlement than the Appalachians, until Americans learned to cope with the treeless, subhumid environment. A series of technological advancements, among them irrigation projects, have supported a reassessment of the agricultural potential of the Plains. (Courtesy of U.S. Army Corps of Engineers)

the late Cretaceous times. The flat-lying sediments that had covered the area were pushed upward with accompanying large-scale volcanic activity during what has come to be known as the Laramide Revolution. Much folding and faulting occurred in the process.

On the eastern edge of the Rockies the disturbance resulted in two parallel ridges running north-south. They are known as the Front Ranges and are composed of uptilted sedimentary rocks in the Canadian and Colorado Rockies, although occasionally granitic rocks dominate, especially in the southern Rockies. They have been much modified by glaciation, sharpened and scoured into horns reminiscent of the Alps. Their abrupt rise from the level Great Plains adds to their visual grandeur. The peaks of these Front Ranges vary from 10,000 to 14,000 feet (3,000 to 4,500 meters) in elevation.

Immediately behind the Front Ranges are a series of scattered mountains and high plateaus. For most of their length the Rockies vary from 100 to 300 miles (160 to 480 kilometers) in width. In their Canadian portion, they are strongly sedimentary in origin and heavily metamorphosed. Rich oil and coalfields line their eastern flank. A huge fault line, running from western Montana to the northern border of British Columbia, results in the broad Rocky Mountain Trench, a fault valley nearly 1,000 miles (1,600 kilometers) in length.

In the section stretching from southern British Columbia to southern Idaho, the mountains are formed of a huge volcanic batholith, a rock mass resulting from the slow cooling of lava. This portion of the Rockies is rich in metallic minerals and is eroded into a difficult topographic stretch of great width. Copper, lead, zinc, and silver are mined in this district. The Bitterroot and Selkirk Ranges are the highest portions of this difficult country. Glaciation is still actively eroding on the Canadian side of the border in the Selkirks. This portion of the Rockies culminates in Yellowstone Park, where the heat of molten material underground creates geysers, hot springs, and other related phenomena amidst splendid mountain scenery.

South of Yellowstone National Park, the Rockies become an alternation of plateaus and basins with impressive, glacier-sharpened peaks. The largest of these basins, the Wyoming Basin, is underlain with rich fuel deposits. It is separated from the Great Basin and the Colorado Plateau by the Wasatch Mountains on the west and the Uinta Range on the south. The classic Rockies, the glacier-sharpened peaks of Colorado, really only form the central, minor portion of the total range. They are separated from the Colorado Plateau by a series of lesser but still spectacular ranges that are rich in metallic minerals, where formed of volcanic rock, and containing huge coal deposits where of sedimentary origin. It is in this part of the Rocky Mountain Overthrust that geologists have uncovered vast new deposits of oil and gas.

The southern Rockies are narrower and lower. Most of the mountain country is composed of lava flows incised

The Canadian Rockies at Banff, Alberta. The spectacular Rockies of North America are an important influence on climate regions and boundaries as well as being a major recreation and conservation area. Particularly rugged sections of the system, such as here in Canada, were once formidable barriers to land transportation. (Courtesy United Nations/Canadian Govt. Travel Bureau)

with deep valleys by rivers that rise in the wetter central Rockies but quickly evaporate in the dryland climate of New Mexico.

Intermontane Basins and Plateaus   The Arctic portion of the intermontane plateaus in Alaska and the northern Yukon is a low lying, broken, and eroded surface that is hill land more than mountain. Several sizeable river plains and topographic basins have developed along the Yukon River and its tributaries. In its Canadian portion, volcanic lava flows have filled in the depression between both the Eastern and Western Cordilleras. Erosion by both water and ice have created a landscape of hills and mountains interspersed with canyons. It is one of the last pieces of true wilderness in North America.

In the Columbia Basin, south of the U.S.-Canadian border, broad lava flows spread out over almost the entire basin. Covered with rich loess in eastern Washington and northern Oregon, the land takes on the appearance of desert south of the Blue Mountains of Oregon. The loess has been eroded into deep valleys, called *coulees,* by torrents of glacial meltwater in the past. Lava flows continue eastward into the Snake River Valley, and, generally, into northern California and Nevada.

The southern portion of this intermontane basin is known as the Great Basin. It is truly desertic in climate and characteristically desertic in its landforms. Known as the Basin and Range Country, it consists of fault block mountains, oriented roughly north-south, alternating with sediment-filled valleys. Large areas of salt flats intervening between the ridges are the remains of old lake beds; large lakes once occupied much of Utah and Nevada during wetter climatic periods. The great Salt Lake is the residue of a once much larger freshwater lake. The Great Basin narrows at the southern end of Nevada only to open up again as a repetition of the same landscape over the desert country of southern California and southern Arizona and New Mexico. Death Valley, at 280 feet (90 meters) below sea level, is the lowest point in the United States. It is located at this constriction between the northern and southern portions of the Great Basin.

In the southwest of this series of plateaus is the Colorado Plateau, which is composed of thousands of feet of horizontally bedded sedimentary rocks. Another great storehouse of hydrocarbons, it is best known for the wonders of the Grand Canyon, which has eroded a meandering channel of great depth into the plateau surface, exposing millions of years of geologic history while sculpting a fantastic and beautiful landscape.

The Western Cordillera   Essentially, the Western Cordillera consists of a line of volcanic peaks, such as Mt. St. Helens, and uptilted blocks. In the Alaskan and British Columbian portions, the valleys once eroded by glaciers have come to be drowned by the sea in a series of long, steep-sided bays known as fjords. The coastal ranges appear only as a series of peninsulas and offshore islands, while the intervening lower areas are submerged beneath the sea. South of Vancouver, alluvium-filled lowlands separate the Western Cordillera from the coastal ranges. The Puget Sound lowland, the northernmost of the three, is a mixture of land and water features. The Willamette Valley is its drier extension in the state of Oregon. The largest is the Great Valley of California, where coalescing alluvial fans from both the Sierras and the Pacific Coastal Ranges have created a huge valley with gentle relief and high agricultural productivity.

Along the eastern edge of this series of basins is a chain of mountains that rival the Rockies in both elevation and scenery. The Coast Mountains in British Colombia are a series of ice-eroded volcanic peaks (not to be confused with the far less prominent Pacific Coastal Ranges). Their Alaskan counterpart is called the Alaska Range and contains North America's highest peaks. Diminishing in altitude westward, they are eventually submerged, in part, beneath the Pacific where they become the Aleutian Islands.

In the Pacific Northwest, this chain is known as the Cascades. The combination of glacial erosion on volcanic cones has created a fanciful landscape of often snow-capped craters perched on a jumble of lava flows.

The Sierra Nevada Mountains extend northwest-southeast along the eastern side of California. Mainly a series of large block mountains, they are quite steep and difficult of access along their eastern side. The western side of the Sierras is known for its ice-carved valleys, falls, and canyons.

Hawaii   The Hawaiian Islands are composed of a chain of active and recently active peaks that have risen above the floor of the sea to form the islands themselves. The mammoth outpouring of lava here represents a "hot spot" in plate tectonic activity associated with a mid-ocean rift.

LAND-SEA RELATIONSHIPS

Unlike Europe, there are few large penetrations of the sea into the North American continent. Hudson Bay, by far the largest, is icebound for much of the year. Similar to Europe, there are large navigable river systems that penetrate deep into the continent. Drowned river valleys from the

Carolinas north to Newfoundland create access inland to the very foot of the Appalachians, while excellent harbors abound. The West Coast, south of the Columbia River, has a paucity of good harbors with the outstanding exception of San Francisco Bay. Northward, the fjorded coast offers excellent harbors, but there is little productive hinterland (in most areas) to have stimulated traffic.

The absence of a direct water route to the U.S. West led to the building of the Panama Canal and the expansion of U.S. interests in the Caribbean. Trans-Pacific trade arose with the development of the West Coast. The St. Lawrence–Great Lakes Seaway has extended oceanic access inland to interior portions of both the United States and Canada, while the Canadians have gradually enlarged the maritime functions of Hudson Bay. Viewed originally as a buffer against outside invasion, the surrounding seas are now rather more the source of connections with the rest of the world and an aid to intraregional transportation in states of enormous physical size.

CLIMATE

Three quarters of the region has an east-west trending zonation of climate. The southwestern quarter experiences a north-south climate boundary orientation largely as a result of the juxtaposition of landforms and the ocean. There are no truly tropical areas except for Hawaii and the very southern tip of Florida. Overall, then, most of the region is humid (receiving adequate moisture), continental (receiving but limited moderating influences from the ocean), and seasonal in climate. (See Figure 1–2.)

The southeastern one fourth of the United States has a subtropical climate with year-round distribution of rainfall and a long frost-free season. Cyclonic storms bring most of the rainfall as high- and low-pressure systems move across the area every few days, bringing variable temperature, humidity, and rainfall conditions. Only a few miles from the sea, the moderating effects of the ocean are largely lost as seasonal and daily temperature ranges reflect the continentality (rapid heating and cooling of air over the even more rapidly heating and cooling land surface) of an interior location.

The northeastern quarter of the United States and the St. Lawrence lowland experience a more intense winter. The East Coast and the Maritimes experience some oceanic moderation, but the rigors of winter intensify rapidly inland. Summers are moderately long, but grow rapidly shorter north of the edge of the Canadian Shield; and the northern two thirds of Canada, as well as most of Alaska, experience long, cold winters and short, cool summers. The Arctic fringes of the entire continent have no frost-free season, forming the largest area of tundra (tree-less, slow-growth vegetation) climate in the world.

A broad swath of steppe (semiarid grassland) fronts the eastern side of the Rocky Mountains south of the fifty-fifth parallel of latitude and west of the 100° meridian of west longitude. This grassland area varies only in length of summer from north to south, experiencing hot summers almost throughout its length and intensely cold winters everywhere except the portions south of Kansas.

West of the Rockies, the land becomes a desert south of the fortieth parallel. There is not a total absence of rainfall; the U.S. deserts are comparatively wet, supporting a varied cover of vegetation. North of the fortieth parallel, the west coast of the continent has cool, rainy-year-round weather. South of the fortieth parallel, California has a Mediterranean climate with parched summers and winter rains. No area of the U.S. West Coast itself is truly hot at any season of the year because of the modifying effect of the westerly winds, which pass over the cool waters of the California current before reaching land.

Almost three fourths of the United States has sufficient average rainfall for unirrigated agriculture, while virtually all of it has sufficient warmth for agricultural utility—the exceptions occur in the highest mountain areas and most of Alaska. Canada, however, is less favored. Over two thirds of that country has very limited or almost no potential for crop agriculture on the basis of the length of growing season alone. Overall, however, the region is one of the world's most favored climatic areas in terms of the potential for agricultural productivity.

DRAINAGE PATTERNS

Ten major drainage regions account for most of the area of the region, but five carry the bulk of the runoff. The largest of these systems, the Mississippi-Missouri-Ohio, drains most of the interior of the United States between the Rockies and the Appalachians (see Figure 2–1). The St. Lawrence-Great Lake system covers less area but carries a volume of water that is also exceptional. Two northern systems, the Yukon and MacKenzie, and the Columbia-Snake system of the Pacific Northwest, account for most of the rest of the volume of water carried from the continent to the sea. Though carrying a lower volume of water, the Colorado system is extremely important for irrigation.

The largest two systems penetrate to the heart of the continent and are effectively joined through a canal from Chicago to the Illinois River. The Mississippi-Missouri-Ohio system is one of the world's most important navigational systems. It drains the richest agricultural portion of the United States as well as the western half of the Manufacturing Belt. While not suited to ocean-going traffic beyond Baton Rouge, Louisiana, armadas of barges ply its waters carrying grain, construction materials, raw materials, and fuels over channels improved to a nine-foot minimum navigational depth. Most of the improved portion of the system is navigable for ten or more months of the year. The western, drier, more rural portion of the basin, however, is primarily used for irrigation and has little utility for navigation. The Tennessee and Cumberland rivers, tribu-

Locks on the Welland Canal near St. Catherines, Ontario. The St. Lawrence Seaway system, an international project, makes ocean ports of the Great Lakes cities of the United States and Canada. Although too narrow and shallow for the most modern and efficient ocean carriers, this inland waterway remains vitally important during its ice-free season. (Photo by Stansfield)

taries of the Ohio, as well as other Appalachian tributaries of that river, have been developed as multipurpose water projects with considerable hydroelectric generation as well as significant recreational usage. The greatest usage of the eastern half of the system, particularly the Ohio, however, is industrial—including cooling for thermal-electric power generation and other industrial functions.

The St. Lawrence system, in contrast, is open to navigation by moderate draft ocean-going vessels (28-foot [8.5 meter] draft) over its entire length. Serving the Canadian industrial heartland and the huge industrial cities strung along the Great Lakes, navigation is its most important single function, although it is icebound for three to five months each year. Even before the creation of the St. Lawrence Seaway, the Great Lakes functioned as an important internal navigational system linking the Appalachian coalfields, Mesabi iron ranges, and the grainlands of the Corn Belt. The Seaway created new possibilities for the development of an international export function, which has supplemented this still important internal trade. Lesser navigational improvements, carrying barge traffic only, connect the Great Lakes and the lower St. Lawrence to the Hudson and the port of New York.

The hydroelectric potential generated by the relatively steep grandient of the river and the large reservoirs of the lakes themselves has only been partially tapped, though the electricity generated thereby has resulted in an unusually heavy concentration of energy-consuming industries along the St. Lawrence and its tributaries, as well as in the Toronto-Niagara Falls district.

Little development of any kind has been done on the Yukon and the Mackenzie systems. Flowing through lightly settled and essentially undeveloped hinterlands to northern seas, they represent a largely untapped resource that could become important in the development of Alaska and northern Canada.

The Columbia-Snake system generates proportionately the largest amount of hydroelectric energy of any of the systems. A vast area in eastern Washington and Oregon and large parts of southern Idaho are also irrigated by the waters of this system.

The Colorado River, while over 1,400 miles (2,200 kilometers) long, has a lower volume of flow than the Delaware, only 390 miles (630 kilometers) in length. However, the Colorado is the "master stream" of the entire Southwest, the largest in drainage basin and in importance. Its waters are so heavily used for irrigation, then drained back to the river with a burden of salts, fertilizer residues, and pesticides, that the Colorado is hardly "fresh" as it enters Mexico to exit into the Gulf of California.

The Sacramento and San Joaquin rivers, which drain the northern and southern parts of California's Great Cen-

tral Valley, are of great importance within that state. Other river systems of subregional importance include the Rio Grande-Pecos, the Salt-Gila tributaries of the Colorado, and the many shorter rivers draining eastward from the Appalachians to the Atlantic, such as the Delaware, James, Susquehanna, and Savannah.

In general, the most important use of western rivers is irrigation, while eastern rivers are used primarily for industrial and navigational purposes. Despite such major power projects as Grand Coulee and Hoover dams in the West, the amount of electricity generated by rivers in the eastern half of the continent is much greater. This is particularly evident in Canada where large new hydroelectric projects in Quebec and Labrador generate an enormous power supply in the eastern portion of the Canadian Shield.

VEGETATION

The vegetational cover of the region as "discovered" by Europeans in the fifteenth and sixteenth centuries was already considerably modified by human activity. The hunting-based culture of some of the plains Amerindians spurred repeated burnings of young forest growth to enlarge the grasslands for the habitat of the bison (buffalo), an important food source. Maps of the region, therefore, are often entitled *potential vegetation* rather than *natural vegetation*, as the correspondence to climatic regions is not always close. Grasslands, which would be expected in areas of streppe climate, actually extended almost to the Appalachians in the interior of the United States, while large areas of scattered grasslands were also found in the South where something like a shrub savanna was commonly encountered.

The forests of North America were found in three broad zones: the Western Mountain Complex (in particular the Western Cordillera), the Canadian Shield, and most of the eastern one third of the United States. Spruce and fir are the commonest trees on the shield proper, while a transitional zone of spruce, pine, and hemlock occupied the southern fringes of Canada and the northern portion of the United States east of the Mississippi. The forests of the rest of the eastern United States tended to be hardwoods and mixed forests with a heavy incidence of oaks. Western forests contained such rapidly growing and spectacular species as the Douglas fir and, in a small part of its southern extensions, the redwoods and giant sequoias.

The southern forested portion of the United States has seen remarkable fluctuation in both area and species. Vast acreages of exhausted and abandoned farmland have been planted to rapidly growing types of pine to support the South's large and growing paper and pulp industry.

Native varieties favored by human planting include many flowering deciduous trees like magnolia, the sweet gum, and tulip trees. Where the growing season exceeds 250 days, live oak and other broadleaf evergreens may appear. Hickory, pecan, and other nut-bearing trees have been selectively encouraged. In swampier areas the cedar has commonly grown, and cypress appears from Delaware on south.

Massive lumbering operations in the northern United States heavily modified the native forests. Softwood forests, cut during the industrial and building boom of the late nineteenth century, were replaced by a growth of hardwoods, which may have been a natural response to warmer climatic conditions or perhaps to exposed lower horizons of soils that resulted from post-lumbering soil erosion. At any rate, hardwoods have all but replaced the original pine, fir, and hemlock forests of this part of North America, although these species are being replanted in some areas.

The prairies of the Midwest present a similar problem of modification. Indians (and nature) maintained the grasslands by periodic fires. The so-called "natural prairie" near Madison, Wisconsin, for example, could only be maintained with repeated burning.

The deserts of the United States have an unusually rich flora and an unusually thick vegetational cover in their natural state. This is at least in part attributable to the fact that there was virtually no grazing in the area until the twentieth century, unlike many of the others of the world's deserts. Sage brush, mesquite, creosote bush, and some spectacular cacti give a relatively densely vegetated appearance to the landscape. There are few areas of shifting dunes, sand flats, or desert pavement in comparison to the great deserts of the Old World.

Human modifications in societies with advanced technologies have been profound. Wind breaks have invaded the steppe and commercially valued species have replaced native types in all but a few forested areas.

SOILS

The relatively complex soil patterns of the region have resulted from wide subregional differences in climate, an extreme variety of parent material, a changing vegetational cover, induced changes in drainage and fertility, and the forces of continental glaciation. Some of the soils of North America have been changed from their original form through intensive use and modification by people.

No classification of soil is fully satisfactory, since soil forming processes are intensely complex and related to climate, vegetation, parent material, and drainage. Since modifications of a striking and relatively rapid sort and degree can occur through human usage, so soil categories, too, become less meaningful. For example, the "poor Champagne" district of France was converted from rough pasture to one of that country's most productive farming districts by dumping garbage, offal, and human waste on the soil for a hundred years. There are many striking examples of even more rapid modification of soils in North America; nearly worthless acid bogs in the Upper Great Lakes area have been converted into rich soils through drainage and the massive application of agricultural lime, both to increase fertility and to modify soil structure. Large acreages in the U.S. South actually became more fertile with the erosion of exhausted topsoil and the consequent exposure of richer subsoils, which had a higher content of plant nutrients. In that case, misuse indirectly improved the soil. Even crop selection can play a role, whereby tree crops, for example, are able to tap deep soil horizons packed with minerals through an essentially infertile surface layer. Most notably, the repeated burning of the vegetation in the Midwest added potash to the soils, while generations of dead grass roots increased the humus content (and nitrogen) to great depths creating rich prairie soils where less fertile forest soils likely would have occurred in nature.

Despite this complexity, five broad soil regions can be distinguished (see Figure 2–2): the northern zone, the drylands zone, the subtropical zone, the transitional zone, and the western mixed-soils zone. The northland zone can be considered agriculturally marginal. Whatever agricultural potential these northernmost, tundra soils possess is virtually irrelevant in the face of severe climate. The more southerly parts of the district, some of which is underlain by permafrost, is covered by heavily leached acid soils of low fertility with little calcium, phosphorous, nitrogen, or potassium (minerals necessary for plant growth). Where glacial erosion dominated, the soils are also thin and rocky; where glacial deposition occurred, they are of varying thickness but of overall low fertility.

Drylands soils are always rich in calcium but can contain poisonous concentrations of soluble minerals. The familiar story of the Nile often leads students to think of desert soils as inherently rich, lacking only water for enormous yields. Poor in humus, large amounts of nitrogen must be added each year to gain even reasonable yields unless, like the historic Nile, the alluvium brought by streams adds it naturally. In all dryland areas, even steppes, the danger of **caliche** formation is present whenever irrigation is used. Caliche is a poisonous concentration of mineral salts in a hardpan (tough, concretelike layer) at or near the surface, making the soil unusable. The soils of the steppes vary from thick black chernozems (where the

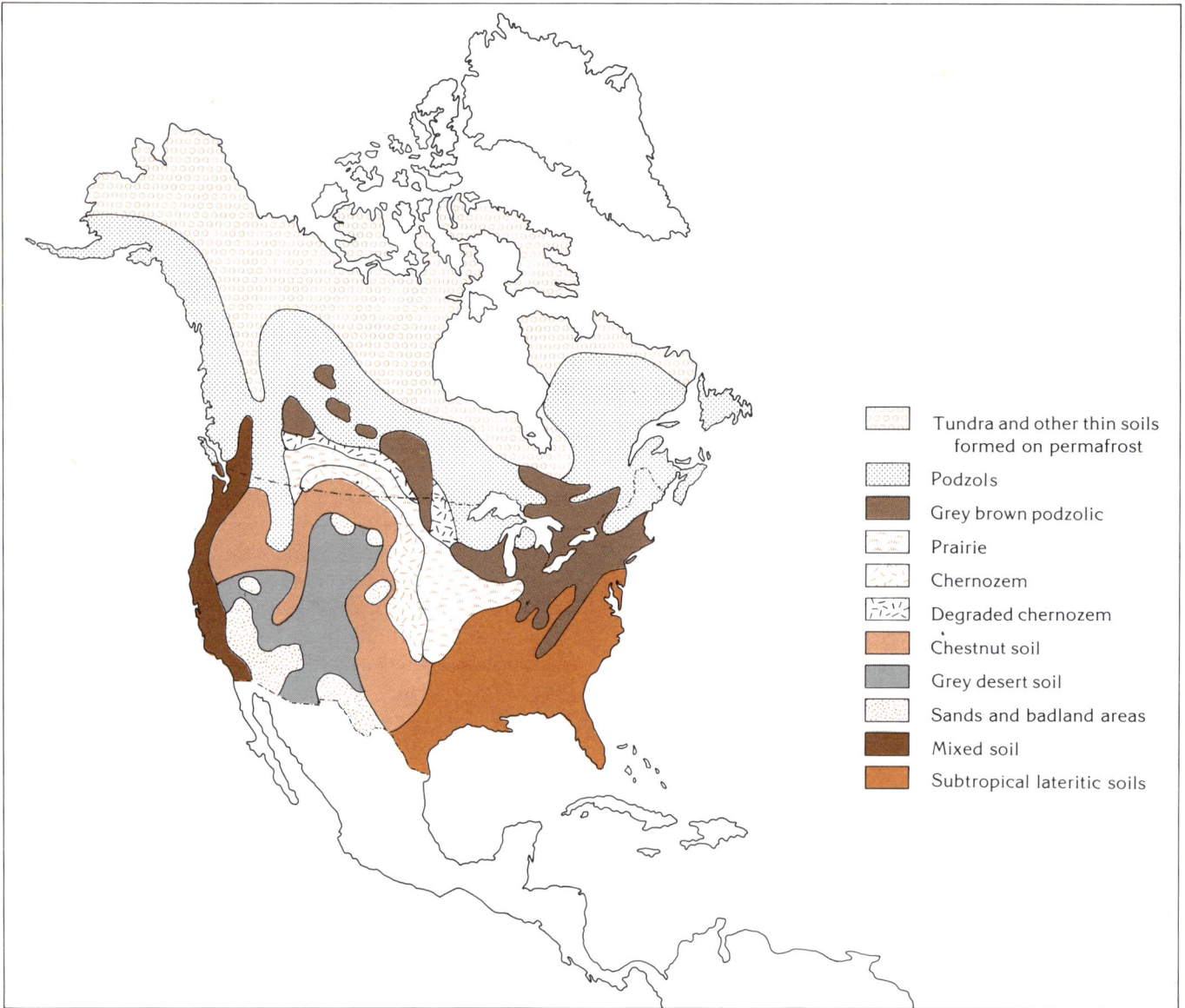

FIGURE 2–2
Generalized Soil Regions. Soil classification systems can become quite complex and, to the nonspecialist, more confusing than helpful. These broadly generalized soils regions have been devised primarily on the basis of their agricultural potential and the set of problems they present to human utilization.

soil water balance is not excessively low) to chestnut-colored soils (at their drier western margins) to brunizems (at their wetter eastern margins) and somewhat less fertile, degraded chernozems (where forests have invaded the original grassland cover). All categories are relatively rich in humus (nitrogen) and calcium.

Subtropical soils are thick and deep, but often badly *leached* (drained of water-soluble minerals). Long, hot summers intensify the tendency toward the leaching of nutrients. They are often red or yellow in color, fairly low in

humus, almost devoid of calcium, and clayey in texture with resulting poor drainage properties. Length of growing season, rather than yield, is what attracted farmers who traditionally grew crops that required a long growing season. Soils that were exhausted by constant cropping were often abandoned for newer, unfarmed areas. Much of the Southern Atlantic Coastal Plain was abandoned through this process. Soil bank programs, leguminous crops (to add nitrogen), grazing, fallowing, liming, and green manuring over the last forty years have regenerated and improved many of these soils to a level of fertility never known before. Wise practice and heavy investment in fertilizer have created (or recreated) soils of reasonable fertility throughout much of the South.

The transitional zone is perhaps most complex. Most soils therein resulted from glacial deposition. Where excessively sandy or gravelly, they are quite infertile. The area's clay-loam soils, however, are relatively fertile. Where the parent material is lime enriched, the soils are highly productive. Dense settlement and years of careful use have encouraged large inputs of fertilizer. Proximity to large urban markets has rendered such large-scale soil improvement profitable and the soils, though moderately leached, are very productive when fertilized and properly drained. Where the original soil was formed under lakes that developed along the margins of the ice, there is a natural humus content that contributes to a superior soil.

The western zone varies greatly in fertility. Much of the soil is thin in areas of slope and almost all is considered immature—lacking the three characteristic layers or horizons. In the Pacific Northwest they are similar to the weathered clays of the Appalachians—stony and of relatively low fertility. In California they are often enriched by volcanic or calcareous (lime-rich) parent material, but may be thin and stony. In the Great Valley of California they are alluvial and their fertility depends on the nature of the parent material in the areas originally eroded. As in the South, climate rather than fertility is often responsible for their use. As in the deserts, much of the area of California requires irrigation.

An amazing percentage of the United States is covered by usable agricultural soil. The original crop surpluses developed capital whereby the extent of the farmable area could be increased and virtually all soils could be economically beneficiated. In Canada west of Lake Superior, only the best soil has been used. Though a much smaller proportion of Canada has relatively good soil, large areas of acceptable soil have not yet been brought into use. Soil is one of this region's most important natural resources and one of the most important keys to understanding its progress and development. Currently, it is the chief surplus-food-producing area of the world, and can continue as such with careful management of soils, minimizing erosion.

THE STRUCTURE OF SUBREGIONS

The United States and Canada region is subdivided into ten subregions, six within the United States and four within Canada. (See Figure 2–3.) The northeastern quadrant of the United States, which coincides closely with the classic Manufacturing Belt, is the old industrial heartland. Population growth rates are generally low, with the central cities of metropolitan complexes in marked decline. This region is still the core, economically, but its preeminence has declined relative to the dynamically changing South and the West Coast. The energy surpluses of the South, in combination with rapidly advancing industrialization, is transforming that region's economy. The agricultural and mining base of the western interior is being augmented by new energy finds; an expanding population (together with more mining) is severely straining water resources there. The growth rates of the West Coast are dropping proportionately, but the subregion, one of the most diverse ethnically, is still growing. Two very different frontiers, Alaska and Hawaii, round out U.S. subregions. Canada's Atlantic fringes form a distinctive subregion, followed by its "divided heartland," the result of a potentially disruptive clash between Canada's French-heritage citizens and the majority culture. The Canadian Plains and West Coast constitute another subregion, followed by the various frontiers of the Canadian Northlands.

THE AGING AMERICAN CORE

The northeastern quadrant of the United States, from Chesapeake Bay west to Kansas City north to the Canadian border, contains the core of the American population and economy. It includes four distinctive geographical areas—New England, the northeastern Megalopolis, northern Appalachia, and the midwestern heartland. Each of these areas has had strong and continuing economic interaction with the others, and together they constitute a remarkably diverse and important subregion.

The nature and qualities of the resource base have played an important part in regional development, both by their presence and absence. New England, one of the earliest European-settled parts of the continent, has a very short list of natural resources, yet was in the forefront of American industrialization. Its magnificent forests once were dominated by huge white pines, 100 feet (60 meters) in height and valued as ship's masts. Two hundred years of cutting with little thought to conservation, however, left an inferior "second-growth" forest by 1850. Although three quarters of the land is still forested, the slow-growing trees are more important for pulp and paper than lumber. New England has no fossil fuels (coal, petroleum, or natural gas), though offshore exploration holds promise. High costs of imported fuel oil have brought a new appreciation of the abundant firewood resource. No significant deposits of metal ores are found in New England. The general lack

FIGURE 2–3
Subregions, with Place Names. The scale and complexity of the United States and Canada suggests
the recognition of subregions for both countries. These subregions are based on general similarities
of physical and economic factors.

of resources has helped produce an interesting modification of industrialization here.

The natural resource base of the Middle Atlantic coast and neighboring Piedmont of the Appalachians is only slightly more impressive. As in New England, the forest resource was more important in the past than the present. Small iron ore and copper resources were largely worked out by the early twentieth century; natural gas and oil offshore have just been discovered and are not yet in full production. This area's real resource is its location on the seaboard, encompassing the historic heartland and with ready access to the coal and other minerals of northern Appalachia.

The steam-powered early maturity of the industrial age in America was fueled by the coal resources of Pennsylvania; later exploitation moved westward to West Virginia, Ohio, and Illinois (see Figure 2–4), supplemented by coal from the Upland South (Kentucky, Tennessee). The first oil well was drilled in western Pennsylvania (1859) and that state remained the largest producer until 1895. Although Pennsylvania, New York, Ohio, Indiana, Illinois, and Michigan all produce some oil and/or gas, their pro-

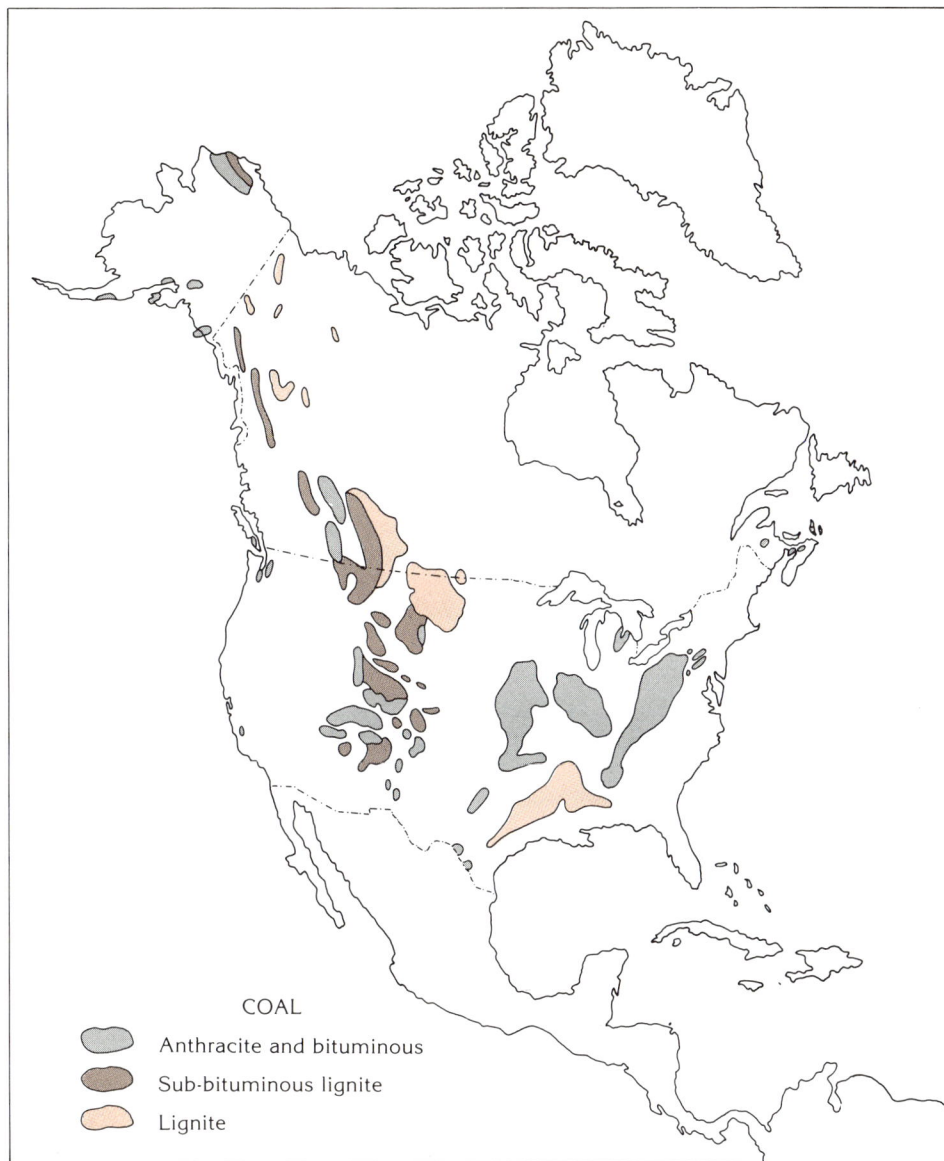

FIGURE 2—4
Fossil Fuels. The location and areal extent of fossil fuel deposits is clearly related to both present industrial locations and, to some extent, currents of population movement and economic development.

duction is tiny compared to their present consumption. The Adirondacks of New York have long produced iron ore, as has eastern Pennsylvania, but the iron that supported the huge expansion of America's industrial output in the late nineteenth and early twentieth centuries was from the Upper Great Lakes (see Figure 2–5).

It is in population distribution that the core is obviously the core; the U.S.'s first (New York) and third (Chicago) ranking metropolitan areas are here, along with other major cities like Philadelphia, Boston, Baltimore, Detroit, Pittsburgh, Milwaukee, St. Louis, Kansas City, Min-neapolis–St. Paul, Cleveland, Columbus, Cincinatti, and Buffalo—the list is the longest of any American subregion and illustrates the industrial power concentrated here. Although densely built-up urban areas occupy a minute fraction of the total area, their low-density, sprawling suburbs tend to reach out toward their neighbors, creating the appearance of city strings or constellations. Most of the people, money, and productivity of the region are concentrated in these enormous urban-dominated regions.

Megalopolis, "giant city" or "super city," was the name applied to a new urban phenomenon by geogra-

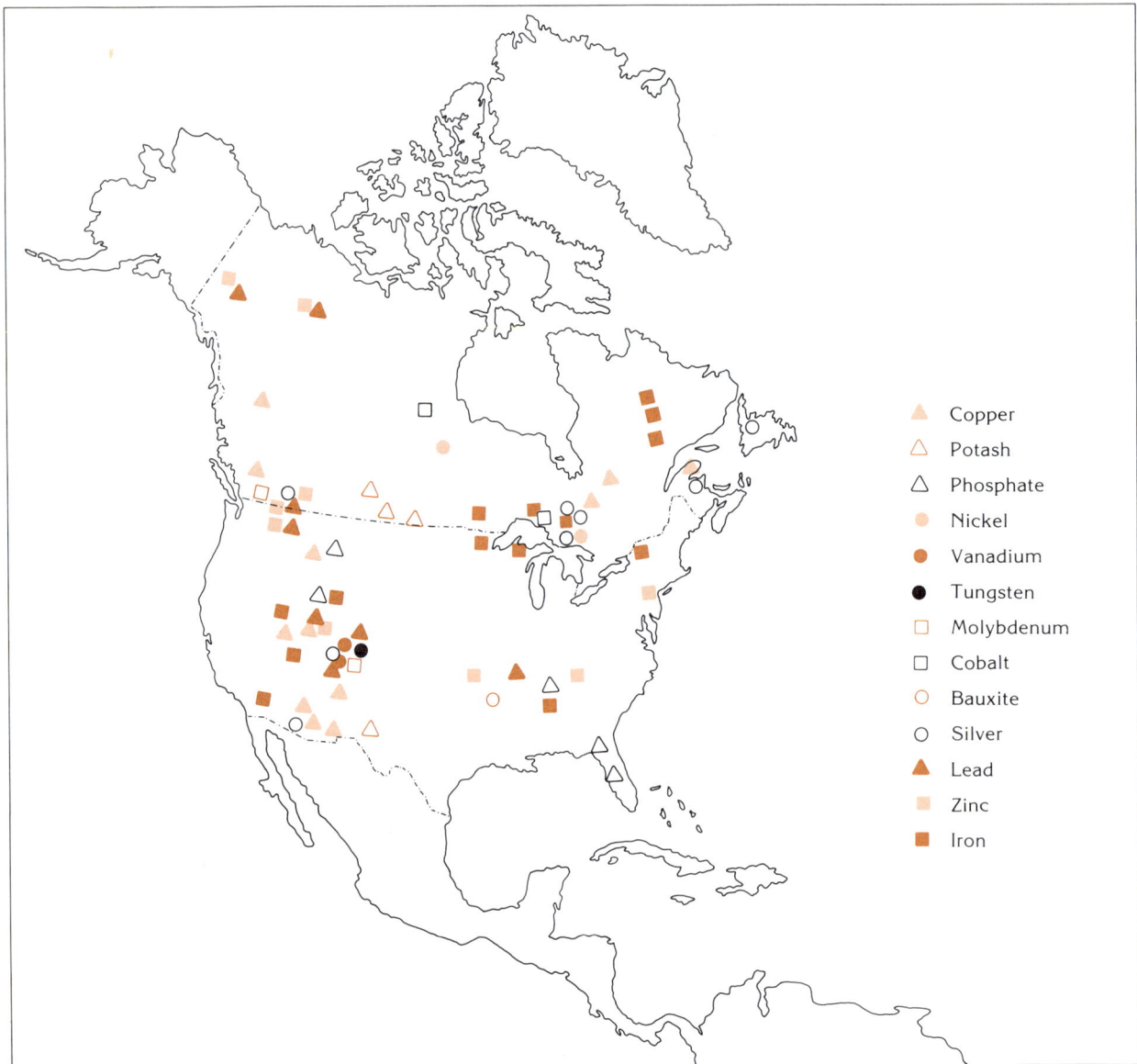

FIGURE 2–5

Mineral Resources. As with other natural resources, metallic mineral ores are defined by current technology, demand, and prices of substitutes. Major economic resources are indicated by a larger symbol than relatively minor ones.

pher Jean Gottmann in a landmark book published in 1961.[4] While certainly one great city expanding outward was not new, what *was* new was a giant urban-dominated region in which a series of great and small cities were growing towards one another along their dense webs of transport arteries (see Figure 2–6). The northeastern Megalopolis, prototype of others to follow, was first identified as the region stretching between metropolitan Boston

southwestward and metropolitan Richmond. Gottmann did *not* mean a continuous urban region—a 300-mile-long Manhattan-like growth. Only about one fifth of the Megalopolis is in urban use, and woodland has been *increasing* in the area (due to farm abandonment). Because urban-suburban development tends to follow highways, many of which radiate outward from the urban centers, there is a large amount of open space between the spoke-like highways. Between New York and Hampton roads the more concentrated development does not fringe the coast, but parallels it 50 to 100 miles (80 to 160 kilome-

---

[4] Jean Gottmann, *Megalopolis: The Urbanized Northeastern Seaboard of the United States* (New York: The Twentieth Century Fund, 1961).

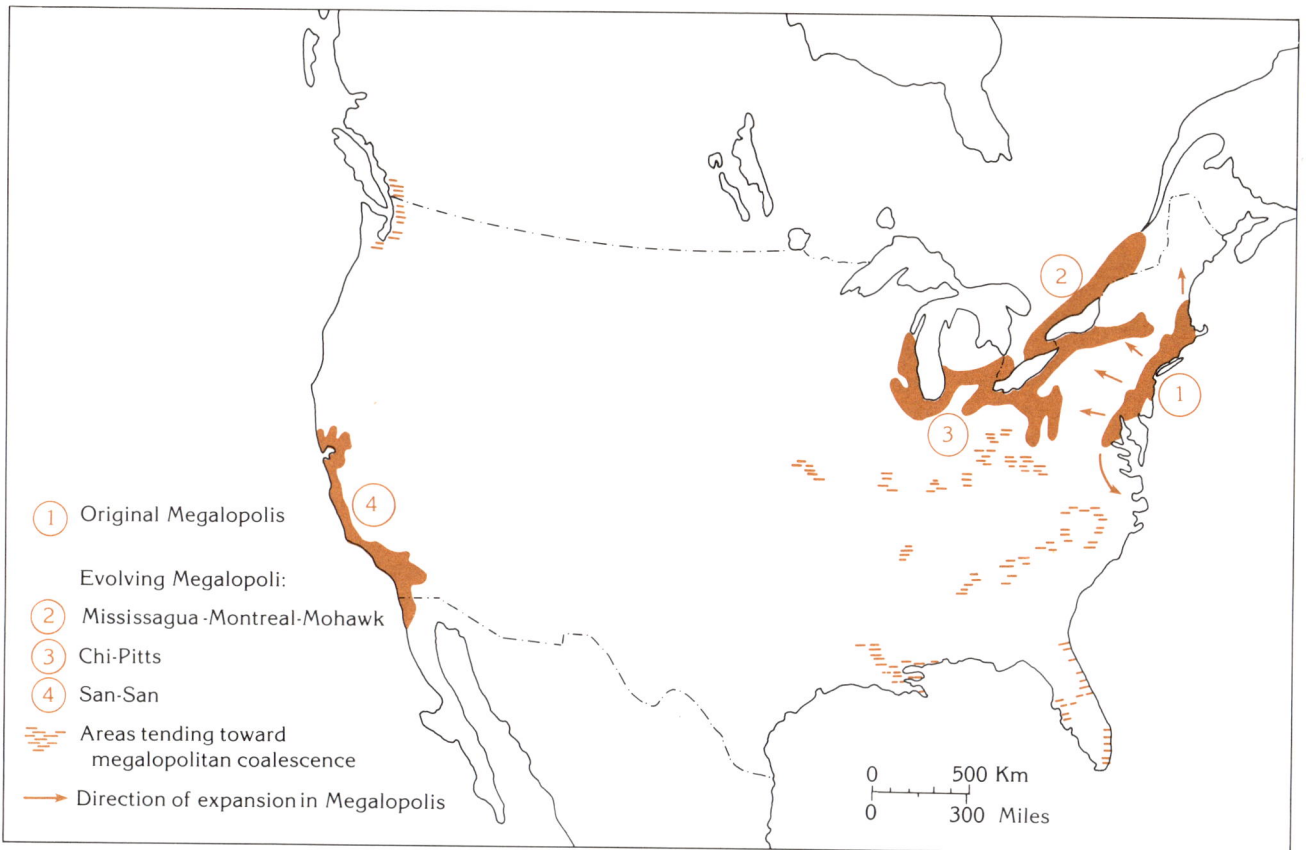

FIGURE 2–6
Megalopolis, Present and Future. The original Megalopolis, along the northeastern seaboard of the United States, is the forerunner of similar urban dominated regions elsewhere in the United States and Canada.

ters) inland. Large "empty" (lightly populated) spaces exist in southern New Jersey's pine barrens, rural Delmarva peninsula, the Appalachians to the west and north, and the Adirondacks.

Most of Megalopolis' cities are seaports; their historic growth impetus was that of **hinge functions**—they connected the dissimilar, complementary economies of the developing American core with the rest of the world, especially with Europe. Although New York, Philadelphia, Baltimore, and Boston are still great ports, their industrial functions are more important, and their service functions still more so.

The great cities of the core were primary benefactors of the great age of European migration to the New World, giving rise to the strong ethnic flavors and mixtures of their neighborhoods. Their magnetic appeal continues, although proportionally diminished, as the in-bound streams of displaced farm labor and discontented poor continue. The source areas of migrants have shifted from Europe to the rural South, Appalachia, and the Caribbean. Once in place and adjusting to the urban-industrial soci-

ety, the new arrivals begin to plan their "escape" to the less crowded outer rings of urban-surburban expansion. The move to the suburbs has been an American dream for generations, but only since World War II has it become possible for the great majority of the middle class to leave the old city behind for the newer type of low-density city we call *suburbia*.

Agriculture is highly varied in its specializations, productivity, and prospects throughout the region. New England's peak farm population was reached 150 years ago; many rural areas steadily lost population for a century before the overspill of nearby towns or cities reversed the trend. Cultivated fields gave way to hay or pasture as New Englanders could not compete with midwestern grain production. The New England physical environment—short, cool, damp summers and thin, stony soil resulting from glacial deposition—is unfavorable to grains. Its farm economy has shifted to dairying and such specialty crops as potatoes in northern Maine, cranberries on Cape Cod, and poultry in New Hampshire and Maine. Cool summers and rolling topography are no problem for cows (although feed must be stored or imported for the long winter), and the Megalopolis nearby is a good market for fresh milk. If Illinois and Iowa can easily outproduce New England in grains, only acid bogs can produce cranberries, which command a higher price per acre's production. The fringes of suburban development in Megalopolis are in a good market position to supply fresh fruits and vegetables to the 42 million people of the region, and they do.

Before refrigeration and in the very infancy of canning, producers of highly perishable fresh fruits and vegetables had to be close to markets in order to survive. This would be predicted by the **von Thünen model,** Figure 1–19. They also earned more per acre than beef producers. Cattle raisers could drive the cattle considerable distances to market; slaughtering would be done *in* the market, reducing the perishability factor. Obviously, conditions have changed since von Thünen's time, altering the details of his model. The basic premise remains true, however: land use, whether in rural or urban areas, reflects land values and the relative ability of potential users to compete for the most attractive or accessible locations.

Food preservation technologies have lessened the importance of close-in location for fruit and vegetable producers, but the advantage remains, as vegetables and fruit delivered fresh to the market command a higher price than those sold in bulk for canning or freezing. The borders of Megalopolis are thus still on the migrant labor circuit as pickers move from crop to crop, season to season. Some enterprising farmers in suburban areas have even decreased their reliance on migrant farm labor (increasingly regulated by states) by advertising "pick your own"—having the customers do their own harvesting as a family outing. High-value crops are a must for farmers on the urban fringes, as they must frequently pay high real estate taxes reflecting the potential market value of their land far more than its agricultural productivity. The suburban areas constitute a large market for young trees and shrubs for transplanting, as well as cut flowers, flower bulbs, and other horticultural specialties. This type of market occurs around any growing metropolitan area, not just Megalopolis. Poultry is important in the Delmarva peninsula, eastern Connecticut, and eastern Long Island.

The farms of Appalachia have traditionally been rather small; both northern and southern uplands have had cropland go out of production. Lengthy, irregular, perhaps unplanned "rotations" of cropland, pasture, and woodland occur in the more general farming and livestock areas of the mountains. There are many specialty areas like the grape, fruit, and vegetable area of New York's Finger Lakes and the apple orchards of the Great Valley of the Appalachians from Pennsyvania to Virginia. One of the most productive and picturesque areas of **general farming**

(a wide variety of crops and livestock) is in a three-county area of southeastern Pennsylvania known for the "Pennsylvania Dutch" (really German in ancestry), who, shunning many modern conveniences, have created a charming cultural landscape reminiscent more of the eighteenth-century Rhineland than modern America. Pressures of megalopolitan fringe expansion and large-scale tourism are countered by an extremely conservative, thrifty, and closely cooperative society intent on maintaining its traditions.

It is the Midwest, of course, that is the premier agricultural area within the subregion. The fact that Americans are well-fed on average and are the world's largest donors of food to the hungry of other lands (in addition to being major exporters) is largely the result of incredible midwestern productivity. The heartland is as much responsible for the American lifestyle as are the industrial and service centers of Megalopolis or the farms and cities of California. Indeed, without the prodigious outflow of corn, hogs, cattle, wheat, soybeans, and other farm products from this area, the United States would be a far different, less affluent culture. There are other vital agricultural regions, of course, but the American heartland is the most astonishingly productive in the world.

The changing nature of (and pressures on) farming in America are nowhere better illustrated than in this classic farming region. (The Midwest, particularly in its western portion, has the highest proportion of regional income from farming of any comparably sized area in the United

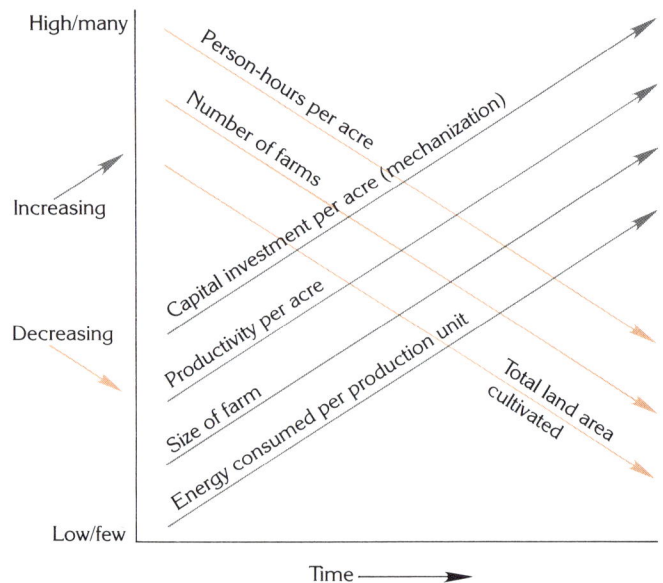

FIGURE 2–7

Trends in American Agriculture. American farmers have been producing more food on less land, using some of the world's highest inputs of energy, capital equipment, and fertilizer.

Farm in South-Central Iowa. The phenomenal productivity of the Corn Belt contributes not only a high American standard of living, but also helps provide a major share of American exports. (Photo by Stansfield)

States.) A survey of trends (see Figure 2–7) in American farming shows an industrialized agriculture with huge investments in machinery. Mechanization has freed millions of acres from the production of feed for draft animals, greatly increased the area that one family can handle successfully, and increased productivity per acre—but it has also greatly increased the capital requirements of commercial farming. Industrialization has also affected the farmer by providing efficient chemical fertilizers, cheaper irrigation technologies (pumps, pipes, drainage systems) and generally efficient, if somewhat controversial, pesticides. (Some pesticides are persistent in the environment and have proven harmful to beneficial insects, birds, wildlife, and even people.) Scientific breeding of plants and animals has produced wheat that is less susceptable to fungous diseases, corn that grows faster, vegetables less vulnerable to damage by mechanical picking, cattle that gain weight faster, hogs with less fat in proportion to meat, and turkeys with bigger breasts. All of this technology requires that modern farmers be familiar with, if not masters of, plant and animal genetics, soil chemistry, soil-water balance management, weather forecasting, marketing, and financing. Nor can they ignore a growing list of federal regulations and programs that present opportunities as well as frustrations. Mechanization has gone hand-in-hand with the increasing size of farms; it makes larger units possible, and using mechanization efficiently requires large units. The economics of farming and inheritance taxes combine to encourage the incorporation of family farms. This minimizes taxes and eliminates the need to sell or subdivide the farm on the farmer's death. Truly corporate farms, **agribusiness,** owned not by members of a family but by a large corporation with other investments and properties, is an increasing phenomenon in the heartland, but more common in the Southwest and California.

Subregions Within the North American Manufacturing Belt The Aging Core corresponds closely to the traditional American Manufacturing Belt. Certainly, there are other manufacturing regions, but the North American Manufacturing Belt (NAMB, which also includes portions of Ontario and Quebec), still contains about 60 percent of total U.S. factory production and over half its twenty largest industrial centers. It is a zone of land in which, while manufacturing is a minor land use in the total, industrial employment per county is significant. Manufacturing in the NAMB is found in small cities and towns as well as metropolitan areas; major centers like Detroit or Chicago are simply large nodes in an industrial matrix. A series of internal subregions (see Figure 2–8) have developed within the NAMB, each specializing in a type or complex of industry.

New England Southeastern New England is the oldest unit within the NAMB. The area has numerous small rivers, easily dammed in the early days of the **Industrial Revolution** to provide direct waterpower (but so did many other areas). New England did have a relatively large population, forming a market, and had a potential labor force of those leaving farming. Textile machinery was fairly simple at first, and most women already had developed relevant skills at home in spinning, weaving, and design. Shoes, based on local leather and home-learned skills, were another early factory product. When the adolescent Industrial Revolution switched from waterpower to steam, the region imported

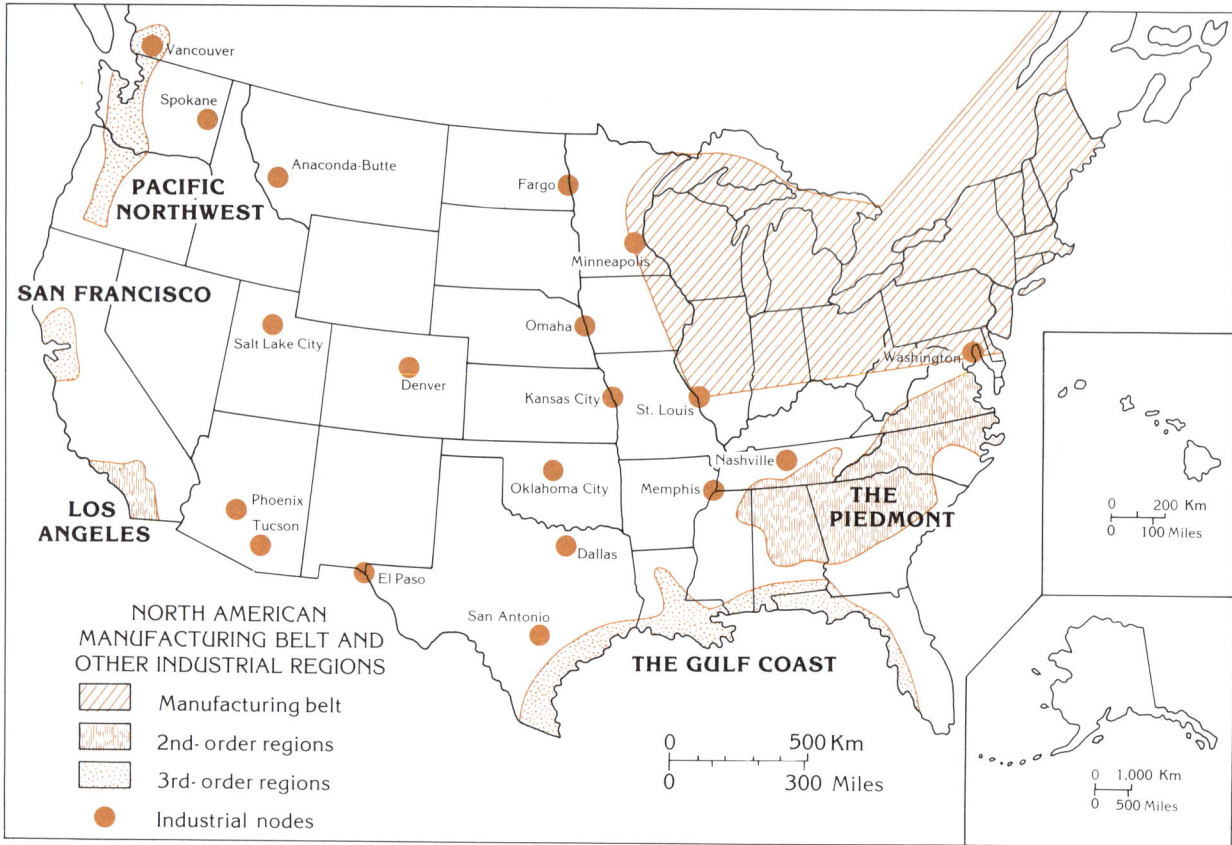

FIGURE 2–8
The North American Manufacturing Belt and Subregions. The North American Manufacturing Belt is not continuous, but consists of a series of multi-city districts and isolated nodes imbedded in a rural matrix.

coal. The eventual obsolescence of plants, locations, machines, and transport systems combined with high taxes and unionized wages to shift the textile industry to the southern Piedmont. By the 1940's, the South led in textiles and New England's remaining factories specialized in fancy and special-purpose goods.

The new and growing industries of the area are in electronics fields. Here, skill is important; access to research labs, libraries, and university consultants may be critical, and high inputs of metals and energy are unimportant, in proportion to the weight or value. **Value added** (difference in value of raw materials and finished goods) is a common measure used to evaluate the importance or regional impact of manufacturing. High-value-added industry is based on human skills and engineering more than on energy—a chronic deficit requiring expensive imports for New England.

Western New England is a complex section that early developed a metal-working specialization. Colt revolvers are a typical early product. Weapons, aircraft engines, scientific instruments, and tools are still important here. **Machine Tools,** the machines that make other machines, are an example of the production of an established industrial region with accumulated skills. Jewelry is also an outgrowth of skills in metalworking. Nuclear submarines, produced at New London, Connecticut, are both a holdover from shipbuilding days and a case of fine skills in demanding, precision work.

New York—Northeastern N.J. Of nineteenth century origins rather than New England's eighteenth century, this area was based more on transportation and market rather than local raw materials. The 1825 opening of the Erie Canal gave New York an important advantage in serving a developing Midwest **hinterland,** although the canal was more important in handling regional exports of agricultural produce rather than imports. The region is quite diverse, with only primary metals absent. The huge market and port functions combine to support a wide array of consumer goods and import processing. From its inception, the section was poly-nuclear; Paterson-Passaic, Jersey City—Hudson County, and Newark-Elizabeth were all early industrial centers in neighboring New Jersey. New York continues to decentralize outward to both New Jersey and southwestern Connecticut; space-consuming and polluting industries led the way, followed eventually even by office functions.

Delaware Valley   Very nearly in the center of the northeastern Megalopolis, the Delaware Valley has one of the best balanced and diversified industrial bases of any major region. Literally everything from missile components, explosives, pharmaceuticals, and autos to oil refining, steel, food processing, garments, ship repair, machinery, paper, and synthetic fibers are produced in this area from Trenton, New Jersey, down both banks of the Delaware to Wilmington, Delaware. Several industries have survived a shift from local or regional resource bases and markets to national and international scales of both. Iron and steel, originally supported by local ores and fuel, has emerged as a major industry in the modern era, now dependent on imported ores from Venezuela and coal from Appalachia.

Oil refining (this is the largest oil refining complex on the East Coast) has likewise shifted its resource base from western Pennsylvania sources, to the Gulf Coast, and then to foreign imports. As the center of gravity of Megalopolis shifts slightly southwestward (the southern and Piedmont fringes of Megalopolis are growing faster than the northeastern end), the Delaware Valley will become even more central to markets, enhancing its locational advantages. (See Table 2–2.)

Baltimore-Washington   Never as dependent on manufacturing, Baltimore's port functions have affected its industrial specialties—an emphasis on processing imports. The second largest single steel works in the United States is located at Sparrows Point, Maryland, near Baltimore. It is based on Appalachian coal transported in rail cars directly (or via rail to Norfolk and barge up the Chesapeake) and foreign ores brought by ocean carriers. Shipbuilding in turn is a customer of the steel plant. Metal fabricating and food processing round out the picture along with air-

TABLE 2–2

Value added by manufacturing by states

State	Percent of National Total	Value Added ($ billion)	State	Percent of National Total	Value Added ($ billion)
Alabama	1.5	7.6 billion	Nebraska	.53	2.7 billion
Alaska	.09	.5	Nevada	.05	.3
Arizona	.57	2.9	New Hampshire	.37	1.9
Arkansas	.85	4.3	New Jersey	4.05	20.3
California	9.24	46.3	New Mexico	.11	.6
Colorado	.77	3.9	New York	7.76	38.9
Connecticut	2.	10.1	North Carolina	3.15	15.8
Delaware	.31	1.6	North Dakota	.06	.3
Florida	1.65	8.3	Ohio	7.52	37.7
Georgia	2.21	11.1	Oklahoma	.71	3.6
Hawaii	.13	.7	Oregon	1.07	5.4
Idaho	.29	1.5	Pennsylvania	6.42	32.2
Illinois	7.2	36.1	Rhode Island	.45	2.3
Indiana	3.99	20.	South Carolina	1.43	7.2
Iowa	1.55	7.8	South Dakota	.09	.5
Kansas	.97	4.9	Tennessee	2.13	10.7
Kentucky	1.71	8.6	Texas	3.51	17.6
Louisiana	1.67	8.4	Utah	.33	1.7
Maine	.39	2.	Vermont	.17	.9
Maryland	1.33	6.7	Virginia	1.85	9.3
Massachusetts	2.87	14.4	Washington	1.45	7.3
Michigan	6.46	32.2	West Virginia	.71	3.6
Minnesota	1.69	8.5	Wisconsin	2.97	14.9
Mississippi	.87	4.4	Wyoming	.06	.3
Missouri	2.21	11.1	Washington, D.C.		NA
Montana	.13	.7	(Puerto Rico)		3.3
TOTAL					500.8

craft and machine tools. Washington remains a center of government with little industrial development.

Hudson-Mohawk-Lake Ontario Lowland This area has capitalized on its location astride major transport arteries connecting the evolving northeastern Megalopolis to the agricultural-industrial heartland via the "water-level route" through the Appalachians. Textiles, machinery, electrical appliances, chemicals based on local salt mines, and ceramic products based on local clays have all developed, though textiles have since shifted southward. Surplus power helped attract electricity-consuming industries such as aluminum refining, while highly skilled labor works in plants producing photographic products, optical goods, scientific equipment, and photocopying machines.

Niagara Frontier The Great Lakes and Lake Ontario—Mohawk-Hudson routes converge here. Traditional industries are flour milling, iron, and steel, reflecting the ease of access to both raw materials and markets via cheap water transportation. Power from Niagara attracted electrochemicals, alloy refining, and fertilizer production. The completion of the St. Lawrence Seaway has enhanced the location of Buffalo and its satellites.

Pittsburgh-Cleveland This heavy-industry section extends from the Pittsburgh suburbs through Youngstown and Akron to Cleveland. It has added other related specialties such as chemicals from coke and coal. Glass, ceramic, and cement production were attracted early by ample fuel. Heavy machinery, such as mining machinery, locomotives, and heavy trucks, are manufactured to meet the demands of industrial customers. Machine tools have advanced, partly taking up the employment slack of declining, obsolescent steel mills and railroad equipment shops. The locational advantages of the area have changed negatively as old, inefficient steel mills had to compete with newer plants at tidewater locations, mills more accessible to the increasingly important imported ores.

East Lakes—Detroit This is one of the least diversified major sections—its fortunes ride with the demand for new cars. Several national economic trends combined to depress the auto industry to the verge of bankruptcy: public preference shifted repeatedly from big cars to small cars and back again as "oil shocks" rocked the markets and erratically shifted the "mix" of small, medium, and full-sized models; government regulation of car mileage averages and air pollution levels demanded massive investment in new engine and body designs and technologies. The Japanese reputation for careful attention to assembly

details and appearance took away customers. The area is so dominated by auto production (including parts, rubber and plastic products, auto glass, and such automotive chemical products as paints, undercoatings, and upholstery foams), that a national recession, coupled with the above economic changes, can cut deeply into auto markets, erasing profits.

West Lakes Metropolitan Chicago-Gary-Milwaukee acts as a "hinge," similar to the functions of New York (and of the whole megalopolis); Chicago funnels the exchange of imports and exports between much of the U.S. West and Southwest with the East (and the rest of the world). Early industries were based on agricultural processing and were related to its transport center functions. Its concentration of transport junctions continues to be highly attractive to industry. The Seaway has made Chicago (and its lakeshore neighbors) a seaport. It is a major lakeport, is connected by a canal with the enormous Mississippi-Missouri-Ohio-Tennessee-Arkansas river systems, is a major convergence point for both rail and highway traffic, and it has the busiest airport in the United States. Thus, water, rail, highway, pipeline, and air transport place Chicago in the center of a vast and efficient transport web. Diverse products include iron and steel, appliances, farm machinery, transportation machinery, machine tools, food processing, furniture, and clothing.

Kanawa-Ohio Valley A heavy-industry node emphasizing raw material-consuming industries, this area is particularly famous for its chemical industries based on coal, natural gas, salt, relatively cheap electrical energy, and cheap water transport for raw and processed materials. Newer additions to the industrial base include electrometallurgical (aluminum) and electrochemical enterprises. The area's handicaps to further expansion include cramped valley sites, high pollution levels in both the river and the subregion's air, and a declining raw material base.

Miami Valley Ohio's Miami Valley stretches from booming Columbus through Dayton and Springfield to Cincinnati. Human ingenuity has played an unusually important role here as the valley's machine shops gave birth to new types of cash registers and business machines, vacuum cleaners, tools, and the Wright Brother's aircraft. Cincinnati, once a major center of hog slaughtering, developed by-product processing such as soap, leather goods, paintbrushes (hog bristles), and lubricants and cooking fats.

Minneapolis-St. Paul The "twin cities" were established on the upper Mississippi River each for a different use of the river—St. Paul grew as a port just below the falls of St. Anthony, and Minneapolis was established to apply the power of the falls to flour milling and other industries. Grain processing and food products have remained important, while companies of international stature have grown up here making thermostats and control devices, abrasives, tapes of all kinds, and plastics. This major transport and service center has a hinterland that extends well into the Canadian Plains.

St. Louis   This city grew as the "Gateway to the West," close to the junction of the Mississippi and Missouri rivers. Slaughtering and meat packing, grain milling, and breweries are important, supplemented by steel and aluminum. Aircraft manufacturing has been important since World War II, when such defense plants were deliberately moved to the interior to safeguard them against the relatively short-range bombers of the day.

Urban Dynamics and the Megalopolis   The low density sprawl of contemporary North American cities (a tendency also observable in other developed countries and some developing countries) is intimately related to changes in transport technology and associated changes in lifestyles. For most of urban history, there has been a sharp distinction between city and countryside. No more. Where once cities were bounded by defensive walls, which encouraged high densities and congestion, walls no longer exist except as museum relics. Most U.S. and Canadian cities never had walls at all (except in the infancy of some settlements in hostile Indian territory). But wall or no wall, cities tended to be very compact with high-density development, due to the costs of commuting. Urban historian Sam Warner characterized the growth stages of Boston as moving from a "walking-scale" city (very compact; most living near their work) to the "streetcar city" (linear, compact strips of outward growth as horsecars, then electric street–cars brought commuting costs within the means of most urbanites) to "automobile cities" (the filling in of low-density areas between transit lines, and sprawl much further into the countryside).[5]

Just as streetcars followed fixed routes and concentrated urban growth in parallel, accessible strips, railroads represented high investments in fixed routes, encouraging industrial development near freight terminals, at sidings, and near urban train assembly yards. A shift to truck transport for light industries was associated with cars (and buses) in making commuting easier, resulting in the further sprawl of the city.

As the growth dynamics of cities have encouraged outward growth in concentric patterns except where channeled by topographic barriers and as modified and constrained by the relative cost of transport, the dynamics of Megalopolis emphasize the advantages of locations on transport axes between cities. Accessibility to market is one of the most powerful locational factors for modern industry. Of course, the proportionate ranking of many locational factors (labor, raw materials, energy, transport costs and availability, taxes and government regulations, and waste disposal are other major factors besides market) varies with the nature of the industrial activity or even wholesaling, retailing, or recreational activities. Metropolitan areas are more than markets, though; their pools of skilled, semiskilled and unskilled labor, the range of services available, the presence of related industries, and their commanding positions within transport webs are all additional advantages for locations close to them.

For half a century, light industries, warehousing, wholesaling-retailing, entertainment, and even office functions have been moving towards the outward-growing edges of the metropolis. Even earlier, space-consuming, polluting industries (oil refineries, chemical works) had sought peripheral locations. Megalopolis's linear series of cities essentially doubled the incentives of suburban location; a position *between* two big cities, astride the transport routes connecting them and accessible to both their markets and other locational factors, was very nearly ideal for many economic activities. While some costs related to transportation might be somewhat higher a few score miles outside the central city, cheaper land, spacious facilities with no parking problems, lower taxes, and access to an interstate highway usually far outweighed any negatives. While growth will generally spread outward from a city, there are thus special advantages to locations *between* cities.

This accelerated growth in the "connector zones" between cities snowballs; that is, development and growth tends to attract more development and growth. The original Megalopolis of the northeastern seaboard, sometimes called "Bos-Wash" (Boston to Washington, D.C.), is a prototype. A southern Great Lakes to Appalachia megalopolis, "Chi-Pitts" (Milwaukee-Chicago-Detroit-Toledo-Cleveland-Pittsburgh), is developing (see Figure 2–6) and growth trends indicate the possibility of future super-megalopolises or city-chains connecting the Great Lakes and northeastern megalopolises via both the Ontario Peninsula of Canada (Windsor-London-Hamilton-[Toronto]–Niagara Falls) and the southern Lake Erie shore (Cleveland-Erie-Buffalo) and the Mohawk Valley–Hudson Valley. Interestingly, the original Megalopolis has a parallel smaller version of its growth dynamics along its seashore

---

[5] Sam Bass Warner, Jr., *Streetcar Suburbs: The Process of Growth in Boston, 1870–1900* (New York: Atheneum, 1971).

fringes, particularly in New Jersey, where a series of once-separate resorts are growing towards one another in a **leisureopolis.**

A major business of Megalopolis is decision making; it has far more than its proportionate share of "brainpower"—government and business executives, research scientists, and other highly skilled and highly educated people. It serves as headquarters for a third of the 500 largest corporations in the United States, contains the national capital, and has more than half of the largest banks in America. Jean Gottmann's epic study of Megalopolis also identified a new category of economic activity to explain its functions. Traditionally there were three broad employment categories: primary (production of raw materials—agriculture, mining, forestry), secondary (processing raw materials into useful forms and products-manufacturing), and tertiary (all services such as distribution, retailing, entertainment, medical and other professional services, and administration). The third, services, category was much too broad. It included those performing routine and largely physical services that require relatively brief training and little intellectual creativity or judgment (warehouse workers, retail clerks, waiters, and business machine operatives). It also included the highly educated, specially trained professionals and executives who do not perform a tangible or physical service (except as part of the application of their professional skills and judgment—surgeons, for example); but who give advice, make decisions, or educate (lawyers, accountants, medical and dental personnel, teachers, and executives of all kinds). Clearly, that last group is different in fundamental ways from the preceding groups, and so Gottmann labeled the decision makers the "quaternary" (fourth) category, noting Megalopolis's significance in this employment category.

A serious problem for the northeastern Megalopolis, as well as other urban areas' "growing edge," is the set of pressures placed on farmers and farmland on the suburban fringe. In the great majority of cities, their original founding and much of their growth was partly attributable to the quality of agricultural resources—soils-terrain-water balance in their vicinity. Obviously, cities grow in river valleys, fertile plains, or irrigated oases, not on barren mountaintops. The physical spread of the city is almost always at the expense of good quality farmland. Since residences, shopping malls, and industrial parks can pay far more for land per acre than farmers, not only does suburban growth make room for expansion of individual farms prohibitively expensive, but farmers are pressured to sell out by a combination of rising prices and especially rising taxes (see Figure 2–9). To help farmers survive on the edge of Megalopolis, some states tax farmland at a special low rate with the understanding that, if that land is sold for development, the state or local government can "back figure" taxes at the developable land rate rather than at the permanent farmland rate. Other state or local governments may purchase future *development rights* from a farm owner, making it sellable only as farmland and thus qualifying it for lower taxes.

Environmental Problems and Potentials   Environmental problems tend to be higher in areas of heavy industry (particularly long-established industrial areas based on fossil fuels or raw materials) and in areas of dense population. The Aging Core qualifies on both counts. In Megalopolis, sheer densities of people and industries have seriously polluted several major rivers; it is asserted by ecologists that the major use of rivers in the United States is the dilution-disposal of wastes. The case of the Hudson River illustrates the problem. Carrying one of the largest volumes of water of any river east of the Mississippi system, the Hudson is so polluted as it reaches New York City that the city plans to use the water only in extreme emergency. Rather than tap the Hudson upstream, which would require very expensive pollution treatment, New York City reaches over to the relatively clean headwaters of the Delaware River and pipes that water *under* the Hudson to the city. This limits the downstream users and potential users of the Delaware's water, requiring interstate agreements (and litigation) to allocate water. There is no shortage of fresh water in the Aging Core, but there definitely is a shortage of *clean* fresh water.

Strip-mining of Appalachian and Illinois coal, prior to the more stringent restoration laws now in effect, has left scores of thousands of acres desolate and unproductive. In the heartland, there is growing concern that intensive farming may be "mining" the soil, depleting its fertility, and contributing to an erosion problem, which could diminish productivity in the future.

At least three of the core's cities qualify as **world cities** in rank—New York, Chicago, and Washington, D.C. As mentioned in the Prologue, New York and Chicago are two of the three major rivals for "primate city" functions; and Washington, D.C., qualifies on the basis of its political influence in the world.

THE DYNAMIC SOUTH

The South is one of the most distinctive and generally recognized subregions of the United States. Its approximate outlines correspond with the old Confederacy—plus Kentucky and minus western Texas.

It is customary to refer to the contemporary South as the "New South" or "Dynamic South" to contrast the pres-

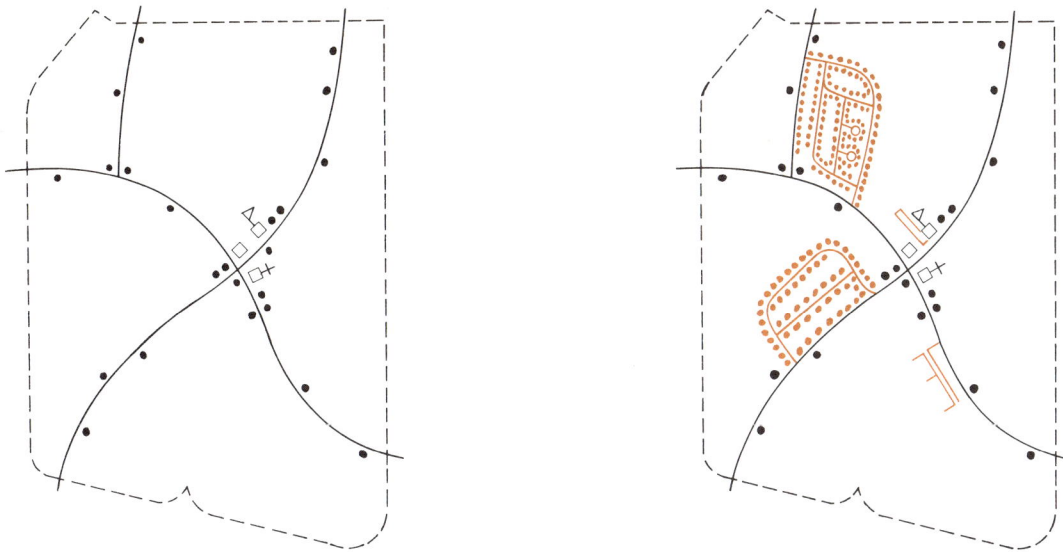

BEFORE URBAN EXPANSION: Rural township, local school, few local government responsibilities, and low taxes on farmland. (● indicates house.)

AFTER URBAN EXPANSION: Rising population means new addition to school, sewer treatment plant, sanitary water supply, traffic lights, more police, new fire trucks, and consolidated high school. Rising taxes pressure remaining farmers to sell for development.

FIGURE 2–9
Suburbanization and Land Values. Most great cities grew within a productive agricultural hinterland. Urban expansion commonly is at the expense of high quality farmland, whose owners are often forced to compete with more intensive land use as the tax rates escalate.

ent with the image of the depressed past, for the Old South (1865 to 1940) was an area of economic and psychological depression. The Civil War had destroyed much of the transport **infrastructure** (the physical structures and related facilities) in the South, had wiped out capital in the form of Confederate currency and bonds, and seized, as war preparations, warehoused cotton. The occupation of the South was much less generously farsighted than the U.S. occupation of Japan or Germany eighty years afterwards. Northern business tended to treat the South as having the kind of submissive colonial status that the British had attempted to impose on their American colonies. The South was to exchange bulk agricultural and other raw or semiprocessed resources for the relatively more expensive manufactured goods of the northeastern United States. The South's resources were to be selectively developed for the benefit of established Northern industrial centers and not necessarily integrated into an expanding, industrializing regional economy in the South. The West, although portions were largely populated by Southerners seeking a fresh start after the destruction resulting from the Civil War, was more "Northern" than "Southern," economically and politically, and the South did not attract new migrants on anything like the scale of the booming, industrial North.

If World War I began the economic revitalization of the South, World War II's demands on the economy greatly accelerated the emergence of the New South. Industry, particularly the textile industry, had already begun the move south before 1917, attracted by milder climates (less heating cost), cheaper labor, weaker or nonexistent unions, lower cost of living, and varied resource base. (Iron ore, phosphates, oil, and natural gas were among the resources exploited in the South by the early twentieth century.) The southern pine forests became more valuable as a pulp and paper resource when a new sulphate process made it possible to produce better quality paper from the trees by dissolving out the tarlike gums in their sap. The South has a longer growing season, and "genetically engineered" trees reach pulp-market size in as little as ten or twelve years; it is possible for landowners to grow trees as long-term rotation crops, cutting 8 or 10 percent of their total forest each year and replanting with fast-maturing pines. The phosphate mines of Florida provide material for fertilizer and chemical use; reserves are adequate for many decades and some phosphate is exported to Japan. A series of major oil and gas fields has been found in the western portion of the region, including the great East Texas Field, the largest ever found in the United States. Offshore wells tap a huge series of fields extending from the Mississippi Delta west and south to the fabulous new offshore fields of Mexico. Although it is unlikely that another East Texas bonanza will be discovered, steeply rising prices in world markets helped trigger a federal "decontrol" (phasing out of artificially low, non-market-controlled price limits). Regional production will be higher than otherwise possible because higher prices support more investment in obtaining oil from deeper, smaller pools or high-risk, very deep exploratory wells and in repressuring of old fields to force more oil into wells already drilled. Similarly, higher prices for natural gas crossing state lines (and thus subject to federal price controls) may eventually bring into production vast but expensive supplies from deep, "geo-pressurized sands" in Louisiana and offshore areas.

There are strong and obvious reasons for an increase in supply of oil and gas (or any other natural resource) following a price rise. A natural resource is simply any material or energy source occurring naturally in the environment that people have identified as economically useful and retrievable. If very sharp price rises were to affect the iron mining industry, for example, many areas with reserves of earth materials just below current economic minimum definitions of *ores* would enter production. It is the same with oil and gas. Rising prices *redefine* the resource to include that which was too expensive to produce before but is now within the economic range. This change over time in the qualitative and quantitative definitions of economic resources is quite common and is related to the phenomenon of creaming a resource. *Creaming* a resource refers to the tendency to exploit at first only the richest, easiest to mine, most convenient to market parts of a total resource base. Later, as demand escalates, prices rise, and the technology of exploitation advances in efficiency, what was overlooked or discarded before is redefined as an economic source. Exploration is also accelerated. The South will share in this new energy boom to the extent that known, but difficult to extract resources will be exploited, exploration carried deeper and into less promising (but possible) areas, and old fields "rejuvenated" by repressuring.

Escalating energy prices will also give some advantages to the rich coal fields of the Southern Appalachian Highlands; coal prices rise as plans for nuclear plants are delayed or abandoned, and as the possibility of coal liquefaction techniques for synthetic gasoline production comes closer to reality. The concentration of coal, limestone, and iron ore in north-central Alabama led to a minor (by world-standards) steel industry at Birmingham.

The population of the South remained heavily rural and small-town long after the rise of the megalopolises in the mid-Atlantic and southern Lakes. This reflects the long dominance of agriculture in the region and its slower industrialization. A consequence was a prevalence of poverty and an outward flow of people, which amounted to a human hemorrhage in some severely eroded and impoverished rural areas. These internal refugees from declining mining areas or mechanization and other agricultural revolutions sought better lives in the big cities, as had earlier generations who left farms in other areas.

There are signs that the rural exodus has begun to reverse, and that blacks in particular have reduced or even reversed their trek out of the South. One of the greatest migrations in history had been sustained (with few temporary reversals) by blacks responding to a powerful set of **push-pull factors.** Among the "push" (negative) factors were decreasing demand for agricultural labor, poor housing conditions, poorly funded social welfare programs for the poor of rural areas, and generally bleak prospects for improving life. "Pull" (positive) factors included access to industrial employment, superior quality housing in cities (even in slums), less pervasive discrimination in jobs (particularly federal government jobs), dramatically more generous social welfare programs available, and a generally optimistic outlook for improving one's life and especially that of one's children. It must be remembered that the same set of attractants and motivations applied to Southern whites, minus most of the discriminatory patterns.

Once the first waves of northward-bound migrants had settled in, located housing and jobs, and familiarized themselves with the urban area and urban lifestyles, they were in a position to ease the way for relatives and friends, frequently providing temporary housing as well as other assistance. Much the same pattern had existed in the waves of European migration to America.

Now the migration is at least partially reversing, partly for the same set of reasons that motivated a general resurgence of small town America everywhere. Some of the push-pulls here are universal, for white and black alike. Life in the great metropolitan centers and their immediate suburbs is perceived as unacceptably costly, pollution-ridden, insecure from street crimes and burglary, and "not a nice place to raise children." Small cities and towns further removed from metropolitan orbits usually offer lower housing costs and lower cost of services, lower taxes, friendly atmosphere, less congestion and pollution, and better recreational opportunities. The interstate highways, sharply reducing travel time and distribution costs, have helped encourage a movement of industry to small cities and towns, providing the jobs for these "outward-bound" (from big cities) migrants. Small cities and towns throughout the United States have stopped losing (and even tend to gain population, often faster than big cities).

The South's metropolitan areas have also grown impressively, partly because the South of twenty years ago, with its slow start in industrialization, still had less than its share of really big cities. In his fascinating book on *The South,* John Fraser Hart observed that most of the big cities of the South were peripheral to the South; they were

Atlanta: The Regional Capital of the Dynamic South. Few metropolitan areas personify the new dynamism of the South as does Atlanta. An important transportation center from before the Civil War, Atlanta serves as regional headquarters for much of the southeast. (Photo by Stansfield)

"hinge cities" connecting the South as a subregional economy with the Northeast (Baltimore, Washington, D.C.), the industrial heartland (Cincinnati, St. Louis), or the West (Kansas City, Dallas, Houston). New Orleans was a large city primarily because it functioned as a port for much of the highly productive Midwest, not simply as a Southern port. Similarly, Miami was *in* the South, but not really *of* the South—its citizens and functions being quite atypical of the South. Atlanta is the best example of a truly (in economic and cultural terms) Southern city; it functions as a **regional capital** for much of the Southeast, just as Dallas-Ft. Worth is a regional capital for the South-West transition area.

The transformation of southern agriculture provides a good insight into the geographic changes that have recently occurred in that area. Cotton and corn no longer rule southern farming as they did until World War II. Diversification, along with many changes in the southern economy, has long since smashed the "Cotton Belt" into a few highly localized cotton regions. Cotton has retreated into a few, favorable areas of the South and to nontraditional new cotton producing areas in California, Arizona, and west Texas. The push factors included soil erosion and soil depletion after a century or so of cotton production; the Piedmont was particularly ravished by erosion. The outflow of farm labor raised the cost of production on

the smaller, nonmechanized farms in traditional areas. The newer, highly mechanized and irrigated cotton lands to the west were far more efficient. At the same time, federal programs, state universities, and county agents were advocating crop diversification, particularly the switch of worn-out cropland to pasture. Regional markets for beef and dairy products surged upward with industrialization.

The Three Souths   If defined in terms of cotton cultivation in the nineteenth century, the South would have been a discontinuous cultural region with three distinctive subregions that together occupied the approximate quadrangel shown in Figure 2–3. The "three Souths" are the traditional cotton-culture, plantation South of the Atlantic Coastal Plain, the Piedmont, and the Mississippi Valley northward to southern Illinois (sometimes called the "Lower South"); the Southern Appalachian Highlands (the "Upper South";) and the subtropical Atlantic-Gulf coasts and Florida. It was the Lower South that developed the cotton kingdom, maintained African slaves as a labor force, and led the Confederacy in its brief, bloody rebellion against an industrializing, urbanizing North intent on abolishing slavery and imposing the national will on the South. The Upland or Appalachian South was a less enthusiastic participant in the Confederacy as its small farms had neither cotton nor slaves and, indeed, western, upland Virginia seceded from Virginia as a Union state (West Virginia) while Kentucky pursued a neutral course before supporting the Union. The subtropical coasts and Florida have developed into a very distinctive region, one that is not southern in the traditional context.

The Upland South   Development patterns and strategies vary, of course, within the "three Souths." The Upland South is benefitting from the resurgence of "king coal"; production increases for Kentucky, Alabama, and Tennessee keep setting new records, while older producing regions in West Virginia and Virginia have had minor decreases in the last decade.

While underground mines are heavy users of machines, surface mining is even more efficient in production per labor-hour. Unfortunately, the strip mining of coal has high potential for environmental degradation, a potential that is now limited but not totally overcome by federal and state regulations concerning restoration of the landscape and the minimizing of damage. New legislation has been successful in that much of the restored forest and farmland is at least as usable as before strip mining, but Appalachia still has some 380,000 acres of unreclaimed land, much of it in the Upland South.

The rejuvenation of the depressed Upland South's rural and mining communities will not be easy or cheap, but there are some bright trends and historical examples. The Tennessee Valley Authority, a federal corporation created in 1933, has demonstrated the positive contributions to the regional economy possible through coordinated conservation, energy development, flood control, and navigation improvement schemes related by a series of some forty dams built by TVA or coordinated into its system. Thanks to TVA, Knoxville, Tennessee, is a river port connected to the Ohio-Mississippi system and a large and growing industrial cluster. Cheap electricity generated through the dams attracted industry, including the Atomic Energy Center at Oak Ridge, and helped convert an impoverished part of southern Appalachia into an economically healthy one. Flood control was combined with a program to control erosion through technical assistance to farmers, along with cheap fertilizer manufactured with hydro power. The contemporary TVA, however, has apparently strayed from its conservation championship by buying huge tonnages of strip-mined coal to fire its thermal generating plants (demand for electricity has long since outpaced hydro potential in the area). The "Great Lakes of the South" impounded by the dams have supported a large tourist industry, and the image of TVA within its service area is generally positive.

An impressive highway-building program (Appalachian Access Roads) has helped overcome the **barrier and channel effect** of the mountains on transport. (This effect is the tendency to seek the easiest way through rather than the route most beneficial to regional development).

Following waves of exploitation from the "outside" seeking to exploit its timber and then its coal, the Upland South now faces another influx of outside entrepreneurs seeking profits from its other resources. This time the land suited to recreational use is being bought up on a grand scale by outside corporations and, piece-by-piece, by urbanites looking for a peaceful mountain retreat. As in the timber and coal booms, the tourism-recreation boom pits well-financed outsiders against the mountaineers' meager funds, outbidding them and inducing an economic and cultural change that raises everyone's taxes to provide services to the newcomers. As in timber and coal exploitation, the profits tend to "drain downhill" while the "opportunities" generated for the locals are mostly low-paying seasonal jobs in service trades.

The Lower South   The Lower South's development continues to emphasize diversification of agriculture as tree crops, vegetables, and soybeans expand along with beef. Timber and pulp production should continue to expand, supporting an important component of the regional industrial base. The growth of medium-size industrial cities continues, such as the Carolina constellation of cities from Spartanburg-Greenville, South Carolina, through Charlotte, Winston-Salem, and Greensboro to the famed "research triangle" of Raleigh-Durham-Chapel Hill in North Carolina. This loose grouping of cities with new industry growing along their highway connectors and near regional airports is a phenomenon related to the megalopolises, if on a smaller scale, and without the obvious degree of loose suburban growth connecting them.

The Gulf Coast and Florida   The Middle-American connection is very important to the entire Gulf Coast and Florida. The flows of Caribbean minerals (oil, bauxite) and agricultural products (bananas, sugar) are helping to stimulate major port improvements at Houston-Galveston, New Orleans, and Mobile, while Miami becomes a major center of Latin American culture and a prime attraction to Latin Americans visiting the United States. If political conditions in the North Africa–Southwest Asian and Africa south of the Sahara regions make U.S. reliance on their exports far less secure, a (western) hemispheric self-sufficiency policy could greatly increase the importance of Gulf Coast-Caribbean and Latin American ties.

The subtropical coast sector of the South will continue to attract both seasonal tourists and permanent residents (largely retired), but some intraregional shifts in growth are evident. Fewer retirees can now afford Florida's

Naples, Florida: The Tropical Dream. The sunbelt-bound flow of wealthy retirees has helped Florida become one of the faster-growing states. Apartments and condominiums like these line miles of Florida's coastline. (Photo by Stansfield)

rising living costs, real estate prices, and taxes; the steep rise in Cuban and Haitian immigrants to metropolitan Miami, with its attendant social costs, may alter some perceptions about the desirability of southern Florida, sending more retirees to the Gulf shores of Texas, Louisiana, Mississippi, and Alabama, and to the Florida panhandle. Miami can be expected to become a link city between the United States and its Latin neighbors; its wholesale-retail and service functions and light industries will reflect the growing importance of this Latin American orientation.

Water—fresh, clean and plenty of it—has become a major asset of the subtropical coast region as chemical and pulp and paper industries grow on the basis of the other material assets of the area. Conflicts over or involving water management, from the endangered Everglades to the pollution-threatened Texas coast, will capture regional interest for some time, as will the "developers versus preservationists" struggle over Padre Island, a long sandy barrier beach off the south Texas coast.

THE WESTERN INTERIOR

The Western Interior subregion includes the Rockies and intermontane basins, along with most of the Great Plains. Lightly settled in comparison with the core, the South, and West Coast regions, the Western Interior is nonetheless one of great change, vitality and significance to the American economy. The coal of the plains, the oil and gas potential of the "overthrust belt" of the Rockies, and the

oils shales of the Rockies basins could prove essential to the energy needs of the United States. The subregion also generates huge agricultural surpluses, primarily wheat, for export, helping to balance the expensive imports of OPEC oil and Japanese manufactures. Without the potential and present food and fuel productivity of the Western Interior, the United States would be much poorer and the world less adequately fed.

The Resource Base The resource base was once dominated by gold. Gold in the central Rockies, discovered by returning unsuccessful California "Forty Niners," drew much attention to Colorado. The gold rushes appear long over, though a rising world market stimulated new prospecting and thoughts of large-scale mine reopening. South Dakota's fabled Homestake Mine, in production for a century, makes that state first in gold production, but the most important minerals are fossil fuels (see Figure 2–4). Conventional oil wells have been producing in the subregion for many years, but new fields, deeper wells, and production from formerly known but then uneconomic sources have all boosted production. Wyoming, along with other states (and Canada's prairie provinces), has a boom atmosphere, with rapidly growing oil and coal towns rivaling uranium towns. Natural gas is also produced in Wyoming, Kansas, and the panhandle area of Texas. Geologists long has known that enormous volumes of relatively low quality coal underlie the northern Great Plains. Little attention was paid to this reserve until the 1970's due to both geographic location and low quality.

The Grand Canyon of the Colorado. The Grand Canyon, in one of America's most visited National Parks, is one of the world's most famous drylands erosional features. The Colorado River, the "master stream" (largest river and drainage basin) of the southwest, is so heavily used for water supply and irrigation in this water-short region that little flows south into Mexico. (Photo by Stansfield)

The geographic concept of **intervening opportunity** is applicable here. It makes no sense to transport anything to market across or through a producing or source area that is closer to that market (see Figure 1–19), unless there is some special quality or other advantage. The major markets for coal, the great industrial-urban centers of the southern Great Lakes and the Northeast both had higher quality coal closer in the Appalachian and Eastern Interior coal fields. Great Plains coal is not of metallurgical (coking) quality and its heat energy content is low; while 70 percent of the U.S. coal reserves (in tonnage) lie west of the Mississippi, 55 percent of the coal measured in energy content lies to the east (not including Alaskan coal). Several factors have redefined northern plains coal as an economically retrievable resource. The OPEC cartel has, by multiplying the cost of imported oil, made other energy resources more attractive and indirectly raised the market value of competing fuels as well. Technological advances in surface-mining machinery (power shovels are more efficient) and in the transmission of electricity now make it possible to use plains coal to generate power near the mine and ship electrical energy to distant markets.

Enormous new strip mines and power generating plants are now rising in Montana and Wyoming. A negative impact on the environment seems inevitable as the coal stripping itself tends to lower water tables, and regenera-

tion of vegetation in the semiarid lands is not as readily achieved in reclaimed stripped areas as in much more humid Appalachia. Air pollution, even with the use of the expensive (and energy-consuming) pollution-control equipment required, will be high just by reason of the mammoth scale of the new generating plants.

The economic pressures on the plains ranchers and farmers are staggering. In areas of Montana so dry that 36 acres (15 hectares) are required to support one cow for one year without overgrazing, those same 36 acres could conceivably produce 1.25 million tons of coal. At average royalties, the landowner would receive about a third of $1 million. When it is remembered that, precisely because of the low agriculture productivity per acre of these areas, average ranches top 1,000 acres (400 hectares), some ranchers' initial resistance to these quick payoffs from mining cannot last.

The oil shales of the subregion, the richest deposits of which are in Colorado, Wyoming, and Utah (see Figure 2–4) could free the United States from dependence on imported oil, but at a very high cost of production and environmental degradation. To extract the kerogen or shale oil (a hydrocarbon similar to petroleum), it is necessary to crush the shale and use very high temperatures to retort (extract as a hot vapor) the kerogen. Shale can be mined, and the rock crushed and heat treated in surface plants or retorted underground. The process is expensive and minimizing environmental damage would add still higher costs. The "spent" shale occupies an even larger volume than before it was mined and processed. The process of kerogen extraction uses water, and mining lowers subsurface water tables; in an already water-short area, these may prove the most serious problems. The attraction lies in the huge volume of the potential resource. As with petroleum or coal, the total known quantity cannot be retrieved, as some will be too deep; too fragmented into small, thin, or low-quality seams; or too difficult to bring to the surface. If relatively thick, rich shale oil deposits (at least 10 feet thick, at least 25 gallons per ton yield under current processing technology) are considered, these shales could yield 600 billion barrels of oil. If thinner, "leaner" shales proved economical to mine and process, the resource could be redefined to over 2 *trillion* barrels.

One major obstacle to rapid development is the reluctance of oil companies to invest billions of dollars in shale processing plants when environmental regulations yet to be written could increase the already high risk. The "overthrust belt," a geologic region running the approximate length of the Rockies, has major oil reserves at great depths. Such possibilities are another risk for high cost shale production. Shale oil was produced profitably in the 1920's, but could not compete with cheap oil from the great East Texas fields, discovered in 1930. The lesson for oil companies was that shale oil is profitable only when future markets are certain to continue upward, price controls unlikely, and environmental restraints eased.

Agriculture and Population Migration: The Changing Plains The repeated and dramatic changes in people's perceptions of the semiarid and sub-humid plains of North America, the "brown midriff of the continent," are related to the changing economy and to technological levels available to aid in their settlement and economic use. The physical environment of the plains—flat to gently rolling terrain, deep soils rich in soluble minerals, covered by a thick heavy sod of intertwined grass roots, subsurface water usually available only at great depths, grass cover ranging from 6 feet high on the eastern margins to bunched, short grass on the western extreme, and surface streams shallow and frequently intermittent (water in them only after local rains)—was first viewed negatively by early European explorers. Finding no gold and only nomadic Indians living at a primitive level, the Spanish explorers of the seventeenth century would have agreed with early nineteenth century Americans that the plains were an unfortunate barrier to western expansion.

For people used to relying on ample wood for houses, furniture, farm buildings, fences, and fuel, the almost treeless plains were a nonsupportive, even threatening environment. The irontipped wooden plows of the first half of the nineteenth century could not turn over the heavy sod of the plains, and lower precipitation seemed to equal inevitably lower yields.

A revolution in land use occurred just after the Civil War when the "cattle kingdom" spread quickly up the plains from Texas as railroads entered the edge of the plains, providing the connection of the immense pastures with the burgeoning cities farther east. The cattle kingdom flourished only a few decades before being partially displaced westward by the second great revolution in land-use systems, the wheat-farming frontiers. Steel plows, mechanical reapers, deep-well-drilling equipment, and barbed wire fencing (to keep out cattle) all combined with railroads to transform the economic possibilities of the great grasslands. Homestead lands and inexpensive purchases from railroads (which had been given government

Coal Mine Near Gilette, Wyoming. The vast energy reserves of the western interior, including oil, natural gas, uranium, and oil shales in addition to coal and lignite, is a major reason for this subregion's economic boom. (Photo by Stansfield)

land as subsidies to construction) made it possible to acquire larger farms than were average back east, partly compensating for lower productivity per acre. Hybrid seed, better adapted to drought, also boosted production per acre.

Unfortunately, settlement of wheat farmers pushed westward into semiarid lands that would better have been left in pasture. A feature of semiarid environments, discovered the hard way by pioneering farmers, is the unpredictability of precipitation from year to year. Long-term averages mean little, as erratic cycles of drier than average years alternate with wetter cycles, both of which are interrupted by atypical years and are of uncertain length. Optimistic expansion of wheat lands in wetter periods was followed by serious droughts, which sent recent in-migrants back east or to the West Coast as their farms literally blew away. Such expansion-retraction cycles have occurred several times as wheat prices fluctuated.

Wheat remains the major crop (although more land is in pasture than under cultivation), while sugar beets, vegetables and, in the Texas panhandle, cotton, are alternatives where irrigation is available. Small grains and oil-seeds are the basis for diversification in non-irrigated areas. Relatively little wheat is irrigated, and the uncertainties of precipitation are minimized more by improved hybrid seed, alternate year cropping, and crop insurance underwritten by the federal government.

The enormous scale of agriculture is a striking characteristic of the plains landscape—huge grain elevators, cotton gins, storage bins, and machinery sheds, combined with the grand geometry of field boundaries and circles of pivot-irrigation. There is a larger-than-life aura to the subregion reflected in its cultural geography as well.

The Rockies and intermontane sectors of the subregion both are characterized by scattered energy booms, continuing summer tourism complemented by rising winter tourism, and grazing and forestry industries. Some of the subregion's cities are booming as Americans become aware of the great natural beauty of the area and move there. Population then, as market and labor force, becomes an attractive factor for some industries, especially electronics and defense and space-related industries, which can bear the high transport costs of location here between major population nodes. As has happened earlier in California, in-migrants attracted by the amenities of the area spurred economic growth, rather than economic opportunity attracting people.

In Nevada, Reno and Las Vegas may be the largest cities to be so completely dominated by resort functions in the United States. A political-cultural amenity, legalization of quick marriages and divorces, virtually every form of gambling, and even prostitution (in some counties) en-

abled Nevada to capitalize on its accessibility to the California metropolises and its position astride important east-west transit routes in luring tourists. Retirement to the dry sunshine of the southern intermontane has also spurred growth through its "import" of savings and pensions earned elsewhere and brought here on retirement. Shortages of fresh water will be the important depressant of growth rates in the future unless further large-scale water transfers are funded by the federal government.

THE WEST COAST

California, Oregon, and Washington constitute the subregion, but the dissimilarities among the units leave proximity and coastal location as almost unifiers of convenience. The two states of the Pacific Northwest have a cooler, more humid climate in their coastal reaches than does California. Pacific Northwest agriculture is divided between production of wheat and fodder in eastern drylands areas, geared to an export market, and humid area specialty crops and dairying geared more to the markets of California and western Canada. Lumbering, aluminum production, aircraft, and wood products industries dominate in an economy far less developed than that of highly varied California. Yet, the whole subregion is Pacific in its orientation, and all three states share in the markets of Alaska, Japan, and, now, China. As California retains a strong Mexican cultural influence and contact, the Northwest seems to be developing a similar relationship with Canada. As California has become a center of innovation and a mecca for migrants, Washington and Oregon will undoubtedly share in the decentralization of California's population, industry, and functions—a process already in progress. As strikingly different as the three states may be, there are similarities and interactions there, and commonality of interests are already in the process of binding the three into a recognizable subregion.

California: The Image and the Reality What people perceive to be true about an area is always an important factor in settlement inflows; it can be critical in rates of regional growth. The problems of **perception,** trying to sort out the various popularly held images of a region in relation to people's cultural background and values, has long fascinated geographers. While it is problematic whether any objective reality can be distinguished from culturally conditioned perceptions, it is generally recognized that California has a vividly positive image to the overwhelming majority of Americans. This very positive image, or rather kaleidoscope of many images, has changed in emphasis over the years but remains powerful.

California is a special place perhaps because its physical and cultural landscapes appeal to, and reflect, popular American ideals about desirable landscapes.

It is said that the most enduringly popular picture postcard scenes of California show the edge of the Los Angeles basin with orange groves in fruit in the foreground and snow-capped mountains behind, all under the bright sky typical of Mediterranean climates. That scene is now more nostalgic than representative. The air temperature inversions common over the Los Angeles basin trap a noxious haze of pollutants so that clear skies are a rare treat. Many of the orange groves have been cut down to make way for freeways, industrial parks, shopping centers, and housing. Even the pines of the fringing mountains have suffered blight associated with high levels of atmospheric pollution. Clearly, the reality has changed faster than the cherished image. But, the image, if altered and dimmed, is still a positive one. Growing awareness that increasing environmental pollution and sheer weight of numbers are putting deterioration pressures on the physical environment is counterbalanced partly by the glittering cultural environment. California, specifically the "Southland," (metropolitan Los Angeles–San Diego), is a very exciting, innovative place.

Southern California has gone from a relative backwater to the largest metropolitan area in the western half of the country in less than a century. The state capital (Sacramento), the largest city (San Francisco), and the state university (Berkeley) were all clustered in the San Francisco Bay area of central California, which boomed following the gold rush. Los Angeles' first important boom was in the 1880's following completion of the transcontinental railroads into the basin. The population again surged rapidly upward in the 1920's as oil derricks and movie studios sprouted, followed by the sustained boom originating in World War II as aircraft and defense industries attracted still more people.

The dispersed nature of urbanization in the Los Angeles Basin, featuring many small centers rather than a single major core, is related to the 1880's real estate booms and consequent settlement pattern. The polynuclear structure of contemporary Los Angeles reflects the formerly separate towns, commonly each with a different agricultural specialty, now embedded in a matrix of automobile-fostered suburban sprawl.

California Agriculture   With only such exotic exceptions as coffee (Hawaii), limes (Florida Keys), and cane sugar, any agricultural product grown in the United States is grown in California. The range of climate and soil types in the Golden State supports a full range of temperate and subtropical plants. California is first in total value of farm products; it is the leading producer of thirty crops and the only producer of some.

This great diversity and prosperity did not always exist. Colonial California's major agricultural export was cowhide; there were then no practical means of preserving and efficiently transporting its potential production of fruits and vegetables. The successive developments, following acquisition by the United States, of transcontinental railroads, refrigerated boxcars, commercial canneries, freezing plants, and refrigerated trucks travelling interstate highways all transformed California's agriculture. The Mediterranean climate, with its relatively warm winters, supports a specialization in winter-season fresh fruits and vegetables. California, like Florida and Texas, can ship fresh salad vegetables to northeastern and midwestern markets at times when their fields are snow-covered.

Distribution Canal, Southern San Joaquin Valley, California. The rapid growth of southern California has severely strained the Southwest's entire water supply. Some of the water in this irrigation system has been transported hundreds of miles from northern California in one of the largest engineering projects ever undertaken by a state. (Photo by Stansfield)

Crop specializations around the state tend to reflect climate and soil qualities, but other, culturally-based considerations are important. The Salinas Valley, for example, specializes in lettuce. Many other parts of the state are physically suited to lettuce production, and the Salinas area could readily produce other crops. Such a regional specialization makes sense for the growers because *collectively* they can attract many rail cars and trucks at harvest season. They can establish marketing cooperatives to stabilize prices and purchasing cooperatives to buy their supplies, machinery, and fuel at wholesale prices. Banks in the area understand the lettuce business and are willing to make loans; state and federal agricultural agents are likely to be, or become, specialists in this crop. The problems of such areal specializations are that lettuce diseases or predators can spread quickly and that harvest labor is needed by everyone at the same time, but economic-cultural location factors tend to be more positive than negative.

California leads the nation in the use of irrigation water, and it has a long tradition of large land units; in these two characteristics, California again demonstrates leadership in American economic trends. Large land holdings were favored under Spanish and Mexican rule. Some of these huge landgrants, confirmed the treaty ending the war with Mexico in 1848, have continued intact into the twentieth century.

The reshaping of California by people has taken place on a massive scale, even for North America. The California Water Plan is one of the greatest engineering works ever undertaken by an American state; it supplements extensive water engineering systems built by the federal government. California has a massive imbalance in water availability and water demand. Northern California, north of Sacramento, has most of the precipitation but little of the population. Two thirds of the total flow of water in the Central Valley is in the northern half, the Sacramento system. Federal and state water systems both transfer "surplus" (not needed for irrigation) Sacramento Valley water southward to irrigate semiarid San Joaquin Valley. (See Figure 2–10) Some of the nation's most valuable farmland now is in the San Joaquin Valley. State-source and federal-source water flows in the same canals and aqueducts, some of it used to replace water no longer available from local sources as deep wells draw down the subsurface supply and diminish or end surface flows.

A second important irrigation project is in Imperial Valley–Coachella Valley east of San Diego. (See Figure 2–10.) This is the last major oasis supplied by the much-used Colorado River before it flows across the Mexican border. The All-American Canal feeds this lush subtropical "winter garden" where three crops a year are sometimes

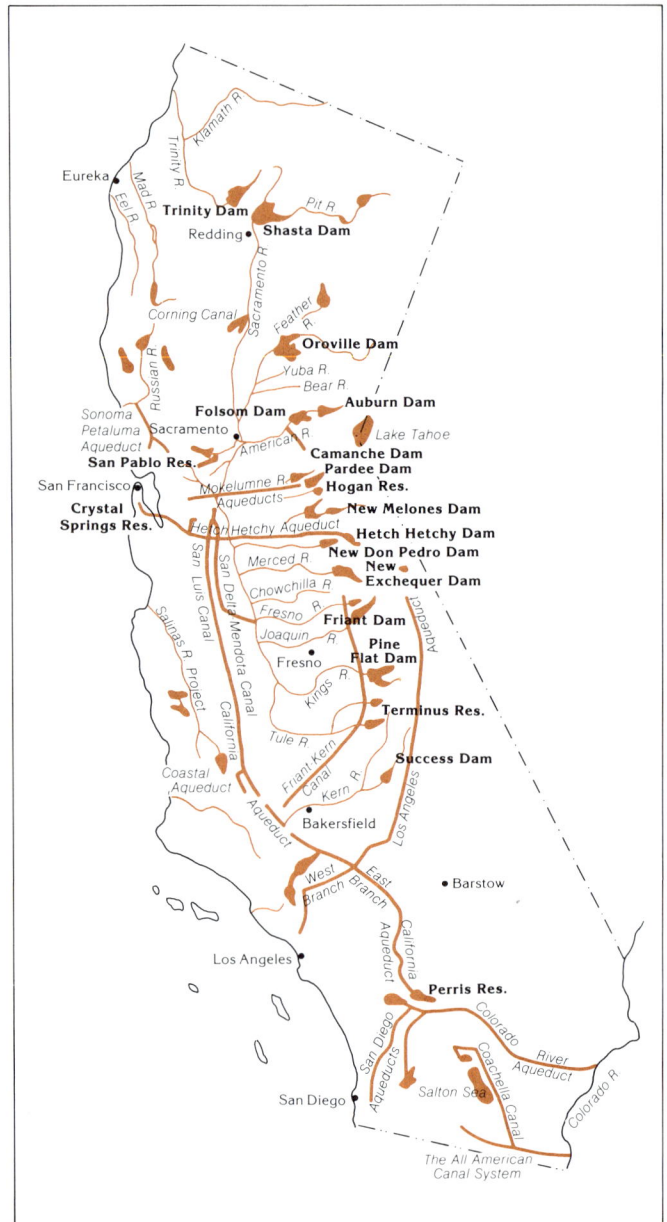

FIGURE 2–10

The California Water Plan and other Major Western Irrigation Projects. Both surface water and groundwater resources of the dry and subhumid west are diminishing under the combined demands of agricultural irrigation and expanding industrial and urban usage. Water is being transported long distances and reused to an unprecedented degree.

produced on the same irrigated land. Mexico has taken the United States to international arbitration over the allocation of Colorado River water. At times, only a trickle of not-very-fresh water reached Mexico, which now has a guaranteed volume.

Oregon and Washington   Agriculture in the northwestern Pacific coast region shares California's emphasis on fruit and vegetable production (though of a different range of crops) and has huge irrigation projects behind the rain-shadow—inducing Cascades. Oregon and Washington orchards specialize in apples, pears, nuts, and cherries, whereas the interior Snake River plains specialize in potatoes (one quarter of the total United States crop), and the eastern portion of the Columbia Basin, the Palouse, is a major wheat section.

Oregon and Washington are relatively less urbanized than California (Oregon has less than the national average urban and Washington is about average). These northwestern states are notable for their enthusiasm for environmental protection: a desire that has become a determination here. An Oregon liberal would say "Visit but don't stay"; a radical would say "Don't visit!" This attitude of controlled growth may have been inspired by the spectacle of rapid growth accompanied by some environmental deterioration in California. However, the forest-products industries and defense-related industries (notably Seattle's Boeing Company) will sustain growth, if at a lower rate than the Southwest.

West Coast Industrial Growth The West Coast subregion, however important its agriculture, has become an increasingly more important component in the total fabric of U.S. industry. Food processing, the oldest branch, has long since been surpassed in importance by the aircraft-aerospace, chemical, and clothing industries. Industrial growth becomes increasingly evident in the smaller communities, but the five major metropolitan areas still dominate. Important factors encouraging industry include: a local, relatively cheap energy supply, the increasing trade ties with the Orient, Alaskan development, the large local market provided by the subregion's burgeoning population, the attractive force of climatic and other amenities, the growing pool of technical and research personnel, and the growing economic and political influence of the subregion's inhabitants. As a center of innovation, it also generates inventions, fashions, and fads that in turn lead to industrial production.

By far the largest industrial center is metropolitan Los Angeles. The orignial impetus to industrial development there was the discovery of oil. Recently discovered new reserves supplement older fields, and Los Angeles remains a major center of oil refining. The related petrochemical industries have led to the development of fertilizer plants, production of artificial fibers, and a diverse set of plants that use plastics as raw materials.

The film industry, not really an industry as much as an entertainment service, has indirectly led to the development of two other industrial branches. Early films often used planes for thriller sequences, and pilots were attracted to the area. It soon became evident that near perfect flight weather, the year around, made Los Angeles an ideal place to test aircraft. Almost at once, southern California began to attract aircraft research and testing functions—while the aircraft industry was in an embryonic stage. Over the years, Los Angeles has become a major producing center for aircraft and aeronautical components. World War II saw that function enlarge radically because of the role of aircraft in the Pacific campaign. The postwar air traffic boom in long distance travel, with California as the normal terminus, further enhanced the industry's growth. The advantages of the area soon became those of skill rather than climate. Bolstered further by space industry contracts, the region's aircraft industry has continued to grow.

Another offshoot of films was a full-fledged clothing industry. The dress of Hollywood stars became the fashion norm for much the the U.S. public. Such Hollywood innovations as the sports coat, the sport shirt, swim trunks, and other leisure wear were not only worn locally, but, eventually, produced locally and shipped throughout the country. Los Angeles is a major garment-producing center for both males and females—manufacturing under- and outerwear as well as specialized sports clothing.

The third offshoot of the film function came later. As celebrities of the entertainment world grew to be more numerous in California than in New York, television shifted its corporate headquarters and programming facilities to metropolitan Los Angeles. Over time that area has become a major manufacturer of television cameras, transmission equipment, and related manufactures. This, coupled with innovation in electrical components and systems for planes, has given birth to a full-fledged electronics industry, one of the largest in the country.

Interaction with Japan has led to large-scale Japanese industrial investment in the region. The most frequent type of facility is an assembly plant using Japanese-manufactured components.

The size and affluence of the local market has attracted assembly industries of all kinds. Automative plants are representative of the market draw. The gradual increase of the industrial market itself has attracted such basic industrial functions as the Fontana steel plant. Far from raw material resources, it functions solely in response to the large and growing metals market generated by southern California's industry.

Los Angeles is industrially diverse, as would be expected of a city of its size. Nonetheless, electronics, aircraft, clothing, and petrochemicals still dominate over other types of industrial production. An unusual facet of this area's industrial mix is the large number of small specialty plants that produce packaging, gimmicks, and

San Francisco. Cosmopolitan San Francisco is an important benefactor from the increasingly important trans-Pacific "connection"—the cultural and geopolitical as well as economic interactions between the United States–Canada and East Asian regions. (Photo by Stansfield)

highly specialized consumer items. None is important by itself, yet, collectively they form a major segment of the city's industry.

San Francisco overshadows Los Angeles as a port and seems to be better at attracting regional offices and financial functions. It is not, however, nearly as important an industrial center. Food processing still forms an enormous segment of its total industry. Its position as the natural outlet for the Great Valley of California will likely result in a continuance of this function. The presence of famed institutions of higher education in the area has led to the establishment of research oriented industries. Pharmaceuticals and electronics are the most noteworthy types of such research oriented production.

San Francisco still has a major garment industry, much of it found in the Chinatown district, some of it still exploiting illegal migrants as cheap labor. Not reputed as a center of fashion, it has long produced work clothes, raincoats, and such specialized clothing as fisherman's garb. Compared to other industrial segments, it is a slow growth sector in the face of foreign competition.

As a major port, metropolitan San Francisco requires a full array of maritime industries, oil refineries, metal foundries, and other heavier industry. Such functions tend to collect in Oakland, with its cheaper land values and greater supply of level land.

San Diego thrives on government military contracts from nearby armed service bases and assembly industries using low skill labor supplied by recent migrants. The aircraft, chemical, and electronics industries are fairly well represented, but assembly industries now outweigh them in importance. It functions as a major entrepôt for raw materials and semimanufactures from Mexico as well as a production point for components that are shipped to Mexico for assembly and ultimate sale in that country.

Portland functions mainly as a manufacturer of lumber, paper, and a large array of wood products. It has a considerable food-processing industry, but it has failed to attract the electronics and aircraft industries so important elsewhere. Stringent laws do much to prevent expansion of chemical or other polluting industries. Small size of market restricts its ability to develop consumer goods industries to any great extent.

Seattle, Tacoma, and their suburbs constitute a major and growing industrial complex. Cheap power from area hydroelectric installations has attracted electroplating and metal refining industries. The area is a major factor in U.S. aluminum production, an industry attracted by cheap power. Boeing, a giant of the aircraft industry, is synonymous with Seattle. In itself, it constitutes a major market for aluminum. Assembly and the engineering-production of aircraft bodies is the major function of that facility.

Woodworking industries are still of great importance in this area of superb forest resources. Backed by the great grain lands of the Columbia plateau and with excellent access to Great Plains production, Seattle has continued to enlarge its food processing function. Alaskan development, the growth of nearby markets in British Columbia, and proximity (plus a tradition of interaction) to Japan all seem to favor continued industrial development.

If agriculture and raw material production are still important on the West Coast, the maturation of that subregion's economy becomes more evident yearly as industry expands and diversifies in what is no longer an area isolated from the mainstream of the American economy.

ALASKA

Historically, perceptions of Alaska's resource base have fluctuated widely. Russia was willing to sell Alaska to the United States in 1867 for both political-strategic and economic reasons. Strategically, the Russians apparently feared that they would not be able to defend Alaska against an aggressive British imperial presence in North America. British seapower and the great distance of Alaska from the Russian heartland would combine against a successful Russian defense. Additionally, though, the Russians knew that Alaska's fur resources, at least those accessible from the coast, had been seriously overhunted. The controversy in America surrounding the Alaskan purchase also focused on this destruction of the only known resource—furs. Alaska was a "sucked orange" in the words of one American critic of the purchase, drained of its value. This dreary image of a worthless, remote frozen wasteland was dramatically shattered by the gold rush of the 1890's. Gold production began in the 1870's, boomed in the 1890's, and reached a peak in 1906, although production

still continues. The oil boom touched off by the Prudhoe Bay discoveries led to the most recent new appreciation of Alaska (although Alaska was already the seventh largest oil producing state before Prudhoe Bay was discovered).

Unlike the gold rush, however, the oil boom, in association with on-going expansion of logging, fisheries, and metallic ores, seems to have achieved a major permanent increase in the states' economic growth. As late as the 1960's, less than one percent of Alaska had been professionally surveyed for minerals, and yet the federal government had recognized the vast mineral wealth potential of Alaska for many decades. The current struggle between developers and conservationists is a contemporary echo of an earlier determination to treat Alaska like a giant storage freezer where its mineral wealth would be stored against future need.

If there is a common theme in Alaska's recent history, it is frustration with the "big brother" role and attitude of the federal government. Prior to statehood (1959), the U.S. government exercised control over the territory much as a distant power controlled a frontier colony. The federal government owned 99 percent of Alaska. After statehood, Alaskans became uncomfortably aware of the limited power of a lightly populated state against what many regarded as excessive regulation. Alaskans are learning, however, to use their political clout, and Alaska will as a result develop in a manner quite different from its north-

Tanker Loading Alaskan Oil at Valdez. The oil being loaded here at the southern terminus of the Alaska Pipeline was pumped on the North Slope at Prudhoe Bay. The pipeline, long-delayed by serious environmental concerns, has helped boost Alaska's state revenues to the nation's highest, per capita.

land neighbors, Yukon and Northwest territories of Canada, which are still directly administered from Ottawa much as Alaska was from Washington prior to statehood.

The gigantic scale of Alaska carries over to the problems and opportunities of the state and its citizens. On the positive side of its economic development issue, Alaska will doubtless benefit from the financial resources of both the U.S. government and American corporations. The state of Alaska received a "birthday present" on statehood of its choice of 103 million acres (42 million hectares) from federal lands (equivalent to the whole area of California). While federal ownership of land remains very high (the U.S. government intends to retain most of Alaska after its land and transfers to the state and to native Alaskans is completed), federal ownership is proportionately higher in Nevada, Utah, and Idaho. Naturally, the state of Alaska is slowly choosing and claiming its land heritage as mineral exploration knowledge proceeds. Alaska is also in the happy position of receiving huge oil revenues relative to its population; great surpluses are a feature of recent state budgets. In 1971, the U.S. government enacted the Alaska Native Claims Settlement Act, which created twelve regional and twenty-two village corporations whose stockholders are 80,000 Alaskan Indians, Aleuts, and Inuit who were at least one-quarter native. These corporations were given title to just under 44 million acres and $962 million. The corporations are encouraged to make money by any legal means approved by their stockholders (no nonnative can buy these stocks until 1992). Native corporations can and do sell mineral rights, timber, fish, land, and leases, and operate fishing fleets, canneries, hotels, and timber enterprises. Alaska has the highest proportion of original Americans of any state.

Alaskan lands long have been open to homesteaders by both federal and state programs, but the state has less than four hundred farms. It produces the smallest proportion of food relative to its population of any state (about 10 percent). Alaska's best agricultural land is in the Matanuska Valley, near Anchorage and close to the site of the new state capital. Although the long days of the subarctic summer can produce some impressively large fruits and vegetables (30-pound turnips and bushel-basket size cabbages are common), the short growing season, low soil temperatures, and thin, acidic soils severely restrict the range of crops.

The Alaska population has the second youngest average age among the states. This reflects both an inflow of people in their twenties to work in construction, mining, forestry and fishing, all physically demanding jobs, and an outflow of older people. Older Alaskans tend to retire to warmer climates and virtually no older people are among the in-migrants. Alaska's population is primarily urban and it is likely that Alaskans will continue to flow into the state's largest city, Anchorage. No other major city seems likely to evolve and the "last frontier" will be a very different kind of frontier. Rather than the wavelike advance of farmers and ranchers into the plains, the Alaskan frontier will be one of widely scattered mineral exploitation sites embedded in wilderness. The harsh realities of the Alaskan frontier will result in only temporary incursions by long-range or seasonal commuters into truly wild country, while the few cities continue to function as support-supply bases for this extractive economy. Exceptions will be many small settlements along the coasts serving forestry and fishing activities.

The "center of gravity" in population, economic activity, and political power has shifted rapidly from the panhandle to Anchorage. Sitka was the Russian colonial capital and Juneau was the American administrative capital from 1900, becoming the first state capital in 1959. However, these panhandle capitals made sense only in the context of coastal development of fur, forest, and fish resources. Juneau is accessible to Seattle by sea, but no road or railroad connects it to any other population center in Alaska.

Anchorage boomed with World War II military spending. Between 1940 and 1950, the metropolitan area's population increased by 750 percent. Oil discovered nearby in the 1950's continued the boom. The 1964 earthquake, the strongest ever experienced in North America, caused $200 million in damages in five minutes. All of coastal Alaska, from the panhandle through the Aleutians, is part of the Pacific "ring of fire"—an unstable zone of frequent earthquakes and many volcanoes associated with the movement of tectonic plates. Aided by federal relief funds, Anchorage rebounded from destruction and even benefitted from the earthquake, when the quake destroyed Seward's port facilities but left Anchorage's port operable.

The rise of Anchorage as Alaska's chief port, major airport, and banking, wholesaling, and retailing center will continue to lower the traditionally high cost of living associated with virtually everything being imported. Economies of scale and the appearance of "lower-48" chain stores make Anchorage by far the most preferred business center. The sheer size of Alaska will continue to support subregional centers like Ketchikan and Juneau, but Anchorage has such an unchallenged position of leadership that even an earthquake could not retard its growth for long.

HAWAII

America's fiftieth state lies more than 2,000 miles (3,200 kilometers) west of San Francisco and occupies a chain of great volcanic mountains built up from the sea floor, a depth of as great as 18,000 feet (5,500 meters) below sea level. The western and central portions of this immense mountain chain barely break the surface. Coral reefs have been built around the edges of the volcanic rock in a process described in Chapter 11. Most of the western two thirds of this state's territory and territorial waters is uninhabited and Midway Island, geographically part of the Hawaiian chain, is administered by the U.S. Navy and is not part of the state. Only in the east have the outpourings of volcanic rock built up far above sea level and created large habitable lands. The easternmost, largest (bigger than Rhode Island and Delaware together), and highest (Mauna Kea is 13,796 feet [4,000 meters] above sea level) is Hawaii, the "big island" that gave its name to the entire chain.

The Hawaiian Islands were discovered and populated by seafaring Polynesian peoples coming from the South Pacific near Tahiti between 600 A.D. and 800 A.D. Their European discovery was in 1778 by Captain James Cook.

Hawaii is the only U.S. state in which Caucasians are not the largest racial group. The native Hawaiians are a tiny minority now compared to the 30,000 native Hawaiians occupying the islands at initial discovery by the Europeans. Their number is now estimated at 12,000, with as few as 500 pure blooded. The impact of the larger world was catastrophic for the first Hawaiians in several ways. Diseases for which the Hawaiians had no natural resistance were introduced accidentally with devastating effects. Well-intentioned introduction of cattle and goats as gifts from the Europeans overgrazed the natural vegetation, and the islands' limited agricultural areas suffered serious soil erosion, which reduced food supply.

The tremendous expansion of sugar plantations in the late nineteenth century (their number went from twenty to sixty-three between 1875 and 1880) was associated with rising imports of Chinese, then Japanese, labor. With the prestige and the influence of the American missionaries rising in the early nineteenth century, many became royal advisers and confidants. They engineered a critical land reform in 1848, which transferred communal lands under royal stewardship to the monarchy (one third), the government (one third), and to the common Hawaiians (one third). In 1850, for the first time, foreigners were allowed to purchase land. The children of the missionaries intermarried with the Hawaiian aristrocracy and formed an oligarchy, which effectively ruled Hawaii for half a century. Interracial marriages became common, producing a society in which no ethnic group has a majority. The largest group according to the census (60 percent) is "mixed." Statehood has ended the political power of the white-Hawaiian oligarchy, which influenced the Hawaiian monarchy, established a republic from 1893–98, and lobbied

successfully for United States territorial status in 1898. An economic legacy of the plantation society has been slower to decline. Plantation money established conglomerate trading companies that controlled the islands' shipping, banking, insurance; real-estate development, hotels, and other services. Some of these old companies have been taken over by "mainland"-based corporations, and new, mainland-financed businesses have challenged their power. Another relic of the plantation oligarchy, one that represents a serious problem to the state and its people is that almost half of Hawaii's land is owned by less than a hundred private landowners. Within the privately owned sector, ten estates, ranches, and corporations own two thirds of the privately held land. The state owns 38 percent of the total acreage, and the federal government, 10 percent. Small private owners hold less than 5 percent. The huge real estate holdings of the individual and corporate descendants of the plantation oligarchy continue virtually intact because they seldom sell any land, but lease it for long terms.

Hawaii's current economic development problems are related to the very desirability of the islands. Population pressure is all too evident on Oahu, where metropolitan Honolulu has far outstripped the rest of the state in attracting new "mainland" immigrants as well as rural Hawaiians from the other islands. Industries other than agricultural processing are almost entirely service industries based on tourism, retirement, and military expenditures. The tourist revolution coincided approximately with statehood. Relatively small numbers of wealthy cruiseship passengers began to be augmented by airborne tourists. Commercial jetplanes, beginning in the early 1960's, reduced fares and travel time, democratizing tourism and bringing literally an avalanche of tourists, most of whom stayed an Oahu, the site of the major aiport. Hawaii, conscious of the over-concentration of tourism on Oahu, has begun to shift new facilities to the other islands. Military spending is likely to remain high, guaranteeing an inflow of money even if the tourist boom should slacken.

CANADA

Canada, at over 3 million square miles (nearly 10 million square kilometers) is the second largest country in the world in territory. Its 24 million people, however, are concentrated near its southern border with the United States, while the Northlands are almost empty. The Yukon and Northwest Territories together form nearly 40 percent of Canada but have 0.2 percent of its population. The concentration of population in the south is not in the form of a continuous belt, but rather is clumped in four distinct zones. (See Figure 2–11.) Canada is a country of vast distances, formidable physical barriers, and large tracts of nonagricultural land separating these major settlement regions. The mainly coastal populations of the Atlantic Provinces are separated from the main concentration, the upper St. Lawrence Valley-Ontario peninsula, by densely forested, thinly settled lands, while to the west of the St. Lawrence-Ontario heartlands lies an even more formidable barrier. The great Canadian Shield is glacially eroded, rugged terrain that forms a gigantic crescent around the southern coast of Hudson Bay, dipping as far south as the northern peninsula of Michigan in the United States. Its scraped rocky surface supports agriculture only in isolated pockets of clay soils originally deposited in lakebeds. Its rugged but not particularly high surface has been a major obstacle to east-west development. Until 1960, for example, when the trans-Canada highway was extended across the shield, trans-Canada highway traffic had to detour south across the U.S. border. The Canadian Rockies separate the western coastal population concentrations from that of the Canadian Plains, which in turn lies on the other side of the shield from the heartland.

CANADA'S ATLANTIC PROVINCES: A BYPASSED SUBREGION OR UPWARDLY DYNAMIC?

Much of Canada's dynamic economic growth has been concentrated in Ontario, Alberta, and British Columbia.

The four Atlantic provinces, New Brunswick, Newfoundland, Nova Scotia, and Prince Edward Island, seem to be relatively stagnant backwaters. The Atlantic Provinces (a term coined in 1949 when Newfoundland joined Canada; the other three provinces had been known collectively as the Maritimes) are at the bottom of a list of average provincial incomes (see Table 2–3). Only Quebec, among the other provinces, has an unemployment rate higher than an Atlantic province. The Atlantic Provinces' average incomes are 40 percent below Ontario's and 60 percent below Alberta's. Federal government transfer payments ("equalization payments") contribute 17 percent of average personal income for the Atlantic Provinces, Canada's highest proportion, while these provinces have the lowest (except for Yukon and Northwest Territories) average proportion of personal income from interest and dividends, only 7 percent. Among Canada's most recent immigrants, half go to booming Ontario, while less than 5 percent choose the Atlantic Provinces.

There are two fundamental geographic reasons for the relative poverty and slow growth of the Atlantic Provinces; there are also some geographic factors that suggest a brighter future. The location of the Atlantic Provinces relative to transport routes and to better quality land in the interior has resulted in their bypass during most of Canada's non-Indian settlement period. This subregion compares with New England and Virginia in America's settlement; it was the early beginnings. Unlike the early colonies of America's seaboard, however, the Atlantic

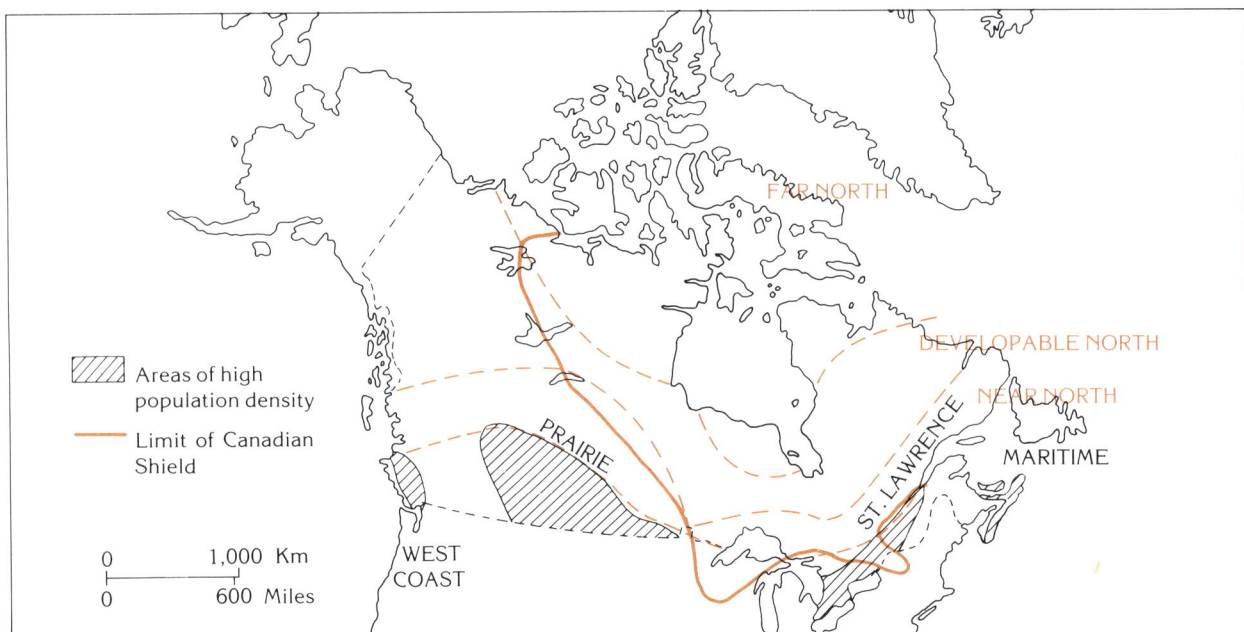

FIGURE 2–11
Canada's Ecumene and the "Three Norths." Canada's settlement ecumene forms four major nodes along the U.S. border. The "three norths" are successively less settled and more frontierlike, with little prospect of much permanent settlement in the far north.

Provinces did not lay astride the routes westward. They did not control the all-important hinge function of connecting sea routes with interior routes, and thus did not benefit from their headstart. The great St. Lawrence Valley was the obvious route to the interior, so that the Atlantic Provinces lay to one side of the major European penetration westward (see Figure 2–12). With some important exceptions, notably Prince Edward Island, the Atlantic Provinces have little good quality agricultural soil. The people of the Atlantic

tions are significant, the volume of bypassing sea traffic accelerates for the spring opening of the Seaway. In one respect, the forward location of Nova Scotia remains important. Port Hawksbury is one of North America's greatest ports for Ultra Large Crude Carriers (ULCC). These giants (some over 400,000 tons) require unusually deep channels and plenty of room to maneuver. Since land transport of their cargo to interior locations is generally by highly efficient pipelines, the normal economic rule that ships carry freight as far into the heart of the market as possible does not apply here.

The Atlantic Provinces average less than 10 percent of their total area in farmland; about three quarters of the land is still forested, despite upwards of four centuries of settlement. Paper, pulp, and lumber have been mainstays of the economies of all except Prince Edward Island, whose 60 percent of land in farms provides potatoes and hay. Both agriculture and forest products are expected to be slow growth industries, however. Potatoes are declining in per capita consumption per year in both Canada and the United States. Beef production is being increased but long winters mean that a great amount of fodder must be kept in storage. A tree-destroying insect, the spruce budworm, is a major problem in New Brunswick and Nova Scotia. Environmentalists have pressured both provinces to stop spraying DDT, the most effective (but environmentally hazardous) insecticide; the current approach apparently is to let the budworms eat all the spruce available and then die

TABLE 2–3

Canada's provinces: relative economic status

	Per Capita Income '78 (dollars)	Percent Unemployed '78	Net Migration '77–'78
Ontario	8,109	7.2	+ 29,658
Quebec	6,903	10.9	− 45,042
Atlantic Provinces			
New Brunswick	5,552	12.6	+ 1,537
Newfoundland	5,039	16.4	− 3,101
Nova Scotia	5,887	10.6	+ 540
Prince Edward Island	4,975	9.9	+ 948
Prairie Provinces			
Alberta	7,738	4.7	+ 33,973
Manitoba	6,899	6.5	− 4,634
Saskatchewan	6,829	4.9	+ 2,074
British Columbia	8,162	8.3	+ 19,159
Yukon and Northwest Territories	7,078	(NA)	− 384

Provinces relied more on their development and use of sea resources, their forests, and their mines.

While Halifax is Canada's largest ice-free, deep-water port, it does not dominate Canadian trade to the degree that would seem logical. (See Figure 2–12). Because sea transport is much cheaper than land transport, though no longer faster, the eastward thrust of the Atlantic Provinces does not necessarily attract cargos to and from Canada's major industrial and population centers. Although seriously handicapped by winter freezing, the St. Lawrence Seaway means that the head of navigation into Canada has advanced from Montreal to Thunder Bay.

In the great days of trans-ocean passenger liners a **forward port** position such as Halifax might have been busy because passengers were eager to transfer to even faster railroads. Freight is rarely in enough of a hurry to transfer to faster land transport at a higher price per mile. Nova Scotia's peripheral position relative to most of the Canadian population and industry means that while winter port func-

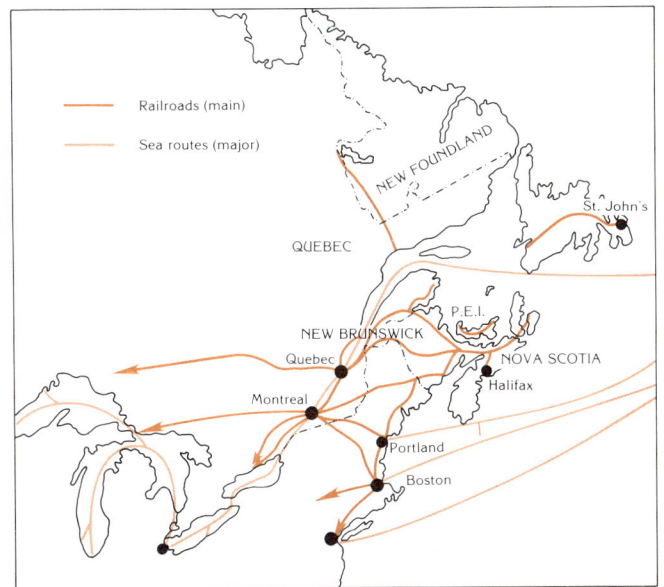

FIGURE 2–12

Atlantic Canada: Sea Routes and Railroads. Atlantic Canada is that nation's bypassed "front door"—the St. Lawrence estuary permits easy penetration of the heartland and Atlantic Canada's outports handle little more than ice-season and supertanker traffic.

Peggy's Cove, Nova Scotia. While highly attractive to tourists, the Atlantic Provinces of Canada have a narrow resource base that is reflected in their relatively lower incomes. Long "bypassed" by traffic inbound via the St. Lawrence, these provinces now hope that oil and gas revenues hold the key to renewed prosperity. (Courtesy of United Nations/J. Isaac)

out by starvation, which is hard on forests and foresters. Many of the rich fisheries of the region, which first attracted and sustained European settlement, had experienced some declines in catches; however, Canada has modernized fishing fleets with grants to fishing cooperatives and fisheries are reviving after Canada expanded its jurisdiction over fishing grounds to a 200-mile (320-kilometer) limit. Sizes of catches should continue increasing and their value will increase even faster.

Government involvement in the economy has had mixed, but generally beneficial results. Newfoundland's provincial government participated in financing an oil refinery that went bankrupt within a few years; it may be reopened when newly discovered oil and gas fields offshore are commercially exploited. Nova Scotia's Cape Breton Development Corporation failed to develop a profitable prefabricated housing industry but has succeeded at expanding mining. Substantial new coal reserves have been discovered at Cape Breton. Although Nova Scotia's peak coal production was in 1917, a major new mine was opened in 1974 and rising markets encourage production. The steel plant in Sydney was taken over by the province in 1968, modernized, and is apparently viable now. The New Brunswick government's encouragement of mineral production was successful. Antimony, a very rare metal, has been produced since the mid-70's; silver, lead, zinc, and copper are also mined. Oil exploration off Nova Scotia and Newfoundland has produced encouraging finds. After twenty years of unsuccessful drilling off

Canada's east coast, oil was discovered in 1979 under the Grand Banks, 168 miles southeast of St. John's, Newfoundland. In an interesting political initiative, Newfoundland's premier sent a scuba diver to place a plague on the Grand Banks proclaiming Newfoundland ownership, but Canada's federal government has not agreed that offshore resources are provincial rather than federal. Oil exploration has already pumped money into the Atlantic ports that build and service drilling rigs and supporting service ships. Optimistic evaluations of the offshore fields project a possible "second Mexico." Such a field would, of course, greatly accelerate an economic recovery, which is already gradually underway. Even bleak, almost unpopulated Labrador, the mainland portion of Newfoundland, contributes income through the sale of hydroelectric power. The largest hydrogenerating station in the world is located at Churchill Falls, almost twice as high as Niagara Falls; it generates 7 million horsepower. Energy is exported via the Quebec Hydro system. In addition, Labrador shares a major iron ore resource with Quebec at Schefferville.

It must be remembered, though, that moderate expansion of fishing, forestry, and onshore mining of metals and coal will not lead to an economic growth rate matching that of Ontario or British Columbia. Even a major oil boom would employ relatively few people permanently, once wells and pipelines were in place. An oil bonanza would presumably increase provincial revenues for at least two of the Atlantic provinces (Nova Scotia and Newfoundland) and reduce their current dependence on federal aid. Meanwhile, federal equalization benefits remain an important prop; in geographer Richard Thoman's words, the Atlantic Provinces alleviate their poverty by "mining Ottawa" for aid.[6]

THE DIVIDED HEART OF CANADA

The heartland of the upper St. Lawrence Valley, westward from the city of Quebec through the Ontario peninsula to the U.S. border at Detroit and Port Huron, dominates Canada's cultural, economic, and political life.

Quebec, nearly twice the size of Alaska, is Canada's largest province. It contains one of Canada's two largest metropolitan areas, Montreal, and accounts for about 26 percent of the country's population. Ontario has more than one third of all Canadians and an even higher proportion of Canada's economic activity. In manufacturing, Ontario dominates the rest of Canada to an almost unbelievable degree with 52 percent of the national total value added by manufacturing. (See Table 2–4.) No single U.S. state approaches the concentration of economic power within the national economy. Together, the top eight states in manufacturing—California, New York, Ohio, Illinois, Michigan, Pennsylvania, New Jersey, and Texas would control the same proportion of national manufacturing as does Ontario (see Table 2–2). Even when the much broader, more inclusive measure of gross domestic product of the provinces is used as an index of relative economic power, Ontario and Quebec remain the same twin centers of activity (see Table 2–4). Not only the two rivals for largest city, Toronto and Montreal, are located within this heartland, but the national capital, Ottawa, whose metropolitan area is fourth largest (after Vancouver), and Quebec City, the seventh largest metropolitan city, are here.

While both Ontario and Quebec are net losers in internal migration of citizens (Quebec's loss is greater, especially as a ratio of total population), Ontario is a heavy gainer in receiving new immigrants to Canada. Fully half of new Canadians initially chose Ontario, while 15 percent choose Quebec. This in-migration follows a cultural cleavage. Immigrants from France and Italy favor Quebec, while Ontario attracts a more cosmopolitan array including East Europeans, Southeast Asians, Caribbean blacks, and Chinese.

Canada's most serious problem lies in the cultural-political geography of its great heartland, for the heart is divided. Quebec's voters defeated a 1980 referendum on continuing a drive toward complete independence from Canada, but the province seems determined to assert a very high degree of autonomy within the Canadian confederation. Quebec is North America's only example of a **national minority** in political control of a state or province. The reasons for Quebec's drive to assert its own identity and its serious threat to the integrity of Canada are cultural. French settlement in North America began early in the seventeenth century; Quebec City was founded in 1608. The climate of "New France," though, was considered quite harsh by immigrant Frenchmen, who generally agreed with Voltaire's dismissal of Canada as "just so many acres of snow." At most, about 500 French settlers had immigrated to Canada on their own. The others, mostly soldiers relesed from military duty, indentured servants, (engagés), petty criminals released from prison, orphans, and paupers, went there under various degrees of persuasion or coercion.[7] These French in Canada, who were to later develop a distinctive French-Canadian culture,

[6]Richard Thoman, *The United States and Canada: Present and Future* (Columbus, Ohio: Charles E. Merrill Publishing Co., 1978), p. 246.

[7]R. Cole Harris and Joh Warkentin, *Canada Before Confederation: A Study of Historical Geography* (New York: Oxford University Press, 1974), p. 19.

TABLE 2–4
Provincial shares of Canada's national economy

	Value Added By Manufacturing		Gross Domestic Products	
	Percent of National Total	Billions of Canadian Dollars	Percent of National Total	Billions of Canadian Dollars
Alberta	4.2	1.8	10.9	23.48
British Columbia	9.6	4.1	12.2	26.24
Manitoba	2.7	1.17	4	8.68
New Brunswick	1.5	.626	1.8	4.03
Newfoundland	.6	.261	1.3	2.76
Nova Scotia	1.7	.719	2.4	5.14
Ontario	52	22.1	39.4	84.65
Prince Edward Island	.1	.041	.2	.559
Quebec	26	11.2	23.7	50.94
Saskatchewan	1.1	.469	3.8	8.35
Total		42.42		214.82

numbered only about 65,000 at the end of the French rule. French immigration to Canada virtually stopped under British rule. Thus, most French Canadians today in Quebec and the other provinces (and the more than half a million who migrated to New England just in the nineteenth century) can trace their ancestry in the New World back to at least 1763. The French Canadians have, historically, maintained a high birthrate, although their rate of natural increase now is below the national average.

The French descendants in Canada have resolutely maintained their culture and language, despite military conquest by Britain, for two fundamental reasons. First is the inherent strength of ethnic pride, reinforced by a language different from that of the majority of Canadians and most of the neighboring Americans. Another factor is the British recognition of French-Canadian culture in the early agreement that French Quebec could maintain its identity through controlling its educational system and guaranteed freedom of religion and equality of language. The bitter resentment of the French Canadians, which may yet dismember Canada, is based on their allegation that the "equality" of languages agreed to has not been maintained.

Internally, Quebec has had to cope with a slow-growth economy, large-scale abandonment of farms, and sizeable out-migration of French Canadians to the other provinces and to the United States. The heavy involvement of U.S. corporations in the Canadian economy has strongly favored English as the language of commerce. The "new Canadians," recent immigrants from the Ukraine, Russia, Poland, Italy, China, the Caribbean, and elsewhere, are most likely to immigrate to "English" provinces and are then certain to learn English first, French either later or never. The strong influence of American popular culture is expressed in radio and television (most Canadian households can receive U.S. stations directly or see and hear American shows on Canadian stations), movies, and magazines. These strong economic and cultural ties have favored English-speakers ("Anglophones") over French-speakers ("Francophones"). To the French Canadians, it seems clear that while they are pressured to be bilingual to get good jobs, most Anglophones do not bother to learn much French. In Quebec, for example, before that province determined to be officially and exclusively French-speaking, about 80 percent of the population claimed French as a mother tongue, while about 13 percent listed English. But, while 61 percent of the population spoke *only* French, 11 percent spoke *only* English, and 27 percent spoke both. Clearly, there were proportionately more bilinguists among the French Canadians.

The compulsory use of French in Quebec has already produced a flight of those offices and service industries that serve national markets. Many of these jobs have moved to Toronto. Industries with heavy investments in purpose-built structures such as oil refineries are not, of course, as "footloose" as insurance offices and cannot respond nearly as quickly to a changing political climate. It has been service industries, however, that have been growing fastest in the Canadian economy. This is typical of a country whose economy is maturing. If the Quebec insistence on the supremacy of the French language induces a continued outflow (and discouragement of potential inflow) of service industries except those based entirely on the provincial market, French Canadians may pay dearly for so vigorously upholding their ethnic pride. While a diminished economic growth could be the short-term result of insistence on exclusive use of the French language, a separate Quebec would not necessarily flounder. An independent Quebec would still be graced by a major world city, and its geographic position astride the important St. Lawrence Seaway would give it bargaining clout with both the United States and Canada. Compromises all around would most likely ensure the common prosperity and stability of the already closely interlinked economies of the United States, Canada, and a possible independent Quebec.

Resource Bases of Quebec and Ontario   Hydroelectric power is a major resource of Quebec. Provincial government-owned Quebec Hydro produces huge amounts of power from the rivers that flow toward the St. Lawrence from the shield and from the seaway project. Another newer source is the network of rivers draining westward across northern Quebec to James Bay. One of the largest hydro-power projects in the world is being constructed on La Grande Riviere; these four power plants will produce about triple the annual output of the Grand Coulee Dam in the state of Washington. This hydroelectric energy is particularly significant to the Canadian heartland as the great St. Lawrence Valley has no oil or coal of its own. Hydro power is also important in Ontario, although neither province has yet fully developed its potential. (See Figure 2–13.) Canada, especially the heartland, is proportionately more dependent on hydro power than is the United States.

Quebec has large iron ore deposits, mainly near the Newfoundland (Labrador) border. Ontario's iron ore resources are not as huge as those of Quebec, but they are being exploited. Asbestos is another mineral product of Quebec, which is largely exported to the United States. A variety of metal ores, including nickel, copper, lead, zinc, silver, and gold are known to exist in isolated, rugged terrain. Exploitation in most cases awaits higher world market prices to support expensive transport development. Ontario has the world's largest single source of nickel at

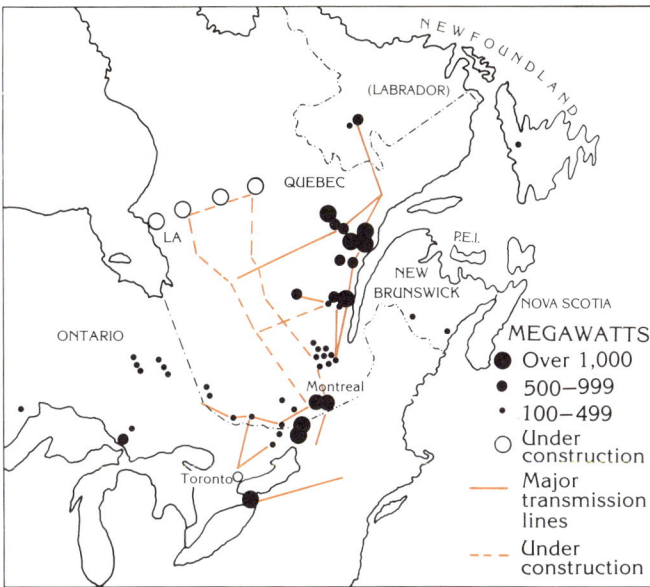

FIGURE 2–13
Eastern Canada: Hydropower Projects. If poor in fossil fuels, Quebec, Ontario, and Newfoundland are rich in "white coal," regularly exporting surplus hydroelectricity as far as New York City.

Sudbury, which also produces smaller quantities of copper, lead, zinc, gold, and silver as by-products.

Logging is a significant activity in both Quebec and Ontario. Pulp and paper are more important than lumber and veneers, and the vast areas in forest are partly counterbalanced by slow growth. Trees in northern Quebec and Ontario may well take a half-century to grow big enough to harvest for pulp, while southern pines in Georgia could be cut at ten to twelve years growth.

It is in agricultural land that Ontario holds an enormous lead over Quebec and the Atlantic Provinces. In an attempt to compensate for climatic disadvantage, limited agricultural area, and distance from markets, the farms of the Atlantic Provinces are being consolidated into larger units and are beginning to emphasize high-quality products, such as seed potatoes and pedigree dairy and beef cattle. Beef production is up and some tobacco is grown on Prince Edward Island.

Quebec has a major advantage—a large urban market—which the Atlantic Provinces lack. Montreal is a customer for dairy products and fruits and vegetables. Quebec-produced butter and cheese are marketed throughout Canada. The agricultural "frontiers" of Quebec are in retreat. Marginal farms are being abandoned (although the farmhouse may remain occupied by "rural nonfarm" people who work in forestry, mining, or manufacturing, or it may become a seasonal home for urbanites). Apples and maple syrup are other Quebec specialties.

Ontario has Canada's best agricultural land outside the prairies (which contain almost four fifths of Canada's farmland). The Ontario peninsula, south of a line from Georgian Bay to the Thousand Islands, is similar to the Central Lowland of the United States in geological structure. It has been glaciated, but the effects of glaciation, as in much of the American Midwest to the south, have generally favored agriculture. The Great Lakes, which flank the peninsula, moderate its climate; the water acts as a reservoir of warmth in the early fall and helps to provide a longer growing season and a lower seasonal tempera-

Toronto, Canada. Toronto, which shares with Montreal the functions of primate city for Canada, shares most of the problems of great cities across the U.S. border. Toronto's transit system is one of the more efficient in North America, helping to maintain the viability of its downtown core. (Courtesy of United Nations/Toronto Transit System)

ture range than neighboring regions. South of a Toronto-Goderich line, corn, soybeans, fruit, and tobacco are grown along with hay and oats. The lakeshore and hilly edge of the Niagara escarpment (over which flows the Niagara River in the famous falls) are excellent orchard lands, which are disappearing under suburban and urban expansion in the "Golden Horshoe" from the Niagara frontier with the United States to Metropolitan Toronto.

This "Golden Horseshoe" is a prospering industrial region, which is, in many ways, a virtual continuation of the U.S. Northeastern Manufacturing Belt. As in the U.S. Midwest, lower Ontario's relatively dense, prosperous farming population helped support agricultural machinery industries along with farm product processors. Canada's auto assembly industry is concentrated in metropolitan Toronto and in Windsor, with the most recent expansion taking place in Montreal. Highly accessible to the huge markets of the U.S. Midwest and northeastern megalopolitan regions, the Ontario peninsula is well-served by rail and highway routes with international connections and by the St. Lawrence Seaway.

CANADIAN PLAINS AND WEST COAST

An advancing frontier moved through the U.S. Midwest, hesitating, but then thrusting forward into the plains once technological and economic changes had made the settlement of the plains feasible. The Canadian Plains, however, had no such "advancing wave" settlement from the Ontario peninsular heartland of Canada. The great Canadian Shield, pitted, gouged, and scraped by glacial erosion, has considerable local relief here. The shield dips below the international border in the upper peninsula of Michigan and in northern Wisconsin and Minnesota (see Figure 2–11) so that the easiest route between the already settled Ontario lowlands and the plains lay south of the Great Lakes, through United States territory. Not surprisingly, almost half a million Americans migrated northward into the Canadian Plains in the late nineteenth-early twentieth century (many returned, though, following severe droughts) to take advantage of Canadian homesteads after the American homesteads were virtually used up. A railroad from the U.S plains reached Winnepeg in 1878, seven years before the Canadian Pacific Line linking Winnepeg with Ontario was completed. Canadian plains farms tended to be larger in the early days than those in the United States, an example of prior U.S. experience benefiting Canada, although the same expansion-contraction of farming versus ranching occasioned by precipitation fluctuations occurred again on the fringes of cultivation in Canada.

The mineral resources of the area are also considerable. Vast deposits of coal and lignite underlay vast portions of the plains. Major oil and gas deposits are already exploited, and large new reserves have been found in the last few years.

The Canadian West Coast bears strong physical resemblance to the American Northwest, as would be expected, but it also is culturally similar to California in some ways. British Columbia is a relatively wealthy province,

Wilcox, Saskatchewan. The Canadian Great Plains. The Canadian Plains, first settled by wheat farmers in the 1860's, have become one of the world's great "bread baskets" along with their counterparts south of the United States border. The North American plains supply huge grain surpluses, which are exported to several other world regions. (Courtesy of United Nations/Canadian Government Travel Bureau)

attractive to migrants from the other parts of Canada, and shares some of California's reputation as a culturally innovative, exciting place. Vancouver, like Los Angeles, is a city whose growth occurred primarily in the auto age; founded only in 1886, it outpaced Victoria, the provincial capital, within a decade. The rivalry of older, established Victoria with its brash upstart neighboring mainland metropolis is reminiscent of the San Francisco–Los Angeles duel for cultural leadership.

Hydroelectric power is impressive in British Columbia, both developed and potential; the abundant power and scarcity of competition for it has attracted a huge aluminum smelter at Kitimat, near Prince Rupert. Like its U.S. West Coast counterparts, British Columbia has outstanding timber resources; more than half of Canada's softwood reserves are here. Large reserves of coal, at present inaccessible, and some oil and gas along with relatively minor deposits of metallic ores round out the resource picture.

THE FAR NORTH

Canadians perceive several successive zones of the Northlands approximately paralleling the U.S. border to the east while trending more northwest-southeast in the west. These zones range (in economic utility and settlement density) from the Canadian archipelago of Arctic islands practically to the northern suburbs of Toronto (see Figure 2–11). The "near north," which is adjacent to the Canadian ecumene, includes the northern sections of provinces from Newfoundland and Quebec to British Columbia. It is an established, aging pioneer zone whose settlements include agricultural activities. The "middle north" is a zone of even thinner settlement, almost all of whose pioneering population is in mining towns. The "extreme north" is almost uninhabited, with isolated groups of original Americans (Inuit and Indians) and very small numbers of military personnel keeping watch over the transpolar potential trajectories of intercontinental missiles. This last, most remote, and economically least significant area could be the most affected by radical change in areas of potential mineral exploitation, especially fossil fuels.

The environmental handicaps of short, unpredictable growing seasons, permafrost, and lack of summer heat are compounded by summer droughts. Much of the far north is characterized by very low precipitation throughout the year. The low availability of moisture becomes critical during the short growing season. When these climatic problems are accompanied by very thin, poorly developed soils over the shield, agriculture is practically eliminated as an economic possibility. The farming fringe advances into

the northern margins of the near north only in the extremes of the plains in the famous Peace River district. Even here, in the most favored portion of the far north for agriculture, success reflects the Canadians' careful attention to good transport facilities. Settlement was deliberately concentrated in a smoothly advancing frontier; parcels of land were made available for farming as the railroad advanced. It had been determined earlier that farms more than a few miles from a railroad were not economic.

In the "new frontier" of the middle north, mining towns are the major modern intrusion. About two thirds of the population of the far north is Amerindian, Inuit, or Metis (half-Indians). The tundra vegetation of the far north has proven to be very easily damaged. Regrowth is agonizingly slow, so that bulldozer tracks, for example, remain clearly visible decades afterwards. The animal life of the Arctic, both land and sea, is relatively sparse and can be locally eradicated by overhunting or overfishing. The biological processes that cope with decay and dispersal of waste operate slowly. The implications of these environmental constraints are several. Sizeable permanent settlements of "southerners," or Canadians and Americans of modern industrial-urban lifestyles, are unlikely and probably should be discouraged in any event. The Inuit and Amerindian populations will continue to grow at a pace outstripping the capacity of the environment to support them in the traditional lifestyles.

The extreme north has high potential for oil and gas exploitation. Geological conditions similar to Alaska's Prudhoe bay extend eastward along the Arctic coast of Canada to the Atlantic. Given the fragile nature of the environment and the extremely high costs of establishing temporary settlements, much of the work force of future oil and gas fields may be long-distance commuters rather than residents of communities whose lifespan might be measured in years rather than decades. It could prove cheaper to fly workers to Arctic sites for an intensive three- or four-day work-week and then return them to their homes and families by air rather than construct complete communities in the Arctic oil and gas fields. Such environmental hazards as sewage disposal and large fresh-water demands thus could be minimized.

In the meantime, the Inuit and Amerindian-Metis groups seem to be advancing further into a welfare-state relationship. The question of maintaining a humane and realistic relationship with the far north's original inhabitants is a serious one for both Canada and the United States. The contact of a high-technology society with one essentially in the stone age has resulted in a massive intrusion into the lesser advanced. Inuit, armed with rifles instead of harpoons or spears, began to kill more of the sparse supply of sea mammals. Amerindians, along with those Inuit that based their food supply on land animals, overhunted those animals also. Under these circumstances, perhaps it was inevitable that some of these people would slip into a dependent relationship in welfare. Since most refuse to leave their home environment, they may form the permanent labor force for the coming oil and gas production boom.

Political-strategic occupation is another type of settlement on the Arctic frontiers. Joint Canadian-U.S. defense forces man radar installations and other military bases.

SUMMARY

The tensional relationships and "world view" of the United States and Canada are quite complex for two reasons. While the United States and Canada have strong political and cultural similarities, as noted, they are not as unified in their outlooks as some Americans naively assume. Also, the relationships of this region with other regions are seldom passive or insignificant. As political geographer Saul Cohen observes "the United States occupies the primary and central position within the Trade-Dependent Maritime geographic region. Further, the U.S. is the world's leading power, when the combination of economic and military strength within a unified central political framework is considered."[8]

TENSIONAL RELATIONSHIPS WITH OTHER REGIONS

Tensional relationships is not necessarily a negative interpretation of interregional relationships; *tensional* as used here refers to active, mutually significant, perhaps changing political, economic, and cultural relationships. Although Canadians emphasize that their international relations are neither dictated by, nor copies of, U.S. views, the differences must be regarded as relatively minor. Canada, for example, anticipated later U.S. diplomatic and trade relationships with the Peoples' Republic of China, and never broke relations with Cuba. It seems clear however, that geopolitical reality binds the two as one in event of any aggression against North America. An independent, democratic Canada could not exist at the side of a hostile, conquered United States, nor could the United States long tolerate hostile dictatorship or external control in neighboring Canada. Just as the sources in foreign investment in Canada's growing economy shifted dramatically from

Britain to the United States during the twentieth century (accelerated by the liquidation of British investments to help pay for two world wars), so too did Canada's ultimate security shift to a closer relationship with the United States. Any exchange of intercontinental ballistics missiles between a warring United States and USSR would almost certainly take place over the polar routes (the shortest routes between most major industrial centers in each country), which would also cross Canadian territory. This reality led to the joint U.S.-Canadian North American Air Defense Command. This fact, combined with their close investment and trade relationships, ensures that U.S.-Canadian divergences in international relationships will remain minor and fundamentally similar in mutual self-interest.

The region's tensional relationships with West Europe are strong and positive, originating in historical and cultural relationships and maintained by alliances and still important trade relationships. There are strong raw material dependencies between the U.S.-Canadian region and the North Africa–Southwest Asian and Africa south of the Sahara regions. While much less dependent on energy imports than the United States, Canada shares American reliance on African metal alloys. Also, American allies and supporters are critically dependent on African and Middle Eastern oil. While about half of the U.S. oil consumption must be imported, the figure for West Europe is closer to 85 percent and Japan, virtually 100 percent. If the Persian Gulf falls under Soviet hegemony, the consequence for the United States, Canada, and their allies could be devastating. The situation in metal alloys reveals an even stronger dependence on, and thus strategic interest in, stable and pro-Western governments in Africa south of the Sahara. Along with the energy resources of the Persian Gulf, North Africa, and Nigeria, the metals of South Africa, Zimbabwe, Zambia, and Zaire are absolutely necessary to the economic activity and survival of the "Western alliance" of the United States and Canada, West Europe, and Japan. For example, 92 percent of U.S. chrome consumption must be imported; 96 percent of the world's proven preserves lie in South Africa and Zimbabwe. A single jet aircraft requires nearly 1.5 tons of chromite ores (a necessary ingredient in stainless steel and jet engines). Central and southern Africa are vital storehouses of strategic minerals—copper, cobalt, manganese, platinum, gold, asbestos, industrial diamonds, and uranium along with chrome; the U.S.-Canadian region could not long survive as a major industrial or world economic military power without continued access to these minerals.

A relationship with the USSR ranging from uneasy détente to dangerous confrontation has helped foster an emergent if tentative and unofficial American-Chinese

---

[8]Saul B. Cohen, *Geography and Politics in a World Divided,* 2nd edition (New York, Oxford University Press, 1973), p. 93.

(PRC) alliance. China clearly hopes to use U.S. technology in its hoped-for rapid modernization.

Unfortunately, Middle America must be regarded as an increasingly unstable southern flank to the United States and Canada. This could endanger U.S. imports of both Middle American bauxite and South American oil and iron ores; a raw material dependence second only to the North Africa–Southwest Asian and Africa south of the Sahara dependence.

THE WORLD VIEW OF THE UNITED STATES AND CANADA

The United States cannot pretend to be another Sweden or Switzerland, going about its business neither seeking nor accepting a leadership role in the world. Neutral democracies survive precisely because the United States has accepted a leadership-protector role against totalitarianism, left or right.

The United States was a reluctant heir to power; it has not consistently sought a world leadership role, nor consciously accepted that position until World War II. Perhaps it has never grown comfortable in this role.

From independence through the end of the nineteenth century, the United States was intent upon internal consolidation of economic development and continental expansion at the expense of militarily weaker neighbors or "power" vacuums (the technologically and numerically inferior Amerindian tribes).

The war with Spain (1898) initiated a more maritime orientation, as U.S. interests shifted from "rounding out" its continental holdings and integrating the continental economy and transport-communications systems to a Caribbean and western Pacific empire. The U.S. sense of security now requires adequate naval and air power to safeguard worldwide inflows of oil, liquified gas, ferrous and nonferrous ores, and outflows of food, forest products, coal, manufactured goods, and high-technology products. The American economy has advanced in scale and technology so that even the vast and varied resources of the North American continent, accessible by land transport systems, no longer provide all necessities, and present systems of world trade interdependence are balanced on the Western alliance's determination and power.

case study

THE CHANGING PERCEPTION OF AMERICA'S NATIONAL PARKS: CONSERVATION, TOURISM, AND ENVIRONMENTALISM.

The interpretations of landscapes, their possible human uses, even their attractiveness, change over time as society's lifestyles and values change. Perceptions of landscapes evolve as a society's values evolve and reflect the contradictions and values conflicts apparent within a society. Americans have repeatedly changed their assessments of the proper use, or nonuse, of their national parks; indeed, the argument as to the best management philosophy continues.

The first official national park was Yellowstone, created in 1872, although in 1864 Congress transferred Yosemite Valley to the State of California as a public park. According to a leading scholar of the origins of the national parks, nationalism was a leading motive in setting aside specific natural wonders.[9] It was important for early Americans to find evidence that the New World was superior to the old. Americans were proud that such phenomena as Niagara Falls were more spectacular than anything comparable in Europe. Thomas Jefferson proclaimed that the view at Harpers Ferry, where the Potomac River cuts through the Blue

[9] Alfred Runte, *National Parks: the American Experience* (Lincoln: University of Nebraska Press, 1979).

Ridge Mountains was "worth a trip across the Atlantic" in itself. Conscious that America could not hope to match the great cultural monuments of antiquity of which Europe was so proud, Americans were particularly enthusiastic about their natural wonders. This combined with an often short-sighted practicality in the phenomenon known as "monumentalism." This landscape philosophy sought to avoid setting aside for public recreation large tracts of land that might be otherwise useful. It emphasized rather isolated, spectacular landscape items. For example, when Congress first set aside the Yosemite Valley, they designated only 40 square miles within the valley itself, failing to protect, initially, the surrounding peaks and watershed. Advocates of park bills before Congress tended to stress the nonutility of these lands except as scenery. Snide European criticism of the tacky commercialism that quickly surrounded Niagara Falls was another catalyst to national park status for nature's spectaculars.

Practical economic considerations were seldom far from the nineteenth century American's perceptions. Among the lobbyists in Congress for the creation of such national parks as Yellowstone, Grand Canyon, and Glacier were railroad owners whose tracks ran close to the proposed parks and whose passenger revenues would benefit from tourism. A prevalent theme among park enthusiasts was the "recapture" of tourist dollars flowing to Europe: "See America first." The boosters agreed that not only did American scenery outrank in scale everything Europe had to offer, but America's natural exotica even mimicked and outdazzled Europe's cultural attractions! The pillars and spires of eroding rock in Bryce Canyon, Utah, for example, were pictured as suggesting cathedrals, and Americans were frequently told that Sierra redwood trees were living contemporaries of the Roman Empire.

Many national parks bills specifically permitted ongoing mineral exploration, as in Alaska's Mount McKinley Park, and even timbering in parts of Glacier Park. Although area reductions would be extremely unlikely today, in the past, national parks and monuments were not regarded as "forever." In 1915 for example, President Wilson reduced the size of the Mount Olympus Monument to allow lumbering.

Largely because the earlier parks tended to be in rough country in the thinly settled High West, the numbers of visitors were originally quite small. As recently as 1908, only about 13,000 visitors a year saw Yosemite Valley, now one of the most visited parks. It was this very small number that helped advocates of the Hetch-Hetchy Reservoir. Hetch-Hetchy Valley is a neighbor of Yosemite and was regarded as just as beautiful. San Francisco needed a large new reservoir and engineering studies pointed to Hetch Hetchy. Essentially, the monumentalist argument for preservation is based on unique, spectacular landscapes. If Yosemite must be saved as a unique landscape for parkland, why did we have to preserve a "second Yosemite" in Hetch Hetchy? The "benefit to the greater number" principle, increasingly used to modify or obliterate earlier established rights in the allocation of water resources in the dry West, appears to have been applied to Hetch Hetchy. It was a landmark decision for park enthusiasts because it gave new dimensions to the old "elitist" versus "right of citizen access" debate. To some conservationists, the lesson of Hetch Hetchy was that the rising tides of visitors must be encouraged by easier access and better accommodations. Only large numbers would suitably impress politicians that recreational uses were important. Only large numbers of citizens with personal experience of the parks' grandeur would have the political clout to forestall transfers of public recreational lands to lumbermen, miners, or dam-builders.

"Everything in the universe is related to everything else" was the guiding principle of pioneer environmentalist John Muir, the founder of the Sierra Club. In arguing for the protection of the environs of Yosemite as well as the valley itself, he observed that the upper tributaries of the streams flowing through Yosemite must be protected also. Thus, a generation after the designation of Yellowstone National Park, there was a shift in philosophy from saving isolated monuments to conserving entire ecological systems, drainage basins, and surrounding environments. It was another generation, however, before a national park was established to preserve a unique wildlife ecosystem in an unspectacular area from the scenic viewpoint, Everglades Park, in 1934.

The automobile age presented many problems to park planners and managers; large numbers of people were now coming to the "peoples' parks" and demanding ease of access for their cars. The older style park visitation, in which almost everyone arrived near the park entrance by train, was based on public transport within the park. Excepting hikers, visitors thus had little individual mobility and their potential for inadvertant environmental damage was quite limited. The automobile age changed all the rules. The democratization of travel associated with rising incomes and car ownership brought demands for more roads and larger parking lots. It also brought many whose recreational tastes supported more elaborate and artificial entertainments.

The Park Service catered to these tastes through such "shows" as the "Bear Cafeteria" in Yellowstone. Within an enclosure fenced off from surrounding bleacher seats, trucks regularly dumped garbage, which attracted scores of bears. This debasement of wild animals through encouraging dependence on human's garbage outraged environmentalists and was stopped several decades ago.

Two themes now seem to dominate the Park Service's management and acquisitions policies. The emphasis has shifted from merely "saving" natural landscape phenomena to preserving intact entire ecosystems. Huge tracts of Alaska, for example, have been designated as public parks and wilderness preserves. National Grasslands on the high plains are a good example of recognizing the ecological value of unspectacular landscapes.

Another theme is the emphasis on acquiring recreational lands much nearer the major population centers, even if these lands are less than spectacular. These market-oriented sites are frequently tiny compared with those of the High West or Alaska, but they are also much closer to the average American's home. The "gateway" park, which includes the Statue of Liberty monument, is an example of this emphasis on developing parklands close to urban populations.

REVIEW QUESTIONS

1   Why has the trans-Atlantic cultural interaction been traditionally more important than the trans-Pacific counterpart? How is this changing?

2   What are the cultural, economic, and political factors contributing to the "good neighbor" relationship of the United States and Canada?

3   Why has the character of the trade relationship between the United States and Canada changed in the past decades?

4   Contrast New England's industrial assets in the early industrial revolution with its present industrial assets.

5   Briefly describe the basics of, and applicability of, the von Thünen model of land use, accessibility, and land value.

6   How did the industrialization of the United States and Canada reshape the nature of agriculture in this region?

7   What are the economic problems of the "Aging Core"? What developmental strategies can revitalize the core?

8   Why is the "Dynamic South" developing at a relatively fast rate now?

9   Why does the long-term migration outflow from rural and small-town America seem to have at least partially reversed?

10   How did the Interstate Highway network revolutionize location requirements for industry, wholesaling, and retailing?

11   Where are the "three Souths"? What are their natural resource bases and developmental strategies?

12   Briefly describe the sequential changes in Great Plains land use from their first exploration by non-Amerindians.

13   What physical and cultural geographic factors underlie California's special appeal to many Americans?

14   In what ways is California agriculture an innovative, pioneering fringe of U.S. agriculture in general?

15   Briefly describe the role of Ontario in the Canadian economy.

16   Contrast the resources, population, and developmental strategies of Alaska and Hawaii.

17   Why is Canada's heartland a "divided heart"? What are the implications of this split?

18   What geographic factors have contributed to the "slowdown" in Quebec's economy?

19   Is British Columbia the "Canadian California"? Compare their economic development and migration rates.

20   Why were Canada's Atlantic Provinces not able to build on their early settlement to become "hinges" for the support of western expansion in Canada?

21   What are Canada's developmental strategies with regard to the "near north" and "middle north"?

SUGGESTED READINGS

1   BRIAN BERRY, *The Changing Shape of Metropolitan America.* Cambridge, Mass.: Ballinger, 1977.

2   STEVEN BIRDSALL and JOHN FLORIN. *Regional Landscapes of the United States and Canada.* New York: Wiley, 1981.

3   HARRY CAUDILL, *Night Comes to the Cumberlands.* Boston: Little Brown, 1962.

4   JOHN FRASER HART, ed., *Regions of the United States.* New York: Harper & Row, 1972.

5   TRUMAN HARTSHORNE, *Interpreting the City: An Urban Geography.* New York: Wiley, 1981.

6   ROBERT IRVING, ed., *Readings in Canadian Geography,* Toronto: Holt, Rinehart and Winston, 1972.

7   RALPH KRUEGER ed., *Regional Patterns: Disparities and Development.* Canada Studies Foundation/Canadian Association of Geographers, 1975.

8   A. G. MACPHERSON ed., *The Atlantic Provinces.* Toronto: University of Toronto Press, 1972.

9   DONALD MEINIG, *Southwest: Three Peoples of Geographical Change, 1600-1970.* New York: Oxford University Press, 1970.

10   JOHN H. PATERSON, *North America.* New York: Oxford University Press, 1979.

11   ALFRED SIEMENS, *The Americas: A Comparative Introduction to Geography.* North Scituate, Mass.: Duxbury, 1977.

12   Statistics Canada, *Canada Handbook.* Ottawa, Canada: Statistics Canada, 1979 (48th edition).

13   JOHN A. STOVEL, *Canada in the World Economy.* Cambridge: Harvard University Press, 1967.

14   JOHN WARKENTIN, ed. *Canada: A Geographical Interpretation.* Toronto: Methuen, 1967.

15   WALTER WEBB, *The Great Plains.* New York: Finn, 1931.

16   C. LANGDON WHITE, EDWIN FOSCUE and TOM MCKNIGHT, *Regional Geography of Anglo-America.* Englewood Cliffs, New Jersey: Prentice Hall, 1979.

17   WILBUR ZELINSKY, *The Cultural Geography of the United States.* Englewood Cliffs, New Jersey: Prentice Hall, 1973.

KEY TERMS

- infrastructure
- tectonic activity
- acculturation
- mainland-rimland
- complementary resources
- *latifundium*
- *tierra caliente*
- intertropical convergence
- vertical zonation
- *tierra templada*
- *tierra fria*
- *paramos*
- cultural hearth
- labor intensive
- *ejido*
- core
- slash-and-burn
- hidden export

3

MIDDLE AMERICA

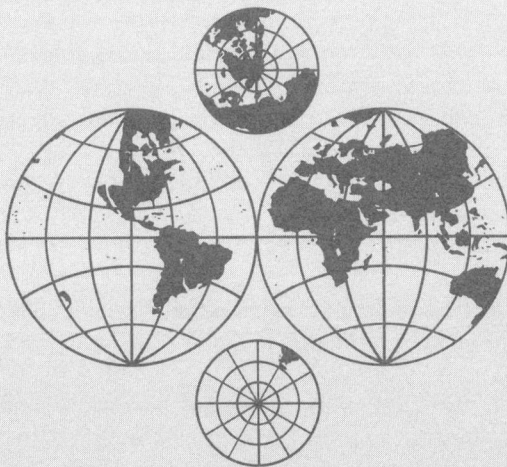

PROLOGUE: TWO VIEWS OF A REGION

Middle America is a region of many small units (both in area and population) of remarkable diversity. Middle America consists of Mexico, the Central American republics, and the islands of the Caribbean. The states of the region are characterized by a locational access to North American markets, a focus on the Caribbean and Gulf of Mexico, and economies that tend to be dominated by tourism. Middle America has traditionally been viewed as a region whose economies are tied to precarious world markets for one crop or another.

Its independent states range in size from tiny island republics of a little over 100 square miles (260 square kilometers) to Mexico, which dwarfs any state in western Europe, with an area of 760,000 square miles (2.0 million square kilometers). Populations of these units range from less than 100,000 to over 70 million.

Although some North Americans may view most Middle American countries as small, Cuba has more people than Sweden; Nicaragua is three-and-one-half times larger than the Netherlands (area); the Dominican Republic has more people than Switzerland; and Honduras is 60 percent larger than the Irish Republic.

Sandwiched in between the two large land masses of North and South America, both filled with impressively large political units, many Middle American states may appear visually unimportant on maps. The total region, though, contains more than 1 million square miles and is roughly the same size as all of western Europe. With 125 million people, it has five times the population of Canada. This gives the region's importance a different perspective.

Some units have shown considerable political instability, which is sometimes considered a characteristic of the region. Others, like Costa Rica, are noted for political tranquility. Conflicting power groups within units have vied for control many times in most of the region's states. Complex issues of land tenure and perceived discrimination against native groups have led to periodic civil unrest. The basic issues involved in Middle American political unrest are quite real.

Fluctuations in commodity prices on the world market often have contributed to political instability. The states of Middle America do not produce simply one commodity. However, climatic conditions in combination with foreign demand patterns often limit the range of export crops. Most are plagued by an imbalance of trade as imports constantly exceed exports. Governments are frequently dependent on taxes on exports for a large portion of total revenue. Depression of world market prices, then, does not simply depress one phase of an economy. It limits the ability of a government to pay debts and to continue developmental projects. Virtually every government in the region has invested heavily in projects for diversifying both agriculture and exports. All have broadened their governmental revenue base. The problems have not been eliminated, but their implications have been gradually minimized.

Many of the region's units have sought to diversify through the development of tourism. One of the commonest means of redressing a trade imbalance is the sale of services by the deficit economy (the developing state) to consumers from the surplus economy (the industrialized states). The apparent wisdom in this formula derives from the developed nations of northwestern Europe, many of which are net importers of food, fuel, and raw materials. Virtually all of western Europe "sold" tourism to Americans from 1950 through 1975 as a means of acquiring hard currency and redressing imbalances of trade. This, it was thought, could be done in Middle America as well.

Yet, there are problems. Regional economies supply the climate and labor—little else. Foreign investors build the hotels and recreational facilities in the absence of domestic capital. Tourism requires an **infrastructure** that developed Europe already had but less developed Middle America essentially did not have. Profits from tourism often leave the economy to return to foreign investors. Taxes on tourism and monies paid for labor are often the only gain; they may not even match necessary capital costs for support facilities. The cruise ships and airlines that bring the tourists are often foreign owned. Tourism as a source of revenue must be closely scrutinized for a fair evaluation. Yet there are some regional economies that have almost nothing else to offer.

Oil and minerals frequently have supported Latin American development. Not all regional states, however, are rich in minerals. Oil-refining facilities, support base functions for oil-drilling crews, and supply of food or materials may allow some regional economies to benefit from another state's mineral strikes. Occasionally, labor shortages allow the temporary movement of migrant labor to a mineral-producing area. Overseas remittances from migrant labor are a source of income, but a temporary one. Few oil-rich economies allow the export of crude oil indefinitely; one of their own first steps in development is generally the building of refineries for the export of petroleum products rather than crude. Supply and support bases only function at full capacity during the stages of drilling and exploration. If it is not a country's own mineral bonanza, the benefits to be derived are few and temporary.

Minerals, tropical commodities, and tourism, the basic triad of development in the region as a whole, vary enormously in their significance among individual states. Singly or in combination, these factors are not necessarily the best solution to problems of development. Entirely new roads to development may be necessary to building sound economies. It is time for a new look at Middle America.

CHARACTERISTICS OF THE REGION

It has been common to link all of the Americas south of the United States into one unit—Latin America (as opposed to Anglo-America, the region north of that boundary). Just as French-speaking Canadians do not consider themselves Anglos, many millions of Middle Americans would not consider themselves Latins. While total homogeneity is not necessary to a region, it is the differences between Middle American and *both* the neighboring regions that justify a separate region.

Physiographically, Middle America consists of a gradually tapering isthmus, or land bridge, and a collection of islands in between two large continental masses. Plate tectonics theory views this region as at the junction of five separate plates (see Figure 3–1). It is a zone of tremendous **tectonic activity** subject to frequent earthquakes and outbursts of volcanic activity. This tectonic activity has resulted in a very complex landscape—hundreds of Caribbean islands and scores of separate mountain basins on the mainland. There are few areas of continuous, level, broadly similar landscape. Even small political units are usually compartmentalized into sharply differentiated, smaller physiographic subunits.

Both North and South America are composed of large political units whereas Middle America (excepting Mexico) is a collection of small states. Each independent unit has developed its own variations in law and government; they are seldom broadly similar to one another or to North or South American models. While Spanish is the official language of most of the region's countries, French, English, and Dutch also are official languages in some of the region's units. Many Indian dialects are spoken and large numbers of people in officially Spanish-speaking countries often know little Spanish. More than anywhere else in the Americas, three major cultural inputs (African, Amerindian, and Mediterranean European) exist in an amalgam. It is difficult to say that they have blended, since a differing one dominates at virtually every location. The **acculturation** process has not produced a uniform regional culture. Regional culture has become far removed for its original European, Amerindian, or African roots.

One might view Middle America as composed of two halves: the land-dominated west and the water-dominated

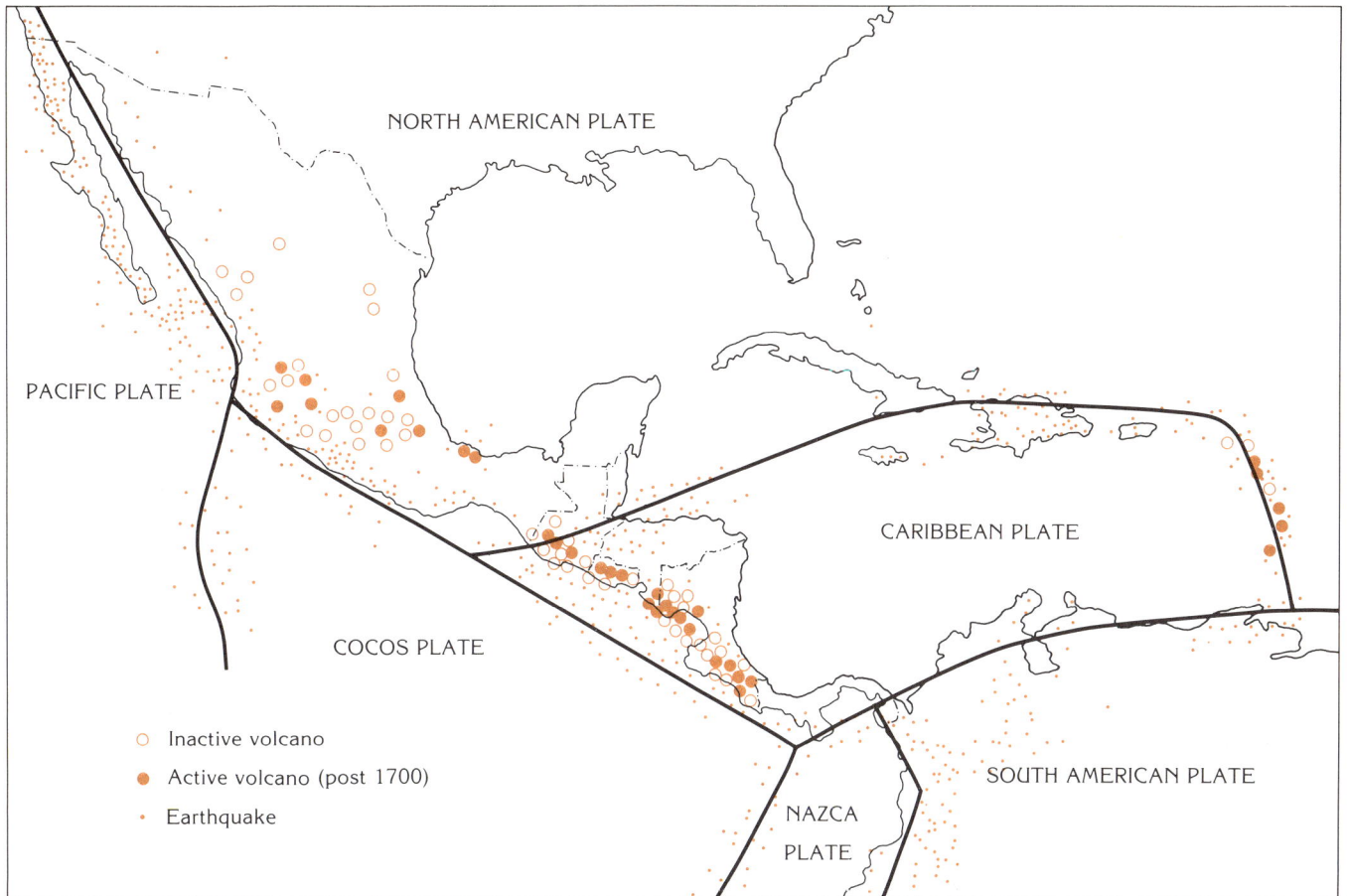

FIGURE 3–1
Tectonic Plates and Volcanics in Middle America. This region is one of the most complex, tectonically, as two small plates are caught between three larger ones. The zones of crustal stress, buckling and faulting, have volcanoes associated with these lines of weakness.

east. The densely inhabited areas are most often mountain basins or high plateaus in the land portion, while concentrations commonly are on coastal or interior plains in the island (water) portion. Geographer J. P. Augelli distinguishes a **mainland-rimland** division—a Euro-Indian mainland and a Euro-African rimland composed of the Caribbean islands and the eastern (plantation) coast of the mainland south of Yucatán.

Common economic problems are in large part rooted in colonial experience. The abundance of rain and sun in an area of reasonably fertile soil offered the opportunity for plantation production of export commodities destined originally for European markets. Amerindian or African agriculture survived in its subsistence format alongside, but it was effectively divorced from the commercial economy. This separation of agriculture from the economy applied even in Mexico, where the commercial aspect was more largely mining than agricultural. Most South American states never developed this sharp dichotomy to the

same extent. Regional character, then, is most sharply demonstrated on the basis of shared economic problems rather more than on cultural similarity.

THE INFLUENCE OF THE U.S. ECONOMIC PERIMETER: THE UNITED STATES AS "BIG BROTHER"

Another aspect of economic similarity may be found in the strong role of the United States in the regional economies. Geographers are often fond of drawing comparisons and contrasts among physical and cultural features that have approximate similarities to one another. Thus, the Caribbean–Gulf of Mexico area was sometimes likened to the Mediterranean. There are many obvious differences, but a comparison is still useful. The Mediterranean links two Northern Hemisphere areas—Europe and North Africa; the bulk of the continent of Africa lies south

Chichicastenango, Guatemala. The cultural imprint of Spanish colonialism throughout most of Middle America has been both marked and long-lasting, though not uniform in spatial distribution or cultural significance. (Courtesy of United Nations)

of the Sahara, which, until modern times, was a much more effective barrier to exchange, both economic and cultural, than was the interior sea between Europe and Northern Africa. Repeatedly, from Phoenician and Roman times forward, empires and alliances have straddled the Mediterranean, connecting portions of the continents. Only in the second half of the twentieth century have European colonies in North Africa finally achieved freedom, and economic links remain strong. But, while the Mediterranean frequently has been an area of competition among major, frequently nearly equal, powers, the "American Mediterranean," the partially enclosed, island-dotted Caribbean-Gulf, long has been under the dominance of the United States without any regional countervailing power. Similarly to the Mediterranean's situation, the Caribbean-Gulf provides a focus on economic and cultural interchange to the northern section of the southern continent, in this case South America. Again, in some ways similar to the old world counterpart, a physical feature (the Amazon Basin) proved a much more effective north-south cultural-economic barrier than the sea to its north, which was more a highway than a barrier. In both the "new" and the "old" Mediterraneans, the industrial states to the north have instigated development of supplementary and **complementary resources** within their southern neighbors across the narrow seas.[1]

---

[1] Saul B. Cohen, *Geography and Politics in a World Divided,* 2nd ed. (New York: Oxford University Press, 1973), pp. 134–36.

The Area as a Transition Zone and Corridor of Contract

Unlike European powers in the Mediterranean region, the United States has been disinclined to expand direct colonial rule. There can be little doubt within Middle America, however, as to "big brother's" interests in the area. Throughout this century, the United States has exercised a strong leadership role in the area, following a century in which it actively discouraged European establishment of major military bases in the area, or any extension of empires. Since the early days of the republic (Jefferson advocated acquiring Cuba, for example), the United States has gradually expanded its economic interests, political-military power, and territory deeper into the Caribbean. The acquisition of Florida (1819) and Texas (1845) rounded out U.S. interests on the Gulf begun with the Louisiana Purchase (1803). This was followed by the Spanish-American War (1898) in which the United States acquired Puerto Rico and began a long and close relationship with Cuba until the Castro revolution. The Panama Canal Zone (1903), following the "independence" of Panama (actively aided by the presence of the U.S. Navy) from Colombia, was followed by the purchase of the Virgin Islands from Denmark to help defend the approaches to the canal. Too, a naval base was leased from Cuba at Guantanamo Bay to safeguard the Windward Passage into the Caribbean.

To defend its interests in the region against regimes or conditions perceived as unfriendly, the United States has sent troops to occupy Nicaragua (1912), Veracruz, Mexico (1914), Haiti (1915), Mexican border areas (1916), and the Dominican Republic (1916); has supported an abortive invasion of Cuba (1961); and has occupied the Dominican Republic a second time (1965). The United States also "destabilized" a Communist regime in Guatemala in the 1950's, and temporarily acquired bases on Caribbean islands during World War II in "lend-lease" deals with Britain. (See Figure 3–2.)

Within the last two decades, the United States has been confronted with an anti-American, aggressively pro-revolutionary Cuba, a temporary break in relations with Panama over the rewriting of the Canal Treaty, and the actual and potential rise of governments in Central America distinctly unfriendly to American interests. The United States is extremely sensitive to political conditions in an area it has come to regard as its "backyard."

THE ETHNO-CULTURAL CONFLICT

In both mainland and rimland Middle America there is a degree of class differentiation based on ownership of the land. In Spanish Middle America, Indian lands were seized and given to Spanish settlers as a reward or incentive from the crown. The new settler-owners proceeded to operate

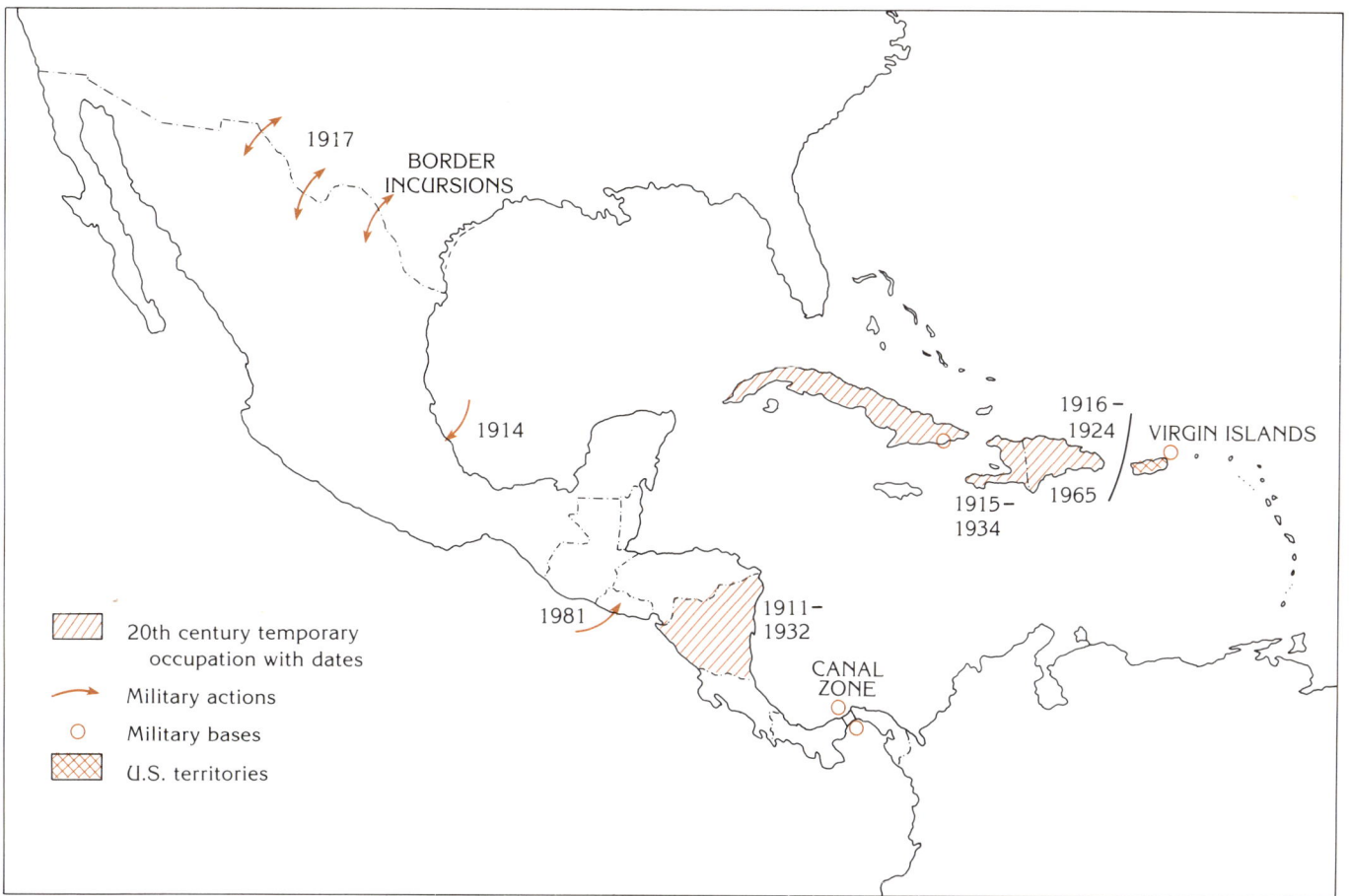

FIGURE 3–2

U.S. Bases and Military Occupations. The strategic importance and economic relationships of Middle America to the United States sometimes have led to a conception of an "American Lake," with military occupation of unstable countries supplementing military bases designed to safeguard both the Panama Canal and the U.S. mainland shores.

their new farms on the *latifundium* system so common in Mediterranean Europe. The term derives from Latin and means broad estates; the new farms were exactly that. Many of the estates included the right to use the Indian inhabitants of the lands as agricultural labor. The Spanish termed such a large estate a *hacienda.* Workers live in villages and generally farm small portions of the estate; rent is paid as a share of the crop or in labor in the fields of the owner. The owner either lives in a rather imposing dwelling at the center of the estate or may be an absentee landlord.

The traditional role of the owner was inspector and, socially, that of patron. Field bosses actually supervised labor; the owner did little but accept the profits, arbitrate disputes and dispense gifts and favors. Families with problems sought his aid and protection. Additional labor was often hired at periods of peak demand. Yields were low, as minimal investment (other than labor) was ever put into the operation. Land was not used efficiently, nor was labor.

Independence commonly brought little change. The government continued to be run and influenced by the landholding class. Indian field labor was kept in poverty and had little or no education. Those living outside the system often had too little land for subsistence and became hired, temporary labor on the hacienda. The result was poverty on the parts of two large classes: the landless peasantry and the Indian subsistence farming community. These social conditions created a small, powerful caste of European descent, which controlled land, wealth, and government—effectively disenfranchising the overwhelming bulk of the populace, usually Amerindians on the mainland.

The populations of the islands and the Caribbean coast share much the same problems. There, the land was viewed as a producer of lucrative tropical crops rather than grains, particularly sugar. The land was sometimes deeded to individual Europeans but more likely to commercial corporations. The labor force consisted of African slaves. The Indian population that resisted control was simply liquidated, if they had survived European diseases.

Plantations were set up to grow highly specialized tropical crops. Ownership was viewed as a business; profit was the exclusive motive, and there was no pretense of social concern. Subsistence was provided in return for labor. Ultimately, after slavery ended, a small wage was added to subsistence, and labor worked by contract. In fact, little changed, since the laborer was still unable to support himself outside the plantation economy.

Plantation labor, sometimes used more efficiently than that of the hacienda, has also come to be present in oversupply. Surplus plantation labor from Caribbean islands sometimes was shipped to the U.S. slave markets. Still others were shipped to mainland coasts to provide labor for new plantations. Even given this movement of labor, the plantations were destined for overpopulation. In some places, plantation corporations have become simply purchasing and marketing organizations for cash crops grown on the small holdings that resulted from division of the plantations. The wealth and real power is still in the hands of a class of entrepreneurs overseas; the small farmers are still at the mercy of economic decisions made abroad. In some cases an upper class of domestic bureaucrats and officials has come into being as a replacement for the old planter class. Sometimes class is defined racially, as in Haiti. In many cases, the results are the same— a large, poor powerless class that is the majority and a goverment that is too frequently unresponsive to their needs and problems.

THE PHYSICAL FRAMEWORK

Just as in its cultural framework, the physical frame of the region possesses great diversity. At its extremes Middle America contains both desert and rainforest. Of the dozen-and-a-half major climatic types known worldwide, ten are regionally represented, along with a full altitudinal range from the hot, humid *tierra caliente* (literally, "hot land" of the coastal plain in the wet tropics) to the mountain peaks that support permanent ice and snow fields. Every conceivable seasonal rainfall distribution is represented.

Too, almost every landform type, tectonic or erosional, is present in the region. At the contact zone of five of the world's plates, it is a jumble of mountain forms, basins and plains, which repeatedly change orientation. Vegetation varies from lush tropical forest to conifers, through natural steppes and savannas to areas without vegetation. Almost no other area of the world is so diverse in its physical environment or contains so many exceptions to the generalizations. It is both a zone of transition and a zone of exception.

TOPOGRAPHY

In its northern reaches, the topography of Middle America can be thought of as an extension of North American physiographic units. The peninsula of Baja California in Mexico is a line of fault block mountains, a continuation, virtually, of southern California's Peninsular Range. Fringed by sporadic coastal lowland toward the Pacific side, the steeply tilted blocks plunge to the Gulf of California as a series of cliffs along the eastern side of the peninsula. The Gulf of California itself is a continuation of the trough that frames the Imperial Valley of California and the mouth of the Colorado.

Eastward, the landscape is a continuation of the basin and range country of the intermontane basin. Most of the northern two thirds of Mexico is a high plateau with basin-and-range features superimposed upon it. The eastern edge is called the Sierra Madre Oriental; it is a continuation, topographically, of the eastern ranges of the Rockies. The plateau edge, deeply eroded by stream valleys toward the wetter south, does not present a major obstacle to transportation. The western edge, the Sierra Madre Occidental, presents a different picture. There, the edge of the plateau becomes a zone of folded and faulted mountains from 100 to 200 miles (160 to 320 kilometers) in width. Streams eroding headward into this barrier from the Pacific form steep-sided canyons that dead-end in longitudinal mountain valleys between almost impassable ranges. The bordering Pacific—Gulf of California lowland is quite dry, lightly settled (except in some valley oases) and in some respects physically isolated from the plateau. The plateau itself becomes higher southward, and more plateaulike as lava flows and sediments fill in the basins. The plateau, densely settled in its southern portion, terminates abruptly in a transverse volcanic range. This range contains many peaks over 10,000 feet (3,000 meters) in elevation as well as the "new" volcano Paricutin, which formed in 1947.

The Gulf Coast Plain is a narrower version of its U.S. counterpart. With the exception of a few outliers of the plateau and some local volcanics, it stretches from the Texas border to the Yucatán peninsula, narrowing from a width of 350 miles (560 kilometers) in the north to less than 50 miles (80 kilometers) in the central portion and again widening southward.

Just north of the eighteenth parallel, there is a striking reorientation of trend. The north-south trending mountain axes, similar to those of North America, are intersected by an east-west tectonic belt that extends westward from the Caribbean islands to which it is geologically and tectonically related. This east-west trending series of ridges continues to Honduras and Nicaragua as line after line of ridges repeats this directional emphasis. The north-south trend, with occasional reversals, continues in the mountains of the rest of Central America until, in subdued form, they appear as the Pacific coastal range of South America, trending parallel to the Andes.

These sharp directional changes are associated with two small tectonic plates, the Cocos and Caribbean, which are caught between the larger Pacific, American, and Nazca plates (see Figure 3–1). The result is a zone of impressive vulcanism and earthquake activity that sits astride the entire midsection of the region.

The Caribbean islands are a classic island arc extending from Cuba through Puerto Rico to Grenada. Like the islands of Indonesia and the Philippines, they are bordered by deep sea trenches—the Puerto Rican Trench and the

Irazu Volcano, Costa Rica. Tectonic (mountain-building) activity, earthquakes, and associated volcanoes are common features of Middle America. (Courtesy of United Nations)

Bartlett Trough. At the northern edge of the arc there has been a considerable uplift of ocean bottom. Florida, the Yucatán peninsula, and the shallow seas off them represent the uplift of sub-sea limestone sediments. The Bahamas, too, are low coral and limestone islands that rise above a shallow sea platform forced upward by neighboring tectonic activity.

The major islands follow the east-west trend. Cuba represents an east-west trending arc; the Sierra Maestra in eastern Cuba are an extension of mountains in Guatemala. A second ridge, forming a volcanic spine in Honduras, comes above the sea to form Jamaica. The two "ridges" are separated by a deep oceanic trough. The island of Hispaniola combines the Cuban and Jamiacan trends. The combined series of ranges, greatly subdued, form Puerto Rico.

Beyond Puerto Rico there are two chains of islands that follow the eastern edge of the Caribbean plate. Both are volcanic, and both trend north-south. The outer line of islands is generally smaller and lower; it is composed of older volcanics. The inner island chain is the opposite on all counts. The islands of the southern edge of the Caribbean (Trinidad, Barbados) were formed by the drowning of the Venezuelan Andes.

CLIMATE

Climatic patterns are also very diverse. The extension of the North American deserts southward terminates inside Mexico. Most of northern Mexico is rather more steppe than true desert. Only the peninsula of Baja California and the state of Sonora are largely desert; the states of Chihuahua and Coahuila are only really desertlike in those parts shielded from rains by mountain barriers. The orographic lifting caused by the altitude of the high plateau and its surrounding mountain rim serves to increase rainfall at the same time that altitudinally decreased temperatures lower evaporation. All but the northwesternmost regions of Mexico receive more than 10 inches (25 centimeters) of rain annually.

South of the Tropic of Cancer, most of Mexico is seasonally dry, but annually it receives quite heavy rainfall. Tropical wet and dry climate (winter is the dry season) prevails in lowland Mexico south of the transverse volcanic ridge. Portions of the southernmost provinces experience year-round rain and are of the equatorial climatic type. Outside a small area of steppe in Yucatán, the rest of Middle America is rather wet on the average. There is, generally speaking, contrast between east and west coasts. Most of the area is in the belt of the Northeast

Trade Winds. In consequence, the eastern coast of Central America receives year-round rain, while the Pacific coast receives adequate rainfall only in summer, the period in which the **intertropical convergence** moves northward, following the direct rays of the sun, bringing equatorial rains to the areas between 8° and 25° north latitude. The amount and seasonal regime of rainfall within the mountain basins depends largely on aspect, rainshadow effects, and the degree to which the orographic effect is felt.

The islands experience a similar duality from southern Cuba through Puerto Rico, receiving more frequent rains and greater annual totals on their Atlantic (as opposed to Caribbean) coasts. In these eastern and northern coastal areas, there is a marked dry season, but a heavy rainfall over nine months of the year supports a tropical evergreen forest. Coasts facing the Caribbean are seasonally dry. Smaller islands have a much drier climate with marked winter drought.

Perhaps a more important concept in understanding the climate of this region is what is called **vertical zonation.** (See Figure 3–3.) Most of the population of the mainland lives in highland areas where temperatures are modified by altitude. Generally speaking, temperatures decrease at a rate of 2° to 3.5°F (4° to 6°C) for every 1,000 feet (300 meters) of elevation. While dense populations can and do occur even in lowlands, both the pre-Columbian Indians and the later European settlers tended to prefer the highland basins. Each range of elevation has a different kind of climate, a fact that has led to the emergence of different crop patterns and lifestyles in each of the vertical zones. The lowland zone from sea level to about 3,000 feet (900 meters) is the *tierra caliente,* or hot land. It is a zone of tropical crop production and was often permanently settled rather than the highlands. Frequently it is a zone of plantation agriculture and, in the past, slave labor was often imported to farm there. From elevations of 3,000 to 6,000 feet (900 to 1,800 meters) the climate is more temperate; the zone is called *tierra templada.* Frost free, yet pleasantly cool, it is a land that can grow corn and wheat well; it is also the zone of coffee cultivation. From 6,000 to 10,000 feet (1,800 to 3,000 meters) or even higher near the equator, the high country is known as the *tierra fria* (cold land). Potatoes, barley, cabbage, onions, oats, and other cold-tolerant plants are the staple crops. Above this is the *paramos,* a year-round grazing area too cold for tree growth, topped by permanent ice in its highest reaches. The same altitudinal zonations are found in tropical highlands everywhere, though rarely do highlands concentrate such dense populations as they do in Middle and South America.

While droughts (or late-arriving rains) present problems on the islands and the Pacific coast, it is too much rain rather than too little that creates more havoc on the Atlantic coast. The large islands and the east coast of

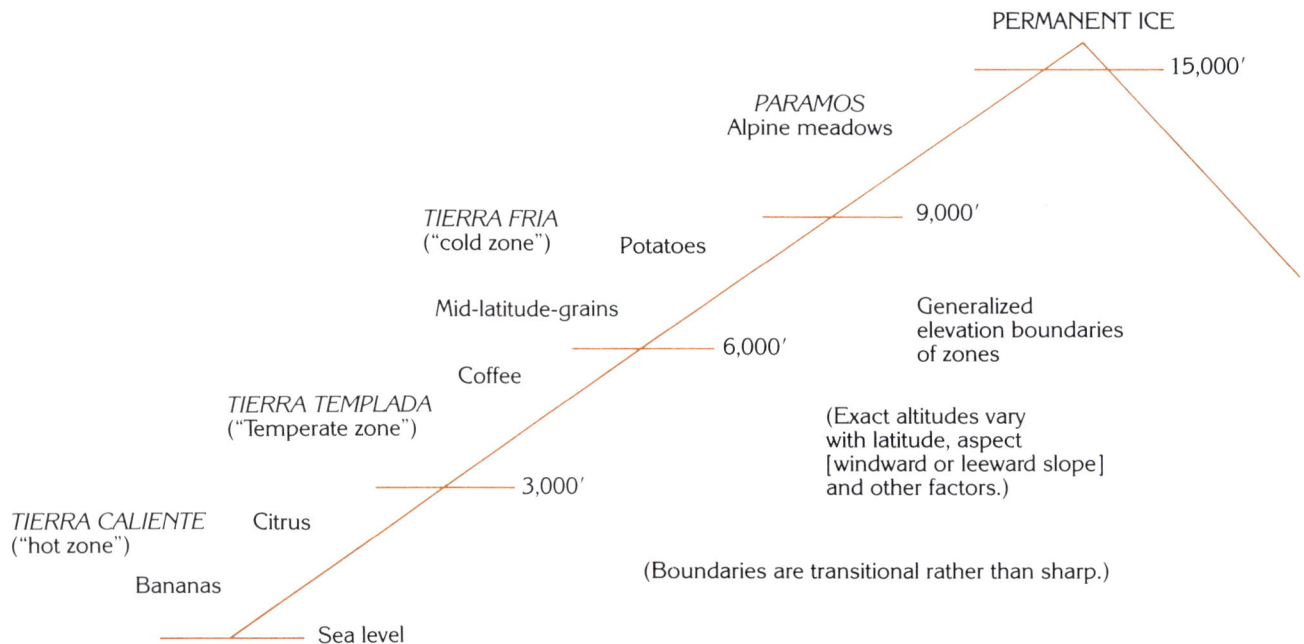

FIGURE 3–3
Vertical Zonation. The regular decrease in temperature associated with increasing altitude means that most Middle American mainland states (and many South American ones) have different climates, and thus different arrays of crops possible, at different altitudes.

Mexico have often been referred to as *hurricane alley* because of the great frequency of disastrous tropical storms. Hurricanes (intense tropical storms) have winds at speeds over 75 miles per hour (120 kilometers per hour) and inflict great damage and some loss of life. They can be accompanied by tidal waves that create a more localized but even greater amount of damage. Unfortunately, too, the peak season of occurrence is August through October, the normal period in which crops ripen and harvest takes place. Serious hurricane damage occurs at several places in eastern Middle America every year. Much less frequently, hurricanes lash the Pacific coast.

LAND-SEA RELATIONSHIPS

At one time the greatest regional importance of the seas surrounding Middle America was linked to transportation. This importance stemmed from the colonial era export of goods to Europe and the role of the Spanish fleet in defending its prize colonial territories. Extension of control by other European states to portions of the area was also by sea. Piracy was common from the seventeenth to mid-nineteenth centuries. Even until recently, the seaborne trade with North America and the very important connection of the U.S. coasts, by sea through the Panama Canal, gave dominance to the maritime transportation function.

The role of the sea in the area has recently changed. The surrounding seas are becoming more important as a source of food and minerals. Recent offshore oil discoveries have given the sea (or seabed) new importance in the Mexican portion of the Gulf. Exploration is now proceeding in Yucatán and Mexico has extended its territorial claims seaward to insure ownership of this valuable offshore resource. Mexico is an exporter of sardines, shrimp, tuna, and shellfish; over a half million tons of fish and seafood are caught yearly. Like Peru, it has developed a large fish meal industry; the meal is used as both fertilizer and animal feed.

Intense population pressures and limited possibilities for agricultural expansion have aided the development of a fishing fleet and fish-processing industry in virtually every Caribbean economy. While the Caribbean fish resource is considerably less rich than that of Middle America's Pacific coast, its contribution to the diet of these overpopulated, one crop islands is quite important. Sport fishing is an increasing source of revenue. Large species like marlin, swordfish, and other "trophy fish" form the basis of an entire segment of the tourist industry.

There is no doubt that the sea, after the warm climate, is the single greatest attraction to tourists. Second home communities, retirement settlements, and convention centers have begun to develop along Middle America's coasts as auxiliary functions to traditional seashore tourism.

There is no doubt that tourism, fishing, and mineral exploitation associated with the seas now outweigh the importance of maritime shipping. Once viewed as strategic to American defense, the development of aircraft and missiles have downgraded the military role assigned to the waters of Middle America, although "quick strike" forces still need advance-base facilities.

DRAINAGE PATTERNS

Despite the heavy rainfall in much of the area and the high average elevation, Middle America has relatively moderate hydroelectric power potential. Streams are short and swift. Mexico has by far the best sites and has developed some 20 percent of its capacity, including some major projects in the Balsas River depression of southern Mexico and in the rainy reaches of the Sierra Madre del Sur. Smaller projects exist on both sides of the plateau, but the irrigation function is often far more important.

The seasonally dry, coral (limestone) islands of the Caribbean sometimes lack surface water entirely. Large numbers of islands in the Bahamas lack settlement because of the lack of a permanent water source. In the Yucatán peninsula, underground drainage in limestone is the norm and sinkholes (surface collapse over caves) trace subsurface drainage courses.

Much of drier northern Mexico—including the basin of Mexico City—has interior drainage. Mexico City itself occupies an old lake bed. Enormous amounts of water necessary for its rapidly expanding population and industry are drawn from groundwater. An unfortunate side effect of this situation is the gradual sinking of the central city as water is drawn from the ground underneath at a rate faster than it is replenished.

There are only three large rivers in all of Middle America: the Balsas, the Rio Bravo del Norte (known to North Americans as the Rio Grande), and the Colorado. All are in Mexico at least partly, and only the first is completely within Middle America. Upstream withdrawal of water from the Colorado (for U.S. farms and cities) prevents large-scale use in Mexico. In most years so much water is withdrawn in both the United States and Mexico that the Colorado does not reach the sea. Erosion of the delta lands and periodic water shortages on Mexican farms in the delta area, combined with the poor quality of reused irrigation water, have led to Mexican protests. In order to redress this grievance, the United States has done little to further develop irrigation along the lower Rio Grande. Mexico draws most of the water from that river and its Mexican tributaries south of El Paso as a kind of compensation for the loss of the waters of the Colorado.

Short swift streams along the dry Pacific coast of Mexico are used to irrigate vast areas. A lucrative and intensive form of oasis farming, supplying fruits and vegetables to both U.S. and Mexican markets, has made these rivers some of the most economically important to Middle America. The combination of terrain and seasonality of precipitation precludes navigation on all but very short stretches of the region's rivers.

The Isthmus of Tehuantepec has been considered as a canal site. This relatively narrow neck of land 125 miles (200 kilometers) in width has often been posed as an alternative to the Panama Canal. Such a Tehuantepec canal would cut the sea distance between the U.S. coasts by several thousand miles. The recent agreement to give up U.S. control over the Panama canal has caused renewed interest in this possible route, although the best alternatives, in engineering terms, are within Panama.

VEGETATION

The Central American vegetational cover exhibits its greatest variation within Mexico. Contrasts decline and disappear southward as rainfall becomes heavier and more uniformly distributed. Comparatively small areas are farmed on the mainland portion, so that the vegetational cover there, however modified by human activities, is readily apparent.

Mexico's desert areas have a regionally differentiated plant covering. In the northwest, the desert landscape exhibits a fairly dense covering. Wetter highlands in Baja California support scrub forest at higher elevations. Only in the salt deserts south of the great bend (of the Rio Bravo) country does vegetation become sparse.

Within the Mexican plateau itself, the vegetational cover is a combination of scrub and steppe. The edge of the plateau forms a striking climatic divide; the higher slopes of both the western and eastern Sierra Madre ranges support dense forests. The lower altitudes support a tropical covering of thorn forest or other semi-deciduous trees. South of the Tropic of Cancer on the wetter Atlantic side and Acapulco on the drier Pacific side, the wetter conditions result in a transition to true tropical rainforest. The drier soil conditions of the northern Yucatán bring about a regional reversion to scrub.

Within the mountain spine of Central America, rain-shadow areas are characterized by a series of scattered tropical grasslands while trees dominate on higher slopes. The vegetational pattern of the islands differs little. Higher peaks and windward facing slopes tend to support rain-forest, while savannas (areas of scattered trees interspersed with grass, giving a parklike appearance to the landscape) and grasslands are the norm in sheltered valleys and on leeward coasts. Densely settled and intensively cultivated, little natural vegetational cover remains on most of the smaller islands.

SOILS

Intense volcanic activity in the Mexican Plateau and the Central American Highlands (as well as some islands) enriches those soils. Brown steppe soils and desert soils dominate in the drier parts of Mexico that extend beyond the volcanic influences. The limestone parent material, which forms the base of many island soils, though rich in calcium, is often of only moderate fertility. Few truly poor soils are found, and these are generally confined to the wetter Atlantic coasts of Central America. The only other area of the tropics with such overall favorable soil conditions is found in Southeast Asia.

THE SUBREGIONS OF MIDDLE AMERICA

Geographic tradition and popular terminology separate Central America and the Caribbean islands from Mexico. Small states in all cases, they share both physical and economic characteristics that make them nearly ideal subregions. Central America is Indian-mestizo-Hispanic in language and culture. Highland agriculture dominates the economies of most of the subregion's states; coffee and bananas are important export crops. The islands developed as commercial plantation economies more than did the mainland, where some variation of the Spanish grain and cattle estate was the dominant commercial land use (other than coffee). The islands tended to emphasize sugar and, after World War II, bananas in their production. The use of slave labor introduced an African cultural element that is quite strong, even dominant, on most of the smaller islands. Indian elements have all but disappeared from the island culture.

Mexico itself is too large and too diverse to form one subregion. It has had a distinctly different history from the other subregions, and there are strong internal differences. The Toltec-Aztec Indian cultural area was quite different from that of the Mayan, although these differences among Indian groups are less vivid than their contrast to European culture. Though the second Mayan empire had ended (c. 1200) before Spanish conquest, it left a decidely different cultural heritage (and languages) than those de-

Tikal, Guatemala. Middle America contains several of the world's ancient cultural hearths. This Maya temple is being studied by archaeologists. (Courtesy of United Nations)

veloped in central Mexico. Today's Mexico incorporates both these **cultural hearths.** Mexico is divided into dry and wet portions, roughly along the Transverse Volcanic Range south of the plateau. Differing economies evolved on either side of that climatic divide. Vast differences between highland and lowland Mexico and people's activities have created a further dichotomy between underdeveloped and quite modern, well-developed portions of the state. As a result of this multiple diversity, Mexico is dealt with as three subregions.

MEXICO—THE "SUPERSTATE" OF MIDDLE AMERICA

Mexico has 71 percent of Middle America's total land area and 56 percent of the regional population. Mexico was a dazzlingly wealthy Spanish colony, so rich, in fact, that some earlier Spanish colonies in the Greater Antilles were partly depopulated and certainly ignored after Cortes' fabulous discoveries. Mexico is the largest Spanish-speaking nation in the world.

Three times the area of Texas, contemporary Mexico is only 60 percent of the state that existed before its collision with a strongly expansionist United States in the 1840's. Its 70 million people are expanding at a natural

increase rate of 3.1 percent, over four times the rate of the United States. In some ways there is an "expansion" of Mexico today, as Mexicans flock across the border (sometimes illegally) into the very portions of the United States that were once a part of Mexico. Like the United States, Mexico is a federal republic; it has thirty-one states and a federal capital district.

This large and diverse Mexico has been sectioned into three subregions on the basis of population density, general level of economic development, and physical-cultural landscape. It should be remembered that in another important sense, there are also "two Mexico's," that of the rich and of the very poor, found throughout all subregions. Although disparaties persist, great economic strides have been made in the last four decades. Mexico's economy has grown at a rate of 5 percent or more per year (adjusted for inflation) since 1938. The cumulative effects of this healthy growth rate places it among those few so-called developing nations that are unquestionably developing. Mexico has achieved almost a 100 percent increase in industrial output *per capita* in a single generation.

Mexico has enjoyed internal stability since 1929, with only one very minor "rebellion" (1938). This has been achieved without strong dictatorial control and without huge military expenditures to pacify a resentful citizenry, a pattern found in some other parts of Latin America. The state has minimized the concentration of power in the hands of the oligarchy or the military. While Mexico has been governed by one political party since 1928, this governance apparently has been by consensus.

This stability and tranquility have supported impressive economic gains. In 1940, only about 14 percent of the total active work force was employed in manufacturing. By 1980, the figure was 29 percent. Investments of foreign capital in manufacturing increased by a factor of sixty-five between 1940 and 1970, though the impact of foreign investment has declined in recent decades as the role of Mexican government and private capital increases sharply. Mexicans save more than any other group in Latin America, and a significant share of the industrial growth and expansion has been financed by Mexican savings. This sharp rise in manufacturing, coupled with an ongoing (if incomplete) program of land reform, has alleviated, but not eliminated, the problems of unemployment, underemployment, landless peasants, and the rise of migrant slums in and near the large cities (especially *the* city, the capital).

In 1910, it is estimated that 1 percent of the Mexicans held 97 percent of the land. By 1940 a reform-minded government had distributed land to over 1.5 million peasants. The pace has continued, and over one half of all the arable land in Mexico has been redistributed since 1917. In addition, new agricultural colonies have been developed in both the dry north and the wet south as irrigation, flood control, and drainage have extended agricultural frontiers. While the proportion of the Mexican work force employed in agriculture decreased from 71 percent to 37 percent (1910–80), the total number of farm workers has actually risen in that same time frame as the population has more than doubled. Despite this rapid population growth, the economy has grown even faster.

In 1940, two thirds of Mexico's people were rural, one third urban. By 1980, these ratios had almost reversed. The highway system was enlarged from 6,200 miles (9,900 kilometers) of paved road in 1940 to nearly 120,-000 miles (200,000 kilometers) by 1977. The literacy rate went from 33 percent (1930) to 84 percent (1979), and in 1982 Mexico will have nearly a million students in higher education. Production of corn increased from 3.1 million metric tons in 1950 to almost 10 million tons by 1980. Wheat production increased from 600,000 metric tons to over 3 million metric tons in the same period, and virtually all other crops doubled or tripled in output. Infant mortality, a measure of children other than the stillborn not surviving to their first birthday (a key indicator of the quality of life as it reflects medical care availability, diet and to some extent, education), had dropped from 294 per 1,000 in 1909 to 49 per 1,000 in 1980.

As impressive as these gains are, they are very unevenly distributed. Industrial, urban, rising middle-class Mexico is a different nation from rural, poorly educated and underfed Mexico. Two nations within one could portend serious trouble if these differences are not progressively minimized by equable economic growth in both sectors. Uneven progress among regions could also present problems. After decades of land reform, 12 percent of the landowners still control over 40 percent of the farmland. A rural population of 3 million farmers and their families still own no land. An equal number hold only enough land for the barest survival. In the late 1970's, the top 5 percent of Mexicans received 25 percent of the income, while almost 40 percent of the "economically active" population earned less than the government-estimated minimum for purchasing necessities. There are obviously still great disparities.

Despite these problems, Mexico is on its way. It has achieved near self-sufficiency in basic foodstuffs, whereas exports of commercial crops like sugar and coffee have increased. The export of meat, processed foods, pineapples, bananas, fish, and winter vegetables have risen sharply. While imports exceeded exports by twice the value in the period 1974–76, they were only 25 percent greater in 1978. Per capita income almost doubled from 1975 to 1980, even when controlled for inflation. Income from large-scale tourism and remittances from family members in the United States more than make up for any negative trade imbalance. The recent discovery of vast new oil and gas reserves could present the answer to many of Mexico's problems. Birthrates have begun to fall, following the now general trends noted in other rapidly developing Latin American economies.

THE NORTHERN DRYLANDS

Northern Mexico has large areas of semi-desert, dry steppe, and long-dry-season tropical grassland. The region includes over 60 percent of all Mexican territory and just under 30 percent of the population. Climate and terrain impose decided limitations on the expansion of agriculture. Nonetheless, it is Mexico's most rapidly growing major region. Only the capital and the new oil fields exceed northern growth rates. It contains fifteen of Mexico's thirty largest cities, including Monterrey (the third largest), and its rapidly growing border towns. Most of the provinces in the subregion are highly urbanized by Mexican standards. Rural densities vary from 2 to 10 people per square mile (5 to 25 per square kilometer) except in the intensely irrigated areas. (See Figure 3–4.)

The subregion contains many of Mexico's important mineral deposits, including most of its coal, iron, and copper as well as major deposits of gold, silver, lead, and zinc. Mining has become proportionately less important to the regional economy as manufacturing and irrigated agriculture expand.

Agriculture is concentrated in two major areas of irrigation: the lower Rio Bravo del Norte (Rio Grande) and its tributaries and a string of riverine oases along the Gulf of California stretching from Mexicali on the U.S. border to Tepic, just northwest of Guadalajara. Cotton, corn, and beans are the specialties of the eastern district, while tobacco, tomatoes, sugar cane, and winter vegetables account for most of the commercial crops in the western district. Despite this strong specialization, the western district is also a major producer of wheat, rice, and vegetable oils. Citrus production has been increasing rapidly as well. High yields as well as high-value crops combine to create a general air of rural progress and prosperity except in the plateau, still dominated by grazing despite increased irrigated acreage. The Laguna district, near the city of Torreon, is a major producer of high-quality, long-staple cotton. It is one of Mexico's most prosperous farming areas and one of the most successful *ejido* projects, although hampered by insufficient irrigation water. (The *ejido* is a communal farm settlement developed to coop-

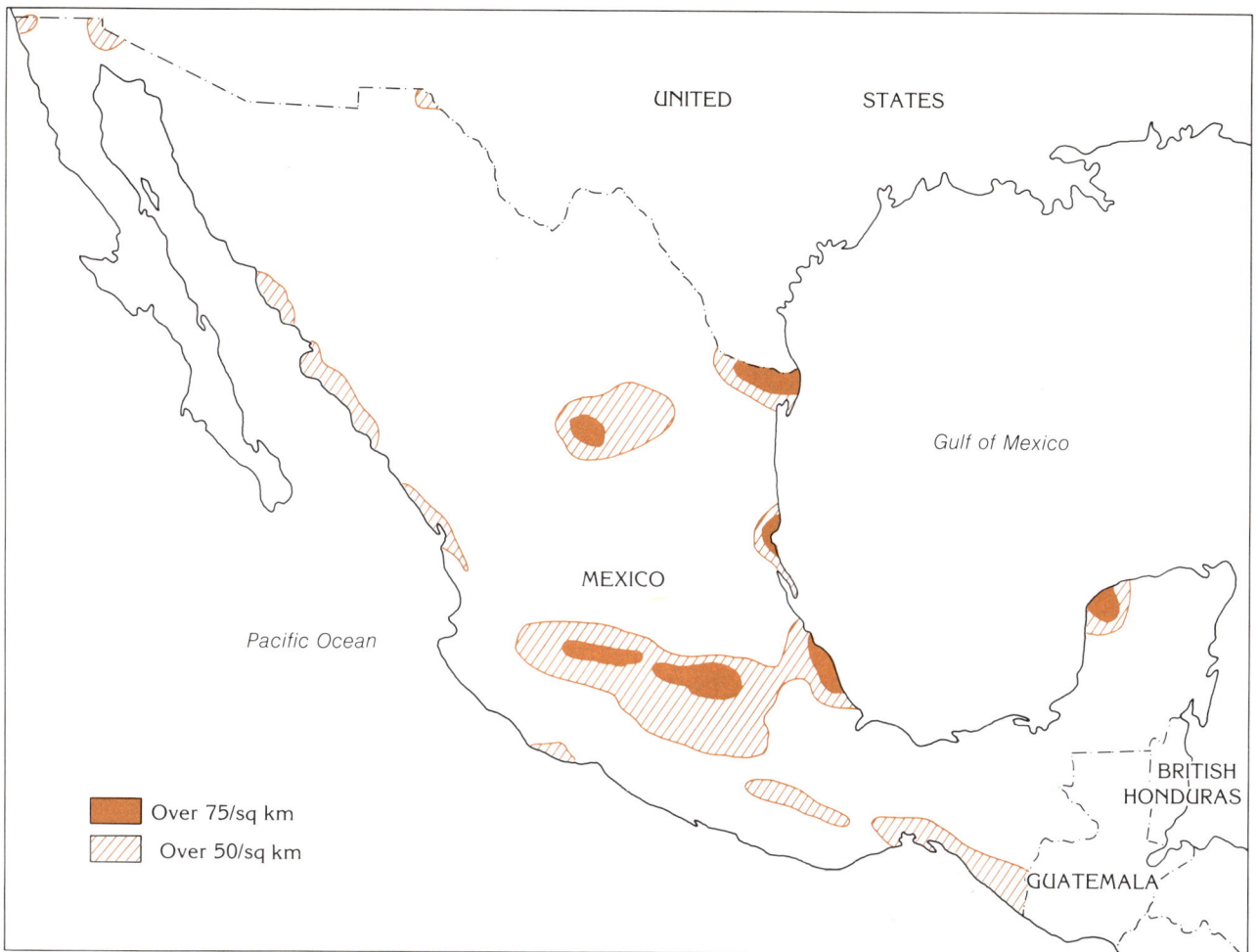

FIGURE 3–4

Population Density—Mexico. Pre-Columbian Mexico's core, the Aztec cultural hearth, remains the heartland; although Mexico is actively developing its disparate frontiers, both north and south.

eratively farm land that was taken away from estate landlords and redistributed to peasants. Similar to cooperatives, their purpose is to aid peasant education and to prevent a return to subsistence agriculture after land reform has taken place.)

One of the earliest industrial ventures of modern Mexico was the building of a steel complex at Monterrey. Iron ore from Durango was combined with coking coal from the coal field near Monclova. Both deposits are fairly distant, but Monterrey had plentiful water and excellent transportation, both absent at the raw material sites. Monterrey has grown into Mexico's second largest industrial city. It has diversified its base with alloy smelting, engineering, chemicals, glass, and clay products—the normal "partner industries" of a coal and steel economy.

The profusion of metal ores in the subregion lead to major metal smelting complexes at several centers. Torreon produces zinc metal and sulfuric acid as well as cad-

mium. San Luis Potosí, Chihuahua, and Durango support similar industries.

New phases of mineral industry are now further adding diversity. Large gas fields near Reynosa in the Rio Grande valley supply a new source of energy as well as a raw material for the rapidly expanding chemical sector. Extension of oil pipelines westward from the gulf will allow for even more rapid expansion.

The greatest success, by far, is registered in a series of border towns that are entrepôts for Mexico's imports (largely from the adjacent United States) and handle an imposing amount of the export trade (legal and illegal) as well. While day-trip tourism, shopping, and entertainment are the functions for which they were originally noted, they have now become primarily large manufacturing centers. These are the centers of Mexico's "export only" and "in-transit" industries. In the former type, foreign investors are allowed to produce semiprocessed goods, using Mexican

Irrigated Fields, Yaqui Valley, Mexico. An important part of Mexico's strategy of development is expansion of food supply; many important irrigation projects are underway in the northwest coastal districts. (Courtesy of United Nations)

raw materials, for final assembly or finishing in the United States or to assemble finished products in so-called free trade zones. In either case the industry uses cheaper Mexican labor in labor intensive industrial processes, exporting all or most of the product to the U.S. duty free. In the latter case, goods are processed in transit on their way from one portion of the United States to another in interim facilities in Mexico. Growth rates in these towns transcend even the capital district. Juarez, the largest (750,000), is Mexico's fourth largest city. Tijuana and Mexicali, both close to the 500,000, mark rank eighth and tenth respectively. Reynosa, booming from gas, chemicals, and a progressive regional agriculture, has developed into a city of a quarter million almost overnight.

The subregion's future is exceptionally bright. New, if lower-grade, iron deposits will extend the economic life of the steel mills in Monterrey and Monclova. Antimony, rare metals, uranium, and copper deposits are opening or expanding in the northwest. Mexico has only begun to tap its fish and seafood resources offshore. There is a fair amount of arable land that can be added with new irrigation projects at only moderate expense. It is exceptionally well served with both rail and highway transportation facilities. There is a growing regional pool of skilled workers. Most importantly, it is adjacent to two of the most rapidly expanding market areas in the United States. Progressive, modern, mechanized, and growing, it provides a sharp contrast to the other two subregions of the country.

THE CENTRAL BASINS OF MEXICO

This subregion is the most densely populated and intensely used portion of Mexico; it supports over one half of the total population. (See Figure 3–5.) As the core area of many of Mexico's great cultures of the past, it has always been the dominant area of Mexico. An area associated with mineral wealth during the period of Spanish control, it has witnessed a decline in the regional importance of mining. The rapidly growing urban industrial centers that are associated with modern Mexico contrast sharply with the small, inefficient subsistance farms that crowd the rural countryside, reminiscent of a much older Mexico.

Mineral deposits are not exhausted, though gold and silver production is declining. The oil, gas, lead, zinc, copper, iron, and coal of the other subregions, however, are more important to modern development. The agricultural base, while rich, is in some senses limited by rural overpopulation and inefficiency of use. The cooler climate does not favor high corn yields, yet tradition keeps it the dominant crop. Constant cropping of corn without adequate fertilization depletes soil fertility. Irrigation could increase yields greatly, but surface water is in short supply over most of the basin country.

The ejido system and the government program of land reform have been most thoroughly carried out in central Mexico. There is no doubt that land reform has fostered political stability, and the ejido system provides a mechanism for the dissemination of seed, fertilizer, and improved farming techniques. New seed, adapted to the cool dry conditions of the region, has resulted in gradually increasing yields. Farmers have been convinced to increase acreages in wheat and fodder crops—a more practical use of the environment than corn crops. The rapid growth of cities has provided a ready market for vegetables and dairy products, resulting in further diversification of rural land use. Major irrigation schemes are improving

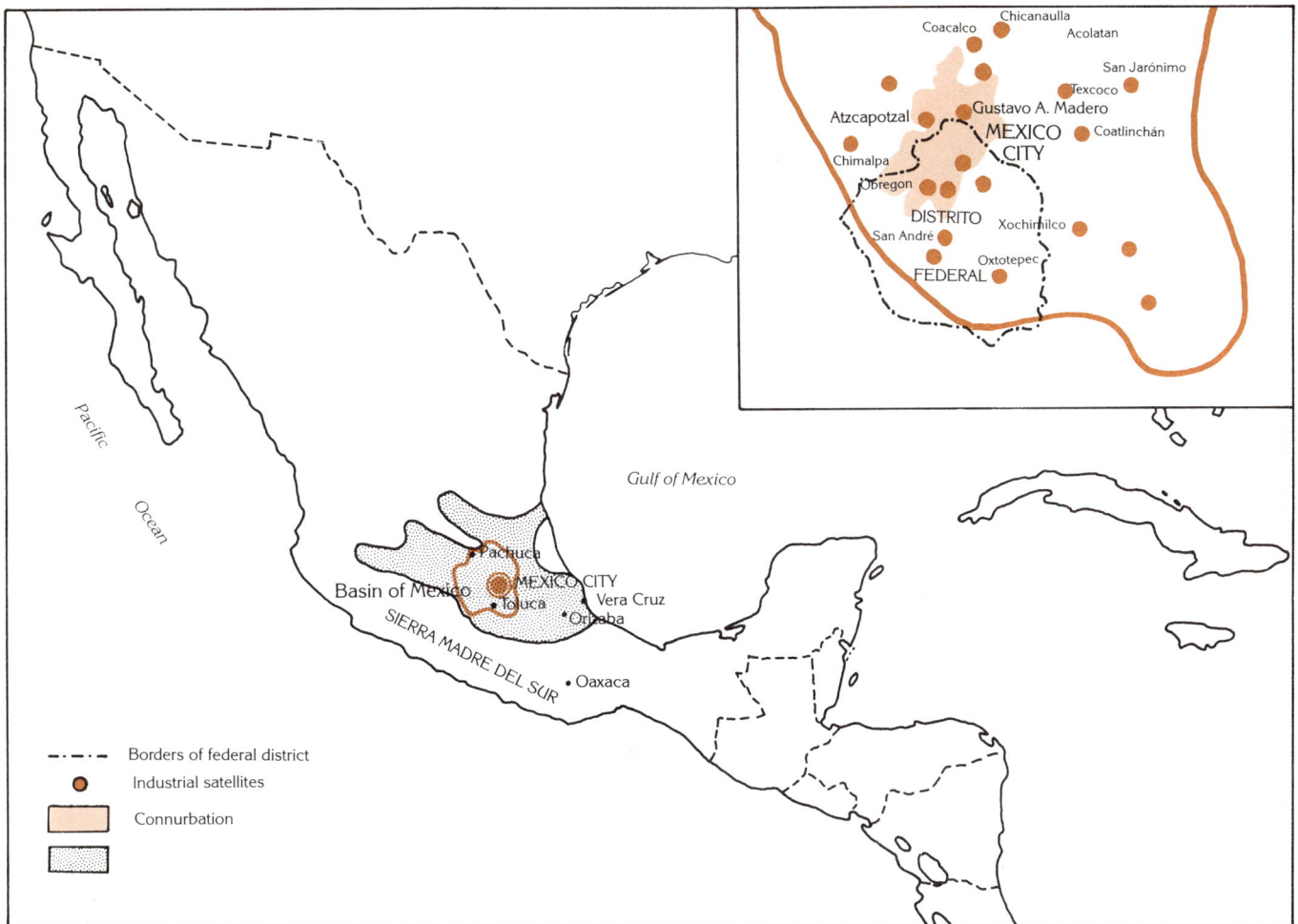

FIGURE 3–5
Basin of Mexico. A constellation of expanding cities is making a modernizing industrial heartland in Mexico's historic core.

regional water supplies and stabilizing yearly harvests. Despite these improvements, high overall density and rapidly increasing population still result in the region having to import food.

The greatest growth and development are evident in the industrial sector. Central Mexico is served by a well-developed network of both highways and railroads. It is Mexico's largest single market, a decided locational advantage for industry, since over half the Mexican buying public can be served within a distance of 200 or 300 miles (300 to 500 kilometers) of a number of points centrally located within the basin country.

The eastern sphere is dominated by Mexico City, the national capital and one of the largest cities in the world. Conservative estimates place its population at over 10 million. It is also the most rapidly growing metropolitan area of the country, despite attempts to disperse industrial investment.

Like other great metropolitan centers, a large part of Mexico City's industry produces consumer goods for the city market itself. Alcoholic beverages, clothing, shoes, construction materials, soap and detergents, furniture, and processed food are the typical products of such urban market-oriented production. It is the largest producer of paper, chemicals, machinery, and pharmaceuticals; for these areas of production, the entire country forms the market. Production varies in sophistication from a step above native crafts through automobiles and household appliances to sophisticated machine tools, scientific equipment, and medical devices.

The rapid growth of Mexico City has multiplied its problems as well as its living standard. Air pollution can reach disastrously high levels during periods of weather stagnation. Congestion approaches a perpetual traffic jam. High costs of living result in high wage structures, and skyrocketing growth rates have inflated land values. Slums engulf the city on several sides as the flood of migrants from rural areas exceeds the ability of even the most rapidly expanding economy to employ all. To cool off this overheated economic growth, the Mexican government has placed restrictions on further expansion. No new plants are allowed to build in the city itself, and plant expansions are strictly controlled. After 1980, this rule was applied to the entire metropolitan area. Special exceptions are made and growth continues, if at a slackened pace. New satellites are developing, but not sufficiently far away to alleviate the problems of congestion and pollution. (See Figure 3–6.)

The power of Mexico City is so great that no other city of any size has arisen within the whole Valley of Mexico. At a distance of 50 to 80 air miles from the capital city, however, a series of cities of considerable size (many of them mining centers and/or state capitals) are becoming industrial centers of importance. Much of their industry consists of branch plants of firms located within the capital or industrial investments that have located there because they are prevented from building in Mexico City itself. The largest (and most nearly independent) of these outer-ring satellites is Puebla, a city of over a half million people. It is located in a densely populated basin some 80 miles southeast of the capital. Not just a local market center for its large agricultural hinterland, it is a major industrial center specializing in textiles. Cotton cloth is still the major output, but a burgeoning Mexican chemical industry now supplies synthetic fiber to add diversification. Chemical fertilizer and machine industries, all using hydroelectrical power, are now gradually outpacing textiles as the city diversifies its industrial base. Puebla is virtually midway between the Gulf Coast oil fields and the capital city. It is also on the main transportation routes from Mexico City to the all-important port of Vera Cruz.

Cuernavaca, with over 400,000 people, occupies the center of a narrow basin perched on the southern edge of the Mexican Plateau. It is one of Mexico's most rapidly growing cities; the population has quadrupled in the last twenty years. Its industrial functions are quite varied. Tra-

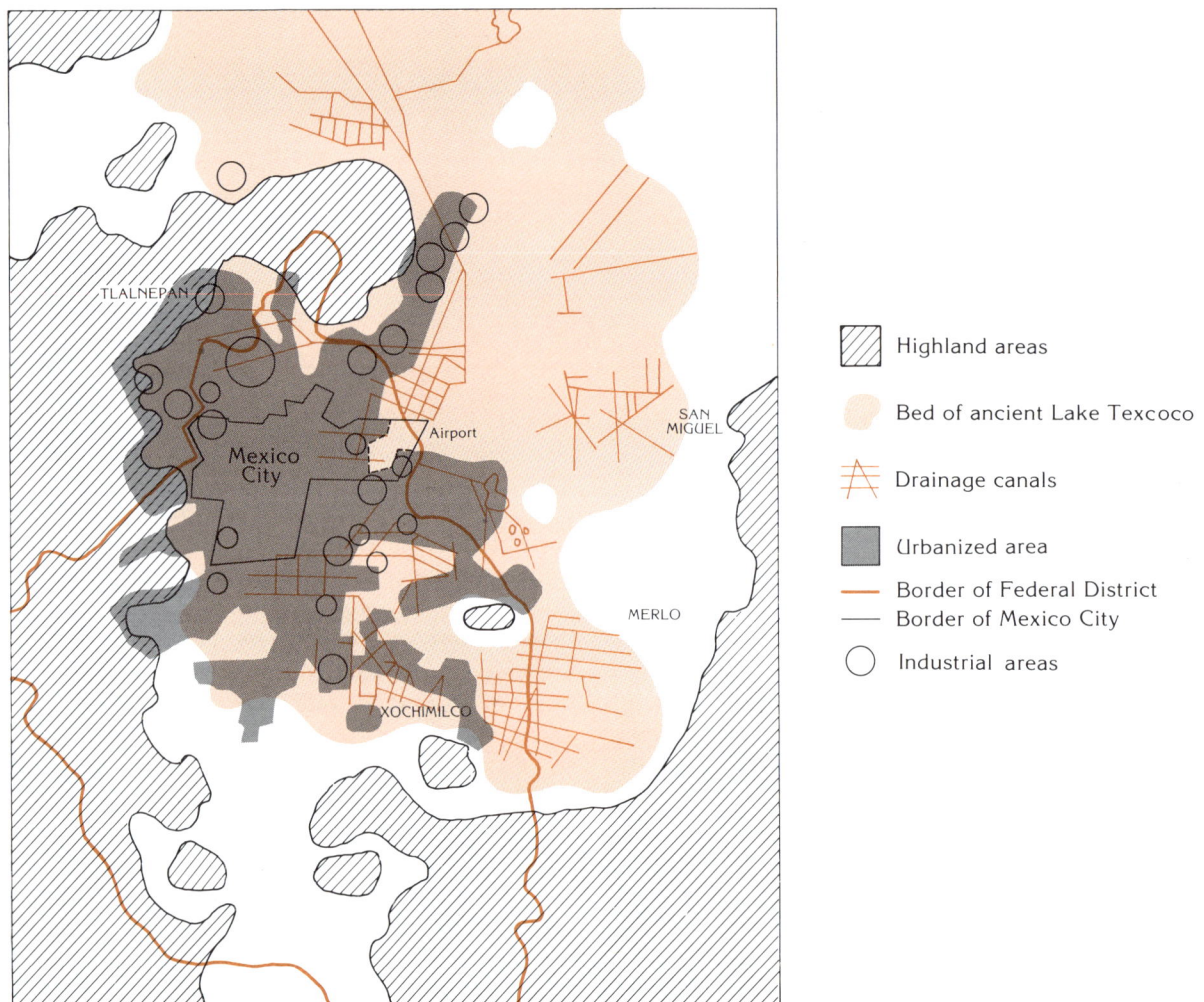

FIGURE 3–6
Metropolitan Mexico City. One of the world's largest and fastest growing metropolitan areas, Mexico City has added problems of concentration of atmospheric pollution within its mountain-encircled basin and a sinking of the city into its former lakebed site.

ditional industry entails the processing of sugar and other tropical crops for the capital city market. Branch plants out of Mexico City find the location advantageous because of proximity, and labor is much cheaper there than in the capital. Cuernavaca also has a pivotal location midway between the capital and the rich metal mining areas of the Mexican South. Like Puebla, it is at the hinging point of the tropical and temperate agricultural economies. It is on the highway to Acapulco, increasingly the most important port on the Pacific coast. In addition to its industrial role, Cuernavaca serves as an important winter resort.

The western sphere of economic influence is tied to Guadalajara, Mexico's second largest city (over 2 million people). Overall, the rail and highway networks of this portion of the central basins are more sparsely developed. Guadalajara draws its importance from its superb agricultural hinterland. It is relatively level land covered with rich volcanic soil; crop patterns include citrus and other subtropical crops in addition to the traditional corn and beans. Guadalajara is a major textile center and a quality producer of glass and ceramic items.

East of Guadalajara is the exceptionally rich basin El Bajío, the most productive agricultural district of this entire subregion. The conversion to wheat (from corn) has been quite successful here. Temperate fruits (peaches, pears, and apples) are a regional specialty. Cattle and pig rearing are very well developed and the small towns of the district often contain meat-processing plants.

In addition to this rural prosperity and air of plenty, the district also contains several large and growing industrial centers. León (600,000) is a major center of milling and food processing; it is now adding major chemical and machine components to its industrial base. Morelia (250,000), Irapuato, and Querétaro (each well over 150,000) have followed similar lines of development on a smaller scale. Each commands a portion of El Bajío's resources and markets. The orientation of the whole district is towards U.S. markets or those of northern Mexico. Guadalajara funnels most of the trade of the area to foreign markets, especially California.

Guadalajara is essentially at the juncture of wet and dry, tropical and temperate climatic regions. If its Pacific port (Manzanillo) is of little importance at the current time, it offers an outlet for a potentially rich trans-Pacific trade in the future. Already Japanese investments have begun to enter the region and Japanese markets absorb some regional exports. The growing California connection is even more promising.

THE MEXICAN SOUTH

The Mexican South is ethnically different from the rest of Mexico in that it concentrates a large number of pure-blooded Indians. Until recently it was peripheral to the economy of the rest of the country. Indeed, it was far less integrated into the economic mainstream of the rest of the nation than ever was the case with the U.S. South. Like the U.S. South, its ports were its chief cities, and trade and production were oriented more to export than to the local economy. Overwhelmingly rural (even at present), it contained large plantations—though most of the populace were small subsistence farmers. Like the U.S. South, it has rejuvenated its economy on the basis of oil and gas, diversification of farming, and climatic advantage. This parallel, of course, is easily overdrawn; there are great differences as well. Growth and development are relatively newer, slower, and definitely more localized. In some ways it is a frontier area.

The area specializes in sugar cane, coffee, cocoa beans, coconuts, bananas, and tropical fiber crops in its plantations. Increasingly, the subsistence farmers cultivate these items as cash crops to supplement corn and beans. This is the first time that the commercial and subsistence sectors have met; in the past they existed as if of two different totally isolated worlds.

The most developed portion of the region is the Gulf Coast, and the most developed sector of that coast is the state of Veracruz. The state contains Mexico's two most important ports, Tampico (250,000) and Vera Cruz (350,000). Mexico's largest oil field is located here (Poza Rica), and new offshore finds of oil and gas have greatly enlarged prospects and reserves. Further discoveries onshore at Cotaxtla insure the continued primacy of the province in fuel and energy production. (See Figure 3–7.)

Oil and gas deposits continue southward into the province of Tabasco (roughly 20 percent of total oil reserves), Campeche (in Yucatán), and across the isthmus in Chiapas on the Pacific side of the subregion. The pace of exploration is increasing, and the Mexican government feels it has only begun to tap the potential. Sulfur and salt, frequent companions of oil and gas deposits, round out the raw material base of the burgeoning chemical industry. Major hydroelectric projects developed along the eastern edge of the plateau generate enormous supplies of cheap power. Fertilizer plants, electro plating, metal refining, cement, electric steels, and a variety of other electric-power-consuming industries are expanding rapidly. The latest in a series of large hydro projects are located on the Papaloapan River in Vera Cruz and the Grivalja-Usumacinta system in the states of Chiapas and Tabasco. These are multipurpose projects intended to control floods, increase irrigation water supplies, drain waterlogged lowlands, eliminate malaria, provide a recreational resource, increase industrial production, and, generally, supply the basis for a massive colonization and development scheme in the sparsely populated territory between Vera Cruz and the city of Merida.

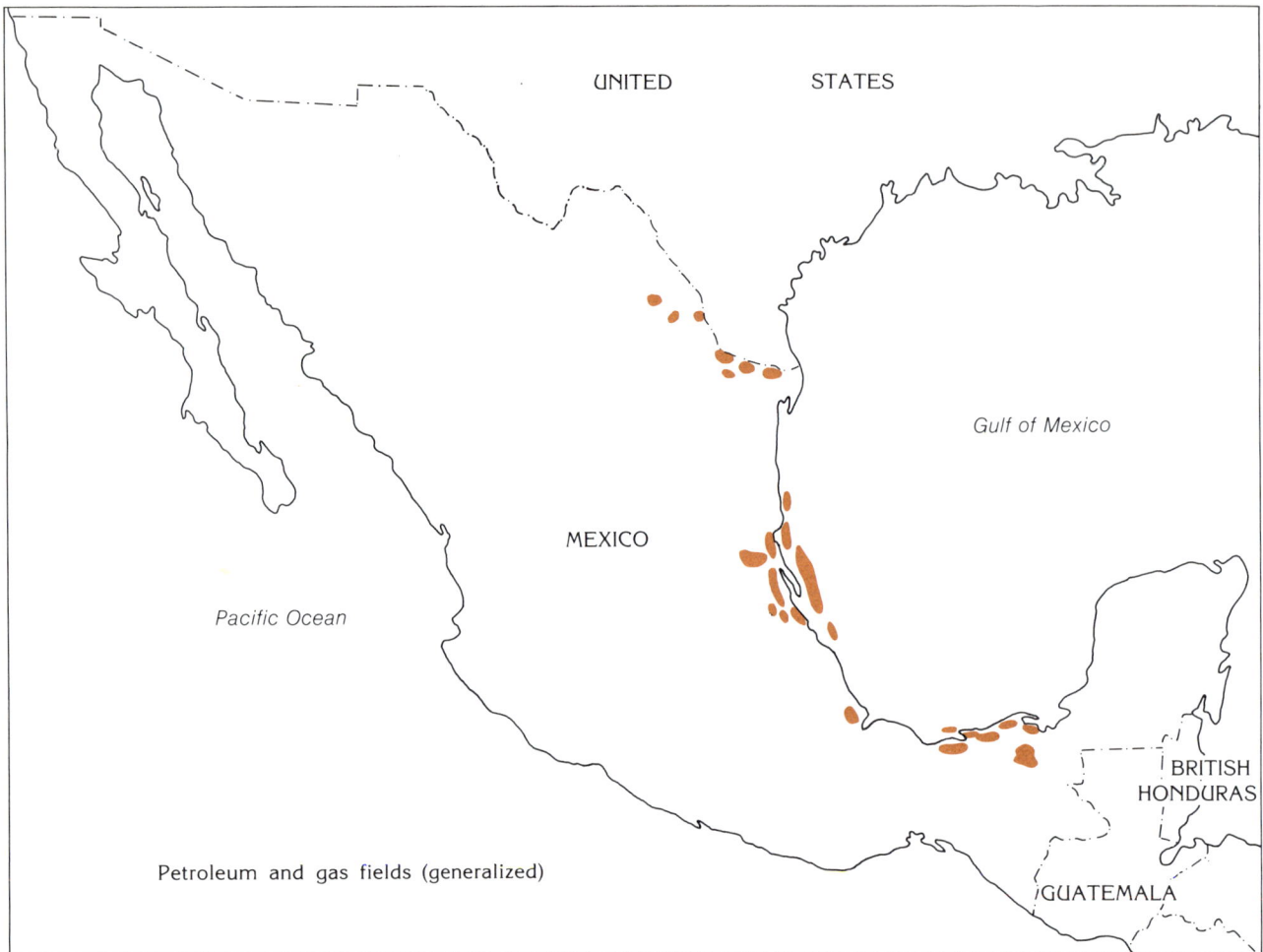

FIGURE 3–7
Mexican Oil Fields. Early in this century, Mexico was one of the world's leading oil exporters; recent
major discoveries make Mexico again a world energy power.

The two major industrial centers are the two port cities of Tampico (serving primarily northern Mexico) and Vera Cruz (serving the central basins). The metropolitan population of both exceeds half a million, and petrochemicals are the lead industry in a rapidly expanding (and diversifying) industrial base. Poza Rica (200,000) is the very center of oil and gas development onshore; it is a major chemical and refining center. The lack of a good port site has discouraged similar developments in the states of Campeche and Tabasco, despite the large-scale exploitation of oil and gas there.

Outside Vera Cruz State there is surprisingly little industrial development despite a relatively rich resource base of both agricultural and mineral components. A series of hydroelectric dams on the Balsas River, however, are expected to create future industrial development in the western half of southern Mexico.

Acapulco (500,000) and Merida (270,000) are the only other cities of note. The former is Mexico's premier tourist center, a resort of world-scale importance. Its lack of rail connections to the interior hampers the growth of its port function, though a superior highway connection to the central basins has been completed. Merida is the regional capital of the Yucatán state; fish processing, the manufacture of sisal fiber and rope, cement, and sugar refining are major industries. The relatively isolated nature of most of southern Mexico is demonstrated by the fact that Merida, while still growing, has slipped from tenth to twentieth place among Mexican cities.

Outside the industry of Vera Cruz State and the tourism of Acapulco, the development of this subregion seems to hinge more on agricultural programs. Densities are under 50 per square mile (20 per square kilometer) almost everywhere in the region, and the government sees this as an ideal area for the desired resettlement of rural populations from the farm districts of the overcrowded center. Possibilities for the further expansion of agriculture are excellent. Volcanic and limestone bedrock results in better than average tropical soils over much of the region.

After centuries of neglect, the Mexican government is now seeking to modernize and integrate this region with the rest of the country. Immense reserves of fuels, minerals, and water should provide impetus to development in a Mexico growing progressively richer.

THE CENTRAL AMERICAN REPUBLICS

The seven countries of Central America, south of Mexico and north of Colombia, exhibit a degree of cultural diversity worthy of a larger region. Five of these countries which founded the Central American Common Market (CACM), regard themselves as truly Central American (Costa Rica, El Salvador, Guatemala, Honduras, Nicaragua). Belize,

formerly British Honduras, remained a colony into the modern era; as the only part of Central America not independent after 1821 and the only predominantly non-Spanish speaking territory in the subregion, it was (and is) very different. Panama, administered as a province of Colombia both during the Spanish empire and afterwards, did not become independent until 1903, following Colombia's rejection of a treaty enabling the United States to build an isthmian canal.

The "five" were all part of a Federal Republic of Central America from 1823 until 1838, when they separated as completely independent. This fragmentation into several small units reflects historic settlement patterns within the rugged mountains as separate **cores** of settlement developed in Pacific coastal areas and interior basins or faulted trenches. (See Figure 3–8) Each of the present "five" was a province of the Captaincy General of Guatemala under Spanish rule; only Yucatán and Chiapas provinces of this imperial captaincy became part of Mexico. The historic federation remains a political ideal of some in the area.

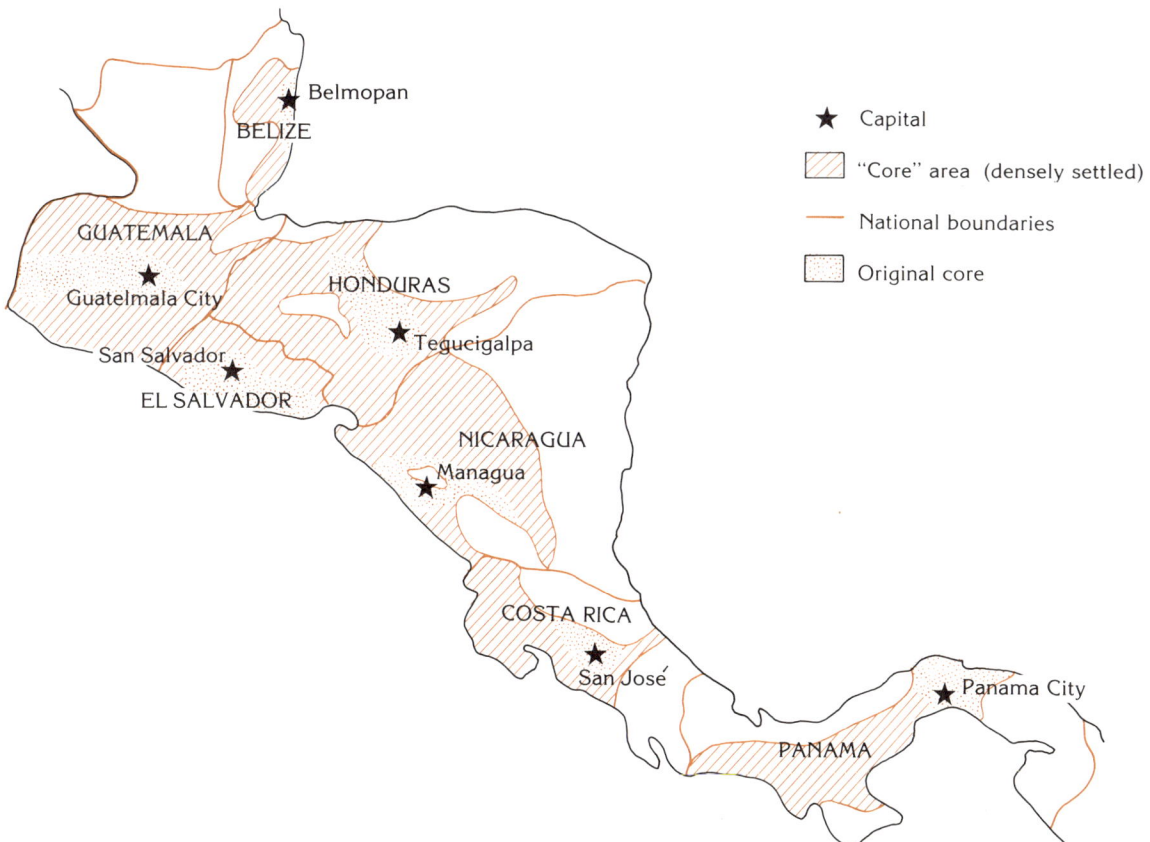

FIGURE 3–8

Central America—National Cores and Capitals. When the short-lived Central American confederation fragmented, states evolved from the separate population cores that had grown in favorable agricultural districts or mining centers.

This is not to say that the "five" are homogenous, culturally or peacefully cooperative. The only recent war in the subregion, brief as it was, occurred between Honduras and El Salvador in 1969. As will be seen, the seven countries that comprise Central America are quite distinctive culturally and economically. Their political-economic distinctions may well increase rather than recede in the near future.

Panama has always been regarded as South American rather than Central American, and has not associated itself with the "five" in any of their sporadic attempts at confederation nor in their common market (see Table 3–1). Belize, English-speaking and possessing an ethnic flavor more Caribbean than Central American, is claimed by Guatemala; as recently as 1977, Britain sent in troops to forestall a rumored Guatemalan "liberation."

Guatemala   Guatemala is the most "Indian" of the Central American states; almost half its citizens are descendants of the Maya. Guatemala shares with its regional neighbors an economic emphasis on agriculture and light consumer goods and assembly industries rather than on

local mineral resources. Hydroelectric power potential is generally good in the region, and Guatemala's Pacific-oriented drainage has good potential. A nickel mine was opened in 1978 and minor deposits of chromite may become profitable as world prices escalate for this steel alloy. (See Figure 3–9.) Despite intensive exploration and favorable natural conditions, no significant oil or gas has been found to date.

Agricultural products provide nearly 90 percent of the value of exports. It has long been customary to refer to the Central American countries, patronizingly, as *banana republics;* the term, which had taken a figurative meaning of unstable, is not only derogatory, it is inaccurate. Coffee is the most important crop in Guatemala, as in most of its neighbors. Coffee alone provides three quarters of the national export earnings. Coffee, bananas, and cotton are raised primarily on large landholdings operated by a *Ladino* (Hispanic) aristocracy, by the national government, or, decreasingly, by foreign fruit companies. Throughout Central America, banana production has become proportionately less important as other export crops were developed, and the major growing areas have shifted to the Pacific

TABLE 3–1
Comparative data for Central America

	Population	Population Growth Rate (per thousand)	Population Density (per square kilometer)	Per Capita Income (U.S. dollars)	Major Ethnic Groups	Language(s)	Exports	Economic Organization[1]
Belize	135,000	3.0	15	750	African Mestizo	English	Sugar citrus Lobsters fish	Caricom
Costa Rica	2,100,000	2.7	105	1400	Spanish	Spanish	Coffee bananas sugar	Cacm
El Salvador	4,400,000	3.3	504	600	Mestizo	Spanish	Coffee sugar cotton	Cacm
Guatemala	6,670,000	3.1	155	850	Mestizo Indian	Spanish	Coffee cotton sugar	Cacm
Honduras	3,100,000	3.5	70	580	Mestizo African	Spanish	bananas coffee lumber	Cacm
Nicaragua	2,500,000	3.4	43	900	Mestizo	Spanish	bananas cotton fruit	Cacm
Panama	1,850,000	2.2	64	1200	Mestizo African	Spanish English	bananas sugar petroleum products	—

[1] Cacm = Central American Common Market, Caricom = Caribbean Community.

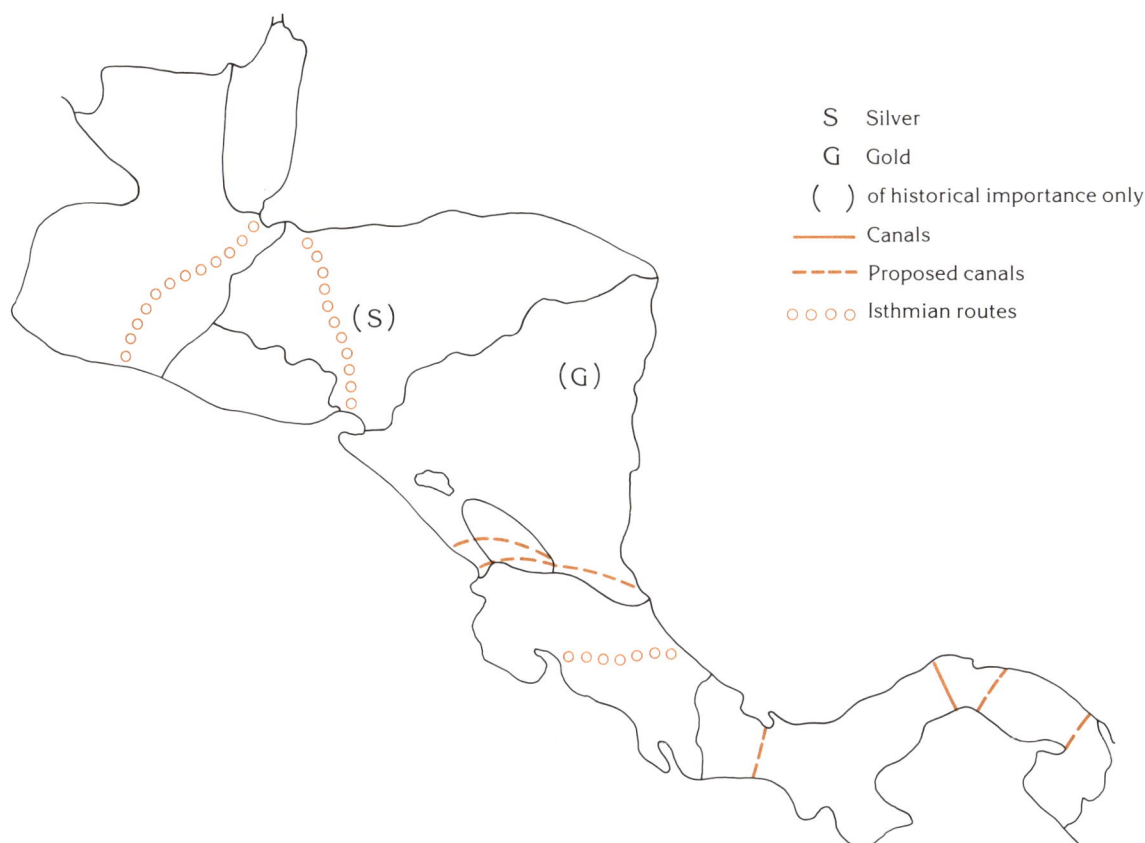

FIGURE 3–9
Central America—Minerals and Corridor Functions. Central America's natural resources feature relatively few economic minerals but an important locational resource. The narrowing isthmus has long had significant "corridor functions," between Pacific Latin America and the Atlantic trade routes and between the Atlantic and Pacific coasts of the United States and Canada.

coastal areas from the Caribbean littoral. The hot, wet Caribbean coast was important first for banana plantations, because climate and soil conditions were generally excellent and the development of refrigerated ships made possible large-scale exports to the eastern United States via Caribbean ports. The Caribbean coastal banana plantations prospered from 1900 to about 1930; then production dropped rapidly due to disease, causing abandonment of many thousands of acres. In the late 1930's, a banana leaf blight also spread through the area. The Central American banana industry then moved across the mountains to the Pacific coastal lowlands. Unfortunately, production costs were then higher as the major markets were still the eastern United States and Europe, and the diseases did spread to the new plantations. Experimentation with disease-resistant new varieties of bananas had benefited both flanks of the mountain spine, but bananas have never recovered their former supremacy in most Central American economies. Foreign fruit companies, sensing

the "winds of change" in the region, have sought a "low profile" and preferred to concentrate on marketing and providing technical assistance and financing to local growers where feasible rather than extending or even maintaining their land ownership.

Guatemala's rate of natural increase approximates the regional average (see Table 3–1), the highest of any region in the world. The population is a young one (45 percent under fifteen) and is projected to double in twenty-three years. The Indian population tends to occupy the highlands west and north of the capital, Guatemala City. Fully acculturated, Spanish-speaking Indians join the Euro-American culture of Ladinos and mestizos; thus the Ladinos expand at the expense of Indians culturally. Some Indian subsistence farmers still practice slash-and-burn[1]

---

[1] In this land-use system, a portion of forest is cut and partially cleared, then the dead, dried vegetation burned to provide ash fertilizer. After a few crops, this plot is abandoned due to decreasing fertility, and another portion of the forest is "slashed and burned."

agriculture and seldom produce a marketable surplus; others have shifted toward commercial production of vegetables. Communal, village-owned land holdings survive from pre-Spanish days, but are commonly too small to produce enough food for a family, as are most private plots owned by Indians. There are still many landless, rural Indians, a social problem with explosive potential.

The rapid growth of cities (Guatemala City now has over 1.5 million inhabitants) is closely related to the plight of landless laborers; the cities offer their only hope, admittedly slender, of economic progress outside of the pioneering farm areas in the eastern provinces. Providing jobs for recent arrivals whose only skills are agricultural is a major problem for Guatemala as well as its Middle American neighbors. Guatemala plans to diversify exports by supplementing its high-quality coffees with more meat and shrimp production, continuing exploration for oil, and continued emphasis on light industries such as textiles, pharmaceuticals, and processed foods. Its balance of trade with its Central American Common Market (CACM) partners has been highly favorable because of its successful export of light industrial products. Its very success has created stresses within CACM as less successful exporters maneuver to renegotiate tariffs and incentives.

Guatemala's main problems appear to be the growing dissatisfaction and impatience of the Indians, who wish a more equitable share in the economy, and the long-standing claim to Belize, which may not be settled in a manner acceptable to Guatemalan nationalists.

Honduras Honduras, in contrast to Guatemala, has a population that is 90 percent mestizo (mixed Caucasian and Indian) with only small minorities of Indians, Africans, and Caucasians. Honduras was, traditionally, less dependent on agricultural exports, as its combination of favorable geology and paucity of good soils resulted in an economy dominated by mining. Silver was the most important export until World War I, when old, declining mines were countered by a booming banana plantation economy. Some silver is still produced, along with lead and zinc, but coffee has replaced bananas as the leading export. Honduras is the poorest state in the region (see per capita income in Table 3–1), and has been long regarded as the most backward state of the region. If any Central American country truly merited the designation of "banana republic," it was Honduras in the 1920's, when a third of the world's bananas were produced on its Caribbean coast. When disease drastically cut production, the United Fruit Company (an American corporation) introduced new crops such as oil palm and gave abandoned banana lands to farmers producing food crops, sugar cane, and livestock.

Newly Harvested Bananas, Honduras. Although many Central American republics rely more now on coffee exports than bananas, the problems of "one crop economies" have not disappeared. (Courtesy of United Nations/J. Frank)

For almost two centuries, Honduran mahogany was a valuable export. Unfortunately, lack of conservation has destroyed most of the mahogany. Honduras is attempting to develop a pulp and paper industry based on its still extensive pine resources.

Hondura's rate of population increase, 3.5 percent, outpaces the rest of the world excepting a very few countries. Fortunately, Honduras has a relatively low overall population density (although concentrated near the Salvadoran border) and an expanding agricultural frontier to help absorb a population that likely will double in twenty years. It has Central America's lowest proportion of urban population. Economic development strategies feature state management and marketing of forest products and bananas and the improvement of transportation facilities. An agrarian reform act (1975) has been implemented slowly, partly in an attempt at minimizing any negative impact on the high productivity of large land units.

Honduras fought a brief, bloody war with El Salvador in 1969. Salvadorans, whose nation's population density is more than five times the regional average (see Table 3–1), had been illegally entering Honduras and squatting on unused lands. The cease-fire (after a five-day struggle) required Salvadoran withdrawal from Honduran territory. Honduras has since built the largest air force in Central America, although it is least able to afford heavy military expenditures.

El Salvador   El Salvador, the second smallest state in the region, lacks a two-ocean frontage as does Belize. Its high population density is more typical of Caribbean islands than Central America. El Salvador has had to cope with being on the "wrong side" of Central America in terms of accessibility to its major markets (United States and Europe). Alone among the Central American republics, El Salvador lacks unsettled, cultivable lands to act as a "safety valve" for its rapidly expanding, predominantly agricultural population. It has the highest proportion of settled land (23 percent) of any Central American state. The high rate of natural increase, just under twice the world average, and lack of suitable land for expansion help to explain its poverty.

Half the total number of farms are less than five acres; these comprise only 5 percent of the total farm acreage. An essentially feudal pattern of land ownership has put the best farmland into plantations producing export crops; the gap between rich and poor has fueled a guerrilla-style revolution. Coffee and cotton, which provide over half of the export income, take the best lands; food production is so low that foreign exchange earned by exporting plantation crops and shrimp must be spent on basic food to supplement locally grown corn, beans, and sorghum. Soils are heavily eroded as the desparate need for more food production pushed cultivation onto steep slopes exposed to heavy seasonal rains. Seasonal unemployment is high because poor Salvadorans plant only one crop per year (the growing season would support two) so that they can migrate to the uplands to work on the coffee harvest for some cash income.

In a way, El Salvador is largely responsible for Central American independence of the Mexican Confederation. Following independence from Spain in 1821, the Central American provinces joined with Mexico, but El Salvador insisted on autonomy. After a brief military struggle won by Mexico, El Salvador petitioned the United States for statehood. Before the United States could act on this wholly unsolicited offer, a revolution in Mexico left Central Americans free to form their own short-lived federation.

El Salvador's industrial growth has been spurred by its acute population pressure as well as entrepreneurial skills and enthusiasm. It is hardly an industrialized economy, but oil refining (based on Venezuelan crude) and cement and fertilizer plants have helped industrial production double in twenty years. The country's compact, densely settled territory is well served by transport systems (by developing-nation standards). Railroads, the Inter-American Highway, and paved feeder roads provide a good network.

As with other Central American states, the wide fluctuations in world coffee markets have had serious impacts on the balance of trade, unemployment, and government revenues based on coffee exports. These states are in the uncomfortable position of relying heavily on coffee markets to provide tax revenue and investment funds with which to diversify the economy and make it less dependent on coffee.

Belize   Belize has by far the lowest population density in Middle America, the official language is English, and half the people are of African or part-African stock. Nearly a third live in Belize City, the former colonial capital and the main seaport. Europeans were first attracted to Belize by the commerical possibilities of mahogany and tropical cedar. The swampy, mangrove coast with its many tiny islands, shallow channels, and coral reefs (hazardous to navigation but favorable to abundant sea life) attracted pirates who hid in the mazelike coastal swamps and islets. English-speaking blacks from the Caribbean islands were imported by the British as forestry labor. Black-Carib Indians are the second most important ethnic group, followed by Spanish-speaking migrants from Guatemala and Mexico.

Belize has decided to move its capital from the hurricane-damaged colonial center at Belize City to a new, more central location at Belmopan (see Figure 3–8). Forestry continues as an important economic activity, although the best tropical hardwoods have been virtually eliminated. Emphasis has shifted to pine lumber for the wood-short Caribbean islands. So little surplus food is produced that towns rely on imported food. The rich fisheries offshore have only begun to be developed. It is hoped that Belize's dismal record in forestry conservation will not be repeated in the spiny lobster and shrimp fisheries. North American markets pay such a high price for these luxury foods, though, that shellfisheries have expanded beyond the natural replenishment limits in most of Central America. Sugar has become an important export recently, most of it produced in the northern, Spanish-culture areas near the Mexican border. Citrus production, primarily for British markets, is also expanding, while rice and beans for local food supply are receiving more emphasis.

If its population were not so dramatically different in culture from that of its neighbors, a merger with Guatemala would be more feasible. Sharp cultural differences have reinforced a determination in Belize not to be submerged in an ethnically and linguistically alien Guatemala. This midget among small states will most probably continue its separate way.

Nicaragua Nicaragua has the unfortunate distinction of having been repeatedly occupied militarily and administered directly by the United States (the last time from 1926 to 1933). Effectively, though not officially, Nicaragua was a protectorate of the United States and is generally mentioned first in any discussion of "Yankee Imperialism." American interest in Nicaragua is related to the great Nicaraguan Rift, a trenchlike valley slicing northwest-southeast across the highlands and mountains of the narrowing isthmus (see Figure 3–9). Nicaragua has the second best routeway across the Central American isthmus. A Nicaraguan canal has been discussed sporadically for more than a century; unfortunately, the same geologic forces that created the rift provide frequent earthquakes and volcanic eruptions in the area.

Volcanic soils (periodically enriched by more ash), in the rift valley and lake lowlands support dense popula-

Shoe Factory, Nicaragua. As both an "import replacement" and potential export item, consumer goods are a logical step in industrialization for developing nations with few resources other than labor. (Courtesy of United Nations)

tions. Three quarters of Nicaraguans live in this zone near the Pacific coast, which includes the capital, Managua, with 300,000 people.

The present, highly uneven population distribution reflects the pre-Spanish pattern, wherein advanced Indian cultures densely peopled the lake lowlands and much more primitive hunter-gatherer tribes lightly settled the central highlands and Caribbean littoral. Nicaraguans are largely mestizo. A 10 percent African-ancestry minority occupies the Caribbean coast. Reflecting a pattern common in Central America, a small minority of people who claimed direct descent from the Spanish colonials held most of the land while the bulk of the mestizo population were landless laborers. The extremely uneven distribution of land and wealth provided considerable popular support for the Marxist "Sandinist" guerrilla war against a corrupt dictatorship. The Sandinists took power in 1979. Unfortunately, they have not honored a commitment to hold free elections after overthrowing the previous dictatorship.

Nicaragua's coffee production was initiated by German and British colonists in the 1890's; they also established the pattern of moderate-size coffee estates or *fincas,* which continue to produce about half the crop. Thus, huge plantation-style coffee producers were never as predominant in Nicaragua as in most other Central American states.

One of the least industrialized Central American states, Nicaragua's industry is concentrated in the capital and emphasizes food processing, textiles, and lumber along with a modern oil refinery and steel-tubing mill.

Costa Rica Costa Rica's inhabitants have gradually spread outward from a single dense cluster in the central highland basins. About 80 percent claim to be unmixed descendents of Spanish colonists. Colonial Costa Rica lay outside the Meso-American Indian culture area; its scattered Indians disappeared rapidly following Spanish conquest. The Spanish colonial emphasis on huge estates owned by Spanish and worked by Indians thus could not materialize here. The result is a pattern of small holdings owned and operated by individual farmers. Costa Rica has the most evenly distributed national income, the highest per capita gross domestic product, and the longest and strongest traditions of democratically elected governments.

No significant mineral deposits have been found, but Costa Rica has been able to build relative prosperity by pioneering new farming areas on both the Caribbean and Pacific flanks of its central core (see Figure 3–10). The tropical climate of the Meseta Central is moderated by elevation so that a wide range of tropical and midlatitude crops can be produced; Costa Rica is the only state in the subregion to have a large dairy industry. The reputation for

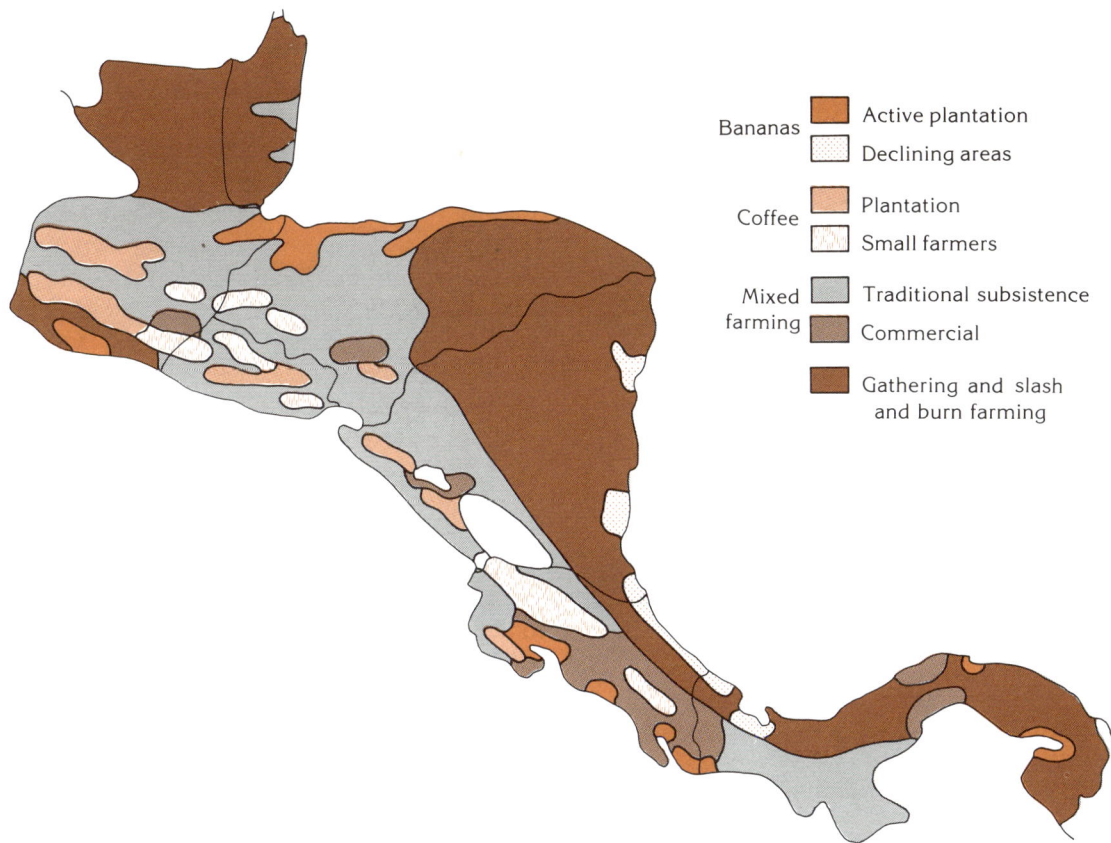

FIGURE 3–10
Central America—Agriculture. Crop specializations, now more likely to feature coffee than bananas, have evolved as each Central American nation has sought foreign exchange through the export of commodities, most commonly tropical commercial crops.

political stability has encouraged foreign financing of light industry. Hydroelectric potential is excellent and, once developed, could further encourage light assembly, and consumer industries.

Panama Panama still tends to hold itself apart from Central American politics and economic cooperation schemes. Until 1903, Panama was a province of Colombia. Nearly impassable rainforests made the connection to Colombia (both economically and politically) tenuous. All that was necessary to ensure Panamanian independence after Colombia moved more cautiously on a canal treaty than Panama wished, was for the United States Navy to interpose its ships between Panama and the Colombian navy.

Panama has a much larger proportion of Indian heritage in its population than Costa Rica. It also has an English-speaking black minority in the Canal Zone, descendants of the labor force recruited from Jamaica and Barbados to build the famous canal under the engineering supervision of Americans. Panama now has the lowest

rate of population increase in Central America, following decades of very high rates. Panama's greatest resource has always been its location at the narrowest portion of the isthmus connecting North and South America. Since Balboa crossed Panama to "discover" the Pacific in 1513, Panama has profited from servicing transit trade. The canal remains its major asset, though it is too narrow to admit the supertankers and bulk carriers that make up a large proportion of international shipping. Completed in 1914, the canal was designed for different scale ships. The canal played an extremely important role in the accelerated development of the United States west coast; its inavailability would still cost American consumers heavily.

The somewhat controversial Panama Canal Treaty (1978) provides a new basis for United States-Panamanian cooperation on the canal. The 1903 treaty had become a political liability for the United States throughout Latin America. The canal obviously would be highly vulnerable to sabotage if Panamanian nationalism and resentment continued to focus on what Panamanians perceived to be a highly unequal and demeaning treaty.

Gatun Locks, Panama Canal. The Panama Canal plays as important a role in trade between the United States' east and west coasts as it does in Latin American trade. The canal is too narrow for many modern ships, especially tankers, and may be supplemented by a paralleling, wider canal. (Courtesy of United Nations)

The new treaty reaffirms the United States' primary responsibility for the defense of the canal until 2000 A.D. The American jurisdiction in the Canal Zone has ended, eliminating the major irritant to the Panamanians.

Panama is really two countries, culturally. The sophisticated urban populations of the "zone's" two cities (Panama City and Colón) contrast sharply with the provincial, agricultural populace of the Pacific lowlands. Bananas, pineapples, cocoa, and sugar are grown for export, but the real props to the Panamanian economy are oil refining and its **hidden exports.** These intangible services, in addition to canal revenues, come from international banking and liberal laws governing the registration of merchant ships. The Panamanian flag flies over one of the world's largest merchant fleets because foreign owners prefer Panama's safety and labor laws, as well as its low taxes. Panama uses the United States dollar as currency; this, in combination with its favorable banking laws, excellent communications and transport facilities, and absence of exchange controls, has multiplied the number of banks licensed in Panama. It has become the principal Spanish-language banking center, especially attractive to depositors seeking refuge from South American inflation and from instability anywhere. There are also clear advantages to tax dodgers throughout the New World.

THE GREATER ANTILLES OF THE CARIBBEAN—CUBA, HISPANIOLA, PUERTO RICO, AND JAMAICA

The larger islands of the Caribbean were among the first, and richest, colonies of Spain. Later in the colonial period they were neglected in favor of the fabulous mineral wealth of Mexico and Peru. Cuba, Puerto Rico, and Hispaniola were at first prized because both gold and densely settled Amerindian populations could be exploited there. Jamaica had little gold, and received much less attention from the Spanish; the English conquered the island in 1655. When the gold of the large islands was quickly mined out, many resident Spanish left for the mainland, taking their supplies, tools, and horses with them. The islands' Spanish population fell so quickly that Spain decreed settlers attempting to leave would have a leg amputated. Even that didn't stem the outflow. The Amerindian population (about 1 million before Columbus) had been largely destroyed, and African slaves began to be imported.

French interests in the western part of the large island of Hispaniola were linked to its possibilities for sugar cane plantations. The French colony of St. Dominigue (later, Haiti) was enormously successful, economically. However, a slave revolt had begun in northwestern Haiti (1791), and by 1804, it was an independent republic.

An interesting sidelight to the Haitian revolt was that it helped the United States acquire the Louisiana Purchase at fire-sale prices. Outnumbered by their former slaves twenty to one, the French in Haiti pleaded for support from France, then entering the Napoleonic period. Locked in a struggle with Britain, France could afford but one military thrust towards the New World. A fleet with an army on board was sent to Haiti to quell the revolt, and then proceed to New Orleans, to strengthen the small garrison there against possible British attack. The French force did not survive Haitian resistance combined with malaria. New Orleans was almost defenseless and, when Jefferson's envoys showed up wanting to buy the east bank of the Mississippi to ensure American trade the use of the river, Napoleon rushed to sell the whole Louisiana territory before it could be taken by conquest.

Cuba and Puerto Rico, unable to join the mainland of Latin America in freedom from Spain in the 1820's, were finally freed as a result of the Spanish-American War (1898). Cuba became a theoretically independent republic, but with strong economic ties to the United States; Puerto Rico became a U.S. commonwealth territory. These political-economic associations have been extremely important in the development of modern Cuba and Puerto Rico. Jamaica became independent only in relatively recent times.

Cuba   Cuba, by far the largest of the Caribbean islands, stretches almost 800 miles (1,300 kilometers). Its strategic location within the Americas has been very important since Columbus. To its west-southwest is the Yucatán Channel between the Gulf of Mexico and the Caribbean, to its east-southeast the Windward Passage lies between it and Haiti, and to its north lie the Straits of Florida. Spain recognized Cuba's key location by making Havana the assembly point for its homeward-bound treasure fleets, using the Straits of Florida to swing west and north of the treacherous shallow water and coral-limestone islets of the Bahamas. (See Figure 3–11.) Cuba's resource base includes one of the world's largest deposits of nickel ores, a key steel alloy. Cuba also has some minor deposits of copper, chromite, and manganese and considerable iron ore reserves. Small oil deposits have been producing for many years; only recently has systematic exploration for possible larger pools been undertaken.

Cuba's 10.5 million people are about 40 percent black or mulatto; the rest are mestizo or white. After the "gold fever" exodus to Mexico and Peru, a second wave of Spaniards was attracted by the developing sugar plantations of the nineteenth century, but, ironically, the largest number of Spanish arrived after Cuban independence. Africans arrived as slaves from 1520 to 1887 (abolition of slavery). A second wave of blacks came as free laborers from Haiti and Jamaica after 1900. Out-migration from Cuba has never been important except in times of internal political stress. The largest emigration, upward of half a million, was of refugees from the increasingly coercive Castro regime after the 1959 revolution, mostly to the United States. As all too common in parts of Middle Amer-

ica, social-economic class tended to be strongly associated with skin tone, lighter on top of the social pyramid and darker on bottom. Cuba's African ethnics tended to be more enthusiastic about the income-leveling effects of Castro's revolution since they had the least to lose and most (including good quality, free medical care) to gain. Cuba has the lowest population density of the larger Caribbean islands, and could be the most prosperous with its mineral reserves, relatively good ratio of cultivable land per person, and accessibility to the American market.

Cuba's population explosion, from 1.6 million in 1900 to 4 million by 1930 and over 10 million now, accompanied the very rapid expansion of sugar output (from less than 500,000 tons in 1900, following decades of revolution against Spain, to 4.5 million tons by 1930). The climate and terrain of Cuba are nearly ideal for sugar cane, with large areas of gently rolling to level land in a tropical wet-and-dry climate. The heavy rains of the wet season are necessary to rapid cane growth, and the dry season is necessary for harvesting. When, after a brief American administration, independence was granted (1902) with the proviso that the United States had the right to intervene to preserve stability, American capital flowed in to boost sugar production. The older style, family-owned plantations with their inefficient sugar mills were replaced by foreign-owned corporations, which consolidated large blocks of acreage, constructed modern *centrales* (large sugar mills), and built miles of narrow-gauge railroads to deliver cane to the mills. These "sugar railroads" give Cuba the highest ratio of rail mileage to population in all of Latin America. The combination of proximity to American markets, heavy American investment in sugar plantations, and

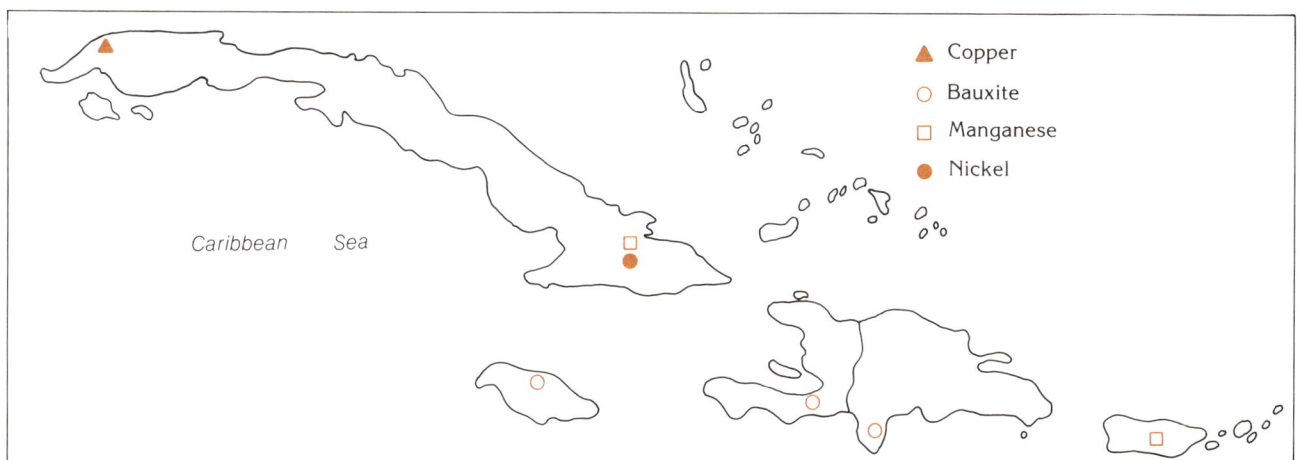

FIGURE 3–11
Greater Antilles: Minerals and Colonial Convoy Routes. The metal ores of the Greater Antilles were important early in the colonial era, then replaced in importance by the gold and silver of Mexico and Peru, whose shipments to Spain made the fortified harbors of the subregion more important than their local minerals. Minerals became important in the modern era, particularly in Cuba and Jamaica.

United States paternalism toward Cuba resulted in Cuban sugar being included in United States crop stabilization quotas after 1933. At the time of the Castro takeover in 1959, Cuba had 95 percent of the United States sugar import quota. This guaranteed Cuban sugar sales at the United States market price, which was almost always far above the world market level (a result of the American decision to subsidize Florida and Louisiana cane growers).

The tragedy of the Castro revolution was that it did not eliminate the latifundia (large landholdings worked by landless workers), but rather reinforced their fundamental effects on the economy. Luckless Cuba has never been free of economic colonialism. No political or economic freedoms existed under the Spanish Empire (Cubans were not even citizens), and this was replaced by exploitive "economic colonialism" imposed by the American-Cuban sugar connection. The break with the United States has placed Cuba in still another, even more exploitive, colonial relationship with the Soviet Union, which now purchases much of Cuba's sugar. Instead of distributing land to peasants, Castro simply nationalized plantations, keeping them intact as "state farms."

Sugar still supplies nearly 85 percent of total export earnings, although cigar production is up, and pineapples, citrus, and other fruits are growing in importance. Still, Cuba must import many of the basic foods—large amounts of wheat, rice, corn, and beans—as its best land is in sugar production. A major trade deficit has given Cuba the largest per capita foreign debt in Latin America (mostly owed the USSR, which also accounts for two thirds of Cuba's trade).

Just as Cuba's neighbors in Middle America scrambled for its former 95 percent of the U.S. sugar market quota, its neighbors eagerly picked up shares of Cuba's formerly lucrative U.S. tourist trade.

Puerto Rico   Puerto Rico, less than one tenth the area of Cuba, has a population density of 985 per square mile (380 per square kilometer). Its very high population density in a mountainous island with severe soil erosion problems and no important minerals led to its unfortunate nickname, "poorhouse of the Caribbean," by the 1930's. Three fourths of the surface is hilly; it has fewer harbors than Cuba and is further from American markets.

Yet it has managed to achieve one of the highest per capita incomes in Middle America, largely thanks to its special relationship with the United States. Puerto Rico is a self-governing commonwealth associated with the United States ("Estado Libre Asociado"—"freely associated state"), which gives it many of the benefits of United States citizenship but no federal income tax nor direct representation in the Congress. There are no tariff or im-

migration barriers into the United States. Political stability, despite a small but active minority of *independistas,* attracts United States investment. Tax advantages and lower wages than "mainland" have brought in many garment, electronics, pharmaceuticals, medical supplies, and assembly industries together with petrochemicals based on Venezuelan and African crudes. While lower than United States' average income, Puerto Rico's is high when compared to the rest of the region. Puerto Rico's economy is still not dominantly based on manufacturing. Agriculture still employs more people, and processing agricultural products is a major part of its industry. Natural resources include only stone, gravel, sand and lime, but a prosperous cement industry is based on these.

A wide range of climate and soil types supports a variety of tropical crops (led by sugar cane), which enter the lucrative United States market on a preferential basis. Cane dominates coastal plains and interior valleys; high prices have even pushed its cultivation into lower mountain slopes. Tobacco, pineapples, and coffee are other export crops. Mechanization on farms was long retarded by fears of displacing too many rural laborers, but unrestricted access and cheap air fares to the "mainland" have reduced some of the economic pressures of overcrowding. The United States–inspired (and supported) "bootstrap" program, started in the 1940's, was as necessary as it was largely because U.S. occupation had turned a country of small farms into one of a mixture of small farms and large plantations, creating a large class of landless *agregados* (hired hands). When Puerto Rico was first acquired, the United States Congress had attempted to prevent precisely this social-economic problem by enacting a 500-acre (200-hectare) limit to any one individual or corporate owner. Unfortunately, the law has widely ignored until Governor Luis Muñoz Marín began a reform. The commonwealth government purchased about half the land held in illegally large units, selling most of it to farmers in 25-acre (10-hectare) units. Government-owned land is also leased to communities of farmers. Along with the per capita incomes, "bootstrap" industrialization has helped improve the material quality of life. Five-and ten-year *tax holidays,* exemptions from corporate and personal income taxes and property taxes, are effective lures, as is a *foreign trade zone* near Mayagüez, where merchandise may come and go without customs taxes. Interior locations, on good highways but farther from ports, are also attracting industrial plants, which are compensated for higher transport costs by being given bigger tax breaks. Tourism has grown considerably, but Puerto Rico suffered briefly from a reputation for high prices and indifferent service; it seems to have been self-corrected by a temporary slump in tourist arrivals. The island's people are predominantly white and mestizo; a 20 percent black minority is the lowest proportion of any of the islands.

There is a considerable movement back and forth between the island and the big cities of the eastern United States, so that American popular culture and ideas have reached virtually every village. Still, Puerto Rico is not "New York in the sunshine"; its people are very proud of their Spanish heritage and determined that the island will retain its distinctive culture.

The Dominican Republic The Dominican Republic shares, somewhat uneasily, the island of Hispaniola with Haiti. Their mutual boundary is also a sharp cultural-ethnic divide. (See Figure 3–12.) The Dominican Republic's per capita gross national product is over triple that of Haiti, its population density is little more than half, and its quality of life is far superior.

The republic has had a trying existence. Virtually ignored by Spain after its alluvial gold was worked out, the colony was encouraged to take up cattle raising. The western third of the island was ceded to the French, who stocked it with an eventual 600,000 African slaves. Following their successful revolt against France, the Haitians invaded the Spanish-culture east (it had been transferred to French control in 1795), and held it until 1844, when they were repulsed by an uprising under Juan Pablo Duarte. Political instability and problems in meeting foreign debt payments led to an occupation by the United States Marines, 1916–24. The United States intervened again in 1965 when it appeared that a Communist takeover was likely. The border with Haiti has been a tightly controlled zone during periods of Dominican stability because the

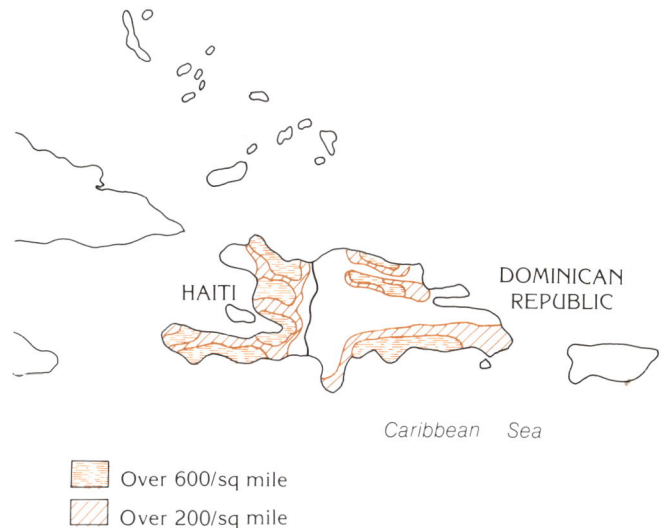

Over 600/sq mile

Over 200/sq mile

FIGURE 3–12
Population Density in Hispaniola. The Haitian-Dominican boundary on the island of Hispaniola is a sharp divide in culture and population density. Historic animosities and a much higher population pressure in Haiti make this a potentially troublesome boundary.

Dominicans have bitter memories of the Haitian occupation and are fearful of gradual Haitian encroachment (by illegal migrants), into their sparsely settled western mountains. Organized colonization of both native Dominicans and recent European immigrants near that border was a policy of the Trujillo dictatorship (1930–61).

The Trujillo dictatorship was a time of economic progress, though at the expense of political freedom. Long a country of small, self-sufficient farmers on their own land, the republic entered the plantation era belatedly as a

Santo Domingo, Dominican Republic. The rapid urban in-migration experienced throughout this region (and the developing world in general) puts great pressure on these governments' abilities to provide decent housing. The public housing in the background was erected to empty the makeshift housing in the foreground, but continued inflows of people outpace housing construction. (Courtesy of United Nations/M. Guthrie)

kind of modern feudalism under Trujillo. Cropland has been increased substantially since 1930 thanks to irrigation, reclamation, and colonization schemes. Sugar, cocoa, and coffee have become the primary export crops, supplemented by rice, corn, beans, peanuts, vegetables, and fruits.

The Dominicans have never been forced to emigrate in large numbers by high population to land ratios, and have received immigrants rather than emigrated. The population is overwhelmingly white and mulatto (mixed Caucasian and black), much of the latter tracing to the Haitian occupation. The Dominican Republic's traditionally favorable ratio of land to people is changing for the worse as population increases, though at a slightly lower rate than the regional average.

A generally good transport infrastructure and the fact that the Republic is a modest exporter of ferro-nickel ores, bauxite, and meat (in addition to the usual tropical plantation crops) should give a good chance for progress. The Republic was a major benefactor of Cuba's loss of preferred access to the United States market, and tourism is increasing with rising cruiseship calls.

Haiti   Haiti is Middle America's poorest country; its infant mortality rate (130 per 1,000 live births) is the region's highest, and its outlook for the future the least encouraging. Almost 80 percent of Haiti is mountainous, and the frantic search for firewood, cultivable land, and livelihood has contributed to horrendous erosion in steep lands where rainfall averages range up to 100 inches (250 centimeters) per year on windward slopes. Haiti's population growth rate has dropped slightly recently, but is still above the world average for developing nations. Haitians are not able to feed themselves on an acceptable level of quantity and quality now, and their population will take only twenty-six years to double at current growth rates. There is no agricultural frontier for this nation of farmers (over three quarters of the people are working in agriculture) into which to expand. Any usable land is already used, indeed, *unusable* land *is* being used—too steep, too infertile—with resulting erosion and decline of soil quality and quantity. Haiti's land resource for agriculture is poor and getting poorer. Less than a million tons of bauxite is exported every year; no other valuable minerals have been discovered.

Haiti is the only Middle American state in which French is the official language, but only about 10 percent of the Haitians speak it. Creole (a mixture of French, Spanish, English, and some traces of African and Amerindian languages) is the majority language. A small elite of mulattoes proudly adhere to European cultural values, including Catholocism, while the bulk of the population, nominally Christian, follow a unique mixture of Christianity and traditional African beliefs.

The landscape is dotted with the ruins of eighteenth century French sugar mills and grand estates, all destroyed as symbols of slavery in the slave rebellion. While such symbolic overthrow must have been very satisfying to an enslaved people, its practical consequences were the destruction of much of the economic **infrastructure.** Haiti quickly went from the Caribbean's richest colony to its poorest republic. Peasant plots in the hills replaced plantations. Coffee production is more a gathering of wild berries than a plantation crop. Sugar and rice grow on irrigated lowlands, coffee on mountain slopes, cotton on semiarid plateaus, and food crops anywhere that will produce a crop. Coffee is the main export crop in value, and the past wisdom of Haitian leaders in respecting the property rights of small farmers has resulted in few neo-plantations for coffee. In sugar and sisal production, though, the modern plantation has become important. Haiti is one of a long list of Caribbean states to have been occupied by the United States Marines (1915–34). During that period, near-chaotic political conditions were stabilized, roads built, sanitation facilities improved, and the treasury built up to a surplus. Laws against foreign ownership of land were also repealed, paving the way for American investment in plantations.

With a suspicious, historically hostile Dominican Republic sharing its only land boundary and very little realistic hope of emigration on a scale large enough to relieve pressures at home, Haiti's chances of improving its citizen's quality of life would seem to lie in increasing manufacturing employment. The illegal immigration to the United States, mostly by small boat to Florida, reached high enough levels in 1981 to spur United States determination to control this rising flood of unskilled and impoverished Haitians.

Port-au-Prince, the capital (650,000), has been attracting light industry that depends more on semiskilled labor than on raw materials, which would have to be imported. Textiles, clothing, and assembly of imported components for re-export, mostly to the United States, predominate. This light industrial development is encouraged by no controls on foreign capital flows or "repatriation" of profits; its currency converts readily to dollars, and new industries are given tax exemptions. If the present looks bleak, it should be remembered that Puerto Rico, the ex-"poorhouse of the Caribbean," used much the same tactics in its successful "bootstrap" efforts. A critical difference, though, could be Puerto Rico's relative stability and democratic government compared to Haiti's elitist dictatorship.

Jamaica   Jamaica's people (75 percent African, 15 percent Afro-European) includes many small minorities such as Chinese, East Indians, and Europeans. Currently, Jamaica is under considerable stress as unemployment

Alumina Plant, Jamaica. Jamaica is one of the world's largest miners of bauxite and exporters of alumina. This plant is operated by a Canadian aluminum producer. (Courtesy of United Nations)

reaches 25 percent and the unemployed, underemployed, and undereducated crowd into sprawling shantytowns with high crime rates. About 15 percent of Jamaica is cultivable or in orchards, 20 percent is in pasture, and 12 percent is worthless, due to severe erosion or excessive drainage in limestone areas. Nearly a third of Jamaica is idle land considered potentially usable with scientific management.

Jamaica's karst topography (limestone honeycombed with underground drainage, caverns, and sinkholes) is a hinderance to agriculture but facilitates bauxite mining. Most of the island's huge reserves of bauxite are found in shallow hollows that resulted from the solution of limestone. Ore is easily produced from these limestone "pouches" by cheap open-pit methods. Power shovels can scrape out the ore and load it for shipment to local processing plants. The aluminum oxide content is low, but huge reserves (the world's largest) and low production costs combined with ease of water shipment to the North American market guarantee exploitation. Reserves will last eighty to ninety years at current rates of exploitation.

Sugar, once helped by the availability of guaranteed markets in Britain under commonwealth preference, has declined in importance. Banana growers have experienced the usual Caribbean-area producers problems—diseases and hurricane-damage; production fluctuates wildly. A new, root-disease-free variety must still be sprayed regularly against leaf disease and requires such elaborate packaging that small producers are switching to other crops.

Population pressures have resulted in a continuing outflow for a century. Both French and American canal engineers in Panama relied on Jamaican labor, and Ja-

maicans have also migrated to Costa Rica and the United States. Migration to the United Kingdom was cut off by new restrictions in 1967, after having reached 30,000 a year. Tourism has boomed; Air Jamaica connects the island with many United States cities to both increase tourism and the share of the tourist dollar retained by Jamaica. Jamaica's prospects are at least as bright as those of any of the Greater Antilles, but short-term fluctuations in bauxite, sugar, and banana production, combined with extraordinary population pressures, will challenge the ability of this democratic government to survive.

THE SMALL ISLANDS OF THE CARIBBEAN

The "Lesser Antilles," the smaller islands of the Caribbean, lie in an arc between Puerto Rico and the South American mainland. To this scattered chain are added the Bahamas to the southeast of Florida, and the Cayman Islands south of Cuba (see Figure 3–13.) The islands are extremely varied in physical structure, from the low, flat Bahamas and Caymans to the volcanic peaks of most of the Lesser Antilles. Only their colonial histories and cultures provide a semblance of regional unity, and even here, the picture is one of an extremely complex mosaic in which a few cultural-economic themes predominate.

Christopher Columbus discovered most of the islands, but Spanish colonization was not important on these lesser islands. They lacked the gold of the Greater Antilles and the mainland, and Spain ignored most of them, excepting a small settlement on Trinidad. Northern European powers were attracted to the smaller islands as bases for regional exploration and for their timber. Britain

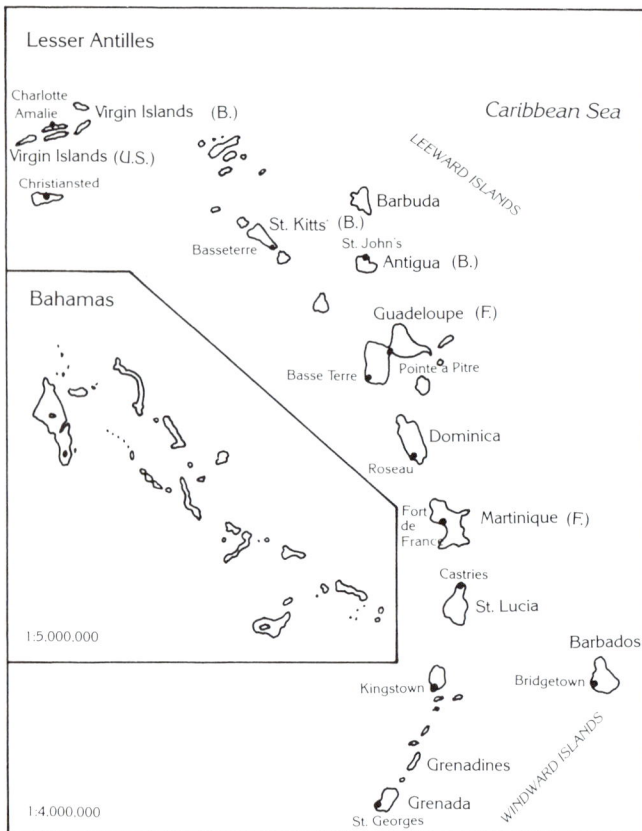

FIGURE 3–13

The Lesser Antilles and the Bahamas. The smaller islands, initially ignored by Spain, became lucrative sugar plantations later in the colonial era. Whether their "crop" is still sugar, or bananas or tourists, their economies have narrow bases, and thus they are considered overpopulated in relation to their resource bases.

and France later attempted to establish colonies of independent farmers on the volcanic islands of the Lesser Antilles. (The Bahamas' thin, coralline limestone soils were not very productive.) Enthusiasm for settling into the life of small farmers on the tiny islands so far and so different from home was distinctly limited. Britain resorted to kidnapping "recruits" for the islands; *to be barbadoed* became a verb describing being kidnapped and forceably transported to the islands.

The real revolution in the settlement and economy of the islands was precipitated by the rapid spread of sugar cane cultivation (mid-seventeenth century). Aboriginal inhabitants of the smaller islands had virtually disappeared under the European onslaught, and European labor was both unwilling and expensive. The lucrative European markets for cane sugar inspired large-scale importation of West Africans. This produced the prevalently black ethnic makeup of all the smaller islands except Trinidad, where blacks (45 percent) are almost matched by East Indians

(40 percent) brought in as "contract" (indentured) plantation labor, though not as slaves.

The "sugar islands" became enormously valuable to the Europeans, quickly becoming one-crop economies; other corps were limited to subsistence foods for slaves or coffee on mountain slopes that could not produce cane profitably. There were exceptions to this "sugar island" scenario. The soils of the Bahamas and Caymans were not suitable to sugar, and the Dutch possessions off the Venezuelan coast were always more important as trade centers than plantation-crop exporters. Export crop diversification has been relatively slow. Sugar was so profitable that it dominated available lowlands and interior valleys. Nutmeg, introduced into Grenada in 1782, was an early replacement for hurricane-destroyed cane plantations. Bananas became important after World War II. Some cotton is grown, especially in Antigua. Barbados and St. Kitts are the main one-crop economies (sugar) in the islands; most production is from large estates. Bananas are still expanding into any land still available.

Industry throughout the islands is based on crop processing (cane sugar and its derivatives, molasses and rum, are the main products), refining of and transshipment of oil products, tourism, and creating receptive political "climates" for international banking. The list of natural resources is dismally short. Limestone is manufactured into cement on several islands, primarily for local markets. Curacao mines some phosphate under heavy subsidy. The long-term persistence of direct colonial control helped encourage European and American investments in oil refineries to process Venezuelan and, lately, African and Middle East crude. Much of the northeastern United States' fuel oil supply is processed in the islands, primarily at Aruba (Exxon), Curacao (Shell), and Freeport, Grand Bahama, as well as in Puerto Rico and other Greater Antilles islands.

Trinidad-Tobago Trinidad, by virtue of its large size and diverse economy, is something of an exception to the generalizations applicable to the Lesser Antilles. Trinidad is rich in natural resources. Geologically, it is a detached fragment of South America; a series of three mountain ranges trend east-west across the island separated by flat, sometimes swampy lowlands. Geologic similarity to nearby Venezuela is reflected in oil, gas, and asphalt reserves. Oil has been pumped since 1910; declining production has meant that Trinidad refineries now rely more on imported crudes. Natural gas reserves provide relatively cheap power for industrialization. Trinidad's Pitch Lake is the world's largest source of natural asphalt. Prized in the colonial period for caulking wooden ships, it was later used in street paving as far away as London. Almost all asphalt paving material is now made as a by-product of oil refining, but Pitch Lake is still mined.

Trinidad and Tobago, a smaller island to the northeast, are associated politically but are quite different ethnically and economically. East Indians were imported by the British to work on Trinidad's sugar plantations. Smaller numbers of Venezuelans, Chinese, Syrians, and European Jews arrived, along with many blacks from the more overcrowded British-controlled islands, especially Barbados. Sugar, coffee, citrus, and bananas are all exported along with refined petroleum, cement, and rum, so that Trinidad-Tobago is one of the region's more prosperous states. This is fortunate for overcrowded, predominantly black Tobagans who have unrestricted access to immigrate to more prosperous, more diversified Trinidad.

Tourism in the Lesser Islands   Tourism is virtually the only industry in the Bahamas, and a leading industry in almost all but the tiniest Lesser Antilles. The Bahamas benefit from accessibility to the United States and a willingness to permit casino gambling. Casinos, thrown out of Cuba by the Castro revolution, moved to the Bahamas. Tourism, though, is a very "footloose" economic phenomenon. Civil disturbances, especially those with racial overtones, can cause dramatic drops in tourism. Strikes at ports, airports, or hotels can quickly redirect tourists to other destinations, with long-term effects on "revisit" trade.

Tourism can be a very deceptive industry for developing countries; much of the apparent income goes right back to the developed countries that are the source of tourists. Tourists place high demands on fresh-water supplies, sewage systems, and transport facilities, yet they are there on a very seasonal basis. Locally-owned, smaller inns and guesthouses tend to receive only the "overflow" when the big hotels are filled. Developed countries' citizens or corporations own the hotel chains, car rental companies, airlines, cruise ships, and casinos. Tourist tastes trend toward prime meats, frozen vegetables, and alcoholic drinks, which are mainly imported. Islanders make up the seasonally employed, low-paid service occupations—waiters, maids, bartenders, taxi drivers, and "beach boys"— but not the managers, who are usually North Americans or Europeans. While seasonally unemployed, islanders can enjoy those beaches not restricted to hotel guests, if the water hasn't been too polluted by the concentration of large hotels.

The Bahamas and Cayman Islands both have become "offshore" banking centers by virtue of laws strictly limiting taxes and guaranteeing secrecy of financial transactions. Over two hundred and fifty banks are legally headquartered in the Bahamas. This political hospitality to money generated within and travelling among developed nations ensures some government revenues and minor white-collar employment without placing any significant demands on space or other resources. Its long-term success, though, depends on political stability and a continuity of political philosophy.

The Caribbean has several demographic and economic trends that may favor instability. Economic opportunities are quite limited in the generally crowded little islands. Occasionally hurricanes and stiff competition in foreign markets for the islands' agricultural products combine with the seasonal, low-pay status of most tourist-industry service jobs to present a discouraging picture for economic expansion. Independence has reduced or eliminated former welfare receipts and subsidies from "parent" countries. It is questionable whether some islands like Guadeloupe can afford complete independence. Britain no longer accepts immigrants from its Caribbean commonwealth partners, and the United States is unlikely to continue as a long-term haven for Caribbean citizens seeking opportunity there. Life may appear care-free to the casual tourist in the islands, but hidden social-economic tensions are surfacing with increasing vehemence.

SUMMARY

Revolution is a key concept in understanding Middle America—revolution in its economic and social senses as much as political. The revolution overturning colonial status was protracted over a century and a half throughout differing parts of the region. The earlier revolutions seldom achieved permanent, thorough equality in political life and economic opportunity. This more complete revolution was not consolidated in Mexico, for example, for a century and a quarter; in some of Middle America's states, this final achievement is yet to come. The Industrial Revolution has been equally slow and erratic in its spatial distribution. Only Mexico, Cuba, and Puerto Rico can be categorized as being in the middle stages of development, and many small islands have barely begun, and hardly have any resource base on which to build. Perhaps more than most other world regions, Middle America is likely to be characterized by vast, growing disparities in economic development.

TENSIONAL RELATIONSHIPS WITH OTHER REGIONS

Middle America is very much in the middle—its location between North and South America is overwhelmingly significant to its economic, cultural, and political interactions with those regions. While European colonial interests have all but faded away, the Soviet Union's acquisition of a client state in Cuba has challenged the United States' hegemony in an area it considered should be free of competing superpowers. There is an unfortunately high probability of further subversion by Communist revolution in some impoverished, rather feudal states of Central America and the Caribbean. Trade with West Europe (East Europe for Cuba) and East Asia (especially for Mexico) will remain distinctly secondary to North American linkages for most of the region's states. Mexico is most likely to become more active in international affairs beyond the New World as its growing economic power bolsters self-confidence and commands new respect.

REGIONAL WORLD VIEW

It is improbable that some of the region's ministates, struggling to advance their economies with almost-nonexistent resources, have much conciousness of global trends and tensions; others, like Mexico, the giant of this region, have progressed far beyond a simple client-patron relationship with the United States and can be expected to play an active part in shaping Middle American understandings of the larger world beyond.

case study
MEXICAN OIL

To understand Mexicans' intense nationalism concerning their oil resources, it is necessary to consider the history of the oil industry there. International oil companies initially found and developed Mexican oil; early exploitation of this resource coincided with the Porfirio Díaz dictatorship, which actively encouraged foreign investment. The Díaz regime, it is claimed, was almost anti-Mexican in its eagerness to favor foreigners. The international oil companies, with small minority participation by Mexicans, were later accused of "skimming" the oil resource; wells had been pumped for maximum short-term production rather than managed for long-term, sustained yields, and natural pressure underground was dissipated wastefully by pumping too fast. Mexican oil fields did show a phenomenal leap in production between 1910, when foreigners had acquired huge leases at supposedly "giveaway prices" under Díaz, and 1921, when Mexico was in the first ranks of oil exporters in the world. Mexican wells were said to be three hundred times as productive, on average, as U.S. wells, showing an average gross profit of over $1.5 million per day. One Mexican official asserted that an oil company had paid only $50,000 in Mexican taxes on an accumulated production of 40 million barrels. Mexicans also claimed that oil companies were reluctant to hire any Mexicans above the laborer level, and it is apparent that no Mexican had executive status in the oil industry before nationalization in 1938. Also, because Mexico exported mainly crude petroleum and imported refined products, gasoline made from Mexican crude cost more in Mexico than in the United States. The Mexican governments of the 1920's and the oil companies struggled over taxes, production levels, and prices for a decade and a half. The oil companies were accused of deliberately cutting production to threaten the government, which had come to rely heavily on its oil revenues. The 1920's and 1930's also saw collapsing prices for Mexico's other mineral products, especially silver and zinc (see Table 3–2). Finally, in 1938, the oil industry of Mexico was nationalized, despite protests from the U.S., British, and Dutch governments.

The response of the international oil companies to nationalization was to press for immediate payment in cash for their nationalized properties. Although Mexico agreed in principle to compensate the companies, cash was short and there was no agreement on the value of seized property. Oil companies claimed ownership of all oil still in the ground while Mexico contended that only oil "captured" (brought to the surface) had belonged to the companies.

Mexicans claim that the international oil industry tried to "freeze" them out—tankers belonging to the major companies would not touch Mexican oil; independent tankers and refiners were made to understand that dealing in Mexican oil would mean no future contracts with the major companies. Tankers delivering Mexican oil to foreign ports were served with legal papers claiming that their cargo had been illegally siezed from its rightful owners, and chemicals and equipment vital to the oil industry could not be sold to Mexico without risking a boycott from the most important customers—the international oil corporations.

The legacy of this bitter struggle has been twofold. The nationalized Mexican oil industry (Petroleos Mexicanos or "Pemex") is committed to a policy of conservative resource management; the excessive pumping and dissipation of natural pressure that characterized the first boom will not be repeated. Secondly, the Mexicans are determined to be very hard bargainers in dealing with the United States and West Europe in oil and gas sales, as this means dealing with many of the same companies with which the Mexicans had a long and acrimonious dispute in the recent past. Mexico's oil and natural gas reserves may be second only to Saudi Arabia's; U.S. oil industry estimates are lower in the belief that Mexicans overoptimistically include *possible* reserves rather than just proven and probable. Recent large-scale discoveries, however, would tend to substantiate Mexican claims. Mexico's economic development pace may well rest on its increasing output of oil and gas and its sale to eager customers like the United States.

TABLE 3–2
Mexico: Petroleum Production

Year	(Million Barrels per Year)	
1910	3.6	
1917	55	
1921	193	Mexico produced nearly ¼ of world supply.
1932	33	
	—	Oil industry nationalized, 1938.
1950	67	
1963	125	
	—	Contracts with foreign oil companies ended, 1969.
1970	177	
1975	294	
1979	483	

SOURCES: Charles Cumberland, *Mexico: The Struggle for Modernity* (New York: Oxford University Press, 1968).
U.S. Department of State, "Background Notes—Mexico," Washington, D.C., 1979.

REVIEW QUESTIONS

1   Why is tourism sometimes a "deceptive industry," in that little real profit can remain in the "host" country?

2   How does *Middle America* differ from *Latin America?*

3   Critically evaluate the mainland-rimland culture region concepts as an aid to understanding Middle America.

4   Contrast the Mediterranean region with the "American Mediterranean"—the Gulf of Mexico–Caribbean.

5   What were the characteristics of the land tenure system transferred to much of this region by the Spanish? What are its lasting effects?

6   How has the United States asserted its geopolitical and economic interests in Middle America? What has been the region's response?

7   Describe briefly the major trends in the Mexican economy over the past forty years.

8   Why has Mexico been especially sensitive to the problems of controlling foreign investment in its economy?

9   How would you characterize the development strategy and growth potential of Mexico's northern drylands?

10 Why do labor-intensive rather than capital-intensive industries concentrate near the U.S. border of Mexico?

11 Is the Mexican South more or less likely than the northern drylands to become a rapid growth area? Why?

12 Why has Panama never been quite accepted by the other Central American states as being in that subregion?

13 Which Middle American international borders are most likely to be hostile or unstable? Why?

14 How did the high labor demands of sugar plantations on the Caribbean islands restructure their societies?

15 What political, cultural, and population distribution factors provided a basis for the fragmentation of the one-time Republic of Central America?

16 Why was Puerto Rico's special relationship with the United States instrumental in its "bootstrap industrialization"?

17 Why did Haiti's revolution against its colonial power have much more negative effects on its economy than the region's other struggles for independence?

18 Why did Spain have so little interest in the Lesser Antilles? What effect did this have on their subsequent development?

19 How did the 1960 Cuban revolution affect the region's tensional relationships with its two neighboring regions?

SUGGESTED READINGS

1   CHARLES CUMBERLAND, *Mexico: The Struggle for Modernity.* London: Oxford University Press, 1968.

2   DAVID LOWENTHAL, *West Indian Societies.* New York: Oxford University Press, 1972.

3   FRANKLIN PARKER, *The Central American Republics.* London: Oxford University Press, 1964.

4   G. ETZEL PEARCY, *The West Indian Scene.* Princeton, N.J.: Van Nostrand, 1968.

5   RAPHAEL PICO, *The Geography of Puerto Rico.* Chicago: Aldine, 1974.

6   CARL SAUER, *The Early Spanish Main.* Berkeley: University of California Press, 1966.

7   ROBERT WEST, and JOHN AUGELLI, *Middle America: Its Lands and Peoples.* Englewood Cliffs, N.J.: Prentice Hall, 1966.

KEY TERMS

- world language
- commercialization
- *indigenisimo*
- push-pull mechanisms
- friction of space
- complementarity
- settlement nucleus
- sensible temperature
- intertropical convergence
- vertical zonation
- *tierra caliente*
- *tierra templada*
- *tierra fria*
- *paramos*

- outports
- import replacement
- reorientation
- intervening opportunity
- time-place utility
- core area
- low-intensivity agriculture
- growth pole
- take-off
- economic maturity
- *estancias*
- beneficiate
- *selva*
- green rush

4

SOUTH AMERICA

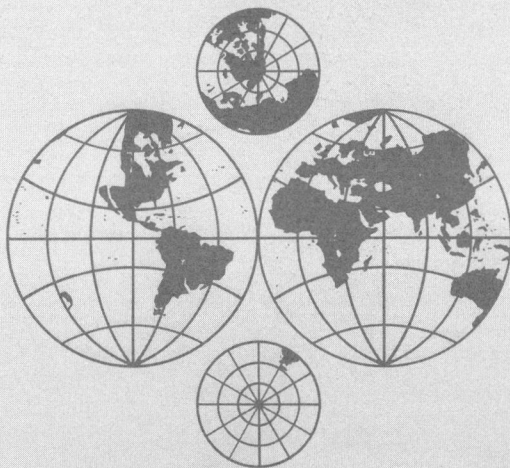

PROLOGUE: VISIONS AND REALITIES OF EMPIRE

Within a century of Columbus's voyages of discovery, the Spanish and Portuguese had explored at least the outlines of both Middle and South America and major portions of what was later to become the United States. The fabulous wealth of Mexico and Peru, literally tons of gold and silver surrendered to the Spanish conquistadores, was rivaled only by the rumors and legends of still greater bonanzas. If it is less than fair to attribute *all* the Spanish explorers' motives to "greed, gold and God," these were certainly driving forces that propelled armies and adventurers vast distances across some very difficult terrain.

These dreams of boundless wealth, available for the taking, did more than motivate exploration. Symbolically, they characterized an attitude towards resources, economic development, and life itself that may still have cultural significance. One legend was of El Dorado, "the gilded one," a chieftain in the mountains of Colombia, who periodically covered himself in gold dust and plunged into a sacred lake. His subjects tossed gold objects into the lake as well. No one ever found this lake, but not for lack of trying. An even more durable legend was of the fairy-tale-like Isle of Brazil. The present Brazil was named for a mythical, paradiselike island, the Isle of Brazil, whose legend of wealth and effortless living was probably two millenia old when the Portuguese explored the east coast of South America. Ironically, the present United States of Brazil, surging forward to economic development partly boosted by recent, huge gold strikes, has come closer than ever before to justifying its ancient name.

Vast portions of the earth came to be dominated by Spain and Portugal, two states closely related linguistically and culturally. The present pattern of states in South America is in large measure the result of the initial division between them and the imperial administrative units they created. Portugal, earlier free of Moorish domination than Spain, had decided on a course of expansion via seaborne exploration. The Portuguese were especially interested in the possibilities of sailing around Africa to reach fabulous India; in 1497, they succeeded in sailing to India via the Cape of Good Hope. By 1500, they officially discovered Brazil, although there is speculation that they may have known about that coast of South America even earlier. The Treaty of Tordesillas (1494), in which papal mediation divided the world beyond Europe into Spanish and Portuguese spheres of exploration and colonization, conveniently awarded, before it was "discovered," the great eastern salient of South America to Portugal. This assured the Portuguese of naval bases on both coasts of the South Atlantic. Although originally limited to that portion of the continent east of the Treaty of Tordesilla's demarcation line

The Natural Riches of South America, Brazil. The early stimulus to the conquest and settlement of South America was its fantastic array of natural resources. Rare woods for dyes and furniture, precious metals, sugar, rubber, tropical food products, and fruits were exported from large plantations or estates. South America continues to maintain the production of these early specialties, as it diversifies its economy with growing industrial and service functions. (Courtesy of United Nations)

(approximately 50° West longitude) Brazil became the largest single colony on the continent when Spain transferred a large portion of the Amazon Basin in Portugal in exchange for the Portuguese colonies in the Phillipines. Portuguese Brazil could use the great Amazon River to extend its control throughout the basin far more easily than the west coast Spanish colonies could extend across the Andes and down into a drainage basin whose only logical outlet for trade was eastward through Portuguese lands. The Spanish colonies along the La Plata-Paraná rivers were also in a difficult position to attempt settlement and exploitation of the Amazon Basin interior.

This Spanish-Portuguese "condominium" of all newly discovered lands across the Atlantic from Europe did not go unchallenged. The King of France is said to have asked sarcastically to see "Father Adam's will leaving the world to Spain and Portugal!" The French, Dutch, and British were most successful at incursions into Portuguese territories, where there were few major mineral-producing areas to attract the military and settlers. Portuguese colonial priorities were elsewhere, and Portugal itself was ruled by Spain between 1581 and 1641; during this time the Dutch, French, and British attempted to move into lightly settled, poorly defended Portuguese claims along the coast. Portugal was finally able to drive the northern Europeans out of their territories south of the Amazon. Britain, Holland, and France did each manage to retain colonies to the north of the Amazon, the Guianas, because overland connections and control from the Portuguese Brazilian core were made so difficult by the great river basin. The Guianas became the only non-Latin colonies on the South American mainland; in this, as in some other respects, the Guianas are *least* typical of South America.

Spanish administration of their immense New World empire, stretching from north of 40°N latitude to south of 40°S latitude (over 6,500 miles or 10,400 kilometers), was accomplished through four viceroyalties, each subdivided into captaincies, presidencies, or audiencias. The viceroyalty of New Spain, from the northern frontiers of Spanish America into Central America, was administered from Mexico City. The second most important viceroyalty, that of Peru, was administered from Lima. The viceroyalty of New Granada, headquartered at Bogotá, and the viceroyalty of La Plata, based on Asunción, were created later in response to the difficulties of administering huge territories via primitive land communications across often difficult terrain (see Figure 4–1). These viceroyalties were in turn subdivided into units with considerable local autonomy; most of the successor states that later emerged corresponded to these imperial administrative units.

The states of South America, except for the Guianas, achieved independence from colonialism between 1811 and 1826. Although this followed some three hundred years of colonial status, these independence dates antedate the independence of most African states by a century and a half. This relatively long independence has had important cultural and economic, as well as political, influences. As in Central America, some early unions and confederations fragmented under the negative pressures of poor land transport and communications and the positive pressures of isolated nodes of settlement focused on a single city, which commonly was a colonial capital (Lima) or subsidiary administrative center (Quito or Santiago). Thus Gran Colombia, held together primarily by Simón Bolívar's leadership and personality, was able to consolidate control among many scattered settlement nodes in what became modern Colombia, but even Bolívar could not hold the more distant parts of his original state, which broke away as Venezuela and Ecuador. Brazil has been a rather consistent winner in territorial expansion; current Brazilian territory includes lands ceded it by Venezuela, Colombia, Ecuador, Bolivia, Peru, Paraguay, and Uruguay, all of its neighbors excepting Argentina and the Guianas.

The United States' Monroe Doctrine, promulgated in 1823, stated that any attempt by European powers to

FIGURE 4–1
Colonial Administrative Areas.
Spain's imperial administration was related to geographic considerations such as resources, population, transport-communications accessibility, and physical regions. Thus, it is not accidental that emerging national states utilized some of the same administrative boundaries as had Spain.

Map labels:
AUDENCIA OF SANTA FE
● Bogatá
CAPITANCY GENERAL OF CARACAS
DUTCH GUIANA
FRENCH GUIANA
Line of Tordesillas
VICEROYALTY OF NEW GRANADA
AUDENCIA OF QUITO
AUDENCIA OF LIMA
VICEROYALTY OF PERÚ
● Lima
AUDENCIA OF CUZCO
VICEROYALTY OF BRAZIL
AUDENCIA OF CHARCAS
VICEROYALTY OF LA PLATA
● Asunción
● Rio de Janiero
AUDENCIA OF CHILE
AUDENCIA OF BUENOS AIRES
INDIAN TERRITORY

COLONIAL ADMINISTRATION CIRCA 1790

—— Border of viceroyalties
- - - Borders of viceroyalty subdivision (Spanish Audencias)
● Capitals of viceroyalties
------ Borders of Brazilian capitancies

reimpose colonial control on independent states anywhere in the Americas would be viewed as an "unfriendly act" toward the United States. Britain also used its powerful navy to prevent this reimposition (and a potential upset of the post-Napoleonic balance of power), undoubtedly helping British economic interests, especially in Argentina and Uruguay. (Britain even helped achieve Uruguayan independence by mediating an Argentine-Brazilian territorial dispute in the area and setting up Uruguay as a buffer state.)

The commonality of interests achieved by these early struggles for independence from colonial control resulted in a hemispheric concept of unity, which has influenced the relations of all the states of the Americas to this day. Regardless of the linguistic and cultural differences that separate subportions of the hemisphere into Norte and Latino America, or those that led to separate national units within each sphere, there is a sense of being American, of being something different from Europe, and even some tendency to think and act as a regional bloc. Though the degree of cooperation and interaction has varied both temporally and areally, this hemispheric view is as real an influence in the policy decisions of the states of South America as ever.

CHARACTERISTICS OF THE REGION

South America, with the exception of the three Guianas and the Falkland Islands, has developed a degree of regional cultural cohesion based on language, religion, and common colonial experience. In all states but Brazil and those small exceptions mentioned previously, Spanish is the official language, which has led to its increasing importance as a **world language.** Despite attempts to standardize the Spanish taught in South American Schools, dialects have evolved, though all are mutually intelligible. This uniformity of language represents a potentially powerful cohesive force throughout South America, facilitating trade and the exchange of culture and technology.

Within South America there are still areas where native Indian languages dominate. Aboriginal groups in the frontier areas of Brazil and southernmost Argentina and Chile form small islands of dominantly Amerindian speech in sparsely settled backlands. A similar situation exists in the Amazon Basin portions of Colombia and Peru, the upper Orinoco Basin, and the Guiana Highlands. In all these cases, the peoples (and languages) involved are a small minority in the larger Hispanic (or Portuguese) millieu. The other area of Amerindian speech is a more important exception, that of the large numbers of Indians resident in the Andean republics and Paraguay. Almost half of the population of Peru is of purely Indian stock, and Quechua (the most widely spoken Indian language) is virtually a second language there. (See Table 4–1.) In Ecuador, Bolivia, and Paraguay, roughly one half or more of the population is of Indian stock. In each of these countries there is a large group that speaks an Amerindian language, though Spanish is the language used in schools. Paraguay does officially recognize Guarani, an Indian language. In these four states, the characteristic unifying force of language is less than fully developed.

In the other countries, however, it forms a powerful unifying force, or at least the absence of a divisive force, in the quest for national unity and distinction. Border disputes in South America have little or nothing to do with language or dialect.

The Portuguese spoken in Brazil has virtually become its own (Brazilian) language. An exceptionally rich national literature and even the medium of song have created a linguistic pride that is the very basis of Brazilian national-

TABLE 4–1
Ethnic groups and languages in South America

Ethnic Group (Percentage of Total Population)				
Country	Indian	Mestizo	White	Black	Other
Ecuador	40–60	20–40	10	10	—
Peru	45	43	11	0.5	0.5
Bolivia	55–70	25–30	5–15	—	—
Paraguay	50–60	10–90	5–10	—	—

Language (percentage of total population)				
Country	Exclusively Spanish	Bilingual	Exclusively Indian	Quechua, Aymara, Guarani	Other
Ecuador	25	67	8	—	—
Peru	40	30	30	22	8
Bolivia	20	20	45–50	35	23
Paraguay	5	40–75	20–55	90	—

NOTE: Estimates of ethnicity vary greatly in Bolivia and Paraguay where the character of mestizos is overwhelmingly genetically Indian with only a small Caucasian admixture. Official language statistics vary greatly as well, thus the variable ranges indicated. In terms of contemporary culture, Bolivia is the most "Indian" of these countries, and Paraguay, the least.

ism. In this case, language very definitely distinguishes a Brazilian from other South Americans, even though the language locally shades into Spanish as one approaches Argentina and Uruguay. Its speakers see Brazilian as the virile language of today and, increasingly, the colonial heir is rapidly overshadowing the original source language with its greater range of expression.

The overwhelming majority of South Americans are adherents of Roman Catholicism, and in some states it is the official religion. Virtually every South American state has undergone a period of anticlericalism in which church properties were confiscated and/or the clergy and the membership were persecuted to some degree. Nonetheless, the church remains a powerful moral influence and a force for internal nationalism in virtually all states. Church administrative jurisdictions are along national lines. Increasingly, the political role of the church has undergone change, and it has become an influential lobby on social reforms.

Three racial-cultural elements have had strong impact on South America: the native Indian, African, and European. While the Europeans originally came as conquerors, large numbers of settlers followed into those areas that lacked a large, native population. The Guianas and the four Indian republics attracted the fewest European settlers overall. A European-commercial zone, in which European settlers and commercial interests dominate, includes most of Argentina, Chile, Uruguay, and southern Brazil, an area with minimal Indian or African cultural input. Therein the population is 80 percent or more of European stock and/or totally assimilated mestizo groups. There is also a tropical plantation area where African cultural input was most heavily felt, an Indo-subsistence core area in the Andes, and a zone of mestizo-transitional culture developed in an effort to reconcile racial characteristics and economic-cultural attributes (see Figure 4–2). Today's South America is becoming more complex through internal migration as the lure of urban employment areas shuffles populations. The booming

Brazilian states of Saõ Paulo and Minas Gerais are increasingly commercial if not so totally European in ethnic makeup. Surely the Colombian small planter and the Venezuelan oil or industrial worker are entering the modern commercial world.

African racial and cultural input is most strongly marked in Brazil where the plantations of the east coast imported larger numbers of African laborers from the sixteenth through the nineteenth centuries to produce sugar, cacao, and tobacco. Roughly 10 percent of the Brazilian population is composed of blacks, and up to 20 percent

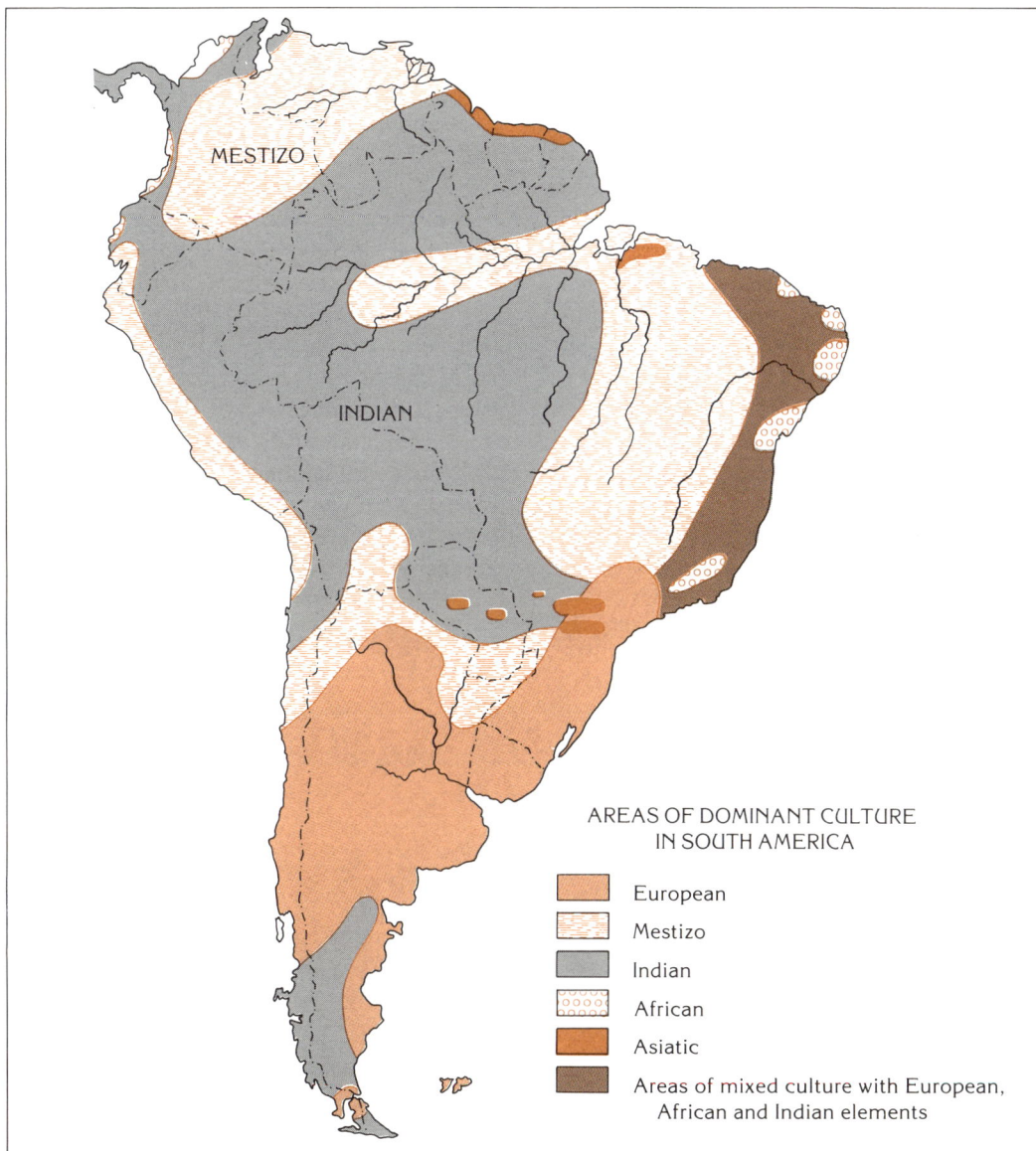

AREAS OF DOMINANT CULTURE
IN SOUTH AMERICA

European
Mestizo
Indian
African
Asiatic
Areas of mixed culture with European, African and Indian elements

FIGURE 4–2

South American Cultural Areas. Contemporary South America features an interesting array of cultural areas, showing the various economic levels and amalgams of European, Amerindian, and African cultures.

more are of mixed racial origins. Blacks dominate in coastal areas of the Brazilian northeast, but they are found in all parts of the country. Slavery in Brazil was rather more like feudalism than U.S.-style slavery. Too, the public attitudes toward racial differences evolved differently. Racial relations appear to generate less tensions there, and though blacks are poorer as a group than nonblacks, there has been a relatively higher degree of social mobility, though not to the highest levels. Income, admittedly still related to race or ancestry, determines status in a rapidly evolving, upwardly mobile society. Black elements in Ecuador (10 percent), Colombia (5 percent), and Venezuela (8 percent) tend to be farmers engaged in commercial, tropical agriculture on small and medium holdings. In these three countries they are far from the poorest element in society. By far the greatest impact of African culture, however, is found in Brazil, where art, music, and agricultural methods often draw on African cultural influences regardless of the origins of the practitioner. African cultural influence and practices are most largely confined to the group itself in the other three countries where they are highly localized in coastal enclaves. Despite this localization, however, racial differences have no effect on national unity or consciousness.

Indian influences are most strongly in evidence along the western side of the continent, where the indigenous population was numerically greatest and where the most advanced Indian cultures had developed by the time of European conquest. Two advanced cultures (the Inca in Peru and Chibcha in Colombia) and a somewhat less so-phisticated one (the Araucanian or Mapuche in Chile), were encountered by the Spanish. The most advanced of these cultures was that of the Inca, whose empire extended from their headquarters at Cuzco (now in Peru) in the Andes north to Quito (now in Ecuador) and south to middle Chile. They worked metal, developed and engineered irrigation works, created farmland by terracing the steep slopes of the Andes, and domesticated crops and livestock.

The Inca Empire consisted of a chain of highland basins and valleys interconnected by a series of stone-paved foot paths or roads. The term *Inca* originally referred only to the rulers. Their ability to hold together this Andean empire with its difficult terrain is often attributed to their exceptional administrative talents and their feats of road engineering, which facilitated rapid communications and movements of troops and functionaries. The success of the Spanish against this mighty empire was less a question of numbers and technological superiority and more the result of internal dissension within the empire. The Incas left a legacy of Indian cultural attributes: the tradition of communal ownership of land, the acceptance of a rigid hierarchy with a powerful ruling class, and the almost complete obedience to government functionaries. Spanish political control was easily attained by simply replacing the Inca rulers with Spanish.

These traditions also handicapped modern development. There was no status associated with land holding; there was, therefore, little pressure for land reform. The acquisition of wealth and possessions was simply not a

Harvesting Potatoes in the Bolivian Highlands. The intrusion of European culture into South America has radically modified the areas's culture, yet much remains of traditional Indian language, attitude, and even agricultural practice. There are great regional disparities in wealth and development within each of the region's countries. In many areas native groups are not integrated into the economy and are engaged in subsistence farming. (Courtesy of United Nations)

cultural drive. This is changing as farm laborers recognize the need to own land. The attachment to the village of one's birth and the family or communal group is inordinately strong, making physical mobility as difficult as occupational or social mobility. Even with these common traits as a basis, the Indians display great cultural diversity, probably because of the long isolation of one basin from another. The effect of Indian cultures outside the Incas' territory has been minimal except in isolated reaches and backlands and in Paraguay.

The impact of the Europeans varies throughout South America. The uniformity of language and religion is largely a result of this colonial experience, quite obviously, but other European cultural impacts may have had a more deleterious effect. In some cases, the Spanish simply wiped out indigenous peoples through protracted warfare. Where little organized resistance was offered, the natives were literally enslaved or placed in peonage, a form of feudal serfdom. The Spanish created and controlled great estates, haciendas where Indians labored, while enslaved Indians worked in the mines to secure the gold and silver that attracted the invaders.

The Portuguese, on the other hand, came to a land that was nearly devoid of settlement. Colonists were less often drawn from the ranks of nobility and the military than the Spanish were. The Portuguese were early divided into two groups. Those with capital sought the rich lands of the northeast for plantations, which they stocked with slave labor. The other nucleus of settlement was São Paulo, a successful settlement composed of poorer Portuguese elements who received small grants of land. Evolving in a part of Brazil more isolated from Portuguese control, they became a pioneer group of fortune seekers that developed and colonized interior Brazil in a fashion similar to North American pioneers. Gold, acquisition of slaves from among the Indians, gem stones, and new farmland attracted settlers and adventurers to new locations. While the staid planters remained entrenched on their slowly eroding estates, the *paulistas* roamed the back country in search of success. They were unlike the land- and status-conscious Spaniards. In the process they colonized much of Brazil and uncovered great new sources of mineral and other raw material wealth. With such an expansionist cultural inheritance, the exceptionally rapid development of modern-day São Paulo state is more readily understood.

Missionaries often acted as the protectors of Indians, especially in Brazil, and introducers of European technology to the native peoples. Their legacy is one of exceptionally great importance today, the assimilation of native peoples to what has become the dominant national culture.

Late-arriving Europeans have also had their impact, creating a zone of surplus grain and meat to supply the plantation areas as well as the overseas markets. Their role has often been that of introducing modernization and **commercialization** into what had become a subsistence economy over vast areas. Large numbers of latecomers (Italians, Iberians, and Slavs) served as tenants on great estates in long-term rotational crop systems in Argentina and the nearest interior of Brazil, clearing land, planting crops on a share basis, and thereby preparing the land for longer term use as rich pasture.

Germans, Slavs, and Italians in southern Brazil have become the bulk of that country's middle-class farmers, supplying the domestic market. Many of their children and successive waves of migration from these European source areas to the rest of South America have become the technicians, scholars, scientists, and engineers necessary to further development. The European cultural input, therefore, continues in a different form until this day.

The mestizo element is frequently assimilated to European language and culture. Mestizo is a lifestyle as much as a biological amalgam. Mestizos form a bridge between native and European cultural elements as well as an economic bridge between traditional and modern practice. These peoples tend to be the small farmers whose holdings are upgraded beyond subsistence to include commercial cash crops.

It is difficult to assess the role of each group in creating a South American culture. The inputs have varied greatly over the region. However, in the areas of strong Indian influence, most national cultures have undergone a period of *indigenisimo*, glorification of the Indian roots of the society and emphasis on pre-Hispanic culture. The European influence has changed form. African influences have blended with those of Indian and European groups into hybrid elements of a new national culture. As both economies and national consciousness develop, new cultures that are truly national emerge. Because of the commonality of historical experience, these national cultures complement one another and blend into the fabric of truly identifiable regional culture.

Economic Characteristics

Population is growing rapidly in all but a few of the South American republics. The southernmost three have entered a period of declining growth rates, which normally accompanies development; while the Guianas, Bolivia, and Paraguay have not yet entered into the period of maximum growth. The first signs of a downturn in growth rates are appearing in Venezuela and Brazil. Gradually, rapid population growth will cease to be a regional characteristic.

Increased urbanization, however, is expected to continue. Latin American states have been characterized as being dominated by a single city, the "primate city," usually the political capital, which contains a unusually high percentage of the country's total population and most of its urban dwellers. This model is currently far more applicable to Middle America than to South America, where polynucleated economies seem to be emerging in most of the region's developing countries (see Table 4–2). However only Brazil and Ecuador have capitals that are *not* the largest city.

Higher urban growth rates than might be expected in countries of a comparable level of development are the result of large numbers of unemployed and underemployed living in the city. Mechanization and modernization of agriculture, a shift from traditional tenancy systems, high rural birthrates, and higher urban wages act as a series of **push-pull mechanisms,** unleashing massive rural to urban movement in South America. With some exceptions, generally in the southernmost three countries, shantytowns of the urban poor arise around most large South American cities. These sprawling slums lack most (or all) urban services and have become pockets of crime and poverty. As some individuals move on when assimilated into the urban economy, they are replaced by new migrants from rural areas, people whose limited education and lack of skills make them ill-suited to urban employment. Having been displaced from their rural functions by machines or changing production patterns, they arrive in the city only to find the same occurrences there—even

before they can get a job. They are landless, unskilled, and ultimately, rootless. Many eke out a living through occasional day labor, subsistence gardening on tiny hillside plots, running errands, prostitution, or whatever earns food or money.

Still, migrants continue to flow in towards their *perception* of greater opportunity. The dwellers in urban shantytowns live in extended family, friendship, or home-village groups, sharing income. Since they are squatters on the land, their shacks may be demolished and their land expropriated at any time for office buildings and apartments spreading out from the city's center. They must seek a new location, again at the city's expanding edge. These shantytowns rank among South America's greatest social problems.

Another common misconception is the hacienda-peon nature of agriculture. Almost no country in South America has gone totally without land reform. Even ultra-conservative Paraguay has developed a land redistribution program, however limited. Virtually all South American states have more land that can be colonized and brought into production. This safety valve may yet contain social unrest and contribute to the eventual elimination of the problem of a rural landless peasantry. However, this remaining land is costly to develop. It requires irrigation, large-scale drainage, vastly improved transportation networks, or great inputs of fertilizer and other forms of agrotechnology in order to become productive. Housing, services, large-scale health-hazard control measures, and a variety of other investments are necessary to insure livabil-

TABLE 4–2
Urbanization in South America

Country	percentage urban dwellers (1)	metro area population (in millions) (2)	population percentage in largest city (3)	number of 1 million cities (4)	number of cities 500,000 to 1 million (5)	number of cities 100,000 to 500,000 (6)
Argentina	75	9.0	33	1	4	8
Bolivia	26	0.7	13	0	1	4
Brazil	65	10.4	8	9	7	37
Chile	80	3.7	33	1	—	10
Ecuador	44	0.9	11	0	2	4
French Guiana	47	0.03	47	—	—	0
Colombia	67	4.4	16	3	3	8
Guyana	43	0.2	22	0	0	1
Paraguay	41	0.7	23	0	1	0
Peru	65	5.0	28	1	1	10
Surinam	50	0.2	45	0	0	1
Uruguay	85	1.4	47	1	—	2
Venezuela	77	3.5	25	1	3	10

NOTE: Table controlled for redundancy so that cities of the second and third rank that appear in a metropolitan (million city) area do not appear in columns 5 and 6. Largest cities appear in the appropriate column.

ity and utility. Such steps require massive government investments, and governments are torn between industrial, transportation, housing, and agricultural sector demands on limited budgets.

There are some bright spots. Chile and Brazil have developed homesteading projects that have had moderate success, though new European migrants have often used these opportunities more frequently than domestic elements who are immobilized by poverty. Colombia has increased its farm acreage by extending roads to areas of good soil that lay unused because of inaccessibility, although building roads in difficult terrain is both slow and costly. Brazil has developed a successful rice-farming area in the state of Rio Grande do Sul by partially draining riverine flood plains and resettling landless farmers. Even there, the capital costs are enormous. South American countries share a need for large-scale investment in their attempts to develop new lands, which all have available for settlement.

Venezuela has begun to develop the Llanos, its great interior savannas along the Orinoco. The discovery of rich iron ore at the southern margins of the Llanos, the large new oilfields in the Orinoco Delta and Plain, and the development of new steel, aluminum, and hydroelectric plants create a local market. The additional advantage of the navigable Orinoco has aided in development.

Peru has increased irrigable area by diverting Andean streams from Amazon drainage to the headwaters of the ephmeral desert streams that flow to the Pacific in a series of multipurpose hydrologic projects. In La Montana, the country's eastern interior, a highway is gradually opening up temperate farmland along the eastern-facing Andean slopes. Oil discovered in the interior is now piped to Pacific ports. These massive investment programs have been reasonably successful, but they have strained the finances of the Peruvian government.

For most South American states, the development of most of these unused lands is still in the future. South America remains an area in which population and development are clustered around the periphery (see Figure 4–8). The interior is relatively empty; low population densities prevail in most national units. What is the degreee of utility of those remaining empty areas? That is a question to which the answer is not yet fully known.

Another frequently held misconception assumes U.S. dominance in trade and economic dealings with all of Latin America, including South America. Table 4–3 indicates the dominant American role in the nearest republics (Venezuela, Colombia, and Ecuador), all producers of oil, coffee, sugar, bananas, and cacao, traditionally exported to the United States. A second tier of countries on either side of this core, largely producers and exporters of metal

ores, indicates a strong, if not dominant, U.S. role. Overall, U.S. trade diminishes with distance as would normally be expected, a phenomenon geographers may term **friction of space.**

Table 4–3 indicates some other trends in South American trade. The European Common Market is equally as important as, or surpasses, the United States in South American trade. The former colonial powers, Spain and Portugal, play only a small role in area trade. Japan and West Germany are particularly important trade partners, and the overwhelming amount of trade, export and import, is with the world's most developed countries. The Soviet Union and its political allies have a relatively limited South American trade; only Peru has any significant trade with the USSR, while Poland trades with Peru and Brazil—largely the import of coffee and cotton to Poland and the export of fishing vessels. The partners listed in Table 4–3 accounted for some 65 to 90 percent of each country's total trade. The Guianas alone trade heavily with the Caribbean islands, and only Ecuador sends significant exports to Panama.

What is truly astounding is the sharp rise in intraregional trade that has taken place over the last decade. Brazil and Argentina, the continent's two giants, are beginning to become major regional trading powers. Argentina and Brazil, in an attempt to extend their hinterlands, are vying for the trade of landlocked Paraguay and Bolivia as well as adjacent Uruguay. Chile, too, has actively begun to develop trade with the other states of the Pacific coast. It is the **complementarity** of temperate and tropical goods among these South American states that has enabled trade to develop. The production of Colombia, Venezuela, and Ecuador is very nearly duplicatory of that of Brazil (except for oil), effectively minimizing Brazil's trade with these countries.

While U.S. economic commitments to South America are quite important and industrial investments are heavy in Colombia and Venezuela, the United States could hardly be considered the dominant economic power region-wide. Politically, however, the region's nations are tied to the United States through the Rio Pact, a mutual defense organization, and a long tradition of hemispheric cooperation. South American states have resented United States direct intervention in Central American and Caribbean republics. With some exceptions, the U.S. record in South America is less sullied. Nonetheless, this past record is viewed by South American states as a matter of concern.

The United States has been able to elicit cooperation on virtually all crucial questions, though agreement at times is grudging or participation belated or incomplete. Disparity in size and power has often caused South Amer-

TABLE 4–3
South American trade 1977/78 (expressed as a percentage of total imported [top] or exported [bottom] by South America)

	United States	EEC	West Germany's share of EEC	Japan	South America	Argentina's share of South America	Brazil's share of South America	Arab oil producers
As an Importer								
Argentina	18	39	(14)	8	15	—	(12)	—
Bolivia	26	15	(2)	11	33	(15)	(14)	—
Brazil	23	18	(8)	8	9	(6)	—	18
Chile	22	14	(6)	7	18	(6)	(5)	7
Colombia	43	23	(10)	9	5	—	—	—
Ecuador	40	18	(10)	13	3	—	—	—
French Guyana	4	72	(1)	2	3	—	(1)	—
Guyana	29	29	(2)	2	1	—	—	—
Paraguay	10	25	(6)	3	40	(21)	(17)	13
Peru	32	20	(7)	8	14	—	(2)	—
Suriname	33	28	(2)	2	3	—	(1)	—
Uruguay	8	22	(8)	1	29	(12)	(15)	18
Venezuela	48	30	(9)	8	3	—	(1)	—
As an Exporter								
Argentina	7	28	(3)	3	28	—	(12)	2
Bolivia	34	25	(2)	1	31	(23)	(4)	—
Brazil	18	28	(9)	7	8	(4)	—	4
Chile	5	32	(16)	12	25	(11)	(7)	—
Colombia	32	30	(15)	2	2	—	—	—
Ecuador	47	9	(2)	2	17	—	—	—
French Guyana	2	10	(—)	1	69	—	—	—
Guyana	22	36	(3)	1	1	—	—	—
Paraguay	12	35	(11)	5	20	(10)	(8)	—
Peru	25	27	(11)	14	8	—	(1)	—
Suriname	39	33	(10)	13	1	—	—	—
Uruguay	13	26	(9)	7	20	(5)	(12)	—
Venezuela	33	20	(11)	9	2	—	—	—

ican states to act with caution. The United States is generally viewed as a "good neighbor," but one that is too close for comfort at times. The community of interest appears to be South American, then Latin American, and only lastly hemispheric.

Virtually every South American country has or has had a dispute over borders with neighboring states. Chile, Peru, and Bolivia, in the War of the Pacific 1879–80, fought over the Bolivian corridor to the sea. Bolivia lost its outlet, a situation that may be reversed if a Bolivian-Chilean agreement for the reinstitution of a small corridor along the Peruvian border reaches fruition. Bolivia also lost a part of the Chaco region to Paraguay (1932–35). Brazil is actively developing roads and railroads to both these countries in an effort to draw them into its economic orbit.

The most recent border flareup, 1980–81, is on the Ecuador-Peru border in the Amazon. Peru's active campaign to develop its interior has apparently revived this long-standing dispute. Virtually all countries surrounding Brazil have aspired to a larger share of the Amazon Basin and, in particular, access to navigation. The peculiar appendage on Colombia (at Leticia) is the result of such a desire. Figure 4–3 shows the areas involved in border disputes, both currently and historically. Only the Argentinian-Chilean border appears conclusively settled. Brazil's massive Amazonian highway system currently under construction is thought of not only as a developmental strategem but also as a means of firmly consolidating Brazilian control over its interior.

Internally, wide disparity in income levels and the need for land reform are frequently thought of as the causes of political instability. Most of the region's countries exhibit wide ranges in income levels, with a small, wealthy elite and a large base composed of the poor. Until recently,

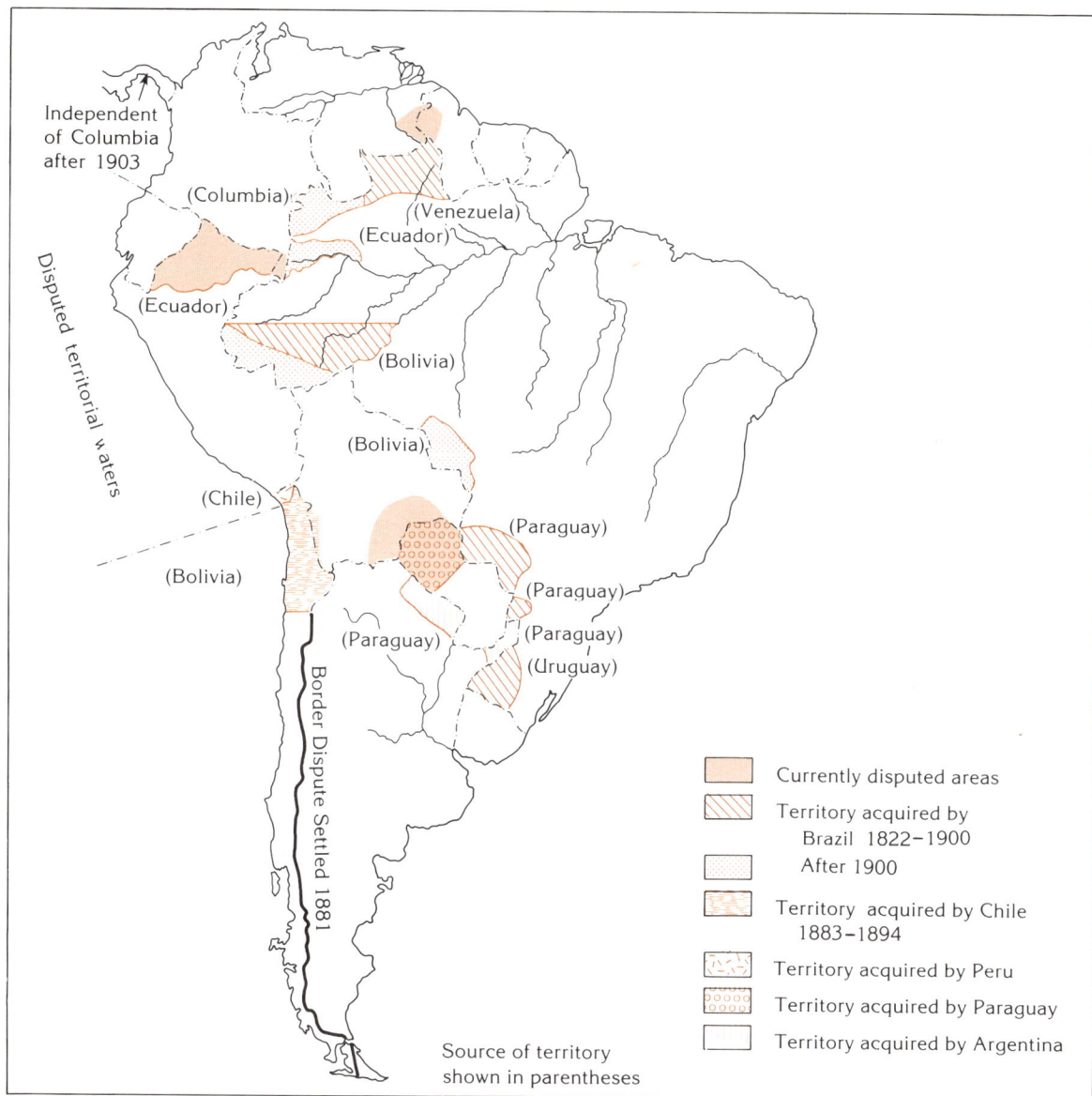

Independent
of Columbia
after 1903

(Columbia)

(Venezuela)
(Ecuador)

(Ecuador)

(Bolivia)

(Bolivia)

(Chile)

(Bolivia)

(Paraguay)

(Paraguay)

(Paraguay)

(Paraguay)

(Uruguay)

Disputed territorial waters

Border Dispute Settled 1881

	Currently disputed areas
	Territory acquired by Brazil 1822–1900
	After 1900
	Territory acquired by Chile 1883–1894
	Territory acquired by Peru
	Territory acquired by Paraguay
	Territory acquired by Argentina

Source of territory
shown in parentheses

FIGURE 4–3

Border Disputes and Territorial Transfers. Post-independence border disputes and wars in South America seldom had the extraregional significance of European wars, but their occurrence and consequent territorial transfers have been quite important within the region.

a middle class was very small. The rapid expansion of industry and even governmental administration has created or enlarged the middle class over the last three decades. Nonetheless, instability in government is still characteristic.

The military has traditionally been a road to social and economic advancement where other roads were absent. It has been one of the most democratic institutions in most countries; in the past, officers were most often drawn from the families of the elite, but advancement for the rank and file was possible. Loyalty to one's officer, however, worked both ways with an expectation of loyalty in return from subordinates' extended families. In this

way, military leaders who came to political power often commanded a surprising amount of popular support. The military often represented specific families or specific economic interests. Threats to a family or interest resulted in open revolt and, if successful, a government takeover.

Today, the size and scale of the military has changed. Larger numbers of troops means less personal contact and a much greater number of recruits from the lower economic groups. Wider literacy has opened officer ranks beyond the economic elite. Today's military sees its role as keeping internal peace rather more than the discouragement of threats. Prolonged battles and guerrilla campaigns have all but disappeared. Coalitions (known as *juntas)* rather than individuals govern, and elected assemblies often continue to function after a military takeover. Public addresses of military leaders emphasize domestic peace, a time to let things evolve during an era of rapid change, rather than a stop to this program or an end to a perceived threat. While the system is unfamiliar to outsiders, it is not always received unfavorably by the public of the states involved. The term *dictatorship,* while widely applied, seems to have evolved into a new and different type in parts of South America. In its newer format, political stability does not necessarily seem to prevent or preclude economic and social change.

RELATIVE ISOLATION

In terms of relative isolation, South America is more distant from Europe than is North America; Chicago is 700 miles (1,100 kilometers) closer to London than is Caracas and almost 2,000 miles (3,200 kilometers) closer than Rio de Janeiro. The breadth of the Pacific isolates South America to some extent from the rapidly growing East Asian economic area; it is almost 10,000 air miles (16,000 kilometers) from Tokyo to Lima, and over 10,000 miles from Melbourne, Australia, to Lima. When measured in sea distances, the only practical means for the transport of most trade goods, distances are even greater. For most of Europe, Africa and Asia became closer sources of tropical products, particularly for those powers with colonies there. The Monroe Doctrine and political disputes engendered by rapidly changing governments (who refused to pay the debts of prior regimes owed to European firms and governments) contributed to minimizing European contacts and to maximizing hemispheric relations. It is only in the late nineteenth and early twentieth centuries that Europe came to be involved in South American investment and trade to any great extent. This relative isolation has placed South American states at something of a disadvantage in trade, encouraging (however indirectly) an emphasis on a few crops and commodities readily marketable in Europe and forcing sale at low prices to aid in overcoming the transportation costs.

On the other hand, this relative isolation has proven to be an advantage in some respects. Intensified by the world trade depression of the 1930's, relative isolation from the rest of the world has encouraged the development of domestic food supplies and allowed for the development of an embryonic industrial structure based on local raw materials and domestic capital in some of South America's states. With improving overseas transportation, this domestic industry is able to export. The diminishing effects of isolation have apparently come at the right time. The Middle East, with its oil-generated surplus wealth, is as close to Brazil as is the United States. Wealthy South Africa is much closer. Brazil, Argentina, and even Chile

have begun to explore these markets, while Japan, most commonly the third most important trading partner of most South American nations, has become a new market for South America's raw materials.

Internal isolation possesses another set of problems. There are few links, other than sea and weak air links, among the region's states. Each has developed in relative isolation because of the lack of transportation links. Indeed, most countries have internal transportation problems and have had several **settlement nuclei,** often unconnected, throughout their history. Only now, for example, is Brazil extending its rail routes to interconnect its many separate local networks. Only over the last ten years have most railroads conformed to one gauge. The long-planned Inter-American Highway system remains incomplete, yet major portions have long been in operation. In the most ambitious scheme yet conceived, Brazil has begun construction of a national highway network that would connect Brazil with most South American countries.

Several trans-Andean pipelines now exist, and a series of roads and railroads cross the Andes interconnecting Argentina, Bolivia, and Chile. With roads already completed, Peru expects to extend rail connections to Bolivia. With its portion of the Inter-American Highway completed, future plans include a highway along the eastern edge of the Andes (in part completed), highways to Iquitos (deep in the interior and at the head of navigation for deep draft vessels on the Amazon), interconnection with the Brazilian highway network, and full connection of its isolated rail lines. Currently, only the section from Cochabamba to Santa Cruz is incomplete in what will become South America's first transcontinental railroad at a point of considerable continental breadth. South America gradually appears to be overcoming the difficulties of distance and internal isolation that have so long precluded intra-regional interaction and a rationalization of production and trade.

THE PHYSICAL FRAME

The continent is overwhelmingly tropical or subtropical in climate. Altitude, or aspect, rather than latitude chiefly determines local climatic conditions and land use. Only the high Andean valleys and the extreme southern "cone" of the continent are temperate. Lacking the truly vast desert areas of Africa or Australia, it is somewhat more habitable than the other southern hemisphere continents. The high Andean mountain spine, composed of multiple ridges, and related to plate tectonics, forms the western side of the continent. The rest is a plateau surface of crystalline rock (much of it below 1,000 feet) covered with a sporadic layering of sedimentaries. There are three large riverine lowlands; the Paraná-Paraguay, the Amazon, and the Orinoco. These separate the Andes and plateau, or, in the case of the Amazon, divide the plateau itself.

The river valleys, which would seem to provide routes of unity and access, in effect divide the population clusters along the western and eastern continental margins. The deceptive simplicity of pattern hides the reality of one of South America's greatest problems—the inaccessibility of the empty interior.

TOPOGRAPHY

The Andes form a continuation of the subsea mountains that are the Caribbean islands and connect, via a second looping arc, to the mountains of Antarctica through the Palmer peninsula. They are the world's second highest mountain chain though their width is comparable to the Appalachians in most cases. Their height, coupled with a structure that consists of two to three parallel ranges, sometimes separated by deeply dissected valleys, has made them an extremely effective barrier, separating the coast lands from the interior. Individual peaks reach heights of 18,000 to 20,000 feet (5,000 to 6,000 meters), while the range averages over 10,000 feet (3,000 meters) for most of its length from Ecuador to central Chile. (See Figure 4—4.)

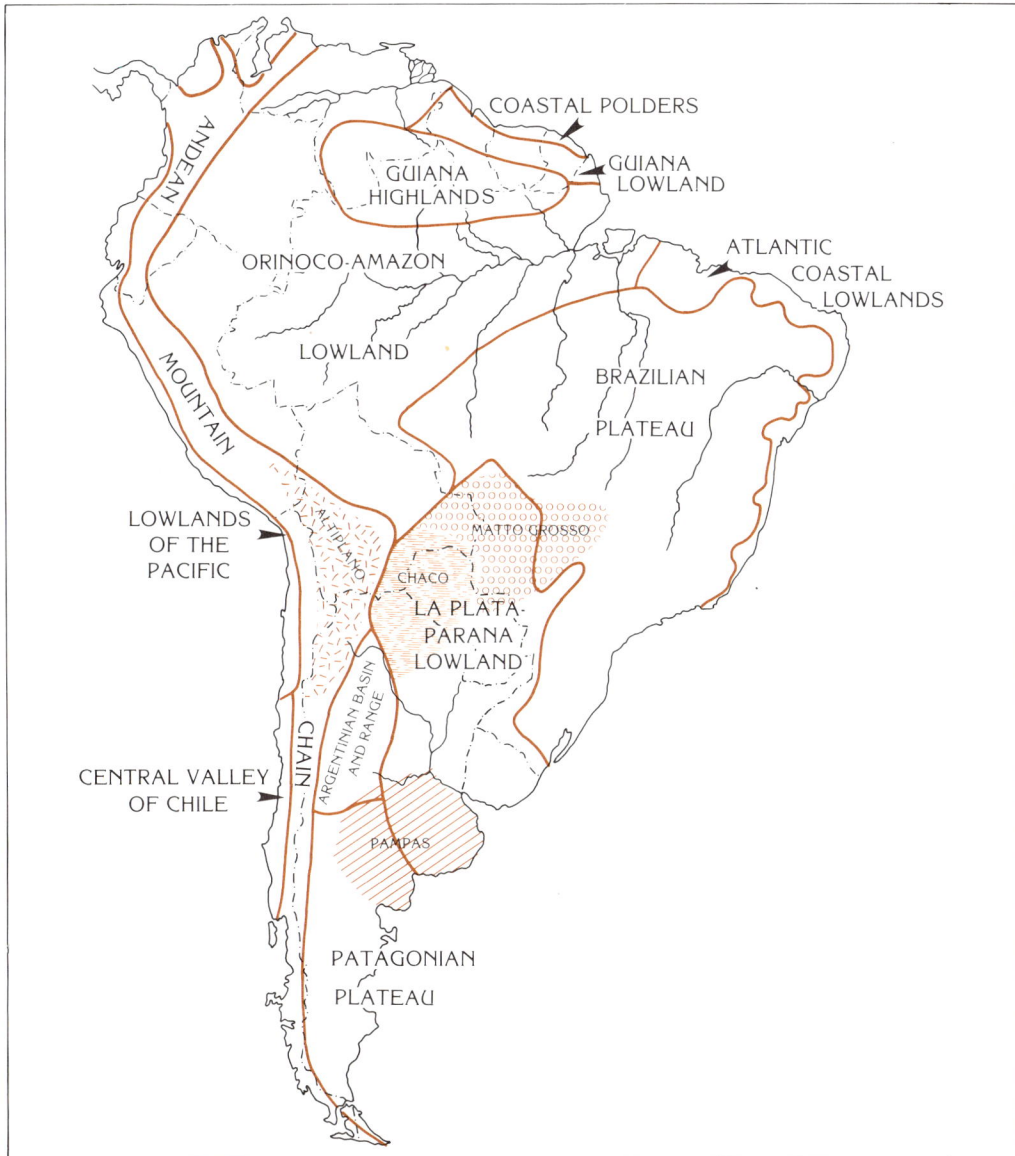

FIGURE 4—4
Physiographic Regions of South America. Deceptively simple in generalization, the landform geography of South America is more complex in closer examination. The significance of uplands and mountains is great in South American settlement, providing temperate regions in otherwise tropical areas.

The Andes are at their lowest elevation and have their least complex structure in the south, generally a single ridge sculptured by glaciation. Northward of central Chile they increase in height and split into two ranges, the westernmost of which is higher and steeper. The highest peaks of the range occur along the Argentinian-Chilean frontier from Mendoza north to Bolivia. In their Bolivian section, the two ranges deviate sharply from their original north-south orientation at the bend in South America, and the ranges diverge to form a high plateau, the Altiplano, between the two rows of peaks. This Altiplano is high and inhospitable; much of it is arid and floored with coarse debris or salt flats, though it contains freshwater lakes at its northern end.

The Altiplano continues into Peru where the form of the Andes changes again. The two ranges become three. While the mountains begin to lower in altitude, they steepen in slope as the upper tributaries of the Amazon incise steep canyons into long parallel troughs between the ridges. Portions of the basins between the ranges are filled with volcanic debris that has weathered into rich soil. While tectonically active throughout their length, vulcanism is most prevalent in the central Andes from middle Chile through Peru to Ecuador as the South American plate moves against the offshore trench. In Peru, the Andes are located nearest the coast; the western cordillera presents a steep face toward the Pacific rising steeply from the narrow coastal plain.

The Andes change direction of trend again at the border of Ecuador; northwest trending ridges abruptly shift to a northeast direction. At this point, they become two ridges again and turn inland, allowing the development of a progressively wider coastal lowland. In Colombia there are again three ridges, widely spaced. The intervening valleys are lower and much broader than those of Peru.

In a final turn to the east, there is only one range that continues into Venezuela, paralleling the coast and terminating in Trinidad. In this section, the mountains are much lower, yet quite complex. Splitting, forming basins, faulted throughout, they form a topographic patchwork to the delta of the Orinoco. In most of this section of Venezuela, the coastal plain disappears.

As along the western coast of North America, there is often a coastal range paralleling the major mountain chain at a lower altitude. Most of it is partially drowned in southern Chile, forming offshore islands. The central Valley of Chile, like the Great Valley of California, is a sediment-filled trough between these coastal ranges and the Andes. The Valley of Chile narrows northward and becomes drier until it forms the broken surface of the Atacama Desert squeezed between the Andes and the plateaulike coastal range.

In Peru the coastal range becomes a series of low hills, all but squeezed out as the Andes approach the sea. Northward in Ecuador a series of discontinuous coastal hills alternates with lowlands and broad river basins and the sculpture of the surface changes from angular to rounded under the influence of increased rainfall. The Guyas River lowland of Ecuador, the Magdalena-Cauca lowland of Colombia, and the Maracaibo Basin are the three largest lowland areas.

The Orinoco lowland is crescent-shaped and broad; it is filled with sediment from both the Andes and the Guyana Highlands, a piece of the shield north of the Amazon. The Amazon lowland is huge, the largest single feature on the whole continent. It is triangular in form with the broad western base against the Andes and tapers to a narrow extent at its mouth. The shifting sedimentary debris and remaining interfluves create an undulating surface.

The lowland of the Paraná-Paraguay river system is best divided into two parts. The northern part, the Chaco, is not totally drained by the river, as much of the surface has underground drainage. The southern part, the Pampas, is a loess plain that is also incompletely drained. As a result, the lowland is much larger than the drainage basin.

The crystalline shield country can be divided into three parts: the Patagonian Plateau, the Brazilian highlands, and the Guiana Highlands (see Figure 4–4). They are all ancient crystalline shield areas—old continental blocks. In most cases the land rises abruptly a few miles in from the coast. These serras or scarps have made movement into the inland relatively difficult, though they are much lower than the Andes.

In the Patagonian Plateau, rivers have incised steep-sided valleys into the plateau surface, allowing east-west movement while complicating the construction of north-south routes. Northward it fades beneath a cover of loess in the east while rising to become the Andean piedmont in the west. This Andean piedmont portion of the plateau is broken basin and range country similar to that found in the American Southwest.

North of the Paraná-Paraguay the shield reaches its maximum extent as a huge triangle between that river system, the Amazon, and the Atlantic. It tilts westward so that the highest elevations are in the east. Large parts of the southern portion are covered by diabase, a volcanic material that results in exceptionally fertile soil. Most of the north and northeast consists of exposed, resistant shield material, part of the ancient platform. Sediments cover the platform in a large lobe between the Araguaid and São Francisco rivers; they also form the cover of the Matto Grosso Plateau in Brazil's interior and the highlands on either side of the Paraná River valley. This portion of Brazil is plateau country, often with an altitude of over 2,000 or 3,000 feet (600 to 1,000 meters).

In the Guiana Highlands, the western portion is higher and more rugged than the Brazilian highlands. A very narrow coastal plain (10 to 30 miles [16 to 48 kilometers] in width) fringes the Atlantic. Though the steep edge of the plateau presents an abrupt face to the sea with little coastal plain, there is a broad continental shelf along most of the Atlantic side of the continent; whereas the western (Pacific) side is bordered by a deep trough, associated with the tectonic plate movement of western South America.

THE CLIMATE

As with most generalizations on South America there is a real gap between popular conception and reality. To many, South America is tropical, implying heat and humidity. It is a wet, rather than dry, continent. It also contains larger zones of temperate climate than either Africa or Australia.

South America does contain the world's largest zone of the tropical rainforest and monsoon forest climate with short (or no) dry season, high temperature and humidity levels, and high rainfall. (See Figure 4–5.) The basin of the

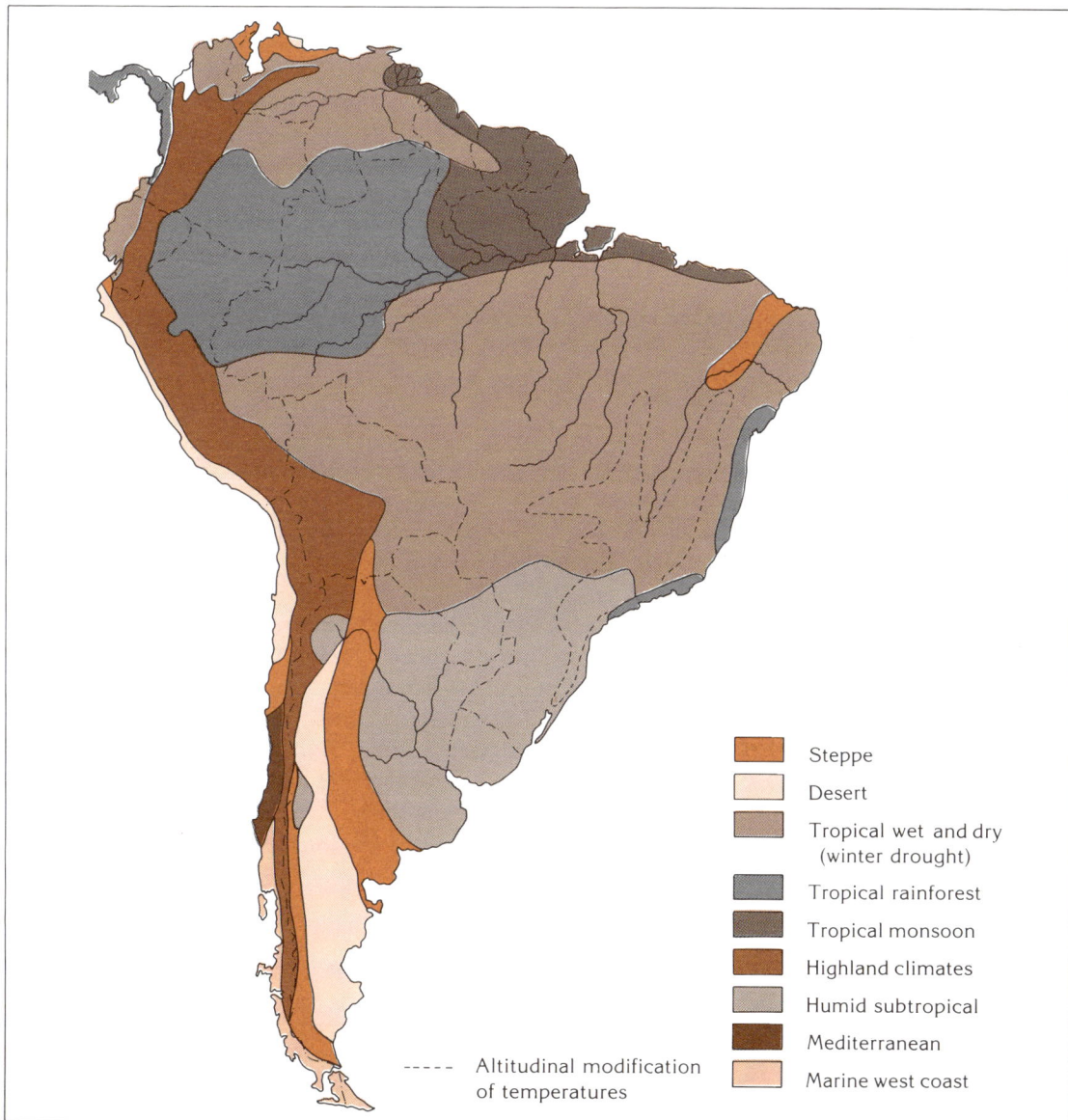

Legend:
- Steppe
- Desert
- Tropical wet and dry (winter drought)
- Tropical rainforest
- Tropical monsoon
- Highland climates
- Humid subtropical
- Mediterranean
- Marine west coast
- ----- Altitudinal modification of temperatures

FIGURE 4–5
Generalized Climate. The popular perception that the wet tropics are undesirable is hardly universal, yet such perceptions may have been involved in the settlement of the tropical interior of the Amazon Basin. It is coastal and/or temperate South America that is the most developed.

Amazon, the Guiana Highlands, and some of the Brazilian and Colombian coastlands have such a climate. Daily temperature variations exceed monthly variations, and rain is a near daily occurrence in the area. Trade winds and seabreezes modify the humidity and **sensible** (human-perceived) **temperature** in limited areas. Temperatures in the high 70's and low 80's F (23 to 27°C) prevail, and the breeze, while gentle, is nearly constant. It is only deep in the interior, in the upper Amazon Basin, that the stereotypic, unvarying tropical climate prevails. Along the Atlantic coasts temperatures may even dip below 68°F (20°C) at night and rainfall totals are much lower than those in the interior.

The bulk of Brazil, interior Venezuela, eastern Bolivia, and northern Paraguay—indeed more than half the continent—experience a climate that is seasonally dry as the **intertropical convergence,** with its accompanying rains, shifts north and south of the equator, following the seasonal migration of the direct rays of the sun. Drought occurs during the winter period, though temperatures are hardly wintry. Most of the area receives 30 to 60 inches (750 to 1,250 millimeters) of rainfall concentrated in a wet period of six to nine months duration. These two belts (Southern Hemisphere and Northern Hemisphere) of savanna climate (see Figure 4–5) have winter (and drought) at opposing seasons of the year. Typically, the warmest temperatures occur during the winter dry season in the Venezuelan savanna, where the absence of clouds and near equatorial location allows maximum radiation.

The higher plateau areas of Brazil experience a similar rainfall regime but cooler temperatures. In part because of latitude, but more because of altitude, the area between the states of Paraná and Minas Gerais, inland from the coast, experiences a delightful climate with temperatures that are rarely below freezing. Temperatures at São Paulo, for example, average 64°F (18°C) with little day-night variation and only 10°F (5°C) variation from the coldest to the warmest months. South of the Paraná state, frost becomes a yearly occurrence, though pleasant subtropical conditions prevail most of the year. Winter months average over 50°F (10°C) and summers may be quite hot and humid, as in the U.S. South. Seasonal extremes are not great, however, and cold weather is never intense or of long duration.

South and west of the temperate climatic areas, the climate grades into steppe and even desert in the belt of prevailing westerly winds on the rainshadow sides of the Andes. In many respects the climate is like that of the Great Plains and great basin areas of the United States. In northern Argentina the conditions are like those of western Texas, New Mexico, and Arizona as one moves west from wetter to drier margins. In Patagonia, the conditions are similar to those found in the Dakotas, Montana, and Utah—only the wet to dry progression is from west to east, the reverse of the U.S. conditions.

The cold Peru current off the Pacific coast creates stability in air masses passing over it, chilling the lower layer of the air and creating a belt of extremely arid desert (the Atacama) that stretches the length of Peru and over the northern one third of Chile. Almost devoid of rain, what plant life exists subsists mainly on fog and dew for moisture. The effect of the current is such that temperatures are much lower than one would expect at similar latitudes.

South of the desert the climate shades very quickly through steppe conditions to a dry-summer subtropical (Mediterranean) climate that coincides with the Valley of Chile, that country's populous core area. Winters are mild and summers hot and rainless. Beyond 40°S latitude, where Chile becomes a maze of islands and peninsulas, the climate becomes rainy year round and virtually always cloudy and cool. Conditions are similar to those of coastal British Columbia in Canada. Stormier and windier than comparable climatic areas of Europe, rainfall is as high as that found anywhere in the tropics—some 75 to 120 inches (1,900 to 2,500 millimeters) annually. With all the monotony and humidity of the rainforest, it has little in the way of sun or warmth.

Two additional climatic features are worthy of note. In the northeast corner of Brazil, inland from the coasts, there is an extremely drought-prone area of land that covers much of the sertão, or backland, in that district. Rains are capricious, in some years causing intense flooding, in other years totally absent. The weather is hot year round, but convectional storms are relatively rare. During the period from September to November, when the intertropical convergence is in the neighborhood, there is often intense drought—the opposite of the expected effect. Rainfall irregularity has led to crop disasters and even famines.

Vertical zonation of climate occurs everywhere that mountains exist. Temperatures decline 3 to 5°F (1° to 2°C) for every 1,000-foot (300-meter) increase in altitude. Mountains that run at right angles to prevailing winds have a wet (windward) and dry (leeward) side, though altitude tends to increase rainfall in all cases by lifting and cooling passing air masses.

The concept of vertical zonation is important here because of the large numbers of people living in South America's highlands and the productivity of those highlands. Altitudes below 3,000 feet (900 meters) are hot and humid, classified as *tierra caliente,* the hot lands, by their inhabitants. Above 3,000 feet to 7,000 feet (2,100 meters) is the *tierra templada* (temperate), a land of perpetual spring. The *tierra fria* (cold land) exists at higher altitudes. Some grain crops and potatoes can be grown, though pastures are the most frequent land use. Above the *tierra fria* is the **paramos,** a land of perpetual alpine pasture, with frost, but generally below the snow line. Above the snow line is the *tierra helada,* "frozen land." The various maximum and minimum altitudes vary with latitude, so that Tierra del Fuego has virtually only the *paramos* and tundra. In the tropics, however, the full range is attained and various climates appear perpetually in one season or another. Because of this, what appears on maps under the bland category of "undifferentiated highland climate" contains a microcosm of all the world's climates.

VEGETATION

As in all other areas of the world, climate coincides strikingly with vegetational patterns. There are exceptions, however. The *selva,* or rainforest, has an open floor here, far less of an obstacle to movement than its counterparts in Asia and Africa. It contains some of the most commercially valuable species in the world. Cacao, Brazilnut, and the rubber tree are native and grow in mixed forests with tropical hardwoods valued as furniture wood. The forest grows in three *stories* whose combined canopies almost exclude sunlight from the floor.

In the Andean areas, the tropical rainforest produces a variety of palm fibers that have uses as fiber, including straw hats. Cinchona, which yields quinine for treating malaria, is a native plant of value, and coca trees, whose leaves yield cocaine, are a common species. In eastern Brazil, the *matta,* a lower variant of rainforest, coincides with the more valuable agricultural soils to a large degree. In consequence, it has been largely removed.

The savannas are grasslands with a limited, but valuable, sprinkling of trees. Characteristically, the grasses can stand long drought, and several have been domesticated for use as lawn grasses because of it. At least one native grass, the Pará, is highly nutritious. Drought-tolerant trees, interspersed with the grasses, often have dual root systems for tapping both runoff and ground water. Tanbark, waxes, fibers, resins, dyes, and various chemical raw materials are derived from these trees.

The temperate grasslands of South America, mostly in the eastern Argentina–Uruguay–southern Brazil area, have all but disappeared, much as their North American counterparts, having succumbed to the extension of cropland areas. Some, offering pasture to sheep, are still preserved in Patagonia, where the land is more properly termed bushland than grassland.

The *caatinga,* or dry forest, of northeast Brazil is unique. The carnauba palm is its most valuable species, but native tree cottons, rubber-yielding plants, and fleshy cacti are all intermixed in a tangle of shrubs and thorny trees.

The temperate forests, much as those of the selva, remain largely untouched. Many of the species are evergreen broadleaf trees reflecting the milder climate. Hardwoods dominate on the Pacific side. The subtropical and temperate forests of the Atlantic yield yerba maté, a species used for a tealike drink, and the valuable Paraná pine.

The Atacama Desert, the world's driest, has virtually no vegetation, while desert shrub occupies much of west-

Pressures on a Limited Land Resource, the Cauca Region of Colombia. South American countries exhibit some of the most rapid rates of population increase in the world. Though averages would show the continent to be relatively lightly populated, there are large areas which cannot be easily utilized. Increasing populations has forced farmers to clear and plant steep slopes, a practice which can lead to destructive erosion. (Courtesy of United Nations)

ern Argentina. Scrubby, drought-resistant plants form a transition from the Atacama to wetter climates.

SOILS

The comprehensive soil classification system has developed ten large groups. Much of tropical South America is covered by one of these groups known as oxisols, heavily leached red soils with high levels of iron and aluminum and low amounts of humus. Traditionally, they were known as laterites and latosols. They are generally thick but of low fertility and lose whatever they have after a crop or two. In savanna they are often underlain by hardpans, which impede drainage.

In the tropics, fertile soils are generally associated with alluvium or volcanic parent materials; they may also form on calcareous rock and at least possess lime and a reduced level of acidity. The rich volcanic soils of the Andes (from Peru to Venezuela) and the terra roxa of Brazil and Paraguay are among the continent's richest. Alluvial deposits of the valley of eastern Brazil and Colombia are fertile, but those of the Amazon and the Chaco area (upper Paraguay) are not universally so. The fertility of alluvium depends on the material from which it is derived.

Soil fertility in South America could prove to be a limitation to the expansion of agriculture. Vast areas of tropical soils appear to be infertile for shallow-rooted field crops, yet can produce very satisfactory yields when put to tree crops. More important than natural soil patterns may be soil depletion and erosion. Traditional agriculture in many parts of South America has proven damaging to soils, and many formerly productive areas have been abandoned after depletion through constantly cropping the same plants or using slopes that are too steep. The hoe, the traditional farm tool, did little damage to soil structure. Mechanization, however, has shown itself able to unleash powerful erosive forces through deep plowing and clear tillage. In some areas, then, mechanization may do irreversible damage.

As in the southern United States, there are large areas of so-called ultisols in South America, tropical or subtropical soils that are less heavily leached. With care, rotation, periodic fallowing, and large inputs of fertilizer, they can give decent crop yields. Much of interior Brazil has such soils, and plans for development rely on cultivation of these less than fertile soils. The success or failure of agriculture in these areas could well depend more on other economic developments taking place in Brazil than on the level of natural fertility.

DRAINAGE PATTERNS

The Amazon, Paraná-Paraguay, and Orinoco rivers form three potential highways into the interior of South Amer-

ica. The Amazon, by far the largest, is the most readily navigable stream in the world. Ocean vessels can reach Manaus, deep-draft river steamers can navigate in 15-foot (4.5-meter) depths all the way to Iquitos in Peru, and even huge tankers can reach the port of Santarem in a river that carries a larger volume of water than any other. Flow is maintained at all seasons since its tributaries span both sides of the equator. It is raining somewhere in the basin at virtually all times. Water depth fluctuations of up to 30 feet (9 meters) do little to hamper navigation. The flood plain is up to 100 or more miles (160 kilometers) wide in many places, a morass of bog and oxbow lakes that store surplus water to feed into the main channel.

The hydroelectric potential of the Amazon is almost immeasurable. In its southern tributaries, steep-sided valleys in solid rock provide excellent dam sites. If gorges along its Andean tributaries are more spectacular, the volume of water and earth stability associated with its southern and northern tributaries is potentially more productive. The actual connection of the Orinoco with the Amazon through natural *stream capture* provides an easy potential route for extending navigation through the very center of the continent. It is the low economic demand, rather than any physical difficulties, that has led to minimal use of these great rivers for navigation.

The La Plata-Paraná-Paraguay system has achieved some degree of economic importance. The broad estuary of the La Plata is difficult to navigate because of silting, but a deep channel is maintained to Buenos Aires and Montevideo, while **outports** to service tankers have been built further downstream. Currently, a 24-foot (7.3-meter) channel is maintained to the Argentinian industrial centers of Rosario and Sante Fe. Commercial river vessels ply the waters as far north as Asunción in Paraguay. Above its confluence with the Paraguay River, the Paraná has lower use. A joint Brazilian-Paraguayan project is developing the tremendous power resource of this river in the area of the Iquassú Falls.

Navigation and power are being developed on the Orinoco, which has a natural 40-foot (12-meter) channel for almost half its course. Iron ore is shipped by both ocean vessels and barge from the Cerro Bolívar mines to Venezuela's plants, as well as overseas. Massive new hydro-power projects on its Guiana Highland tributaries generate power for aluminum plants, paper mills, alloy smelters, and other power-consuming industries. As agriculture develops, the river has proven its worth as a transporter of the surplus of the Llanos to domestic and foreign markets.

The São Francisco River has provided the traditional inland link between southeastern Brazil and the northeast, areas whose rail networks are only now being connected. The Guayas River (Guayaquil) is navigable for 200 miles (320 kilometers); it is almost the only important stream for navigation of the west coast. Virtually all others, however, though short, shallow, and seasonal in flow are usable for irrigation in their lower reaches and hydroelectric generation in their source areas. Almost all these short streams from northern Peru through Antofagasta in Chile support irrigated agriculture. Argentina is developing a similar duality of use on some of the streams in Patagonia.

A classic example of transportation problems in underdeveloped areas is the Magdalena system of Colombia. It is shallow and seasonally unusable, but it is navigable for several hundred miles above Barranquilla. Railroads and road portages, even rope and pulley systems, were installed to get over the problem areas; there are great losses in time and great costs in labor involved as goods are unloaded and reloaded a half-dozen times on the route to and from Bogotá. Improvements, including the ultimate canalization of the system, are part of the total development plan of Colombia.

However difficult and costly, the potential for a full-scale development of internal water routes exists. In terms of natural waterways into the interior, South America has perhaps the greatest potential of any of the world's continents.

THE STRUCTURE OF SUBREGIONS

A grouping appears logical for the Andean states of Peru, Bolivia, and Ecuador—states that are not only Andean, but also largely Indian in culture. However, if Peru and Bolivia are largely mineral economies, Ecuador is agricultural. Paraguay, a largely Indian society, is also agricultural. These four states are grouped into a single subregion of dominantly Indian culture. (See Figure 4–6.) The Caribbean littoral states include Colombia, Venezuela, and the Guianas; they belong nowhere else, though as their trade indicates, they are more closely linked to the Caribbean than to South America. Brazil, with over half the continent's area and population, is necessarily subdivided. Perhaps the most obvious subregion is that of the developed southern tier—Argentina, Uruguay, and Chile.

Each subregion is based on a different set of criteria. Nonetheless, the basic commonality of one factor is often enough to create a subregion with clarity and coherence.

THE CARIBBEAN LITTORAL: COLOMBIA, VENEZUELA, AND THE GUIANAS

Of all South American states, Colombia and Venezuela are most directly tied to the economy of the United States as suppliers of raw materials and tropical products as well as being importers of that country's technology, capital, and capital goods. Despite the recent colonial heritage of the Guianas, Suriname and Guyana are almost as firmly tied. Both are heavy importers of goods from the United States; and, while still trading heavily with the former colonial power, aluminum ore (bauxite), their major export commodity, goes primarily to the United States. Only French Guiana, severely underdeveloped and officially an overseas department of France, does not fit the pattern. Even in this case, primary exports (food items) go to Suriname to feed the bauxite miners there and seafood (shrimp) goes to the United States.

Colombia   Colombia's 26 million people rank it third in population size in South America. Its degree of development as measured by a per capita GNP of $1,010, how-

Coffee Plantation in Colombia. Most South American states have suffered from overdependence on export of a few crops or commodities. Fluctuating world market prices have caused severe economic disruptions periodically. The emphasis on plantation or estate production has also led to problems of land tenure and a landless peasantry. (Courtesy of United Nations)

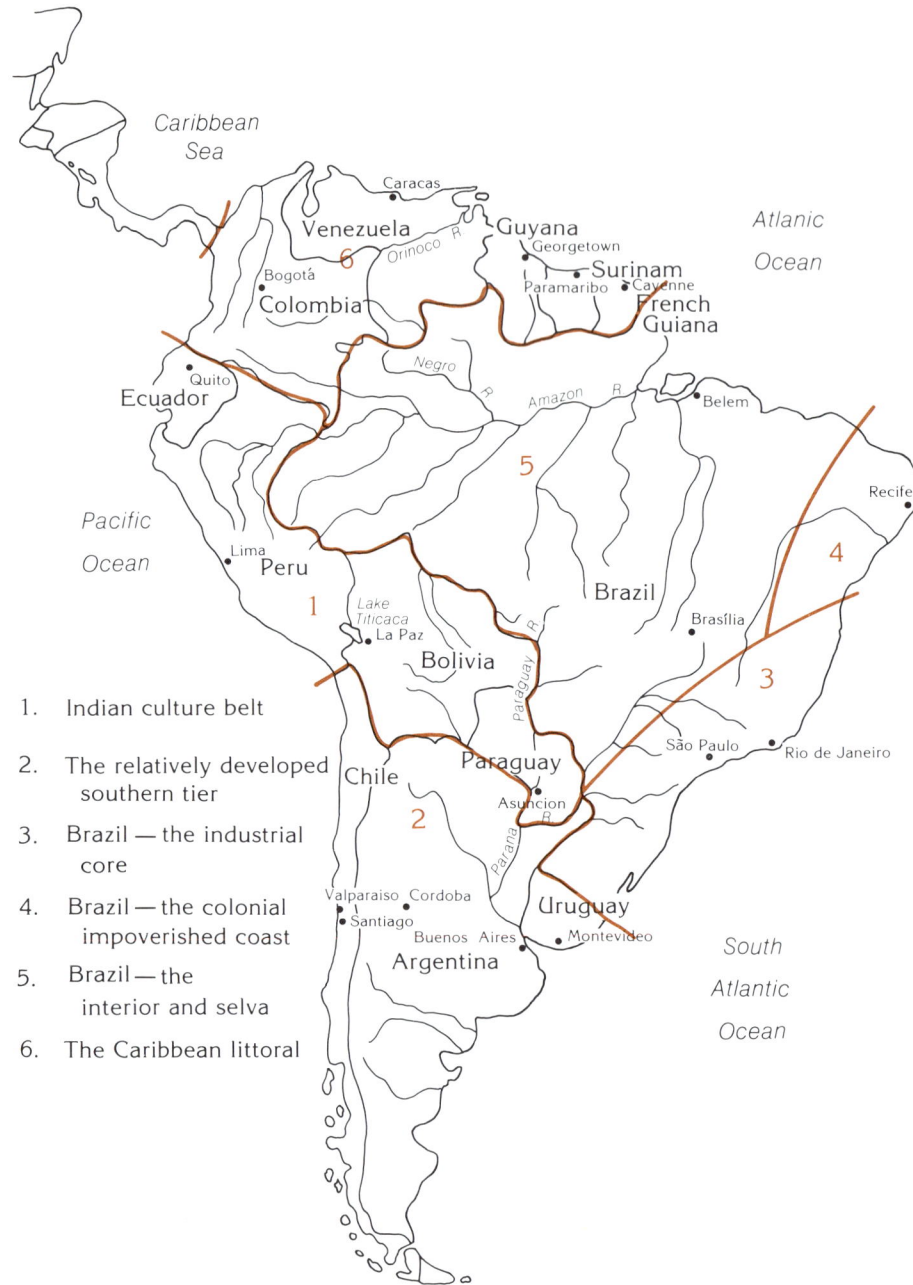

1. Indian culture belt

2. The relatively developed southern tier

3. Brazil — the industrial core

4. Brazil — the colonial impoverished coast

5. Brazil — the interior and selva

6. The Caribbean littoral

FIGURE 4–6
Structure of Subregions. One of the largest countries on earth, with over half of South America's area and people, Brazil is considered as four subregions. Other states are grouped on the basis of similarities in culture, economic development, and international trade orientations.

ever, would rank it only eighth. The natural resource base, while large and varied, is much less of an economic bonanza than that of neighboring Venezuela. Nevertheless, Colombia's economic progress has been steady and impressive since the late 1960's. Colombia, until 1976 a net exporter of oil, has increased domestic consumption through industrialization to the point of becoming a net importer. Exploration has been intensified, and major new natural gas discoveries will undoubtedly help cushion the impact of rising energy prices and demand.

Colombia also has the largest coal reserves in the region (over 30 billion tons), but large-scale investments will be necessary to significantly increase production. Ninety-five percent of the world's emeralds are mined in

Colombia; the government controls the largest mines, but many emeralds appear in "uncontrolled markets." Colombia is also the region's largest gold producer (see Figure 4–7).

Official statistics on foriegn exchange earnings are certainly underestimated due to Colombia's large-scale supplying of illegal drugs to the American markets. This marijuana-cocaine connection to the North American markets has grave potential for "destabilizing" the government through the huge potential for bribery and corruption associated with millions in illicit profits.

Colombia has been plagued by political unrest associated with the large-scale rural to urban migration that has created twenty-three cities of over 100,000 population

FIGURE 4–7

Mineral Resources of South America. From colonial times, some parts of the region have been noted for mineral production. Contemporary patterns of mining show an apparent reversal of early association of economic development with the fabled mines of Peru and Bolivia rather than the other subregions.

including the capital, Bogotá, at 3.5 million. Most of this urban growth is recent and not all can be readily absorbed by even the most industrialized country in northern South America. The high proportion of young people in the population have added demands on such public sector functions as educational and social services. A terroristic, guerrilla war has flickered periodically; "la violencia" of 1948–58 cost at least two hundred thousand lives. Any Colombian government must fulfill rising expectations, maintain order, and balance a precarious budget—a set of heavy demands indeed.

Officially, half of Colombia's foreign exchange is earned by coffee; it is the world's second producer after Brazil. The coffee, renowned for its quality, is produced largely on small farms rather than on estates. Any fluctuation in world market prices can adversely affect the economy. As a result, Colombia has encouraged a drive toward export diversification twinned with **import replacement** of textiles and other consumer goods. Cut flowers are an expanding crop, and large-scale industrialization has created many new jobs. Colombia manufactures consumer chemicals, processed food and beverages, cement, and metal products. United States firms have built over one hundred fifty joint stock plants in Colombia in the last decade.

Despite its seeming dependence on coffee, Colombia's agriculture is incredibly diversified. The combination of the High Andes valleys and slopes with tropical lowlands makes the production of a full range of crops and commodities feasible. If it grows in South America, Colombia is a producer: cocoa, sugarcane, bananas, tobacco, coffee, cattle, citrus, corn, wheat, potatoes, pineapples, and every vegetable imaginable. Agricultural colleges have different courses of study for "cold climate" and "warm climate" farming. There is a great potential for expansion of agriculture as much fertile soil remains yet uncultivated. With a declining annual growth rate of 2.1 percent, Colombia can provide for more people. In contrast to Venezuela, few Europeans have come in recently, but like Venezuela, the population is largely of mestizo and European descent, with very few Indians and a black population of 5 percent.

Among the many migrants to Colombia were the Antioqueños, descended from Christianized Jews and Moors, who settled near Medellín. Skilled in crafts from their occupations in Spain, they began the first industries in the country. Today, Medellín is a center of diverse and expanding industry, producing leather goods, textiles, and machinery. Overshadowed now by rapidly growing Bogotá, it still ranks as the second most important Colombian city and industrial center.

Botagá, the capital and cultural center, has attracted much foreign investment in the form of assembly plants whose production is geared largely for the export market under special reexport agreements. It also boasts a large, domestically owned clothing industry, which is equally successful at export.

Cali and Bucaramanga are the other industrial centers in a district that is rapidly becoming a major industrial district in the very center of Colombia.

Venezuela   With its great mineral wealth, Venezuela has by far the highest GNP per capita in South America: $3,130 per year, a full $1,000 per person above that of second-ranked Argentina. Venezuela, a founding member of OPEC, nationalized its oil industry in 1976, placing it in the hands of a government corporation, Petroleos de Venezuela. Oil accounts for 90 percent of the country's foreign exchange earnings, two thirds of government revenue, and 30 percent of the GNP. About half of Venezuela's oil is exported to the United States. Because Venezuela has twelve refineries, including one of the world's largest (Amuay), it exports over a third of its oil as refined products. Other OPEC members are also constructing refineries, following Venezuela's lead. Profit from refined products is much higher than from crude, although the profit margin thus generated was relatively higher in the pre-OPEC days of cheap crude.

Oil production in Venezuela peaked in 1970, declining through the 1970's as the long-producing Maracaibo fields (see Figure 4–7) have been gradually depleting; an OPEC strategy, emphasizing "more for less," has been raising prices and holding down production to prolong the life of the resource. Recently, drilling at much deeper levels

Venezuelan Iron Mine at Cerro Bolivar. Oil has provided the capital for development, but Venezuela has diversified its economy in the last two decades. Mines, steel mills, hydroelectric projects, aluminum mills, and chemical works have been developed in the Orinoco Valley and the Venezuelan segment of the Guiana Highlands. These projects represent not only diversification but the development of the country's interior region. (Courtesy of United Nations)

under Lake Maracaibo, together with exploration of the "Orinoco Tar Belt," has discovered what may be the world's largest deposits of "heavy oil"—thick, almost tar-like oils that cannot be retrieved through traditional oil wells. Steam injection, an expensive process, may be necessary to recover this oil, but high prices now justify this process. Thus, Venezuela is likely to remain a major oil power for many decades.

Venezuela is also a major producer of iron ore; again, Venezuela has nationalized the industry and the largest customer is the United States. Gold is a less important mineral in value, along with relatively minor deposits of copper, coal, nickel, manganese, and diamonds (over 1.5 million carats yearly). Hydroelectric power potential is yet another energy resource of Venezuela; one of the top four hydro power producers in the region, Venezuela's Guri Dam will eventually generate 9 million kilowatts, ranking it above all but a handful of power projects in the world. There are also large deposits of sulfur, phosphates, nickel, and asbestos in which exploitation has begun.

Part of the explanation for Venezuela's impressive prosperity (though incomes are extremely unequal) is the relatively low ratio of people to this fabulous resource base. Venezuela was a population of 14.5 million in an area the size of Texas and Oklahoma; it has one of the lowest population densities in the region. The annual growth rate, however, is 3 percent, above the regional average (2.7 percent), and almost twice the world average. The population is very unevenly distributed as most Venezuelans live in the Andes basins and along the Caribbean coast (see Figure 4–8). While about half of Venezuela lies south and east of the Orinoco River, that area contains only 4 percent of the people. Venezuelans are mostly mestizo (70 percent), European-descent (20 percent), or Africans (8 percent), with only 2 percent Amerindians. The last great influx of Europeans came when Venezuela was among the first New World states to welcome displaced persons from World War II. Venezuela's booming economy has attracted many Colombians across the border, both as legal and illegal migrants.

Agriculture employs one fifth of the work force, testifying to the rapid industrialization and urbanization of the country, but it produces only 6 percent of the GNP. Coffee and cocoa are exported, but they are far overshadowed in importance by mineral exports. Largely due to the combination of lucrative jobs in minerals and manufacturing and the rapid increase in numbers of consumers (at Venezuela's growth rate, the "doubling time" of its population is under twenty years), food output has not kept up with demand, and food imports have been necessary to fill the gap. Venezuela can afford food imports, but this is cutting into funds otherwise available for industrial and infrastruc-

Downtown Caracas, Venezuela. Venezuela's booming economy has created strikingly modern cities, where, however, the income gap between rich and poor shows few signs of diminishing. (Courtesy of United Nations)

ture development. Venezuela is attempting to reduce food imports by funding irrigation and water storage projects and by making credit available for farm improvements. Clearly, Venezuela has the physical and financial-technical resources to become self-sufficient in basic foods.

The rapid growth of manufacturing, just under 10 percent per year, has led to severe shortages of trained workers and managers, so that skilled craftsmen and technicians must be recruited abroad at the same time that Venezuelan unemployment rates are at about 4 percent. Much of the unemployed and underemployed (part-time work and/or "sharing" a full-time job with another) workers are recent arrivals to the cities who are functionally illiterate and equipped only with agricultural skills—a phenomenon common to all developing countries. Manufacturing emphasizes oil refining, iron and steel (over a million metric tons per year), aluminum (400,000 metric tons per year), auto assembly, and consumer goods. A new $4 billion city,

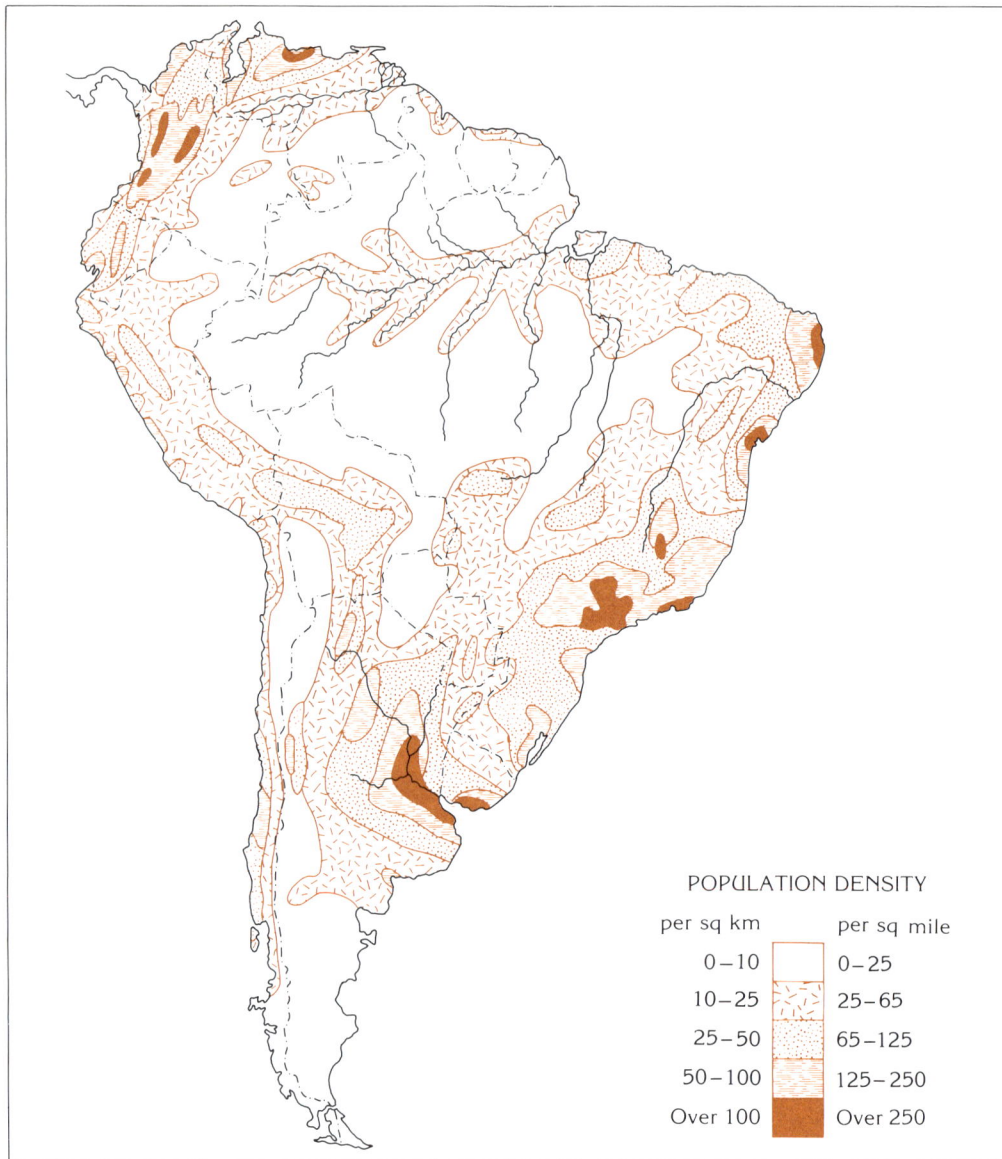

POPULATION DENSITY

per sq km		per sq mile
0–10		0–25
10–25		25–65
25–50		65–125
50–100		125–250
Over 100		Over 250

FIGURE 4—8
Population Density. South America's population distribution is only now beginning to move from a peripheral (Andes basins and valleys and seacoast) location pattern toward one reflecting the potential of the interior.

Ciudad Guyana, is being completed 300 miles southeast of Caracas to help spur development of the "empty South."

Among other developmental thrusts, Venezuela has set about developing the Llanos, as mentioned earlier. Cattle ranching is the major form of agriculture, but rice has been introduced in the delta area. The new mining and industrial areas of the Guiana Highlands form a local urban market for overproduction. Large areas are to be colonized in conjunction with a land reform program nationwide. Farmers are settled on new holdings in the interior at government expense. Long-term, low-interest loans and credits are extended to the colonists. Ultimately some 100 million acres (40 million hectares) are to be settled.

Following a history of political instability and military dictatorships (Venezuela has had twenty-six different constitutions), the country has entered an apparent period of democratic rule. Clearly, Venezuela's future is one of the brightest in the region and indeed the world.

Guyana, Suriname, and the French Guiana   The only mainland South American colonial territories remaining after the dissolution of the Spanish and Portuguese colonial empires in the region were in the Guianas—British, Dutch, and French. British Guiana became independent Guyana in 1966, Dutch Suriname was granted independence in 1975, and French Guiana became an overseas department of France in 1946, which means that it is administratively part of France and sends elected representatives to the French National Assembly and Senate the same as any part of France. Population densities are light; the total population of these three states (1.6 million) is less than that of metropolitan Atlanta. In addition to their non-Iberian colonial status and culture, the Guianas stand out from the rest of South America in their ethnic makeup, which is related in turn to their former colonial economies.

In several economic and cultural senses, the Guianas have more in common with the Caribbean islands than with the rest of mainland South America. They were viewed by their colonial masters as extensions of Caribbean "sugar island" economies, if with much larger territories. Britain, the Netherlands, and France each at one time controlled the territory of all three present units. Holland was confirmed in its Guiana claims by Britain in exchange for the British takeover of New Netherlands (New York) and was probably pleased with the trade-off of a not-particularly-profitable colony in North America for a potentially great sugar plantation. As the three Guianas were but sparsely inhabited by primitive Amerindian groups, all three colonial nations imported labor for sugar (export) and rice (subsistence) production. East Indians are the majority in Guyana, the largest single group (37 percent) in Suriname, and are a minority in French Guiana. Africans, likewise imported for plantation labor, form the next largest ethnic groups in Guyana, but are a tiny minority in Suriname, where Javanese supplemented East Indians. French Guiana has a "creole" society of mixed Europeans, Africans, and Asians, with a tiny minority of Amerindians. Sugar remains an important crop and export of Guyana and French Guiana but a minor export of Suriname. Suriname's bauxite deposits rank among the richest in the world; the country mines, processes, and exports both bauxite and alumina, and also manufactures aluminum using hydroelectric energy. Guyana also mines bauxite for export and plans a huge hydroelectric project to produce higher-valued aluminum for export. Forest products industries could be expanded significantly.

Despite these mineral resources, the three countries remain largely undeveloped. Population is confined to a narrow coastal strip of land, much of it diked and reclaimed from the sea. The interior in each case is sparsely settled by Indians or descendents of runaway slaves who live in primitive conditions as hunters and gatherers. Vast mineral and hydroelectric potential in the interior highlands remain almost totally untapped, though Guyana is

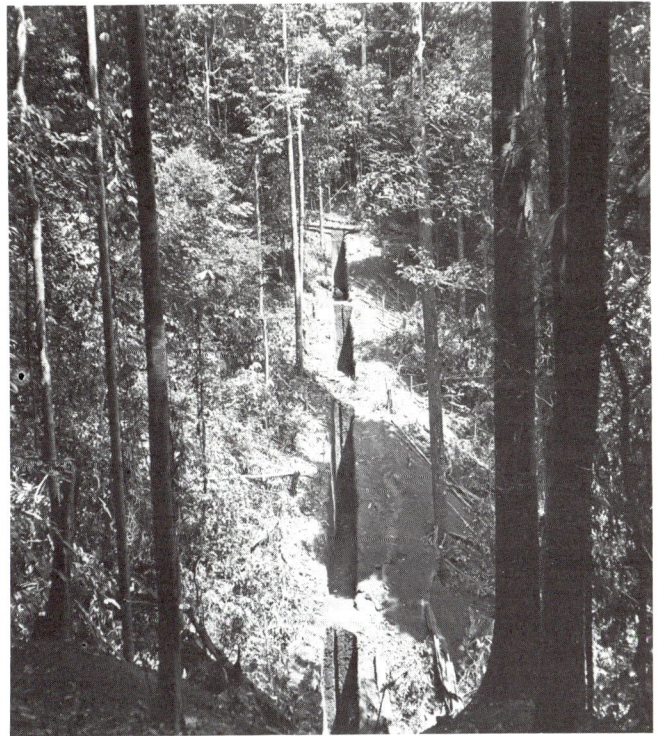

Geologic Prospecting in the Rainforests of Guyana. Vast areas of the continental interior are covered by thick forests and remain virtually uninhabited. Many of the soils found in such areas are virtually useless for agriculture, but mineral resources offer a potential for development. Under the aegis of the United Nations Development Program, large parts of Guyana were surveyed by air, and certain more promising individual areas were prospected with drilling and geochemical soil survey. Full development of South American countries will require the integration of these interior regions with the already settled wastelands. (Courtesy of United Nations)

attempting planned settlement and both Guyana and Suriname are involved in major hydroelectric development schemes in the interior.

THE INDIAN CULTURE BELT—ECUADOR, PERU, BOLIVIA, AND PARAGUAY

Of the four great Amerindian civilizations that developed in the New World prior to the European occupation, two (the Chibcha and Inca) were developed in the Andes of South America. The Inca Empire, by far the most important of the two, stretched 2,000 miles (3,000 kilometers) from present-day Ecuador through Peru and Bolivia to central Chile and northwestern Argentina (see Figure 4–9). At the time of the European conquest, the population of all of South America is estimated to have been about 4 million. Three million were believed to be in the Peruvian-Bolivian highland core of the Inca Empire. The

FIGURE 4–9
Ancient Empires and Culture Regions. Prior to European exploration and conquest, South America had one of the New World's most advanced cultures along with vast lands very lightly settled by groups that remained among the world's most primitive until this century.

Incas had developed elaborate terracing and irrigation systems, knew the uses of fertilizer, and had domesticated llamas, alpacas, ducks, guinea pigs, and dogs. These peoples had also domesticated potatoes and corn, their principle gifts to the rest of the world. Their largest domesticated animal, the llama, could not carry a person (its maximum load is about 80 pounds [36 kilograms]) and they had no animal-drawn plow but used digging sticks instead. Despite these seeming handicaps, they supported a dense population (for the time), and had achieved a sophisticated division of labor into specialized classes of priests, administrators, and warriors. A system of footpaths, sometimes miscalled *highways*, interlinked the empire. Apparently they knew about the wheel but made no practical use of it; the extent of the empire is even more remarkable considering that food production and transport and communication depended so heavily on human power.

The conqueror Pizarro arrived with fortuitous timing, just after an internal power struggle, and subdued this huge empire over a period of a decade. The stunning output of gold and silver from the Andes made Peru the most valued Spanish colony in South America and Lima the most spendid colonial capital. Spanish colonial policy was directed as safe-guarding this magnificent prize and the routeways to it. Spanish Peru's trade flowed eastward and south to the Atlantic via tributaries of the Paraná system, through Asunción and Buenos Aires, or went by ship to Panama, then across the peninsula to an Atlantic port (see Figure 4–10).

Thus, during both the preconquest and colonial periods, the "Indian" subregion was the center of wealth and population for the entire continent and contained its most progressive cultures. Now, ironically, it is the once less advanced and less productive sectors of the continent that have advanced, or have shown stronger signs of advancing, into more prosperous (and more democratic) societies. The "southern tier," Chile-Argentina-Uruguay, long known as the most industrialized, most prosperous part of the region, is being challenged by mineral-rich Venezuela, booming Brazil, and high-potential Colombia. Economically and culturally, the Peruvian-Bolivan highlands are now a relatively poor backwater of rather limited prospects. (See Table 4–4.)

FIGURE 4–10
Colonial Trade Routes. Much of Spain's colonial efforts were directed toward developing and safeguarding the trade routes from their mineral-rich colonies back to Spain.

TABLE 4–4
"Indian" South America—selected comparative data

	Percentage of Population American Indian	Percentage of Population Urban	Birthrate (per thousand per year)	Percentage of Labor Force in Agriculture	Per Capita GNP (dollars)
Westernizing "Indian" Culture Subregion					
Bolivia	55	—	44	—	510
Ecuador	40	43	42	—	910
Paraguay	45	40	34	—	850
Peru	46	63	39	43	740
Relatively Well-Developed Southern Tier					
Argentina	7	72	25	—	1,910
Chile	5	80	22	—	1,410
Uruguay	(negligible)	—	20	8	2,090
Caribbean Littoral					
Columbia	1	65	29	—	1,010
French Guiana	—	—	—	—	—
Guyana	3	40	28	—	550
Suriname	2	—	30	—	2,110
Venezuela	20	75	36	—	3,130
Brazil	—	62	32	32	1,570

Ecuador   Ecuador, on the northern fringes of Inca culture and control, has three distinct physical-cultural geographic zones, which the Ecuadorans call *costa, sierra,* and *oriente.* The sierra, the Ecuadoran portion of the Andes system, contains the capital, Quito, but the costa has surpassed the sierra as the country's most populous and productive zone in both agriculture and mineral wealth.

Ecuador has the relatively low per capita GNP characteristic of the Indian culture subregion despite a varied resource base featuring oil, copper, iron ore, and minor deposits of lead and coal. Important oil fields, though not in the same league as those of Venezuela, are found both on the Pacific coast and in Oriente province, Ecuador's slice of western Amazonia. A pipeline transports oil from Oriente to the coast; total reserves are estimated at over a billion barrels.

Ecuador, more impoverished than Paraguay, has the highest annual growth rate in South America, 3.1 percent. Although residents of the sierra have shown a willingness to move to the richly productive farmland of the costa, migration to Oriente province has been too little to fully develop that area's potential for food and export crop production. Jívaro Indians, still pursuing a hunting and gathering existence, successfully repulsed organized colonization efforts in the sixteenth century, and their reputation apparently is still a discouraging factor. The crowded sierra basins, populated mostly by Indians and mestizos of frac-

tional European ancestry, are likely to continue to send migrants to the black-, Indian-, and mestizo-inhabited coasts rather than the frontier lands of the Oriente.

The costa's lowlands around the Gulf of Guayaquil support a quarter of the nation's population and produce the world's largest export crop of bananas along with large crops of rice and cocoa. The intermountain basins of the sierra produce complementary "mid-latitude" crops in response to the cooling effect of higher altitude as well as some tropical crops in protected, deep valleys. Corn, wheat, potatoes, and pasture are the predominant land uses of the sierra. Agriculture tends to be commercial in the costa, subsistence in the crowded sierra basins, and virtually nonexistent in the oriente. Guayaquil, Ecuador's largest city and leading port, is about 50 percent larger than Quito.

Ecuador lost a large portion of its oriente to Peru's aggression in 1941. A war again broke out in 1981 as Ecuador's long resentment over this issue surfaced.

Peru   Home of the original Inca culture and exceptionally wealthy in minerals (both variety and abundance), Peru is economically the most promising of the states of the Indian-culture subregion. It is by far the largest and most populous state as well. A series of moderately large oil fields is located along Peru's coastal plain, though it had become a net importer of oil by the early 1970's. However, the probability of more major strikes is quite high and a large new field began production in the Amazon Basin in 1976. A trans-Andes pipeline has now been completed, and exploratory drilling is taking place offshore.

A large deposit of high-grade iron ore, fortunately not far from sea transport, is used for both export and a growing domestic steel industry, at Chimbote near some sizeable coal deposits. Peru also has important reserves of copper, lead, gold, and zinc to round out its mineral base.

The cold Peru current, sweeping close inshore and transporting mineral nutrients to support the base of the oceanic food chain, sustains one of the largest, most prolific fisheries in the world. Long before commercial fishing arose, however, the fish indirectly contributed another major resource—guano, the shore zone's accumulated layers of bird manure deposited by the seabirds feeding offshore. The very dry climate, with almost no rain, allows deep layers of bird guano to develop. This rich source of nitrate, easily acquired, was important in the munitions industries of the world before nitrogen-fixation from the atmosphere was developed. The guano is still very desirable as fertilizer, and a government monopoly regulates production. Thus, the fisheries contribute both directly and indirectly to Peru's economy. During the 1970's, however, the fish catch plummeted when the current changed direction temporarily, and overfishing further contributed to decline. The milling of anchovy fishmeal was banned entirely to permit fish stocks to rebound.

As in Ecuador, the areas of cooler climate at high altitude formed the historical core under the Incas. Peruvians, however, were quicker to develop their Pacific low-lands than were the Ecuadorans, even though they are arid. The very narrow coastal plain of Peru, south of Chiclayo (see Figure 4–4) contains a series of long, narrow valleys reaching back into the Andes at right angles to the coastline. This pattern leads to a series of irrigation-based ribbons of cultivation and settlement, separated by either steep mountains or patches of a narrow desert coastal plain. A series of "miniature Egypts" produce cotton, sugar, rice, and basic foods in these coastal oases. The water is so heavily used that little actually flows into the Pacific.

Approximately in the center of Peru's narrow coastal plain is the capital, Lima, founded by the Spanish in 1535. With its nearby port city of Callao, the metropolitan area contains 4 million people, about one fifth of the total population. Lima is important as an import-distributing center and a manufacturer of consumer goods along with its administrative functions. It is a major South American air transport node.

Peru's mountain valleys and basins support an important grazing economy and grow temperate zone crops, mainly corn and potatoes. While mestizo settlement and commercial agriculture dominate along the coast, purely Indian culture and subsistence farming dominate in the mountains. The only significant industry, outside the textile and leather works at Cuzco, is mining, which centers around Cerro de Pasco—a mineral district in production for hundreds of years.

Where Peru's Amazonian interior was long empty, the government has publicized if not implemented a concerted effort to colonize and integrate it with the rest of

A Copper Mine Near Arequipa in Peru. Mineral resources are the bulwark of the Peruvian economy. The export of ores supplies much of the capital necessary for internal development on other economic fronts. (Courtesy of United Nations/J. Frank)

Peru. Recent oil strikes have done much to hasten the process. Not only the trans-Andean pipeline but also several major power lines from new hydroelectric plants are carrying energy and power to the mountains and the coast. Diversion of water from the Amazonian headwaters has added to the meager supply of the coastal streams, allowing an increase in irrigated acreage. A railway to the coast parallels the pipeline. The Andes have posed some challenging engineering problems. Iquitos, the regional capital, is an inland ocean port; Brazil has declared the Amazon an international river, allowing unrestricted Peruvian trade.

Agricultural settlement has begun to inch down the easternmost range of the Andes from the mountain basins above. The government is stimulating the development of coffee on the intermediate slopes and tropical crops on the lower slopes. Progress is slow but steady as the frontier advances. Several roads have been built across the Andes to facilitate the movement of crops to the more developed areas of Peru, but the routes are long and hazardous. The most ambitious project yet conceived is that of the Marginal Forest Highway projected along the eastern slope of the Andes the length of Peru. Only about 20 percent of the route has been completed in difficult terrain. Supposedly it would link the Amazonian areas of Ecuador and Bolivia with Peru while also serving as a route for colonization and the transport of developmental materials into the area as well as its surplus production out to world markets.

These ambitious schemes could, if fulfilled, enable Peru to house, feed, and employ its rapidly expanding population while adding diversity to its mineral-dominated economy and export trade. Ultimately, Peru could become a surplus producer of food, manufactured goods, and energy, as well as metallic minerals, *if* these plans and projects are completed. Progress, however, is slow, and such giant investments have severely taxed the Peruvian economy. The rate of growth has had to slow down while many investments have been temporarily abandoned until the economy is returned to stability, debts are paid, and the trade deficit is lowered.

Yet the potential for development is great. The paved, 1,500-mile-long (2,400-kilometer) Pan American Highway already provides a north-south link through virtually all the coastal oases and a connection to Chile, Bolivia, and Ecuador. Rail and highway links connect this artery and the country's more important ports to the highland basins. A north-south highway interconnects the most important mountain basins, while several links extend across the remaining range to the navigable tributaries of the Amazon in La Montaña. Only the Marginal Forest Highway is needed to form a relatively complete transportation network integrating three diverse physical zones.

Time (and market trends) are on the side of Peru, and as stability returns, projects will be completed. Of the four states in the subregion, it is most likely to advance and develop.

Bolivia Although Bolivia is a large country in area (equivalent to France, Spain and Portugal combined), its 5.5 million people (roughly comparable in size to metropolitan Philadelphia) are concentrated in the high plateau called the Altiplano (see Figure 4–8). Relatively dense ribbons of population follow irrigated valleys or occupy small, somewhat lower basins with almost empty space between them on the arid plateaus and among rugged mountains. The area around Lake Titicaca has long been occupied by dense populations taking advantage of the deep lake's moderating effects on temperatures (wheat and corn ripen here despite elevations up to 12,800 feet (3,900 meters). An ancient civilization centered here was conquered by the Incas moving out from their Peruvian core.

Present-day Bolivia was a prized part of the Spanish South American Empire, second only in importance to Peru as silver flowed out of the Potosí district. Copper was known to the ancient civilization here as it occurred (as it only rarely does) in "native" or pure metallic form. Potosí, on virtually a mountain of rich ore, including silver, tin, and tungsten, continues as a major mining center despite the unusually high costs of processing and transporting ore in Bolivia.

Bolivia has lost territory to several of its neighbors within the span of a century. In the War of the Pacific, 1879–83, Chile took Bolivia's only ocean port and its nitrate (guano) deposits (see Figure 4–3). In 1932–35, Paraguay pushed its territory deeper into the Gran Chaco district at Bolivia's expense. During the rubber boom, Bolivia lost Amazonian territory to Brazil. In each case, Bolivians had made little attempt to settle these relatively remote, lowland territories. Remaining Bolivian territory east of the Andes contains few people and, it would seem, attracts little attention from the Bolivians, except for some promising discoveries of oil, iron ore, and manganese in the lowlands near the common borders of Bolivia, Paraguay, and Brazil. While oil is not produced in great quantity, natural gas is more abundant and is important in fueling developing industries (mainly metals processing, cement, and consumer goods). Bolivia currently imports food it probably could produce itself, partly because Bolivia's population and producing centers are so isolated from one another and because only 3 percent of the land is suitable to agriculture.

Landlocked Bolivia has rail connections to Arica and Antofogasta, two Pacific ports in Chile, and Argentina has made Rosario a "free port" to lure more Bolivian trade. A railroad links Santa Cruz with the Brazilian system. Sucre is the judicial seat while La Paz functions as the administrative capital. About two thirds of Bolivians speak either of two Indian languages (Quechua or Aymará), the highest such proportion of non-Spanish speakers in the region.

Government instability and social unrest have plagued Bolivia. Overdependence on mining has resulted in economic fluctuations as world market demands for tin, tungsten, and silver move up and down. Much of the Altiplano is barren, arid salt flats, or inhospitable tundra, not developable for agriculture and forming an economic wasteland between its core and the Pacific coast. Much of Bolivia's eastern area has low developmental potential. Equatorial forests cover exceptionally poor soils in the northeast while much of the northern interior lowland is a clay plain that is inundated with water for half the year. The Chaco country is almost a semi-desert for nine months of the year and a lake for the other three in a zone of fluctuating climate and highly developed subsoil hardpans. In between is Santa Cruz, the only area with promise and the target for colonization from older established agricultural areas. Cotton and sugar farms are being developed here in a small, but relatively fertile and reliably watered area. Connected by rail and highway to the Brazilian coast, a road now reaches westward to the Altiplano—a parallel link planned for the near future would effectively complete a **reorientation** of Bolivia's economy away from the Pacific and the mineral areas and toward the Atlantic and new agricultural frontiers. Steel and petrochemical plants are planned (or under construction) in Santa Cruz. Gas, limestone, and salt deposits round out the raw material base for a varied chemical industry that, it is hoped, will change Bolivia into a modern manufacturing economy. A joint Argentinian-Bolivian railroad now connects Santa Cruz to the Argentinian rail network as Brazil and Argentina vie for Bolivia's trade. Sugar cane, rice, and cotton production are rising rapidly as agricultural development expands in the Santa Cruz district.

With poor connections by unpaved roads to Peru and Paraguay, with a vacilating Chile not quite restoring the promised corridor to the Pacific, Bolivia is attempting to reorient itself away from the world of the Andes and tradition. Curiously, the prosperity of the colonial era too was associated with the road to the east rather than the routes to the west.

Paraguay Paraguay's 3.5 million people (less than Santiago, the capital of Chile) occupy a country with little known mineral wealth but ample agricultural potential. Nearly the entire population is classified as mestizo, but this may have more to do with social aspirations than European genes; Indian heritage, if not lifestyle, is clearly

dominant. The population is the smallest of any Spanish-speaking South American country, a fact related to both long-continuing transport difficulties and to one of the most disastrous wars ever fought when considered in the light of the proportionate loss of people. In 1865, Paraguay began a war designed to provide it with an ocean port. Brazil, Uruguay, and Argentina joined in alliance against Paraguay and fought for five years until an exhausted Paraguay surrendered. Paraguay lost nearly half of its original population of 525,000 people, finishing the war with only 22,000 males. Paraguay's second adventure in territorial expansion was more successful, the Gran Chaco War with Bolivia in 1932–35. With extensive water engineering works, the Gran Chaco could become a prosperous agricultural district. However, at present, none of the four nations controlling portions of it (Paraguay, Bolivia, Brazil, Argentina) have effectively settled their Chaco lands and brought them within their respective national economies.

Landlocked Paraguay's access to the world is complicated by the fact that its rail connections to Argentina cross the maze of shifting channels of the Paraná River via ferries rather than bridges. The costs for shipment to the port of Buenos Aires are quite high. Bridges elsewhere encourage traffic to flow eastward through Brazil rather than southeastward through Argentina. Forest products and tobacco join meat and live cattle as major exports. Citrus, cotton, and other crops could be greatly expanded as transport efficiency to potential markets increases.

Hydroelectric development, including a huge, joint project with Brazil at the Iquassú Falls on the Paraná River, dramatically decreased the need for oil imports. Surplus power is exported to Brazil and Argentina, earning foreign exchange. New hydroelectric projects with both Brazil and Argentina are in the planning stage. Small oil finds in the Chaco produce a limited supply; prospecting continues as a major thrust of government developmental programs.

Industry remains in an embryonic stage—a few textile mills and cement plants besides the saw mills and meat-packing plants built for the first-stage processing of traditional exports. Close to 30 percent of the population is illiterate. Most roads are unpaved and the rivers are only seasonably navigable. Paraguay is the ultimate backwater country of South America south of the equator. In a region where remarkable economic strides are being made on all sides, Paraguay remains virtually stagnant.

CHILE, ARGENTINA, AND URUGUAY

These three countries are often treated as a unit, less because of their similarities and more because of their collective differences from the rest of South America. All three economies have been tied more firmly to western Europe (or, lately, Japan) rather more than to the United States. While many Chileans have some Indian blood and some Indian cultures still exist in Chile and Argentina, these three countries have the most completely European populace and the most totally European culture of all Latin American countries. All three have undergone economic readjustments during the last two decades. Industrialization took place early in all three, though it has not been characterized by even growth, either regionally or over time. The farm economies of all three have moved toward greater intensiveness and diversity, away from wheat and cattle for the export market and toward industrial crops and the needs of the domestic market. All but Uruguay have vast, undeveloped frontier areas. All have a reasonably high standard of living, but they no longer lead the continent. Change, adaption, and the search for a new economic niche are characteristic of all three. Energy costs and supplies have seriously disrupted traditional ties. These areas have great unrealized potential, and, with great strides taking place elsewhere in Latin America, the next few years may be crucial in determining whether they lead or are left behind in regional economic development.

Developing region countries closer to Europe, Japan, and the United States represent an **intervening opportunity** that acts to this subregion's detriment. **Time-place utility** is the key to understanding. Increasingly, Europe produces more of its own food and buys from the most competitive supplier, often the United States and Canada. Those countries' proximity and, therefore, lower transportation costs may be the only difference in price, but it is significant enough to have reoriented the grain trade. Meat is increasingly produced in Europe itself as a means of rationalizing high agricultural production costs for grain—meat brings more profit per acre than grain.

Radical changes in world markets have left these countries with outmoded specializations and difficulties of readjustment. Once the most distant and least desirable part of the Spanish Empire, they become the most prosperous of the successor states after independence. Once again, they could become economically dormant. To avoid this, governments have looked to diversification of agriculture, self-sufficiency in resources, industrialization, and the increasingly lucrative regional market.

Chile   Chile is an elongated political unit that spans 2,650 miles (4,260 kilometers), 57 degrees of latitude, and at least six climatic zones. A collection of basins, islands, peninsulas, and oases, it would appear, superficially, to be the least likely place to achieve national unity. Yet, Chilean nationalism is well developed, and a relatively dense network of roads, railways, and water and air routes have created a reasonably well-integrated unit. The Andes form a well-demarcated eastern boundary that grows more stable with time. Political stability is challenged *internally* rather more than *externally.*

The people of Chile are an amalgam of Spanish settlers with Araucanian Indians, augmented by latter colonization from Italy, Germany, and other parts of western Europe. The advanced Araucanian culture area was incorporated into the Inca Empire shortly before the Spanish arrival. Unlike Peru or Bolivia, the mixture of Spanish and Indian culture was complete and thorough; there is no large Indian group outside the commercial economy. Later migrants have assimilated to the Spanish language and Chilean nationality and culture relatively rapidly and completely.

The population is most heavily concentrated in the central zone of Mediterranean climate, the fertile and reasonably well-watered Valle de Chile, giving the country a single, central, well-outlined and prosperous **core area,** a significant factor in national unity. To the north, the desert zone is not well suited to irrigated agriculture, but is based on mining, fishing, industry, and some transit trade to and from landlocked Bolivia. South of the core is a zone of cooler, wetter, less-fertile land that has a reasonably high agricultural potential. Containing a coal and iron resource, suited to dairying, and rich in timber, it was a pioneer zone of advancing settlement frontier until the last decade. The fjorded southern coast is similar in climate and appearance to Norway. Agricultural potential exists in scattered valleys, on the leeward sides of islands and is, in all cases, relatively isolated from the core area. The exploitation of this territory's hydroelectric potential and rich timber resources is only beginning.

Further south, the cool and windswept grasslands are only lightly used for the grazing of sheep. Recently, oil resources in the area of the Strait of Magellan have created a new economic resource in the area. Like all other areas south of the Valle de Chile, it is oriented toward the domestic (rather than international) economy.

The northern deserts were once Chile's most important economic asset. Nitrates for explosives and gunpowder occurred here in large deposits, preserved by the area's aridity. Sought after by the European powers for military purposes, it resulted in rapid economic growth for the whole nation's economy. The development of synthetic nitrates depressed the economy for a while, but large deposits of salt, sulfur, and especially copper quickly revived the desert-area's economy. Copper now represents 30 to 50 percent of all export value in normal years. Small but expanding production of lead and zinc will soon make Chile self-sufficient in these minerals. A variety of alloys, large deposits of fertilizer raw materials, high-grade iron ore, coal deposits of moderate grade, and rich gas fields give Chile the most well-rounded mineral base in all of Latin America.

Industry is well developed in Chile. The country has one of South America's few *integrated* steel mills; it operates almost entirely on domestic resources. Cellulose, wood pulp, and paper industries are growing rapidly under the impetus of German, Italian, and Japanese, as well as domestic, capital investment. With 80 percent of the population living in urban areas, one of the highest urbanization rates in the world, Chile has developed a large range of consumer goods industries geared to both foreign and domestic markets.

Despite fifty years of attempted land reform, agriculture is still dominated by the large, often underproductive estates of the central valley that have survived since colonial times. In a climate similar to that of California, a wide variety of crops can be produced in that district. Despite government pressures, large areas are still devoted to grazing, dry farming of wheat, and other forms of **low-intensivity agriculture.** Gradual reforms and great increases in productivity were implemented in the 1960's. The election of a Marxist president in 1970 led to a military takeover; under conditions of internal chaos, the economy had faired poorly, though inflation now has abated somewhat.

Chile now imports food and carries a heavy yearly trade deficit. New investment projects have virtually ceased since 1970. The economy stagnates while the population continues to grow, albeit at a relatively low rate by South American standards. Chile, like Peru, is in a stage of economic pause. Relatively well developed already and possessed of a magnificent resource base, Chile's regional importance and income have suffered relative decline. Currently, a country that should be going places rapidly is going nowhere.

Argentina While suffering the same subregional syndrome of an economic slow-down, the situation in Argentina is somewhat brighter. Argentina encompasses over 1 million square miles of territory (3 million square kilometers) and, with 27 million people, it has the second largest population after Brazil. (Rapidly growing Colombia, however, may surpass it in rank.)

Argentina came to be the most prosperous state in all of South America by the close of the nineteenth century. Oil-rich Venezuela has now replaced Argentina as number one in per capita income in the region, but Argentina has no close contenders for the second rank spot as well as a much better distribution of income across the population. Rocked by the most intense inflation found virtually anywhere in the world, it has managed to survive and even to grow. Its high degree of self-sufficiency and its inherent natural riches are largely responsible for this apparent economic resiliency.

The greatest single resource of the country is its rich soil; almost one fifth of the country is included in the Pampas, an area of rich prairie and steppe lands of incredible fertility. The Pampas is in many ways similar to parts of Canada and the United States. It has a flat to gently

Meat-Packing Plant in Buenos Aires. In sharp contrast to many other portions of South America, the temperate South is a land of relative prosperity, strongly Europeanized culture, extensive agriculture, and food surplus. Late to develop, the extensive grasslands of the Pampas are a major contributor of world food supplies. (Courtesy of United Nations)

rolling terrain originally carpeted in thick, rich grass stretching as far as the eye can see. Occasional clumps or ribbonlike strips of trees line the relatively few permanent streams. It was settled rather late in the postcolonial era as fiercely hostile Indians successfully repulsed attempts at European-culture settlement long after European migrants had taken control of other portions of the continent. The Pampas was to become fabulously productive of both cattle and grain, but it was at first largely ignored by people of European culture.

In the finer details of physical geography, of course, the North American and South American mid-latitude grasslands are not mere mirror images of one another. The Pampas is considerably flatter than the Great Plains, which have much more local relief than nonresidents usually imagine. The rivers of the Great Plains have cut well below the average surface, while those of the Pampas have less pronounced valleys and often dead-end in salt flats after flowing sluggishly across the virtually flat surface. The similarities of the two continent's grasslands in appearance and even settlement history are amazing, if their similar human history is coincidental. Both areas were initially reconnoitered by Spanish explorers, who were similarly unimpressed. In both cases, the climatic transition is drier to the west, wetter to the east, and the agricultural products tend to flow eastward to centers for processing, distributing, and consumption. However, whereas the U.S. and Canadian Plains together have many east-west major transport routes and many medium-sized cities engaged in processing and marketing, the grasslands of Argentina and neighboring Uruguay have but one major focus each (see Figure 4–11).

In both great grasslands, the climate is seasonal, with wetter summers characterized by thunderstorms and cyclonic storms in spring and fall. The Great Plains, however, have far more severe winters, even in their southern portions, than do the Pampas. In each grassland, there is serious question as to how "natural" the grassland is, or how much they may have been enlarged through deliberate use of fire to eliminate trees and herd game for killing. The Plains and Pampas Indians used remarkably similar strategies to kill meat—buffalo in North America, guanaco, deer, and rheas (ostrichlike birds) in South America.

As noted in Chapter 2, the reassessment of the Great Plains came suddenly; there was rapid change in the Pampas, and it, too, was related to the same changes in the world economy and in agricultural and transport technology. It was only a little over a century ago that the military power of the Indians in both areas was finally crushed. The Pampas Indians were practically exterminated, as the Plains Indians were reduced in numbers and confined to reservations in generally undesirable lands. A frenzy of railroad building occurred in each area; British capital helped create a dense rail net on the Argentine Pampas, clearly

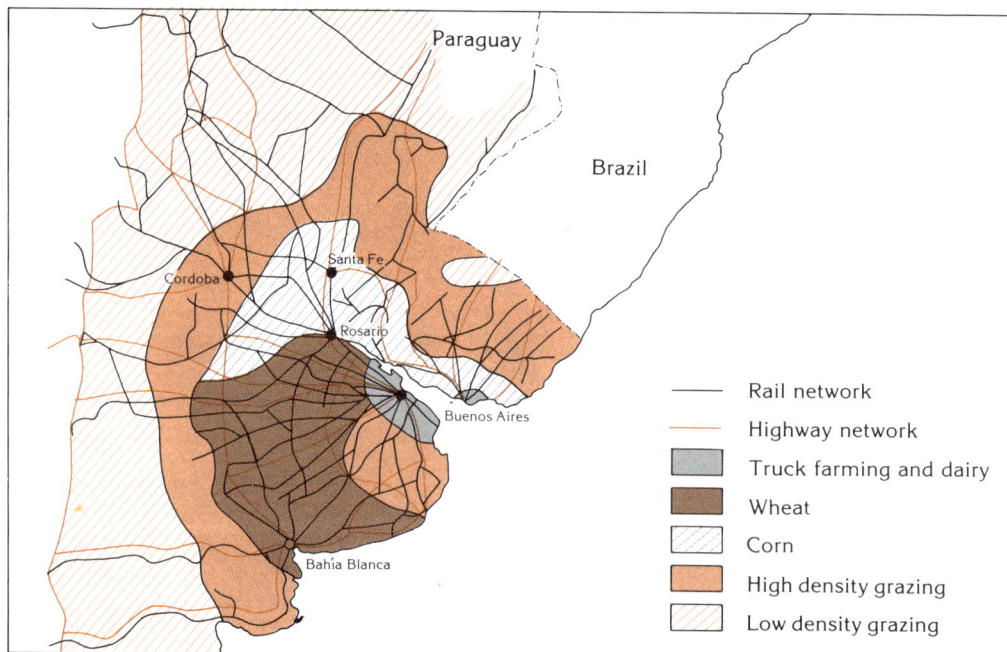

FIGURE 4–11

The Pampas: Land Use and Transport. In few other areas of the world was the engineering of railways so easy or their developmental impact so marked. The dense rail net evolved to serve (and create) one of the world's most productive agricultural regions.

focusing on Buenos Aires (see Figure 4–11), while fewer lines were built in Uruguay.

Foreign capital was attracted by a situation in which railroad construction costs were among the lowest ever achieved (virtually flat land with few streams), the potential for agricultural production was great, and the government had stabilized. As on the North American grasslands, the second half of the nineteenth century saw a technological revolution in farm machinery, transport, commercial canning, and refrigeration, which changed land use on the Pampa drastically. In the late nineteenth century, purebred cattle grazing cultivated alfalfa pastures replaced scrub cattle on uncultivated coarse native grasses. Commercial wheat farming then partially displaced cattle on the wetter fringes. Corn later displaced wheat in areas closer to Buenos Aires and in the wetter north and then experienced land-use competition from market-oriented fruit and vegetable production and dairying. The resulting pattern is roughly one of concentric circles of different land uses outward from Buenos Aires, resembling the theoretical land-use zones of decreasing intensity propounded by von Thünen, the classic scholar of land-use theory (see Figure 1–16).

An immense proportion of Argentina is usable for agriculture, some 40 percent is in pasture, and about 12 percent is in cropland. It is the fourth largest producer of cattle in the world and the single largest meat exporter. It is a major producer of wheat, barley, corn, flaxseed, soybeans, sunflower seed, wool, mutton, and pork. When the United States has embargoed grain sales to the Soviet Union, Argentina has filled the gap in grain trade.

In addition to its rich agricultural base, Argentina possesses a sizeable mineral resource, which is only now beginning to be exploited on a large scale. Small coal reserves in Patagonia are mined for the generation of electricity and use as a chemical raw material. The Andes foothills produce gold, silver, copper, iron, tin, and other minerals. While deposits are not large, they form a varied raw material base for the country's rapidly growing industry. Oil, long a crucial import, is now sufficient for the domestic market—largely from fields around Comodoro Rivadavia in Patagonia. A vast hydroelectric potential is being rapidly harnessed to serve industrial needs. Its forests yield quebracho for tanning leather—a product in which it dominates world markets.

As in Chile, about 80 percent of the population is urbanized, and almost one third of the population lives in metropolitan Buenos Aires—making it one of the world's largest cities. That city is Argentina's largest and most diverse manufacturing city, producing a full range of consumer goods and machinery in addition to processing agricultural production. Over one sixth of the labor force is employed in industry in this highly advanced economy.

North of the Pampas proper is a much wetter, though nonetheless fertile, area designated Entre Rios, the land between the rivers. Drainage has gradually been implemented to extend the area of cultivable land. Corn, and now rice, are the major grains. Rosario (1.1 million) and Sante Fe (275,000) are the large cities that dominate the area. Both are large industrial centers with chemical, automotive, and agricultural machinery industries, and Rosario has a sizeable steel industry.

North and northeast of the Pampas, the land is lightly settled and not used to its fullest advantage. This is the warmest part of Argentina. In the Chaco areas, forestry (the cutting of quebracho trees for use in making tannin as well as logging) vies with cattle grazing. The northeastern two provinces, neglected until recently, are now being settled by more recent migrants from Europe.

The Argentinian northwest is a land that is much drier. Topography is similar to that of the Basin and Range Country in the western United States. Originally settled by colonies of Europeans from Chile and Bolivia, it was long associated with those areas more than with Argentina. The extension of transportation links from Buenos Aires has effectively tied the scattered oasis and valley settlements to Buenos Aires instead.

In the northernmost portion of the district, near the Bolivian border, there are rich mineral-bearing districts in the Andes and the high plateau. Tucumán, the most densely populated rural district in Argentina, is a major sugar cane producing area. The city of Tucumán is a rapidly growing industrial center designated as a **growth pole** by Argentine planners in an effort to decentralize function and population from the single dominant center of Buenos Aires.

Córdoba, at the divide between the Pampas and the drier west, is a city of almost one million people. Like Tucumán, Córdoba is sheltered by mountains from the climatic severity associated with the Andes. It is a noted leather goods center, a producer of glass and ceramics, as well as a major automotive center.

The other major oasis is Mendoza, an area of semi-desert with winter rains and mild winter temperatures. The extension of irrigation has created vast orchards and vineyards in the countryside in a landscape of Mediterranean flavor. Most Argentine wines and olives and major amounts of the country's soft fruits (peaches, cherries, plums, and apricots) are produced here. Well tended and picturesque, the district is a favorite resort for both Argentine and Chilean tourists. The city of Mendoza is industrializing rapidly and the whole district constitutes one of Argentina's most rapid growth areas.

Patagonia remains the country's last frontier. This vast triangular portion of southern Argentina is a flat plateau dissected by deep river valleys at fairly evenly spaced intervals. Most of the area is desert or steppe; a natural grass cover is the dominant vegetation. Sheep herding is the principle economic function, and the cool climate produces a thick coat of first quality wool on purebred sheep. Valleys offer both shelter and water, enabling a more intensive agriculture of grains and fruit. Fewer than a million people inhabit the area, though its economic importance is much greater than the low population density implies. The government has targeted this area for rapid in-migration. Argentina's rapidly growing fishing industry is based here, and the country's most important coal, oil, and gas reserves are all located in Patagonia. Argentina has begun a program of basic investment in power-generating facilities, petrochemicals, aluminum-refining plants, and fertilizer works to use the area's power and mineral resources. Like Siberia in the USSR, however, distance and poor connections with the core area limit its potential. Export of the area's riches, rather than direct settlement and intensification of agriculture, has been chosen as the route to development.

The enormous diversity and agricultural riches of Argentina have placed that country in an enviable economic position. Yet, rampant inflation, labor troubles, and government instability have hampered progress. The gradual reorientation of production and markets, the very successful drive for self-sufficiency, and the extension of Argentine economic influence to much of southern South America are keeping the economy growing. Competition with Brazil is friendly and cooperation between the two states is increasing. The stability provided by the rich agriculture of Argentina is apparently sufficient to overcome any other potential destabilizing forces. Unlike Chile, there is growth, despite internal problems. Unlike Brazil, much of the capital investment in infrastructure is already completed. Generally considered far more staid and conservative than Brazilians, Argentines seem to have developed the same sort of taste for progress, grand schemes of development, and belief in a national destiny. Not only has the public accepted growth and change, they demand it in a nation that has clearly passed the stage of **take-off** and is well on its way to **economic maturity.**

Uruguay   Uruguay is physically an extension of the Pampas on the other side of the Plata estuary. Culturally, it is a transition area between Argentina and Brazil. Indeed, its very existence is the result of conflict between those two states that resulted in the creation of Uruguay as a buffer. Like Argentina, its population is largely European in origin. While its wealth is almost entirely based on agriculture, only 8 percent of the work force is directly employed in farming. Industry, like that of Argentina, consists of food processing and the production of consumer goods for the domestic market.

The economy of Uruguay is even more centralized in the capital city. Some 85 percent of the population is urban, and almost 60 percent (1.6 million) of the country's people live in metropolitan Montevideo.

Uruguay is South America's smallest country, about the size of the state of Washington. The country is a low-lying, gently rolling plain with a few low hills. Uruguay has an excellent supply of water and a temperate climate in which frost occurs only once every decade or so. The soil is exceptionally fertile and gave rise to a natural cover of rich, nutritious grasses. Stock raising is the most important occupation in a land with ten times as many stock animals as people. Sheep rearing is most important, though cattle raising is rapidly overtaking it.

Uruguay is prosperous, with a yearly per capita income comparable to that of Brazil and just slightly lower than that of Argentina. While virtually everyone speaks Spanish, fully a quarter of the population is of Italian descent and almost 40 percent of the total is of non-Spanish ethnic origin. It has a high rate of literacy, a large middle class, a fairly equitable distribution of wealth, and a reasonably high standard of living. Meat and other basic foods are so cheap that the per capita income of $2,090 is really deceptively low in terms of actual purchasing power.

With a 60 percent yearly inflation rate and a rapidly aging industrial plant in its food-processing sector, Uruguay has recently experienced intense economic problems. A costly program of public health care, pensions, guaranteed minimum income, and other social benefits has often been blamed for economic chaos. It is far less these programs per se, however, and more the question of an overlarge administrative bureaucracy. One worker out of every four is a government employee in the world's most cumbersome bureaucratic establishment!

The lack of investment in the food-processing industry, as government and private investors alike hastened to build new, diverse manufacturing establishments in imitation of Argentina, led to a recent cancellation of contracts for meat by Britain and other nations. Spoilage and high bacteria counts, as well as lowered inspection standards, led to this curtailment; all are indirect results of this aging, outmoded, poorly-maintained meat packing industry. Despite new plants producing cement, clothing, chemicals, plastics, and textiles for the domestic market, there is economic stagnation. The greatest single problem, however, is the cost of importing petroleum.

The antidote to the energy problem has been a series of hydroelectric dams built to create huge reservoirs in the relatively level terrain. In the area of domestic manufactures, high protective tariffs have been created, but plants are monitored for efficiency of production. Taxes are used as a weapon against those entrepreneurs who resist modernization. Much has been done to increase the efficiency of government. Even agriculture is beginning to benefit. Cropland is scheduled to increase to 15 percent of the total as opposed to the current 10 percent. Land reform is taking place as inefficient *estancias* (estates) are nationalized, subdivided, and resettled by farm families. Landlordism has almost disappeared, in part through mechanization of many of the estates. As more land is devoted to corn, pork production is increasing rapidly. Rice and soybean acreage has increased rapidly. Rice is now exported. Some 10 million fruit trees have been planted, and oranges and orange juice are a new and lucrative export.

With very few raw materials at hand and a small domestic market, Uruguay's industrialization has been severely handicapped. The forests, rare as they are, yield one million cubic meters of softwood yearly under a program of sustained-yield forestry. This is sufficient to supply a domestic paper industry and a part of building material needs. Imported petroleum is refined into products in turn used as chemical feedstocks. Both chemicals and refined petroleum products are important re-export items. Rolling mills for steel and aluminum place at least some processing of metals within the country, and most sheet steel used in manufacturing is supplied domestically. If parts are not produced locally, at least assembly takes place in Uruguay. The very successful wool and cotton textile industries, both using domestically produced raw materials, are major exporters.

Tourism is expanding rapidly. With its pristine beaches, lovely climate, and excellent hotels, Uruguay is attracting droves of tourists from Argentina and increasing numbers of vacationing Europeans. The huge inflation rate indirectly creates many bargains for international tourist-shoppers as retail trade booms.

A booming Brazil now sends both tourists and investments. Conscious of its dependence on fluctuating world markets for its commodities, Uruguay is trying to carve itself a niche in the area of intraregional trade in order to become a necessary part of the economic boom found in the countries on either side of it.

BRAZIL

Brazil has been divided into four subregional units: the colonial Interior, the Northeast, the Southeast, and the South. The Northeast section stretches from Belem at the mouth of the Amazon to the borders of the state of Espírito Santo. It is the longest settled part of Brazil and is characterized by fluctuating climate, relative overpopulation, and an obsolescent economic structure. The Southeast section is dynamic, growing, partially industrialized, and still in the final phases of settlement expansion. The Interior, whether rainforest or savanna, is a lightly peopled frontier district of apparent potential for development but with inherently great obstacles to rational development as well. The South, temperate Brazil, is overwhelmingly geared to grain and meat production for the domestic economy. Overall, it contains the most modern mechanized agriculture in Brazil, if it is still a pioneer area and still far less industrialized than the Southeast.

THE NORTHEAST

The story of the northeastern subregion is one of boom and bust. Beginning as a sugar plantation economy, slaves were imported from Africa to do the work. The proliferation of sugar cane plantations to other areas and the evo-

The Sertão of Brazil. As a part of the program to develop its poorer Northeast subregion, the Brazilian government is developing irrigated agriculture and improved pastures in this dramatically unstable part of the country. Periodic droughts, floods, and outbreaks of plant and animal diseases have added to the area's economic instability. Of all of South America's countries, Brazil has made the strongest commitment to the development of its interior. (Courtesy of United Nations)

lution of Britain, France, and others into colonial powers in the eighteenth century soon brought the Portuguese monopoly to an end. Various lesser booms in cacao, tobacco, and cotton followed, each bringing temporary prosperity and ultimately ending in decline. The succeeding booms were shorter lived, yet each brought a new wave of settlers. The better watered coastal areas continued in production, but expansions into the drier back country, the *sertão*, often never reached full potential before drought brought an untimely end to the boom. On its interior side, then, the border of settlement has fluctuated constantly.

As each crop lost its position in world markets, the production remaining went increasingly to serve the domestic market and the leftover, unserved corners of the world market. Production was and is exploitive, notoriously inefficient, and unable to compete with the higher quality, cheaper production of other areas. Out-migration has been quite heavy; the inhabitants of this subregion have come to be the colonizers of other frontiers and the source of unskilled labor for Brazil's cities.

Where irrigated, agriculture has stabilized. Modernization proceeds at a slow, steady rate, but this very process results in increasing unemployment. Land reform has been suggested as an alternative. The resulting small units, however, would either degenerate into subsistence farms or fail to compete against large-scale plantations. Even diversification of the agricultural economy presents problems; the very labor-intensive nature of traditional sugar culture would result in unemployment and lower farm income were it to be replaced by other crops.

In an effort to stem the economic decay of this area, the government has begun an intensive campaign to industrialize the cities and to **beneficiate** agriculture through irrigation, fertilization, and capital investment. Generally, light industry is emphasized with food processing, assembly, and textiles as the leading items produced. A depressed area for over one hundred years, it was long the most important section of Brazil. With a per capita income of one half that of the national average, economic redevelopment is its most pressing need. Several large projects have been undertaken to achieve some level of stability. The world's largest petrochemical complex has been built outside Salvador in Bahia state. A capital-intensive type of industry, however, it requires far fewer employees to operate it than it did to build it. The choice of the site was not based solely on economic need. Brazil's largest producing oil field is located in Bahia state and promising new fields have been discovered offshore of the northeastern states (see Figure 4–7). Other large investments include several large hydroelectric projects, major port improvements, some large-scale irrigation schemes, and two huge cement plants. It is planned to link the existing isolated links of the northeastern railroads (largely single lines from each coastal port to the edge of the sertão) to the rest of the system. The highway system of the Northeast has been pushed ahead rapidly and is almost completed. In this one aspect of transportation, the Northeast possesses perhaps the best developed road system in the country. It has been fully linked also to the road network of the Southeast; it has recently been linked to Brasília, and, through it, to the rapidly growing southern Interior. A third important link to the Interior will be completed shortly (see Figure 4–12).

Despite this program of intensive investment, the Northeast lags behind the rest of the country on almost all fronts. Birth- and death rates are the highest in Brazil, yet the edge of excess births is sufficiently high to sustain rapid population growth. The subregion contains three of Brazil's "million cities," yet they are not yet fully industrialized and much of the urban growth (in large measure a result of migration from the sertão or overcrowded rural backlands) cannot be absorbed into the labor market. Irrigation projects can locally ameliorate the effects of drought, but the bulk of the sertão is still not irrigated. Prolonged droughts would render irrigation useless as water sources became exhausted. New lands have been opened up to settlement in the interior of Maranhão, relieving land pressures to a minor extent. Still other farmers have begun to settle the lands bordering the highways to Brasília and Manaos. Tens of thousands have resettled in the industrial areas of São Paulo and Rio de Janeiro, now that transportation improvements have opened the road to the rest of Brazil. Yet notwithstanding all outlets and improvements, the developmental lag remains as the rest develops even more rapidly. The Northeast is no longer stagnant nor its situation hopeless, yet its problems are great. Offshore oil, should it prove to be a major field, however, could sharply reverse the subregion's fortunes.

THE SOUTHEAST

The Southeast (or East, as it is sometimes designated) subregion contains over 40 percent of Brazil's total population and its two largest cities, Rio de Janeiro and São Paulo. Of the 5 million industrial workers in Brazil, over half are employed in São Paulo, which contributes over 58 percent of all Brazil's industrial production by value. The states of Rio de Janeiro and Minas Gerais rank second and fourth in the nation, making the Southeast the dominant industrial district of the country. Despite its overall industrial nature, it is also the second most important agricultural district. It is the very heart of Brazil.

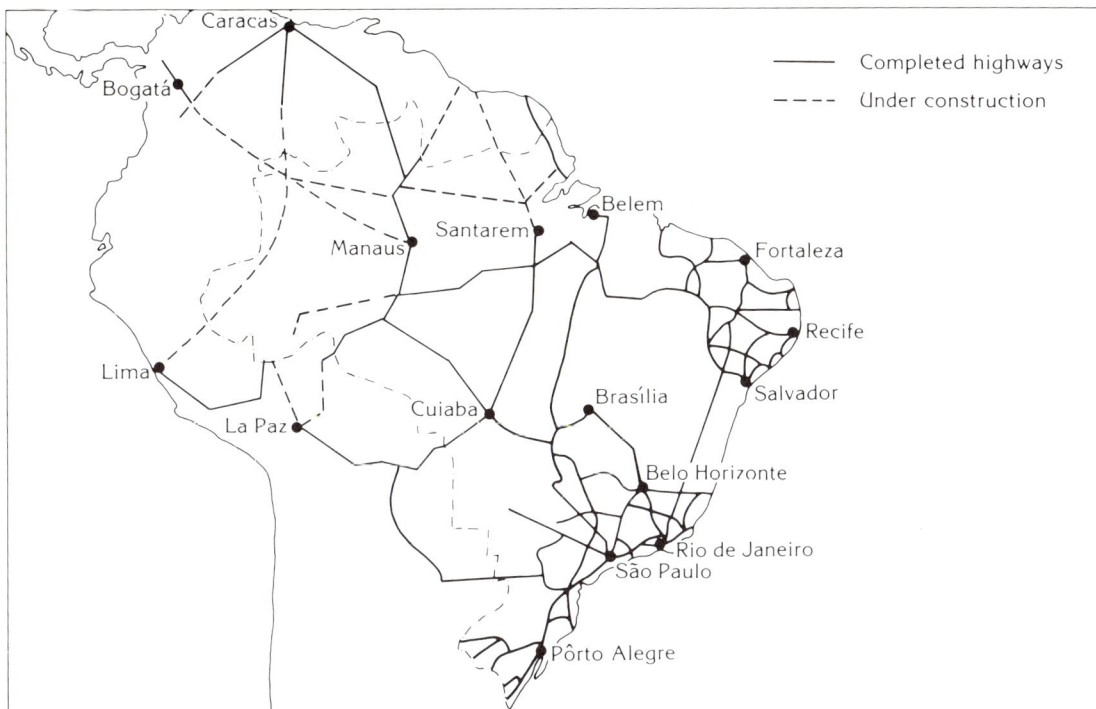

FIGURE 4—12
Brazil—Transport and Development. Brazil's long-term concentration of population and development in its coastal fringes, plus its recent drive to effectively incorporate the interior into the national economy, is reflected in its transport system.

Like most of eastern Brazil, it has a narrow coastal plain, which rarely exceeds 100 miles (160 kilometers) in width before it ends at the steep scarpland, the edge of the Brazilian plateau, and almost disappears just south of Rio de Janeiro. Under the relentless tropical rains, it has weathered in places into the famous sugar-loaf hills, which make the entrance to Rio's harbor such a spectacular sight. Yet the plateau country, rather more than the coastal plain, possesses the true agricultural riches of the subregion with its vast areas of thick, fertile soil developed on a base of old volcanic material.

Surprisingly, the Southeast was both late and slow to develop as trade, plantations, and colonial development first centered on the Northeast. The first Portugese settlers did not arrive until the sixteenth century. They were cattle herders who led a life similar to the familiar U.S. cowboys. Known as *bandeirantes* ("flag bearers"), they tended toward a much more active role in exploration, settlement, and development, however, than the average cowboy. They essentially roamed the land freely, seeking wealth and adventure. They discovered deposits of gold, gem stones, and metals, which were to become the beginnings of Brazil's massive mineral wealth. Their exploration and settlements also gave credence to Brazil's claim over half the continent. Their tales of riches and the fertility of the land attracted planters and migrants to the area; these

latter establishing a sufficiently dense population over the subregion to wrest the political capital and the economic momentum from the Northeast. Rio developed first as a port for the export of gold and diamonds; it ultimately became the capital until Brasília was founded in 1955.

The placer deposits of gold and diamonds were exhausted by the early nineteenth century, but the planters who had arrived in the subregion soon found another source of riches in coffee. The coffee boom dates from the 1830's. A plant native to Ethiopia, it was imported to Brazil via Haiti where the French had grown it as a monopoly crop. Two crucial things happened to unleash the coffee boom. Coffee houses became the social rage of Europe. At the same time, disease was attacking the French, British, and Dutch plantations in Asia. The stage was set for another Brazilian boom as world demand soared and world supply shrank. Coffee plantations, which took only five years to reach production after planting, raced up the Paraiba Valley inland from Rio de Janeiro and onto the plateau of São Paulo. The fertile terra roxa soils developed on the volcanic material produced rapid growth of trees and excellent grades of coffee. The huge fazendas (plantations) had large labor requirements for clearing, planting, and harvesting of coffee beans. The labor demand unleashed a great overseas migration that brought large numbers of Italians, Portugese, and even Spaniards to the new agricultural lands of Southeast Brazil. Coffee became the chief crop and chief source of income for Brazil, but the Southeast dominated production overwhelmingly from the start. Erosion and exploitive techniques ruined much land in the process, but the boom went on uninterrupted until the oversupply of the 1920's and the Depression of the 1930's gradually diminished the role of coffee in the Brazilian economy.

It was the depressed coffee market that gave rise to the industrial boom. A government faced with economic collapse was forced to erect tariff barriers against imports of manufactured goods, limit coffee production, create a source of domestically produced food, and create an infrastructure for the needs of industry where none existed. Short of fuel, Brazil turned to the development of hydroelectric power. The first basic industry was cement, needed to realize the planned governmental construction projects. Shortages of cloth, clothing, and shoes were met with small entrepreneurial investment in the first plants producing these commodities for the domestic market. Traditional exports were partially processed (e.g. wood into lumber) before they were allowed to leave the country. The first steps in industrialization were completed by 1940; World War II saw the second step. Brazil, a U.S. ally, was blockaded by German submarines. Consumer goods and foods, more than ever, had to be produced at home. Under these conditions, the U.S. government was pressed to give aid to Brazil in building a national steel industry (government owned). Using the incredibly rich ores of Minas Gerais and some local coal from southern Brazil as raw materials, a major steel works was developed at Volta Redonda, midway between São Paulo, Rio de Janeiro, and Belo Horizonte. These three cities anchor the major industrial district of Brazil to this day, and Volta Redonda at its center still produces most Brazilian steel. Brazil now shares eighteenth rank in world steel production with Canada.

The greatest drawback to Brazilian industrialization remains fuel, but the country is rich in metallic resources. Brazil produces about 125 million tons of high-grade iron ore yearly, mainly from the state of Minas Gerais ("general mines") near the town of Itabira. Reserves of recoverable iron ore are estimated at over 100 billion metric tons, a virtually ineshaustible supply. This state also contains large reserves of bauxite; copper, lead, zinc, silver, gold, and rare metals are found in minable quantities in the same area. Minas is an important source of industrial diamonds and high-grade quartz crystals as well. This vast mineral wealth provides a solid industrial base as well as a series of lucrative exports, which earn foreign currency.

Industrialization has proceeded rapidly in the Southeast, an area now proceeding beyond the takeoff stage to

The Paraiba-Pirai Hydroelectric Project. Brazil's enormous hydroelectric potential and varied mineral base are being developed rapidly, contributing to one of the most rapid economic growth rates found anywhere in the world. (Courtesy of United Nations)

full diversification. There are three important industrial states in all of Latin America: Argentina, Brazil, and Mexico. Basing its original development on supplying domestic needs, Brazil has now entered world and regional markets as an exporter of manufactured goods, most of which are produced in the Southeast. Despite its basic lack of petroleum resources, Brazil now refines over 2 percent of the world's petroleum products. One of its two large refining centers is in the Southeast. It is by far the largest producer of electricity on the continent. The latest project, the Iquassú Falls power complex on the Paraná River, will almost double Brazilian production upon completion, and most of the power will be shipped to the Southeast. Brazil's aluminum production is now in a league with that of western European countries. Its growing automotive industry produces about one half million units a year. Possessing South America's most important shipbuilding industry, the yards of Southeast Brazil produce 4 or 5 percent of the world's tonnage yearly—a truly remarkable accomplishment when it is considered that it out-produces France, West Germany, and even Great Britain.

As the Southeast was the first area to enter into industrial production for the domestic market on a significant scale, it is not surprising that the shoe, textile, and clothing industries are well represented there. Indeed, the subregion dominates the country even in these lines of production. The difference of late is the scale of production, the emphases on synthetic fibers and cloth, and the obvious export orientation. While factories in the Northeast are generally small establishments producing cotton cloth from locally grown cotton, the mills of São Paulo and Rio de Janeiro states produce synthetic cloth and fiber in large modern mills.

The latest industrial push in the Southeast has been in the production of appliances, electronics, and chemicals. Brazil now ranks ninth in the world in the production of television sets. Beginning with simple plants producing washing soda and bleaches, the chemical industry has developed the production of plastics, paints, solvents, detergents, fertilizers, and synthetic fibers. About 40 percent of the nation's chemical industry is located in the Southeast. The original home of the rubber tree, and once the center of a natural rubber boom, Brazil now produces almost 4 percent of the world's *synthetic* rubber. Huge cement works, dominantly in the Southeast, have increased production almost 800 percent in the last two decades. It is a net exporter of that commodity supplying much of the market for South America. As the home of some of the world's most innovative and spectacular architecture, the Southeast produces (and exports) plate glass, anodized aluminum sheeting, structural steel, and even prefabricated homes as well as construction equipment.

A measure of the upgrading of exports is illustrated by the traditional wood industry. Since 1970, plywood, pressed board, cellulose, pulp, cardboard, and newsprint have come to the fore in exports, while both timber and board exports are decreasing. Despite the fact that the forests of the Southeast have been largely cut over, the processing of timber into these secondary and tertiary products takes place largely in the Southeast; the South and, recently, the Amazon Basin are also major producers of wood products.

With a sustained average economic growth rate of about 10 percent per year for the last two decades, Brazil is progressing toward **economic maturity.** The Southeast accounts for most of this gain. Industry has spread to suburbs and outlying cities at an exceptionally rapid rate. Once simply driven by economic nationalism, the industrial complex is now self-sustaining and searches out new markets beyond national borders. Smog and congestion may obscure the horizon of booming São Paulo, but Brazilians see quite clearly where their economy is headed.

THE SOUTH

The Brazilian South is a land of cultural transition. The most thoroughly "European" area in terms of the origins of its settlers, the South opened late as an agricultural frontier. The South is in some ways analogous to the Middle West of the United States in an earlier era. A land of rich prairies, it has become Brazil's agricultural heartland. This subregion is still filling in its last frontiers of settlement, cutting its virgin forests, developing its mines at a rapid rate, and gradually moving away from the processing of agricultural raw materials, as its main industrial thrust is into more diversified and complex industries.

Unlike the American Middle West, it is peripheral rather than central, and it is not yet well served by transportation facilities. It is very much central, however, to the developed portions of Atlantic South America and very accessible indeed to the expanding export markets that Brazil has developing in Paraguay, Uruguay, and northern Argentina. The climate is really subtropical and frosts are rare except at higher elevations. While it is Brazil's chief supply area for grains and meat, it is only now beginning to export its surplus production abroad.

The three major European ethnic groups to enter the area were the Germans, Italians, and Slavs. Most came as colonizing pioneer farmers during the late nineteenth and early twentieth centuries under government-sponsored settlement programs.

The pastoral economy, while still represented by scattered elements throughout the subregion, is primarily confined to the southern and western portions of the state of Rio Grande do Sul, adjacent to the borders of (and similar economic endeavors in) Uruguay and Argentina. The wool and hides produced are used as the raw materials in considerable wool textile and shoe and leather goods industries, which have developed in that state.

Germans and Swiss produce a mixture of European and American crops (corn, dried beans, and the rye-potato-pig crop livestock combination so characteristic of much of Germany), which enter the home market. Farms are moderate-sized family affairs with a reasonably high degree of mechanization. The Italians have developed vineyards producing wines for the Brazilian market. In drier areas, even olive groves are found.

The richness of this hinterland has made the city of Porto Alegre (1.3 million) Brazil's sixth largest and one of its most important ports. Slaughter, meat packing, brewing, tanning, milling, and like industries are major employers here. There are nearby coal and lignite deposits that are now being mined, and a new steel industry has been built nearby. Similar to the Great Lakes cities, it has begun to develop the manufacture of farm and transportation equipment on a large scale, creating a local demand for steel.

Santa Catarina is a land in between the plains and hills of Rio Grande do Sul and the fertile plateau country of the state of Paraná. The broken, hilly nature of the landscape has resulted in rather small, scattered farms with limited prospects. Florianopolis, the capital and port, is isolated on an offshore island. Other than short local rail lines, communication is north-south. The area's farmers have turned to dairying and market gardening, producing specialty and high demand crops for the urban markets of the South and Southeast. Industry is not very well developed, consisting primarily of small textile mills and food processing plants. Industrial possibilities are great, however, since Santa Catarina has the largest reserves (and highest grade) of coal yet discovered in Brazil.

The state of Paraná is, surprisingly, a rapidly growing agricultural frontier at the same time that the Brazilian industrial revolution is encompassing the area, resulting in stupendous population growth. With over 10 million inhabitants, the population has come close to doubling almost every decade since 1940. As with the other two states in the subregion, Germans and Italians established colonies in the late nineteenth century. However, Slavic elements, Poles and Russians, formed a major colonizing force as well. Farming patterns are the same, but farms are often larger and occasionally more prosperous because of proximity to the urban markets of Rio de Janeiro and São Paulo. In the last forty years, rapid colonization of the western and northern frontier areas has taken place, as coffee farming has spilled over from neighboring São Paulo. Paraná state has now become the major coffee-producing area of Brazil; yields are great and the quality is high, though the risk of growing coffee has been demonstrated by severe frosts.

The South essentially represents the new Brazil—diverse, growing, industrially oriented, and working more toward the fulfillment of Brazilian needs. The area still contains rich forests, and the tapping of hydroelectric resources along its western edge promises new stimuli to industry. The South, as much as the Southeast, represents the new, developed, and powerful Brazil.

THE INTERIOR

The last of Brazil's frontiers, the Interior, really consists of two parts—the dominantly forested tropical lands of the north and the scrub-savanna lands of the south. The north encompasses 1.4 million square miles (3.6 million square kilometers), over 40 percent of Brazil's territory, and has a population of some 5 million people. Most of the development is confined to the delta of the Amazon and the coastal areas of Pará state. The south, larger than Mexico, contains several centers of development, including the capital, Brasília. With almost 9 million people, it is one of South America's most rapid areas of growth.

The north and the *selva* (tropical rainforest) are not coextensive. Many portions of the north are grassland or savanna, while the forest ranges from scrubby woodland to magnificent stands of timber. However, over most of the area, the dry season is either absent or of short duration, and a monotony of high temperatures and high humidity are the rule. After a brief rubber boom around the turn of the century, the north retrogressed into the economic background. Always isolated, the Amazon was its only route of transportation until the development of the Brazilian network of highways. This investment in roads has dramatically changed the orientation of the north, which is, for the first time, connected with the rest of the economy. A major and continuing problem, however, is the difficulty and expense of road maintenance.

As of yet, there is little apparent difference in its economy. While the isolation of old has been almost eliminated, the shortage of local labor (the other traditional handicap to development) remains. Rubber is still harvested, but attempts to create plantations have met with failure; disease and labor problems have hampered production. Medicinal herbs, nuts, roots, and fibers are still gathered to supplement the income of farmers on slash-and-burn, subsistence plots. Some plantations and specialty crops have succeeded. Japanese colonists have become successful pepper and spice producers in the state of Pará, and jute production is expanding in the wetlands bordering the Amazon. Mineral resources are slowly being uncovered. Large commercial deposits of manganese are being exploited in the territory of Amapá, and some oil has been found in the Amazon Valley. Gold and bauxite reserves are known to exist in the territory of Roraima. Manaus, turned into a free port, has succeeded in attracting some industry, and a large paper and pulp complex is being built along the Amazon with the aid of German capital. Nonetheless, progress is still slow and the north remains essentially undeveloped outside a few enclaves.

The southern portion of the Interior offers much more developmental promise. It now contains some 8 percent of Brazil's population and five discernable poles of growth. Major in-migration has occurred since 1950, and the area grows more rapidly by far than Brazil itself. The five growth poles are Brasília, the farmlands of southeastern Goias, the mining districts of both northern and southern Matto Grosso, and the wet rangelands of the upper Paraguay River, called the Pantanal.

The improved transportaiton network that was necessitated by Brasília's creation and the large market of the capital itself has reversed the fortunes of the area, elimi-

Brazília. After some initial growing pains, Brazília is effectively carrying out the functions for which it was intended—a market center and developmental pole for the ultimate settlement of Brazil's interior as well as the seat of the government. (Courtesy of United Nations/ J. Frank)

nating isolation as a detriment, and creating a lucrative local market. The city has grown more rapidly than expected, as thousands of migrants from the Northeast and the sertão throng to its environs. The official, planned city contains only half the population as temporary barracks for construction workers, hastily constructed slums, and self-built farmsteads house the rest of the federal district's population.

The farmlands of southeastern Goias state are a continuation of the Brazilian highlands with a climate modified by altitude. Coffee production is of increasing importance, but wheat for the capital market is also a major crop. Market gardening has been developed by squatters, while cattle rearing spreads over the savannas of the southern half of the province. Goiana, the state capital, has grown to a population of 600,000 while two other centers of over 100,000 people have developed as district centers. The capital generates industrial demands that are best met by the nearby districts; therefore, food processing, clothing, and printing plants have already sprung up in what promises to become a new light-industrial base. The railroad has been extended to Brasília and will ultimately reach Belém at the mouth of the Amazon. New highways already reach each of the country's major districts. This intensification of the transportation network will undoubtedly enhance the possibilities for further development. Even mineral wealth is developing as tin and titanium mines have been opened in the district.

Growth in Matto Grosso is also proceeding apace. Traditionally, it was the land of the *mamelucos,* mixedbreeds of largely Indian culture, who herded cattle in the mosquito-ridden marshes of the Pantanal and the tickridden scrublands of eastern Matto Grosso. Diamond and gold rushes attracted only temporary settlement, and the state was more like the north than Goias in terms of development.

Matto Grosso, however, presented a very real potential for development. Much of the area is plateau and mesa country 2,000 to 3,000 feet (600 to 900 meters) above sea level. Summers are hot but never unbearable. Winters are delightfully cool but frost free, and nights are quite comfortable for nine months of the year. Rain is seasonal, but the totals are quite high and prolonged drought is almost unknown.

The higher areas of the southeast are gradually coming under the plow, as the agricultural frontier spills over from the neighboring states of Paraná and São Paulo. Large deposits of manganese, iron ore, and nickel are known and mined, while diamond deposits continue to be exploited. An asbestos mine has recently been opened in the southeast. Cattle still remain the chief product, however. Little industry has developed as yet, but the "Bolivian connection" has already created a market for Brazilian goods. As in Goiana and Paraná, the expansion of the agricultural frontier is quite likely to spawn the almost simultaneous growth of urban industrial centers. The Interior, at long last, is moving toward development. This movement is very slow, though, as Brazil's orientation is still coastal.

SUMMARY

The traditional solidarity of the Western Hemisphere, once the keystone of American foreign policy, was really far more a feature of the nineteenth rather than the twentieth century. Rising differences in the degree of development and standard of living between the United States and other New World states slowly introduced a note of discord. By the turn of the century, North America was viewed as less of a friend and protector and more of an exploiter by many South American states. It seemed, even to those states who had little direct economic interaction with the United States, that the United States had grown closer to Europe and farther from its old allies. Despite a variety of programs and policy changes, U.S. relationships with South American governments have been cool, if not overtly unfriendly, for much of this century.

World War II, the perceived Soviet threat after the Cuban affair, and a waning domestic resource base have all spurred U.S. efforts to improve relationships with South American countries. Aid has helped improve the U.S. image. Still there is the fear of intervention by the United States in domestic affairs. Gradually, there appears to be a renewal of the recognition of a commonality of interests on both sides. Perhaps the greatest reason for its occurrence, however, is not aid, but a renewed self-confidence on the part of South American states. As growth and development occur, there is seemingly a marked willingness to engage in trade, joint projects, discussion, exchanges of personnel, and joint solution of problems. As with siblings, a certain amount of stature and independence is necessarily attained before harmony and trust replace disputes.

TENSIONAL RELATIONSHIPS WITH OTHER REGIONS

South American states have had considerable tension over borders with one another. Tensions with other regions, except North America, were remarkably few after the end of colonialism despite disputes arising out of unpaid debts to European powers and their nationals. Nonetheless, the relations between South American and European states have not been hostile overall.

There are disputes, however, Argentina claims the Falkland Islands, a British colony. Both Argentina and Chile lay claim to a portion of Antarctica that is also claimed by the British. Until recently, several states most notably Ecuador and Peru, impounded European vessels (as well as U.S. and Japanese vessels) for violating territorial waters.

Relationships with the Soviets are less than cordial. Some South American states have outlawed domestic Communist parties, and few welcome Soviet trade or visitations.

THE REGION'S WORLD VIEW

By virtue of the dominance of Euro-American markets, the relationships of South America with the rest of the world, other than Japan, are distant, not because of animosity, but rather a lack of interaction. Venezuela, through OPEC, has enlarged its Middle East contacts. Most of the others have less favorable relationships because of the rapidly rising prices for imported oil. For the time being, it appears that South America is beginning to improve its continental relationships, to expand its export markets wherever possible, and to renew its relationships with North America on what it sees as more equitable terms.

Paramount among the ambitions of many South American states is the development of their internal economies. Those that have attained a measure of development appear ready to embark on the road to higher goals. Brazil, in particular, aspires to a position of equality with the world's superpowers. The next few decades will reveal whether that superpower status will be achieved. The potential is obvious, and the momentum of development has thrust Brazil forward. Currently, it would appear that Brazil is one of the few candidates that could make it to that goal.

case study
ECOLOGICAL PROBLEMS IN THE AMAZON BASIN

The Amazon Basin, an area nearly as large as the contiguous forty-eight U.S. states, is one of the largest single ecosystems on earth. It contains the largest tropical rainforest in the world—2.7 million square miles (7 million square kilometers) (intermixed with some savanna lands). The Amazon is a super-river with the world's greatest volume of flow; 1,000 miles (1,600 kilometers) upstream at Manaus, a *tributary* of the Amazon (the Rio Negro) is 4 miles (6.4 kilometers) wide and 200 feet (60 meters) deep. (By comparison, the Mississippi River at Vicksburg, 200 miles (320 kilometers) from the sea, is "only" a third of a mile (one-half kilometer) wide, about 70 feet (20 meters) deep, and carries about one thirtieth the water volume.) The Amazon is so huge that its first European explorers, the Portuguese, called it the O Rio Mar, the "river sea." It has comparably great ecological significance to both the basin and to the fisheries of the Atlantic (at least as far away as the Grand Banks off Newfoundland), due to its nutrient-laden flow into the ocean. This flow colors the Atlantic 20 miles (32 kilometers) outward from the mouth of the Amazon, and ocean currents carry some nutrients into the Caribbean, supporting an abundance of life. This transfer of nutrients continues up the East Coast of North America into the Gulf Stream.

A thousand tributaries feed the Amazon in its flood-plain portion alone; the main stream is navigable for 2,300 miles (3,700 kilometers) by ocean-going vessels. The Brazilians have designated the Amazon an international waterway, and it is becoming a major artery of commerce.

An ill-considered, now abandoned proposal to dam the main stream of the Amazon would have had adverse effects on the rich fisheries supported partly by its discharge of nutrients into the Atlantic. The impending destruction of the rainforest of the basin may have other indirect effects on the rest of the world, but the adverse effects on Brazil could be catastrophic. Data collected by orbiting satellites document the destruction of rainforest at some 60,000 square miles (155,000 square kilometers) a year in the late 1970's. Unfortunately, removal of the forest is likely to mean *permanent* elimination of the forest and rapid impoverishment of soils. At current rates of forest destruction, the basin's rainforest will have disappeared entirely in less than a quarter of a century. This would be an ecological, biological, and economic tragedy of major proportions if it happens (such "straight-line" projections rarely come true).

In the words of a noted anthropologist specializing in the region, the Amazon rainforest is a "counterfeit paradise."[1] It is counterfeit in the sense of having a deceptive appearance that causes people to misjudge its value or potential. In midlatitude lands, a lush forest growth normally is an indicator of fertile soil that can be converted to good-quality agricultural land. In tropical rainforests, however, the fertility is more in the forest itself than in the soil. The very high levels of metabolism of everything in the tropics—bacteria, fungi, termites, ants, and other animals—means that the daily rain of debris to the floor of the forest in the forms of dead vegetation or dead insect or animal life is quickly decomposed. There is such a rapid degeneration of decaying matter that little remains once the forest is removed. Additionally, the soluble minerals near the surface have long ago been carried away (or deeper) by the plentiful water, so that only large trees with deep roots can recycle these minerals up to the surface. An estimated 2 percent of the basin has soil rich enough to support agriculture once the forest is cut.

The Amazon forest, two thirds still intact, supports over one hundred thousand species of plants and animals; the rainforest is a giant "nursery" of species, many of which originated there and then emigrated elsewhere, adapting to different environments as they evolved away from their tropical "home." Destruction of the forest will likely result in extermination of much of this genetic diversity. Many of these plants and animals have unknown or unappreciated traits that could be used to develop new varieties of familiar food sources or entirely new ones.

The timber reserves of the Amazon would meet all the world's timber demands for twenty years at present rates of consumption. Amazingly, much of the tree cutting going on in Amazonia is simply to clear land for other uses—the wood is burned to get rid of it, not harvested as timber. An estimated billion dollars worth of wood is burned every year to clear land, mostly for cattle grazing.

[1] Betty Meggers, *Amazonia: Man and Culture in a Counterfeit Paradise* (Chicago: Aldine Atherton, 1971).

But, while people could do without beef, they cannot do without food. It might make more sense to investigate carefully the food potentials of the rainforest's myriad forms of life than to eliminate the forest for possibly short-lived pasture or cultivated land use.

Clearly, interrupting the continuous recycling of nutrients within a mature rainforest on inherently infertile soil can be a very poor idea. Many times, people have misjudged the rainforest's soil potentials. One of Brazil's oldest **green rush** frontiers, for example, was Bragantina, an area the size of Belgium. Opened up to farming at the turn of the century as a model of tropical development, Bragantina's soil was so exhausted by the 1940's that its settlers were resettled near the Bolivian border. Their experience there was the same as at Bragantina, except that the soil "wore out" even faster.

The highly varied plant life of the rainforest tends to be scattered rather than concentrated in one place. The rapid spread of plant disease, fungi, and insect predators may be a factor in this dispersed pattern. Attempts at artificially concentrating a species in plantations have generally not succeeded. Brazilnut trees, when grown in groves to make harvesting easier, did not produce nuts. It was thus discovered that insects that pollinate them make their base in a different species of tree. A more famous example is the "Fordlandia" rubber plantation failure. In 1927, the Ford Motor Company purchased some 2.5 million acres (1 million hectares) of land along a tributary of the Amazon. A modern town was built, and high standards of housing, free medical care, and high wages were used to lure labor into an area unpopular with most Brazilians. Plant diseases wiped out many trees. The hilly site experienced severe soil erosion as the original forest cover was removed and replaced by rubber tree saplings. Iron compounds in the soil, exposed to pounding rains and strong sunlight, oxidized and caked into a bricklike surface that radiated heat up to the young rubber trees, weakening their resistance to disease and insects. Part of Fordlandia was exchanged for a nearly level site on which machinery could be used more effectively, but even here production was not high enough to justify the huge investment; Ford abandoned its plantations after World War II, returning them to the Brazilian government. Here again, "lackadata" proved a crippling handicap; too little research had been carried out before thousands of acres of rainforest were destroyed to no permanent gain.

Brazil's Trans-Amazon Highway (see Figure 4–12), for which 8 million acres were cleared, has opened up the interior to exploitation on a grand scale. The mistakes of the past may now be repeated on a still larger scale, as the technological means of destroying forest are more efficient now. The developing countries in general, not just Brazil, may be destroying their future resource base for short-term gain. Multinational corporations may be the major benefactors for this exploitation, and the developing countries may bear the permanent scars in their ecology and economy.

It need not be. The developed world has proven, repeatedly, that forests can be managed as a "flow resource," continuing to produce trees under scientific management following careful study of the trees and their ecology. Ironically, while the developed world has helped instigate widespread destruction of tropical forests through its advanced technology (bulldozers, draglines, transport systems) and its rich markets, it may also provide the means of dramatically documenting the damage (satellite photography) and developing long-term management techniques, hybrid trees, and new species that minimize destruction and even reverse the degradation apparent now.

REVIEW QUESTIONS

1 How did the motivations and cultural attitudes of many Iberian explorers and settlers affect settlement patterns?

2 What are the evidences of challenges to the Spanish-Portuguese "condominium" in South America by other European powers?

3 Describe the functions of topography and drainage in relation to transport that helped shape the colonial and contemporary political boundaries of South America.

4 What are the major cultural unifying factors within South American states?

5 What is the significance of *indigenisimo* in South American cultures?

6 What are the push-pull mechanisms that propel South America's generally high urban in-migration rates?

7 How does vertical zonation contribute to agricultural diversification?

8 In what senses do the states of the Caribbean littoral fit a Middle American pattern more than a South American one?

9 Compare Colombia and Venezuela in terms of their natural resource bases, economic development levels, and economic prospects.

10 Briefly describe the relative economic development and prosperity status of each subregion.

11 What are the problems of economic development of their eastern Amazonian lowlands faced by Ecuador and Peru?

12 How has Brazil acted to capture more international trade from many of its Amazonian basin neighbors?

13 Contrast the economic development problems and potentials of Chile's northern and southern "pioneer" areas.

14 In what ways can the Pampas be compared with the North American Great Plains in natural environment, settlement, and economic development?

15 What historical-geographical factors contributed to Brazil's pattern of population distribution?

16 What economic development strategies is Brazil applying to the Northeast?

17 Why was the creation of Brazilia termed a *bold gamble?* Did it pay off?

18 What are the environmental risks associated with the exploitation of the selva in Brazil?

19 Briefly describe the modern challenges and tensions of "hemispheric solidarity."

20 What is meant by the *green rush?* Why has the implied prosperity frequently failed to materialize?

SUGGESTED READINGS

1 J. P. COLE, *Latin America: An Economic and Social Geography.* Washington, D.C.: Butterworth, 1975.

2 A. GILBERT, *Latin American Development: A Geographical Perspective.* Baltimore: Penguin, 1974.

3 PRESTON JAMES, *Latin America,* 4th ed. New York: Odyssey Press, 1969.

4 JOHN SAUNDERS, *Modern Brazil.* Gainesville: University of Florida Press, 1971.

5 RUDOLFO STAVENHAGEN, ed., *Agrarian Problems and Peasant Movements in Latin America.* Garden City, Anchor Books, 1970.

6 RICHARD THOMAN and RICHARD CONKLING, *Geography of International Trade.* Englewood Cliffs, N.J.: Prentice Hall, 1967.

7 CHARLES WAGLEY, ed., *Man in the Amazon.* Gainesville: University of Florida Press, 1974.

8 KEMPTON WEBB, *Geography of Latin America.* Englewood Cliffs, N.J.: Prentice Hall, 1972.

9 ERIC WOLF and EDWARD HANSEN, *The Human Condition in Latin America.* New York: Oxford University Press, 1972.

KEY TERMS

- superpower
- infrastructure
- European Economic Community (Common Market)
- Industrial Revolution
- maritime orientation
- continentality
- expatriate worker
- decentralization
- Sun Belt tourism
- complementarity
- demographic transition
- shatter zone
- rationalization of holdings

- location strategy
- cyclical industry
- overdeveloped economy
- developmental strategy
- plant obsolescence
- new town
- green belt
- rump state
- corridor function
- high-value-added
- machine tool
- use-pressure
- finite resource
- geothermal energy

5

WEST EUROPE

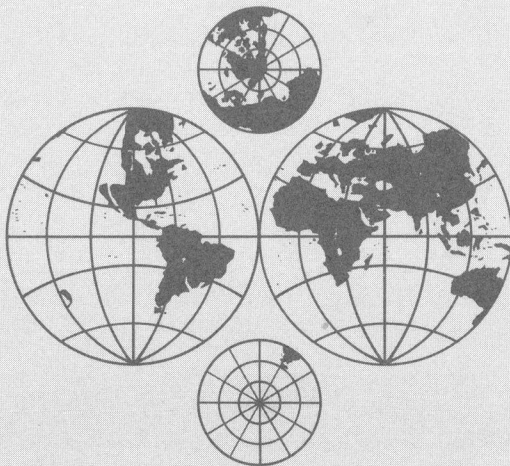

PROLOGUE: A PAST OF IMPERIAL GRANDEUR, A PRESENT OF DEMOCRATIC PROSPERITY

A map of colonial empires in 1914 (Figure L) shows the zenith of West Europe's political domination over large parts of the world. Great Britain controlled one fourth of the earth's surface; its navy ruled the world's oceans, aided by control of narrow seas connecting the oceans. France ruled an empire scattered from the Caribbean to Southeast Asia. Even the "newcomer" colonial powers, Germany and Belgium, controlled African territories much larger than their home states; the fading empires of Spain and Portugal were still present.

Colonial empires tell only part of the story; West Europe also led the world in industrial technologies and productivity. By almost any measure, one or another West European state was then first in the world's production of steel, coal, ships, or any other industrial commodity. True, the United States, Japan, and Russia were all expanding industrial states not to be underestimated, but economic and political geographers looking at the world in mid-1914 could hardly have been expected to foresee the destructive, nearly suicidal effect of two world wars on Europe.

Within the memory of a single generation, this political domination has almost disappeared. Colonial territories directly administered by the home country have disappeared, except for minute remnants. Seemingly, economic leadership and industrial power have been eclipsed too. It is not surprising that many non-Europeans view individual West European states as second-class powers, shadows of their former glory. They each seem almost pygmies in comparison to **superpowers** like the United States and the Soviet Union. Each has been surpassed in the customary rankings of industrial productivity by the super-states or Japan. The end of World War II saw an exhausted, largely ruined continent of Europe a pawn in the new struggle for world leadership between the United States and the Soviet Union. Just as the "obvious" geographic interpretations of Europe in 1914 would have been a long-term continuation of economic leadership and political domination, the reasonable projection of Europe's potential in 1945 would have been predominantly negative. Much of Europe's industrial and transportation **infrastructure** was wrecked, including whole cities like Rotterdam and Hamburg. Much of West Europe's accumulated wealth and overseas investment had been liquidated to finance wars. The enfeebled colonial powers clearly could not long hold their colonies as independence movements gathered momentum. *Is* West Europe a collection of "has-beens" overshadowed by the new giants?

Former Colonial Offices, London. The former colonial powers of West Europe have had varying success in readjusting their economies and their views of the world to the loss of empires. (Photo by Stansfield)

Perceptions of West Europe change significantly, and almost reverse, if the region is viewed as an integrated unit. The **European Economic Community,** the proper name for the Common Market, is the world's largest single market for imports. (It is abbreviated either as EEC, or more commonly in Europe, the EC.) As a unit, the EC outproduces the Soviet Union and ranks second only to the United States in overall economic-industrial power. With 272 million people, its population exceeds that of the United States or the USSR and is more than twice that of Japan. It is the world's second largest manufacturer of steel and cars. Clearly, as a unit, the European Community has superpower status. But is it more than a statistical unit; is it a real, functioning unit?

The answer is complex. The EC, whose full members are the United Kingdom, West Germany, France, Belgium, Netherlands, Luxembourg, Italy, Eire, Greece, and Denmark, is *not* a federal state like the United States, Canada, or Brazil. Although some of the *forms* of federalism exist, like the Assembly or European Parliament, they function more as consultative bodies than legislative ones (see Figure 5–1).

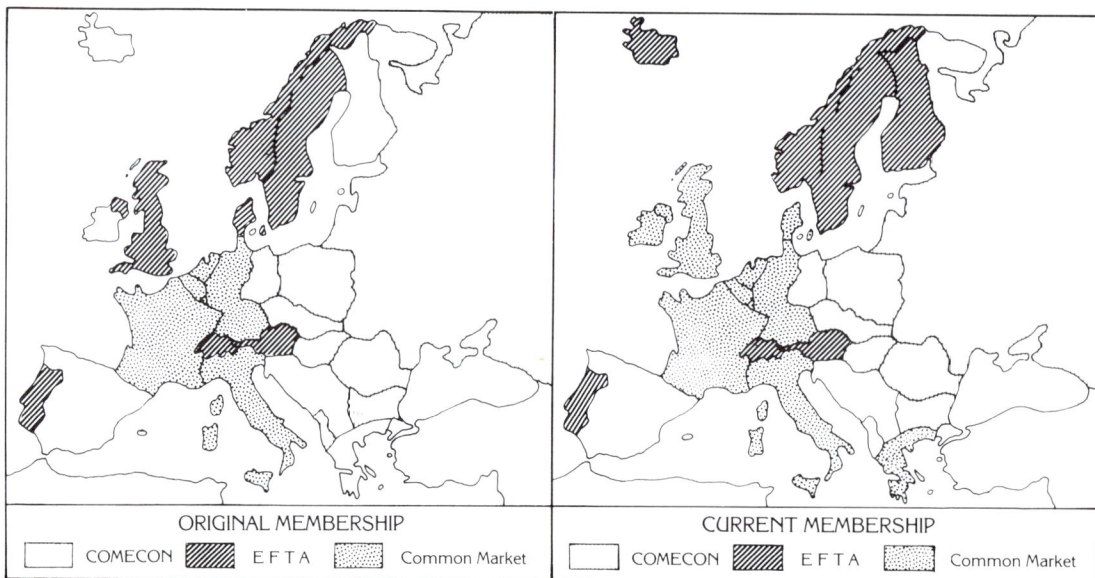

ORIGINAL MEMBERSHIP	CURRENT MEMBERSHIP
COMECON E F T A Common Market	COMECON E F T A Common Market

FIGURE 5–1

European Economic Community. With the United States and Soviet Union as examples of the advantages of large economic units within which goods, labor, energy, raw materials, and capital flow unhindered by tariffs, some of the states of Europe voluntarily limited their sovereign powers to create an economic union that has been successful.

The two superpowers have demonstrated the economic power, vitality, and versatility of huge units. These great states grew with an unfettered flow of raw materials, finished goods, capital, labor, and energy. All could be freely interchanged unhampered by tariff barriers or other political border restrictions. An economic union, to be followed eventually by some degree of political union, looked like a solution to the very serious recovery problems of Europe after World War II. Prosperity through cooperative effort, eliminating the economic effects of national borders, could also help build stability and reduce old nationalist rivalries and traditional enmities.

The United States, facing deteriorating relations with its wartime ally, the Soviet Union, sought to rebuild the industrial democracies of West Europe as quickly as possible. A strong, stable, and prosperous West Europe would reduce the threat of domestic Communist parties in the West and would counterbalance the threat of Soviet invasion. It was this happy blend of self-interest and charitable desire to help Europe recover that led to the Marshall Plan of 1947. Europeans were to allot the aid and organize recovery. This challenge was met by the Organization for European Economic Cooperation (OEEC), a forerunner of the Common Market and the European Community. The EC's political integration has been disappointingly slow for many advocates of a true "United States of Europe." There is no doubt, however, of the success of economic unification.

THE DISTINCTIVENESS OF WEST EUROPE AS A REGION

In purely physical terms, Europe is not a separate continental landmass, but rather a western, peninsulalike extension of the great landmass of Eurasia. West, or non-Communist, Europe is the personification of these peninsulalike qualities with a complex intermeshing of land and sea. (See Figure 5–2).

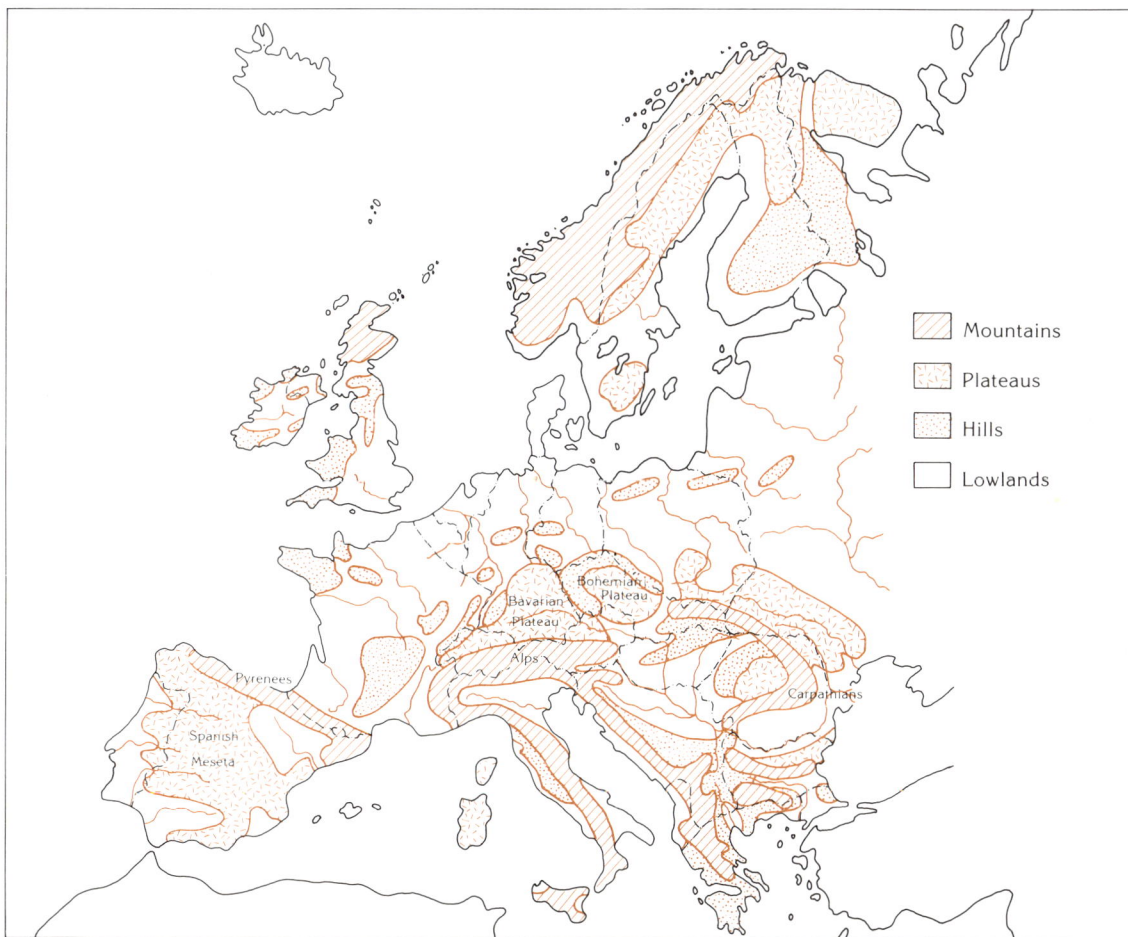

FIGURE 5–2
Generalized Landforms and Drainage. Europe, in physiography not a continent but rather the westward peninsulas and islands off the great Eurasian landmass, is characterized by a complex intermingling of land and water. Seas penetrate far inland in the Mediterranean and Baltic with great significance to climate and to transport accessibility.

The **Industrial Revolution,** that complex association of significant and rapid changes in economic, political, social, and technological developments, was born here; West Europe felt its profound effects first. This great revolution in the way people used raw materials, energy, transportation, and technology to improve the average quality of life is one of the great unifying factors for this region. Not all the states of West Europe have made the same level of progress through the industrialization-modernization process, but all have been affected by it.

The human and economic interchange over the centuries, the common historical and cultural currents to which all parts were subjected, and the complementarity of resulting development create a region by any standards. The long-standing existence of most of its member states and their general **maritime orientation,** coupled with its success as a center of innovation and leadership, have created a stability on one hand and a climate of change on the other. Little more is needed to justify Europe as a region. Yet the diversity of its components and the uncertainties of politics now have resulted in two Europes. The realities of survival have fostered the internal integration of each half. The disparities in development, far from clear cut, are less meaningful than politics in dividing Europe in two. West Europe now is associated with a set of ideas and principles that is quite different from those of East Europe. Time encourages further differentiation of the two. Yet, the two were always different, much as siblings who share the same parents do embark on different lifestyles and careers. The longer they are apart, the more clearly defined the regional differences become.

West Europe has again emerged as a potent economic force. Still dependent on imports for raw materials and food, it has developed a positive net balance of trade. Prosperity of an unprecedented level has been reached, with some countries, notably Sweden and Switzerland, exceeding the per capita income level of the United States.

HISTORICAL AND CULTURAL CHARACTERISTICS

In West Europe, Germanic and Romance (Latin-based) languages prevail, providing another unifying factor. Erse (Irish Celtic) is the official language of Eire (although most Irish speak English), and this is the major exception to the Germanic-Romance domination. Smaller groups of Celtic languages users are found in Scotland, Wales, and Brittany. Basque, an ancient language, is spoken by a minority population in both Spain and France. A Finno-Ugric language is spoken in Finland, though many Finns also speak Swedish, another Germanic language. (See Figure 5–3.) Two western European languages, English and French, have become "world languages," languages widely used throughout the world due to colonial influence, scientific writing, and trade.

West Europe, along with East Europe, has shared the cultural heritage of Greece and Rome, blended with important contributions from Teutonic and Saracenic cultures. Roughly half of West Europe was at one time part of the Roman Empire, and almost every part of this region was influenced to some degree by Roman trade and culture.

Christianity, in its Roman Catholic and Protestant forms, is almost the universal religion, at least nominally, of West Europe. Judaism remains the most important minority religion despite the tragic holocaust and large-scale migrations to Palestine-Israel. Relatively small minorities of Moslems are found in Britain, France, and the Netherlands; like Britain's small Hindu minority, these people are primarily products of recent immigration from former colonies.

West Europe shares a strong maritime orientation. Excepting a few small landlocked states, West European states have developed ports of international rank. (Although Iceland lacks a truly major port, it is clearly a maritime state.) Most have aspired to naval power and are heavily involved in ocean fishing; many are both major shipbuilders and operators of extensive merchant fleets.

One of West Europe's salient characteristics is its continuing aspirations toward world leadership, not only economically and politically, but in cultural affairs. European art, ancient through contemporary, still carries prestige. Rome remains the administrative center of Roman Catholicism with over 500 million adherents worldwide. Canterbury remains an important, guiding (though not controlling) influence on worldwide Anglican church communities. The World Council of Churches and the International Red Cross have central headquarters in Switzerland. The World Court is based at The Hague, the Netherlands. Switzerland performs many international conference functions, and the capital cities of West Europe have served as the scenes of countless international peace conferences.

ECONOMIC CHARACTERISTICS

Even in economics, there is some degree of unity. West Europe is characterized by a range of modifications of capitalism, by heavy investments in transport technology and systems, and by an unusually high ratio of international trade in its individual economies. Although all of West Europe has state-owned railroads, state-owned or

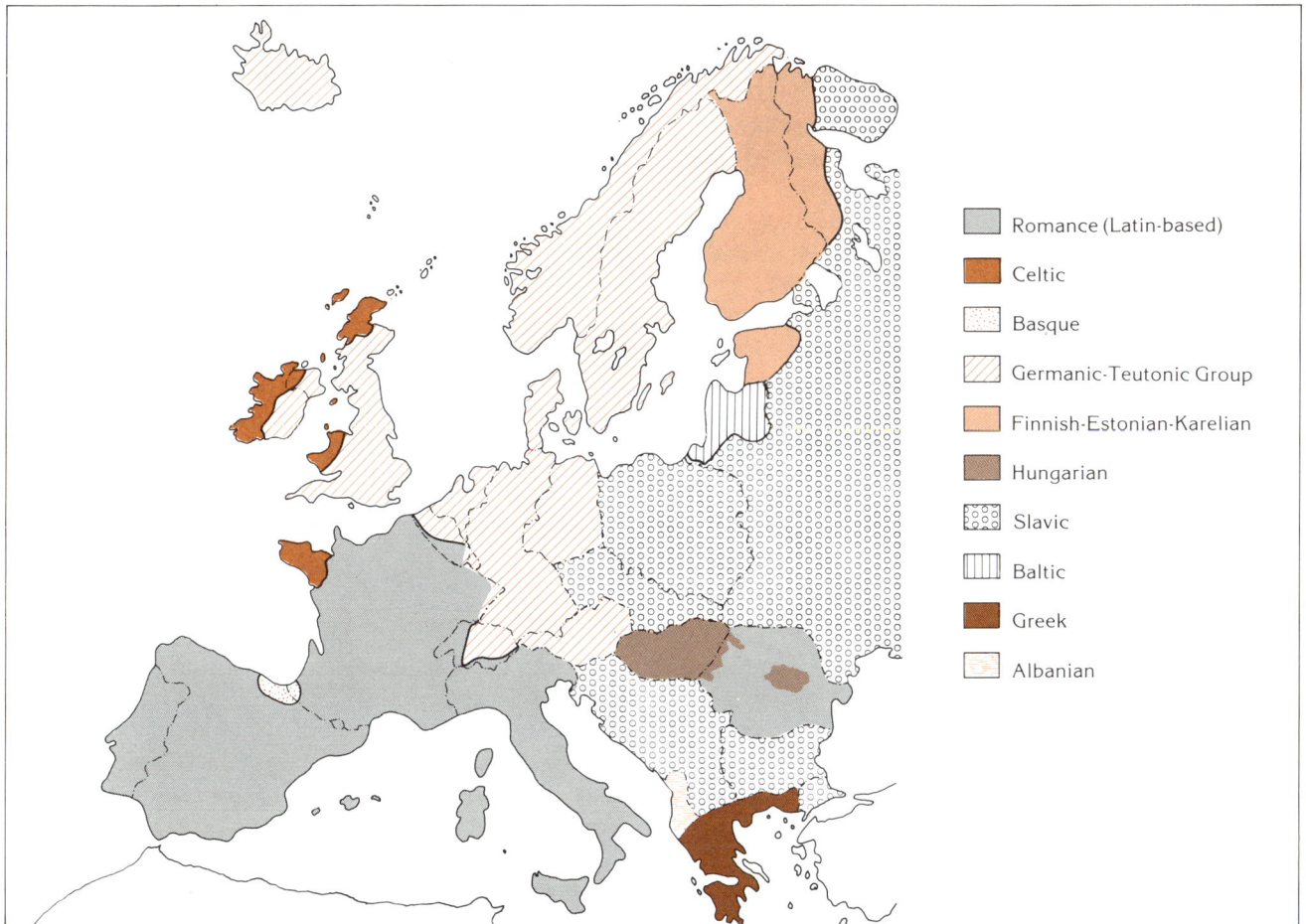

FIGURE 5–3

Languages of Europe. Latin-based (Romance) and Germanic languages dominate in southwestern and northwestern Europe, respectively, while the Slavic group prevails in the East. In each of these major language areas, exceptions persist, frequently as historic minority groups in peripheral areas.

state-subsidized airlines, and varying degrees of ownership of basic industries like electric generation, steel, and coal mining, there remains some degree of reliance on traditional entrepreneurial capitalism. Remaining privately controlled businesses and corporations may be subjected to comprehensive regulations, sometimes onerous in degree, but only selected parts of the economy are directly owned and managed by governments. Private ownership of housing, farmland, and retail business remains lawful and encouraged. Democracy is the universal ideal.

The economic integration of much of West Europe, with the unattained long-range goal of some type of political unification, is greatly facilitated by the superb transport networks that link the densely populated, heavily industrialized, and urbanized heartlands of the region. The heavily used, internationalized Rhine River is symbolic of the close interconnections of national and subregional econ-

omies. Tunnels under the Swiss Alps, channel crossings by Hovercraft, fast international express trains,—all illustrate the long-term emphasis on international communications and transport. Electrical energy is interchanged internationally, and long-distance pipelines constitute a recent addition to international transport.

PHYSICAL CHARACTERISTICS

In addition to its "peninsula and island" characteristics, the marine west coast climate is prevalent for more than two thirds of the region. The Mediterranean climate provides a complementary agricultural area as well as a tourist magnet during the long winters of the north. Most of this southern two thirds is adequately watered, has mild winters, and a long growing season. What climatic differentiation occurs is a subtle gradation, yet enough to encourage differences in specialization of agricultural commodities.

Over one third of its extent, West Europe is a level plain; even its mountain ranges now rarely act as barriers to movement to any great degree, although their "barrier" effects were considerable in the past. The surrounding seas were ever available as an aid to movement. Much of the area is usable for agriculture or at least pasture. The physical components of the landscape are all interconnected by land corridors, by sea, by river systems—all of which have acted more to enhance movement and interaction than to deter it, although ease of movement is far greater now than in the formative period of this mosaic of cultures.

THE PHYSICAL FRAMEWORK OF WEST EUROPE

Despite its relatively small size and the overall similarity of its surface landscape features, West Europe is physiographically complex. The long narrow body of the whole continent of Europe is oriented east-west, and to this core are appended a series of islands and peninsulas around the three edges of West Europe. Though lowland areas are common, there is an alternation of mountains, hills, basins, plains, and plateaus strewn across the landscape that almost defies orderly categorization. Blocks of land alternate with bodies of water, adding to the complexity, as seas and bays penetrate far inland. As a result, West Europe has an unusually high ratio of coastline to total area.

Unlike its physiography, Europe's climatic patterns are relatively simple. Unusually warm, considering its northerly latitude, maritime influences are felt throughout the continent to some degree. Temperature ranges, both seasonal and daily, increase with distance inland from the sea. Conditions are almost everywhere humid in the north, becoming sub-humid in the south. Rainfall is greatest in mountain areas and along the west coast. Sheltered valleys and basins in the north receive less precipitation as do the lands of southern Europe. Winter precipitation maxima occur in the Mediterranean lands and in the mountains of the British Isles, as well as along the Norwegian coast. Summer maxima occur in the lands along the Baltic Sea and in the Fenno-Scandian Shield. Only the Mediterranean lands have a definite dry season, occurring in summer. The rest of the continent receives precipitation throughout the year; some of it with monotonous regularity. Total rainfall generally decreases eastward.

THE TOPOGRAPHY

The features of Europe can be viewed as a series of arcs, each oriented a little differently, each representing a different age and set of features. Four physiographic areas correspond with this orientation and include the Alpine system, the Central Highlands and central massifs, the European Plain, and the Northwestern European Highlands. Each unit is itself a complex area containing regional variations; none is as simple as these highly generalized names might imply.

The Alpine system is a highly complex association of mountains with bordering lowland corridors and enclosed basins (often of great size). Platforms and plateaus were also uplifted at the same time and became a part of the Alpine complex. Not a single chain of mountains, the Alps include many individual ranges. They are the most recent mountains of Europe (about 70 million years old) and are composed of folded sediments with a crystalline rock core. In western Europe, the Alps occupy an arc that stretches from the French and Italian rivieras to the eastern borders of Austria. Since the mountain heights are frequently used as borders, they seem to follow along the common boundaries of France, Italy, Switzerland, Germany, Austria, and Yugoslavia. Sharpened into peaks by mountain glaciation, it is the highest portion of the Alpine system that is referred to simply and categorically as the Alps, the most rugged part of Europe.

Lower but related chains spread out in several directions. The Appenines, forming the central spine of Italy, the Sierra Nevada of southern Spain, and the Pyrenees, which form the Franco-Hispanic border, are all parts of the same system in western Europe. The Pinaus of Greece are a related system.

Four major lowland areas are associated with the Alpine system. In Spain, the lowlands of Andalusia and the Ebro Valley are shallow basins located between the Alpine ranges and the old crystalline block that forms the Iberian massif. Still larger and more level is the basin of the Po River of northern Italy, a former arm of the sea now silted in by alluvium. The lowlands flanking the western side of the Appenines are piles of sediment covering a now submerged ancient crystalline massif. The small lowlands of Thessalay and Salonica are their counterparts in Greece.

A number of plateaus and platforms were uplifted at the same time, as in the Apulian area of southeastern Italy and the Swiss Plateau between the Alps and the much lower Jura Mountains. The Balearic Islands of Spain, the northern peninsula of Corsica, and the remainder of Sicily are portions of the Alpine Mountains that rise above the floor of the sea.

Just to the north of the Alps is a series of lower features often called the Central Highlands. They are a folded, partly metamorphozed remnant of a much older mountain system, flanking the Alpine system on its western and northern edges. Four major highland areas are the bulk of the Spanish Meseta, the Massif Central of France, the Franco-German highlands (stretching from the Ardennes to and beyond the East German border) and the Bohemian massif, the western edge of which stretches into West Europe beyond the Czech border.

After the Alpine uplift, rivers entrenched deep valleys in these upland areas. Stresses accompanying uplift often fractured these areas into a series of fault blocks, some faulted up, others dropped down. (See the more complete discussion of plate tectonics in Chapter 1.) This highland physiographic area contains most of Europe's coal reserves. Where zones of weakness allowed, volcanoes formed or lava flows reached the surface. These are the most complex geologic features of Europe. Isolated uptilted fault blocks form the Vosges of France and the Bladsford Mountains of Germany. Downdropped blocks form large, linear valleys like the Rhine Graben (Trench) and the valley of the Rhone. Though later covered with Alpine sediments, the Bavarian Plateau is a part of this grouping. The deeply faulted grabens, which are so characteristic of this physiographic area, form major corridors of trade.

The European Plain stretches from the Pyrennees to the Urals, widening out at the Polish-Soviet border to encompass the width of the entire continent. In the Southwest are the unglaciated, rolling plains of the basins of Acquitaine, Loire, and Paris. Even the basin of London, across the English Channel, is a part of this system.

North of the delta of the Rhine and the London Basin, the plains are composed of glacial deposits left by the continental ice sheets of Pleistocene times. Old glacial spillways form a series of east-west valleys stretching in a series of gentle arcs from the North Sea to western USSR. In places they are interconnected by short north-south spillways oriented at right angles to the major valleys. Many have been excavated to form West Europe's dense network of canals. Along the northern edges of the plain are found gravely morainal hills. In western Europe they form the Danish islands, the eastern edge of that country's mainland peninsula, and the hills of the Baltic Coast. Small outliers of the Plain are found in southern Sweden and the Swedish islands.

The oldest mountains of Europe, the Northwestern Highlands, are really two sets of mountains developed at two different times. The older forms most of Sweden and

Finland. Over a billion years old, repeatedly eroded by glaciers and constantly eroded by water, the mountains were leveled to a plateaulike surface. Known as a shield area, it is similar in age, origin, and landscape appearance to the Canadian Shield. Only along the Norwegian borders do the features rise to a significant height. The region is known as the Fenno-Scandian Shield.

The Caledonian Mountains had been eroded almost level. Later tectonic activity uplifted these old remnants into low mountains. Glaciers deepened the valleys, and extended lowlands occur where blocks were down-faulted. Uplifted blocks form the Scottish Highlands and the mountains of Norway. Iceland, a recent volcanic creation, dates to the time of great volcanic activity elsewhere in Europe.

The extreme complexity of this landscape is reflected in the diversity of European land use, mineral wealth, and crop patterns.

THE CLIMATE

Three major types of climate cover most of West Europe. The Iberian countries, Italy, Greece, and the south coast of France are typically Mediterranean in climate, with mild wet winters and hot dry summers. Areas north of the Alps and south of the Baltic, the British Isles, and the Norwegian coast have a maritime west coast climate, cool, cloudy, and wet virtually all year. The Scandinavian countries, the mountains, and sheltered interior portions of Germany are subject to a more continental climatic regime with larger daily and seasonal temperature regimes, warmer summers, and sharply cold winters.

The Mediterranean Climate This type of climate is sunny and pleasant throughout the year, part of the reason for the intensive development of tourism in the area. Most rainfall occurs between October and May, though even then the skies are sunny between brief showers. In summer drought is the norm. Winter temperatures are mild and frosts are infrequent. January temperatures average over 40°F (14°C) everywhere except the highlands and in the Po Valley of northern Italy. Sheltered or coastal areas are generally warmer than interior or exposed areas like the Spanish Meseta or the Po Valley. Even in winter the nights are cool rather than cold, and snow is rare.

Destructive cold winds of gale force invade the area on rare occasions, with heavy crop (and even physical) damage. On occasion hot, desiccating summer winds blow over from Africa. Generally, the Alps protect southern

Europe from winter cold much as, to a lesser degree, they protect northern Europe from summer heat. By all standards the climate is pleasant, although rainfall fluctuations can cause problems of both seasonal flooding and drought.

Some interior corners of Spain and its southeastern coast are so much drier than Mediterranean climate that they become true steppe. The northern and northwestern coasts of Spain are transitional to the marine climate of northwestern Europe. The Po Valley, more sharply seasonal and continental, has yearly frosts, a distinctly colder winter, and more summer rain. Summer heat is most intense (and drought most pronounced) in the Spanish Meseta, southern Italy (including Sicily), and Greece.

Marine West Coast Climate   If Mediterranean conditions are pleasant, those of the more northerly European countries are somewhat less so. Generations of environmental determinists in geography lauded the marine west coast climate. Advanced levels of development were attributed to this climate, which was described as stimulating, changeable, and temperate. Similar achievements in nineteenth century North America caused determinists to even erroneously equate the very dissimilar climates of the two areas.

Few would call the climate of northern Europe "pleasant." There is no doubt that it is temperate. Seasonal and daily temperature ranges are small. Winters are rarely bitterly cold, but they are damp and rawly uncomfortable. Summers are never hot; they are damply cool. Rains can be seemingly endless, if seldom intense. The skies are cloudy—virtually all day. There is snow, though the cover is not lasting. Winter skies tend to be dull and overcast. Rain comes as a mist or drizzle.

Most of the area west of a line from Denmark to Munich has a January average of freezing or slightly above. East of that line temperatures in that month average slightly below freezing. Isotherms in winter are oriented north-south, indicating the powerful temporizing influence of the sea. Fog, present at all seasons, is most frequent in winter.

Summer skies have few sunny days. July temperatures average 57°F (14°C) in Scotland and coastal Norway, 60°F (15°C) over most of England and Germany, 64°F (18°C) in London and Paris, 70°F (21°C) in southern France. Summer isotherms in Europe mirror latitude, running east-west. **Continentality,** with its diurnal extremes and summer-season heat, is exhibited in only a few areas.

Total rainfall is surprisingly light, some 20 to 40 inches (500 to 1,000 millimeters) except in the mountains and along the northwestern coast. There are no dramatic seasonal changes. Spring creeps inperceptibly forward. In fall, the leaves turn from green to dull yellow, to brown and disappear in the drizzle and fog, and it is winter again. Marx described the climate as "tubercular," rather closer to the truth than the determinist's "invigorating."

A few areas fare better. The southern half of France, transitional to Mediterranean conditions, is much more sunny (and considerably warmer) in summer. Bright, sparkling weather does occur in the Alps in winter. Southward facing slopes, the lower Rhine, and the Rhone corridor all have somewhat more pleasant conditions. Any southward-facing slope is a little warmer in summer. Any leeward (facing away from prevailing winds) area is somewhat drier and a little less cloudy.

There are advantages to this climate, however. There is a six- to nine-month growing season almost everywhere except in higher altitudes. Weather disasters and hazards are few and infrequent.

The Continental-Transitional Climates   The remaining climatic area of West Europe has a climate that is somewhat more typical of this latitude. Yet even here, the modifying influences of the ocean are not absent. The warming influences of the West Wind Drift (the "remainder" of the Gulf Stream) penetrate as far as the Kola peninsula of the Soviet Union, keeping Arctic ocean ports such as Murmansk ice-free the year around and warming, however weakly, the fringes of the Arctic shores. The shallow Baltic, more brackish than salt and frozen for over half of its extent in the winter season, still has a tempering effect. The result is a climate that is more nearly continental, yet not as extreme as that of similar latitudinal areas in Canada or Siberia. It is more similar to the northern Great Lakes states, an area considerably to the south.

The temperature extremes noted in the area are intensified with altitude and distance away from the sea, even though such distances are quite small. Rainfall is relatively light, with most areas receiving between 15 to 25 inches (380 to 630 millimeters) and all areas having a pronounced summer maximum.

The Arctic fringes of the area pass to a tundra fringe with high altitude and/or increased elevation. The southern half of the area has a cool continental climate, the northern half truly subarctic—not unlike the climate of the Canadian Shield. The transition from one to the other is not sharp, so that the division, while reflected in population density and land use, becomes quite vague.

VEGETATION

In few areas of the world have we so completely modified nature as in Europe. The distinctly Mediterranean areas apparently produced a forest of oak, cypress, and pine. Our use (or misuse) often reduced that forest to a cover of drought-adapted shrubs. The olive, generally described as characteristic, occupies an area that is not entirely co-incidental with Mediterranean climate. The maquis and garrigue vegetation types cover a larger area than that which is coincident with this climatic type.

The second identifiable zone is that of the northern forest. The boreal forest seemingly consisted of an association of pine, spruce, and birch, with oak probably a late invader. People have planted broadleaf deciduous trees, wherever they can survive, as decorative covering, a source of food or fodder, or even as furniture wood. Commercial scale plantings have tended to encourage spruce because of its rapid growth and value for pulp and paper.

The zone in-between, often called temperate forest, is a matrix of broadleaf deciduous trees with islands of pine or mixed forest. Altitude produces montane conifer forests.

Heath and moor can be swampy or dry, on flatlands or in rolling and hilly areas. Where wet, they can and have been reclaimed for agricultural use. Where dry, they are generally grazing land of the lowest grade or simply wasteland. They extend discontiuously across northern Europe in areas where glaciation occurred. Both are associations of low, scrubby vegetation. Heath implies a shrubby, dry complex of heather and other shrubby plants. Moor is generally found in rolling, broken countryside and contains bogs in hollows and lower spots. It is probable that the spread of these vegetational types over large areas is the result of land misuse—akin to the spread of maquis over the Mediterranean landscape.

DRAINAGE PATTERNS

As might be expected in an area of relatively heavy rainfall, the European drainage network is quite dense. Several factors are of importance:

1. A high degree of navigability is noted throughout West Europe. Canals and dredging have often increased such navigability.

2. Rivers are generally short and drainage is outward from the continental center.

3. Rivers with their origins in the Alpine system and the northwestern highlands tend to carry the greatest amount of water.

4. The volume of water discharged and size of individual drainage basins is least in Mediterranean Europe.

5. Political boundaries and considerations have been extremely instrumental in hampering the use of rivers

for navigation as well as in determining which rivers receive navigational improvement.

SOILS

The complex interrelationships of climate, vegetation, drainage, and parent rock material that make soil have been greatly modified by thousands of years of human use. Heavy population and land pressures encouraged the clearing of forests, terracing of sloping areas. fertilization of poorer soils, drainage of swamps, and even reclamation of land from beneath the sea. Perhaps only in East Asia have people modified the original soil to a comparable degree.

In general, the soils of West Europe are of moderately natural fertility. The fertility-leaching process known as podzolization is ongoing here, as in any area where precipitation exceeds evaporation. Podzolization has advanced most completely in the cold, moist climates of northern Europe and along the overwatered western fringes.

Secondary forces, such as glaciation, have modified soils by drainage changes, transport of soil material, and selective erosion and deposition.

Two large areas of fertile soils stand out—one in the southeastern and one in the west central portions of the continent. The superior soil types consist of lime-rich soils, some alluvial soils, wind-blown loess (a fossil of the great ice ages), humus-enriched black earths, solution deposits in wet/dry limestone (terra roxa), and recent volcanics. Soils developed under a deciduous forest in somewhat drier areas and/or on fertile parent material are generally above average fertility. Some bog soils, if drained and cared for, may be of reasonably high fertility.

In West Europe the large area of fertile soils constitutes an almost continuous zone located within the unglaciated European plain and some of the surrounding hills of the Central European Uplands. France's self-sufficiency in foodstuffs is largely a result of the high incidence of fertile soils found in that country. The loess hills of central Germany support high population densities. They constitute a narrow and erratic westward extension of loessic soils in West Europe.

Alluvial deposits vary greatly in fertility. Areas of alluvium with higher fertility occur in the Po Valley, the lower courses of the Rhine and Rhone, and many of the lesser rivers of Europe. Recently uplifted marine alluvium and some areas of drained bog soil are included in this category. Mediterranean soils are often thin and stony, but recent volcanics, alluvial floodplains, and terra roxa soils are important exceptions.

The poorest soils of Europe are coincident with northern locations, with heavy rains, and/or poor drainage. Frequently the soils of the shield and of mountain areas are also extremely thin and stony with areas of barren rock. Areas of sand dunes are also of extremely low fertility; glacial outwash plains of sand and gravel have similar limitations.

The cultural consequences of soil fertility for Europe are amazing and are mirrored in any number of distributions from lines of urbanization to population density and areas of food surplus generation. Each of Europe's more populous countries contains a core of superior soil. It frequently becomes the economic and political core of that individual country as well.

Faced with limited supplies of land in relation to population, Europeans have resorted to technical efforts to improve land quality, to increase the arable area, to improve yields, and to correlate crops grown with land-use potential. The results are stunningly high food yields and the ability to support large populations with the produce of relatively small areas. The ability of most European states to hold down imports of food to a relative minimum is a tribute to European technology in particular and human ingenuity in general.

LAND-SEA RELATIONSHIPS

Perhaps nowhere else in the world are land-sea relationships as important. Two enclosed bodies of water extend east-west, deeply into the interior of the land masses; the North-Baltic incursion and the Mediterranean basin. Rivers, often navigable, reach inland to the very center of the continent. Virtually no part of western Europe is more than 300 miles (480 kilometers) from the sea. The narrow entrances to the seas and important mountain passes have at times enabled certain states to control access to other areas of Europe, and to enrich themselves or increase their power in the process.

THE STRUCTURE OF SUBREGIONS

History has taught us to think in terms of national units in this home of nationalism and nation-states. Regional geography, another concept originating in West Europe, has taught us to think in terms of smaller units of homogeneity within national territories. Any attempts to devise "natural" groupings based on physiographic or climatic similarities results in the violation of logical cultural borders, yet a regionalization is desirable in an ordering of thought. Proximity, history, cultural similarity, and developmental levels have all been used in subdividing the major region into more manageable parts or subregions (see Figure 5–4).

CULTURAL FOUNTAINS— GREECE AND ITALY

Cultural leadership in times past and its legacy of a continuing major impact on the political and economic thought of West Europe characterize both Greece and Italy. Ironically, these fountainheads of Western culture, which long served as vital links between Eastern and Western civilizations, are both relatively young as modern nation-states, having been fragmented and dominated by contending foreign powers for centuries. The modern state of Italy was born in 1870; Greece achieved independence in the modern era in 1830. In both countries, economic progress is impressive if occasionally erratic, though both countries have had a measure of instability since the restoration of democratic governments following World War II.

The Resource Base   Greece, the second poorest country of West Europe after Portugal (see Figure 5–5), has a fairly favorable resource base. Although there is no bituminous coal, Greece has relatively large deposits of brown coal or

A Small Temple on the Acropolis, Athens. Ancient Greece and Rome served as fountainheads or sources of much of Europe's culture; this heritage is also a salient characteristic of the region. (Courtesy of the United Nations)

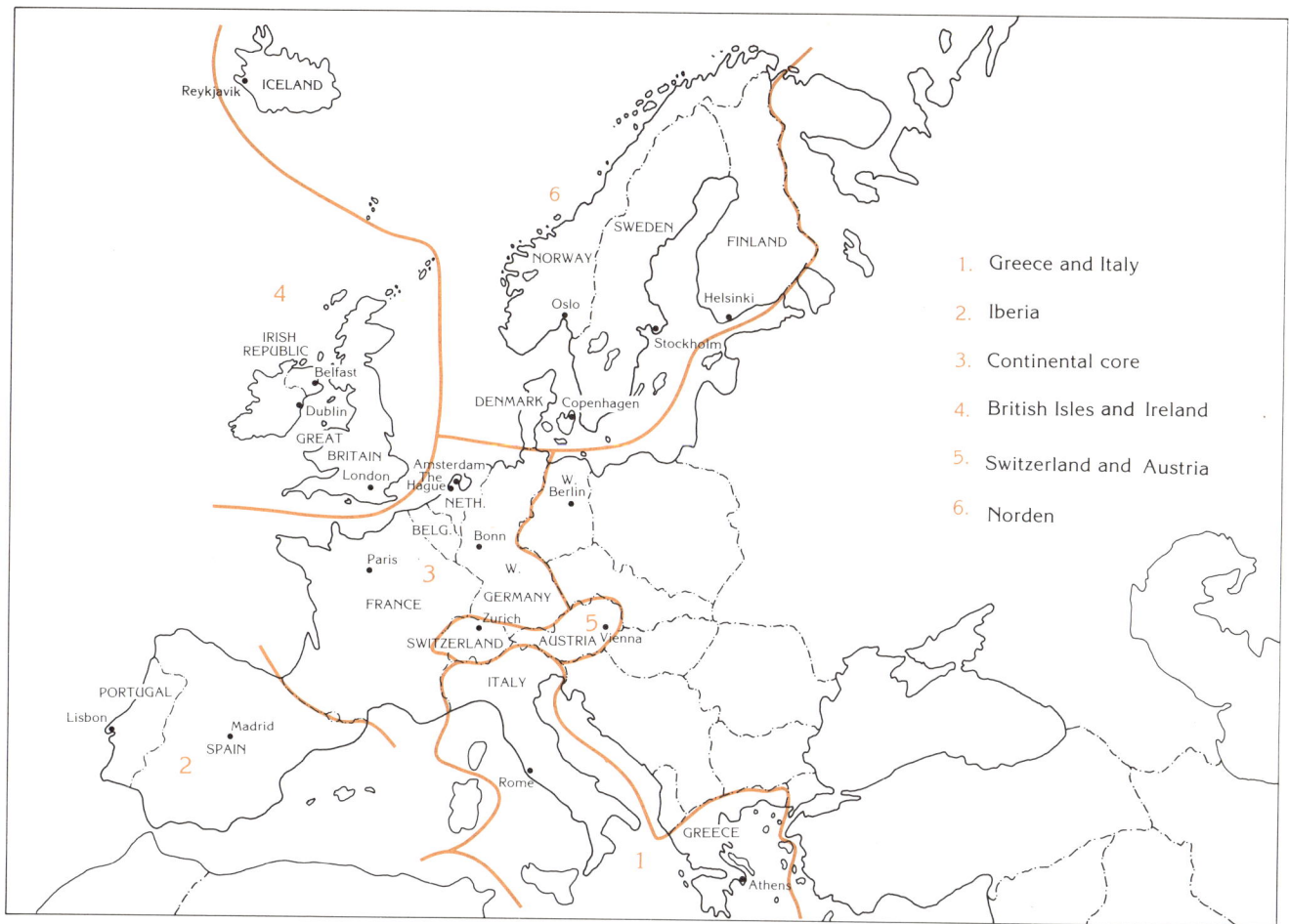

FIGURE 5—4

Structure of Subregions. The complexities of this crowded, culturally varied, immensely productive region are best studied through a system of subregions. Subregions reflect level of economic development, cultural similarities, and, frequently, historical association.

Rome. Once the most important city in the region, Rome is still a "world city" in its cultural leadership and religious administrative functions. (Photo by Stansfield)

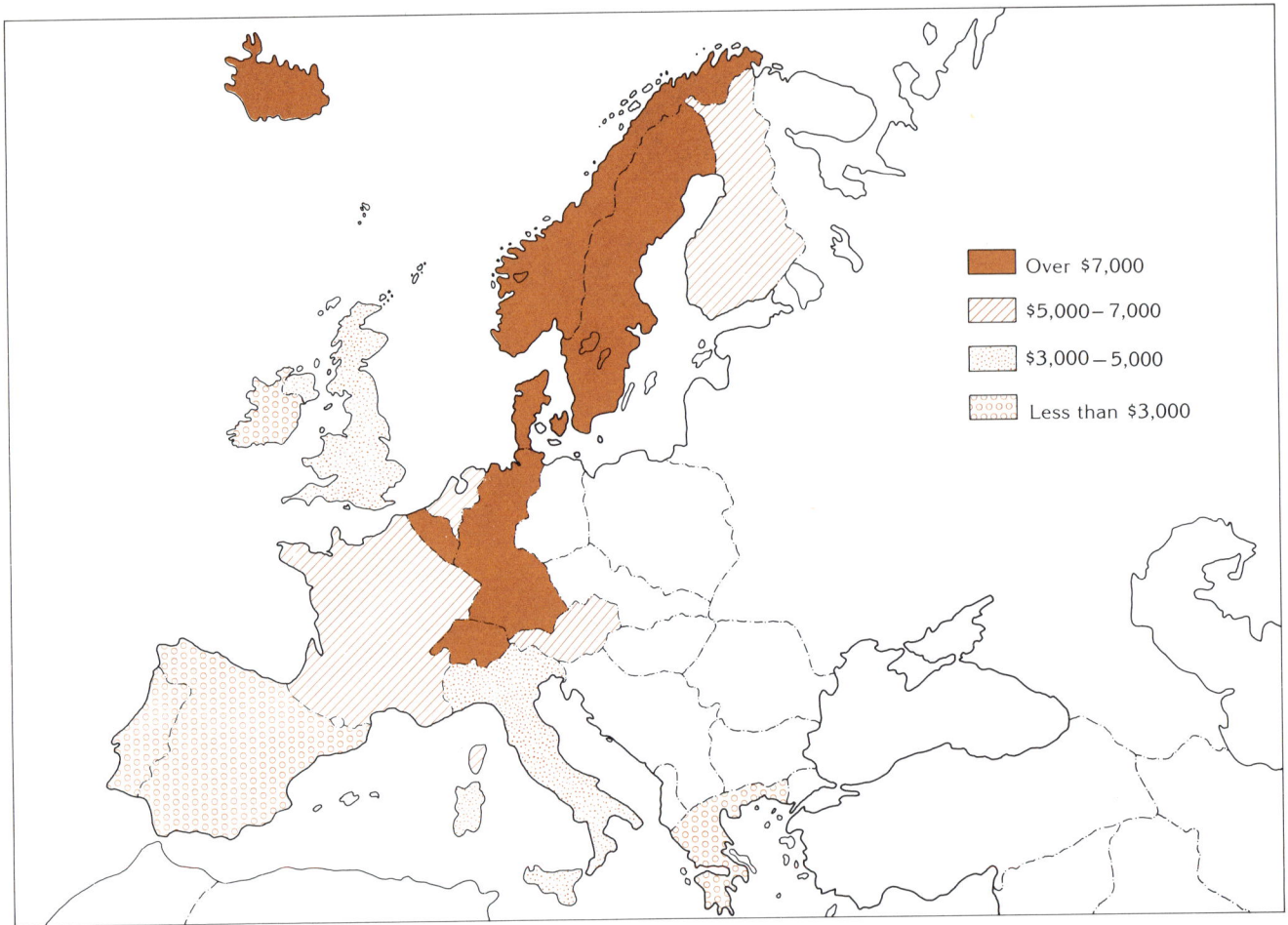

FIGURE 5–5
Per Capita Incomes, West Europe. Per capita incomes in Europe show a north-south axis of high income from the Scandinavian peninsula through Switzerland, flanked by somewhat lower incomes to the west and south and much lower incomes for most of East Europe (not shown).

Legend:
- Over $7,000
- $5,000 – 7,000
- $3,000 – 5,000
- Less than $3,000

lignite; reserves of peat are even larger. More than half of Greece's electric energy requirements are supplied by these domestic reserves. Although oil from Greek portions of the Aegean Sea now supplies less than 10 percent of their consumption, there is optimism about future exploration. Some natural gas has also been discovered. (See Figure 5–6.)

Greece also has at least a billion tons of bauxite reserves. This ore is processed into aluminum for export as metal and metal products. Major mines produce an ore containing both nickel and iron, and minor deposits of lead and silver are exploited.

Italy is the fourth largest producer of both hydroelectric energy and natural gas in West Europe. Unfortunately, there is little potential for further expansion of hydro power, while natural gas deposits (mostly in the Po Valley and in Sicily) are being tapped at such a fast rate that they are

unlikely to last beyond the end of the century unless new discoveries are made. Oil fields, mostly in Sicily, are small and provided only about one percent of Italy's consumption in recent years. There is almost no coal and only a small lignite mining industry. Iron ore production is minor, and bauxite production is insufficient for domestic needs. Italian mercury production ranks among the world's highest, and lead-zinc production is significant. Export of mineral products from Italy is even lower than that of Greece, especially on a per capita basis.

Population   Greek population has expanded from less than three quarters of a million at independence to about 10 million currently. Over one fourth of the total lives in metropolitan Athens, while the mountainous areas have exceptionally low densities. As in Spain, there are many densely populated small nuclei separated by vast areas of

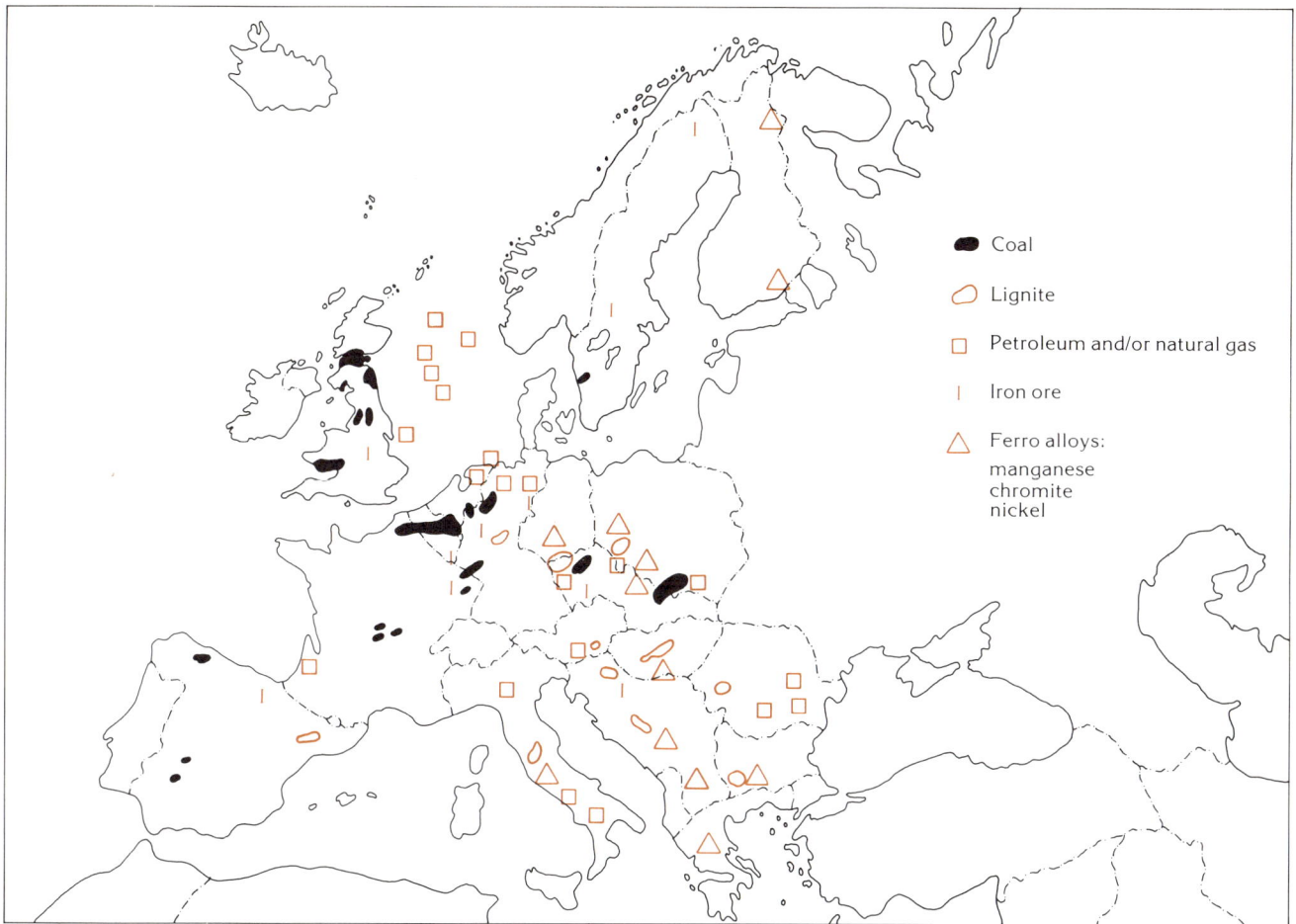

FIGURE 5–6

Mineral and Fossil Fuels, West Europe. The coal of northern and central Europe powered its Industrial Revolution, and the region is reasonably well supplied with metal ores; however, some states achieved industrial power with few local resources, and only a handful of minerals enter extraregional markets on a significant scale.

low density. Heavy out-migration in the first two decades of this century went primarily to the United States. Greece has now joined the "southern tier" of labor-exporting countries, along with Portugal, Spain, Italy, and Yugoslavia. The long-term rural-to-urban migration continues both internally and internationally. About 400,000 Greeks work in other EC countries, mostly in West Germany. As with the other "exporters" of labor, Greece's economy could ill-afford the sudden return of these **expatriate workers** if West Germany's economy slows to the point of sending more "guest workers" home. (See Table 5–1.)

Italy's population, approaching 60 million, is densely settled over most of the peninsula. Huge concentrations live in the great industrial cities of the Po Valley and in central Italy where Rome has a population of 3 million. The natural increase rate is low by world standards and

even for West Europe. The reunification of little more than a century ago seems to have been successful in that there is relatively little pressure for local autonomy. People of different cultural traditions such as Sicilians or Sardinians are not notably secessionist-minded compared with provincial *centrifugal forces* in Spain. Emigration continues to relieve population pressures but takes place on a much smaller scale than the outflow earlier in this century. Internal migration flows remain high, the south being the sender and the north and Rome being recipients. Rome, by virtue of its immense historical importance, its continuing international role as headquarters of the Roman Catholic Church, and its capital function would be considered a "world city." Milian, headquarters of multinational corporations and a leading industrial design center, is also a "world city."

TABLE 5–1
Population characteristics, by country

	Population (millions)	Population Density (per square kilometer)	Growth Rate (natural)	Percentage Urban
Austria	7.5	90	−.08	52
Belgium	9.9	324	.06	52
Denmark	5.1	119	.11	70
Eire	3.4	48	1.11	55
Finland	4.8	14	.45	63
France	53.5	98	.39	74
West Germany	61.3	245	−.21	83
Greece	9.4	71	.71	67
Iceland	.2	2	1.12	89
Italy	57.0	189	.29	59
Luxembourg	.4	138	−.15	70
Netherlands	14.0	341	.45	79
Norway	4.1	13	.25	49
Portugal	9.9	107	.69	38
Spain	37.5	75	.81	42
Sweden	8.3	18	.06	85
Switzerland	6.3	153	.24	60
United Kingdom	55.8	229	.03	74

Agricultural Patterns   A higher proportion of Greeks (some one third) are engaged in agriculture, forestry, and fishing than in any other western European nation. Agriculture, though declining in relative importance and in work force, provides one fourth of Greece's exports by value. Less than one third of mountainous Greece is cultivable. Fortunately for Greece, precipitation induced by air masses rising against the highlands provide heavier precipitation than would be expected in a Mediterranean country, and the runoff is used in irrigation projects. Despite the handicap of many very small farm units and the pressing need to rationalize holdings by consolidating scattered fields, Greece is self-sufficient in cereal crops. Cotton and citrus production is rising, while exports of fruit, vegetables, wine, and tobacco increase.

Italy has 15 percent of its labor force in agriculture, a much lower figure than Greece's, but still representing the largest single numerical group of farmers among western European nations. Despite a high proportion of total land area in steep slope, more than 40 percent of Italy is cultivated land, and almost two thirds is used for some kind of agriculture. Sharecropping, once common, is being phased out. Government policy is aimed at enlarging the many tiny, inefficient holdings but must then contend with an increased flow of displaced peasants into cities with already crowded slums and high unemployment rates. Government involvement in, and funding of, agricultural

reform is impressive. More than $2 billion were spent during the 1960's to compensate landowners for expropriated land for subdivision among landless farmers, to drain marshland, and to develop irrigation as a means of supplying more arable land to small farmers. Mechanization is increasing rapidly. The flow of poor farmers to the industrial cities has been so great that in some areas, particularly Sicily, there is actually a labor shortage in agriculture and some land is not farmed as intensively as it had been.

Large injections of capital and technology from the prospering industrial cities of the subregion have benefited northern agriculture. Drainage projects, fertilization, and irrigation projects have all transformed the once marginal agricultural lands of the Po Delta to among the best in Europe. As is common among industrial versus developing countries, heavily industrialized northern Italy's agriculture employs a smaller proportion of the labor force, but these fewer farmers on larger farms produce more per land unit than those of the less industrialized south. Although Italy is West Europe's second largest producer of both wheat and corn (after France), production costs are high. Italy is the largest exporter of wine, by volume, in Europe, but a fair amount of the wine is of the cheaper varieties. The Italian wine industry is now trying to build a higher priced market for quality and specialty wines. A major thrust of government policy is now to increase the size and efficiency of Italy's animal husbandry industry.

Improved pasture and selective breeding are designed to increase Italy's meat production, an area in which it lags far behind such nations as West Germany or Britain.

Considering their high ratios of coastline to area, neither Greece nor Italy emphasizes a fishing industry. Total catches are low, perhaps reflecting the notoriously high levels of pollution of the Mediterranean.

Industrial Development and Strategies   As would be expected in a country so dominated by agriculture, Greece's industrial strategy emphasizes processing and packaging of agricultural products. Other main industries are textiles and chemicals. Government policy favors **decentralization** of industry from Athens into smaller cities and towns as well as domestic production of consumer goods to reduce

imports. The two policies are related, resulting in small, but modern factories scattered through the country. Greece's four oil refineries produce as much petroleum products for export as for domestic consumption. A steel industry has been developed to reduce imports, and three large shipyards produce ships for Greece's large merchant fleet as well as specializing in repairs. (See Figure 5–7.)

Industry in Italy is so heavily concentrated in the north that two thirds of all industrial workers are located there, while only 50 percent of the people live there. The Italian government has tried, strenuously and continuously, to shift industrial growth to the south and to relieve unemployment and reduce internal migration. Although Italian industry includes such giants as Fiat, ENI, Montedison, Dunlop-Pirelli, and Olivetti, there are also large numbers

FIGURE 5–7
Major Industrial Regions, West Europe. No other world region of comparable size has such a dense concentration of industry. These are the cultural hearths of the Industrial Revolution and, collectively, this region ranks with the "economic superpowers"—the United States, Soviet Union, and Japan.

of very small companies. The Italian government has moved into the economy in a major way, taking over failing, inefficient firms and attempting, through consolidation and modernization, to make them competitive. This nationalization has not always boosted profits or productivity; the political goal of higher employment frequently overrides economic considerations. Too, the government bureaucracy is widely regarded as bloated and inefficient itself; this does not foster confidence in its ability to successfully manage industrial concerns. IRI, a state-owned holding company, operates a small auto producer (Alfa Romeo), steel works, and shipyards—all at a loss. The steel industry in general, though, has been thoroughly modernized to meet the challenges of tariff elimination within the EC. Modernization can run at odds with government efforts to provide more jobs in distressed parts of the country. The location of an efficient new steel plant at Taranto, on the "heel of the boot," was supposed to help reduce regional unemployment. Its effect was negligible after construction was completed; efficiency implies a *capital-intensive* operation with relatively few workers. The Italians have been successful in steel despite their having almost no local raw materials.

Italian chemical industries, by contrast, can use a varied domestic raw material base in methane gas, sulfur, salt, limestone, and other commodities. Natural gas is especially important in the manufacture of fertilizer and industrial chemicals. Plastics manufacture has expanded, but expansion may slow since it is dependent on imported oil. Italy is also an important producer of cement and aluminum.

Clothing has long been a large export industry, based on Italy's reputation for fashion design and craftmanship. This industry, however, is extremely competitive and the future is uncertain. Italy ranks third, after the United States and Japan, in output of household appliances like refrigerators and washing machines, dominating EC markets. Olivetti typewriters and office machines are sold around the world and are also assembled overseas. Fiat supplies about one fifth of the entire EC auto market. It is the most international of all auto manufacturers, having set up plants in Yugoslavia, Spain, Turkey, and even Libya. Fiat has built entire auto plants for Poland and the Soviet Union, so that Fiats are the most familiar cars in the world.

Environmental Problems   Greece apparently is making great progress on its environmental problems. Reforestation (to hold back water on steep slopes and reduce soil erosion) has been very successful in Greece. New species of fast-growing trees, such as eucalyptus from Australia, have been established in "tree plantations" to both control erosion and provide a long-term "crop" for pulp produc-

tion. Outside reforestation, Italy's record in conservation and pollution control is not good. Almost every bathing beach in Italy, for example, is dangerously polluted from untreated sewage and industrial wastes. One of the related problems is tourist pressure. Millions of foreign tourists continue to flow to Italy's Mediterranean sunshine and huge and varied stock of cultural treasures, contributing inadvertently to pollution pressures. Tourism is still a major support of the Italian economy, although congestion levels in summer at popular attractions seriously annoy Italians. Government policy is to spread the season, emphasizing the winter ski resorts and the less crowded times, and to direct tourism more into the south, and to Sicily and Sardinia. Tourism in Italy could well be at a critical turning point. Pollution of natural amenities, severe congestion at the great cultural monuments, and, worst of all, political unrest could adversely affect future tourism.

Like Italy, Greece enjoys a combination of cheap prices, abundant sunshine, and an array of cultural artifacts high on every tourist's list. Tourism boomed after World War II. Too many tourists crowd into Athens; the already badly congested capital can barely cope with its resident population. The famed Parthenon has been fenced off due to heavy wear and some vandalism from visitors. As with Italy, the Greeks are attempting to spread tourism more evenly across both calendar and country.

Political Stability   Italy has been ruled by almost forty different governments since the overthrow of the fascist regime during World War II. General strikes repeatedly paralyze the economy. Capital flows (illegally) across the border to Switzerland as the wealthy cope with one of Europe's worst inflations, least stable currencies, and highest tax rates. A rising tide of terrorism, kidnapping, assassinations, and rioting threatens the whole structure of Italian society.

Greece, too, has had a turbulent political history and less than a decade ago overthrew a military dictatorship that had ruled for seven years. Rising standards of living should contribute to stability, but Greece must cope with being West Europe's outpost in the eastern Mediterranean. Bordered by Communist countries and long-term traditional enemies, like Turkey, Greece is in a precarious position. Tensions with Turkey over their respective national populations in Cyprus and over division of potential oil fields in the Aegean are serious problems indeed.

IBERIA

The Iberian peninsula is shared by Spain, with nearly 38 million people, and smaller Portugal, with a little less than 10 million. Spain is a relatively poor nation by West European standards, but has a per capita income about 70 percent higher than that of Portugal, West Europe's poorest country. The two countries shared in the cultural heritage of Moorish occupation, the battle to expel that control, and the race for world trade and colonial empires. Related in language, culture, and history, they form a compact subregion.

The Resource Base   From the time of the Phoenicians, Spain has been considered a storehouse of minerals (see Figure 5–6). It is an important producer of mercury, copper, lead, and silver, and a relatively minor source of iron ore, zinc, and bauxite (aluminum ore). Spain managed to export iron ore before its own iron and steel industry grew to absorb total domestic production; it now purchases additional ore from overseas. Spanish coal mines, handicapped by difficult geologic conditions and relatively poor quality coal, have been taken over by a state-controlled company, which is attempting to modernize production. Coal output has fallen as imports are cheaper, despite the industry's assured market in state-owned steel and generating plants. Some oil has been found near Burgos, in the Ebro River basin, and offshore; but this is expected to supply less than 10 percent of Spain's annual consumption. Natural gas strikes have been limited, supplying under 10 percent of demand. Spain does possess large supplies of uranium and has embarked on a nuclear power program.

Portugal's variety of minerals, unfortunately, is not matched by commercially exploitable quantities in most cases. Tungsten ores are important, and large reserves of iron ore could support higher production. Minor copper and tin deposits together with limited supplies of coal complete Portugal's mineral resource base. No oil or natural gas had been discovered by the early 1980's, but exploration continues.

Population   Spain's population is projected to grow to 45 million by 2000 A.D.; it has one of West Europe's higher rates of natural increase. Nearly 1 million Spaniards have emigrated, at least temporarily, in search of jobs. Internal migration is also high, flowing from less developed rural areas of the interior to the coastal industrial and tourist centers. Spain has long had serious problems of strong centrifugal forces, cultural and political. The fifteenth century unification under Ferdinand and Isabella, Columbus's patrons, has produced a rather uneasy alliance more than union into a single society. The Catalans of the northeast, with their "capital" at Barcelona, consider themselves very different from the people of northwestern Asturias or southern Andulucia. The choice of Madrid, a geographically central location, as capital (to override the conflicting claims of the great cultural and economic centers like Barcelona, Seville, and Zaragoza) has not unified the contending provinces sufficiently to let a central government relax. The most serious contemporary threat to Spain's stability and civil peace is the Basque independence movement. The Basques are a culturally distinctive group who speak a language unrelated to Spanish. (See Figure 5–3.) Their ancient homeland straddles the border of France and Spain on the western side of the Pyrenees. The Basque desire for regional autonomy has been partly met by Madrid, but not fast enough for the Basques. The central government is sensitive to the potential fragmenting of power among the historic provinces.

Portugal does not have the serious cultural and provincial splintering of Spain but has had to deal with the consequences of losing the last European colonial empire in Africa, the huge territories of Angola and Mozambique. Nearly a million returning colonists from Africa, or about 10 percent of the country's population, had to be absorbed in the late 1970's. Portuguese living standards, while higher than world averages, are low for western Europe. A strong outflow of job-seekers led to a temporary decrease in the population during the 1960's. These Portuguese workers outside Portugal sent home more foreign exchange than Portugal earned through tourism. Foreign workers are always first to suffer from recession abroad. Faltering economic conditions elsewhere are sending thousands of Portuguese back to the home labor market. The same is true for Spain, West Europe's largest "exporter" of labor after Italy.

Agricultural Patterns   About 45 percent of Portugal is in cultivated land, with one third in forest and most of the remainder in meadow and pasture. Overall, precipitation is seasonal. Droughts are common in the south where precipitation is only one fifth the northern average. The land tenure situation is varied, with small family farms dominant in the north and large estates in the sparsely populated south. These estates were taken over during the 1974 revolution, resulting in at least temporary drops in production. Even though Portugal's proportion of work force in agriculture (28 percent) is high by regional standards, the country must import most basic foods. Portugal is a major wine producer, exporting large quantities of its famous port and other wines throughout Europe and North America. Wine production could increase with scientific management of vineyards and a rational policy of land redistribution.

Spain has almost as high a proportion of land under cultivation as does Portugal. There is more pasture and meadow, as the Spanish have not preserved their forests as carefully. Low precipitation over the interior and south has led to large areas of extensive farming combined with smaller irrigated areas of intensive use. There is a general pattern of very small farms in the better-watered north, trending to large estates in the drier south. Spanish agriculture suffers from underuse of some lands, particularly those in large estates, and undercapitalization. Mechanization levels in all of Iberia are much lower than in northwestern Europe.

Industrial Development   Spain is one of the most rapidly modernizing economies of West Europe. Industrial production roughly doubled in the 1960's, and growth continues, aided by the Spanish decision to abandon their autarky policies in 1960. Spanish import tariffs remain high on many consumer goods, an import policy that will have to be extensively revised if Spain's application to the EC is implemented. Only in shipbuilding is Spain's industry on a scale equal to that of the northwestern European economies. As in other West European countries, the government has acquired control of or significant interests in a broad range of industrial enterprises. Among those sectors of the economy in which INI, the government holding company, has at least a one-third interest are petroleum refining, coal mining, automotive production, and chemicals. INI also owns almost all of the shipbuilding industry and controls the nation's airlines.

Steel production has risen rapidly since the 1950's, but consumption rose even faster, necessitating imports. Large quantities of raw materials for steel making must be imported. Spain's chemical industry has been growing rapidly also and is associated with oil refineries and local raw materials. Shipbuilding and auto production are both healthy industries with up-to-date physical plants and a skilled, productive work force.

Portuguese industry is far more concentrated in the highly competitive areas of textiles and clothing. Very strong competition from such industrializing nations as Brazil, India, and the Philippines is posing serious problems for Portugal. A small steel industry must import coking coal and is handicapped by the use of poor quality domestic ores. Like Spain, Portugal has developed a significant shipbuilding industry with ship repairs as a growing specialization. Lisbon's deep, spacious, and well-protected harbor adjacent to the main shipping lanes for oil tankers serving West Europe is an advantage. The Portuguese government has nationalized large companies and is investing heavily in building whole new industrial complexes to reduce unemployment rates. Portugal has applied for full membership in the EC.

Tourism   Both Spain and Portugal have major tourist industries. Spain leads Europe in net total foreign exchange receipts from tourism; it is its most important single industry and supplies more than half of Spain's foreign exchange. There is a high, positive "balance of tourism earnings" as the Spanish spend much less on international tourism than they earn. Iberian tourism is a fine example of **Sun Belt tourism** observable elsewhere in the world. The warm sunshine of southern Spain and Portugal is a powerful attraction for the residents of the highly industrialized northwest European countries. There, gloomy, short winter days are a burden that increasing numbers can afford to escape for a winter holiday. Even in summer, the marine west coast climates of Britain, Scandinavia, and other areas produce overcast, drizzly days in sharp contrast with the almost cloudless skies of the Mediterranean.

Rising incomes in highly industrialized countries, progressively cheaper air fares, and the "bargain" hotel and restaurant rates of relatively poor Spain and Portugal have all contributed to the boom. Spain has aimed at "mass market" tourism, emphasizing lower costs. The tourist trade also helps support traditional Spanish crafts industries for souvenirs. Internal transportation infrastructure has been greatly improved and expanded, and the Costa del Sol and the Costa Bravo have become linear cities with wall-to-wall hotels and vacation-home condominiums. Tourism is heaviest in summer, the traditional (and only) holiday time for working class and lower middle-class Europeans. Land speculation and apparently uncontrolled building have marred some of Spain's most beautiful coastlines. The tourist industry in Spain is expected to continue expansion, but not at the hectic pace of the 1950's and 1960's. Portugal's tourist trade is only one tenth that of Spain as it has not so actively sought mass-market tourism.

Economic Problems and Prospects   Spain's preferential trading agreement with the EC, its heavy tourist inflow, and remittances from Spaniards working overseas have been instrumental in maintaining a viable economy throughout most of the 1970's. However, high oil imports severely penalized the economy during the late 1970's. If a policy of government subsidies to evidently inefficient industries continues, and tourism does not continue growth, Spain could come under serious financial stress.

Portugal used to rely on surpluses generated by its huge African colonies, plus remittances home from workers abroad, to balance its high rate of imports. The shock of losing the colonies has not yet been fully overcome. There is room for an expanded tourist industry to take up some of the slack employment, but Portugal will suffer proportionally more than Spain from OPEC price increases as it has no known domestic fields. Portugal must complete the revolution towards a democratic society, drastically modernize its agriculture, and expand its industrial base in order to improve living standards.

Spain is making a determined effort to increase its export markets in Latin America, building on common language and cultural ties. Spanish heritage is a strong component of Latin America cultures, and the various revolutions against imperial Spain early in the nineteenth century are so far in the past that an amicable relationship prevails with its former colonies.

THE CONTINENTAL CORE—FRANCE, WEST GERMANY, AND BENELUX

One of the greatest concentrations of urban populations and industrial centers of the world lies in northern France, West Germany, and the Benelux countries (Belgium, Netherlands, Luxembourg). To a significant degree, this complex is the geographical, economic, even cultural core of West Europe. France has long occupied a leadership role, for centuries *the* leadership role, in European culture. West Germany, strongly resurgent after the wartime destruction and postwar division of Germany, is one of the world's foremost industrial states even without its European Community partners. Together with the Benelux countries on their North Sea flank, France and Germany formed the core of the European Community (only Italy is both an original member and not in this subregion). The nucleus of the EC was formed by the European Coal and Steel Community, in which the two historic antagonists, France and (West) Germany, set aside their titanic struggles for mastery of Europe and cooperated in its economic recovery and resurgence into a world leadership role. While major West European industrial powers (Britain, Italy, Sweden) and smaller industrial economies (Spain, Austria, Switzerland) lie beyond the core, this heartland is the greatest concentration of economic power in this important region (see Figure 5–7).

The Resource Base   The importance of international flows of raw materials throughout the subregion is underlined by the geographic pattern of the resource base. Although geologically diverse France has a fairly large array of mineral resources, large quantities of coal must be imported from West Germany. French coal production has dropped to less than half the mid-1960's peak. Iron ores are plentiful; the largest fields (in Lorraine) are well situated for interchange with West Germany whose **complementary** surpluses of good quality coal are not far from the French border. This geographic juxtaposition suggested the idea of the European Coal and Steel Community of 1951. French statesman Robert Schuman saw the eco-

nomic logic of this coal-iron ore exchange, a potential benefit to both French and West German steel industries. (See Figure 5–6.) In addition to its coal production, West Germany ranks as one of the world's largest producers of lignite (low quality, low thermal energy content "brown coal"). Not useable in steel manufacture, it can be used to generate electricity in place of imported oil. Neither France nor Germany has any immediate or foreseeable chance of following Britain and Norway into petroleum self-sufficiency. France produces less than 5 percent of its oil needs. Germany's share of the North Sea fields is tiny; its government is appealing the 1958 Geneva agreement on dividing the floor of the North Sea for oil and gas production. France's natural gas fields, like its oil fields, are already in declining production. West German oil production, third in the region after Britain and Norway, is still less than 5 percent of its consumption. In natural gas production, Germany is again third, after the Netherlands and Britain. Prospects for further discoveries of gas in Germany are far better than for oil.

Like other long-industrialized nations, Belgium's coal deposits have been worked for so long that production has been in decline except for new, deep mines made possible by new technology and rising energy prices. Belgium's gas supply is mostly in the form of by-product gas from the coke ovens processing coal for the steel industry. Netherland's coal production, too, has been falling, but natural gas is a major resource. These deposits (at Groningen) fuel its economy and earn foreign exchange through gas exports via pipeline to Switzerland, France, West Germany, Belgium, and even Austria. Gas sales are so large that the Netherlands also imports natural gas from Norway (via Britain) and from Algeria.

Luxembourg's iron ore is its major resource; production is down from the peak of the 1960's, and French ores are now imported on a large scale. While the Netherlands has no important resources after its fossil fuels, Belgium is little better off, with only a minor iron ore industry. France is a major source of bauxite and potash, used in fertilizer and chemical industries. West Germany is a major producer of potash also, along with zinc, but is only a minor source of lead, bauxite, and copper.

Population Distribution and Characteristics   France, once regarded as the premier example of a nation that had reached the very low growth stage at the end of the **demographic transition,** has begun to grow more recently. Between World Wars I and II, France's population growth rate was one of the lowest anywhere. After 1945, the birthrate rose and remained fairly high until the late 1970's. As with Britain, the end of empire for France not only saw a return of colonials, but also an influx of citizens of the former colonies. Algerians make up a large percentage of the unskilled labor force in France. There are also groups of Arab peoples from formerly French Lebanon, Syria, and North Africa, along with Southeast Asians from former French Indo-China.

West Germany's population expanded after 1945 largely through in-migration attracted by the booming economy and, for East Germans, personal freedom. The Federal Republic's territory went from a 1946 population of 46 million to 62 million by 1971. Nearly 2 million fled East Germany before the infamous wall shut off the "escape valve" of West Berlin. Jobs have attracted inflows of Italians, Spaniards, Greeks, Yugoslavs, and Turks. Rising social problems and economic slowdowns have led to legislation controlling the inflow of foreign workers (*gastarbeiters,* "guest workers"), but EC countries only reluctantly modify the right of "open borders" to workers. Italy is thus not restricted as a source of workers, and as agreements between the EC and Spain, Greece, and Portugal mature towards full membership, these "sender" nations will resume their traditional source roles. West German birthrates are now so low that the government is expressing concern for the future of the German nation. The population has actually declined since 1975.

Belgium's high density population, one of the highest in Europe, is unfortunately badly split culturally. Belgium lies along the **shatter zone** of Latin and Germanic culture and language. Unlike Switzerland, whose multilingual population has achieved complete harmony, Belgium has a potentially very serious division. A relatively sharp, east-west line separates the Flemish-speaking (a language closely related to Dutch, itself a close relation of German) majority in the north from the 45 percent of the population who speak French (including bilinguals). Brussels, the capital, is approximately astride the linguistic-cultural divide.

Luxembourg's third of a million residents have the second highest rate of population decrease, after West Germany. Almost 20 percent of their work force is of foreign origin.

Over the last one hundred years, the Netherlands have had one of Europe's highest average growth rates. Over 14 million people are crowded into the Netherlands, with a projected 16 million at the end of the century. A numerically small, but highly visible minority of Indonesians from the former empire have carried internal political struggles, particularly over the autonomy of the Moluccas, into terrorist activity within the Netherlands. As elsewhere in West Europe, these former subject peoples are employed in unskilled service jobs.

Agricultural Patterns France's relative wealth and power over the centuries can be traced, at least in part, to its variety and quality of agricultural resources. Almost a third of France is under cultivation, with another quarter in pasture and meadow. Thanks in part to both a **rationalization of holdings** program (consolidating former scattered plots) and a continuing flow of people from the land, France averages larger farms than most of its continental neighbors. France's wheat production is so high that it is among the top ten wheat producers in the world, growing almost half of the wheat supply of the original six-country nucleus of the EC. The Mediterranean environment of the southeast provides winter fruits and vegetables, olives, and rice, while the more continental climate of northeastern France produces apples and dairy products, and the almost subtropical conditions of the southwest can grow the crops requiring a hot, wet summer, such as corn or tobacco. Corsica provides citrus fruit. This variety and the productivity of France's broad range of soil types places French agriculture in a very strong position within the EC.

West German farms average little more than half the size of the French. As with France, West German agriculture is far more productive now than a few decades ago, with larger inputs of fertilizer and greater use of machinery. Despite much less favorable environmental conditions than in France, West Germany manages to supply about 80 to 85 percent of its food consumption. West German agriculture emphasizes grains, sugar beets, and animal fodder; livestock products bring in most of German farm income.

As in West Germany, Belgian agriculture occupies a great deal of land but supplies little of the total gross domestic product. The livestock industry is well developed on the cool, wet coastal plains and hilly southeast plateau as well. Luxembourg's agriculture pattern is similar to Belgium's; livestock products supply 80 percent of farm income.

More than half of the Netherlands is agricultural land, and more than half of this is pasture. Netherlands' exports to the rest of the EC include beef, butter, eggs, and cheese. Almost half of the cultivated land is used to produce food crops and root crops, such as beets and potatoes. Horticulture, commercial gardening of fruits and vegetables, is well advanced in the Netherlands, which has half of Europe's total greenhouse horticulture.

Urban Industrial Development and Development Strategies France's iron and steel industry is moving towards tidewater, as is Italy's. This location enables them to import raw materials at the cheapest transportation costs and ship finished products to world markets. Japan has long demonstrated the desirability of such coastal locations. The general surplus in steel capacity throughout Europe, as each industrial nation has expanded capacity, has retarded French plans for further expansion of its tidewater

Dairy Cooperative, Friesland, Netherlands. The highly developed economy of the Netherlands involves the production and processing of high-quality farm products such as this factory for condensed milk. (Courtesy of United Nations)

mills. The French aluminum industry, like those of Norway or Canada, is attracted to inexpensive hydroelectric power in mountain valleys where competition for the energy is minimal. The French ship concentrated ores to either the Alpine valleys near the Swiss and Italian borders or to the Pyranean valleys near the Spanish border. The highly diversified chemical industry is spatially associated with raw material sources, such as the potash beds of Alsace, the petroleum refineries of the lower Siene valley, Bordeaux, and Marseillies and the hydroelectricity of the Alpine valleys. The French aerospace industry, in addition to cooperating on the *Concorde,* is involved in consortiums

building the much more successful "airbus," an intermediate-range, high-capacity airliner. Military aircraft are a major export; France sometimes seems to specialize in supplying countries and regimes out of favor with (and therefore unable to purchase aircraft from) the United States, Britain and/or the Soviet Union. The French reputation for quality and innovative design is excellent. France's automobile industry and electrical engineering are concentrated in metropolitan Paris.

Paris has so long dominated French political, economic, and cultural life that the French government has taken active steps to decentralize both industry and service

Paris, France. In many ways in highly centralized France, Paris is *the* city, with such an overwhelming lead in many functions that it is an excellent example of an unchallenged "primate city." (Photo by Stansfield)

functions (including government) outside the Paris region. Industrial building permits are deliberately restricted for Paris but easy to obtain outside that metropolitan area. Industries willing to locate or relocate in high unemployment areas can get up to 20 percent of the cost of relocation or expansion from the government. The first phase of decentralization seemed to favor the outer suburbs of Paris, a phenomenon of location similar to that experienced in North America and in Britain. Recent French government policy allocates relocation-expansion aid almost in direct proportions to distance away from Paris. Paris is an excellent example of a *world city*—a city of international economic, cultural, and political importance.

French experiments in comprehensive planning also emphasize the expansion of the port at Marseilles and the development of entirely new resort facilities along the Mediterranean coast. Marseilles is to become the southern European version of Rotterdam's *Europort*—a capacious, highly efficient port serving a multinational hinterland. Genoa is Marseille's chief rival for this multinational port function. The long-term and accelerating growth of tourist and vacation land use along the Mediterranean coast has led the French to attempt to divert further tourist resort development from the almost too popular Riviera, lying to the east of Marseilles towards the Italian frontier. New resorts, some of spectacular modern design, are being built west of the Rhone estuary in a previously non-tourist-oriented area. In this way, mounting pressures on the Riviera can be reduced, and income diverted to a lower-income area with as yet uncrowded beaches. New ski resorts are also being built in the French Alps. This massive capital investment and comprehensive planning, which

preserves much of the beauty of the physical environment, is largely responsible for the continuing growth of international tourism to this, the largest tourist recipient in western Europe in terms of total income. (Spain's *net* income is higher as the French themselves spend much money as tourists abroad.)

West Germany's industrial economy is heavily geared to export and to heavy industry. Unlike the steel industries of most other industrial states, West German steel plant expansion and new sites have not emphasized coastal location. Instead, a strong orientation toward coal fields is maintained in the Ruhr and Saar areas. German chemical technology ranks among the world's first and best. German leadership in the development of coal tar derivatives, for example, introduced many new synthetic products from this one source—dyes, pharmaceuticals, and artificial fibers. The West German chemical industry remains one of the largest in Europe and features three huge corporations that rank with the largest in the United States. The research and market rivalries of these three have helped produce a productively competitive situation. The "Big 3" (Bayer, Hoechst, BASF) have become multinational companies, marketing and packaging their products through the world and establishing manufacturing facilities in many foreign countries. This **location strategy** helps overcome import restrictions and tariff barriers; it also reduces labor costs and avoids further concentration of potentially polluting industries in West Germany.

The Volkswagen auto plant at Wolfsburg, started before World War II but greatly expanded after the war, is the largest single auto plant in the world. VW was the first mass-produced European car to invade the American

Ski Resort in the French Alps. The "Leisure Revolution" in France, as throughout the developed world, has led to the creation of more tourist facilities, many in formerly marginal areas in the geographic and economic senses. (Courtesy of United Nations/Orr)

Barges Loading Coal at Duisburg, West Germany. The highly developed transport systems of West Europe, such as its inland waterways, support international transfers of raw materials, energy, and manufactured goods. (Courtesy of United Nations)

market on a large scale. The fantastic growth rate of the 1950's and 1960's are behind it, but VW now is an international producer with plants in Mexico and Brazil as well as the United States. On the other hand, U.S. companies (GM and Ford) operating in West Germany hold about a third of the domestic West German market.

Precision instruments and optical products (cameras, microscopes, telescopes) are traditional German specialties now under severe competition in world markets. Shipbuilding is a problem industry for West Germany as for other nations. Overcapacity of shipyards and strong competition for contracts make it an uncertain sector of the economy. Shipbuilding is highly **cyclical,** that is, the demand fluctuates greatly from year to year reflecting swings in employment and profit levels.

Although West Germany ranks second only to France in total foreign tourist receipts, the Germans are such enthusiastic tourists themselves that West Germany has a net tourist receipt deficit of billions. In areas outside West Europe, Germans are likely to be first or second in numbers of tourists from Europe, even in such places as Thailand or Tanzania. Within West Europe, the West Germans are the most important source of foreign tourists for most of their immediate neighbors.

West German transportation system development has given it one of the highest densities of transport routes in the world. The superhighways (autobahns), begun in the 1930's, are among the finest anywhere but are also very heavily travelled. The West Germans have also saturated the extensive canal network that links practically every major city and even connects the Rhine-Main system with the Danube (Donau) network. With highways and canals both unable to take much more freight load, the

Germans have modernized their rail network for both freight and fast passenger service. The national airline (Lufthansa) handles large numbers of domestic as well as international flights.

Belgian industry has suffered the destruction of two wars in this century but, paradoxically, this very destruction meant that there was no way to maintain obsolescent facilities. Modernization has insured high efficiency. Metallurgical industries are handicapped, however, by a lack of domestic ores and a small local market. Many multinational companies have chosen Belgium as a final assembly point, especially for cars, due to its central location in West Europe. The inflow of EC and North American corporate investments has helped make Brussels one of the most expensive cities to visit, as hotels and apartments are in very high demand. Belgium's northern province of Flanders was one of the pioneers of the Industrial Revolution, specializing in textiles. Britain's rise in the Industrial Revolution can be traced partly to this growing market for British wool and the technology source provided there. Textiles are still an important industry but have shifted from imported natural fibers to synthetics. Like West Germany, Belgium has a net deficit in tourism. Tourists are attracted both to North Sea beaches and to Belgium's historic cities.

Luxembourg, once almost totally dependent on the local iron-ore based steel industry, has diversified. Aluminum, chemicals, and rubber tires are among the new plants attracted to Luxembourg since World War II.

The Netherlands' economy is closely tied to its important port functions and trans-shipment activities. The Dutch control the Rhine Delta; that river is Europe's busiest waterway, serving the industrial heartland of West Germany and even supplying Switzerland with a port. The same facilities that handle much of the international trade also serve the Dutch industrial complex. The long-term trend in ocean shipping has been for ships to get larger. These larger ships increase economic efficiency, but require deeper water, more spacious harbors, and larger freight volumes. The multi-national hinterland of the largest port in the world, Rotterdam's Europoort, thus helps support the Dutch industrial base. Steel and chemicals both benefit from tidewater locations in the Netherlands. Shipbuilding has the usual problems, but the Dutch have been able to maintain a viable aircraft industry by specializing in smaller aircraft. The huge Philips electrical appliance firm, headquartered in the Netherlands, makes everything from electric razors to x-ray machines. It is a giant, even when compared with U.S. and Japanese competitors. The Dutch share German enthusiasm for touring abroad; there is a negative balance of tourism receipts, and the Netherlands is an increasingly expensive place to visit.

A common problem of developmental strategy must be faced by West Europe's industrial heartland and much of the rest of the region. In a sense, the region, and especially this subregion, is **overdeveloped.** While much of the world must cope with problems of underdevelopment (in essence, the inadequacy of technological levels and industrial and transport infrastructure to fully develop the resource potential), the crowded, older industrial nations must deal with a diminishing resource base and heavy dependence on imported raw materials. The Netherlands is perhaps the best example of this phenomenon in which human resources of skill and efficiency are developed to the maximum. The Holland Randstadt (Holland "ring-city") and the agglomeration of heavy-industrial constellations in the Ruhr Valley are two unusual world cities, particularly significant in that they represent a multinuclear form of urbanization that seems to be growing rapidly in Europe just as in the "megalopoli" of North America (see Figure 5–8).

West Europe has evolved several different development strategies to cope with overdevelopment. One approach is to import cheap grains and agricultural byproducts to convert into high-value, high-quality exports such as Dutch cheese or Swiss chocolate. English candy, Scotch and Irish whiskey, and Dutch and Danish beer are other examples of paying for bulk, basic food imports by high-value processed agricultural exports. Another strategy is intensive development of exports of high-value-

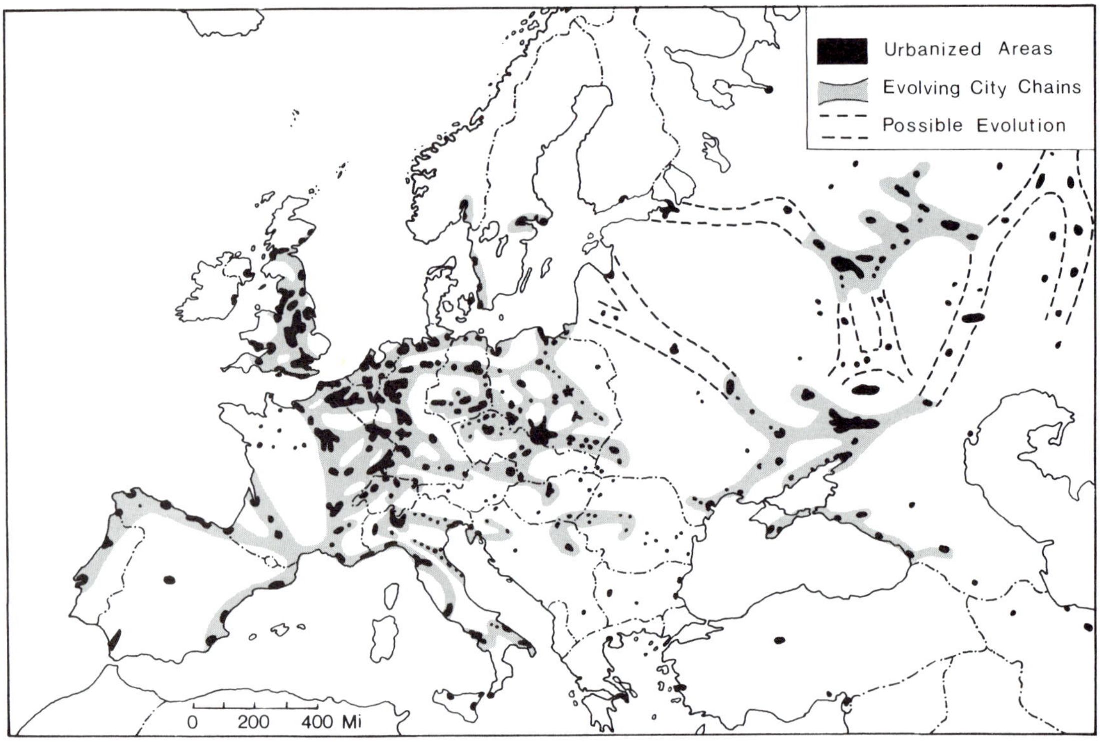

FIGURE 5–8
City Chains of Europe. Industrial development spawned by coal fields, other mineralized areas, and river valley's transport advantages have shown a tendency to lead to linear urbanized strips. Locational advantages of low density land between cities and astride connecting transport lines also spur the phenomenon of city chains.

added manufactured goods such as Dutch electrical apparatus, Swedish telephones, or Italian refrigerators. Another common economic adjustment is the *hidden export*—the sale of services rather than goods. Tourism is probably the most common hidden export; others include banking, brokerage and insurance services, ships crews, and rental of facilities.

Political Stability   Within a range of variation, the countries of the continental core are more stable than the world average. While all except Luxembourg have some cultural minorities and/or provincial centrifugal forces of some divisive potential, the national governments concerned seem capable of dealing with these tensions through compromise solutions acceptable to all. In France, the Celtic-heritage people predominant in Brittany and parts of Normandy press forward with varying zeal their claims to recognition of their language and culture, with more provincial autonomy a possible outcome. West Germany is a federal state in which the ten *lander* have some measure of local control. The Bayern Land (Bavaria) has traditionally considered itself less subservient to the central government and asserts a Bayerish culture as somewhat separate from the rest of Germany. However, this provincialism is not a threat to the continued existence of the Federal Republic. West Germany's major problem, either an international or domestic problem depending on the viewpoint, is the 1945 split of Germany into occupation sectors that became the German Federal Republic (West) and the German Democratic Republic (East). Although both Germanies seem to have reconciled themselves to the loss of territory to Poland and the USSR following the war, the split of Germany and Germans will remain *the* question for the duration of the split.

Belgium can be considered stable only if the north-south split of Flemish and Walloons can be peacefully resolved. The two language-cultural groups, if led by extremists, could eventually split the country. Cultural differences are sharpened by the different economic outlooks of the two areas. The Walloons of the south must cope with the challenge of modernizing an obsolete steel industry and phasing out old, inefficient coal mines. The new investments have gone to the booming ports and port-related industries of the Flemish north. Also, the Walloons have been losing the "cradle race" to the more prolific Flemish.

Luxembourg's population, by contrast, is essentially homogeneous culturally, except for a resident foreign labor force that is one of the highest percentages in western Europe (18 percent). Beyond small, sometimes violently demonstrative minorities from the former colonies, the Netherlands is quite stable. The major challenge the Dutch face is controlling land use and environmental pollution in such a heavily industrialized, heavily populated, small country. The corrosively polluted Rhine must be cleaned up; this environmental problem is compounded by the international status of that river basin. With an already great urban constellation, the Holland ring-city (Randstat), the Dutch are planning their crowded land to avoid becoming a huge megalopolis with some agricultural areas imbedded within. The challenge of effective planning is seldom as pressing as in Holland. Fortunately, the Dutch experience in long-range planning, gained in surviving the hazards of flood and storm in the swampy delta areas, as well as in reclaiming extensive areas of shallow seabed in the polder projects, indicates both capability and determination.

BRITAIN AND EIRE

Placing Britain and Eire in the same subregion may seem to some like assigning dogs and cats to the same cage. More than eight centuries of English colonialism in Ireland have left a legacy of hatred and mistrust between the Irish and English. Its nadir has been reached in the tragic civil war in Northern Ireland. However, the very fact of British domination for centuries and its consequent effect on the development of contemporary Eire, plus the very close ties of these two in trade, tourism, and migration, make this a logical subregion.

There is a confusing abundance of political and geographical names for the components of the state known officially as the United Kingdom of Great Britain and Northern Ireland. The United Kingdom includes England, Scotland, Wales, and Northern Ireland, together with quasi-independent units like the Isle of Man and the Channel Islands. *Great Britain* refers to the island on which are located the once-separate states of England, Wales, and Scotland. *Britain* and *British* are used interchangeably with the lands and residents of the island, sometimes implying inclusion of Northern Ireland. The entire political unit is sometimes misnamed *England.* It is neither accurate nor advisable to refer to the inhabitants of Scotland or Wales as *English.*

The United Kingdom (UK) has had to adjust its economy, internationalist philosophy, military expenditures, and self-image to the rapid devolution of empire. The largest empire the world had ever seen presented the British with both the problems of huge expenditures for immense naval forces and colonial administrations and the potentials of enormous markets and diverse raw material supplies. As in its construction, the end of empire has presented both problems and potentials. The British have a record second to none in consciously preparing colonial peoples for self rule. The resulting independent states have not all honored the model presented by Westminster. The transition from colony to fully independent, equal, and voluntary members of the British Commonwealth has not always been smooth for either the ex-colony or the parent country.

The economy of the UK has been the slowest growing among the West European states. Its transition from imperial splendor, with guaranteed imperial markets and financial partners, to a rather small state by superpower standards has been handicapped by four factors. These are (1) Long insistence on retaining preferential trade relationships within the Commonwealth. (2) The associated failure of the UK to join the Common Market at its outset. (Australia and New Zealand pressured to retain their preferred status in British markets while the personal antagonism of General DeGaulle also resulted in delaying entrance into the Common Market.) (3) The hardship of operating a largely obsolescent industrial plant. (4) An economy besieged by a bitter, sometimes irrationally self-destructive class warfare. The psychological transition to the late twentieth century's realities has not yet been fully made. This fact must remain in the forefront of any geographical analysis of the UK. Similarly, Eire (Republic of Ireland) has not yet recovered from its long colonial status, although its evolution of more suitable economic and political policies may outpace those of the UK.

The Resource Base   The resource base of the island of Britain is not particularly impressive for a state that led the first Industrial Revolution. Coal has been mined for some seven centuries in Britain; it has been exploited on an industrial scale for three centuries, and it is projected that a two-hundred-year supply exists at present rates of mining. Obviously, the preceding centuries of mining have removed the most accessible coal and the least expensive to exploit. The remaining coal lies deep and in narrow, broken seams. Mechanization was very slow in many pits. Government takeover under the Labor (socialist) government did not mechanize any more enthusiastically than private owners due to both shortage of investment money and unwillingness to mechanize many miners (and voters) out of a job. Still, mechanization is progressing and Britain's coal production is at a cheaper overall cost than Germany's. Tin has been mined in Cornwall for several thousands of years; high prices recently have rejuvenated some mines to produce about one fifth of Britain's needs. Iron ore was sufficient to supply Britain's early industrialization, but the remaining stock is of rather low iron content, with many impurities.

The brightest parts of the resource picture are natural gas and petroleum. By 1976, Britain was already the second largest European producer of natural gas (after the Netherlands), and production is expected to quadruple to nearly 200 billion cubic meters by the early 1980's. Production was already so high in the early 1970's that the British government required households to shift from burning coal for home heating to natural gas. This not only guaranteed a market to sustain heavy investments in gas exploitation, but reduced air pollution levels in the cities. Oil discoveries have been most encouraging. The UK's section of the North Sea (see Figure 5–6) includes three large, proven fields. These hold at least one billion barrels of oil and make the UK the only Western industrial leader self-sufficient in oil. Optimistic reports of a possible huge oil basin in southwestern England could make the UK a significant oil exporter by the mid-1980's. Extensive test drilling has been carried out in the south of England, the channel, and the *western approaches*—the shipping lanes leading from the open Atlantic to the channel.

Eire's natural resource base is less encouraging as that Republic makes its long-delayed entrance into the modern industrial world. Some natural gas has been discovered, and exploited, off the southwestern coast near Cork (see Figure 5–6). Exploration is accelerating in the Irish Sea. Eire has little coal but uses large quantities of peat (turf), compacted vegetation matter taken from bogs, which generates about one fourth of Eire's electricity. Historically, Ireland mined some gold, but metallic minerals had not been exploited on an industrial scale for centuries before strikes of copper, lead, zinc, and silver were discovered in the 1960's. Eire now is one of the largest European sources of lead and zinc.

Population Distribution and Characteristics   The population of the UK is about 56 million. The UK's slow population growth rate and low birth and death rates identify it clearly as being in the last stage of the demographic transition. Over 16 percent of the population has passed retirement age. The birthrate of 12 per 1,000 is considered rather low. Eighty percent of the UK's populaiton live in towns or cities, and seven giant *conurbations* (urban areas that have grown towards one another, creating a chain of urbanized areas or a large city expanding outward to include older, once-separate cores) house about 30 percent of the population. In common with other mature industrial-urban economies, the UK has had slow growth or decline in population in these huge central cities.

Eire was the twentieth century's only example of a continuously declining population for over a half a century. (East Germany's population loss, likewise due to out-

Collecting Peat for Fuel, Eire. Peat is a traditional domestic fuel for cooking and heating in Eire. It remains competitive due to the high price of imported oil. (Courtesy of United Nations)

migration, but for different motivations, did not last as long.) The population had reached 6.25 million just before the infamous potato famine of the 1840's. Population had expanded after the introduction of the potato from South America, as Ireland's climate, poor for most grains, was suitable for potatoes. A blight killed most potato plants and a huge out-migration began. The out-migration was sustained, long after the potato blight problem was resolved, by a lack of industrial jobs in Ireland. In 1961, Eire's population was only 2.8 million after more than a century of heavy migration to Britain, North America, and Oceania. Population began to grow again in the 1960's and is presently 3.5 million. About half of Eire's people live in towns, and one fifth of the nation lives in Dublin, which is far larger (580,000) than Cork (130,000), the second city of the Republic.

In addition to the steady inflow of Irish to the UK, the UK has received a large immigration from India, Pakistan, Jamaica, and Trinidad. Commonwealth passports allowed these citizens of former colonies unrestricted access to Britain. The sudden surge in nonwhite, non-European culture arrivals caused stricter immigration laws by the late 1970's. At first, resentment against Indians and Pakistanis was higher than that for Caribbean blacks because the Indians and Pakistanis were more likely to be competing for middle-class jobs. The initial resentment against Indians and Pakistanis has now largely subsided as these immigrants demonstrate that they are hard working, ambitious, and generally strong on law and order. Few Asian immigrants are accused of violent crimes. However, black resentment against very low-paying jobs and the growth of ghettoes has exploded into violent demonstra-

tions. Although Britain has long offered a haven to persecuted minorities such as the Huguenots (Protestant French) and Iberian Jews, the sharper cultural differences and much larger number of commonwealth emigrants have strained the British reputation for tolerance.

EC membership opens entry for workers from other EC countries for both Britain and Eire. Of course, it also opens new migration opportunities for the British and Irish. EC migrants from Holland and Belgium enjoy the warmest welcome, although little friction is traceable to any EC workers.

Agricultural patterns   About 80 percent of Britain's land is in agriculture; the figure for Northern Ireland is 85 percent. Only one third of that land is cultivated, with the balance in pasture and meadow. It is lowland Britain that is cultivated in barley, wheat, oats, potatoes, sugar beets, and hops (used for flavoring beer). Highland Britain, which is most of the Pennines, Wales, and Scotland, is mainly pasture for sheep and cattle. Britain produces about half of its total food requirements, an impressive figure considering its very high population density, high proportion of land not suitable for cultivation, and a farm population of only about 2.5 percent. Productivity has been significantly increased since World War II. Beef production has doubled and hog production tripled since 1946. If tropical and subtropical commodities are subtracted from consideration (Britain could not possibly produce these anyhow), Britain grows two thirds of its food requirements.

Although, as indicated by a voter referendum, the British generally favor membership in the EC, the EC's agricultural policies are a main point of disagreement.

British farmers would be in an excellent competitive position if French and German farmers were less insulated from marketplace realities. France refuses to allow British lambs into its markets in defiance of an EC ruling.

Eire uses about 70 percent of its land in agriculture; three fourths of this is in pasture. Agriculture employs over 20 percent of the Irish and accounts for 18 percent of Eire's Gross Domestic Product, much higher than the industrial nations of West Europe. Irish farms tend to be much smaller than those of the UK. In export terms, Eire is practically a one-crop economy agriculturally. Cattle dominate food exports, and Eire is highly vulnerable to steep cycles of cattle prices in the EC.

Urban-Industrial Development Patterns "British and Best" was once a proud boast of the quality of British manufactured goods. Allowing for some patriotic overstatement, it was largely true up until World War I. The UK was the first industrial nation and the British take justifiable pride in this. There is a penalty attached to being first, however. Unless care is taken to maintain a sufficiently high rate of modernization, the first becomes the oldest in industrial plant, and the least efficient. First in existence can then mean first in obsolescence. In Rostow's scheme, Britain had reached the final phases of industrialization (that is, the country had fully matured) by 1914. But it was too dependent on coal mining, steel manufacturing, textiles, and shipbuilding. In 1914, Britain launched over 60 percent of the whole world's total commercial tonnage of ships. It now supplies about 4 percent. Except for one in Belfast, the whole shipbuilding industry has been nationalized. Obsolescence of both plant and thinking are handicaps. While the Japanese concentrated on building highly profitable supertankers and container ships through the 1960's, the British were launching a heavily subsidized transatlantic liner, the *Queen Elizabeth II*. While a beautiful engineering work, the *Queen Elizabeth II* is an anachronism in the age of jumbo jets, as much a source of pride as profit.

The textile industry, of course, is one of the first established by developing countries. British textile production, a mainstay of the economy, has slumped drastically. Only the high quality, specialized textiles retain a future in a highly competitive world industry.

The dissolution of empire has meant that British goods no longer enjoy protected markets. Adjustment to the Common Market or EC (Britain entered in 1973) has not been easy. While membership opens up the entire market to British exports without tariff, it works both ways. Inefficient manufacturers in Britain will be forced to close. Supporting high-cost French and German farm products, while sealing off the former Commonwealth food suppliers, is highly unpopular and costs over $2.5 billion per year.

The chemical industry is apparently thriving. Partly British-controlled Imperial Chemical Industries (ICI) is one of the largest in the world, and partly British-owned Shell Oil has large petrochemical plants in the UK. British Petroleum (BP), partly owned by the British government, is another major factor in this third most important export industry.

The small size of the British domestic market led government-owned British Aircraft Corporation to agree to jointly produce a supersonic aircraft with France's Aerospatiale. The resulting *Concorde* is an unfortunate example of costly mistakes in market analysis coupled with superb design and engineering. Research and development costs in aircraft manufacturing are huge and must be spread over a large "model run" or number of units with that design. Competing American aircraft manufacturers can count on a large domestic market and profitable military contracts to help underwrite at least part of the research and development costs. Britain and France jointly spent some $2.5 billion to produce the first *Concorde*. Very few (nine) have been sold to date. Americans are particularly concerned about the alleged damage to the upper atmosphere by supersonic aircraft and the effects of sonic booms generated when the aircraft accelerates beyond the speed of sound. The *Concorde* was initially a very noisy aircraft when taking off at subsonic speeds. The Americans decided not to build their own supersonic commercial transport; without access to lucrative American markets, the Concorde was extremely unattractive to airlines. The eventual lifting of American bans on *Concorde* landings has hardly helped, as the *Concorde* is an "energyhog." Its "payload" (passenger capacity) of only one hundred is considered too small in relation to operating costs. The commercial failure of *Concorde* has been a very bitter experience for both the British and the French.

Ireland's industrialization began very late. Peripheral to industrial Europe, it remained almost untouched by the Industrial Revolution. Even by 1976, only 30 percent of the Irish work force was in industry, compared with 57 percent of British employment in manufacturing plus other fields related to industry. Eire's per capita income is lower than the UK's and is comparable more to Mediterranean than northwestern Europe. (See Figure 5–5.) Irish wage rates, though rising, are still lower than most highly industrialized nations. This, along with Eire's policy of "tax holidays" (no taxes on profits earned by exports until 1990) should lure more factories from EC corporations. Eire's very attractive combination of tariff-free access to the whole EC, low wages, and shorter distance to North American markets continues to boom its industrial growth.

Value of exports increased 150 percent in seven years in the 1970's. Food processing remains the largest employer, but probably not for long. Electronic equipment, engineering, and textiles are now prominent. Chemicals are growing quickly, partly because of Gulf Oil's huge supertanker port, oil storage facility, and petrochemical plants at Bantry Bay. Pharmaceuticals are another growing branch. A major aluminum plant is planned near Shannon. A large industrial park near Shannon Airport is subsidized by the government to attract high-value products like industrial diamond production that can logically use air freight.

Changes in Britain's industrial structure can be examined by the experience of the auto industry. Although the internal combustion engine was largely developed in Britain, the British did not expand their auto industry as quickly as the Americans in the early twentieth century, even considering the difference in size of their domestic markets. Again, as in so many other sectors of industry, the size of the domestic market in the United States supported far more efficient mass production. Many economists and political scientists assert that high rates of taxation seriously reduced the availability of investment capital in Britain and an ill-advised high valuation of British currency in a return to the gold standard (1925) helped reduce foreign markets during a critical decade for auto industry expansion. Also, Britain's heavy reliance on international trade (Britain ranks with the much larger economies like Japan and the U.S.—each has about 10 percent of total international trade), made its auto industry, along with other industries, slump alarmingly in the Great Depression of the 1930's. The British auto industry has gradually shifted location by building new plants in Wales, Scotland, and Lancashire, de-emphasizing the older locations of the midlands, Oxford, and metropolitan London. Production is dominated by four large firms, three of which are subsidaries of American or French companies. Cars are the most valuable single item of trade among EC countries and competition with the large German, French, and Italian companies has been fierce. Many EC car manufacturers, including branches of Ford and GM, produce standard models or "Eurocars." Whether actually assembled in Britain, Germany, or Italy, parts flow freely among countries to assemble interchangeable cars. Even Britain's sole big automaker (still under British control and nationalized), BL Industries, assembles some cars in Belgium. Production continues at a high rate, but mainly for the domestic market. British cars should have a bright future in EC and other world markets if a sliding reputation for quality control can be reversed and if the notoriously high number of days lost to strikes can be reduced. Co-operation between labor and management seems to be more of a problem in Britain than in Germany and France.

In contrast to Eire's successful blend of tax holidays and subsidized industrial parks, the UK's **developmental strategies** seem to be poorly coordinated and erratic. (Of course, Eire started with a different set of developmental problems but was not handicapped by extensive obsolescence of plants.) Of Britain's traditional industries, coal, steel, and automobiles seem reasonably modernized and productive. It is questionable whether healthy industries like chemicals, machinery, electronics, oil refining, pharmaceuticals, and clothing should pay excessive taxes to subsidize obsolescent industries like shipbuilding (except profitable off-shore oil platforms) and finance high risk, very high research and development cost products like *Concorde*. Britain's industrial future may lie in those high-technology industries in which the expensive research is available cheaply through licensing from U.S. or Japanese firms or through consortiums with these and other sources. Innovation flourishes in Britain as evidenced by developments like the Hovercraft and advanced technology nuclear plants. The export of "pop culture" consumer goods, fashions, and entertainment has been remarkably successful in the last decades.

Problems and Prospects   The outlook for both Britain and Eire can be described as cautiously optimistic. The UK's long-drawn-out decision, twice frustrated by France, to join the EC should prove more realistic, economically, than retaining Commonwealth trade preferences. British competence in banking and insurance can aid the entire EC. Tourism to Britain should continue to grow; this expansion must be controlled and seasonal peaks smoothed out if possible. Even though the pressure of mass tourism in summer London is distasteful to many Britons, foreign tourism must be encouraged to counterbalance the British tourists' outflow of money. Eire's tourist industry is capable of much larger growth.

The most serious threat to a burgeoning Irish tourism, and to the political stability of both the UK and Eire, is the civil war in Northern Ireland. Part of the problem is economic; an unemployment rate of 11 percent is at least as important as the centuries-old cultural-religious split. Considered separately, the six counties that make up Northern Ireland have a 2-1 Protestant majority. The entire island has an overall Catholic majority. Roman Catholics in Northern Ireland complain of pervasive discrimination, politically, socially, and economically. Working-class Catholics tend to suffer higher unemployment in declining textile and shipbuilding industries. Northern Ireland, sometimes called Ulster, was the only part of Ireland to industrialize in the nineteenth century. (Actually, "Ulster" as a historic designation would include three counties in the Republic). It shares the **plant obsolescence** handicaps of the rest of the UK. Protestant Irish are fearful that a political merger with the Irish Republic would submerge them as a religious-cultural minority and that they then would suffer discrimination. The British army has been in Northern Ireland for more than ten years in an apparently fruitless attempt to put down the war of terror being waged by both sides.

This ongoing civil war, with little realistic hope of resolving the conflict, is hardly the environment to attract badly needed new industrial investment. Both sides need jobs. The economic drain on the UK is serious in terms of welfare costs, subsidies of all kinds, and military expenditures. The Republic, although advocating the union of the divided island, disavows the terrorist activities that are bleeding the people and economy of the north. It is not impossible that terrorism could spill over on a larger scale to the Republic and even destroy the democratic government in Dublin. Clearly, the "Irish question" must be solved for both the UK and Eire if they are to advance at rates comparable to their continental partners in the EC.

The environmental problems of the UK would seem all too familiar to North Americans. The sheer density of urban-industrial populations living at fairly high standards by world averages generates traffic congestion and deterioration pressures on scarce recreational space. The quality of much of the workers housing of the Victorian Era is quite low. The coal-based industrialization of a century and a half has left a scarred landscape in many areas.

The British have earned a reputation as skillful and imaginative planners in their development of **new towns** and in their innovative "recycling" of formerly industrial or transport landscapes for recreation. The first industrialized society also produced the first great industrial cities with their dreary rows of closely-packed brick housing. By the end of the nineteenth century, Britons were experimenting with comprehensively planned, self-contained communities called *new towns,* specifically designed to avoid the poor environments of the largely unplanned industrial cities. Before World War II, the national government had designated a **green belt,** a zone of no-expansion around London, to contain its outward sprawl. This was followed in 1946–47 by the New Towns and Town and Country Planning Acts, which gave the central government wide powers of planning. London, as other "world cities," tends to attract a disproportionately large share of big city-bound internal migration. Eleven new towns have been built on the edge of London's green belt to channel population and industrial expansion in that metropolitan region. Twelve more have been built (or are planned) for England, five for Wales, five for Scotland, and four for Northern Ireland. While there are aspects of monotony to the new towns, in general they have been very successful in meeting their goal of providing a safe, efficient, and humane environment.

SWITZERLAND AND AUSTRIA

Physically very similar, Switzerland and Austria are quite different culturally and economically. Switzerland, whose core was established by a defensive league of three cantons in 1291, is Europe's oldest independent republic; it has not been involved in a foreign war since 1515. Modern Austria, in contrast, is the **rump state** left from a once-vast empire that controlled much of central and southern Europe and ended only in 1919. Much more prosperous Switzerland relies on its control of important north-south transit routes, its highly skilled work force, and its long-standing neutrality and political stability to buttress its intensely private capitalist economy. Austria, more than twice the size of Switzerland but with only about a million more people, has one of the largest publicly owned sectors of the economy in any noncommunist state (the result of a complete economic reorganization after the disaster of World War II). To tourists seeking picturesque mountain scenery and superb skiing, Switzerland and Austria might seem virtually interchangeable, but in many important respects they are distinctively different.

The Resource Base Both Switzerland and Austria are dominated by the great Alpine mountain system; however, their natural resource bases are quite different. While Switzerland has no significant mineral resources under current exploitation, Austria has a considerable range of minerals. Oil fields, small by world standards but significant within Europe, supply nearly one fifth of Austria's needs. However, Austria will have exhausted its local oil reserves within a decade unless new strikes are made. Domestic production of natural gas supplies about half of domestic demand. Some of Austria's small coal fields have ceased production. Lower quality lignite (or brown coal) is currently mined in large quantities. Austria's iron ore has been mined for over two millenia; it too is falling in production and supplies less than one quarter of Austrian consumption. Small quantities of nonferrous metals and chemical minerals are mined.

In both countries, hydroelectric power is an important energy source. Swiss hydro potential is almost completely developed; climbing consumption will be met by adding five new nuclear plants to the three already in production. Seasonal fluctuation in water flow produces seasonal fluctuation in hydro-power generation. In summer, Switzerland exports electricity to France, Italy, and West Germany. In contrast, Austria's hydro potential is little more than half used. Austria exports electric energy and can continue to do so if the potential is further developed.

Population

Switzerland's population of some 6.5 million includes about one million foreigners, mostly workers drawn by the booming Swiss economy. This imported work force is generally employed in lower-skill, lower-paying jobs (construction, maintenance, and tourist service). Minor fluctuations in employment levels are greatly magnified for these "expendable" foreign workers and their compatriots who daily cross the borders to work in Switzerland. The Swiss are often multilingual. Two thirds speak German as their native tongue, nearly one fifth French, and most of the rest, Italian. The population is just about evenly divided between Roman Catholics and Protestants.

Austria's very slowly growing population, currently about 7.6 million, includes a much smaller contingent of foreign workers (about 200,000). Both Austrians and Swiss are predominantly urban. The Ticino (Italian-Swiss border region) and western Switzerland are growing in population faster than eastern Switzerland and the Zurich metropolitan area. In Austria, the largest city and capital, Vienna (Wien) has been declining in population since the loss of empire after World War I.

The Agriculture Base

Only about 25 percent of Switzerland is suitable for cultivation of crops; the rest is too steep, too rocky, or in permanent ice and snow cover. More than a quarter of the country is forested, with the rest of its productive land in pasture. One quarter is incapable of any kind of production. Agricultural production has almost doubled since World War II, despite a decrease in number of farms, due mainly to increased fertilization and more scientific agriculture. Family farms still prevail, supplying about 60 percent of total food production. The Swiss supply all of their own milk, pork, and potatoes and nearly all their beef. Like other European countries, Switzerland subsidizes its agriculture, directly and indirectly, especially by land tax regulation and agricultural product tariffs. There is both strategic logic in this (no nation wants to run short of food in wartime) and a desire to maintain a rural society and landscapes as part of the tourist-attracting milieu.

Less than half of Austria is agricultural land; of this, about 40 percent is cultivated and the rest is pasture. Austria manages to supply nearly 85 percent of its own food needs from this limited land base. The high percentage of pasture land makes Austria, like Switzerland, both self-sufficient in dairy products and even a net exporter. Wheat, rye, barley, potatoes, and sugar beets are grown along with fodder crops. Very small farms are decreasing in number, a phenomenon found throughout West Europe.

Urban-Industrial Development Patterns

Switzerland is probably the world's premier example of human resources overcoming the handicap of a poor raw material and limited energy base. Switzerland was one of the earliest West European states to enter the Industrial Revolution; it still has one of the world's highest proportions of the labor force engaged in industrial production. The Swiss took full advantage of their position astride major north-south routes and significant east-west routeways within Europe. Landlocked, the Swiss worked successfully to internationalize the Rhine River. The Rhine routeway links Basel with the world's greatest port at Rotterdam and with the extensive West European canal network. This transport linkage is as vital to the Swiss economy as is the superb railway system linked with France, Italy, West Germany, and Austria. The Swiss are still building Alpine tunnels to enhance its **corridor functions** for both rails and highways. Pipelines link the Swiss oil refineries with Italy, France, and West Germany.

The early pattern of industrial plant location in Switzerland was one of scattering throughout rural areas and small towns. This reflected the early dependence on direct water power (leading to scattered site development) and the "cottage" industry nature of two of the first industries, watchmaking and textiles. Work in these industries was commonly done at home; entrepreneurs might even subdivide the work and have different parts or processes carried out in different cottages. The shift from direct water power to hydroelectric power did not necessarily concentrate these enterprises in cities, even as small factories replaced cottage labor. Skilled labor generally attracts industry to it, rather than the opposite.

Textiles are now relatively less important. Severe competition has driven the Swiss from low-priced textiles into a specialization in very high quality specialized and fashion textiles such as silk ribbons, lace and velvet.

The Swiss watchmaking industry once dominated world markets with over two thirds of the total world market. Watches are the best example of **high-value-added** goods, as the high price of a fine timepiece is due largely to skilled workmanship and design, rather than any intrinsic value of raw material used. The Swiss could overcome having to import raw materials and fossil fuels by specializing in such high-value-added products. Swiss supremacy in watchmaking has been challenged recently, especially by the Japanese. The new technologies of electronic and digital watches were not adapted by the Swiss soon enough. Swiss labor is also very high priced, as befits its skill, but the high skill required in assembling mechanical watches could not produce electronic watches cheaply enough. The Swiss share of the world market for watches has slipped below half.

The Swiss reputation for quality of design and workmanship is reflected in the success of their machinery and pharmaceutical industries. Electrical machinery, instruments, surgical applicances, and electric locomotives are exported. **Machine tools,** that is, the machines that shape, press, drill, and cut metal and other material to make other machines, are a Swiss specialty. In a hierarchy of industrialization, machine tools would occupy the pinnacle. (See Figure 5–9.) The first step above handcrafts would be simple, human-powered machines like small textile looms. The next step is an increase in scale of this machine and the application of inanimate power. Following these more complex machines is the evolution of an industry specializing in making the machines that make machines.

The Swiss chemical industry, like its metal-fabricating industries, is oriented to high-value-added products. High-bulk, low-value-added chemicals must locate near raw materials, but pharmaceuticals are very high in value, low in bulk, and can be transported economically over large distances. Research and quality control are keys to success in drugs, and the Swiss control a surprising fraction of the world's ethical drug markets. Branch plants and packaging centers distribute Swiss brand names throughout the world.

Fancy food products, based at least partly on imported materials, are also major factors in the Swiss economy and have spawned huge, worldwide corporations. Swiss milk surpluses have been used in the manufacture of fine chocolate and cocoa for a century and a half, using cocoa beans and sugar from the tropics. Cheese manufacturing also consumes large quantities of milk in producing another expensive specialty food for export.

In contrast to free-enterprise dominated Switzerland, Austria's basic industries are nationalized. Profits have frequently been low and productivity stagnant, unfortunately not uncommon characteristics of industries controlled by government bureaucrats. Steel making is the largest single industry in Austria, specializing in high quality steels from an oxygen-blast process invented in Austria. Like neighboring Switzerland, the rest of Austria's industry emphasizes high-value products as most of the raw materials must now be imported. Chemicals, pharmaceuticals, wood pulp, textiles, machinery, and metal consumer products are other important industries. Electronics industries, concentrated in metropolitan Vienna, produce television sets and communications equipment. Unlike Switzerland, Austria has had to overcome the war-time destruction and postwar stripping of its plants as "war reparations" to the USSR.

Both Switzerland and Austria have been able to convert agriculturally unproductive or marginally productive mountains into economic advantages as tourist attractants. The Swiss have developed tourism into not only a major industry, but an art and science to be taught in hotel, restaurant , and tourist service schools to both Swiss and foreigners. Despite a very high-value currency, which makes visits expensive for most foreigners, the Swiss tourist business continues to thrive. West Germans, whose own currency is highly valued, are the largest group of foreign tourists to Switzerland. Austria is one of western Europe's premier tourist areas, with a larger volume of

Technician Adjusting Measurement Device, Geneva, Switzerland. Resource-short Switzerland has long specialized in high-value-added products, such as scientific instruments, to overcome its lack of cheap fuels and domestic ores. (Courtesy of United Nations)

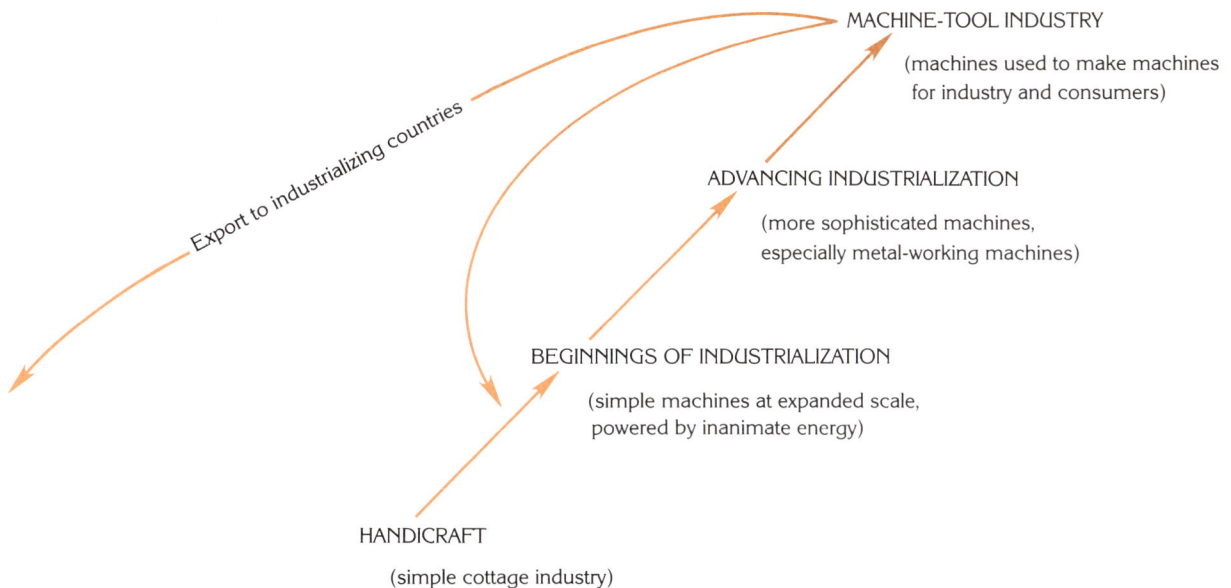

MACHINE-TOOL INDUSTRY

(machines used to make machines
for industry and consumers)

Export to industrializing countries

ADVANCING INDUSTRIALIZATION

(more sophisticated machines,
especially metal-working machines)

BEGINNINGS OF INDUSTRIALIZATION

(simple machines at expanded scale,
powered by inanimate energy)

HANDICRAFT

(simple cottage industry)

FIGURE 5–9
Hierarchy of Industrialization. The key to industrialization is the shift from cottage to factory production: applying inanimate power through machines of increasing scale and sophistication. The highest form of industrialization features a machine tool industry, manufacturing the machines that in turn are used to make machines that produce consumer goods.

tourists than Switzerland. Austrian tourism grew very rapidly during the period 1950–75, as it was perceived as a cheaper version of Switzerland. However, the Austrian currency has recently risen in value, making it less of a bargain. Shared language and proximity, both important factors in tourist trade, explain the predominance of West German tourists in Austria.

Environmental Problems Although the dimensions of the problem are greater in Switzerland, the two alpine countries share a concern to protect the rural environment from ill-planned resort and second-home development. Too-rapid growth of tourist facilities can put unbearable **use-pressures** on the fragile environment near the tree line or above it. Pristine mountain lakes may be fouled by pollution. The farming economy may be pressured out by the competition for land; ski chalets and ski resorts can pay more for land than can a farmer wishing to expand his meadows to remain competitive. Large corporations moving into the hotel business can drive out small family operations, and, by importing seasonal labor, eliminate the part-time jobs that helped make small farms viable. Switzerland has special problems with lake pollution on those lakes that serve as international borders.

Obviously, countries that rely on tourism for earning foreign exchange cannot afford, literally, to allow the environment to deteriorate, biologically, or aesthetically. The Swiss and Austrians are both sensitive to the need to foster

orderly, planned growth of tourist facilities without endangering rural charm.

Political Stability Swiss neutrality, strictly observed and jealously guarded, served the Swiss well through two destructive wars. To be sure, this neutrality served the interests of all combatants, too, as it preserved a safe exchange point for prisoners of war and a meeting ground for diplomatic contacts, official and unofficial. The policy of armed neutrality, coupled with an impressively stable democratic government, has helped make Switzerland a haven for bank accounts from the wealthy of less stable countries. There has been such a strong inflow of money into Switzerland that some Swiss banks began charging "negative interest" on foreign-owned accounts; a charge was levied on the account rather than interest payed. This international banking function helps balance Swiss purchases of foreign raw materials and food and supports an international re-insurance industry (the practice of insurance companies, in effect, purchasing insurance on their higher risks; this reduces their outlay in the event of unusual disasters).

Austria is now a peaceful, stable democracy. The two major political parties effectively share in government, and industrial-labor relations are good. Austrian neutrality is a product of the peace treaty that ended the postwar occupation, and the Austrians have no intention of violating this neutrality in action or spirit. The Austrians are not likely to forget that Soviet tanks are only fifty miles from Vienna. Soviet-Austrian trade is important, with the Soviets supplying natural gas by pipeline. Vienna makes an excellent base for Western business corporations interested in trade with the Soviet bloc. Austria has become adept at balancing their close relationships with both the USSR and the capitalist democracies that have become its major trading partners.

In Switzerland, the neutrality that the Austrians are now trying to emulate is under extensive reconsideration and adjustment. The Swiss are sensitive to foreign opinion that considers their neutrality more of a smug isolationism than a necessary policy to avert disaster. Certainly this criticism is neither universal nor completely fair, but the Swiss have involved themselves with the EC in an economic (if not political) relationship and point to their service to international understanding and well-being through their neutrality.

SCANDINAVIA AND ICELAND (NORDEN)

The five northernmost nations of West Europe, known collectively as "Norden," have had an interwined history and share some economic and cultural traits. At various times, Denmark or Sweden, the most powerful and aggressive states of the subregion in different eras, have dominated the others. The Swedes gained independence from Danish kings in 1523 and became a major European power in the next century. Sweden ruled Finland from the twelfth century to 1809, when Finland became a grand duchy of the Russian Empire. Norway was ruled by Denmark between 1381 and 1814, when Sweden took it over; independence was finally achieved in 1905. Iceland was an independent republic until 1262, when it joined with Norway and then was associated with Denmark from 1360 to 1918. Only in the twentieth century have all five states become independent, politically, and their cultures have been strongly influenced by long association.

Scandinavia   Norway, Sweden, Denmark, and Finland are all very different in their economies. While each has been politically linked with at least one other, and some of their cultural heritage is shared, their resource bases vary enormously. Denmark, whose peninsulas and islands are mostly glacial outwash and debris from the great glaciers that eroded the Scandinavian peninsula to its north, has the poorest resource base. Except for minor peat and lignite deposits, now abandoned, Denmark's only fossil fuels are small, barely commercial deposits of natural gas and oil in its small portion of the North Sea. Its low-lying, sandy, rolling terrain offers practically no hydro-power potential. The Danes' only domestic raw materials are food products that are processed there and a cement industry based on limestone and chalk deposits. About 9 percent of the Danes are farmers; they produce one quarter of the country's exports. In fact, Denmark produces enough food, most of it very high quality food, to supply triple its own population. Two thirds of the land is cultivated, producing wheat, barley, sugar beets, and animal fodder. Denmark has specialized in high-value-added animal products like butter, cheese, eggs, hams, and bacon. Excellent quality control has earned Danish products premium prices throughout northwestern Europe.

Norway, in contrast, has recently struck it rich in its large section of the North Sea oil and gas fields. When the North Sea was first being actively explored for oil and gas, there was some quesiton as to whether Norway was entitled to any share of the shallow sea's resources because a deep sea trench thousands of feet deep separated Norway from the shallow platform of the North Sea bed. Norway's claim was upheld despite the lack of a continuous continental shelf outward from its coast. (See Figure 5–6.) Until about 1970, Norway had no fossil fuels other than some coal production in Svalbard (Spitzbergen), an Arctic archipelago far to the north. Norway has suddenly become an oil-rich country; it was self-sufficient by 1975 and the only European country that could export a surplus of oil by 1980. Due to the trench, oil and gas from Norwegian fields cannot be pipelined directly to Norway; oil is delivered by tanker to Norway but piped directly to Britain. Gas is piped

Fifteenth Century Castle in Finland. Nationalism and nation-states were largely European contributions to political science. This castle once defended Finland's border with an expanding Russia. (Courtesy of United Nations)

to both Scotland and West Germany. Less than 3 percent of Norway's share of seabed has been opened to exploration. Norway is determined to produce the **finite resource** slowly, to stretch it out over generations and minimize inflationary stresses at home. The Norwegians are so adept at hard bargaining for their low-sulfur, high quality oil that they are called, not always admiringly, the "blue-eyed Arabs."

Norway also has an excellent hydroelectric potential created by heavy rainfall along its mountain spine. Although Norway has one of the world's highest produciton rates of hydro power per capita, only half has been harnessed. The remaining half, however, will be more difficult and expensive to exploit. Iron is mined near the Soviet border in the far north; a surplus is exported after Norway's own steel industry is supplied. Copper and limestone are other natural resources; Norway, like Denmark, exports large quantities of cement. Very little of Norway is warm enough to produce grain (2.7 percent is cultivated); output on this small area has been increasing due to better fertilizers and farming techniques. Cattle and sheep are pastured and fed fodder crops. Norwegian agriculture is heavily subsidized to maintain some domestic production.

Sweden is relatively rich in metallic minerals. Iron ore is mined at several locations; the largest mines are at Kiruna, Gallivare, Svappavaara, and the Bergslagen district. Copper and lead are also mined. In fossil fuels, though, Sweden's economy is highly vulnerable. Sweden is one of the world's largest importers of oil. To date, prospecting in Sweden's offshore waters has been disappointing. Like Norway, Sweden has great hydro-power potential, half of which is developed. Low reservoir levels in winter and occasional drier than average years are supply problems partly overcome by international interchanges of electricity. Sweden and Norway export electric energy (via undersea cables) to Denmark in summer and import coal-generated energy from Denmark in winter.

In less than a century, Sweden's agricultural population has gone from 75 percent to 6 percent of the total. Main crops include wheat, barley, sugar beet, and potatoes. More than three fourths of farm income is derived from animal products—milk, beef, hogs, and sheep. Skane, in southernmost Sweden, has the best land as well as the most favorable climate.

Finland's fossil fuels are limited to some peat. Finland lacks the large hydro-power potential to partly compensate for a lack of fuels. Hydroelectric plants do supply about one third of the electric energy but are handicapped by uncertain water supply. Unlike Sweden, which has adapted a "go-slow" attitude on nuclear power and has very serious reservations on its safety factors, Finland intends to develop nuclear power to take at least 20 percent of the energy demand. Two plants were built by the USSR

and two by Sweden in a classic example of Finland's delicate maneuvering between the USSR and the West.

Finland's glaciated lowland character, very similar to Canada's "Shield," has relatively little agricultural land. Less than 10 percent of Finland is used for food production, but the Finns have been successful in pushing northward the limit for crops such as wheat, barley, and sugar beets by scientific plant breeding. The average size of farms is slowly increasing and the number of farms is declining.

The population of Finland, less than 5 million people, is less than metropolitan Chicago. Finland has experienced recent out-migration, mostly to Sweden, in search of jobs. Sweden controlled Finland at one time, and Swedish is still an official language. The majority of the people speak Finnish, a language related to Hungarian and Estonian; it is not a Scandinavian tongue.

Industry and Development Strategies   Denmark has had to develop highly specialized industries whose reputation for excellence of design and quality of craftsmanship support the high prices resulting from the Danes poor raw material and fuel situation. Shipbuilding remains important, though Japanese and Polish competition is severe. Machinery (such as diesel engines), stereo components, and fine furniture are among their most successful exports. Denmark is also the largest beer exporter in West Europe and is a major exporter of specialty and high-quality foods.

Denmark is highly dependent on foreign trade with one third of its total production exported. Denmark is the most visited of the Scandinavian countries, although like most West European countries, a heavy outflow of tourists comes close to eliminating the favorable balance of tourist expenditure. Denmark's population of a little over 5 million is relatively homogeneous, with only a small minority of Germans in the south.

Norway is West Europe's least densely populated country. Much of its industry would be considered small scale by the major industrial nations, and most of it is related to abundant hydroelectricity. Aluminum is produced with large amounts of electricity; Norway is a large supplier of this metal whose world-wide markets should continue to grow. Surplus electric power has lead to the creation of a large-scale chemical industry in Norway; "heavy water," fertilizer, and a variety of electrochemicals are the main products.

Norway earns much of its foreign exchange by tourism and by providing transportation services. Nearly as many Swedes as there are Norwegians visit Norway annually, as well as large numbers of West Germans and Americans. Norway's sparse population, spectacular scenery, and largely unpolluted environment will make it a continuing tourist lure. The Norwegian merchant marine fleet is one of the world's largest, including tankers, container ships, liquefied gas carriers, and highly specialized cargo-carriers of all kinds. The Norwegians also operate a large fleet of cruise liners in the Caribbean and Mediterranean as well as along their own beautiful coastline. Their huge fleet makes Norway especially vulnerable to any sudden changes in the volume of international trade. The Norwegians will probably continue to invest their oil wealth in diversifying their economy by such purchases as a major share of Volvo, Sweden's largest industrial corporation.

Sweden, whose population of about 8.5 million approximates that of New York City, has an amazing variety and complexity of industrial structure. It is an important auto manufacturer and exporter, aircraft manufacturer (but under license with foreign designs), and telephone-equipment manufacturer (one of the world's largest exporters). Sweden, like Japan, has actively encouraged industrial consolidation to improve their competitive advantage in world markets; unlike Japan, it has also embarked on a program of nationalization of industry. Swedish steel manufacturing specializes in high-value specialty steels, like stainless steel and steel for machine tools. Its modernization of very competitive industries is illustrated by their shipbuilding industry. A covered yard was built to facilitate shipbuilding in all kinds of severe weather. Huge prefabricated sections are welded together and pushed out of the covered area. The assembled ship is "launched" in a drydock. Specialty goods include ball bearings, electrical appliances, and typewriters. Sweden is a net importer of steel because of its huge consumption of steel in the manufacture of export products. In common with its neighbors, Norway and Finland, Sweden has a very large forest products industry reflecting its high percentage of forest in total land area.

Finland's forest product industry is its largest single industry; two thirds of the country is in forest, mainly privately owned. The industry is handicapped by a short growing season and relatively high production cost. Steel and metal fabricating industries are next in importance. Finland has specialized in the production of papermaking machinery, exporting whole factories. Finnish shipyards are likewise geared to both domestic and export markets; they specialize in ferries and icebreakers. Finland also has one car assembly plant to build their own version of Swedish Saabs.

Iceland   Iceland is a very special case, geographically and economically, although cultural and historical ties with Scandinavia remain important. Iceland is one of the most homogeneous nations in the world; Icelanders are descendants of Norwegian settlers who arrived in the ninth and tenth centuries and absorbed the earlier Celtic settlers from the British Isles. They number less than a quarter million, and their population growth rate is one of the lowest in the world (0.9 percent). Iceland boasts one of the world's most literate populations (99.9 percent) as well as one of the highest average longevity statistics, seventy-four years. Infant mortality rates, a classic measure of the quality of life, are only a little over half (9.6 per 1,000 live births) that of the United States.

The Icelanders have managed to build a reasonably prosperous economy (per capita income is $5,500, higher than that of the European average) on a largely barren island the size of Virginia with very few natural resources. Iceland is of recent volcanic origin. About three quarters of the island consists of glaciers, lakes, a lava desert, and other wasteland. Iceland has been among the pioneers in using **geothermal energy.** Hot water and steam from hot springs and geysers have long been used to heat buildings and greenhouses. Iceland now generates some geothermal electricity from the interior heat of the earth to supplement its hydroelectric power. These sources of energy are exceptionally valuable on a volcanic island with no fossil fuels. Diatomite, the tiny skeletons of algae found in uplifted seabed portions of the island, is mined and used as filtration material; perlite (volcanic glass) is another resource of minor importance. Hydro power is abundant enough to power an aluminum smelter near Reykjavik and help extract chemicals from seawater.

Iceland's major resource is the rich fishing grounds around the island. Eighty-three percent of the value of Iceland's exports are supplied by fish, over 1.5 million metric tons caught per year. Iceland's repeated extension of its exclusive fishing waters and its territorial sea (a concept more fully developed in the last chapter), attempting to reserve more and more of this resource to their own fishermen, has led to several short but sharp conflicts with Britain. Because only 4 percent of Iceland is cultivable and climate limits crops to potatoes, turnips, and hay, Icelanders consume large amounts of fish as well as relying on fish for export income. For this reason, Icelanders have been quite aggressive at zoning out foreign fishermen. Britain asserted "historic rights" to use of fishing grounds off Iceland, contesting the further extensions of Iceland's exclusive fishing zone. While Iceland had claimed a 16-mile (26 kilometers) exclusive zone as early as the seventeenth century, a 1901 agreement with Britain had established a 3-mile (5-kilometer) zone. A 4-mile (6-kilometer) zone was proclaimed in 1952, followed by 12 miles (19 kilometers) in 1958.[1] By 1972, Iceland expanded its exclu-

---

[1] Lewis Alexander, *Offshore Geography of Northwestern Europe* (Chicago: Rand McNally, Association of American Geographers Monograph Series, 1963), p. 109.

sive fishing zone to a total of 50 miles (80 kilometers) offshore and its territorial waters to 200 miles (320 kilometers). British gunboats escorted British trawlers inside Iceland's 12-mile limit, 1958–1960, but withdrew under international pressure. The dispute had threatened to seriously weaken NATO by an Icelandic withdrawal. Iceland has no military forces of its own (its defense had been guaranteed by Denmark up until 1941 when the United States assumed responsibility), but Iceland has important base facilities for the control of the North Atlantic. The presence of a U.S. Air Base at Keflavik (just outside the capital, Reykjavik) has periodically been a major issue in domestic politics. A 1974 agreement between the United States and Iceland calls for U.S. defense of the island as requested by the Icelanders.

SUMMARY

West Europe has, within a century, declined from political-military master of the world and leader in industrial development and technological innovation to a set of second- and third-class countries in a world dominated by superpowers. Still, West Europe is an immensely important region in the world's economic and cultural affairs. As an economic unit, the EC ranks among the superpowers in productivity and invention. Psychologically, there has been decline; statistically, there has been growth, but at a lower rate than that of the new giants. The average West European is more prosperous, healthier, and enjoying the prospect of a longer life span and higher quality of life than ever before. Especially considering the terrible destruction of World Wars I and II, it is amazing the West Europe's recovery has been so complete, that its industries and cities have not simply recovered, but surged on to new triumphs.

A certain sad unease, however, can be traced to the general feeling that West Europe is no longer in control of its destiny. The very split of the continent into a West and an East, each dominated (but to very different degrees) by one of the potentially warring superpowers, emphasizes the relative demotion of Europe from power center to pawn. There seems little likelihood that this chasm between Communist and non-Communist Europe will disappear except in the aftermath of a major war—something Europeans dread. While trade and tourist restrictions ease, the fundamental split remains. It is not comforting to West Europeans to know that the literally vital decisions affecting them are now made in Washington, Moscow, or even Beijing or Tokyo.

THE REGION'S WORLD VIEW AND TENSIONAL RELATIONSHIPS WITH OTHER REGIONS

The unwillingness to accept, meekly and unquestioningly, the postwar situation of second-rate status is evident in France's decision to build its own nuclear weapons and to withdraw, for the most part, from NATO, the alliance of the United States with its West European partners. The United States had guaranteed West Europe a "nuclear umbrella," a shield against the threat of Soviet invasion, but would the United States unhesitatingly launch a nuclear war to defend West Europe? Once the Soviet Union had developed its own extensive nuclear arsenal, would the United States accept the certain retaliation of Soviet nuclear forces by using the "ultimate weapon" first? Or might the United States attempt to limit the war to a nonnuclear one, at least until the continued existence of the United States was at stake rather than the defense of West Europe? The expensive development of their own nuclear weaponry was a reiteration of France's "independence" from reliance upon the United States and its "umbrella."

As satisfying to the French as this accomplishment may be, it remains true that western Europe has been displaced from the pinnacle of world domination. Acceptance, if not resignation, has evolved over the decades since 1945. There remains the satisfaction that, in many measures of the quality of life such as longevity, some West European countries outrank either of the superpowers. Aspirations to cultural leadership or equality with the superpowers are not impractical. There must be some satisfaction in noting that enormous portions of the rest of the world are off-shoots of European culture, as extensively modified and adapted as they may be. The Americas and Oceania were largely populated from West and East Europe; the Russians are a predominently European culture, and European culture has exerted a strong influence in portions of Africa and even sections of Asia. Perhaps the Europeans look upon the United States and Soviet Union with that mixture of admiration, disappointment, and alarm with which aging parents view the activities of their affluent, very independent, sometimes insensitive children.

West Europe should not be underestimated. The region remains a potent force, economically and culturally, if not in military might. The next century may be the "American century" or the "Japanese century" or even the "Chinese century," but the Europeans will be an active part, a prospering part, of the new world to come.

case study

SITE AND SITUATION FACTORS IN THE GROWTH OF LONDON

London, one of the largest cities in the world, is also one of the oldest. Why did such a great city arise exactly where it did? What aspects of that location were so clearly and permanently superior to a multitude of alternative locations? The analysis of the location of cities has long been a favorite topic of geographers. *Site* and *situation* must both be considered in interpreting the reasons for city growth and city functions. Sometimes a poor site can be overcome by engineering projects if the situation is superior; an example would be Leningrad. More commonly, though, both site and situation considerations must be good in order for a great city to develop.

The site of London's original core is on a bed of gravel lying atop a layer of blue clay in the approximate center of the London Basin. The London Basin is a structural basin in gently down-folded sedimentary rocks. The successive exposed "rings" of eroded sedimentary layers form low, outward facing ridges, or cuestas, much like a nest of saucers of diminishing size. The gravel bed was the most convenient place to cross the river Thames as the tidal action almost ceased at that point. Here, the river was relatively narrow compared with the downstream estuary. There was a settlement at London when the Romans arrived there in 43 A.D. It is less certain as to whether a bridge preceded the one built by the Romans. The Roman Wall around the city, roughly a squared-off semicircle, did jog in one corner to take advantage of an already built wall. The London Bridge of the Romans had a simultaneous effect on both land and water traffic. Because there was no bridge further downstream, and few upstream (bridges were very expensive and difficult to build then), the Roman road network of southeastern England focused on that bridge, channeling land transport through the growing city. The bridge also formed the upstream limit of ocean navigation as sea-going ships could not pass under it. (See Figure 5–10.)

The porous gravel bed allowed the use of primitive sewer arrangements without unusual health hazards. The low, eroded, but outward-facing ridges of the basin could be used to advantage in defense. The Romans established the major fortifications of their town, Londinium, on the downstream river bank where the wall came to the river. This location was to protect the city from pirates and other sea-raiders. Later, the Norman French built the Tower of London at the same place for the same reasons.

The situation of London was a superior one with regard to the island of Britain. Generally, western and northern Britain are less desirable for crop cultivation due to both rugged topography and cooler, wetter climate. The largest expanse of relatively flat land, and the normally drier and sunniest part of the island, are in the southeast. The Thames dominates the drainage pattern of this better agricultural land. In a preindustrial, agricultural society, this concentration of good farmland was a definite asset; it supported the densest population and richest cities. In Roman Britain, Wales and Scotland were hostile borders, so that London enjoyed the security of location well within Roman-controlled lands. The Thames

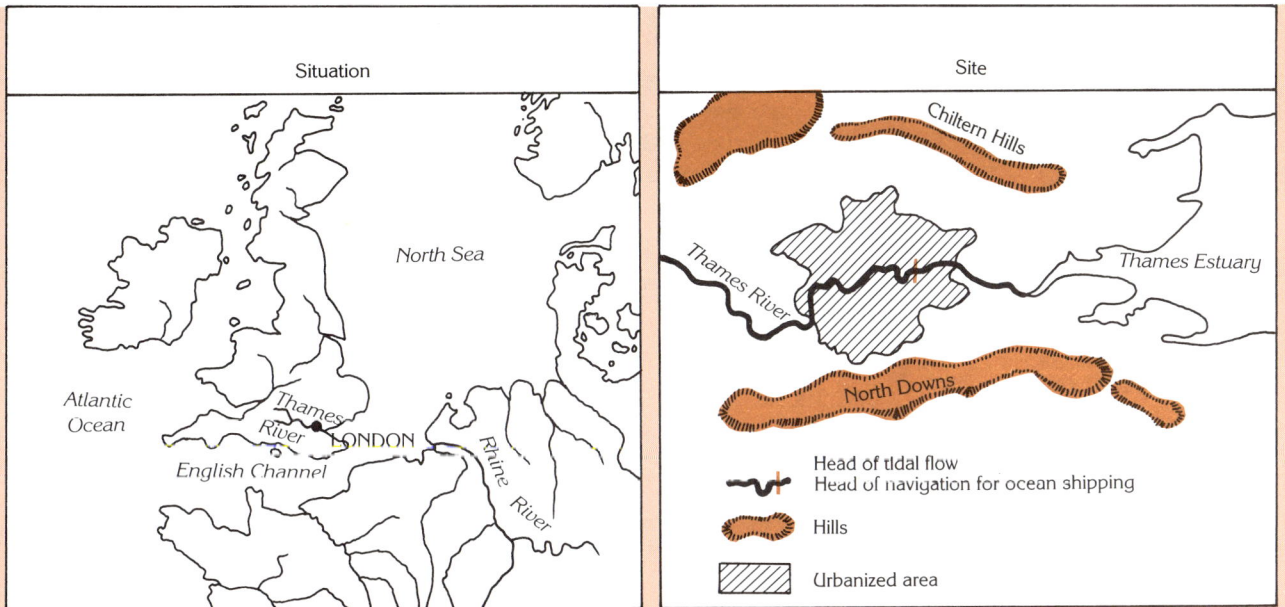

FIGURE 5–10

Site and Situation of London. The persistence of urban functions through two thousand years and the rapid growth of nineteenth century London, together with its continuing if relatively diminished world leadership functions, suggest an advantageous site within southeastern England. London has a superb situation within the region and along interregional trade routes.

estuary is perfectly suited for trade with the continent of Europe, aimed as it is at the Rhine Delta. The Rhine Valley has been an important continental trade route for millenia, and the Romans naturally emphasized trade contacts with the continent.

Roman control lasted for four centuries, after which London may have temporarily lost much of its population and trade functions during the political chaos that followed. However, by 1066, the city was once again a thriving, prosperous trading center. William the Conqueror led his victorious armies northwest from Hastings towards London but did not attempt to invade the city. He burnt Southwark, the suburbs around the southern fortifications to the bridge, but then marched west up the Thames Valley. He crossed the river near Oxford and returned down the north bank, establishing camp at Westminster, then several miles outside the old walled city of London. An emissary under a white flag was sent to William from the city; he had good news for William. The city of London had just held an election for king, and William had won! There was no other likely candidate of course, but officially London was an unconquered city. William had avoided destroying the city by invasion because he recognized that this wealthy merchant city was a great asset to his new kingdom. London gained by having William reconfirm its local autonomy in trade and finance.

This mutually beneficial and face-saving arrangement with London did not earn London the title and functions of royal capital, though. London had never been the political capital of the entire political unit of England, neither under the Romans nor the various Saxon kingdoms. It has always been the commercial capital, though. William established his capital at Westminster, partly to avoid the government being too influenced by the merchant interests or the urban mobs. Thus the city had two distinct nuclei at an early date. The metropolitan area has grown to combine and submerge these once separate centers, but their different functional identities remain. As the city continued to grow, other distinctive, specialized centers arose in different parts of the metropolitan region.

Site factors continued to influence urban development. When the gravel layer, or "lens," had been built up, it was difficult to extend built-up dense settlement onto the exposed clay that would not absorb and naturally filter the effluent from sewage pits. Expansion outward atop the clay layer awaited the development of sanitary sewage systems. Once these systems were built, the city grew outward explosively. The blue clay was an advantage, however, in building the world' first subway system, as tunneling through the clay was relatively easy.

As the city continued to grow, the port functions spread downstream towards deeper water and wider channels. Industrial functions and worker's housing tend to be located on the eastern, downriver side associated with the port. Partly because the prevailing westerly winds carry industrial pollution in the atmosphere downriver to the east, the western portions of the city tended to attract upper-class housing, which also were attracted by proximity to the glamour of the royal court.

REVIEW QUESTIONS

1 Why do many Europeans feel that their culture area has been demoted in world significance? Are they correct?

2 What are the cultural and political relationships of the new superpowers with West Europe?

3 List some positive and negative characteristics of West Europe's leadership in achieving the Industrial Revolution.

4 Why is the Mediterranean-type climate an economic asset to both agriculture and tourism?

5 Why is it ironic that Greece and Italy were among the last nations to achieve independence in the modern era?

6 Many West Europe states have official "decentralization" policies. Why are these policies considered necessary?

7 What are the economic dislocations that follow the end of colonial empires?

8 Some historians regard Germany as the "natural master" of Europe, politically and economically. Is there any geographic basis for this alleged leadership?

9 Using France as an example, review the stages of the demographic transition.

10 What geographic factors support France's drive toward agricultural self-sufficiency?

11 Describe the factors of location that are the basis for Rotterdam's importance as an international port. What are Rotterdam's chief competitors for this international entrepôt function?

12 What are this historic political and cultural roots of the "northern Ireland question"?

13 How does the *oncorde* reflect the handicaps of relatively small domestic markets for the research and development of high-technology aircraft?

14 Why was Switzerland not invaded in either World War I or II?

15 In what senses did World War II prove "suicidal" for West Europe?

16 What environmental problems must small, densely populated, heavily industrialized states like Britain and the Netherlands face?

17 Why are machine tool industries characteristic of very highly developed industrial economies?

18 What developmental strategies have the Danes used to overcome their severe shortage of industrial raw materials?

19 Why does Norway's developmental strategy feature tightly controlled rates of oil production?

20 Why has Iceland been a leader in extending its territorial waters frontiers?

21 Why has France insisted on its own nuclear weapons development? How is this development related to superpower strategy concerning West Europe?

SUGGESTED READINGS

1 T. S. ASHTON, *The Industrial Revolution, 1760–1830.* London: Oxford University Press, 1948.

2 M. A. BUSTEED, *Northern Ireland.* London: Oxford University Press, 1974.

3 ROBERT DICKINSON, *The West European City.* London: Routledge and Kegan Paul, 1963.

4 AUBREY DIEM, *Western Europe: A Geographical Analysis.* New York: John Wiley and Sons, 1979.

5 JEAN GOTTMANN, *A Geography of Europe.* New York: Holt, Rinehart, Winston, 1969.

6 GEORGE HOFFMAN, ed., *A Geogrpahy of Europe: Problems and Prospects.* New York: The Ronald Press, 1977 (Fourth Edition).

7 TERRY JORDAN, *The European Culture Area.* New York: Harper & Row, 1973.

8 V. H. MALMSTROM, *Norden: Crossroads of Destiny.* Princeton, N.J.: Van Nostrand, 1965.

9 WARREN NYSTROM and PETER MALOF, *The Common Market: European Community in Action.* Princeton, N.J.: Van Nostrand, 1962.

10 NORMAN POUNDS, *An Historical and Political Geography of Europe.* London: HARRAP, 1947.

11 DUDLEY STAMP and S. H. BEAVER, *The British Isles.* New York: St. Martin's Press, 1971.

KEY TERMS

- buffer
- march area
- Comecon
- shatter zone
- successor state
- irredenta
- collectivize
- developmental goal
- satellite
- moraine
- cultural crossroads
- developmental enclave
- developmental gap
- agricultural-industrial complex

6
EAST EUROPE

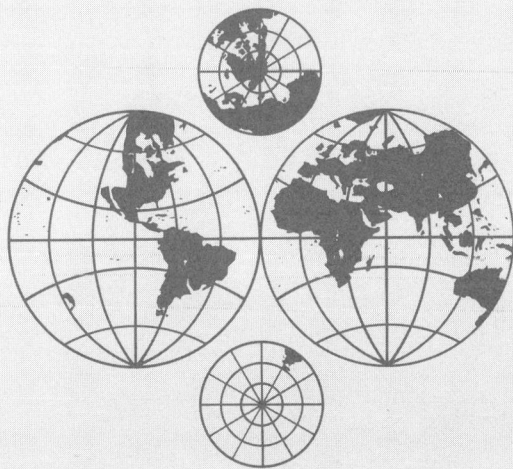

PROLOGUE: THE LAND IN BETWEEN

East Europe is not a new region, though it was the advent of Communist control throughout that area that has conditioned people to think of it as a separate region. It has been viewed as somewhat separate from western Europe since at least the eighteenth century. Seen now more as the transition zone between an economically unified West Europe and the giant Soviet state rather than just an extension of the latter, it was always viewed as a kind of "frontier Europe." The zone of Moslem-Catholic-Protestant-Orthodox contact, the linguistic meeting ground of Romance, Slavic, and Germanic languages, the traditional **buffer** area against attack by non-European elements (and thoroughly varied because of this contact and transit function), the area has always displayed a high degree of heterogeneity. It has been thought of as an "undistributed middle"; separate largely because it was neither West Europe nor Russia, neither Scandinavian nor Mediterranean. It is a part of Europe and peopled by Europeans, but it is somehow unlike the rest of Europe. Involved in every major European war, it has been the recipient of or had contact with every major European cultural movement, ideology, influence, or idea—as well as many non-European cultural inputs. Always along the path of cultural diffusion, the area itself has also engendered innovation. The cultural blend that has resulted, while differing among its various component areas, has itself become sufficiently different to merit a separate cultural status. It is definitely European culture and the area has been more thoroughly and completely in contact with *all* elements of European culture than some parts of West Europe. It is just a different amalgam of these elements that has resulted.

Traditional texts on Europe, even world geographies, in the eighteenth and nineteenth centuries lumped the area's diverse states and cultures into a general pot labeled East (or eastern) Europe. West European unfamiliarity and lack of first-hand contacts were responsible for its conceptualization as a region. The geography of an age that set physical limits to regions could find none in the area. The Alpine system (traditionally dividing northern and southern Europe in the West), splits into several chains that wander and loop, changing direction throughout the area. Drainage basins are of no use as physical limits—the Elbe, emptying into the North Sea, rises in eastern Europe, while the Danube, emptying into the Black Sea, has its sources deep in western Europe. It has often been described as Europe at its widest point, farthest from the sea, yet even this is not necessarily so. The distance from Malmo to Hammerfest in Scandinavia is greater than the distance from Gdansk to Athens; the distance from Szczecin to

Trieste is less than that from Rotterdam to Venice. The Alpine system here is lower, with numerous passes, and more easily crossed than elsewhere in Europe. The area is *not* isolated; it is open to contact and passage from and to all directions. Most of it is physically closer to the Rhine than to Moscow.

The reasons for its distinct regional character are related more to its openness than to its isolation. It sat squarely astride the major routes to the Crusades and trade with the Near East as well as important east-west routeways. The Norse (and later Hansa) north-south trade route to the Byzantine Empire and its Moslem successor states passed through the area. It was the western terminus of Chinese caravan routes at the same time that it contained the easternmost extensions of Flemish manufacturing and trading outposts. Traditionally a land of food and resource surplus, major parts of it were incorporated into the Roman, Byzantine, Holy Roman, and Ottoman empires for lengthy periods of time. The Reformation arose here and then spread to the West. Often thought of as a land of estates and serfs, feudalism actually replaced freehold farming only after conquest from the outside. Elected monarchs, free cities, and assemblies of nobles with a system of checks on rulers (all primary level experiments in democracy) predate similar occurrences in the West. Despite all this, geographies are full of clichés about the area that imply isolation, economic backwardness, low level of cultural attainment, and autocratic rule. These clichés were the very factors of assumed homogeneity on which generations of European geographers from the six-teenth to mid-twentieth centuries based their concept of East Europe as a region.

Out-of-date volumes describe the role of physical barriers and sheer distance in isolating the area from Western thought and culture. Inhabitants were all lumped together as one group, Slavs, regardless of their linguistic and cultural propensities. The region's culture was viewed only as "folk culture." (Students were subjected to the stereotype of an illiterate, head-scarf-clad, rural folk laboring endlessly in fields, their only respite being folk dances.) Poverty and anarchy were often described as the chief attributes of the citizenry. Yet its obvious natural riches and strategic trade importance were such that Rome, Austria, Germany, Sweden, Greece, Persia, Denmark, England, France, Italy, Turkey, and Russia each attempted to control all or a part of it at various times. Caught between the greatest powers of history, it was the **march area** of almost every significant empire of the Old World, including the Mongols, the Moslems, and Napoleon.

It was the near-constant attack or control from outside the region that eclipsed native political control and resulted in poverty for the region's inhabitants. Denied its own national aspirations, the area was the ultimate source of and impetus to German and Russian nationalism. Its inhabitants provided the grain surpluses that built much of western European urban culture until the mid-nineteenth century. Its scientists discovered that the sun (not Europe) was the center of the universe, while its production and ingenuity gave variety to northern European cuisine. Its native music gave zest to a precise, highly formal

Mostar, Yugoslavia—The Turkish Quarter. East Europe has long been an area contested by major powers that surround it. As such it is a region of marked cultural contrast and ethnic heterogeneity. (Courtesy of United Nations)

western European musical tradition, and, some feel, something of soul to a continent enshrouded with too much of Puritan reaction. Its core was the Austrian Empire, the epitome of European culture.

The constant struggle and change has produced a distinct culture. Not only do the inhabitants possess a certain resilience, but also, as might be expected, a highly developed cynicism. All are fervently nationalistic, yet the nationalism of each is tempered by the political realities of size and position vis á vis more powerful neighbors and world forces beyond their control. Each of the countries involved has obviously undergone a great deal of recent Soviet influence, adopted a Communist form of government (although these governments *function* more as socialist ones), devoted much of its energies to the rebuilding of economies after war damage, and pursued intense developmental programs that tax total national resources. The drive for improvement of living standards, both national and individual, is a strong motivating force. The individual motivation factor is surprisingly strong, considering the position that traditional Marxism takes on individual material gain. Many (but not all) of the traditional intraregional animosities have disappeared or weakened over time. As societies become more urban and industrial, individual cultural traits are submerged, to some degree, in a larger, more homogeneous East European culture. Intra-bloc travel has increased understanding and mutual familiarity. Cooperative investment programs foster a kind of areal economic unity, as do **Comecon** (Com-

munist East Europe's version of the Common Market) trade agreements.

Yet, strong differences *do* persist, and a picture of a uniform, Communist-influenced lifestyle and culture would be a dangerous oversimplification. Perhaps the most dominant note of similarity is the universal reordering of the economies and culture from a rural peasant orientation to that of an industrial urban type.

CHARACTERISTICS OF THE REGION

East Europe is composed of eight small political units, many of which contain more than one major ethnic group. Some of the more colorful terminology of political geography has its origins in this area and its political problems. The term **shatter zone** was coined to characterize the zone of **successor states** that emerged after 1918 in the area formerly controlled by the disintegrating empires of Germany, Russia, Austria-Hungary, and Ottoman Turkey. It implies the lack of power in the region's individual states, which were viewed as residual fragments of once larger units in this geological analogy. It was further implied that the zone would remain one of instability and weakness, much as a fault zone in an area of tectonic activity. The instability was not caused simply by the apparent power vacuum in the area, but also by the potential border con-

The Old Town of Warsaw. Built in the thirteenth century, destroyed during World War II, and reconstructed over the last three decades, the Old Town of Warsaw symbolizes the endless struggles to which East Europe has been subjected and embodies the strength of nationalism present in the countries of the region. (Courtesy of the Embassy of the Polish People's Republic/P. Krassowski, Sport I, Turystyka)

flicts, **irredentas,** and the large number of national and ethnic minorities found in most countries.

While virtually all the region's states contained minorities, two, Czechoslovakia and Yugoslavia, are actually amalgams of national groups. In general, ethnic complexity reached its greatest intensity in the Balkans where all fourteen nationalities represented in the Austrian Empire were resettled in areas seized from the Turks. This intense complexity, when viewed in the light of Woodrow Wilson's post-World War I policy of self-determination of nations, could have resulted in a jigsaw puzzle of ministates and noncontiguous, fragmented political units. The term *Balkanization,* referring to the division of territory into many small units, was coined in reference to this situation.

Changes in borders and population exchanges during the last forty years have done much to simplify the ethnic picture, but they have not totally eliminated the problems. East Germany remains separated from its historic core area; Yugoslavia is still a poly-national state; and all of the region's states have made some adaptions for the cultural autonomy of resident minorities. Borders have been finalized by treaties, but the number of changes over time still leave a great potential for conflicts over historical, if not clearly ethnic, territorial claims (see Figure 6–1).

A second regional characteristic is the dynamism of industrial and urban growth. Prior to 1945, only Berlin and Saxony in East Germany, Silesia and a few of the larger cities in Poland, and the Czech portion of Czechoslovakia had developed any significant amount of industry. Today, seven of the region's states have developed a primary metallurgical industry, six are surplus producers of textiles, shoes, and clothing, five have fairly well-developed automotive industries, and four are significant large-scale producers of chemical products. Urbanization and industrialization have taken place rapidly throughout the region, but the intensity of both tends to decrease from northwest to southeast, reflecting the general decrease in development along the same directional lines.

Characteristically, agriculture has been **collectivized** in most cases, and the level of investment in that sector has been low. Poland is the most important exception, where 80 percent of the farms are still individually owned. Yet all states have made compromises with the peasantry in implementing their particular type of governmental

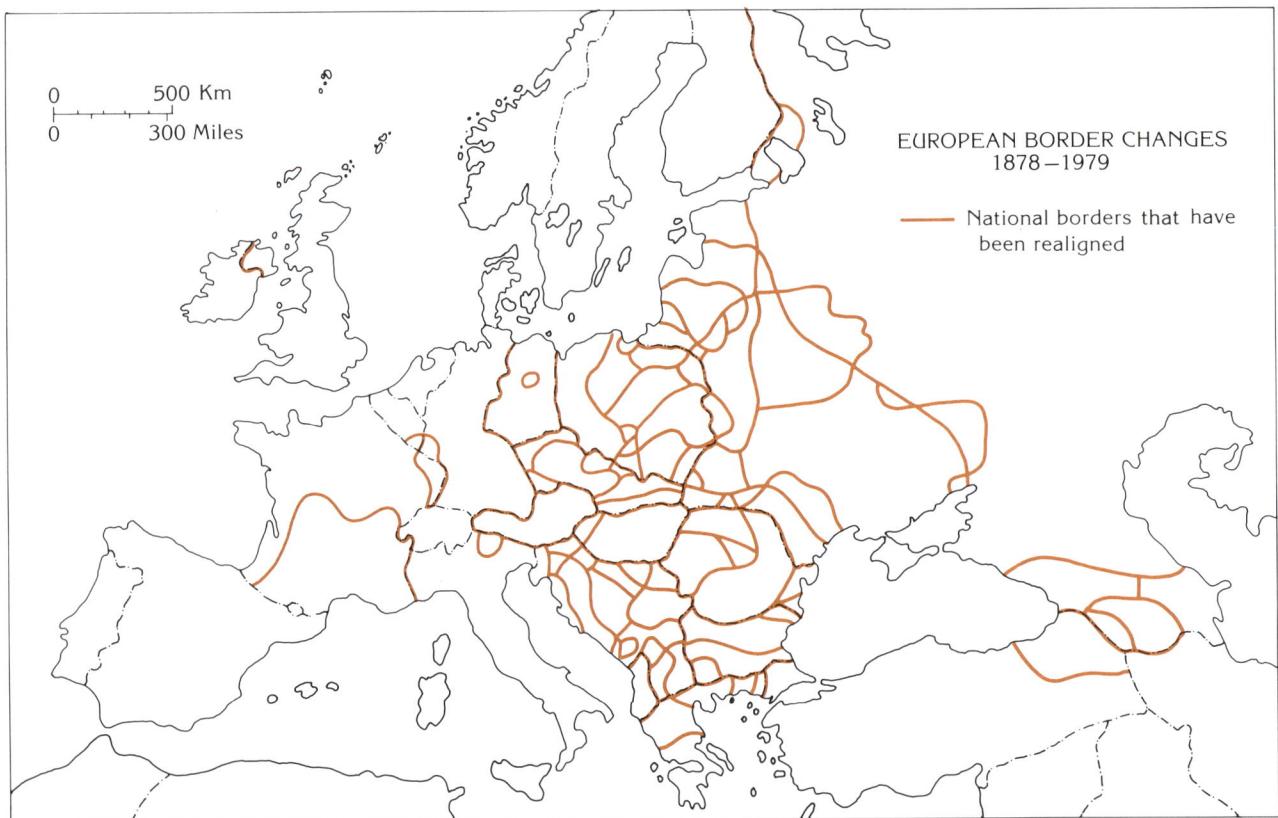

EUROPEAN BORDER CHANGES
1878–1979

——— National borders that have
been realigned

0 — 500 Km
0 — 300 Miles

FIGURE 6–1
Frequency of Border Changes, East Europe. A characteristic of this cultural and political shatterbelt is the extraordinary number of border changes, involving sizeable areas of political realignment, that have occurred relative to border changes in more stable West Europe.

ownership and direction in the farming component of the economy.

Two conflicting **developmental goals** have arisen because of the changing emphasis on the nature of industrial investment as handed down from the Soviet Union. During the Stalinist era from the onset of Communist control to 1953, individual self-sufficiency and basic industry were emphasized. In response, each East European state attempted to develop a heavy industrial base as well as a full range of other industries to ensure self-sufficiency. Later programs emphasized specialization, and, duly, each state attempted to develop a series of export-oriented specialties in which it would have a bloc-wide monopoly. The result has been a highly varied industrial base in each country except Albania as the need to avoid imports on one hand conflicts with policies geared to spurring exports on the other hand. Demands for increased availability of consumer goods has led to expansion in certain industries (notably textiles) to the point where the region's nations must seek export markets either in the third world or through selling to developed countries at less than the cost of production in an attempt to obtain hard currency.

Three economic patterns have emerged in foreign trade from these dichotomies of economic interest. There is increasing trade with the capitalist nations of the West; it does not even fluctuate downward noticeably with the cooling of official relations. Intraregional trade, which was almost nonexistent before 1947, has become exceptionally important as complementary economies and cooperative efforts develop under the aegis of CMEA (the Communist Common Market). The Soviet Union, meanwhile, in a reversal of the traditional colonial trade pattern, has become the major supplier of raw materials to East Europe's industries while purchasing finished goods and sophisticated manufactures from its so-called **satellites.** In the most recent decade there has been a brisk trade in licenses and patents purchased from capitalist countries and firms. Certain foreign firms have been invited to make investments within the region, while a surprising number of satellite country firms subcontract work for foreign enterprises. (For example, "British" woolens were observed being worn in Poland, and several dozen West German firms subcontract the production of machine parts in six different East European countries.)

While surpluses of manufactured goods are increasingly in evidence, most of the region's states now have agricultural deficits. There is a temptation to relate this to bureaucratic inefficiency and to popular resistance to collectivization. In reality, however, it also reflects rapid population growth in some of the countries, while in virtually all it reflects the low level of agricultural investment as well as the shift of large acreage to nonfood crops (flax, cotton, oil

seeds, etc.) that serve as industrial raw materials. Inefficiency and bad planning do play a role, but state and collective farming per se is not the cause of lowered food supplies.

THE PHYSICAL FRAMEWORK

We have previously reviewed the entire European continent (see Chapter 5). In general, this region has a large percentage of its area in level, usable land. As in the realms of politics and culture, so, too, in climate East Europe is a transitional zone between maritime and continental influences and climatic regimes. Seasons are more pronounced than in West Europe, and temperature ranges are generally more extreme. The region is relatively well watered, but rainfall is excessive in only a few mountainous areas. Soils run the entire gamut of fertility, from worthless to exceptionally rich. Drainage patterns have their most overriding implications in the way in which they have tended to channel development and trade.

TOPOGRAPHY

Most of the northern one third of East Europe is composed of the North European Plain. It is a nearly level, glaciated terrain characterized by poor drainage and a gently rolling landscape. Three rows of morainal hills screen East Germany and Poland from the Baltic coast proper: the Mecklenburg, Pomeranian, and Masurian hill districts. Not high or imposing, they nonetheless form significant and readily visible features in the landscape. Riddled with lakes, they form important tourist districts in the respective countries. The Baltic coast itself often consists of high terraces with steep seaward-facing slopes backing narrow fringing beaches, though there is a remarkable development of sandspits where the Vistula enters the Baltic. South of the **moraines,** hummocky glacial debris is interspersed with ancient glacial spillways that once carried melt waters away from the retreating ice. These spillways have come to be used as the easily excavated channels for a well-developed system of canals.

A series of ancient massifs and low mountains bounds the plain on the south from central Germany to the Moravian Gate between Czechoslovakia's Sudeten and Carpathian Mountains. This is a country of mountain, basin, and low plateau alternating across the landscape and covered with a rich coating of **loess** (wind-deposited, fine-grained material) soil in many areas. The Harz and Thuringian mountains of southwestern Germany enclose a low limestone plateau that has become one of East

German's new industrial districts, despite the lack of surface water. Between the Harz and the diamond-shape block that gives the characteristic shape and outline to western Czechoslovakia is the rich Leipzig Basin. The Bohemian Block is a mass of ancient crystalline rock whose steep sides form the Sudeten, Ore, and Bohemian Forest mountains, all of which are rich in ores and minerals and have collectively formed an important European mining district since prehistoric times.

A broad, open corridor, the Moravian Gate, separates this western mountain and basin country from the Carpathian Alps and the plateau country of southern Poland. This plateau is composed of limestone covered in part with glacial debris, waterborne sediments, or wind-blown loess. Occasional scarps and the folded Holy Cross Mountains are the only distinguishing features on this landform to distinguish it from the northern European Plain. Low-grade iron deposits are found in these scarp and hill areas, while the valleys at the foot of the Carpathians hold small deposits of oil and gas.

Lower and less grand than the Alps, the Carpathians form a reverse crescent outlining the eastern side of the Hungarian or middle Danube Basin. Two mineral-rich blocks, the Slovak Ore Mountains and the Bihor Massif of Romania, are found inside the crescent at either end of the Carpathians. Along its southwestern edge, the middle Danube Basin is flanked by the Dinaric Alps, a broad zone of folded limestone ridges and plateaus with solution basins, caves, sinkholes, and underground streams—characteristic of landscape that results from surface collapse into voids eroded by underground solution of limestone. The Dinaric Alps continue as folded ridges and valleys into Albania, where, not composed of limestone, they are known as the Pindus Ranges.

The Romanian Plain is really a continuation of the Podolian Plateau in the north, becoming a true sedimentary basin only in the south. Following the reverse S-curve formed by the Carpathians, the Transylvania Alps, and the Balkan Mountains, it, too, is a rich and productive agricultural area.

The southernmost part of the region is occupied by two ancient blocks of crystalline material. Known as the Dobrudja and the Rhodope mountains, they are faulted and contain volcanic intrusions in many areas.

Two large basins and the North European Plain, then, contain most of the level land of the region. The approach to the region from the south is made difficult by rough mountain country, while penetration of the plains, plateau, and hill country of the northern two thirds of the region is easily accomplished from any direction.

LAND-SEA RELATIONSHIPS

Maritime power is so dominantly a trait of western Europe that little attention has been paid to the role of the sea in eastern European development. With access only to the landlocked Baltic, Mediterranean, and Black seas, rather

State Farm in Hungary. Much of the region consists of vast plains and large, often very fertile basins. Except under unusual circumstances, the region produces a surplus of food. It once functioned as the granary of Europe, one of the reasons that it has been so frequently subjected to invasion. (Courtesy of United Nations/Interfoto, Hungary)

than open ocean, there is little question that seapower was less important to the region's states. However, from certain perspectives the sea has been an exceptionally important factor in the region's history and politics.

Access to the sea has often been considered one of the most important goals of the foreign policy of individual states in East Europe. The case of the Polish corridor is probably the most noteworthy. In 1918, Poland was awarded a corridor of land along the lower Vistula to guarantee maritime access. The heavily German port city of Danzig was detached from Germany and given the status of "free city" to insure that revisionist elements could not block Polish trade as a means of pressuring the new state into border revisions or economic concessions. This maritime access was deemed so important to the survival of Poland that it was one of Woodrow Wilson's original "fourteen points" in the post-World War I peace plan.

The corridor in effect divided Germany into two parts without direct, contiguous land connections. The Poles, fearful of German control of Danzig, built their own totally new port within Polish territory at Gdynia, almost adjacent to Danzig. The Germans, also uncertain of Danzig's status, invested much in developing a port for East Prussia at Elbing, immediately adjacent to the free city's borders, but within definitely German territory. The corridor became one of the pressing issues in Polish-German relations and ranks as one of the causes of World War II. The border settlement after World War II awarded Poland a lengthy coastline on the Baltic. Further, Poland's western border became the navigable Oder River, which provided access by water from the Silesian coalfields to the Baltic. In addition, Poland was awarded the port of Szczecin (Stettin) on the western side of that river and a small part of an island to insure Polish control of the mouth of the river and, thereby, access to the port. Szczecin had had excellent water and rail connections with Berlin, which it had traditionally served as a port facility. When the port was awarded to Poland, despite guarantees of access, East Germany developed a new port complex at Rostock.

Similarly, Yugoslavia's access to the sea has been an issue. While that country had a long coastline on the Adriatic since its inception in 1919, it had no overland access (due to topographical barriers not overcome) to any of the small ports it controlled. Italy's control of certain ports, peninsulas, and islands along the Dalmatian coast effectively gave them control of the entire Adriatic. Fiume (Rijeka) was given free city status, much as Danzig, to handle Yugoslavia's trade; it was one of the few ports with connections to the interior. Trieste, together with the entire Istrian peninsula, was awarded to Italy, and much of Yugoslavian trade was forced to use Italian port facilities. Following Poland's example, Yugoslavia built a port at Susak,

next to Fiume. The claims of Italy to the Dalmatian coast were based on ancient Rome's control of the area and significant (but still a minority) numbers of ethnic Italians living in the region's cities. The very term *irredenta,* signifying nationals who are resident outside the national territory, was coined by an Italian nationalist, born in Fiume, who resisted the awarding of that city to Yugoslavia.

Again, after World War II, the problem was eliminated by shifting the international border; the two countries agreed to the awarding of Trieste to Italy, but the awarding of the rest of Istria to Yugoslavia. Most Italian nationals emigrated; the rest have a protected legal status within Yugoslavia. Trieste, essentially a port with no hinterland, is kept alive by government contracts and investments. Most of its unskilled labor functions are performed by Yugoslavs who cross the border daily on special work permits. Industry has been attracted to Trieste by this cheaper migrant labor and special arrangements that allow duty-free access to the Yugoslav market. The Yugoslavs now control Rijeka (Fiume) completely. Like Gdansk (Danzig), it is really a series of politically created, once-competing ports. Yugoslavia is now developing the port of Split by enhancing its connections to the interior.

Similarly, Bulgaria has fought multiple wars over the issue of direct access to the Mediterranean in Thrace. Romania and Bulgaria have disputed control of the Black Sea port of Constanta. The Soviets reclaimed Bessarabia in 1940 to give them access to the Danube (and acquire membership on the Danube Commission) and to control access to the Black Sea from the Danube.

Landlocked Czechoslovakia and Hungary have been guaranteed the free use of certain ports on the Baltic and Black seas and have the theoretical right to free navigation on the Elbe, Oder, and Danube to facilitate trade. Some Czechoslovakian patriots once felt that Trieste could be claimed by that country on the grounds of having once controlled that port in the ninth century, while Hungary never officially abandoned its claims to Rijeka (Fiume) until 1945.

Despite the somewhat meager maritime tradition, the region's states have obviously been driven by the desire for access to the sea. Poland, since acquiring the Baltic coast, has become a major power in shipbuilding and has developed a large maritime fleet. Yugoslavia and Romania are following suit. The Polish government has invested huge sums of money in developing their portion of the Baltic coast as a resort complex for Scandinavian as well as domestic tourists. Yugoslavia, Romania, and Bulgaria have done even more to create international tourist resort complexes on their coasts. Even Albania, with its exceptionally low level of development and its xenophobic attitudes, relied on the sea as its contact media for relations with China. This now defunct alliance with China enabled Albania to leave the Soviet orbit and to pursue its independent course of action.

CLIMATE

Most of East Europe has a climate best described as humid continental with moderate maritime modification. Far removed from the Atlantic, the winters of East Europe are much colder than those of West Europe, and the seasonal and daily temperature ranges are also greater. Nonetheless, the general maritime influence is felt, and the area has a much warmer climate than might be anticipated at that latitude.

The northern climatic zone includes East Germany, Poland, and most of Czechoslovakia. This northern climatic subzone experiences relatively mild winters with January averages between 22° and 32° F (−5° and 0° C). Cold winters are rare; though in almost every winter there are short cold snaps as Siberian air masses intrude. Temperatures decline eastward, indicating the very real significance of the maritime effect. Summers are relatively cool, while the transitional seasons are very long. Summer rainfall maxima occur, but rain is fairly evenly distributed. Precipitation is really quite low (20 to 30 inches [500 to 750 millimeters] annually), though the high number of cloudy days retards evaporation. Severe droughts affect eastern Poland on rare occasion. More debilitating to crops are the cool, wet summers that occur when maritime influences prevail and crops rot in the fields for want of dry harvesting weather.

The southern subzone is much warmer in summer, although winter temperatures differ little from the northern subzone. Summers are long and hot with precipitation peaking in spring and early summer. The climate is very nearly ideal for winter wheat and, except in occasional drought years, it is reasonably suited to corn production.

There are three exceptions to this general pattern. The Adriatic coastal fringes of Yugoslavia and Albania experience a truly delightful Mediterranean climate with winter rainfall and summer drought. Shielded by the Dinaric Alps, the winters are as mild as those of Italy's coasts. Certain Mediterranean specialties cannot be grown here, however, because of the occurrence of intense, cold winds called *boras;* these occur a few days each winter when continental cold spills over the Dinaric barrier. These winds are not only subfreezing in temperature, but also tree-flattening in force.

The Dinaric Alps themselves are oriented at right angles to prevailing winds. They receive among the highest rainfall totals in Europe, often in excess of 80 inches (2,000 millimeters). The other exception is eastern Romania, which experiences true steppe conditions—evaporation exceeds the total precipitation. Generally, the Balkan countries, astride the Mediterranean–cold winter continental climatic divide, experience the greatest fluctuation in weather conditions, both rainfall and temperature, from year to year.

DRAINAGE

Three river systems, the Elbe, Oder, and Vistula, drain the northern portion of the region. Almost everywhere covered by glacial debris, much of the drainage is poorly integrated with swamps, lakes, and shifting river courses strongly in evidence in the landscape.

Most of the central portion of the region is drained by the Danube and its tributaries. The Danube is navigable for most of its length; a series of rapids at the "Iron Gate" is the single major obstacle. A joint Yugoslav-Romanian power and navigation project will eliminate the hazards to water traffic in the Iron Gate area. In its middle course the Danube meanders and shifts its course repeatedly. Strong flood control measures have been taken and most of this middle course is now regulated. Similar conditions, as yet unregulated, occur in the lower course of the Danube.

The Dinaric plateaus of western Yugoslavia lack surface drainage altogether in many places. No streams of any significance flow into the Adriatic. The intense faulting that has taken place in the Balkans has developed a series of hills and valleys that tend to channel streams as well as important corridors of land transportation. A few down-dropped fault blocks form valleys that contain large lakes.

SOILS AND VEGETATION

Oak, beech, and birch are by far the commonest trees throughout East Europe. There are major forest reserves only in Yugoslavia and Romania. In an effort to produce pulp wood, large acreages of swamps and mountains in all of East Europe have been planted with spruce. The barren grasslands of the Yugoslav karst country are a steppe caused by the absence of surface water. Sparsely wooded steppe was the normal vegetational pattern over most of the Danube Basin.

A belt of very fertile brown and black earths has formed on the loess belt north of the Carpathian and Sudeten mountains. Indicative of a general human upgrading of soil in the region, however, the best crop yields in Poland are obtained on the poorer glacial soils of the districts of Poznan, Opole, and the lower Vistula.

True black earths of exceptional fertility are found in the eastern halves of both Romania and Hungary. Even where not black earth, the soils of the middle and lower Danube are highly productive. The soils of the mountains of the Balkan peninsula are often thin and stony, but pockets of the rich, red, solution-formed soils known as terra rosa are scattered throughout the mountains in pockets of exceptional fertility. Overall, the soils of eastern Europe yield well with proper management.

THE STRUCTURE OF SUBREGIONS

The region can be divided into three subregions based on cultural, economic, and even physical similarities. The three northern states experience the highest income levels, living standards, and degree of industrialization. East Germany contains one of Germany's oldest industrial districts in Upper Saxony. Poland combines the heavy industry of the Silesian coalfields with the old Sudeten textile district, inherited from Germany in 1945, and a rapidly expanding industrial center. Czechoslovakia, at least the western portion, was the primary industrial district of the Austro-Hungarian Empire. All three units have well-developed specializations, though each is also relatively self-sufficient in many types of industrial production. Together they form the primary industrial zone of East Europe. Agriculture is both productive and technologically advanced, but all three states are food-deficit areas.

In the second region, the non-Slavic center, Hungary and Romania constitute an area currently undergoing industrialization yet still moderately agricultural in orientation. This is the richest farmland in the region, and both countries produce food surpluses. Though heavy industry is represented, lighter types of industrial production dominate. Russian influence here once was notably weak, while Austrian and French influence has been quite strong. The Danube itself forms a strong intraregional link. Though the languages are totally different and the respective religious traditions are also different, there has been a great deal of contact between the two states. Hungarians constitute the largest minority in Romania, and fully one third of today's Romania was long a part of a Hungarian state. There are strong historical similarities in land-use patterns and land-holding systems. Vital lines of transportation have always bound the two states together.

The third subregion consists of three very mountainous states (Bulgaria, Albania, and Yugoslavia) historically linked through the bond of Ottoman Turkish control over centuries. The least developed and most agrarian areas of

Katowice Steel Works, Poland. The northern subregion is fueled by the great coal deposits of Upper Silesia and vast reserves of lignite. It produces over 40 million tons of steel yearly and contains a diverse collection of industry, giving it world rank among industrial regions. (Courtesy of the Embassy of the Polish People's Republic/J. Morek, Sport I, Turystyka)

East Europe, they are also plagued with problems of internal communication and transportation difficulties. Singled out to remain agrarian states within the framework of the CMEA, they have each rebelled in a different manner against this plan for maintenance of the status quo. All three lay claims to Macedonia, though Yugoslavia controls most of that district. Albania is quite backward, while the other two states are advancing rapidly. Above all, the mountainous topography and their orientation toward the Mediterranean and Black seas provide the strongest basis for subregional unity.

THE NORTHERN INDUSTRIAL ZONE: EAST GERMANY, CZECHOSLOVAKIA, AND POLAND

Industrial and mining areas of long standing form a core of old industry along the common border of the three countries. The percentages of population employed in industry are equivalent to those found in West Europe and are still growing. Industrial production is already high and continues climbing (see Table 6–1). Diversity is the key and all branches of industrial endeavor are represented. Trade is increasing and exports of industrial commodities are not limited to the Communist bloc states.

World percentage data indicate that this zone is of industrial significance on a worldwide scale. Table 6–1 establishes that a degree of comparability exists and that the area is truly industrialized and developed. In large measure, this is because the region was already industrialized before it was drawn into the Soviet orbit.

The East European industrial district is spread out along the common border of the three states and contains almost the full range of industrial types. The coalfields of Upper and Lower Silesia, the ore-producing districts of the Ore and Sudeten mountains, and the massive lignite deposits found under the adjacent hills and lowlands form the raw material base. In 1980, the district produced over 230 million tons of coal, almost 400 million tons of lignite, and 40 million tons of steel. This was in addition to 4 percent of the world's copper, large amounts of lead and zinc, a wide range of alloys and rare metals, and a huge production of mineral products of lower value such as glass, clay and ceramics products, cement, and brick. It is one of Europe's leading textile-producing districts and a world-scale producer of chemical products; it even produces over 1 million cars and 2 million television sets annually. It is anchored by the cities of Leipzig, Krakow, and Prague, but it also contains dozens of other sizeable cities and hundreds of smaller industrial centers. A series of newer investment areas encircle this core in an incomplete, secondary industrial arc surrounding the core, while a scattering of ports and other outlying areas represent the final frontier of industrial development. (See Figure 6–2.)

The lowland areas found within the core and this peripheral, secondary industrial area also constitute the primary agricultural districts of the three countries, though the agricultural core of East Europe lies farther to the south.

Each of the three countries in this region has different problems, potentials, and production specializations. Nonetheless, their economies are to a large degree complementary, and there has been a relatively high degree of integration of production. All three are tied to the Soviet economy, yet trade heavily with the West. Each seeks to enlarge its role as a supplier to underdeveloped third world states, yet, basically, they are among each other's best customers and suppliers in what could become a highly integrated economic unit.

TABLE 6–1
Industrial production in the northern industrial subregion of East Europe

	1949	1960	1979	1949	1960	1979	1949	1960	1979
	Steel (million tons)			T.V. Sets (thousands)			Passenger Automobiles (thousands)		
East Germany	0.8	3.3	7.0	—	417	584	3.5	64.1	171.0
Czechoslovakia	2.8	6.8	14.8	—	263	482	20.8	56.2	182.0
Poland	2.3	6.7	20.0	—	171	915	—	13.0	363.1
	Electrical Energy (billion kilowatt hours)			Cement (million tons)			Artificial Fertilizer (thousand tons)		
East Germany	16.7	40.3	97.5	1.2	5.0	12.3	200.0	529.3	1,305.2
Czechoslovakia	8.3	24.3	70.0	1.7	5.1	10.3	64.0	263.5	1,046.1
Poland	8.3	29.5	119.0	2.3	6.6	19.2	236.9	840.1	2,596.0
	Textiles (all types of cloth) (million meters)			Paper and Cardboard (thousand tons)			Shoes (million pairs)		
East Germany	183	448	715	277	515	1,023	N.A.	26.2	40.0
Czechoslovakia	420	562	918	275	429	1,146	N.A.	44.1	61.3
Poland	514	853	1,459	253	457	1,326	N.A.	39.0	73.5
	Synthetic Rubber (thousand tons)			Tractors (thousands)			Transistors (millions)		
								1965	
East Germany	N.A.	86.8	155.0	N.A.	4.4	4.0	N.D.	N.D.	N.D.
Czechoslovakia	N.A.	0.0	59.3	N.A.	32.5	35.3	—	3.0	38.0
Poland	N.A.	20.2	130.0	N.A.	8.7	59.5	—	3.0	76.5

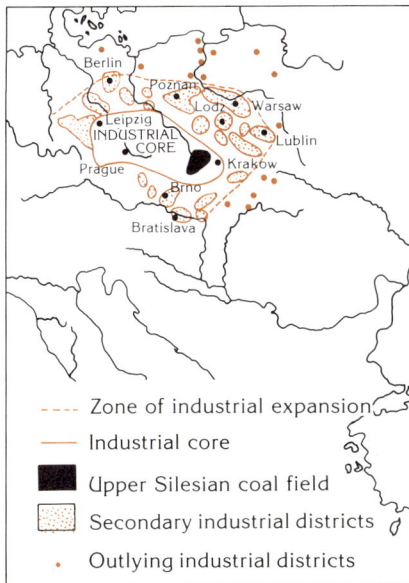

FIGURE 6–2
Industrial Zones in the Northern Industrial Subregion of East Europe. The "northern three" included the first industrial zones of East Europe, with modern industrial complexes in place long before the advent of Communist regimes.

Poland With an area of approximately 120,000 square miles (300,000 square kilometers) and a population of over 35 million people, Poland is the largest of the East European republics. With firm cultural ties to the West and large emigree colonies in North America, Poland has also been able to act in a more independent fashion than most of the region's other states. Its most noteworthy deviations from the Communist norm are the open practice of formal religion, the dominance of a peasant, freehold farming system, and the development of an independent trade-union movement. The ties of the people to land and religion are deeply entwined with the national mystique, and the Soviets are extremely aware of the fact that the violation of Polish nationalism ultimately precipitated Western involvement in World War II. The country has always suffered a precarious existence between Germany and the Soviet Union. At times, however, this location can be an advantage. The present may be one of those times, as East-West trade linkages increase.

The central lowland forms the historical and political core of Poland. The surface is generally a level-to-rolling plain with great regional variations in soil fertility. The sandy outwash plains south of the morainal hills are notoriously infertile; they became one of the two great source areas for Polish migrants to North America between 1863 and 1925. Further south are the rolling till plains, the most intensely used part of the lowland. Pockets of favorable soil support wheat and sugar beets, but most of the district has soils of limited fertility.

The southern plateaus and valleys are the most productive and densely populated areas. An upland of limestone stretches from Upper Silesia eastward to the Russian border, forming a foreland of the Carpathians but separated from them by a valley. The Carpathian and Sudeten mountains and their immediate forelands contain most of Poland's known mineral wealth. The mountains are pierced by many low passes and contain broad, sometimes fertile basins.

Agriculture While the country has only limited areas of good soil, agriculture was the mainstay until recent times, and it still supports about 30 percent of the population. Over half of Poland is under cultivation. In normal climatic years, Poland is self-sufficient and even produces a small, exportable surplus. In bad years, grain must be imported, while contracts with the USSR for meat, dairy products, and produce must still be fulfilled. Eighty percent of all farms are privately owned. Most farms are small, and rapid rural depopulation is still going on. State or collective farm restructuring, so staunchly resisted since 1947, will probably come to pass by default as rural to urban migration continues at a high rate. The rate of mechanization on these small farms is quite low. However, cooperative ownership of machinery is encouraged and farmers accept new techniques and ideas readily. Creation of chemical fertilizer production complexes in Silesia and at several cities along the Vistula has increased the available supply. However, while most farmers use chemical fertilizer, inputs are only moderate by most of West Europe's standards, and yields are less than the maximum possible. The low native fertility would require about a 40 to 50 percent increase in application to obtain yields equal to those of the Benelux countries or the Germanies. The rapid intensification of animal husbandry in recent years has added to the general fertility level.

Rye still covers the largest acreage, but wheat is sown over an acreage about two thirds as large. The combined acreage of wheat and barley is greater than that of rye, and rye acreage declines yearly. Potatoes are still a staple and very important, but fodder crops now surpass potatoes in importance, and industrial crops (mainly flax, sugar beet, and oil seeds) occupy an acreage about half that of potatoes. Commercial dairying and meat production are the areas of greatest increase in importance.

Six farming districts can be identified in Poland (Figure 6–3). The loess lands of the south, together with areas of rendzina soils and reclaimed marsh, emphasize wheat. Dairying's importance in this district reflects the interaction of mountain pastures with the grain fields of the valleys. In the western portion, farms are larger and more mechanized; barley is grown as a rotational crop, and the best

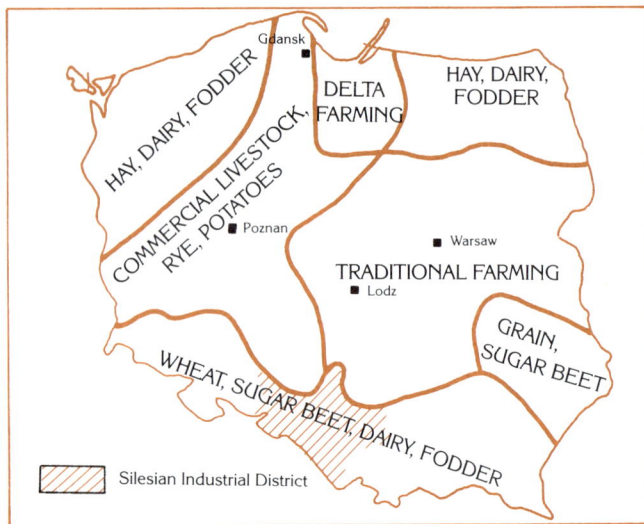

FIGURE 6–3
Crop Livestock Farming Districts in Poland. These crop-livestock districts, fairly complex for the territorial size of Poland, reflect terrain and soil conditions. They are evidence of development strategies for high-quality food export and of efforts towards self-sufficiency for domestic consumption.

lands are used for industrial crops. The small farms of the eastern, more mountainous portion are hay and dairy farms with the most favorable land devoted to wheat. Farms here are also less specialized and have lower overall yields. The upper Silesian portion of this district is largely given to market gardening and the production of dairy products for the large urban market there.

In the area of Poznan, commercial livestock farming and intensive dairying are the chief endeavors. Rye is still the most important grain, but hay and fodder crops dwarf the acreage sown to rye. Virtually all the farms greatly exceed the national averages for both swine and cattle. This district is truly commercial with an intensity and productivity that compares favorably to farms in West Germany and Denmark. Farm cooperatives started here over one hundred years ago. Most farms classified as "collectives" in this district (in government statistics) are really cooperatives. The cooperatives are loosely organized and the productivity is such that government interference is minimal.

East-central Poland is the district of least change. A land of small farms, it has undergone the greatest rural-to-urban shift and greatest out-migration of any portion of Poland. Over 80 percent of the land is still in small private holdings. The traditional grain, rye, leads all acreage with potatoes a close second. The highest yields are found in the zones surrounding Lodz and Warsaw. Extensive land-use types, like the grazing of sheep, dominate on the poorer lands south of those cities. The recent construction of fertilizer plants at Plock, Wloclawek, and Pulawy on the Vistula have helped increase yields by simply increasing the availability of fertilizer at an affordable price. It has become the target of recent government study and invest-

ment, as it is destined to become the meat-supply area for Warsaw and its ever-growing number of industrial satellites. It has suffered as much from industrial investment (and commensurate agricultural underinvestment) as it has from any resistance to change. The decision to maintain a large part of this area as agricultural, rather than to industrialize, has redirected government investment into farm improvement.

The southeastern grain–sugar beet district is another example of redirection of government investment. During the Stalinist period, one of the goals of agriculture was self-sufficiency in wheat. Lands formerly held by Ukrainians and Germans removed during population transfers were used to enlarge peasant holdings; large estates were converted into highly mechanized state farms. Many other small farmers were shifted west, receiving land grants in the recovered territories. Wheat and sugar beet productions are subsidized and area farms receive priorities for investment in mechanization and fertilizer. The area's state farms are characterized by high yields, with among the highest yields of both wheat and sugar beets in the country. Popular generalizations about private versus public sector farming are severely tested here.

The delta district is a highly specialized agricultural milieu that is also a recent recipient of state investment for improved farming in both private and public sectors. Fully one third of the area is in meadow and pasture. Pasture and fodder crops are paramount, but wheat acreage is increasing. Public sector holdings account for about 60 percent of farm acreage; dairying is well developed, but commercial beef breeds dominate.

The low fertility of the soil in the morainal district results in large farm units, even in the private sector. An unusually large percentage of the farms are in state or collective holdings, reflecting not only the fact that this district is largely formed from the recovered territories (where state holdings as a percentage of total are higher by far than the national average), but also the low rates of in-migration to lands known to be of low utility. In an effort to use all land as quickly as possible, both for reasons of food needs *and* justification of occupation, the Polish government set up large state farm units. This original pattern still persists (see Figure 6–4). Seed production, animal breeding, and experimental farming are functions of many of the state farms. Large state farms grow, process, pack, and ship fodder and commercial feed. Cattle are bred in the northeast, pigs in the northwest. Grains are confined to the best lands; dairy cattle are omnipresent. Specialized industrial crops occupy significant acreages. In many respects, however, this area is the least intensively used in Poland.

In general terms, Polish agriculture has greatly increased its variety and productivity over the past three decades. The government sees its problem as too many

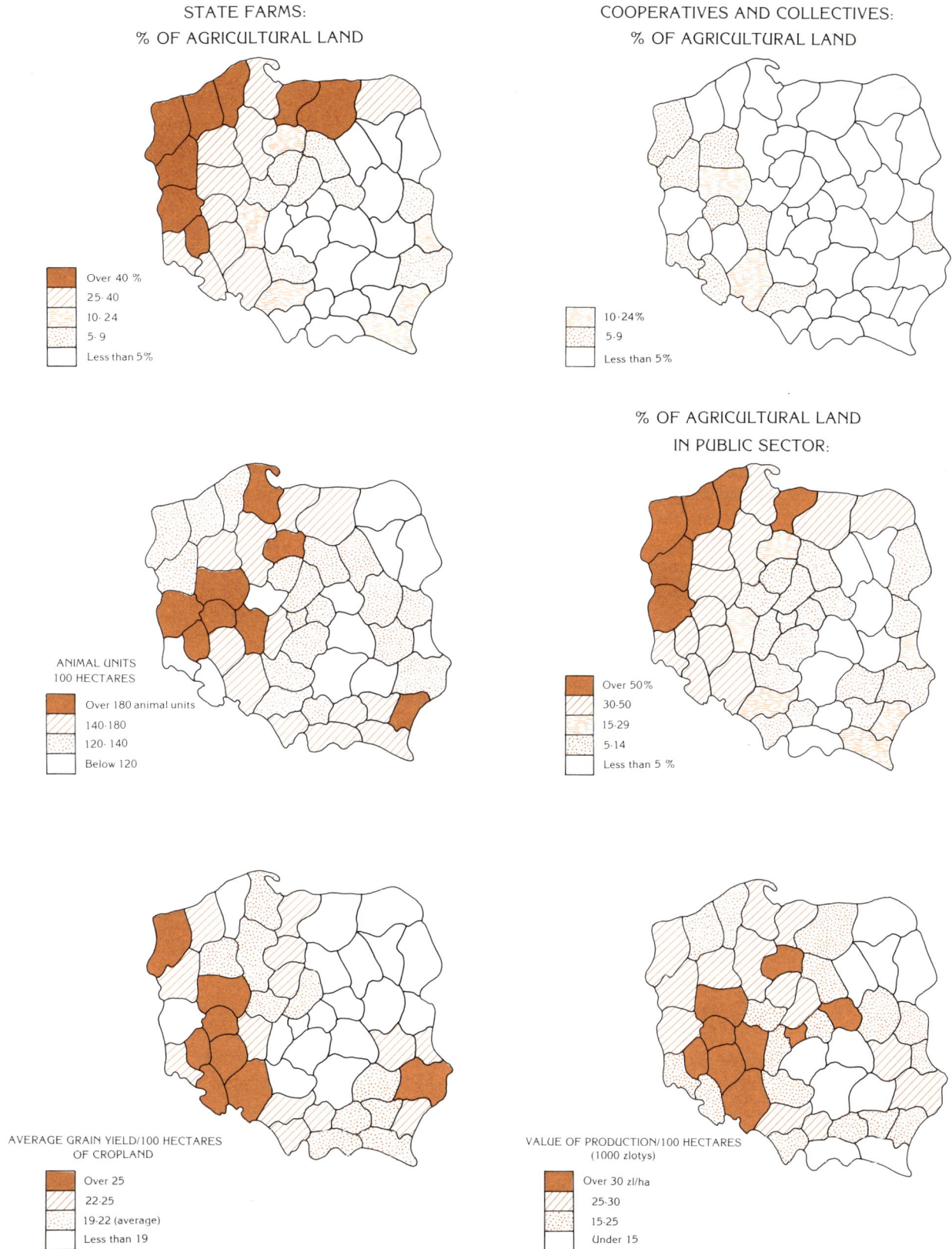

STATE FARMS:
% OF AGRICULTURAL LAND

Over 40 %
25-40
10-24
5-9
Less than 5%

COOPERATIVES AND COLLECTIVES:
% OF AGRICULTURAL LAND

10-24%
5-9
Less than 5%

ANIMAL UNITS
100 HECTARES

Over 180 animal units
140-180
120-140
Below 120

% OF AGRICULTURAL LAND
IN PUBLIC SECTOR:

Over 50%
30-50
15-29
5-14
Less than 5 %

AVERAGE GRAIN YIELD/100 HECTARES
OF CROPLAND

Over 25
22-25
19-22 (average)
Less than 19

VALUE OF PRODUCTION/100 HECTARES
(1000 zlotys)

Over 30 zl/ha
25-30
15-25
Under 15

FIGURE 6—4
Poland: Percentage of Land in Public and Private Farming. Unlike the USSR, Poland's agriculture is
characterized by a mix of public (state farms and collectives) farming and private. Public ownership
tends to be prevalent in those territories resulting from the postwar border shifts westward into former
German lands; obviously, these lands did not have Polish farmers already in place.

small units incapable of full-scale commercial production. The private sector sees low commodity prices and high costs of fertilizer and machines as its greatest hindrances to production. Where investments are lacking (or sporadic) in both the public and private sectors, one observes a general backwardness in agriculture. Roughly half of Poland could experience great increases in productivity if already successful programs were followed in districts of lower intensity farming. One of the hidden negatives in public sector farming is the over-bureaucratization of the farms. On many state farms, 30 to 40 percent of all personnel are managerial. The ultimate solution to Poland's problems may lie in a mixed-economy type of farming. Already, private farmers are allowed (even encouraged) to increase the size of their holdings through purchase or rental of land. With a relatively high population density and a large negative balance of payments, not a single piece of land can lie idle without detriment to the economy, and already producing land must yield to the fullest.

Public sector farm wages are quite low, and the overall opportunities and benefits of industrial employment encourage youth to leave for urban centers. City housing shortages have only a minor effect on retarding rural to urban flows. One of the newer aspects of Polish agriculture is the commuting workers who reside on the farm. Generally one marriage partner commutes to an industrial job while the other farms. In some ways, this is the best of both worlds, especially where the journey to work is kept artificially cheap, lest factory labor fall short of needs. Rural space and food supply coupled with industrial wages and fringe benefits allow such commuters the best of all living standards. In an effort to stem the outflow of farmers, free medical care, pensions, and other fringes have been extended to full-time private sector farmers during the last decade. What the ultimate result of all these conflicting trends will be is an open question.

Resources and Industry   Poland is regarded as the mineral storehouse of East Europe. Upper Silesian coal production, now over 200 million tons yearly, fuels East Europe's power plants and steel mills as well as earning foreign credits through export. A new coalfield near Lublin is soon to be put into production. Lignite deposits are scattered throughout the midsection of the country, and four major fields are in production. Large amounts of investment have been channeled into the search for oil and gas, though only small producing fields have resulted. The large Polish petrochemicals industry is dependent, overwhelmingly, on Soviet-supplied petroleum.

Poland, a major steel producer but minor iron ore miner, uses imported ores for most of its needs; Soviet ore shipments are very high priced and of variable grade. Postwar geologic research has uncovered major deposits of copper in the southwest and huge deposits of high-grade natural sulfur in the southeast.

Poland's industry is oriented more toward basic, heavy industrial production than that of either Czechoslovakia or East Germany. Its portion of the industrial core is the most intensely industrialized area of the country. Upper Silesia is a Ruhr-like concentration of steel mills, metal refineries, and chemical works that create a polluted, if prosperous, industrial district of world rank. In an attempt to decentralize industry from the old cities at the heart of the coalfield, a peripheral ring of industries has been developed just beyond the farthest extent of the coal reserves. Krakow, an intensely diversified industrial city on its eastern edge, emphasizes machine and engineering industries and is the site of the large Nova Huta steel works. Czestochowa, a religious shrine city intimately entwined with Polish nationalism, is a center of iron mining that acts as the district's industrial entrepôt from the north. Steel and engineering industries dominate in the city itself and a host of rapidly developing satellites. The cities to the west produce chemicals and cement on a massive scale, while Beilkso, near the Czech border, produces textiles, automobiles, and machines tools. New mines have been sunk in the southwestern portion of the coalfield, tapping higher-grade coals that are at considerable depths and in geoglogically complex areas.

The Lower Silesian district is one of the country's two traditional textile districts. The textile towns stem from a medieval tradition and are scattered the length of the Sudetens on both sides of the international border. Their growth has been limited in the last twenty years. There has been new investment, however, in small machinery and electronics plants, which increasinly dominate the economies of the mountain towns. The greatest industrial growth in Lower Silesia has come in the towns and cities of the Oder Valley. The river itself is navigable and major rail and highway facilities parallel its course. Clothing, engineering, and chemical industries combine the products of Upper and Lower Silesia into technically complex industrial goods; Wroclaw (600,000) is the dominant city and a major center of engineering and electronics.

Three cities (Warsaw, Lodz, and Poznan) dominate the industry of central Poland. Warsaw specializes in consumer goods and technical equipment, Lodz (a nineteenth century textile city) has diversified recently, though textiles still dominate output. A recent new lignite and power complex nearby is expected to provide the cheap power necessary for further diversification. Poznan is best known for railroad equipment and armaments, but it also posesses huge pharmaceutical, cosmetics, and detergent industries that export throughout the Soviet bloc. Lignite, at Konin, provides the regional power supply; gas deposits at Ostrow are expected to enlarge the fuel base. Small plant expansion in the satellites of these three cities and in intervening towns is gradually creating an industrial belt.

Two other areas are noteworthy. The lower Vistula, once dominated by food and forest processing, is rapidly growing into a diversified industrial area. The Baltic ports of Gdansk, Gdynia, and Elblag are now major centers of maritime engineering. Plock and Wloclawek, receiving oil from the Soviet pipeline, are major refining and petrochemical centers. Southeastern Poland, once targeted for industrialization in the 1930's, is finally reaching that goal in the 1980's. The huge new Lublin coalfield, recently discovered gas deposits, enormous reserves of sulfur, high-grade glass sands, and pottery clays are its new resource base. Agricultural machinery, aircraft parts, trucks, mining equipment, appliances, and a variety of factory machinery dominate production.

Population and Migration   Virtually no other country in the region has experienced such a transfer of population. In 1945–47 some 8 million Germans were expelled or migrated from the formerly German territories awarded to Poland after World War II (Figure 6–5). At the same time, some 3.5 million Poles were transferred from the western USSR after border changes in the east. The gap between expellees and immigrants was filled by armies of volunteer migrants from rural central and eastern Poland, so that by

FIGURE 6–5
Oder-Niesse Territories. Following World War II, Poland experienced a westward "shift," as formerly German territories in the west and the southern portion of former East Prussia became Polish, but traditional Polish territories on its eastern frontier were absorbed by the Soviet Union.

1960, Poland could declare "the western territories" fully repopulated. High birth rates also accomplished much of the repopulation in one of the major baby booms found anywhere in Europe. The population of the so-called recovered territories now exceeds prewar levels by about 15 to 20 percent.

Urbanization has taken place at an even more spectacular rate, as over 60 percent of the population is urban as compared to 20 percent prior to 1939. Rural depopulation continues at a rapid rate in the southeastern and eastern provinces, whereas the farm population declines more slowly elsewhere. Metropolitan Warsaw, with 2.2 million people, remains the prime attraction for migrants, while most of the rest pack into the port cities and the high-wage industrial areas of Upper Silesia. Mass immigrations characterized the new copper district over the last decade, while the Lublin coalfields are expected to undergo similar migration pressures in the 1980's. The cities of the Baltic combine scenery and climatic attractions with the best opportunities to buy foreign-produced luxuries and consumer goods—a kind of unofficial amenity in a society where many items are still scarce.

Some of the ethnic Poles who remained in the recovered territories (about 1.0 million) after the border changes of 1945 and their descendents have chosen to migrate to West Germany over the last twenty-five years. This migration has been arranged officially. Their place is almost immediately filled by rural migrants in what has to be the most mobile of all societies in East Europe.

The changes in borders and consequent transfers of people have eliminated a major problem for Poland. In 1939, some 30 percent of Poland's citizenry belonged to a different ethnic group. Today the country is 99 percent Polish. There are some Poles still living outside the country, some 1.6 million in the USSR, and a few tens of thousands in Romania and Czechoslovakia. Millions of emigree Poles and their descendants live in the United States, Canada, France, Britain, West Germany, and Australia.

While the borders of current-day Poland have been officially accepted by treaties with both East and West Germany, the territorial question could conceivably be reopened at some future date. Polish-German relations are officially cordial, but Polish public opinion is still decidedly aware of World War II. More volatile now, however, is the potential for a Polish-Soviet conflict stemming from Poland's persistently independent domestic policies and internal unrest.

East Germany   The German Democratic Republic, as it is officially known, has the highest standard of living of any Soviet bloc nation. The traditional characterization of East Germany was that of the agricultural portion of the country, while what became the Federal Republic of Germany was considered to have the mineral wealth and the industry. This was an overgeneralization. East Germany does contain the largest area of superior soil found in prewar Germany. Nonetheless, it was thoroughly industrialized and produced no food surplus of note.

Population and Movement   The East German state has an area of 41,000 square miles (108,000 square kilometers); it is slightly smaller than the state of Pennsylvania and has a population of almost 17 million people. The country, for which no historical tradition exists, is the former Soviet zone of military occupation, a leftover from the quadripartite division of Germany among the allies after World War II. Some 4.5 million German expellees from other East European countries, including the Oder-Neisse territories of Poland, entered East Germany between 1945 and 1950; yet the population remained stagnant, or even declined, as some 2.8 millions migrated westward between 1955 and 1961, and unknown numbers made the move before 1955. This heavy emigration led to the construction of the Berlin Wall in August 1961. Currently, some 20,000 migrants (largely the aged and infirm), are allowed to legally emigrate to West Germany yearly. Others use more complicated routes, such as visiting Yugoslavia (on vacation) and seeking asylum in the West German embassy there.

As is the case in the Federal German Republic, deaths exceed births in a now-aging population that suffered lower birthrates in the immediate post–World War II period due to the heavy wartime losses of males. Both Germanies record declining populations, and, in both cases, immigration falls just short of redressing the declines of natural growth.

Agriculture   Over half the country is arable. Meadows and pastures cover another 15 percent and are intensively fertilized and even irrigated. Collectivization takes an unusual form in East Germany; land may be collectively owned, but each collective is divided into lands farmed by individuals rather than cooperatively farmed lands. The independence of decision allowed is rather broad. Yields are comparable to those of western Europe, the only such case in a Communist economy. In an attempt to increase self-sufficiency and to reduce imports, much land has been switched from rye and other grains to wheat and sugar beet. To insure higher yields of these crops, there is heavy fertilization. Livestock numbers have increased radically (especially pigs and beef cattle) in the last fifteen years in an effort to reduce the imports of meat. Per capita production of pork and poultry now exceeds that of West Germany. However, imported grain and livestock feed is

necessary to maintain this high level of production, and the country remains a net importer of food and agricultural commodities.

Industry and Resources   East Germany is the world's leading producer of lignite (brown coal) with a production in excess of 250 million tons yearly. There are large deposits (and production) of potash, though West Germany received the bulk of the famous Stassfurt deposit by the positioning of the border. Rare metals, including uranium, are produced in the Ore Mountains and Thuringia. The mineral base is not large, nor varied, but it is sufficient to meet most of East Germany's fuel needs and some critical raw material needs for its exceptionally well-developed chemical industries.

A higher percentage of the population is employed in manufacturing than in any other country in the world (with the exception of city-states like Singapore and Hong Kong). Despite the lack of a domestic supply of coking coal or iron ore, East Germany produces over 7 million tons of steel annually. The large market formed by its metal-fabrication industries justifies this large investment despite the need to import raw materials.

The chemical industry leads all other branches in terms of value of production. There is a huge chemical fertilizer industry, and myriad firms produce both consumer and industrial chemicals for export and domestic markets. Lignite, with the cheap power it generates, is the single most important domestic resource for industry. Soviet oil, brought by the Friendship pipeline, supplies the other main ingredients. East Germany has come to specialize in plastics, synthetic resins, solvents, vinyls, and urethane products—shipping these products throughout the Soviet bloc.

The East German textile industry concentrates in Saxony. Karl Marxstadt (formerly Chemnitz) is the leading center for the production of synthetic fibers and cloth. Knit goods, artificial fur, velvets, and other high-quality, high-value items increasingly dominate production as the domestic market for any lower-priced items is increasingly supplied by imports.

Machine manufacturing is almost ubiquitous, as every major type of industrial or consumer machinery is produced somewhere in East Germany. Carrying forth its prewar tradition, East Berlin is the major center for the production of electronics and office equipment as well as appliances. Leipzig and its satellites produce lenses and scientific-medical-laboratory equipment as well as machine tools.

The two major cities (apart from East Berlin), Dresden and Leipzig, have never recovered their prewar population sizes. Dresden, once a famed residential city with fine theaters, museums, and one of the world's greatest collections of art, has become more of an industrial city under the Communist regime. The famous porcelain and china, with which its name is so closely associated, are still made. Its textile industries still produce velvets, laces, brocade, and high-value materials. However, it is now a major center for chemical and machine production as well as optical goods, control devices, and machines tools.

Leipzig still holds its annual trade fair, a holdover from medieval times. Its great fair was originly based on the agricultural productivity of its hinterland, perhaps the most fertile soil area in Germany. Harvesting was accomplished by Polish seasonal migrant labor for centuries, and Leipzig, unlike many of the other areas of Germany, had very strong ties to East Europe throughout its history. The Leipzig Fair today is a showcase for Communist bloc industrial technology, and, like Poznan in Poland, a place for the exchange of goods, machinery, technology, patents, and processes between East and West. Machinery, indeed entire factories, are engineered and manufactured in its suburbs. It is still a major center for fur production, now using imported Russian skins. Printing and publishing, its most ancient industrial tradition, is still a major employer. Fine lithographs and reproductions of art works are produced here.

Some small cities in Thuringia date their industrial traditions to the Middle Ages. However, during the last thirty years the East German government has revitalized and expanded Thuringia into a major industrial area. Many of the newer lines of industrial specialization, such as the automotive industry, are located here. Jena, the original home of Zeiss photographic equipment, maintains many of the patents and processes (and even the name) of the firm, even though the Zeiss family moved its private operations to West Germany.

A curious effect of the post-1945 border changes has been the development of Rostock as a port. This ancient Hansa city, long stagnant, has become East Germany's major port and, through modernization, is seeking to attract Czech trade away from the Polish port of Szczecin.

The Future   There is one serious question remaining—that of ultimate German reunification. Former West German Chancellor Willy Brandt had as one of his goals the normalization of relations between the two Germanies, a program he referred to as *Ostpolitik*. To achieve this goal, it was necessary for the Federal German Republic to recognize all post–World War II border changes and to enter into nonaggression treaties with the Soviet Union and the various countries of East Europe. Further, West Germany extended large interest-free credits to East Germany, paid some outstanding indemnities to individuals and to the

East German state, recognizing that entity as an independent sovereign state. To avoid any disruption of the rest of the treaty provisions, the question of reunification was left open. Both states are members of the United Nations and have a full range of diplomatic relations with each other and most of the world's other states. West Germany is the most important trading partner of East Germany after the USSR and the other states of East Europe, which together account for about 60 percent of East German trade.

Several factors either enhance a continuation of separate status or block reunification. It is a decided advantage to the USSR to maintain the current situation; a divided Germany is viewed as less of a military threat, while a sophisticated East German industrial plant continues to supply Soviet needs on very favorable terms. The East German state enjoys a monopoly on certain items of trade within the Soviet bloc under CMEA agreements—in effect a protected market. The Communist party, solidly in control in East Germany, would become a minority party in a united Germany. Membership in the European Economic Community, so intimately linked to West German prosperity, could be threatened by Soviet refusal to allow it as a price for reunification. Precedent for this was set in the settlement unifying Austria. The Rapacki Plan, repeatedly introduced in the UN by Poland, advocates a neutral, unarmed Central Europe consisting of Switzerland, Austria, Poland, Czechoslovakia, and both Germanies—outside any collective security agreements or any cooperative economic organizations. The net effect of any such agreement poses many unanswered problems of both political and economic nature.

There is a considerable body of opinion in both Germanies that favors military noninvolvement. Again, there is some element of public opinion that feels that West Germany has become too "Americanized" or too similar to other areas of western Europe, and that only in East Germany has the culture of Germany been preserved unspoiled. There is, also, a tradition of separatism. Until the mid-nineteenth century, Germany was many states rather than one. Separation, then, is not new, and it could conceivably be thought of as normal. Currently, the prospects for reunification are not good. However, the economic prognosis for the separate Germanies continues to be excellent. Each, in its own way, is the economic power of its own respective group of associated states. There are powerful forces in both states who see the status quo as beneficial, and there are even larger numbers who fear that any change might have detrimental effects.

Czechoslovakia   Czechoslovakia was a 1918 creation that united two Slavic-language groups. The Czechs, long a part of the Austrian portion of the empire, occupied a highly developed and heavily industrialized district. The Slovaks, governed under the Hungarian portion of the dual monarchy, were largely farmers or small-town artisans and service workers. Czechs were descended from the oldest of the Slavic states, and Czechs once sat as kings (or emperors) in both the Holy Roman and Austrian empires. There had been no tradition of cooperation or union between the two peoples. Despite some animosities between the groups, however, the state was one of the most successful creations, economically, of the Treaty of Versailles (1919).

This success does not imply that there were (or are) no problems. Like Poland, Czechoslovakia contained large ethnic minorities. Some 3.3 million Germans occupied the rimlands of Bohemia and Moravia, which the Nazi government of Hitler referred to as the *Sudetenland* and claimed in 1938. In 1939, that same government extended a protectorate to the remaining Czech territory, while making those portions of Slovakia not directly annexed by Hungary a protectorate of that state. Together, the Sudeten Germans, the Hungarians, and some half-million Ukrainians accounted for some one third of the total population. Since 1945, Czechoslovakia has become more ethnically uniform. Most Ukrainians were contained in that portion annexed to Russia. Some 200,000 Hungarians were exchanged for 80,000 Slovaks, and, while there is still a sizeable (500,000) minority, there is less friction. All but 100,000 Germans were expelled from the Sudetenland. Today, only some 6 percent of the population is neither Czech nor Slovak. Nonetheless, it remains a coalition of two distinct nationalities.

There are still twice as many Czechs as Slovaks, despite the higher Slovak growth rates. Many Czechs are Protestants, while the overwhelming number of Slovaks are Roman Catholics. Most importantly, despite heavy government investment in Slovakia, the Slovak portion is still largely rural and definitely less developed than the Czech portion. Unity, apparently, is now accepted by both groups as other problems have taken precedence.

Agriculture Only some 12 percent of the population is now employed in agriculture compared to almost half in 1939. Nonetheless, it is an important segment of the country's economy. Four sizeable areas of fertile, fairly level land account for the bulk of farm production. The Bohemian Basin was the core area of the early Czech kingdom. Rich loess-covered hills and valleys yield heavy crops of wheat, barley, and sugar beet, while the meadows support herds of choice dairy cattle. West of Prague, the slopes grow hops, reputedly the finest in the world. The Moravian lowland district is the other important Czech agricultural area. Its southernmost portions are warm enough for wine grapes and corn, while its northern portions specialize in malting barley and sugar beets. The two remaining districts, both in Slovakia, are the Danube lowland and the valleys formed by the upper tributaries of the Tisza. They produce corn, sunflower, and tobacco in addition to vines and wheat. The remaining hill lands have a much more general farming pattern with rye, potatoes, pork, and dairy products as their staples of production.

Virtually all of agriculture is collectivized, though some rural districts remain dominated by private agriculture in the more mountainous areas of Slovakia. Despite mechanization, agriculture suffers labor shortages as youth migrate to the city.

Although the land is rich, with a history of careful husbandry and a relatively high level of efficiency, the country must still import food. Large areas sown to industrial crops further impinge on food production. Yields of grain are higher than in the United States, except for corn, yet only three fourths those of West Europe. Animal husbandry is well developed, though meat is often in short supply because of contracted exports to the USSR and East Germany. If the land does not exactly flow with milk and honey, it literally overflows with wine and beer—both major export commodities.

The Resource Base The country is more fortunate in this respect than East Germany if less so than Poland. The greatest sources of fuel are large deposits of lignite in and adjacent to the Czech Ore Mountains as well as scattered across lowland Slovakia. Much of it is high grade; over 100 million tons are mined annually to supplement (and conserve) the 30 million tons of bituminous coal produced yearly, mainly from the Czech portion of Upper Silesia.

The ancient mines of the Czech Ore Mountains have long since ceased to yield any significant quantities of metals, though there is continuing production of uranium. The Slovak Ore Mountains, however, still produce significant quantities of iron and even small amounts of gold. The rather large deposits of low-grade iron ore in the Slovak Ore Mountains form the supply for the large new steel mill at Kosice. Two old traditions persist; graphite for pencils and high-grade kaolin for fine china are still mined and exported. There are minor deposits of oil and gas, though the USSR supplies most of the demand for both. Fully one third of the land is covered with some of Europe's best managed, highest yielding forests.

Industry This is the dominant employer. The country has three major steel bases, one in each of its major divisions: Kladno, near Prague, Upper Silesia (Ostrava), and Kosice in eastern Slovakia. With a yearly production of over 15 million tons, Czechoslovakia consumes and produces more steel per capita than any other country in the world, except Luxemburg. It leads all nations in East Europe in the production and consumption of electrical energy, and it has developed a significant hydroelectric-generating capacity in Slovakia to ease that area's fuel shortage while increasing its industrial base.

Transportation equipment (including cars) and armaments are two of its most important lines of production. The world-famous Skoda Works at Plzen (Pilsen) and other cities produces over eight hundred types of metal products and machines, though it is best known for its cars and light armaments. Prague manufactures a full line of metal products as well, but aircraft parts, buses, motorcycles, and machine tools are its best known products. Most of this industrial production enters the export market.

Chemical industries are geared almost exclusively to the domestic market, as raw materials must be imported and transportation costs would be quite high. Textiles, clothing, and footwear are oriented to both domestic and foreign markets. Always known for quality, high-priced lines of production are shipped to the Soviet Union and West Europe, while low-priced items are sent to third world markets.

Long renowned for quality glass, Czechoslovakia still produces and exports crystal, laboratory glass, Christmas tree ornaments, and costume jewelry. Continuing the glass tradition on a more Soviet-style line in the last four decades, Czechoslovakia also manufactures plate glass and insulated storm windows.

Population and Migration Despite the intense industrialization of the country, there are few large cities, with Prague the largest city by far, dwarfing the other five cities with over 100,000 people. It is a splendid city, not destroyed by wars, a museum of all types of architecture. Population is evenly distributed across the countryside in picturesque villages, while dozens of small regional and manufacturing centers (20,000 to 50,000 each) actually concentrate the bulk of the population. Bratislava, sprawled along the Danube, has become the second largest city in the country under the impetus of Slovakian industrialization. Without the high birthrate or population transfers that aided Poland in repeopling the recovered territories, the Sudetenland remained partially empty. Government revitalization of industry and tourism in that area has at last led to its rehabilitation. Much of today's citizenry, however, is Slovak rather than Czech, as large amounts of surplus labor were only available from Slovakia.

Long one of the most conservative and obedient of Soviet satellites, Czechoslovakia underwent a political liberalization in the late 1960's after a long period of economic stagnation. Dismayed by this public display of independence, Soviet troops intervened in 1968. Despite animosities (which still survive) with Germany and its other neighbors, the Soviet threat is perceived as most immediate. Since 1968, the economy has moved sluggishly forward with almost imperceptible change.

HUNGARY AND ROMANIA: THE NON-SLAVIC CENTER

While non-Slavic elements are present throughout East Europe, it is in this subregion that they overwhelmingly dominate—effectively dividing the Slavic states of East Europe into two separate parts. The Romanian language is Latin-based, a cultural residue preserved over more than fifteen hundred years since the end of Roman control. The language of Hungary, Magyar, is an ancient Asiatic tongue not related to any Indo-European language. (See Figure 5–4.) In both cases, the peasantry has become heavily intermixed with Slavs, and Slavic words are present in both languages. In such cultural expressions as farm tools, folk costume, food, and music, the Slavic influence is even more obvious. Yet, despite these similarities, truly distinct Hungarian and Romanian cultures have emerged, and the national unity of both states has in some ways been built on the perception of being different from surrounding Slavic groups.

Both states suffered long periods of dominance by other political units. While the Turkish occupation of Hungary lasted only a little over one hundred years, it left much of the Danube Basin depopulated and destroyed, since it was a major battlefield area in the Islamic-Christian contest for control of the Balkan peninsula. The defeat of the Turks was followed not by a resumption of independence but by subjugation to the Austrian Empire. Romania spent almost four hundred years under Turkish control. Unlike Hungary, it was isolated from the cultural trends and technology that emerged in West Europe over that time period. Whereas Hungary emerged as an agrarian, but fairly well-developed state, Romainia embarked on its career as an independent state as one of the most underdeveloped in Europe.

As in all cases in East Europe, there are disputes over borders, irredentist claims, historical claims, and a general lack of coincidence between the boundaries of the states as now constituted and the distribution of each country's nationals. Hungary is peopled 97 percent by ethnic Hungarians. There are a quarter million Austrian Germans in residence, but these are residents of long standing and do not form the basis of any ethnic claim by either Austria or the Germanies. Some 50,000 to 100,000 Slovaks are gradually being exchanged for Hungarians resident in Czechoslovakia. Lesser numbers of Serbs, Croats, and Romanians live around the country's fringes but are counterbalanced by much larger numbers of Hungarians resident in Romania and Yugoslavia. Indeed, it is Hungary that has irredentist claims, as some 1.7 million Hungarians live in Transylvania and the western borderlands of Romania, while 500,000 live in Czechoslovakia, 400,000 in Yugoslavia, 150,000 in the USSR, and a like number in Austria. A sought-after redress of the 1919 borders was the main reason behind the Hungarian-German alliance of 1940.

Romania has both internal complexity and external ethnic claims to complicate its national unity. In 1939, about 30 percent of Romania's population was non-Romanian, but postwar border changes, repatriations, voluntary migrations, and population exchanges have simplified the ethnic picture; some 88 percent of its residents are Romanians today. Large numbers of Hungarians (almost 8 percent of the total population) justify a grant of cultural autonomy. Some 400,000 Germans remain; residents for over seven hundred years, they are gradually decreasing in numbers as they voluntarily migrate to West Germany. Most of the once large Jewish population has emigrated to Israel, though a considerable number fell victim to the holocaust (the mass murders of minorities and dissidents by the Nazis). Yugoslavia and Romania have exchanged minorities on an amicable basis over the last five years, while the cession of territory to Bulgaria removed most of that minority. The other, smaller minorities are gradually becoming Romanized, though the repatriation of the small Turkish minority has been the subject of negotiations.

Some 14,000 square miles (over 35,000 square kilometers) of Romanian territory was seized by the Soviet Union in 1940. Much of it now constitutes the Moldavian People's Republic within the Soviet Union wherein live some 2.5 million Romanian-speaking people. Long a part of the Russian Empire (until 1918), the Moldavians write in the Cyrillic alphabet (essentially the same used by the Russians) but speak the Romanian language.

The two countries are otherwise something of a cultural transition zone. The Hungarians are Roman Catholics or Protestants as are the northern Slavs, while the Romanians are largely Orthodox Catholics like the Russians, Greeks, and most South Slavs. The Hungarians, regardless of language differences, have had strong cultural ties with Poland, Austria, and Germany. Indeed, the German language is widely spoken and understood there. The Romanians, long linked to the Russians as allies and protectors, have traditionally looked to France as a culture source and Germany as an economic partner. Both agricultural economies originally, Hungary and Romania have sought to develop industry at a rapid pace in recent dec-

ades. Long adversaries of one another, both have tended to pursue courses of relative independence, creating distinct and innovative versions of Communism that suit national needs and realities rather more than official Soviet programs and dictates. Both perceive themselves as something of a bridge between East and West. They occupy the center of East Europe, the zone between the Balkans and the North European Plain. They are at the contact zone of Islam and three varieties of Christianity. They control some of Europe's most important traditional trade routes and occupy some of the most fertile and productive of that continent's lands. Every important cultural entity that ever existed in East or Central Europe aspired to (and conquered) some part of the area, from Rome to the Soviet Union. Linked by the Danube, astride the steppes that brought Asian conquerors and Euro-Asiatic trade, these countries are the consummate **cultural crossroads.**

Long the food supply area for western Europe, Hungary and Romania constitute a veritable sea of grain on rich loess or black earth soils. Each is overwhelmingly dominated by a capital city of disproportionate size. Over 10 percent of all Romanians live in the capital, Bucharest. That city contains over 25 percent of all Romanian industry and fulfills the role of *primate city* despite its eccentric (off-center) location within the country. The old original core area of Transylvania lost all but its historical significance as it came to be occupied by other nationalities. Budapest, the capital of Hungary, contains a quarter of all Hungarians and over half the country's industry. Like Vienna, its size and disproportionate influence reflects its past as the seat of a much larger state. The old core, the Little Alfold Basin, passed from importance as Hungary spread to the east and south, just as Transylvania lost its leadership role when the Romanians set out to colonize the Danubian plains. As in Romania, the old core came to be peopled by others, Austrians and Slovaks, as the new frontier areas attracted the majority group.

The capitals of both countries have long constituted **developmental enclaves,** areas of intense and advanced development far beyond that found in their respective hinterlands. One of the great problems of the last forty years has been the development of other, outlying areas as a means of achieving universal, statewide development. In both cases it is the mountain zones that have been chosen for investment because of their potential as producers of minerals and other raw materials. The sharp rural-urban differential has gradually begun to disappear in Hungary, but it persists in the landscape as well as in other cultural attributes in Romania. Both have reopened Western trade contacts as a means of economic expansion while unable to forego the economic ties to the Soviet Union. Both have

New Residential District in Budapest. The rapid industrialization of East Europe has led to an even more rapid migration from rural to urban areas and consequent pressure on housing. New construction techniques have been developed to increase the tempo of building. Budapest, Hungary's largest single industrial center and the goal of most migrants, houses over one fifth of Hungary's population. (Courtesy of the United Nations/Interfoto, Hungary)

made enormous strides in industrializing and are increasingly more oriented toward the developed northern three countries than to the less developed states of the Balkans. Even in this aspect, they form a transition zone.

Hungary Hungary became an independent kingdom in the year 1001. Hungarians have generally thought of themselves as the easternmost outlier of West European culture. The country's parliament predates any found in the West by at least a century. Hungarian nationality was subjugated within the greater Austrian Empire as a result of the Turkish invasions, emerging strongly once again in the mid-nineteenth century when Austria was forced to grant equality to Hungary in the so-called dual monarchy.

On the losing side of the Central Powers in World War I, it was reduced in size and population by the treaty that followed. In one aspect this was positive, as it left a

solidly Hungarian state with few minorities. On the other hand, large numbers of Hungarians were left outside the homeland, leading to animosities and potential border disputes with all surrounding states. Again a German ally during World War II, Hungary temporarily expanded into areas it had controlled historically, only to be defeated again and forced back to the central core. As a defeated axis power, they came under complete Soviet domination in 1945. An abortive revolution came in 1956 when a rapidly liberalizing Hungarian regime was quashed by Soviet tanks. Since that time, change and innovation have occurred at a slower tempo.

Population and Movement An estimated 500,000 Hungarians left during the 1956 revolution, a blow from which Hungary has never fully recovered. The country's growth rate has averaged less than one-half percent in any year since that time; Hungary has a relatively high death rate due to an aging population. Some 1.5 million emigrees live outside the country, while almost 3 million Hungarians live in the surrounding states once controlled by Hungary.

Migration from the countryside to the city has been going on at a very rapid rate, so that some 55 percent of the population is now urban. With a population density of 296 per square mile (114 per square kilometer), the country is densely populated, reflecting its high fertility and exceptionally high degree of agricultural utility.

Unlike the rural populations of western Europe who live in small villages, Hungarian farmers dwell in large sprawling settlement units that are more like towns. Frequently, farmers must have smaller second dwellings amidst the fields to cut travel time during peak labor-demand periods.

Agriculture Hungary generates an agricultural surplus. Almost three quarters of the land is in farms and almost 60 percent of the total area is in cropland. Corn is the largest single crop in both area and yield, with wheat as a close second. There is a large surplus of sugar, not easily exported and far too large for the domestic market. Sugar-beet pulp is used to feed herds of swine, and Hungary has surplus meat production—a rarity in East Europe. Horses have all but disappeared, replaced by over seventy thousand tractors. Sheep, once the dominant type of livestock, have decreased radically in importance in recent decades as land has been converted to more intensive use.

Agriculture has been almost completely collectivized or put under state control. This was fairly easily accomplished in a country where baronial estates occupied most of the land and where a landless peasantry was the norm. Small holdings were created in 1945, but collectivization began almost immediately in 1950. State-owned farms constitute only 11 percent of the farmland, while loose cooperatives occupy some 20 percent of the land. Collectives, by far the dominant type of farm, own their own land. Each individual is guaranteed a private plot, which in Hungary can be unusually large, and some 10 percent of agricultural land is in private plots. Statistically they are a part of the collective, but in reality they are not. Depopulation of the countryside has led to some unusual experiments in semiprivate farming, and some 6 percent of the farmland is held in such fashion. Mortgages and loans are guaranteed by the state in return for fulfilling long-term contracts to farm lands that have been abandoned or underused.

Horticulture has taken on a new importance in recent years. Large acreages have been converted to orchards, vineyards, and truck crops for export to CMEA nations. Hungary is rapidly becoming the processed-food supplier for much of East Europe. Astute at business and marketing, their agriculture (like their industry) is geared to an urban consumer market in which wives with jobs outside the home have little time for shopping or preparation.

Industry and Resources   Hungary has the poorest resource base of any country in East Europe. There is some oil and gas produced, unfortunately of insufficient quantity to meet domestic needs. About 80 percent of all oil is imported, though Hungary produces almost 70 percent of its gas needs. There are large lignite deposits if insignificant supplies of hard coal. Virtually all coke and coking coal for its steel industry must be imported, although lignite supplies most of its thermoelectric generating plants. While there is little potential for hydroelectricity in a country that is quite flat, much of that limited potential has been developed. A nuclear generating plant has been built with Soviet aid, but much power is imported from the USSR, which has linked Hungary to its power grid. Two pipelines feed Soviet oil into Hungarian industrial enterprises, while a gas pipeline connects the Volga-Urals gas fields of the USSR with Hungary.

There are minor deposits of lead, zinc, and iron, but all must be augmented with imports. Bauxite is the single mineral resource produced in oversupply, and the aluminum industry has been developed as a joint Soviet-Hungarian enterprise using Hungarian ore and Soviet surplus power at locations in both countries. The Hungarian aluminum industry is one of Europe's most important.

A small steel industry is a leftover from the era of Stalinist economic policy. It does not come near meeting the domestic need generated by such large-scale consumers as the machine and appliance industries. Official statistics often emphasize heavy industrial production in the list of products, but it is consumer goods that have become dominant. Hungary produces the highest quality

Hungarian Food Exports. As part of its specialization within the CMEA, Hungary has a highly developed food processing industry with worldwide as well as bloc-wide markets. (Courtesy of the United Nations/Interfoto, Hungary-MTL)

television sets in the bloc; their export is an important earner of foreign currency. Refrigerators and small kitchen appliances are other well-developed specialties.

Lovers of luxury and masters of craft, the Hungarians have identified important markets overlooked in the plans of other CMEA economies. Hungarian busses, complete with reclining plush seats, air conditioning, and carpeted floors are used bloc-wide for long-distance passenger travel. Hungarian furniture is considered superior in quality and design to that of all other East European production. The wines, at first neglected by the Communist government, have reestablished themselves in European markets. Musical instruments, a long-established tradition, are marketed throughout Europe, while sound systems and other electronics have virtually no competition within East Europe. Clothing and shoes are major items of production and export. In an almost unprecedented action in East Europe, Hungary has reestablished a private fashion clothing industry.

Although consumer products are dominant, some areas of producer goods production have received heavy investment. Machine tools, for example, virtually all imported before 1950, now constitute a major category of exports.

While Budapest still dominates, each county seat has received some industrial investment, and a line of industrial development extends along the highlands from Lake

Balaton through Budapest to Miskolc. The rapidly growing chemical industries, requiring large amounts of water, are developing along the Danube in a north-south axis that intersects the highland zone at Budapest.

The NEM   Hungary essentially scrapped centralized planning in 1968 in the face of an economic slowdown and renewed domestic unrest. State ownership is retained under this new plan, the so-called New Economic Mechanism (NEM), but factory management and production is left in the hands of production units. State production guidelines are only of the most general type, while a more nearly market economy is allowed to direct the investment, production level, and price structure for each factory. Factories are more or less free to set prices, to buy parts from any source, to introduce technological changes, to introduce new lines of production, and even to increase wages as long as they show a profit. Competition among these state-owned enterprises is not only allowed but is encouraged. Under this system, personal income has risen rapidly, though increasing oil prices and worldwide inflation have recently reduced economic growth rates.

Of all the East European countries, Hungary is most dependent on foreign trade. Over half is still with Soviet bloc states; and the Soviet Union, its major supplier of raw materials, still accounts for a quarter of Hungarian imports and 30 percent of its exports. Nonetheless, a brisk trade is carried on with Austria, West Germany, Switzerland, and Italy. The real dynamics of Hungarian industry, however, are exhibited in its aggressive marketing of consumer goods, luxuries, and technical equipment to East European economies. Emphasis on quality craftsmanship and fulfilling consumer needs throughout a changing East European society have yielded remarkable success.

Romania   Romania traces its origins to 200 B.C. when it was first colonized by a Thracian tribe, the Dacians. Its Roman conquerors, who called it Felix Dacia (happy Dacia), left an indelible mark on the language, an isolated pocket of Latin-based speech surviving at some distance from the rest of those related languages. Not so happy were the succeeding centuries in which invading Asians pillaged the lowlands, forcing the Roman-culture colonists into the safety of the Transylvanian Basin, an area surrounded by protective mountains and forests—isolated from the fertile grasslands that surrounded it on all sides. There in the mountain fastness they evolved as a people called Vlachs or Wallachians.

Since the ninth century, these people, under population pressure, have spread out from the old core. At first they left to become hired shepherds on mountains lands that could not be farmed. The greatest movement occurred, however, with the advent of Turkish control. Not farmers, but fighting men and landlords, the Turks encouraged the Wallachians to settle the grasslands of the Lower Danube when they had effectively sealed off further invasion from Asia. Thus rather late in history, the early Romanians came to reoccupy their traditional homeland.

The impetus to nationalism, however, remained in the old Transylvanian core. There a local noble, Vlad the Impaler, defended independence in an area never fully under Turkish control. He was called *the Impaler* because of his practice of displaying the bodies of Turkish troops and tax collectors along the roads and passes into this natural fortress. Each victim had a stake driven through the heart. Immortalized in a corrupted version of history as Count Dracula (his actual title), he was actually a national hero who managed to stave off Turkish control by a clever, if brutal, display, to use rumor to spread the message of fear and invincibility—fully aware of the fact that he lacked both the troops and technology to defend against a full-scale Ottoman invasion.

This medieval holding preserved a national identity and culture that was gradually extended to the entire unit. As Turkey weakened, autonomy was enlarged and extended to a greater area, so that by 1878 an independent Romania, one third the current size, had come into existence. On the winning side in World War I, the country was enlarged to include almost the maximum of its territorial claims. On the losing side in World War II, it was forced to relinquish considerable territory and came to be dominated by a victorious Soviet Union.

Since 1964, disappointed with Soviet and CMEA plans to maintain its role as a supplier of food and raw materials, Romania has pursued a progressively more independent policy, foreign as well as domestic. Reforms in planning and an aggressive policy of development have been characteristic ever since. Cooperation with China and Yugoslavia, criticism of Soviet intervention in Hungary and Czechoslovakia, trade with (and investment from) the West, and the limited acceptance of both Warsaw Pact and CMEA dictates have all been indicative of this attitude of independence. Yet, the government remains officially Communist, economic policies are kept relatively orthodox Marxian, and no overt actions have been taken toward the USSR. Romania's chief goal is development; economic and political liberalization has not accompanied these policy changes. Theirs is a different kind of "independence" than that demonstrated in Hungary, Yugoslavia, or Poland.

Population and Movement   Once one of the most rapidly growing states in Europe, population increase has now slowed to 0.9 percent yearly, a figure only slightly higher than that encountered in the rest of Europe. In the mid-1970's, the government toughened abortion laws to prevent depopulation, as the population had actually declined for a few years.

Despite its reputation as one of Europe's less developed areas, infant mortality has dropped dramatically and health clinics are well staffed and ubiquitous. In recent years Romanians have made a business of health spas and rejuvenation centers geared to improving the health and condition of senior citizens from foreign countries. Devoted to dietary awareness and exercise, they have also become masters of cosmetology and cosmetic surgery; they have become the mecca for Europe's aging (of better-income level) who wish to preserve their youth.

With a density of 235 per square mile (91 per square kilometer), the area is less densely populated than most of Europe. The country occupies an area roughly the size of Illinois and Indiana, while the population is about 15 percent larger. The richness of soil is comparable and there are similar levels of land utility. The differences, however, are striking on several points. While Illinois and Indiana are large industrial states, Romania remained overwhelmingly agrarian until the last two decades. Even in agricultural potential, the capricious and overall low rainfall renders Romania naturally less productive. Lastly, the low level of technology and agricultural investment has left Romania even less productive than it could be.

Thus two areas of comparable size, population, and utility represent almost the antithesis of one another, with Romania as backward and seemingly overpopulated as Illinois and Indiana are advanced. The actions of the Romanian government since 1964 have been geared to reducing this **developmental gap.** Slow growth is considered desirable, but no growth was seen as a danger in an economy where men retire at sixty-two and women at fifty-seven and where the labor demands of rapidly developing industry could only be met by siphoning off personnel from a yet unmechanized agriculture, thereby reducing food production.

Faced with this dilemma, Romania has proceeded to attack all problems and to develop on all fronts—an impossible task at which they have had remarkable success to date.

Agriculture   Almost 65 percent of the area of Romania is usable for agriculture, though only a little more than 40 percent of the country is sown to crops. Meadow and pasture occupy a disproportionately large area and dry-farming or other long-term fallowing practices further reduce the total. There has been little in the way of irrigation, despite an adequate water resource, and much of the Danube Valley and Delta could be converted into highly productive farmland with adequate drainage and flood control measures. The full agricultural potential of Romania has by no means been tapped.

What had been a slavish imitation of Soviet agricultural policy is now being corrected, though agricultural investment still has a much lower priority than that assigned to industry. Following the Hungarian example, private plots have been enlarged and peasant production for the free market encouraged. State investment has been channeled into experimental stations, breeding, and seed production facilities and farms producing only for the export market. The government has effectively replaced animal power with some one hundred thousand tractors—at least in the level, grain-producing plains.

Some 10 percent of all farmland is in individual hands; much of this is in marginal pasture and meadow. Fully 10 percent of the truly productive farmland, however, is now allocated to private plots.

Because of the fluctuating rainfall conditions, yields are highly unreliable, though produciton has increased an average of 5 percent per year during the period 1974–80. Corn, to which much of Romania is only marginally suited, is the chief crop. Wheat production is generally sufficient for domestic needs, and some is exported in most years. Recently, vast acreages have been devoted to oilseed crops and sugar beet; also increasing rapidly is the area devoted to orchards and vineyards. Growth in wine production has been rapid yet carefully managed. The best foreign and native grape stocks have been combined to produce wines of relatively high quality and virtually all types, allowing Romanian inroads into West European markets.

Animal husbandry is far less well developed than in Hungary. The shepherd tradition remains strong, and Romania raises over 15 million head of sheep. Romania raises only a third the number of cattle or pigs raised in Poland on a comparable agricultural area, yet four times as many sheep. Poultry raising has received the greatest impetus in recent years, both on private plots and on government-run farms. Eggs are processed and shipped as a lucrative export product. Chickens are being commercially produced on a large scale.

Despite progress, there are many remaining problems. The productivity of agriculture remains quite low. The immediate solution to be employed will be larger inputs of chemical fertilizer. This, however, awaits the completion of several large and expensive chemical complexes to supplement the existing moderate production (about half that of Poland, if double that of energy-poor Hungary). The agricultural labor force has dropped from 70 percent to 30 percent of the total. However, it consists largely, now, of older men and women as the young have sought more lucrative factory employment. Grain production is up, but more and more of it is siphoned into the production of alcohol, vegetable plastics, and animal feed—leaving less for export at a time of record imports needed for industrialization. Still, some 3 to 4 million tons of grain are exported each year, some 15 to 20 percent of total production. Despite enormous industrial investments, Romania remains primarily an exporter of agricultural products and raw materials.

Resources and Industry While productivity in agriculture is much lower than in Hungary, Romania posesses an immense reserve of natural resources. Some 12 to 15 million metric tons of oil are produced annually in Romania, one of the world's oldest oil-producing states. The Ploesti fields, which played such an important role in World War II, are all but exhausted. However, five newer, if smaller fields, come close to maintaining the level of 1940 production. The difference is the Romanian economy, which now demands more than can be domestically produced. Romania, traditionally Europe's major exporting nation, must now import Soviet oil and some Arab oil as well. The search for petroleum, a major area of investment, has yielded only moderate finds to date. Exploration has uncovered, however, one of the world's greatest gas fields in Transylvania. Production is about 10 percent of the Soviet Union's and has become an important raw material resource for the burgeoning chemical industry.

Huge deposits of low-grade coal underlie much of the country, but limited deposits of high grades are insufficient for the metallurgical industry's needs. Nonetheless, some 30 million tons of coal of all grades are mined annually, adding a significant domestic energy resource. Five million tons of salt, a vast supply of wood, millions of tons of chemically-pure limestone, and sulfur from a variety of sources round out one of the best of all possible bases for a chemical industry. (See Figure 6–6.)

Romania must import 80 percent of the iron ore required for its steel industry. Convinced of the need to develop heavy industry, Romania now has an annual capacity of over 15 million tons of steel. Rivaling the production of Czechoslovakia and near that of Poland, Romania now

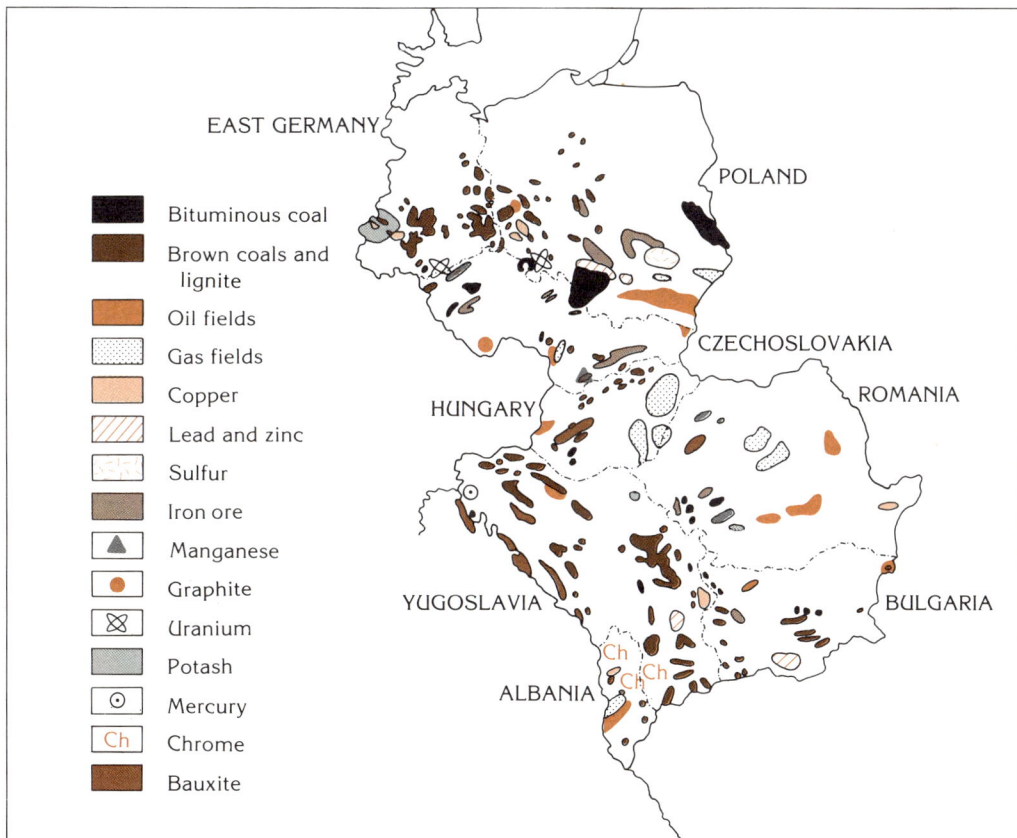

FIGURE 6–6
Natural Resources in East Europe. Despite lingering Western myths about economies characterized by technologically deficient agriculture and little else, East Europe has a varied, and reasonably productive, natural resource base.

The Iron Gate Hydroelectric and Navigation Scheme. This joint Yugoslav-Romanian project is one of the largest hydroelectric generating facilities in the world. Joint economic projects such as this are providing mutual benefits to economies of states in an area where traditional animosities often prevented cooperation in the past. (Courtesy of the United Nations)

ranks third in East Europe in steel production. By comparison, it produces over half the steel produced by a much larger Britain. Much of it is converted into pipe, a major export as well as a basic need in the chemical industry.

Prospecting has uncovered major deposits of bauxite, and a full-scale aluminum industry has been partially constructed. The first limited production of that metal is already underway. Copper is mined at several locations, while Romania is a major producer of gold and silver by European, if not world, standards, and there are apparently large reserves of uranium. Crowning the list of raw materials is one of East Europe's last remaining reserves of high-quality forests, which produce everything from pulpwood and sawed timber to fine hardwoods for violins. Even the reeds of the Danube Delta are used for paper production.

Of all elements of industry, chemicals have received the most significant investment. Large plants in Transylvania complement those located in the oilfields, while new complexes are coming into production at the country's three ports, Braila and Galati on the Danube and Constanta on the Black Sea.

In an effort to maximize the value of its resources, Romania has adopted a policy of doing at least primary processing before export. About 25 percent of its consid-

erable cement production is exported, some of it as prefabricated modular building units. Sawn timber, pulp, and paper, (rather than logs) are primary exports. Other export specialties include tractors (almost forty thousand units yearly), oilfield equipment, and prefabricated chemical plants.

Industry in Romania is still at a moderate level of complexity; there has been little investment in electronics, machine tool production, or sophisticated equipment—all of which must be imported. Despite absolutely herculean strides, foodstuffs, wood products, and petroleum products are still the leading exports. The gradual increase in the level of raw material processing, while requiring much capital investment, has supplied a sound base for further expansion.

Currently, Romania trades more with non-Communist countries than with the bloc. Furs, clothing, knit goods, and petrochemicals form the bulk of the exports to the West—cheaper goods of medium quality for mass consumption. The Soviet Union is still its chief supplier of raw materials. As with the northern three, the traditional colonial role has been reversed. Prefabricated factories and oilfield equipment move to the third world in a lucrative and growing trade, while agricultural products move to other states in East Europe. Fully 20 percent of Romania's trade now moves to third world nations, following the Yugoslavian pattern of trade with nonaligned states.

After a long tradition of distrust and political animosity, Romania has sought a normalizaiton of relations with a similarly oriented Yugoslavia—both are advocates of a strongly independent "national Communism." Minorities, never a pressing issue in either case, have been exchanged. Both nations are developing a joint hydroelectric and navigation scheme at the Iron Gate on the Danube, the most serious navigational impediment on that river. Trade between the two states has increased rapidly. Contacts and trade with both Germanies have been increased, and foreign investment in joint stock corporations is actively sought.

The strains of such a sustained high level of investment are beginning to show, but so are the results. In an uneasy political position, they have sought close relations with China, the states of western Europe, and even the United States. The ability to have accomplished all this is less than twenty years, and without incurring overt Soviet displeasure, may well be the greatest accomplishment achieved by any state in East Europe.

THE BALKANS

There has never been complete agreement among cultural geographers on just what constitutes the Balkans.

Khremikovtsii Steel Works, Bulgaria. Once considered the most backward portion of Europe, the Balkan subregion is gradually developing an industrial base of major proportions. Much resistance was offered to Soviet plans for a continuance of its traditional function as a supplier solely of food and raw materials. (Courtesy of United Nations)

Physical geographers, however, normally gave that name to an area south of the Sava and Danube rivers, from the source of the former in the Julian Alps to the mouth of the latter on the Black Sea. Thus constituted, this area excluded most of the productive Danube lowlands, leaving a Balkans characterized by mountains, generally low land utility, and difficulty of access. It also included the area controlled longest and most completely by the Ottoman Turks. Cultural geographers would generally agree to the inclusion of all the areas south of this physical border, but would often add Romania while excluding Greece.

The subregion within East Europe includes Yugoslavia, Bulgaria, and Albania. They are each governed by Communist party regimes, although each has developed or accepted a different brand of Communism. Two of the three countries are overwhelmingly Slavic in speech and culture, yet Slavic culture is definitely not the basis of the subregion. Economic backwardness might have once provided a basis for designation of the area as a unit, but while less developed than the northern three, Yugoslavia and Bulgaria cannot now be classified as underdeveloped.

Even the mountainous nature ascribed to the Balkans is not universal. Much of Bulgaria consists of fairly level plateau and basin units, while the productive core area of Yugoslavia is the Danubian plains and adjacent hill lands.

Although the traditional cultural complexity of the area has been simplified over time, ethnic diversity holds real potential for further disputes. Borders have stabilized to some degree, though many claims and counterclaims remain unsolved. Nationalism is a potent force in the subregion, but nationalities are not uniformly well developed. There are many cores, often mountain or valley basins, but large areas of disputed hinterland separate them, and one nationality may occupy all or a part of several cores. Historical states of the Balkans have often ceased to exist as political entities. If there is unity, then, it is a unity of diversity. The Balkans remain that part least integrated politically as well as with the greatest diversity of ethnic groups. It is also the area with the greatest intraregional disparities of economic development among its various parts—even within single political units.

Yugoslavia   Yugoslavia has the largest area and population in the Balkans. It is a composite for which there was no historical precedent prior to 1919. Its name means "land of the South Slavs," and it does indeed include the major portion of South Slavs. Each major group within Yugoslavia has had its own separate history and in the past its own separate state. Serbs (40 percent) and Croats (22 percent) are the two largest ethnic groups. They speak the same language, but use different alphabets in accordance with their past religious contacts and traditions. Five other major ethnic groups are recognized by separate autonomous republics or districts, and seventeen other minorities are still acknowledged by linguistic, educational, and other accomodation. Table 6–2 presents a simplification of the ethnic complexity.

The country is so culturally diverse that it has had to institute a form of ethnic federalism not unlike that found in the USSR. There are six ethnic republics and two autonomous districts within the Serbian republic. It has been the explicit policy of the government to reduce such tensions by allowing for maximum cultural autonomy even at the lowest (village and commune) level. The personality of

TABLE 6–2
Yugoslavia: ethnic and cultural diversity

Ethnic Group	Percentage of Total Population	Language	Alphabet	Religion	Autonomous Designation	Historical Political Status (independent existence)
Serbs	40	Serbo-Croat	Cyrillic	Orthodox	Republic	950–1060, 1169–1356, 1815–1918
Croats	22	Serbo-Croat	Latin	Roman Catholic	Republic	903–1102
Slovenes	8	Slovenian	Latin	Roman Catholic	Republic	never independent
Bosnians	8	Serbo-Croat	Cyrillic	largely Moslem	Republic	1150–1250, 1360–1465
Macedonians	6	Macedonian	Latin-Cyrillic	Orthodox	Republic	908–1025
Albanians	6	Albanian (non-Slavic)	Latin	mainly Moslem, some Orthodox	Autonomous district	
Montenegrans	2	Serbo-Croat	Cyrillic	Orthodox	Republic	1356–1918
Hungarians	2	Magyar	Latin	largely Roman Catholic	Autonomous county and village units within Vojvodina	
Turks	1	Turkish	Latin	Moslem	none	
(others)	5	—	—	—	—	—

long-time Yugoslav leader Marshall Tito was effective in holding the unit together.

Countering this governmental attempt to conserve unity is a series of cultural and historical claims made by surrounding states (Figure 6–7) and the national ambitions of certain Croatian elements. Religious groupings essentially follow ethnic lines, although several separate Orthodox churches exist. Perhaps even more disquieting is the tendency for economic development to conform to ethnic lines, with the Slovenes and Croats more highly educated and skilled than other groups. In an attempt to reconcile economic disparities, each individual republic has received some major government investment. Despite this effort, the initial industrialization of the two northern republics plus the centrality and transportation advantages of Serbia have tended to contribute to the maintenance of a developmental gap among the republics.

Position and Potential Yugoslavia controls the most important land routes from western and eastern Europe to the Aegean, Adriatic, and Black seas and the Turkish Straits. The Danube River, the Morava-Vardar corridor, and several critical passes through the Alps, Rhodope, and Balkan mountains are all located within Yugoslavia. These same paths were traveled by trade and transportation in ancient times. The railroads of the nineteenth century, including the famous Orient Express, now have been supplemented by highways to maintain the viability of these traditional land routes.

While the physiography is difficult, it is not impassable. Wide, ample corridors, low passes, broad river valleys, and linear fault troughs serve to channel movement in all directions from certain key locations that control strategic crossroads. One of the great problems of Yugoslavian development was that it controlled the through routes but not the ports. Before 1945, almost all ports with links to the interior were in foreign hands. Postwar border realignments and a virtually all-Communist East Europe would seem to have been an advantage, creating a level of homogeneity of political control that should have encouraged movement. However, Yugoslavia's break with the bloc in 1948 worked against this tendency.

Five rail routes and nine highways now link the Adriatic Coast with the Danube Basin. National animosities and borders cause many routes to dead-end abruptly or to have limited use. The rail network, built to service the export trade, has been replaced by a highway net designed more to serve and integrate the domestic market. A six-lane north-south motorway forms the major transport line. It is paralleled by the narrower Dalmation coastal highway along the Adriatic coast. Major links between them now create the frame of an integrated network. A new railroad

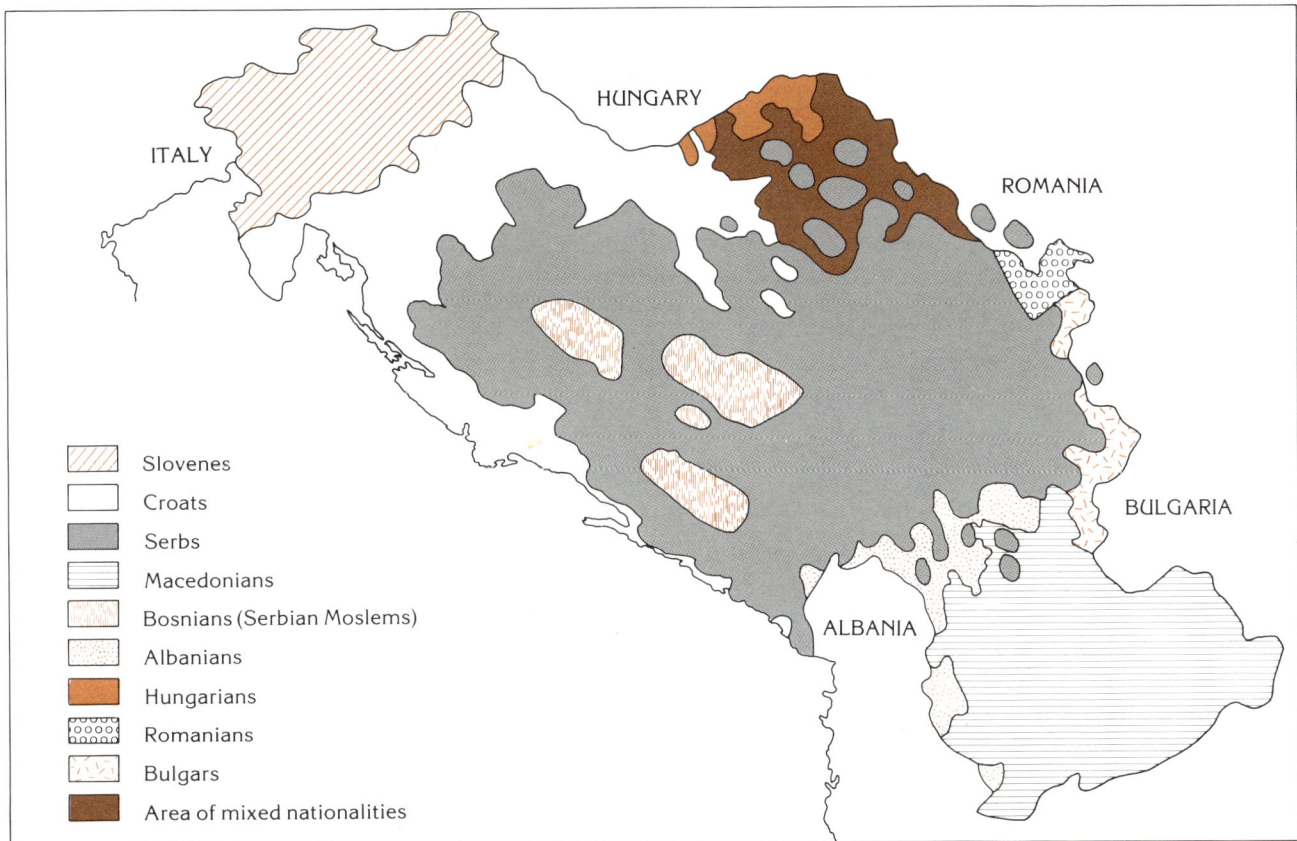

FIGURE 6–7
Yugoslavia: Ethnic Diversity and Disputed Areas. Yugoslavia has the most complex ethnic mix within the region; its system of ethnic republics within a federal frame, patterned after that of the USSR, is an attempt to defuse the high potential for national minorities to seek independence.

connects Belgrade with the port of Bar, providing a shorter link from the rich Danube basin to the sea.

Agriculture   Roughly 40 percent of Yugoslavia can be cultivated, while some 30 percent each is in pasture and forest. As in all the countries and areas south of the Carpathians and east of Vienna, corn is the single most important crop, with wheat second. As in Romania and throughout the Balkans, sheep are more important than other livestock, but pigs are rapidly replacing them in all but the roughest, least cultivable areas.

Yugoslavia has chosen to increase its specialization in termperate fruits and wine grapes, with heavy production of grapes, apples, pears, and plums and a series of wines and brandies, which increasingly enter the export market. Farming is not collectivized. Though peasant cooperatives and state farms still exist, decollectivization took place essentially in the late 1950's. There is an upper limit (10 hectares or 25 acres) on the size of private holdings.

The Yugoslavian climate is mild, similar to that of Virginia in the interior, but with a Mediterranean climate on the Adriatic coast. The growing season is long enough for two crops annually along the coast and in the southern half of the country. Severe droughts occur every four or five years, but their effects have been reduced through improved seed and better fertilization. Yugoslavia is relatively self-sufficient in grain and produces a surplus of meat, sugar, and vegetable oil. Fresh fruits and vegetables are grown out of season, marketed more in northwestern Europe's urban centers rather than domestically.

Despite improvements in farm product prices and living standards, rural people still flock to the city. Large acreages of farmland have been abandoned in many marginal areas, while terraced vineyards and orchards along the Adriatic coast were slowly decaying until lucrative local tourist markets and government subsidies rejuvenated them.

Raw Materials   Yugoslavia possesses a wide variety of mineral resources, but energy resources are present in only moderate supply; lignite and semi-bituminous coals are present in fairly large reserves scattered throughout

A.

B.

Rural Yugoslavia and the Camp-grounds on Lake Balaton in Hungary. Some of the past remains, but even in the country-side there is change. Industrial-ization is considered the route to prosperity and affluence as shown in these two, contrasting scenes. Rural life remains hard work, while urban occupations offer a guaran-teed vacation and other amenities of lifestyle. (Courtesy of the Unit-ed Nations)

the country. Low in caloric value, these coals are still the chief source of thermal energy. The most important mining districts are in central Bosnia (near Zenica, the large metallurgical base), northern Serbia (just south of Belgrade), and the eastern half of the Slovenian Republic. There is a large hydro power potential, as the Dinaric Alps have a heavy, if seasonal, rainfall. This potential is the sec-ond largest in all of Europe after Norway, and about half the electricity generated is hydroelectric.

It is in metal ores, however, that Yugoslavia is richest. Some 2.5 million tons of bauxite are mined annually, al-most exclusively along the Adriatic coast. It is a major producer of copper. Chrome, lead, zinc, and mercury are produced in sufficient quantities for export. Major investments are continuing to open up large reserves of iron ore.

Industry The domestic supplies of metal ores have led to the development of a fair-sized metallurgical industry. Spared the Stalinist era emphasis on steel, Yugoslavia has developed an iron and steel industry smaller than that of any other country in East Europe except Albania. The lack of a domestic coal resource led to this decision, while the presence of metal ores of all kinds encouraged diverse metallurgy instead.

Several unusual features characterize Yugoslavia's industry. Unlike that of other East European countries, it is consumer oriented, run by elected workers' councils, and produces in response to a market-oriented economy. Industry is quite diverse and virtually all major branches are represented. Despite attempts to decentralize investments, two districts still dominate: the northwest (Slovenia and Croatia) with textiles, clothing, electronic, and engineering industries; and the Danubian district with food processing, the chemical industry, and the manufacture of farm implements and food-processing machinery.

Newer industrial districts are being developed in Bosnia and along the Morava-Vardar corridor. Italian, American, German, and Japanese firms have invested in joint enterprises in Yugoslavia. Exports to West Europe tend to be inexpensive clothing, footwear, and furniture; those to East Europe tend to be more sophisticated—appliances, electrical equipment, and high-value canned foods and wines. Much of its manufactured goods enter third world markets where Yugoslavia has been an important source of aid, technology, and credit since the mid-1950's.

The most interesting point of Yugoslavian industry is the decentralization of management into the hands of elected workers' councils. This is far closer to the orthodox interpretation of Marx than the Soviet industrial model, which establishes professional managers, technicians, and production planners. Industry in Yugoslavia is profit-motivated, and even unemployment is allowed—unlike the situation in the other East European countries. Large amounts of surplus industrial labor are employed in Austria, West Germany, Italy, and Switzerland. Remittances of money from these workers to their families do much to reduce what otherwise might be a serious trade imbalance.

Population Yugoslavia's annual growth rate has dropped below 1 percent per year for the first time in its history. Growth rates are now lower than those experienced in the United States, Canada, and the Soviet Union. At the same time that demographic growth has slowed, the GNP and real income have been increasing at rates of 3 to 4 percent per annum, allowing for a steady increase in the level of living. Urban dwellers are 42 percent of the total, and the declining percentage of labor employed in agriculture (45 percent) indicates the strides made in economic development. The series of relatively large cities and the absence of a large and dominant capital city reflects the federal administrative system more than any dispersion of industry.

Oil Refinery at Rijeka, Yugoslavia. The race for development has strained many of the national budgets of East European countries to the breaking point. Environmental problems have begun to arise, and new dilemmas over the best use of the land and the resources confront the region's governments. (Courtesy of the United Nations/G. Palmer)

Ethnic diversity continues, but the balances change. The tendency for Serbs, Croats, and Slovenes to form the bulk of international migrants is reflected in their decreasing importance in the total ethnic makeup of Yugoslavia. Higher birthrates among the less developed peoples have gradually increased their relative importance, while such ethnic groups as Italians and Germans, already shrunk in importance through post-1945 repatriation, continue to decline in importance.

While the overall tendency is for the relative importance of the Yugoslavian nationalities to diminish, the decline is not drastic. On the other hand, those who identify as "general Yugoslavian" have increased, and migrants to the nation's industrial centers often tend to assimilate to the language and culture of the ethnic group dominant there. Romanian (65,000) ethnics are to be exchanged for a roughly equal number of Serbs from that country.

The ethnic hodge-podge of the Vojvodina has tended to decrease as Poles, Czechs, Slovaks, Germans, Russians, and Ukrainians have been repatriated from this district, which was settled by people from virtually every national group in the Austro-Hungarian Empire after expulsion of the Turks. A similar tactic was employed after the annexation of Bosnia in 1908. Yugoslavia has been sorting out this resulting ethnic patchwork in rural areas ever since; redistribution of the population to cities is creating something of a new ethnic diversity in these areas, one that is proving to be more rapidly assimilable.

Bulgaria   Balkan in location, Slavic in speech and culture, Asiatic in origin, and most obedient of the Soviet allies, Bulgaria is in many ways atypical of East Europe. Bulgarians are one of the South Slavic nations, yet they reside outside of Yugoslavia. Historically, two great Bulgarian empires once included much more than present-day Bulgaria, and in 1878, the then re-emerging national state included most of Macedonia and a port on the Aegean coast—two foreign policy goals that Bulgaria has never lost and territories that they have sought to regain.

Bulgaria, like the other Balkan states, has several cores: the Balkan Platform, the Plain of Thrace, the coastal lowlands, and the western valleys and basins (Figure 6–8). Yet, unlike Yugoslavia, it is relatively uniform in ethnic composition, with 86 percent of all people Bulgars. Originally,

FIGURE 6–8
Core Areas of Bulgaria. Bulgaria's relatively small territory is fragmented into a series of separate population-economic cores, primarily by the east-west trending Balkan Mountains.

the Bulgars were a Turkic people who overran the Slavs of the present area in the seventh century. The name remains, but the conquerors were in time absorbed by the more numerous Slavic settlers. Later Turkic peoples, the Ottoman Turks in particular, did not assimilate and now constitute a fairly large and unassimilated ethnic group within the country.

Agriculture   The combination of vast stretches of near-level land, fertile soil, and mild climate results in a strong set of agricultural advantages. The country is of a size and fertility similar to the state of Ohio, but it is less level and also less populous.

Despite its southern location and proximity to the Mediterranean and its lesser seas, the country has a somewhat more continental climate, with colder winters. Alternately, sharp continental winters and hot Mediterranean summer droughts may periodically interrupt the mild average climatic patterns.

The Danube Platform is drier than average and colder in winter. It is a country of grain culture, with corn and wheat dominant, and large mechanized farms. Livestock are raised primarily for meat. The southern and eastern lowlands, with their milder climate and drier summers, support a more varied agriculture with irrigated rice, the famous Balkan tobaccos, cotton, silk culture, attar (perfume essence) of roses, and high-quality fruits and vegetables. The western basins and valleys emphasize dairying, sugar beets, and industrial crops, while mountain pastures everywhere support large herds of sheep.

Bulgaria underwent extensive land reform before World War II. Small farms were grouped into productive cooperatives that produced in part for the export market, emphasizing high quality horticultural products. Bulgarian agriculture then was neither backward nor unproductive. This early tradition of cooperative agriculture may have made collectivization somewhat easier; it was completed in 1958. Over 15 percent of the arable area is irrigated. Fertilizer input has increased radically since the development of a domestic chemical industry, and yields are only slightly lower than those found in western European countries.

Recently, in an attempt to improve the systems efficiency, state and collective farms are being integrated with industrial-processing firms and consumer outlets in what are termed **agricultural-industrial complexes.** Agriculture now employs only 25 percent of the work force, a figure quite similar to that of the northern industrial countries, but thought not to include many categories of employment that are primarily farm work or work done on farms even though classified as nonfarm work.

Resources and Industry   Bulgaria, like Yugoslavia, relies on brown coal and hydroelectric power for most of its energy supply. Yearly production is some 30 million tons from a half dozen fields scattered throughout the country. Bulgaria has constructed a large refining and chemical industry based on imported Soviet oil. Lead, zinc, copper, and iron ores round out the raw material base.

The largest metallurgical works are located at Pernik and Kremikhovtsii, on either side of Sofia. The former plant is based on local, often low-grade coal, while the latter is based on a large deposit of low-grade iron ore. Bulgaria meets most of its steel needs with a domestic production of 2.5 million tons. The integrated plants supply metal for Sofia's engineering and machine plants, which dominate those lines of production nationwide.

Bulgarian Development Policy   Bulgaria has doggedly resisted its assigned role of raw material and grain production within CMEA. Without straying from the ideological lead of Moscow, Bulgaria has quietly built up its industrial strength. Almost 25 percent of all industrial employees are now employed in machine building. A cigarette and tobacco industry has world rank, while wineries, canneries, and other processing plants still account for a huge portion of the volume, value, and employment in industry. Bulgaria is increasingly importing Soviet raw materials and exporting finished goods to that country. The USSR supplies over half of Bulgaria's imports and takes almost half of its exports.

Tourism   Yugoslavia, Romania, and Bulgaria rival one another in tourist trade, each with over 6 million visitors annually. Each combine sunny climate, excellent beaches, and low cost into a vacation package with broad consumer appeal. While Yugoslavia caters more to West Europeans, Bulgaria has also opened its doors to nonbloc tourists on a large scale. The sandy beaches stretching northward from the ports of Varna and Burgas form the bloc's official "riviera"—outdrawing the more crowded and far less opulent Soviet resort beaches.

Albania   Last and obviously least important of the Balkan states is Albania. Long classified as the most backward corner of Europe, it is still an agrarian state after almost forty years of Communist rule.

Albania has a population of 2.5 million people in an area a little larger than Vermont. Some 1.5 million Albanians live in Yugoslavia and a large number live in northern Greece. Albania was only an independent state for thirty-five years between Byzantine and Ottoman Turk control. The people have a somewhat uncrystallized nationality, and tribal groups (and dialects) distinguish the peoples of

Budva, Yugoslavia. Central planning has gone beyond industry and agriculture to include all phases of the region's economies. Tourism, once thought of in terms of the domestic resort function only, has become international in its outlook. It is a major earner of hard currency for all Balkan states except Albania. (Courtesy of the United Nations/Villani)

the north and the south. Religious differences have split the country, but the current regime has diminished religious influence. In the last thirty-five years, a standard language has evolved, and the literacy rate has risen from 20 percent to 75 percent, yet portions of the country remain outside the modernization programs despite government efforts.

Economy   It is difficult to obtain any data on the Albanian state. It is a known exporter of oil, producing a surplus since the late 1930's. Large deposits of chrome, copper, and ferro-nickel ores are exploited, and concentrates of these ores (and some refined metal) are exported. There are large deposits of brown coal and a superior hydroelectric potential, yet per capita income is thought to be the lowest in Europe.

One of the hindrances to economic development is the rapid population growth rate (2.4 percent annually). Further, a disproportionate share of national income is channeled into defense spending in a country that perceives itself as surrounded by hostile states.

In 1961, Albania broke with the Soviet Union, espousing an economic and defense alliance with the People's Republic of China. It is unsure of its relationship to China since the Sino-American improvement in relations.

Alternately receiving developmental funds from Italy (1930's), Yugoslavia, the USSR, China, and now some West European countries, Albania has developed oil refining, petrochemical, textile, tobacco, cement, and farm machinery industries. Drainage of coastal marches, irrigation

of the coastal plain and of alluvial fans inland, and improvement of seed and stock have led to an improved agriculture. Citrus is raised around the southernmost shores of the Adriatic, while cotton and other subtropical crops occupy increasing areas of the coastal plain. With little contact now beyond its immediate neighbors, Albania still seeks its own road to development.

TENSIONS AND TROUBLES

Few areas of the world encompass so many traditional enemies within such a limited area, yet animosities are more past than present. Poland and Hungary have revived their long-standing friendship, while Czechoslovakia has actively sought to reduce any tension involving its relations with those two states. While Yugoslavia and Romania draw toward one another, they (and the rest of the region's states) have disputes with virtually all surrounding states. This has been one of the world's most frequently war-disrupted areas. While tension have been reduced, they have not been eliminated.

Pressed between Germany and the USSR, most other East European states still retain some animosity toward both German states. Bulgaria, Romania, and Hungary have the lowest level of anti-German public feeling; it is perhaps highest in Poland. The Soviet "threat"—now a reality—remains an issue as each of the region's states seeks its own road to development and improvement of living standards. Anti-Soviet (or anti-Russian) sentiment is felt virtually everywhere in the bloc except Bulgaria. Anti-Russian feeling has been strongest in Czechoslavakia and Hungary. The Polish see the Soviet threat to Poland as real, yet little has yet happened to reverse Poland's outspoken labor movement and economic protest.

The world view of the region is unclear and changing. Increasingly, East Europe has looked westward for trade while pursuing an official "world view" that was tied to that of Moscow. In most cases, neither the West in general, nor the United States in particular, is viewed as a direct threat. The realities of Soviet presence are understood; the power of the Soviet Union makes an independent world view less than likely. Progress and change are expected, but always within strict limits.

case study

EXPERIMENTS IN DECOLLECTIVIZATION

Despite all attempts at collectivizing Polish agriculture, independent farming never disappeared in Poland. In 1956, the Gomulka regime reversed the official government stand, and much land was returned to private hands. Even confirmed Communists who had willingly joined collectives had to accept the return of the land. In 1980, 68 percent of all agricultural land was in private hands, 19 percent was in state farms, and the rest in collectives, cooperatives, or other forms of farm ownership not clearly of the private type.

It has often been stated that independent ownership and free decision making are the missing ingredients in Communist agriculture. Of the eight most productive provinces in Poland, however, only one is clearly dominated by private holdings (see Figure 6–4). On the other hand, only one is clearly dominated by state holdings. The rest are divided almost evenly into public and private sector. It is known that official policy has often favored collectives and state farms over private holdings with delivery of fertilizer, choice of breeding stock, better seed, and almost anything else that might improve production.

However, natural fertility presents some limitations. Certain areas of state-dominated holdings cannot yield heavily no matter what sort of capital investment is made.

Improvements in Polish agriculture under a return to free farming were less than anticipated. Yields of grain have approximately doubled since the 1956 de-collectization but fluctuate wildly from year to year and district to district. Yields from state and collective farms are consistently slightly higher than those in the private sector except for a handful of hand-labor intensive crops.

The conclusions drawn are somewhat conflicting. The government claims that Polish farms are too small to be efficient. The Polish farmer blames low-market prices (no incentive) and difficulties in obtaining fertilizer, fuel, and building materials. Weather has been poor over the last few years.

Yugoslavia's program of decollectionization has been fairly comparable. Yields have increased to a level commensurate with Polish yields despite lower original yields, but also perhaps due to better lands and a warmer climate. In neither case do yields differ measurably from those East European countries that are still dominated by collective and state farms. For whatever reasons, some popularly held notions do not bear statistical scrutiny (see Table 6–3).

Capital investment supplied to Yugoslavia has apparently been responsible for much of the increase in yields wherever they occur. Since 1960, Poland has increased application of fertilizers 400 percent, while Yugoslavia has increased it

TABLE 6–3
Production data for Polish farming pre- and post-decollectivization

	Pre-decollectivization (averages 1950–55)			Post-decollectivization (averages 1975–79)		
	State Farms	Collectives and Cooperatives	Private Farms	State Farms	Collectives and Cooperatives	Private Farms
Pigs per 100 Hectares of Agricultural Land	33.0	37.5	50.5	107.3	147.5	108.1
Wheat Yields (quintals per hectare)	15.7	15.9	16.2	30.2	29.8	27.5
Rye Yields (quintals per hectare)	13.5	13.7	14.7	22.7	21.2	18.9
Potato Yields (quintals per hectare)	117	128	132	204	198	203
Average Yearly Milk Production (kilograms per cow)	2,900	3,160	3,350	3,150	2,850	4,053
Meat Production per 100 Hectares of Agricultural Land (quintals)	210	90	340	292	490	363
Artificial Fertilizer Used (kilograms per hectare of agricultural land [1979])	47.0	23.5	20.7	316.9	277.2	150.3

by 350 percent. Both have incorporated modern techniques and intensified farming, yet neither has outstripped productivity in those fully collectivized countries of comparable climatic and soil conditions. Technology, rather than landownership, appears to hold the key to understanding higher levels of farm productivity.

REVIEW QUESTIONS

1 On what bases, other than Communist control, is East Europe a distinctive region?

2 Summarize both advantages and disadvantages of East Europe's "shatterbelt" position.

3 What were the cultural and political implications of East Europe being a "marche area" of many great empires?

4 What are the goals and organizational systems of Comecon? Is this a successful effort?

5 Why has the degree of maritime orientation in East Europe been rather consistently underestimated?

6 Briefly describe the extent, from country to country, of modifications and national adaptations to the rigid Marxist approach personified by the USSR.

7 Which is the most sophisticated, industrialized economy within East Europe? Which is the least so?

8   To what degree do East and West Germany maintain trade relationships? Is there any realistic hope of a peaceful German reunification?

9   Briefly describe East Europe's mineral and fuel resource bases.

10 What economic role did the USSR envision for its southeast European satellites, Romania and Bulgaria? How have these satellites altered the original plan?

11 What special internal problems does Yugoslavia's ethnic mosaic present to its stability?

12 Considering the direction of international flows of raw materials and manufactured goods between the USSR and East Europe, which is the colony and which the parent, or developed country, economically?

13 How did Yugoslavia's pursuit of a uniquely Yugoslavian communist internal development and foreign relations policy help Albania to escape confrontation with the USSR over its onetime alliance with the People's Republic of China?

14 Identify the "least typical" of the states of East Europe and defend your choice in terms of its economic, cultural, and political geographic factors.

15 Why does the present status of most of East Europe preclude a genuine "world view" for most of its states?

16 Why has Poland permitted such a high degree of private versus public farm control?

SUGGESTED READINGS

1   VACLAV BENES and NORMAN POUNDS, *Poland.* New York: Praeger Publishers, 1970.

2   GEORGE HOFFMAN, ed., *Eastern Europe: Essays in Geographical Problems.* New York: Praeger Publishers, 1977.

3   GEORGE HOFFMAN, *Regional Development Strategy in Southeast Europe: A Comparative Analysis of Albania, Bulgaria, Greece, Romania and Yugoslavia.* New York: Praeger Publishers, 1972.

4   ROBERT KAISER and DAN MORGAN, *The Soviet Union and Eastern Europe: New Paths, Old Ruts.* New York: Foreign Policy Association, 1973.

5   HUEY KOSTANICK, ed., *Population and Migration Trends in Eastern Europe.* Boulder, Colo.: Westview Press, 1977.

6   KURT LONDON, ed., *Eastern Europe in Transition.* Baltimore: Johns Hopkins Press, 1966.

7   IAN MATLEY, *Romania: A Profile.* New York: Praeger Publishers, 1970.

8   ROY MELLOR, *Eastern Europe: A Geography of the Comecon Countries.* New York: Columbia University Press, 1975.

9   R. H. OSBORNE, *East-Central Europe: An Introductory Geography.* New York: Frederick Praeger, 1967.

10 STEVAN PAVLOWITCH, *Yugoslavia.* New York: Praeger Publishers, 1971.

11 NORMAN POUNDS, *Poland Between East and West.* Princeton, N. J.: Van Nostrand, 1964.

12 _____, *Eastern Europe.* Chicago: Aldine Publishing Co., 1969.

13 THOMAS WOLFE, *Soviet Power and Europe, 1945–1970.* Baltimore: Johns Hopkins University Press, 1970.

KEY TERMS

- taiga
- successor state
- *kombinat*
- complementarity
- Virgin Lands Program
- continentality
- permafrost
- chernozem
- orientational bias
- Siberian River Reversal Scheme
- green belt
- closed city
- growth pole

7
USSR

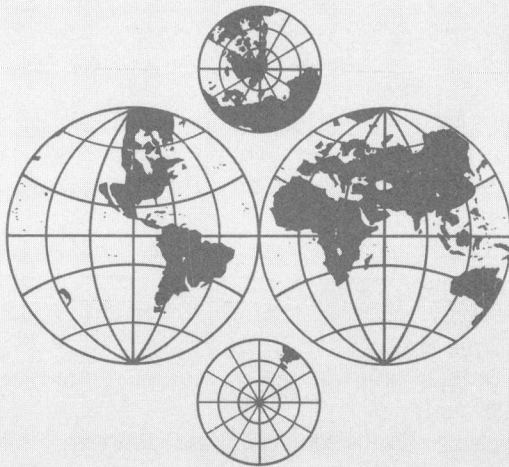

PROLOGUE: THE LAST EMPIRE?

Technically both in Europe and Asia, the Soviet Union has participated in regional organizations and meetings that deal with the affairs of both continents. By virtue of its Asiatic and Moslem minorities it has attempted to claim the right to participate in the Moslem League, the Asian games, and any number of other activities geared to regional or ethnic interests. In language and culture, the Russians are definitely Europeans, but the state is no longer Russia—it is the Union of Soviet Socialist Republics, a title that reflects its ethnic and cultural diversity. (See Figure 7–1.)

The borders of the USSR are approximately the same as those of the Russian Empire of pre-revolutionary times; with rare exception, the ethnic composition is virtually the same. The land and peoples that fell to Russian conquest in the sixteenth through the nineteenth centuries are a part of the USSR. Western observers often claim that it is the last surviving colonial empire. Russia was indeed an empire; it is legitimate to ask whether the successor government has changed this situation.

There are 108 official nationalities recognized in the Soviet Union; they speak over 180 languages and dialects. Most of these groups are quite small; many are scattered over large, noncontiguous areas. Many seem never to have had a state of their own, and a national consciousness was not fully developed except among a few ethnic groups. Nonetheless, some groups now included in the USSR have had a clearly developed nationalism at one time or another.

Two nations, Finland and Poland, were never reincorporated after their independence in 1918; there is no doubt as to their separate statehood. Formerly independent Lithuania, Latvia, and Estonia were small independent states in the modern era from 1918 to 1940. There remains a question of how well these units were able to develop national feelings among their citizenry during this brief time; yet, clearly, among the older generations there must remain some legacy of past independence. The Moldavians are Romanian in speech and culture, though long association with the tsarist empire left a legacy of the cryllic alphabet. Incorporation into a highly nationalistic Romania (1918–40) must also lead to questions of their actual "separateness" of nationality from the Romanians.

Briefly (1919–23), an independent Ukraine appeared in the aftermath of the revolution and the civil strife in Russia. Similarly, each of the three Transcaucasian republics (Armenia, Georgia, Azerbaydzhan) declared their independence at the time. A coup temporarily established two Turkic language entities in Soviet Central Asia during the 1920's, though their level of public support is not well known.

FIGURE 7–1
Member Republics of the USSR. Constitutionally, if not realistically, each member republic could withdraw from its voluntary association with the other republics. Each major national minority, many of which have been separate states at one time, has an ethnic republic; the Russian Federated Soviet Socialist Republic, by far the largest, contains many minor ethnic groups as well.

Pressures for assimilation are strong in the USSR. Advancement may depend on knowledge of the Russian language; higher education, with rare exception, uses Russian as the language of instruction. Over 15 million people who listed themselves of non-Russian nationality in the 1979 census also listed Russian as their native tongue. Yet over 90 percent of most ethnic groups tenaciously cling to their native tongue, in particular those still in their native area.

Ethnic Russians constituted 55 percent of the total population in 1959, but only 53 percent in 1970. No comparable figure for the 1979 census has been released, but it is known that many non-Russian groups have growth rates that are double or triple the rates for Russians. It may well be that Russians have become a minority in their own country. Heavy assimilation pressures may well be countered by non-Russian growth pressures.

Russians are virtually omnipresent in the Soviet Union. They are the overwhelming majority in their own republic (the Russian Soviet Federated Socialist Republic, or RSFSR), the largest in both area and population within the federation. They also form the largest single group in the Kazakh Republic, where they significantly outnumber the native group after whom the republic is named. They are the plurality, even the majority, in many of the smaller autonomous republics and districts that are subunits within the larger republics. They are a significant minority in virtually all the republics; and, in the areas east of the Volga, they are the majority in virtually all cities—even in the non-Russian republics. Russians have been the most active colonizers and are the most widely distributed ethnic group.

Despite their areal and cultural dominance, it has not been necessary to be a Russian to advance to the top governmental or party ranks. Stalin was a Georgian, Lenin had some recent Tartar ancestors, and most major national groups have had representatives at the most influential levels.

In truth, Russia of 1918 was faced with a dilemma. The Communist party was only loosely in control and the entire country was racked with civil strife. National ambitions on the part of non-Russians could have destroyed this tenuous control. Lenin sought an answer that would keep the state intact without inflaming nationalist tendencies among non-Russians. Stalin supplied the answer; his success in dealing with the ethnic question advanced his career in the party. The system that he created was one of ethnic federalism with (ultimately) fifteen republics based on ethnic groupings. Each would have the theoretical right to secede. Other national groups (those who didn't meet the requirements of population size or a common border with a foreign country) were given autonomous units of lesser stature.

The apparent idea was the removal of the sting of subjugation by soft-pedaling Russian nationalism while retaining (even encouraging) the trappings of nationalism among non-Russian groups. Each group received schooling (through eight grades) and the right to trial in its own language. Native customs were virtually glorified. Every ethnic group had its own museums. Native literature (where it existed) was republished and often translated into Russian for nationwide dissemination. Where no literature existed, it was carefully developed. Where no alphabet or written language existed, Russian linguists created one and introduced it through the education system. In short, the very things of which nationalism is often built were enhanced, not forbidden. As Stalin observed, it was the denial of such trappings that actually fanned nationalism among the minority groups in the old empires of Europe. It was a gamble designed to defuse nationalistic separatism, and apparently it has worked.

Russia, in effect, had expanded into a power vacuum once it had consolidated the control of Moscow over all the Russian principalities. The advance across Siberia was rapid and without much resistance. Expansion to the west and south in Europe was generally the result of wars with other empires, not necessarily the subjugation of all or part of other nation states. Expansion in the Caucasus and Soviet Central Asia was done essentially to secure frontiers against perceived threats from other powers.

Whatever the motives for expansion, the results are clear; the USSR is a polyethnic state. However, the consequences are not totally clear. Nationalist movements could conceivably arise in any number of areas; many important resources and industrial investments are located in areas peopled by non-Russians. Their loss could do irreparable harm to Soviet economic progress or greatly diminish Soviet power.

Soviet retention of the old tsarist domains is now a must. The wheat supply, crucial to survival, comes in large measure from the Ukrainian and Kazakh republics. The Ukraine has important iron and coal reserves as well as an impressive heavy industrial base. Much gas and oil comes from Soviet Central Asia or the areas along the Volga that are peopled by Tatar, Finnic, or Turkic peoples.

The myth of the "search for a water port" is not a crucial issue. (Indeed, it never was, as ice-free Murmansk has been Russian for centuries, even before there was such a town.) Economic survival is hardly dependent on trade in this most nearly self-sufficient of countries. Conquest of most of the lands took place a long time ago. In a relentless push eastward, the Soviets (and the tsarist Russians before them) developed agriculture, forestry, and industry through colonization of lands that were lightly settled and only extensively used. On ethnic grounds, 70 or 80 percent of the territory of today's Soviet Union could be claimed as Russia.

Yet the problem is not solved. An expansionist Iran or Turkey could develop *irridentist* claims to territory peopled by groups that are often closely related in language, culture, and religion. The Chinese have never officially recognized Russian (or Soviet) control over Far Eastern Siberia. Ukrainian nationalist groups in exile may reflect a more deep-seated nationalism among that ethnic group than even the Russians have suspected. More, rather than fewer, Byelorussians list their national language as their native tongue. Soviet deportation of certain nationalities deep into the interior of the country during World War II betray's an uneasiness about the strength of national identity and the degree of loyalty (among certain ethnics) to the Soviet government. The question of whether the USSR is a nation, federation, or empire is still open.

THE UNITY AND DISTINCTIVENESS OF THE USSR AS A REGION

The Soviet Union is the only country given the status of a region by itself. It is certainly not the only political unit governed by a Communist philosophy and system. It is of European culture, yet it differs strongly from western Europe; it is sufficiently different in scale and culture, too, to differentiate it from Communist East Europe. The population of the USSR represents only about 6 percent of the world total, yet it is larger than that of many other regions. Area alone (15 percent of the earth's total land surface) would justify separate regional status. It is larger than four of the seven continents and larger than the United States and Canada combined. Occupying portions of two continents, it includes a multitude of ethnic and cultural groups; yet it is a product of European technology and economic and political ideology; its political system gives it a certain degree of cohesiveness, despite internal cultural differences.

An overriding problem faced by the Soviet government has been the political and economic integration of all parts of such a huge and diverse territory. The fact that it has more or less succeeded in this task provides the necessary unity for regional status. These very problems have created a distinct outlook and set of practices that are not operative in any other area governed by a similar political system.

Despite the fact that Soviet culture has clear and distinct roots in an older Russian culture, the post-revolutionary government has gone beyond the inherited tradition. Following an interpretation of Marx peculiarly suited to the scale of the country and the level of development inherited from the past, they have created a new cultural hybrid that is recognized, even in the West, as distinctive. Acculturation has proceeded apace. The collective, the party, the Five-Year Plan, even the monotonous architecture have created a common experience. The government has attempted to refocus the loyalty of the people beyond the nation to a set of theoretical ideals and practical goals; it

has produced a rich cultural amalgam. The culture of today's Soviet Union is distinctly different from the Russian culture of the past. The state is now modern, urban, and technologically advanced. The controls on religion have divorced many Russians from one of their great sources of traditional culture. Much of inherited culture has been discarded in favor of something new. Influences of the distant past have their place, but the society has become conditioned more to present and future.

This homogeneity of experience and outlook provides the necessary ingredients for designating the USSR as a region—a formal region based on relative uniformity. The all-pervasive centralization of the economy, government, and ideology in Moscow supplies the rationale for declaring it also a functional region. The distinctly national cultures and attitudes of surrounding Communist states

Red Square and Lenin's tomb—Moscow, USSR. The Soviet government of the USSR has determined to replace old loyalties and ethnic nationalism with a new ideology and loyalty to the Communist state. Lenin's tomb is, in a sense, a shrine to the Soviet state. (Courtesy of United Nations)

has succeeded at least to some extent. Regardless of regional differences in language, dress, or food preference, all Soviet citizens share many common experiences and have developed similar attitudes and perceptions. Foods, music, farming techniques, and even clothing styles have passed from minority cultures to the majority. The reverse has happened on an even larger scale. The citizens of the USSR have become intranationally cosmopolitan, though their contacts with other nations (even those of Communist East Europe) are limited. Even selective inputs from the West are allowed, but the emphasis is on *selective.*

If the Soviet interpretation and administration of Marxist ideology has produced an often dull uniformity throughout the whole country, the diversity of the citizenry

(and their citizenry) separate the USSR from them. The role of old cultural roots in the current culture of today's Hungary, China, or Poland—as opposed to the USSR—should make their regional distinction equally clear. Sixty-odd years after the revolution, few still alive remember Russia as it was—almost all grew up in the Soviet Union.

PHYSICAL CHARACTERISTICS

There is little doubt as to the physical diversity of the USSR. The longitudinal extent of the USSR dwarfs the latitudinal spread considerably; continentality helps minimize climatic differences. The long, cold winter experienced over 90 percent of the country provides a degree of climatic similarity. The Volga and its tributaries provide a degree of integration within European Russia, but the south-to-north flowing rivers of Siberia tend to segregate more than unify. It has been left to technology to integrate both European and Asian USSR with railroads and highways that cross the grain established by the rivers.

Most of the population occupies a limited belt of land of relatively high utility. Composed of steppe (natural grassland) on the south and grading through wooded steppe and mixed forest to the **taiga** (dense, coniferous, boreal forest) on the north, it stretches across the Soviet Union from one end to the other, narrowing eastward. Level to rolling throughout, it provides a similar range of climatic and physiographic milieus. The lack of sharp breaks gives it a degree of uniformity. Only areas outside this belt, generally beyond intervening physical barriers of low utility, are markedly different. The flatness of most of the *inhabited* area is another physical characteristic; it has never impeded movement, either of an imperial (long-term) or travel (short-term) nature.

HISTORICAL UNIFIERS

The Russian presence (and control), for centuries uninterrupted, has been the greatest historical unifier. The Russian core area (essentially the European portion of the RSFSR) has been centrally controlled by one government since roughly the time of Columbus. Most of Siberia has been under the same control for three hundred years or more. It is only the peripheral areas (where all the federal units are located) that came under Russian control later. By the time of American independence, only limited fringe areas of the current state were not a part of tsarist Russia. (See Figure 7–2.)

Historically, the route to unity under the tsars was a cultural one, involving the spread of both Orthodoxy and Russian language. Overt russification (the Russianization of culture) was official policy, and church and state worked together toward this goal. The world *faithful* (in its collective sense) made no distinction between loyalty to church and state. The Orthodox liturgy asked God's blessings on

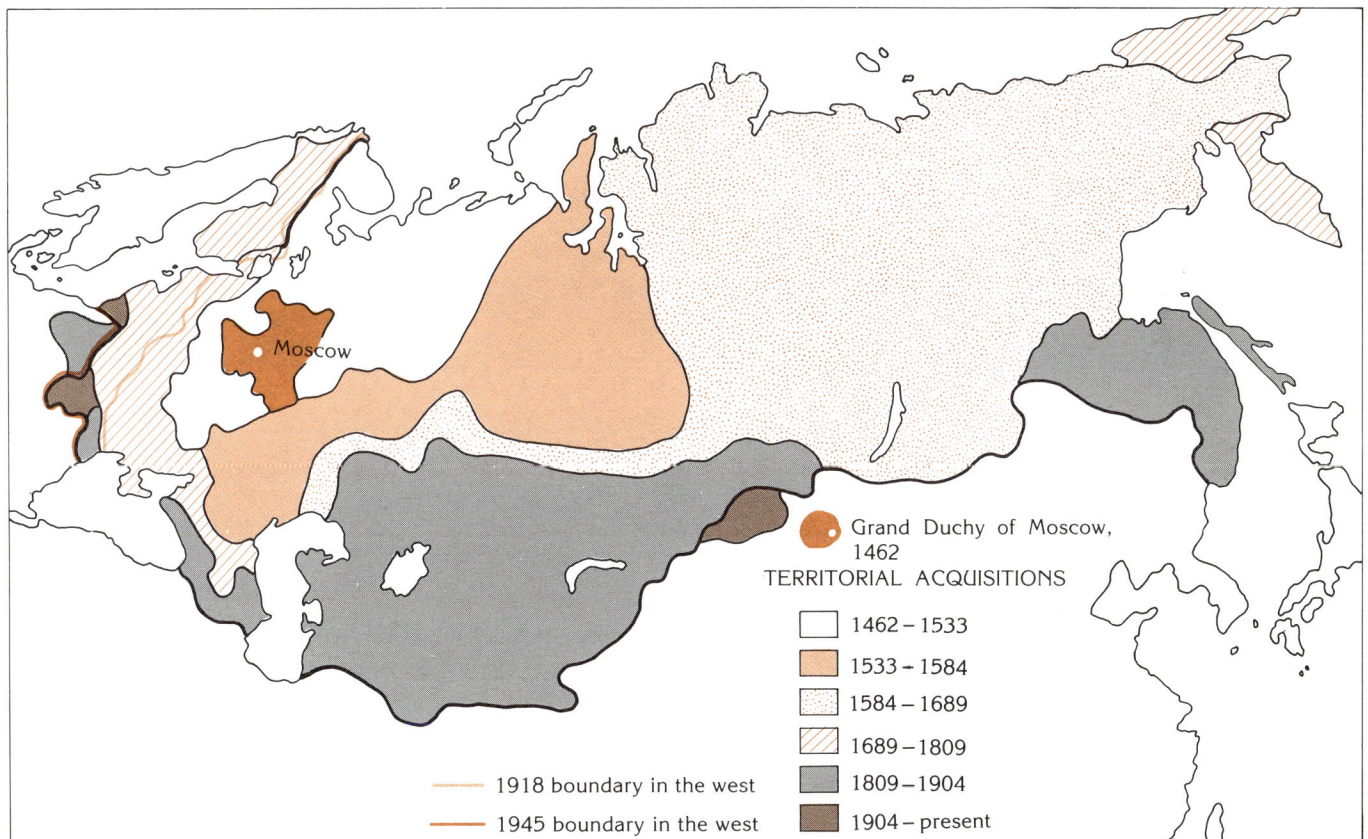

● Grand Duchy of Moscow, 1462

TERRITORIAL ACQUISITIONS

□	1462 – 1533
	1533 – 1584
	1584 – 1689
	1689 – 1809
	1809 – 1904
	1904 – present

——— 1918 boundary in the west
——— 1945 boundary in the west

FIGURE 7–2

Expansion of the Russian State. Moscow, near the divides among many river valley routes and deep within the forest (raiding Asiatic horsemen preferred the grassy steppes), formed a focus for the subsequent expansion of the Russian state as the power of surrounding states was successfully challenged.

the rulers as well as the people. The emphasis on community, the collective faithful as opposed to the individual, that is found in the Orthodox liturgical service is striking. The designation of the country as *Mother Russia* and the tsar as *the little father* throughout Russian literature is a manifestation of this all-encompassing drive for unity. The advent of Communist control in 1918 was a change in the philosophy and leadership of government, not necessarily the interruption of a political continuity.

ECONOMIC UNIFIERS

The drive for self-sufficiency and economic development has been the central guiding theme at least since 1918, though the economic unification of the realm was also a tsarist goal. It was the decision of the rulers of the **successor state** after 1918 to supplant the traditional set of cultural unifiers with economic unifiers, bonding together, thereby, the increasingly disparate rural-urban, farmer-industrial worker groups. It was also their aim to integrate the far-flung holdings of inherited empire into one powerful economic whole.

An early tsarist attempt at economic unity was the Trans-Siberian Railroad. Yet, as with its percursor, the tsarist system of post roads, its primary purpose was military rather than economic. It was the Communists who saw its use as an economic unifier; it functioned as an economic corridor only after 1918. The rivers, which crossed it at virtually right angles, served as collectors and distributors for the mainline of the Trans-Siberian. The railroad network of European-USSR essentially follows the rivers and the trade routes established in ancient times, focusing on Moscow, the traditional center of power from the fourteenth to the eighteenth centuries. It focuses only secondarily on Leningrad, the "latecomer" capital founded by Peter the Great as St. Petersburg in 1703. Even though the railroad net of this part of the country was built when Moscow was not the capital, the focus shows the strong

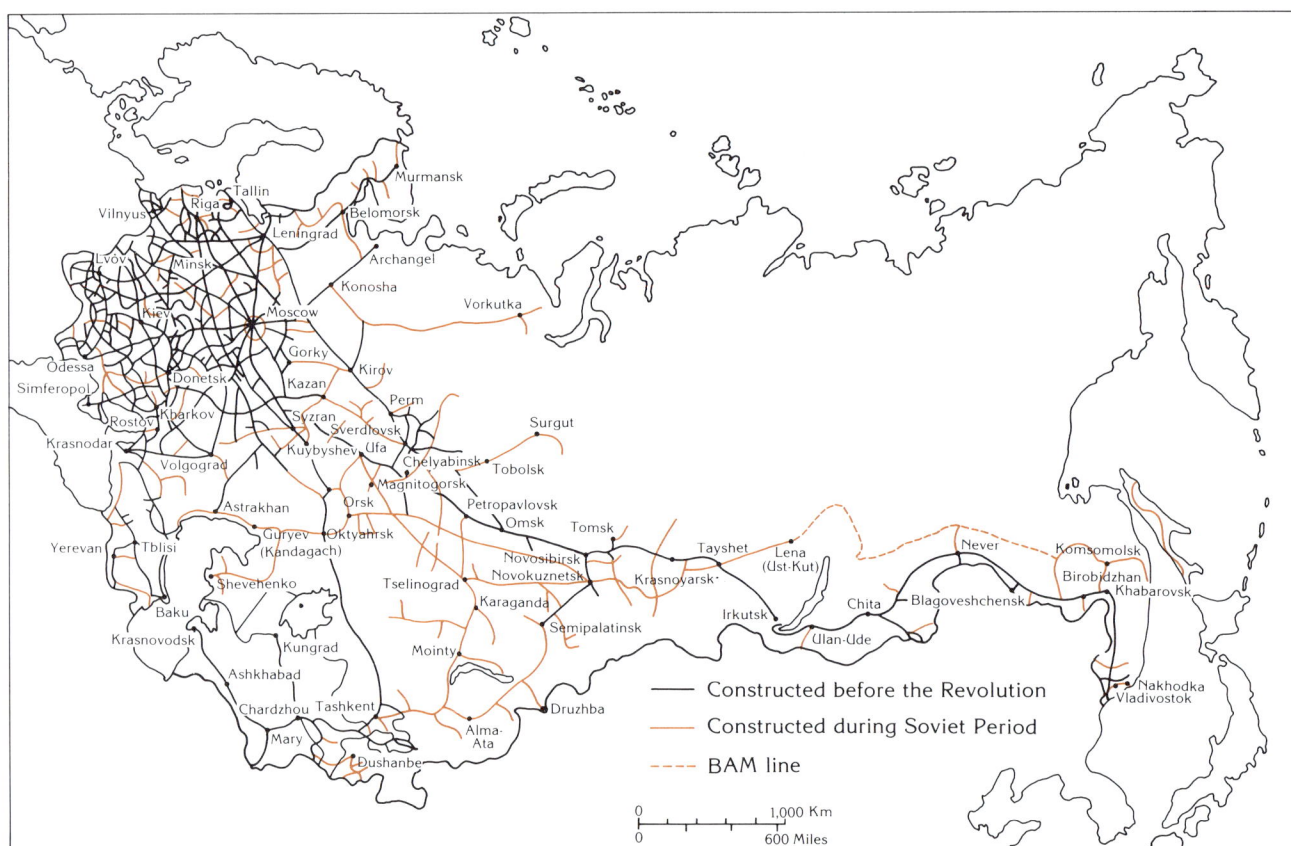

FIGURE 7-3
The Railroads of the USSR. The Soviet Union is far more dependent on its railroad system than is the United States, despite a determined development of internal waterways and the beginnings of a modern highway system. Vast distances between natural resources, development nodes, markets, and strategic centers have led to heavy investments in rail lines. Traffic is quite heavy on main lines, such as the famed Trans-Siberian.

unifying effect on Russia that Moscow had come to possess through years of centralized rule.

The Trans-Siberian came to be the official mechanism for tying the lightly settled Asiatic domains to the Moscow economic core. The proof of Communist intent can be seen (Figure 7–3) in the flurry of post-revolutionary railroad building. Several new lines across the Urals tied European Russia to Western Siberia. In turn, the building of the Turk-Sib (Turkestan to Siberia) Railway (1931) linked Soviet Central Asia (earlier linked to European Russia) to the Siberian lines. New lines linked all the republics of European USSR with each other and with Moscow. Economic regions were created and production specializations were assigned; new rail links were constructed to insure the flow of raw materials to manufacturing or marketing regions. Thus the system of economic planning and the rail network combined to create a new economic unity, one which replaced the older concept of virtual local self-sufficiency.

Subprograms of the main planning goals added further unity through economic integration. So-called ***kombinats*** were developed for the exchange of complementary raw materials to maximize the utilization of freight cars. Beginning in the Ukraine, the system shipped iron from the central Ukraine to the Donbas coalfield and steel complex (Figure 7–4). The reverse haul carried coal to the then newly developed steel base of the central Ukraine. The **complementarity** of resources, then, was exploited to the fullest. The shipment of empty railroad cars (rolling stock were a scarce commodity) over the already overbur-

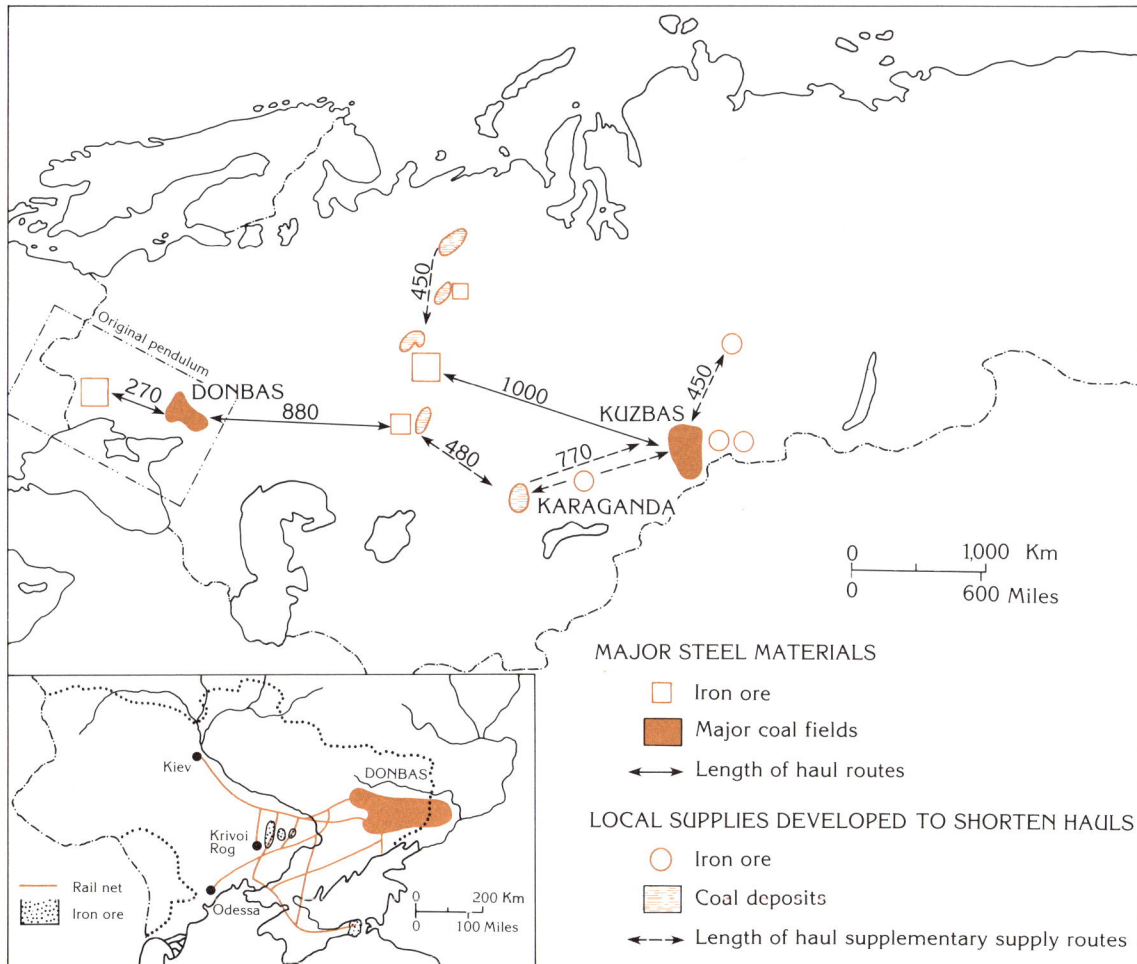

FIGURE 7–4
Mineral Resources and Kombinats. The USSR has one of the world's greatest stores of minerals, in both quantity and variety. Among the handicaps to their effective exploitation is the problem of distance. Transport costs can be excessive where bulky raw materials are hauled long distances. A Soviet solution to the problems of long-distance raw material flows is to "combine" or pair two industrial regions, each based on a different, complementary raw material.

dened rail network came to be thought of as unconscionable waste. After a time kombinats were set up all over the country, regardless of the distance involved. However wasteful this may have been of both time and energy, it served to integrate the country's economic regions.

Similarly, at a later date, unified power grids and oil-gas pipelines were created to shift fuel and power throughout the populated portions of the Soviet Union. The river network, however seasonal in utility, is gradually being developed to the same end. New canals and even river reversal schemes may integrate the entire economy by yet another mode of transportation.

Even the often neglected agricultural production system is contributing to national unity through interdependence. The ambitious **Virgin Lands Program,** first interpreted as a colonization venture to increase grain production, has had a unifying effect. These lands, now thought of as a second grain base, now ship their surplus throughout the country as the traditional grain base of the Ukraine shifts to other crop specialties. Planned programs to reverse Siberian rivers and increase irrigated acreage in Soviet Central Asia would have an even more startling effect, creating a contiguous agricultural core that would span both sides of the Urals and encompass almost equal areas. Of all the factors helping to unify the USSR, economic unification may be the most important.

THE DEVELOPMENT OF STATE AND COLLECTIVE FARMS

Three basic aims seem to pervade all planning in Soviet agriculture: (1) increase in total food production, (2) increase in the production of technical (industrial) crops, and (3) the dominant use of organizational remedies (as opposed to technological ones) in improving productivity. Generally, attempts by the government to improve *production* involve two types of schemes: colonization of new (and therefore more marginal) areas, and the improvization of new schemes for increasing production in established areas through organizational changes or improvement of the land itself. Agricultural investment is assigned one of the lowest priorities, hence the tendency toward extreme innovation rather than slow, sound investment. Planners and government workers who emphasize industry are in charge; they know little of agriculture. Thus, some almost disastrous programs appear from time to time. Ideologically, Marx saw labor as the only determinant in production costs; philosophically, he envisioned society as able to overcome environmental problems and to exist essentially independent of the natural environment. Marx, an urban sort, knew or cared little for or about farms and agriculture. He and Engels were extremely vague as to the

farmers' role in the new society they expected to emerge. Lenin, interpreting Marx to fit Russia's situation, was also an urban being. As a result, Soviet agrarian policy evolved over time as a curious, often conflicting, set of principles—all compromises between philosophical aims and physical or cultural forces.

In tsarist times, not all, but much of the land was in large estates farmed by near-slave laborers called *serfs.* Feudalism of a sort, it ended in 1863, leaving many free but without land or work. Others received land but at high prices with long-term, high-interest mortgages. A communal system of landholding also existed in ancient Russia, and, in a revised form, succeeded serfdom in some areas; this was the ownership of the land and operation of the farm by the farm village community, or *mir.* These two factors, land-hungry peasants and the tradition of communal ownership, were to eventually shape Soviet land tenure policies. The Marxian tendency to lump industry and agriculture together and his admonition to "eliminate the differences between country and city" led to unusual innovations in the new Soviet state.

The first "answer" to the problems of Soviet agriculture was found within the framework of the N.E.P. (New Economic Policy), that brief return to capitalism under Lenin (1921–28). Most farms were privately owned and operated; large ones were nationalized or reduced in size, and landless peasants, or those with small holdings, received lands from this government land bank. Lenin resorted to this policy to gain the support of farmers (75 percent of the total population). Inefficiency of farming techniques, wartime destruction of equipment, and the reversion of many peasants to subsistence farming left the city workers either without food or paying enormous food prices. The proletariat, supposed to be the primary beneficiary of the revolution, was thoroughly annoyed with the high prices and the scarcity of food in the cities. It remained for Stalin (the first rural-origin leader of note) to innovate further. His was the program of mechanization and collectivization. A crash program for building tractors was instituted in 1928. It failed to increase yields; few could use or maintain them. Fuel was scarce and so was the general farm machinery they were supposed to power. There was virtually a total absence of spare parts and mechanics. Collectivization was even a worse failure, at least at its inception. The program began with the holdings of *kulaks* (a name given to the class of owners of the larger, more successful farms who had emerged under N.E.P.). Smaller farmers at first supported the program, but by gradually reducing the maximum size limit of private farms, virtually all farmland was collectivized or organized into state farms by 1940.

Theoretically a voluntary association, collectives were actually forced on the peasantry. Resistance was rife as livestock were slaughtered, farmers refused to plant or harvest, and city dwellers starved. But Stalin, with the aid of force, succeeded in carrying out the plan. The aims behind collectivization were several in number: mechanize farms, increase efficiency of farms by increasing their size, substitute rational planned production for haphazard practice, and maximize the efficiency of labor input by reducing the number of laborers on farms—thereby liberating a work force for expanding industry. The unannounced (but most important) aim was the formation of capital for industrial investment from the farm profit. Not only was the collective supposed to insure planning and to control production, but also to regulate marketing. The government acted as the intermediate agency, buying crops at low prices and selling at high prices.

There are conceptual differences between state and collective farms. A state farm is a state-owned enterprise operated by wage labor. A collective is a group-owned enterprise of member farmers guided by state directives and plans. The original collectives were based on a kind of primitive peasant cooperative that had evolved in the villages of western Russia centuries ago. Land was communally owned by the village, and fields were assigned to members for cultivation. Production was sold by the village council and the profits distributed to members based on a combination of the amount of work done and the needs of each household. Collectives, though incorporating vast areas and many villages, operated in much the same way.

State farms are quite different. They are frequently found in areas of difficult environment or in pioneer areas; each economic district of the USSR has several state farms that serve as seed farms or livestock-breeding stations. Overall, state farms are larger in size than collectives, but the major difference between the two is in wage structure. State farm workers are paid flat hourly rates. Collectives pay in shares of profit; wages on a collective, therefore, fluctuate with farm productivity. Both sets of farms are increasingly specialized (in particular the state farms) in type of production. Soviet agriculture has changed many areas to a more specialized farming similar to that of the United States or Canada. The earliest attempts to increase production per worker took the form of nonmaterial rewards, like medals, peer group pressure, and prestige. The mediocre results of nonmonetary rewards eventually pointed the way toward the development of wage differentials. Excess production beyond norms is rewarded by cash bonuses, termed *Socialist incentive.*

Both state and collective farm workers have the use of private plots. All collective members and most state farm workers till a piece of ground for their own food needs, though each receives a share of grain, potatoes, dairy items, or other foods from the production of the collective or state farm itself. These private plots produce a seemingly disproportionate share of certain commodities, reflecting a great intensity of production on a small area—brought about by hand-intensive, high labor input techniques, and selection of crops (those which bring high prices, yield very well, and are not grown by the state). Much of this private plot production (originally intended for family subsistence) is sold at the free bazaars. Collectives emphasize grain; cattle and other livestock have remained largely in private hands so that 40 percent of meat and milk, 80 percent of potatoes, 80 percent of eggs, and 40 percent of vegetables still come from private plots. Differences in productivity are not explainable solely in terms of "private ownership." Workers could not afford to grow these commodities for sale were they not fed by the state or collective farm. The private plot has become a fringe benefit to generate extra cash income for low-wage farm workers; it also extracts extra production from them at the same time. As in Oriental agriculture, no mechanized farm (private, corporate, or public) could produce as much food per acre as a hand-intensive horticulture under *any* economic system.

The percentage of the work force employed in agriculture has decreased from 75 percent in 1913 to 17 percent at present, thus liberating the work force needed for industry as planned. The industrial base has grown enormously, so that the Soviet Union is now the world's second largest industrial producer; the capital for this growth was obtained largely from the agriculture sector. Total food production has increased. Grain once exported is now consumed at home. There is not only more grain, but there are also more Soviet citizens, and all of them have a better diet than formerly. The grain exports of tsarist times were drawn out of the public diet, not from any greater productivity of farms. Production is greater than ever. The Soviets produce more wheat per person than Americans; they simply consume far more bread. Meat production per person is about half that of the United States. Their production of fruits and vegetables, while much lower, is increasing, but the diet is not inadequate by any standards.

The USSR has radically increased its acreage in industrial crops and is self-sufficient in most items. It also produces large exportable surpluses of such items as flax, linseed oil, sugar, hemp, cotton, and other industrial raw materials. Fertilizer usage is now about 75 percent that of U.S. farms. There are about half as many tractors per unit area of farmland in the Soviet Union as in the United States, but many Soviet tractors are larger and used more intensively. Productivity on Soviet farms is lower than that of U.S. farms, but climatic conditions are often responsible.

The greatest handicaps to Soviet agriculture remain capricious weather, a poor distribution system, and, above all, the low priority assigned to investment in the agricultural sector. Collectives have increased in size, efficiency, and productivity. Planning reforms, increased autonomy in decision making, and improved prices for farm products have all led to greater production. Increased capital investment is the likely key to even greater productivity.

Despite all these positive changes, distribution is still a very weak point. Marketing facilities are extremely poor, and storage facilities in short supply. The speed of the system is incredibly slow. It is poor distribution that results in regional shortages even when the commodities available are adequate.

THE PHYSICAL FRAME

The sheer size of the USSR makes generalization difficult. However, the climatic diversity is less than one might anticipate in a unit of its size. While the subsurface geology is amazingly complex, it is not reflected in diverse landforms. The smoothing actions of glaciation and relatively recent marine and stream desposition have hidden the traces of past tectonics from view over much of the country. At the same time the sheer scale of the topographic features tend to make it easy to categorize the country into large, relatively homogeneous topographic units. Conveniently, too, the soils and natural vegetation zones exist in broad, continuous belts where they correlate to a remarkable degree with one another and with climatic zones. It is only with a firm understanding of the physical landscape that the Soviet Union's limitations and economic prospects can be fully understood. (See Figure 7–5.)

TOPOGRAPHY

There is less topographic variety than one might expect within the 8.5 million square miles (22 million square kilometers) of the Soviet Union. Three large plains cover more than half the territory. In the west, the North European Plain widens to encompass virtually all of the European portions of the USSR, from the Arctic to the Black Sea. The northern half of this plain has been glaciated and is generally rolling, boggy country with occasional strings of morainal hills (ridgelike glacial deposits) and a few low structural mountains. The southern, unglaciated half is more of a platform covered with rich loess soil, deeply eroded along stream valleys.

A large plain occupies the depression from east of the Caspian Sea to the mountain lands at the Chinese, Afghan, and Iranian borders. The West Siberian Plain occupies the area between the Urals and the Yenesei River; it is a flat, sodden, poorly drained area, totally flooded during the season of thaw. These three plains are separated from one another by the narrow, folded mountain chain of the Urals, the Caspian Sea, and the Kazakh Plateau, which stretches eastward at right angles to the Urals.

Further eastward, the great rivers of Siberia have eroded the Central Siberian Plateau into a rough countryside that was legendarily difficult to cross. The Lena River drains a large lowland basin at its eastern edge, while the Soviet Far East is composed of impressive rows of parallel mountain chains that reach down to the very coast of the Pacific.

Most of the southern border area is mountainous in the extreme. The Caucasus and related mountain systems stretch from the Crimea through the Turkish borderlands to eastern Iran. The jumble of mountain ranges at the core of Asia, known as the Pamir Knot, extends into Soviet Central Asia, with strings of related mountains forming parts of the Soviet-Chinese border. An intensely folded area of mountains and high plateaus, quite similar to the difficult country of the Soviet Far East, extends from Mongolia to the headwaters of the Amur River, also giving rise to the headwaters of the great Siberian rivers. Ringed with mountains on its Asian frontiers, the region has been most vulnerable to attack from the plains of the west. To some extent, this fact has conditioned Soviet military and economic thought.

LAND-SEA RELATIONSHIPS

One of the oldest myths of western European reasoning has been the Russian "drive" for ice-free ports. Russia essentially always had them. Openings to seas other than the Arctic or the Black Sea in *other* directions was far more the reason for Russian expansion. It is only in this century that the Russians have become sea-oriented in their thinking or military reasoning. Some of the seas surrounding Russia are singularly unattractive. The Arctic and its seas are navigable for only some thirty to sixty days east of Novaya Zemlya, the island extension of the Urals. The fish resource of the White and Barents seas, while considerable, has never been a major attraction, nor even capable of meeting the demands of the internal market. The Caspian and Aral seas are giant salt lakes that receive the waters of important rivers, but go no farther.

The western and eastern seas, however, have great potential importance. In the past, the Baltic was the scene of active trade. At times, Germany and Sweden or Denmark so dominated trade there that Russia was effectively squeezed out of the maritime picture. Leningrad (then St. Petersburg) was built, however, to give access to the Baltic. Russian conquest of Finland and the Baltic states enlarged this foothold, but at a time when the importance of the Baltic was rapidly waning.

The Black Sea is essentially "dead" in terms of a fish resource. A layer of sulfuric acid below the surface, a kind of natural pollution, limits marine life to a few species and

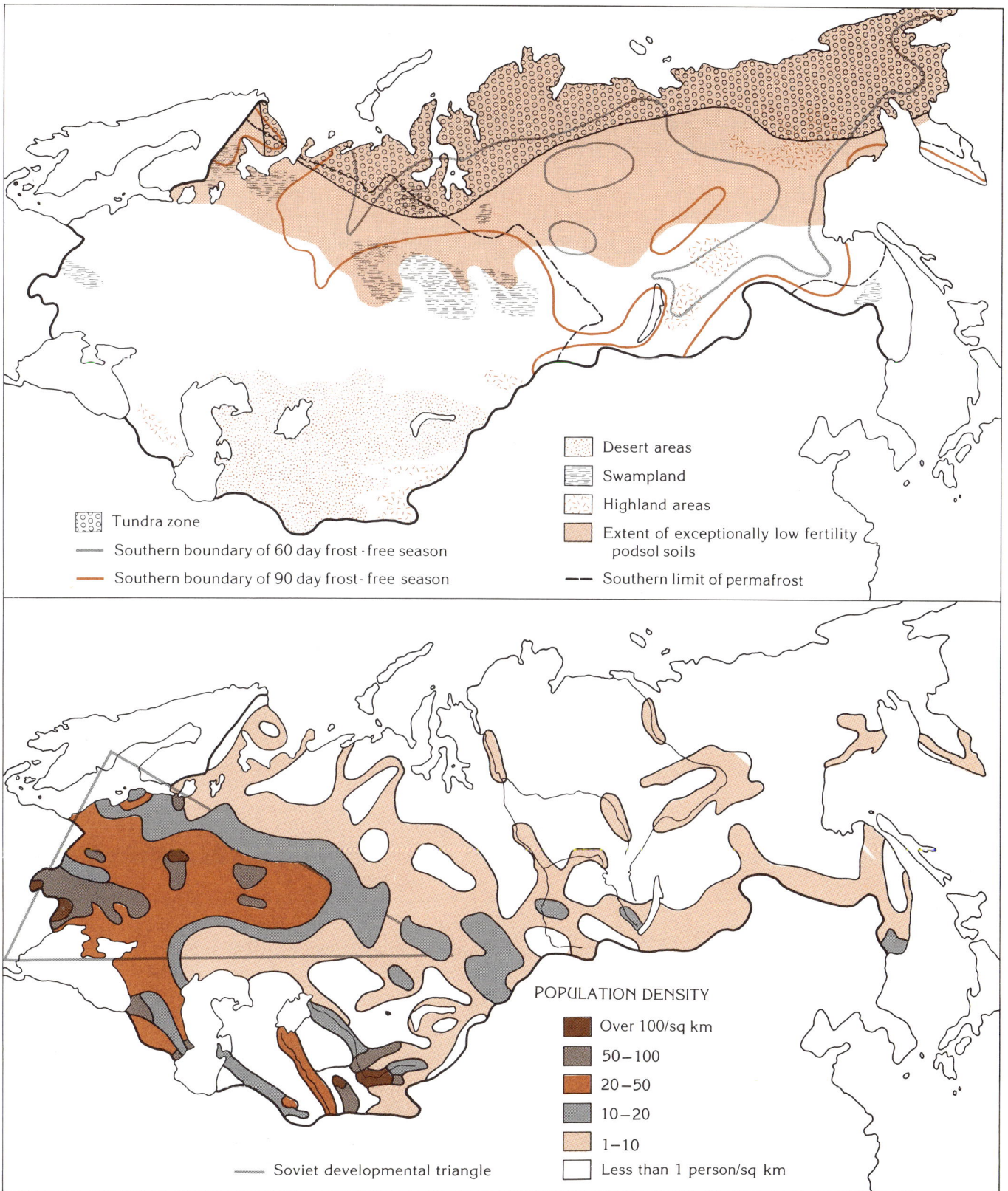

Tundra zone

Southern boundary of 60 day frost-free season

Southern boundary of 90 day frost-free season

Desert areas

Swampland

Highland areas

Extent of exceptionally low fertility podsol soils

Southern limit of permafrost

POPULATION DENSITY

Over 100/sq km

50–100

20–50

10–20

1–10

Less than 1 person/sq km

Soviet developmental triangle

FIGURE 7–5

The USSR Ecumene—Topography and Climate. The settled, agriculturally productive, and industrialized portion of the USSR takes the form of a huge triangle, whose one base is the western border from Leningrad to Odessa with sides converging at approximately Novosibirsk along the Trans-Siberian "lifeline."

no great number of fish. Almost enclosed on the southwest by the Turkish Straits, it has been used more for domestic, rather than international, shipping. A major Russian foreign policy objective has always been the by-passing of the straits through either territorial acquisition in the Balkans or Iran or the development of friendly allies in those areas. Since 1918 the straits have been open to trade in times of peace, though the Turks are still in control of the crucial waterway and less than friendly toward the Soviets.

The Pacific coastal waters are open to navigation for varying periods of time. In most years, Vladivostok can be kept open all year with icebreakers. Japan's home islands and the Kurile Islands once formed effective gates that could limit access to Soviet Pacific ports in the warmer southern portions of the Seas of Japan and Okhotsk. Border revisions after World War II awarded southern Sakhalin and the Kuriles to the USSR, along with clear access to the Pacific. The westward extension of the Aleutian Islands (Alaska) remain as an American-controlled constriction to the Bering Sea and the Arctic beyond.

The Soviet Union now possesses the world's largest fishing fleet, a powerful navy including the world's biggest armada of submarines and a considerable merchant marine. Soviet ships traverse (and fish) all oceans. The Arctic route is now of less importance to a nation that has become a major sea power. Increasing Soviet trade with western and third world nations has taken Soviet interest in the sea far beyond any search for ports. Their military naval presence is felt in all oceans. Nonetheless, the economy of the USSR is still relatively self-sufficient, and domestic movements (largely by land) of goods far overshadow international marine traffic. The seas around Russia have been far less influential in that country's development and outlook than they have been in the United States or the countries of western Europe.

CLIMATE

One of the primary facts about the Soviet Union is the low degree of utility of much of the country. Most of the population lives within a triangle whose base is the western border from the Black Sea to the Gulf of Finland (Leningrad) and whose apex is at the city of Novosibirsk in Siberia. Population east of this point tapers to a narrow, winding ribbon that parallels the Trans-Siberian to its eastern terminus. (See Figure 7–5.) Only two concentrations of any size (the forelands of the Caucasus and the oases of Soviet Central Asia) exist outside this triangle of development. Nothing better illustrates the climate of the Soviet Union than population distribution. North of the triangle, the land is generally too cold for sustained commercial agriculture; the region south of it is generally too dry.

Of the five major categories of climate, only three have any great areal extent in Russia: humid microthermal, polar, and arid—in a word, cold, colder, and dry. Most Russians live, in effect, at the warmer margins of the cold zone and the wetter margins of the dry zone; in neither case highly desirable, but in both cases at least liveable. Both these zones narrow eastward as **continentality** increases and moderating maritime influences decrease.

The humid microthermal variant that is most usable occupies most of that triangle of development. It is characterized by long, sharply cold winters and short, often cool, summers. Continentality increases eastward with greater seasonal and daily temperature ranges and greater extremes. Precipitation declines both southward and eastward, grading into the wetter fringes of the dry climatic zone that extends along the triangle's southern side.

The polar climatic type known as *tundra* occupies the Arctic fringe and many areas of higher elevation, while a subarctic climatic zone forms the transition between tundra and the triangle. Deserts occupy most of the lowland in Soviet Central Asia. Only a few sheltered areas along the Black Sea experience a warm, subtropical climate with a long growing season and plentiful rain.

Moscow is fairly typical of the more humid parts of European Russia. The average January temperature is 13.5°F (−10.3°C), rather similar to Winnipeg or Edmonton in Canada. In July, the temperature warms up to the mid-60's F (18°C), a degree of warmth similar to London or Quebec. Only a little more than four months are frost free. Because of the Atlantic influence, temperatures are more moderate than average at that latitude; for the same reason, skies are frequently cloudy and overcast (80 to 100 percent cloud cover on three quarters of the days of winter). Snowfall is relatively light, but it stays on the ground for five months.

Summer features bright, sunny days. Most rain falls in late summer or early fall, unfortunate in that it coincides with harvest time. Rains often occur in brief, but heavy showers between extended sunny periods. The northerly location brings long hours of summer sunlight whereas winter days are extremely short.

Temperatures warm southward, so that winter is shorter and less intense. Kiev, near the border of the steppe (semiarid climatic zone) has winter and summer temperature averages similar to those of Chicago, 23°F (−5°C) and 72°F (22°C) respectively. Precipitation is light, 18 to 20 inches (450 to 500 millimeters) annually. Skies are clear and sunny on a majority of days in both seasons. Despite the obviously warmer average weather, seasonal extremes are almost as great as those experienced in Moscow.

The subarctic areas possess a climate even more extreme. In Irkutsk, a large Siberian city, the January temperature averages −12°F (−21°C). Areas near Oymyakon have reached −90°F (−68°C) in winter and the average for January is −44° on either scale. Summers are fairly hot; Irkutsk has the same July average as Moscow, but many other locations are even higher. Oymyakon has experienced a temperature range of 185°F (104°C) from the hottest to the coldest day of the year. Mid-summer frosts can occur, and the growing season varies from two to four months. Cloud cover is negligible in any season, and precipitation is light. Most of the area is dominated by the Siberian high pressure system in winter. Winds move from the cold land outward to the continental margins. With no significant water source from which to draw moisture and the very 'ow moisture holding capabilities at such low temperature, it is obviously quite dry. Summer rains are brief, heavy thunderstorms in much of the area, but the Pacific coast has an almost monsoonlike quality to the summer rains.

The tundra is cold. By definition, no month averages above 50°F (10°C) and virtually every month experiences some frost. Precipitation is extremely light, but when it is that cold, evaporation cannot exceed what little precipitation falls.

In the steppe areas, cold winters and hot summers are characteristic. Rainfall is light but comes in the best possible season for grain crops, early and mid summer. Evaporation exceeds precipitation, so that crops are dependent on stored moisture from the spring thaw for germination. Skies are cloudless on almost all days and a few torrential thunderstorms bring what little rain occurs. By definition, there is too little rain for trees. Climatically the steppes of the USSR are similar to the Dakotas, Montana, and the Canadian Prairies. In the west, temperatures are similar to those experienced at Kiev; in the steppes of Kazakhstan or of Western Siberia, the temperatures at both seasons are a few degrees warmer than at Irkutsk. In Barnaul, for example, the January average is 0°F (−18°C), while the July temperature average is 68°F (20°C).

In the mid-latitude deserts, rainfall is everywhere less than 8 inches (200 millimeters) yearly. January temperatures average below freezing except in a few favored spots. Summer heat, however, is intense, and the more southerly settlements average over 80°F (27°C) in July. Temperatures of over 100°F (38°C) are common during summer afternoons. Most precipitation falls in winter in the south, in summer in the north. Everywhere, it is intensely dry; the low humidity levels and high temperatures mean that evaporation greatly exceeds precipitation. Only in a few favored locations in the foothills of the mountains is there sufficient rain to approach steppe conditions.

There are three small enclaves of subtropical climate: the Crimea, southeast of the protecting coastal mountains; the eastern Black Sea coast; and the lowlands along the southern Caspian Sea. The use of the word *subtropical* here is relative. January temperature averages are more like those of Seattle or Richmond than like southern California; they all average two to three degrees above freezing, unlike the rest of the USSR. By comparison, then, winters are quite mild. The Crimean coast has a Mediterranean regime with a dry summer. The other two have more evenly distributed rainfall and exhibit some very high total annual rainfall. Batumi, on the coast of Georgia receives 100 inches (2,500 millimeters) of rainfall. These areas have developed extensive resort functions and have come to specialize in subtropical crops, regardless of the marginal nature of the area and the frequency of frost hazards.

In sum, the Soviets have had to develop their economy in an area that is subject to climatic extremes and is characteristically marginal. Virtually every developed country contains some such areas, but few other than the USSR have no area that is truly favorable for agriculture.

VEGETATION

Vegetation patterns here follow zones of climate rather exactly. Each zone of vegetation has characteristic species and the vegetative associations are relatively simple and unvarying. The country contains one sixth of the world's forests, and a surprising amount is still in its natural state because of difficulty of access.

The tundra zone contains a vegetational complex of little economic value—mosses, lichens, and a bush of dwarf willow and birch. Much of the area consists of barren rock or standing water. All species must tolerate drought, poor drainage, extreme winter cold, acid and shallow soils, mid-summer frost, and a long season of dormancy. Where protected from wind, facing southward and better drained, the land supports stunted trees. Even grasses are limited to hardier types. This zone seems better adapted to raising mosquitoes than vegetation; the former constitute a plague in summer.

Covering a vast extent in Siberia and the northern one fifth of European Russia, the taiga is the most important vegetational type in the USSR. The taiga is a forest of coniferous (cone-bearing, needle-leaf) trees; because of the very cold climate and the **permafrost** that underlies the area, the forest grows slowly and contains few species. Bog covers about one half the taiga. Spruce, pine, and fir extend over wide areas. Larch, a conifer that loses its needles in the winter, is the dominant species in eastern Siberia and the Soviet Far East. Weather conditions are so dry and cold in winter that the complete dormancy of the larch makes it more competitive than the other conifers.

Farther south is a zone of mixed forest. The soils are less acid and the winters less severe. Hardly luxuriant, the vegetation at least forms a continuous cover. With no

Harvesting Grain on a Collective Farm in Western Siberia. Mechanization and the organization of vast areas into huge farms have enabled Soviet planners to extend the frontiers of farming to marginal areas, providing a nearby food supply for major industrial and mining complexes located outside the traditional heartland. More importantly, the use of marginal climatic areas has helped to stabilize Soviet grain supplies to some degree, though imports are still necessary. (Courtesy of United Nations)

permafrost, drainage is better, and trees are more deeply rooted. Much of this area has been cleared for agriculture; forest remains only in poorly drained areas, on steep slopes, and in abandoned fields on weaker, sandier soils.

The mixed forest grades into steppe over a discontinuous and irregular belt known as the wooded steppe. Previously grassland, the warming of climate over the last few hundred years has allowed trees to invade the steppe. This area has been virtually converted to 100 percent agricultural use and few examples of the natural vegetation remain.

The steppe itself is a belt of almost endless grass. The high humus content of the soil results from accumulation of the decayed roots and stalks of annual grasses. Soils are neutral to basic and calcium compounds collect at or near the surface in many areas. Trees occupy valley bottoms and a few areas of high water table, but it is grass that dominates over 95 percent of the surface. Where rainfall is heavier, the grass is tall and the vegetational cover is complete. As it decreases southeastward, the grass becomes shorter and the cover discontinuous.

The steppe grades into semi-desert where rainfall goes below 8 or 10 inches (200 or 250 millimeters) annually. Short bunch grasses predominate and less than half the surface area is vegetated. Sagebrush and xerophytic (drought-adapted) shrubs are the commonest cover in the desert proper. Vast areas of the Central Asian desert have shifting dunes or such sandy or rocky soils that little vegetational growth is possible. After the thaw and the early spring rains, the desert flowers and turns green, leaving patches of nutritional grass that support herds of sheep.

SOILS

Each vegetational type has its corresponding soil type occupying the same zone (Figure 7–6). The most widely used soil classification was developed by a Russian, V. V. Dokuchaev, and his Russian soil type names are still in general descriptive use. Soils generally reflect a combination of parent material, vegetational cover, climatic processes, and drainage. With continuity among these factors over immense areas, the soils of the USSR are reasonably similar in fertility and other characteristics over broad regions as well.

Tundra soils are more like partially decomposed rock with an admixture of peaty, semi-decayed vegetation. Lichens grow on bare rock, serving to break down rock materials. Where even the shallowest depression or crevice exists, dead lichens and coarse rock form a thin, fragile layer of soil. Mosses add a layer of decayed materials. Decay is slow because of cold, standing water, and naturally preserving acids in the soil and water. The name *tundra* is used to describe the vegetation, the climate, and the soil, showing the close association.

Taiga soils are somewhat thicker but not necessarily more productive. The acid-loving conifers shed needles that decompose slowly, yielding little humus. Abundant ground water percolates through the soil leaching almost all nutrient value. Ashen white, highly acid, rich in iron and

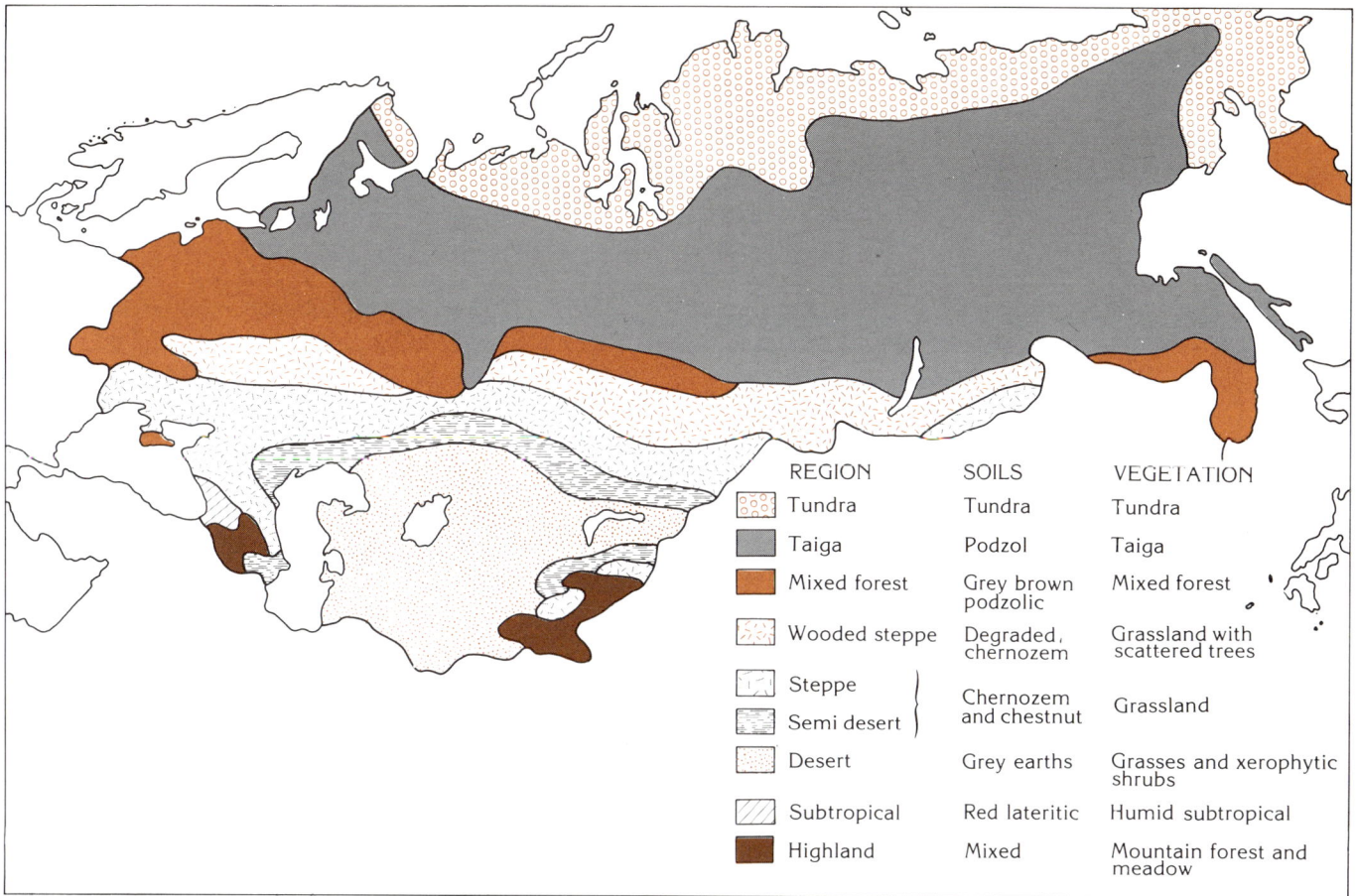

REGION	SOILS	VEGETATION
Tundra	Tundra	Tundra
Taiga	Podzol	Taiga
Mixed forest	Grey brown podzolic	Mixed forest
Wooded steppe	Degraded, chernozem	Grassland with scattered trees
Steppe	Chernozem and chestnut	Grassland
Semi desert		
Desert	Grey earths	Grasses and xerophytic shrubs
Subtropical	Red lateritic	Humid subtropical
Highland	Mixed	Mountain forest and meadow

FIGURE 7–6

Vegetation and Soil Regions. Russian soil and botanical science have contributed the terms *chernozem* (black earth prairie soils) and *taiga* (slow-growth coniferous forest) to the international vocabulary of these sciences. The great size and climate range of the USSR, together with its great topographic variety, have produced a varied complex of soil and vegetation types.

silicon, low in humus, devoid of calcium—these are the podsols. Agriculturally, they yield poorly under most circumstances. Intensive liming several times a year, addition of nitrogen, and the spring burning of plant refuse (to add potash) will force them to yield moderately if carefully tended and artificially drained. The net expense involved is incredible; it comes close to using the soil only as a neutral medium for growth. Chemically, it is akin to growing garden plants in ground glass, shredded steel, and aluminum beer cans.

The soils of the mixed forest zone are podzols as well. Where the vegetational cover was that of deciduous (seasonal leaf-losing) trees, considerable humus was added. Leaching is less intense and soils are thicker and better drained. The Soviet Union is fortunate in that much of this area has been enriched by glacial action. Ice-ground soil and rock particles transported from distant source areas added desirable chemical nutrients. Where broadleaf forest humus, volcanic, or calcareous (calcium-containing or

limey) parent material or alluvial deposits have enriched the podsols to a considerable extent, or where leaching is less complete, they are called *podzolic* ("podzol-like") soils, indicating the lessened degree of leaching.

The wooded steppe yields a moderately leached brown earth, mildly acid, rich in humus, moderately endowed with calcium, and frequently rich in potash. Soils are high yielding if supplied with sufficient water, a problem in years of drought. Mainly composed of fine-textured loess (wind-blown soil particles of indirect glacial origin), they are easily eroded by both wind and water when disturbed through plowing. Poorer in fertility and drier than the prairie soils of the United States, they are richer by far than podzols.

Under steppe vegetation, the generations of unleached humus create a thick, dark waxy soil of incredible fertility—the famous **chernozem** or black earth. These soils are naturally rich in calcium, nitrogen, phosphorous, and potash—virtually any mineral a plant needs for growth. They are deep and generally well drained, and they have the additional advantage of good retention of ground water. In all aspects they are the equivalent of the best soils in the North American Great Plains. They have the potential to yield enormously but the absence of sufficient water, the very condition that keeps them fertile, is a detriment to plant growth. Caliche (a mineral concentration of poisonous proportions) forms at the surface where water tables are high. Irrigation tends to increase this tendency and is not necessarily the answer to higher yields. During prolonged droughts, wind erosion is a problem.

Toward the drier margins of the steppe, soils developed under a more sparse vegetational cover are reddish brown (chestnut) in color. Application of fertilizer increases yields, but the climate is even drier, making farming more hazardous. Most of the Virgin Lands colonization program took place in these soil areas.

Chestnut soils grade into grey desert soils that are calcium rich and humus poor. The mineral content is often dangerously close to toxic levels; they are usable only with careful irrigation in some areas. Most of the Soviet Central Asian desert, therefore, will remain unusable.

The small areas of subtropical climate possess red and yellow lateritic (predominantly iron-oxide compounds) earths. Poorly drained, they are used more because of climatic advantage rather than for their dubious fertility. Only where alluvial did they yield well. Now, with chemical fertilizer, they can give unusually good yields. They are a small, but precious asset in a country characterized by extreme climates.

DRAINAGE PATTERNS AND RIVERINE UTILITY

The broad, flat plains areas of Russia allow the development of mighty streams with far-reaching tributaries. The Volga is by far the largest river in Europe, and the rivers of Soviet Asia are among the largest in the world. Even short streams, like the Neva of the Leningrad area, may carry enormous volumes of water—a fact not suggested by their length or breadth, but rather hidden in the depth and speed of flow. The USSR possesses an enormous hydroelectric potential, great irrigation possibilities, and significant transportation advantages in its riverine system.

Yet, many of the rivers are icebound for ten months of the year, limiting navigation. In spring they flood vast areas, hindering plowing and seeding at a crucial time in a short growing season. In summer, many rivers are shallow and depleted by the lack of rain. The strong seasonal fluctuations in flow reduce their energy generating utility as well. Most even flow the "wrong way." The giant rivers of Siberia dead-end in a frozen, almost useless Arctic Ocean. They thaw first in the south (headwaters) towards ice-jammed mouths in the north, creating a backup that floods incredible acreages. The Volga (which flows southward) empties into the Caspian Sea—a salt lake with no outlet. The Soviet Central Asian rivers, fed by glacial meltwaters derived from the border mountains, die out in the sands or the shallow, salty Aral Sea. The rivers in general flow due north or south in a country where the **orientation bias** (dominant traffic direction) is largely east-west.

Coal, oil, ores, and other bulky commodities from the south are shipped in barge trains that must fight the current on their way north to Moscow and the Central Industrial District, while empty barges reap the advantage of current on the return trip. It is quite the opposite of the advantageous Mississippi-Ohio system in the United States. Trade *followed* rivers, rather than *used* them, during much of Russian history.

The Communist era has reversed this situation sharply. Water transportation improvement has become a major goal, and the USSR is now a world leader in fishing, hydroelectric power generation, irrigation, maritime traffic, and naval might. The investments necesssary to reach this position have been enormous; the results are impressive.

The navigational possibilities of the Volga River have been greatly enhanced through a series of massive dams and canals. Dams built at cities along the Volga have created a series of Great Lakes that extend in an unbroken chain from Volgograd on northwards to Kineshma, north of Moscow. The Volga-Don canal has now connected the Volga to the Sea of Azov, allowing direct access to the Black Sea. Smaller projects have enhanced the navigability of the upper Volga, Oka, and Moscow rivers, allowing navigation by vessels of 20-foot (6-meter) draft.

The old Marinsk canal system, which connected Leningrad with the White Sea, has been revitalized and upgraded to the same standards. The giant Rybinsk reservoir on the upper Volga has linked the two systems so that navigation from the Black Sea to both the Arctic and the Baltic are possible.

The smaller, but critically located, Dnieper has also been converted into a series of lakes. The hydroelectric project at the rapids of the Dnieper bend was one of the great projects of the 1930's. It has since been overshadowed by other larger projects and is incorporated into a chain of water steps that allow navigation well above Kiev, the capital of the Ukraine.

Two remaining links in the overall navigation plan remain incomplete. The upper Don River and the tributaries of the Dnieper are scheduled for similar projects now that the rich iron reserves of the Kursk area are in production. Major new investments in the iron and steel industry are being located in the district between the Ukraine and the Central Industrial District. Industrial water needs and cheap water transportation are both considerations in implementing this major new industrial base. The Dnieper and Don will be linked to the Volga and its tributaries near Moscow. In turn, it is planned to link the Soviet river system via both Poland and the Western Dvina—Baltic to the pan-European canal and river system. The costs involved will likely be less than was already spent on earlier projects; the plan is obviously not an idle dream, as the USSR further integrates its economy with those of East Europe and increases its trade with West Europe.

The second European linkage not yet completed involves the Urals. The Kama River, a major tributary of the Volga, has been rendered navigable for much of its length. It is planned to link the Kama to two northward flowing rivers and the Arctic. This would give the Urals two outlets to the Arctic, water connections to a source of timber (in short supply locally), a new source of coking coal (the Pechora-Vorkuta basin), and an all-water route to both Leningrad and Moscow. Should all these plans be realized, all major raw material resource producing areas and all major industrial districts in European Russia would be linked by cheap water transportation. The already significant hydroelectric capacity of European Russia would double. Large-scale flooding would virtually cease to be a problem, the millions of acres of additional farmland would be added or improved through drainage and irrigation. Significantly, the entire European continent, with all its markets and resources, would be directly tied by water to the Soviet Union.

However, there are problems. The shrinkage of the Caspian Sea is in part attributed to the projects on the Volga. The shallow, northern end of the sea is now navigable only by shallow draft vessels. Scientists have opposed the northern canal links, fearing the unknown effects on the water table, groundwater supplies, and underground mining. The large lakes that have resulted stay frozen longer than the rivers. Violent summer storms occur over the new lakes, a new climatological phenomenon. Agricultural lands and entire cities have been inundated by reservoirs, and no one knows how much damage is being done by the increasingly polluted rivers that now disperse their waters all over the European part of the USSR. Despite these disadvantages, the program will likely continue. Now alerted to environmental concerns, the progress may be slower and definitely better planned.

If the sheer scale of the European program of river engineering is staggering, that of the **Siberian River Reversal Scheme** is even greater. (See Figure 7–7.) To date, three major steps have been taken. The first was control of the headwaters of the Yenesei along its tributary the Angara. A dam now backs up the waters of the Angara River to the city of Irkutsk. The second step in this water stairway is already completed. The Bratsk Dam on the Middle Angara (1961) was the largest dam in the world with a capacity of over 4 million kilowatts; it created a lake over 300 miles (500 kilometers) long to the bottom of the Irkutsk Dam. A third dam of even larger power capacity has been built at Ust-Illimsk, farther downstream. Dams on the Yenesei proper have been constructed in the headwaters and at the city of Krasnoyarsk. Ultimately, the entire river is to be tamed and utilized in this fashion. Power generated is giving rise to local, large-scale, capital-intensive industry. Surplus power is shipped westward over the national grid. Lake Baikal, the world's deepest lake, insures a steady flow of water, even during the intense cold of winter.

Inland Water Transport in the USSR. One fo the most difficult tasks confronting the USSR is the integration of its far-flung resources into an economic unit. Much of the drainage network of the European USSR has been canalized and improved to facilitate the long distance shipment of low-value raw materials by water, the cheapest possible form of transportation. (Courtesy of United Nations)

Phase 2 of the scheme is the irrigation of the deserts. Many small dams already built are being superseded by large ones on the Amu Darya, Syr Darya, Chu, Ili, and other rivers of the region. Fed by glacial meltwaters from the world's highest mountains, the hydroelectric potential of these streams is quite large. Irrigated areas have been greatly enlarged, and plans for a further extension of irrigation are being implemented yearly.

The third phase is planned to be the development of the Ob-Irtysh river system, already partially accomplished. Ultimately, the Yenesei system would be linked to that of the Ob and surplus waters would be reversed through the low-lying Turgay gate to Soviet Central Asia. Waters of all three systems would drain into the Caspian and link the western two thirds of the Asiatic USSR to the almost completed network of the European USSR. It is not impossible; given the climatic limitations of the Asiatic USSR and the enormous costs and distances involved, the real question is whether it is economical.

Once before, work was abandoned on many of these massive Siberian schemes. The recent emphasis on redeveloping agriculture in northern European USSR and the decision to develop the new industrial base south of Moscow serve to indicate another demotion in emphasis on Siberia. Immediate problems of grain supply and consumer demands may cause the planners to shelve these grandiose schemes again. If the past is any guide, however, the pendulum could reverse itself at any time. Pragmatically, the Soviets now appear to have designated Siberia as a hinterland for the old European core, exporting its surplus power and riches to further develop the core. Even such an official policy, however, does not preclude further investment in hydroelectric projects or irrigation schemes. Each new construction is a further link in the planned water utilization system. When enough links are in place, the completion of the entire plan will appear more feasible.

THE STRUCTURE OF SUBREGIONS

The heartland versus hinterland, the fifteen ethnic republics or the nineteen economic regions are potentially all legitimate bases for subregionalization, regardless of cen-

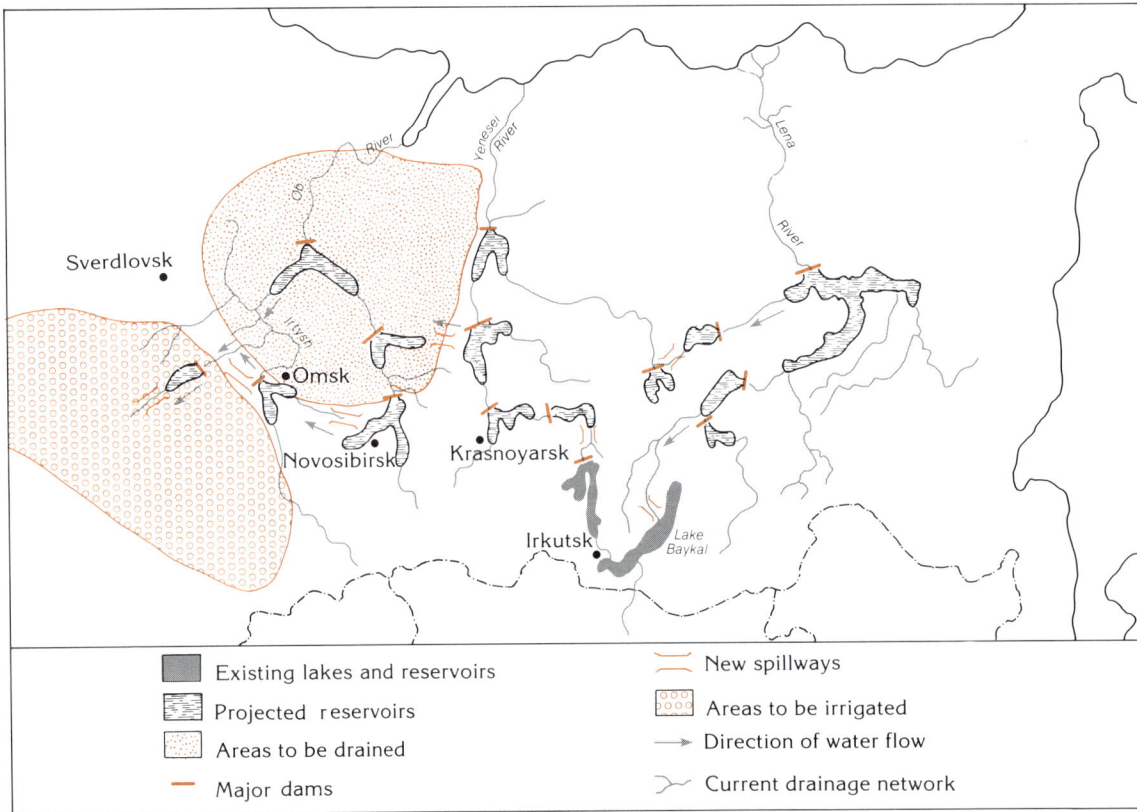

FIGURE 7–7
Siberian River Reversal Scheme. One of the largest water engineering and management projects ever undertaken, the Siberian River Reversal is only partly completed. Designed to divert Arctic Ocean-bound fresh water southwestward to warm, but dry, areas for crop irrigation, this scheme is intended to greatly expand Soviet crop production while generating hydro power and improving navigation.

tral planning and the extreme centralization of authority. The problems of regionalization are indicated by the frequent changes in administrative regionalization that have been brought forward by the government of the USSR over the past sixty-five years. The official economic planning districts, as they are designated by the government, have been combined into larger subregions that exhibit similar characteristics, problems, and prospects. (See Figure 7–8.)

The *Central Industrial District* designates the European core area of Russian culture and early industrial development. It contains the largest single industrial district in the USSR as well as the agricultural hinterland that serves it.

The subregion of the North and Northwest represent the Baltic hinterland. The four ethnic republics there are being developed on the industrial model of New England and as an industrial-agricultural hinterland for Leningrad. The vast resources of the northern portion, largely underdeveloped, have been traditionally linked to Moscow since the seventeenth century. However, the coal, metal, fertilizer minerals, oil, gas, and timber of this area have been definitely reoriented toward Leningrad in the most recent twenty years. This reorientation of the North to the Baltic

Coast has a historical precedent in the founding of the early state of Novgorod, once a rival of the Moscow of the Middle Ages. Historically and economically, this association is quite natural.

The subregion of Ukraine and Moldavia represents the agricultural heartland of the Soviet Union. Its regional unity is based on its commercial agriculture, its emphasis on industrial crops, its ethnic differentiation from the Russian core, and its major role in Soviet industry. Its borders extend eastward to include related agricultural and industrial areas with similar cultures and economies.

The Volga-Urals subregion is given continuity by two parallel linear features, the Volga River and the Ural Mountains. The Volga valley is rich in oil and power, whereas the Urals contain vast deposits of metal ores and other minerals. The two are complementary sources of industrial raw materials and are strongly linked economically.

Ethnic diversity, oil and gas, Islamic culture and contacts, specialized agriculture, climatic similarities, and even the Caspian Sea serve as unifying characteristics for a subregion that includes the Caucasus Mountains, its forelands, and the republics of Soviet Central Asia. These are more recently conquered parts of the old Russian domain, and they maintain something of the aura of the frontier

FIGURE 7–8

Structure of Subregions. The subregionalization of the USSR primarily is based on economic and physical criteria, with some consideration to ethnic-cultural factors.

and the exotic to most Russians. They share a growing tourist-retirement-health resort function, which serves the entire country. Their relationship to the core area (including movie making, the Soviet equivalent of cowboys and Indians, and even something of an innovative lifestyle and culture) is not unlike that of the American Southwest to the U.S. core area.

The last subregion is that of Siberia. Vast and only beginning to develop, it is a frontier land by any standards. The vast reaches held together by the Trans-Siberian Railroad and the rivers constitute a unit by virtue of its problems and prospects. It is frequently treated as a single unit even by Soviet planners. Northern Kazakhstan is included because of similarity; it is now peopled overwhelmingly by Russians rather than the native Kazakhs. Developed in conjunction with Western Siberia and along the same model, adjunct to the Kuzbas and Eastern Siberia in its development of raw materials and agriculture, it is similar to Siberia, more so than to Soviet Central Asia. Only its southernmost reaches, the Syr Darya River valley and related oases, are properly a part of Central Asia; that por-

tion is dealt with in the Soviet Central Asia–Caucasus subregion.

CENTRAL INDUSTRIAL DISTRICT

Ethnically uniform, the Central Industrial District is the home of Russian culture and the heartland of what came to be the modern Russian state. Moscow is not only the national capital, but the subregion's capital. The road and rail networks focus on that city, as does the subregion's economy. No other Soviet subregion focuses quite so completely on a single urban center. Viewed in the light of the theory of urban hierarchy, it is almost an ideal of Christaller's model. This is no accident, nor a confirmation of the theory, since the Soviet's have deliberately used that model as a guideline in centralized planning (see Figure 7–9).

Moscow, the primate city of the Soviet Union, has 8 million people. Again borrowing from Western planning theory, it is surrounded by a **green belt** of farmland, parks, and forests—an area in which development is restricted. It

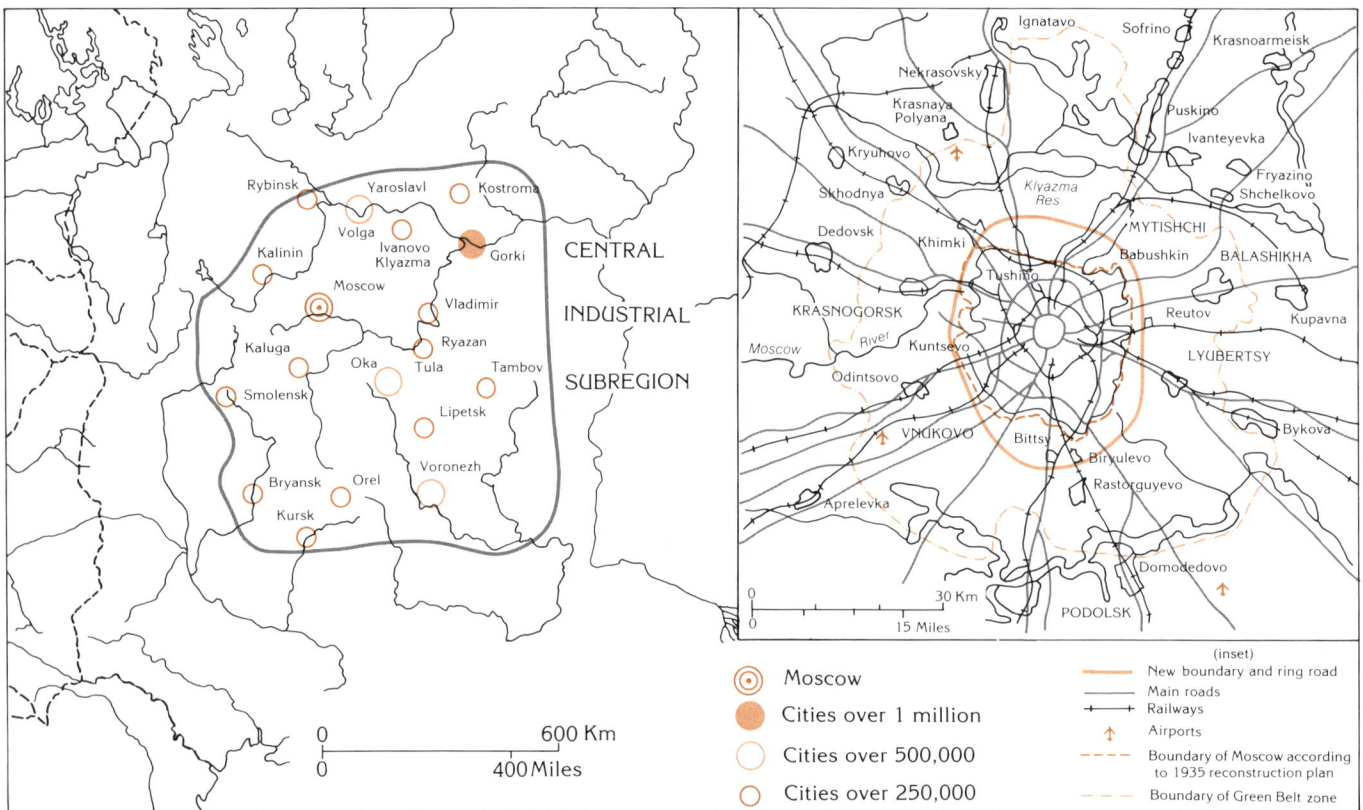

FIGURE 7–9

Moscow and the Urban Hierarchy. Moscow's attractive power for both facilities and people has led to an official determination to control its growth rate by decentralizing some functions (and locating new plants) in the medium-sized cities within Moscow's metropolitan orbit. Moscow's growth, felt to be approaching that of diseconomies of scale through congestion, has been difficult to slow due to the capital's amenities, especially in shopping.

serves the "day-trip" recreation needs. Beyond this are a ring of satellite towns, generally of 50,000 to 100,000 or more people. These serve to partially process goods for finishing and final assembly in Moscow, or as specialized suburbs (scientific, technical, or educational) to serve the highly specialized needs of the primate city. They are on an encircling railroad originally built as a by-pass around the busy Moscow transportation node. Beyond this is an incomplete second ring of semi-independent industrial cities of 200,000 to 500,000 population, located at a distance of 90 to 125 miles (150 to 200 kilometers) from Moscow—places like Vladimir, Kalinin, and Tula. These are regional trade centers for their own hinterlands, local administrative centers and specialized industrial centers in their own right. Nonetheless, they are completely overshadowed by Moscow.

In the farthest reaches, 200 to 300 miles (300 to 500 kilometers) from the center of Moscow, there is a third ring of industrial and administrative centers of roughly the same population size. These cities are more widely spaced, have developed satellites of their own, are highly specialized, and are more loosely linked to Moscow. Their relationship to that city is comparable to the linkages of such mid-size cities as Scranton, Albany, and Hartford to the megalopolitan core of the eastern United States. This third ring dies out northwest of Moscow in the low-utility farming country of the Valdai hills and in the direction of a competing Leningrad.

Some of the cities of the third ring, like Yaroslavl (600,000), Gorki (1.3 million), or Voronezh (790,000) are major centers in their own right. They service needs of the entire country, not just those of Moscow. Yet, they are still tied to that city's economic pull. All other million-size cities (except Gorki) and all major industrial centers of the USSR exist beyond this third ring. Moscow exerts its administrative function throughout the country, but its economic impact is primarily limited to the Central Industrial District.

Moscow produces almost 10 percent of the Soviet Union's industrial goods by value. It is also the largest educational center, the home of the government, a major port, the largest transportation node, and the dominant center of Russian and Soviet culture.

Its fortified center, the Kremlin, is its nucleus, though most of the buildings within its walls are now museums and tourist objectives. It is still the governmental nerve center, though most of the bureaucracy works outside its walls. Adjacent Red Square, with Lenin's tomb and GUM, the giant department store, is the focal point for parades, state occasions, and even shopping.

The city, as inherited by the Communists in 1918, was little changed from its eighteenth century form. The skyline was dominated by the Kremlin and the splendid onion-domed churches. The first step in modifying it (1930–40) was the development of broad boulevards radiating from the city center, lined with new contruction of an ornate, imposing, pseudo-classical style approved by Stalin himself—his concept of traditional opulence. Seven large towers (in a style known as Stalin Gothic in the West) were constructed to give a new skyline, symbolically low-

GUM—Moscow's Largest Department Store. Two outstanding problems still face the Soviet consumer despite years of rapid industrial growth. Many consumer goods are in short supply and of poor quality. Inadequate distribution networks result in regional shortages in certain goods. One of Moscow's prime attractions to migrants and tourists is the availability of such consumer items in this, the capital and primate city. (Courtesy of United Nations)

ering the importance of the church and raising that of the state.

Parks and stadiums were liberally sprinkled through the new city. Beyond the city center, progressing slowly because of the low priority assigned to housing, are row upon row of high-rise dwellings. Each development is designed to be relatively self-sufficient, with schools, workplaces, medical services, and shopping for the entire neighborhood. The whole city is interconnected by a splendid, ornate subway system, itself a tourist attraction.

Within the city are giant industrial complexes. East and southeast of the city center are concentrations of heavy industry. Lighter industry, including consumer goods, is scattered throughout the city. New industrial and research suburbs, where it is hoped that everyone "talks shop," have been developed at the outer edges. Many emphasize chemicals, plastics, appliances, and precision engineering—the newer branches of Soviet industry.

Moscow is the place where goods are most readily available (in part to serve the emerging bureaucratic bourgeoise, in part to impress foreign tourists and dignitaries). While wages are only slightly higher than the national average, it is the pull of amenities, real or imagined, that is the draw to migrants from all over the USSR.

Moscow has long been a **closed city,** with migration by permit only. Yet, despite its low birthrate, it continues to grow. From 1959 to 1979, it grew by almost 60 percent— an exceptionally rapid rate. Many illegal migrants come to the city on forged I.D. cards. Others simply rent a room illegally. Thousands live there on "temporary" permits that never seem to expire. The demands of industry for labor are in direct opposition to government directives that advocate a no-growth policy. No new industry is allowed to locate there, but expansions are not forbidden. The burgeoning bureaucratic establishment demands new labor constantly. Old plants add and diversify functions. The citizenry of Moscow demand better services and more consumer goods, swelling labor demands. As a result, Moscow grows, despite official wisdom.

In the most recent decade, the growth has slowed to a rate of about 1.3 percent per year, allowing Moscow to begin to meet the demand for housing. Only Novosibirsk, among the twenty largest cities in the Soviet Union, grows more slowly.

The other cities of Moscow *oblast* (county) have none of Moscow's investment priority status. Many retain the log cabin homes of old; services are grossly inadequate, adding to the throng of Moscow-bound commuters and shoppers. The oldest have drab nineteenth century textile mills or foundries at their center; a few have well-planned high-rise communities linked to some rapidly growing, high-priority industry. They are often temporary stop-offs on the road to Moscow, halfway houses for migrants from the rural areas to the big city.

This district of Moscow and its immediate satellites are industrially diverse. Machine building and light engineering industries are now most important, having surpassed the traditional, if still important, older base of textiles, clothing, and food processing that began in the nineteenth century. The newest and most rapidly growing industrial segments are appliances, consumer goods, and chemicals. The rapidly growing chemical industry is geared to plastics, detergents, and synthetic fibers. The raw materials are oil and gas now brought in by pipeline. The end market is the Central Industrial District consumer.

Moscow still produces automobiles and trucks, but the major production has shifted elsewhere. Paper and wood processing, an original regional specialty, has shifted nearer to raw materials.

Highly attractive **growth poles** are now being established at some distance from Moscow in the second and third rings of satellite development. Special housing priorities and the assignment of Moscow-produced consumer goods to these poles will likely lessen the Moscow-bound craze, as planners seem finally to have reached a partial solution to the problem.

The second ring of Moscow satellites consists of old regional trade centers whose industrial specializations date

A Machinery Plant in Moscow. The relatively small and primitive industrial base in existence before 1918 has been broadened and improved during the Soviet era through massive industrial investment. The Central Industrial District (Moscow in particular) now produces a wide variety of industrial machinery for both domestic and foreign markets. (Courtesy of United Nations)

from tsarist times. They received notable investment and increase in their industrial function during the early Communist drive for industrialization. The new Soviet government chose to expand the national industrial base by localizing new investment in the areas nearest the center of government during the 1920's.

In each of the two outer rings of such industrial satellites, one city overshadows the others. In the inner ring, that city is Tula. Tula's original function was lignite mining supplemented by a small iron and steel base. Tula and its hinterland have since developed an important chemical producing area, particularly in the production of nitrogen fertilizers. This function enlarges continuously with the increased availability of gas as a raw material, supplied by pipeline. A series of machine-building industries were established to add value to the end production, thereby overcoming the high cost of locally produced iron and steel. Now that a new regional source of iron ore has begun to be exploited (the Kursk magnetic anamoly), the iron and steel industries, as well as associated metal engineering plants, have begun to develop rapidly. The other cities of ring 2 have exhibited less dynamic growth over the last twenty years.

The third ring contains three larger, more fully independent cities (Gorki, Yaroslavl, and Voronezh) in addition to the cities of the old textile region along the upper Volga and the ancient fortress cities that guarded the historically important river routes. Of all these urban centers, Gorki is by far the most important.

Located at the junction of the Volga with the Oka River, Gorki is the location of the oldest (and largest) truck factory in the country, the Volga automobile factory, the largest Soviet bus factory, and dozens of engine- and auto-part factories. Despite the location of new plants elsewhere, it is still the largest center of automotive production in the USSR. Ships, barges, boats, and rail and airplane parts and components are manufactured there. Large steel works produce pipes for the expanding pipeline network of the USSR and rolled steel for a variety of industries in the area. An expanding chemical industry produces artificial fertilizers and synthetic livestock feed. Paper and woodworking industries are of great importance as is a growing consumer goods industry. The city and its suburbs are now growing more rapidly than Moscow. Gorki serves as the contact point between the Central Industrial District, the Volga Valley, and the Urals—three of the Soviet Union's largest agglomerations of industry.

The largest city in the upper Volga valley and the economic capital of a large industrial district, Yaroslavl is a city of 600,000 people. Once a major textile center, it has now developed an even stronger specialization in factory machinery, engines, electrical machinery, and a full-scale petrochemical and oil-refining industry. The original impetus to its chemical industry was the conversion of potatoes to alcohol and synthetic rubber.

Most of the textile centers are strung along an axis from Yaroslavl to Gorki. Ivanovo, the largest, is still a giant cotton mill town. As the extreme northwest of the district is Rybinsk, a city located at the site of the great Rybinsk Reservoir. At the contact zone with the taiga, it specializes in lumber, paper, and woodworking as well as power generation for the factories of the district.

South and east of Moscow the cities of the third ring are more widely spaced. Kursk, in the extreme southwest, is the site of a long-known magnetic anamoly that caused extreme compass deviation. Exploration since the 1930's has uncovered huge deposits of iron ore of all grades, and the district has now surpassed the Urals, becoming the second most important iron ore mining center in the Soviet Union.

Lipetsk, like Tula an old iron center, has a population of 400,000 and a renewed steel industry. Expanded old mills and newly constructed ones will swell area steel production to more than 15 million tons yearly; specialties are high-quality steels, electrical steels, and galvanized metals.

Voronezh is the dominant city in the southern part of the outer ring of satellites. Halfway between the Donbas and Moscow, it has capitalized on its locational importance. Near to Kursk, it produces ore concentration equipment for the up-grading of ores from that and other districts. It manufactures agricultural equipment, food processing machinery, electronics, and machine tools and is a center for aircraft production. Using natural gas piped in from the Ukraine, it produces synthetic rubber and a wide variety of other chemical products. No other center in the USSR has been the recipient of so many new types of investment in recent years.

The cities of the southern half of this third ring of satellites are scheduled for major investment during the last twenty years of this century. They are virtually all located on major routes focusing on Moscow, and this part of the subregion itself will be the site of a major new metallurgical base, a crash program to improve agriculture, and a transit-distributional function that interconnects the Ukraine, the industrial districts of East Europe, the Volga Valley, and the gas and oil resources of Central Asia and the Caucasus with the Central Industrial District. Long-term regional depopulation trends are now in the process of reversal.

In general, this oldest (and largest) of Soviet manufacturing regions is undergoing a process of diversification (and redevelopment). Short of resources, other than iron, the network of oil and gas pipelines that pass through the subregion make expansion both profitable and possible.

Plate Mill in the Metallurgical Complex at Lipetsk. After years of economic neglect, the Central Black Earth portion of the Central Industrial District has begun to receive large-scale industrial investment. The development of iron-ore deposits at Kursk and the decision to use Siberia as a raw material base for the more populous Soviet regions have combined to partially reverse the long-established trend of extending development beyond the Urals. (Courtesy of United Nations)

Consumer goods and chemical industries, high priority investment areas at this time, will be the leading developmental sectors. The southern half, with its giant new metallurgical base, will be the major area of growth.

The agricultural picture has traditionally been less bright. In the north, summers are short, cool, and damp. Farms (even collectives) were small, and fields were often widely scattered among the forest. Drainage was always a problem, and the poor agricultural prospects in juxtaposition to growing industrial cities lead to long-distance commuting and widespread rural depopulation.

This area is scheduled for agricultural revitalization. Drainage, erosion control, and consolidation of farms are planned. Massive liming to neutralize acid soil, seed improvement, and irrigation projects will improve yields. The plan is to intensify and commercialize production through investment. Dairying, feed lot meat production, and a renewed emphasis on market produce are expected to revive local agriculture.

The central black earth portion (see Figure 7–10) is characterized by unspecialized general farming, though wheat is the dominant crop. For an area that is naturally rich (with excellent soil and a fair availability of water), it is surprisingly neglected. Poor farming techniques and past rural overpopulation have led to severe erosional prob-

lems. Sunflower and sugar beet are major crops, and yields are moderate, even with limited application of fertilizer, despite the bad farming practices and conservational neglect of the past. Government programs to extend the acreage of sugar beet and corn have been coupled with investment in local fertilizer factories. The expansion of dairy herds has led to the introduction of rotational fodder crops on a large scale. As a result, the productivity of the area is gradually improving.

Rural overpopulation has gradually cured itself through massive out-migration and the development of large-scale commuting to the area's growing cities. Workers here are less anxious to live in city apartments, since the rural food supply is much better. At harvest time, city workers help on the farms after working hours. As often as not, pay is received "under the table," and a kind of extra-legal, symbiotic rural-urban relationship is more prominent here than in any other area of the USSR.

Even the Central Industrial District, virtually the core of the country and the best developed area, exhibits the problems generally felt throughout the Soviet Union. The relative neglect of the agricultural sector is particularly evident here. It is a poor agricultural landscape. The inefficient distribution system is particularly visible here where millions make periodic treks to Moscow for goods and services. Newly developing industry and urban centers will improve the overall regional picture, but currently there are striking differences between burgeoning city and unkempt countryside.

THE NORTH AND NORTHWEST

This area is peripheral to the Soviet core, but in a changing and specialized sense of that term's meaning. Over time, both historical Russia and the USSR have changed economic orientation from an internal focus, emphasizing domestic development and self-sufficiency, to a focus on external trade and contact with areas outside its political boundaries. During the Stalinist era, the major goals of the country were self-sufficiency, internal development, and defense. At that time, this subregion took on the character of a backwater. The Volga-Urals, the Ukraine, Siberia, and Soviet Central Asia received the bulk of developmental funds in an inward-looking economy. In the eighteenth and nineteenth centuries, the North-Northwest had been a forward position, intermediate between the Russian core and western Europe. It received the innovations and technology of the outside world, diffusing them from its important contact position throughout Russia. As the capital and chief port, St. Petersburg (Leningrad) became the most sophisticated and technically advanced manufacturing center.

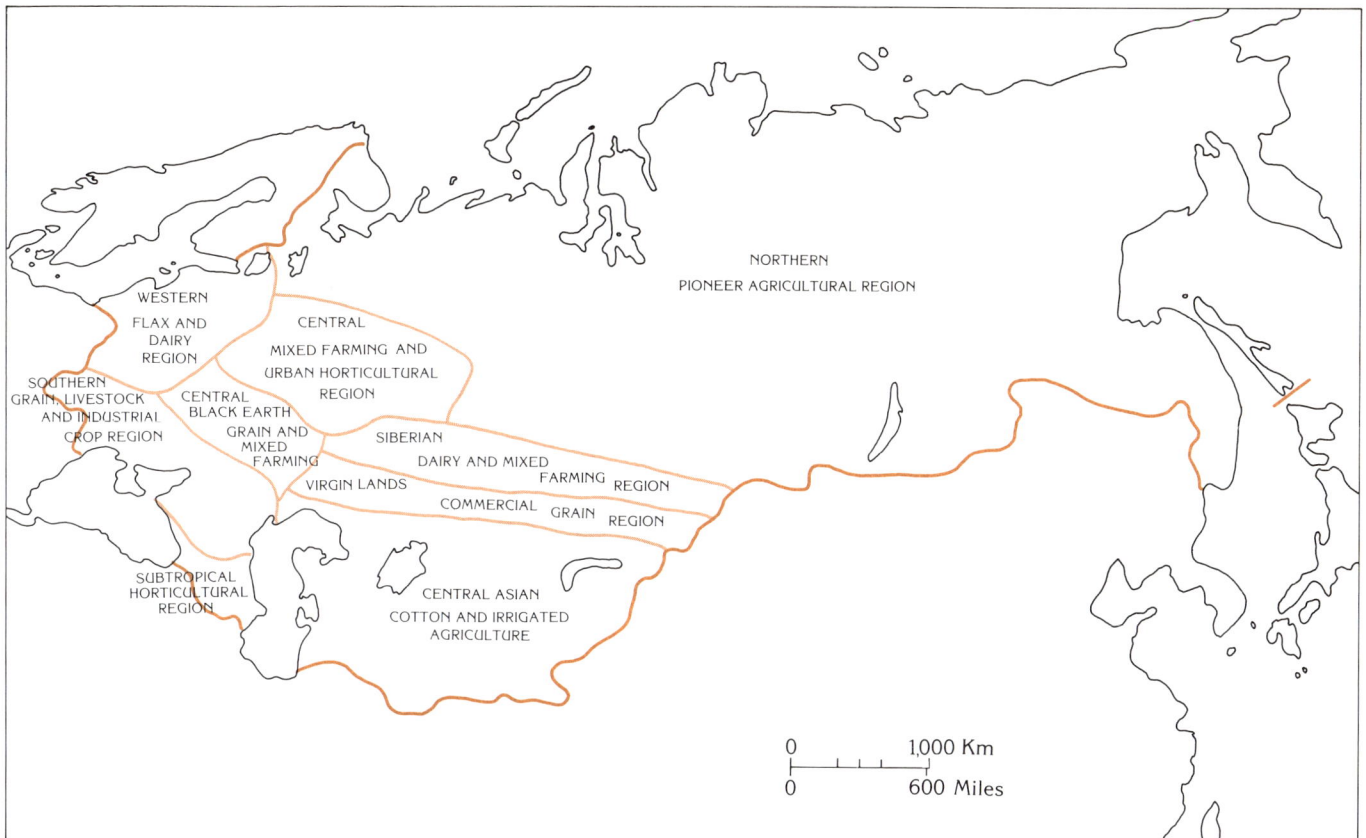

FIGURE 7–10
USSR Agricultural Areas. The USSR is attempting to increase both industrial and agricultural production and improve the quality and variety of food available, all within the natural limits imposed by terrain and climate. Agriculture continues as a weak spot in the Soviet economy, though there is little proof that an alternative land-tenure system would produce markedly better results.

Once again, the area enjoys an intermediate positon. The USSR has seemingly entered a new period of large-scale contact with the outside world. The growth and redevelopment of the Central Industrial District has bolstered this subregion's economy. The development of a Soviet merchant marine, fishing fleet, and large-scale export trade return it to a position of importance and growth. Facing the rapidly developing and relatively wealthy markets of both eastern and western Europe, deeply involved in Soviet contacts with the third world, backed by the redeveloping Central Industrial District, it once again flourishes on trade. Its economic positon has shifted once again from the periphery to the zone of contact.

Leningrad, with over 4 million people, is often described as Russia's most Westernized city. It is indeed a great cultural center, second only to Moscow. Located at the northern extreme of commercial agriculture, it suffers a deficit in food. The forests of its immediate hinterland, long overexploited, are no longer a major asset. Its port is icebound for three or four months of the year. It is a fuel-deficit city that has limited raw material resources in its immediate hinterland. It received little attention and investment during the Stalinist years.

The traditional industrial specializations of the city developed during the tsarist era with high-quality textiles, luxury goods, machine tools, shipbuilding, and engineering (both metal and electrical). These specialties remain the same, and Leningrad still accounts for some 5 percent of total Soviet industrial output.

The city occupies a series of low, marshy islands at the mouth of the Neva River. It is a pleasant city with an unpleasant climate, possessing a fine collection of architecture from the eighteenth and nineteenth centuries. It houses one of the world's great art collections in the Hermitage Museum.

The city uses almost 10 percent of the Soviet steel output. Most of it is produced at centers a long distance away. A moderate-sized mill in the area, at Cherepovets, produces high-quality specialized steels. Iron ore comes from fairly low-grade deposits in Karelia and the Kola peninsula, and coal is hauled from the distant Pechora basin, over 700 miles (1,100 kilometers) away. Production costs are extremely high, but the demands of the nearby Leningrad market supply an economic justification. The products of most Leningrad industry are of exceptionally high value, which aids in amortizing the high raw material assembly costs at Cherepovets and Leningrad itself. Leningrad still produces the highest quality machine tools, scientific and medical equipment, measuring devices, and industrial controls. Even its textile and clothing industries specialize in the highest priced items and the latest in fashions. Increasing amounts of the subregion's industrial production enter export markets. The manufacture of hydroelectric turbines is a specialty that serves the entire country.

The citizenry of the city possesses an elite mind set; Muscovites are still viewed as less-than-cultured people, and even factory workers pride themselves on dress, educational advancement, and other status symbols. Townspeople have perhaps the highest level of knowledge about things Western.

North and northeast of Leningrad there is an almost endless stretch of taiga broken by only a few agricultural clearings. Near to the city, the forest has been virtually destroyed through over-exploitation, but the quality (as well as the quantity) increases with distance. Lumbering, woodworking, furniture, paper, cellulose, and wood chemicals (including rayon fiber) are the chief industrial products of the area's towns. A few large cities concentrate most of the population in a district that is surprisingly heavily urbanized and very sparsely inhabited in rural areas.

Archangel, a port on the Arctic, was the chief Russian port before the conquest of the Baltic coast. Wood industries and fish processing are the dominant employers. Closed by ice for five months of the year, it still ships a reasonable tonnage. Murmansk, the second largest city in the north, is virtually ice-free because of the last vestiges of warmth from the North Atlantic Drift (the northernmost extension of the Gulf Stream). With over 350,000 people in an extreme physical environment, it handles much of the winter trade of icebound Leningrad and Archangel. Shipbuilding and a naval base supplement metal processing as industries. The metal-rich Kola peninsula contains copper, nickel, and iron ores, and large new iron deposits of a lower grade are being developed in Karelia.

South of the Kola peninsula, the forests provide a mediocre wood resource in Karelia, an area with a Finnish-speaking minority. New iron deposits, nearer to Cherepovets, are under development. Low-grade bauxite ores support a local aluminum industry. Along the southern edge of the taiga, the merciless exploitation of the forest has cleared vast areas, some of which are being developed for agriculture in a very marginal climatic area.

The Pechora basin, at the subregion's northeastern extreme, is gradually developing since a railroad was built to tap its resources. The loss of Donbas coal production during World War II spurred its rapid development, but local labor supplies are scarce and further expansion proceeds slowly. Reserves are large and high grade, but mining costs are high, and the distances to markets complicate the economic prospects. Oil and gas finds are beginning to outline what may be one of the world's largest deposits. Most of the production will be shipped to other areas and little development beyond mining is anticipated.

The Baltic Coast presents an altogether more prosperous picture. Poor in resources, but with a strategic location and excellent ports, it is developing a well-balanced and technically advanced industrial sector. Different in culture and blessed with excellent beaches, it has become a Soviet tourist mecca.

The Baltic Coast consists of three ethnic Republics and a conquered piece of former German East Prussia, now a part of the RSFSR. The three republics were independent from 1919 to 1940, and possess a high degree of national consciousness. The Estonians, long a Swedish vassal state, developed a prosperous commercial agriculture in a not-too-fertile environment. The Latvians occupy an area where Russia, Poland, and the Teutonic Knights long vied for control. Riga, the capital, has long been an important Baltic port and was once a great Hansa trade city. Lithuania's people, like the Latvians, speak a Balto-Slavonic language that is not a Slavic tongue. It was once a great empire stretching from the Baltic to the Black seas. The entire coast is peopled by advanced, highly educated and quite sophisticated peoples whose attitude toward the Russians is a mixture of patronizing tolerance and uneasy acquiescence to the reality of power.

Unlike the north and northwest, agriculture here has some bright prospects, though only about 40 percent of the land area is usable. Hay and fodder crops occupy the largest area in a dominantly dairying economy. Milk yields are high, and collectives specialize in cheese and butter for the Soviet and, increasingly, export markets. Livestock production receives major emphasis, and the high price of meat in the Soviet Union ensures regional farm prosperity. This part of the country uses the greatest amount of fertilizer per acre, and the Soviets have done much to improve drainage and the quality of pasture.

Peat and oil shale in Estonia are the only significant mineral resources. Small hydroelectric projects contribute to the energy base, but it is the oil and gas pipelines from the interior that have solved the energy dilemma. Oil and gas-bearing formations are being explored under the Baltic, but no results have been published. Amber, fossilized pine resin, has been exploited as a semiprecious gemstone since Roman times, and a considerable jewelry manufacture has grown up around it.

It is not the resource base but the ports and position that have stimulated industry. The interwar independent states had developed new industries and expanded old tsarist era investments. Textile, clothing, paper, furniture, and construction material industries were well developed before 1940. The Soviets sought to develop the area along the lines of industry emerging in New England in the 1950's. High value metal goods, electronics, and sophisticated consumer items became dominant. While wood products and paper are still produced in export proportions, their comparative importance has decreased. Quality is not neglected, and Baltic republic-produced appliances and furniture are in high demand.

Russians migrate into the Baltic republics in large numbers. They constitute 10 percent of the population of Lithuania, 30 percent of Latvia, and a quarter of the people in Estonia. Improved living standards are the draw, but the Soviet government also prefers to relocate Russians there in sufficient numbers to insure regional loyalty.

Riga, with almost a million people in its metropolitan area, is by far the largest city. It is a major port and contains a variety of industries. With a splendid medieval city at its center, it is one of the few Soviet cities with a significant night life.

Two Lithuanian cities, both once capitals, are major urban centers. Vilnius, the current and traditional capital, has a half million people. It is an important university city. Long the poorest of the three republics, Lithuania is industrializing rapidly and Vilnius is a major center for consumer goods production. Kaunas, the interwar capital, specializes in electronics, quality textiles, and machine tools; it is a major center of Soviet medical and agricultural research.

Tallinn, the capital and port of Estonia, functions almost as an industrial suburb of Leningrad. Association with the Soviet Union has been a mixed blessing, but the access to the large Soviet market is booming the regional economy, and trade with the West is increasing demand even further.

Byelorussia was an economic dead end until the last twenty-five years. The home of the original Slavs, it has not developed a clear-cut nationality, nor has it any history as an independent unit. What seems to make it different is its long historical association with Poland and Lithuania as well as its long isolation from the Moscow core area. The name, which means "White Russia," has no political connotation; it is an old designation from the ancient state of Kievan Rus, which was divided into "white," "red," and "black" portions as indicative of the color of the soils of each portion. This is white (Byelo) Rus, the land of ashen white, infertile podsol soils.

The area is a blend of moraine and swamp. Long an obstacle to invading armies, both Napoleon and the Germans (twice) suffered large losses on their retreats through the area. It is a classic Russian military move to force the retreating enemy back through the Byelorussian mire. This morass of bog and sluggish streams interspersed with gravel hills is hardly a fortuitous environment for agriculture.

Climatically, Russia begins here. This is the farthest westward penetration, in most winters, of the Siberian high with its intense cold and bone-chilling winds. The summer is cool and rainy, like that of northern Europe. A Byelorussian scholar once described the climate as "the worst of both worlds." Until recently, there seemed to be little in the way of mineral resources, and even the forest (of mediocre quality) was exceptionally difficult to exploit in this waterlogged land.

Bad climate, poor soil, and scattered farmland notwithstanding, the Soviets have attempted to develop a commercial farm economy here. The shortages of meat, nationwide, lead to the development of beef, hogs, and poultry as regional specialties. Vast deposits of potash supply a local source of fertilizer. Wherever limestone comes near the surface, huge open pit mines have been developed to give lime for neutralizing the acid soils. Huge amounts of fertilizer, most of it locally (and cheaply) produced, are applied to the soils. Both drained marsh and sandy moraine yield potatoes, which, together with skim milk, are fed to hogs. Smoked pork is a well-developed commercial specialty of the area. Flax for fiber is grown (25 percent of Soviet production), though hay and pasture are the dominant use of land. Poultry are fed on small grains and artificial feed in a U.S.-style broiler industry that is a recent innovation.

Several million acres have been drained over the last ten years. Yields of most crops exceed Soviet averages and the processed food products of the region are known for high quality.

More important than its agricultural progress is the area's industrial growth. The population was 90 percent rural in 1918, but by 1979, more than half the population was urban. Minsk, the capital, has a population of 1.4 million. It is the ninth largest Soviet city and has grown more rapidly than any of the other ten largest Soviet cities. Unlike Moscow, its growth is based on industrialization much more than the growth of administration or services. On the rail and highway routes to Poland, Vienna, and Berlin, it is often the first impression a foreign visitor receives of Soviet cities. New "skyscrapers" of up to twenty stories have been built to give the town an impressive skyline. Not to be outdone by Moscow, an ornate subway is being built. More importantly, not to be outdone by Poland, a series of high speed highways attempt to give the city a Western look.

Behind this new, opulent Minsk is an impressive array of industry. The first factories, dating from the 1920's and 30's, were truly Soviet in scope and production. Heavy dump trucks, giant excavating machinery, and tractors were the products of some of the world's largest factories of that type. But even industry has taken on a new look as Minsk produces a huge share of Soviet motorcycles, bicycles, and now, tractor trailers. Giant new appliance works turn out refrigerators and washing machines, often on foreign license. Electronics industries are developing rapidly, and Minsk manufactures increasingly sophisticated computers and hand-held calculators.

The dozen other major cities are far less varied in their industrial output. There are a half-dozen synthetic fiber plants making polyester yarn. Over one fifth of the polyethylene produced in the country is from Byellorussian cities located along the gas pipelines. Woodworking, cellulose, and paper industries are prominent in virtually all towns, but chemicals and electronics are rapidly overtaking older specialties.

This massive industrial and agricultural investment in Byelorussia represents a hybrid between the consumer-oriented industries of the Baltic coast and the chemical and machine emphasis in the Ukraine. It is a functional link in a westward-facing facade of the Soviet Union, quite deliberately designed to impress the arriving tourist or functionary. It is also very strong evidence of the shift in official Soviet policy to an outward-facing, export-oriented contact with Europe and the world beyond.

MOLDAVIA AND UKRAINE

This subregion is the richest agricultural area of the Soviet Union as well as its second most important industrial area. The combined mineral assets (including coal, oil, gas, iron ore, salt, mercury, manganese, potash, sulfur, uranium, and yet others) of the area are staggering. Without a doubt, it is the most productive part of the USSR. The subregion occupies most of the land settled primarily by Ukrainians and the Moldavian SSR.

The term Ukraine means land at the edge (in the context of the Russian core). The area was the original

Russian state (Kiev Rus) from the ninth through the thirteenth centuries. Overrun by Tartars, it became part of Lithuania (and then Poland) from the fourteenth and fifteenth centuries until the time of Peter the Great and Catherine the Great, when it was gradually absorbed into the Russian Empire. The peoples are descended from the Cossacks (Slavic paramilitary tribesmen) who farmed the land and acted as a defense against Asiatic tribes. Out of diverse beginnings, a Ukrainian nationality has developed. The nation has its own language, literature, culture, and mythology. The Russians have tended to treat Ukrainians as "almost equal" partners, hoping to minimize any separatist tendency. The nation declared itself independent in 1919–21, and there was some support for German-inspired "independence" during occupation. More people speak Ukrainian than ever before, and a strong cultural revival is apparently in progress.

The Moldavians are Romanians who use a cyrillic alphabet. With no physical or linguistic differences separating them from the Romanian province of Moldavia, the ethnic designation is largely a matter of convenience to the Soviet government, which reinstituted control over an old province (Bessarabia) of the tsarist empire when they reincorporated Moldavia in 1945.

Economic, rather more than cultural, similarity is the basis of regionalization. This is the old "bread basket" of Russia; it is also the Russian "southland," an area of warm temperature climate with an increasingly different type of agriculture from that found in the rest of the country.

Almost the whole subregion consists of steppe or wooded-steppe soils. Only the northwest corner and some isolated swampy areas have podzolized soils. The brown, black, and chestnut earths have a natural fertility that is legendary. The western half of the subregion is a series of low, but sharply dissected plateaus. East of the Dnieper, the country is a rolling plain except for the Donets ridge—a dissected plateau that contains the rich Donbas coal resource. In the Kuban, the farthest eastern portion of the subregion, the relatively level land is a piedmont plateau in the foreland of the Caucasus.

Climatically, the area is warm by Russian standards. Winter temperatures average from the mid-20's F ($-5°C$) to slightly above freezing in sheltered locations. Summers are long and hot; the growing season is generally six months or longer. Rainfall decreases from northwest to southeast, though the small area of Black Sea coast in Krasnodar Kray has heavy rainfall.

Agriculture is diverse. Traditionally, wheat has been the dominant crop, but corn covers an increasing acreage. After his visit to the United States in the mid-1950's, Nikita Khrushchev, impressed with the prolific cornfields of the Midwest, declared the Corn-Livestock Program in the Soviet Union. Most of the Soviet Union is too cold for the ripening of grain corn. Those areas sufficiently warm (170 days or more) are generally too dry for the crop. Many areas that meet both the moisture and growing season requirements lack the hot nights absolutely necessary to corn. Of all the areas still planted to corn, this subregion is the most productive.

One of the greatest problems of the subregion is the dessicating winds from the southeast. Shelterbelts and windbreaks have been planted to reduce this hazard and to help control wind erosion. A series of canals leading from the giant reservoirs on the Dnieper are used to irrigate an increasing acreage in the southern Ukraine; this will help to increase total and average yields as well as to stabilize annual production in this, the most drought-prone part of the Ukraine.

The level of mechanization is exceptionally high, even by Soviet standards. During the periods of time when the official goal of increasing production emphasizes improving regional agriculture (rather than pioneering new areas), the Ukraine is generally the recipient of the largest share of investment.

Crop-livestock patterns are regionally differentiated to match production with regional climatic and soil capabilities (see Figure 7–10). The northern podzol soil areas engage in dairying and hog raising. Potatoes are widely planted as feed, while hemp, hogs, flax, and low-grade tobacco are grown as cash crops. The central Ukraine is most typical, with vast acreages in wheat, sugar beet, and barley (as a second crop). Meat production is the most intensive in the USSR, with large herds of stall-fed cattle and swine. Sugar-beet pulp is used as animal feed, and oil seeds of various kinds are a major industrial and cash crop. The southern area emphasizes corn on wetter and irrigated lands, though wheat increases in acreage east and south. In the area beyond the Don, wheat and sunflower dominate, though corn acreages are high if yields are risky. In three areas, Moldavia, the Crimea, and the Transcarpathian Ukraine, a kind of market-produce agriculture is dominant. Vineyards produce table grapes and wines. Cooler and higher slopes are planted to orchards. Vegetables are grown for national fresh produce markets. Sheep tend to replace cattle and swine as the chief livestock. Population is exceptionally dense in these areas and labor intensive corps are favored. Farming tends to be more general in the western Ukraine and more highly specialized in the eastern and southern Ukraine.

The oldest industrial development is associated with the coalfield of the Donbas; major developments took place in the late nineteenth century, largely financed by foreign capital. Iron ore at Krivoi Rog, 150 miles (240 kilometers) to the west, and local limestone and man-

ganese ores within 125 miles (200 kilometers), meant that all raw materials necessary for the manufacture of steel were located in close proximity.

While the coals are of coking quality, mines are deep and seams are faulted, so that mining is expensive. Nonetheless, the cheap costs of raw material assembly made the Donbas a natural choice for investment in steel. Coking coal by-products and local rock salt deposits became the resources for a chemical industry, now augmented by natural gas from local and long distance sources. Lead and zinc ores, transported from distant deposits, are smelted here for use as alloys and in galvanizing.

Begun in the 1880's, this most important of all Soviet heavy industrial complexes has been growing ever since. Its relative importance has declined, but it has grown in absolute terms and continues to grow, if at a much slower rate.

The coal basin itself is the location of heavy industrial plants that manufacture pig iron, steel, chemicals, metal products, alloys, and machinery. The configuration of settlement (many towns of roughly equal size) is similar to that of the Ruhr in Germany. Coal, raw chemicals, rolled and bar metal, and semifinished products leave the area in the direction of other manufacturing areas—the Dnieper Bend complex, the Sea of Azov complex, and the cities of Kharkov and Rostov. The latter two locations are major metal fabrication and engineering centers located on crucial arteries leading to other industrial areas. The former two are complementary iron and steel bases that are near to iron resources.

The simplest relationships are those involving the iron deposits. The Krivoi Rog iron beds have given rise to a second heavy industrial center in the central Ukraine. Three large plants (see Figure 7–11) have been set up at river crossing points on the Dnieper. The fourth, built in the 1930's and expanded in the 1960's, is located at Krivoi Rog, virtually on top of the largest iron producing area in the USSR. The so-called pendulum kombinat was designed to utilize transportation to the maximum by shipping coal on return trips to the iron district for use in a new steel base there. The addition of electrical power as a resource (available from giant dams on the Dnieper) gave impetus to diversification. Dnepropetrovsk (1.1 million), Zaporazhye (800,000), Krivoi Rog (700,000), and a half dozen other cities of over 100,000 now form a full-fledged industrial complex. Zaporozhye is a major center of aluminum and automotive production. The rest are major centers of metal engineering, and all have an increasing role in the production of consumer goods. Kremenchug, a major center for heavy equipment manufacture and oil refining, is now scheduled for a new iron and steel complex and major investment in chemicals. Collectively, the

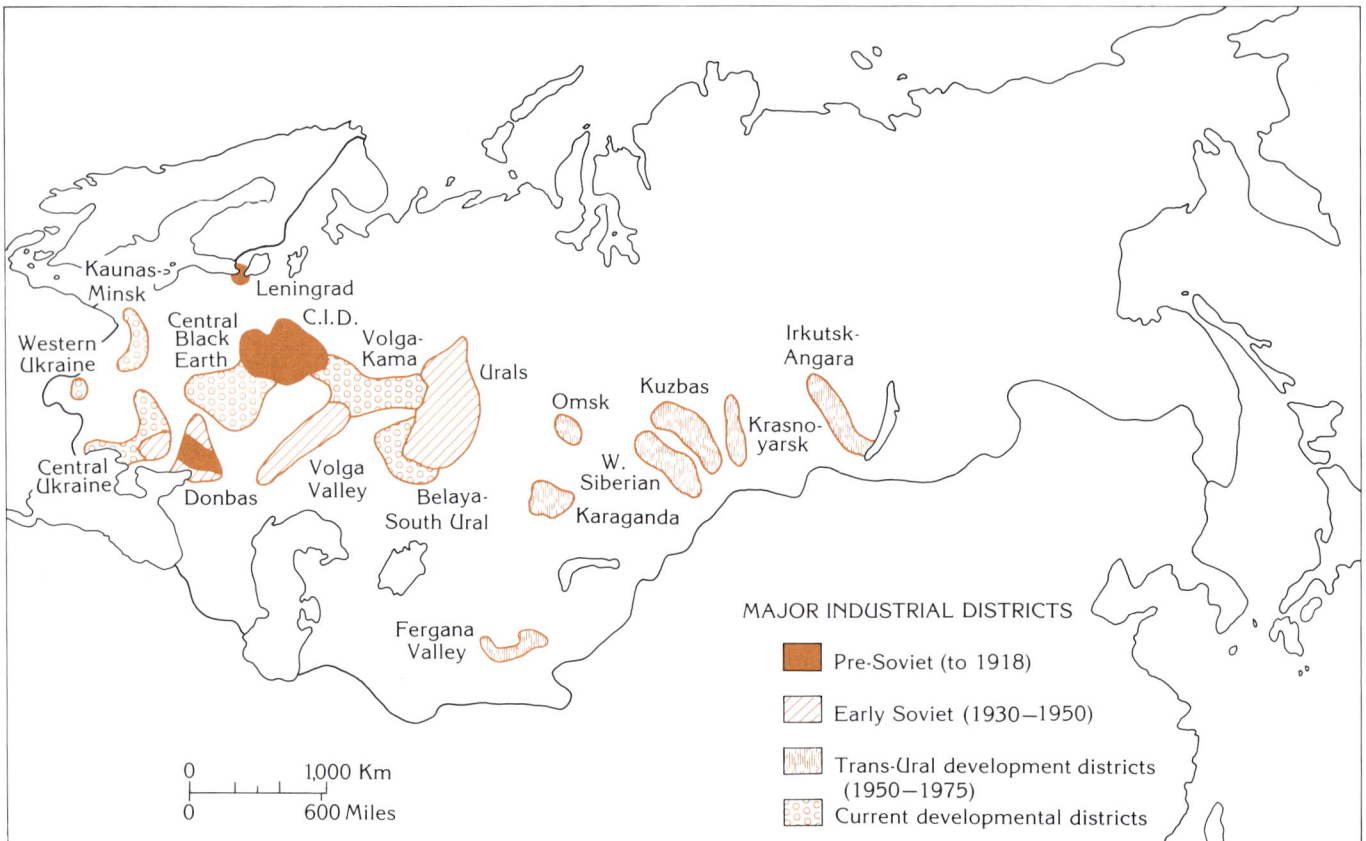

FIGURE 7–11

Industrial Development Districts. Soviet strategies of development have oscillated between national integration and regional self-sufficiency. Industrial development now favors expansion and modernization of such early Communist era raw-material-based industrial zones as in the Ukraine and European Russia.

production of the Dnieper Bend is equally as important as that of the Dongas.

In the 1930's, the Soviets built a new metallurgical and chemical base on the Sea of Azov at the port of Zhdanov. Iron ore (of low grade) was to move from Kerch on the Crimean peninsula to Zhdanov and the Donbas, while coal was to move in the opposite direction.

Kharkov and Rostov have functions similar to those of Cleveland and Chicago, though unlike those cities they are not themselves primary producers of steel. Kharkov is on the main rail route from the Donbas to Moscow, while Rostov is on the navigable Don River, with access to the Volga, as well as on main north-south rail routes. Both cities have excellent access to fuels, major Soviet markets outside the region, and a cheap, nearby supply of metals. As such they are major engineering centers of enormous scale. Kharkov (1.5 million) manufactures turbines, agricultural machinery, and transportation equipment, in addition to factory machinery of all types. Rostov specializes in tractors and combines at two mammoth complexes. As a major port, it builds and repairs ships and processes agricultural products imported from abroad as well as the

produce from its own rich hinterland. Both cities convert metals, chemicals, and semimanufactures into finished products on their way to the Central Industrial District, the Volga-Urals, and the Caucasus—Soviet Central Asia.

Kiev, located farther up the Dnieper at the contact between the black earth and mixed-forest agricultural zones, performs a series of functions more analagous to Kharkov as well as being the capital of the Ukrainian SSR. Founded in the eighth century, Kiev was a defensive site where the important trans-European, east-west route met the north-south water route of the Dnieper. As the chief point of control on early trade routes, it grew to enormous relative size at a time when London and Paris were villages. Destroyed in the thirteenth century by Mongols, it was not reincorporated into Russia until the eighteenth century. In the intervening years, it was an important administrative and trade center under the empires of Lithuania and Poland. It was the regional cultural center and was also an important religious center.

When added to the Russian domains, it became the center of the richest agricultural and, eventually, industrial domain of the country. It is now the third largest city in the

Soviet Union and receives an almost preferential treatment in investments as a means of insuring Ukrainian cooperation. Like Kharkov, it is the northern gateway to an important industrial district. While Kharkov specializes in metal engineering industries, Kiev is a model of diversity, manufacturing machines, clothing, textiles, chemicals, consumer goods, precision equipment, and processed food. It has a major tourist function, both internal and international. It is a center of nationwide importance, while Kharkov is largely a regional center.

Flanking these industrial agglomerations on either side are two districts with a greater dependence on agriculture. The western Ukraine and Moldavia constitute similar, yet complementary, halves of the western agricultural district. To some degree overpopulated (and intensively farmed because of it), this portion of the subregion developes slowly. Sugar beet and livestock replace grain as the main agricultural products. The less fertile northern portion is still heavily geared to the rye-potato-pigs and dairy pattern so characteristic of general farming in northern Europe.

The southern half of the district is warm enough (and wet enough) for growing corn for grain in most years. Intensive vineyard and vegetables production yield extra income for collectives engaged in general farming. As one travels south, the landscape takes on a Mediterranean aspect with its white homes with tiled roofs, walled farm yards, and ubiquitous patches of vineyards and orchards. It is a pleasant land with less severity than the steppes of the eastern Ukraine. The "southern aspect" is everywhere prominent, with shuttered windows and outdoor cafes, night-time crowds out strolling or shopping, and well-stocked coffee houses.

The resources of the area include gas (moderate quantities), some potash, a little oil, and some coal—hardly sufficient for an industrial base. Yet, new industrial enterprises are springing up. Small consumer industries, fertilizer works, and plastics plants dot the newer sections of the cities as the Soviets seek to modernize and develop their western frontier. Lvov (700,000) is an old medieval town that has dominated the western Ukraine since its founding. It was a great center of learning and the arts in the Polish Empire; its dialect became the standard Polish language. A largely Polish city, its rural hinterland was clearly Ukrainian in speech and culture. It is the marshalling yard and chief shipping point for Soviet trade with East Europe. A diverse industrial city, its plants have now begun to decentralize functions and develop branches in surrounding towns and cities. The home of an important university and a polytechnic institute, it is a center of technical research and development as well as a center of diverse engineering.

Kishiniev is its Moldavian counterpart. With a smaller hinterland, the city has something over 300,000 people. Wine, leather, and food processing are its chief industries. The local agricultural collectives emphasize quality produce for the best Soviet hotels and for export.

East of the lower Don River, precipitation increases as the Caucasus are approached. Corn again replaces wheat as the staple grain, though less successfully. Vineyards dot the countryside but wine making is a new function, producing largely cheaper table wines. In the river valleys, irrigated rice has become a prominent crop. Sunflowers brighten up the landscape of harvest season. The soil is rich and comparatively well-watered; the land conveys an air of prosperity. There are fewer people and less pressure on the land.

The area is fairly rich in raw materials. The coalfield of Donets extends beyond the Don though coal mining ends near Rostov. The hills of the Caucasus foreland are quite rich in oil and gas. Most industry is concentrated in Krasnodar (600,000), the regional capital. This city is a large chemical-producing center and a major factor in Soviet food processing.

Rounding out the subregion is a series of resort cities stretching along the southern foothills of Crimea and the Black Sea Coast. Both areas are backed by sheltering mountains that reduce winter wind and cold. Yalta in the Crimea and Sochi on the Black Sea are the most famous and best developed. With extremely narrow beaches, these resort areas appear intensely crowded. Busy all year, packed to overflowing from May to October, they are the premier internal tourist objective in the USSR. Beginning in February, sunbathers in fur coats huddle inside portable wooden windbreaks, soaking up the winter sun. By April, hardier types swim in the chilly waters of the Black Sea. By June, the beaches are a sea of humanity. Away from the centers of the tourist towns are the *dachas* (cabins) of the wealthier bureaucrats, officials, and factory managers—the so-called Red Bourgeoisie.

THE VOLGA-URALS SUBREGION

These two areas, one a river valley and the other a mountain range, are linked by complementarity of both resources and functions. Roughly contemporary in time of their development, they are both truly the products of the Soviet era rather than modifications of an inherited tsarist base. Both were recipients of major new investments from 1935 through 1970, and they were both chosen as sites for the relocation of industries evacuated from the European portions of the USSR during the period 1938–45, encompassing World War II. Growth has slowed since

1975 as major Soviet investments have now shifted to the western portions of the USSR and to new mineral-bearing areas in Kazakhstan and western Siberia.

Many compare the Volga to the Mississippi and the Urals to the Appalachians; in reality dissimilarities outweigh similarities. The Volga is icebound for much of the year; it flows the "wrong" way in terms of the delivery of raw materials to manufacturing and consuming centers and the return of empty barges. Its flow is erratic, and its utility is highly seasonal. Overall, it is a much smaller river than the Mississippi, and navigation was exceptionally difficult until greatly modified by dams and canals. Until the construction of the Volga-Don canal, it terminated in an internal sea located in largely desert country. In all these aspects it differs strongly from the Mississippi.

The Urals are superficially like the Appalachians in that they are a long, narrow range of folded mountains trending north-south. They function as something of a climatic and cultural divide, as do the Appalachians. They are old, not very high, and not much of a barrier to transportation—the same as their U.S. counterpart. However the similarities end there. The region's people have an income much higher than the national average. Unlike the Appalachians, the Urals are fuel poor yet very rich in metal ores, and their economic development has been much more diverse. Together with the Volga Valley they exert an enormous influence on the Soviet economy, enjoying a degree of national importance and productivity roughly comparable to that of the Great Lakes-St. Lawrence corridor within the North American Manufacturing Belt.

Climatic and vegetation zones are skewed northward on the drier, more continental side of the Volga. For historical Russia, Siberia began just across the Volga. Culturally, the valley is an ethnic mixture of Tatar, Turkic, and Finnic peoples scattered broadly through a Slavic matrix. The meeting of European and Asian cultures is everywhere evident.

Both agriculture and industry were late developing. Much of the lower Volga valley and the southern Urals were not put into crops until the 1930's. New cropland was again added during the Virgin Lands Programs (1954–60), and existing agriculture has been intensified through irrigation. It is a land of large, mechanized grain farms except at its northern and western fringes where more nationally typical mixed farming prevails.

The Urals were chosen to be the location of the "Second Metallurgical Base," essentially the duplicate of the Ukraine. With rich, high-grade iron deposits it appeared to be a natural choice. It was necessary to bring in coal from the Kuznetsk coal basin (Kuzbas) at the extreme eastern end of Western Siberia, a distance of over 1,000 miles. An intermediate coalfield was developed at Karaganda (see Figure 7–11) to reduce the long hauls, but high ash content of those coals made them of limited utility. Despite the constraint of fuel scarcity, the region did indeed become a metallurgical complex equivalent to that of the Ukraine.

Four large integrated iron and steel complexes form the nucleus of the Ural's industry. The steel produced, once destined for delivery to the Central Industrial District, is now used locally or in the Volga Valley industries as giant aircraft plants, rolling stock factories, a host of machine shops (large and small), and the demands of a booming petroleum-petrochemical industry (pipe, tanks, structural steel) consume virtually all the steel in an important array of secondary manufactures. Local bauxite ores are refined into aluminum and fabricated into foil, aircraft, kitchen utensils, and a host of other products. Copper refineries, now relying on ores from Kazakhstan, supply arsenals, wireworks, and factories for brass and bronze castings. Manufacturing has long since passed the primary industrial phase, though consumer goods industries are still poorly developed.

Four cities dominate production. The largest, Sverdlovsk and Chelyabinsk (both over 1 million), vie for regional leadership. Magnitogorsk ("magnet mountain") the site of a huge, though nearly exhausted, iron resource is almost purely a city of iron and steel manufacturing. Ores used there now come increasingly from lower-grade deposits at Kustanay, but the steel remains the cheapest produced in the USSR. It ships much of its production to Soviet Central Asia and Western Siberia. As a center for extraregional export, it has developed little in the way of auxiliary industry.

Chelyabinsk, in the south-central Urals, draws its raw materials from the South (Samarkand gas, Karaganda coal, Kustanay iron, etc.) and markets finished industrial goods to Soviet Central Asia and the southern half of European Russia. It is a major producer of armaments and aircraft as well as factory machinery. Sverdlovsk, the largest center of the North Urals, is a mirror image of Chelyabinsk. As local ore supplies deteriorate, it will come to depend on the low-grade, but enormous, iron deposits of Kachkanar. Its supplementary fuels (gas) will come from the new Western Siberian fields, and distant Kuzbas coal will likely be supplemented by production from the Pechora field to the north. The city possesses a full range of engineering industries and markets to the northern half of European Russia and the developing areas of Western Siberia, particularly the new oil and gas fields. Placed at a disadvantage when the Trans-Siberian route passed through Chelyabinsk instead, it will now receive new rail routes connecting it eastward to the new mineral boom areas of Western Siberia.

The cities of the Volga Valley reflect an even greater diversity. All are metal engineering centers, and most have major petroleum refining and petrochemical complexes. Their industries use large amounts of electrical power supplied by the series of dams lining the Volga. Each is a major transportation center where water, rail, pipeline, and roads of national significance meet and cross. In total, there are six metropolitan complexes of over 1 million inhabitants. Like most of the Urals' cities, they are largely the result of investment over the last fifty years.

The largest single urban complex is that located along the great bend of the Volga and centered on the city of Kuibyshev (1.6 million). Industry stretches in an almost unbroken line for thirty miles in either direction along the Volga. Kuibyshev is located where the Trans-Siberian crosses the Volga. As the center of the Volga-Urals oil field, its growth rate and regional importance are similar to that of the Dallas-Fort Worth area.

Kuibyshev boasts a rapidly developing consumer-goods industry. The most recent addition to the consumer function has been the Soviet-Fiat automobile plant at Togliatti, located at the northwestern end of the bend, producing over 750,000 vehicles yearly. A reflection of the city's importance is indicated by the fact that it was to be the provisional capital of the USSR if Moscow fell during World War II. The massive amounts of power generated here by a tunnel that short-cuts across the Volga bend has generated myriad electrochemical and electrometallurgical industries. Even though the Volga Valley has been scheduled for reduced industrial investment in the future, Kuibyshev is likely to continue growing at an impressive rate. It serves as the chief link between the European and Asiatic portions of the USSR.

Roughly equidistant from the Volga bend, respectively north and south, are the urban complexes of Kazan and Saratov-Engels. Kazan is by far the oldest and was the capital of the Tatar Khanate. Unlike many other ethnic groups, the Tatars readily assimilated to Russian language and culture and intermarried freely with the Russians. Less than half the population of the Tatar ASSR (of which Kazan is the capital) is composed of Tatars, but the Tatar physical traits are virtually omnipresent among the region's peoples. The city's location, near the confluence of the Volga and the Kama, its navigable tributary, has insured it an important trade function since early times. Leather, furs, wood-working, soap, felt, and decorative metalwork—all descended from traditional Tatar crafts—were its early specialties. The petrochemical industry has developed on a large scale, even though the city has no refinery. The Tatar ASSR is the largest oil producing area of the Volga-Urals oil field. Nearby, a series of satellites produce automotive components and trucks, so that Kazan is sharing in the rapid growth of the Soviet automotive industry.

The Saratov-Engels complex, with over 1 million people, is located where the Transcaspian railroad line, the

Oil Refinery in the Volga Valley. Huge oil refineries and related petrochemical complexes now line the banks of the Volga. These enterprises are based on local oil supplies from the vast and productive Volga-Urals oil deposits. (Courtesy of United Nations)

major route to the Virgin Lands and Soviet Central Asia, crosses the Volga. It is also a major crossing of oil and gas pipelines. Refining equipment and machinery for the chemical industry (including entire plants for export) are major specializations of the city's engineering industry.

Volgograd (once known as Stalingrad) is most famous for the great battle fought here during World War II. It represented the farthest eastward advance of German troops, whose intention was to cut the Volga, which transported vital oil from the Caspian fields, as well as lend-lease war equipment from the United States via Iran. The city produces rolled steel for the engineering industries of the other cities of the Volga Valley. It is a major producer of tractors and refines aluminum. A major oil and petrochemical complex, it is served by major pipelines. A nearby gas field and the great dam on the Volga supply virtually all power needs. Rapid growth in Soviet Central Asia and the Transcaucasus have favored its recent growth.

The remaining two "million cities" of the Volga Valley are based on raw materials. Ufa, in the autonomous region of the Bashkirs (a Turkic people) is a major refining and petrochemicals center that supplies plastics and synthetic rubber. It is second only to Kuibyshev in refining and petrochemicals. Perm, its northern counterpart refines oil as well, but is better known for its nearby coalfield, salt, and potassium deposits, which form the basis, together with local oil, for a large and diverse chemical complex. It is a major pulp and paper-producing center located on the edge of good timber resources in the north and not too distant from the now-developing forestry of Western Siberia. The planned canal from the Pechora to the Kama would increase the economic advantage of the city.

The Volga-Urals region is now a surplus producer of food, agricultural raw materials, fuel, minerals, and machinery. What was a pioneering area fifty or sixty years ago has now become a major industrial-agricultural complex fully integrated with the older centers of the European USSR. More, it serves as the link between the older portions of the country and the rapidly developing realms of Transcaucasia, Western Siberia, Soviet Central Asia, and the Virgin Lands. It is the supply base for Siberian and Soviet Central Asian development and the market for raw materials now produced in those regions. Increasingly, its industries generate exports for the burgeoning trade between the USSR and third world nations. Despite its inland location, its rapid growth, emphasis on oil and petrochemicals, and industrial orientation toward large-scale developmental projects and third world trade make it more analogous to the American Southwest and Gulf Coast more than to the Appalachians or the Mississippi Valley. This was Russia's "Wild East" until the twentieth century; its scale and specializations are similar to those of the U.S. southwest.

SOVIET CENTRAL ASIA AND THE CAUCASUS

Much, but not all, of this subregion is a desert. The Transcaucasian valleys and some of the southernmost oases of Soviet Central Asia are subtropical, but the bulk of the area has severe winters. A majority of its inhabitants are Moslems, but there are many important minority culture groups. It is exceptionally diverse and complex in ethnicity and culture, yet large numbers of Russians and other Slavs dominate in most of its cities. Intensive, specialized agriculture and the resort and retirement function are exceptionally well developed. Its unity as a subregion is based on its specialized agriculture, its recency of conquest, its pioneering quality, and its distinct cultural heritage.

The subregion includes the North Caucasus Piedmont, the Transcaucasian valleys, four of the Soviet Central Asian republics, the part of Kazakhstan south of (but not including) the Virgin Lands, the lower Volga, and the Caspian coastal zone. It has a population of about 50 million people, growing at a rate almost double the national average though a combination of high birthrates and strong net immigration. (See Figure 7–12.) Its economic potential is not yet fully developed.

It has long been the aim of Soviet planners to open up Asiatic Russia with its great storehouse of mineral and forest wealth and its underutilized agricultural potential. This subregion is a part of that Soviet frontier. Of the two parts (Siberia is the other) the plan has succeeded best here. Despite inducements and regulations of all kinds, Siberia is a land of net out-migration. The USSR west of the Urals continues to house some 70 percent of the total population. What shifts have occurred to the Asiatic portion have gone most largely to this subregion rather than to Siberia. Nowhere, however, except in a part of the North Caucasus and in the region around Alma Ata, do the Russians constitute a majority in rural areas. Despite Slavic in-migration, local birthrates are sufficiently high to insure the dominance of local ethnics.

The western portion of the subregion is one of the most culturally diverse in the world. The ancient Christian peoples of Georgia and Armenia exist side-by-side with Buddhist Kalmucks, a variety of Turkic- and Iranian-speaking Moslems, Russians and other Slavs, and the residues of Asiatic tribes. Occupying an isthmus between the Black and Caspian seas, elevations run from below sea level to over 18,000 feet (25,000 meters). The westward-facing valleys have a humid subtropical climate with heavy rainfall, while eastward-facing valleys are largely desert. Two higher areas, a northward-facing piedmont and a southward-facing plateau are severely continental with steppe-like rainfall patterns, severe winters, and hot summers. Even the physical habitat is diverse, and major changes occur over short distances.

Separating the two portions is the Caspian Sea, the largest lake in the world. Because of the withdrawal of water for irrigation, the damming of the Volga, and perhaps even climatic change, the area of the Caspian has been shrinking. Its level is now about ten feet lower than it was in the mid-1920's.

The eastern portion is a vast expanse of deserts surrounded on three sides by mountains or plateaus. The utility of the desert varies from rangeland suitable to sheep grazing to wasteland; a few areas are suitable to dry farming. Wherever streams fed by the glacial meltwaters from the high bordering mountains penetrate the desert, there is a dense settlement pattern, based on sedentary agriculture rather than grazing.

Cotton, fruits, early vegetables, and industrial crops are the most vital agricultural crops throughout the area. Most of the subregion's agriculture is dependent on irrigation. While isolated from the core of European Russia, it supports a large population that is economically linked to that core, fulfilling an important economic role as a supplier of raw materials. Links among the various parts of the region are sparse; even the Caspian does not act as a major intraregional link. Peripheral, geographically, it is in some senses central to the economy. Most of it was a

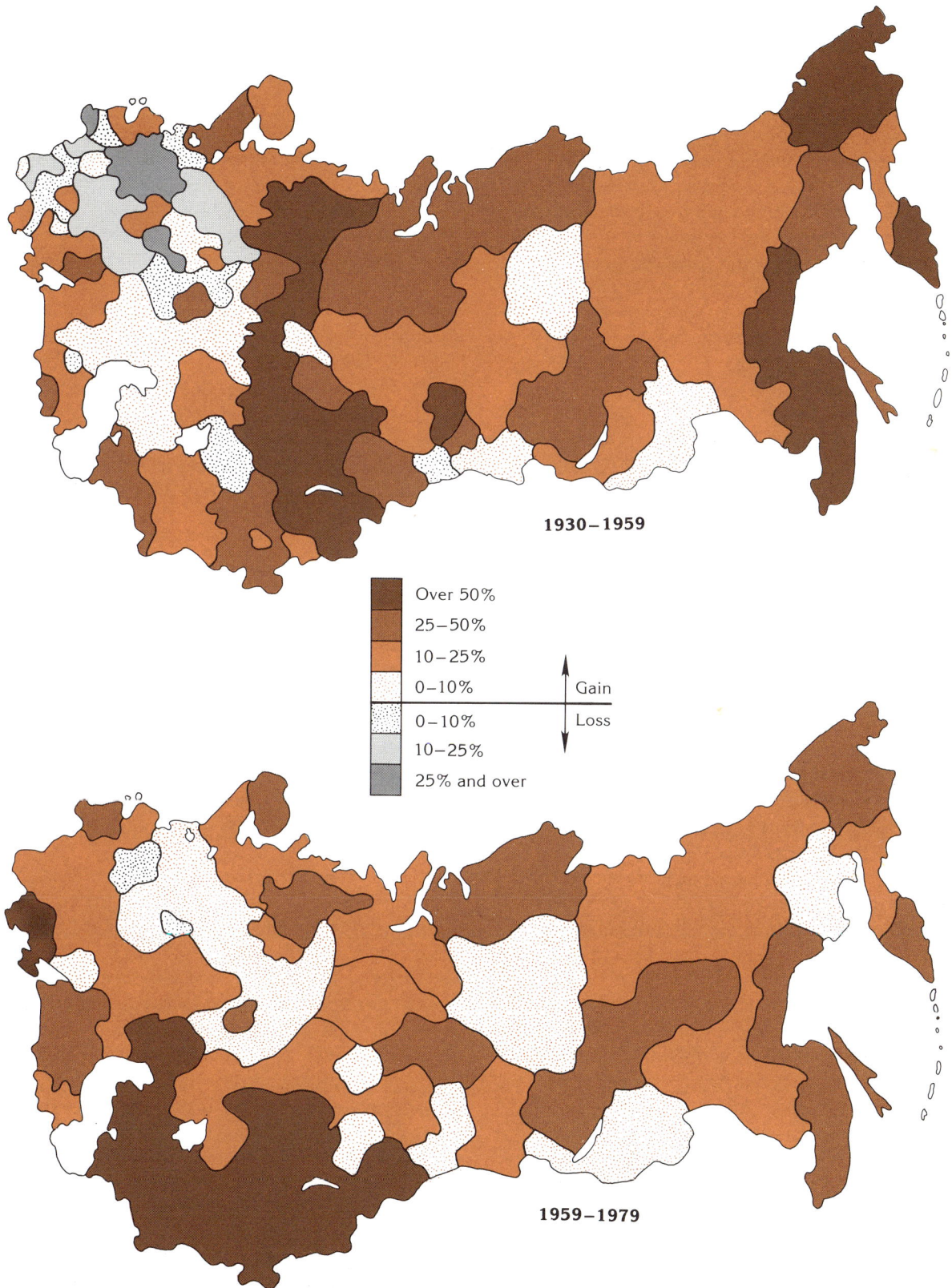

Over 50%	
25–50%	
10–25%	
0–10%	Gain
0–10%	Loss
10–25%	
25% and over	

1930–1959

1959–1979

FIGURE 7–12

Population Shifts in the USSR. Despite an array of special incentives, in-migrants to Siberia seldom make their stay there permanent. It is easier to find willing migrants to the warmer, drier regions and to the better developed Baltic republics. Individual initiative and rule-bending has resulted in a Soviet, muted but still evident, "Sun-Belt" movement similar to that of the United States.

part of various Mongol, Persian, and Turkish empires in the past. The origins of the entire area link it to the classical and ancient worlds, and trade among its various parts is more ancient than Russian control or the Soviet era. It is the Soviet Union's piece of the ancient world, its colonial extension into the vast reaches of Asia.

The western portion of the subregion was conquered between 1750 and 1830, though the lower Volga and north Caspian shores became Russian in the sixteenth century. The original aims of the conquest were subjugation of enemy tribes and the development of a buffer against Turkey rather than any economic gain.

The ethnic diversity is attested to by the range of autonomous jurisdictions. There are three republics (Armenia, Georgia, and Azerbaydzhan), eight autonomous socialist republics (a lower ranking), and several smaller autonomous oblasts. There are more than 20 million people in this portion of the subregion and probably less than 10 percent of the total are Russians or other Slavs.

The Caucasus Mountains are the physical core of the region, though their highest slopes are virtually uninhabited. Population is clustered in two parallel strips on either side of this empty core. It is more dense south of the mountains in the system of transverse valleys that run from the Black Sea to the Caspian. South of the Caucasus, the climate is truly subtropical, at least in the lowlands, but humid in the west while subhumid or even arid in the east. The second less dense line of population follows the northern foreland of the Caucasus.

The agriculture of this western portion is exceptionally diverse. Georgia specializes in tea, citrus, and tung (an oil-bearing nut). Large areas of vineyard and orchard occupy the eastern half of the republic along with silk culture and fine quality tobacco. Subtropical crops are grown on the slopes where the frost hazard is minimal. Rice and corn, the traditional grain crops, occupy the more frost-prone valleys, and livestock are pastured on the higher slopes during summer.

Drier Azerbaydzhan emphasizes irrigated cotton. Alfalfa and corn are irrigated in the dry lowland of the Kura River where some 800,000 acres (320,000 hectares) are irrigated. Even the Armenian plateau produces cotton, despite its shorter growing season.

North of the Caucasus, the climatic conditions are more continental. Wheat, sunflower, corn, and sugar beet occupy most of the land. Even here, though, sheltered areas are given to orchards and vineyards. The wetter western areas graze cattle, while drier eastern pastures support sheep. Irrigation projects serve to increase yields of the temperate crops grown there.

Agriculture (and settlement) decrease in intensity beyond the Kuma River. Wheat is replaced by the drought-tolerant millet, but most of the land is used for grazing.

Sheep, goats and camels are pastured on the thin desert scrub. A thin strip of irrigated land follows the Volga from Volgograd to Astrakhan, but the rest of the countryside is poor quality grazing land.

Oil fields dot the northern Caucasus foreland, culminating in the great oil field at Baku. Long the greatest oil producing region in the Soviet Union, it now accounts for only 10 percent of total production. Oil is found at thirty-two different levels, making this one of the world's most productive fields. Deep drilling has rejuvenated all these older fields to a certain extent. The Stravropol gas fields are among the largest and most productive in the country, and a smaller gas field produces limited quantities south of Baku. Local coal needs are supplied by two small fields in Georgia, and some yet-unexploited lignite deposits are scattered throughout the Caucasus. The Kura and Rioni rivers have great hydroelectric potential and several million kilowatts of energy are generated by these short, swift streams at dozens of small- and medium-sized hydroelectric stations.

Manganese and other alloys exist in fair supply. There are major lead and zinc mines in the area as well as minor deposits of copper, iron, and low-grade aluminum ore.

The major cities and industrial centers are the three republic capitals, the port of Astrakhan, and the mineral producing centers. Baku is by far the largest manufacturing center. The city's spectacular growth came with the oil boom, and its industry reflects that origin. Drilling equipment, floating docks, offshore drilling platforms, transmission pipe, bits, casings, pumps, and pressure control equipment are its major specialties. A second growing specialization is chemicals and machinery for their processing.

In contrast to the industrial jungle of Baku, Tbilisi (the capital of Georgia) is picturesque. Situated along a river gorge and containing a wealth of historical sites and religious architecture, it is one of the USSR's great tourist attractions. There is no heavy industry, but a wealth of consumer goods plants gives it a strong industrial structure. Silk, quality textiles, appliances, food-processing equipment, and excellent wines are representative of its high-value production from small, clean unobtrusive plants scattered throughout the city. Yerevan, the Armenian capital, specializes in aluminum and chemicals based on plentiful hydroelectric power. Textiles, wines, and fruit processing have now become secondary.

The Black Sea coast is lined with resort cities in what has become the Soviet riviera. High demand and limited physical area have caused the Soviets to begin developing a similar string of resorts along the Caspian, south of Baku. Cultural conflicts in this Moslem area have led to misunderstandings, and these resorts are often enclosed, self-contained units with curfews for the guests. Beyond the North Caucasus, there is only one industrial center of note, Astrakhan. The city was once the capital of a powerful Khanate of the Golden Horde, a great trading center on the overland routes to the Far East, and a bustling port on the Caspian. Today it is on the dead end of the Volga, and its port is so badly silted that ships must dock in an open water roadstead miles offshore. Still, it has importance as a port and an industrial center. With 500,000 people, it ranks fourth in size after the three republic capitals (with over 1 million population in each). Leather goods and fish processing (especially caviar) are major industries. Relatively stagnant until recently, it is expected to grow along with the increasing development of the resources of Soviet Central Asia. Various canal schemes, rail, and highway links are planned to enhance its position as the pivotal exchange point between Soviet Central Asia and European Russia.

The realm of Soviet Central Asia is equally as diverse and distinct as that of the Caucasus. Conquest by the Russian Empire came even later, covering the period 1824 to 1895—this was virtually the last frontier, as Russia sought potential cotton growing lands and a sphere of influence in Asia. Putting a stop to British expansion in this part of Asia was an immediate concern.

Most of the peoples speak a Turkic language. However, these languages are not closely related, and a variety of non-Turkic ethnics are found in the area. The Tadzhiks (and several other groups) speak Iranian dialects. Russian and Soviet occupation have increased the diversity. Slavs now constitute a majority in the Kazakh republic. Russians form 10 percent to 30 percent of the population in the other four republics. Volga Germans, and disenfranchised peoples of the Caucasus were shipped here during World War II; many remain. Changing economic opportunities have shifted native peoples from their homelands to other republics. Most republics have a dozen or so nationalities, but few are represented as separate political units.

The physical core of this part of the subregion is the vast desert at its center. Population is concentrated in a crescent along its southern and eastern edge, sandwiched in between mountain and desert. There are two additional ribbons of dense population along the courses of the Amu Darya and Syr Darya rivers that dead-end in the Aral Sea. Except in the extreme south and in sheltered valleys, the climate is severe. It has a great seasonal temperature range coupled with an equally great diurnal (daily) range. Far removed from the seas, it receives little precipitation except in the mountains. Closed off from the benefits of the monsoon by the Himalayas, at an enormous distance from both the Atlantic and Pacific, what little rain arrives is from the Atlantic.

Agriculture is overwhelmingly dependent on irrigation. Virtually every stream has been brought into use. This is the irrigated Soviet Cotton Belt, where cotton is rotated with alfalfa to maintain soil fertility. Some grain (wheat or barley) is dry-farmed in the foothills of the region's bordering mountains. Areas near urban centers specialize in fruits, vegetables, and melons. The bulk of the area is used for herding sheep; the traditional pastoral nomadism has, however, long since been collectivized. Recently, programs for crop diversification have been introduced, but cotton still dominates. Well over half of all Soviet irrigated cropland is located in the region.

Once thought resource poor, the area has recently become the recipient of important mining investment. Gas is the chief energy source. About 30 percent of all Soviet gas comes from the Soviet Central Asian republics; the chief fields are located near the city of Bukhara and in the Turkmen Republic. A series of small oilfields ring the Caspian Sea from the Emba River south to the Turkmen hills. Small fields have been uncovered in the Fergana Valley and near the Afghanistan border. New drilling in the Ural River area claims to indicate large reserves in that general area. Currently, Soviet Central Asia produces only some 5 percent of all Soviet oil, but reserves are thought to be much greater. The area has a moderate hydroelectric potential that has been developed as an auxiliary function of irrigation dams.

Copper, lead, and zinc are found in the mountains of the Uzbek SSR and in eastern Kazakhstan where deposits are huge. Copper is mined at Dzhezkazgan and near Lake Balkhash; the former area also mines manganese, the latter, molybdenum and tungsten. The lead deposits of the Upper Irtysh Valley are among the USSR's largest.

Industry has only begun to develop in Soviet Central Asia. Early plans to create a "second cotton textile base" in the area have not materialized. There is only one great industrial city, Tashkent, now the fourth largest city in the Soviet Union with about 2 million people. Textile machinery, construction equipment, and agricultural machinery are all produced there in addition to some cotton textiles. Food processing is growing rapidly, including the production and packaging of traditional native delicacies. As the developmental center for Soviet Central Asia, its industries are diverse and oriented to farming, construction, and machinery for processing locally produced raw materials.

A few major mineral processing centers have developed in the last thirty years. Chimkent processes phosphate into fertilizer and chemicals as well as being the site of the largest lead smelter in the Soviet Union. Dzhambul is a chemical center of note, while Leninogorsk in East Kazakhstan smelts a variety of metals from the region's rich polymetallic ores.

With industry in its embryonic state and mining in the early stages of development, what is attracting migrants to the area? Exotic cities, cloudless skies, and a superb back-

Irrigated Cotton Farming in Soviet Central Asia. Much of the Soviet Union has little or no agricultural utility. In an effort to expand acreage, to diversify production, and to attain self-sufficiency, the Soviet government has irrigated large areas of the warmer drylands. Once totally reliant on imported cotton to supply its textile industry, the USSR now exports its surplus of this commodity. (Courtesy of United Nations)

drop of snow-capped mountains form an array of attractions and amenities. Agriculture and construction are still the chief sources of employment for migrants, but tourism is rapidly becoming of equal importance. Soviet Central Asia also offers high wages and other inducements. Official policy has long been advocating decentralization of industry, and many government enterprises have placed expansion plants here to reap various benefits offered to managers and employees alike. "Footloose industries" with no great ties to raw material supply areas dominate. While the government planners set limits and guidelines, factory boards and administrative personnel have much to say about plant expansion and relocation. In effect, plant managers receive reduced government taxes on production, larger bonuses and other benefits for agreeing to locate in specific areas of government choice. They also receive larger raw materials quotas at artificially low prices to induce transfer to such frontier industrial areas. Given a choice between this frontier area or some part of Siberia, the choice is quite obvious. Thus textile, light engineering, pharmaceutical, and consumer goods industries have expanded into this region.

Space program facilities, climatic and agricultural research stations, and geologic exploration facilities have established a research component in the local economy. This serves to attract other research facilities that hope to share the brain power as well as the research results. Many firms manufacturing transportation equipment and communications devices have located research facilities in the area. This brain-powered industrial function is a relatively

new endeavor in the Soviet Union and its location could be virtually anywhere in the country. Traditionally a function of Moscow, it has begun to spread rapidly to the Caucasus and Soviet Central Asia.

The subregion then, is characterized by rapid economic expansion, growth and change. Railroad, highway, air, and pipeline linkages to the European USSR, are to be greatly increased. Tourism, health, and recreation are envisioned as large-scale regional functions, serving the entire USSR.

The subregion's prospects are exceptionally bright. Industrial specializations will be in high growth areas and consumer goods. Food production locally is adequate; more favored areas are geared to crop specialization and basic grain sources exist in bordering regions. The energy base is large and diverse, and the industrial function is growing. Most importantly, the area is perceived as having amenities, insuring a continuing influx of migrants to meet the labor requirements of a rapidly expanding economy.

Increased Soviet trade with India and the Middle East will undoubtedly benefit this area as well. Soviet irrigation technology, cotton harvesting machinery, hydraulic engineering, and dryland farming techniques are already being exported.

The pull of amenities cannot be underestimated. Even in a controlled, centrally planned economy, people and agencies find ways to circumvent directives or to subvert intent. Figure 7–12 indicates the strength of amenities to some degree. Outside the Soviet Far East, an area with a low original population base and intense investment in

Textile Embroidery Plant in Samarkand. Soviet investment has created an industrial base in virtually all parts of the country. Soviet technology and Central Asian traditions of design are combined in this factory's production, exhibiting the processes of acculturation in a polyethnic Soviet society. (Courtesy of United Nations)

military and mining enterprises over the last twenty years, all areas of rapid growth are associated with Soviet Central Asia, the Caucasus, the Black Sea shores, and Moldavia—the Soviet equivalent of the Sun Belt. The new oil and gas boom in Western Siberia may alter this pattern to some degree, but the announced decisions to exploit and ship out Siberian raw materials, rather than to develop the total regional economy, and to redevelop parts of European Russia would seem to indicate the contrary.

SIBERIA

The term Siberia implies cold, forced labor, political exile, imprisonment, and a host of other distasteful images. Yet its original conquerors saw it as a land of economic opportunity, replete with gold and furs. The Soviets see it as containing the resources necessary to making the USSR the world's most powerful economic unit.

Two schools of thought have evolved in the Soviet Union concerning the proper way to use Siberia's potential. One sees it as a colonial frontier awaiting colonization and settlement, viewing settlement as essential to development and integration with the rest of the Soviet Union. The other sees it as largely unsuitable for human habitation, envisioning minimal settlement sufficient to exploit the resources, with shipment of Siberian resources to the developed parts of the country. Both schools of thought have periodically been dominant as Soviet investment in Siberia ebbs and flows.

A few years ago, the Soviets spoke of the "Siberian Miracle" and proudly displayed the engineering achievements accomplished there. The latest census (1979) reflects a different picture; the Siberian growth rate (10.1

Housing Complex in the Soviet "Sun Belt." Despite the centralized nature of planning, droves of Soviet citizens are migrating to the Caucasus and Central Asia—a kind of Soviet Sun Belt. New investment to provide housing and employment must follow. (Courtesy of United Nations)

percent) over the ten year period barely exceeded the national average of 8.6 percent, despite the youth of the population and the much higher than average birthrates. While the population grows, there is a net out-migration, and growth rates in the Soviet "Sun Belt" are double and triple those of Siberia.

Only the Soviet Far East and the new oil and gasfields of Western Siberia showed truly high growth rates (see Figure 7–13). The already settled lands showed growth rates at or below the national average; the Virgin Lands (after remarkable growth in the 1960's), showed an increase of only 7.8 percent between censuses. The cherished Third Metallurgical Base (the Kuzbas) has a growth rate of a little over 1 percent, while the oldest and most favorable agricultural areas actually exhibited a small decline. The "miracle," for the time being, appears to be over, or, at least, taking a different form. The answer lies in the factors of distance and rigorous climate, particularly in terms of the way in which they increase the costs of development, production, and transportation.

Siberia as defined here includes the Virgin Lands and all areas north of them and east of the Urals industrial complex. The Virgin Lands are included, though located in part in the Kazakh SSR, because of their Russian ethnicity, economic links to urban areas of Siberia, and location adjacent to similar physical and agricultural areas across the Kazakh border. As conceived and implemented, the Virgin Lands ignored that border. Culturally, it has disappeared as the bulk of Kazakh tribesmen and the Soviet Central Asian economic-cultural area lie far to the south.

The region is characterized by the pioneering aspect of the lifestyle, the harsh continental climate that prevails throughout, and official (and pragmatic) recognition of the area as different from either Soviet Central Asia or European Russia. Physically, climatically and culturally, it is quite diverse. Along its southern border is a belt of dry or wooded steppe that continues almost unbroken, but ever narrowing, to the Pacific Coast. North of this is a narrow zone of birch woodland, also suitable for agriculture. Most settlement concentrates in this farming zone. Still farther north is a zone of boreal forest stretching to the tundra of the Arctic shores. This boreal forest contains over one fifth of the world's forest reserve and is very sparsely settled. It can be broken into four parts from west to east: the swampy lowland of Western Siberia, the East Siberian Plateau, the basin of the Lena River (another lowland), and the Pacific mountain belt.

The resource base is best described in superlatives. Siberia contains 90 percent of Soviet coal, almost two thirds of its natural gas, and 80 percent of its hydroelectric power. It contains the world's largest forest, largest single coalfield (one of dozens), and its second largest gold and diamond fields. There are considerable iron and tin reserves, large deposits of lead and zinc, and many rare metals. Oil has been discovered in promising quantities, and aluminum ores are now exploited. All this is known on the basis of limited geologic prospecting; what is not yet known may be even greater.

Enticing as this may be, production must be shipped out over the world's longest railroad or through the world's longest pipeline. Electricity generated there must travel the world's longest average distance over the world's longest power transmission grid. Siberia contains the world's coldest permanently inhabited city, the world's largest swamp, and its thickest permafrost outside Antarctica. It suffers some of the world's strongest winds and greatest daily and seasonal temperature variations. The resources are there, but getting them out is another matter.

The population is young, composed of fairly recent migrants and enormous numbers of temporary residents just out of school or college and repaying the cost of a free education by accepting duty in Siberia. Males still outnumber females in most areas, despite the remarkable reverse sex imbalance found in the rest of the Soviet Union. Because of this youth, birthrates are almost double the national average. Population concentrations follow the zones of usable agricultural land, essentially paralleling the Trans-Siberian railroad. Each point at which the railroad crosses a major river has become the site of a large city. A secondary (and much less dense) set of population concentrations parallels the major streams as far as the land is usable. In Siberia, access is virtually as important as natural environment in influencing settlement patterns. The whole of northern Siberia is sparsely populated. A few large cities exist in unfavorable environmental areas solely to exploit mineral deposits. Primitive tribes pursue a nomadic lifestyle in the forested areas between the rivers. Some areas with considerable agricultural potential are lightly settled because of the difficulties of access.

Ethnic Russians dominate in all cities and commercial farming areas to the point of virtual exclusion of other groups. Just over a million aboriginal ethnics reside in Siberia out of a total of 34 million people. Ukrainians and Byelorussians live in scattered colonies from the Virgin Lands (mostly in Kazakhstan) to the Soviet Far East. Indeed, Ukrainians are the second most numerous ethnic group in Siberia. Mongols, Turkic peoples, and Finnic tribes are next in importance. With the exception of the Kazakhs and Buryats, the Russians have met little opposition from native peoples in either the past or present. There have been culture conflicts, however. Collectivization of a tribally-owned herd of animals was simply a name change, since traditional groups had communal holding of both herds and grazing land. Attempts to induce nomads to become sedentary farmers is where the conflict lies. There is no well-developed nationalism among any of the groups except perhaps the Kazakhs.

Siberian migration patterns are enormously complex. Migration began immediately after the first portions of Siberia were acquired in the sixteenth century. By 1700 the Russians had acquired most of it, but it was treated less as an area for colonization and more as a land for hunting and trapping. Missionaries followed the adventurers and converted many native peoples to Orthodox Christianity. In the process, many became assimilated to Russian language and nationality, adopting a sedentary lifestyle at the same time, and thus becoming the first permanent agricultural settlers. Small villages grew at fur collection points and in conjunction with a string of defensive forts, much as in early North America. One can see many similarities in the process of settlement, but the comparison is far from exact. First, the frontier was more a series of nuclei strung out east-west rather than an advancing longitudinal line of settlement. Settlement grew out from these nuclei to form a zone at a later date. By 1650, a series of forts was established all the way to the Pacific at Okhotsk. Many of today's large cities are creations of the nineteenth and twentieth centuries, representing a kind of in-filling of the gaps in the original line of settlement. Irkutsk was founded in 1652, for example, long before Omsk (1703) or Novosibirsk (1893) located much farther west. Secondly, the dominant direction of movement in Old Russia was south, not east. The peopling of the Black Earth district, the Ukraine, the Volga-Don steppes, and the North Caucasus occupied most Russians from 1550 through the beginning of the twentieth century. About three times as many people migrated southward as those who migrated east of the Volga.

After the emancipation of the serfs in the 1860's, there was a movement to Siberia of landless peasantry seeking new farms. By 1900, southwestern Siberia and parts of adjacent Kazakhstan had been settled to some degree. The Trans-Siberian, completed in the 1890's, allowed conversion of subsistence farms to commercial production and connected the scattered settlements into a line. A second group of colonists was then attracted to the remaining lands with access to the railroad. New urban settlements, developed along the line further east, gave impetus to the development of agriculture in each urban hinterland.

World War I and the revolution interrupted the flow, but the new Soviet regime adopted a policy of Siberian development and the uniform spacing of industry nation-wide. Between 1926 and 1939, some 4 million people moved to Siberia. Most of this migration, however, was destined for urban centers, mines, construction projects, and new industries.

World War II brought the evacuation of millions from the Ukraine, Byelorussia, and western Russia. Industry was evacuated to the east as well. While most of these refugees (and industries) moved to the Volga-Urals area, some 5 to 7 million people went to Siberian destinations (approximately 30 percent of the total). Despite the fact that most returned, some 10 percent to 20 percent of the voluntary wartime refugees elected to remain in most areas. Deported groups were forced to remain until post-Stalinist rehabilitation (the Volga Germans had nowhere to return as their lands had been occupied by other wartime migrants). Sizeable prisoner of war populations remained as well; though many were repatriated in 1956 and 1959, some still remained until the mid-1960's.

The final large-scale migration came with the Virgin Lands Campaign of 1958–60. This program ploughed up and settled almost 100 million acres (40 million hectares) of steppes in Western Siberia and Kazakhstan. Of those entering the Virgin Lands, however, as many as one half may have come from the Urals or other parts of Siberia, themselves areas of labor shortage. Western Siberia actually suffered out-migration, although the neighboring Kazakh oblasts of the Virgin Lands grew by a startling 42 percent with a net in-migration of 700,000 people.

Migration to Siberia continues, but at a less than healthy pace. The new oil and gasfields (see Figure 7–13) and the mineral development and construction areas in the Yakut ASSR are currently growing rapidly, but small numbers are involved. At the same time, it is estimated that over 500,000 people left the eastern Urals between 1970 and 1979, while 200,000 left the Kuzbas, 100,000 the Virgin Lands, and almost a half million have left the Altai Kray (see Figure 7–12) over the last twenty years. Some of this population is undoubtedly recirculating to other areas of Siberia, but many have gone to the warmer climates of Soviet Central Asia or to the Ukraine and the cities in the west.

One Soviet study has estimated that Western Siberia lost over 500,000 people through out-migration between 1959 and 1970. Another study showed that over half the new migrants to the cities of Eastern Siberia left after three to five years. The lack of housing, little social life, poor services, and sheer boredom were the principle reasons given. Where are people going? It is difficult to get accurate statistics, but some assumptions can be made. Since the rate of natural increase in Moscow and Leningrad is minimal (at times near zero), and since increasing numbers of retired people from these same centers move to the country or to the warmer south, the moderate rates of growth exhibited in these large cities can only be accomplished by net in-migration. A net out-migration of 800,000 people (disregarding natural increase) would reduce the population of Eastern Siberia by 10 percent; if all those people migrated to the Central Industrial District, they would represent only a 2.5 percent increase in that district's population or a little better than 5 percent in Soviet Central Asia, which grew almost 30 percent during the most recent census period. As a result of these movements, most of Siberia remains an area of acute labor shortage. The recent trend toward capital-intensive projects in Siberia and shipment outward of raw materials has undoubtedly been influenced by this migrational pattern. In a given year, Siberia may lose over 10 percent of its natural increase through out-migration.

Agricultural patterns in Siberia have become stabilized in recent years. After a near disastrous flirtation with corn during the Corn-Livestock Program of former Soviet leader Nikita Khrushchev, most of the steppe area west of the Kuzbas is now planted to spring wheat, silage corn, and drought resistant sunflower. After a propitious start, crop failure became a recurring phenomenon in the Virgin Lands. Erosion and depletion of soil fertility through constant cropping without fertilization took their toll. Farms there now use increased amounts of fertilizer and land is fallowed in a short-cycle form of dry farming. Alfalfa is grown as a rotational crop and diversification with livestock is gradually taking place. Bad years are expected, but drought rarely occurs in the Ukraine and the Virgin Lands at the same time. They are complementary in terms of drought cycle.

Farming in Western Siberia is older, more general in nature and usually less risky. Normally, about one third of the land is in grain and the other two thirds in hay and pasture. Dairying is of great importance, in particular along the northern margins. Following the European pat-

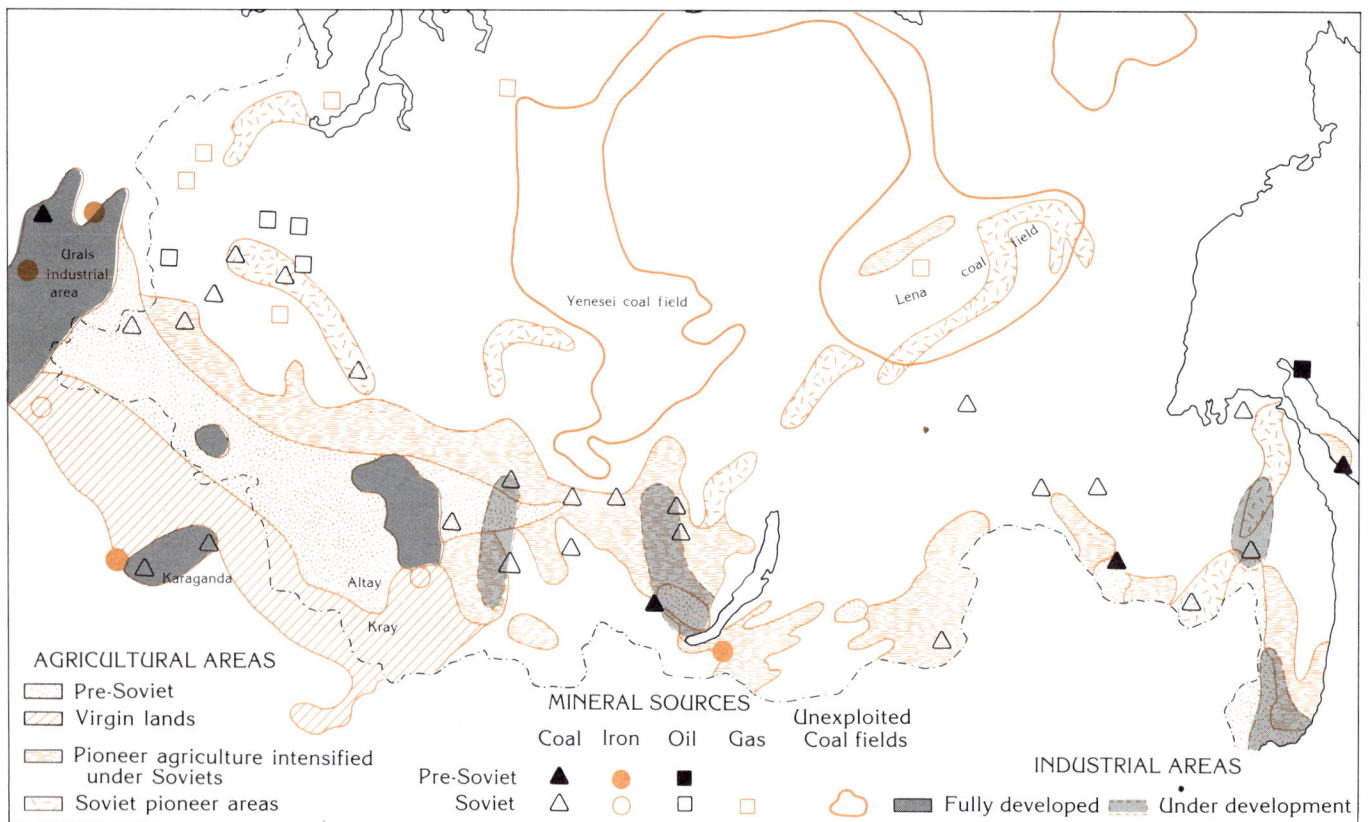

AGRICULTURAL AREAS
☐ Pre-Soviet
▨ Virgin lands
▨ Pioneer agriculture intensified under Soviets
▨ Soviet pioneer areas

MINERAL SOURCES
            Coal   Iron   Oil   Gas   Unexploited Coal fields
Pre-Soviet   ▲   ●   ■
Soviet   △   ○   ☐   ☐   ⬭

INDUSTRIAL AREAS
▨ Fully developed   ▨ Under development

FIGURE 7–13
Siberian Development Strategies. The vast, lightly developed resources of Siberia, so distant from the USSR's ecumene, present special economic development problems of extreme climate and permafrost. Transport development and complementary production-market districts are seen as keys to development.

tern, potatoes and hogs are important components of every farm's crop-livestock mix. Butter is a major export commodity. A series of canals for irrigation has been partially completed in an effort to increase yields and intensify production.

Agriculture becomes less risky, but less productive east of the Yenesei River. Where pockets of steppe exist, grain yields are reasonably high, but most of the area is more suitable to hay, dairying, and potatoes. Some of the steppes remain unfarmed, given over to grazing where native peoples have resisted sedentary agriculture. At the same time, the food needs of new urban industrial centers and mining towns are being met by using the poor soils of the boreal forest zone. Barley and other hardy grains, onions, cabbages, and potatoes are produced in environments with as little as sixty frost-free days. Costs of production are high, but lower than the costs of importing food. Sheep are grazed on the native steppes, while reindeer herds dominate in forested areas.

The southern part of the Soviet Far East has great potential. A drainage program for the Amur Valley could almost triple acreage in this food-short region, but Chinese cooperation is necessary. The Khanka lowland, bordering Manchuria, specializes in soybeans, sugar beet, hemp, fruits, and even some rice in a milder climate. Other areas grow wheat and barley if dry, oats or buckwheat if wet and cool, in the middle course of the Amur. Experimental agriculture is found throughout this chronic food deficient region. The most promising area is the Lena valley around Yakutsk, where northern prairie soils of good fertility are widespread. Quick-ripening wheat, rye, and barley are grown here in the short (sixty-to-eighty-day) frost-free season with its near round-the-clock daylight. Fur farming is a lucrative sideline on many area collectives.

Industry has developed along highly specialized lines in each portion of Siberia. Coalfields and transportation centers concentrate most factory production. Primary production, in particular raw material processing, construction materials, and metallurgy are best developed. The Kazakh republic's industry is located primarily outside the Siberian subregion as defined here. Nonetheless its industrial production serves the Virgin Lands. The low-to-moderate-grade iron and polymetallic ores of Kustanay have given rise to a growing mining industry. The only other significant industry in the Virgin Lands is the processing of grain and foods at Semipalatinsk and Tselinograd.

Industry is surprisingly diverse and well-developed in the southern part of Western Siberia. The western industrial district emphasizes oil refining, petrochemicals, wood in-

dustries, and synthetics. The main centers are Tyumen, Tobolsk, and Omsk, the second largest city in Siberia. The new oil and gas fields of Western Siberia are now the chief raw material source. The western two cities specialize in wood and chemicals, while Omsk specializes in synthetic rubber, plastics, machinery, and food processing. The area is one of the few textile and consumer goods producing complexes in Siberia.

The eastern district is also diverse but more oriented to primary production. The Kuzbas coalfield, the second largest Soviet producing field, is its fuel source. Giant thermoelectric power complexes feed into long distance transmission lines as well as into local plants. A dozen major industrial cities rim the edge of the coal field from Novokuznetsk (550,-000), the major iron and steel center, to Tomsk, a major university and research center beyond the mainline of the Trans-Siberian. Tomsk is now booming as one of the three refining and petrochemical centers (Tobolsk and Omsk are the others) for the new oil and gas fields to the north. Coke, chemical, and metal plants; foundries; and machine shops are found in town after town. Despite the impressive array of industry, however, the Kuzbas is a stagnating economic area that never fully reached its planned scale of iron and steel production. Increased regional demand from the burgeoning oil fields and chemical industries will undoubtedly lead to some expansion.

At the junction of two rail lines is Novosibirsk (New Siberia). It is Siberia's largest city (1.4 million) and the eighth largest in the USSR. Like Chicago, it is a large rail center adjacent to a navigable waterway and at the contact zone between a large coal and metallurgical base and a rich agricultural area. Here the semimanufactures and primary production of both halves of the region are finished and transhipped to other parts of the USSR. While concentrating on metallurgy and machine manufacture, it is really quite diverse.

Integrated by rail and pipeline and soon to be integrated by a canal and river system, these industrial centers are the capstone to a fully developed Western Siberia, perhaps the only portion of Siberia that really is.

Eastern Siberia, with elementary industry and less well-developed agriculture, is decades behind Western Siberia in its scope of development. Distance from market centers and rapid growth areas is the obvious reason as the area is not resource poor. Coal abounds; the small but productive Minusinsk basin is dwarfed by the Tunguska fields, the largest reserves in the USSR. The Kansk-Achinsk coalfields provide open-pit mined lignite from thick, shallow seams at the lowest cost per ton of any mine in the Soviet Union, while the Angara fields reach virtually to the city of Irkutsk. Dozens of small (but potentially productive) fields are scattered across the southern side of the entire region. Thus far, there has been little luck in the search for oil and gas, though rock origin, age, and structure are correct. Oil seeps and tar pits indicate that it is there; the great stores of coal in the area have resulted in only limited prospecting for oil and gas to date. The Yenesei River, which drains the region, has an incredible hydroelectric potential that has been moderately well developed over the last thirty years. Tens of millions of kilowatts are generated by six dams built to date, and others are planned for the future.

Fuel and power set the stage for the functions envisioned for this region. It is to generate cheap electrical energy to feed into the national grid. What is not exported is to be used in a series of energy consuming industries that employ little labor: paper and pulp plants, fertilizer plants, electrochemical works, alloy plants, and electroplating and aluminum reduction plants. Extensive area forests will supply raw material for saw mills and woodworking plants producing a third category of exports—all with the aid of great capital investment and little labor input.

Many large dams and plants have been built. Mining increases rapidly, and more industry is planned. Currently, each dam site boasts two or three major plants, but the two largest cities, Krasnoyarsk and Irkutsk, dominate the subregional structure. Both cities have machine-building industries that currently use steel and metals (other than aluminum) brought in from the Kuzbas. They are the chief developmental and supply bases for industrial construction; both are on the Trans-Siberian mainline. Krasnoyarsk (800,000) is more diverse; a major aluminum refining center, it concentrates on metalworking industries, though food and textile industries are present. Irkutsk is a major center for the production of chemicals, cement, and lumber. It supplies construction materials and some heavy machinery and equipment for mining and construction projects.

Blessed with coal of all grades and even iron deposits, there is only one small outmoded steel plant using scrap and imported pig iron. The huge dams and cheap coal, meanwhile, generate giant surpluses of power that must be used. The fortunate occurrence of low-grade bauxite in the area has produced the aluminum boom, and Eastern Siberia now surpasses the production of the Urals in the country's three largest plants. Local ores are not too abundant, and in the near future ores will have to be shipped in. Transportation costs are enormous, but production goes on and new plants are planned. Ores for the new facilities will come from as far away as Hungary and Africa, much of the distance by expensive overland transport. Exports are contracted for sale as far away as France,

Britain, and Japan—again in large measure by overland transport. Some exports of alumina and metal will be used to pay for imported aluminum ores in an ever-widening circle of costly, poor planning.

Norilsk, a mining center in the north, boasts large mines and a smelting complex that obtains gold, silver, copper, nickel, and a dozen other metals from local ores. A local gas field supplies fuel, and all goods and metals are shipped in and out over the Arctic sea route, which is usable for only thirty to sixty days a year. Despite difficulty of access, it is a highly profitable operation.

The industry of the Soviet Far East is far more limited in scope. Fish processing, forestry, mining, oil refining, and paper are the chief constituents. Vladivostok, with over 500,000 people, is the chief port and industrial center. Hampered by ice in winter, it has been supplemented by two outports to the east. Shipbuilding and repair, military and maritime installations, and a host of light industries add diversity to the woodworking and fish-canning plants that were its traditional employers.

Much cruder processing is done at Khabarovsk, a river port on the Amur where the Trans-Siberian turns southward to Vladivostok. A few chemical plants exist in a forest of lumber mills and woodworking plants. As could be expected, it manufactures chain saws and lumber mill equipment. There is a small consumer goods component. A half dozen cities of over 100,000 duplicate these specialties. Only Magadan, a port that is icebound for seven months of the year, is of note as the entrepôt for the rich Kolyma goldfields that rival those of South Africa's Rand.

There are a host of environmental problems that limit Siberian development, yet the Soviets have shown themselves able to deal with most of them. They have developed special mining, pipeline, and construction technologies to deal with permafrost and have been pioneers of heavy duty trucks that can withstand extreme weather.

The problems of development remain distance and lack of local outlet for production. The Soviets are willing to make the largest investments to develop a plant, area, or region—yet it is not the initial cost, but the ongoing transportation costs that render them often unprofitable. The other great problem is labor supply. It is the lack of willingness to labor under such conditions at any price that proves to be the problem.

SUMMARY

Developmental strategies in the USSR have always favored development on several fronts and in several places at the same time. Small projects are mixed with giant "monuments to Communism." Transportation and housing are often inadequately planned, but quality engineering, design, and multipurpose functions are present in many Soviet industrial and developmental projects.

Much has been written about Soviet goals and aims in international affairs. Its world view is well known and its ambitions have brought it into conflict with many other regions and states.

DEVELOPMENTAL STRATEGIES

Large-scale regional planning has undergone several phases. Originally, strategic defense considerations favored a uniform dispersal of industry. The shortcomings of such a plan, with no regard for raw material supplies, soon became obvious. It was followed, bureaucratically, by overcorrecting the perceived fault. Raw material sites were to become the exclusive location, ignoring marketing costs or the advantages of market location. This was replaced by economic-administrative regions, each of which was to become as self-sufficient as possible within the regional framework. Not without fault, this has become the regional planning model within practical limits.

On a large scale, the Soviets recognize fuel and energy, other raw materials, food supply, iron and steel, construction materials, and secondary manufactures as the chief components of any regional economy. Normally a raw material source or energy supply is identified first. Mining is the first economic endeavor. Transportation is supplied primarily to facilitate the development of the mining venture and the ultimate export of the minerals to other regions. Next is the construction base to produce building materials for further development. No development is envisaged without a metallurgical base of basic structural steel. Where possible, local fuels and iron ores are used, regardless of quality, supplemented by higher quality materials brought in (when necessary) from the nearest possible alternative source of supply. The next step is local food supply. As with all agriculture, generally, it has a lower priority than basic industry. After the basic supply of staples has been developed, diversity is encouraged within the particular climatic limitations of the region. Lastly, industrial crops are introduced as a source of alternative income for post-pioneering collectives. Prior to industrial diversification, the transportation network is improved and integrated to stimulate intraregional exchange, labor movement, and economic integration. Cities are assigned a hierarchical level and supplied with a suitable range of outlets and functions. In the final phase, industry diversifies. When full development is reached, a high-quality specialized line of production may be added—one which is marketed primarily outside the region. After full development is reached, growth takes place largely through expansion of existing facilities unless new resources are discovered.

This plan is followed in a leap-frog fashion. For example, the Urals were developed as an iron-mining area first. To facilitate mining, the rail net was extended to all deposits first and only then were new links built to the European market. In an effort to secure local fuel, lignite, charcoal, and low-grade coals were used to supplement high-grade coking coals brought in from the Kuzbas—the object was the creation of a large metallurgical base built in the early 1930's. Major cement and brick industries, plus forestry, were developed in the mid-1930's to allow construction of housing for the expanding labor force and to build new industrial structures. Local materials were used entirely. By the late 1930's, a food supply base was created on the east bank of the Volga, followed in the 1940's with diversification of the industrial base. In the 1950's, one saw the in-filling of the Volga economic region, first developed as a food-supply area. It reached full development by the mid-1970's.

Each increase in distance from the European base, however, has resulted in a longer time scale. Western Siberia developed its energy sources in the late 1930's, its metallurgical base in the 1940's, its food supply with the Virgin Lands (settlement and staples 1955–1965, diversification somewhat later), and its industrial diversification in the last decade.

Eastern Siberia is still in stage one, developing fuel and raw material resources. The metallurgical base should follow soon, though as yet unannounced. The BAM (Baikal-Amur Mainline Railway) line (see Case Study) may be looked upon as necessary to mining development and the ultimate transportation of ores to that coming metallurgical base. The Soviet Far East, still exploring for its ultimate resources, is in an embryonic stage.

However one may disagree with the Soviet ordering of priorities, the developmental strategy has proven largely workable. In the 1920's and 30's, the Volga-Urals areas were still a frontier. By 1979, they had reached full maturity and become areas of relatively slow growth. The automotive industry of the Volga Valley, constructed during the last decade, represented the final developmental phase of industrial diversification, much as the aircraft and appliance industries of the Urals signaled that area's attainment of full maturity in the 1960's. Until that stage was reached, both were rapid growth areas. They have now begun to stagnate, as development pushes eastward and Western Siberia prepares for its final attainment of maturity over the next decade or two or three, depending on official investment policy.

TENSIONAL RELATIONSHIPS

Today's Soviet citizen recognizes two different levels of enemy. One is the general enemy of "capitalism," an alien economic system. As the chief proponent of that system, the United States is singled out as the representative enemy force. That is the lesson of Marxist theory. On the other hand, history has taught the fear of the nearer, more immediate enemy, with the threat of invasion from the east or the west. The Mongol Hordes and Napoleon's Army differ little in the common mind from the perceived threat of today's China or a reunited Germany. World War II is still vivid in the minds of the Soviets, and the theoretical enemy, while never out of sight, is viewed as a lesser, more distant threat.

Gradually, the Soviet Union has come to terms with Germany, but insists on a continuance of separation. Western European unity is not necessarily perceived as a larger version of the same threat. The two most immediate threats now appear to be a restive, changing China whose potential grows with development and a restive, changing Poland whose actions might lead to internal struggles within the Soviet Union.

THE SOVIET WORLD VIEW

The Soviets long viewed the world through the prism of Marxism, expecting a worldwide revolt of the working classes. Its failure to materialize in the 1920's led to a great deal of theoretical rationalization at home and an isolationist attitude toward relationships with other areas. All non-Communist governments were viewed as a threat. Isolation gave time for the country to develop its internal structure and to consolidate effective political control over the world's largest state. Participation in World War II was viewed as a temporary expediency, a means to survival while waiting for the ultimate class conflict to arise. The Soviets would not have entered that war without being attacked. They saw it as a war among imperial powers in which they should take no part. Many theoreticians and Marxist philosophers thought it would result in the "class struggle" as time wore on.

At the end of World War II, the Soviets sought to surround the USSR with a series of "friendly" states; this could mean only "Communist" states, since by definition, all capitalists are the enemy. In purely political terms it sought buffers. Only when China was added did Soviet success result in new goals—the piecemeal change in the balance of power. The United States, for its part, saw containment

as the only alternative short of all-out war—the creation of a series of military alliances with states surrounding the USSR to prevent its further ideological expansion. Stalin saw it only as a new stage in the struggle—the new status quo was accepted and the Communist bloc, not just the USSR, was what had to be contained.

Khrushchev (premier, 1958–64) viewed the world in the same terms philosophically. By simply stating that unless a state were allied to the United States, it was a "friend" of the Soviet Union, he sought to alter the world balance and inadvertently recognized the third world as a separate entity. Economic competition and skillful diplomacy replaced brush wars as the means for expansion; the Soviet Union had reached a level of development where it felt that it had much to lose in an armed conflict of major scale. It had reached equality in power.

Attitudes since have varied with shifting leadership. There has been a broadening of the internal power base since the death of Stalin in 1953. One man can no longer decree without consultation. Changes in leadership within the USSR have resulted in changes in foreign policy. Vietnam gained little for the Soviets, who may have seen it more as a means of outflanking China than any "next step" in piecemeal world conquest.

The arms competition between the United States and the Soviet Union has moved to advanced technological levels and into the realm of space. Cuba is more a useful thorn in the side of the United States than a strategically located ally. African nations have changed ideologies and allegiance swiftly, and there have been no lasting loyalties or commitments to the USSR as a result. What began in Yugoslavia in 1948 bore fruit in China in the mid-1950's as Communist ideology became a matter of national interpretation rather than uniform dogma.

Straight-forward world conquest and full-scale armed conflict have lost any appeal they may have once had in a nuclear age. Generations of Russians used to an improving living standard find ideological purity outdated and unrealistic. World power is less appealing if it will cost great sacrifices, and it could result in total destruction. The Soviet Union has opted for equality, at least for the time being, in order to face other threats—either internal or from other Communist states that are not necessarily as "friendly" as their acceptance of an economic system and ideology might imply.

case study
THE BAM (BAIKAL-AMUR MAINLINE RAILWAY)

A major new development effort is to be the long-planned, oft-started but never finished BAM project (see Figure 7–14), from Ust Kut on the Lena River to Komsomolsk on the Amur River—an auxiliary route to the Trans-Siberian mainline. It is hoped that it will also be a developmental entry into the Lena River basin as well as a route for the export of surplus Siberian raw materials and semi-manufactures to Japan. Construction is to be done by the Young Communist League in a widely ballyhooed program reminiscent of the colonization of the Virgin Lands. It is to be this decade's (and this generation's) great monument to Communism. As with all such great projects, it is to be multipurpose and the "final answer" to the dilemma of Siberian development.

Its original aim was defensive—building an alternate line in case the Trans-Siberian were sabatoged. In the second revision of the plan, it was to alleviate the overburdened Trans-Siberian, which was jammed with long distance cross-hauls of raw materials, finished goods, food, and supplies shuttling between Siberia and European Russia. In this reincarnation, it is purely a response to economic needs.

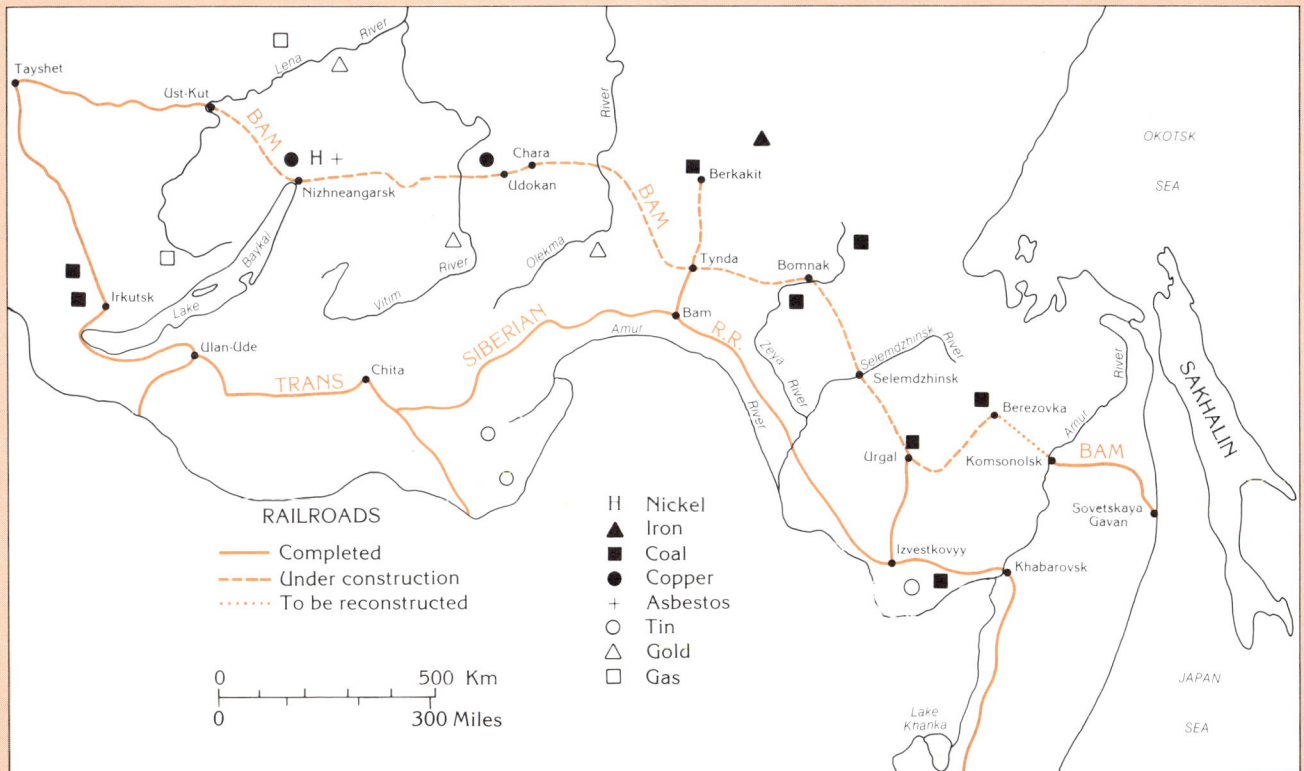

FIGURE 7–14
BAM (Baikal-Amur Mainline Railway). This railroad project, long in the planning stage, is designed to relieve part of the burden of heavy use on the Trans-Siberian line while tapping resources in the regions north and northeast of Lake Baikal. A bypass of part of the Trans-Siberian may have strategic significance in the event of a dispute with China.

The Soviets intend to use it as a "land bridge" for containerized freight moving between Japan and Europe. It is to supply an alternative to pipelines for the movement of oil in tank cars. It will provide access to known nickel and copper deposits en route. It will open up new coalfields whose production will be entirely exported. It will open up timber reserves and perhaps even attract Japanese joint investment capital. Ultimately, it will develop the Soviet Far East as a raw material emporium for Japan and other parts of the Far East. It would aid Eastern Siberian development by placing it squarely in the middle of the European and Japanese market as well as between two well-developed surrounding regions. It would increase Russian settlement in an area disputed with the Chinese, while creating a local market for the planned increases in food production from the Arctic prairies of the Lena basin. It would even stimulate a railroad car industry that could use all that surplus aluminum. Now, could anything be better?

The problems of construction are fierce. The line would be over 1,900 miles (3,000 kilometers) long, and the distance to the coast, with connecting lines, is over 2,500 miles (4,000 kilometers). About a third of the route is to be constructed over permafrost, which buckles and heaves when vegetation is disturbed. The line must cross five major rivers (including two of the largest and widest in the USSR) and myriad streams, gulleys, and gorges. It must also cross or tunnel through a half dozen major mountain ranges and many smaller ones. Four tunnels (at least) and over two hundred bridges and trestles will have to be built. Equipment and materials will have to be shipped in where virtually no roads exist. Some of the countryside along the route is virtually unexplored. The area involved is earthquake prone and subject to landslides, mudslides, and winter avalanches. Temperature extremes with ranges of over 100°F must be withstood by workers, material, and equipment. The project will need one hundred thousand laborers in an area of acute labor shortage; there is no housing available for them. Virtually all food must be flown in by helicopter. Materials used in its construction will undoubtedly delay the completion of other projects. Does all this give pause to the government or the Young Communist League? Never!

All workers get BAM T-shirts and shoulder patches. Foreign students are invited to share in the joys of socialist labor for free room and board and an end-of-contract vacation. Newspapers and T.V. run an endless array of encouraging ads.

The project was announed in 1974, and construction was to begin in 1976 with a completion date of 1980. The completion date has come and gone and BAM remains unfinished. Labor has always been in short supply and housing has been inadequate, despite some innovative plans. Skilled workers and engineers often refused association with the project despite wages almost double their home area base pay. Many youth quickly lost their enthusiasm. After months of wilderness living in crude facilities, they simply went home. Despite extensive permafrost studies, the route (and structures) have not been able to withstand the summer thaw. There have even been reports of sightings of abominable snowmen.

The BAM inches along a little at a time. The projected cost has long been overrun, and inflation moves it upward daily. Communist centralized planning, however, is accustomed to long-range goals with even longer-range payoffs; the BAM is a good example of this kind of thinking.

REVIEW QUESTIONS

1   What is the nature and scope of the USSR's "minority problem"?

2   Why is the Soviet-Chinese border tension a threat to the stability of some of the ethnic republics and autonomous areas?

3   How logical are the *kombinats?* What was their original intent?

4   In what sense was the Virgin Lands Program a calculated risk? Has it payed off for the Soviets?

5   What is the real nature of the supposed Russian "drive for ice-free ports"?

6   Why are the great Siberian rivers said to flow the "wrong" way? What are the implications of *wrong?*

7   What are the potential environmental problems associated with the "river reversal" scheme?

8   By what means do the Soviets attempt to control in-migration to Moscow and some other attractive cities? Are they successful?

9   Criticize the view, popularized by the Soviets, that they took power in a backward, preindustrial society and then rapidly developed it.

10 Why was the creation of a new capital at St. Petersburg (Leningrad) a classic example of a political-cultural reorientation?

11 Contrast the present economic specializations of Leningrad and Moscow.

12 What qualities of the physical environment enhance the agricultural potentials of the Ukraine?

13 Briefly describe the Soviet version of the "Sun Belt." Do its migrational and functional characteristics resemble those of the U.S. Sun Belt?

14 What engineering and environmental problems have been associated with the great dams on the Russian portion of the European Plain?

15 What is the nature of the "minorities problem" in the USSR?

16 How do the Urals and the Appalachians compare in terms of mineral resources, effect on transportation, and nature of their industrialization?

17 Why is Soviet Central Asia expected to develop faster than the alternative "Frontier area," Siberia?

18 While the Russian drive eastward to the Pacific can be compared to the American drive westward to the Pacific, what significant advantages did the Americans experience as contrasted to the Russians?

19 What are the industrial raw material assets of Siberia?

20 Critically evaluate the potential versus the cost of the BAM (Baikal-Amur Mainline Railway). Would such a project likely be undertaken in a capitalist or mixed economy?

21 How has the Soviet "world view" changed over time?

SUGGESTED READINGS

1 GEORGE DEMKO and ROLAND FUCHS, eds., *Geographical Perspectives on the Soviet Union.* Columbus: Ohio State University Press, 1974.

2 W. GORDON EAST, *The Soviet Union.* Princeton, N.J.: Van Nostrand, 1963.

3 CHAUNCEY HARRIS, *Cities of the Soviet Union.* Chicago: Rand McNally, for the Association of American Geographers, 1970.

4 DAVID HOOSON, *A New Soviet Heartland?* Princeton, N.J.: Van Nostrand, 1964.

5 ———, *The Soviet Union: People and Regions.* Belmont, Cal.: Wadsworth, 1966.

6 W. A. DOUGLAS JACKSON, *The Russo-Chinese Borderlands.* Princeton, N.J.: Van Nostrand, 1962.

7 ———, ed., *Natural Resources of the Soviet Union: Their Use and Renewal.* San Francisco: Freeman, 1971.

8 J. F. KARCZ, *Soviet and East European Agriculture.* Los Angeles: University of California Press, 1967.

9 DONALD KELLEY, KENNETH STUNKEL, and RICHARD WESCOTT, *The Economic Superpowers and the Environment: The United States, the Soviet Union and Japan.* San Francisco: W. H. Freeman & Company, 1976.

10 PAUL LYDOLPH, *Geography of the USSR.* New York: Wiley, 1977.

KEY TERMS

- perception
- dynamic adaption
- cultural amalgam
- monsoon
- oil bridge
- shatterbelt
- client state
- cultural hearth
- ethnocentrism
- Oriental intensive agriculture
- commune
- capital-intensive
- Great Leap Forward
- takeoff
- tribute territory
- marche capital
- outport
- successor state
- entrepôt
- irredenta
- high-value-added

8

EAST
ASIA

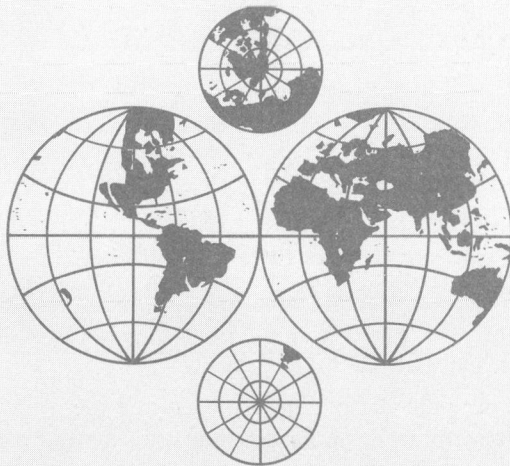

PROLOGUE: CHANGING WESTERN PERCEPTIONS OF CHINA AND THE EAST ASIAN REGION

Our **perceptions** of any particular part of the world change repeatedly over time, as witnessed by the quickly changing American attitudes towards the People's Republic of China. After the diplomatic initiative of the early 1970's, the onetime enemy of Korean War days suddenly began to be looked upon as a potential friend. Long thought of as an alien, unfriendly society, the People's Republic of China suddenly became the focus of U.S. interest. The media took full advantage of this opportunity to satisfy Western curiosity about the world's largest nation and oldest continuous culture. A door long closed was again open. Chinese-made consumer goods became more apparent in U.S. markets; Chinese styles began to influence U.S. fashion, and that nation's customs and traditions became a focus for attention. The resumption of diplomatic relations presented new opportunities for trade, as U.S. business anticipated the opportunity to enter new markets and explore the possibilities of a potential new source of supply.

Western cultures have long been intrigued and fascinated by the Orient. Roman Europe had a small scale but significant trade with ancient China and, ever since, much European economic and political energy has been directed toward developing trade with the Orient. It is alleged that when Marco Polo was asked, on his deathbed, if he wouldn't confess that his account of the Khan's empire was grossly exaggerated, he replied, "I never told the half of it!" Europeans were impressed as trade expanded and they gained access to China's stock of wonders. Chinese technology (through the seventeenth century) clearly equalled or even surpassed that of Europe. In ceramics and metallurgy, Chinese craftsmanship was vastly superior. The rapid expansion of trade relationships with the Orient was perhaps an important impetus to Europe's Renaissance.

By the nineteenth century, European imperial ambition ultimately focused on the China trade as European military technology forged ahead of that of China. Various European nations sought territory and/or trade concessions from the then-weakening Chinese Empire. The British controlled sea routes and acquired Hong Kong; the Russians developed overland routes, climaxing in the Trans-Siberian Railroad and its Manchurian extension. The Trans-Siberian Railroad attempted, in a sense, to outflank British naval power and to secure some of the lucrative China trade to the Russians.

The emphasis on the China trade has shifted focus from China's once-superior consumer wares and luxury items to China's potential as a purchaser of Western manufactured goods and a possible supplier of oil and other raw materials. There was great excitement in America after the Nixon visit to Beijing. China was perceived as a vast, underexploited market. To a consumer-oriented economy like that of the United States, it became the sparkling prospect of nearly a billion consumers. Imagine selling a pocket calculator to each of 25 million students. The sudden "opening" of the People's Republic of China (PRC) can be compared to the famous "opening" of Japan in the 1850's. The prospect for significant shifts in world trade patterns, alliances, and alterations in the balance of power are just as high now as in the 1850's.

THE DISTINCTIVENESS OF THE REGION

One of the five great population concentrations of the world, East Asia is clearly separated by large, nearly empty areas from other major clusters of settlement. It is distinct in language and culture from any of the rest of the world's regions; and, despite an often surprising internal diversity, it has a degree of unity that few other regions possess. It has been one of the world's great centers of innovation; it has developed several major civilizations, which diffused their knowledge and technology over a large area of Asia—creating a high degree of regional uniformity long before it came into contact with the Western world. The impacts of cultural interaction with the Western world were two-way, as both cultures exchanged ideas and technology. Just as Western culture was enriched, yet remained distinct, in the process of culture contact, so the culture of East Asia remained separate, even if some Western ideas, inventions, and behavior patterns were adopted.

HISTORICAL-CULTURAL CHARACTERISTICS

China has been the clear, long-term cultural leader for the East Asia region. A distinctively Chinese culture and a well-established state appeared about 1500 B.C., though the origins of that culture may have even predated 2500 B.C. Chinese tradition and legend begin with the "Yellow Emperor" (about 2700 B.C.). The dynamic Chinese culture had profound impacts on China's neighbors in this region. China dominated the Korean peninsula culturally and politically for scores of centuries before Korea was first invaded by the Japanese (who sought, thereby, to gain military access to China) in the sixteenth century. Korea was clearly a satellite of powerful China for much of its history until the late nineteenth century. Its alphabet, clothing styles, religion, and art show strong Chinese influences, though their origins and language are clearly not Chinese.

Much of Japanese culture was adapted from, or at least strongly influenced by, China. Art, religion, technology, architecture, and other elements of culture flowed from the mainland to the islands of Japan, much as Britain and Ireland received cultural impact from the continental cultures of Europe. Although the spoken languages are quite different, the Japanese adapted Chinese ideographs to express Japanese in written form. Japanese are still somewhat in awe of China as a civilization; they regard it the way western Europeans might honor their Greco-Roman, Egyptian, and Babylonian antecedents. Buddhism came to both Korea and Japan via China, and Confucianism came to strongly influence both other nations. There is a much greater degree of cultural uniformity than in most other world regions, at least in its more general aspects.

ECONOMIC CHARACTERISTICS

Westerners commonly underestimate the extent, longevity, and scale of Chinese maritime contacts. There is little doubt that trade did function to bond the region over centuries. Similarities among tools and household items used throughout the region show the export of Chinese technology as well as goods. The emphasis on paddy rice culture in all regional economies is another feature held in common, though not all parts of the major units grow rice. Each of the region's major states have had to deal in some way with aggressive European colonial ambitions and trade initiatives. Each nation's modern industrialization has been powered to a degree by cheap, disciplined labor during its early stages of expansion.

PHYSICAL CHARACTERISTICS

China is rather neatly defined by physical barriers of impressive scale. Mountain ranges, including the world's highest mountains, and extensive deserts provide what earlier geographers would have categorized as *natural boundaries*. Rugged and lightly populated, these physical features have been used intelligently by regional political and military leaders.

REGIONAL DISTINCTIONS

The preeminent distinction is the unique blend that has resulted from the combination of an ancient, non-Western culture with a **dynamic adaption** of Western technology. In the past, Chinese culture spread to Korea, Japan, and

Taiwan at the region's peripherae. (See Figure 8–1.) Those areas later received the greatest impact of Western technology, selectively adopted portions of it and modified it to fit the realities, limitations, and potentials of East Asia and Oriental society. Now this **cultural amalgam** spreads from the peripheral areas to the ancient Chinese core. A resurgent modernization, begun in Japan, now reaches toward China through South Korea, Taiwan,[1] and Hong Kong. China and North Korea also received a degree of Western influence via their political contact with the Soviet Union. Thus, the Western impact has been received from both sides, from two widely varying interpretations of Western culture. There is no doubt that the Japanese version of the amalgam has been more economically successful, and the opening of China to these influences will likely produce even more adaption and change. The region, then, is characterized by a dynamic combination of Western and Eastern culture; by a productive blend of Western technology and Eastern human energy and disciplined drive. Marxism and capitalism have both had input and impact, yet the resulting regional interpretations of both are decidedly different from their original forms.

As long ago as 2 A.D., the population of China was officially tabulated at 59 million, comparable to the population of the entire Roman Empire at the same time. Japan and Korea had proportionally dense populations early in their histories as nation-states. These relatively dense populations have tended to impress Westerners as *surplus* or overcrowded, a perception frequently noted by the East Asians themselves, and one related to various governmental policies and goals for at least several centuries.

A result of the large numbers of people in lands with many physical barriers to cultivation (steep terrain, flood-prone valleys, climatic extremes) was the evolution of an agricultural system emphasing the most productive use of *land* rather than the most efficient use of *labor*. Labor was plentiful; quality cultivable land was relatively scarce. Intensive agriculture is prodigal with human energy in order to maximize production of food. Traditional Oriental agriculture thus came to be more large-scale gardening than the commercial, highly specialized agriculture that developed in North America, for example, in the nineteenth century. There, the emphasis was on maximizing the efficiency of the farmer through extensive use of machines rather than on concentrating human labor on small patches of land for maximum production per areal unit.

The same prodigious use of cheap labor influenced early patterns of industrial production. The adoption of labor-saving machinery now raises the potential for indus-

---

[1] The Nationalist Chinese government fled to the island of Taiwan (at one time called Formosa) and established there the Republic of China. This state is known familiarly as Taiwan.

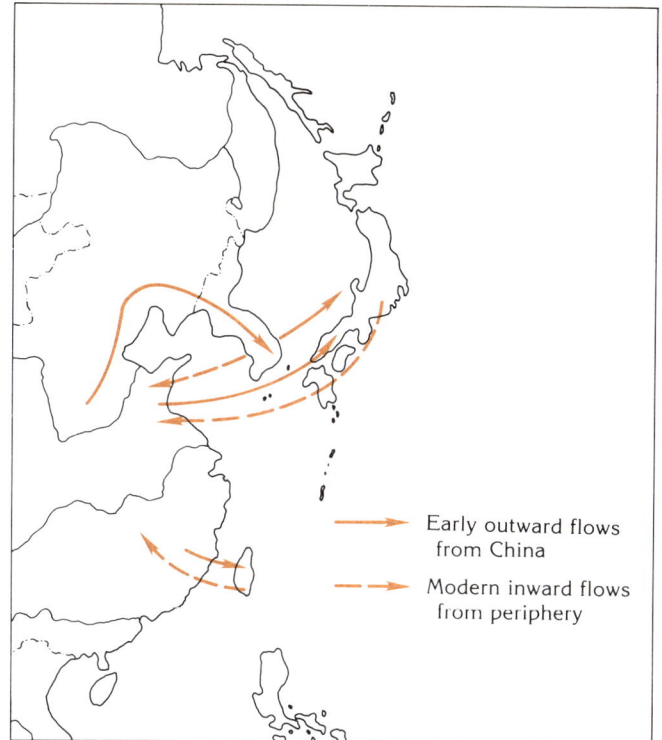

FIGURE 8—1
Core to Periphery, Periphery to Core Flows of Culture-Technology. China's historic core is, in a sense, the cultural hearth of the entire region. Culture flowed outward, historically, but in recent times, the flow of technology has reversed as the more industrialized periphery sends new technology to the core.

trial production in the region to an astronomical level. Japan has essentially achieved this potential. Taiwan, Korea, and Hong Kong are well on their way. The advent of this modernization of industrial production in the PRC is just occurring.

THE PHYSICAL FRAME

The densely populated core area of East Asia is clearly delimited by its physical surroundings. It is often thought of as the well-watered area of level land in East Asia, yet this is a false assumption. Topography was early negated as a factor in delimiting human settlement patterns, as terraced slopes—the product of human labor—conquered one of nature's limitations. Human energies modified the natural environment with regard to water supply through irrigation and drainage, but with a slightly lower degree of success. The boundaries of the area of dense settlement have in a sense been determined more by the capabilities of Oriental society to control and shape nature. Dense settlement ends at the point where it becomes impractical to extend sedentary agriculture any further; yet within this densely settled core, the limitations of slope and water supply have obviously been surmounted by human endeavor. Oriental society has expanded well beyond the most favorable natural environments, creating a favorable environment where none existed in nature. This is perhaps the greatest single significance of the physical frame in the East Asian region.

TOPOGRAPHY

The landforms of East Asia are extremely complex, ranging almost the entirety of geologic history and type. Most of the region is mountainous; much of it has not been adequately mapped or explored by geologists. About 80 percent of China is comprised of mountains and plateaus; this predominance of highlands also holds true for Japan, Korea, Taiwan, and even Hong Kong. China is rimmed by a series of mountain ranges, from the rugged mountains and high plateaus that lie to the south of the Siberian Plain, through the massive Altai and Tien Shan along its western borders, to the Himalayas and Tibetan Plateau of the southwestern border reaches and the steep mountains and plateaus of Yunnan in southcentral China. (See Figure 8–2.)

The prevailing "grain" of China's topography is east-west, including much of its mountain rim frontier and the smaller, but significant, Tsingling range, which is an important climatic divide within eastern China. The Korean peninsula resembles a giant fault-block, or chunk of earth's crust tilted up along its eastern (Pacific Coast) edge with a more gentle, though deeply eroded, back-slope down to the Yellow Sea to the west.

Japan and Taiwan are part of a series of great arcs of islands running off the mainland shores from the Kuriles

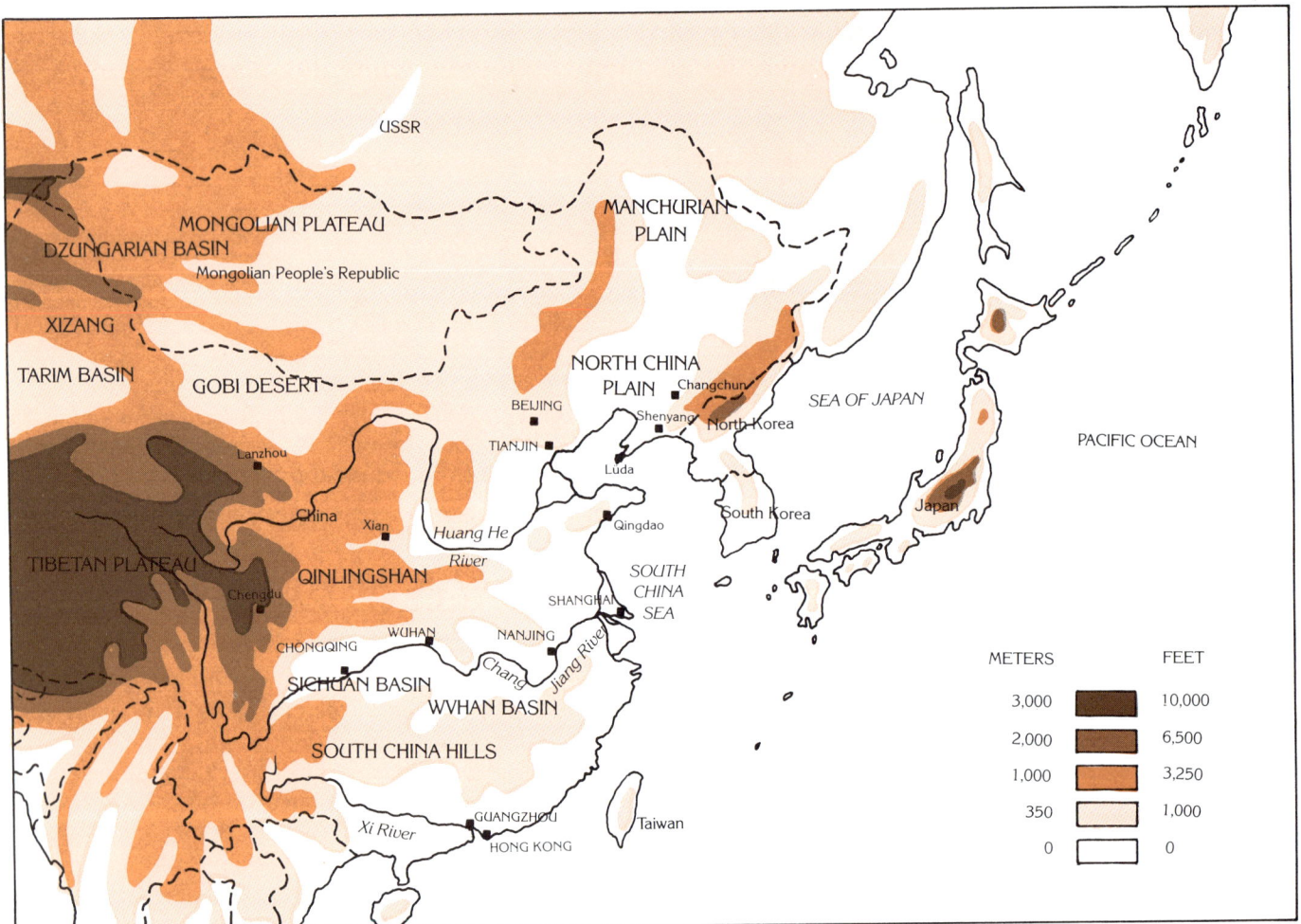

FIGURE 8–2
Generalized Topography and Drainage, East Asia. The region stretches from the dry heart of Asia to the monsoonal east coast, embracing the Korean peninsula, the Japanese islands, and Taiwan. Two huge river systems drain much of China, surrounded on most land boundaries by rugged mountain chains.

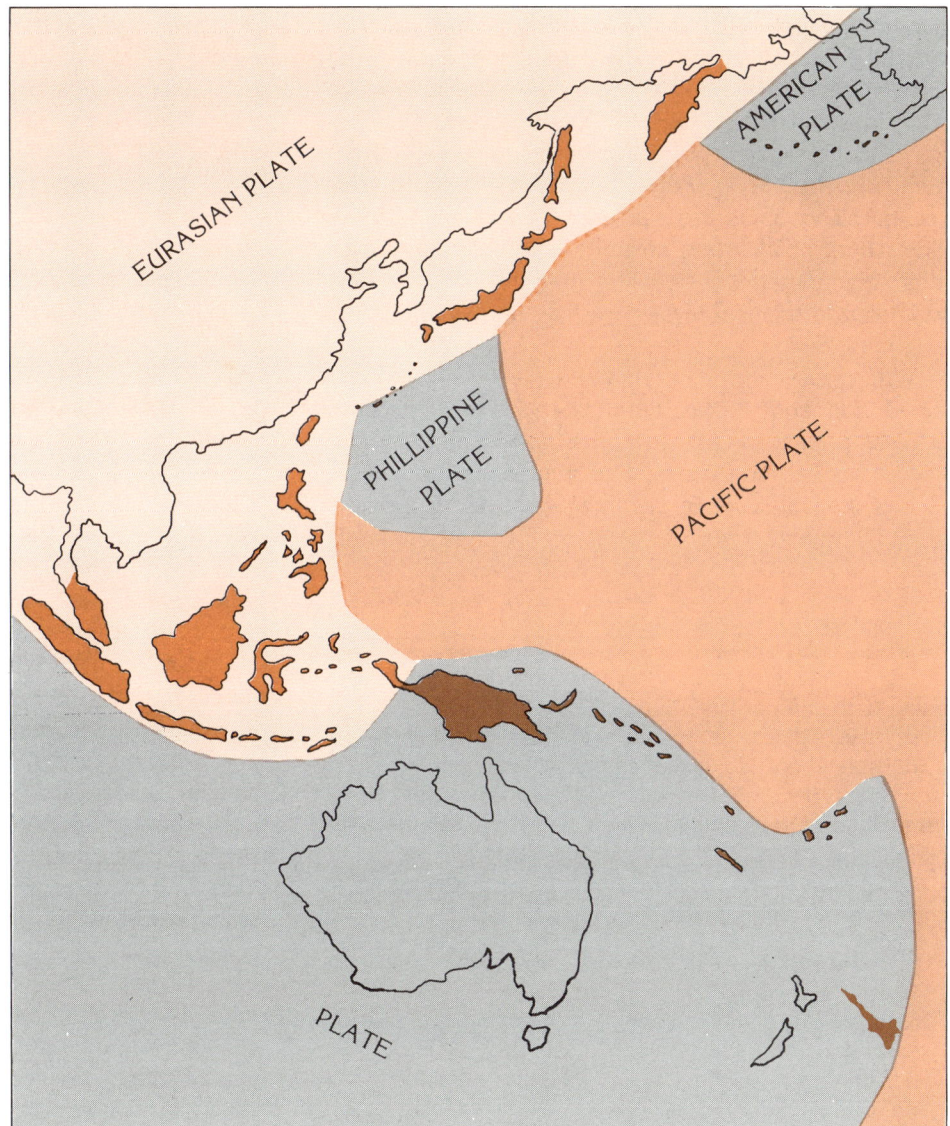

FIGURE 8–3
Island Arcs and Crustal Plates.
The sea floors are gradually
spreading as oceanic crustal plates
diverge from mid-ocean ridges
where the solid crust is exceptionally
thin. Oceanic basaltic crustal plates,
slowly sliding under the continental,
granitic plates, create both deep-sea
trenches just seaward of arcs of
tectonically active (earthquakes,
volcanoes) islands lying just offshore
from the continent.

to Indonesia. These predominantly mountainous islands are, like the mainland of East Asia, geologically complex. The island arcs are geologically unstable—earthquakes and volcanic activity are common.

The entire rim of the Pacific Ocean is characterized by frequent earthquakes and active volcanoes. This is related to the contacts of the great tectonic plates. The continents "insulate" the crust against rapid heat loss as the solid crust is thicker over most continental areas. Giant convection cells within the earth's molten interior are thus concentrated near the edges of the continents. Rising super-heated magma comes near the surface at the edge of the continents, pushing up the mountainous, earthquake-prone island arcs like Japan, and, just offshore of this, "dragging down" the solid crust in huge oceanic

"deeps," which lie just off the island arcs. (See Figure 8–3.) Some magma thrusts up through cracks and lines of weakness in the crust in the unstable islands, emerging as lava from volcanoes like Japan's Mt. Fuji. The island arcs are not completely volcanic; some have older continental-type rocks and sedimentary strata as well. Their natural resource base can be correspondingly varied.

Whether island arc or continental mass, level land is at a premium in East Asia, and not all of that is usable for agriculture. Some 20 percent of China is level, but only 10 percent of that country is arable. Population clusters in dense settlements along arable stretches, in particular in China with its relatively low degree of urbanization. The lowland of East China, composed largely of the delta lands of the Chang Jiang and Huang He rivers, houses an inordinate percentage of China's population.[2] It may be considered the primary core. Another large lowland forms the nucleus of Manchuria and stretches from the Yellow Sea to the Amur, drained by rivers flowing in opposing directions. Smaller, densely populated basins occupy the middle and upper portions of the Chang Jiang. Myriad smaller level to rolling areas are scattered through hilly South China where small rivers create usable delta and valley plains within a matrix of steeply sloping hills. Vast plateaus and basins in the arid west have little agricultural utility. (See Figure 8–2.)

Where possible, the hills have been terraced, swamps drained, and lands irrigated and otherwise reclaimed under great population pressure in a dominantly agrarian society. Even Japan pursued this type of human modification of the landscape in the time period before industry came to dominate that society. All over East Asia, lowlands

TABLE 8–1
Selected place names, new and old style

Chinese place names in this text have been revised according to the official Pin-Yin system. Because the use of this new standard Chinese (as spelled in the Roman alphabet) was not widespread outside of China prior to 1979, a selected list of important place names in both "old style" and Pin-Yin is presented for convenience in using references and maps with the traditional names.

Traditional	Pin-Yin
Provinces	
Sinkiang	Xinjiang
Tibet	Xizang
Kiangsi	Jiangxi
Szechwan	Sichuan
Kansu	Gansu
Yenan	Yan'an
Shensi	Shaanxi
Hopeh	Hebei
Rivers	
Yangtze Kiang	Chang Jiang
Si	Xi
Hwang Ho	Huang He
Cities	
Peking	Beijing
Canton	Guangzhou
Nanking	Nanjing
Tientsin	Tianjin
Chungking	Chongqing

[2] Many Chinese place names, familiar to Westerners and contained in books, atlases, and wall maps published as late as the late 1970's, have been revised according to the Pin-Yin system. This more accurately reflects the preferred, northern dialect official Chinese pronunciation. (See Table 8–1.)

have been used to the ultimate and humans have sought to enlarge the cultivable area through the beneficiation of, and actual physical change in, the physical environment.

CLIMATE

Most of the East Asian region has a temperate climate, but China's extreme south coast and the offshore islands, Hainan and Taiwan, are truly tropical. Northern Manchuria has a climate resembling that of its neighbor, Siberia. The western deserts are seasonally cold and somewhat less dry than other deserts, while the Himalayas and parts of the Tibetan Plateau have a tundra climate or, in the even higher areas, permanent snow and ice. The most important feature of East Asia's climates, like that of South Asia, is the phenomenon known as the **monsoon.** The monsoon is a seasonal reversal of prevailing winds over most of southern and eastern Asia. It is extremely important in understanding the agricultural problems and natural hazards of this densely populated part of the world. Monsoonal air circulation prevails from the mouth of the Red Sea to Japan; the term is of Arabic origin and referred to seasonal wind direction in the Arabian Sea.

The monsoon phenomenon results from the fact that land and water surfaces heat and cool at very different rates; surface temperatures tend to create atmospheric pressure differences. These atmospheric pressures differences in turn set up wind flows. In summer, the land mass heats up faster than the surrounding areas; warm, rising air currents tend to produce a temperature-induced low pressure. The cooler sea surface in summer usually produces temperature-induced high pressures. Air will flow toward the continental low pressure area from higher pressure areas over the sea.

The summer circulation of air around the edges of the continent is, then, an onshore wind. This oceanic origin air coming in over the coasts contains large amounts of water vapor (see Figure 8–4). For most of island and coastal Asia, then, the summers will be a time of heavy precipitation, cloudy skies, and warm, humid conditions. In the winter, however, the reverse causes and effects prevail. The landmass cools off much more quickly than the oceans (which can transfer heat energy within them, horizontally and vertically). The winter sea surface is relatively warm, inducing lower atmospheric pressures than those over the colder land. Once again there is a flow of air from a relatively cool surface to a relatively warm one. This time, however, the origin and destination areas of wind flows are reversed. The prevailing winds of winter are opposite to their summer counterparts. Winter skies for most of monsoon Asia are thus clear, with little chance of precipitation unless an outward flow of air from the continent crosses a

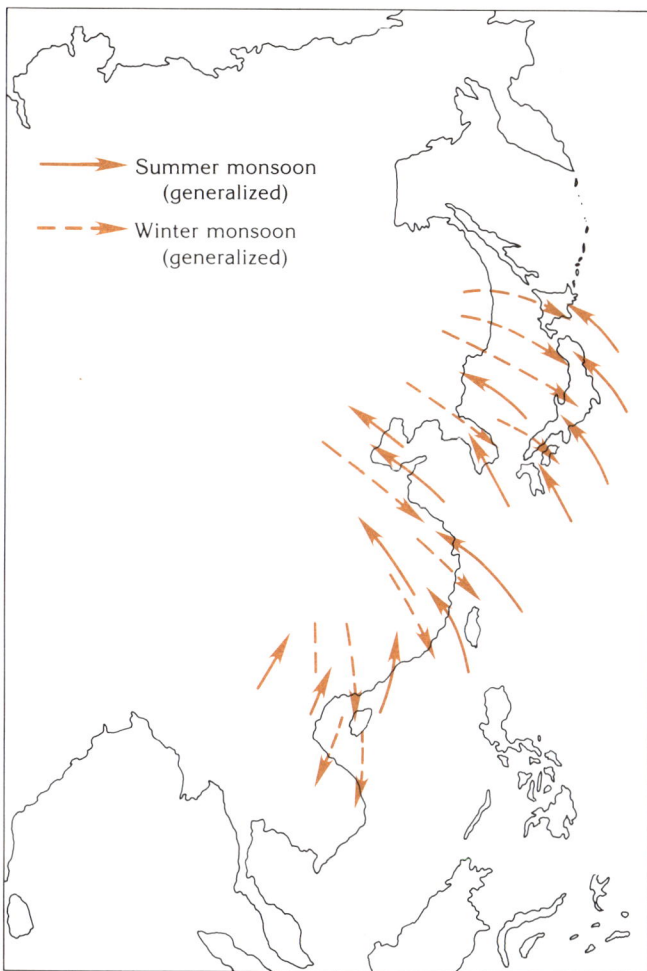

FIGURE 8–4

Monsoonal Circulation, East Asia. The monsoon mechanism of cold high pressures over the continent in winter, replaced by a warm, low pressure area in summer, causes seasonal reversals in wind direction around the fringes of the land mass.

sea surface before coming onshore again. (Western Japan and parts of Southeast Asia yield such examples.)

As will be noted in the South Asia region, the timing of the arrival of the summer monsoon is critical; it can vary greatly and there is a relatively sudden wind reversal over South Asia. Over most of East Asia, the reversal is less dramatic. This concentration of precipitation over China in the summer does have serious consequences in flooding and drought patterns.

DRAINAGE PATTERNS

In simplified form, China's topography is higher in the west, lower in the east, resulting in a drainage pattern that flows eastward towards the Pacific. Two of the world's greatest rivers, the Huang He (Yellow River) and Chang

Jiang flow eastward across China. The Yellow River is named for its muddy color, a product of heavy erosion in the general region of its great bend where it flows through an area of loess (wind-deposited, fine-grained sediment). As the Huang He flows out of its mountain gorges and onto the North China Plain, it moves from a steep narrow valley onto a broad, gently sloping plain on its way to the sea. Its lower valley has an extremely gentle gradient. This river built much of the North China Plain by wandering back and forth across it and depositing silt. The river thus changed course repeatedly through its history, sometimes abandoning one exit to the sea and creating another. The last great shift of the Yellow River occurred in 1852. Coincidentally, a British naval force had blockaded the mouth of the river. There was little Chinese reaction to the blockade, and it was months before the British realized that the river had shifted course and was emptying now hundreds of miles away. The dense human occupancy of the plain could not, of course, tolerate many such shifts in course because of the widespread flooding that accompanied it. People have been in terror of the Yellow River's floods and course changes for all of China's history. In over two thousand years of recorded history, there have been serious floods on the Huang He almost every other year. Diking the river behind artificially raised banks is not the perfect solution, however. Parts of the Huang He now flow on a raised ridge some 30 feet (9 meters) higher than the surrounding plain (see Figure 8–5). When the river breaks through the walls of this ridge of mud, the resulting flooding is disastrous.

By far the most important river of China is the Chang Jiang. Its course of nearly 3,500 miles (5,600 kilometers) in length is navigable over large stretches and has long formed a major artery of trade and transportation for central China; indeed it is navigable by ocean-going vessels to virtually the center of the populous core area. The Chang Jiang is divided into three major basins: upper, middle, and lower, which together contain almost 40 percent of China's population. It is a major source of irrigation water for millions of acres of paddy rice and possesses an enormous hydro power potential that has barely begun to be developed. The Chang Jiang, unlike the Huang He, rarely overflows its banks. The occasional flooding that does occur is normally the result of prolonged rains of an exceptionally heavy nature. When this situation occurs, the resulting floods can be disastrous, in particular given the dense populations that line its banks.

Smaller rivers drain the extreme south of China (the Xi) and lower Manchuria, while the nothern portion of that area is drained by the Amur and its tributaries. Much of arid western China and large parts of the Mongolian People's Republic have interior drainage, where rivers die out

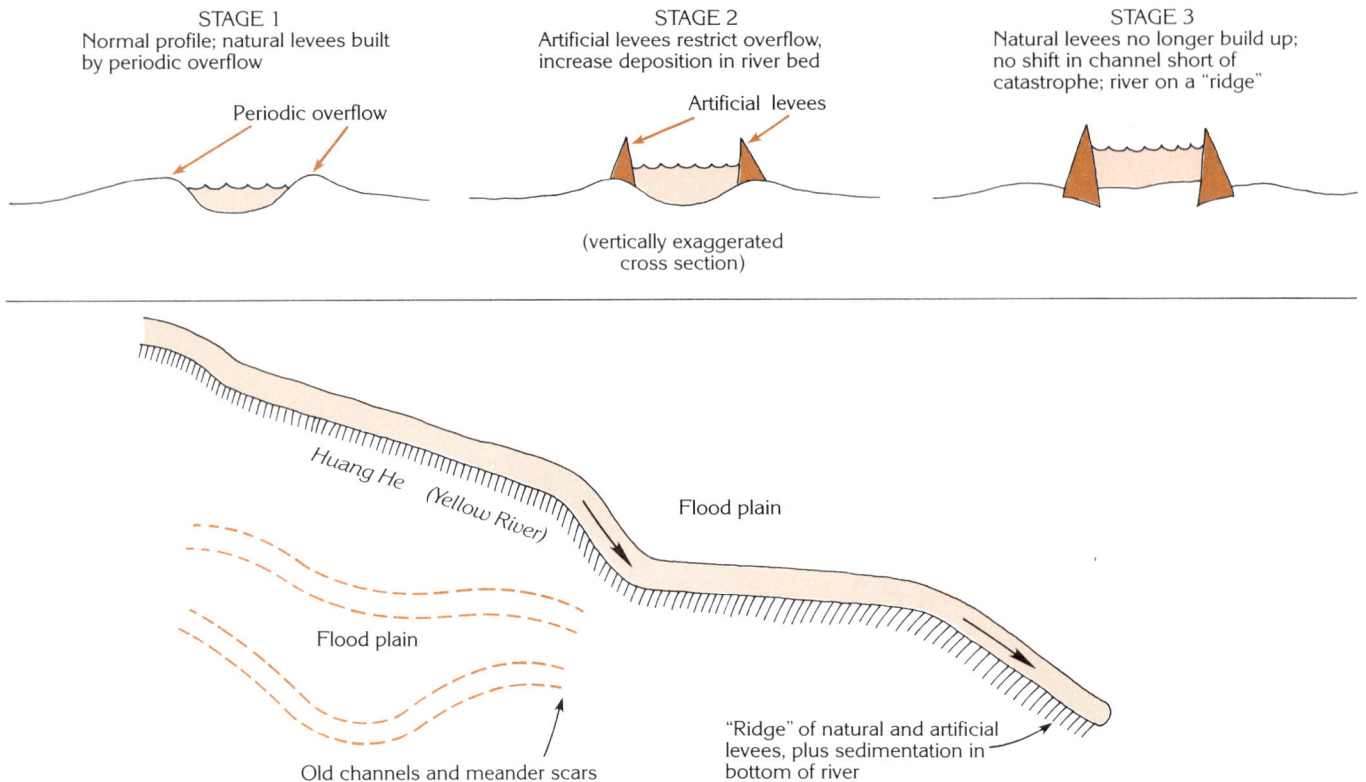

STAGE 1
Normal profile; natural levees built
by periodic overflow

Periodic overflow

STAGE 2
Artificial levees restrict overflow,
increase deposition in river bed

Artificial levees

(vertically exaggerated
cross section)

STAGE 3
Natural levees no longer build up;
no shift in channel short of
catastrophe; river on a "ridge"

Huang He   (Yellow River)

Flood plain

Flood plain

Old channels and meander scars

"Ridge" of natural and artificial
levees, plus sedimentation in
bottom of river

FIGURE 8—5

Huang He on an Artificial Ridge. Unimpeded by people, the Huang He, in its lower course across the North China Plain, would periodically overflow, depositing silt on its banks and building natural levees. When artificial levees are constructed atop the natural ones, the confined river deposits more of its sediment burden in its channel; water levels rise, matched by high artificial levees. Eventually, the river actually flows within a ridge above the surrounding flood plain.

in sands or salt lakes, never reaching the sea. The Brahmaputra flows in a deep structural trough in southern Tibet before entering India. The Huang, Chang, Salween, and Mekong—major rivers of Southeast and East Asia—rise in the Xizang highlands and flow through spectacular gorges before emerging to form the rich lowlands of coastal Asia.

VEGETATION AND SOILS

Vegetation and soil develop together over time, and each is strongly influenced by both physical geographic factors and by people, directly and indirectly. East Asia, whose human population has been relatively dense throughout human history, has experienced profound, long-term human interaction with both vegetation and soils. Natural vegetation would be influenced by climate, solid geology, and soils, and even birds and animals through selective seeding and consumption. Over most of East Asia, however, it would be impossible to discuss natural vegetation because people have altered the vegetation so completely. They have destroyed forests wholesale, introduced new

plants and grazing animals, and drained and irrigated soils. Overgrazing has probably seriously diminished grassland, extending deserts, and of course altered "natural" soil development. Most of China's core and developing fringe would have been forested, as was (and is) most of Japan, Korea, and Taiwan.

Soils have been altered as much as "natural vegetation." Cultivation for upwards of two thousand years has stirred the natural zones or layers of soils. River and canal mud has been added to terraced fields, and both draining swamps and irrigating semiarid or seasonally dry soils have changed them. Oriental cultures have long fertilized soils by adding both animal and human manure. Farmers also add "green manure" or plant refuse and inedible parts of fish. In flooded rice paddies, fish, duck, and frog droppings further enrich and change the soil. The constant plowing and cultivating of some soils have changed their texture by breaking down soil particles. Standing water in the rice paddies has changed soil both chemically and physically. As perhaps nowhere else on earth, East Asian soil would be best classified as human-made.

LAND-SEA RELATIONSHIPS

There are startling contrasts among the states of East Asia as far as their perception of the importance of the sea is concerned. In the modern era, China has not been notable as a sea power. Although there are hints of Chinese determination to become a *regional* seapower, the PRC apparently is not about to join the superpowers at sea. The PRC's merchant marine tonnage (excluding river vessals) is only little more than one tenth that of Japan's. While modern Japan's merchant ships and fishing fleets travel throughout the world, China's trading ships have tended to be coastal, seldom venturing far from the regional waters. Another measure of the perceptions of the importance of sea power is the ratio of Army personnel to Navy/Coast Guard/Marine personnel. In Japan, the Army outnumbers Naval personnel by three to one, while in the PRC, the ratio is approximately thirteen to one. (For the United Kingdom, the ratio is slightly above two to one.)

Japan's seaward orientation compared to land-preoccupied China is related, of course, to its heavy dependence on seaborne trade for raw material imports and manufactured goods exports. Japan, for example, operates nearly five hundred tankers; the regular procession of oil tankers from the Persian Gulf and from Indonesia to Japan has been termed the **oil bridge.** Although Japan has developed most of its considerable hydro power, this contributes only 5 percent of total energy demand. Japan also has the third largest number of nuclear power plants in operation (after the United States and United Kindom), but must still rely on the oil bridge. Thus, Japan's traditional dependence on sea lanes has been strongly reinforced by its current economic position. Its very limited military power, especially its naval and air forces, may be increased as the PRC expands its fleet.

Taiwan and South Korea are both in the process of expanding their merchant and fishing fleets; their maritime orientation would appear to be less than Japan's but more than that of the PRC's. Hong Kong is extremely trade-oriented but relies entirely on British naval and other military units for defense.

Over history, Japan has tended to view the sea as a means of contact with other areas and cultures. The sizeable military fleet of the World War II years attests to its maritime orientation. Despite the early evolution of a brisk coastal trade that extended even to the Arab world, China has never developed a modern maritime mentality. The sea is still viewed as something of a local concern. Taiwan views it as a defense perimeter to a certain extent, while mainland China sees the sea mainly in terms of augmenting its transportation network and as an area for inshore fishing. Recent exploration for offshore oil may expand Chinese perceptions of the utility of its nearby seas.

THE STRUCTURE OF SUBREGIONS

East Asia houses more than a quarter of the world's people. Despite the cultural influence of China on the entire area, many regional cultures are distinctive. This combination of sheer size and diversity justifies a series of subregions, yet there are also the questions of separate nation-states, widely differing political systems, divergent historical evolution of parts, and even contesting cultural elements requiring subregional treatment. (See Figure 8–6.)

The old core area versus the developing fringe and the sparsely settled periphery were chosen as the dividing lines between subregions within China. In effect, Han Chinese (ethnic Chinese) have long dominated the Chinese fringe area culturally and are even the majority population in much of the region. Nonetheless, the land outside the old twenty-eight provinces is or was a pioneer area of China—characterized by in-migration of Chinese, by rapid new development and, historically, a fluctuation in the degree of association with (or control by) the traditional Chinese core.

Five political units constitute an East Asian **"shatterbelt."** The Mongolian People's Republic is distinctive on both cultural and historical grounds. An area of nomadic grazing rather than sedentary agriculture, it gave rise to a great military organization and leadership, which once conquered most of Asia and threatened to conquer most of Europe. The people and their language are distinctly not Chinese. Even today, the Mongolian People's Republic is a **client state** of the USSR, not of China. Mongolia, too, is the remainder of a great past civilization, as the monuments and cities of Tamerlane, Kublai Khan, and other rulers would testify. Rapid assimilators of knowledge and technology, the Mongols were organizers of space and people, military innovators, and, sometimes, superb administrators. They were the one effective challenge to the great cultures of the Medieval world.

The two Koreas share a peninsula, isolated by water from both China and Japan. They are racially different from the Han Chinese and singularly defiant of outside control by any outside power. At times in the sphere of influence of Russia, China, or Japan, they are fiercely independent. Ultimately, they have always expelled the would-be colonial master; split into two by cold-war political fortunes, it is still one cultural entity.

Chinese in language and culture, Hong Kong and Taiwan are poilitically separate from the PRC. The former is a colonial outpost, the latter the refuge of a government in exile. Both are rapidly industrializing, developing economies; both are economically linked to the West. Once dominated, respectively, by Britain and the United States,

FIGURE 8–6
Structure of Subregions. Larger than the United States in area and the first in the world in population, China is studied as three regions. Japan constitutes a separate subregion, while the cultural hinges— the Mongolian People's Republic, the two Koreas, Taiwan, and Hong Kong—make up another.

they can both be thought of now as being within the economic orbit of Japan. They are sufficiently similar as the homes of emigree Chinese to be considered one subregion.

Modern, progressive, urban, and industrialized, Japan is perhaps the most powerful unit in the region. No one is likely to challenge its separateness or importance.

THE CHINESE REALM:
CHINA AS A MODERNIZING COUNTRY;
CHINA AS A CIVILIZATION

Only the Soviet Union and Canada are larger than China, and China surpasses all other states in the size of its human population. Ironically, although China had one of the world's first national censuses (records from the second year of the Christian Era have survived), no one is precisely

sure of how many people now live in China. Informed estimates range from about 850 million to a billion people. This means that almost one of every four people alive today is Chinese. The high rate of agricultural employment (75 percent), relatively minor and recent industrialization, and relatively low standards of living would indicate that it is a developing nation. Clearly, though, it is not an ordinary developing nation. The PRC has re-established firm control over all portions of its territory; this unity and the support it will lend to the development of a modern industrial state had not existed for most of a century. While there is still a pressing need to improve both the quantity and quality of average diet, for the first time in more than a century there is no widespread or serious famine. The PRC has detonated nuclear devices, launched space satellites, and begun the industrialization of what would have been considered, a half-century ago, a technologically backward country. Although their optimistic forecast that

China will be a major industrial state (and military power) by the year 2000 may be premature by a few decades, there can be little doubt that China will become a superpower in every respect during the lifetime of Americans of average college age.

China has had no great or permanent destruction of its territorial state. There has been no large-scale disruption of China as a civilization. China is a relatively young civilization, though, if compared with those of the ancient, but discontinuous **cultural hearths** of Egypt and the Middle East. The Great Pyramid was already two thousand years old at the time of the great philosopher, Kung Fu Tse (Confucius), the earliest Chinese civilization that is dated by written records.

While hardly unique to them, the Chinese have been notably self-centered or **ethnocentric** as a culture. The two old, traditional names for their country, *The Middle Kingdom* and *The Central Flower Country,* emphasize the Chinese view of China as the center of their universe. This ethnocentric view must be placed in a historical context. If late in comparison with Egyptian or Babylonian civilization, Chinese culture *was* far more advanced than that of any of its close neighbors. It is understandable that early Chinese civilization would have seen itself as uniquely advanced compared with the "barbarian" groups that surrounded it (and repeatedly threatened it).

The self-confidence of this great, rich, and expansionist civilization must be understood in terms of a long history of cycles of the expansion and contraction of centralized authority over the vast and varied territories of the Chinese state. The lands now ruled from Beijing are at least as large a unit as ever *directly* controlled by any Chinese central government. While a large, unified China has existed periodically over the last two thousand years, there have been interludes of internal disorganization, of provincial independence, civil war, and temporary invasion-domination by foreign powers. Westerners should not overemphasize, however, the weak disunity and technological inferiority of the last two hundred or so years. Placed within the context of over two millenia of Chinese history, this comparative weakness and vulnerability should be seen as a brief, if tragic, interlude. In terms of its significance to world culture, technology, arts, and economy, China has ranked among the superstates for most of its existence. Inevitably, China will reclaim this major rank in the new form of a modern industrial state.

The Core   The core consists of the provinces of traditional China. At one time (until the colonization of Manchuria by Han Chinese) this may have been designated as agricultural China as opposed to the outer ring dominated by economies based on hunting, herding, or other pursuits besides sedentary agriculture. It is the homeland of the Han Chinese, a people who began their civilization in the valley of the Wei River, a tributary of the Huang He.

Population   China's population has always been considered to be burdensomely large by anyone else's standards. Government awareness of this has led to various programs to control growth. The Chinese annual growth rate of 1.5 percent per year is lower than the world average. The large original base, coupled with the youth of the

Tien an Men Square, Beijing. China has been the cultural hearth for the region and continues as its dominant nation in population, if not industrial technology and productivity. Beijing, the traditional, imperial capital, is now the capital of the world's largest Communist state in population. (Courtesy of United Nations/T. Chen)

population, makes even this moderate growth rate a matter of concern. Birthrates (23 per 1,000 in 1980) are higher than in the United States (14 per 1,000), but they have fallen rapidly in recent decades and continue to decline. Death rates (10 per 1,000 in 1979) have dropped dramatically, much of the reason for continued growth at a more than desirable level. The average Chinese male has a life expectancy of sixty-two years at birth and female life expectancies now exceed sixty-five years. There is no great imbalance in sex ratios.

The youth of the population is reflected in the massive educational enrollments. Some 150 million children attend elementary school. Some 95 percent of the population over fifteen are now able to read and write. This very youthfulness represents a strong potential for continued growth. The government attempts to control growth through a high legal age of marriage (eighteen for females; twenty for males), persuasion (people are encouraged to postpone marriage until age twenty-eight), restrictions of a monetary nature (ineligibility for certain fringe benefits), and indirect pressures (housing and taxes). Growing urbanization and public education programs will probably tend to reinforce the decline in birthrates.

The overall density of population is 265 per square mile (102 per square kilometer), a figure that is placed in perspective when it is realized that the population density of Pennsylvania is roughly the same. Much of China is not usable for agriculture, however, and a scant 10 percent of the total is cultivable. This brings the figure into perspective, particularly when it is realized that the Chinese work force is employed dominantly in agriculture (68 percent).

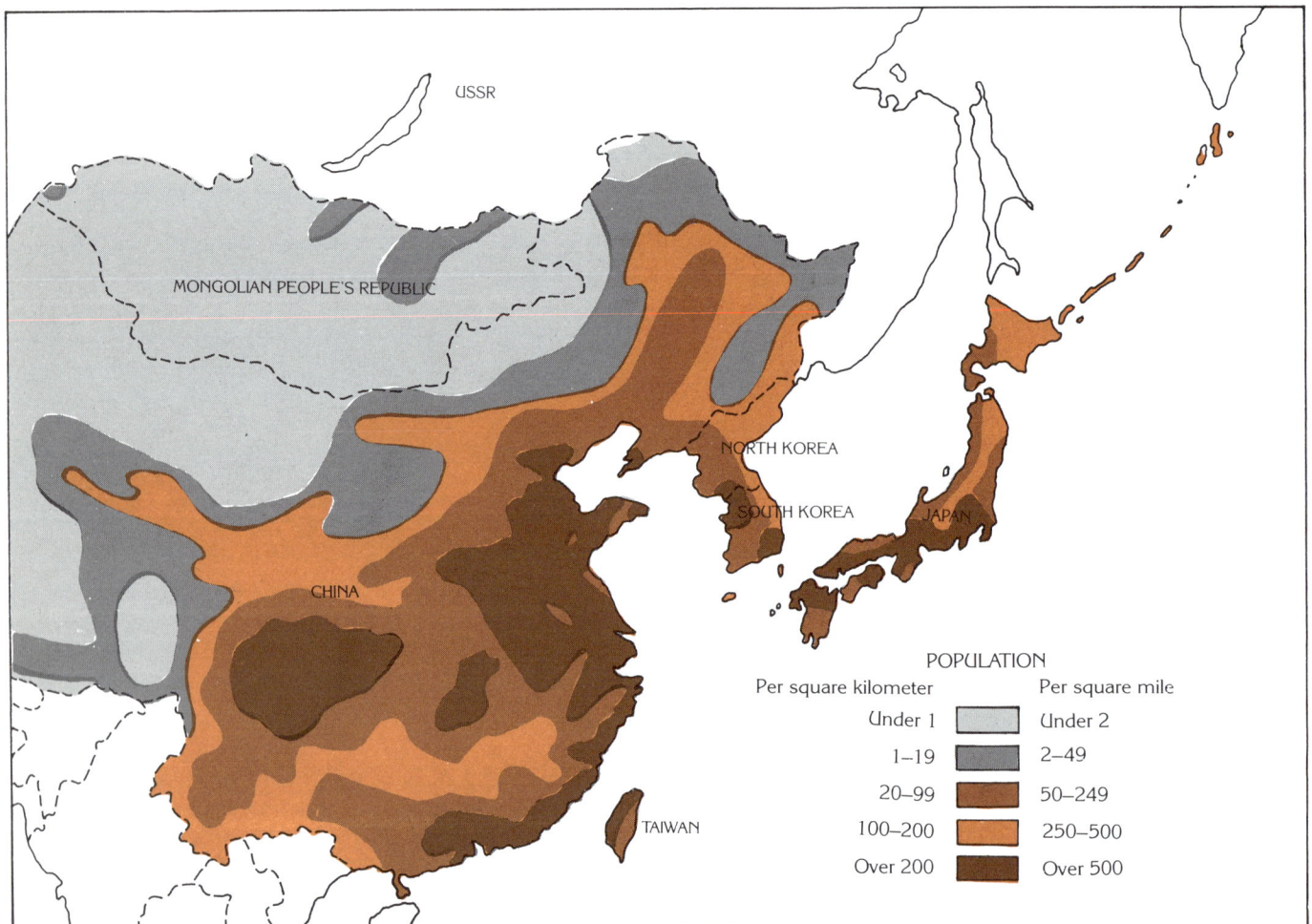

FIGURE 8–7
Population Density, East Asia. While China's overall population density is about one fourth that of New Jersey's, its population, along with those of the other states in the region, is very unevenly distributed. The western deserts of the region are virtually empty, while the city-state colony of Hong Kong has over 11,000 per square mile.

Rural densities of up to 2,500 per square mile (960 per square kilometer) are found in the lower and middle Chang Jiang basins. Densities of 1,200 per square mile (463 per square kilometer) are average in most of the arable country. (See Figure 8–7.) Some 18 percent of all Chinese now dwell in cities. There are fifteen large cities of over 1 million people, the largest of which, Shanghai, has over 10 million people. Chinese cities often contain relatively large rural populations as the government enlarged city limits (c. 1955) to insure self-sufficiency for cities in produce, dairy products, and meats. Incorporation also insures these suburban communes with an adequate supply of labor and a continuing source of night soil (human manure) for fertilizer.

The two great river valleys and their associated lowland or fairly level areas concentrate most of the population. Effectively, most Chinese live on the "wet side" of the 20-inch (500-millimeter) rainfall line. Within the core, the mountains of southern China and the drier western margins of the core have considerably lower densities. The (Chang Jiang corridor with its three basins and large, compound delta is the largest single concentration.

Within the core, the dominant trend of movement is rural to urban. Stabilization of food supply has all but eliminated the massive relocations of people formerly wrought by floods, drought, and other famine-inducing phenomena. Improving conditions in the PRC have reduced emigration to Hong Kong. Manchuria, long a target of planned colonization, is now effectively settled. Youth are still encouraged to migrate to new agricultural colonies and industrial developments in the west and southwest. The overseas Chinese, emmigrants to other lands, total some 30 million, most in Southeast Asia. Recent restrictions (and sometimes out-and-out discrimination) in Southeast Asian countries discourage any further migration, as do exit visas obtainable only after meeting stringent requirements.

The large size of China and language distribution maps might lead one to think of China as ethnically diverse. In fact, some 94 percent of the people are Han Chinese. The 6 percent who constitute ethnic minorities dwell in the fringe areas, where they often constitute a local majority. Mongols, the Uigurs and other Turkic groups, and Tibetans dominate in the western half of the state. Chinese colonization has engulfed the Manchus and Koreans in Manchuria. The various groups of people related to the Thai are strung out across southern China, in particular the areas bordering on the countries of Southeast Asia.

Agricultural Patterns   Chinese agriculture is perhaps the most intense in the world. Virtually all available land is used, including seasonally exposed river beds, roadside verges, medial strips on highways, and urban window boxes. In **Oriental intensive agriculture,** the methods are primitive, but yields are high. *Interculture* (growing additional crops between rows) and multiple cropping of the same land result in an enormous total food yield per acre. For example, individual yields of rice or barley per acre may be quite low when compared to Western commercial, mechanized agriculture. Since, however, barley, sweet potatoes, rice, and half a dozen other crops are produced on the same acre, the overall food yield in Oriental agriculture is higher. Machines save time and labor, but they do not improve yields per se.

The complexity of Oriental agriculture is amazing. Its heavy yield potential is based on a complex system of rotations coupled with the following techniques: (a) greenhousing, (b) seedling selection, (c) irrigation, (d) drainage, (e) selective cultivation, (f) weeding, (g) interculture, (h) multicropping, (i) intensive fertilization, (j) selection of complementary crops, and many others. While all of these techniques are used to one degree or another in Western agriculture, it is the peculiar use of all of them in combination, and the way in which they are used, that make Oriental agriculture unique. Commercial fertilizer may be substituted for human or animal dung with little or no loss in yield, but there is almost no substitute, even on modern collectives and state farms, for massive inputs of hand labor. Chinese production, despite heavy increases in mechanized agriculture in the production of commercial (industrial) crops, in the dryland areas of non-paddy culture, and in the pioneer areas, still relies on the traditional system using hand labor.

A "typical" unit of Chinese agriculture would be hard to identify. A theoretical example from eastern central China would probably follow a regime much like the following:

January/February—Planting of seeds in greenhouse, cold frame, or small, sheltered field covered with plastic tenting. The seedling becomes the unit of planting at a later date; it allows for preselection of good healthy stock. Since rice requires 210 days for growth, the technique saves time, using a part of the season *with* frost occurrence to begin farming.

March/April—Rice seedlings are planted in a series of flooded ditches. Any frost that occurs late can be avoided by "flooding" the whole paddy. Flooding gives rice a guaranteed water supply; nutrients are brought in solution with the waters; most importantly, it allows the development of hybrids with heavy grain yields (big heads) and a low ratio of straw (stalk). The rice will remain in the field (paddy) until harvest, about August 1. The "hills" between the trenches will be used to grow another crop, barley or oats, which are quick ripening grains that like it cool. Planted as seedlings (45 days) or dry sown (60 days), they will yield a grain crop by May 1.

May—Barley or oats is harvested, and the entire paddy is flooded to hold up the now half-grown rice. The paddy becomes the scene of a whole new ecology of interdependent organisms. Water chestnuts float between the rice. The water itself will reduce the need for cultivation; moist earth will not form clods or pans. Fish, freshwater shrimp, or frogs are grown as a water crop. They feed on weeds and plankton. They can be eaten by the farmer, by larger fish, or the ducks. None of these eat or disturb the rice or chestnuts. Duck manure is particularly rich fertilizer; the fish are edible.

June/July/August—The paddy is drained to aid in ripening the rice; the old trench (from barley or oats culture) is now hoed up against the rice stalk to aid drainage and support the grain. The intervening ditch will yield lettuce or Chinese cabbage in 45 days; they are sown as seedlings right after a heavy manuring. The rice is harvested in late July or early August. The newly harvested area is given to seedling cucumber plants, beans, or sweet potatoes. Lettuce and cabbage will be harvested in early September and some pickled for winter use. Cucumbers will be harvested throughout late September and October. Vines from the sweet potatoes will feed the swine, along with rotten and deformed sweet potatoes; others are left in the ground all winter and harvested as needed.

Late Fall—As the cucumbers and early sweet potatoes are harvested, a winter crop of radish or spinach is grown. Where warm enough, field peas are grown. They are legumes that aid in soil fertilization through nitrogen fixation from the air. If they do not ripen, they are still nutritious as a fodder crop. They can also be used for winter silage. Some varieties of winter onion and hardy cabbage are also often grown.

Cows feed on the pea vines and some of the oats or barley. The pigs, on a potato and table-scrap diet, will also fowl off (search for and eat undigested matter in the cow manure) the cow, and chickens (who act as important insect control as well), will fowl off the pig, so that the least particle of food is not wasted through a lack of digestion. The resultant chicken manure, together with human manure, is scattered over the land. Pigs yield meat, leather, bone (for buttons), fat (lard), and bristles for paint brushes, a viable export. Even the rice straw is used for thatch, mixed with mud for building bricks or wattle, for fuel, for paper, or for woven mats. Bones and odds and ends are ground for fertilizer. Not only is the system a heavy yielder of food, but

it provides for most of the needs (other than clothing) of the farmer in a subsistence society. Silk culture, which could be done at home (literally inside the house), or money from the sale of small amounts of food or a cash crop provides for the clothing needs. No piece of land is wasted; no growing day is not taken advantage of.

Chinese agriculture yields a maximum of food, eliminates serious erosion, increases (rather than depletes) soil fertility and does minimal environmental damage. It has evolved over thousands of years and has enabled such countries as China to be self-sufficient (or nearly so) in food needs, despite extremely high population densities. Even Chinese cooking reflects the population pressure and the drive for maximum utilities—the use of sprout, shoot, and pod; the technique of undercooking vegetables to preserve vitamins, or cooking over stoves that require little fuel. It is difficult to foresee tractors and frozen dinners as providing for future improvement in either the quantity or quality of the Oriental food resource.

Despite its large population, China exports some food in most years. Grain imports from the United States and Canada are used mostly to fatten animals. It also enables farmers to grow industrial crops rather than grain. Processed foods and rice are among China's chief regional exports.

Within the country there is a regional differentiation of crops. The extreme south of China can grow two crops of rice a year with careful planning and management. Tea is the specialty of southern hill lands too steep for most other crops. Most of the Chang Jiang valley can grow two crops annually, rice and a winter grain—generally wheat. North China, colder and drier, can only harvest one grain crop (generally winter wheat or some variety of millet), rounding out production with vegetable crops and potatoes. The steppes of the northern fringe, similar in climate to the Dakotas and Montana, grow spring wheat by "dry farming" on a rotational basis with pasture. The hot summers and rich prairie soil of Manchuria emphasize corn and soybeans as do similar soil-climatic areas in the United States. Increasingly, the Chinese seek to diversify their crops—both for home consumption and export. Citrus, bananas, and sugar cane are becoming rapidly more important in southern China. Cotton acreage has increased enormously, and oil seed crops (also used in industry) are replacing grains in some parts of the North China Plain and southern Manchuria.

China, before the completion of the Communist revolution, was primarily a land of tiny farms in a fragmented rural mosaic of field patterns. The average size of a farm in eastern China was only about 3.5 acres (1.4 hectares). While about three quarters of the farmers in North China

Commune in Shanxi Province, China. Terracing of slopes is necessary in this area, which is periodically devastated by floods and droughts. Chinese agriculture has had several cycles of rising and falling productivity as political philosophies became less or more extreme. (Courtesy of United Nations/A. Holcombe)

owned all of their land, in the double-rice-crop South only a little more than a third of the families were not tenants. The lot of these tenants was often one of grinding poverty, as rentals ran as high as 40 percent of the value of the total harvest for the year. While the landlords were comparatively rich, their total holdings seldom exceeded 20 to 30 acres (8 to 12 hectares), divided among many tenant families.

Marxist doctrine reserves special scorn for the "exploitive" landlords who profit from other's work, so the Communist confiscation of landlords' holdings and redistribution to peasant farmers was immediate, and very popular. Tenants at long last had the security of their own plot of land. This initial land reform boosted farmer morale and farm output. State taxes were low at first, and farm production rose by nearly a fourth during the first Five-Year Plan, 1953–57. As in the Soviet Union of the 1920's, however, ideology was more important, evidently, than practical economics. Soon after the Chinese farmers at last enjoyed owning (or at least controlling) their own plots of land, they were persuaded to join "production teams" to coordinate their efforts. Next they were organized into cooperatives of some thirty to forty household units that agreed to pool their land holdings. Uneconomically small and fragmented holdings were abolished and field units become much larger. By 1957, these small cooperatives of neighbors were being consolidated into the first phase of collective farms. These first collectives were about the same size as village units; there were almost three quarters of a million of them. Individual garden plots were retained by the farmers, as well as privately owned animals and small farm implements. The Communist government saw,

however, that these still small-sized collectives had merely reinforced the narrow provincialism of most Chinese farmers. It was determined to "collecticize the collectives," much as had been done before in the USSR. The three quarters of a million collectives were forcibly merged into about twenty-four thousand. Their size ranged from enormous in the pastoral economies of the north and west to an average of about 75 square miles (190 square kilometers) in eastern China. The number of households in each **commune** ranged from less than seventeen hundred in low-density, noncultivated areas to over eight thousand in the eastern plains and river valleys. The size of the communes was so obviously unrealistic that by the mid-1960's, their number had tripled again. The impact on the society was great, and the impact on the farm landscape, even greater. The complex, fine-grained hodgepodge—tiny fields separated by dikes, property boundaries marked by trees and shrubs, even the many small shady graveyards—was gone. In its place was a North-American-plains-like, grand-scale geometry of huge fields stretching off to the horizon.

The destructively experimental and impractical triumph of ideology over common sense and local decision making on choice of crops, timing of planting, and harvesting has had serious consequences for China. Undoubtedly, the familiar natural calamities of flood and drought also contributed much, but the diseconomies of scale in these huge collectives and the resentment of peasants dispossessed of their own land were in some part responsible for the dismal harvest that sent China into world grain markets repeatedly in the 60's and 70's. An example of political decision to ignore traditional crops and agricultural practice was an experiment in Xinjiang cited by Victor Petrov.[3] Army units and demobilized soldiers undertook experimental development of fourteen huge state farms in the semiarid western lands. The winter wheat failed and the cotton never bloomed. The rice was killed by frost. An expensive experiment proved that the traditional crops and methods were also the best.

The new form of communes that has evolved in the post-Maoist era is a somewhat more pragmatic and less doctrinaire approach. Families are no longer separated as they often were in the communes of the 1960's. Farming decisions are no longer centrally made by planners and government officials; instead, "production teams" of twenty-five to fifty families, generally friends and neighbors, make decisions on crops, planting and harvesting time, allocation of resources, and even commune investments. Private plots have been restored. Workers now receive payments in accordance with time spent on the job and job category; rates for each task are set by the decision-making teams. Discipline is really now a matter of social pressure and economic advantage gained through work.

Some 90 percent of China's arable land is in communes, while state farms (with salaried workers) occupy some 8 percent of the arable acreage. State farms are often of huge size and are frequently located in marginal areas. In addition to emphasizing industrial crops and breeding stock, they function as experiment stations, educational centers, seed farms, and laboratories for new techniques. They are heavily mechanized and still receive priority allocations of fuel, machinery, and fertilizer.

The latest phase in commune organization has sought to prepare the rural population for the transition to an urban industrial society. The sporadic nature of seasonal labor demand in farming led government officials to view commune labor as an underused resource. Much as in Japan in the early twentieth century, cottage labor production is being marshalled into team efforts. Knit goods (machine made), hosiery, clothing, basket making, canning, shoe assembly, wickerware, jewelry, farm tools, and electronics components are now being produced and assembled in the villages. Peasants are learning new skills as well as increasing their earnings. With time, the peasants engaged in this program will become fully skilled workers. Work hours are assigned along with farm labor to avoid removing labor from critical farm production and to maximize the usage of each piece of capital equipment. Farms are gradually becoming multipurpose enterprises through this newest innovation.

The Resource Base   For many years, coal and tungsten were China's only known resources of any significance. One of the early emphases of the post-revolutionary government was the search for minerals to aid in establishing the traditional heavy industrial base of Russian-inspired, Communist-style development. The search produced important finds of many crucial resources, a sufficient variety and quantity to sustain a giant industrial state.

Chinese energy resources are impressive. Known coal reserves are equivalent to 25 or 30 percent of the world's total. The largest reserves are in Shanxi and Shaanxi provinces and in the Shandong penninsula (see Figure 8–8). Smaller, but strategically located deposits fuel the heavy industrial complex of Manchuria. Coals of a somewhat lower grade underlie much of Sichuan province, while tens of dozens of smaller deposits have been opened throughout the country as local fuel supplies for home and industry. These local mines have greatly relieved pressure on China's forests, once heavily cut for charcoal to supply domestic needs. Mineable reserves are estimated at over a trillion tons, and yearly production is about 600 million tons, rivaling U.S. production and surpassing that of the Soviet Union. Coal provides almost two thirds of all of China's energy needs.

Known gas reserves and production are small, but the potential for commercial finds, both on and offshore, is excellent. Gas is being sought because of the ease of transportability, and, as among the cleaner of fuels, because of increasing concerns in China about industrial pollution. The search for oil has been more rewarding. Yearly production is now over 100 million tons, about one fourth that of the Unites States and one sixth of the Soviet Union. Traditional source areas were in the dryer, distant western areas—Gansu province and the autonomous area of Xinjiang. New fields were discovered in Manchuria in the 1970's. More than self-sufficient, China now exports oil to Japan. Japanese technology initiated the recovery of oil from oil shale in Manchuria in the 1930's. Production has continued and expanded. Reserves of oil shale are immense if recovery is expensive. Currently, drilling is taking place offshore in both the Yellow and South China seas. Gas production is concentrated in Sichuan, but small, yet important, fields produce near the industrial centers of Shanghai and Guangzhou.

China's huge hydroelectric potential (8 to 10 percent of the world total) is a greatly under-exploited resource. Huge rivers with steep gradients in narrow canyons located in western China provide virtually ideal hydroelectric sites.

Iron ore reserves are abundant, but most deposits are small and the quality of ores is relatively poor. The principal advantage is obtained from their location: (a) iron ore

---

[3] Victor Petrov, *China: Emerging World Power* (Princeton, N.J.: Van Nostrand, 1967), p. 26.

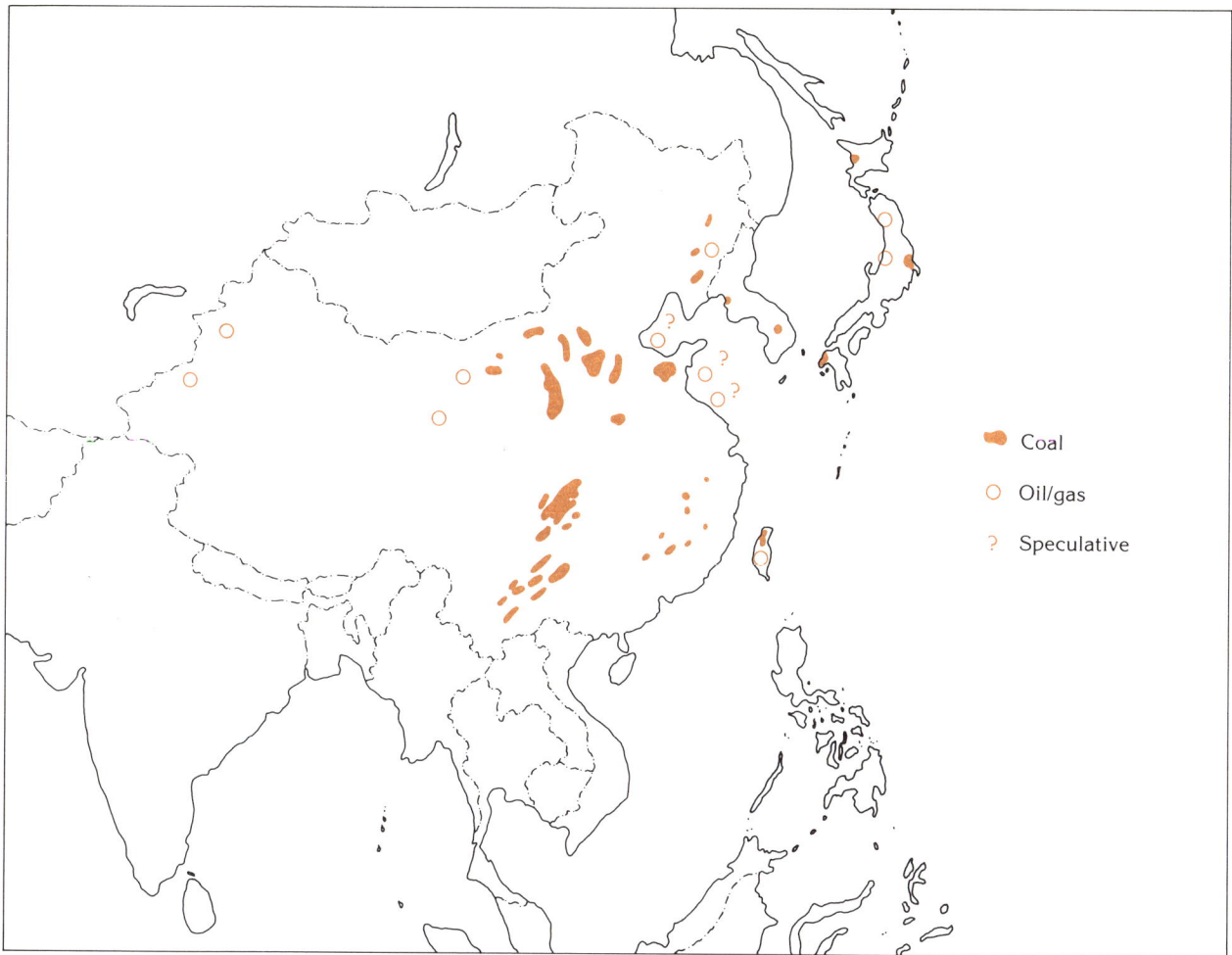

FIGURE 8-8
Fossil Fuels, East Asia. China is one of the world's energy superpowers, with widely distributed coal fields and good oil potential. Japan, in contrast, is a heavy importer of energy, while Korea and Taiwan have minor deposits of fossil fuels.

deposits are widespread, occurring in most provinces; (b) deposits are frequently near to large coal deposits. Shanxi, Hebei, and Shandong provinces have both major coal and iron reserves. Some iron is exploited along with coal in the very same mines in Manchuria. China produces 6 to 8 percent of the world's iron (by Fe content), about 5 percent of the world's known reserves. The Tayeh iron deposits near Wuhan (middle Chang Jiang basin) are both extensive and of high quality.

Tin is produced in southwestern China (Yunnan province) in significant quantities. China is still the world's largest producer of tungsten—a valuable alloy and a frequently used substance in electric-light filaments. Bauxite, copper, lead, and zinc are produced in significant amounts. Significant deposits of phosphate rock form the foundation of a rapidly growing chemical fertilizer industry. There are new discoveries of alloys such as nickel,

chrome, manganese, and antimony. China is proving to be a major mineral storehouse. (See Figure 8–9.)

One of the principal deficit resources, traditionally, has been wood. Land pressures and demand for domestic fuel resulted in the progressive denudation of Chinese forests. During the early 1950's, massive reforestation campaigns were begun to reduce erosion and flooding and to provide a new resource for future generations. Even surfaces eroded to bare rock were blasted, filled with soil, and trees planted; attempts were made to stabilize moving dunes by reforesting them in areas of the dry northwest. The results of the campaign were mixed, but gradually forests have been re-established. In some places wood is cultivated as a crop.

Industrial Development Strategies Modern China inherited a prerevolutionary industrial legacy (of sorts) in

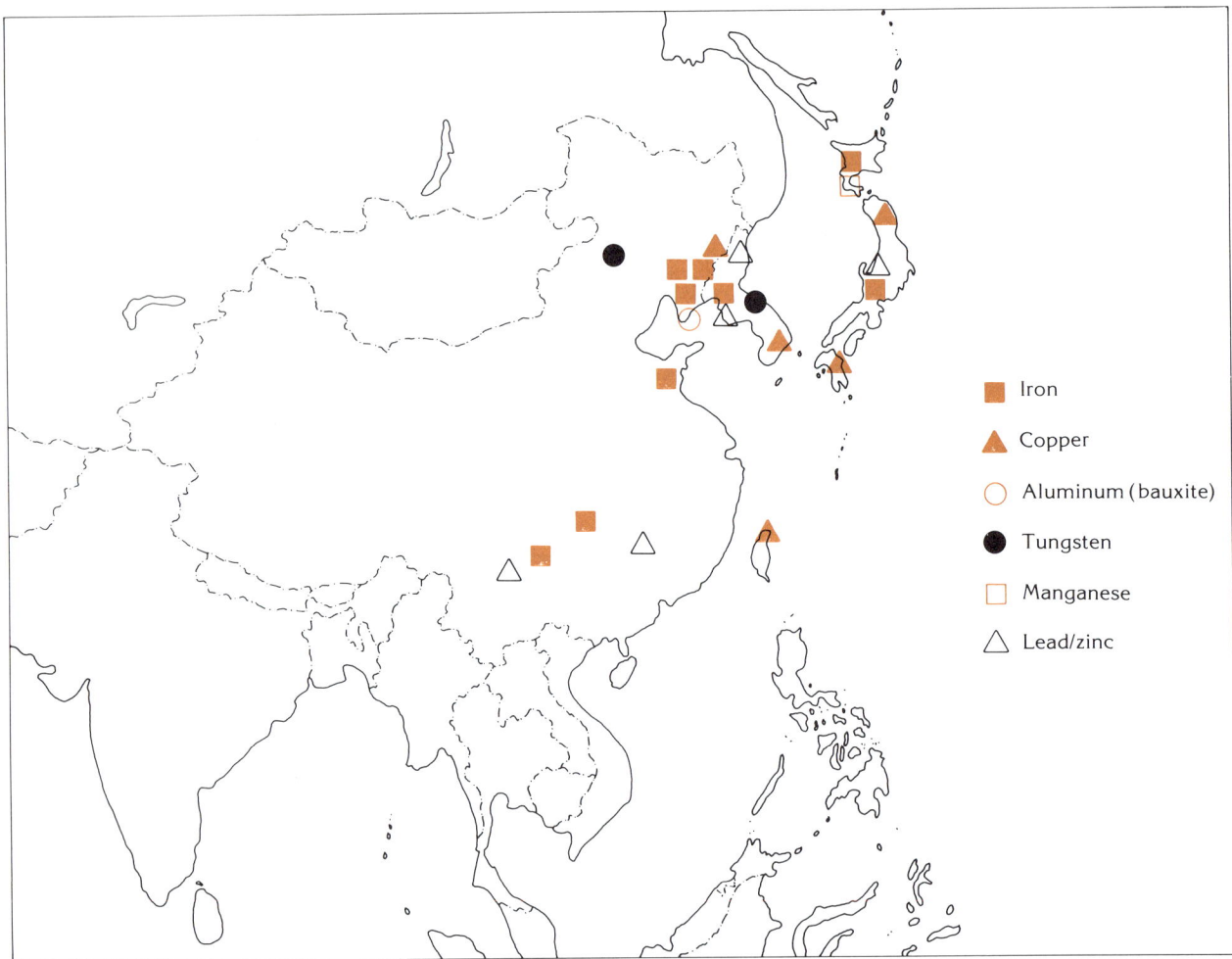

FIGURE 8–9
Mineral Resources, East Asia. China's vast territory has not yet been thoroughly explored; its northeast and south-central areas have many important metal ores, while Japan and the Koreas have a fairly wide variety, if limited quantity, of economic minerals.

1949. Most of this early industrial base, particularly in core China, was focused on light industry. Food processing, textiles, clothing, silk, and tobacco products were the most important elements. Most of the textile industry was foreign owned and the capital plant was generally old and outmoded. A few cities, Shanghai in particular, dominated industrial production. Japan developed a significant steel industry in Manchuria during its occupation of that area (1933–1945), while the Wuhan district was a significant producer of steel. Most of the rest of industrial production was better classified as crafts (jewelry, lacquerware, porcelain, ceramics, and art objects), though they formed an important part of Chinese exports.

The first phase of industrial modernization in China began almost immediately after the conclusion of the revolution. Following the Soviet lead, China embarked on a series of expensive, **capital-intensive** projects geared to

establishing a heavy industrial base. Capital was to be supplied from the agricultural sector. Much of the industry was to be located in the interior to counterbalance what the government viewed as the capitalist era's overdevelopment of the port cities. The costly projects did little to advance China's industrialization and, in effect, resulted in an underfunding of the crucial agricultural sector.

Disenchanted with the Russian-style plan's results by the mid-1950's, Mao initiated his own Chinese plan for development, attempting to capitalize on China's vast armies of surplus labor. The program came to be known as the **Great Leap Forward.** Designed to instantly transform China into a self-sufficient industrial economy, it was to "mobilize the masses," who would substitute labor for capital. The hallmark of the program was the backyard furnace for the production of iron and steel. Outdoor bread ovens became miniature blast furnaces. Iron was mined everywhere; scrap was substituted if no iron was present. Coal or charcoal was used as fuel. Iron and steel production increased rapidly, but much of the iron smelted was of such low quality as to be unusable. Spurred by rhetoric and patriotism, workers left farming tasks undone to tend the backyard furnaces. Agricultural production declined as the all-important ingredient in Oriental agriculture, labor, was occupied with other tasks. The rail system groaned under the burden of *cross-hauling* coal, iron ore, charcoal, pig iron, scrap, and steel. Agricultural commodities rotted in the fields and on loading docks as raw materials and steel had first priority on transportation. Cities began to rebel as food supplies grew short and piles of iron and steel began to mount. The Chinese economy came very near to total collapse.

After this calamity, Chinese industrialization resumed a slow rate of growth. Planners now sought to revive native skills and transform them into industrial output of export quality. Agriculture was re-emphasized, and industries to benefit that sector (fertilizer, implements) received high priority. Smaller scale investments prevailed, and factories were developed in small towns and rural areas. Consumer goods became more important.

Since the early 1970's China has resumed large-scale investments, but in well-planned establishments at carefully chosen sites. Some private enterprise is now allowed in the consumer goods sector. Industry and industrial planning are both deliberately decentralized. Big and small investments are balanced, both traditional and modern industrial sectors are given equal rank, as China continues its policy of "walking on two legs." The pace of growth has begun to pick up in tempo. China has apparently entered the **takeoff** phase as the economy begins to gather momentum.

Today Chinese steel production is about 35 million tons yearly. Over 40 million tons of chemical fertilizer were produced in 1979 as well as 50 million tons of cement. The textile industry is still expanding at a rapid rate. Wood products industries grow rapidly as the reforestation program of the 1950's begins to produce mature timber. Expanded coal and oil production have led to rapid development of the manufacture of chemicals and plastics. There is now a new emphasis on transportation improvement accompanied by heavy investment in industries producing trucks, bicycles, and railroad rolling stock. Shipbuilding has begun to become important in coastal cities, and a major output of specialized farm implements, suited to Oriental intensive agriculture, has recently been achieved.

Despite the emphasis on decentralization of investment, China's dozen largest cities continue to dominate industrial production. Nonetheless, distinct zones of indus-

trial development have begun to emerge. Shanghai, together with Nanjing and Hangzhou, dominate a major industrial district in the Chang Jiang delta lands. This is China's largest industrial district. Traditionally a center of consumer goods, especially textiles, it has become China's most diverse industrial center. In addition to the traditional cotton and silk goods, it is now a major producer of synthetic fibers and cloth. Petrochemical industries have been established near large dockside refineries, producing fertilizers, resins, synthetic rubber, pesticides, and plastics. The largest automotive center in China, it produces trucks, busses, taxis, and motorcycles. In response to expanded commerce, the shipyards run full tilt. Household appliances, furniture, and electronics industries round out the list of fabricated goods. Shanghai itself leads in production of all these commodities. Nanjing has become a major chemical production center while retaining its strong development in the manufacture of textiles and clothing. Electronic components and scientific equipment are rapidly developing specialties. Hangzhou specializes in agricultural implements, food processing, and the manufacture of milling, canning, and other food-processing equipment. There are dozens of small and medium plants scattered throughout the countryside between these three great industrial centers.

To supply the metal needed in this wide array of manufactures, Shanghai produces 6 million tons of steel yearly. New steel mills, already under construction, will very shortly double that capacity.

The second most important industrial complex is that of Manchuria.[4] The original Russian and Japanese investment in iron and steel has been enhanced by the later Chinese endeavors. The Northeast produces over a third of all Chinese iron and steel. Large new oil fields in the area have given rise to major refineries and extensive chemical complexes. As the oldest and largest center of steel making, it has become the major machine building center of China, including machine tools. Anchored by the Taching oil field and the steel-making center of Harbin on the north, it culminates in the dual port cities complex of Lüda, a great refining, petrochemical, and shipbuilding center. Intermediate centers include Changchun (automobiles and tractors), Jilin (fertilizers and synthetic substances), Shenyang and Anshan (steel and machinery), and a host of smaller centers now arising as satellites to these major urban centers. Only recently (and just barely) has this area slipped to second rank in importance. The third largest Chinese industrial area is evolving in North China. The two original nuclei were the treaty port at Tian-

---

[4] The term *Manchuria* is not used by the Chinese, who refer to that region simply as "The Northeast."

jin and the pre–World War I German investment in and around Qingdao. The area is only loosely knit into a region—it remains rather more a collection of separate nuclei in close proximity. German investment centered in three areas: cotton textiles, coal mining (over a billion ton reserve underlies the Shandong Hills), and forest products.

Tianjin is the **outport** for Beijing, and in 1949 had about 10 percent of all Chinese industry. Textiles, glass, shoes, and clothing were dominant, along with flour milling and rug making. European states and the Japanese had investments and treaty concessions there. With the advent of the Maoist regime, it became China's most important port from 1949 to 1960. Coal is mined just northeast of the city. Beijing, the capital, has become a major industrial center in the last thirty years. There is a major integrated steel mill, bicycle factories, enormous cotton textile and clothing mills, and myriad small plants producing electrical equipment, machinery, and a host of consumer goods. Still, the administrative and cultural functions dominate over industry. This industrialization under the Communists has added a new dimension to the city, which now has over 8 million people. Tianjin is now the largest single center of the chemical industry in China. It has a huge iron and steel complex and a major emphasis on heavy machinery. The construction of a new artificial port in 1949 has enhanced both the commercial and industrial functions of the city, which now has a population of over 5 million. As functions begin to extend inland and small satellite industries supplant agriculture as the chief employer, the two cities are gradually becoming one aggregation. The discovery of oil in the Huang He delta has enriched the area's raw material base. Industrial investment is slowly linking Beijing, via Tianjin and the delta, to the Shandong peninsula, forming one large North China industrial region—the country's third largest. The Shandong peninsula, rich in coal and iron, has developed a steel industry to augment its well-developed base of textiles.

Thus, despite government plans to industrialize the interior, it is the coastal cities of old that still dominate. The hinterlands have been enlarged and major industrial districts have developed, but the old treaty ports and early investment areas are still of major importance.

Much of the rest of China's industries is in scattered nuclei in the interior and the south. The premier examples of large investments in the interior designed to develop the countryside and to integrate the country are Baotow in Inner Mongolia and Lanzhou in remote Gansu province. Baotou is a major center of iron and steel production on the great bend of the Huang He, north of the Drdos Desert. Symbolically, it is beyond the Great Wall and in lightly settled, drylands China, outside the core area. The other major center is Lanzhou—the gateway city to the dry west at the contact zone of fringe and core China and within sight of the Great Wall. The site of a major oil field, Lanzhou is a major center for refining, petrochemicals, and the smelting of nonferrous metals. Both cities are on extensions of the railway network built since 1949. (See Figure 8–10.)

Xian and Taiyuan in the loess hills are the capitals of the provinces with China's major coal reserves. Taiyuan is the more important center, with a large steel complex and machinery plants. Chemicals are increasing in importance in the manufacturing complex, and new consumer goods industries develop to supply the needs of workers. Xian, in the original culture hearth of the Han Chinese, came to be a major center of steel production during the backyard furnace era. Today it has a more rational development that emphasizes machine production, chemicals, pharmaceuticals, and transportation equipment.

Zhengzhou, the capital of Henan province, is another area of major coal reserves. It is a rapidly developing center of diverse industry. Though each of the five cities discussed is quite separate and distant from the other, they roughly outline a developmental district—west of the North China industrial region, which, it is hoped, will become a new industrial region.

There are three other centers of note: the Wuhan complex, the Sichuan Basin, and the industrial district of Guangzhou. Wuhan, in the middle Chang Jiang Basin, is the center of vast iron reserves, some of good quality. The city is really a cluster of cities where the Han River enters the Chang. Midway between Beijing and Guangzhou (and at the midpoint between Shanghai and the Sichuan Basin), this is one of the great crossroads of China—a major rail, water, and highway junction. The iron and steel industry here predates the Communist government, but it has been greatly enlarged since 1949. The district around Wuhan produces roughly 15 percent of the national total of iron and steel. Nearby coal is not of good coking quality, but cheap water transportation provides adequate supplies from more distant fields. Major engineering industries, including large-scale factory machinery, use the steels produced in this urban complex of over 5 million people.

The Sichuan Basin contains two large cities, Chengou and Chongqing. Supplied amply with coal, gas, and oil found throughout the basin, they are growing centers of heavy industry. Food-processing industries are now developing rapidly in this rich, but formerly isolated, agricultural area. Chongqing is generally considered as being the head of navigation on the Chang. Since 1949 it has been connected to the main Chinese rail network. Chengpu is at an important junction on the north-south interior route

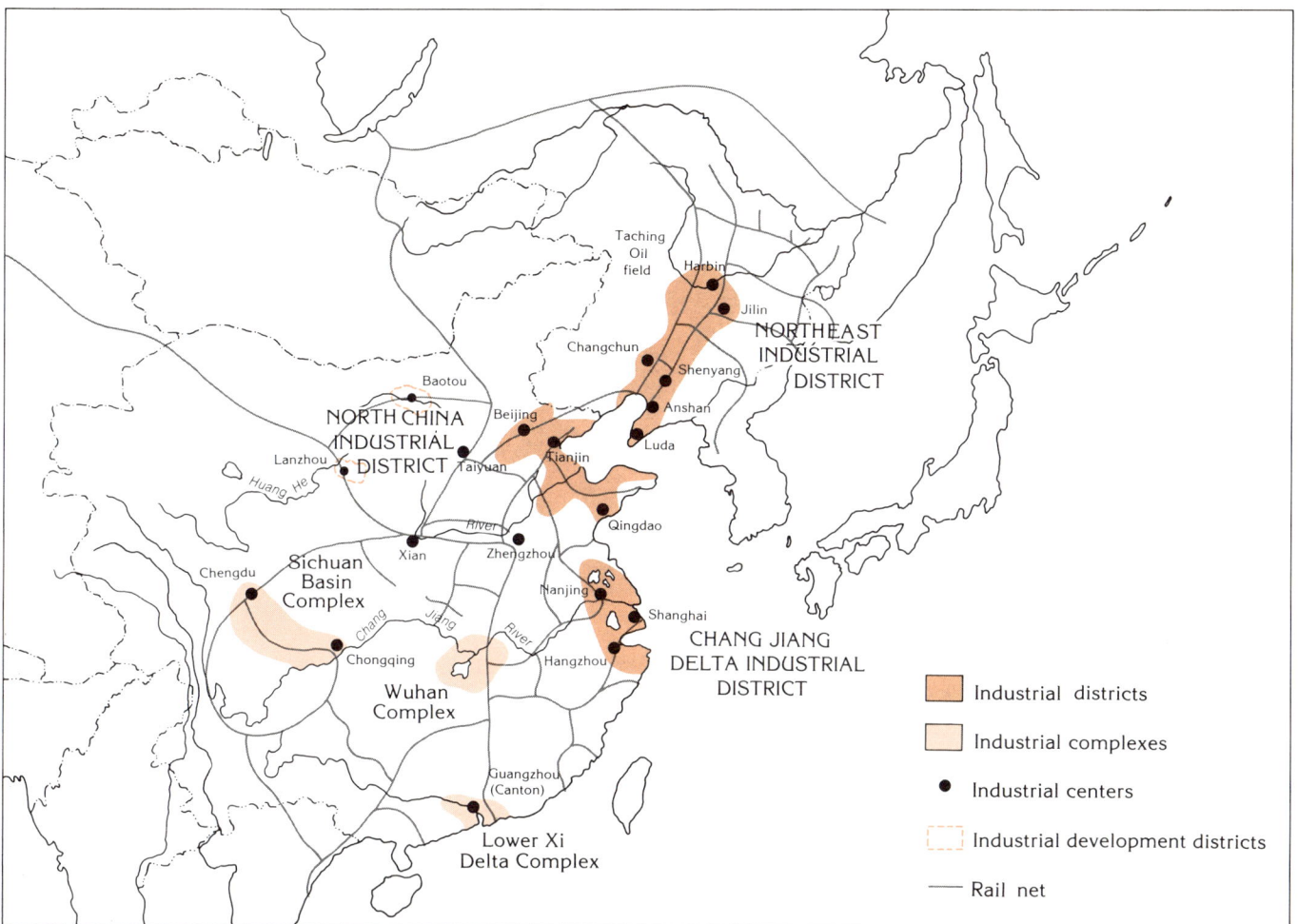

FIGURE 8–10
Industrial Zones and Development Areas of China, Showing Railways. China's initial industrialization was fostered by foreign investment and technology, concentrated in coastal cities and in the Northeast (Manchuria). Following wartime destruction and postwar Soviet dismantling of some Manchurian facilities, China has attempted to both rebuild and modernize these early centers and create new centers in the interior.

(see Figure 8–10). The Sichuan and Middle Chang Jiang basins are viewed as the logical location for inland expansion of the lower Chang delta complex.

Guangzhou, a major treaty port in the nineteenth century, is the regional capital of all of south China. Lacking fuel and hemmed in by steep hill country, it is a center specializing in light industry for domestic consumers and traditional exports. Food processing is becoming very important as Chinese specialty foods increasingly enter the export market. The highly productive, subtropical, and tropical agriculture of southern China forms the major raw material base. Specialty textiles like embroidery, knit goods, brocades, and upholstery material enter the export market. Minerals produced in the area have led to the development of nonferrous metallurgy and fertilizer plants.

Farm implements and supplies are produced for the intensive local agricultural sector. With almost 5 million people, it is a major urban center. There are two keys to its industrial growth: the potential for hydroelectric power (which would provide a major energy source) and the development of industry to supply ports and semiprocessed raw materials to the burgeoning industry of Hong Kong. As labor costs rise in that city, Guangzhou offers the potential for taking over the assembly functions of the toy, clothing, and small machine industries of Hong Kong.

Developmental Strategies   Faced with a large and growing population, yet endowed with considerable mineral wealth, China now embarks on a full-scale drive toward industrialization. The legacy of the *treaty port* and the ex-

Guangzhou, China. The city of Guangzhou, near Macao and Hong Kong, was traditionally one of China's "contact points" with foreign trade and culture. The large new hotel, on the right, continues this tradition after the end a period of minimal contact with the West. (Courtesy of United Nations/T. Chen)

port-oriented industry, plus domestic consumer goods, which developed there, were viewed as a relic of colonialism. The exploitation of cheap labor and the foreign orientation were both anathema to the Maoist government, which sought to develop Chinese self-sufficiency.

The government planned to build a series of totally new, heavy industrial centers at raw material sites in the interior. Industry was planned to focus inward and to emphasize producer goods for furthering Chinese development. The failures of certain programs, the withdrawal of Russian capital, and increased interaction with the West have ended in a rejuvenation (and expansion) of the coastal centers. The developmental strategy of the 1970's was rather more one of enlarging the existing bases in the three major districts. Investment in the interior has not been abandoned. The improved transportation network and the discovery of new mineral resources has increased the economic viability of most of these centers. With renewed emphasis on export and the reorientation of trade from the Russians to the Euro-American markets and Japan, however, the older eastern centers are more favored.

Environmental Problems and Potentials Western visitors to China are impressed by the cleanliness of urban environments. The *use* of what Westerners would consider waste greatly reduces many of what Westerners perceive as pressing environmental problems. The advent of industry, however, may bring water and air pollution problems not fully anticipated by a government bent on industrial development.

Political Stability Apparently there is now a series of highly pragmatic programs geared to reconciling public needs and desires with developmental initiative. Since the Great Leap Forward failed, agriculture has been targeted for major investment. The government has proven to be responsive to rural needs and complaints.

The decentralization of decision making in agriculture and the renewed emphasis on consumer goods are both likely to draw public support. Improved coverage by mass media and tremendous strides in education are enormously helpful in building national unity. After over thirty years of existence, the government now perceives itself as stable and less threatened by outside intervention. The death of Mao (who used an almost personal allegiance in order to obtain unity of action) and the strides already made in development, plus the long historical existence and the pride it engenders, have paved the way for the development of a firm nationalism. Minorities are too small to pose a threat, and government programs of cultural autonomy may be sufficient to defuse any separatist movements.

Cultural and Economic Capitals Core China contains two great world cities, Beijing and Shanghai. The former is the greatest center of Chinese culture and education. With an area of over 6,000 square miles, it incorporates hundreds of thousands of farmers within its borders. The capital of the Khans, as well as the Manchu dynasty, it has often been the Chinese capital. A city of 8 million, it is renowned for its beauty and interest. Its name means "northern capital" and its importance as the center of the

Huang He lowland, as well as its intermediate position between China's two largest industrial districts, enhances its domestic importance.

At Beijing's center is the Forbidden City, once open only to the emperor and his court, now a museum of international fame. Around this was the Manchu city, walled as a defense parameter around the imperial court. Beyond this was another walled city, built by the Tatar Khans, with its wide boulevards and splendid parks (often mistakenly believed to be the work of the Communist era government by those who see its similarities to Russian boulevards and squares). Farther to the south is the Chinese city, built to house the Chinese who were forbidden to reside within the other walls when non-Chinese leaders ruled. Beyond this is the fifth city, the new city of modern China built to house the burgeoning population of industrial and office workers during this most recent thirty years of spectacular growth. Filled with splendid architecture and museums, carefully landscaped and maintained, home of China's finest academic and technical institutes, it is the very center of modern Chinese culture; resplendent with history and tradition, it is a memorial to China's past. Capital of the most populous state in the world and the center of an important branch of Marxist thought, it is a city with worldwide impact.

Shanghai is the largest city in China but was never a political capital. Shanghai grew rapidly after 1843 when it was first opened as a *treaty port*—one open to foreign ships, merchants, and consulates. Shanghai tapped a richly productive, heavily populated hinterland. Shanghai was several cities, side-by-side, with European residential quarters. European-Chinese commercial and manufacturing zones, and traditional Chinese urban areas all crowded together on a distributary of the great Chang, the Hwangpu. Its sizeable and cosmopolitan Western population made it a "foreign" city to traditional Chinese eyes and in fact, European influence was once so strong that many hotels, restaurants, and clubs, while they had Chinese employees, forbade Chinese guests. It is not surprising that many Chinese regarded it as an evil reminder of Western, exploitive imperialism. The Communist regime at first tried to restrict the rebuilding and continued growth of Shanghai, finally relenting when it was obvious that, after all, the imperialist image (and fact) had disappeared long ago, and Shanghai was a major industrial and commercial center. One reason for its persistent growth is the generally superior *infrastructure* of transport, communications, electrical energy supply, and support facilities installed during the "bad old days" of Western dominance. In many ways, Shanghai was China's most Westernized or modernized metropolis at mid-twentieth century, and it continues to benefit from its superb situation. As the PRC moves out from a period of intense self-examination and internal consolidation towards a more internationalist political and economic outlook, Shanghai will take the lead again in economic, while not political, administration.

The Developing Fringe   It is difficult in some ways to justify the second largest industrial area of China, the Northeast, as part of a developing fringe. However, the area has been colonized by Han Chinese largely during the last one hundred years, and its industrial development began only forty-odd years ago. Active agricultural colonizations of its fringes is continuing and industrial development, while now more a question of diversification, still proceeds apace. It was the cold area of the north, not suitable to rice culture and protected as almost a private park (by the Manchu dynasty) from Chinese settlement. The rest of the fringe is essentially the drylands/wetlands contact zone—the land beyond the Great Wall, or the areas of the southwest, peopled by non-Chinese minorities and only lightly used for agriculture until recently. Except for the Northeast, now a part of China's economic core, the development of the fringe is confined largely to agricultural settlement and the search for minerals.

The Northeast (Manchuria)   This is the greatest heavy industrial center in China, but its relative significance can be expected to decline as the industrial development continues in other sections of the "inner ring" of China. The Northeast is nearly rimmed by mountains averaging more than 3,000 feet (900 meters) in elevation. The climate is transitional to that of neighboring Siberia, with extremely cold winters in the north followed by hot summers (daily temperatures average in the upper 60's to the mid-70's F (20° to 24°C). The much cooler average temperatures and the associated lower agricultural productivity per acre meant much lower population densities for the Northeast than were found in the North China Plain. Most Chinese did not consider it a very desirable place until population pressures mounted sufficiently in the seventeenth century to begin intensive settlement of the plains in the southwest of the subregion. The bulk of the Northeast remaining was left to nomadic tribes until about three quarters of a century ago. The last dynasty, the Q'ing of the Manchus, was not eager to settle its traditional homeland and power base with larger numbers of Chinese either. The relatively sudden in-pouring of Chinese into the Northeast in the last days of the dynasty must rank among the great migrations of modern history. There is still some room for expansion of agriculture in the drier and colder north. Northeastern farms tended to be larger than those typical of the North China Plain, before the consolidation under the Communists. It usually produces an exportable surplus of grains.

The Northeast's rank among China's industrial regions is more a product of foreign investment than of any unique qualities of natural resources. It was Japanese investment and technology that led to the rapid development of the Northeast in the 1920's and 1930's. Russian interests there early in this century conflicted with a growing Japanese interest, helping to precipitate the Russo-Japanese War. The Russians had built a railroad across the Northeast as a short-cut from central Siberia to their Pacific coast port and naval base, Vladivostok. (See Figure 8–10.) The Chinese Eastern Railway was in effect an agency of the Russian imperial government. The Russians had full rights of policing the rail corridor, together with mineral exploration and development rights. At the time of the Boxer Rebellion, 1900, the Russians were pressuring the Chinese to cede the Northeast to them. Only the Japanese victory in their war with the Russians, 1904–05, removed the threat of Russian domination. The Russian threat was followed by the reality of a Japanese take-over; Japan set up a puppet state, Manchukuo. The rapid movement of Chinese into the Northeast (or Manchukuo after 1931) continued even under Japanese rule. The population went from about 17 million people at the end of the Russo-Japanese War to 34 million by 1930 and reached 47 million by 1953. The Japanese built their South Manchurian Railway after the victory over the Russians, and, by World War II, the Northeast had more rail mileage than the rest of China together.

The Japanese constructed a vast iron and steel complex in Anshan. Relatively small compared with the rest of China, the Northeastern coalfields are still impressive. At Fushun, for example, a deep open-cut mine produces more than 20 million tons per year from a coal seam averaging 240 feet (70 meters) thick. This coal seam lies below a layer of oil shale, which must be removed to exploit the coal. The oil shales are processed by a refinery originally built by the Japanese. The Northeast also contains about 4.5 billion tons of iron ore, although most of the ore is low-grade.

During World War II, the Northeast's highly developed transport net, coal and iron ore mines, oil shales, and nonferrous minerals helped to power the Japanese economy. Anshan steel works had reached a capacity of more than a million tons of steel by 1945. Just as in eastern Europe, victorious Russian armies were followed by teams of dismantlers of plants—the Anshan works were almost completely dismantled and shipped back to Russia. Soviet technical assistance and materials did, however, aid the Chinese in rebuilding Anshan during the late 1940's and early 1950's. It would be interesting to speculate on who got the better deal—the Russians who carted off a steel plant dating back to 1919 or the Chinese, who presumably got a technologically more advanced plant by the 1950's.

The recent diversification of industry is a prelude to the demise of reliance on local coal and iron reserves. Within easy reach, by both rail and water, of the reserves of Shandong and North China, it will continue to produce large amounts of iron and steel economically. The profitability of this industrial segment will be further enhanced, however, by the current proliferation of metal-using industries. The discovery of China's largest (to date) oil reserves here have resulted in the rapid enlargement of chemical production. Recent discoveries of bauxite, molybdenum, lead, zinc, and manganese will further enhance metallurgy.

Great Wall of China. China is one of the oldest nations in continuous existence as a people and culture. In the long run, it has successfully resisted all invaders, absorbing external forces when it could not repel them at the border. (Courtesy of United Nations/T. Chen)

Petroleum, magnesite, and by-product sulfur enrich the potential for even greater development of chemical industries.

This combination of agricultural settlement and industrialization has raised the total population to almost 100 million. There is room for further expansion. New deposits of high-grade iron and coal have been discovered in northern and eastern frontier districts. Most plains of reasonable fertility could be brought under agriculture if drained (such a project, however, would require cooperation with the USSR). The rich forests of the Great Khingan Mountains have not been fully exploited and the areas beyond are only lightly grazed—well below their carrying capacity.

As evidence of its full incorporation into China, the Northeast's politically separate status has been removed and its administration replaced with provincial status for three new provinces of China. The western portion, lightly populated, is now attached to the Inner Mongolian autonomous area. The dense population now extends, unbroken, from the North China Plain, through the Manchurian lowlands, almost to the Russian border (see Figure 8–7). The Northeast, then, is only a fringe area in the sense of its newness and its separate status until recent years.

The Inner West   The frontier between Mongolia and China has changed so rapidly and so frequently over the centuries that Mongolia is more a physical geographic designation than a cultural region or a nation-state. The Great Wall of China is sometimes regarded as the border, or at least as a Chinese attempt to demarcate and stabilize that border. Obviously, it did not as the Mongols continued their invasions by simply bribing or threatening the gatekeepers to allow passage. Too, there were (and are) several Great Walls, also reflecting change and fluidity.

Among the striking features of the Great Wall, other than its scale and architecture, are its proximity to Beijing and its historical record of the flow and ebb of Mongol strength. Corporate Beijing now includes a part of the Wall within its territory, and in some places it is only 30 miles (48 kilometers) away from its center. The **marche** nature of the historic capitals is well demonstrated in this fashion. It is an existing record, too, of the push of the agricultural frontier westward and the advance of Chinese colonization.

Inner Mongolia, now reduced to a small portion of its former administrative extent, is really the core area occupied by the few remaining Mongols within China. Most Mongols dwell in the USSR or in the (Outer) Mongolian People's Republic. The term *Inner Mongolia* as used here refers to the wetter grasslands between the traditional Mongolian semi-desert environment and the wetter areas of grain culture. It is short grass steppe, for the most part,

but with a continuous vegetational cover. It extends from the Amur lowland to the foothills of the Tien Shan. Its southern and eastern limits are the Great Wall and the Great Khinghan Mountains. Its northern border is delimited by the territorial extent of the (Outer) Mongolian People's Republic.

Two of China's newer provinces Gansu (new in the sense of relatively recent enlargement) and Qinghai can be properly thought of as fringe China. The southwestern provinces of Yunnan, Guizhou, and Guangxi, though long conquered by the Chinese, also have something of the frontier aspect and are more properly considered a part of this subregion. (See Figure 8–11.)

Inner Mongolia   The enlarged Inner Mongolia described above can be subdivided into three parts: the inner slopes of the Khingan range, the developing center, and the western desert and semi-desert.

The easternmost portion presents a mountainous aspect only from the northeastern plain. The western slopes are a gentle, undulating, gradually sloping plateau surface covered with grass. Forests have not been totally destroyed; small clearings indicate the presence of the Chinese farmer and the attempt to extend the frontier of agriculture into the region. The area is not isolated, as two major railroads and many roads link it to the eastern plain. Two small oilfields and a coalfield of local importance are the known mineral wealth. It would likely have been cleared and settled under population pressures from a thickly settled Northeast had China remained a purely agricultural state. It was saved from earlier settlement by the actions of the Manchu dynasty, which preserved it as a private hunting ground. It shows little promise as a solution to Chinese food supply problems. Near the disputed frontier with the USSR and still peopled largely by Mongolians, it now has the aspect of a military frontier zone more than anything else.

The middle or developed portion is, if anything, drier than the portion already discussed and, therefore, seemingly less developable. This has not been the case. It has the official designation of the Inner Mongolian Autonomous Region, but the Chinese form the overwhelming majority. Here, true desert is intermingled with steppe, but the northern bend of the Huang He and other water sources present the possibility of irrigation.

Some 6 million people live in the region but only 600,000 to 900,000 are Mongols—the rest are Han Chinese. The Chinese have attempted to sedentarize the Mongols as the area becomes a major grain-producing region under the impetus of irrigation.

More economically important is the city of Baotou, a major new Communist investment area with a giant, inte-

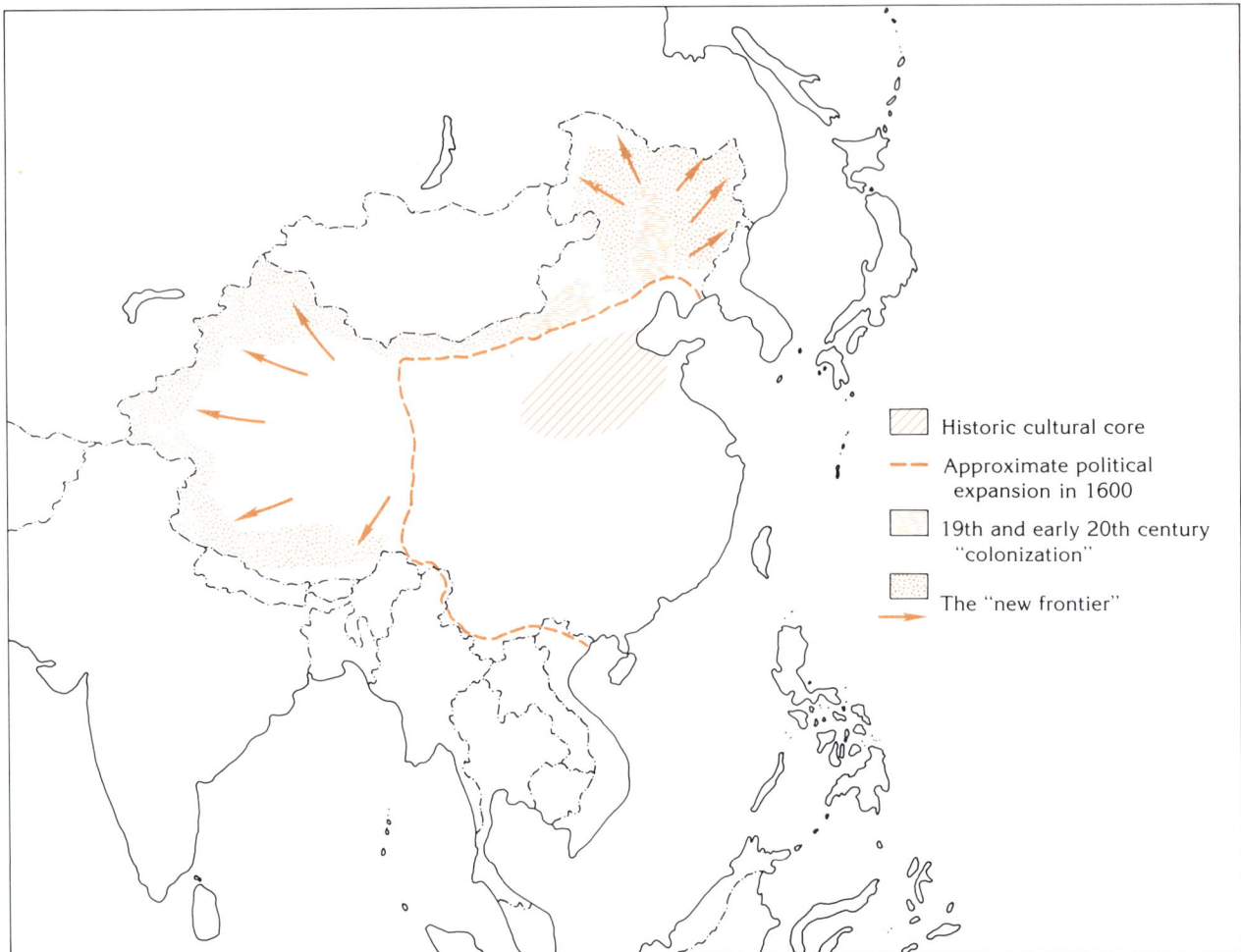

FIGURE 8–11

Expansion into "Frontier China." The Han (ethnic Chinese) have been expanding into other parts of what is now China proper for many centuries. Late nineteenth century colonization of Manchuria was followed later by more migration to the peripheries, particularly to Manchuria and the semiarid west.

grated steel mill—a virtual symbol of the government's determination to develop the interior. With both iron and coal nearby, it is a logically located investment in terms of raw material assembly costs. Its purpose, is as "seed industry" for further development and the purveyor of structural steel for construction.

The western, almost unpopulated third is largely desert. With little water available for irrigation, it derives its importance from recent oil discoveries virtually just inside the border. The Hui, the ethnic element from which that autonomous region derives the name, are Moslems. Many are converted Han Chinese in Gansu province, but others (some 3 to 5 million) are descended from Turkic tribesmen who migrated from central Asia.

Gansu province represents an early Chinese advance to the west. It is effectively a penetration of Chinese settlement separating Mongol from Tibetan. Hemmed in by mountain and desert, it is surprisingly well watered and has a milder than anticipated climate given its latitude and interior location. The soils are rich, wind-blown loess. Rice, cotton, and tobacco are grown under irrigation, once serious erosion has been stopped by the use of strip-cropping, terracing, and contour plowing. The area is traditionally known for its apricots, peaches, and melons, but the agriculture is quite diverse. Irrigated areas (and settlement) are being expanded by tapping underground waters.

An ancient caravan route has been paralleled by an important railroad that extends westward to within 200 miles (320 kilometers) of the Soviet border. The province is rich in oil and gas, and it has developed a rather large chemical industry to use that resource. It is the development of industry, rather than increased cultivable area, that will most likely be responsible for the growth anticipated in the area.

The southwest is a land that has been Chinese for centuries, yet it is not typically or thoroughly Chinese. It is limestone country in wet, almost tropical southern China.

The karst topography (limestone eroded by underground water) yields a landscape of sinkholes and solution valleys interspersed with rounded hills and residual rock contorted into strange shapes by a combination of tectonics and erosion. This fertile country is often difficult of access and was not thoroughly incorporated into China until this century, though Han Chinese migrants to the area long ago came to be the dominant ethnic group. Once famous for its opium (one of the few crops of sufficiently high value to bear the difficult journey and consequent high transportation costs to market), it grows two crops of rice a year and produces sugar as well as a wide variety of fruits and vegetables. Recent large-scale irrigation projects have increased the arable area and greatly improved yield on existing farms. High-grade deposits of tin, tungsten, antimony, bauxite, copper, lead, and zinc make it a veritable mineral storehouse. There is even coal and iron, and a local steel industry has developed. Huge water power potential promises a bright future in the development of metallurgy.

The Guizhou Hills, east of Yunnan, are dissected into tortuous slopes. There is little level land and virtually all slopes have been cleared and terraced. Little land is wasted. The Miao, Yao, and Thai minorities constitute a large percentage of the population. Forced into the hills by Chinese in-migration, they pursue an extensive form of crop agriculture. During the Communist period of control, new crops and techniques have been introduced into the native agriculture, resulting in higher regional food production. Reforestation of some slopes has checked erosion, improved water supplies and created a new regional resource in an area of rapid tree growth. Vastly improved rail connections are paving the way for ultimate industrial development.

The Guangxi region and the island of Hainan represent truly tropical China. Peopled largely by Thai-related peoples in rural areas (if Chinese in the city), the area is among the most ethnically diverse in China. Intensive Chinese rice culture in the area yields three crops yearly. Sugar, bananas, citrus, and a wide variety of tropical fruits and industrial crops provide high-quality, hard-currency-earning exports. Intensification of agriculture has brought an influx of Chinese into one of the last colonizable areas (or, rather, intensifiable) of China.

Collectively, then, the Chinese fringe represents an expansion of the core area into the colder, drier, and hotter margins, respectively, of the country. Intensification of agriculture and new irrigation schemes have enabled all the areas involved to absorb migrants from the overcrowded core area. At the same time, new employment has been created by mineral exploitation and industrialization. Part of what Mao saw as a new Chinese heartland, this area has benefitted from massive investment in the agricultural,

transportation, and industrial sectors. At least the provincial capitals have been industrialized on a major scale. This subregion is gradually becoming an outer industrial crescent providing raw materials and semimanufactures for the Chinese core as well as a base of developmental supply for areas farther west.

Frontier China   China has a "Wild West" comparable in some respects with that of the nineteenth century U.S.'s Wild West. In one extremely important respect, though, they are not comparable. The Americans could cross a wide belt of rugged mountains and plateaus of arid and semiarid climate with the goal of better-watered, good-quality farmland on the Pacific coast. For the Chinese, their western territories of desert and semiarid lands, mountain chains, and plateaus ends in political boundaries across these rugged drylands, not a potentially productive and very attractive ocean shoreline.

China's western territories are not, of course, mere wastelands. Mineral prospecting is not yet complete, but there are promising finds of oil and metallic minerals. There is some opportunity for irrigation projects to add badly needed agricultural lands. But, as noted earlier, the overwhelming bulk of Chinese live in the eastern heartland or core, and the inner ring. Until recently, however, the Chinese have considered these largely barren lands lightly populated by non-Chinese ethnics as **tribute territories** of the Chinese state. Little attempt was made to assimilate these groups.

The Chinese did not garrison and effectively administer many parts of outer China despite official territorial claims. The last imperial dynasty, that of the Manchus, asserted control over the largest territories ever claimed as part of the Chinese Empire. The varying degree of actual control over these fringe territories is illustrated by the political divisions of *inner* and *outer,* applied to both Mongolia and Tibet. Outer Mongolia, mostly the Gobi Desert and semiarid grasslands near the Siberian frontiers, was poor in resources and too remote from China proper to justify much military or administrative effort on the part of the Chinese. Outer Mongolia historically was left pretty much alone as long as the official overlordship of the Chinese emperor was acknowledged. In contrast, Inner Mongolia was really governed by the Manchu emperors, and Han Chinese farmers were encouraged to settle there under the protection of the Chinese military.

Inner Xizang (Tibet) is that part closer to China and long effectively under Chinese control. Outer Xizang (Tibet to Westerners), was the more remote and rugged part of the plateau. Claimed as part of the Chinese Empire, Tibet effectively governed itself as the Chinese presence in Lhasa, the capital, was a handful of Chinese who were usually ignored. The British presence in Lhasa was stronger than the Chinese for the first four decades of the twentieth century. Tibetan trade, for example, flowed southward to India over the 15,000-foot (4,600-meter) passes of the Himalayas because the longer routes to China proper were infested with bandits. Tibet's "port" for its relatively small international trade was Calcutta rather than some Chinese coastal city. Had a powerful and determined British Empire remained in India longer, it is not impossible that Tibet would have become a political and economic satellite of India, much as "Outer" Mongolia has become such a satellite of the USSR.

The Low Utility West An area of low utility and sparse population, lies in Xizang and Xinjiang, extreme western Sichuan, and most of Qinghai and Gansu provinces; these areas have periodically been independent and sometimes controlled by powers other than China. The high plateaus and mountains of Xizang and Qinghai are the highest land on the earth's surface. Most of Xizang has a tundra climate or is covered by permanent ice and snowfields except in a few sheltered valleys and lower basins. Much of the surface is bare rock or has a comparative dusting of infertile soil. The agricultural prospects are anything but promising. Much of Xinjiang is a desert basin, one of the driest in the world. Spots favorable to agriculture have been long settled, and expansion of arable area is a risky and costly process.

Since neither area is close to core China and both have scant transportation networks, these territories remain remote—beyond the fast-paced development associated with the rest of China. Now firmly controlled and integrated politically and administratively with the rest of the state, they remain peripheral to the economy.

Xizang (Tibet) Xizang's population of 1.7 million is still largely composed of natives. Only about 7 percent of the people are Chinese, largely administrators and military. Some one hundred thousand Tibetans live in exile in India and Nepal, while an additional 2 million live in southwestern China and parts of Xinjiang. The distinctness of ethnicity results in its government as an autonomous region. The traditional religion is the Lamaist variant of Buddhism. The monasteries controlled much of the wealth and the limited land; nationalization of both took place almost immediately.

The government has attempted to raise the standards of development in Tibet with a number of massive investments in irrigation and built a skeletal, but modern, system of roads. Textiles, leather, cement, fur, paper, and fertilizer industries have been established. A number of small plants produce farm implements and equipment. A coal mine has been opened, and a few hydroelectric plants

provide electricity to limited areas and power to the first elements of a planned fertilizer and chemical industry. The area is now self-sufficient in grain (largely barley), and dairying has been introduced. There is a forest resource in the extreme southeast of some value. Salt lakes, which abound on the high plateau, could ultimately supply valuable chemical salts. The numbers of yaks and sheep have increased sharply under Chinese control, and hides and wool now move into the Chinese commercial economy. Much of China's hydroelectric potential is in Xizang.

Xinjiang At times this area has been a virtual satellite of Russia. During the period of amicable Soviet-Chinese relations, this region was seen as a vital link between the two governments. A railroad, which extends as far as the capital city (Urumchi), was to link core China and the Soviet core area via Xinjiang and Soviet Central Asia. More promising than Xizang in terms of accessibility, it develops at a more rapid pace.

The largest group, the Uighur, a Turkic people, form about 45 percent of the total 12 million. The Chinese now constitute the second largest group (35 percent), where before 1949 their numbers were negligible. Most of the Uighur are Moslems. Most of these border peoples have tribal, linguistic, and cultural affinities across the Soviet border—a potentially dangerous situation for China (and for the USSR).

The area is completely encircled by mountains. The alluvial fans at the botton of the slopes are irrigated and intensely farmed. These oases, on both sides of the desert, were important watering places for the caravans of ancient and medieval time, which brought silk and tea westward.

The country is composed of two large basins. The larger (Tarim) basin of the south is usable only with irrigation. Alpine pastures are grazed in summer and intermediate slopes provide grass in winter. Camels, goats, and sheep are the major livestock. The northern basin is better watered and is rather more steppe than desert.

Chinese horticulturists and agronomists have done much experimentation in this area. New irrigation techniques and new hybrids, coupled with a tripling of the arable land (on a small beginning base), have brought great increases in food production.

Large oil fields and moderate gas deposits are the most important mineral production. Coal, gold, copper, and molybdenum are produced in small amounts. A pipeline now flows oil eastward.

Despite evidence of progress, the area is still a frontier region. The dead-end nature of the location (due to the Sino-Soviet dispute) and the remoteness from market, as well as the limited usable land, will likely limit further development for some time to come.

THE EAST ASIAN SHATTERBELT

The term *shatterbelt* describes an area containing many small political units—**successor states** to empires that formerly dominated the area. The great colonial empires of Britain and France, once active in the area, have all but disappeared; the great empire of Japan is dissolved. Russia's influence in the region has waned. Several new, small states have appeared to replace imperial holdings. A power vacuum exists where once the great political forces of an era contested for trade privileges and colonial holdings.

The successor states in East Asia seem to have become more economically powerful than their predecessors. Hong Kong, while still a colony, booms and grows into an industrial giant from a miniature base. Taiwan, ostensibly a rump Nationalist China in exile, is proportionately more developed than mainland China. Korea, split into two states by cold war politics and nearly destroyed by a civil war supported by contending great powers, prospers in two halves—each oriented in a different economic and ideological direction.

Only Mongolia, caught between the Soviet Union and China, remains economically quiescent and politically without influence. If this is related to physical isolation and distance from markets, the better fortunes of the other successor states are explained by their very openness and accessibility. At the outer edge of East Asia, they are open to contact. Unable to recede into self-sufficiency and purely domestic concerns, they must reach out to the rest of the world for survival. They have discredited the myth that densely populated countries, heavily reliant on agriculture, cannot hope to develop.

Position, then, can be viewed as extremely important. Domestic initiative has certainly been more important than superpower guidance and investment. Japan, deprived of much of its imperial land and resources, almost devoid of a military establishment, has surged forth as the region's economic superpower. Perhaps its example has been as important in the growth of regional economies as anything else.

The Koreas In common with Germany, Korea is a cultural, national unit split by "cold war" politics. As in Germany, the splits grew out of what was thought to be a temporary division into military zones of occupation. The Soviet Union entered the war in Asia only shortly before the surrender of Japan, which had occupied Korea since 1895. Both the Communist state (with its capital at Pyongyang) and the Republic of Korea (which uses the traditional capital at Seoul) claim jurisdiction over the entire peninsula. Doubtless many Koreans yearn for a reunification under an elected government to reestablish the long history of the Korean state. There is, however, little likelihood of peaceful reunification.

Korea is not particularly rich in natural resources. There is a minor deposit of low-grade iron ore in North Korea (Democratic People's Republic of Korea), along with small scattered deposits of gold, copper, and iron alloys and both anthracite coal and lignite. (See Figures 8–8 and 8–9.) The very considerable hydroelectric potential of the Yalu River (the boundary with Manchuria) was largely developed by the Japanese during their imperial control.

South Korea's (Republic of Korea) resource base is even poorer than that of North Korea. Until 1948, coal and electric power flowed south across the thirty-eighth parallel. A small anthracite coal field and even smaller deposits of tungsten, gold, silver, copper, lead, and manganese exist, but South Korea's remarkable industrial growth has occurred despite, rather than because of, its resource base. Japanese investment had concentrated in what became North Korea, so that the South started with very little industrial *infrastructure.*

The Korean War, 1950–53, was disastrous for North Korea's population and only slightly less traumatic to the South. Korea's population had risen quickly under the Japanese occupation. Investments in industrialization, the growth of transport systems, and the expansion of cities had spurred employment and improved the standard of living to some degree. About 13 million Koreans in 1900 had grown to 26 million by 1944. In that year, some 8.8 million lived in North Korea and over 17 million lived in the South—about a two-to-one ratio. The dramatically larger loss in North Korea is evidenced in the 1960 figures—South Korea had attained a population of over 25 million, while the population of North Korea had declined to 8.2 million, increasing the ratio to three to one. As both economies recover, the disparity has lessened (see Table 8–2).

TABLE 8–2

Population of Korea in selected years (in millions)

	North Korea	South Korea	Total
1900	—	—	13.0
1944	8.8	17.5	26.3
1949	9.5	19.2	28.7
1960	8.2	25.4	33.6
1978	16.6	37.0	53.6
1980	17.9	38.2	56.1
2000 (projection)	27.4	51.1	78.5

Despite their geographic position between two much larger, occasionally aggressively expansionist nations, the Koreans are a distinctive people with their own language, society, and rich cultural heritage. They may have originated in the forests of central Asia before migrating to the Korean peninsula. Some migration from China (extending for many centuries into the modern era) completed the melding of the Korean people.

Agricultural output and growth rates show a sharp contrast between North and South. Rice is the predominant crop in both Koreas, forming more than half the total tonnage of farm products. Other crops include barley, millet, soybeans, and sweet potatoes. North Korea has had a serious problem in feeding its population. Despite minor concessions like private gardens, collectivization into "cooperatives" has not produced the surge in productivity precipitated by South Korea's incomplete land reforms. South Korea's agriculture is becoming commercial and shifting to much greater emphasis on livestock raising.

View of Seoul, South Korea. Seoul's recovery from wartime destruction has been phenomenal, as American and Japanese investments helped the South Koreans achieve one of the world's fastest growth rates. (Courtesy of United Nations)

South Korea's urbanization and industrialization can only be described as explosive. Seoul has a population of over 8 million and is expanding rapidly. The industrialization of South Korea has set new world records in terms of pace of development. While Japan already possessed an industrial base and large skilled industrial labor force on which to build its postwar "economic miracle," South Korea has zoomed from a largely preindustrial stage in 1945 to an economic power by the 1980's. South Korea's progress from 1965 to 1980 equals a half century of development in older industrial nations. Within the present decade, South Korea will probably become the third largest shipbuilder in the world, and its steel industry will produce double that of Britain's. The total economy could match that of West Germany well before the close of this century. The electronics industry is already one of the world's largest. This success story is based on high rates of capital in-flows and shrewd government economic planning.

The stability provided by the South Korean government and U.S. defense forces, together with the strongly pro-growth attitude of both government and people, attracted heavy investment from Japan, the United States and overseas Chinese interests. Japanese investment and even trade was at first discouraged due to bitter memories of the long occupation, but is now rising. South Korea's burgeoning tourist trade rests largely on Japanese tourists. The South Korean economy has recently shown some signs of the strain of being the fastest expanding in the world. Inflation and rising wages have resulted in the loss of some markets for cheap consumer products to Taiwan and Hong Kong.

As would be expected in a country undergoing massive industrialization and explosive urban growth, environmental pollution is growing. Potentially controversial is the government's decision to rely very heavily on nuclear power generation to reduce dependence on OPEC oil. By the mid-1980's, eight nuclear generating plants should be in operation. South Korea also operates a tidal generating plant on the west coast where 30-foot (10-meter) tides are common.

Seoul, the traditional capital and now a world city, is clearly the economic and cultural "capital" as well as the seat of government. Its growth and corresponding congestion have meant the construction of two subway lines in a city that was almost destroyed in the Korean War. Clearly, any future reunification of the peninsula logically would focus on Seoul as its capital.

North Korea's rate of economic growth has been comparatively less spectacular. By the late 1970's, the North was producing 50 million tons of bituminous coal annually and about 15 million tons of lignite—represent-

Export Processing Zone, Kaohsiung, Taiwan. In this combination of a free-trade zone and industrial park, over 40,000 workers use the latest technology to expand export and attract still more industry, using the zone's transport and industrial material advantages combined with tax benefits. (Courtesy of United Nations)

ing a growth rate of over 500 percent in twenty years. The country is a major producer of tungsten. Large zinc deposits accounted for 3 percent of world production, a major accomplishment for a small country. True to the Marxist format, it has emphasized the production of heavy industrial goods, though there is significant development in textiles. A major producer of electrical energy, it consumes roughly double the energy per capita of South Korea. A rapidly expanding chemical industry produces large amounts of fertilizer, some of which is exported to China. Intensive use of fertilizer from this new industrial branch has increased rice yields by about 30 percent since 1975, and the general agricultural picture has brightened considerably in recent years. Though North Korea has fewer people to feed from a larger area, much of its area is mountainous and ill-suited to agriculture. Fully 70 percent of its area is in forest.

North Korea is in the unenviable position of being the neighbor of both the Chinese and Russians at a time of poor relations between those two countries. It has moved deftly, maintaining trade and an amicable relationship with both. It has capitalized on its machine and metallurgical base, supplying these commodities to Vladivostok and the Soviet Far East. China purchases machinery in addition to electrical power, fertilizer, paper, and lumber.

The Republic of China (Taiwan)   Taiwan, an island 100 miles (160 kilometers) off the coast of mainland China, is about one third the area of South Korea. Coal and abundant natural gas comprises the industrial resource base,

supplemented by salt and a variety of construction materials. The island is about 60 percent forested. A mountainous "spine" dominates the east coast, while the west coast has some coastal plain well suited for agricultural production.

The population of some 18 million includes about two hundred thousand original Taiwanese, the descendents of Chinese who had migrated there before the Japanese took over in 1895, and about 2 million mainland-born Chinese who moved the capital of Nationalist China to Taipei following the communist victory on the mainland.

Following the loss of control over the mainland, the Chinese nationalist government introduced a successful land reform in Taiwan. Tenant farmers could buy land at 2.5 times the value of annual yields, payable over ten years. Landlords cannot hold more than 7.5 acres (3.0 hectares). Landlords were compensated for the full amount received from tenants; many landlords whose wealth was then liquid became entrepreneur industrialists. Agricultural propserity supported industrialization by reducing food imports and supplying raw materials for a growing food-processing industry. Subtropical and tropical Taiwan harvests two rice crops a year and is now more than self-sufficient in rice. Sugar, canned asparagus, canned mushrooms, canned pineapple, bananas, and tea are exported. Intense agriculture is necessary in very high density Taiwan, whose land supports more people than all of Australia, two hundred times its size.

In addition to food processing, leading industries include textiles, electronics, electrical appliances and machinery, motorcycles, and autos. Taiwan's shipbuilding industry is capable of building tankers of 500,000 tons. Industry accounts for about 85 percent of exports in value.

Taiwan's industrialization was spurred by the inflow of capital and skills with the arrival of the Nationalist Chinese. Political stability and the guarantees provided by the U.S. Seventh Fleet in the Taiwan Straits attracted investment from Japan, the United States, and Southeast Asia's sizeable "overseas Chinese" business community, who seek stable capitalist countries in which to invest.

A growing petrochemical and petroleum refining industry is based on local natural gas and imported oil. Taiwan expects to have at least five nuclear generating plants in operation by the mid-1980's. The Republic of China was bitterly disappointed at the diplomatic recognition by the United States of the Communist regime at Beijing. However, trade relations between the United States and Taiwan continue largely unaffected, and so far the shock has been more psychological than economic. It may be possible for the PRC and ROC to coexist in a loose arrangement that would save face on both sides and maintain Taiwan's autonomy. Certainly the Republic of China, which out-produced the entire mainland's industrial plant during the early 1970's, could be a valuable asset, whether under full political control or not, to the planned economic expansion of the PRC.

Hong Kong Politically, the British crown colony of Hong Kong is an antique—a leftover from the age of European colonial imperialism. Hong Kong is partly a prize of war— the island of Hong Kong and a small tip of the Kowloon peninsula were ceded to Britain by China after losing a minor skirmish called the Opium War, 1839–42. Britain fought the war to open China's markets to opium produced in British India. The opium would pay for Britain's imports from China. The original cession of some 33 square miles (85 square kilometers) was later augmented by the leasing of the adjacent 365-square-mile (945-square-kilometer) "New Territories"; this lease expires in 1998.

Hong Kong's original function, like those of the many treaty ports in which Europeans and Americans enjoyed special privileges, was as an **entrepôt,** or transshipment, warehousing, and wholesaling point. In the face of a largely incompetent and corrupt civil administration in China under the last dynasty, the Western powers sought the security and trade advantages of their own little spheres of control. It was the Westerner's law and order that prevailed in the treaty ports. Trade could be negotiated under Western laws and military protection; the treaty ports were run by Westerners for the benefit of Westerners. The products of China were gathered into the ports for warehousing and wholesaling to Europeans and Americans.

Hong Kong's trade relationships expanded to important contacts throughout the Orient as the volume of its trade increased. It became a market for both Chinese and Western goods for Indochina, Malaysia, the Philippines, and Indonesia.

During World War II, Hong Kong was controlled by the Japanese, who also controlled most of eastern, coastal China. Nationalist China did not envision a continuation of colonialism in postwar China, but a local British garrison's initiative raised the flag after the Japanese surrendered, and all sides accepted that Hong Kong was still British. The civil war in China, which ended in the Communist victory, had several far-reaching effects on Hong Kong. Chinese fleeing the civil war and the repressive new regime boosted Hong Kong's population to 4 million from under 1 million in the early 1930's. Many, but certainly not all, of these new arrivals were Chinese businessmen and entrepreneurs whose status was in jeopardy under Communist rule. Sometimes these immigrants brought some capital along with managerial talents and industrial skills.

Within a few decades, Hong Kong was transformed from a predominantly trading economy to an industrial one. Trade was greatly restricted with China as the Communist government concentrated on internal reorganization problems. The long nonrecognition of China by the United States also affected trade. Curiously, though, the official ban on U.S.-China trade made Hong Kong even more important as a neutral trading point. Chinese materials and semifinished goods were shipped to Hong Kong, finished and packaged, and sent on as made in "British Hong Kong" and thus acceptable in U.S. markets. Similarly, American technology could be exported to China via Britain and Hong Kong. Trade between China and the Western nations could be financed through Hong Kong's banking facilities, which included both the Beijing government's Bank of China and branches of important British banks.

Hong Kong has no industrial raw materials within its borders. Most of the colony is mountainous; only about 12 percent of its land is in crops or pasture. The high population density precludes self-sufficiency in food. Most of the fresh food, together with most of the water supply, flows across the border from China. Just by shutting off the water supply, Beijing could bring the colony to submission in a few hours. There are only about twenty thousand British in Hong Kong; it is a Chinese city whose unique political status offers advantages to the Chinese even more so than to the British. This explains its continued existence despite its origins in the humiliation of the last dynasty and its symbolization of Western domination.

Hong Kong's industrialization is based on abundant, cheap, and hard-working labor, and on capital in-flows from refugees and overseas Chinese. Textiles and clothing are major products. Plastic consumer goods, especially those requiring hand-assembly (such as plastic flowers) are a Hong Kong specialty, along with electrical goods and transistor items. Hong Kong is the world's largest "shipbreaking" center where obsolescent ships are dismantled into scrap and reusable parts. It is also the world's largest producer of toys.

Hong Kong, Taiwan, and even South Korea to an extent, can be viewed as examples of the potential of disciplined labor, high savings rates, and good long-range planning that could be effectively harnessed for the modernization of the PRC. Whether the Beijing government can pragmatically override traditional Marxist philosophy sufficiently to fully use this impressive human energy and talent still remains to be seen.

Mongolia Mongolia, wedged between the Soviet Union and the People's Republic of China, has been alternately dominated by each of its far more powerful neighbors for the last several centuries. Known as Outer Mongolia, it was a Chinese province from the late seventeenth century to 1911 when, during the turmoil of the overthrow of the imperial Chinese state, Mongolia became an autonomous state under Russian protection. This Russian "protection" dissolved in the Russian revolution, and Mongolia was briefly a Chinese province again (1919 to 1921). Independence was again declared and a treaty signed with the Soviets. A 1946 plebiscite overwhelmingly reaffirmed Mongolia's independence of China. Since then, Soviet political and economic influence have intensified, with Soviet troops stationed in Mongolia since the 1960's. Ironically, Mongolia at one time was a world power that had conquered most of present-day USSR and China. The Mongols once ruled from the coasts of China to Poland and Hungary.

Outer Mongolia's physical and economic geography is related to its alignment with the Soviet Union. The only really usable lands of Mongolia are in the northern grasslands and forests of the Siberian border. This inhabited part of Mongolia is separated from Chinese settlements in Inner Mongolia by several hundred miles of desert. Economic ties, as a result, are much stronger with the USSR than with China, although the Mongolian capital of Ulan Bator is connected by rail with both China and the USSR.

Mongolia's nearly 2 million people are predominantly Mongol ethnics with a 5 percent Kazakh minority and some Chinese. The population growth rate is 3 percent, one of the higher increase rates in the world, reflecting a dramatic shift in the economy from nomadic herding to an industrializing society. The USSR and various East Eu-

ropean states have provided the technical assistance and financial aid to fuel Mongolia's rapid modernization.

The resource base is fairly impressive considering the relatively small population. Coal production is over 3.5 million tons per year, and there are large deposits of copper, molybdenum, phosphorite, and tin. A minor oil field ceased production in the 1970's but geological exploration continues. Industry, mostly food processing, textiles, and consumer chemicals, already accounts for a larger share of the GNP than agriculture, which still employs half the labor force. Exports, however, are primarily agricultural—cattle, horses, wool, meat, hides, and grain. Eighty percent of Mongolia's foreign trade is with the USSR.

The Soviet military presence and virtual control of Mongolia's economy have established a great salient in the border with China. The PRC regards Mongolia as an **irredenta;** this may prove to be a major point of contention between the USSR and the PRC.

JAPAN: THE RISING SUN CONTINUES TO RISE

Japan is unique among the world's developed and powerful industrial states: it is the only such industrial state that is non-Western in culture. Japan is the third most productive modern economy. In many categories of economic production, Japan ranks first or second. It is first in shipbuilding, first in automobile production. Yet, Japan is slightly smaller than California. The other two economic "superpowers," the United States and Soviet Union, have huge territories and resource bases in comparison with Japan. Japan is the only economic superpower that is *not* presently a major military power. If population density is expressed in terms of cultivable land rather than total land area, then Japan has the world's highest population density, excepting only the city-states of Hong Kong and Singapore. It has 118 million people crowded into a few coastal lowlands and highland basins. Much of the mountain country is virtually empty.

If anyone believed that there is a direct cause-and-effect relationship between the physical resource base and level of industrialization, Japan would be the best counterargument. Japan's economy has averaged twice the growth rate of the United States through the 1960's and 70's. It accounts for nearly 10 percent of total world trade; its recent $3 billion a year trade surplus with the United States is the greatest bilateral trade imbalance of all time. Yet Japan must import most of its coking coal, almost all its iron ore and petroleum, and all of its raw cotton and wool. The volcanic origin of portions of the islands has meant that Japan has plenty of sulfur. Thin, broken seams of coal fueled early industrialization, but now two thirds of consumption is imported. One sixth of its copper and one third of its lead and zinc demands are supplied by Japanese mines. There is very little prospect for offshore oil development and no significant home island source of uranium.

Population distribution in Japan is closely related to the limited availability of reasonably level, and hence easily cultivated, land. Much of Japan is made up of rugged forested mountains with narrow ribbons of agriculture and population in the valleys. Japan's largest plain, the Kwanto Plain around Tokyo, is only roughly the size of the Los Angeles basin, about 120 miles (193 kilometers) in length. Much of Japan's population is concentrated in the southern two thirds of Honshu, the largest island, and on the two southern islands of Kyushu and Shikoku. About two thirds of Japan's people are located on 31 percent of its total area. (See Figure 8–12.) Even preindustrial Japan was relatively heavily urbanized; Tokyo had a million people in 1700, making it the largest city in the world even then.

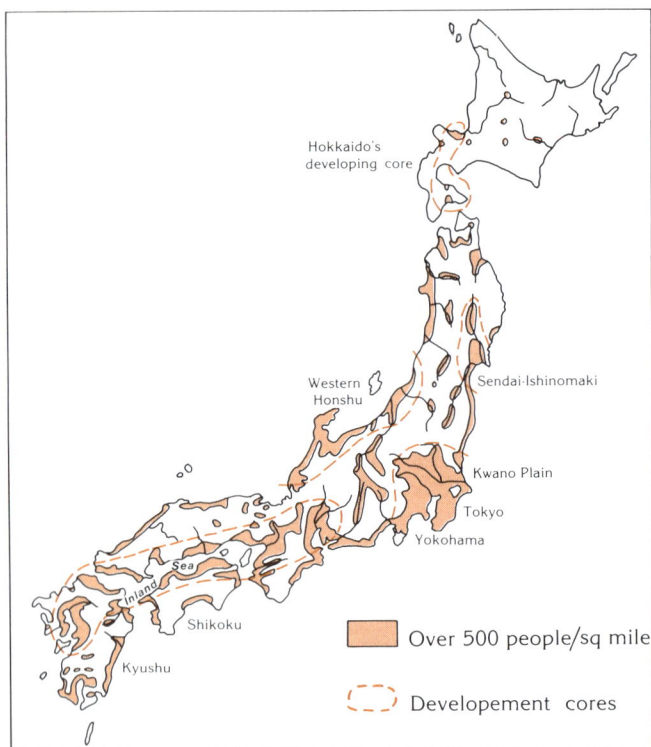

FIGURE 8–12

Population and Development Cores in Japan. Japan's population is heavily concentrated in the coastal pockets of lowland, leaving most of the mountainous areas virtually empty. Industrial development has likewise concentrated in coastal locations, particularly the "inland sea" between southern Honshu, Shikoku, and Kyushu, while Hokkaido is still something of a frontier.

Population control has been a prevalent feature of public policy since the end of World War II. Japan's population had tripled in less than a century from the "opening of Japan" until 1945. The birthrate had begun to fall slightly by the 1920's, but the shock of losing the war precipitated a drive to reduce it further. In 1945, Japan had lost an empire and shrunk to its mid-nineteenth century territorial status. Three and a half million returned to the home islands from the lost empire. There was a brief baby boom associated with returning veterans after the war. The birthrate in 1947 was 34 per 1000. By 1952 it had been reduced to about 20 per 1000. This meant that, during their great leap in industrialization, the Japanese population had relatively few young people to educate and care for; their elderly dependent population was also relatively small.

The Japanese population is almost homogeneous ethnically. There has been very little in-migration since 750 A.D. The Ainu, once dominant through the Japanese islands, are on the verge of cultural absorption. The only sizeable group of non-Japanese resident are six hundred thousand Koreans, the remainder of a large group imported as labor during World War II.

A curious group called the *eta* or *burakumin* are physically indistinguishable from other Japanese but are regarded as outcasts. Equal under law for a century, this continuing social prejudice may date from discrimination against a clan of butchers and tanners, much as India's Untouchables also necessarily violated religious proscriptions on taking life and handling carcasses.

Agriculture in Japan might better be described as gardening. The land units are minute by Western standards (the average Japanese farm is under three acres (1.2 hectares); 40 percent are less than 1.5 acres), and the productivity per acre is probably the highest in the world. Japanese agriculture is not as efficient per worker-hour as in the more mechanized United States, but yields of rice per land unit are at least 50 percent greater than in the PRC, and twice those of India. Large tractors would make little sense on very small units, but the Japanese have developed a small tractor that they walk behind. The American occupation government, led by General Douglas MacArthur, pushed through a massive and thorough land reform that forbade ownership of more than 7.5 acres (except in Hokkaido's New England-like climate). This reduction in landlordism, coupled with small-scale mechanization, has resulted in such high rice productivity that, with production increasing and per capita consumption falling, Japan must cope with a rice surplus. This surplus, as in many industrialized European nations, is, however, dependent on strict import controls and heavy subsidies. American rice could be delivered in Japan at about half the cost of raising it there.

New Tokaido Line ("Bullet Train"), Osaka, Japan. Japan has the world's fastest train service linking four of its largest cities, which are so close that air service is not as efficient as rapid rail service. Japan has clearly outgrown its onetime reputation as a copyist to become a leading innovator of technology. (Courtesy of United Nations)

Japanese agricultural imports emphasize high quality and luxury foods, especially proteins. Japan has only about 2.5 percent of its land in pasture; beef cattle are stall-fed. From the 1950's through the 1970's, Japan's dairy cattle population went from 140,000 to 2 million and broiler chickens from 18 million to 70 million.[5] Japan imports about 20 percent of its food; however, if imported animal feed were also considered it would reach 50 percent. Japan, again like European industrial states, accepts the higher food costs that result from subsidies and import restrictions in order to maintain a stable rural society and to avoid potentially disastrous reliance on imported food. Japan's proportion of population engaged in agriculture is now less than 15 percent (less than the Soviet Union's) and will stabilize at about 10 percent.

Agricultural productivity is enhanced by double-cropping in the southern half of Honshu and the southern islands. Rice is produced in summer, and a hardier grain or vegetable is grown in winter.

In the absence of a large and varied physical resource base, the Japanese industrialization has emphasized products in which human skill represents most of the value of the finished goods. Such products are termed **high-value-added** and are typical of resource-short industrial strategies such as that of Switzerland; high-quality cameras are an excellent example. Likewise, a finished automobile is worth far more than the value of the raw steel, glass, plastic, and rubber that went into it. The Japanese industrialization strategy has been obviously successful; among its key strengths are a prevalent group spirit of cooperation, a long-term beneficial interaction of corporate and gov-

ernment planning, and the internal flexibility of giant conglomerate corporations. (These concepts are more fully developed in the Case Study.)

Japan was never entirely cut off from the rapidly expanding technology of western Europe during its supposed isolation from the 1630's to the 1850's. During the late eighteenth century, the Japanese determined to acquire European technology selectively without the risk of associated colonial domination and/or trade exploitation. A few Dutch traders were allowed to establish themselves on a very small island offshore. The Japanese exported silk fabrics and porcelain to pay for illustrated encyclopedias, industrial models, and other sources of information on European technology. The government underwrote "pilot projects" in applying this technology, and as a result, when Commodore Perry "opened up" Japan, the Japanese were already experimenting with, and using, steam engines, power looms, metallurgical techniques, and other Western technology.

Government-fostered infant enterprises were sold off to reliable families for further development, starting a tradition of very close government-business cooperation that has persisted. Corporate size and concentrated power are encouraged, as they represent as advantage in world markets.

To praise Japanese labor as highly disciplined and motivated is almost an understatement. Japanese productivity per worker-hour would delight European, American, or Soviet managers. Production efficiency keeps increasing; production lost to strikes is one fourth that of Britain. Japanese workers of all ranks commonly are employed by only one company during their working life. Their pay scale is largely determined by their number of years *with*

[5] Robert Hall, *Japan: Industrial Power of Asia* (Princeton, N.J.: Van Nostrand, 1975).

that company, not their age or experience. Japanese workers are very loyal. In return for a practically guaranteed lifetime job, rising salary, and abundant fringe benefits, they sing the company song as they begin work and recruit their children to work at the same place. The average Japanese worker's buying power has historically (since 1950) increased at nearly 10 percent a year, so that loyalty and hard work pay off. There is, of course, a real possibility that worker enthusiasm would drop considerably if living standards ceased their upward climb.

Japanese workers get 20 to 30 percent of their pay in special bonuses at New Year's and midsummer, in addition to continuing weekly salaries. This system, together with the generally high rate of increase in buying power, facilitates a very high rate of savings, thus fueling business expansion with ready capital from banks fat with savings accounts. Japanese savings rates average from three to four times those of Americans. Japanese tax rates are somewhat lower than in the United States and much lower than in most West European countries; this also fosters savings.

Even Japan's mountainous, island geography contributes to efficiency of plant operation. Large tracts of flat land suitable for industrial location are almost inevitably on the seashore. Shallow water offshore from crowded, narrow coastal plains encourages new industrial expansion by dredging deep ship channels close inshore and filling in adjacent tidal lands, providing industry with ocean shipping facilities. Coastal location using imported raw material and supplying distant markets by sea is an extremely efficient transportation system compared to land transport system for long-distance freight movements as in the United States and USSR. (See Figure 8–13.)

Japan's "economic miracle" of rapid postwar expansion also owes much to American and European technology. The ubiquitous transistor, for example, was invented at the Bell Telephone Labs in northern New Jersey; it is difficult to imagine the Japanese economy without this piece of American ingenuity. Similarly, the German invention of the Wankel rotary engine was first mass-produced by the Japanese. Up to 1970, the Japanese had spent about a billion U.S. dollars on licenses to use the other's technology; they got a bargain. Much of American and European technology is a "spin-off" from very high-cost military-objective research. Its true cost of development would be hard to measure. Japan's very low profile military establishment spends a much smaller percentage of GNP than any other major industrial nation. Japan is an innovative industrial society, however, and Japanese technology is licensed to the West as well as the reverse.

Environmental pollution is a serious threat to high-density, higly industrialized Japan, which gets so much of

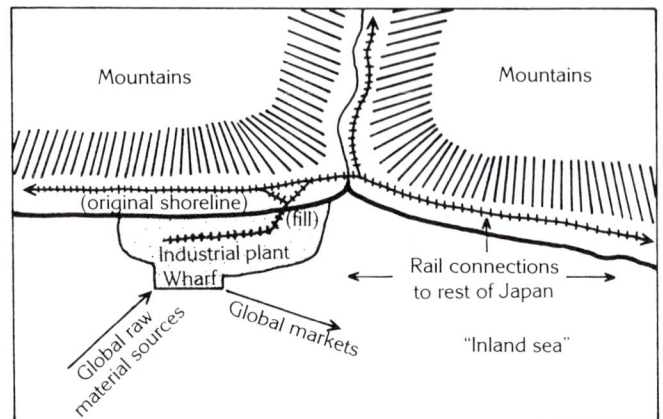

FIGURE 8–13
Schematic Map of Typical Industrial Site in Japan. The narrow, discontinuous coastal plains of Japan, backed by rugged mountains, favor coastal industrial locations often enhanced by dredging ship channels and filling shallows for plant sites. International raw material imports and large-scale exports of manufactured goods can thus directly use efficient ocean shipping.

its food from everyone's favorite dump—the sea. The Minimata Bay tragedy of the late 1960's is symbolic of the environmental poisoning that followed rapid industrial expansion. Mercury wastes from a pulp and paper mill's effluent permeated the sludge at the bottom of Minimata Bay; shellfish from the bay, consumed by local residents, had poisonously high concentrations of mercury. The effects were particularly tragic for the unborn children of mercury-contaminated mothers. Other heavy metals including calcium are present in many offshore areas; the effects of some of the pollutants are not always as immediate and drastic as at Minimata Bay. As Japan's economy matures, more money will be necessarily diverted to environmental protection.

Japan's education system deserves much credit for its success in adapting and innovating technology and in expanding international trade as well. A capsule definition of Japan's educational system has been given as "European quality, American quantity." Japan's dependence on a highly skilled and innovative labor force requires a superb, if rather rigid (by American standards) educational system. It is generally agreed to have the highest functional literacy rate of any country.

Traditional Japanese society did not develop concepts of inalienable rights of citizens, of representative government, or any of the philosophical foundations of democracy. Japanese feudalism committed the followers to obedience and loyalty, and granted the leaders almost unquestioned authority. This was tempered by a long tradition of group rather than personalized leadership. It was made difficult, deliberately, for one person to exercise au-

Steel Plant, Wakayama, Japan. In common with most Japanese heavy industry, this steel plant, dependent on imported ores and fuels, is located on tidewater, a location that also facilitates exports of the finished product. (Courtesy of United Nations)

thority; group discussion would lead to a consensus of leaders, which seldom was at variance with what the population as a whole would accept. Group decision making was prevalent and remains characteristic of the economy and government both. The 1947 Constitution, largely the effort of General MacArthur, functions quite well, and Japan is a true democracy although many Western-imposed concepts of government have been turned to strictly Japanese applications and functions. There are occasional anti-government demonstrations and some small, troublesome dissident groups. However, there are no internal cleavages of note, and neither government nor social instability is a problem as long as Japan grows and prospers.

Tokyo as a World City The aggregation of Tokyo-Yokohama-Kawasaki is the quintessence of the concept of a world city.[6] Depending on exactly where the planning region boundary is drawn, this great area contains between 25 and 30 million people (in bounding most metropolitan areas around the world, determining just how far out into the surrounding sprawl of suburbs and satellites one carries the official area is a complex problem compounded by varying political and economic definitions of *metropolitan area*).

By both Japanese and European standards, if not those of the New World, Tokyo is a fairly recent city; the first permanent nucleus of future Tokyo was only estab-

lished in 1456. The site of Tokyo is on a well-protected bay, backed by the largest plain in the islands. Its situation is on the largest island, Honshu, approximately central to the four main Japanese islands. (See Figure 8–14.) Less than a century and a half after founding, it was the de facto seat of power in Japan under the Tokugawa regime. Tokyo became the official capital with the restoration to full power of the emperor in 1868. By 1920, Tokyo City had 3.3 million. The 1923 earthquake did not halt growth; rather, it accelerated the decentralization of the city already then under way. Heavy industry moved south along the bay shore toward Yokohama, while residential areas moved toward higher land. Similar decentralization phenomena can be observed in London and Los Angeles, among others.

Tokyo's growth in the modern era has been powered by heavy in-migration. Japan's natural increase rate has fallen in almost every year since the 1930's, as birthrates fell faster than death rates. Internal migration explains Tokyo's growth as employment shifted from agriculture toward manufacturing and services. The services sector accounts for almost two thirds of the city of Tokyo's employment (the administrative unit, not the metropolitan area). Tokyo's renowned congestion and overcrowding of public transport (official statistics show that rail cars and subways commonly carry 200 percent or more of their design capacity) has led to a large subway expansion program.

Housing problems reached nightmarish proportions during the period of rapid postwar growth (4 million new metropolitan residents added in ten years); some companies resorted to building apartment houses for exclusive

[6] Peter Hall, *The World Cities* (New York: McGraw Hill - World University Library, 1966).

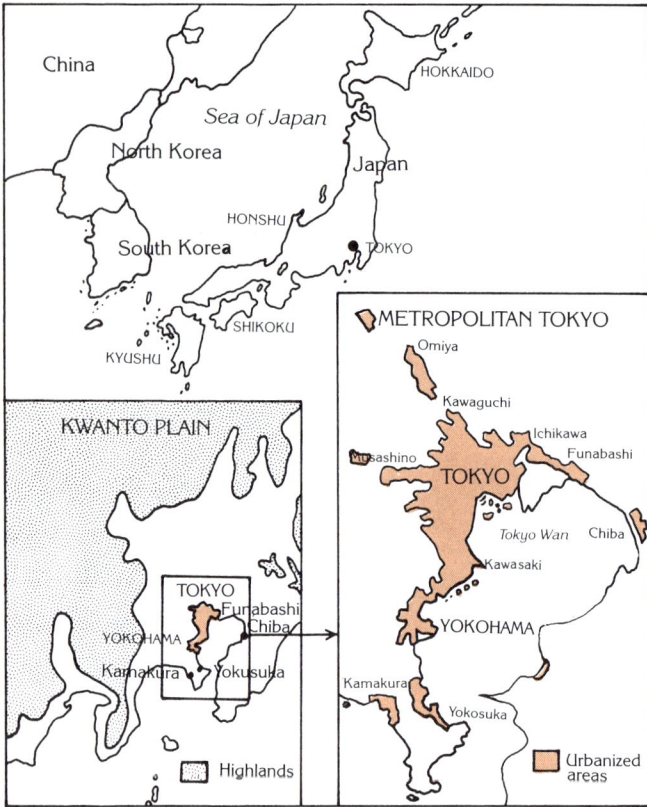

FIGURE 8–14
Metropolitan Tokyo. Tokyo claims the title *Largest City in the World*; it almost certainly was the largest city in the late eighteenth century. (As elsewhere, definitions of *largest* depend on the choice of a boundary for the metropolitan area.) Tokyo now is clearly a world city in economic and cultural significance.

rent to their employees. Many Tokyo families occupy a total housing space of less than 400 square feet (37 square meters), the equivalent of a single room, 20 feet (6 meters) square. The explosive growth of the metropolis has severely strained sewage, water supply, refuse disposal, and surface traffic control services. The pragmatic Japanese are decentralizing some 80,000 government jobs to the far suburbs. Filling in large portions of shallow Tokyo Bay and building up (Tokyo has a relatively "low profile" among the world's great cities—a fact not unrelated to the frequency of earthquakes there), the city is able to continue its growth despite the scarcity of land.

SUMMARY

From a global viewpoint, the East Asian region is far from stable. The existence of "two Koreas" and "two Chinas" points out the potential instability of the region. North Korea is constantly probing for weakness or failing resolves in South Korea; this could be the birthplace of another war. It is by no means clear what relationship will develop between the two Chinas. Despite their diminutive size in

area and population, the nationalist Chinese have near-equivalent economic power until the mainland fully industrializes, a process that may well take decades. As Hong Kong's importance as an exchange point dwindles with the U.S. recognition of the PRC, Hong Kong's status could be changed in a few hours by a Chinese invasion.

Japan is a superpower economy and a very influential nation in world cultural and trade affairs, but it is not a great power in the military sense. There can be no doubt, however, that Japan could easily and quickly mount a full military establishment if it resolves to do so. Its enormously productive and sophisticated economy, heavily dependent on imported raw materials, requires free and secure access to global shipping lanes. If Japan should sense a threat to its economy by rising tension, and if the certainty and effectiveness of the U.S. alliance were questioned, Japan could be a resurgent military power. Japanese economic interests are paramount in any survey of the East Asian region. While some Japanese see China as a "natural" trading partner, with its great need for technology, its still incompletely exploited resource base and its huge potential markets, others would prefer to concentrate on North American raw material investments, Australia's coal and ores, and Siberian development schemes in cooperation with the USSR.

TENSIONAL RELATIONSHIPS WITH OTHER REGIONS

Large-scale Japanese involvement with the PRC could endanger their limited, but growing economic relationship with Soviet Siberia. A "trade war" with the United States is not impossible. The Japanese appear unable to appreciate Western resentment at Japanese insistence on free-trade access to world markets while maintaining formidable barriers to Western penetration of Japanese markets. A serious recession in Japan's North American markets for manufactured goods coupled with continued price gouging in petroleum (Japan is the world's largest single importer), could lead to labor unrest as buying power ceases its heretofore dependable increase. Any instability in Japan could be a tragedy on a truly world scale.

The Japanese share with China, on a much smaller scale, the claim to national territory once controlled by them but now "temporarily" under another state—the USSR. The Japanese would like to regain the Kuril Islands, lost in the last days of the Second World War. (Japan also lost its southern half of Sahkalin Island but appears to have resigned itself to that loss.) China claims a much larger territory in the Soviet Far East. An aggressive tsarist empire acquired large areas of the weakening Chinese Empire in the eighteenth and first half of the nineteenth centuries. The Chinese have regarded these territorial transfer treaties as unequal ones forced on a temporarily

Tokyo-Kobe Expressway, Japan. This toll expressway is designed to supplement the New Tokaido Line as a major artery in Japan's most densely populated, industrialized area. The transport infrastructure of developed, as well as developing, nations must be maintained at the highest level of technology to support continued growth. (Courtesy of United Nations)

enfeebled China. The PRC has published maps showing the area between the Manchurian border and the Pacific coast (including the Soviet's naval base at Vladivostok) as being "currently under Soviet administration." It is not impossible that a Japan that may surpass Soviet economic output by the turn of the century and an expanding, nationalistic China with a major grudge to settle, could be, in combination, the most serious threat facing the Soviet Union. A possible, if not probable, merger of Japanese technology and industrial power with Chinese manpower and raw materials could eventually form the world's most powerful alliance since the victorious allies of World War II.

THE REGION'S WORLD VIEW

Optimistically, the East Asian region could reach and maintain a mutually beneficial economic and cultural in-

teraction with their Pacific basin neighbors. The "Greater East Asia Co-Prosperity Sphere," which Japan once sought to build with conquest and colonial control, exists now in peaceful trade. International trade, investment flows, and tourism now link most of Southeast Asia, Oceania, and the East Asian shatterbelt with Japan. If the war-born animosities and suspicions about Japanese intentions can be minimized, it is probable that Japan and its trading partners could create a kind of "Asian Mediterranean," a region of close cultural and economic interaction that could evolve into a dynamic new hybrid civilization. A stable and prospering East Asia could strengthen its links with Western culture in Oceania and North America to make the Pacific a new focus of economic and cultural vitality surpassing even that of the North Atlantic.

case study
BUSINESS AND GOVERNMENT IN JAPAN: CONTROL AND COOPERATION

The astounding success of the Japanese economy, despite the presumed handicap of domestic shortages of virtually every industrial raw material, has already been described. The vigor, adaptability, and flexibility of the Japanese economy and society would suggest that Japanese organizational goals and systems, specifically the relationships of government and private enterprise, can be studied profitably by others. If the Japanese have paid Westerners, especially Americans, the high compliments of adopting many of their technologies, styles, and popular culture, Americans should not lose sight of the fact that the United States is moving toward a society with many of the problems familiar to the Japanese.

The United States is becoming more strongly influenced by international trade and is no longer largely independent of large-scale imports of natural raw materials. The United States is no longer, actually or psychologically, living in an era of abundant resources with limited incentives for conservation. Many of the challenges to America in its third century are similar to the challenges that the Japanese have met successfully. Modern Japan is clearly a distinctive culture, nation, and economy. It is not an Oriental version of the United States, no more than the United States is a Western mirror of Japan. There is little possibility of an overall comprehensive copying of cultural adaptations to problems of economic development, resource management and conservation, environmental pollution control, and maintaining and increasing qualities of life; nor is there a need to. The United States can learn from the success of Japanese institutions and economic/political philosophies without copying them but rather by selectively adapting them.

The obvious differences between U.S. and Japanese cultural, economic, and political philosophies and systems should not blind Americans to significant similarities. Both are prosperous, highly industrialized nations. Both have had to deemphasize labor-intensive industries under increasing competition from, among others, the East Asian shatterbelt. Both emphasize capital-intensive, research-oriented industries. Both value the goals of universal education. Capitalist free enterprise dominates each countries' economy. In both, environmental pollution controls are successfully minimizing the degradation resultant from rapid expansion of and crowding of industry. Japan and the United States have each invested heavily in foreign countries to insure a continued flow of raw materials to their economies. Both are functioning, if not perfect, democracies. Both have established foreign branch plants to take advantage of cheaper labor.

Since the middle of the nineteenth century the Japanese have consciously embarked on an extensive redesign of their society, specifically their economy. The well-known adaption of Japan to the then-superior Western technology from the 1860's was matched by the drastic reorganization following World War II and its loss of empire. The Japanese economy has twice been focused upon "fast catch-up"; twice the pragmatic Japanese have designed systems of rapid assimilation of information and technologies. The result has been the rise of an industrial and technological prodigy. For example, Japanese watches outsell the Swiss product; the Japanese expanded faster into new technologies like digital electronic watches than did the long-term quality leaders of Europe and the world. Japanese cameras and optical equipment have surpassed German products, even within Germany. Only a decade ago, the American market's major imported car was the West German-made Volkswagen, but now VW is fourth behind the Japanese makers. (American-made VW's are not, of course, considered an import.) Japan annually exported about 2 million cars to the United States by the late 1970's.

As noted elsewhere, it is not a case of cheap labor that explains Japan's successful penetration of American and European markets. Although difficult to measure in terms of buying power, tax burden, and quality of life, Japanese workers earn wages roughly comparable to those of Americans. Efficiency and high productivity in Japan account for their success in international markets. It is estimated, for example, that Japanese auto workers produce about five times as many autos, by value, in the same time span as their British counterparts.

There are cultural reasons for the high morale, high productivity, and outstanding loyalty of Japanese workers. The Japanese emphasis on communitarian approaches to labor management and incentives, productive involvement of labor in decision making, and identification of labor's interest with corporate success is not necessarily uniquely Japanese nor alien to U.S. society. The earlier history of Japanese industry exhibited motivational problems and high turnover in some cases; Japanese owned and managed plants in the United States show some of the same worker loyalty and high standards of productivity among their American workers as among their Japanese workers. The Japanese stress on seniority in wage rates, rewarding loyal service, would not be alien to traditional U.S. labor movement policies. Strenuous efforts to maintain the employment of their employees, through retraining and shifting to other facets of the corporate structure, pay off for employer and employee alike. The Japanese policy of early retirement for the managerial elite opens up promotion opportunities.

It is in business-government relationships, however, that the Japanese have worked out a highly effective system of mutual support and interaction. The Japanese conception of the range of activities engaged in by one corporation is much broader than that characteristic of Western culture. The Japanese have no narrow restrictions on corporate enterprise. For example, Japan has a nationalized rail network serving the entire country. Privately owned railroads are encouraged to serve some of the commuter routes around big cities. Their routes and operations are planned in conformity with those of other private railroads and of the state-owned systems. The railroad operations of these private corporations usually do not make profits. But, these companies also own huge department stores and shopping complexes, perhaps including restaurants and offices, atop their central city station. The people they deliver by rail to the central location help make that location very profitable, more than making up railroad operating losses.

The relationships between big business and the national government in Japan are based more on a concept of common interest and national goals rather than on a suspicious, adversary relationship. The Japanese recognize the worldwide, competitive value and powers of large corporations. Consolidation of companies into fewer giants with larger shares of the market is viewed as desirable. The Tokyo government, for example, has attempted, unsuccessfully so far, to encourage Japan's six major auto manufacturers to consolidate into two or three. Fewer but larger, richer corporations would give Japan an edge in the increasingly highly competitive world auto markets. In contrast, in the United States, the Justice Department has viewed General Motor's share of the domestic market (about 50 to 60 percent) with trust-busting alarm. In Japan, successful businesspeople, especially in export industries, are heroes. Information on international markets and economic trends is shared by corporation and government to mutual benefit as their common goal is a stronger Japan, better able to compete in world markets.

If there is a "Japanese miracle," perhaps it is their ability to screen out ideology and focus on pragmatic analysis. Problems are solved the most efficient and profitable way. Their organizational genius is directed at exacting the maximum effort from each to the maximum benefit of both the individual and the society. Their amazing success deserves study and suggests selective emulation.

REVIEW QUESTIONS

1   What evidence exists in the non-Chinese cultures of the region of China's cultural dominance?

2   Where was the original core of the Chinese state? How did it spread outward?

3   How does China's "Wild West" compare with that of the United States? What are the important differences between these Wild Wests?

4   Japan's relationship to mainland Asia has been compared to Britain's relationship with mainland Europe. What are the critical similarities and differences?

5   What are the major characteristics of Oriental intensive agriculture?

6   Cite evidence for the apparent supremacy of ideology over practical economics during part of the Communist regime in China.

7   How have the Chinese communes been modified recently to encourage greater production?

8   Briefly summarize China's raw materials base for further industrialization. Where is necessary technology likely to come from?

9   How have China's developmental strategies changed from just after the consolidation of Communist control to the present?

10   What were the obvious inefficiencies of the People's Republic of China's Great Leap Forward?

11   What historical and cultural geographic factors contribute to the potential instability of the Russo-Chinese border, particularly in the east?

12   Compare the PRC and Japan in terms of their present and potential military and economic power.

13   Why did North Korea start with an industrial infrastructure superior to that of South Korea? Why has South Korea far outdistanced North Korea now in industrial output?

14   What are the implications for Taiwan (Republic of China) of the U.S.'s official recognition of the PRC?

15   Briefly describe Taiwan's developmental strategy.

16   Why has the PRC refrained from reclaiming the British Crown Colony of Hong Kong?

17   Why did Hong Kong's economy make a rapid transition from a predominantly trading center to an industrial one? What are its industrial assets?

18   What were the key factors in Japan's postwar revision and expansion of its industrial strategies?

19   Why do many Asians think that Japan has built a kind of economic empire throughout parts of East and Southeast Asia?

20   What cultural factors are significant to Japan's reputation for high productivity in quantity and quality?

21   Briefly describe Japan's domestic raw materials base.

SUGGESTED READINGS

1   KEITH BUCHANAN, *The Transformation of the Chinese Earth.* London: Bell, 1970.

2   RAFE DECRESPIGNY, *China: The Land and Its People.* New York: St. Martin's Press, 1971.

3   ROBERT HALL, *Japan: Industrial Power of Asia.* Princeton, N.J.: Van Nostrand, 1973.

4 HERMAN KAHN, *The Emerging Japanese Superstate: Challenge & Response.* Englewood Cliffs, N.J.: Prentice Hall, 1970.

5 OWEN LATTIMORE, *Inner Asian Frontiers of China.* New York: American Geographical Society, 1940.

6 SHANNON MCCUNE, *Korea: Land of Broken Calm.* Princeton, N.J.: Van Nostrand, 1966.

7 VICTOR P. PETROV, *China: Emerging World Power.* Princeton, N.J.: Van Nostrand, 1967.

8 FORREST PITTS, *Japan.* Grand Rapids, Mich.: Fideler, 1974.

9 EDWIN REISCHAUER, *The United States and Japan.* New York: Viking Press Compass Books, 1965.

10 _____, *The Japanese.* Cambridge, Mass.: Belknap Press of Harvard University Press, 1977.

11 THEODORE SHABAD, *China's Changing Map: National and Regional Development, 1949–1971.* New York: Praeger, 1972.

12 GLENN TREWARTHA, *Japan: A Geography.* Madison: University of Wisconsin Press, 1965.

13 YI-FU TUAN, *China.* Chicago: Aldine Publishing Company, 1969.

14 EZRA F. VOGEL, *Japan as Number One: Lessons For America.* Cambridge, Mass.: Harvard University Press, 1979.

KEY TERMS

- Pax Britannica
- caste
- village autarky
- cultural assimilation
- nation-state
- iconography
- circulation
- demographic transition
- infant mortality rate
- monsoon
- infrastructure
- salination

- Green Revolution
- planned economy
- regional growth pole
- development enclave
- march (advance) capital
- takeoff
- plebiscite
- cultural hearth
- developmental strategy
- protectionist tariff
- ministate
- nonalignment

9

SOUTH ASIA

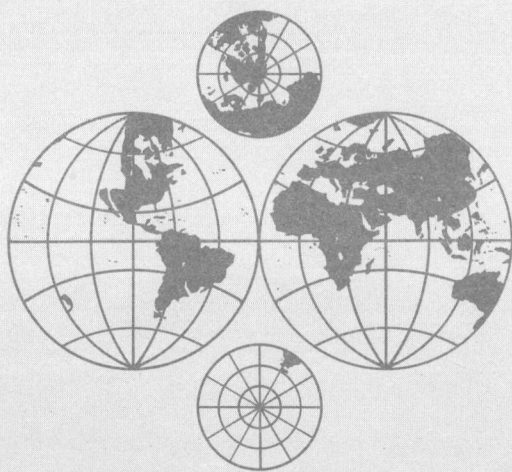

PROLOGUE: INDIA AND THE LEGACY OF COLONIALISM

India was, and remains, the clearly dominant state of South Asia economically and politically. Until 1947, the Indian Empire, Nepal, Bhutan, and Ceylon (Sri Lanka), all controlled by the British, were the only sizeable states in the region. Fabulous India was a giant magnet attracting European traders to this region a few centuries ago. The immense importance that Europeans placed on securing trade routes to India is evident throughout the history of European exploration. The Portuguese, in their quest for a secure route to India, circumnavigated Africa and established their claims to various African territories as convenient way stations. Similarly, the Dutch and then the British established themselves at the Cape of Good Hope largely to have a service port for shipping in the India trade. Even the European discovery of the Americas was an accident of the race to India.

India was renowned for vast wealth; it seemed a dazzling place to Europeans of three or four centuries ago with its near-monopoly on diamonds. Sapphires were another Indian export, along with a variety of spices needed to preserve foods. Rare and beautiful woods complemented elephant ivory in furniture and decorative pieces. Indian metallurgy was unsurpassed; its fine steel weapons and cutlery were world famous, as was its brassware. Indian cottons and silks were the highest quality available. The princes of India were conspicuous in their lavish display of luxury goods.

This image of wealth and superb craftsmanship did not reflect the realities of life for the vast majority of Indians. India was not a single, unified state, and never had been. The Empire of the Moghuls, in decline by the seventeenth century, had never conquered all of the Deccan while its own territories were collapsing into a chaos of small states plagued by guerrilla warfare. Internal trade was insecure and deteriorating; death rates were rising. The gradual assumption of control by the British undoubtedly was made easier because the Indians wanted and needed "law and order," even if imposed from without.

For the ninety years prior to 1947, *India* refers to the area now divided among the states of India, Pakistan, and Bangladesh. Nepal and Bhutan were strongly influenced by British India, while the island of Ceylon (the name was changed to Sri Lanka in 1972) was part of the British Empire until 1948. Thus, during the colonial period, the term *India* referred to almost the entire region.

THE ADVENT OF THE BRITISH

The English were late getting started in the race to establish trade centers in India. By the late 1600's, however, the Portuguese presence in India had been weakened by losing several sea battles to the English. The Dutch were concentrating their attentions on the islands of Southeast Asia. The French colonies in the south, strong before 1740, were reduced to tiny coastal settlements by 1760; Portuguese holdings were soon limited to a few coastal colonies. By the middle of the eighteenth century, there were no major competitors blocking British control of India.

The frequent inability of local rulers to maintain safe conditions for trade led, inevitably, to the British East India Company's generally becoming a political as well as an economic force. The Company prospered, sometimes returning a 200 percent dividend in one year. Such profits led, naturally, to a very strong desire to remain in control of trade, which in turn meant both putting down internal rebellion and safeguarding hostile frontiers. The British government began regulating the political activities of the Company in 1773, assuming full authority after the Indian Mutiny of 1857. The princely states, still under native Hindu, Moslem, or Sikh rulers, were also incorporated into the empire. Self-rule was permitted within strict limits of cooperation with the British. Few princes rebelled and none succeeded. The troublesome northwest frontier was defined by the end of the Second Afghan War in 1880 and the Indian Empire continued in relative peace, excepting the Japanese threat in World War II, until 1947.

The British Empire in India dominated the entire region, including Ceylon. It unified India by direct economic and political action, and, unwittingly, by being the focus of the independence movement. In the almost century of empire between crushing the Mutiny and granting independence, Britain achieved a remarkable degree of economic development in India. To be sure, India itself literally paid for this progress, through taxes, exploitation of its resources, and the high profits made in trade between industrialized Britain and developing India. Nonetheless, the progress was real and unprecedented.

THE ADMINISTRATION OF THE INDIAN EMPIRE

British India was an accidental empire. Trade remained a paramount concern of the British after the government replaced the Company as ruler and pacifier. Prior to British control, wealth was achieved through conquest. Warrior castes conquered a village, took over its land, rented it back to the villagers and thus became relatively rich. This militaristic quest for land was one of the leading causes of the continued flair-ups of invasion and war that bled village India for centuries. Military strength produced wealth; un-

less control were ruthlessly maintained, the land was soon transferred to other military victors. The **Pax Britannica** (the period of peaceful stability enforced by British military power) put an end to this chaos and reordered the hierarchy of Indian society.

There were amazingly few British in India to rule the 300 million Indians in 1858, or 400 million by independence. An average of two thousand British bureaucrats were employed in the Indian Civil Service. Ten thousand British officers led the two hundred thousand Indian troops of the Indian Army, augmented by sixty thousand British troops. A few tens of thousands of army dependents and similar number of business people were the only other British in the polyglot sea of Indians. It says much for both British policy and administration and Indian desires for peaceful achievement of independence that no bloody rebellion against the British occurred for nearly ninety years.

GANDHI'S SPINNING WHEEL: POLITICS AND ECONOMICS INTERWOVEN

The textile industry of India has had both economic and political aspects since British involvement in the seventeenth century. In this early colonial period, the quality of hand-made Indian cottons was world-renowned. British legislation designed to protect the developing cotton textiles industry of Lancashire, England, restricted the import of Indian cotton cloth at the same time that cheap, factory-made cotton cloth from England began to flow to India. British India could not erect similar tariff barriers, and British textiles drove higher-cost hand-loomed cotton out of this market. As early as 1851, an Indian entrepreneur imported machinery from Britain and started a cotton mill at Bombay. That city's merchants had developed business administration skills over a centuries-long trading tradition. By independence, there were over four hundred cotton mills spread across India, with Bombay the leading center. Thus, Gandhi's famous campaign against factory-made cloth was directed at British imports and against Indian industrialization as well.

A peculiar element of Indian society, probably related to the strong traditions and avoidances of Hindu **caste** customs, is the close coincidence of certain religious groups with entrepreneurial talents and ambitions. Business people tend to be from groups outside traditional Hinduism (Jains, Sikhs, and Parsees). Most of India's political leaders are from upper castes who consider themselves superior to the business-oriented merchant castes.

At least three different strands of political philosophy are woven into Gandhi's "spinning wheel" revolution against the British and the Indian capitalists. One was the genuine fear that industrialization and urbanization, the twin results of Western-style "progress," would destroy the Indian social fabric of self-contained traditional villages. Gandhi saw the human misery of the urban slums and rejected industrialization; he saw industrialization and urban poverty as cause and effect. Gandhi's vision was of a peaceful, traditional **village autarky;** his socialism was one of egalitarian cooperation among villagers rather than the Western-style socialism of an urban proletariat running huge factories. Another theme was the identification of industrial capitalism with the colonial ruler. Spinning one's own cotton and rejecting factory-made cloth was a symbolic rejection of Britain, and also a way of cutting British profits and tax revenues.

INDEPENDENCE AND PARTITION

Mohandas K. Gandhi (*Mahatma* is an honorary title meaning "great soul") was one of the world's least likely revolutionaries. A nonviolent pacifist, whose ultimate weapon was the threat to starve himself to death, he led one fifth of the human race to freedom. Gandhi's father was the hereditary prime minister of a tiny state near Bombay, and Gandhi was sent to England to study law in preparation for inheriting the position. In London, Gandhi had a brief fling with **cultural assimilation**— he bought Western clothing, tried to copy a British upper-class accent and even took dancing lessons. Unable to find work as a lawyer in India, he migrated to South Africa. There he was introduced to the racial segregation of public facilities, and there he developed his ideas and techniques for nonviolent protest.

In 1920 Gandhi began his long struggle to achieve an independent India. He was characterized by an intriguing mix of forthright practicality and, to Westerners, a cheerful determination to ignore the realities of culture, politics, and human failings. Gandhi appeared to underestimate the depth and rigidity of the fundamental religious split within India and to overestimate the average human's capacity for saintly behavior. Gandhi's now-famous tactics of passive resistance, featuring nationwide "strikes" in which everyone was supposed to stay home or visit a temple for prayer, probably would have failed in almost any other circumstances than in British India. The indigenous population was so immense compared with the small number of British, and the Empire so exhausted and sensitive to democratic public opinion at home, that

independence did come with no blood shed between ruler and ruled. The tragedy of independence was the warfare between Hindu Indian and Moslem Indian, not between Indians and British.

Territorially, the subcontinent was not composed of a few massive blocks of Moslem land flanking a huge Hindu territory. The pattern was more one of an incredibly complex mosaic of tiny, interwoven Moslem or Hindu parcels of land, buildings, or businesses. In many of India's hundreds of thousands of villages, both Moslems and Hindus, sometimes in company with a few other religious sects, lived out their lives almost literally side-by-side. Rioting between the two groups became unfortunately common; economics was a basic reason. India before the British had been controlled mostly by Moslem rulers in the north and center. Under the British, the Moslems were not able to maintain their former educational superiority over the Hindus. To Hindus, British control and introduction of Western technology and economic systems presented a much greater opportunity than it did to most Moslems. As independence approached, British India's Moslems were not about to be submerged numerically in a Hindu-dominated state. Although Gandhi, with his characteristic mix of shrewd foresight and impractical generosity, suggested that the Moslems be reassured of their status within a united India by letting them run the new government, the Hindu majority understandably was adamant about one person, one vote.

Mohammed Ali Jinnah emerged as the leader of a movement for an independent Pakistan, a Moslem state to divide British India with an independent Hindu India. *Pakistan* was a created name, formed from the names of Moslem-dominated provinces of the Punjab, Kashmir, and Sind. The violence that swept the subcontinent when independence was promised by Britain precipitated an incredibly short timetable for British withdrawal. The decision was made to grant independence to India and Pakistan quickly, so that a civil war might be averted.

Boundary lines were drawn under the pressure of a deadline, by British bureaucrats who knew little about the cultural and economic complexities of India. Had the boundary makers been more knowledgeable and had more time, though, the boundary would still have been an impossible job in terms of equity to Hindus and Moslems. Millions of people fled across borders that did not exist a few days before; between 200,000 and 500,000 were killed in violent riots against former neighbors. This tragedy was compounded by the Kashmir question. Kashmir is a strategically situated state where China, India, and Pakistan meet. Located in the Karakorum Mountains west of Tibet

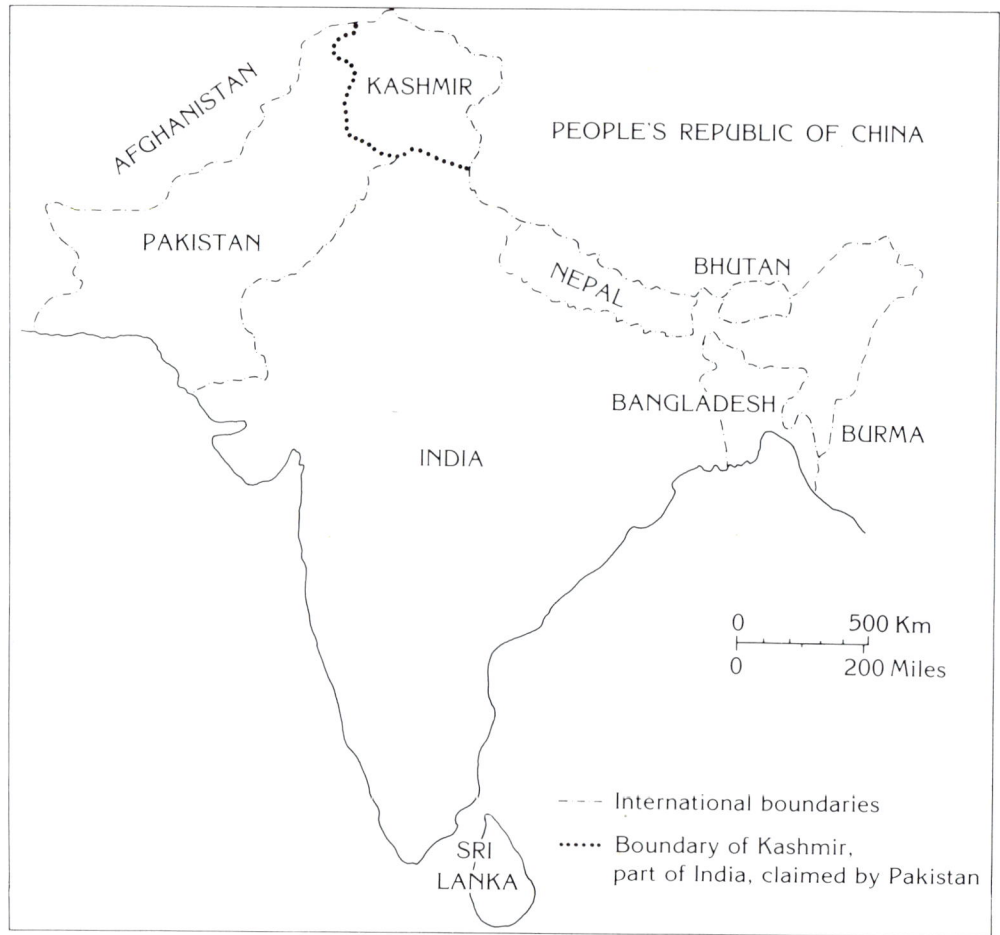

FIGURE 9–1
Partition of British India and Kashmir. At independence the former British Indian Empire was split into two states, a Hindu India and Moslem Pakistan. As the two peoples were intermixed, spatially, millions found themselves on the "wrong" side of a border. The Hindu ruler of predominantly Moslem Kashmir insisted on joining India, creating a dispute that still persists.

and (except for a small portion) north of the great alluvial plains of the subcontinent, Kashmir had a hereditary Hindu maharajah who ruled over a Moslem majority. (See Figure 9–1.) The future leaders of India had at first agreed with the British that Kashmir would join Pakistan. The maharajah, though, prevailed on India to back his decision to take the state with him to Hindu India. Kashmir, together with the legacy of bitterness occasioned by the partition of India, has been the cause of several India-Pakistan wars.

THE DISTINCTIVENESS OF THE REGION

Unity is a basic ingredient in nationhood. Without it, there may be no nation, only a country struggling for survival, unable to turn its attention to domestic and international problems and opportunities. While India is an independent **state,** it is not yet a **nation-state** in the sense of a Sweden or Japan. Some social scientists would compare the In-

dian subcontinent with Europe rather than with a single country.[1] Pakistan and Sri Lanka both have also experienced problems of unifying their different ethnic groups, but their problems hardly approach those of India in scale and divisiveness.

HISTORICAL AND CULTURAL CHARACTERISTICS

Many Indians speak more than one language and some of India's 782 languages are spoken by only a few thousand. The largest single language and first official language, Hindi, is spoken by less than one third of all Indians. There are four "major" languages in the south—the Dravidian languages of Telegu, Tamil, Kannada, and Malayalam, but these are more distinctly different than are the northern languages. The "major" northern, Indo-European lan-

[1] Walter Neale and John Adams, *India: The Search for Unity, Democracy and Progress* (Princeton, N.J.: Van Nostrand, 1965).

guages are descended from Sanskrit—these are Hindi, Punjabi, Rajasthani, Marathi, Gujarati, Pahari, Kashmiri, and Oriya. Each of these is as different from the other as are the Latin-based languages of Spanish, Rumanian, or Italian. This basic Sanskrit-Dravidian divide follows the borders of various empires of the past. The communications problems brought about by multiple languages is illustrated by the continuing use of English, the language of the departed colonial ruler. Although only about 2 percent of the population are literate in English, these tend to be the educated elite, as the university system developed under the British used English as the language of instruction. Thus, India, which hardly needs another language, continues to use English as an "associate" language in which, in fact, most government business is transacted.

To the complex Indian language mosaic must be added a very fundamental cultural factor—the variety of religions. About 85 percent of Indians are Hindus, but the Hindu religion contains at least as many different sects and denominations as does Christianity across the world. About 10 percent of Indians are Moslems, with 2 percent Christians and nearly 2 percent Sikhs, a group concentrated in the Punjab. Small numbers of Buddhists along the Himalayan frontier and Jains and Parsees are other small minorities.

The fundamental conflict in the subcontinent was, of course, between Islam and Hinduism. The Hindu religion is considered native to India, its written forms having originated in the Indus valley about four thousand years ago. There is little in the way of specific philosophy or dogma; Hinduism is very tolerant of a wide range of individual beliefs and practices. It may have grown and prospered in this culturally fragmented land because it was able to absorb many different cultural traditions without forcing homogenization.

Islam, introduced into the region by invasion and conquest after the eighth century, is about as different from Hinduism as is possible. Islam, the youngest of the three great Western religions, is philosophically much closer to the other two, Judaism and Christianity, than it is to Hinduism. Like Christianity, Islam is a proselytizing religion—it seeks new converts; Hinduism does not actively seek new adherents. Islam is strongly monotheistic (it recognizes but one God) as opposed to Hinduism's large numbers of gods and goddesses. Islamic religious rites feature solemn, austere ceremony and contemplation, while Hindu ceremonies are exuberant, noisy affairs with bells and firecrackers. Islam preaches the essential equality of all people, while Hinduism included a social system of strongly stratified castes.

The strong fractionalization of India's culture—its deep divisions of religion, its large number of languages,

none numerically dominant, and its racial and other cultural fragmentations—has presented many obstacles to unification. The primary historical and cultural forces have been Islamic conquest, British imperialism, and the struggle for independence. Each of these successive factors has had a greater impact upon unification than its predecessor. The fact is that India was never a unified state until 1947; even the split of Hindu India and Moslem Pakistan (and, later, Bangladesh) created fewer major states than had ever occupied the subcontinent until then.

Political geographer Jean Gottmann categorizes state-building factors as **iconography** and **circulation.** *Iconography* is the set of ideas, beliefs, interpretations of history, heroes and heroines, and concepts of the state's role and goals that ties together people into a nation. A strong iconography shapes a strong, unified state. In Eastern Orthodox Christianity, *icons* are two-dimensional religious pictures; in the political geographic sense, icons are symbols of shared beliefs that focus on a state and loyalty to that state. *Circulation* refers to the physical communications and transportation systems and structures that literally tie the country together. A strong, well-developed circulation system is one in which ease of communications and transportation is better from any part of the state to any other part of the state than it is from any part of the state across an international border.

A state with more than a dozen major languages, a sharp division philosophically between the two largest of many religions, a variety of cultural-racial heritages, and a history of political fragmentation has serious problems. The political unification problems of India illustrate the reasons for the lack of prior unity.

ECONOMIC CHARACTERISTICS

The railroad system, a legacy of colonialism, reflects both the positive and negative aspects of British imperialism in India. India has the fourth greatest total track mileage in the world. It has the next best system in Asia to Japan. The system inherited from the British in 1947, however, had several serious handicaps, and much effort has been directed at modernization.

Because the railroads were designed to expand the major port hinterlands and thus extend the lucrative trade between Britain and India, the rail lines radiated out from Bombay and Calcutta, and to a lesser extent, Madras and Karachi. Facilitation of trans-oceanic trade with Britain, rather than the fostering of internal development, was the primary goal. A secondary role of the railroads was to move troops quickly within India and especially to its borders. Because direct British internal rule never extended over all of India, the rail lines were constructed mainly in those parts of India ruled directly rather than in the princely states. The British saw to it that the main lines connecting major cities and administrative/garrison centers were broad gauge (5 feet 6 inches or 1.6 meters). However, several narrower gauges were constructed in the princely states and in areas of difficult terrain where there were construction cost advantages to narrower roadbeds and tighter curves. If cheaper to build, in the long run the narrow gauge lines are very expensive for the country because they form entirely separate systems. (See Figure 9–2.) Freight must be reloaded onto a car of another gauge when goods move from one gauge to another, and passengers must change cars. About half of India's track mileage of 35,000 miles (56,000 kilometers) is broad gauge; the rest is meter gauge or even narrower.

This hodgepodge of different gauges is only part of the problem; other difficulties were antiquated equipment and inadequate maintenance. The Republic of India has nationalized all railroads and modernized them enough to have quadrupled the 1947 freight volume. India's passen-ger rail figures are also impressive because few Indians can afford to use the domestic airlines and very few have private cars. Despite the problems, the railroad system acted (and acts) as an economic unifier, tying together (if with difficulty) all parts of the subcontinent, including the now-separate rail nets of Pakistan and Bangladesh.

PHYSICAL CHARACTERISTICS

It is not an accident that the Moghul Empire, like the earlier empires, was more successful in dominating northern and central parts of the subcontinent than the South. From the highlands of western Pakistan to the heavily forested Assam hills on the Burma frontiers, a great alluvial plain stretches for some 1,200 miles (1,900 kilometers). The Indus River drains the northwestern fifth of this plain, while the central and largest portion is in the Ganges and Jumna systems. The easternmost region is drained by the Brahmaputra system, which merges with the Ganges in its

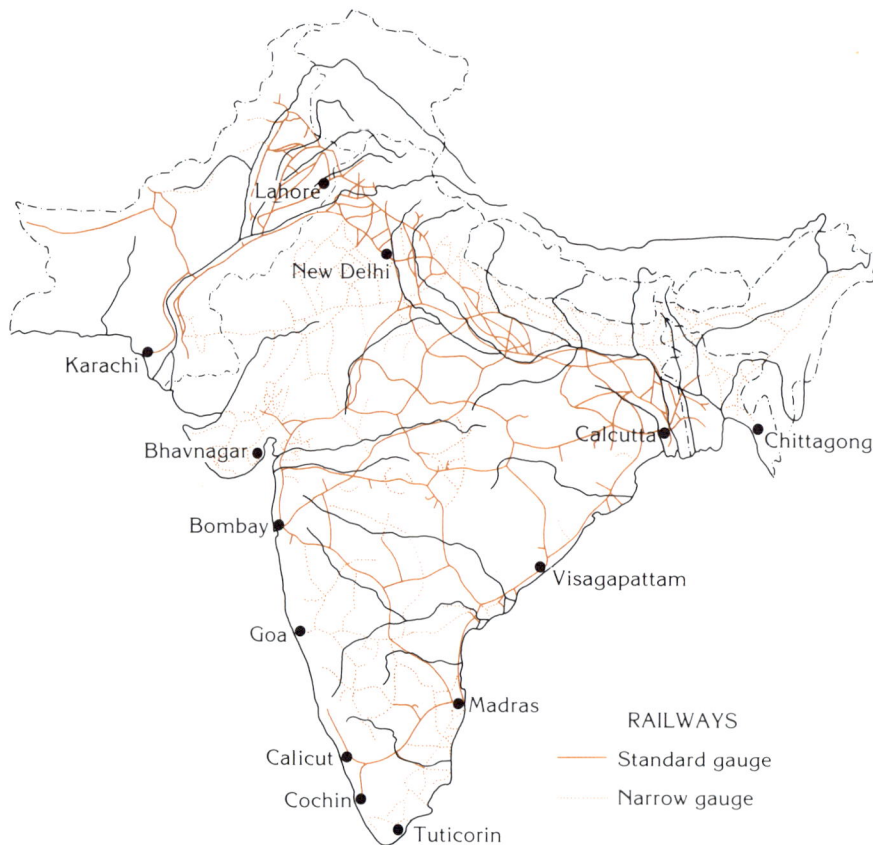

FIGURE 9–2

Major Rail Lines in South Asia, Showing Narrow Gauge Lines. British colonial investment provided South Asia with a dense rail net, but one whose utility is diminished by being of different gauges; trains cannot move onto a different gauge track. Narrow gauge lines, cheaper to build, sometimes were developed in areas of lower military-strategic importance.

great delta at the head of the Bay of Bengal in modern Bangladesh. Successive empires have proven that it was easier to extend military and administrative control over this vast plain with its peripheral hill lands than to extend that dominance southward across the Vindhya Hills to the Plateau of Deccan, an ancient block of the earth's crust. Tilted higher on the west, this block forms an escarpment, the Western Ghats, averaging five thousand feet in elevation. The eastward, down-tilted section of this plateau of igneous rocks is heavily dissected by stream erosion that follows faults and zones of weakness in the plateau. In between is a rugged country, not impossible to penetrate, but certainly more difficult in terms of establishing transport-communications circulation. Post-independence India and Pakistan split this great plain between them, with East and West Pakistan occupying the opposite ends of the plain. (See Figure 9–1.) There is a natural physical unit in the great peninsula of land southward from the high mountains of the Hindu Kush and Himalayas, but it has never supported a single, unified state.

POPULATION GROWTH AND DEVELOPMENT: THE PRESSURE OF PEOPLE

Although there are other densely settled areas and certainly other very poor countries, South Asia has acquired an image of both poverty and high human density. This poverty image has been compounded by the assumption (often untrue) that high density and the prevalence of poverty are cause and effect and, furthermore, that significant alleviation of this problem is unlikely.

There is little doubt that the size and growth rate of its population is the central problem of the region. Clearly, the area has not completed the **demographic transition** (a model, introduced in Chapter 1, that links population growth rates with economic development). The picture is not one of complete, inevitable disaster. A survey of vital rates (see Table 9–1) indicates that at least India's natural increase rate, the "surplus" of births over deaths, has begun to drop.

While India's birthrates are still very high when compared with those of the developed world, they are lower than those of the rest of South Asia excepting Sri Lanka. They are considerably below some of tropical Africa's and Latin America's exploding populations but, significantly, far above China's. (A determined effort there by a nondemocratic government has reduced long-term, traditionally high rates.) India's natural increase rate currently would lead to a doubling of its population in 36 years, assuming that death and birthrates remained stable. Other "doubling times" are 58 years for China, 99 years for the United States, and 1,386 years for Sweden. Kenya, at 18 years, has the world's shortest doubling time.

Vital rates alone do not illustrate the magnitude and nature of India's population problems. India's population under fifteen is 41 percent. In contrast, that of China is 32 percent, the United States, 22 percent, and Sweden, 21 percent. In modern industrial societies, those under fifteen (and over sixty-four) are likely to be nonproducers while still being consumers. A very *young* population (one with a large proportion of under-fifteens) will have correspondingly high expenditures on education. However, while persons in their early teens are almost invariably dependents in industrial, urban societies, in traditional India they would be active contributors to the family's income and food supply. This illustrates one aspect of the dilemma of developing nations: overcoming the traditional, agricultural-based, conservative cultural pressures to have many children. Although there is a complex of reasons for high birthrates, two outstanding factors are economic necessity and historically high death rates.

In India, where more than three quarters of the population are classified as nonurban (generally, those living in communities of less than 5,000 population with no extralocal administrative functions), children are an economic asset in agriculture. Quite young children can guard fields against wandering cattle, tend livestock, collect dung for fuel, weed, and generally make themselves useful. Older children can approximate an adult's economic contribution, so that poor farmers are encouraged to have many "nonpaid" family workers. The alternative to

TABLE 9–1
Vital rates, South Asia

	Population (millions)	Population Density (per square mile)	Natural Increase (percentage)	Percentage Urban
Bangladesh	87.5	1,510	2.14	13
Bhutan	1.4	65	2.31	NA
India	642.0	512	1.93	24
Nepal	14.3	248	2.26	4
Pakistan	81.2	224	2.40	28
Sri Lanka	15.6	560	2.18	26

a large family would be either (or both) a lessened capacity for working the land or the necessity of hiring outside labor. Also, children provide "social security" by helping to support and care for aging parents.

To these practical considerations must be added a historically high death rate. India's **infant mortality rate** (children, not including the stillborn, who do not survive to their first birthday) is still ten times that of the United States and sixteen times that of Sweden, although it has declined markedly over the past two decades. Indian parents tend to compensate, conciously or otherwise, for a lower survival rate by having more babies than they can realistically expect to see reach maturity.

Across both time and space, poor people tend to have more children than rich people. Which is the cause and which the effect is a classic "chicken and egg" question. Some social scientists assert that very poor people are most prone to live in the present psychologically. Their problems tend to be very immediate, such as securing tonight's dinner, whereas wealthier people's thoughts might focus on long-range economic problems, such as saving for a child's college tuition. Poor people, it is alleged, have been forced to cope with so many immediate and pressing problems that they tend to be oriented to the present rather than the future. If this present-orientation thesis is correct, then the overwhelming majority of Indians cannot be expected to voluntarily restrict the number of children in the interests of future food supply-population ratios.

India, with a 1.9 percent rate of natural increase, must cope with over thirty-five hundred net additional Indians *per day*. This huge increase reflects the large population base to which the relatively modest rate of increase is applied.

Given India's cultural and agricultural-economic pressures against small families, the frustrations of family-planning advocates can only be imagined. Whatever its shortcomings, India is still far more democratic than the majority of its neighbors; thus there was a general outcry against the government's direct pressures on government workers to restrict family size, whereas China's official campaign to lower family size has been obviously successful. A democratic India is most likely to experience a slowly dropping birthrate in association with progressive industrialization and urbanization. It must be remembered, also, that in a country with a *per capita* GNP of about $180, it is not likely that much of this average product can be directed into elaborate birth control programs.

THE PHYSICAL FRAME

A large physical area combined with a large population of varied language and culture apparently inspired the term

Indian subcontinent. The compactness of this physical unit, its rather sharp physical boundaries, and the areas of low population density that surrounded this high density core area all lent credence to the term. It was a culture region as different from that of China or the Middle East as it was from Europe. Bounded on the landward side by the high mountains of the Himalayan system, adjacent to the Indian Ocean, it was of itself a distinct physical unit of near-continental scale.

Time and cultural differences have resulted in not one but eight political units coming into existence in the area. Cultural differences place the eastern margin, Burma, in the realm of Southeast Asia and Afghanistan in the Southwest Asia-North Africa region.

Peninsular India is composed of an ancient block of crystalline, continental material referred to as a *basement complex.* It has not been disturbed in recent times, nor has it undergone inundation and uplift. Technically a plateau or shield, it has the appearance of hills. Enormous amounts of basaltic lava have poured forth from fissures in the earth in more recent times, covering much of the northwestern portion of the block.

North of this ancient continental massif are two troughs that have been filled in with alluvial sediment in recent times. These are the fertile and populous Indus and Ganges river valleys. This huge lowland is known as the Indo-Gangetic Plain.

North of the plain is a relatively young series of complex folded and faulted mountains. Beginning as a series of hills, they rise in rows, higher and higher, culminating in the mighty Himalayas. Despite the relatively few passes and extreme difficulty of passage, these mountains have not functioned as an impenetrable cultural or economic barrier. Nonetheless, they have seemed to demarcate the Indian subcontinent from other cultural and political entities, allowing it to develop a somewhat different character. They function as a climatic divide to some extent as well.

Despite this seemingly impressive physical isolation, wave after wave of new cultural impacts have come to the region both by land and sea, through the passes on the one hand or via boats driven by monsoon winds on the other. The area's culture is a product of outside influences amalgamated with native concepts. Thus the seemingly neat and definite physical frame has not acted as a wall.

TOPOGRAPHY

The landforms of South Asia are easily categorized into five broad regions: the Indo-Gangetic Plain, the Plateau of Deccan, the Himalayan Mountains, the island of Sri Lanka, and the Ghats, the last being a series of mountains parallel to the coasts of peninsular India. The very large percentage of level to rolling land is one of the physiographic hallmarks of South Asia, yet only the compound delta of the Ganges and Brahmaputra rivers and a narrow coastal plain seaward of the Ghats, plus much of coastal Ceylon, are truly level. Erosion has created a rolling landscape over most of the region, including broad parts of the Indo-Gangetic Plain.

The Indo-Gangetic Plain is a large area of riverine alluvium. The Indus Valley continues as a plainlike erosion surface into the Thar Desert of northwestern India and Pakistan. Thousands of feet thick, the alluvium creates a gently rolling uniform surface of great agricultural value. Fed by monsoon runoff and by glacial meltwaters, the rivers never run dry, creating a reserve base of irrigation water even in the driest years. At its mouth the Ganges Delta is subject to destructive inundations. The Thar Desert is a true desert, whose level surface is covered with salt flats, playas (salt lakes), shifting sands, and sparse vegetation. The Cutch area at its southern extreme is a silted-in arm of the sea with semi-desert conditions.

The so-called Plateau of Deccan is not a tableland surface. The northwest portion consists of black, tabular basaltic lava flows, while the rest of the area is an ancient mass of metamorphic and igneous rocks. Weathering and erosion have created a rolling to hilly surface except where alluvium has created level flood plains along occasional smaller rivers. Since the block that is peninsular India tilts eastward, most streams flows in that direction.

The Ghats, the edges of the plateau block, are identified as the Eastern and Western Ghats as a geographical convention. The Western Ghats are truly mountains with elevations of 3,000 to 8,000 feet (1,000 to 2,500 meters). It is really the crest of a scarp with a steeply sloping western edge and a gently sloping eastern (landward) edge. Few gaps cut through this elevated area and the effects of orographically heightened rainfall include a massive potential for hydroelectric power. By comparison, the Eastern Ghats are discontinuous hills. Drier than the Western Ghats, they are yet heavily dissected. With less original height, a less steep slope and most of the drainage, a wider bordering coastal plain has been developed. (That bordering the Western Ghats is 15 to 70 miles [24 to 113 kilometers] in width). Headward erosion of the larger east flowing rivers has extended flatter areas many miles inland while at the same time creating large, near-level delta plains. These fringing lowlands are known as the Malabar and Konkan coasts in the west and the Coromandel and Golconda coasts in the east. In the island of Sri Lanka, the high mountains of the south central area are fringed by dissected hill lands in turn surrounded by a broad coastal plain.

There are three parallel Himalayan ranges, the Outer, Lesser, and Greater Himalayas, from south to north. Rivers have entrenched steep-sided valleys and canyons into these ranges. Glaciers have sharpened the mountain tops to characteristic horns or peaks. Over twenty-five peaks in the Himalayas exceed 25,000 feet (7,600 meters) in elevation. There are few passes through the system and most are at very high elevations.

CLIMATE

South Asia, while possessed of a varied climate, is characterized by the alternation of pronounced wet and dry seasons. The rainy season is termed the **monsoon**. Rainfall in winter is rare except in the extreme northwest of the region and in Ceylon. Beginning in April, the prevailing winds change direction, reversing the dominant land-to-sea trend of winter. (See Figure 9–3.) Precipitation moves gradually inland, reaching a maximum in July and August, and then a gradual retreat of the intertropical convergence zone follows. The intertropical convergence is the general zone in which surface winds come together from northern and southern subtropical high pressure cells; winds then become vertical as air rises in the equatorial low pressure. By November, most of South Asia is again dry. What makes this regime different from the standard tropical wet-and-dry climate is the amount of rain that falls during the wet season. Sri Lanka, the Western Ghats, and the Ganges Delta area receive the greatest amount of rain for the longest period of time. In oversimplified terms, the rainy season is so wet as to provide sufficient moisture for tree growth throughout the year.

Temperatures in South Asia are also seasonal. The north has a greater temperature fluctuation, with mild comfortable winters and intensely hot summers. The south is warm, though not unbearable, year around. Elevation creates a few perenially cool and pleasant areas scattered throughout the region. Only southern India, Bangladesh, and Sri Lanka are truly tropical in every respect.

The date of arrival of the monsoon, the intensity of the rain, and the degree of penetration inland vary greatly. Droughts, with accompanying famine, generally result from late arrival of the monsoon, with less rain for a shorter period of time and a significantly lower degree of inland penetration. An early arrival and a prolonged rainy season creates flooding. Total annual rainfall fluctuates greatly and may exceed that associated with areas of tropical rainforest in Latin America and central Africa. (See the Case Study.)

DRAINAGE

The drainage pattern of South Asia contains many more minor streams than major ones. The Indus, Ganges, and

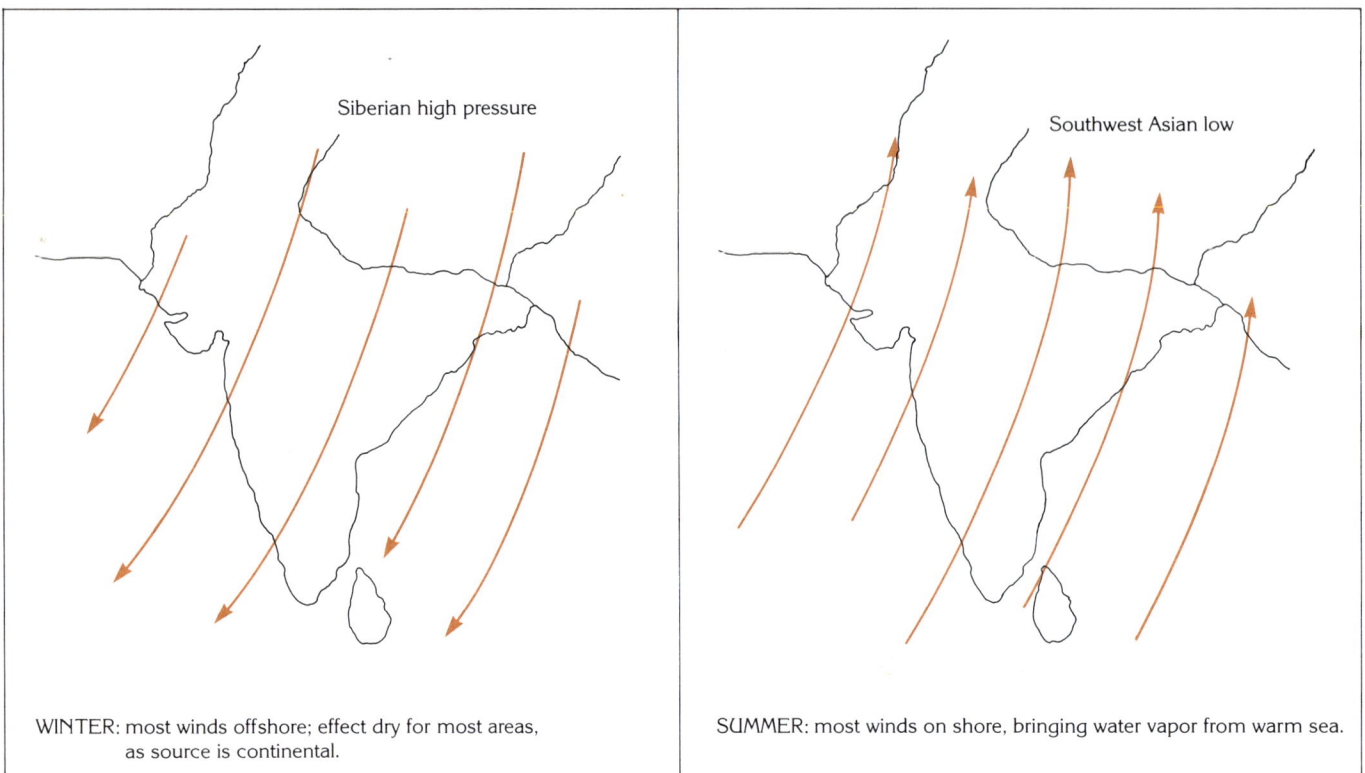

Siberian high pressure

WINTER: most winds offshore; effect dry for most areas, as source is continental.

Southwest Asian low

SUMMER: most winds on shore, bringing water vapor from warm sea.

FIGURE 9–3
The Monsoon. The phenomenon of the monsoon, although present in lesser degree in other continents, is the most dramatic impact of the physical environment for most South Asians. The unpredictable timing of its arrival is the crucial question for most of the region's agriculture.

Brahmaputra rivers, the largest, all have their sources in the Himalayas. Thousands of short tributaries enter the Indus and Ganges from the Himalayas. The lesser incidence of tributaries from peninsular India is strikingly obvious on any drainage map.

In peninsular India, most rivers flow eastward, and most have their sources in the Western Ghats on the extreme western side of the peninsula. Two rivers, the Narbada and Tapti, flow westward along a fault line and empty into the Gulf of Cambay to the north of Bombay. Northwestern India, like many deserts, is an area of interior drainage (streams do not reach the sea). Sri Lanka has a typical radial drainage pattern with many short streams flowing outward from the mountain core to the fringing shore by direct routes, much as spokes from the center of a wheel.

The large volume and relatively steady flow of the Indus and Ganges provide an excellent and reliable source of irrigation water in those valleys. Most rivers of peninsular India suffer erratic and seasonal flow with commensurately limited opportunities for irrigation. In the areas of peninsular India covered by lava flows, the water table is too deep to be penetrated by the primitive wells of peasants. In consequence, storage tanks, ponds, and small reservoirs dot the landscape, providing some water for use during the dry season.

VEGETATION AND SOILS

Few places on the earth have been occupied by such a dense population for so long. Even where the land has not been cleared for cultivation, grazing animals and wood gathering (for fuel) have greatly modified the original cover. As near as can be ascertained, a variety of tropical wet-and-dry forest occupied all but the wettest areas. Monsoon species, able to anchor themselves in the muck of the wet season, yet with natural adaptions against drought and fire (periodic burning), predominated. Teak, banyan, and sandalwood have notable economic value. Constant pressure on the resource has reduced vast areas to scrub forest and bamboo. In the northeast (Assam) there are stands of truly tropical rainforest.

Vast areas of alluvial soil fill the valleys of the three major rivers. New alluvium arrives with each flood, but the

Primitive Irrigation System, Bangladesh. Water—too little, too much, or poorly timed rains for crop growth—is a critical factor in South Asian agriculture. This outdated, human-powered water pump can be replaced by a more efficient system only through outside investment. (Courtesy of United Nations/Carl Purcell)

practices of farmers and the availability (locally) of manure are more important as determinants of fertility. In general, the use of plant stalks and animal dung as fuel and building material, coupled with constant cropping, have measurably reduced the original fertility in many areas of the Indo-Gangetic Plain.

The soils of peninsular India and Ceylon fall basically into two categories: tropical "black earth" (northwestern portion of Deccan) and red-yellow latosols. The famous black soil inland from Bombay, rich in calcium and phosphates if low in nitrogen (humus), is one of the world's great areas of naturally rich soil. It is deeply weathered volcanic rock, with good yields despite constant cropping of cotton.

The rest of peninsular India has typically impoverished tropical soils. Where enriched by careful aplication of lime and fertilizer they can yield fairly well. As in similar areas of wet-and-dry climate, they bake hard during the dry season, suffer serious erosion during the wet season, and contain subsurface hardpans. Overall utility, except in river valleys and a few other favored areas, is quite low.

Northwestward, soils take on dryland characteristics, including lower humus content. These soils vary from chestnut earths in the Upper Ganges to light grey desert soils with overconcentrations of calcium and salt as one aproaches the deserts. Unlike the almost totally man-made soils of the Chinese river valleys, South Asia soils have been rather more depreciated in fertility, than enhanced, by the activities of the farming population.

THE STRUCTURE OF SUBREGIONS

A country as large and diverse (physically, culturally, and economically) as India must be subdivided into several subregions. The other, smaller states of the region are considered here as either separate subregions (Bangladesh, Pakistan, Sri Lanka) or grouped into a subregion (Bhutan and Nepal).

Real differences have developed between the more traditional Indian heartland, or Ganges Plain, and the more dynamic Deccan coastlands. As development proceeds apace, however, the investment of both public and private funds in industry and **infrastructure** has spread development from the coastal cities and traditional urban centers that served as administrative centers under the British to the interior of peninsular India. India, as such, has been divided into the following regions:

1. The Indian heartland—including the Ganges Plain, the city of Calcutta, the Chotta-Nagpur hills (heavy industrial district adjacent to Calcutta), and the lowlands of Orissa,

2. The peninsular south—including the dynamic coastal ports and the more traditional (but rapidly changing) lands of the peninsular interior,

3. The peripheral lands—including the mountainous border districts, the drylands of the western frontier,

and the wetlands of Assam; all essentially under-utilized, potential pioneering areas of the subcontinent. (See Figure 9–4.)

Although rural life is slowly being transformed throughout India, the pace of change is slowest in the heartland; the primary discussion of traditional, rural Indian culture, thus, is included in the heartland segment.

THE INDIAN HEARTLAND

The identifying characteristics of the Indian heartland include very high population density, agriculture based on canal irrigation, a high proportion of land under cultivation, a relatively dense transport network, the earliest heavy industrial center, and a physical unity contributed most largely by the Ganges Plain. India's largest metropolis, Calcutta, and its fourth largest city, Delhi, are located within this subregion. The heartland contains 55 percent of all of India's population and densities over 1,000 per square mile (400 per square kilometer) are not unusual.

Land Use in the Heartland The lower, easternmost part of the Ganges Plain is used for rice, while the upper, drier section (toward Delhi) is primarily a wheat area. In the wheat area, rice is a common second-rank crop, and wheat is a common second crop in the rice region, along with corn and, close to the Bangladesh boundary, jute. India, the probable original source of sugar cane, is the largest grower of cane in the world, with most production centered in the heartland. Because much Indian sugar cane is low in sugar content and not refined to Western standards, sugar output is behind Cuba and Brazil. The rather low sugar content is partly a result of the fact that northern India is outside the tropics; sugar cane requires a long growing season with very high humidity except at harvest.

The westward transition to wheat is related to diminishing rainfall as the monsoons move away from the warm sea. India's primary means of increasing agricultural production is irrigation. At independence, India had about 50 million acres (20 million hectares), one sixth of the total cultivated area, under irrigation. By the end of their first

1. The Indian Heartland
2. The Indian South
3. The Indian Periphery
4. Pakistan
5. Bangladesh
6. Sri Lanka
7. Nepal and Bhutan

- - - International boundary
——— Subregional boundary within India

FIGURE 9–4
Structure of Subregions. All of this region was once part of, or strategically dominated by, British India. The subregions reflect political realities of the successor states as well as India's size and diversity.

five-year plan, 1956, the Indians had expanded irrigated lands to 66 million acres (27 million hectares). By the early 1980's, 120 million acres (48 million hectares) should be irrigated. Irrigation schemes in the heartland have been, in the past, larger scale and more efficient than in the Deccan because of the plains environment. Only low dams, *barrages,* were necessary to impound large quantities of water in the Ganges Plain. Newer engineering projects are more expensive because dams must be built further upstream in hilly country. As everywhere, the best sites, those easiest to use and most efficient in terms of a benefits-to-cost ratio, tend to be the first ones used. Further expansion means developing progressively less desirable sites. An educational campaign emphasizes to farmers that irrigation water must be drained off to avoid water-logging of soils and to minimize the salination process. **Salination,** or "salting" of irrigated soils, occurs when formerly dry soil with soluble minerals dispersed through it is flooded with irrigated water. Water percolating deep into this soil picks up the minerals in solution. When irrigation ceases at the close of the crop season, the surface dries; soil water, carrying the minerals, comes back up to the surface by capillary action, then is evaporated leaving behind crystals of minerals. A crust of soluble minerals can thus accumulate in the upper layers of soil, effectively poisoning it for plant growth. Irrigation, without careful long-range soil management, can be a temporary boost to agriculture but a long-run disaster.

Village Life in the Indian Heartland   Nearly three fourths of the people of India depend directly upon agriculture, and agricultural products provide about 40 percent of the gross national product of this thirteenth largest economy in the world. Approximately 80 percent of all Indians live in the more than one-half million villages. India is likely to remain an agrarian-based, village-dominated society for some time, despite the fantastic growth of its great cities. India's population has been growing at an annual rate of about 2 percent; the average annual increase in agricultural production has been running at 2.6 percent, so that India *is* making progress in one of its most critical areas—the race between increasing population and increasing food supply.

Though progress is real, the enormity of the problems of Indian agriculture and the huge number of people still on the verge of starvation suggests the need for a close look at the economic, cultural, and physical problems inherent in this sector of the economy. While the problems of overcrowded land, erratic monsoonal rainfall, uneconomic fragmentation of holdings, and shortage of fertilizers are common throughout India, they are most seriously felt in the heartland.

Even after the rising productivity of Indian agriculture in recent decades is taken into account, average productivity per land unit is much lower than in developed countries or China. Beyond the relatively low productivity of land under cultivation, there is the problem of unused or fallowed land. In a land where population pressure on cultivable land is immense, an estimated 40 million hectares of land (almost 100 million acres) is officially classified as "wasteland or other land which has the potential for cultivation." There are a variety of reasons for this "waste" or fallowed land not being currently used—lack of traction power, irrigation water, or fertilizer. Some land is fallow at least temporarily because the landowners have not made satisfactory rental agreements with farmers. Traditionally, the different castes are landlords, farmers, and moneylenders, whereas in many Western capitalist societies two or three of these roles will be combined in the same person. It would "break" **caste** to actually cultivate the land if one was an upper-caste landlord. Similarly, money-lending would not be a suitable occupation when one owned land and rented it to farmers. The cyclical nature of almost all categories of farming means that the cash return is not continuous through the year but some expenses will be ongoing. For farmers with little or no savings, this means borrowing money to live until the crop is harvested. A government survey showed that more than 6 percent of the rural households had no land at all while almost half those sampled occupied, but did not necessarily own, "farms" of 2.5 acres (about 1 hectare) or less. These tiny farms represented only about 6 percent of the total cultivated land. On the other hand, over a third of all cropland is occupied by only 4 percent of the households. Some, but by no means all, of the tiniest farms are worked by people who have an urban or industrial job as well. Both the Hindu and Moslem laws of inheritance allow the subdivision of property among all the sons. This means that even a large holding can be reduced to mere patches of land within a few generations. In one survey of a village in the Punjab, it was found that 12,800 acres (5,200 hectares) of productive land around that village had been divided into some sixty-three thousand separate parcels. One landowner may have twenty or thirty separate plots of land. To people who are desperately poor, inheritance rights are taken seriously even when the amount of land involved can be measured in feet rather than acres. It is not unusual for someone to inherit a half-interest in the production of a single fruit tree.

The traditions of inheritance are not the only reason for excessive fragmentation. Another is the desire to provide fair shares of different kinds of land to all local villagers. It was once customary to assign a farmer one portion of upland and one of valley land to grow different

Oxen Threshing Rice, Uttar Pradesh, India. Crop production per land unit remains lower in South Asia than the region's potential, largely due to relatively inefficient techniques. However, rapid modernization of farms would displace many millions of rural poor into the cities, a potential social disaster. (Courtesy of United Nations/C. Srinivasan)

types of crops. Obviously, a farmer trying to use two dozen separate plots of land will spend a lot of time "commuting" from one to another and will find it almost impossible to purchase fencing for all these small parcels. Wandering cattle will "harvest" his crops for him unless kept out by fencing or constant vigilance.

The solutions that are suggested frequently by Westerners would not be acceptable to the Indians. Mechanization, a common suggestion, does not necessarily increase productivity *per acre;* it uses *labor* more efficiently, yet using agricultural labor more efficiently in the Indian heartland would make millions of farmers "surplus" labor. The urban labor markets of heartland cities hardly need millions more unskilled laborers; unemployment and underemployment (a worker holding only a parttime job or sharing a fulltime job with several others) are already serious problems, and they are growing worse. Mechanization would mean increasing imports of high-priced oil, which is already the largest drain on foreign exchange.

The interwined nature of culture, custom, and economy are nicely illustrated by the "sacred cow" in India. The role of the cow in the Indian agricultural economy is quite complex and easily misinterpreted by non-Indians. Westerners touring India see apparently homeless cattle wandering about, foraging for food. These cattle seem to be totally useless; the Hindu religious ban on their slaughter seems born of ignorant superstition. Closer examination of the role of these cows in the Indian economy shows that the animals are useful, however. Almost always, someone does own these wandering cattle; they will return home at night. They have been turned loose to scavenge food for themselves, much as pigs and chickens of earlier Western culture farms were permitted a range of freedom to find their own food. Indian farmers certainly cannot afford to feed their cattle grains, as is customary in Western farming. Indian cattle eat mostly field stubble, weeds, and vegetable refuse that people would not eat anyway. If

they manage to break into a richer farmer's field and consume grain, the poor farmer can be forgiven for not regarding that minor redistribution of resources as a calamity. Indian cattle are not needed fulltime on the farm. Their main job is providing the seasonally necessary traction power so that the poor farmer may plow his tiny, scattered fields. The cow also provides fertilizer. Much of the manure is dried and used as cooking fuel. It provides a clean-burning, slow heat, which can be safely left alone while the housewife is working elsewhere.

Replacement of the all-purpose cow with a tractor would have several economic drawbacks. Tractors are expensive, need costly spare parts and use increasingly expensive diesel or gasoline fuel. They could not be used very efficiently on the small separate plots of Indian farms. They do not contribute fertilizer or cooking fuel. A cow is also a "tractor factory," calving draft animals for the future; a machine just wears out. Contrary to Western belief, the cow does become beef eventually. Untouchables are untouchable largely because they deal in death—they haul away the carcass of an animal dead of natural causes, tan the hide, process the bones for bonemeal or charcoal and eat the flesh. India is a major exporter of hides. Even the milk production, low by Western standards, is an important addition to diets normally low in fats and proteins. It is probable that, given the low investment in feeding and caring for their cattle, Indians use the animals far more efficiently than in the Western world. Considering that the cow is absolutely necessary for plowing the fields and produces important "by-products," the Hindu prohibition on slaughtering them can be seen as a way of making maximum use of the animal.

Agricultural Conservatism in the Indian Heartland A common frustration to would-be leaders and innovators, from Gandhi to visiting Western experts, is the intense conservatism of most Indian farmers. Various efforts to introduce new crops, new varieties of plants, chemical fertilizers, cultivation techniques, or other departures from the traditional seldom succeed quickly, if at all. Fertilization is one of the greatest deficiencies of Indian agriculture. After a millenium or more of constant crop production, even the rich alluvial soils of the heartland need heavy fertilization, deeper plowing, and/or crop rotation. Indians have, for some reasons related to caste, not used human waste as a fertilizer as fully as in traditional East Asia.

While such conditions are typical of much of India, they are particularly characteristic of the heartland, where care of the land, improved techniques, and better seed could produce greater yields. With less than half an acre per person of arable land and a very low cash income, heartland farmers have little room for experimentation. Where Western farmers might spend $50 to $100 per acre in fertilizer, a small relative sum, their heartland Indian counterparts would be investing their entire annual income. The promised gain in crop yields, assuming it does materialize, will not feed the family and hold off creditors until the coming harvest. Similarly, the Indian farmer can rarely afford to plant a soil-enriching crop to plow under rather than harvest. Even though this may be a relatively cheap way to fertilize the fields, few can forego a year's income in hopes of increasing future yields.

Only the largest farmers and/or landowners (those with a "cushion" of savings) can afford to gamble with new techniques. The **Green Revolution,** based largely on specially developed hybrid seeds and on large applications of fertilizer, is thus most effective at boosting yields for the largest, richest farmers, not the smallest and poorest. Although the Green Revolution is real, it has its costs, and its initial costs favor relatively prosperous landowners.

Southern India presents a contrast. Frequently, local industry produces fertilizer relatively nearby and at a somewhat cheaper cost. Traditionally, much land has been left in fallow; densities of population are much lower. Each year the farmer, without reliable irrigation, gambles on the monsoon. Two crops are sown together; the first will not survive, grow and mature if the rains are late. With fallow land and a tradition of the "long-shot gamble" in crop production, these farmers can and do experiment to a greater extent. Proportionally more farmers own their own land.

In the heartland area, fragmentation of already tiny holdings continues as families subdivide lands among remaining heirs. Tenancy rates are much greater, and the need to "make the rent" forces a more conservative attitude. Alternative employment opportunities, either full- or part-time, are fewer and, most frequently, farther away.

Industrial Development in the Heartland The relatively slow pace of investment from the private sector and the need to establish a balance in foreign trade spurred the Indian government to invest in industry on a very large scale. A **planned economy** was felt to be essential in an economy where wealth was concentrated in the hands of a small, tradition-bound upper class. In an attempt to avoid regional rivalry and to alleviate rural unemployment, the government has attempted to disperse industry. Yet, rational economic planning and the realities of transportation, raw material distribution, and assembly cost have favored certain areas.

The heartland reflects some of these divergent "pulls." There is no doubt that it has a large surplus of labor, yet most of it is unskilled. Rural areas here are intensely orthodox in their respect for Hinduism's religious and cultural practice. Industrial employment in some ways would violate caste—both in terms of occupation itself and the intermixture of castes under one factory roof. It is a seeming paradox that the heartland receives less industrial emphasis than the traditional rimland, the peripheral area of divergent culture and, formerly, lower economic and political influence.

Yet there are sound reasons for this lack of industry. The South has greater mineral resources except for fuel. In the heartland, the exceedingly thick alluvial cover of the Ganges Plain would render most mineral wealth found underneath it far too expensive to mine. The dense regional railroad net, most of it broad gauge, would appear to be a locational advantage. Yet, it is overburdened with passenger traffic and the cross-hauling of agricultural commodities. The dense population of the heartland would appear to form the largest, most compact market in the country, yet many in this market area are poor and engaged in subsistence farming, almost wholly outside the commercial economy. The area is central to the Indian subcontinent, but peripheral to the ports. Since industrial development hinges on needed imports and the need to raise currency through exports, it is the rimland, not the heartland, where the developmental action is concentrated. As in any developing economy, much of the impetus to the generation of economic activity is external so it is that the coastal regions of India are developing first.

Nonetheless, the official government plan is to establish regional **growth poles** and to disperse development throughout the country. The growth pole concept takes a very positive view of uneven growth, such as that in **development enclaves,** discussed elsewhere. Rather than attempt to spread development capital throughout a lagging region, centers are chosen for more concentrated investment and development. While an early effect is to further exaggerate the differences between the growth pole and less developed areas, activity in the growth pole later stimulates raw material production, related industries, marketing facilities, and transport infrastructure throughout the entire region.

The Port of Calcutta. The heavily congested port of Calcutta will require considerable capital improvements to maintain its economic position as the industrial heart's port. (Courtesy of United Nations)

The heartland contains the largest single industrial region of the country at its eastern extreme (Calcutta-Damodar), and there is a new and growing industrial complex centering on Delhi, the national capital.

Calcutta is a name evocative of strong, largely negative, reactions. The city was founded by the British as a trading settlement in 1690; in less than a century it had a half million people. The Hoogly River is the best available harbor on the east coast of India. Calcutta was sited to provide not only a deep-water anchorage safe from typhoons, but also to provide security in the early colonial days. At the city's back is a complex drainage network of poorly drained delta, providing a barrier to invasion in much the same way that Venice is protected. Being on the east bank of the Hoogly gives Calcutta some protection against invasion from the west, but also hinders its ability to serve as the port for the most densely populated part of India—the Ganges Plain. This huge productive area, with its enormous work force and market and proximity to important industrial raw materials, is India's greatest hinterland. (The trade hinterlands of Calcutta and Bombay meet at Delhi.) Calcutta's explosively rapid growth has been fueled by a series of crop failures and famines in fairly distant provinces; as a result, its population is composed of many different ethnic and linguistic groups. Within 150 miles (240 kilometers) to the west are most of India's iron ore and coal reserves. In addition to its serving as the commercial, financial, and manufacturing center for most of eastern India, Calcutta is also the port for Nepal and Bhutan. Up until the 1960's, Calcutta alone accounted for almost half of India's imports, nearly a quarter of its exports, and one third of its financial transactions. This high

degree of dominance has been reduced, but Calcutta is still very important in India's domestic economy and international trade. It is estimated that by 1986 there will be at least 12 million people in metropolitan Calcutta. The century and a half of rapid, uncontrolled growth in the urban region has produced a planner's nightmare—almost half the population lacks clean drinking water; and in the central city, only 6.5 percent of the land is used for roadways, compared with an average 25 percent for U.S. cities.

Calcutta and its suburbs, in particular Howrah, have long been established centers of industry. Jute milling was the major endeavor under British rule. Competition from Bangladesh (and the manufacture of plastic bags) has seriously cut into the market for jute. The 1947 division of India left most of the factories in India and most of the jute acreage in what was East Pakistan (now Bangladesh); this disoriented the jute industry from the inception of independence.

Since that time there has been much diversification of industry; light manufactures and consumer goods have become particularly important, largely as a by-product of nearby heavy industrial development. Iron and steel, heavy chemicals, alloys, and energy-generating facilities on the nearby Damodar Valley in effect supply the raw material needs for railway equipment, rubber goods, light machinery, paper, glass, metal products, plastics, and pharmaceuticals produced in metropolitan Calcutta. A considerable segment of the jute industry has shifted to cotton and synthetic textiles. Rapid expansion has witnessed development of industry far beyond the city. Many nearby towns and even villages now have small assembly and packaging plants. Despite impressive growth, however, the city and region are still typified by massive unemployment as migration from the countryside exceeds employment opportunities.

In the Damodar Valley, a mixture of private and government capital has created India's major heavy industrial base some 140 miles (225 kilometers) west of Calcutta in and around Jamshedpur. Four major coalfields, accounting for over 90 percent of India's total reserves, are found in the vicinity of the steel center of Asanol (see Figure 9–5). South of Jamshedpur, another steel center, are the great iron ore deposits of the Singhbhum Hills. The fortunate coincidence of coking-quality coal and high-quality iron ore gave an early boost to India's iron industry. India's iron ore reserves represent some of the largest and richest deposits in the world. In iron ores, 55 percent iron content would be considered quite high enough to exploit; Some Indian ores run as high as 70 percent iron. Such ores are now mixed with lower quality ores to "stretch" the resource. Other iron ore fields, including some beyond the heartland, are being developed to support both an expanded Indian steel industry and to supply exports to Japan. Discoveries since World War II of new iron ore fields have placed Indian reserves so high relative to consumption that India has literally thousands of years worth of ores in reserve. India is also self-sufficient in coal and limestone.

The original mill at Jamshedpur is still the largest steel producing center. New centers have developed at Ranchi, Asanol, Bokara, Durgapur, and Rourkela. By-products of coking support an immense chemical industry while basic metals are forged and cast into an impressive array of metal goods and machinery, from nails to locomotives, industrial presses, and military tanks.

Iron and steel, along with coal, flow as far east as Calcutta on the rail network; but the rails do not form a continuous net in the delta east of Calcutta, due to difficulties in bridging the many distributaries. For the same reason, water craft can collect and distribute materials such as jute throughout the delta, but not westward of Calcutta. This concentrates many industrial materials and fuels at Calcutta, helping to make it a major manufacturing center.

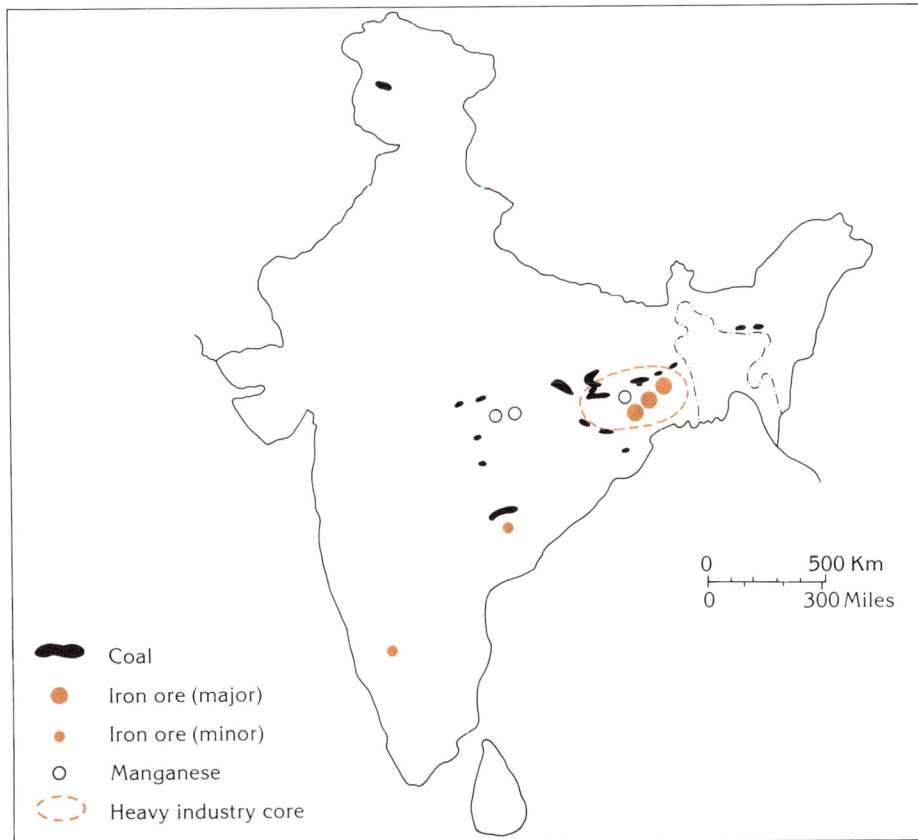

FIGURE 9–5
India's Heavy Industry Base. India is a major industrial nation, a fact sometimes obscured by the Ghandian "homespun" philosophy. India's iron ore reserves are among the world's largest, and support a significant steel industry.

Bicycle Factory, Asanol, India. This bicycle plant is typical of the metal fabricating and consumer goods industries of India's older industrial core. (Courtesy of United Nations)

Delhi, like most capitals, is a city of bureaucrats. The market is relatively affluent since government employment pays reasonably well by Indian standards. Clothing, pharmaceuticals, prepackaged food, furniture, and household appliances are manufactured for the local and national markets. Delhi, Meerut, and surrounding suburbs, however, rank a poor fifth in the hierarchy of Indian manufacturing centers.

New Delhi (also commonly referred to as just *Delhi*) is a world city by virtue of its being the administrative center for the second largest state (in population) in the world. The multi-million populations of the commercial and industrial centers of Calcutta and Bombay make them both potential world cities, yet their importance is regional, not international. Delhi, South Asia's largest inland city, unlike Bombay and Calcutta, was an important center long before the European colonial ambitions created coastal trading cities. India's capital is generally known as *New* Delhi because a new urban core was created by the British in 1911 when the capital of British India was moved there from Calcutta. New Delhi is the eighth capital of India to be constructed in that vicinity.

Delhi occupies an important position within the subcontinent because it stands at the place where routes converged between the Himalayas and the Thar Desert and Aravalli hills to the south. It is also near the watershed of the two great river systems, the Indus-Sutlej and the Ganges. Delhi is a classic **march** or **advance capital,** located as it is near the traditional invasion routes into the subcontinent. Four times the history of India has been changed on the battlefields to the north of Delhi. In some ways, it is a curious choice of a capital for a Hindu India,

as its older portions are Moslem in architecture and historical significance, and its newer area is the monumental symbol of the splendor and power of the British *raj.* Both the superb location of New Delhi and the in-place collection of administrative offices and communications facilities installed by the British mean that it will continue to dominate the political life of India.

There is a scattering of very large cities in the plain that are targeted for future industrial development. Lucknow and Kanpur, each over a million people, and six others over five hundred thousand, would almost be guaranteed to be industrial centers in the Western world by sheer dint of size. In India, however, large agglomerations need not be. They are primarily market centers with some food processing, crafts, and a transportation and administrative function.

THE INDIAN SOUTH

A number of factors differentiate the South of India from the other parts of that state. Historically, the area has been that last or least frequently conquered by those seeking to unify the subcontinent. Even the British granted a degree of autonomy to a number of native states in the area.

The people of the peninsula are shorter, darker, and of a somewhat different culture, the product of a different set of cultural inputs and the residue of earlier Indian peoples and cultures. The South (particularly south of 20° N) is the stronghold of Dravidian languages. These are not at all related to the Indo-European dialects spoken elsewhere. A separate culture (including a distinct architecture) arose in the centers of the South.

Just as the Indo-Gangetic North developed two large regional capitals (Delhi and Calcutta) at either extreme of the region, the Indian South has developed two major cultural centers (Bombay and Madras) at the opposing extremes of that subregion. Overall the population density is lower, but so is the utility of the land.

The South is a land of truly tropical climate with no cool season. The topographic impression is one of hills rather than plains. Yet the South, too, possesses some areas of rich soils rivaling or even surpassing the fertility of the Indo-Gangetic alluvium in some areas such as the black earth plateau country inland from Bombay.

The Strength of the Resource Base   There is a variety of mineral wealth, but it is scattered in many small, often uneconomic deposits. In fact, peninsular India is fuel poor. The greatest available energy locally is the hydro power generated in the rainy Western Ghats. Much of the rail system in the region of Bombay has switched from coal to electricity for this reason. The extreme variability of rainfall over most of the rest of peninsular India reduces the hydro power potential.

One of the world's most imposing iron ore reserves of high quality is found near Salem, inland from Madras. The absence of coal and some technological difficulties have retarded its development. High-grade deposits are currently mined in what was the Portuguese treaty port of Goa, virtually at tidewater. It is the quantity, quality, and distribution of fuel, not iron, that acts to retard an even more rapid expansion of the iron and steel industries.

Manganese, a steel toughening agent in high demand, is a major Indian export. Peninsular India, while not the sole source, contains the largest and best grade deposits. Mica, a material used in insulation and, therefore, electrotechnical manufactures, is produced in Madras province.

In recent years large deposits of bauxite have been uncovered in the regions of Cutch and the Gulf of Cambay. Among the major thrusts of Indian investment in recent years has been the development of increased electrical energy output to expand aluminum production and the making of chemical fertilizer. While petroleum resources are slim, recent finds offshore in the Indian Ocean (near Bombay) offer some hope for the future.

The natural and agricultural resource base of peninsular India is somewhat more varied and better developed that that of North India. India ranks fourth in world cotton production after the United States, China, and the Soviet Union. Cotton is grown throughout India, but the black earths of Deccan are the overwhelmingly dominant region. The district around Madras is another major producing area.

In an attempt to reduce imports, India has developed plantations for both tropical crops and temperate crops in high demand. Bananas, rubber, and coffee are grown in the peninsular southwest, the last in the hill country. Tobacco is a specialty crop of the southeast coast, where varieties similar to those of Brazil and Cuba are grown.

New export crops such as oranges, plantains, and medicinal herbs are receiving increasing emphasis, mainly in the peninsular interior. Renowned for seasonings since the days of the spice trade, South India (in particular the west coast) grows ginger, mace, pepper, cardamom, cinnamon, nutmeg, and other spices for both domestic use in the highly seasoned Indian cooking and for export. While Ceylon, Darjeeling, and Assam are renowned for quality teas, the hills of South India near Madras are also a major area of production.

Climatic differences, cultural preference, and water availability contribute to startling regional crop differentiation. Rice is a major crop only in the riverine delta areas of the South and some better-watered districts. Nowhere does it approach the dominance characteristic of the North, and considerable southern production is in non-paddy, upland varieties of rice that are lower yielding. Wheat acreage is very small. Millet is the dominant grain crop. Often interplanted with rice, cotton, or other crops, it can withstand drought to a remarkable extent and insure some food production in even the worst of years. Peanut acreage has increased radically in recent years. Together with sesame and cotton seed oil, these are the major sources of fats in an essentially vegetarian diet. North India is dominated by rice, barley, wheat, and sugar cane while South India is dominantly a region of cotton, peanuts, millet, and tropical crops. Of the two areas, the latter is much more important for industrial and export crops.

While all of India experiences a shortage of wood, portions of peninsular India have developed commercial lumbering and wood export. Teak and ebony in particular are grown in the Western Ghats for export.

Population   South India is definitely overcrowded in proportion to the available land. Agricultural densities vary greatly from one region to another; water availability, more than inherent soil fertility, seems to affect the distribution most. Concentrations of 750 per square mile (300 per square kilometer) are average over much of the Indo-Gangetic Plain; in South India such densities are reached only in the delta plains of the major rivers and in the coastal plains of Kerala state. Large areas of lower density (less than 125 per square mile or 50 per square kilometer) occur only in the hill country. Southern India contains a slightly higher proportion of urban dwellers. Seven of India's eleven cities of over one million population are found in the region (Table 9–2), including Bombay, its second largest city.

A characteristic of note is the strong male-female imbalance in the cities of South India. The temporary (if often long-term) migration of males to the cities seeking employment creates a very strong female dominance in the area's rural villages and an overwhelming dominance of males in the cities.

The Booming Industrial South   Three of the four well-developed industrial districts of India are located in the South (see Figure 9–6). Two, Bombay-Poona and the district of Madras-Bangalore-Madurar are centers for the manufacture of cotton textiles and the processing of tropical goods and in some ways are the legacy of British colonial investment policy. Bombay-Poona is the second most important manufacturing region of India. Bombay was the most important colonial port, exporting raw materials and semifinished goods as part of the colonial trade.

Bombay grew as an international trade center. Like many example of European "contact points" with potentially hostile, numerically superior foreign cultures, Bombay was a combination of the location considerations of security and excellent harbor. Seven small islands of lava, soon joined by natural and artificial accumulations of silt

TABLE 9–2

Population rank of India's cities (metropolitan areas)

City	Population (millions)
Calcutta	9.1
Bombay	7.3
Delhi	6.0
Madras	3.4
Hyderabad	2.4
Ahmenabad	2.1
Bangalore	2.0
Kanpur	1.4
Poona	1.3
Nagpur	1.2
Lucknow	1.1

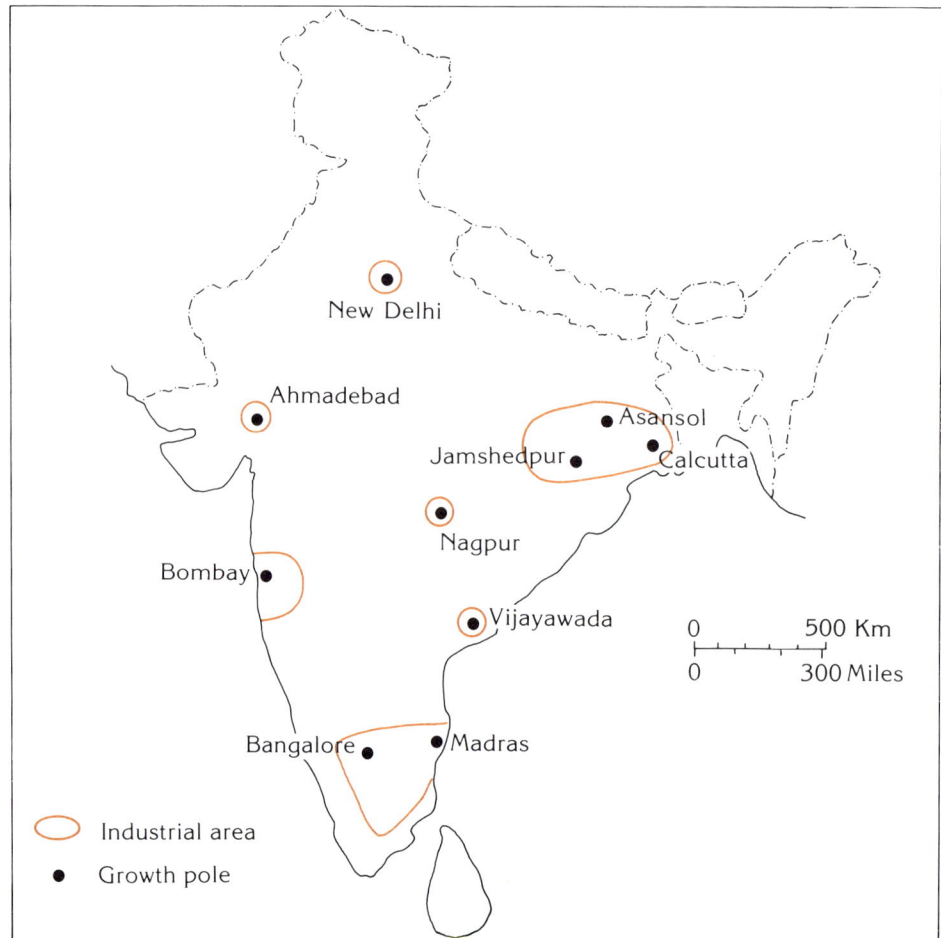

FIGURE 9–6

India: Industrial Areas and Growth Poles. India's industrial development is accelerating in the South, partly as a result of raw material advantages and partly reflecting centralized economic planning's emphasis on encouraging "growth poles."

Port Improvements, Madras. New port facilities under construction at Madras testify to the more dynamic growth of the South of India in contrast to its historic heartland. (Courtesy of United Nations)

and sand, are separated from the mainland by a belt of poorly drained swamplands and salt marshes that provided some security from surprise attack. The harbor is one of the finest in the world.

A more cosmopolitan city in architecture and society than is Calcutta, Bombay leads in motion picture production (India produces more films than any other country) and is the most diverse manufacturing city in India. Centered on the black earth cotton district, it has long been the major cotton textile producing center of India. Water power from the Western Ghats supplies the energy source. A new nuclear plant now supplements this supply as does oil. Bombay is the largest oil port and refining center in India. Recent offshore finds will enhance the area's attractiveness as an industrial location. Petrochemicals, synthetic fibers, plastics, chemical fertilizers, paints, and varnishes are some of the newer industries that have developed around oil refining. With a food surplus in its hinterland, the region has developed an important food-processing industry. Diversification since the 1950's has added automotive, machine tool, electronics, aircraft, and engineering industries to this most diverse of all Indian industrial centers. Expansion to the interior has been spurred by superior regional transportation advantages and the development of skills among villagers who once commuted or temporarily migrated to Bombay; an industrial district now extends through dozens of hinterland towns and villages to Poona. The government plans to develop the old Portuguese port at Goa and extend broad gauge rail lines to that city; these plans plus Goa's high quality iron ores and existing small manufacturing plants

have recently added to the attractiveness of that location. It is envisioned as the third pole in a triangular industrial district of Bombay-Poona-Goa.

The second of the old traditional industrial districts is Madras-Bangalore-Madura. Madras is the fourth largest city of India and its third most important port. Cotton textiles formed the basis of its industrialization. The region has since diversified; consumer goods, aircraft, food processing, leather industries, and light chemicals have all received intensive investment, in particular around the interior city of Bangalore. Machine tools, precision engineering, scientific equipment, and electronics are centered in and around Coimbatore, making it India's chief center of technical goods production.

Madras, the regional port, has added automotive and engineering industries in recent years. Located in an intensely populated district, it is scheduled for continued industrial growth. Nearby ores at Salem will likely lead to the development of a heavy industrial base in the district, rounding out the total regional industrial spectrum.

A third district of the South is centered around the Gulf of Cambay. Ahmadabad and Baroda are the chief cities of the area. It now functions as the *entrepôt* district for Delhi and the populous upper Ganges valley. Cotton textiles have been expanded, but the manufacture of chemicals and related products has burgeoned since 1950. Second to Bombay in oil refining, it is a growing center of plastics and petrochemical manufacture. One offshoot of its cotton textile industry is ready-made clothing for domestic and export markets. The region is now the third most important manufacturing region in India.

Development Strategies In the most recent decade, India has sought to develop other new industrial districts in the peninsula. The state of Kerala has been expanding its food and tropical products processing industries, a government attempt to cope with serious regional overpopulation and unemployment. Chemical plants at Cochin are adding diversity. Zinc smelting, bauxite processing, and mining of a dozen minerals in the district will add to the potential for development. A new triangular industrial district is growing with its apex at the Hyderabad and its port at Visakhapatnam.

South India marks itself as an area for investment due to its raw material resources, port facilities, higher regional educational-technical standards, improved food supply through irrigation, better highway network (if poorer rail facilities), proximity to the growing markets of East Asia and the Middle East, a tradition of trade and manufacturing of some duration, and even pressures set up by regional separatist possibilities.

Problems and Potentials The French-British-Portuguese struggle for control of the India trade resulted in the development of at least a dozen ports, as well as rudimentary manufactures. This early colonial legacy formed a commercial orientation and an industrial beginning. After independence, a major road network was built in peninsular India. This has enhanced regional transportation coverage and greatly improved regional accessibility.

Now being developed are lignite and bituminous coal deposits in the peninsula and more hydroelectric sites in the Western Ghats (in particular, in Kerala state). Improved rail and intracoastal shipping now make the considerable Indian coal resource of the Chotta-Nagpur hills accessible to peninsular India. Thorium and other rare earths exploited in the extreme south of peninsular India supply a domestic resource for the generation of nuclear energy.

To improve agricultural production, the Indian government has intensified investment in irrigation. New reservoirs in South India and improved tank irrigation have helped stabilize regional food supplies. Recent good national harvests are in part due to this regional stabilization and investment.

As regional markets demand more metal in manufactures and require more sophisticated production, the region acquires even more diversity. Far beyond the earliest step of development, peninsular India has met most of the preconditions for **takeoff.**

Japanese imports have greatly expanded the markets for South India's raw materials, citrus fruit, and tropical products. Japanese industrial investment in the area is increasing as well. On the other hand, Japanese exports are threatening certain handicraft industries and are slowing the growth of such industries as shoes and clothing.

INDIA PERIPHERAL

It is difficult to think of teeming India as having regions suitable to expansion, yet there are frontiers. The mountain valleys and slopes of the Himalayas, rain-soaked Assam, and the Thar Desert district together form the third subregion of India. Exceedingly dissimilar in climate and topography, they have the common factors of low population density, unexploited resources, and nontraditional attitudes.

Assam Almost cut off from the rest of India except for a narrow corridor, Assam is a classic borderland in that it reflects intermingled but distinctive ethnic groups; many Assamese are most closely related to the Chinese and to the Shan of Burma than to the Hindus. Assam is also atypical for India in that it has large tracts of river valley land that could be cultivated but are not. The Brahmaputra Valley, the easternmost extension of the Ganges plain, is bounded on the north and east by rugged hill country. Rice and jute are produced in the lowlands while tea is grown on the hill slopes. Assam has more land in forest than any other Indian state; this resource, along with hydroelectric potential and presently noncultivated lands, give Assam a growth potential unusual for India.

The Northwest and Divided Kashmir The northern bulge of India, directly north of Delhi and flanked by Pakistan and China, is one of the most troublesome parts of the region and the world. Kashmir has been disputed since the partition of British India in 1947; it has been the major cause of war between India and Pakistan in 1947–48 and 1965. Kashmir became a secondary topic of contention in the Bangladesh (East Pakistan) crisis and brief war of 1971–72, but with the independence of Bangladesh, Kashmir's unresolved status resumed its role as the major issue separating India and Pakistan. China also controls territory to the northeast of Kashmir proper that India claims.

In 1947, the "princely states" of imperial India were encouraged, or pressured, to voluntarily join Hindu India or Moslem Pakistan. The choice was usually obvious and based on the majority religion/culture of each state. The Hindu ruler of Kashmir opted to join India; India provided an army, on request, to defend the throne of Kashmir and has refused to consider a UN-administered **plebiscite** (a poll of the citizenry on possible change in affiliation). The cease-fire line through Kashmir leaves most of the disputed territory within India and cuts across the westward-flowing rivers, whose valleys are the traditional trade routes out of Kashmir. Kashmiri timber used to be a very important export to the lower Indus Valley, now in Pakistan, but the border interrupts this trade relationship in much the same way that East Pakistan (Bangladesh) jute was cut off from Calcutta mills.

Kashmir is not likely to be forgotten by Pakistan, and China is unlikely to relinquish its occupance of land claimed by India. The northern frontier is thus likely to provide problems for decades. India has managed to "normalize" relations with both China and Pakistan despite these unresolved, conflicting territorial claims.

The Himalayan Hill District   The Himalayas possess a high potential for hydroelectric energy development. The lack of transportation facilities renders development of even the best sites difficult at this time.

Mid-altitude slopes have a valuable forest resource. The upper slopes are totally barren, while lower slopes and valleys have long since been cleared for agriculture. The mineral base is unknown, though small deposits of oil, coal, and gas have been uncovered. There is little room for agricultural expansion because of slope. Outside the densely populated Vale of Kashmir, the low densities reflect the rigors and realities of agricultural development in mountain areas. Pastoral activities dominate now, but some intensification of use can take place in valleys. Power and industry, not agriculture, is where the potential lies.

The Dryland West   The dryland West is composed of the states of Rajastan and Punjab, areas of steppe and desert climate. At its center is the Thar Desert, an area of migrating sand dunes and wind-blasted, bare rock surfaces. Much of it is salt flats associated with the typical interior drainage. There is little rain at any season. Around the edges of this desert, the steppe regions can support agriculture without irrigation, though irrigation is used wherever possible.

Hard-bread wheats are the most general crop of the region. In the early twentieth century British investment here helped create a new food base for India. Mechanization was introduced here early, as were the techniques of dry farming. Population densities are quite low, less than 100 per square kilometer (250 per square mile) everywhere except in the intensely irrigated oasis of the Punjab. Less than half the land is cropped in any given year except where irrigation facilities are present.

Petroleum has been found, but in disappointingly small deposits. There is a small, but promising, copper resource. Any future development of mineral or agricultural resources will require improvement of transportation.

This district represents something of an internal problem area for India. There are large numbers of Moslems in the region that borders directly on Pakistan. The Sikhs, a people of a religion that is a modified offshoot of Hinduism, are the dominant group in Punjab; borrowings from

Islam that are a part of that creed have not brought it closer to that religion. The Jains, people of a strictly orthodox, ascetic offshoot of Hinduism, are also concentrated in this area. Thus the dryland West is atypical in religion and culture, in some ways a potential threat to Indian unity. Much of the expansion of agriculture that has taken place has been on state farms using hired labor. The possibilities for expanding irrigated agriculture are very good, yet they run into oposition from local groups who fear an influx of culturally different outsiders.

PAKISTAN

Pakistan represents a transition zone between the worlds of Islam and South Asia. The people of the sparsely settled southwest of the country speak an Iranian dialect; those of the rest of the country, the overwhelming majority, speak Urdu or other languages related to Hindi and the other tongues of India. The alphabet and script are derived from the Arabic; the religion is Islam. Like most countries of Southwest Asia and North Africa, it has a desert climate and a dependence on irrigated agriculture; like drier India, it has a wheat-dominant agriculture and is characterized by dense rural populations. A part of British India for much of recent history and also part of the empire of the Moguls, it had been attached to many of the great empires of the Middle East in the more distant past. An ancient **cultural hearth** itself, it has been invaded by alien cultures from all sides; the cultural impacts of ancient Greece (Alexander's empire), the Persians, the Caliphs, the Mongols (and through them, the Chinese), the Hindus of India, and the British have all been felt.

Its separation from India in 1947 resulted in a split territory whose two parts were almost a thousand miles apart. Unified only by religion, it was perhaps too diverse to survive. The creation of an independent Bangladesh from East Pakistan resulted in a more homogeneous state, but the new Pakistan still lacks any solid basis as a national unit. The national identity is still building; its success or failure as a nation-state is still in question.

Natural Resource Base   The resource base of Pakistan is best described as mediocre. There have been no great oil finds, but petroleum is present (reserves of some 300 million barrels are documented). There are extensive gas reserves, and natural gas has been designated as the national fuel and energy base. Gas fuels most electrical generating stations and is the raw material base for Pakistan's expanding chemical fertilizer industry. Oil production meets only 15 to 20 percent of domestic needs in an economy that uses relatively little oil. There are some small deposits of low-grade coal, but none is of metallurgical quality. Hydro power, moderately developed and with significant potential, rounds out the energy base. Electrical energy production is increasing through a crash program of investment in power generation facilities.

Small amounts of low-grade iron ore, salt, gypsum, sulfur, and chrome round out the mineral base. Prospecting is in its infancy and geologic conditions indicate the potential for a much greater variety and quantity of mineral production.

Population Characteristics Pakistan, with 80 million people, is one of the ten largest countries (population) in the world. Punjabis make up two thirds of Pakistan's population, though Urdu (spoken by only 9 percent) is the official language. Almost a quarter of the population speaks unrelated languages. (Less than 20 percent of the people can be classed as literate in any language.) English is still widely used among the educated and (as in India) is an associate language.

At 2.4 percent, Pakistan's annual growth rate is greater than that of India, but somewhat lower than most Islamic nations. The average life expectancy of fifty-one years is rapidly rising as infant mortality decreases. Densities of almost 100 people per square kilometer (265 per square mile) are really much higher when viewed in relation to *arable* land, since most of Pakistan's area is in mountain or desert. Almost 30 percent of the population is urban; two large cities (Karachi and Lahore) account for almost 10 percent of the total population.

Migrational Patterns Migration has been critical in Pakistan's development. Millions of Moslems left India for Pakistan in the civil wars following independence. A repeat migration took place on a smaller scale after the Bangladesh split in 1971, with some 2 million Bengalis being repatriated from (West) Pakistan to Bangladesh, and a much smaller number repatriated in the opposite direction. The capital, located at Karachi in 1947, was temporarily shifted to Rawalpindi (near the disputed area of Kashmir) and then to the newly created city of Islamabad. (See Figure 9–7.)

The Hindu minority in Pakistan has been reduced to less than 2 percent of the total population. Nonetheless, the sizeable group of Moslems in India represents, along with Kashmir, a possible source of conflict in the future.

Agricultural Patterns Larger than Texas, much of Pakistan is too dry for cultivation. Paradoxically, though, much of Pakistan's farmland is too wet—it is waterlogged after a half-century or more of continuous irrigation. Inadequate drainage in these fields raised the water table too close to the surface for many crops; salination, combined with waterlogging, took 100,000 acres (40,000 hectares) out of production each year by the late 1960's. A total of 16 million acres (6.5 million hectares) of formerly good farmland had been abandoned at the same time that new irrigation projects were under construction in the Indus Valley. Managing the older and newer irrigation areas alike is made more difficult by the very high evaporation rates prevalent in summer. It is estimated that less than half the water entering irrigation canals ever reaches the fields. Yet irrigation is virtually the only route to a high yielding agriculture.

Gudu Barrage on the Indus River, Pakistan. This barrage (low dam) on the Indus provides irrigation water for some 2.7 million acres of land north and east of Karachi. (Courtesy of United Nations)

FIGURE 9–7
Pakistan: Industry and Cities. One of the world's largest Islamic nations, Pakistan's economy appears to be recovering from the civil war that split off East Pakistan as Bangladesh.

Agriculture employs about 57 percent of the total labor force, producing 45 percent of national income and half of all exports. It is conceivable that Pakistan will become an industrial economy in the future. However, agriculture is the current economic mainstay. Between 25 and 30 percent of the total area is in farmlands, despite the limitations of climate. Pakistan has the world's largest single irrigated food production system. It has developed the Indus and its tributaries for large-scale irrigation; land reclamation schemes, desalination projects, and even deep well irrigation have greatly increased the available arable area. Grain and cotton production occupy most of the new areas, the former contributing to dietary self-sufficiency, the latter to export earnings. Now a net food importer, Pakistan expects to reach self-sufficiency by 1990.

Increased availability of water and fertilizer, improved seed, and a more nearly adequate distribution system have all contributed to increased agricultural production. Rice and cotton crops have doubled production in the last decade; over 8.5 million metric tons of wheat are produced yearly. Rice dominates the lower Indus Valley and the delta country, while northern Pakistan is an extension of the wheat belt of northwestern India. Cotton dominates the zone between the two grain crops but increasing acreages are being sown throughout the country. Oilseeds, sugar, and tobacco are grown as industrial and cash crops, while dairying and horticulture are expanding near urban areas.

The Indus Basin irrigation system is not yet completed, though it should be fully operative by 1990. Increasing availability of domestically produced fertilizer will undoubtedly increase yields in the future. Unlike most of the rest of South Asia, the food supply picture is reasonably bright.

Urban Industrial Development Patterns   The expanding energy base (gas and hydroelectric power) has led to a respectable growth rate in Pakistan's industry. Currently, 14 percent of the labor force is employed in industry and 17 percent of the GNP is contributed by that branch of the economy.

Early industries were mainly geared to the processing of agricultural materials. The milling of flour and ginning of cotton were most important; locations were scattered

Industrial Development Core at Iskanderabad, Pakistan. A planned new industrial city in Pakistan, Iskanderabad specializes in cement, food processing, and pharmaceuticals. (Courtesy of United Nations)

throughout the country near production sites. Since 1952, the government has made large-scale industrial investments and large concentrations are beginning to emerge.

Karachi, the seaport, largest city, and former capital was selected as a heavy industrial development area, with chemicals and metallurgy featured as base industries for further industrialization. Textiles, paper, fertilizer, and surgical instruments have been developed to fill local needs; these industries use cheap labor for export production. It is still the largest and most diverse of Pakistan's industrial centers. Recent large-scale investments are extending industry in the direction of Hyderabad, an old agricultural processing center (Figure 9–7), creating an Indus Delta industrial district.

The two other manufacturing regions are found in the north. Available hydro power (developed in conjunction with irrigation projects) and local raw materials combine in the production of the two northern districts. The larger, centered on Lahore, is dominated by light industry. More diverse than Karachi, this region's industrial installations are also less concentrated—spread over dozens of villages and towns, which complement (and supply) the central and dominant center at Lahore. The Northwest Frontier Industrial district can be characterized as an emerging industrial region. A dozen major and moderate size hydroelectric installations fuel the industrial economy. Appliances, simple agricultural machinery, printing, an embryonic electronics industry, fertilizer production, and oil refining form that basis of regional production. Peshawar, Islamabad, and Rawalpindi are the major regional centers.

Developmental Strategies and Problems The **developmental strategy** for Pakistan is based on the following guidelines:

1. The development of large-scale multipurpose water projects that supply hydroelectric energy and munici-

pal water supply source as well as water for industrial processing and irrigation.

2. The development of industry based on local raw materials, especially fertilizer, textiles, and leather goods.

3. Self-sufficiency in grain and export of processed cotton, oil seeds, and tobacco products.

4. Elimination of unemployment through industrial development.

5. Intensified geologic prospecting.

To date, the developmental progress of Pakistan has hinged on foreign aid—some $10 billion over the last twenty years. Unlike India, large amounts have not had to be siphoned off into grain purchases. However, a large amount has been spent on military programs. Private entrepreneurs are still reluctant to invest in industrial projects so that public sector investment is dominant.

Pakistan's growth in food production and GNP exceeds population growth. However, continued high growth rates are a concern. A long history of internal disorders, the instability of Iran's regime, and an unfriendly government in Afghanistan all contribute to a lack of confidence on the part of foreign investors.

BANGLADESH—THE MOST IMPOVERISHED STATE?

Bangladesh is the eighth largest country in the world in population. Its 90 million people live in an area slightly smaller than Wisconsin; this population density, over 1,500 per square mile (580 per square kilometer), makes it one of the most crowded parts of the world. The conterminous forty-eight states of the United States could hold the entire population of the world at that level of density. Bangladeshis are concentrated in the east central part of their nation, in the areas around Dacca and Comilla (see Figure 9–8). The Chittagong hills of the southeast and the Sundarbans forests of the southwest are relatively lightly populated.

Unfortunately for the Bangladeshis, their small overcrowded country has a very short list of natural resources. However, there is a very substantial quantity of natural gas in the delta area. One offshore field and eight inland fields contain, among them, an estimated 9 trillion cubic feet of natural gas. Exploration is under way for petroleum. There are also large coal deposits known, but these are so deep that exploitation will be difficult. Some limestone deposits are the only other known mineral resources.

Nearly 98 percent of the Bangladeshi are members of the Bengali ethnic group. They speak Bangla (Bengali). Some non-Bengali Moslem immigrants from India and some tribal groups along the southeastern borders make up much of the remainder.

Until December of 1971, Bangladesh was East Pakistan. In the partition of British India, the predominantly Moslem areas near the eastern and western ends of the great riverine plain of northern India were designated Pak-

istan, although the two parts were separated by more than a thousand miles of (Hindu) Indian territory. Although united in their adherence to Islam, little else was held in common between the citizens of East and West Pakistan. A civil war broke out in the spring of 1971 largely as a result of Bengali demands for more provincial autonomy, and Bengali claims that national development expenditures and opportunities in the national armed forces and civil service were disproportionately in favor of West Pakistanis. India saw an opportunity to weaken its historic enemy by supporting the Bengali nationalists. The Indian government hosted the "government in exile" of the future Bangladesh, aided refugees, and provided reconstruction aid. Just as India and Pakistan had to divide the assets and liabilities of British India, down to railroad cars and filing cabinets, Pakistan and Bangladesh had to agree on a similar division.

Agriculture Agriculture is the key to the Bangladesh economy as 90 percent of the Bangladeshis live on the land. Although very densely populated, Bangladesh has generally fertile soil and ample water for agriculture. Indeed, its food productivity explains its dense population in the first place. Although Bangladesh is sometimes regarded as very poor and with a high probability of remaining poor, it *is* possible to expand food production there. The major crop, rice, can be harvested three times a year. Better flood control and irrigation projects could support more food production. India and Bangladesh have agreed to jointly develop the water resources of the delta area. A major problem in boosting food production is that developing nations can seldom afford the chemical fertilizers needed for increasing yields. Bangladesh's natural gas resources are being used to manufacture fertilizers.

Urban-industrial development patterns Dacca, the capital, has over 2 million people and, as in India and other developing countries, it is growing faster than the employment base in industry or services. The industrial sector, mostly nationalized, is not considered very efficient. The main industry, processing jute into burlap and carpet backing, is Bangladesh's major earner of foreign exchange but is not very profitable. Customers complain of poor quality control, and synthetic substitutes have made inroads in foreign markets. Cotton textiles industries suffer lack of local cotton fiber and protective tariffs in potential market countries. Jute, sugar, and textile mills that are government owned have had economic problems, while government-encouraged private investment in pharmaceuticals has produced a thriving industry attracting considerable foreign investment.

Although there is a strong probability of oil offshore of Bangladesh (also a strong probability of a boundary

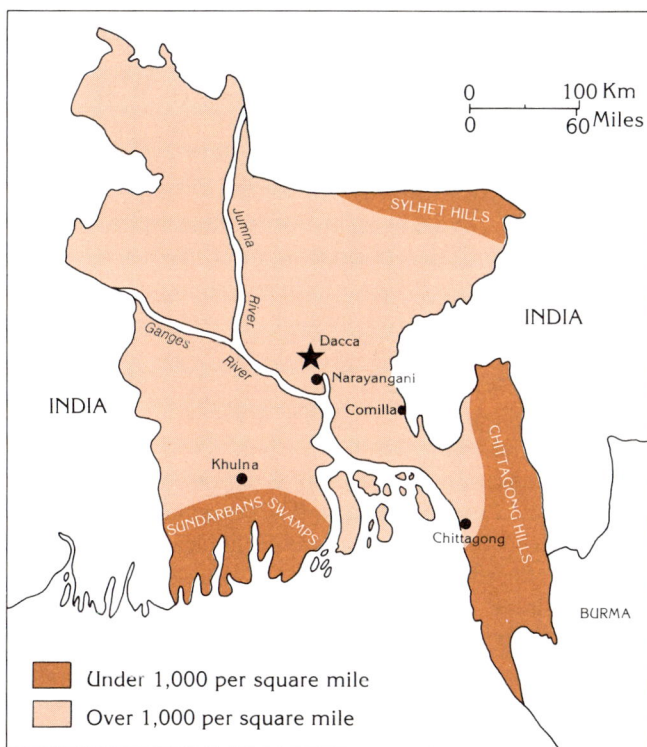

FIGURE 9–8

Bangladesh: Population and Cities. Bangladesh, in the fertile, densely populated delta of the Ganges-Brahmaputra, is one of the poorest nations on earth. Its development prospects hinge on its ability to support a crowded, rural population expanding faster than the economy.

by its gas-based fertilizer factories could draw Bangladesh back from the brink of human disaster by starvation. If the population growth rate can be lowered, rising industrialization may be able to absorb enough of the surplus labor force to relieve pressure on the crowded farmlands where most plots are both tiny and inefficient.

SRI LANKA

Sri Lanka is a republic occupying the pear-shaped island known until 1972 as Ceylon. Only 18 miles (29 kilometers) from India, Sri Lanka is about the size of West Virginia and has a population of 15 million. Its population density is about one third that of Bangladesh and slightly higher than India's. The northern part of the island, and the southern coastal areas, are lowland plains with a hilly and mountainous core in the south. About 40 percent of the island is under cultivation; tea and rubber are the main export crops. The natural resource base is narrow, with very few minerals present.

Population density is greatest in the southwestern part of the country, which has the heaviest rainfall produced by the summer monsoons rising against the highlands. Columbo, the capital, is approaching the million mark. For decades, the population growth rate was 2.4, the rate at which a population will double in twenty-five years. Fertility rates have begun to drop recently but are still high enough to dilute development gains. The government has recently increased the availability of birth-control services. About 70 percent of the people are Sinhalese, with about 22 percent Tamils, and 8 percent Moors (Moslems descended from sailors and traders originating in the Persian Gulf). The Sinhalese are Buddhist, while the Tamils are Hindu and the Moors, Moslem. This cultural divergence has been a cause of ethnic strife in the past and some militant Tamils have pressed claims for a separate Tamil state. About half the Tamils are "Indian Tamils" whose ancestors arrived last century as plantation labor when both India and Ceylon were part of the British empire. These "recent" arrivals, in contrast to the "Ceylon Tamils" who had been established there earlier and who were full citizens with votes, were not offered citizenship after Ceylonese independence in 1948. India also refused repatriation of these Tamils, claiming they were not Indian citizens either. India and Sri Lanka have gradually divided these stateless, hopeless people into repatriated Indians and Sri Lanka citizens, but much bitterness remains among Tamils in both nations. Sinhalese remains the sole official language despite agitation to recognize Tamil. As in India, English was widely spoken among the educated and official circles. Literacy is about 85 percent, far above the average for South Asia. Political power has been transferred from the English-

Dacca, Bangladesh. Bangladesh ranks among the world's poorest states, with a narrow resource base and dense population. While not hopeless, the Bangladeshis' progress, not to say survival, appears to depend on international development aid. (Courtesy of United Nations/Philip Teuscher)

dispute with India over the division of these offshore areas), the Bangladeshis currently must spend a third of their foreign exchange earnings on imported oil. Hydroelectric power is fairly well developed, and the government is expanding the rural electrification program to take advantage of this ample source of energy. An important source of foreign exchange is the remittances of Bangladeshis living overseas. Skilled and semiskilled workers are "exported" to labor-demand areas throughout the Moslem world. The United States has provided nearly $15 billion in foreign aid and the Soviet Union is the second ranking donor to Bangladesh.

Despite the serious problems of coping with a very dense population and high growth rate (the number may double by 2000 A.D.), the future need not be disastrous. Maintenance of good relations with India, especially concerning the equitable division of water, the good chance of striking oil, and the increasing food yields made possible

Sri Lankan Fishing Boat. One reason for generally low catches per fisherman in this protein-short region is lack of modern fishing technology. This Sri Lankan fishing boat has just been equipped with a diesel engine. (Courtesy of United Nations)

speaking urban elite to a broader base, reducing the reliance on the colonial language.

Agriculture   The economy of Sri Lanka is dominated by agriculture; tea earns 40 percent of export value and rubber and coconut accounts for another 30 percent of exports. Traditionally, Sri Lanka has relied on foreign exchange earned by tea and rubber to purchase food, as normally half its food requirements were imported. For years, this exchange of high-value tea and rubber for lower-value rice worked well, and living standards were superior to the regional average. The government began an extensive land reform in the 1970's, nationalizing both foreign and locally owned plantations. Productivity has not risen as fast as expected, and an expanding population has far outpaced increased food production. Food imports now use three quarters of the country's export earn-

ings as prices received for exports stagnated while food prices rose. This serious problem is compounded by rising energy costs, and disaster is averted only by large infusions of foreign aid and food subsidies.

Development Strategies   Sri Lanka is a typical example of the plight of developing countries that are attempting to industrialize by exporting clothing to the developed world. Characteristically, textiles and clothing are among the first industries to modernize in a developing nation. There is a near-universal market locally for cheap, machine-made textiles. Textiles can be made into clothing with the skills already acquired in craft work. In Sri Lanka's case, an attempt was made to develop a clothing industry before a local textiles industry had matured, using imported cloth. It was reasoned that manufacturing jobs should be expanded as quickly as possible, with the lowest capital investment possible, to pay for the huge food imports of this poor country. Rapid expansion into European and North American markets was followed there by a series of **protectionist tariffs** to protect local clothing industries. Sri Lanka's clothing exports are considerably below their projections of a few years ago. A basic question is: if developing nations that are lacking energy resources and relying on food imports cannot effectively use their one real resource—cheap labor—because of tariff barriers to their products, what *can* they do to help themselves?

NEPAL AND BHUTAN

Nepal and Bhutan are landlocked countries on the southern slopes of the Himalaya Mountains between the Tibetan Plateau and the Ganges Basin. Nepal, about the size of Arkansas, has about 14 million people, while smaller Bhutan, comparable to Vermont and New Hampshire combined in area, has only 1.5 million and is even less developed than Nepal. (The small state of Sikkim has been absorbed into India.) In both, peaks over 20,000 feet (7,000 meters) are common. These highlands are very sparsely populated, with most people of both countries living in valleys below 9,000 feet (2,700 meters). The summer monsoon brings fairly heavy seasonal precipitation.

Nepal's population includes ethnic groups that have migrated from India, Tibet, and Central Asia. The third of the population living in the Terai, the Nepalese portion of the great Ganges Plain, are culturally indistinguishable from their neighbor Indians. Ninety percent of the Nepalese are Hindus, with Buddhist and Moslem minorities. There are more than a dozen languages spoken, but Nepali is the official one. The Terai generates a food surplus, which supports the food-deficit highlands and provides a small export trade to India. Only 30 percent of

Nepal is cultivable but 90 percent of the Nepalese are farmers. Rice, wheat, and jute are the main crops. Until the 1950's, Nepal was almost totally isolated due to both difficult terrain and deliberate policy of Nepalese kings. One of the least developed countries of Asia, the Nepalese economy is still dominated by subsistence agriculture. One third of Nepal is forested, and there are plans to exploit this resource, including construction of a paper mill. The hydroelecric potential is great, and both India and China (People's Republic of China, PRC) have provided economic and technical assistance in power plant construction. Mineral resources have not been fully explored; however some coal, copper, iron, zinc, and cobalt have been found.

Although Nepal is not very heavily populated by Asian standards, the ecological damage resulting from mounting population pressure is serious. Deforestation of steep hillsides has led to severe soil erosion and could pose problems for the hydro dams by heavy silt accumulation in the reservoirs. Two thirds of Nepal's foreign trade is with India, and Calcutta functions as Nepal's port for overseas trade. India has made it clear that it will not tolerate any Chinese territorial aggression in Nepal, and both economic ties and cultural relations between Hindu Nepal and India are closer than with the Chinese. However, the Nepalese are determined to maintain excellent relations with both giant neighbors.

Bhutan is even more dependent on India than is Nepal; by some measures, Bhutan barely qualifies as an independent state. Since 1910, Bhutan's foreign relations have been "guided," by Britain until 1947, then by India. Also since 1910, India has provided a subsidy to Bhutan, a responsibility continued by independent India. Bhutan's economy is one of the most primitive in the world; it is only now shifting from barter to the use of Bhutanese and Indian currency. Self-sufficient in food, Bhutan has a high population growth rate similar to that of Nepal. Prior to the seizure of Tibet by the PRC in 1950, Bhutan's trade had been oriented northward. Since 1950, Bhutan has reoriented its trade southward to India. For practical purposes, this small state wedged between China and India is a semiautonomous part of India. The majority of Bhutanese are Buddhist. Ninety-five percent are illiterate farmers.

In both areas, people farm rice on terraced hillsides and in the valleys. Barley and pastoralism dominate in the rigorous climates of higher altitudes. Each has become a tourist stop for those seeking out splendid scenery, unusual architecture, and an array of cultures. Like many other **ministates,** they are following the route of tourism, tax refuge, and highly specialized exports as their route to development—if at a somewhat more primitive level.

SOUTH ASIA—TENSIONAL RELATIONSHIPS WITH OTHER REGIONS

India's dominant position within the South Asia region means that tensional relationships within the region as well as with other regions revolve around India's friendships and foes. Three major themes prevail—India's **nonalignment** policy, the three India-Pakistan wars, and India's rivalry with the People's Republic of China. Jawaharlal Nehru, India's first prime minister and one of the leaders in the struggle for independence, was chief architect of nonalignment in a policy of "neutrality plus." Mere neutrality was passive. India was to be an active force for a peaceful and progressive world. India has become a major voice for third world countries and has played an active role in the United Nations. India made important contributions to various UN peacekeeping operations. India has also chaired various international control commissions established in Laos, Vietnam, and Cambodia. Because many Indian scholars are fluent in English, India has made a disproportionately major impact on American thinking.

Many in the United States have viewed India's nonalignment policy as being biased against the United States. It appeared that India was determined to take a highly moralistic, critical approach to American policy while saying very little about Soviet policy. Popular opinion in the United States viewed India's voluble criticism as churlish and lacking in gratitude for the massive foreign aid supplied India by the United States (over $11 billion by 1979, more than one third of all aid India has received since independence). India's claim to moral leadership is also flawed, in many Westerner's eyes, by determination to retain Kashmir despite the Moslem majority of that state's population, military action in occupying tiny Portuguese coastal enclaves in 1961, and Indian action in Sikkim in the mid-1970's. India's seizure of Sikkim is an example of their determination to dominate the Himalayan frontier states in competition with China. Indian sensitivity to their border with China reflects the major interregional tensions involving South Asia and East Asia. In 1962, Chinese troops drove deeply into Indian territory before unilaterally proclaiming a cease-fire and withdrawing to previous positions. There is still a large area north of Kashmir that is claimed by India but controlled by the PRC.

In this clash of giants, the other nations of South Asia have tended to establish friendly relationships with either India and its Soviet supporter, or with China. (See Figure 9–9.) Opposition to India has helped foster a Pakistani relationship with the PRC, which could conceivably develop as a military alliance. Soviet and PRC foreign aid, technical assistance, trade treaties, and military aid throughout the South Asia region tend to reflect the pro- or anti-India alignments that have developed.

Afghanistan and Iran seem to be replacing India as Pakistan's major concern. Pushtun tribes and their lands were divided between Afghanistan and (then) India in 1893. Pakistan regards this border as "established"; Afghanistan does not. An unfriendly, Soviet-backed regime in Afghanistan could complicate matters. Landlocked Afghanistan is dependent on either Pakistan or Iran for access to the ocean; it has recently begun to demand border revisions again. At the same time, hundreds of thousands of Afghan refugees have fled to Pakistan. Relations with the Soviet Union have worsened because of Soviet military intervention in Afghanistan. The future of relations with Iran is also unclear.

THE REGION'S WORLD VIEW

India's self-confidence can only be increased by the bumper harvests of the late 1970's, reducing its need to import food and thus freeing more foreign exchange to absorb the climbing cost of petroleum. The increase in Soviet naval power in the Indian Ocean may also bolster the confidence of the Soviet's unofficial ally, India. In 1974, India joined the "nuclear club" with an underground nuclear test. The United States reacted with dismay at nuclear proliferation in an area that has experienced repeated wars and also questioned India's priorities in financing nuclear weapons research when most of its people are desperately poor.

Pakistan's world view is geared to survival in what it sees as a hostile environment. Long-standing feuds with India, a weak Iran, and a potential Soviet push from Afghanistan have caused a reorientation of Pakistani feeling. They have recognized Bangladesh (1974) and exchanged prisoners and population. Despite an official policy of "step-by-step" normalization of relations with India, distrust and recent Indian agreements with the USSR have slowed things down.

In a traditional "outflanking" gesture, they have sought allies outside the immediate region. Relations with

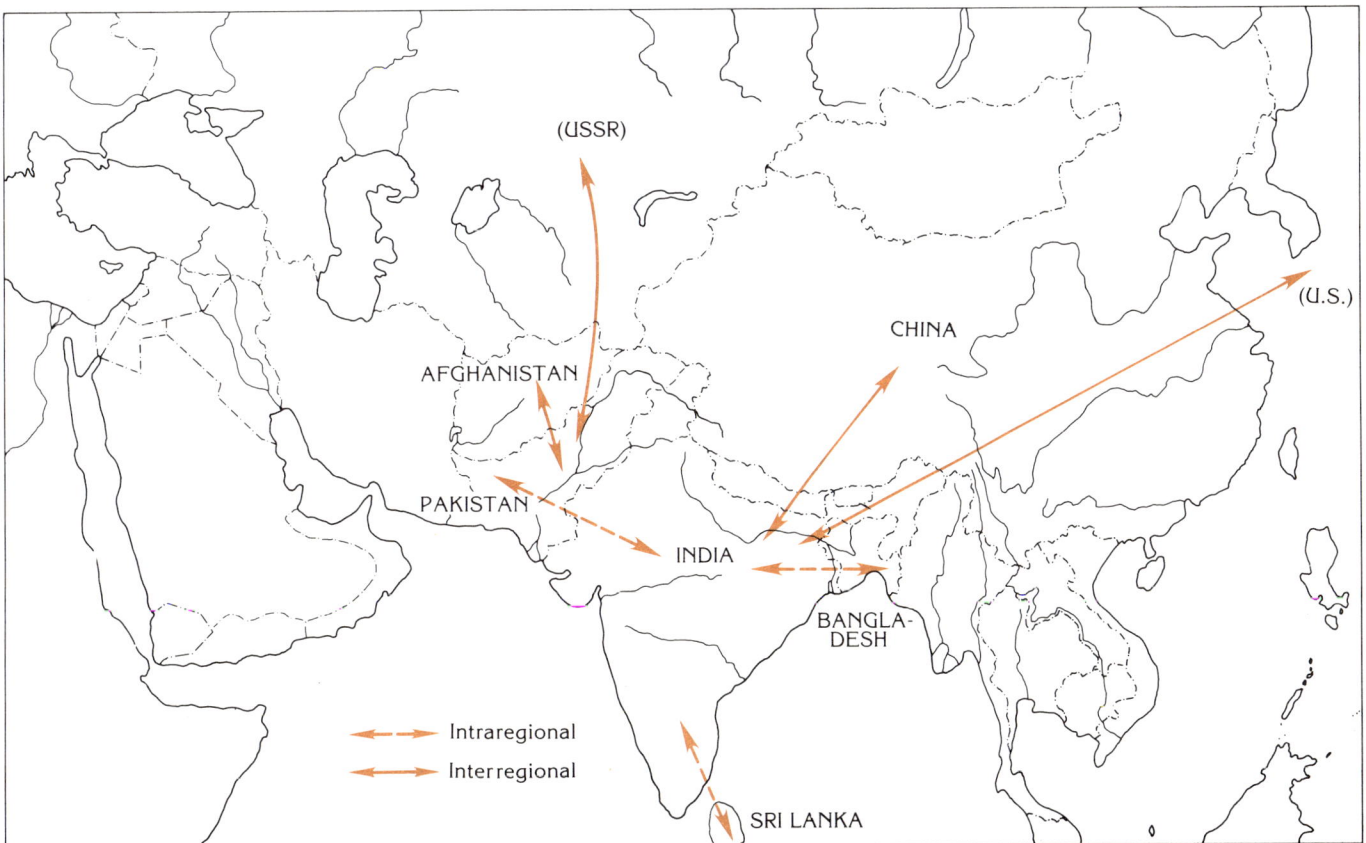

FIGURE 9–9
Schematic Map of Tensions, Intra- and International. Few world regions present such clear, persistent, and potentially disastrous tensions as South Asia. Friendship or distrust of India, or its major opponent, Pakistan, influences policies and alignments with neighboring regions and with the superpowers.

China have grown much closer. The Afghan situation has resulted in increased American military and economic aid to Pakistan and closer (if informal) ties between the two. Ever mindful of its Islamic heritage, Pakistan has sought (and is seeking) closer ties with the Arab world without taking sides in any Middle Eastern disputes. Having purchased a nuclear fuel processing plant from France, they seem to be nearing membership in the still-select club of nuclear powers. In the face of Indian nuclear power, Pakistan feels that it must build an equal deterrent.

case study
THE MONSOON

The monsoon is the key to understanding South Asia. It affects Southeast Asia and East Asia as well, but to a less dramatic degree. There also are monsoonal tendencies around some coasts of the other great land masses, but they are of minor significance compared to that of the Indian subcontinent.

The monsoon, previously mentioned in the section on East Asia, originally referred to the seasonal shifts in wind direction experienced in the Arabian Sea and along the East African coast. Arab sea traders were sensitive, naturally, to the direction and force of the winds that propelled their vessels. The seasonal reversal of wind is commonly sharply defined in India and frequently involves strong winds for months at a time. While very cold air circulates out of the Siberian high in winter to China, north of the Tsingling range, and to the Korean peninsula and Japan, the Indian subcontinent is protected from it by the great Tibetan Plateau and the Himalayas. Nevertheless, high pressure over land in winter does produce a land-to-sea air flow in that season. For India and Bangladesh, the winter air is of more local, warmer origin than that of northern East Asia. For South Asia, the major axis of monsoon air circulation is roughly northeast-southwest. In winter, the weaker flow is from the northeast: in summer, the much stronger flow is from the southwest. This produces two general zones of heavy *orographic,* or mountain-induced, precipitation. One is along the Western Ghats, the western edge of the Plateau of Deccan, from north of Bombay to Cape Comorin; the other is along the flanks of the Himalayas. There is also a large area of heavy summer precipitation in Northeast India, which is partially orographic in nature. The heavy rains produced by warm, moisture-laden air, sweeping in from the Bay of Bengal and then rising steeply against the Himalayas, can reach incredible totals. Over 400 inches (10,000 millimeters), in one year, mostly within four months, have been recorded on the lower slopes of the Himalayas. The long-term averages are less spectacular than the unusual year or season, but even they tell the story of abundantly wet summers followed by rather dry winters as the winds reverse. The Indian city of Darjeeling, just south of Sikkim, for example, has a July average precipitation of over 32 inches (810 millimeters), while December, January, and February each have less than 1 inch (25 millimeters) per month. Thus, Darjeeling's 122-inch (3,100-millimeter) annual precipitation average includes a fantastically wet summer as the onshore winds from the tropical ocean sweep up the slope of the Himalayas, and then a near-desert-like winter as the winds flow from the land toward the sea. Cherrapunji, on the slopes of Assam in the border area with Burma, *averages* 457 inches (11,600 millimeters) a year (July alone receives 107 inches [2,710 millimeters]) and has recorded annual totals of over 900 inches (23,000 millimeters).

Paradoxically, the farmers in India, whether in the almost unbelievably high precipitation areas mentioned above, or in more normal monsoon areas like Calcutta (64 inches [1,600 millimeters] per year) or Allahabad (38 inches [960 millimeters] per year), still are most bothered by drought. It is the *timing* of the onset of the summer monsoon, not the total precipitation, that is most important. There are some parts of South Asia for which the winter monsoon is the rain-maker. These areas, like Sri Lanka (which benefits from both summer and winter monsoons) and the extreme southeast coast of India, have relatively wet winters because the winter monsoon first flows offshore, across warm water, and then onshore again.

For the great majority of South Asians, however, the summer monsoon is the time of heavy dark, low clouds and almost daily downpours, while winter features clear skies and hard, baked brown earth. Crops must be planted before the arrival of the summer monsoon. The seeds must have germinated and the tiny plant anchored itself by its root system before the downpour, which could simply wash away seeds. If the monsoon does not arrive when expected, the soil will not have enough moisture to support the growing plant, which will then wither and die. Since the reversal of wind systems and arrival of the rains depends upon the weakening of the Siberian high pressure as temperatures advance, the development of a Southwest Asian low pressure, and upon relative temperatures over the surrounding sea, the timing is predictable only in a general sense. A late arrival of the rains can mean crop disaster for millions of farmers. In times past, this crop disaster resulted in widespread famine and death. No wonder that Indians look forward eagerly to the gray skies and torrential rains of the summer monsoon. It is their life-support system. While Western-culture cartoons portray persons with bad luck as having a dark cloud over their heads, Indians understandably regard dark clouds as very good luck indeed!

REVIEW QUESTIONS

1   Briefly describe the political conditions in India that led to British control.

2   What cultural and political conditions, unique to British India, favored Ghandi's non-violent protest movement?

3   List some major philosophical and cultural dissimilarities between Islam and Hinduism.

4   Why is India considered to have a severe "population problem" when its growth rates are lower than in many other developing countries?

5   What are the economic incentives for many poor people of this region to have *many* children rather than few?

6   Why is the arrival date of the summer monsoon essentially unpredictable? What consequences does this have for agriculture in much of this region?

7   What cultural factors act to retard modernization of Indian agriculture? Why would rapid modernization induce economic dislocations?

8   What is the rational basis for the Hindu proscription on slaughtering cows?

9   How does the "Green Revolution" tend to favor large landowners rather than the poorest farmers?

10   Why does the Indian heartland seem to have economic growth below that of the Indian South?

11 How did the partition of British India affect Calcutta and the jute industry of Bangladesh?

12 On the basis of raw materials, labor costs, and international markets, which of India's industries have the best export potential?

13 How does India's multicultural, multilingual population pose special problems for democratic government?

14 Why is irrigation in desert areas not always a permanent improvement in terms of soil productivity?

15 Assess the relative chances of this region's states for future success in adequately feeding their people.

16 What cultural and political tensions led to the separation of Pakistan into two states?

17 Of the region's states, which is most likely, in terms of present cultural, religious, linguistic, and/or racial tensions, to experience pressures for regional autonomy or independence?

18 How does Indian-Chinese rivalry affect the foreign policies of the other states of the region?

19 In what ways was British colonialism a positive factor in economic development within the region? Were there negative impacts of colonialism as well?

SUGGESTED READINGS

1 NAFIS AHMAD, *Economic Geography of East Pakistan*. London: Oxford University Press, 1958.

2 S. ARASARATNAM, *Ceylon*. Englewood Cliffs, N.J.: Prentice Hall, 1964.

3 J. FAALAND and J. R. PARKINSON, *Bangladesh: Test Case for Development*. Boulder, Colo.: Westview, 1975.

4 MARVIN HARRIS, *Cows, Pigs, Wars & Witches: The Riddles of Culture*. New York: Random House, 1974.

5 R. JAHAN, *Pakistan: Failure in National Integration*. New York: Columbia University Press, 1972.

6 PRADHUMA KARAN, *Bhutan*. Lexington: University of Kentucky Press, 1968.

7 BEATRICE LAMB, *India: A World in Transition*. New York: Praeger, 1966.

8 WALTER NEALE and JOHN ADAMS, *India: The Search for Unity, Democracy and Progress*. New York: Van Nostrand, 1976.

9 LEO ROSE, *Nepal: Strategy for Survival*. Berkeley: University of California Press, 1971.

10 DONALD SMITH, *South Asian Politics and Religion*. Princeton, N.J.: Princeton University Press, 1966.

11 O. H. K. SPATE and A. T. A. LEARMOUTH, *India & Pakistan: A General and Regional Geography*. London: Methuen, 1967.

12 JOSEPH SPENCER and WILLIAM THOMAS, *Asia, East By South*. New York: Wiley, 1971.

KEY TERMS

- slash-and-burn
- core
- development enclave
- hinterland
- successor state
- hearth
- demographic transition
- irredenta
- tectonic plate
- laterization
- intertropical convergence
- silvaculture
- laterite
- cultural shatterbelt
- cottage industry
- infrastructure
- capital intensive
- import replacement
- physiologic density

10

SOUTHEAST ASIA

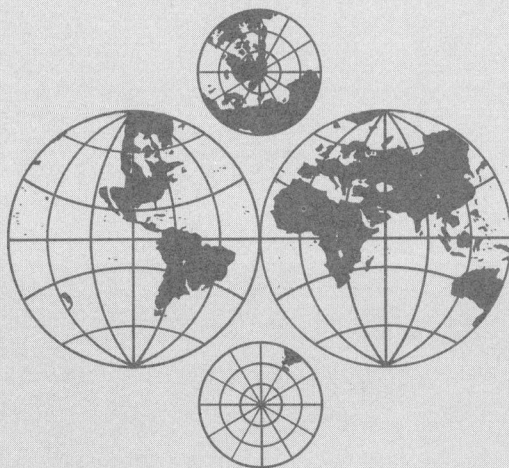

Southeast Asia is very much a "land in between"; for much of its history, its culture has been shaped by a position between the repeatedly expansionist cultures and peoples of India and China. It is a region of sharp cultural differences and contradictory economies—one in which topography plays an unusually important, if passive, role. On average, most countries of Southeast Asia are lightly populated in comparison to East or South Asia, yet averages mean even less here than in other regions. Often, the people of the sparsely settled hill country are of different ethnic background and likely of different religions and cultures than are those of the much more densely populated lowlands. Agriculture in the uplands is likely to be of the low-intensity, shifting, **slash-and-burn** variety, while valleys, deltas, and some lowland plains generally support incredibly dense agricultural populations based on wet (paddy) rice cultivation. Of course, differences in agricultural techniques anywhere in the world are usually related to topography, but the lowland-upland contrasts throughout Southeast Asia are unusually sharp.

A series of great rivers, many of whose headwaters are in the eastern and southeastern flanks of the Himalayas, are channeled southward by steeply folded topography and form wide valleys and alluvial plains as they approach the sea. These fertile alluvial soils support heavy concentrations of people and several have become the **cores** of states. (See Figure 10–1.) Thus, the middle and lower valleys of the Irrawaddy formed the cores of Burma; the Menam Chao-Prao, the Thai core; and the Red River, the original Vietnamese core territory. The central and lower Mekong, one of the largest river systems in all Asia, flows through the densely populated sectors of Laos and Kampuchea (Cambodia), and the southern, secondary core of Vietnam. Many of the most productive soils of the island archipelagoes tend to be in the coastal areas and lower river valleys; thus, this part of the wet tropics, in contrast to those of much of South America and Africa, has always been highly accessible to ocean-borne trade and cultural contacts.

Strong influences from both China and India are apparent in Southeast Asia's people and cultures. The fabled Angkor Wat ruins testify to the power of a great civilization that existed in the lower and middle Mekong Valley from the ninth to fourteenth centuries. They show clear Hindu influences, which also reached to the central Vietnam area in the ancient Cham civilization. The distribution of plows shows the almost intertwined nature of Chinese and Indian cultural penetrations. Indian plow types were common in Java, Sumatra, Cambodia, and Laos, while Chinese plows predominate in Vietnam, the Philippines, and northern Borneo.

FIGURE 10–1

River Valleys and Settlement Cores of Mainland Southeast Asia. These mainland states each have at least one (Burma and Vietnam have two each) densely settled, historic core of prime agricultural land; subsequent national boundaries tend to follow the ethnically dissimilar, much less intensively used hill lands peripheral to the core(s).

There are at least three different "cultural worlds" throughout the region: the isolated, primitive, shifting agricultural realm of the uplands with their distinctive ethnic groups, frequently not integrated economically or politically with the larger society; the crowded, intensively cultivated wet-rice lowlands; and the **development enclaves** of the plantations and cities, especially the capital cities.

The rise of the great trading cities like Singapore, Manila, Bangkok, and Hanoi is largely a product of European imperialism; western Europe began to replace Indian and Chinese trade and cultural influences by the eighteenth century (earlier in the Philippines). The British in India, ever trying to stabilize and pacify the Indian frontiers, pushed into Burma; Burmese rice surpluses, so near to Indian food deficits, were an added attraction. The British and Dutch colonial empires split what was left of the Malayan culture area (the Spanish had occupied the Philippines in the sixteenth century) to acquire coastal trading stations for the lucrative spice trade. Coastal trade centers expanded control into the interior to stabilize the **hinterlands** supplying the spices. The successful transplant of natural rubber trees from the Amazon Basin of Brazil

(using stolen seed to break the Brazilian monopoly) led to still further expansion of political control inland. The French expanded into Vietnam from an initial settlement at present-day Danang (1858). By the end of the nineteenth century they had moved into Laos, which had been loosely controlled by Siam (Thailand), and Cambodia. Thailand managed to remain free by a combination of able kings and the fact that it functioned as a buffer between British expansion from Burma on the west and Malaya on the south and French expansion westward from Vietnam. Even an independent Thailand was literally shaped by imperialism as its boundaries were, in effect, determined by British and French colonial policies.

Rubber to feed Western industrialization instigated more than territorial acquisition; it stimulated trade and migration as well. The demand for plantation labor led to imports of workers from British India and China. The commercial boom generated by rubber (and tin) helped establish great trading cities whose entrepreneurial middle class were almost invariably Chinese. Thus the postcolonial states inherited a situation of ethnic diversity. New rubber plantations in Southeast Asian and African colonies enabled the industrial states of Britain, France, and Holland to supply their own markets, as well as other customers, at prices that they then controlled. Spices, sugar, tea, palm oil, and other plantation crops were added, diversifying the exports but not the domestic economies, which were still

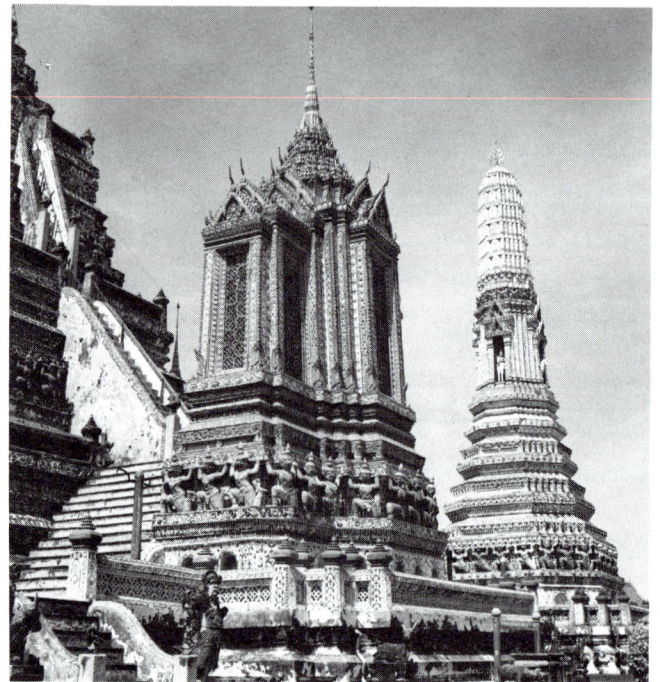

Temple of Dawn, Bangkok. A region of exotic cultural amalgams and contrasts, Southeast Asia is a classic example of a cultural shatterbelt. (Courtesy of United Nations)

entirely agricultural. Plantations and cities, associated with the modern commercial economy elsewhere in the world, exist side-by-side with primitive subsistence economies in the rest of the territory. Thus each of the **successor states** consisted of differing, unintegrated economic portions. Much of the energy of postcolonial governments has had to be devoted to economic integration and to blending different cultures and peoples into one nation.

THE DISTINCTIVENESS OF SOUTHEAST ASIA

Southeast Asia is a region of contradictions and wide divergences from any average. It is both a probable ancient **hearth** of agriculture, with many domesticated plants and animals originating here, and a recent agricultural frontier, with peoples from South Asia and East Asia pushing into lightly settled river valleys, deltas, and coastal lowlands within the last few centuries. It is commercial and subsistence, developed and underdeveloped at the same time. Borders overlap ethnic distributions; claims and counter-

claims keep political uncertainty a fact of daily life. Yesterday's allies are tomorrow's enemies and vice versa. Influenced by surrounding mega-regions, yet distinctly different, Southeast Asia must be a separate region since it is so clearly *not* a part of other regions in the area. All of the area's states share the same basic problems; they are *not* functionally integrated.

HISTORICAL-CULTURAL CHARACTERISTICS

This region has received strong human and cultural influences from South Asia, East Asia, Southwest Asia, and West Europe. On a map of predominant religions, this diversity is immediately apparent (see Figure 10–2). Indonesia is the world's largest Moslem nation, while the Philippines are the only predominantly Christian country in all Asia, and the mainland states have various Buddhist sects with Islamic, Christian, Hindu, or animist minorities. As noted with Thailand, colonialism was not universal, although it was a dominant force in all other Southeast Asian states for a century or more. Colonialism is still a

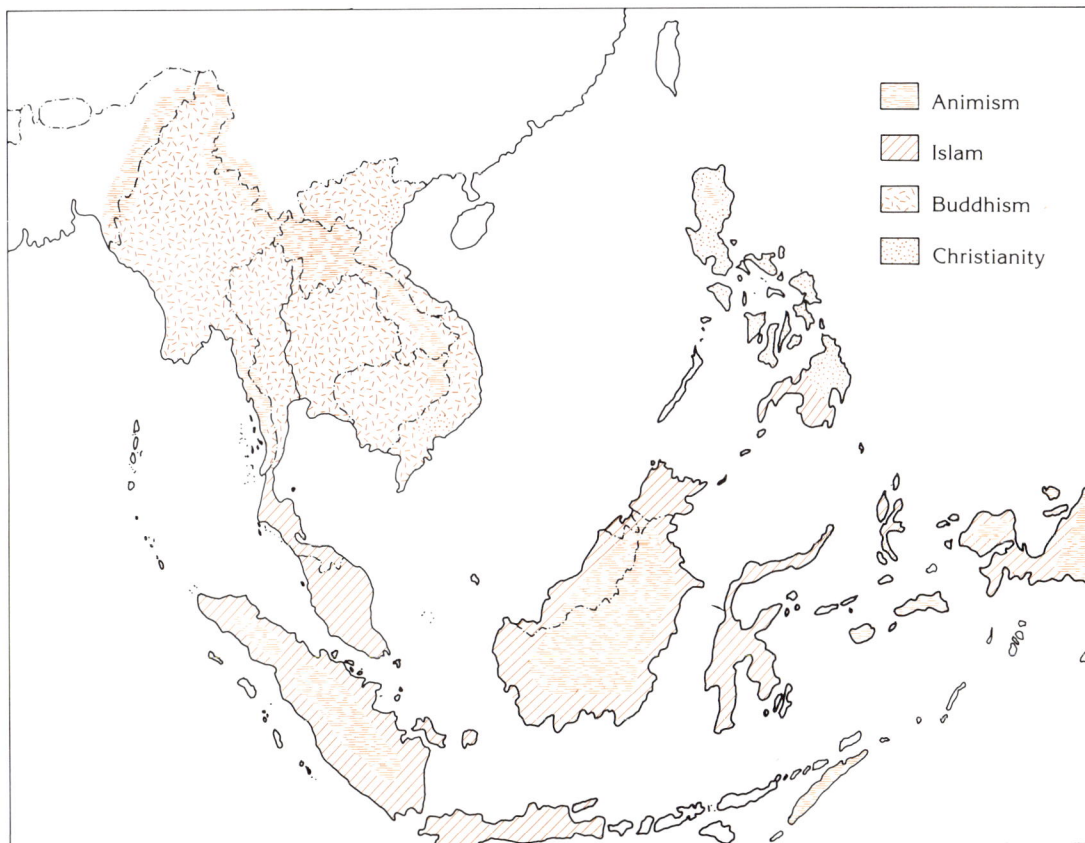

Animism

Islam

Buddhism

Christianity

FIGURE 10–2
Predominant Religions. Typical of a cultural shatterbelt, Southeast Asia's predominant religions show the impact of many different cultural currents from neighboring, and even far distant, regions.

major factor in the region in that many contemporary national policies (and problems) are reactive to the recency of colonialism. Plantation economies were usually highly localized. For example, plantations were very important in Malaya, but almost nonexistent in either former British or Dutch Borneo. Commercial crop production for export revolutionized Java and Vietnam but hardly touched Cambodia or most of the outer islands of Indonesia.

PHYSICAL CHARACTERISTICS

Southeast Asia's peninsulas and archipelagoes may be regarded as an "Asian Mediterranean"; even those cultures not oriented to sea contacts and trade, such as the Burmese, were reoriented to oceanic influences in the European imperial period. The region consists of nodes, separated by mountainous interfluves or surrounding seas. It is everywhere tropical (except in the very heights of mountains), universally well-watered, and often more fertile than comparable tropical environments elsewhere.

ECONOMIC CHARACTERISTICS

The extremely uneven population distribution means that the region includes very heavily populated areas such as Java, along with virtually empty lands, both upland and lowland. Therefore, the region has underutilized economic potential.

The "overseas Chinese" in Southeast Asia, some 12 million strong, are a proportionately small group within the overall population but are economically powerful in virtually every country of the region. Their economic power and strong tendency to retain a Chinese subculture amidst their host cultures has made the overseas Chinese a highly controversial, sometimes persecuted, minority. While it was western European states that acquired direct political control in most of Southeast Asia during the colonial period, it was more a Chinese colony in terms of actual population migration. The Chinese who migrated to the *Nanyang*, "southern sea," constitute the largest group of Chinese living outside of China or Taiwan. These Chinese originated primarily in southern coastal China, particularly the hinterlands of ports. Generally, they formed an urban middle class between the mass of indigenous peoples and the elite and European rulers. Often imported by the European colonialists as indentured servants (people who contracted to work a specific period of time in return for their transportation and maintenance) in tin mines and rubber plantations, the Chinese worked and saved to build small retail businesses. These businesses in turn supported a second generation of professionals and proprie-

tors of larger, more prosperous businesses. Some also became moneylenders. The Chinese of today, then, are typically urban shopkeepers, craftsmen, market gardeners, bankers, professionals, and government bureaucrats. There are very few Chinese peasant farmers in the Nanyang.

Although very few contemporary overseas Chinese were born in China, the Chinese language and culture is studied in community-run schools. Most are multilingual, speaking at least one local dialect or language, a European tongue and, of course, Chinese. Although some degree of intermarriage and acculturation has occurred, particularly in Thailand and the Philippines, the Chinese are frequently regarded as aliens despite their citizenship by birth in Southeast Asian lands. Their virtual control of the rice trade, obviously a sensitive issue throughout the region, contributes to local resentments as both farmers and consumers perceive the Chinese as profiting heavily from this everyday necessity. The internationalist outlook of the urban merchants and financiers among the overseas Chinese is at odds with the often intensely nationalistic people only recently freed from colonial status. Also, the post–World War II involvement of Chinese ethnics in Communist insurgencies in Malaya, plus the fact that Communist party members in Indonesia were most likely to be Chinese, set them in opposition to nationalist governments in those countries.

The overseas Chinese often dominate trade between Southeast Asian nations. The hostility of their hosts interacted with Chinese determination to maintain both their cultural identity and international contacts as opportunities in case of banishment from their "temporary" homes. It was an obvious trade advantage to an overseas Chinese merchant in Malaya, for example, to deal with another Chinese merchant in the Philippines. A shared language, a shared culture, and a knowledge of the other's reputation (and credit rating) within the close, intermarried communities of Chinese facilitates international deals, providing a form of regional economic unity through trade and interaction.

It is not uncommon for overseas Chinese to manage to hold several passports—their official citizenship in their host country, and either (maybe even both) Nationalist China (Taiwan) and People's Republic passports. Understandable in view of jealousy and threats from suspicious host populations and/or governments, this multiple-passport situation is often interpreted by the hosts as evidence of disloyalty and therefore grounds for further harassment. Racist, jealousy-motivated resentments have resulted in expulsions and even mass murders, as in Indonesia, Kampuchea, Vietnam, and in the case of the "boat people." It is tempting for politicians in the region to focus discontent on the highly visible "alien" and prosperous Chinese.

Other economic characteristics are the dualism of the economies—commercial versus subsistence and the dependence on fluctuating world market prices for foreign exchange. The economic problems of each country in the unit, then, are virtually the same.

WHAT MAKES IT DISTINCTIVE

The whole area of Southeast Asia is characterized by rapid population growth, although the regional increase rate of 2.2 per 1,000 is lower than that of Africa south of the Sahara or most of Latin America. High regional birthrates have not yet been matched by a lowering of death rates. The great surge in natural increase characteristic of the second phase of the **demographic transition** is yet to come. Birthrates have already begun to decline in some parts of the region, however. No other area of the world has such an enormous variation in birth-, death, and growth rates among individual units. This may reflect most accurately the vast intraregional disparities in development (see Table 10–1).

Political instability is another distinctive feature. On-going guerrilla rebellions have occurred (and repeatedly recur) in almost every unit. Disputes over borders exist among virtually all states in the region (and some with states outside the region). Each state claims at least one **irredenta,** land controlled now by another state but claimed on ethnic or historic grounds. Regimes have changed with amazing rapidity in most of the region's countries.

The Vietnamese War is a case in point. The guerrilla war against French occupation of Indochina in the 1930's blended into World War II wherein Japanese control was challenged by native groups. The return of French control was met by further local resistance. A U.S. government, unfamiliar with the region's problems and history, saw itself not as a colonial successor, but rather as a source of aid for a beleaguered native government resisting Communist-inspired aggression.

The lengthy Vietnam War did little to change things. Most Westerners assumed peace would follow U.S. withdrawal. Instead, there was an almost immediate resumption of war, this time against Cambodia. Attacks also occurred in Laos, and fighting at times spilled across the Thai border where refugees from Laos and Cambodia had sought asylum.

The first recorded war in Vietnam took place in 111 B.C.; there followed over one thousand years of guerrilla action against the Chinese conquerors before it achieved independence. For the next five centuries Vietnam occupied itself with wars of expansion against the Khmer civilizations (Cambodia), while also fending off (and periodically invading) China. By the end of the eighteenth century Vietnam was faced with European military actions preparatory to winning trade concessions and colonial territory. If France has relinquished its claims and the United States had never intended a lasting occupation, official maps indicate that the Chinese have not. Even if all three successor states in Indochina are Communist ruled, it does not follow that they are friendly. Periodically, the Chinese and the Soviets are asked for aid, but with a bewildering lack of loyalty or allegiance offered in return.

THE PHYSICAL FRAME

A decidedly usable portion of the tropics, Southeast Asia consists of five major river basins separated by long, parallel-folded mountain ridges, a major peninsula, and thou-

TABLE 10–1
Vital statistics in Southeast Asia

	Birthrate (per 1,000)	Death Rate (per 1,000)	Natural Increase (percent of population)
Countries with relatively low growth			
Singapore	17	5	1.2
Kampuchea	33	15	1.8
Indonesia	34	15	1.0
Countries with moderately high growth			
Thailand	32	9	2.3
Vietnam	42	18	2.3
Brunei	28	4	2.4
Burma	39	14	2.4
Laos	45	21	2.4
Countries with characteristic rapid growth			
Philippines	34	10	2.5
Malaysia	34	6	2.7

sands of offshore islands that vary from tiny to islands larger than Great Britain. Most of the mountainous country, mainland or island, is related to (and part of) a giant chain of folded structures that extends from the Atlas of North Africa, through the Alps and Himalayas, to the Malay Peninsula and continuing beyond as a series of island arcs off the Asian mainland.

Heat and high humidity persist year round. Seasons tend to be marked by fluctuation in rainfall rather than temperature. The mainland portion has a distinct winter dry season, but the seasons are better described as wet and wetter in the lower Malay Peninsula, the offshore islands, and even parts of the mainland coast.

TOPOGRAPHY

The riverine basin of Burma is Y-shaped, with the two limbs separated by difficult hill country. The entire lowland associated with it is enclosed by a mountainous horseshoe-shaped rim that culminates only a few miles from the ocean. The Salween creates a canyonlike valley and only widens into a narrow lowland, shared in part with Thailand, at the twenty-second parallel. The Menam Chao-Prao lowland of Thailand has been created by local rivers not of Himalayan origin, while the Mekong basin and its terraced older erosion levels form a multiple stage basin shared by several countries. The short Red River originates in southwestern China and creates a fertile delta lowland as it enters the Tonkin Gulf. Over most of the mainland, except for the Isthmus of Kra and the central Vietnamese coast, there is reasonably good development of a coastal lowland.

In Indonesia, the situation is more complex. The western limb of the Burmese horseshoe continues out at sea as the Andaman Islands, forks, and in turn becomes the mountain spine along the southern edge of the Indonesian island chain. In Sumatra, this spine has a generous coastal lowland eastward. In Java, alluvial fill, volcanic flows, and erosion have created a plateaulike surface, while eastward only the tops of the chain remain above water as a series of islands terminating at Timor.

The other limb of the Burmese horseshoe, after being split in two by the Salween, continues to form the Malay Peninsula before disappearing under the sea and reappearing as the mountain spine of Borneo (Kalimantan). Here the range splits into several other chains, making a series of alluvial basins separated by ridges—a miniature of the mainland. Celebes (Sulawesi) has the same high mountain core with five prongs, but the intervening basins are largely drowned in the ocean.

A single mountain spine with elevations over 15,000 feet (4,600 meters) runs northwest to southeast astride the center of the island of New Guinea. To its south is broad, swampy coastal lowland—similar to Sumatra. To its north a much lower ridge traps sediment in intermontane basins before it reaches the sea. The bottom of the sea, much more than the maze of islands above it, gives us hints to the contortion that has taken place.

This loose and spreading bundle of mountain ranges seems to regroup in forming the Philippines. The ridges of northern Borneo, Sulawesi, and New Guinea apparently collect again, forming the outer parameters of that island chain. Alluvial lowlands, volcanic flows, and coral colonies have connected peaks and earlier smaller islands into larger units.

The complexity of the topography results from the contact of large, rigid rock plates. Some plates are ocean bottom, while others carry continents above them. Where these plates collide, there is much deformation of the crust through folding and faulting. Earthquakes and volcanic eruptions occur as well, as one plate tends to slide under the other.

Southeast Asia is at the contact zone of at least four **tectonic plates:** the Pacific, Australian, Philippine, and Eurasian (see Figure 10–3). Movement of any or all would generate mountain-building activity and evidently has in this complex zone of mountain, basin, and island. Wherever else multiple plates collide (the Caribbean, the Mediterranean) the landscape is also one of peninsulas and islands.

The results in Southeast Asia are not only spectacular, but increase this tropical area's utility via volcanic material and alluvium. Tropical soils that would normally be leached of their fertility by the chemical reactions of **laterization** (aided by intense heat and large amounts of water), are periodically recharged with fertility by the overflow of streams and/or the addition of fresh, mineral-rich volcanic material.

Four major alluvial lowlands, some subdivided into several parts, and thousands of small ones constitute most of the good usable land on the mainland. The weathered soil derived from volcanic rock provides hill, plateau, and lowland surfaces at many locations within the Malay Peninsula and the offshore islands. The intense variation in topography has tended to hinder economic as well as cultural contact. At the same time, this physiographic segmentation is at least in part responsible for the high degree of utility. It would seem that even in topography there is diversity, instability, and the mixture of positives and negatives so characteristic of the region.

LAND-SEA RELATIONSHIPS

The sea provides the most important linkages throughout the area. It was by sea that the great invasions, waves of

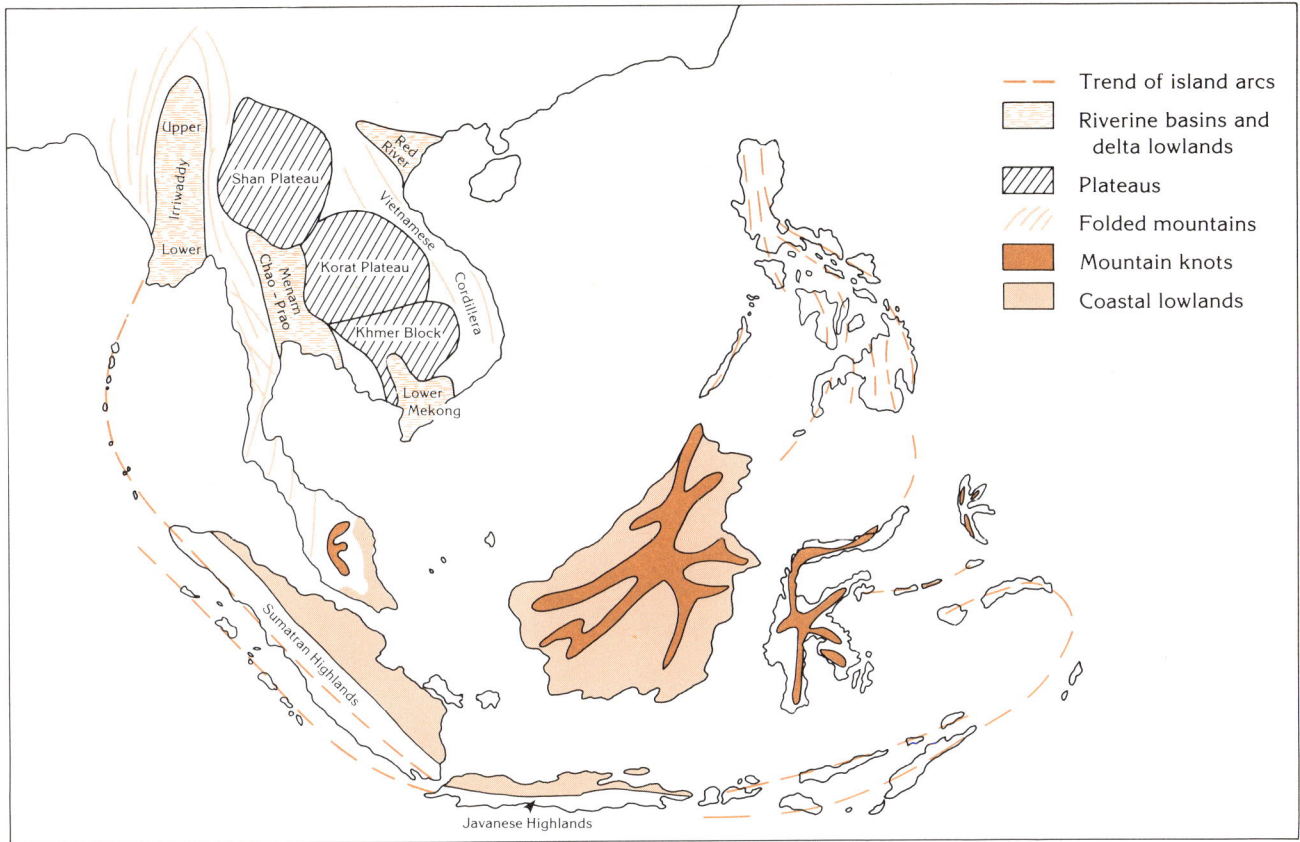

FIGURE 10–3

Generalized Topography and Plate Tectonics. The complex intermingling of land and water in this realm of peninsulas and archipelagoes testifies to the region's position astride colliding plates and peripheral to the "Pacific ring of fire," whose belt of earthquakes and volcanoes branches westward through the Indonesian archipelago.

settlement, and military actions have almost always come. The Malay peoples, dominant on the islands and the peninsula, are known as a great seafaring nation. Little is known of their origin, but they are now thought to be an amalgam of Negroid, Mongoloid, and perhaps Paleo-Asiatic, Australoid, and some Causasoid racial elements. Related elements span much of the Pacific basin and reach Madagascar on the other side of the Indian Ocean.

The mainland cultures—the Thai, Tibeto-Burman (at least the regional subgroups located here), Mon-Khmer, and Vietnamese—were not maritime in orientation. They seem to have spread down the mountains, rivers, ridges, and valleys from points of origin in western and southern China.

Most of the non-Malay cultural influence that came by sea was brought by traders. Indian influence predates the Christian Era. Over two thousand years ago, pre-Aryan cultures from Ceylon and southern India had a great impact on the area. Hinduism was brought to Indonesia, Cambodia, and the Mekong Delta by traders and the migrants who followed. Architectural evidences of this are found through these portions of Southeast Asia. Later and continued contact with India is represented in the dominance of Buddhism on the mainland. The Chinese brought their culture by both land and sea beginning in the third century B.C. Again, the mechanism was traders followed by migrants. Arab traders followed in the thirteenth century. Finally, Europeans began maritime contact in the fifteenth century, ending in a wave of political colonialism, if not settlement. To this day, most of the region's economies are export-oriented and rely on the sea for transportation.

The sea in this region is extremely shallow in the area between western Indonesia and the mainland. Great oceanic deeps extend on the east of the Philippines and the south side of Java and Sumatra. The oceanic area between these two trenches is very deep in the eastern extreme of the region. Exceptionally shallow seas are again encountered between Australia and New Guinea. The Malay Peninsula and the outer islands virtually enclose the South China Sea and a series of smaller seas in the eastern portion of Indonesia. It is an area of intermixed land and water surfaces that separate the Pacific and Indian oceans. (See Figure 10–4.)

FIGURE 10–4
Straits and Entrances to the "Inner Seas." Indonesia's strategic significance is based on the narrowness of the ocean passages from the Strait of Malacca eastward to the shallow seas north of Australia.

A dominant power could easily block a series of straits that control entry. On the north, the Bashi Channel separates the Philippines and Taiwan. To the east, the Strait of Molucca offers entry from the mid-Pacific between the Philippines and New Guinea. The Torres Strait separates New Guinea and Australia. By far the most crucial entryways (and narrowest) are those from the west: the Sunda Strait between Java and Sumatra and the Strait of Malacca between the Malay Peninsula and Sumatra. The former was considered so vital in protecting Dutch interests in Java that they also occupied Sumatra. The British, to protect their routes to China, fortified Singapore and laid claim to the lower end of the Malay Peninsula. Various proposals to build a canal across the Isthmus of Kra were opposed by the British as they already controlled the best route from the west.

The Japanese, between 1941 and 1945, intended to protect their occupied lands in Southeast Asia by controlling the straits. A series of major battles were fought between the U.S. and Japanese fleets to open routes into these inner seas.

Today the strategic importance is just as obvious. Japan's oil lifeline extends through this sea. Indonesia, concerned for its fish resource, controls the size and routes of tankers through the straits.

Three of the nine states cannot reach all their domestic territory without sea routes. Another, Singapore, must receive all supplies, even most food, from overseas sources. Eight of the nine have seacoasts, and all have the need to receive supplies and send exports via water. Thus far no local maritime power has arisen, but most of the region's states desire maritime fleets.

CLIMATE

Most of the area is exceptionally well watered, and no area is subject to extremely high rainfall variability and recurring drought. The circulation pattern set up the the monsoon (discussed in detail in Chapter 9) is such that parts of the mainland portion are characterized by a double maximum, receiving rains from both the winter and summer monsoons. The normally cold, dry air associated with the winter monsoon is modified by the time it reaches Southeast Asia. In passing over the warm waters of the North Pacific and the South China Sea, the air becomes warm, moist, and unstable. Winter rainfall is particularly heavy on the east side of the Philippines, and significant moisture reaches the coastal areas of Vietnam, Cambodia, the Isthmus of Kra, and the upper Malay Peninsula.

This double maximum climatic area is generally classified as monsoonal, though only coastal areas west of the Menam Chao-Prao Delta have the dry winter and truly wet summer characteristic of the monsoonal climate. The coast of Vietnam and the Isthmus of Kra experience two wetter and two drier seasons, but average enough moisture to support monsoon forests.

Interior locations of the mainland are typically tropical wet and dry areas. In large areas of interior Burma, Thailand, and Cambodia, there are two or three months without rain. The downpours of June through September constitute a truly rainy season. Monthly temperature averages are 10°F (9°C) lower during the dry winter season, and seasonal humidity averages vary greatly. The dry season becomes more pronounced and longer from east to west. Indeed, the central Irawaddy Valley of Burma is almost like a tropical steppe because of its combination of distance from a source of moisture and the strong *rainshadow* effect caused by the horseshoe of near-encircling mountains.

South of the region of the double maximum is a region of more tropical weather patterns. The island of Mindanao, the Republic of Indonesia, and most of Malaysia lie within the area of the **intertropical convergence,** and most rainfall is tied to that mechanism. Much of the southern Philippines, Malaysia, and most of Indonesia north of 8°S latitude experience a truly tropical rainforest climate of continuously high humidity and temperature with no marked dry season. Singapore, in many ways typical, has an average humidity of 80 percent and an average temperature of 80°F (26°C) in virtually every month. Rainfall averages 6 to 10 inches (150 to 250 millimeters) per month and rainfall occurs on about one half the days of every month. This monotonous, seasonless climate encompasses most of the area.

The eastern half of Indonesia, from Java to Irian Jaya (New Guinea), experiences something of a dry season—perhaps "less wet" is more accurate. There is a pronounced rainfall maximum in summer (this is in the Southern Hemisphere) from November to April, and a much lower winter rainfall, though no month is totally without rain in most years. A truly wet and dry tropical climate is found in the islands east of Java and in southern New Guinea. There the average monthly temperature cools a few degrees during a brief mid-winter period, humidity levels drop 10 to 15 percent, and rain occurs on only two or three days per month.

In the Philippines, the western edge of the islands receives a summer maximum, while the eastern edge, as mentioned earlier, has a winter maximum. The central belt between has a generally drier climate since it is in the rainshadow of both sets of monsoonal winds. North of Mindanao, the climate tends to be monsoonal, rather than truly tropical rainforest in type, with such heavy wet season precipitation as to negate the brief dry season.

Northern Indochina has a climate rather like that of southern China or the Indus Valley. It is sufficiently cool in winter (except along the coast) to be classified as subtropical. While frosts do not occur, average temperatures fall below the 64°F (17°C) necessary to maintain some types of tropical vegetation. Winter days are mild, but nights can get cool.

Highland areas are everywhere subject to altitudinal moderation of temperatures. In particular, in Indonesia there are rather large areas of temperate, high altitude climate—though with virtually no seasonal variation in temperature and rainfall. The mountainous northern rim of Burma and some of the highest areas of Laos can experience frost.

The Philippines and the east coast of Vietnam are particularly subject to Pacific hurricanes (typhoons). Virtually all lowlands are subject to seasonal summer flooding. The region, however, is not generally subject to either the disastrous droughts or perennially heavy floods so characteristic of South and East Asia.

DRAINAGE

Southeast Asia is one of the great reserves of undeveloped water power in the world. Burma alone has over 3 percent of the world's developable hydroelectric potential, mostly associated with the Salween Valley. The lack of level agricultural land in that valley means that dam sites could be easily constructed without disrupting agriculture or settlement to any degree. The upper valley has many falls and rapids, and the river is confined to a steep gorge. This single resource could supply a sufficient amount of power to supply all industrial and consumer needs even in a future developed Burma.

While there are many small hydroelectric sources in Thailand and the three successor states of Indochina, it is the Mekong River that forms the major potential. Any development here, unlike those in Burma, would require the agreement and cooperation of several countries. Too, this sort of project would require the displacement of considerable segments of agriculture and population in order to fully exploit the potential.

Indonesia is a land of short, often swift rivers that end in swampy deltas and coastlands. Comprehensive hydroelectric development could serve the dual purpose of power generation and the extension of arable land through drainage and flood control. Indonesia's hydro potential is 4 to 5 percent of the world total; as elsewhere in the region, very little has been developed to date.

Most of the Philippine potential is on the mountainous southern island of Mindanao. The Philippines have developed a greater percentage than any other country in the region.

The full impact of this electrical generating potential is realized only when compared to other areas. Eastern and western Europe together possess less than 5 percent of the world's potential, while Southeast Asia has over double that amount. A coal-short Japan relied heavily on a much smaller hydroelectric potential (± 1 percent) to power its early industrial development. While currently mostly potential, hydro power is an extremely valuable asset for this region's future economic development.

Scale of delta formation is a crucial factor. Regional deltas here are larger than that of the Nile, and three of them (the Irawaddy, Mekong, and Menam Chao-Prao) come close to the scale of the huge Ganges Delta. The first two are rapidly extending the land surface seaward while the last is virtually an inland delta. Yearly floods renew the soil, creating an excellent environment for wet-rice farming. Current population densities are one third to one half those of similar areas in China, India, and Bangladesh, implying that further agricultural development and attendant population growth can be sustained without overburdening the area's land resource. The region's rivers, with the exception of the Red River (northern Vietnam) and the rivers of the Luzon plain in the Philippines, have not been fully exploited as sources of irrigation water.

The Tonle Sap, a fresh-water lake in Kampuchea, fluctuates greatly with the wet and dry seasons. It harbors a major fish resource in an area that has been traditionally short of protein. During the wet season, the Mekong floodwaters flow into the lake, while during the dry season, the flow is reversed. Crops are grown on the exposed lake bottom during the dry season. Artificial control of this unusual water resource could vastly improve Kampuchean agriculture as well as aiding in industrial development.

VEGETATION

Unlike South and East Asia, there are still considerable areas of natural vegetation that have remained untouched until the present or the relatively recent past. Virtually all the islands and the wetter portions of the mainland were originally covered with a dense growth of tropical rainforest or its monsoon variation. These magnificent forests were able to exist even on areas of generally poor soil. Along with plentiful rain and abundant sunshine, this was due to a deep root system able to penetrate to nutrient-containing lower soil horizons, forming efficient mechanisms for recycling rapidly decomposed organic litter.

Most of the region's forests are broadleaf evergreen. Typically the rainforests are multistoried, with rapidly growing, diverse species. Climbing plants interlace the network of trees, using the last available sunlight. Mangrove swamps ring the coastal lowlands in many areas. Bananas, citrus, plantains, and coconuts are among the domestic species with food value, but the rubber tree and the oil palms were imported from other areas.

People's intrusions into the environment have reduced the area of original rainforest; however, most of New Guinea, the interior of Borneo (Kalimantan), the northern half of Sulawesi, and the east coast of Sumatra still contain large reserves of tropical hardwood.

The monsoon forests are lower in crown height and less dense. Teak is a widespread and valuable species harvested in Burma, Thailand, eastern Java, and the islands east of Java. Some eucalyptus have cash value and sandalwood, a common species, commands a high price.

The forests of Indonesia, in particular those of the outer islands, form the largest regional reserve. The government owns almost all forest land and has begun an ambitious program of investment and development. Over half the forest area has been granted as concessions to foreign (primarily Japanese) concerns. Current government plans limit the export of logs and favor processing in Indonesia before export. Sawn timber and plywood are the chief wood-industry products. Conservation is largely lacking at present except in Java and Sumatra; this could adversely affect the timber resource as could the current speed of exploitation.

The forests of the Philippines are more carefully cared for. Construction timber, paneling, plywood, lumber, and now even furniture are made from Philippine mahogany (luan). Conservation and professional **silvaculture** have come late and incompletely (post 1950), but they are now firmly entrenched in the system.

Most of the mainland forest has been cleared for permanent agriculture, converted into tree plantations, or degraded by repeated slash-and-burn clearing for agriculture. Northern Thailand has the last large reserve of mainland monsoon forest. Defoliation agents used during the Vietnam War destroyed much of the forest in the hills of the Indochinese peninsula. Their long-term effects on the vegetational cover are as yet unknown.

Grasslands consist of two types, natural and man-made. The natural grasslands of Southeast Asia were savanna or shrubby parkland associated with rainshadow areas. They are frequently burned for shifting agricultural use and at times have been converted into bamboo plantations. Heavy pressures on the land have greatly modified the original forest in the tropical wet and dry areas of the mainland.

Much of the land of the smaller islands east of Java and on parts of Sumatra supports a sparse grassland cover on badly eroded land that has been cleared too often for shifting agriculture. Similar alteration of vegetational cover could occur anywhere that unwise forestry is followed by too-frequent slash-and-burn usage.

SOILS

Of all tropical soil areas in the world, those of this region appear to be of highest potential. While red in color, not all are **laterites** or necessarily infertile. Large areas of Java, southern Sumatra, and the Nusa Tengara Islands have soils developed from basic volcanic materials. Similar soils appear in Sulawesi and the Philippine islands of Luzon and Mindanao.

The high fertility of the alluvial delta plains built up along the major rivers may only be in part "natural." Chinese-style fertilization and cropping techniques have probably done much to enhance the natural attributes of these deltaic soils. Another area of potentially high agricultural utility (and fertility) may be the humus-rich swamps that abound in eastern Sumatra and lowland Borneo.

THE STRUCTURE OF SUBREGIONS

Traditionally, Southeast Asia is divided into mainland and insular portions, but this format ignores some important cultural differences that may be of greater importance in understanding the region as a whole. While the blending of pre-Aryan Hindu and Chinese elements of culture is obvious throughout the region, the dominance of the Chinese influence on the mainland is obvious. A Chinese-related language dominates in only one state, Burma, but Chinese trade and culture, if not imperial control, has influenced all. Many of the region's native cultures were also present in southern China. The Chinese influence on agricultural techniques, clothing, and some cultural behavior patterns is rather striking.

Malaysia, Indonesia, and Singapore are a part of the Malay cultural-linguistic milieu, yet Singapore is simply a Chinese island in the midst of a much larger Malay realm. Most of the Malays are of Islamic faith, differing thereby from the dominantly Buddhist mainland.

The Philippines, while Malay in language and some elements of culture, has been heavily Westernized by fifty years of American colonial rule. Ruled by Spain for several centuries before 1898, the Filipinos are largely Christians. Religiously and culturally, then, they are distinct.

It is obvious that three vastly different cultural worlds exist within the region.

THE MAINLAND

Mainland Southeast Asia is frequently described as a **cultural shatterbelt.** Negrito native peoples may have occupied much of the area. Hindu conquerors mixed freely with the natives, and formed a state known as Funan. The conquest of this state by neighboring peoples, themselves lightly Indianized, brought forth the great Khmer Empire, which included today's Kampuchea (Cambodia), much of Thailand, southern Vietnam, and even parts of Burma. Beginning with a core in the Red River Delta, the Annamese spread their empire along the Vietnamese coast and eventually into Laos. A series of wars were fought with the Khmer, a traditional enemy. The power of both was eventually eclipsed by China.

The Thai, whose homeland may have been in southern China, were probably pressured into moving south by Chinese migrations from beyond the Chang. Little is known of early Thai history, but a state is thought to have existed since the twelfth century. The Laotians are culturally and linguistically related to the Thai; the areal extent of Thai linguistic groups (from south China to the Malayan coast and from eastern Burma to the Red River valley) may give some hint as to their maximum extent.

The Burmese are culturally tied to Tibet. Never spreading beyond its original core area, Burma has been ruled by (in part) Thai and Khmer empires as well as by the Chinese (thirteenth to the sixteenth centuries).

This mosaic of empires, cultures, and conflicts is composed of units that are, consequently, ethnically mixed. The only element of uniformity is provided by the once more widespread Buddhist religion. Even there, beyond the acceptance of Buddhism's simple doctrines, there is regional difference. The primacy of monks and the narrow road to salvation for only a chosen few characterizes the Buddhist sect of the western four states; in contrast, the Mahayana Buddhists of Vietnam are a more liberal, Chinese-influenced sect with a wider variety of deities and an easier route to salvation.

Within the mainland region, the three states of former French Indochina are considered separately because of obvious effects of colonial control as well as the common element of Communist ideology in government.

Vietnam, Laos, Kampuchea (Cambodia) Once united in French Indochina, these three states are as dissimilar as are any others in the region. Poverty and the destruction of war are their shared characteristics. While the cultural influences of India are apparent in Kampuchea and Laos, Vietnam was strongly influenced by China. Chinese expansions from the Chinese cultural hearth in the middle Huang He (Yellow River) valley tended strongly southward. These expansions drove out or surrounded upland pockets of other peoples, most related to contemporary Southeast Asian groups. Southward expansion down the Vietnamese coast was much easier than in the canyonlike river country to the west. The original core of the Vietnamese (the Red River plains) was brought under Chinese control by the second century B.C., and its culture strongly influenced by China. Even the name *Vietnam* means the "southern country," and obviously it is in relation to China that Vietnam is southern.

Vietnam has been likened to two rice baskets connected by a slender carrying pole.[1] This image reflected the two fertile river plains and delta complexes, the Red River to the north and the Mekong Delta in the south. The Vietnamese traditionally have avoided the uplands, so that Vietnamese ethnics occupy the two cores at either end of the country, plus pockets of valley lands facing the sea where the mountain spine meets the sea. The Vietnamese, to whom village life and its social relationships was very important, could not move to the mountains and find enough continuous area for conversion to the rice paddies intended to sustain a whole village; their culture remained,

then, a lowland one. Unable to expand northward into China, they expanded down the coast into the delta of the Mekong. The Vietnamese are the region's best hydraulic engineers, having built an elaborate system of dikes and canals to tame the flood-prone Red River of their primary core. The Mekong Delta has always been a more lightly settled frontier to them. By the mid-twentieth century, the Red River lowlands were so densely populated that the importation of rice became necessary; the southern, secondary core of the settlement was a net rice exporter. This natural *complementarity* was enhanced by the fact that northern Vietnam had the raw materials—anthracite coal, iron ore, tin, and chrome—to support industrialization.

It was relatively densely populated, culturally advanced Vietnam that was the star of French Indochina. Rubber plantations were added to Vietnam's traditional exports of rice. The French made a puppet of the Vietnamese emperor. Nationalism among the 85 percent Vietnamese ethics had been well advanced by the long struggle against the Chinese and reinforced by language and an eccelctic brand of Buddhism, Confucianism, and Taoism. Nationalist activity began against the French within twenty years of their conquest of Vietnam. As elsewhere, the Japanese occupation demonstrated the colonial power's weaknesses and fueled determination to achieve freedom at the end of World War II. An anti-Japanese coalition led by Communists was quickly redirected to an anti-French movement, the Viet Minh.

The implications of the tight, closely contained village structure of Vietnamese society was not quickly evaluated by the French. Traditionally, private land was supplemented by communal land, periodically allocated to villagers for their temporary use. Cooperation in road

---

[1] Robbins Burling, *Hill Farms and Padi Fields: Life in Mainland Southeast Asia* (Englewood Cliffs, N.J.: Prentice Hall, 1965), p. 107.

Digging an Irrigation Canal, Near Hanoi. Two recurrent themes of Southeast Asia are the use of masses of human labor and the dependence on wet-rice culture. These canal builders in Vietnam are office workers volunteering their weekends. (Courtesy of United Nations/G. Cohen)

maintenance and dike repair and communal stockpiles of grain for emergencies demonstrated a strong village society. Village leadership was in the hands of a council of respected villagers, including educated ones, who appointed one of their number to an office that is poorly translated as *mayor.* (This mayor had little prestige and was more a routine clerk and messenger for village leadership consensus than an executive.) The French tended to expect too much from the mayors and thus undercut whatever little real authority they had.

As anywhere in an essentially feudal society, land tenure is the critical question for most people. The European colonial period introduced manufactured goods to the detriment of village crafts. This undermined an important rural source of income because rice culture is extremely seasonal in labor demands. Even very dense rural populations had no surplus labor at harvest time, but, off-season, chronic temporary unemployment resulted from the substitution of European manufactured goods for handicrafts and **cottage industries.** It had become the pattern for villages to specialize in a particular range of products (textiles, iron work, containers, etc.), partly because a skilled villager would share his knowledge of skills only with fellow villagers, not "strangers" from two miles away. The decay of this communal craft industry contributed, as did the colonial regime's taxes, to an increasing indebtedness among the farmers. Land was typically in the hands of a few, with large numbers of peasants without land or with too little land to feed a family.

In the provinces south and west of Saigon (now Ho Chi Minh City), two thirds of the farmers were landless, and nearly half the land was held by one fiftieth of the people. Land rents were 40 to 50 percent of the crop. During the successful struggle to oust the French, the Viet Minh revolutionaries carried out a drastic land reform. They confiscated land from landlords and gave it to the peasants. South of the demarcation line drawn to facilitate French withdrawal (the partition was supposed to be temporary, but a free election to choose leaders of a unified nation, agreed to in the Geneva Agreements of 1954, never took place), the Diem regime instituted its own reform. Landlord influence was strong within the South Vietnamese government. Landlords were compensated for redistributed land. Perhaps understandably, the peasants of the South were not impressed by a reform that sold them land the Viet Minh had promised them free, nor were they suitably grateful when told that the government was lowering rents that the Viet Minh had abolished.

The "temporary partition" became one of the sharpest boundaries in the world, a portion of the line of confrontation between Communism and the West as North Vietnam was a Communist state and the south began receiving lavish economic and military aid from the United States. There is little doubt that much of this well-intentioned aid was misdirected or wasted. The consumption levels of the urban elite benefited far more than the poor farmers. Imports of cars and motorbikes almost equalled vital fertilizer in value, and government corruption flourished. The previous French mistake of trying to control villages through the misunderstood "mayors" was repeated. Just as in the late colonial period, central government control was limited to the cities and some major interurban routes (at least in daylight), while the many-celled, self-contained villages were tied in neither to the national economy nor political life. In 1964, the Hanoi government decided to speed the work of the Viet Cong Communist guerrillas in the South by committing regular North Vietnamese army units in the South. This invasion triggered an escalation in American forces from "advisors" to more than half a million personnel at peak. U.S. troop withdrawal began in 1972, leaving naval and air support forces to aid the South Vietnamese until a peace agreement was concluded in 1973. Infiltration of more North Vietnamese troops into the South finally defeated the Saigon government in 1975.

Vietnamese communization of the South denied the large Chinese minority their traditional trading functions, now nationalized, and long-term animosities led to a mass flight of the Vietnamese-Chinese from the country, helping to precipitate a brief war with the PRC in 1979. The Vietnamese also invaded Kampuchea, alleging Kampuchean attacks on Vietnamese citizens.

Today's Vietnam has not fully recovered from the war or protracted civil strife. The population, now some 48 million, is growing at a rapid rate. There are some sixty minorities in the country and the degree of national cohesion remains unknown.

Following the Chinese model, the current government anticipates the development of cottage industry using agriculturally produced raw materials and seasonally surplus labor. Over 90 percent of the population is still employed in agriculture. There is an attempt to enlarge peasant cooperatives through consolidation, a plan that runs counter to old village loyalties. State farms have been developed for livestock rearing and the production of industrial crops like cotton and sugar.

The North continues mining coal and a few other minerals on a reduced scale. Textile and food-processing industries have begun to resume normal production. All private firms have been nationalized, including holdings of U.S. firms. Only French interests have been allowed to continue to function as foreign investments. Electronics and machine industries that arose during the period of U.S. involvement continue as government-owned operations. As in much of Asia, Japan is rapidly becoming the principal trading partner.

There are probably few states in the world whose nationhood is as shaky as that of Laos. Probably the poorest state in the region (nobody knows just how poor Kampuchea might be), Laos consists mainly of wild hill country flanked to the west and south by the Mekong Valley. Most people living within its boundaries have no concept of loyalty to Laos. The country has but the tiny beginning of a transport and communications **infrastructure.** Few towns have electricity yet, although the foreign-built Nam Ngum Dam on the Mekong north of Vientiane, the capital, exports electricity to Thailand. There is no railway, and a very low ratio of paved roads to area. Industry, limited to the small-scale production of consumer goods (soft drinks, beer, cigarettes, rubber sandals, etc.), is in a depression due to wartime destruction and dislocations. Laos was an unwilling tool in the East-West confrontation; its development prospects are as uncertain as its independence.

Kampuchea (Cambodia), unlike Laos, has had a long history as a distinctive culture and state; the great Khmer civilizations are a direct ancestor of the present state. The French were not as interested in either Cambodia or Laos, with both positive and negative results. These states escaped some of the sociological problems a richer minerals and/or plantation area might have experienced, but a low level of investment in their economic development was also true. Once independent, the Cambodians tried hard to be nonaligned, which was virtually impossible in this area of major confrontation between superpowers. Ninety percent of the people are (or were—no reliable statistics have appeared for over six years) ethnic Khmers, with Chinese and hill tribe minorities. Population density was low by regional standards, 71 per square mile (27 per square kilometer), even before a protracted and exceedingly complicated civil war, which finally ended as Vietnamese forces defeated the Pol Pot regime in 1979.

Premier Pol Pot's Khmer Rouge had instituted an unbelievably harsh regime in 1975. If not actually intended to destroy the country and its people, Khmer Rouge policies virtually had that effect. The country was cut off from all normal contact with the outside world. Cities and towns were forcibly evacuated and their residents chased into the wild countryside to fend for themselves with no tools or food. Money, any kind of money, was officially abolished. Hundreds of thousands of people fled to Thailand; hundreds of thousands more died in the general upheaval and destruction of the economy. Kampuchea is the best example of near national suicide known in the modern world. The infrastructure of the nation—transport, public buildings, warehouses, hospitals, post offices—all were senselessly destroyed along with unknown numbers of people.

BURMA AND THAILAND

Burma and Thailand, the first a British colony conquered in three wars from 1824 to 1886 and freed in 1948, the second the only Southeast Asian country to retain its independence throughout the colonial period, share several characteristics and problems. Each has a sizeable majority of its own national ethnics (the Thai are 75 percent of Thailand's population; the Burmans make up 72 percent of Burma's people), but each has minority peoples in strategic borderlands. This is a result of the region's characteristic valley and river plain cores of densely occupied wet-rice-based cultures, surrounded (almost literally in these two instances) by hill-country tribesmen practicing more extensive agriculture, often of the shifting variety. These minority groups, much less concentrated than the people of the cores, tend to occupy far more territory than is reflected in their proportion of the national population. (See Figure 10–5.) The Burman and (indirectly) Thai states were shaped by the European imperialism that determined their boundaries. Previous boundaries of the two were rather fluid and included tributary states of varying degrees of organization and loyalty. When Burma was attached to British India (it was separated and given limited self-government in 1937), boundaries were established with a view toward defensibility more than recognizing ethnic territories. Similarly, Thailand's boundaries reflect treaties with Britain and France based more on imperial policies and objectives and less on who lived where. Boundaries in Southeast Asia frequently ignore both ethnic and economic units, in common with many in Africa south of the Sahara.

Burma's upper core (centered on Mandalay) and lower core (the more recently settled delta area of the Irrawaddy centered on Rangoon) are occupied predominantly by Burmese-speaking, Buddhist Burman ethnics. The Arakan coast strip is occupied by Burmese-speaking people, but has had a different political history; it has cultural links with Bangladesh, including a large Moslem minority. The Shan states to the north and east enjoy considerable autonomy; the Shans spread across boundaries from southwest China to Laos and Thailand as well as Burma. There is little evidence that the Shan are effectively incorporated in the economic and political life of any of these states. Chinese influence may be strongest, and could eventually cause problems if a Chinese-protegé "Greater Shan State" movement is fostered.

The much older, more advanced cultures of the cores tend to disparage the upland groups. The Burmese label *Karen,* for example, a designation for a group of tribes in the south of Burma, may be loosely translated as "slave-barbarians." These Karen have been in more or less continuous conflict with the central government, unlike the Kachin of the far north who are loyal, if not assimilated.

Thailand faces very similar problems, with a Thai core in the Menam Valley surrounded by largely unassimilated tribes including the Shan (see Figure 10–5). The remote highlands, occupied by ethnic groups loosely controlled by or hostile to the central government, not integrated into the national economy and well suplied with weapons thanks to every war since World War II, are notorious for smuggling and other illicit activities. The infamous "golden triangle" of rugged hills in the area where Burma, Thailand, and Laos converge has been a source of opium and heroin for decades and is representative of the blurred boundary zones of uncertain loyalty between most main-land states. This "twilight zone" of largely autonomous people, legally or realistically, is a simmering threat to most of the mainland states of the region; clearly all their territory is not part of a nation-state.

Burma's economy is heavily dependent on the export of rice as a source of foreign exchange. In fact, this dependence *increased* from the 1930's through the 1970's, making it literally a "one-crop" economy highly vulnerable to fluctuations in world market prices. Burma has the potential for diversification; cotton, timber, rubber, and important (but underdeveloped) lead, zinc, tungsten, and oil reserves could make it one of the more prosperous of developing nations. A growing population will reduce exports of rice by consuming more at home, so that diversification is necessary to even maintain the level of national income, much less raise it. Burma's per capita gross national product, $150, is the second lowest reported in the region, after Laos. Offshore drilling is underway with tracts leased to foreign oil companies, a major departure from a

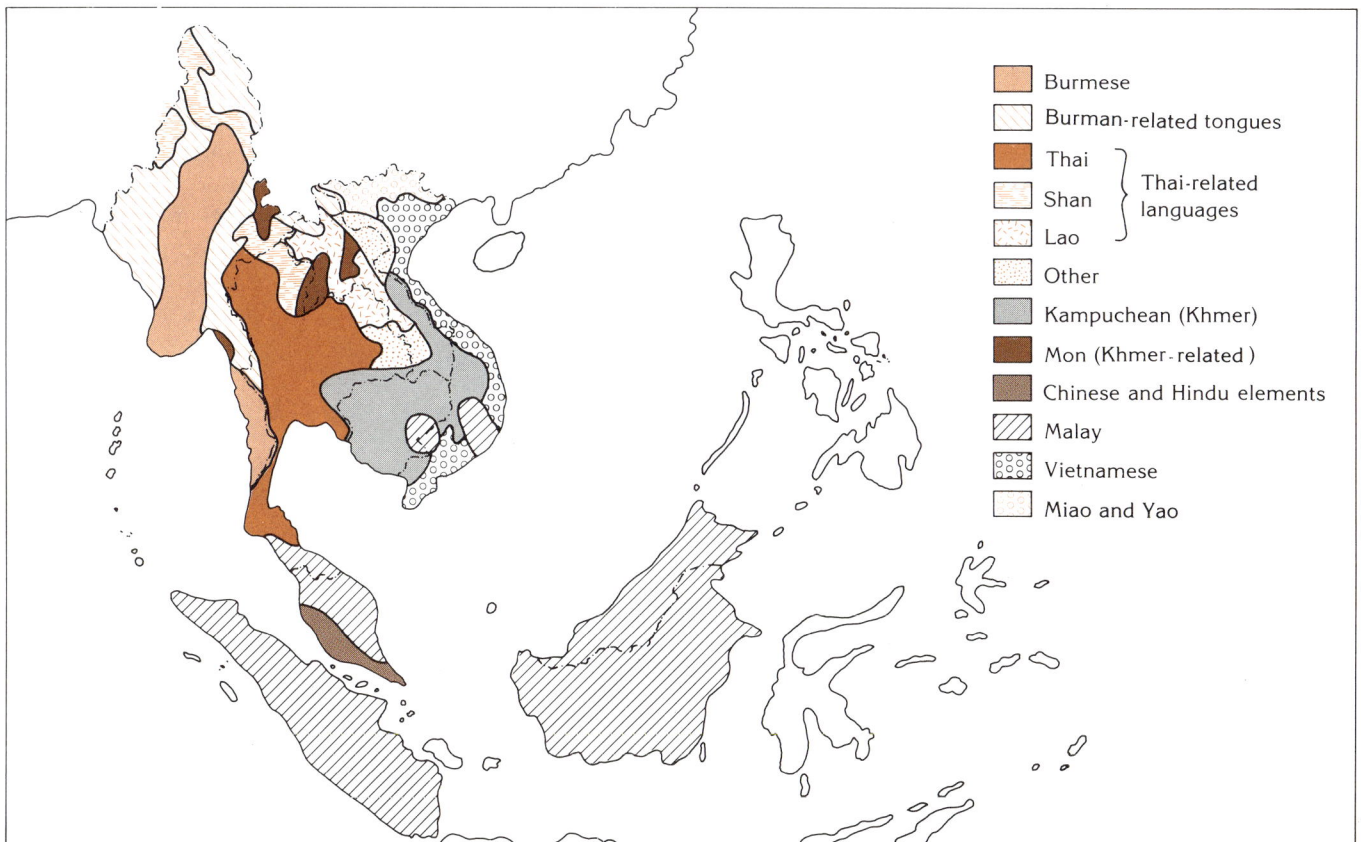

FIGURE 10–5

Ethnic Distributions of Burma and Thailand. A potential threat to the stability of Southeast Asian states such as Burma and Thailand, among others, is the common pattern of a majority, intensive-farming-based culture, virtually surrounded by extensive highlands more lightly settled by minority ethnic groups.

Loading Teak Logs, Burma. Lumbering is an important activity in the more thinly settled fringes of the "rice baskets" of the valleys. Log exports are so high as to raise questions of possible environmental damage. (Courtesy of United Nations)

former policy against foreign investment. Socialist Burma was the first non-Communist country to recognize the PRC and is eager to maintain its tradition of neutrality and nonalignment.

Thailand, in contrast, has been more pro-Western and relies more on private enterprise. A full third of the country is cultivated and agricultural exports (rice, sugar, rubber, corn) are foremost, but mineral products are expected to become much more important in the near future. Several trillion cubic feet of natural gas have been discovered under the Gulf of Siam and will begin replacing expensive imported oil as fuel. Tin dredging is increasing, and forest products production is scheduled to rise sharply. Per capita GNP is three times that of Burma, supporting a higher level of imports and local market consumption. An impressive transport development program (both highways and airports) has helped increase tourism to over a million international visitors per year.

THE MALAY CULTURE SUBREGION

This subregion contains Southeast Asia's wealthiest state in per capita income (Brunei, $10,460) as well as its third and fourth richest (Singapore, $3,260, and Malaya, $1,090). The natural resource base is impressive. Indonesia's per capita income of $360 represents a stable, sizeable income from oil, timber, rubber, tin, and agricultural exports, though it is diluted by a huge population. At 147 million, Indonesia is the fifth largest nation in the world and the largest Moslem state. One receives the impression

Boat Vendors, Bangkok. Bangkok, since 1767 the capital of the only Southeast Asian state to avoid colonialism, is typical of the region's fast-growing, industrializing cities, which still retain a distinctive cultural landscape. (Courtesy of United Nations)

of a densely populated, resource rich, and potentially wealthy portion of the world when analyzing these constituent units. Malayan people, many of them Moslems (see Figure 10–6), form the majority of population in all of these states except the predominantly Chinese city-state of Singapore. The British and Dutch colonial empires effectively divided this Malay cultural-ethnic area among themselves (excepting the Portuguese territory of Timor and the Philippines). As a result, today's independent states essentially have borders conforming to colonial administrative limits. Nationalism, then, follows patterns established during colonialism rather more than ethnic and linguistic uniformity. The subregion consists of two tiny enclaves at one extreme and two larger, but fragmented, political units (Malaysia and Indonesia).

Malaysia, Brunei, and Singapore As originally constituted, Malaysia was several separate colonial units. Malaya was a federation of small states that encompassed the strategic Malay Peninsula and included the fortified base of Singapore. Brunei, Sarawak, and North Borneo were three British colonial units on the northern edge of the otherwise Dutch-controlled island of Borneo.

The Chinese, imported as labor by the British, stayed on after work contracts were fulfilled as businessmen, craftsmen, middlemen, traders, and bankers. Their economic success and relatively large numbers have made them a major concern to the Malayan element. Indeed, counterbalancing the large Chinese population has been a major goal in those portions of the subregion that were once British controlled.

British Malaya was an exceptionally prosperous colony. The mining of tin and the development of extensive rubber plantations used large amounts of imported labor from both China and India. As a result, the mainland portion of the colony of Malaya was almost equally divided between Malay and non-Malay elements. When independence seemed imminent, the question of the Chinese was in the forefront. If Singapore were to be included in a newly independent state, the Chinese would predominate. Singapore was retained outside the first Malay federation as a crown colony. The second Malay federation included the

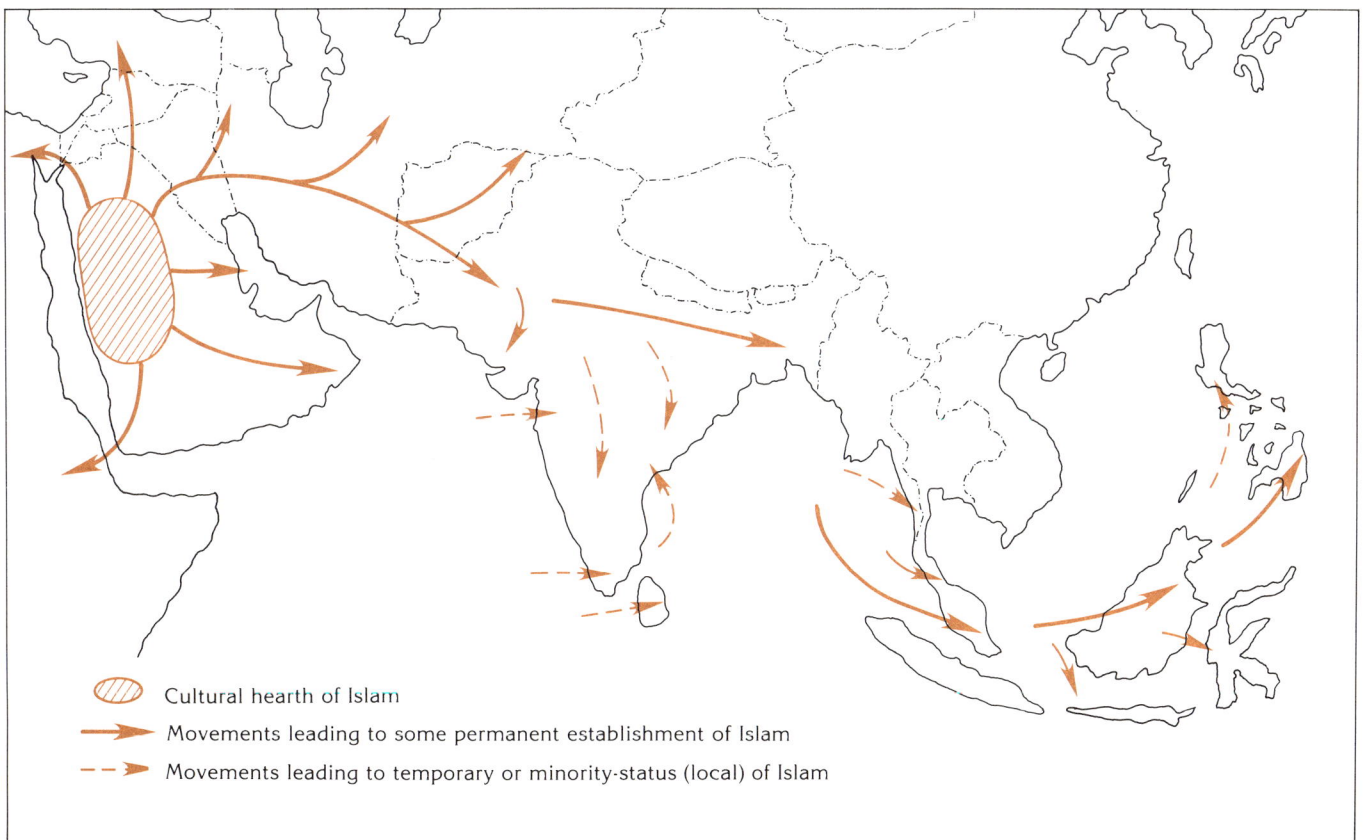

FIGURE 10–6

Islam's Spread Through South Asia and Southeast Asia. While Islam spread through South Asia by both overland conquest and oceanic trade, its strong association with seaborne trade and coastal trading stations is evident in Southeast Asia.

Legend:
- Cultural hearth of Islam
- Movements leading to some permanent establishment of Islam
- Movements leading to temporary or minority-status (local) of Islam

Collecting Natural Rubber, Malaya. The establishment of rubber plantations throughout Southeast Asia, using seed stolen from Brazil, was both a cause and effect of European colonialism in the region. (Courtesy of United Nations)

British North Borneo territories in an effort to "dilute" the Chinese majority in the federation in 1965, two years after it had joined. Malaysia thus now consists of the southern half of the Malay Peninsula and the northeastern quarter of the island of Borneo, some 400 miles (600 kilometers) away across the South China Sea. As currently constituted, Malaysia has over 12.5 million people. Some 36 percent are Chinese and 10 percent are Indians and Pakistani. A variety of other groups are present, so that Malayans constitute a bare 50 percent of the total.

Initially, Indonesia was hostile to the new country on the grounds that it was a relic of imperialism that should have been merged with Indonesia into a single, Malay-culture state. Such a merger would have given Indonesia the foreign-exchange earning power of Malaysia and added much potentially cultivable land. Indonesia's government pursued a policy of "confrontation" (breaking relations, avoiding economic relationships, but stopping short of war) before tacitly accepting Malaysia's existence. Singapore's independence helped avoid a war, as Singapore handles a great deal of Indonesia's (especially Sumatra's) foreign trade. It is probable, however, that Indonesia will continue to covet East Malaysia (northeast Borneo) and Brunei as population pressures mount in Indonesia, outpacing economic development and absorbing much of that country's considerable oil income.

In the meantime, Malaysia continues its independent existence. The mainland is still dominated by the mining

and agricultural sectors. More diverse than formerly, peninsular Malaya produces 350,000 tons of iron ore, large amounts of bauxite and rare metals, as well as gold, in addition to tin (tin production has begun to decline). Rubber production, a traditional export also in decline, is being augmented by the increased production of palm oil, coconut oil, and tea. Rice is in short supply and the government is faced with the problem of whether or not to increase food self-sufficiency at the expense of reduced production of export crops.

There is little industry other than first-stage processing of raw materials and native handicrafts. It is a country without a primate city, without a major port, and without a major manufacturing center. The separate political entity of Singapore still performs all these functions.

The territories of Sabah (once North Borneo) and Sarawak add little to the fortunes of Malaysia other than their function as dilutors of the Chinese minority. Most of their exports duplicate those of peninsular Malaya. Hemp, cocoa beans, and pepper add some diversity to the total economy's exports, and there is some mining of copper and antimony. Oil from Brunei is refined in Sarawak and exported as petroleum products.

Brunei's outstanding prosperity reflects a small population (only about 220,000) in ratio to a large oil reserve, a situation similar to that of some Persian Gulf sheikdoms. It opted not to join Malaysia in 1963 to protect its high standard of living. Brunei would seem highly

Singapore. Singapore, an important trading center for a century, has a predominantly Chinese ethnic population, a fact that resulted in its separate political status from Malaysia. (Courtesy of United Nations)

vulnerable to pressure from Indonesia if British support vacillates.

Singapore remains a city-state; it must import not only food but water (via pipeline) from mainland Malaysia. Food shortages there mean that increasingly more food comes from even farther overseas. A large-scale fishing program has been instituted to help increase Singapore's domestic food supply. Over 75 percent of the population is Chinese. Manufacturing and trade are the greatest sources of employment. Almost one thousand factories employ over a quarter of a million people in manufacturing in this ministate of 2.5 million. Business, services, and transportation employ an additional 200,000 each in an economy estimated to be growing at almost 10 percent per year. Singapore refines and exports petroleum products from Indonesian oil; produces a host of electronic goods (mainly in Japanese-owned subsidiaries); exports crude, Malaysian-produced rubber; builds and repairs merchant and military ships, carries on most of the shipment of goods among Malaysia's scattered parts; and manufactures machinery and transportation equipment distributed throughout Asia. Chemicals, pharmaceuticals, tires, and plywood round out exports, while a considerable range of clothing, textile, shoe, building-material, and food-processing industries cater primarily to the domestic market. Its continued success requires the continuance of an almost free trade privilege with all the states of South, East, and Southeast Asia.

Indonesia   With an area of almost three fourths of a million square miles, Indonesia is by far the regions largest political unit. It is composed of all or part of five major islands and thousands of smaller ones. The archipelago stretches 3,500 miles (5,600 kilometers) from east to west and almost 1,200 miles (1,900 kilometers) from north to south. The distribution of population varies immensely. With over 85 million people in an area the size of New York State, the island of Java averages over 1,500 people per square mile (580 per square kilometer) and is one of the most densely populated areas in the world. The so-called outer islands are much less densely populated, while Irian Jaya (the Indonesian portion of New Guinea) is virtually empty.

This area was under some form of European colonial control since the sixteenth century. Known as the Indies or the Spice Islands, it was one of the most coveted pieces of international trade territory since the inception of European colonialism and maritime power. The Dutch replaced the Portuguese as the colonial ruler in the seventeenth century, gradually extending their control to the outer islands from their original base in Java.

The soils of the outer islands are not particularly fertile. Java, however, presents unusual circumstances. Its soils (as are those of southern Sumatra) are enriched by periodic volcanic eruptions. Erosion is a serious problem on slopes exposed to heavy, seasonal rains, even in areas of better soil. Volcanic soils of Java, however, are only part of the explanation for Java's huge population. While the British set up rubber plantations in Malaya by importing a labor force, the Dutch coerced the Indonesians into producing desired commercial crops. British indirect rule strengthened the power of local rulers, while the Dutch policy of highly centralized administration reduced the former elite to the role of salaried functionaries. A large Dutch bureaucracy oversaw compulsory commercial crop production; Indonesians, especially on Java, were ordered to plant and deliver quotas of crops the Dutch demanded. Javanese peasants saw that large families would provide the necessary labor force needed for both the exploitative commercial crop quota and subsistence food production. The rural areas were thus forced into the commercial economy. This system was never as strong on the outer islands like Sumatra or Borneo as it was in Java.

Indonesia began its independence with considerable prestige among the nations of the developing world as it was the first in the region (1945, formalized in 1949) to achieve its independence through a successful revolution against its former colonial power. The "winds of change" in Southeast Asia were greatly accelerated by the events of World War II. The Japanese invasion demonstrated an unbelievable vulnerability of the colonial powers. The power and splendor of the European colonial powers seemed, in retrospect, to have been a facade, and the victors were another Asian people. The Japanese encouraged nationalist movements in their conquered territories, hoping to channel the movement into collaborationist governments. Three days after the Japanese surrender, an independent Indonesia was proclaimed. The Dutch, exhausted after a brutal and destructive Nazi occupation, could not reimpose control. In 1965, an unsuccessful coup by the predominantly Chinese ethnic Communist party was defeated by the army, and a massive retaliation, apparently spontaneous and born of both long-term resentments and contemporary politics, resulted in the deaths of several hundred thousand Communist supporters, mostly Chinese-Indonesians.

An early focus of the new Indonesian nationalism was western New Guinea which, though ethnically and culturally different, had been part of the Dutch East Indies. The Netherlands had retained control of its half of New Guinea when Indonesian nationalism swept the other islands, finally handing over Dutch New Guinea to Indonesia in 1962.

There is strong sectionalism within the framework of Indonesia's thirteen thousand islands. The lesser-populated, export-earning islands of Sumatra, Borneo (Kalimantan), and Celebes (Sulawesi) resent the fact that they literally export money (as tin, oil, rubber, timber, natural gas, bauxite, and copper) to support densely populated Java, which imports far more than it exports. Java's large population plus the control of the location of the capital (Jakarta) add up to control of the entire Republic, including economic development policies and government spending. Resulting resentments in the other islands weaken Indonesian unity, which has repeatedly been galvanized by nationalistic drives to acquire West Irian (Dutch New Guinea), Portuguese Timor (annexed in 1976), union with Malaysia (unsuccessful), and repeated threats to "liberate" the Australian protegé state of Papua New Guinea.

Despite the overpopulation problems of Java and the difficulties of communication among the scattered islands and peoples who speak diverse dialects, the state is inherently rich. Indonesia is a major producer and exporter of oil and natural gas. Reserves are huge and new discoveries have recently added to the total. Production approaches 2 million barrels per day. Most oil is produced in central Sumatra, but newer fields are producing in New Guinea, western and eastern Java, eastern Borneo, and offshore in the Java Sea. There are large producing gas fields in northern Sumatra and in southeastern Borneo. Much promising territory, both on and offshore, remains unexplored.

Indonesia has large nickel deposits on Sulawesi and new copper mines have opened in New Guinea. Bauxite is mined on a moderate scale and is now domestically smelted in northern Sumatra. Over a half million tons of coal are mined from deposits that could be greatly expanded. Iron sands are exported now, but a domestic steel industry is planned for the near future. By far the most important metal mined is tin on the islands of Bangka and Billiton, off Sumatra, and in the islands just south of Singapore. There is a huge lumber resource that was largely unexploited before 1967.

Manufacturing is slowly beginning to develop. The government has planned a dual aproach to manufacturing. Large plants processing raw materials are to be placed near the exploitation site. These tend to be **capital intensive** and oriented toward primary processing for export. The second part of the approach encourages foreign investment in consumer industries to be located on labor surplus Java. These would serve largely the domestic market. A third, unplanned industrial grouping is developing rapidly in the villages that outlie the dozen large urban centers, eight of which are located on Java. These are small enterprises of a cottage industry nature. They produce consumer items for the urban population. Some villages have become quite specialized. Much furniture, building material, clothing, shoes, and even such items as bicycles and farm tools are being manufactured in this rapidly growing segment of the manufacturing sector.

A considerable textile industry now exists using imported yarns. Large government industrial complexes produce cement, fertilizer, glass, chemicals, and plywood. Major foreign investors produce motor vehicles, tires, chemicals, and pharmaceuticals. Diversity of ownership, scale, and production are hallmarks of industry. Almost 3 million people are employed in industry, but most of those would be regarded as craftsmen rather than industrial operatives in a more developed society. Nonetheless, industrial progress is both real and impressive.

Agriculture has come to be a problem area. Certain of the old Dutch plantations have been retained as government-owned estates that specialize in high-quality export crops and/or industrial crops. Many others have been divided and used to resettle landless peasants or to augment

Offshore Tin Dredge, Indonesia. The largest in the world, this floating tin dredge operates in shallow waters off Bangka Island. Tin is Indonesia's second most important mineral export, after oil. (Courtesy of United Nations)

small individual holdings. Farms in Java are extremely small if highly productive. Irrigation and increasing amounts of commercial fertilizer are increasing yields, but the upward limit of productivity is virtually in sight. There is a domestic food shortage as peasant agriculture cannot cope with the rapid increase in population. Commercial agriculture has been in a state of steady decline while subsistence agriculture has increased.

The government approach to agriculture is also dual, diversification of export crops on one hand and resettlement of population to new areas in the outer islands on the other. The first program has been rather more successful as coffee, tea, citrus, sugar, and palm oil acreages increase. The latter has not been quite as successful. It is estimated that over 1.5 million migrants have been resettled in Sumatra, but less than one half of these have been agricultural resettlers. The rest have sought employment in mining, service, and industry. Fully another 1.5 million

people have packed into the capital district, almost equalling the flow of Javanese to the outer islands. In terms of the islands' population problems, these are largely a rural to urban movement within Java. Only Kalimantan of all the other outer islands seems to have any significant net in-migration.

Overpopulation of Java exists alongside labor shortages in the outer islands. Short food supplies in Java's countryside are met with imported food, while grain and fruits rot in the fields and on the docks of Sumatra and Kalimantan. Solutions may appear simple, but problems, like the country itself, are immense, diverse, and complex.

THE PHILIPPINES

The nearly 50 million Filipinos sometimes boast that they are the third largest English-speaking state in the world; about 40 percent of the population uses English as a sec-

Terraced Rice Fields, Bandung, Indonesia. Terracing of hillsides for paddy rice cultivation represents a huge investment of labor in expanding food production. (Courtesy of United Nations)

Textile Plant in the Philippines. The textile industry is always one of the first modern industries in a developing nation as the market is nearly universal—everyone consumes clothing, and machine-produced cloth is cheaper than hand-made. More advanced industrial nations "export" jobs in textile manufacturing by setting up plants in lower labor-cost areas. (Courtesy of United Nations)

ond language. Pilipino, based on the most widely spoken native language, Tagalog, is taught in all the schools, but English remains important due to the close trade and cultural ties with the United States.

The Filipinos are mostly of Malay racial stock, with about 10 percent intermarried with Chinese (in one of the few instances in which Chinese overseas did intermarry). At least a thousand years ago they were in contact with the Chinese, and later, with Indian and Arab people; their European "discovery" was in 1521, followed by Spanish conquest in 1565. The Spanish introduced Christianity, which remains the religion of more than 90 percent of the people. They also introduced their emphasis on very large land holdings, handed out to reward loyal conformists. These large estates have remained a social problem and have been part of the motivation of the Huk Rebellion.

The United States acquired the Philippines in its war with Spain (1898); an insurrection previously directed against the Spanish was redirected at the Americans, ending when the revolutionary leader Aguinaldo agreed to American occupation with promised eventual independence. The church was disestablished and most church lands were purchased for redistribution; a Filipino-staffed civil service was created and self-governing commonwealth status was granted in 1935. The Philippines distinguished itself as the only "colonial" territory in Asia that remained loyal against the Japanese invasion, and complete independence followed in 1946.

The Communist-dominated Huk Rebellion (at its peak from 1945 to 1953) was focused on land tenure. American reforms had redistributed much land, but two factors worked against an expansion of small peasant holdings: the extension of large-scale cash-crop production, leading to a reconcentration of land ownership; and a 60 percent increase in the Philippine's population between World War I and II, which increased the number of landless farmers, despite American reforms, by outpacing the rate of redistribution. In 1948, almost half the farms, occupying about 40 percent of total acreage, were operated by tenants or part-tenants. The typical split of farm income was half to the tenant, half to the landowner, and as high as 90 percent of the tenants in some districts were deeply in debt. Interest rates ranged up to 200 percent per year. These crushing burdens of debt coupled with a strong sense of helplessness and hopelessness was receptive ground for the Huk rebellion, which centered in the cash-crop, tenant-farmer areas of Luzon. The rebellion was put down as far as a major threat to the existence of the state, but resistance still flickers throughout the countryside as land reform continues at a slow pace. Continued rapid expansion of the population (2.5 percent) strains the ability of the government to provide land for all.

The Philippine economy expanded rapidly just after World War II, due in part to a free-enterprise-oriented economy that was attractive to American investment, particularly in forest products and minerals industries (iron ore, copper, chromite). A "birthday gift" to the newly independent state from the United States was guaranteed preference in American markets until 1974 for such commodities as sugar; thus political independence did not mean immediate or complete severance from the American economy.

Economic development strategy rests on four objectives: attainment of self-sufficiency in basic foodstuffs (rice, corn), accelerated exports of tropical specialty crops (sugar, pineapples, coconut products, forest products—the Philippines is one of the world's largest exporters of logs, lumber, plywood, and veneers), increased exploitation and export of minerals, and further industrialization (**import replacement** of consumer products, diversification into cement, steel, fertilizer, chemicals, and refined petroleum products).

SUMMARY

Within half a century, Southeast Asia has gone from a region dominated by West European and American colonialism to an arena of competition among two superpowers—the United States and the Soviet Union—and a regional power and potential superpower—the PRC. The region is now fragmented into neutralist, pro-Western, pro-Soviet, and pro-Chinese states. These varying orientations and allegiances have been known to change drastically with changes in Southeast Asian governments.

TENSIONAL RELATIONSHIPS WITH OTHER REGIONS

The People's Republic of China shares boundaries with Burma, Laos, and Vietnam, while the other superpowers are more remote, territorially, if deeply involved in regional politics. South Asia, dominated by India, has historically been a significant cultural influence, but its contemporary role is passive. Burma's peripheral hill tribes have some ethnic-cultural counterparts across the Indian border, but there seems to be more of an intranational political problem than international at this point. Australia-Oceania and Southeast Asia would appear to have greater potential for interregional friction, centered on relations between Australia and Indonesia. Irian Jaya (western New Guinea) served as a rallying concern for Indonesian nationalism before the Dutch handed it over. Papua New Guinea, on Indonesia's eastern land boundary, is currently strongly oriented to Australia and not ethnically Indonesian (nor was most of western New Guinea). Indonesia would appear to have little logical claim to Papua New Guinea, but the domestic economic pressures of a huge, growing population in Indonesia could be focused on New Guinea if rich resource strikes are made there. The resources of the outer islands are directed to support Java, and this pattern could be applied to a desired all-Indonesian New Guinea's resources. Indonesia regards Papua New Guinea as a neocolony of Australia and may regard it as a likely field for initiating an Indonesian-backed nationalistic movement to sever close economic ties with Australia. Illegal drugs enter Australia from Indonesia through a poorly policed sea boundary to very lightly populated Australian territories. This hardly helps Indonesian-Australian relations.

China has long had active political interests in Southeast Asia, along with the strong cultural ties maintained by the overseas Chinese. Vietnam is China's major opponent in the region, having fought a brief war with the PRC and established close ties with the USSR, which has the use of the large U.S.-built naval base at Cam Ranh Bay. This naval base is approximately opposite the major U.S. base at Manila Bay across the South China Sea; it is a potential threat to both the United States and China.

THE REGION'S WORLD VIEW

The region's world views range from the intensely neutralist, self-centered view of Burma through the generally pro-U.S. views of Thailand and the Philippines to the virtual absence of a world view in devastated Kampuchea or poorly organized Laos. Vietnam is clearly an ally of the USSR and currently dominates Kampuchea and Laos; political logic would urge the PRC to establish friendships in Thailand, Malaysia, and Indonesia, although racial hostilities toward the overseas Chinese may complicate this effort. Japan has established many strong economic links throughout the region as market for minerals and forest products, source of manufactured goods, and entrepreneur in helping establish light industries, especially assembly, which are integrated with and financed by the Japanese economy. Memories of wartime occupation within Southeast Asia may work toward keeping Japanese interests economic rather than political, but the Japanese were not always considered the enemy by the people of the region's then colonial units. Japanese money is welcome, and individual Japanese are treated politely.

Indonesia, with 40 percent of the total regional product, 78 percent of the region's oil production, and a position astride the sea lanes from the Indian Ocean to the Pacific (sharing the Strait of Malacca with Malaysia and controlling the Sunda and Lombok straits) is clearly the key to the region's harmony with East Asia and Australia-Oceania. U.S. economic aid to Indonesia has again become important. The United States is Indonesia's second most important trading partner, after Japan, and is attempting to counterbalance the Soviet Union's Vietnamese alliance with a Thailand-Malaysia-Indonesia-Philippines combination of active allies and friendly neutrals.

The U.S. relationships with the Philippines have remained close since independence; since 1947 they have received $2.5 billion in U.S. economic aid, and U.S. leases on an air base and naval base will continue through 1990. Japan has recently displaced the United States as most important trading partner, and a Philippine government with eroding popular support is providing some anxiety about future relations with the United States.

At least while the United States and People's Republic of China share an objective of counterbalancing Soviet power, the extraregional political relationships and tensions seem to have decreased in number from three to two. It is unlikely, though, that PRC and U.S. interests in mainland Southeast Asia can remain congruent for long.

Within strictly limited parameters, Southeast Asia can be compared to East Europe—a zone of historic confrontation between major, sometimes contending cultures and states from outside the region itself—a shatterbelt of smaller countries dominated by powerful neighbors.

case study
THE PHILIPPINES AND THE MORO REVOLT

A long-festering internal problem of an apparently unassimilable minority continues to plague the Philippines; sporadically, the Moslem-Christian mistrust breaks out into guerrilla warfare. The reasons lie in the ethnic-religious geography of the Philippines, the islands' settlement history, and attempts at agrarian reform.

Islam was spread into the southwestern Pacific's margins by Arab and Moslem Indian traders. They quickly set up small Moslem principalities, effectively controlling their trading bases, and spread their religion and culture into tributary hinterlands. Islam thus came to dominate the Indonesian archipelago before the Dutch and British colonial period, and also began spreading northeastward into the Philippines (see Figure 10–6). Islam reached the southernmost islands of the Philippines, the Sulu group, Mindanao, and Palawan, by 1480, while the Spanish did not arrive in full force until 1565. Thus, the southern islands had fairly well-established Moslem populations before the arrival of a Christian European colonizer. The Spanish reversed the northward flow of Islam but never succeeded in imposing their control over the established strongholds of the Moslems, known as the Moros (Moors). Spanish control never penetrated beyond the north coast of Mindanao and the northern tip of Palawan. While the colonial economy encouraged commercial agriculture and established the large, aristocratic landholdings typical of Spanish control in Luzon and the Visayans (the central island group of the Philippines), and helped generate higher population densities, Mindanao remained in a subsistence economy, isolated economically from the rest of the archipelago. The American administration extended more effective control over Mindanao and made serious efforts to improve the living standards of all, Moro, Christian, or animist alike. The American policies of separating church and state, starting a public school system, and purchases of church-owned lands were all popular with the Moros, who became more active participants in an emerging Filipino society and nation.

Renewed tensions, however, followed Philippine independence. The Communist-inspired Huk Rebellion, mentioned previously, was countered both by military action and by appeasing some of the landless peasants' quest for land. Homesteading on government-owned lands was encouraged, and the "empty island" of Mindanao was targeted for additional settlement from the more crowded islands. Whether Mindanao was "empty" or not depends on one's point of view. Mindanao's overall population density in 1948, during the Huk Rebellion-inspired resettlement program's initiation, was 104 per square mile (40 per square kilometer), compared to a national average of 166 per square mile (64 per square kilometer). Some Mindanao provinces had densities as low as 20 or

30 per square mile (7.7 to 11.6 per square kilometer), while Laguna, south of Manila on Luzon, had 457 per square mile (176 per square kilometer). However, when **physiologic density** (population per *cultivated* acre, not total area) is considered, the differences between Mindanao and the national average is not so extreme; Mindanao's physiologic density in 1948 was 956 per square mile (369 per square kilometer), while the Philippine average was 1,186 per square mile or 458 per square kilometer. While there was a large acreage of unused, potential cropland in Mindanao, the existing Moro settlement was dense because a population lacking transport and farm machinery but characterized by a relatively homogeneous social group tends to form compact settled areas within a matrix of "empty" lands.

The encouragement of large-scale immigration into Mindanao from virtually every place else in the Philippines meant a rapid change in the religious geography of Mindanao. The Moros perceived themselves as being engulfed by a new Christian majority in *their* island, in which they formerly had a local majority. If Mindanao were to serve as a "safety valve" for the expanding population of the whole nation, future Moro expansion would be cramped. The Moros have sporadically supported a "Mindanao for the Moros" movement, encouraged by Indonesia, whose government anticipates a merger of an independent Moslem Mindanao with Moslem Indonesia. Thus, the Filipinos, in attempting to solve the agrarian problems underlying support for the Huk Rebellion, precipitated a reopening of old tensions in Mindanao.

REVIEW QUESTIONS

1 How was shifting agriculture ("slash and burn") a management technique for dealing with the problems of tropical soils?

2 How have the "overseas Chinese" contributed to economic development in the region? To internal discord?

3 Briefly describe how some mainland states have valley cores surrounded by peoples "outside" the national economy.

4 Where are the important straits into the "Asian Mediterranean?" Why is their control still so vital to industrial powers outside this region?

5 Why is Southeast Asia characterized as a "cultural shatterbelt?"

6 Why were the northern and southern "cores" of Vietnam complementary?

7 What were the geographic reasons for the greater colonial impact on Vietnam than on Cambodia or Laos?

8 Why is the "golden triangle" border area of Thailand, Burma, and Laos essentially outside national control? What are the implications for these states?

9 What political considerations, based on cultural geographic factors, led to the independence of Singapore as a city-state?

10 Briefly review the geopolitical implications of Vietnamese historic (and continuing) animosity towards China.

11 How does the extremely uneven population distribution of Indonesia affect its developmental strategy and viability as a state?

12 How does the intense social and economic interaction of some Southeast Asian villagers act to retard pioneering in more mountainous areas?

13 How did conflicting colonial ambitions enable Thailand to retain independence as a buffer state?

14 Why would a reputation for political stability be essential to Singapore's development strategy? Can Singapore become an "Asian Switzerland?"

15 Which of the region's states is most likely, in terms of population, resource base, and level of development, to assert extraregional influence and power?

16 How can heavily populated, developing states like Indonesia effectively use their populations as development assets?

17 Why were the Philippines the only Southeast Asian colony to remain loyal to the colonial power during Japanese occupation in World War II?

SUGGESTED READINGS

1   L. R. BROWN, *Seeds of Change: The Green Revolution and Developments in the 1970's.* New York: Praeger, 1970.

2   ROBBINS BURLING, *Hill Farms and Padi Fields: Life in Mainland Southeast Asia.* Englewood Cliffs, N.J.: Prentice Hall, 1965.

3   C. A. FISHER, *Southeast Asia: A Social, Economic and Political Geography.* New York: Dutton, 1966.

4   D. FRYER, *Southeast Asia: Problems of Development.* New York: Halstead, 1978.

5   B. HIGGINS and J. HIGGINS, *Indonesia, The Crisis of the Millstones.* Princeton, N.J.: Van Nostrand, 1963.

6   T. G. McGEE, *The Southeast Asian City: A Social Geography.* New York: Praeger, 1967.

7   ALAN MOUNTJOY, *Industrialization and Under-Developed Countries.* Chicago: Aldine Publishing Company, 1967.

8   R. R. RAWSON, *The Monsoon Lands of Asia.* Chicago: Aldine Publishing Company, 1963.

9   HARRY ROBINSON, *Monsoon Asia.* New York: Praeger, 1967.

10 C. HART SCHAAF and RUSSELL FIFIELD, *The Lower Mekong: Challenge to Cooperation in Southeast Asia.* Princeton, N.J.: Van Nostrand, 1963.

11 ALICE TAYLOR, ed., *Focus on Southeast Asia.* New York: Praeger, 1972.

12 F. L. WERNSTEDT and J. E. SPENSER, *The Philippine Island World: A Physical, Cultural and Regional Geography.* Berkeley: The University of California Press, 1967.

13 L. E. WILLIAMS, *The Future of the Overseas Chinese in Southeast Asia.* New York: McGraw Hill, 1966.

KEY TERMS

- ocean island
- ocean trench
- antipodes concept
- mirror-image colony
- aboriginal people
- import replacement
- economic hinterland
- economic heartland
- tectonic plate
- Pacific ring of fire
- atoll
- interior drainage
- exotic stream
- mixed economy
- geothermal power
- Pidgin language
- developmental strategy
- white Australia policy

11

AUSTRALIA-OCEANIA

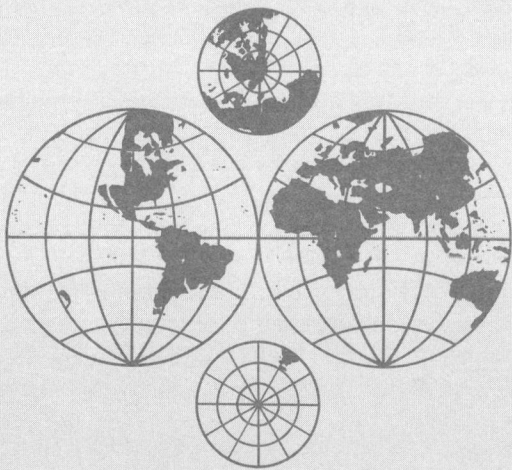

Relative isolation is a key concept in the geographic analysis of Australia and Oceania. The region includes the continent of Australia, the large islands that comprise New Zealand, and the eastern part of the island of New Guinea, as well as *Oceania,* a geographic term that includes the scattered, small islands and constellations of islands that are the Pacific's **ocean islands,** small islands not geologically related to any continental shelf or continental mountain system.

The vastness of the Pacific Ocean, the setting for this region, is difficult to comprehend. Sheer size and distance account for part of the perception of this region's isolation. The Pacific is the greatest single geographical feature on the planet. (See Figure 11–1.) It occupies one third of the area of the world, a proportion that is greater in area than all the lands above sea level. At its greatest width, from Panama to the Malay Peninsula, it extends some 12,500 miles (20,000 kilometers); from the Bering Strait between Siberia and Alaska to the Antarctic Circle is a distance of 9,300 miles (15,000 kilometers). It is the deepest ocean with an average depth of 14,000 feet (4,000 meters), reaching down to 35,000 feet (11,000 meters) in one of its great **ocean trenches** between Guam and the Philippines. In sailing across the Pacific, the world's first circumnavigators, Magellan's crew, sailed for ninety-eight days from Cape Horn to Guam; they spotted only two small islands on the way.

These superlative distances and scales are related to two other measures of relative isolation—the biological uniqueness of the area and the recency of European discovery and colonial activities. Australian native animal life is unlike that of any of the other inhabited continents. Australia and New Zealand form a kind of "dead end" to animal migration—protected, noncompetitive places for the continued or arrested development of some very unusual species. The evidence of the native animal life indicates that Australia has been isolated from Asia since the Miocene Period (some 25 million years ago), and that New Zealand has been separated even longer (since the late Mezozoic Era, some 70 million years ago).

Australian animal life is dominated by the relatively primitive marsupials—mammals in which the partially developed fetus is born long before it can survive unprotected. It develops more fully in a long period in the mother's pouch. The placental mammals, those that nurture a much better developed fetus in the uterus prior to birth, are represented in Australia only by bats, rats, and mice. There is no representation of the great cats, no antelope nor deer, no buffalo nor primates. To complement

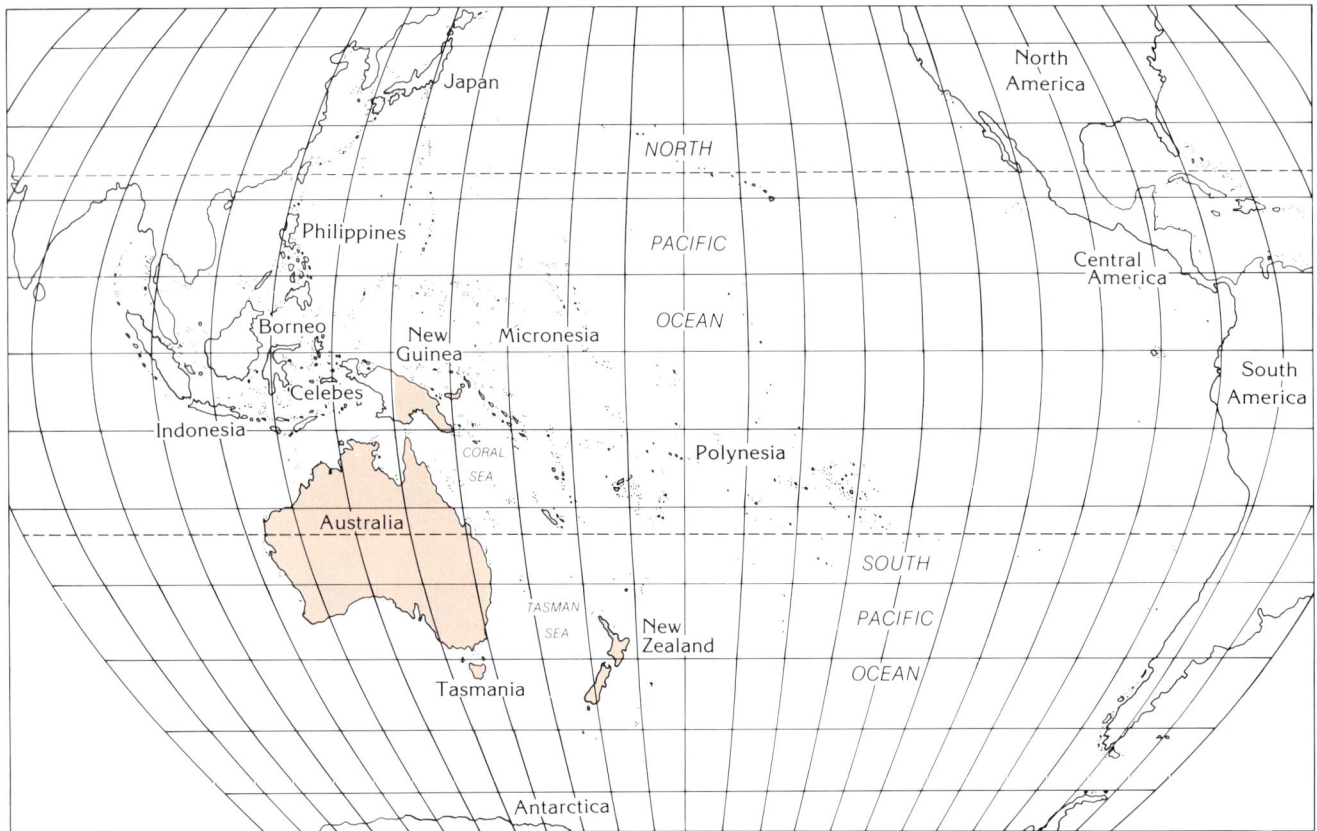

FIGURE 11–1
Regional Setting: The Pacific Basin, Australia, New Zealand, New Guinea, and Indonesia. Australia and New Zealand were the last major land areas to be incorporated in the European exploration and colonization pattern dating from the fifteenth century. Literally at the opposite ends of the earth from Britain, most of this region represents an exclave of European culture adjacent to sharply different Southeast Asian cultures.

the list of missing animal species, there are animals unique to Australia. To the four dozen kangaroo species must be added such oddities as the world's only egg-laying mammals, the duck-billed platypus and spiny anteater. Amphibians and freshwater fish are scarce, but bird species are numerous and varied. New Zealand is so remote from the biological mainstreams that its streams lacked any edible fish except eels, which spend part of their lifecycle in the ocean and can thus migrate from one land area to another.

While this biological evidence indicates isolation over whole geologic eras, the modern history of exploration and settlement indicates an isolation in the cultural sense and in terms of human perception. The ancient Greeks, aware that the world was a sphere and possibly having circumnavigated Africa, guessed at the existence of a great southern landmass. They had no evidence for it; their sense of order and balance suggested that there *should* be one to counterbalance the great known land masses of the northern hemisphere. This imagined land mass was shown on sixteenth, seventeenth, and even eighteenth century maps as "Terra Australis Nondum Detecta" (the southern continent not yet discovered). Despite a firm belief in the existence of an "Australia" or southern land mass, the Pacific basin and Australia remained the last great region to be unknown to outsiders (though of course their local inhabitants knew about them). It wasn't until the seventeenth century that Europeans had any direct knowledge of Australia. The coasts of Australia were so unimpressive to the first Dutch explorers venturing from Indonesia that, perceiving no trade value, they didn't attempt settlement. Exploration proceeded so slowly that it wasn't proven that the islands of New Zealand were not part of Australia until 1769. Throughout the vastness of the Pacific basin the pace of discovery was about as slow. The westernmost Hawaiian Islands were not "discovered" until 1778. Until that greatest of Pacific explorers, Captain James Cook, made his voyages in the 1760's and 1770's, very little was known of the entire Pacific basin. As late as the 1840's most of the Pacific islands were unclaimed; the race for territory among the French, British, Germans, and to an extent, the Americans, did not intensify until the 1870's. Thus, economic and political interest from outsiders in most of the Pacific basin's islands is only about a century and a quarter old. The first European settlements in Australia coincided approximately with the American Revolution. The story of the settlement and exploitation of Australia and Oceania by other than their aboriginal inhabitants is fascinating in its compression of the colonial time span and the unusual natural qualities of this environment.

THE DISTINCTIVENESS OF THE REGION

Australia, New Zealand, and their neighboring islands form the *antipodes,* that is, the extreme opposite portion of the planet, from Europe. The **antipodes concept** was important in European perceptions in that it resulted in this region having a peripheral position in the assignment of priorities in colonization and development. Australia was, literally, a "British Siberia." People were sent there originally as punishment for criminal offenses.

There were many reasons for the various European colonization efforts from the sixteenth through the late nineteenth century. Some colonies were essentially strategic bases. Fabulous mineral wealth was an obvious motivation in others, while some were sought to supply tropical crops and commodities like sugar, rubber, or palm oil. Still others were intended as mirror images of the home country—transplanted populations occupying physically similar landscapes and, in fact, reproducing the cultural landscapes of home. Commonly, colonies reflected some intermixture of these motives. New Zealand and the cooler, more humid portions of Australia seemed like preeminent possibilities for **mirror-image colonies,** though the great distances involved tempered their attractiveness. The discovery of gold in the 1850's, however, only added to an already growing migration from Britain in search of farmlands.

THE "EMPTY CONTINENT"

Not only did Australia have very few **aboriginal people** at the time of British settlement (one quarter to one third of a million), but those people were still at the hunting and gathering stage of societal development. They were thus at lower levels of economic-organizational development than were many Amerindians. Their small number and

very light impact on the landscape reinforced European perceptions of an "empty" land, a fresh canvas on which a British society could be reproduced following the end of the era of the penal colony concept. The Polynesian aboriginal people of New Zealand, the Maori, were considerably further advanced than Australia's bushmen. Relative development level made little difference to British colonization policies toward native peoples, however.

ECONOMIC CHARACTERISTICS

This region has an extraordinarily low ratio of population to area and resources (excepting a few island groups considered in isolation). The continent of Australia has but 5 people per square mile (2 per square kilometer), New Zealand, 30 per square mile (12 per square kilometer) and Papua New Guinea, 17 per square mile (6 per square kilometer). In contrast, Asia has an overall average of 150 per square mile (58 per square kilometer), while Bangladesh has a density of almost 1,500 per square mile (580 per square kilometer).

The combination of overall low density and great distance from its important trading partners (Japan is 4,300 miles [6,900 kilometers] by sea from Sydney; California over 6,000 miles [9,700 kilometers] away) has posed many problems for the region. Industrial production for export has faced two fundamental obstacles—distance from most markets and the much lower labor costs of its closest neighboring regions. New Zealand, for example, cannot hope to sell most manufactured goods at competitive prices in Southeast Asia. An alternative type of industrialization— **import replacement** for the local market—is more logical, but here the low population is something of a handicap. Thus, the two developed, technologically advanced states of the region attained and maintain their high standards of living mostly by exporting minerals and the products of technologically sophisticated, large-scale agriculture.

OCEANIC DOMINANCE VERSUS THE EMPTY CONTINENTAL CORE

Sheer scale of distance, both intraregional and interregional, is a major characteristic of Australia-Oceania. For the Pacific islands the ocean is a unifier, the dominant (sometimes sole) means of trade. Despite their inherent island nature, however, Australia, New Zealand, and Papua New Guinea are more like continental core areas. Both Australia and New Zealand are characterized by development along their fringes; yet even this development supplies a largely domestic market with certain agricultural products and many of the domestically consumed manufactures.

The interior farmlands of Australia, indeed even some of the fringe regions, function as a traditional **economic hinterland.** Raw materials and basic, unprocessed or semiprocessed farm products are the major exports. Wheat, wool, hides, meat, cotton, coal, ores, and refined metals are the major exports, reflecting the hinterland "supply" nature of the economies. Meat, dairy products, animal feed, wool, and wood pulp are exported from New Zealand in large quantity. In short, they are supply areas for a more populous, more diverse **economic heartland** area elsewhere. Japan, the United States, and the United Kingdom are the major customers. The market areas for regional manufactures are largely the respective domestic markets of each other. Obviously, the sea is important in this trade, yet the economies of these two large states are largely self-sufficient.

Exports exceed imports in most years, and, increasingly, domestic industry replaces imports. Tropical food and beverage crops, tobacco, sugar, and rubber are increasingly produced in Australia. Some of these commodities, until recently imported from the commonwealth members of Southeast Asia, are now becoming exports as Australian tropical agriculture expands rapidly. Oil, until recently a crucial import, is now produced in oversupply. The refining and chemical industries are now developing rapidly, again *replacing* imports with exports, not just developing import replacements. Ferrous and nonferrous metallurgy are following this pattern, along with machinery and transportation equipment, areas where skill and mechanization may counterbalance relatively high labor costs. Imports are increasingly relegated to highly sophisticated technical production (optical goods, cameras, scientific equipment) or basic items produced cheaply in developing area economies (textiles, clothing, shoes). Necessities are most often domestically produced or could be produced at home if needed. The one-time isolation now becomes irrelevant; the sea is less a lifeline and more an avenue for prodigious exports. As they grow and develop, the economies of Australia and New Zealand will likely become more integrated with other parts of the world, and, consequently, the sea connections may take on a greater meaning. During this current developmental phase, however, Australia and New Zealand seem to be developing as a new heartland. The decision to increase interaction with the rest of the world becomes more a question of choice than of necessity.

THE PHYSICAL FRAME

The continent of Australia is the smallest of the continents and geologically one of the oldest landmasses. It has a fairly compact form with a relatively smooth coastline when compared to Europe or Asia. For millions of years, the continent has been stable, spared the violent mountain-building activities of great crustal movements and vulcanism. The abrading and smoothing actions of weathering and erosion have been at work without much counterforce of uplift for so long that there are few really spectacular landforms. Only on the east coast of Australia and at a few isolated interior locations have mountain-building activities occurred within the recent past on a geologic time scale. In contrast, New Zealand and the Pacific islands are much more recent, if less complex, in origin.

TOPOGRAPHY

The present surface of most of Australia is one of low elevation; most of the continent is below 1,000 feet (300 meters). The eastern highlands, about one sixth of the total area, are a complex highland of lifted, folded, and warped rocks with a few volcanic traces. These highlands parallel the coast for nearly 2,500 miles (4,000 kilometers). Their relatively low elevations (the highest peak is Mt. Kosciusko, 7,328 feet [2,234 meters]) makes them more comparable to the Appalachians or Urals than to the Andes or Sierras. The mountains reach their greatest heights in New South Wales and Victoria, sometimes plunging directly down to the sea. The name *Australian Alps* is more picturesque than accurate.

The bulk of the continent is composed of a series of plateaus interspersed with lowlands. These lowlands have some low hill ranges but are generally sedimentary basins covered by recent water and wind-deposited debris. Extensive sandy or gravel deserts occupy many of the lowlands. Dry lakes, covered only occasionally by shallow water after local thunderstorms, are the foci of internal drainage networks. The great Western Plateau occupies about half the continent; most of it is above 1,200 feet (300 meters) with relatively small mountain ranges in the middle and west that reach up to 3,000- or 4,000-foot (900- to 1,200-meter) elevations. A few spectacular landform features, such as Ayers Rock, are isolated rock projections above the general plateau level. A small area of faulted mountains with deep, narrow valleys and ocean gulfs occurs in the south-central coastal area. West of this area, along the Great Australian Bight, is an unusual desert landform, the Nullarbor (literally, "no trees") Plain of the southern plateau area. Limestone underground drainage systems mean that practically none of the precipitation received stays anywhere near the surface. Plant life is virtually absent as are stream-deposited surface materials.

The great islands of New Zealand (North and South islands), in contrast with Australia, are tectonically very active. New Zealand is the result of a giant series of earth crust faults or fractures along which blocks of crust have been moved and thrust. The resulting landscape consists of chains of volcanoes where molten material has moved to the surface, taking advantage of these huge cracks or lines of weakness. The immense ocean basin of the Pacific is bounded by a titanic zone of frequent earthquakes, active mountain-building forces, and vulcanism related to the locations of **tectonic plates.** The famous **Pacific ring of fire** is anything but pacific itself. Many of history's most famous and devastating earthquakes, including twentieth century disasters at San Francisco, Tokyo, Long Beach, and Anchorage, as well as countless ones throughout Central and South America, are related to this ring of fire. Sections of the Pacific littoral are quite literally a ring of fire with an unusual incidence of active volcanoes in the Aleutian Islands, much of Japan, the Philippines, the New Zealand islands, and even parts of Antarctica. The plate tectonic theory, described in detail in other chapters, explains this ring-of-fire phenomenon.

Among the ocean islands of the Pacific, the high-profile, steeply mountainous type (like the Hawaiian Islands, New Caledonia, or Bougainville) are volcanic in origin. Others are uplifted coral platforms (such as Naaru), while the very low-profile, commonly ringlike islands or **atolls** are coral reefs usually built upon some submerging volcanic base. The origin of the coral atolls, an interrupted

circle or oval of low relief surrounding a shallow lagoon, is still open to discussion. Polyps that build the coral reefs through accumulation of billions of tiny lime "shells" or exoskeletons are not particularly hardy creatures. They are very sensitive to temperature; living coral exists only in tropical seas. They do not tolerate dirty or turbid (cloudy) water. They cannot live more than 20 or 30 feet below the surface as they need ocean waves to bring them food. It is this last environmental restriction that means that coral in the top layers of the deeper waters must be built on a volcanic base or, if sea levels have changed through tectonic activity or glacial advances and retreats, on a base of older, now dead, reef.

The most widely accepted theory of coral atoll development is that of Charles Darwin, the great naturalist and codeveloper of the theory of natural selection. The circular form of atolls, according to Darwin, results from the fact that the coral first started as a fringing reef growing around the volcanic cone just below sea level. If the volcanic cone subsided back toward the sea floor slowly (the result of diminished molten material pressure beneath it), or was leveled by erosion, the process was matched in speed by the growth of coral, which consequently took a roughly circular form (see Figure 11–2).

These colonies of billions of tiny, primitive life forms have had immense effects on the physical and human geography of the tropical Pacific. Wave abrasion of the

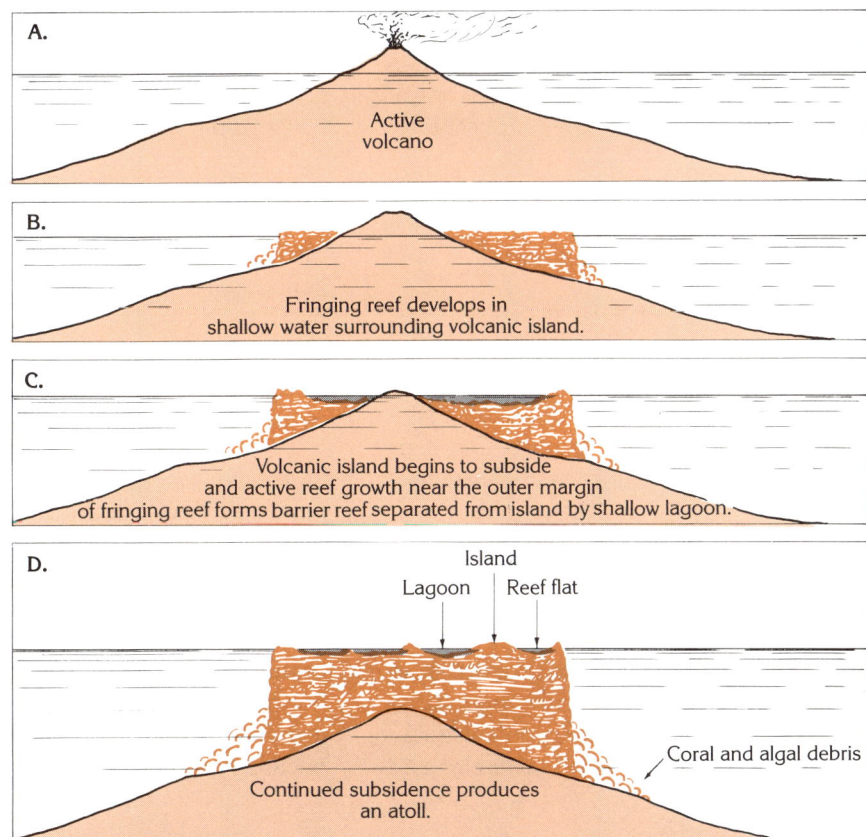

FIGURE 11–2
Formation of Coral Atolls. Thousands of tiny islands owe their existence to the exoskeletons of billions of tiny coral polyps. Living coral does not occur far below the surface, so that living coral capping thick reefs of dead coral on volcanic bases must represent a slow subsidence of the volcanic cone.

coral builds up a sandy cover that can support a few species of plants. The atolls usually have very few species of plants or animals, as only those capable of travelling as seeds in salt water, arriving by air (seabirds), or arriving in driftwood (insects, lizards, crustaceans) could have made the journey from the continents and their fringing islands to the "new" land. The coconut palm, for example, is ubiquitous among the atolls and beaches of the tropical Pacific as the coconut can float over open seas, be washed up on a beach or reef a few feet above water, and take root. Generally, the Island of New Guinea, closer to, and geologically related to, the continental mass, has the greatest variety of animal life. The variety decreases with approximate distance from New Guinea. The animal life of the Pacific islands seems to have migrated primarily from New Guinea and Australia.

European explorers and whalers from North America also contributed their exotic animals to the smaller islands as well. Rats were an accidental "contribution"—a disastrous one for both native animals and plants in that rats have nearly destroyed coconut palms on many islands. Frequently, the discovery of both inhabited and uninhabited islands by whalers and other Westerners would mean the deliberate introduction of goats, sheep, pigs, or cattle. On inhabited islands, the animals were gifts to local people (who may themselves already have introduced an array of nonindigenous animals and plants). Uninhabited islands were "seeded" with some domestic animals as an "insurance policy" against starvation should future crews be shipwrecked on them. On the Hawaiian Islands and many other Pacific island groups, there are populations of feral livestock (domestic species that have long since reverted to the wild).

LAND-SEA RELATIONSHIPS

That part of Australia most desirable to Europeans was (and remains) the more temperate climatic areas—the southern and southeastern coasts. Thus, the initial development took place at "the antipodes of the antipodes"—as far as possible from northwestern Europe. The early sea routes (before Suez) back to Britain were of astounding length (12,000 miles [19,300 kilometers] from Melbourne to London via Capetown, almost half of the earth's circumference), so that seaborne trade back to "home" would be almost the greatest distance possible to travel. Even by more direct air routes, London is 10,500 miles (16,900 kilometers) from Melbourne (San Francisco, in contrast, is just over half this distance). While many other regions of the world are physically closer to Australia-Oceania, Britain remained economically, culturally, and

politically "closest," at least until World War II. Consequently, Australians and New Zealanders perceived themselves as being at the end of the world's longest imperial lifeline. Transport from Britain to Australia and New Zealand (New Zealand is another 1,200 miles [1,900 kilometers] from southeastern Australia—not exactly a close neighbor) has usually been heavily subsidized by all governments concerned. Costs were so high on this extremely long trip that sailing vessels made their "last stand" in the Australia-Europe grain trade. Until the 1920's, the sailing ships' low operating costs (the power is free) made them competitive, if slow.

None of the states in this area, despite their early dependence on overseas trade and water contacts, have developed a significant merchant marine or navy. Perhaps this very isolation, combined with a large domestic resource base and vast areas of unused, potentially productive land, has encouraged self-sufficiency—thereby obviating the need for any great maritime fleet. The major cities are located on harbors and have become important ports, but the bulk of ocean commerce in the region is carried by the fleets of others. Vast stretches of harborless coast backed by unproductive hinterlands are characteristic of large parts of Australia. The Great Barrier Reef of Queensland virtually eliminates shipping along most of that coast. Transcontinental railroads, air service, and a superb road network among its settled parts reduce the need for coastal shipping. The Pacific islands, however, are served primarily by ocean transportation—either by small native craft, which can more easily navigate the shallow entrances to lagoons at the center of atolls, or by commercial craft registered in other nations.

The ocean, then, is an underused resource. Not only navigation but commercial fishing as well is poorly developed. Huge distances between scattered islands or from this region to other major land masses and population centers favor contact, trade, and travel by air rather than by sea. The ocean has been viewed by the Europeans settled in the area more as a buffer than as a connector.

CLIMATE

Except for the great land masses of Australia, New Zealand, and New Guinea, the influence of the sea is dominant, and tropical marine climates are typical. Again excepting Australia and New Zealand, this vast area is characterized by warmth and moisture. The great bulk of this greatest of oceans is within the tropics; even island groups such as the Bonins south of Japan, Midway Island northwest of Hawaii, and Easter Island (Rapa Nui), while technically poleward of the tropics, are tropical in climate because of the warm Pacific. Almost all the small islands of the Pacific basin, except those of the extreme north and south (like the Aleutians), are clearly tropical by any definition.

North Americans and Europeans seem to use the terms *paradise* and *Pacific island* almost interchangeably. The Pacific islands have a dreamlike quality for westerners, who have further romanticized the already abundant physical and cultural charms of the islands. Part of the explanation for this phenomenon may be physiological—that is, related to human physical nature. The human race is physically adapted to warm, moist climates. Without the extensive and elaborate modification of climate that culture has produced, from clothing to air conditioning and central heat, the human body is uncomfortable and perhaps even in danger of adverse physical adjustment (unaided by cultural adaptations) in nontropical conditions. When developed-area residents picture an ideal physical environment for their dream vacation, that imagined scene is most likely going to include palm trees along an ocean beach. The fascination with the "South Pacific" may be reflective of the fact that this environment is close to the optimum for people's comfort. Furthermore, the seacoast may well have been a favorite home of early man, with its rich variety of food and useful natural materials from both land and sea.

The prevalence of warmth and moisture means that all but the tiniest islands are well watered by updrafts. Higher temperatures over land during the day result in air being heated faster over the land, expanding and rising upwards, cooling as it rises. Vertical-development clouds are formed and precipitation commonly follows (see Figure 11–3). Even on small atolls that do not develop these strong updrafts, tropical storms and the pervasive moisture in the air support a good vegetation cover. Thunderstorms are quite common, as are seasonal tropical depressions called typhoons in the Pacific (hurricanes in the Caribbean). Surface winds over the tropical and subtropical Pacific are most frequently the result of vertical air movement over the ocean and originate from over a tropical sea.

In the vicinity of the equator, there are strong updrafts of air triggered by relatively high surface temperatures; air heated near the surface expands, rises, and cools with resulting condensation and precipitation. This primarily vertical movement of air, lifting air off the surface to create a lower atmospheric pressure (the equatorial low), meant that sailing ships made slow and erratic progress in the low pressure area. The vicinity of the equator was labeled the *doldrums* by early sailors due to the high probability of a sailing ship's being becalmed there for days. This rising, cooling air circulating through the atmosphere is a kind of giant convection cell, sinking back toward the surface around the tropics themselves. (All of these pressure and wind systems "migrate" seasonally, following, with a time lag of a month or so, the latitudinal shift in the location of the near-vertical rays of the sun.) The general zone of sinking or subsiding air back to the surface gives us two more areas of prevalent vertical movement of air, one in

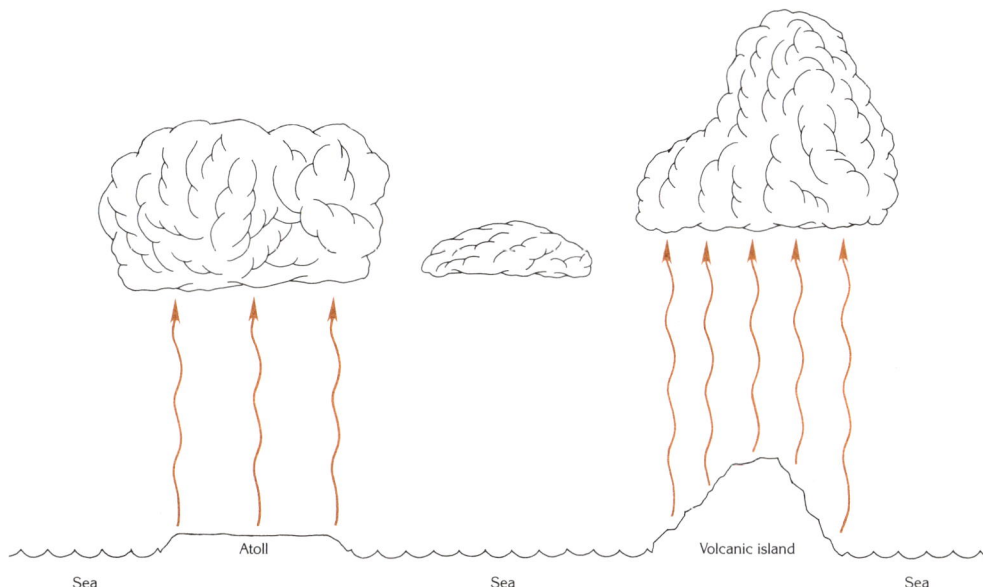

FIGURE 11–3

Vertical-Development Clouds Over Islands. Land surfaces heat faster than water surfaces in high solar energy-input areas; expanding, rising air over islands creates updrafts that frequently cool air to condensation level, forming a cloud marking the island's location on the vast horizons of the open ocean.

each hemisphere. These areas of subsiding, warming air form pools of high pressure rather than continuous belts of high pressure. Surface winds circulating in from the high pressures towards the equatorial low are so strong and dependable that early sailors termed them the *trade winds*. It is these winds that dominate the tropical ocean world of most Pacific islanders.

The climate of the Australian continent can best be described as arid, with an incomplete fringe of more humid climates. In Australia's winter (June-August), high pressure prevails over land, and the resulting winds move primarily outward from the dry land mass toward the coasts. Descending, warming air moving over the dry land of course does not acquire much moisture for subsequent precipitation over that land mass. In summer (December-February), a low pressure dominates northern and central Australia, drawing air in over the southeastern and eastern coasts from the surrounding sea. This flow of moisture-laden air is of little benefit to the arid interior, however, because the mountains of the eastern highlands concentrate precipitation along the coastal ranges, placing the interior in a rainshadow similar to that caused by the Sierras and Cascades for North America's intermontane region.

Australia's far northern coasts experience the effect of the great monsoon atmospheric circulation described in Chapter 9. The summer (which coincides with the northern hemisphere winter monsoon of southern and eastern Asia) is wet, with moist northerly winds coming in over the north coasts from the warm seas. Thunderstorms are common during the summer here. The winter in this region is much drier, although not entirely without rain. The monsoon circulation of air, with its seasonal reversal, is then predominantly offshore.

Australia's east coast has an adequate precipitation pattern year-round, with only an occasional drought. The northern sector is influenced by monsoonal circulation and has, hence, a summer maximum; the southern east coast has a winter rainfall maximum like its neighboring Mediterranean-type climate to the west. Two zones of Mediterranean-type climate focus on the regions dominated by the cities of Perth and Adelaide. The Mediterranean climate type (described in detail in Chapter 5) is characterized by dry summers of bright sunshine followed by mild, rainier winters. The seasonal shifts of subtropical high pressure cells and westerly wind belts account for this, as well as other, Mediterranean-type climates.

New Zealand, named by a Dutch explorer after a province of Holland, is very similar in climate to "old" Zealand. Just as in northwestern Europe, the climate is dominated by the prevailing westerlies sweeping over relatively warm (for these latitudes) ocean surfaces. The rainy, cool summer, mild winter (for the latitude) marine climate is shared by Tasmania. The moderating influence of oceanic air masses tends to be strongest on the windward (west) coast but is strong everywhere.

Snowy Mountains Hydro-electric-Irrigation Project, Southeastern Australia. Water management is an important concern in mostly arid Australia. Here, water is being diverted to the interior via tunnels to both generate power and provide vital irrigation water. (Courtesy of United Nations)

DRAINAGE PATTERNS

There is only one major river system in Australia, the Murray-Darling Basin of the southeast, which drains most of the provinces of New South Wales and Victoria as well as parts of Queensland and South Australia. The rest of the streams are either short, swift torrents running from the eastern highlands (the Great Dividing Range) to the sea or seasonal streams of moderate and erratic flow in the monsoonal and Mediterranean littorals.

The interior of Australia is characterized by **interior drainage.** Streams dead-end in salt lakes or simply disappear into the sands. Most are intermittent.

In contrast to surface drainage, vast underground reservoirs of ground water abound. The largest, the Great Artesian Basin, underlies the northeastern one sixth of the continental interior. Seven other smaller, but still quite important, artesian basins ring the coast from western Victoria to northern Queensland. Only some desert areas of the western interior seem to lack both surface and subterranean water sources.

Winding, mature, swamp-bounded, and sluggish streams dominate the lowlands of New Guinea. Short, swift streams with steep gradients characterize New Zealand—many are fed by glacial meltwaters from the heights of the Southern Alps. The Pacific islands most often lack any significant surface drainage features.

VEGETATION

Scattered areas of tropical rainforest are found in the lowlands and on the lower slopes of Queensland. The weather regime is monsoonal (a dry winter season) and the temperatures more often subtropical than tropical. Yet, without frost and watered by prodigious stream runoff or high water tables, the forest there is composed of broadleaf evergreens reminiscent of tropical rainforests. The northern fringes of the Australian continent and parts of the Queensland interior are a mixture of savanna and shrubby forest.

Eucalyptus varieties are most characteristic of both temperate and tropical climatic zones. Low grasses of the savanna and steppes ring the central deserts of the interior. Many native broadleaf evergreens, with adaptations for seasonal drought, appear in Mediterranean climate areas. Only the driest desert areas lack vegetation to any degree and only the wet cool extremes of the southeast and Tasmania have deciduous trees and any significant number of coniferous trees.

New Zealand's forests are more characteristic of temperate areas. The drier eastern side of South Island is covered with lush grass and shrubby plants. Drier Pacific islands have semi-deciduous forests, while wetter islands, including New Guinea, feature rainforests or grassy savannas in rainshadow areas.

SOILS

Soils of the tropical portions commonly are termed *laterites,* indicating low fertility. Since many Pacific islands are of volcanic or coral reef origin, however, they are relatively fertile and nutrients are naturally replenished despite leaching. Only the northern extremes of Australia, parts of the islands of New Guinea, and the Bismark Archipelago have the leached, largely infertile soils characteristic of the tropics.

Wetter subtropical areas of Australia and New Zealand develop soils with clay pans. They are of only moderate fertility unless enriched by alluvium; they are similar in color, structure, and productivity to the soils of the southeastern United States. Grassland areas of interior Australia, both tropical and temperate, are dominated by reddish prairie soils and chestnut earths not unlike those of the southern Great Plains. They yield well if supplied with sufficient water. The desert soils, often gravelly, are of varying fertility. Large areas of fixed dunes and desert pavement would preclude crop agriculture, even if water were available. Alkaline soils that cannot be used without "rinsing" or chemical alteration are scattered throughout the steppe and desert areas.

THE STRUCTURE OF SUBREGIONS

The sheer size of Australia and the intrinsic climatic and economic differences between its developed, largely temperate fringe and its desert core necessitate its division into two subregions. New Zealand and Papua New Guinea are sufficiently large (and different) to be treated as units, while the small size and high degree of similarity between one small island and another allow the grouping of the thousands of Pacific islands, scattered all over that ocean basin, into one subregional unit. (See Figure 11–4.)

THE DRY INTERIOR

The dryest of the inhabited continents, Australia's great arid center is very lightly populated. Almost all of this vast interior region averages less than two persons per square mile (0.8 per square kilometer); extensive areas are unin-

1. The Dry Interior
2. The Dynamic Fringe
3. New Zealand
4. Papua New Guinea
5. The Pacific Islands

FIGURE 11–4

Structure of Subregions. Australia's peripheral development flanking an "empty heart" is reflected in its subregionalization. New Zealand is distinctively different, as is Papua New Guinea and the island world to the north and east.

habited. (See Figure 11–5.) In this "youngest" of inhabited continents (in terms of its European discovery), the interior remained a complete mystery until the middle of the nineteenth century. The aridity of the interior was forbidding to people of a culture dependent on large domestic animals, as forage and water were known to be very scarce. The usual explorer's habit of following great river valleys into unknown interior lands could not, of course, be used in Australia. The first east-west crossing of the continent was in the early 1840's, but even then little was learned about the interior. The first north-south crossing of the interior (in the early 1860's) added little information. Only one man survived the return trip, and few written records were kept.

Farming and Agricultural Potential in the Interior With less than 15 inches (380 millimeters) of precipitation a year over most of the interior, in combination with high temperatures (average summer temperatures exceed 86°F (30°C) everywhere and even winter maxima are over 77°F (25°C), surface water is largely absent. The combi-

nation of high mountain ranges and on-shore, moisture-laden winds is found in every other continent but Australia. Nearly three quarters of the continent is almost without any permanent streams. Only a few **exotic streams** (those with sources in regions of a different, heavier-precipitation climate) flow into the interior.

Much of the underground water is in acquifers (porous rock) trapped between two impervious rock strata that act as waterproof layers. Some of this water is artesian, that is, it will flow to the surface under its natural pressure. In some places water is as deep as 7,000 feet (2,000 meters) below the surface and is quite hot when it first surfaces. Unfortunately for Australia, the bulk of this large quantity of subsurface water supply is also of very poor quality. It usually cannot be used to irrigate fields or for human consumption because it contains such a high level of dissolved minerals, but some can be used to water livestock.

The soil of much of the dry interior is most kindly described as "impoverished." Naturally, it has little moisture and, because of aridity, very little partially decom-

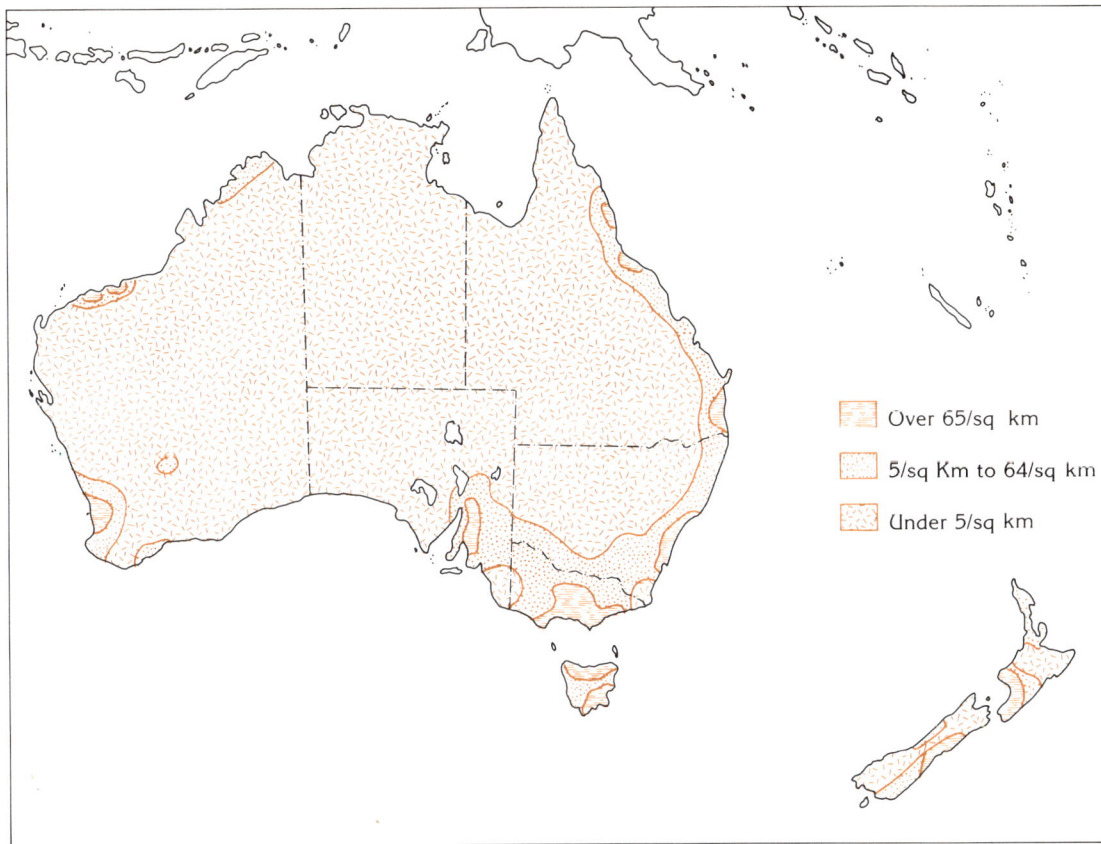

FIGURE 11–5
Population Density, Australia and New Zealand. Excepting important mineralized zones in the interior, the arid and semiarid interior and tropical northern coasts are very lightly settled, as Australians concentrate on the subtropical and temperate coasts. Rugged New Zealand is only relatively more evenly populated.

posed organic matter. Minerals, another component of fertility, may be absent (or worse, present in salty, poisonous concentrations), as so little water has been available to dissolve them and carry them away from the topsoil. Where the natural vegetation is not that of deserts or semiarid grass (mostly found in the transition between the desert and the northern and eastern monsoon forest), it is likely to be shrub. Some of this shrub/low tree country can support cattle, especially if less nutritious shrubs can be replaced by others that support grazing. Prickly-pear cactus, introduced a half century ago, quickly became a major pest, and then was eradicated. Happier foreign plant introductions have included a South American legume (nitrogen-fixing, soil-enriching plant that makes good animal feed), which has reportedly increased carrying capacity on some ranges by 500 percent. Where the climate is transitional from monsoon to desert, cattle raising has increasingly become the dominant land use. As in other tropical areas, Brahman cattle have been crossbred with European

varieties. Beef is shipped to the United States and Japan as well as to domestic markets.

Australia is the scene of a catastrophic example of what American wildlife ecologist George Laycock calls *animal roulette.* European rabbits were deliberately introduced into Australia in 1859 when a rancher imported a dozen pairs to release for hunting. Six years later the rancher had killed twenty thousand rabbits without exterminating them. Five rabbits eat as much as one sheep and yield less meat; they also compete with sheep for the same food. Australia has exported more than 15 million frozen rabbit carcasses per year at times, and has taken strenuous steps to control the furry pests. A 2,000 mile-long (3,200 kilometer-long) rabbit fence was built at a cost of more than $1 million early in this century. The deliberate infection of Australian rabbits by disease drastically reduced their numbers in the early 1950's, but the problem is still far from solved. The lesson was painful, expensive, and still not learned around the world—the introduction of exotic animals into a different environment can be disastrous for that environment's native vegetation and animal life and for a whole region's economy.[1]

It is in the erratic advance (and occasional retreat) of the farming frontier in the borders of the dry interior region and the dynamic fringe in which geographers can study the hazards of misjudging the capricious climate that characterizes the transition zone from well-watered land to desert. The pioneer fringe was a phenomenon of Australian settlement during the 1870's through the 1890's, just as it was in Canada and the United States. In each nation, the subhumid, semiarid transitions were being tested for wheat-growing potential. Around the globe, similar dry grasslands, formerly regarded as usable only in extensive grazing economies, were being re-evaluated as wheat fields. Relatively little was known about them and, as noted in United States and Canada, the cyclic nature of precipitation in these semiarid lands was not thoroughly understood. Much of the experimentation on these potential wheat lands was empirical—plow up the natural vegetation, plant wheat, and either harvest a successful crop or abandon the farm after a few successive attempts. This was an expensive lesson for the farmers involved, and expensive, too, for the whole society. Investments in railroad lines alone were heavy and not remunerative if the farming district failed.

South Australia was founded as an agricultural colony. To minimize speculation and encourage a lasting, orderly settlement, Britain's National Colonization Society was formed in 1830 to sell land, plowing back proceeds to subsidize more colonists, and control the advance of the frontier by selling land only in contiguous blocks, carefully surveyed. South Australia was chosen as the site of the colony because it was then practically empty of Europeans, and it had a Mediterranean-like climate of mild, wet winters and hot, dry summers. It quickly became apparent, though, that aridity increased sharply away from the coast in the vicinity of present-day Adelaide. The colonization of South Australia expanded rapidly in the 1870's. A see-saw movement of people occurred (even in this supposedly carefully planned and orderly colonization) due to bitter experience with variable rainfall patterns. Wheat acreages leveled off in the mid-1880's and two decades of net out-migration followed one of heavy immigration. What was achieved, finally, surely outpaces the setbacks and human tragedies of farm abandonment. The agricultural frontier had advanced 150 miles (240 kilometers) since 1870, and 2 million acres (810,000 hectares)

had come under cultivation, doubling the colony's settled area.[2]

The colony was anything but a failure, despite the serious problems of long-term and unpredictable cycles in precipitation. What was learned was just as valuable as what was produced; this advance of a farming frontier into the "margins of the good earth" must be done cautiously and with adequate experimentation with new technology, new techniques, or new seed. The frontier is as much in the laboratory as in the field.

Most of the dry interior of Australia will most probably not experience revolutionary change in land use. The margins may be areas of minor expansion, but the great bulk of the interior will remain an almost empty land except for the spotty pattern of mining towns and isolated ranches. Large herds of sheep and cattle graze on vast acreages of land with a low carrying capacity.

The Mineral Wealth of the Interior Australia is one of the world's richest nations in mineral resources, both their variety and quantity. Both major subregions of Australia have important mining areas. In the nearly empty interior, they are of course even more important with regard to settlement and transport patterns than in the dynamic fringe.

Gold began the mineral rushes and booms in the interior. First discovered in 1851, there was a second boom in the 1880's. Gold continues to be a major product in Australia, which ranks fifth in world production, most of the gold being produced at the Kalgoorlie-Coolgardie area in Western Australia's interior. Gold helped populate Australia just as it did California; in the decade following the discovery of gold, Australia's population almost tripled. (See Figure 11–6.)

Broken Hill, in the interior of New South Wales, is a world-rank mining center for lead, zinc, and silver, producing three fourths of Australia's output. Mount Isa in northern interior Queensland is a major center for production of copper, lead, zinc, and silver.

Iron ore has been known and mined for a long time on the coast of Western Australia. These mines and those of South Australia could alone support Australia's expanding steel industry. One of the world's greatest concentrations of high-quality iron ore came into production in the 1960's, at Pilbara, Western Australia, in the interior. Most of the production from the huge new source is exported to Japan. Discoveries of these iron ores in large, rich deposits have given a new dimension to the importance of mining in the interior. Australia's iron ore production has skyrock-

---

[1] George Laycock, *The Alien Animals: The Story of Imported Wildlife* (New York: Ballentine Books, 1970), pp. 170–78.

[2] Donald Meinig, *On the Margins of the Good Earth* (Chicago: Rand McNally, 1962), p. 203.

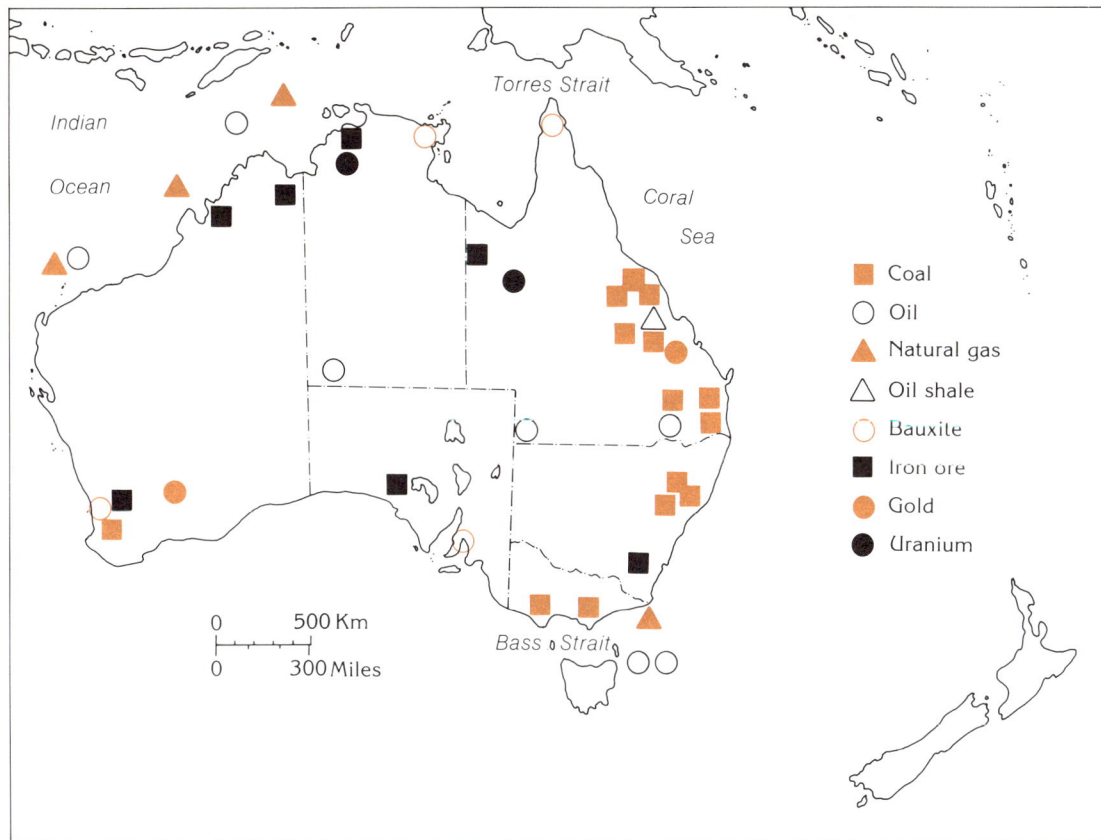

FIGURE 11—6
Mineral Resources. Rich mineral strikes helped populate Australia, and more recent finds of bauxite, iron ore, and gold along with agricultural exports, continue to sustain its economy. Papua New Guinea is exploiting important mineral reserves as well, while New Zealand remains much more dependent on agriculture.

eted since World War II; production was only 11 million tons per year as late as 1967, soaring to almost 90 million tons per year by 1980. Australia is now the third largest iron ore producer in the world (after the USSR and Brazil) and the second most important iron ore exporter. Reserves (of all grades and types) are found largely in the interior and Western Australia leads in production, though all states except Victoria produce some.

Oil, until the last decade, had been a major Australian import. Australia discovered its first major oil field in southeastern Australia (Bass Strait), offshore, in 1967, contemporary with the finding of major new gas fields in central Australia. This oil is being pumped quickly from a modest reserve, and Australia would again be dependent on foreign oil if major discoveries are not made. Drilling and exploration have uncovered new small fields as the search for oil quickens in pace.

New discoveries in the three western provinces show great promise, as do offshore sites along the northern continental shelf. Recently, a series of finds have been made in southeastern Queensland and around the edges of the Great Artesian Basin in the eastern interior. Australia could shortly become a major world producer if any of these prove to be major deposits.

To cap its extraordinarily good fortune in minerals, Australia had discovered the world's largest deposit of bauxite at Weipa (see Figure 11—6) along with more phosphate, zinc, manganese, nickel, and copper in northern Queensland. The Cape York bauxite deposits are the largest in the world, and Australia has become the world's largest exporter.

THE DYNAMIC FRINGE

Australia's population distribution shows a markedly peripheral pattern. (See Figure 11–5.) As in the case of Brazil, this developed, more densely occupied coastal fringe is partly related to Australia's colonial history. Unlike Brazil, the European colonization was relatively recent, and most

Drilling in the Bass Strait, Australia. The Bass Strait fields supply most of Australia's current oil production, although there are excellent oil prospects elsewhere in the continent. Australia also has important coal and oil shale resources. (Courtesy of United Nations/Australian Information Service)

unlikely to ever shift significantly to the interior. The dynamic fringe, as defined here, is more than the coastal areas themselves. Indeed, some coasts, such as those of the Nullarbor Plain, much of the Western Australia coast and the coast from north of Perth clockwise around the continent to the central east coast of Queensland, are not part of the dynamic fringe. In contrast to the very lightly populated interior, the dynamic fringe is home to most Australians. It includes the highest, most scenic mountains of the continent, better watered parts of the variety of subtropical and temperate humid climate areas in the states of Western and South Australia, Queensland, New South Wales, and Victoria, as well as parts of Tasmania.

Population Distribution and Migration Australia's rapid population growth, a 75 percent increase since the end of World War II, testifies to the continuing importance of immigration. From 1947 to the 1971 census, Australia had a net in-migration of 2.6 million. The birthrate is also quite high for a developed nation. The planned rapid expansion by immigration has been slowed down now by the pressure of higher unemployment. Now, the government limits immigration to those sponsored by Australian relatives and to selected professional and occupation groups needed by Australia. Most immigrants (past and present) were destined for the fringe rather than the interior. As mentioned, the earliest migration to Australia was in the form of "transported convicts." The reasoning was that remote Australia was the perfect low-security prison. Their

offenses were generally minor, such as inability to repay debts, and the prisoners were to support themselves through agriculture, presumably reforming themselves in the process and certainly relieving Britain of the cost of maintaining them in prison back home. Like other schemes for reducing the costs of the criminal justice system, in other times and other places, this one did not quite work out as planned. The penal colony at Sidney had to be supplied with food from Britain, halfway around the world, for a decade. Free settlers were much more successful. Taking the hint, the British government began to both free prisoners ahead of schedule and encourage more free settlers. Food shortages were significant in the early colonies, partly because the poorer soils along the coast could not support the kind of concentrated settlement that the government favored. Administratively, it was easier to control a compact, coastal colony. Like administrators everywhere, though, those of the Australian colonies found themselves playing catch-up with the energetic, imaginative pioneers who quickly perceived the possibilities of the uplands for sheep. These "squatters" pioneered beyond the permissible area and the government later confirmed most of their land acquisitions. The introduction of merino sheep early in the 1800's had the same levels of continent-wide impact on settlement and progress as the gold discoveries of the 1850's and the massive multiple mineral strikes of the 1950's and 60's. The first pioneer settlement was in 1788, the largest convict "transportations" were in the 1830's, and even then the number of free settlers arriving was higher than the number of prisoners.

The Australians are a heavily urbanized people (86 percent urban) and fully 22 percent of all Australians live in their largest city, Sydney. Such an overwhelming dominance of one city in the United States for example, would mean that, proportionately, about 49 million people would be concentrated in the greatest metropolitan area. Aside from important mining settlements, extraordinarily huge, low-carrying capacity ranches, and some evolving winter tourist resorts in the desert, the dynamic fringe *is* Australia, demographically and economically.

Cultural-Economic "Capitals"   Highly urbanized Australia does not have a "primate city" in the sense of having one metropolitan area that clearly dominates economic and cultural leadership and significantly outranks its nearest competitor in population size. In some ways resembling the close rivalry of Canada's Montreal and Toronto (but without the cultural-linguistic divide present there), Sydney and Melbourne have maintained growth rates that place Melbourne a consistent, close second. Both are ports, both are state capitals, and both are located approximately in the center of their state's settled coastal areas. Both rank among the top fifty cities in the world. In 1970, Sydney (2.6 million) outranked Melbourne (2.3 million); Sydney contained 58 percent of its state's total population, while Melbourne held 66 percent of Victoria's total population. By 1980, the figures were 3.4 million and 3.0 million, with Sydney still leading. These two great cities can be expected to dominate Australia's economic and cul-

tural life between them; in a sense, they are a "twin" primate city. In a classic example of the location of a created capital between its two preexisting rivals for the capital function, the Australian federal capital at Canberra is between Sydney and Melbourne, but closer to the larger rival, Sydney.

Dynamic Fringe Agriculture   The early free settlers and their merino sheep both multiplied rapidly. By 1851, when the colony of Victoria split off from that of New South Wales, it already had 77,000 settlers and 5 million sheep. The dynamic fringe is still a major producer of sheep and cattle despite a shift to more intensive crop agriculture. While sheep and cattle are still important there, agriculture in the fringe is now quite diverse. The first major grain production began shortly after initial settlement; it was the frontier crop.

The advance of the wheat-farming frontier introduced the second mainstay of Australia's agricultural base with its rapid expansion in the 1870's. Today, most Australian wheat farmers also graze some sheep, and vice versa. Market swings in prices for wheat and wool bring about individual decisions to expand one at the price of the other, so that Australian farmers continually expand and contract wheat acreage and sheep pastures. Wheat now occupies about half the total cultivated acreage and is grown on land with 10 to 20 inches (250 to 500 millimeters) of rainfall per year. The wetter margins of western and southern Australia are important producing areas. The wheat lands are somewhat better watered in Victoria, New South

Sydney—Australia's Largest Metropolitan Area. Australia is an overwhelmingly urban society and has been so for nearly a century, despite its deserved reputation as a specialized and major producer and exporter of agricultural products. (Courtesy of Australian Information Service)

Wales, and Queensland, which also have considerable production. (See Figure 11–7.)

Sugar cane is a major crop in coastal Queensland, produced mostly on small family farms using heavy mechanization. More cane could be grown, but Australia is cautious about expansion in this notoriously cyclical world market. An agency of the State of Queensland sets quotas and prices and handles marketing. Australia became the second largest sugar exporter after Cuba when that country lost many of its export markets in the 1960's. Other subtropical and tropical crops (cotton, coffee, and bananas) have been introduced in Queensland.

Fruit and vegetable production, using only about 1 percent of Australian cropland, accounts for one fifth of total value of crops. Australia's climate range enables it to produce not only mid-latitude fruits such as apples, pears, peaches, and apricots, but also tropical fruits such as oranges and bananas. Vegetables are grown near most big cities, while Tasmania specializes in cool-climate crops such as potatoes and apples. A growing wine industry is based on vineyards near Adelaide.

Australia can dominate world wool markets (it produces twice as much as its nearest competitor) because, in addition to the mixed sheep and wheat farms, sheep are also grazed on the driest margins of usable land, land sometimes so dry that vegetation is sparse enough to require 30 acres (12 hectares) of it to support one sheep.

Dairying is carried on close to all big cities and in the wet highland valleys from Rockhampton on south. The Tasmanian north coast is a traditional area for dairy cattle, while coastal wetlands along the South Australia–Victoria border have been drained and improved for dairying in a seasonally dry area. In addition to the extensive cattle ranches in the north, beef cattle are stall-fed on farms near all major urban centers.

Developed Fringe Natural Resources In addition to hydro power (16 percent of total electric energy), Australia's large coal production relieves some of the pressure from its oil production. Seventy-seven million metric tons of

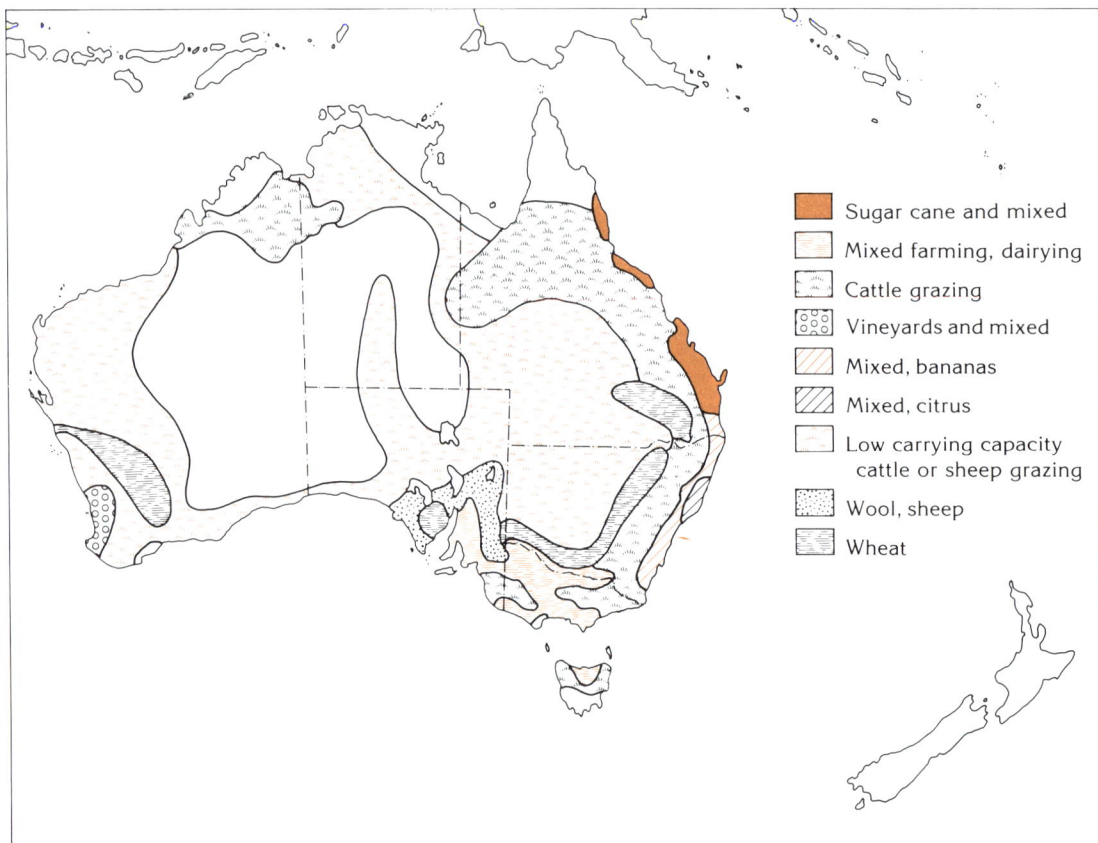

Legend:
- Sugar cane and mixed
- Mixed farming, dairying
- Cattle grazing
- Vineyards and mixed
- Mixed, bananas
- Mixed, citrus
- Low carrying capacity cattle or sheep grazing
- Wool, sheep
- Wheat

FIGURE 11–7

Agricultural Regions of Australia. Australia's size and diversity of physical environments support a wide range of crop specializations. Australia produces exportable surpluses of both tropical and mid-latitude crops and is the world's largest exporter of wool.

bituminous coal are produced each year, together with 33 million metric tons of brown coal (lignite).

Coal, the single largest employer of miners, is mostly a product of the developed fringe, with heavy production in Queensland and New South Wales (see Figure 11–6). Fortunately for Australia, the most significant reserves in quantity and quality are relatively easily accessible from the great coastal cities. Coal had been exported as early as 1801, and exports to Japan have increased rapidly recently.

The diminishing production of the Bass Strait fields has led to an extensive exploration program, on and offshore. Australia has a major deposit of oil shale on the east coast of Queensland. As with the U.S. Rocky Mountain oil shales, there are some serious environmental pollution potentials in large-scale exploitation. The total reserve is estimated at 2.3 billion barrels and is projected to produce 200,000 barrels a day by 1990, about one quarter of Australian consumption at that time.

Australia has less than one tenth the proportion of land in forest when compared to the United States. The timber and pulpwood harvest is strictly controlled by the government to insure continuing production at the regrowth rate. Despite its small area of forest cover, the Australians manage to supply about 70 percent of their lumber requirement through careful management.

Fishing resources have only just begun to be fully exploited. Abundant beef seems to have discouraged a large commercial fishing industry until export markets became accessible with frozen fish products. Historically, Australia has exported pearl shell from its tropical northern waters. Japanese investment and expertise have encouraged a cultured pearl industry in the north. Crayfish tails and tuna have become major fishing industries, as has commercial oyster farming. The Australians have expanded their territorial fishing waters from 3 to 12 miles (5 to 19 kilometers) as Japanese and Russian trawlers began to take large catches offshore. Most aspects of the fishing industry could be dramatically expanded in future.

Industrial Development Patterns in the Dynamic Fringe   Sixty percent of all Australians live in the eight largest cities, of which six are state capitals. The unusually high proportion of population in capitals of states is related to the economic development patterns of those states. Each separate colony or state built a railroad system designed to channel the hinterland production of farm commodities, minerals, or timber to the state capital, invariably a seaport. It was not until much later that a unified national rail system became a goal. Achieving the goal has not been easy, because the early single-focus rail nets were often of different gauge than those of neighboring states.

An entirely standard gauge transcontinental railroad was not achieved until 1969.

The urban economy, as well as that of rural extractive industries, is characterized by a **mixed economy** philosophy of free enterprise combined with strong regulatory and even ownership involvement of the federal government. These federal controls are especially significant in banking, minerals, and energy. Federal and state governments own railroads, utilities, telephone communications, the international airline, and one domestic airline. Australians enjoy some of the highest wage rates in the world; these wages are set by state and federal wage boards.

Isolation and the small size of the domestic market have restrained the development of Australian manufacturing. Its nearest neighbors, geographically, are characterized by either heavy population and cheap wages, as in Southeast Asia, or an even smaller market with its own problems of isolation, as in the case of New Zealand. Isolation makes it difficult to export manufactured goods due to the cost of transport to distant markets. Semiprocessed raw materials are an exception. The small domestic market (Australia has fewer people than California) limits the opportunities for achieving economies of scale in production. Further reducing economies of scale is the rather separate nature of each state's economy, which encourages nationwide enterprises to set up a factory in each capital city to serve that market.

Only fortieth in population among the world's nations, Australia is in the top dozen in world trade. While much of that world trade is the export of raw or semiprocessed materials, Australians would like to further expand the markets for manufactured goods. At present, the processing of raw materials for export is the leading export manufacturing business.

Developmental Strategies   The export of manufactured goods from Australia is expected to increase as Australian production of motor vehicles, heavy machinery, farm equipment, and machine tools increases. The shift toward the export of sophisticated manufactured goods to supplement raw material and semiprocessed materials is uneven, however. A promising expansion of shipbuilding has collapsed to the point that a Japanese firm won a contract for Australian warships; the controversy over this contract largely ignored the problem of high cost, inefficient labor attibutable to the government-set wage policies. It would appear that the very high standards of living and wage rates can be supported in highly mechanized, export-oriented mineral production but not in all export-oriented manufacturing.

Australian policy toward foreign investors has shifted several times in the past two decades. During the 1960's, an open investment policy coupled with fabulous mineral strikes attracted a surge of foreign industrial and commercial investment. In the early 1970's, the government began to screen foreign "takeovers" of Australian businesses. In 1975, a new policy, less restrictive but favoring Australian majority ownership, was enacted. As in many countries, the economic sectors of mass media, banking, and transport are closed to foreign investment. Australia ranks after Canada, the United Kingdom, West Germany, France, and Switzerland in hosting U.S. investment abroad.

As in South Africa, World War II's interruption of normal trade relationships accelerated Australia's development of import-replacement industries. Australia now assembles autos, builds machinery of all kinds from its own steel, and produces a wide range of industrial and consumer chemicals, clothing, processed foods, tobacco, and paper products. Even wine and beer are produced for both domestic and export markets.

Environmental Problems   The environment is a pressing issue because of the scarcity of water and the dependence on the agricultural resource. The new emphasis on mining and industrial growth will present new problems of pollution and new types of potential threats to both urban and rural environments.

A very common image in Australia is a bulldozer grinding across the dry land, throwing clouds of dust into the bright blue sky. Many U.S. citizens visiting Australia are charmed by the open spaces, the dynamic pace of development, and the easy, democratic friendliness of Australians. "Like the United States a generation or two ago" is a common comparison drawn by North Americans. This image of a younger United States has both positive and negative aspects, though. Both the United States and Australia were settled by northwestern Europeans at a time in history when the Industrial Revolution was in its lusty infancy. The new lands had apparently limitless land and resources and were only very sparsely settled by stone-age original inhabitants. The physical environment was seen as a hostile entity that must be tamed.

The exploitation of resources, with little thought of conservation or the future, that characterized the nineteenth century United States seems prevalent in twentieth century Australia. Overgrazing is a serious problem, especially when it is remembered that 58 percent of Australia is in grazing land, with only 5 percent cultivated. Very little land has been set aside as national parks or forest preserves. Poison is a very common "control" method against competitors or predators for domestic grazing animals— sometimes the poison is used indiscriminately. A growing conservation movement may reverse the exploitive tradi-

tion before serious, long-term environmental damage occurs.

Political Stability   Australia is distinguished not only by universal adult suffrage, but also by *compulsory* universal adult suffrage. Democracy is a strong tradition and one in which Australians popularized the "Australian" or secret ballot. The federal constitution closely resembles that of the Unites States, specifying federal powers and leaving others to the states.

Australia has become an important donor of economic aid in its part of the world. This aspect of regional leadership is quite impressive; Australia ranks fourth in the world in the percentage of its national income devoted to economic assistance for developing countries. Naturally, the Australians hope that this enlightened generosity will help achieve stable, prospering regional settings for their prospering, stable nation.

NEW ZEALAND

Quite similar to "home" climatically and virtually "empty" in being very lightly populated by indigenous peoples, New Zealand consciously patterned itself on the home country, politically and culturally. Europeans, primarily British, are 90 percent of the ethnic population of New Zealand. The remaining 10 percent are Polynesians, almost entirely Maoris, the pre-European population. New Zealand, about the size of Colorado, has about 3.25 million people. The Maoris are increasing at a faster rate than those of European heritage. In common with West Europe and North America, the life expectancy is high, the literacy rate is high, and most of the population (70 percent) is urbanized.

New Zealand's resource base, other than its agricultural potentials, is quite narrow. Minor soft coal deposits in the South Island, some lignite on both main islands, and a scattering of nonferrous minerals on both islands constitute the mineral resource base. No petroleum, little natural gas, and no major metallic ore sources other than a fair-sized deposit of iron ore make New Zealand an unlikely location for heavy industry. The hydroelectric potential is excellent in proportion to population and is about one third developed. New Zealand's position on the ring of fire means that earthquakes are common, if usually of minor scale, and volcanic activity has been a major force in shaping the islands. New Zealand is extremely complex geologically, with ancient crystalline rocks and sedimentary areas along with lavas. A few volcanoes have been active into the modern period and there are numerous geysers, hot springs, and steam fumeroles. New Zealand is among the few nations to have begun to harness its **geothermal power** potential. (See Figure 11–8.)

About 70 percent of all New Zealanders, including almost all Maoris, live on the more temperate North Island. The Auckland peninsula of the North Island is subtropical, while the Southern Alps of the South Island and the extreme southeast are subarctic. As with Australia, the European discovery was made by the Dutch, but settlement was under the British. Lumbering, whaling, and sealing attracted small numbers of Europeans before the British formally annexed the islands in 1840 and, that year, began systematic settlement. A series of wars with the Maoris, who were resisting white settlement, ensued in the 1860's. Since 1870, natural increase has been larger than immigration and now accounts for three quarters of the population growth.

Agriculture remains the predominant sector of the economy, although manufacturing is increasing. New Zealand is the world's largest exporter of lamb, mutton, and dairy products and is the second ranking exporter of wool. These products make up almost two thirds of the country's exports. New Zealand is unusually dependent on exports, which account for 23 percent of its gross domestic product (GDP). (The United States, in comparison, exports about 7.5 percent of its GDP.) This is even more remarkable considering the vast distances between New Zealand and most of its trading partners.

The oceanic, very moderate climate of New Zealand with its lack of extreme temperatures for most of the country and the near-universal abundance of precipitation (New Zealand is one of the tourist destinations for which travel agents always recommend taking a raincoat!) makes it ideal for the growth of nutritious pasture grasses. About one third of the country is in cropland or sown pasture, one third is in rough pasture and commercial forest, and one third is in unproductive mountainous terrain. Apart from the South Island's Canterbury Plains, there is little flat land, a factor that also encourages pastures rather than cultivation in this heavy precipitation area with a high risk of erosion.

The relative dominance of agriculture sometimes leads to the assumption that manufacturing in New Zealand is "little and late." Actually, isolation from other industrial areas in the colonial era helped to foster a variety of manufacturing enterprises aimed at the small local market. Textiles and shoes were such early manufactures. Large-scale food processing developed as refrigerated ships made the export of meat and dairy products to distant markets feasible. Meat packing and freezing, butter and cheese processing, and canning have become important industries based largely on export markets.

The government has actively encouraged diversification of both export and local-market-oriented industry in an attempt to cushion the impact of world market fluctua-

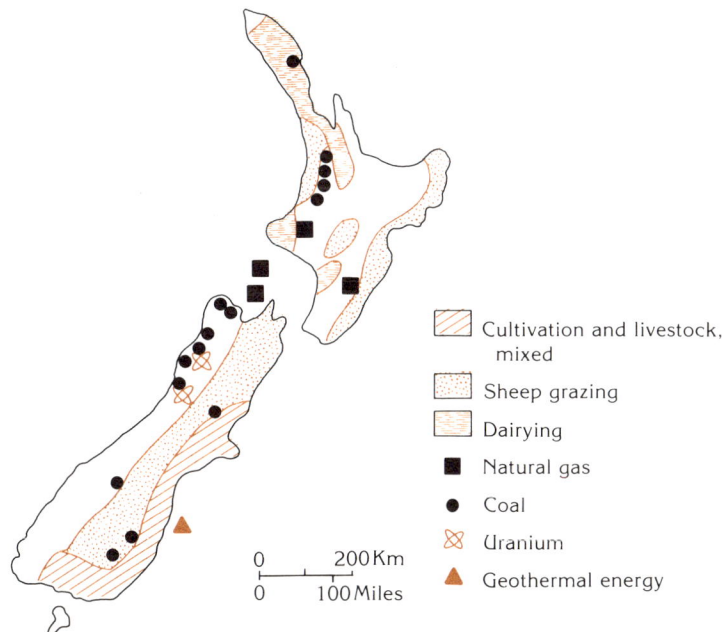

FIGURE 11–8

New Zealand: Agriculture and Mineral Energy Resources. New Zealand's range of mineral and agricultural exports is far narrower than Australia's, although New Zealand is able to exploit geothermal energy to supplement its hydroelectric power.

Wellington Harbor, New Zealand. Like Australia, New Zealand is a largely urban society based on the export of agricultural raw materials, though New Zealand's economy is much less diversified and less prosperous than Australia's. New Zealand also cannot match the mineral wealth of its larger neighbor. (Courtesy of National Publicity Studios, Wellington, New Zealand)

tions on the entire economy. New Zealand has moved rapidly forward in industrialization; its industries now include electronics, auto assembly, chemicals, paper, fertilizers, and printing. New Zealand's economy suffered a major setback in the great world depression of the 1930's, rebounded during World War II, and expanded rapidly afterwards. However, it was faced with a double threat in the 1970's. Britain's decision to join the European Economic Community in 1973, long delayed precisely because of its trade relationship with its commonwealth capital, has drastically reduced that market for New Zealand's agricultural products. The EEC, under British pressure, agreed to phase out New Zealand's share of British markets on a declining quota rather than eliminate it abruptly. Cheese imports were phased out by 1977 and butter by 1980. New Zealand likewise phased out its system of preferential tariffs favoring British manufactured goods on all products except automobiles. The loss of free access to British markets was serious enough but was compounded in the 1970's by the soaring price of petroleum. The government's decision to maintain what amounts to full employment under these trying economic conditions has worsened New Zealand's balance of payment problems. Economic growth has been essentially stagnant, while inflation has gone on at a double-digit scale.

Auckland, with almost a million people, is the largest city. Both Auckland and Wellington, the capital (400,000), are on the North Island. The South Island's largest city is Christchurch (335,000).

The economic problems of New Zealand, together with far superior communication and transportation sys-tems than were available in the colonial period, has led to some serious consideration of a political union of Australia and New Zealand. Closer ties of their economies would probably benefit New Zealand somewhat more than it would benefit Australia. Although Australia and New Zealand are not exactly close to each other, they share language, a cultural heritage, and, importantly, a world view that is probably closer than that of any two other independent countries in the world. The countries *are* close in the context of their relative isolation from Europe and North America, and their sharp distinctions, racially, culturally, and economically, from Southeast Asia. Certainly Australia and New Zealand are close enough in both a cultural sense and in terms of modern transport and communications for a union to be conceivable.

PAPUA NEW GUINEA

Papua New Guinea (PNG), 100 miles (160 kilometers) to the north of Australia, shares the great island of New Guinea with Irian Jaya, the easternmost territory of Indonesia. PNG is included with Australia-Oceania rather than Southeast Asia (which includes Indonesia) because of its close economic and political ties with Australia. It was administered by Australia until independence was achieved in 1975. During the era of European colonialism, the island of New Guinea was subdivided among the Netherlands, which controlled the western half as part of the Dutch East Indies (now Indonesia); Germany, which claimed the northeastern quarter from 1884 to 1914; and Great Britain, which established a protectorate over the southeastern quarter, Papua, in 1884. Britain transferred the administration of Papua to Australia in 1902, and Australian troops occupied German New Guinea, along with the Bismarck Archipelago and the German Solomon Islands, in 1914. The former German territory became a League of Nations mandate, supervised by Australia, in 1920. Administration of Papua, the New Guinea territories, and the neighboring islands was combined following the end of Japanese wartime control in 1945. Australia embarked on a sequence of progressive steps toward self-rule for Papua New Guinea as early as 1951, when a legislative council was established.

A single mine on the island of Bougainville produces one fifth of PNG's gross domestic product and more than half of its exports. Copper, gold, and silver are exported from Bougainville, and potentially commercial copper deposits have been found on the main island as well. (See Figure 11–6.) There are excellent prospects for a major gas and oil strike in the Gulf of Papua, although no large field has yet been brought into production. PNG has the potential for becoming a major forest product exporter; 40 percent of the country is in commercially valuable forest, but transport systems are not yet adequate to support large-scale exploitation. (See Figure 11–9.)

This country of over 3 million is growing at 2.6 percent. Except for about 1 percent Australians (and even fewer Chinese), the population is entirely Papuan ethnically, a Melenesian people intermixed with Negritos. Culturally, however, the country is extremely complex. Separated by steep, mountainous terrain covered with tropical rainforest, highly localized cultures have developed, often in apparent ignorance of other groups a few miles distant. About 650 separate languages have been identified of the island of New Guinea; of these 160 are totally unrelated to any other language. Most of these languages are spoken by only a few thousand people. A **pidgin language** has been evolved from English and native words; this makeshift language of convenience serves commercial relations and government administrations. The small educated elite speaks English.

Agriculture is expanding, with emphasis on coffee, copra, cocoa, tea, and rubber. Cattle are becoming more important as a means of reducing meat imports. Pyrethrum, a natural insecticide, is also an important crop. However, 80 percent of the population is little touched by the commercial economy, remaining in subsistence farming of sweet potatoes, taro, and other root crops. Some of these subsistence farmers do grow small amounts of coffee in order to have some cash income. Coffee prices, notoriously cyclical on world markets, have fueled prosperity in the highlands recently, but a slump in coffee markets would be correspondingly serious. Foreign ownership of plantations was completely phased out by the early 1980's.

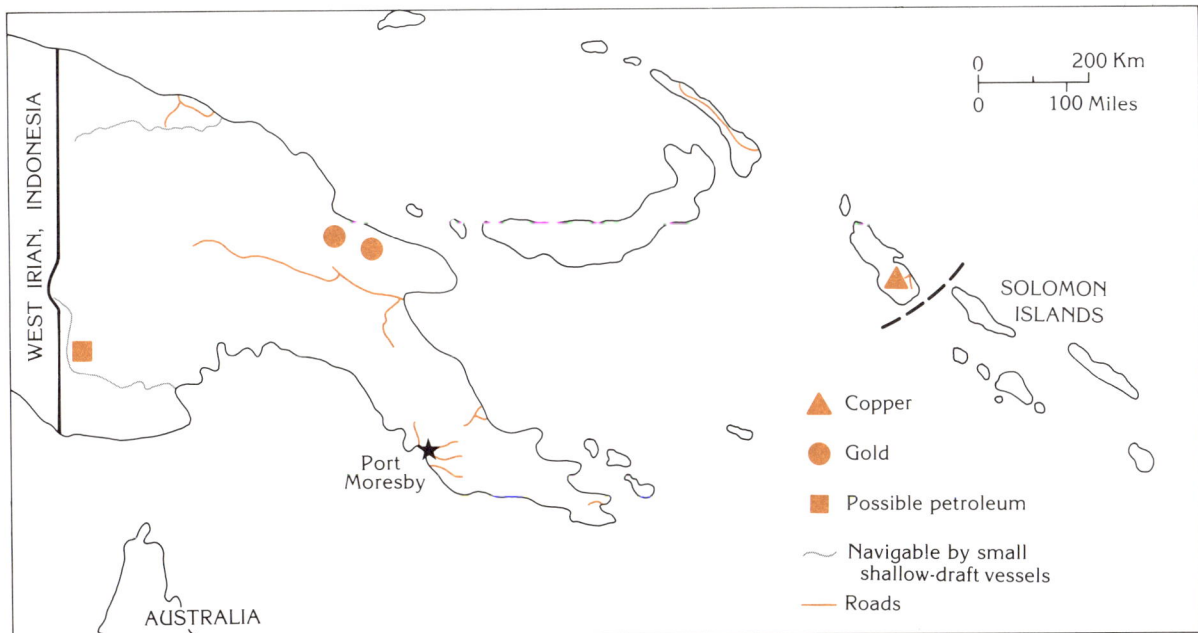

FIGURE 11–9
Papua New Guinea. Papua New Guinea is this region's least developed major land area. Mineral, forest, fisheries, and agricultural sectors of the economy, however, all have potential for expanded output. PNG is one of the best prospects in the developing world.

Crocodile Farm, Papua New Guinea. As crocodile hides bring high prices, Papua New Guinea has established several "farms" for the commercial production of hide, comparable to the "fur farms" of cooler climates. (Courtesy of United Nations/S. Stokes)

Typical of developing nations around the world is the rapid growth of PNG's urban centers. Port Moresby, the largest city at about 140,000, is growing at a rate of 10 percent a year; smaller cities in the interior are growing at 6 percent a year.

PNG's **developmental strategies** must take into account both the cyclic nature of tropical commodity prices and the proximity of Southeast Asia, with its far lower labor costs. One strategy is to continue to diversify agricultural exports. Thus, as in the late 1970's, when copra prices were falling, cocoa and coffee were rising enough to more

than counterbalance falling copra revenues. The tuna fishing industry is being expanded; skipjack tuna catches here rank third in the world.

The decision to legislate a high minimum wage for urban industries means that PNG cannot compete with Southeast Asia in export of manufactured goods. Current government industrialization planning emphasizes import replacement consumer industries.

There is some concern that overly-rapid expansion of commercial agriculture and cattle grazing in the tropical rainforest areas could lead to serious soil erosion prob-

Road Construction in Papua New Guinea. The exploitation of Papua New Guinea's extensive tropical forest, which covers 85 percent of its territory, requires new road construction. Timber exports currently enjoy high markets, but the danger of erosion in such high precipitation areas is serious. (Courtesy of United Nations)

lems. Much of PNG is composed of highlands, with knife-sharp ridges separating narrow valleys. Rainfall averages 80 to 100 inches (2,000 to 2,500 millimeters) a year, and some areas receive more than 200 inches (5,000 millimeters). Once the deceptively luxuriant rainforest is removed, the often infertile soil may not long sustain cropping or even pastures, so that there is potential for some severe environmental degradation.

PNG stands out as a success story among developing nations. Its transition from colony-protectorate through trustee territory to fully independent state seems to have been remarkably smooth. Its economy is expanding and diversifying; its currency is stable and has been appreciating in value, and its outlook is bright if a true nation can be melded from its polymorphous multicultural society. Close and friendly relations with Australia, its former mentor, would appear central to PNG, whose border with Indonesia is not always peaceful. Additionally, Bougainville, with its copper riches, attempted independence from PNG in the mid-1970's. Unwilling to share its copper revenues, Bougainville was kept as part of Papua New Guinea only after violent rioting was controlled.

THE PACIFIC ISLANDS

The remaining Pacific Islands constitute the final subregion. They are traditionally divided into Micronesia, the small islands located largely in the North Pacific, and Polynesia, the islands of the South Pacific. In this case, the larger islands of Fiji, New Caledonia, and the New Hebrides, generally included in Melanesia, are also part of the subregion. Physically they can be divided into high (volcanic) and low (coral) islands. The islands vary in size from a few acres to 210 square miles (544 square kilometers) in the case of Guam and an even larger area in Samoa and Fiji. Western Samoa, Fiji, and Naaru are independent countries as are Tonga, Tuvalu, Kiribati, and the Solomon Islands. The rest of the islands remain colonies of France, United Kingdom, New Zealand, and the United States. Former Japanese Micronesia is administered as a trust territory by the United States.

There is limited development on most of the islands. Copra, coconut, and other fibers are the major commercial crops. Tourism is a major source of income in Tahiti and on some of the other islands. Military bases (such as on Guam and Midway) can be a major source of employment, and military personnel form a major market for tourism and other services. Indirectly, the military are a source of raw material as used and abandoned equipment, packing cases, clothing, and transport equipment become absorbed into the local economy and/or used in crafts.

Population pressure is often great, and local resource bases are insufficiently diverse to encourage new economic endeavors. Outside tourism, a few highly localized mineral deposits, and coconuts, there appears to be little future development possible on most islands.

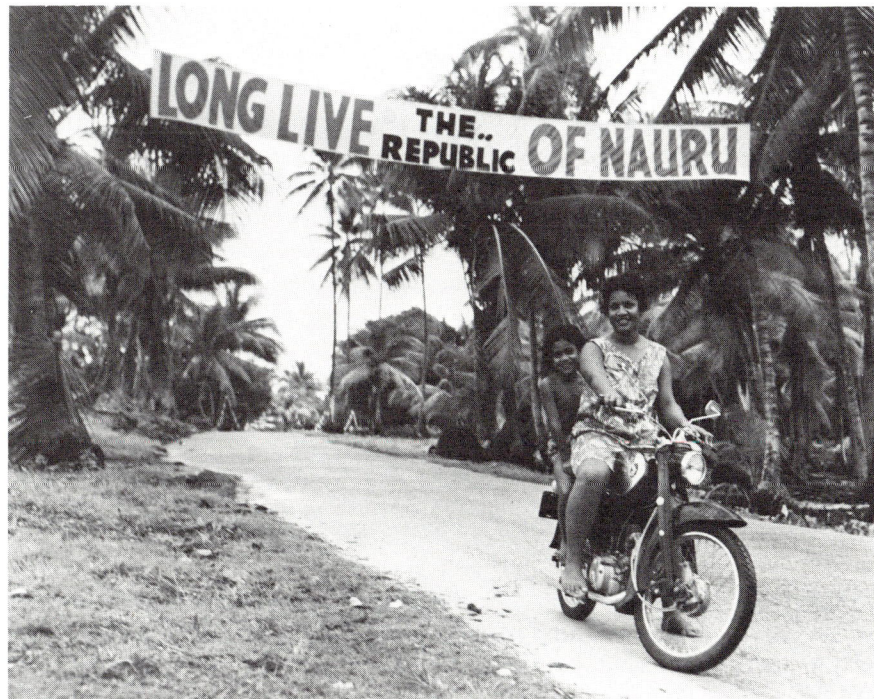

Nauru. Independence was a deservedly joyful moment for Nauru, but, like many of its independent island-group neighbors, the long-term economic prospects may be less happy. Nauruans enjoy a high income from their phosphate mines, but that resource will eventually be depleted, leaving few other sources of income other than accumulated savings and investments. (Courtesy of United Nations)

TENSIONAL RELATIONSHIPS

Distance, isolation, cultural distinctiveness, and relatively sparse population have been dominant features of this region's self-image and relationships with near neighbors (but alien cultures) and distant (but culturally close) "cousins." Neighboring Southeast Asians and somewhat more distant South and East Asians have been viewed, quite literally, as undesirable aliens. Traditionally, Australia and New Zealand's ties have been close to Britain. For most of their history, this region's two largest nations have had minimal trade relationships with their near neighbors; indeed, surprisingly little considering relative distance. Immigration policy long favored Britons and Irish, with exclusionary policies towards Asians. This so-called **white Australia policy** was never totally exclusionary; about 5 percent of new arrivals to Australia come from Asia and Africa. The policy has historic roots in the gold rush days when the Chinese population was increasing at a rapid rate and when the importations of Melanesian and Polynesian cheap labor (*Kanakas*) was disrupting the economy. The small-scale relaxation of this white Australia policy is a gesture of friendly relations toward Asia more than a major shift in policy.

There is no way that Asian population pressure could be significantly relieved by even a "wide open" immigration policy. The image of an "empty" Australia, temptingly close to a teeming Asia, is not realistic, environmentally, if it is sometimes politically attractive within Asia. The continent has quite limited resources in both cultivable land and water. Australia most probably could not comfortably accommodate two or three times its present population on a comparable living standard. Even tripling Australia's present 15 million people by admitting 30 million immigrants would hardly begin to solve the overpopulation problem of Asia, and it would definitely not benefit Australia to have such a sudden surge in population. New Zealand never had the dramatic "invasion" of Asian and Melanesian-Polynesian miners and laborers that so startled Australia; it has maintained an almost homogeneous ethnic population aside from the Maoris. Australia began to admit, and even recruit "new" immigrants (those from Europe not counting the British Isles) after World War II. The greatest number of immigrants is still from Britain, but Germans, Scandinavians, and Italians, all present since the 1870's, are increasing in the stream of migrants. To these groups are now added migrants from the Netherlands, Poland, Yugoslavia, and Greece. Maltese, Hungarians, Spaniards, and Turks have been coming in larger numbers as well. Of the one fifth of Australians who were foreign-born at the 1971 census, 42 percent were from the British Isles, 43 percent from other European countries, and the rest predominantly from Asia.

THE REGION'S WORLD VIEW

Militarily, the dependence of Australia and New Zealand on Britain ended early in World War II. The capture of Britain's main Southeast Asian naval base at Singapore by the Japanese and the Japanese invasion of New Guinea and the Solomon Islands meant that Britain could not defend its dependents in this region. Literally overnight, the United States supplanted Britain as the senior partner in the defense of Australia and New Zealand. The United States fought a bloody and unwinnable delaying action in the Battle of the Coral Sea essentially to give Australia time to complete its defense preparations. The alliance of Australia, New Zealand, and the United States has been close ever since and is basically a nonpartisan policy in the domestic politics of all three nations. There are minor differences of opinion, but the alliance is recognized as key to the area's security. The inability of a faltering British postwar economy to maintain high rates of investment in its commonwealth partners, and growing investment from the United States, especially in Australia, helped seal the shift from Britain to the United States as benevolent "big brother." For New Zealand, the loss of British markets occasioned by Britain's entry into the EEC was more serious than it was for Australia.

The relationship of this region with Japan is a complex and controversial one. While many "new" Australians, arriving after World War II, may care little about the war period in the Pacific area, older Australians vividly remember the Japanese occupation of New Guinea, only 100 miles (160 kilometers) from Australia. Wartime experiences are sufficiently remembered that Japan has an uneasy, if mutually profitable, trade relationship with Australia. As is true of its postwar trade relations with the United States, particularly with Alaska, Japan has developed a kind of economic colonial relationship with Australia. Some of Australia's natural resources have been increasingly exploited with the involvement of Japanese capital and technology and destined for a Japanese market. Japanese manufactured goods are more apparent every year throughout the entire region. The United Kingdom has been a diminishing trade partner for both Australia and New Zealand since the end of World War II, while Japanese trade has recently been on the upswing. In the Australian economy, Japan is the largest overseas market for exports and ranks second as a source of imports. The People's Republic of China is the largest single customer for Australian wheat. The United States supplies 20 percent of Australia's imports.

In the economy of New Zealand, Japan rivals the United Kingdom as a source of both imports and exports, a close second in each instance. While New Zealand's agricultural surpluses and Australia's mineral resources and agricultural surpluses would appear to make them natural trading partners with Japan (the closest heavily industrialized, but resource-poor, state), some unpleasant memories still cloud this relationship. Still, the war is long over; the alliances of Australia and New Zealand with the United States, the United Kingdom, and Malaysia and Singapore are not directed at Japan; and a prospering, democratic Japan is definitely in the interests of Australia-Oceania.

Papua New Guinea's healthy economy, balanced budget, and low external debt is made possible largely by the generosity of Australia and New Zealand who provide foreign aid to the sum of 40 percent of PNG's budget.

Australia considers it essential that its nearest neighbor be a friendly and democratic state. Japan also provides a small subsidy to PNG to smooth the way for its investments in timber, fishing, agriculture, and tourism. Australia and New Zealand share the United States' hopes that PNG will become a regional leader among developing countries and maintain its friendly cooperation with the Western cultures of the region.

Australians and New Zealanders are realigning their global thinking. Their futures would seem to lie within an expanding Pacific basin economy in which Japan and the United States are major partners.

case study
PROBLEMS IN PARADISE—TWO ISLAND COUNTRIES IN RAPID CHANGE

The long-held western perception of the South Pacific islands as an unspoiled paradise is far from accurate. Many of these islands are currently experiencing the problems familiar elsewhere: rapid expansion of population; overdependence on world market prices for a narrow range of agricultural exports; a deteriorating environment due to resource exploitation, erosion, and mismanagement; and escalating prices for imported manufactured goods. Two tiny states serve as samples of the array of problems facing these island countries with uncertain futures.

The Kingdom of Tonga is an archipelago of about 150 islands, of which 45 are inhabited, in the South Pacific. The islands are mainly either uplifted coral platforms or volcanic bases covered with coral limestone. The largest island, site of the capital city of Nuku'alofa, is 99 square miles (256 square kilometers) in size. The Tongans are Polynesians with a very small admixture of Melanesians; there are also a few Europeans and some other Pacific islanders. The Tongans have a royal tradition of 1,000 years of Tongan monarchs, whose power once extended to Hawaii, 3,000 miles (4,800 kilometers) away. The island kingdom was a protectorate of Britain from 1900 to 1970. It is now fully independent with friendly economic relationships with Britain, New Zealand, and Australia. The economy is largely non-cash, subsistence agriculture and fishing. Coconuts and bananas are the main export crops; processing coconuts into copra and dried coconut meat is the only industry other than handicrafts. The copra industry is plagued by wild fluctuations in world market prices; long-range economic planning is very difficult. Banana exports are handicapped by plant diseases, high prices for necessary fertilizers, and high costs of refrigerated long-distance shipment. The annual growth rate of population is 2.6 percent, higher than the world average and especially serious in view of the very limited area. The constitution guarantees each adult male an 8.5 acre (3.44 hectares) tract for subsistence, but population pressures mean that even this small plot either must get smaller or large numbers must emigrate or crowd into Tonga's one urban area, Nuku'alofa, population 25,000.

The Tongans are trying to diversify their economy by developing a commercial fishing industry based on tuna by using their forests and over-age coconut plantations for wood, and by encouraging tourism. Cruise ships now call at Nuku'alofa, and tourism could be greatly expanded. The Tongans are also raising more cattle to reduce beef imports, and there are some signs of minor oil deposits that are being explored. Tonga remains very dependent on New Zealand economically, and New Zealand is responsible for Tongan defense. The present stable royal government may be challenged by a rising sophistication on the part of the people, coupled with a population already outstripping the agricultural support capacity of the islands.

The Republic of Naaru, an island about halfway between Sidney, Australia, and Honolulu, is fabulously wealthy by Tongan standards and even developed world standards. Naaru's per capita income averages about $13,000, the highest of any developing country outside the Persian Gulf oil sheikdoms; Tonga's per capita income is only about $430, and Tonga produces most of its own food, including vegetables, fruits, starches, pigs, and chickens; Naaru has virtually no agriculture. Naaru is essentially a plateau of high quality phosphate rock, used in fertilizers. This is fringed by a sandy beach and arable belt around the island. The sole industry is phosphate mining, which provides the only export. Practically everything is imported, mostly from Australia and New Zealand. The island has a very high population growth rate, 3.8 percent, with two thirds of the people native Naaruans. Once a German colony (1888–1914), the island became a protectorate of Australia, New Zealand, and Great Britain (Australia exercised administrative control). Naaru became independent in 1968, one of the tiniest states in both population (then 8,000) and area (8 square miles [21 square kilometers]). The future of the economy is extremely bleak, as the present rate of exploitation will exhaust the phosphate rock reserves in about a dozen more years. A long-term trust fund has been established to hold the two thirds of mineral income that is being saved to provide future income for Naaruans. The government has also invested in an airline (Air Naaru), and the Naaru Pacific Shipping Line, a modern office skyscraper in Australia. As a country without taxes of any kind, Naaru could become an international haven for corporate offices and banks if its isolation is overcome by modern communication and transport, and if it builds a reputation for a solid and stable political climate.

REVIEW QUESTIONS

1   Why was Australia originally viewed negatively for European colonization?

2   Why have Australia and New Zealand developed technologically sophisticated, large-scale agriculture as export suppliers?

3   How has the significance of distance to Europe changed over time? Distance to East Asia?

4   What is meant by the "empty heart" of Australia?

5   Briefly describe the mechanisms and effects of tropical marine climates.

6   What is the physiological basis of the popular perception of the tropical Pacific islands as "paradise?" Are they an economic-cultural paradise to their inhabitants?

7   In what way is the Australian choice of a new capital similar to the situations of Washington, D.C., and Ottawa?

8   Why are import-replacement industries part of Australia and New Zealand's development strategy? Has this strategy worked?

9   Why does the international trade importance of Australia and New Zealand far out-rank their relative population size?

10   How is the prevalent Australian attitude toward exploitation of the environment related to population density and resource base?

11   Briefly describe the mineral resource bases of the major states of this region.

12   How did Britain's membership in the European Economic Community affect the. trade patterns of Australia and New Zealand?

13   Why are Australia and Indonesia relatively uneasy neighbors? How does Papua New Guinea add to tensions here?

14   Why did Australia strictly control in-migration for many years, strongly favoring Europeans?

15   Why did a close American alliance suddenly replace Australia's and New Zealand's former reliance on a British military shield?

16   In what way is this region an economic hinterland in relation to the developed economies of Japan and the United States?

SUGGESTED READINGS

1   HAROLD BROOKFIELD, ed., *The Pacific in Transition: Geographical Perspectives on Adaptation and Change.* New York: St. Martin's, 1973.

2   H. C. BROOKFIELD and D. DART, *Melanesia: A Geographical Interpretation of an Island World.* London: Methuen, 1971.

3   ANDREW CLARK, *The Invasion of New Zealand by People, Plants and Animals: The South Island.* New Brunswick: Rutgers University Press, 1949.

4   KENNETH CUMBERLAND and J. S. WHITELAW, *New Zealand.* Chicago: Aldine, 1970.

5   KENNETH CUMBERLAND, *Southwest Pacific: A Geography of Australia, New Zealand and Their Pacific Island Neighborhoods.* London: Methuen, 1958.

6   M. LEVINSON, R. WARD, and J. WEBB, *The Settlement of Polynesia.* Minneapolis: University of Minnesota Press, 1977.

7   TOM MCKNIGHT, *Australia's Corner of the World.* Englewood Cliffs, N.J.: Prentic Hall, 1970.

8   DONALD MEINIG, *On the Margins of the Good Earth: The South Australian Wheat Frontier, 1869–1884.* Chicago: Rand McNally, 1963.

9   JAMES PERKINS, *Australia in the World Economy.* Melbourne: Sun, 1968.

10   K. W. ROBINSON, *Australia, New Zealand and the Southwest Pacific.* London: University of London Press, 1974.

11   O. H. K. SPATE, *Australia.* New York: Praeger, 1968.

KEY TERMS

- complementarity
- leaching of nutrients
- hardpan formation
- compressional stress
- centripetal tendency
- development enclave
- neocolonial
- monsoonal
- intertropical convergence
- balkanization
- enclave
- overcapacity

- nation-state
- import-replacement
- transport infrastructure
- centrifugal force
- magnetic anomaly
- irredenta
- exclave
- acculturation
- apartheid
- detribalization
- Bantustans
- developmental differential
- loyalties set

12

AFRICA SOUTH OF THE SAHARA

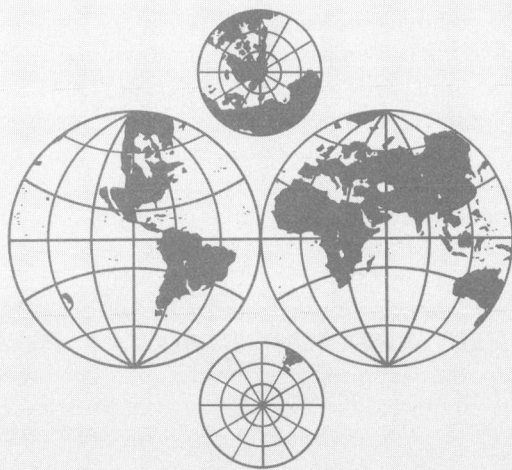

PROLOGUE: FROM COLONIAL SPHERE TO INDEPENDENCE: THE STRESSES OF RAPID CHANGE

Africa south of the Sahara is an extremely diverse region in its human, physical, economic, and cultural geography. Most of the people of this part of the earth, commonly called Black Africa, would be characterized as Negroids, but there are strong Caucasoid elements evident in such groups as the Ethiopians and recent Caucasian migrants to southern and eastern Africa.

The earlier European exploration of the interior of the New World may have contributed to the once-common view that Africa was very mysterious. Topographical and climatic factors functioned as handicaps to easy penetration of the interior from the seacoast. Many of Africa's great rivers are not navigable very far upstream from their mouths; rapids and waterfalls bar the way up the great Congo (Zaire) River, while shifting sandbars and mudflats characterize the sluggish distributaries of most West African rivers. The caravan routes across the Sahara were far too difficult for the novice; the Sahara clearly *was* passable to trade caravans but certainly not an easy route.

By the middle of the eighteenth century, Europeans knew far more about the Great Lakes and Mississippi River than about the Niger, the Congo, or the Nile. The source of the White Nile (Lake Victoria on the Equator) was not known to the Western world until 1862; the Congo Basin was not explored by Europeans until 1876. Well into the nineteenth century, Westerners were confused about which direction the Niger River flowed or where it entered the sea.

A striking reorientation of trade routes and intercultural contacts occurred from the sixteenth to the nineteenth centuries. The effects were as important in northern and western Africa as they were throughout Europe and the Arab world. European exploration refocused trade routes away from the Mediterranean and toward the open Atlantic. The ancient, difficult trans-Saharan routes were superceded by the much faster sea routes, and the trade of the Sahel and the Guinea coast was reoriented to the Atlantic coast, not across the Sahara (see Figure 12–1). The Sahelian empires of Mali and Songhay, based on gold mining and trans-Saharan trade, fell at about the time that trade shifted toward sea routes. The power and organizational and technological achievements of the African kingdoms were unknown or forgotten. An Arab historian had noted that eleventh century Ghana could field two hundred thousand warriors (William the Conqueror needed about fifteen thousand to take England at about the same time). It is probable that a good amount of gold circulating in Mediterranean trade originated in West Africa

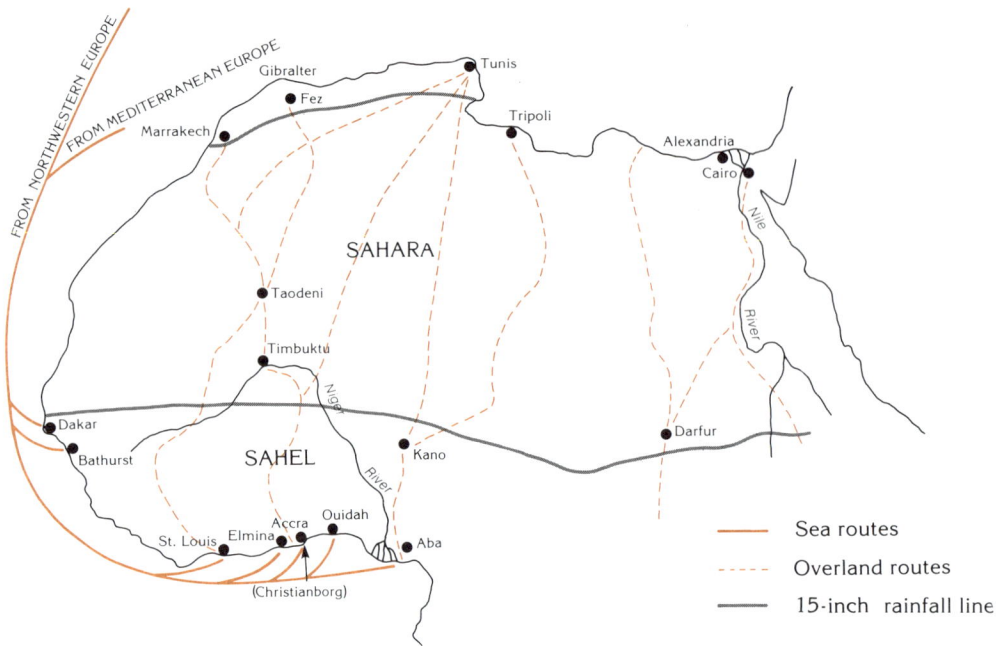

FIGURE 12–1
Sahara-Sahel-Atlantic Coast Trade Routes. The exploration of the western coast of Africa by Europeans, beginning in the fifteenth century, eventually established direct ocean trade routes to the coast between Dakar and Cameroon, which effectively outflanked the earlier established land routes from the Mediterranean across the Sahara.

before the sixteenth century, and Africans certainly knew mining and metal-working techniques. Great African states fell because of the trans-Sahara invasions of Arab peoples, the seaborne invasions of Europeans, and the unprecedented scale of the slave trade after 1600. The power and glory melted away and were nearly forgotten in the ensuing European colonial land-grab. Africa south of the Sahara might now qualify as the least understood major region in terms of its cultural geography and history, just as a century and a half ago it would have been among the least known in physical geography.

THE GRAND IMPERIAL SCHEMES

Each colonizer stationed troops within colonial empires at strategic points. A transportation network was necessary to successful troop deployment. Once such military justification could be proven, funds could be obtained for investment in great highways, railroads, and river improvement schemes. Auxiliary support came from entrepreneurs who envisioned settlement and economic development in the wake of solid military control.

The Cape-to-Cairo Railroad Perhaps nothing else so exemplified the dreams of European imperialism in late nineteenth century Africa as the never-completed Cape-to-Cairo railroad. It was envisioned by British South African

diamond and gold merchant Cecil Rhodes, who had both the wealth and political influence to actually drive a railway north from South Africa into then-wild country later designated as Northern and Southern Rhodesia (see Figure 12–2). Rhodes saw the Cape-to-Cairo as the backbone of an immense African empire controlled by Britain. The two termini were already controlled, directly or indirectly, by Britain, and the rail systems were growing in both Egypt and southern Africa. Britain's (or at least Rhodes') grand design for an African empire conflicted with the imperial ambitions of France and Germany. Rhodes was determined to outflank the evolving French and German territorial objectives, then jelling into firm territorial claims.

Transcontinental railroads were a common tool of imperial control and development; railroads would quickly deliver troops, but would also support colonial settlement and foster economic development.

Considering the scale of the ambition, the problems of terrain and climate along the proposed route, and the fact that Britain did not control Tanganyika until World War I, it is amazing how close the British came to completing their Cape-to-Cairo Railroad. Rhodes' railroad drove to the Congo (Zaire) border, and a railroad was pushed southward in the Sudan from Khartoum. The Cape-to-Cairo is unlikely to ever be completed as the East African empire it was to serve no longer exists, and road and air services can connect the remaining links.

FIGURE 12–2

Cape–to–Cairo Railroad (Proposed) and Major African Rail Lines. British imperial ambitions, specifically those of Cecil Rhodes, envisioned a north-south transcontinental railroad as the "backbone" of a British-dominated East African empire. While never completed, the "Cape-to-Cairo" dream did spur railroad building over much of the proposed route.

PROBLEMS OF REGIONAL UNITY

Africa south of the Sahara is characterized by enormous diversity in cultural, historical, economic, and physical terms. The great number of political units suggests this strongly, yet these units reflect the territorial divisions of European colonial powers rather more than cultural groupings, historically evolved entities or physical regions. In a sense, this region is just beginning to fuse as a region, at least in the perceptions of its people. While animosity toward the colonial power may have temporarily united diverse peoples in the struggle for independence, in the aftermath the basic internal diversity of the new states reappeared. Linguistic, tribal, and religious lines were ignored in plotting colonial boundaries, leading to many potential conflicts, both internal and international. The search for unifying factors reveals the basic diversity of its parts. Yet even the nearly universal problems of national unity and internal conflict are in a sense a common ground for the regional designation.

Accra, Ghana. The Portuguese Fort on the horizon dates from the sixteenth century European contacts that quickly accelerated to colonialism. The impacts of colonialism, cultural as well as political and economic, are still apparent throughout Africa. (Courtesy of United Nations)

THE COLONIAL EXPERIENCE AS A COMMON BACKGROUND

The recency of European colonial domination is a major common experience, and the reaction against it, a unifying factor. The colonial legacy, in both its positive and negative aspects, is still an important influence in the area's economics and politics. A map of Africa in 1948 (see Figure 12–3) would have shown essentially the same independent states, colonies, protectorates, and other externally ruled states as a similar map in 1914. On the 1948 map, only Liberia and Ethiopia were fully independent states in Africa south of the Sahara. (South Africa, a self-governing state in the British Commonwealth at the time, had not extended full citizenship rights to its black majority.) Yet, by 1961, (see Figure 12–3) the bulk of the continent was independent. The suddenness with which most of Africa achieved freedom from colonial control is matched only by the preceding spectacular explosion of European territorial control in the second half of the nineteenth century. Excluding both northern and southern extremities, the African continent was not colonized through direct territorial claim and control until the period 1870 through 1900. For the majority of Africa south of the Sahara, the colonial experience lasted less than a century. In contrast, most of the Americas had a colonial status lasting some two or three centuries or more. To be sure, advances in transport and communications helped make the African colonial experience an active agent of cultural change and economic development despite its shorter span.

Up until 1870, European interests in Africa were peripheral, literally and figuratively. Trade with Asia and the Americas was far more lucrative till then; Africa south of the Sahara was seen as a series of coastal forts and trade stations on the way to India and the Orient before the Suez Canal opened in 1867. The coastal area between the Gambia River and Angola had been brutally exploited in the slave trade; the region's main export from 1500 to 1800 had been people in chains. It was the attitude of ruthless expansion of the slave trade, combined with general ignorance of the geography of the interior, that retarded interest in more comprehensive economic development.

The Role and Scope of the African Slave Trade   It is probable that 20 million people were taken from West Africa alone and some 50 million from the entire continent during the period of intensive European participation in the slave trade (1600–1800). The tragedy of this trade was not restricted to the huge numbers actually exported. Slaving both resulted from and encouraged tribal warfare; prisoners were sold to Arab or African traders who took the slaves to coastal stations maintained by Europeans. The intertribal wars related to the slave trade helped to depopulate whole districts. While Arab slavers had carried off relatively small numbers of Africans, mostly from the north and east of Africa, for a thousand years, the much larger scale of European slaving amounted to a hemorrhage of population from which Africa is still recovering in some senses.

It is ironic that some of the first land claims extending into the interior of West Africa were made on behalf of freed slaves. The end of slavery throughout the British Empire in 1807 was the beginning of the end for the slave

AFRICA — 1948

▨ Independent states

SPANISH IFNI
SPANISH SAHARA
ALGERIA
FRENCH SOMALILAND
GAMBIA
PORTUGUESE GUINEA
SPANISH GUNIEA
UGANDA
RWANDA
BURUNDI
KENYA
N. RHODESIA
NYASALAND
MOZAMBIQUE
ANGOLA

AFRICA — 1961

▨ Non-independent states

S.W. AFRICA
BECHUANALAND
SWAZILAND
S. RHODESIA
BASUTOLAND

FIGURE 12–3
Independent States, 1948 and 1961. Independence came with almost startling rapidity in Africa following World War II. In 1948, independent states were the exception; by 1961, European control had vanished from the bulk of the continent.

trade. Sierra Leone was chosen as a refuge for freed slaves from Britain in 1787. After Britain abolished its own slave trade, it embarked on a crusade to eradicate the trade entirely. British naval vessels patrolled the West African coast, intercepting slave ships, freeing prisoners and setting them ashore at Freetown in Sierra Leone.

In 1816, the American Colonization Society was granted a congressional charter to send freed slaves back to West Africa. The first ex-slaves from the United States arrived at present-day Monrovia in Liberia in 1822. In 1847, Liberia became the first independent republic in Africa.

The African Land Rush   Events in West Europe triggered the race for territory in the late nineteenth century. The triumph of the German Empire at the conclusion of the Franco-Prussian War (1870–71) resulted in German determination to enter the race for tropical colonies. It also induced a humiliated France to seek alternative evidence of power and glory by acquiring huge new colonial territories, primarily in Africa. Also, the major industrializing powers decided to develop legitimate trade to compensate both Africans and Europeans for abolishing the slave trade. Tropical vegetable oils were in high demand for the rising industries of Europe, particularly for soap and candles.

Africa south of the Sahara in 1870 was a temptingly vacant area in the political perceptions of Europeans. European technological superiority in weapons, transport, and communications would make short work of African groups weakened and demoralized by centuries of war and population loss related to the slave trade. The real danger to the Europeans was the possibility that conflicting imperial ambitions in Africa could set off another war among them. For example, France was building an African empire by following the relatively easy route of the navigable Senegal River to the interior, then down the Niger Valley and overland to Lake Chad, with northward penetrations from the Guinea coast. This strategy was in support of a drive to establish a continuous east-west sweep across northern Africa (see Figure 12–4). In contrast, Britain's grand strategy was to link British-dominated Egypt with its Cape Colony in southern Africa, forming a "British backbone" the north-south length of the continent. Portuguese control of the coasts of Angola and Mozambique supported a vague claim to the interior between those opposite coasts, and Germany envisioned an east-west link between its colonies in Tanganyika and Cameroon.

The practice of arranging treaties with "kings" or chiefs (who may or may not have had the right to repre-

sent African interests or understood the implications of the treaty), together with only a vague notion of inland geography, led to an international conference at Berlin in 1885. It was international only in a provincial sense—it was attended solely by European states active in African colonization (the United States sent an "observer" but did not attempt to grab any African territory). No Africans were invited. At this Berlin conference, international boundaries were drawn and spheres of influence recognized. Belgium's King Leopold's, claim to the Congo Basin was recognized by the major European powers largely because it made a good buffer between their conflicting claims. No major power wanted any other major power to control the heart of the continent. (See Figure 12–4.)

The effect of colonial imposition of boundaries by European states has had lasting effects on the now independent states. Many, especially in West Africa, are unrealistically small in territory and/or population. They may have serious problems surviving in a world dominated by superpowers. Africa's large territorial units, such as Nigeria and Zaire, have had problems of internal struggles that led to civil war. Black African nationalism has become a major force, perhaps *the* force, for African unity and cohesion as a world region.

ECONOMIC PROBLEMS IN COMMON

In many ways the economic framework of Africa south of the Sahara is the result of the colonial experience as well. The economy coexists at two levels: one the precommercial or subsistence agricultural economy and the other an export-oriented production of plantation and mine. The former, the traditional African means of livelihood, employs the bulk of the population yet contributes little to economic growth; the latter, introduced under colonialism, employs relatively few yet provides the bulk of capital for development. While this is a normal pattern for underdeveloped areas, nowhere is it so startlingly visible as in this region. Each economy is geared to the outside; transport systems are separated from that of other states and almost solely limited to moving export goods. High demand items from only the richest deposits seem the only commodities shippable because of relative cost and isolation. Commercial agriculture ships vegetable oils, tropical fruits, fibers, spices, and coffee or tea—also high-value, high-demand items capable of bearing shipment costs.

There is no unity of production, nor **complementarity** within and among African states. The unity (or homogeneity) is one of the colonial nature of the goods shipped and the orientation to export markets in developed areas. Even the surplus grain and meat of a relatively modern and well-

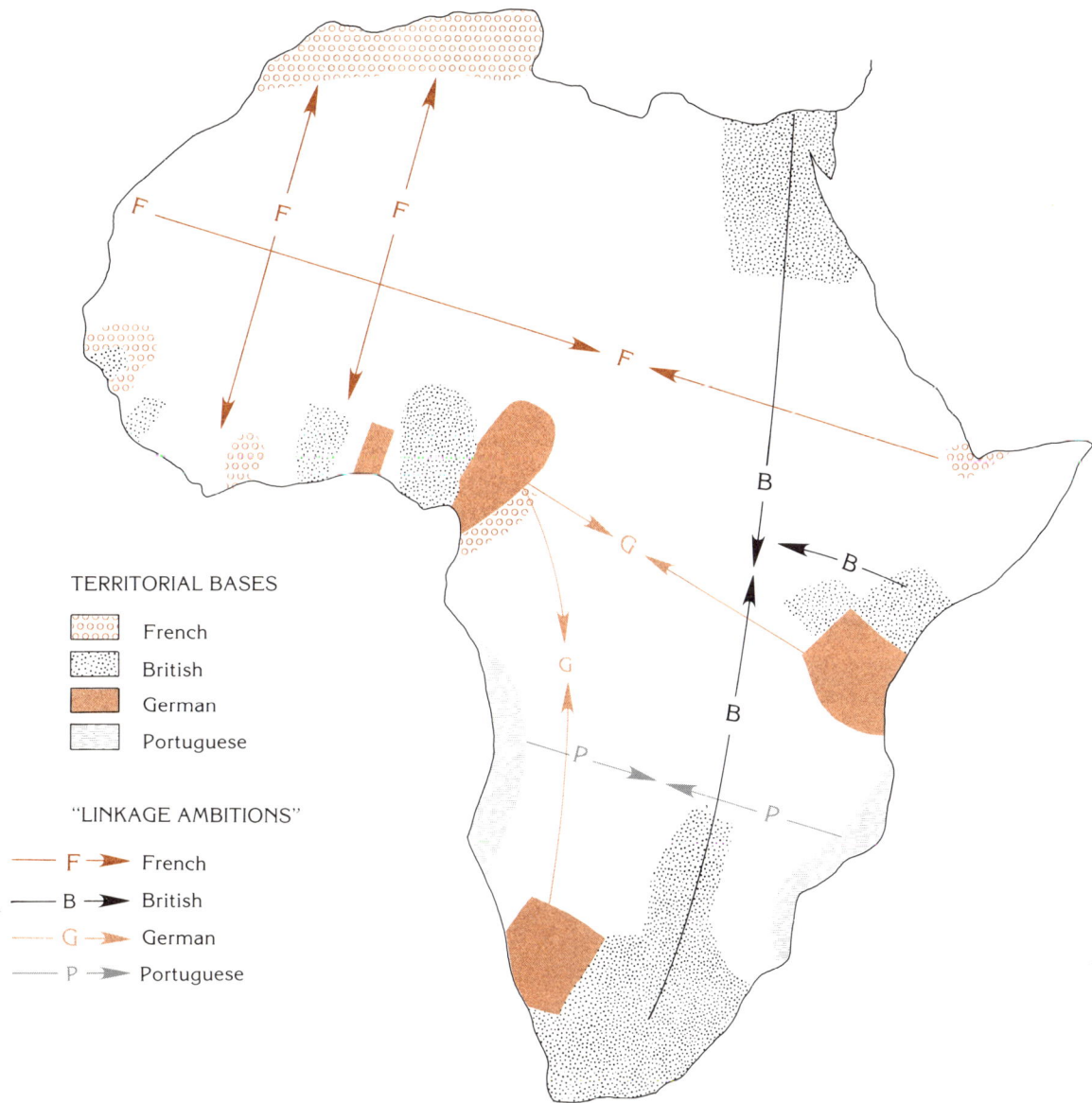

FIGURE 12–4
Imperial Ambitions in Africa, Late Nineteenth Century. The race for territory in Africa became an arena of great power competition. Conflicting ambitions, particularly concerning the Congo Basin, led to an international conference at which the Congo Basin was awarded to Belgium's king as a buffer amongst great power colonial claims.

developed South African farm economy enters the export market, and even there the use of labor and style of farming is distinctly that of a plantation—vast acreages using hired seasonal labor to produce crops primarily for export.

In the realm of tropical agricultural products, these states cannot determine prices; they compete with one another. A rise in prices brings vast acreages of a single crop into production; the oversupply that results in a few years depresses prices in a boom or bust cycle. Imported commodities and goods tend to remain at relatively high prices. African economies are frequently overspecialized in one or two export crops and entire economies fluctuate radically with crop prices.

Another disadvantage of overspecialization is the tendency to increase disease and insect damage. By creating ideal conditions for crop production, producers inadvertently create ideal conditions for parasites who thrive on that crop as well as for bacteria, molds, and viruses that attack those crops. If the dip in world prices doesn't ruin such an economy, insects and disease frequently will.

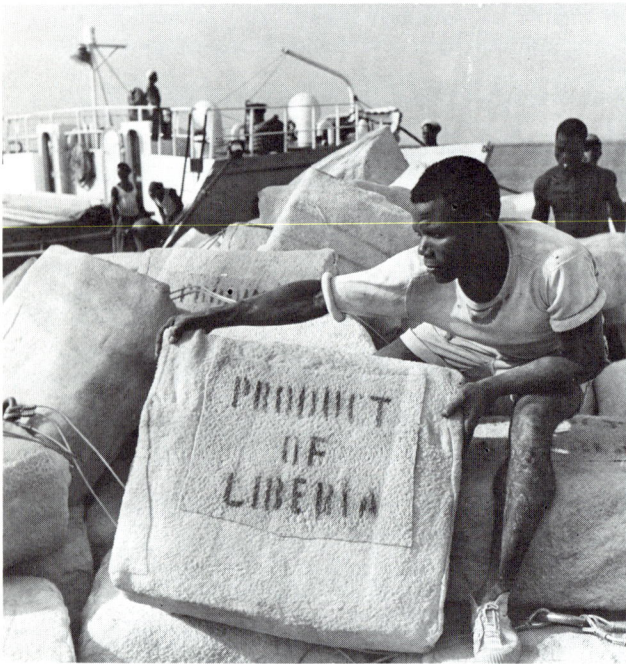

Loading Crude Rubber at Monrovia, Liberia. Tropical commodities, such as natural rubber, are often produced on plantations; entire national economies may be vulnerable to price fluctuations in foreign markets. (Courtesy of United Nations)

PHYSICAL CHARACTERISTICS

While diversity of physical landforms and climatic type are the rule, some physical similarities are obvious and relatively uniform throughout the area. One is a near universal poverty of soils. In the areas of constantly high rainfall, soils are impoverished by a constant **leaching** (rinsing) **of nutrients** from the upper levels where plant roots can reach them to lower soil levels where they are unavailable to crop plants. In areas of alternating wet and dry seasons, there are soil impoverishing problems of **hardpan formation**—a subsurface concretion of minerals, which disrupts wet season drainage and interferes with soil water storage properties during the dry season.

In either case, soils are rich in iron, silica, and aluminum—elements not particularly needed for plant growth, and poor in the calcium, potassium, nitrogen, and phosphorous that constitute plant food. Precommercial agriculture traditionally solved this problem by long periods of fallow between crops and periodic burning of vegetation (shifting agriculture). Increasing population reduces the length of fallow (noncropping) periods and, inadvertently, decreases the availability of plant nutrients and contributes to erosion.

WHAT MAKES THIS REGION DISTINCTIVE?

The relative recency and swift decline of colonialism in this region sets it apart from all others. The intense, all-encompassing influences of colonialism are all too obvious. Here, history appears to be compressed in time. Things happen, and have happened, rapidly. Whereas nationalism and a system of states have evolved over centuries elsewhere, the entire tribe-to-colony-to-state sequence of events has occurred in less than one hundred years. The result of these **compressional stresses** has been

Conakry, Guinea. Africa south of the Sahara is one of the world's least densely populated, industrialized or urbanized regions. All of these factors are changing rapidly, however, subjecting the region's people to compressional stresses. (Courtesy of United Nations)

Manganese Mine in Gabon. Many African states' economies are based on the export of minerals developed through foreign investment or foreign loans. Many Africans perceive a "neocolonial" relationship with the developed world, and resent it. (Courtesy of United Nations)

many states with diverse populations that have no clear sense of loyalties to state, government, or even one another.

Too, the developmental disparity between well-developed enclaves and their matrix of primitive economic level is nowhere more obvious. With it are found accompanying **centripetal tendencies.** Each **development enclave** is less related to any other enclave within the state and more related to the developed world outside.

Lastly, the area suffers a kind of **neocolonial** existence. Most African states are deeply indebted to developed countries and to international agencies that supply developmental funds. The inability of the domestic economies to generate capital, plus the dependence on conditions and markets outside Africa south of the Sahara is nearly uniformly felt. Technically independent, they are far from

sovereign in economic terms. This is best shown in the continued dependence of most African states on former colonial markets and sources of supply. Even where new outside markets and supply sources are achieved, there is the tendency for those new sources to interfere in domestic affairs—economically, politically, and even militarily. Any citizen of Africa south of the Sahara might well wonder what the differences really are between colonial control and independence.

THE PHYSICAL FRAME

Africa south of the Sahara is a huge shield area that rises abruptly above the sea in most places to a high inland surface. Almost totally within the tropics, it is characteristically hot except at higher elevations. From its equatorial center toward north and south, the precipitation decreases in total and increases in seasonality. Aspect and elevation modify climates over rather large areas.

Less is known of African geology and environmental conditions than of any other continent. A deceptively simple surface and regular climatic regime contain myriad exceptions.

TOPOGRAPHY

Most of interior Africa south of the Sahara is a plateau surface that averages 1,000 to 2,000 feet (300 to 600 meters) above sea level north of the equator and somewhat higher (2,000 to 5,000 feet [600 to 1,500 meters] in elevation) south of it. The northern, wetter section has been more thoroughly dissected, resulting in rolling hill country over most of the area with occasional portions that qualify as mountains. The plateau is made of ancient crystalline rock; it has apparently been geologically stable for long periods of time.

Along the northern edge of the region are a series of basins—depressions in the plateau—stretching west to east at the border of the Sahel and savanna vegetational zones. They are the basins of the Upper and Middle Niger, Lake Chad–Bodele, and Bahr el Ghazal. At the juncture of wet and dry climatic zones they are filled in part with swamps, salt lakes, or other water features of shifting, changing size and location. Only their southern margins are located fully within this region.

South of these depressions is a thoroughly dissected plateau country of relatively rugged hills. In the west they are called the Guinea, in the center the Nigerian plateaus, and in the east, the Ubangi-Shari upland. Dissection (and, therefore, relief) is progressively less pronounced from west to east. The Futa Djalon highlands of the western extreme (Guinea) and the Bongos Massif (Central African Republic) in the east are the highest points and the chief source areas of major rivers.

The coastal lowland is fairly well developed along the Atlantic and Gulf of Guinea coasts. It varies from 50 to almost 400 miles (80 to 640 kilometers) in width and is an unusually (by African standards) wide strip of fairly level land.

Interrupting the pattern at the change in coastline orientation from east-west to north-south, there is a diagonal chain of rugged volcanic mountains, the Adamawa highlands. In their southern portion they are submerged under the sea, forming a series of islands from Annobon to Fernando Poo. On land they extend along (or parallel to) the Nigeria-Cameroon border, almost to Lake Chad.

South of the equator the plateau surface is higher, frequently less dissected and somewhat saucerlike in that the edges are higher than the center. Indeed, the center consists of two immense sedimentary basins, the Congo (Zaire) Basin, much lower and older, and the higher basin occupied by the Upper Zambezi and the Kalahari Desert. Along the Atlantic coast the lowland is confined to a narrow coastal strip that rises abruptly to a high plateau surface.

The simplicity of African topography changes abruptly along the eastern and southern edges of these two huge inland basins. Along the eastern side is the rift country, a classic proof of the continental drift (plate tectonic) theory. The continent of Africa is apparently pulling apart, giving rise to a feature known as the Great Rift Valley. (See Figure 12–5.) With its associated bordering highlands, it extends from Mozambique to the Gulf of Aden and continues as the Red Sea to the Sinai peninsula. At the top of Lake Nyasa, the valley divides into two sections; the western is occupied by a series of lakes, the eastern is lined with East Africa's great volcanoes. The intervening plateau area is covered with sediments and in part occupied by Lake Victoria. In its Ethiopian section the highlands spread out to cover most of the country. In the southeast, after disappearing briefly, the rift surfaces again as the Drakensberg Mountains of the South African coast.

Two fringing lowlands edge the coast of eastern Africa, one extending from Durban to Zanzibar, the other from that island to the tip of the African horn. The width of these coastal plains varies from 50 to over 400 miles (80 to 640 kilometers).

The island of Madagascar is a piece of the African continent that has fully separated from the main continental mass. The high mountain core is surrounded by coastal lowlands, broad and well developed on the western side, extremely narrow on the eastern side.

LAND-SEA RELATIONSHIPS

Over much of the coastline of West Africa, mangrove swamps are extending the shoreline seaward. This tangled growth in shallow water yields few good harbors. Most of the best ports of West Africa today are artificial. The mouths of rivers are often silted and suited only to shallow draft vessels. Even along the drier shores south of the Congo (Zaire) River, the proximity of the interior plateau and the lack of good natural harbors hampered trade and penetration. The best harbor development occurs from Cape Town (South Africa) to Maputo (Mozambique), where the plateaus and mountains reach almost to the shore—areas from which penetration into the interior is exceptionally difficult. The eastern coast had sufficient harbors to develop ports, and trade developed largely with the Arabs.

The early European view of Africa was that it was something to "get around" on the way to the Orient. Ships circumnavigating the continent were serviced and supplied from a few strategic harbors and offshore islands.

For Africa south of the Sahara, the sea has been a means of contact with the outside world only in recent times. The closing of the Suez Canal (1967–75) and the consequent reorientation of the oil trade around Africa (many tankers now are too big for Suez) has done little to develop new African sea trade or related functions. The few landlocked African states have come to agreements with surrounding states for the use of ports and transit routes. The volume of trade from most African states is relatively small.

CLIMATE

Little of Africa south of the Sahara extends into the zones of subtropical or temperate climates. However, large parts of southern and eastern Africa are of sufficiently high elevation to experience the cooling influence of altitude. All of the area is warm over most of the year and few areas experience frost; only the West African coast, the Congo Basin, and parts of the coast along the African horn are truly oppressive in heat and humidity.

The rainforest climate with its double seasonal rainfall maximum, high heat and humidity levels, and high yearly rainfall totals occupies a relatively small area from the mouth of the Niger to the mouth of the Congo (Zaire) and inland to the edge of the Great Rift Valley. Annual rainfall totals of from 60 to 120 inches (1,500 to 3,000 millimeters) are common and dry periods are really simply less wet.

Similar conditions are found on the Guinea Coast from Guinea to Abidjan in the Ivory Coast. Here the con-

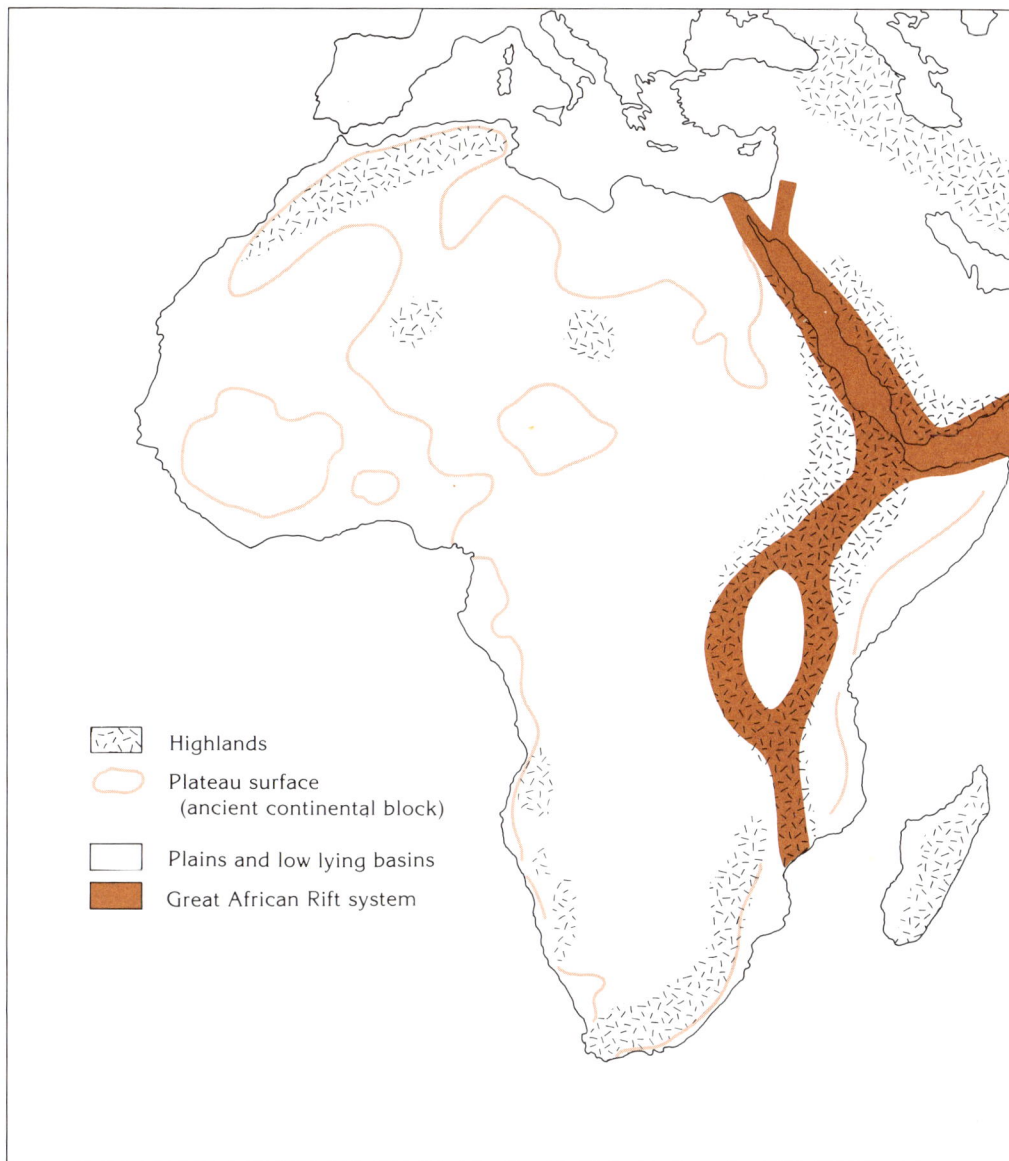

FIGURE 12–5
Generalized Topography. Relatively little of Africa south of the Sahara is in coastal plain; the major exception is in Mozambique. Commonly, the plateau escarpments come close to the sea, and much of Africa has a relatively simple coastline with few natural harbors. Its rivers are seldom easily navigable as mangrove swamp and sandbars mark their mouths, and rapids and waterfalls block navigation further upstream.

ditions differ in that they are **monsoonal.** The dry season is pronounced but brief, and rainfall totals compare with those of the rainforest proper.

On either side of this narrow belt of perpetually hot and humid climate is a belt of tropical savanna climate with a dry winter and hot-humid summer. Rain is brought by the poleward movement of the **intertropical convergence** following the migration of the direct rays of the sun. The dry season is longer and more pronounced the farther

removed from the equator. Along the northern edge of this belt, the climate is transitional into steppe and even desert conditions in an area of highly irregular precipitation. On the southern side of the rainforest the savanna climate penetrates farther poleward. The coasts are dry, but the interior plateau receives sufficient radiation to develop convectional storms in the summer. Rainfall totals vary from 20 to 80 inches annually (500 to 2,000 millimeters), and rainfall is more reliable than in the northern savanna even if it is still generally limited to a three- to five-month period. Altitude (south and east of Zaire) modifies the climate sufficiently to alleviate some discomfort of heat. Monthly temperature averages range from 60°F (15°C) in the cool, dry season to the not uncomfortable levels of the mid-70's F (22°C) in the warmer summer season of the rains. Only in Zaire, Mozambique, and the coast of Tanzania or in lower valleys do the heat and humidity normally associated with this climate type become the average condition.

South of the Angola-Zambia-Zimbabwe border the climate becomes steppelike. Rainfall totals fall below 20 inches (500 millimeters) yearly and the rainy season is compressed into a period of two to four months. Cloudiness is rare (10 percent of the days) and humidity levels are quite low at all times. Unlike the Sahel, rainfall is less variable. The Kalahari Desert is more a semi-desert; truly arid conditions are limited to the coast and the northwestern portion of the Republic of South Africa.

The Republic of South Africa, south of the Tropic of Capricorn, experiences truly temperate conditions. There is a definite winter with some frost danger over a three-month period. Even the higher areas, however, are sufficiently close to the sea to experience moderating maritime effects. The Cape of Good Hope area has a Mediterranean regime with dry, hot summers and mild, rainy winters. The eastern highlands and the eastern coast of South Africa have humid subtropical conditions with year-round rain; short, cool winters and hot summers on the coast, if pleasant ones in the higher interior.

The African horn often appears on maps as an area of either deserts (coastal) or undifferentiated highland climate (interior). Rugged mountains in Ethiopia exhibit a vertical zonation of climate, similar to that found in the highlands of Middle and South America. Aspect, as much as altitude, influences the source and amount of rainfall. At times (and in certain places), monsoonal winds bring moisture in off the Indian Ocean. More commonly, the northward movement of the intertropical convergence brings heavy summer rain. Seasonal and yearly rainfall variability is great.

The hot, humid but almost rainless Danakil coast of Eritrea is often classified as desert. It has at least a discontinuous vegetational cover that makes parts of it appear more like semi-desert.

Madagascar, an exception, has an east-to-west zonation of climate. The windward eastern coast has rainforest conditions, the mountains a highland climate, the western coast a savanna climate, and even some areas of steppe climates are found in the extreme southwest. Aspect, elevation, and maritime effects are dominant there, divorcing it almost entirely from the regular climatic regime of Africa south of the Sahara.

VEGETATION

Vegetational cover most often reflects climatic patterns, but in Africa south of the Sahara the degree of coincidence of the two is not especially great. The modification of natural vegetation through overgrazing and increasingly intensive cropping in marginal areas has probably changed the extent of original natural vegetation zones. Unlike the Brazilian rainforest, which extends well beyond the limits of the tropical monsoon and rainforest climates, the African rainforest occupies only the core of those climatic regions.

The savanna vegetation, consisting of a grass matrix of open parkland and occasional trees, is the norm over much of northern tropical Africa. The forest-grassland distinction in Africa is less clear than in other areas. In the wetter savanna, grass often dominates over trees because repeated fires tend to reduce tree growth. A normal savanna, however, is typified by acacia trees scattered sparsely over a grassy landscape of not very nutritional grasses. It covers a zone of transition along the savanna-Sahel border and much of eastern Africa.

As the northern border of the savanna is reached, grasses occur in clumps rather than as a continuous cover; thorny shrub and bush replaces trees. South of the Congo basin, as with climatic transition, the zonation is less sharp and the vegetation more varied. Much of the vegetation of wetter South Africa is more forest than savanna. Despite the long dry season, trees rather than grass dominate.

The transition southward into areas of steppe climate is marked by a transition to thorn forest and bush savanna before grasses come to dominate completely in the South African veld (termperate steppe). The deserts of South Africa and Somalia are more steppelike and grassy than those of the Sahara or Danakil coasts.

DRAINAGE PATTERNS

The equatorial core of Africa with its intense rainfall is the source area for most of that continent's major drainage systems. Total rainfall decreases and the seasonality of its occurrence increases poleward from that core with rare exception. River systems are fewer, smaller, and have less stabilized flow in a rough approximation of this general rainfall pattern. The desert areas are characterized by intermittent streams (those that contain water only after storms) and interior drainage.

The river with the largest volume of flow, the Congo (Zaire) originates in the rift highlands of East Africa. The volume of flow is not only enormous but extremely stable, due to the heavy total rainfall distributed more or less evenly over the year and the stabilizing effect of the system of African Great Lakes, which are the sources of many tributaries. The river drains a large, shallow depression before descending over a lengthy series of rapids and falls on its way down the escarpment to the sea. With tributaries on both sides of the equator, it receives rain in some of its catchment area at all times. The basin covers over 1.5 million square miles (3.8 million square kilometers), and in some places the river is 8 to 10 miles (13 to 16 kilometers) wide. Large stretches of the river and its tributaries are navigable in its central section, but falls and rapids impede such use in its upper and lower reaches. The Congo (Zaire) is one of the most important potential hydroelectric resources in the world, but little has been developed to date.

Even the Nile, so intimately associated with Egypt, has its sources in this region. The river flows over 4,000 miles (6,400 kilometers) to its mouth over six cataracts between Aswan and Khartoum. The flow actually diminishes as it reaches drier climatic areas with high evaporation, and the hydroelectric energy potential is a fraction of that of the Congo (Zaire).

Rising in Sierra Leone and Guinea, an area of extremely heavy rainfall, the Niger travels north into the Sahel-Sahara borderlands where it forms a large, swampy inland delta. Much diminished in flow, it winds southeastward back into the wetter West African areas where it is joined by the Benue before it reaches the sea in Nigeria. The Niger is navigable in the lower 500 miles (800 kilometers) of its course, as is the Benue for most of its length. Portions in the Sahel are seasonally navigable.

The Zambezi is a typically African stream with multiple sources and a variable flow. Victoria Falls, much higher than Niagara, occur where the river plunges from a shallow, inland basin through a series of gorges on its way to the sea in Mozambique. The Kariba Gorge below the falls has a huge hydroelectric project.

A series of smaller rivers drain small individual sections of the rest of Africa south of the Sahara. Most are not navigable and only a few have any significant hydroelectric potential. Noteworthy is the Volta, in West Africa, which has been developed for hydroelectric energy; a major aluminum works in Ghana is associated with this development. The fluctuating, partially fresh, partially salt-water Lake Chad occupies a large interior basin at the common border of Chad, Cameroon, Niger, and Nigeria. The Limpopo, which forms the northern border of the Republic of South Africa, is known more for the development of the lands along its course than for itself. The Orange, which drains the interior of the Republic of South Africa, is an important irrigation source; it dries up before reaching the sea.

Most of the rest of Africa's streams are short, unnavigable, and of only local importance. However, many of these short, swift streams could provide energy to the oil-poor economies of some West African countries and valuable irrigation water to the arid lands of coastal East Africa.

SOILS

The intense heat and high humidity levels of this region combine to favor rapid breakdown of particle size and to initiate chemical reactions. Parent material is exceedingly varied and often at great depth beneath the soil. Parent rock material varies greatly over small areas. It would seem that drainage, slope, and seasonal water regime have more effect on soil than do vegetational cover or parent material.

In general, African soils are of widely varying fertility and are easily ruined if not carefully used. They do not lend themselves to European-American farm machinery and agricultural techniques as witnessed by many failures to apply them in an African millieu. Yet, with careful use, some African soils produce crops of high quality.

The soils of the equatorial core are generally reddish or yellow-red in color, indicating that they are acid, high in iron and aluminum oxides, low in calcium and humus, and generally heavily leached. Nonetheless, where the soils are alluvial or where they result from volcanic material, they can possess a reasonable potential. Much of this soil area is only periodically cleared for shifting agriculture. Plantations occupy the better soils capable of sustained yields.

Soils of the wet and dry tropics are on the average somewhat more fertile. The difficulty of using them is associated with water retention and a concretion or hardpan (a layer of minerals cemented together) beneath the surface. In the wet season the top layer of soil is saturated with water and the countryside is flooded. During the dry season, the water quickly evaporates and the soil becomes a baked, bricklike surface. Heavy machinery can pack it into a macadamlike surface. Some theorize that suspended dust particles in the air reduce insulation, retard updrafts, and in turn cause further drought by reducing the chances of rain. Fertilization, crop rotation, and fallowing enable some soils of this zone to produce moderate yields.

South of the Congo Basin, the grasslands of the savannah and the thorn forest areas contain soils of moderate fertility. The commonest type is a reddish brown or chestnut-colored soil. Not as severely leached, the content of calcium and humus is somewhat higher than average for tropical conditions. These soils, however, can suffer hardpan of enormous thickness. In some areas they are similar to prairie soils where developed under a grass cover. The tropical prairies possess considerable fertility, and soils of this type in the cooler highlands can give remarkable yields. The Orange Free State and Transvaal in South Africa, parts of Zimbabwe, Mozambique, Uganda, Tanzania, and Kenya possess these highly fertile soils.

The volcanic highlands of Ethiopia and the Great Rift Valley area of East Africa possess unusually fertile soils, as do the slopes of the Adanawa highlands in Cameroons. They are capable of constant cropping without serious damage if soil erosion is controlled. The desert soils of the Kalahari and Southwest Africa are calcium rich if humus poor. Currently used for ranching and nomadic herding, they could produce reasonable yields if supplied with water.

THE STRUCTURE OF SUBREGIONS

This region is subdivided into six subregions: West Africa from Guinea to Cameroon; the Congo basin and its western margins; the "horn" of Africa; East African highlands; the south-central thorn forest—plateau from Angola to Mozambique, plus Malagasy (Madagascar); and southern Africa. More than in most such subdivisions of a major world region, the subregions reflect more the need to subdivide for increased comprehension than any marked degree of cultural, economic, or physical homogeneity within these subregions.

WEST AFRICA SUBREGION

West Africa is a region in which European colonial interests were early attracted by gold and slaves. Britain and France were the dominant colonizers; Portuguese Guinea (Guinea-Bissau), independent Liberia, and two German colonies, Togo and Cameroon, were the exceptions, and German control ended in 1914 after only thirty years.

Natural Resource Base   Gold has been mined in parts of West Africa for over a thousand years. Africans were accomplished metallurgists long before colonization, smelting lead, tin, and iron as well as gold. Ghana, once called the Gold Coast, still produces some gold, but reserves are diminishing rapidly after centuries of exploitation. The same is true of the famous tin ores of northern Nigeria. Diamonds are produced in Ghana, the Ivory Coast, and Sierra Leone, the most important West African producer. The most important mineral resources in the subregion, by total value, are aluminum ore (bauxite), iron ore, and oil. Guinea has one third of the world's high-grade bauxite reserves. Ghana hopes to develop its bauxite in order to feed its large aluminum-smelting industry, which presently relies on imports. Sierra Leone mines some bauxite, and

Cameroon and Guinea-Bissau have known reserves. Iron ore was first mined in Liberia in 1951 and now provides 60 percent of that country's exports; it is the third ranking iron ore exporter after Canada and Australia. Iron ore is also produced in Sierra Leone and may soon be exploited in Guinea.

One reason for West Africa's late industrialization has been a shortage of coal, on which nineteenth century industrialization was based. Nigeria has mined some coal since 1915, and this fuel was important in its early industrialization. Far more important than Nigerian coal, however, is Nigerian oil. Nigeria rocketed from virtually no production before 1958 to the fifth largest exporter of oil in the world; by 1975, oil accounted for 90 percent of Nigeria's foreign earnings. Nigeria refines its own oil for domestic markets at three refineries. Huge reserves of natural gas exist and Nigeria hopes to establish fertilizer plants, electric power plants, and liquefied gas plants to take better advantage of them.

Population Characteristics   Characteristic of the early stages of economic development, the West African states tend to have higher than average population growth rates. The Ivory Coast has an astonishing 4.2 percent growth rate, followed by Liberia and Benin. Urbanization is proceeding rapidly, with at least four "million plus" cities in the region. There is very little *official* international migration among these states, but it should be remembered that many boundaries, cutting across tribal areas, are lightly patrolled.

National Economic Problems and Prospects   The **balkanization** of West Africa into thirteen states heightens the significance of international boundaries in economic development. There is little interchange among the states. Duplication is almost inevitable, and small national budgets set limitations on the number and scope of developmental projects.

Senegal   Senegal is an exception to the generalization that African rivers are not navigable; it has four navigable rivers including the Gambia. With only 5.5 million people and few natural resources, Senegal has maintained a high (for the region) per capita income by exporting agricultural products to France and the Common Market. Dakar, the capital, now nearing 1 million, was once the colonial administrative capital for all of French West Africa. Its excellent harbor and airport facilities make it internationally important. Typical of the drier fringes of tropical "wet and dry" climates, peanuts are a major crop for export; the oil is used in cooking in Europe. Excellent fishing grounds offshore are a major resource; Dakar exports large quantities of canned fish. Tourism is expanding, partly in response to the superb sport fishing available. Phosphates are the only significant mineral export.

The Gambia   The Gambia, an **enclave** within Senegal, is a relic of colonial competition. The first British colony in West Africa, the Gambia is a narrow strip of territory on both banks of the navigable Gambia River. The international boundary cuts this superb river off from its natural hinterland, so very few ships make use of this great natural waterway. The French built a railroad paralleling the river but within Senegalese territory. The Gambia's only resources are fish and peanuts. The logical merger into Senegal became a near certainty in 1981, creating Senegambia. Gambia has only about 600,000 people.

Guinea-Bissau   Guinea-Bissau only achieved independence in 1973; Portugal was the last European state to free its African possessions. One of the subregion's poorest states, Guinea-Bissau may have some exploitable bauxite deposits, but its exports are now peanuts, palm oil, and timber. The revolution severely disrupted the economy.

Guinea   Guinea is about the size of Colorado and has some 5 million inhabitants. It has the potential of becoming one of the subregion's most prosperous states as it has a varied and impressive stock of natural resources including bauxite, iron ore, diamonds, gold, and a large hydroelectric potential. Guinea was the only French colony to reject membership in the French community in favor of immediate and full independence in 1958. France and its allies withdrew all investments, forcing Guinea into closer trade ties with the Communist bloc, although it is officially nonaligned.

Sierra Leone   Sierra Leone has about 3.5 million in an area the size of West Virginia. Like the Gambia, Sierra Leone has a natural asset in trade that is underused because its hinterland is restricted by boundaries created during the colonial period. Freetown, the capital, has the finest natural harbor in West Africa. It is lightly used and was only provided with a deep-water quay in 1953. Sierra Leone, like Guinea, has badly leached, infertile soils. Sierra Leone shares Liberia's curious social-cultural makeup reflecting its origin as a refuge for freed slaves. The "repatriated" freedmen, many of whom had not been born in Africa, were *detribalized;* that is, they knew virtually nothing of their tribal heritage. They spoke English, were probably Christian, and came from a variety of original homelands all through West Africa. Settlements such as Freetown and Monrovia were culturally isolated from the interior tribes, which the freedmen regarded as inferior.

Liberia   Liberia was in some ways disadvantaged by never having been a colony. It lacked the usual colonial investments in transport and communications infrastructure, mineral exploration and exploitation, and plantation development. The United States provided little help to its offspring before World War II as it did not wish to be accused of colonialism in Liberia. No sizeable Western investment arrived until Firestone Rubber acquired the largest rubber plantation in the world in the 1920's. Its 12 million high-yield rubber trees provide the second most important export after iron ore. Liberia, which does not mine any diamonds, manages to export them, thanks to large-scale smuggling from its neighbors. The economy got a large boost during World War II when American military engineers built a deep water port at Monrovia and a major airport. Liberia, which uses American dollars as its official currency, maintains close trade relations with the United States and is very receptive to U.S. investment. Goodrich and Uniroyal have joined Firestone in rubber growing, and timber production is expanding. The 1980 overthrow of the Americo-Liberian (descendants of freedmen) party rule had little immediate effect on Liberia's economy or its special relationship with the United States.

Ivory Coast   The Ivory Coast, a little larger than New Mexico, has such a prosperous economy that there are as many as 1.5 million noncitizens in its total population of 8 million. Many of these migrant workers are from Upper Volta. A lack of any natural harbors along a coastland made hazardous by heavy surf and inhospitable by mangrove swamp helped retard European penetration. French "pacification" of the interior (the elimination of organized resistance) was not completed until 1915. Abidjan, now a million-plus city, was made a seaport by dredging a canal across a sandbar that protected the lagoon on which the city is located. The Ivory Coast is predominantly agricultural; coffee, cocoa, sugar, bananas, and palm oil are exported in large quantities. Other than some low-grade iron ore, the sole mineral resource is a moderate reserve of oil offshore. The Ivory Coast's policy of welcoming foreign investment has helped give it a favorable balance of trade with France, West Germany, and the United States, its main trade partners.

Upper Volta   Upper Volta's very high (by African standards) population densities in the better-watered south sends many Upper Voltans to the Ivory Coast or Ghana to find work, seasonally or permanently. Upper Volta is one of the poorest countries in all Africa. It is primarily agricultural and very vulnerable to the fluctuations in rainfall of the Sahel-savanna natural region. A French-built railroad links the capital with Abidjan, which serves as Upper Volta's port.

Abidjan, Ivory Coast. Those states in Africa south of the Sahara that have a more balanced array of exports and whose stability attracts heavy foreign investment appear to have a bright future. (Courtesy of United Nations)

Ghana Ghana was the first colony to achieve independence in sub-Saharan Africa. It has a good balance between mineral resources and agriculture and has the potential for becoming a prosperous modern state. Its status as the world's largest exporter of cocoa has been both an asset and a handicap. As with other tropical-world exporters of specialty and luxury crops, Ghana has no realistic hope of completely controlling prices through market mechanisms such as the oil producer's OPEC. If Ghana or even all of West Africa were to curtail production to force prices up, there would be a predictable increase in cocoa plantings in other tropical areas to take advantage of rising prices. While West Africa dominates cocoa production (Ghana is first, Nigeria second, and Ivory Coast fourth in world production), Brazil is the third most important producer and could readily expand acreage and cut into Ghana's markets if it became more profitable.

Cocoa in Ghana, unlike rubber in Liberia, is not a plantation crop, but is produced by independent farmers. Unfortunately, there have been a series of plant epidemics that seriously affect production. Cocoa prices tend to fluctuate wildly on world markets, making a gamble of long-range planning for cocoa planting and marketing. As with other West African states, there is a large production of other crops for domestic food, not exports. These include corn, rice, plantains, and peanuts. There is a sizeable fishing industry and Ghana is nearly self-sufficient in livestock.

Ghana inaugurated West Africa's largest hydroelectric project, the Volta River Dam, in 1966. Nearly half the energy produced is used by a large aluminum works at Tema. (Unfortunately, the worldwide aluminum industry has had problems with **overcapacity** relative to demand over the last decade. Power from Volta Dam is exported to Benin and Togo and also supports light industries in southeastern Ghana.

Ghana's compact area of cocoa production, industrialization, urbanization and modernization (the area between Tema, Accra, Kumasi, and Takoradi [see Figure 12–6]) is an example of the development enclave, a zone or region of relatively advanced development level within (usually on the coast of) a significantly less developed country. The capital tended to be a seaport in the colonies. The administrative infrastructure of buildings, communications centers, transport facilities, and military bases were all in place at independence. It was easiest and most efficient for the new state to use the colonial capital as its capital too. The initially superior transport-communications facilities and other amenities attract new investment to the capital and nearby regions. Development snowballs in this enclave of supporting facilities, while the underdeveloped hinterland generally attracts investment only for mineral exploitation. In Liberia, for example, the capital city is also the most modern port. It is near the international air field and has modern water supply, sewage, and electric facilities. It has the best health care facilities and hotels. Small wonder that business people prefer to locate new enterprises (and themselves) in the capital rather than in the interior. Ghana's development enclave is larger than

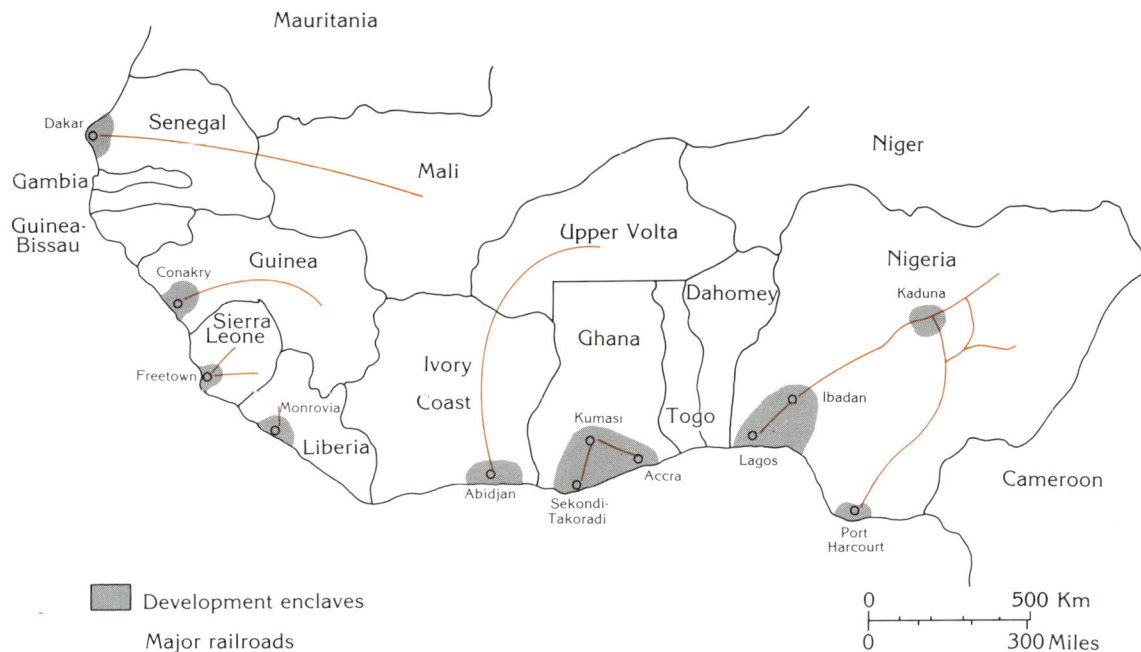

FIGURE 12–6

Development Enclaves in West Africa. Development enclaves—"islands" of modern transport, communications, and energy supply infrastructure with commercialized agriculture, modern mining, and some industrial development—were commonly on or accessible from the seacoast, as they date to colonial investment policies.

those of many of its neighbors, but Ghana shares their long-range problems of encouraging development in other areas.

Togo Togo is the remainder of a small German colony divided between Britain and France after World War I. Britain took the western third and added it to Gold Coast colony; the French sector became modern Togo. Smaller than West Virginia, and with 2.5 million people, Togo is struggling for self-sufficiency. Phosphates and limestone are mined, and cocoa and coffee are exported. Oil prospecting is active but unrewarded so far. The transport infrastructure was above average because of a high level of German investment that had made Togo their only self-supporting colony.

Benin Benin, formerly Dahomey, was the last West African native state to participate in the slave trade. The last Portuguese slave ship sailed from it in 1885. Oil palms are grown on African-owned plantations first planted to produce revenues after the lucrative slave trade ended. Little other development of importance exists.

Nigeria Nigeria is the superstate of West Africa. With 68 million people, it has the largest population on the entire

continent, including Egypt. Nigeria's size, physical diversity, impressive resource base, and oil revenues make it potentially the most successful African state if it can achieve a truly united citizenry. Nigeria, the only federal state in the subregion, created twelve provinces in 1967 to further decentralize the former Eastern, Northern, Western, and Midwestern states. While all West African states have some internal problems associated with their multicultural, multilingual, multitribal status (Ivory Coast alone has sixty different tribal groups), Nigeria alone suffered a prolonged and devastating civil war. Nigeria is not a **nation-state** in the political geographic sense. A close correlation of a nation (a people with a shared, distinctive culture and a general consensus that they have a common destiny) and a state (a political organism occupying a defined territory) has not been achieved. The territorial coincidence of a nation and a state cannot be assumed, and even such long-established nation-states like France may have dissident cultural minorities who seek some degree of self-rule. Nigeria never existed as a country until 1914. The British navy first established a base at Lagos in an effort to eliminate the slave trade centered there. As happened in India, control was extended over much of the country by transferring political power from the private Royal Niger Company to the British Crown.

Nigeria has three regions of high population density (see Figure 12–7) that coincide roughly with the Western, Eastern and Northern regions created by the British as administrative units. Islam is long established in the Northern savanna zone and such cities as Kano are recognized cultural centers of Islam. The agriculture, natural vegetation and climate, cultural history, and languages of the North sharply differ from those of the South.

In the South, while physical factors such as climate and vegetation are not markedly different from east to west, cultural differences are critical. While many southerners are of traditional animist religions, the dominant tribe of the Eastern region, the Ibo, had been strongly influenced by Christian missionary activity and took advantage of mission schools. Hard working and eager for both more education and wider opportunity, the Ibo had

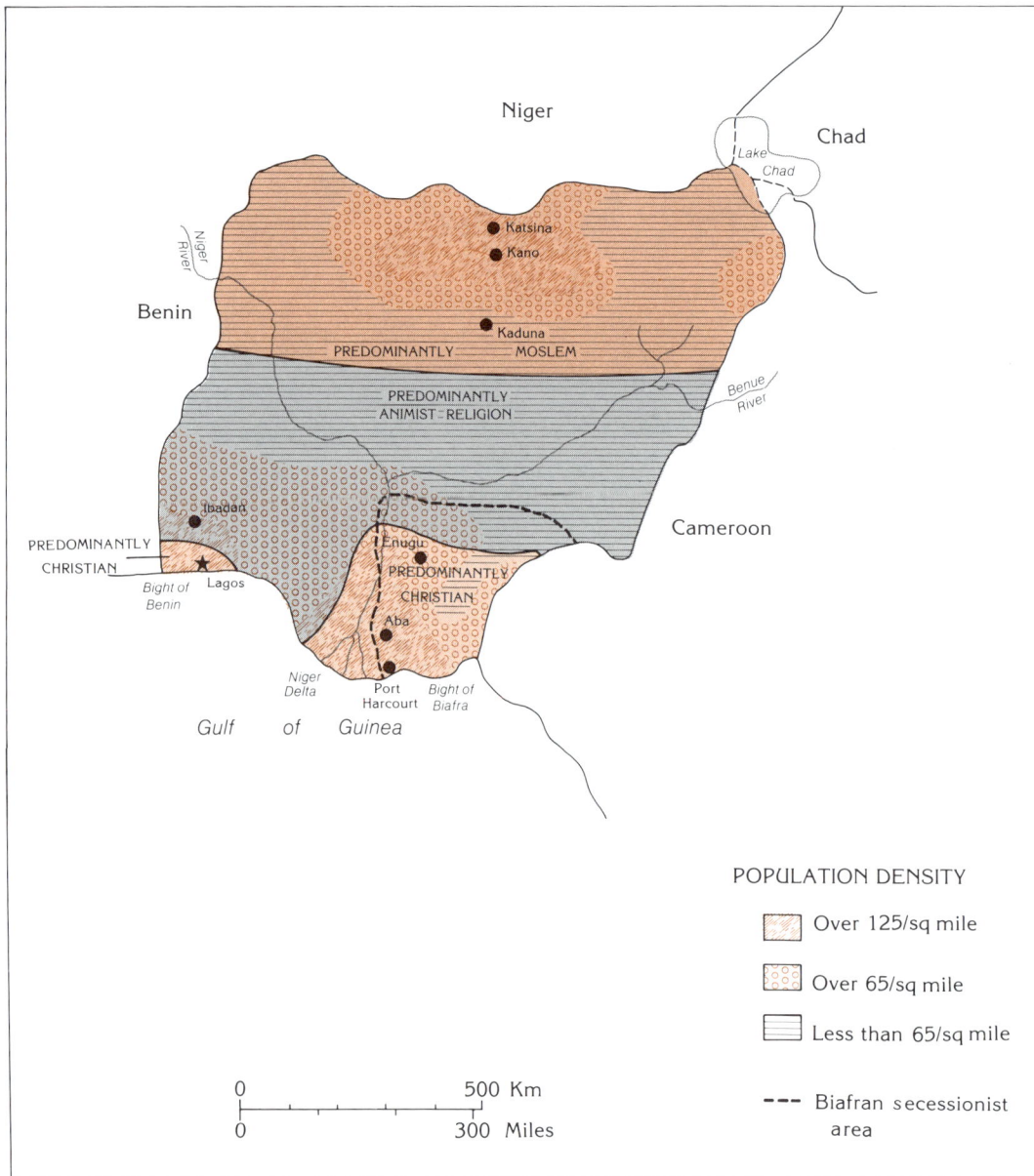

FIGURE 12–7

Population Density and Ethnic-Religious Affiliation in Nigeria, Showing Biafra. Africa's largest state in population, Nigeria has bright prospects if it can create a unified nation from the ethnic and religious diversity that led to civil war, 1967–70, as the eastern region seceded as the state of Biafra. The economic development levels and land use systems differ greatly within Nigeria, especially between the northern semiarid grasslands and the tropical rainforest of the south.

impressed the British with their adaptability to administrative work in both the civil service and the military. Northerners and westerners in Nigeria accused the Ibo of perpetuating themselves in federal administrative positions and the officer corps by favoring other Ibo at hiring and promotion time.

Oil was first produced in the Niger Delta west of Port Harcourt in 1959. The oil fields tend to be in mangrove swamp or offshore; production costs are high but the quality is excellent. For the Eastern region, the oil was a bonanza to what had been Nigeria's poorest region—dependent on subsistence agriculture and palm oil exports. Many easterners resented having to share this new wealth with the rest of the federation, and the federation had never been particularly strong.

In 1967, the Eastern region seceded as the independent state of Biafra. A civil war followed, lasting until 1970. More than 1 million people died, mostly in Biafra, when a federal blockade cut off outside food aid. During the civil war, oil production practically stopped in Biafra, but exploration was increased in the neighboring midwestern state. By 1974, oil production had rebounded.

Nigeria has a brilliant future if the bitter legacy of the civil war can be overcome. Thanks to oil revenues, the damage to the economy related to the civil war has been erased. Eliminating the intertribal and interregional mistrusts engendered by the war will take much longer. The blockade and starvation tactics employed to end the war seemed to some a kind of "final solution" to the Ibo problem. The "giant of Africa" is taking steps to ease tensions and reduce tribal-based discrimination patterns.

Cameroon   Cameroon, like Togo, was divided between British and French administration after German control ended in 1914. The bulk of the former German Cameroon was administered by France with a smaller portion in the west coming under British control and added to Nigeria. The former French portion became an independent republic in 1960, together with a formerly British-administered province.

Although 70 percent of Cameroon's export earnings are based on agriculture, the country is not as vulnerable to market fluctuation as are many other West African states. Agricultural production is highly diversified and coffee, cocoa, bananas, rubber, cotton, peanuts, and palm oil are all exported. The government has an active program of farm services that provides credit, fertilizers, and insecticides. It also controls marketing. There is also an active and expanding industrial sector, featuring **import-replacement,** consumer goods, and an aluminum plant using hydroelectric power to process bauxite imported from Guinea. Cameroon is a modest oil producer.

CONGO BASIN SUBREGION

This subregion consists of the states of Congo, Gabon, Equatorial Guinea, Zaire, and the Central African Republic. These states range in size from Equatorial Guinea, the size of Maryland, to Zaire, which is ninety times larger and the largest country in central Africa. The three largest units (the Central African Republic, Congo, and Zaire) are all largely within the drainage basin of Africa's greatest river, the great Zaire or Congo River. The Central African Republic stretches north across a low divide to the Chad basin, and Gabon and Equatorial Guinea are oriented to their Atlantic seaboards.

The people of this area have had widely divergent colonial experiences related to the timing of their first contacts with Europeans and Arabs. The Bakongo peoples of the area around the mouth of the great river were once united in a kingdom that exchanged ambassadors with Portugal in the sixteenth century. Arab traders and slavers penetrated to extreme eastern Zaire in the nineteenth century. Many of the tribal groups of the central basin, however, had no contact with outsiders until the end of the nineteenth century.

Zaire   Zaire is the third-ranking state in the entire continent in size and fifth in population. If it can overcome the shortcomings of its inadequate **transport infrastructure** and resolve internal dissension among its varied peoples, it could be the "Brazil of Africa"—a large, resource-rich, economically diversified power of the twenty-first century.

Zaire was once the world's largest private plantation; it was not transferred to the Belgian state as a colony until 1907. This transfer in power was the result of a worldwide scandal when particularly vicious means of exploiting the country and its people were exposed. Because Zaire's boundaries are entirely the result of conflicting European colonial ambitions that ignored tribal areas, and because Belgian administration was least effective in preparing the Congolese for freedom, Zaire has strong potential for further replays of the civil war that erupted in 1960, weeks after independence. This war was essentially repeated in 1964 and again in 1967, 1977, and 1978. The persistence of the **centrifugal forces** is related to both internal disunity, as discussed in the Case Study, and to attempts by the Soviet Union, via its Cuban ally's troops in neighboring Angola, to subvert the Zaire government. This effort is directed at one of the richest mineralized zones in Africa in order to deny its minerals to the West.

The strongly divisive, centrifugal political and cultural forces within Belgian Congo were recognized, but perhaps encouraged, by the Belgian colonial administration's creation of a federal system, which gave much power to the provinces. The 1967 constitution reasserted centralized power by placing the provincial administrations under direct control from Kinshasa, the capital.

Belgian policy had been to encourage large monopolistic companies to take responsibility for developing the vast resources of Zaire. The Belgian government retained shares in these corporations. One of these powerful companies, for example, mined copper and uranium, operated river boats, plantations, and a brewery, and controlled an airline. The combination of vast mineral wealth and official cooperation with giant monopolies had propelled Zaire's economy rapidly forward by independence.

Enormous plantations are the largest in Africa outside Liberia. About 80 percent of Zaire's agricultural exports—palm oil, rubber, coffee, cocoa, and tea, are produced on plantations, while small African-owned farms contribute most of the cotton and peanuts.

Zaire ranks first in world production of industrial diamonds and cobalt, sixth in copper, eighth in manganese, ninth in tin, and tenth in gold. It also produces silver, lead, zinc, and uranium. Copper alone provides more than 40 percent of Zaire's exports by value. Zaire also has some iron ore, coal, and oil. Most of the oil is offshore, but exploration is active onshore as well. (See Figure 12–8.) Most industry is located either in the Copperbelt's provincial capital of Lubumbashi or in the booming (population 2 million) capital of Kinshasa. Zaire, then, has more than one development enclave.

Most of Zaire's 28 million people are still cultivators. Population densities are so light, however, that only about 2 percent of the land is cultivated. It is estimated that about half the country's acreage could be cultivated, so that Zaire is among the African states whose potential for food pro-

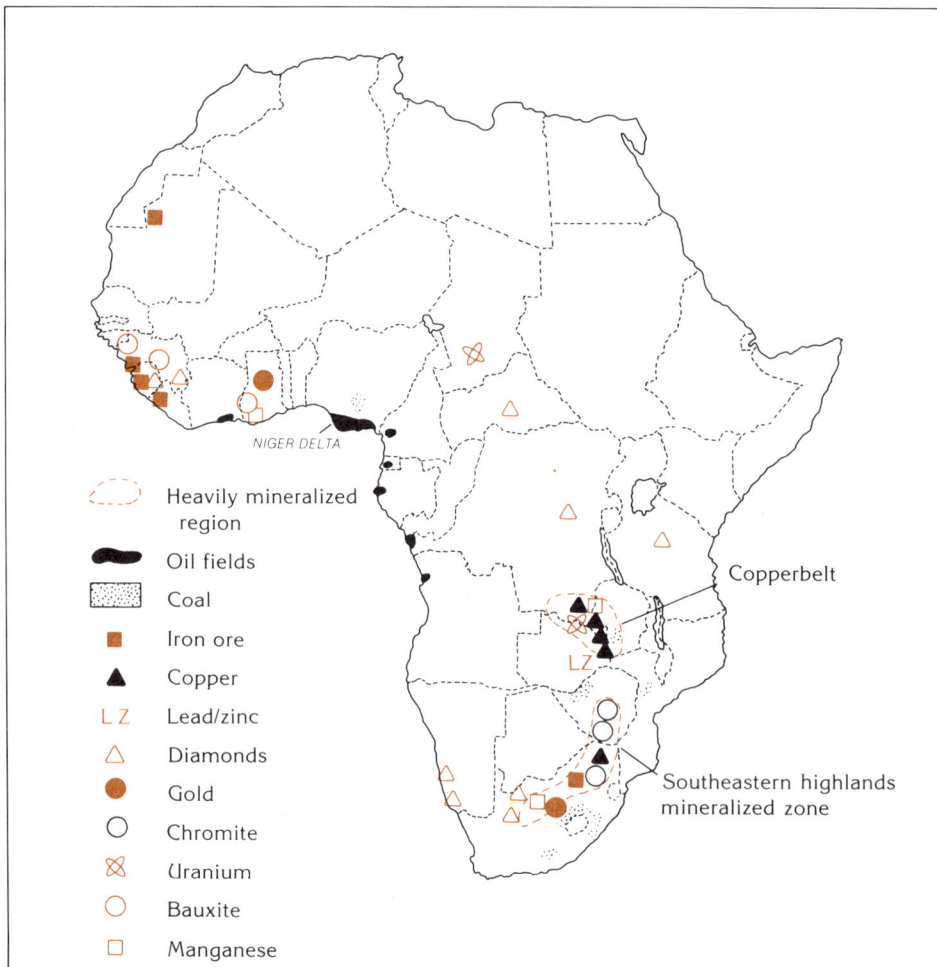

FIGURE 12–8

Mineral Resources of the Region. Africa south of the Sahara has several heavily mineralized zones of international significance. The Copperbelt of Zaire and Zambia is matched only by the phenomenal quantity and variety of metal ore in South Africa and Zimbabwe. This region's steel alloys are essential to modern aircraft technology, and Nigeria is a major exporter of oil.

duction is hardly touched. Forest product industries could also be expanded many fold.

Zaire accounts for 13 percent of the world's hydroelectric power potential, since the enormous volume of the Zaire (Congo) River plunges through the rim of its saucerlike basin to the Atlantic through a narrow gorge. A complex of dams and generating stations is being completed at Inga on a paralleling gorge and on the Zaire itself. Zaire's foreign trade is predominantly with Belgium and the rest of the European Economic Community, although the United States is an important customer. An interesting political reaction to Zaire's cultural fragmentation and thin veneer of European colonial culture is a determined, comprehensive program of "Zairization." The state and river both were to be known as Zaire rather than Congo, and colonial place names were replaced. A new flag and national anthem were introduced, and all individuals were legally required to replace foreign names with African ones. The Zairans are trying hard to develop a distinctively African, Zairan culture—and with it, a loyalty to the idea of a Zairan **nation-state.** Zaire's fabulous potential is as yet unrealized; it has the lowest per capita income ($175) of the subregion, and one of the lowest in the world.

Congo   Congo, formerly French Congo, flanks Zaire to its northwest, extending 800 miles (1,300 kilometers) inland from the Atlantic. A little larger than New Mexico, Congo has only 7 people per square mile (3 per square kilometer); its 1.5 million people are divided among 75 tribes.

Fortunately for Congo, its administrative capital, Brazzaville, became the colonial capital of all of French Equatorial Africa. This induced large capital investments in the city and in transport and communications facilities. As a result, Congo, one of the poorest countries in mineral resources and cultivable soils, has prospered. Brazzaville, a river port opposite Kinshasa, became the terminus of a railroad from the Atlantic port of Pointe-Noire in 1945, so that its transport connections are excellent. Riverboats connect Brazzaville with some northern river towns, but the north in general remains practically empty. Some 75 percent of the population is located in the vicinity of Brazzaville, Pointe-Noire, and the savanna lands between them. Pointe-Noire handles both Congo's imports and exports and much of the international trade of the Central African Republic and Chad.

Most Congolese are subsistence farmers, producing a wide variety of export crops such as palm nuts, sugar, bananas, peanuts, tobacco, coffee, and cocoa. Tropical wood is the most important export item, although a potash mine has opened near Pointe-Noire, which is also the center for offshore oil exploitation.

Central African Republic   The Central African Republic's capital, Bangui, is at the head of navigation upstream from Brazzaville. There are no railroads at all, and until this century, there were no urban places. Now towns are growing so rapidly that parts of the countryside are virtually depopulated. Diamonds account for about 40 percent of export receipts, but production costs have been rising faster than diamond prices. Some uranium ore is mined and it is believed that there are exploitable deposits of iron, nickel, manganese, gold, tin, and copper. Many of these minerals are located in a great **magnetic anomaly** recently detected by satellite reconnaissance.

Gabon   Gabon is one of the wealthiest countries in Africa in terms of per capita gross domestic product. With less than three quarters of a million people in an area the size of Colorado, Gabon has an average per capita gross domestic product of $2,800, more than twelve times that of Zaire. Manganese and uranium ores are exported via Pointe-Noire. Oil and natural gas are produced offshore and there are plans to extend a railway from Libreville, the capital, to the eastern border. Gabon has a large trade surplus and the government encourages foreign investment in further diversification.

Equatorial Guinea   The Republic of Equatorial Guinea consists of the two former Spanish colonies of Rio Muni on the coast between Cameroon and Gabon, and the volcanic island of Fernando Poo. This small country's only resources are the rich agricultural productivity of Fernando Poo (cocoa, bananas, coffee, pineapple) and the forests of the mainland portion.

AFRICAN HORN SUBREGION

Ethiopia, Somalia, and Djibouti form this subregion. Ethiopia is the oldest independent state in Africa, while Djibouti, a former French colony, is one of the newest independent states in the world (1977). The third unit, Somalia, is a merger of former British Somaliland and Italian Somalia. Somalia and Ethiopia are among the most impoverished states in the world, with per capita incomes of about $80 and $100, respectively. Djibouti, the size of New Hampshire, has a per capita income of about $400, but no natural resources other than a good harbor. The three states have widely varying means, strategies, and chances of advancing the living standards of their people.

Ethiopia   First described by the Greek historian Herodotus in the fifth century, B.C., Ethiopia is commonly cited as an example of the significance of topography to defense, isolation, and independence. The rugged Ethiopian plateau consists of volcanic lava on top of sedimentary strata. It has been split by the trenchlike Great Rift Valley. The East African rift system is related to other sharply defined landforms, like the Red Sea and Arabian peninsula, the gulfs of Suez and Aqaba and even the Dead Sea and the Jordan Valley (see Figure 12–5). There is ample geologic evidence that the entire Arabian peninsula was torn away from the "horn" of Africa during continental drift. Much of the area is characterized by earthquakes and other indications that Africa east of the Great Rift may eventually split away as the bulk of the continent drifts westward, rotating very slightly clockwise.

Ethiopia, the historic state, and Ethiopia, the rugged volcanic plateau, have long been synonymous. The Christian kingdom of Ethiopia was long under pressure from Moslem peoples, who, occupying the lowlands, surrounded and isolated it. The present boundaries of Ethiopia with the Sudan and Kenya show a high correlation with elevations over 3,000 feet (900 meters).

Ethiopia was a true empire—it contained many different people and regions joined with the original highland core by conquest and held together by the power and authority of the emperor. Modern Ethiopia began with the successful military expansion carried out by Menelik II, who recognized Italian, French, and British colonial claims to portions of the Red Sea–Gulf of Aden seacoasts in exchange for their recognition of him as emperor of Ethiopia. Menelik also agreed to a French-built railroad linking his new capital with the port of Djibouti in French Somaliland. A long struggle between Christians and Moslems for political power is related to the balance of religions in the population, about 35 percent Christian and 45 percent Moslem, with 20 percent animist; it climaxed in the 1974 revolution, which deposed the last emperor. Fascist Italy conquered Ethiopia in 1935–36, creating a vast empire with Eritrea, an older Italian possession on the Red Sea coast, and Italian Somaliland on the Indian Ocean coast, both contiguous with Ethiopia. Ethiopia was liberated by British forces in 1941, along with their conquest of Italian Somaliland and Eritrea. The modern history of the three states is thus interlinked. A further, potentially dangerous interlinkage is the manner in which ethnic groups of strong national ambitions straddle international boundaries, and/or lie within the control of an alien group. The "horn" of Africa is one of its least stable areas, both in physical (tectonic-volcanism) terms and in political-cultural terms.

In the outcome of World War II. Ethiopia was awarded Eritrea. This province is heterogeneous, culturally, with a great variety of ethnic groups. The UN, in awarding Eritrea to Ethiopia, gave Eritrea a degree of autonomy that Ethiopia was not prepared to honor. The continual erosion of Eritrean local autonomy resulted in an independence movement. By the time of the overthrow of the emperor (and perhaps contributing to that revolution), much of Eritrea paid little attention to Addis Ababa.

Although this is one of the earliest centers of domesticated plants, contemporary agricultural techniques are very inefficient. The volcanic soil is generally superior and the altitude moderates temperatures, but primitive implements and severe soil erosion combine to limit production. The light, steel-tipped wooden ox-ploughs used on many farms do such a poor job of breaking up the soil that each field may be ploughed three or four times before planting. Although Ethiopia is the probable origin of coffee trees and can produce some of the finest quality coffees, the value of part of the crop is reduced by a lack of quality control.

Ethiopia is self-sufficient in food, except in drought years, but production could be greatly increased with more scientific agriculture. More than half the country is good quality grazing land, and cattle exports have a bright future as agriculture in general is modernized. Natural resources include copper and some gold, platinum, salt and potash, but Ethiopia's biggest potential natural asset is water. The plateau is the source of the Blue Nile; the hydroelectric potential is enormous and only beginning to be developed.

Any economic development plans must first consider transport development. Almost half the Ethiopians live more than one day's walk from a paved road. Industry is in its initial stages of development, featuring food processing, textiles, and cement.

In addition to its potential breakaway province of Eritrea, Ethiopia faces serious problems in its relationships with Somalia and Djibouti. Somalia apparently regards Djibouti's 300,000 people as an **irredenta,** ultimately to be joined into a greater Somalia. Somalia has waged a brutal war in Ethiopia's Ogaden region (see Figure 12–9) in an attempt to bring that territory, occupied primarily by Somali nomads, into Somalia. Somalia also regards part of northeastern Kenya as properly part of a Somali ethnic state. Somalia, in short, has a high potential for starting multiple wars in this part of the world.

Somalia Somalia as now constituted is a little smaller than Texas and has 3.5 million people, 60 percent of whom are nomadic or semi-nomadic pastorialists. Less than 1 percent of the land is under cultivation, producing bananas, corn, peanuts, sugar cane, and cotton. Somalia is a rarity among African states in the homogeneity of its population; 98 percent are ethnic Somalis. There are as many camels and cattle as there are people, and sheep

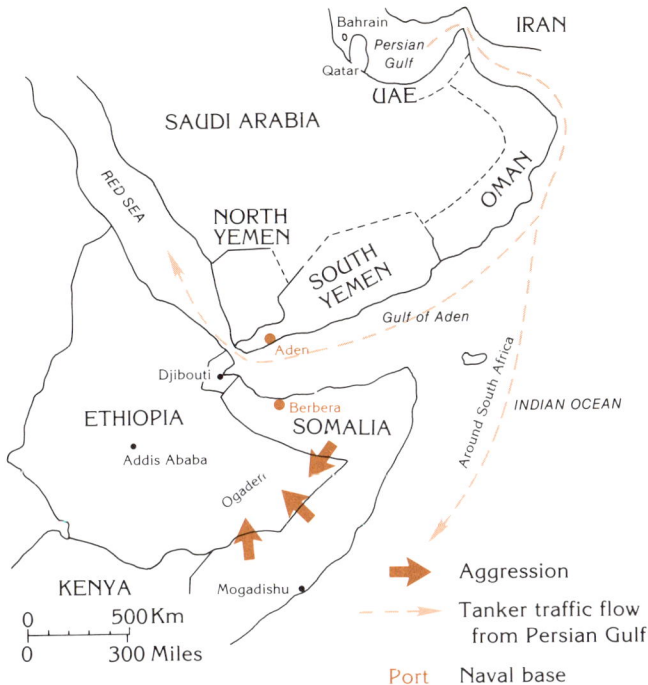

FIGURE 12–9
Territorial Conflicts and Strategy in the "Horn." Somalia has asserted territorial claims against Ethiopia and Kenya and may press claims against Djibouti. However, the dispute with Ethiopia over the desolate Ogaden region is the most serious. Somalia's position adjacent to the oil lifelines of Europe, both via the Gulf of Aden and those tankers bound around the African continent, makes it a desirable ally of potential opponents of the West.

and goats outnumber people three to one. The ethnic Somali are traditional nomads—they appear to disdain the drudgery of cultivation and those who cultivate. Some former nomads were encouraged to become agriculturalists during the Italian colonial period. The Italians drilled wells and introduced irrigation systems, but when they departed, many Somali cultivators promptly went back to nomadic herding in arid and semiarid country.

Somalia's mineral resources are little known and not developed. Other than livestock, exported live and as hides and canned meat, Somalia's basic asset is its 1,700-mile (2,700-kilometer) coastline in the strategic area where the oil of the Persian Gulf flows either up the Red Sea to Europe via Suez or around Africa to Europe and North America. This strategic significance is not unknown to the Soviets, who have donated a new deep-water port at Berbera (see Figure 12–9), directly south from Aden. Its transformation into a major refueling base for the Soviet fleet patrolling the economic lifeline of the west is a distinct threat.

Djibouti   Djibouti, a small pocket of former French territory surrounding a superior harbor that is the logical port

for much of Ethiopia, has no resources other than its trade services to Ethiopia. The Addis Ababa Railway makes a profit because Ethiopia's own ports are not connected by rail to Addis Ababa. (Perhaps this is because Djibouti had the foresight to present the Ethiopian government with a large share in the railroad company.) Djibouti is 89 percent desert wasteland and would appear to have a bleak future, economically, and a short one, politically, if Somalia moves against it with force.

EAST AFRICA SUBREGION

The East Africa subregion includes Tanzania, Kenya, Uganda, Rwanda, and Burundi. The resource base of this portion of the African region is much poorer than those of other, neighboring subregions. There are no mineral-rich areas comparable to the Rand, the Copperbelt, or Nigeria's "oil delta." The five countries of East Africa are primarily agricultural and comparatively poor. Burundi and Rwanda each have minor deposits of low-grade and underexploited minerals. Uganda has a minor copper mine, and Tanzania has undeveloped iron ore and coal reserves to complement dwindling outputs of gold and a variety of gem stones.

This subregion in general is a zone of contacts among major African ethnic groups—the Bantu, who predominate south of the equator; the Nilotic, Nilohamitic, and Sudanic peoples of the upper Nile Valley area, and Pygmy groups in Burundi, who may represent the last remnants of the aboriginal population of a large area of East Africa. Tiny Rwanda and Burundi are the least complex, ethnically, each with Hutu majorities (89–85 percent) and Tutsi (Watusi) minorities of 10 percent and 14 percent, respectively. Uganda's largest single group, the Baganda, in contrast, forms only one twelfth of the total population, while Tanzania's 18 million people are divided among 130 ethnic groups, only one of which has more than a million. Kenya is the most homogeneous of East Africa's larger states, with the Kikuyu forming 20 percent of its 15 million population. With the important exception of a narrow coastal strip and offshore islands, East Africa had remained the most "African" subregion, the least influenced by either Europeans or Arabs until the late 19th century.

Rwanda and Burundi   The remote, mountainous lands that become Rwanda and Burundi, long protected from invasion by combination of sheer distance from the coast, rugged terrain, and lakes and swamps, had no recorded exploration by Europeans until the 1890's. In both territories, each about the size of Maryland, the Tutsi had brought cattle into the area and traded them to the larger group, the Hutu, for land. Eventually the Tutsi ended up with most of the land and established a feudal system in which the Hutu traded their labor for cattle and grazing rights from the ruling Tutsi. German control, ended in the 1916 invasion from the then Belgian Congo, resulted in a League of Nations mandate granted to Belgium for these two remote provinces of former German Tanganyika.

The high, cool mountains of the Zaire-Nile watershed in central Africa suffered little from either of the great depopulators of Africa south of the Sahara—the slave trade or the disease-bearing, wet-lowland–infesting tsetse fly. Rwanda and Burundi are both characterized by some of the highest population densities in tropical Africa, over 400 per square mile (150 per square kilometer). As about 95 percent of each country's people are in subsistence agriculture, these crowded areas of high relief are being intensively farmed by people who lack the knowledge and tools of scientific farming to minimize erosion. Severe erosion and erratic rainfall have led to famines and wide variations in coffee production, the major export crop. Rwanda has an ideal climate for tea and, with government encouragement, tea exports are expected to diversify the "one-crop economy." Methane gas from the bottom of Lake Kivu on the Zaire border could become an important fuel for the light consumer and import-replacement industries now being developed. Burundi is also expanding tea acreage and will soon begin exploiting a high-grade nickel deposit recently discovered. Long-range development plans are hampered by already dense populations growing at a rate higher than the world average, a general lack of transport infrastructure, and distance from international markets. Both states experienced post-independence conflicts between the Hutu and Tutsi, which led to hundreds of thousands of deaths and the flight of several more hundred thousands. Poverty and a bitter legacy of inter-tribal civil war will probably continue to undermine their stability.

Uganda   The Republic of Uganda has had so troubled a decade that its per capita income, once the highest in East Africa, has experienced a rapid decline. The people of Uganda, a country about the size of Oregon with 12 million people, have suffered one of the most murderous dictatorships in the modern world; economic and social recovery can be expected to be slow. Uganda had been thought to have a bright future. British colonial policy had early forbidden large-scale white land ownership, preventing the kind of bitter civil war that plagued Kenya and Zimbabwe. The relatively cooler uplands support a fairly dense population. Most of the country lies between 3,000 and 5,000 feet (900 and 1,500 meters), although the densely populated shores of Lake Victoria are swampy, giving an impression of lowlands. A copper mine at

Kilembe supplies 5 percent of the national revenues, and some of Africa's best agricultural soils are found in Uganda.

The shallow lake is a major water resource, and a source of the Nile. The great dam at Owens Falls, the outlet of Lake Victoria, generates enough power for an industrial enclave at Jinja. This includes a copper smelter, steel rolling mill, textile factories, processing plants for peanuts, and a brewery. Kampala, the capital, is linked by rail with the Kenyan port of Mombasa, although relations with Kenya have sometimes deteriorated to the point of closing the border. In short, Uganda has at least average physical resources and a better than average economic infrastructure for East Africa. Its negative economic growth in recent years is entirely attributable to governmental mismanagement.

The largest and most progressive tribe in Uganda, the Baganda, occupy the fertile and productive shores of Lake Victoria. More than a century ago, the Baganda had established a powerful military state that demanded (and got) tribute from surrounding peoples. They had organized a good road system and set up a system of chiefs loyal to a "chief of chiefs," the fabled Kabaka of Buganda. This feudal system made the British deal with the Kabaka and his chiefs as a formidable power.

As independence approached, the Baganda were determined to safeguard their traditional leadership. The 1962 Independence Constitution created a special federal relationship between Uganda and the Kingdom of Baganda. The hereditary Kabaka (King) of Buganda was elected President of Uganda but was overthrown in 1966, when the traditional kingdoms were also abolished.

In 1967, an "economic war" was declared to place all sectors of the economy in Ugandan hands. About 50,000 Asians, mostly Indians, were abruptly expelled. Unfortunately for the Ugandan economy, the confiscated Indian shops, small businesses, and textile factories did not prosper in unskilled hands. Indian technicians had also run many enterprises such as the hydroelectric plant. Production fell in all sectors of the economy except government services.

Recovery since the overthrow of the Amin regime has been erratic. Rising prices in the notoriously unstable coffee markets could contribute to recovery in Uganda as it is normally the third largest coffee exporter in Africa. However, Ugandan coffee is mostly a cheaper variety. Kenya and Tanzania produce most of the finer quality coffee, which commands higher prices. While large plantations produce most of the coffee exported by Kenya and Tanzania, small freehold farmers prevail in Uganda, Rwanda, and Burundi and also produce much of Tanzania's cotton crop.

Kenya Kenya, with its narrow mineral base (one mine recently opened near Mombasa, producing lead, silver, and zinc) has but one major resource—agricultural land. Almost all of the southwestern third of Kenya is above 4,000 feet (1,200 meters) in elevation, moderating the climatic effects of location astride the equator. These richly productive highlands have been both positive and negative in their effect on Kenya's economy. The 1895 establishment of a British protectorate soon resulted in the fertile highlands being opened to white (mostly British) settlers. The Kikuyu and Masai, who occupied much of the highlands, had been decimated by disease among both humans and the cattle on which the Masai depended. The almost depopulated highlands looked empty to the incoming whites; they assumed that their incursion would have little effect on Africans. A 1933 law set aside 50,000 square miles (130,000 square kilometers) as native reserve in the highlands as against 12,000 square miles (31,000 square kilometers) of "white highlands." However, the white highlands coincided with most of the best farmland and became highly productive. Diversified farms produced both tropical-subtropical commodities (cotton, coffee, sisal, tea) and crops usually associated with the midlatitudes (wheat, corn, dairy products) as well as fine beef cattle. In 1952, the Kikuyu rebelled in the bloody Mau-Mau uprising. One million Kikuyu, who had lived amongst the white homesteads, were forcibly resettled in an attempt to break the revolt, but the Mau-Mau revolt eventually achieved independence in 1963. The British government bought most of the white-owned farms and redistributed the land to Africans. Further diversification has added rice, bananas, sweet potatoes, and peanuts to Kenya's major crops.

Kenya's population distribution closely reflects that of agricultural land; much of the north and northeast is lightly populated desert. Kenya's economic development features important hydroelectric installations that power an expanding industrial sector. Food processing, brewing, clothing, and cement are supplemented by a paper mill and an oil refinery at Mombasa, the second industrial city after Nairobi.

Kenya's tourist business has thrived because of its varied and picturesque scenery, its reputation for political stability, and the foresight of Kenya in setting aside 6 million acres (2.4 million hectares) in ten national parks and four game preserves, most of which are equipped with luxurious visitor accommodations. In this way, Kenya's wild animal life is converted into an economic asset, although there is considerable pressure on the government to convert some park and game land into farms. Only 10 percent of Kenya is suitable to cultivation and another 6 percent is good pasture. Kenya has repeatedly managed

a trade surplus and encourages foreign investment in its mixed economy. A potential threat to its internal stability and good relationships with its neighbors are the irredenta territorial claims advanced sporadically by both Uganda in western Kenya and by Somalia in the eastern border zone. Nairobi, an unusually attractive city with an excellent climate and a major international airport, is becoming a tourist and convention center.

Tanzania Tanzania, East Africa's largest state in both area and population, has an unusual, peripheral distribution pattern to its population of 18 million. The high, arid plateaus of the nation's center are sparsely settled compared with the Indian Ocean coast, the lakeshores, and the slopes of the volcanic mountains with their superior soils. This pattern of far-scattered population nodes places special significance on Tanzania's transport network, which is heavily reliant on railroads. Railroads (over 1,600 miles [2,600 kilometers] in length, not counting the "Tanzam" line to Zambia) have much greater mileage than paved roads (about 900 miles [1,400 kilometers] in total length). (See Figure 12–10.)

Tanzania is a result of the voluntary merger of the former British mandate of Tanganyika and Zanzibar, consisting of the islands of Zanzibar and Pemba about 20 miles (32 kilometers) offshore. These islands had a very

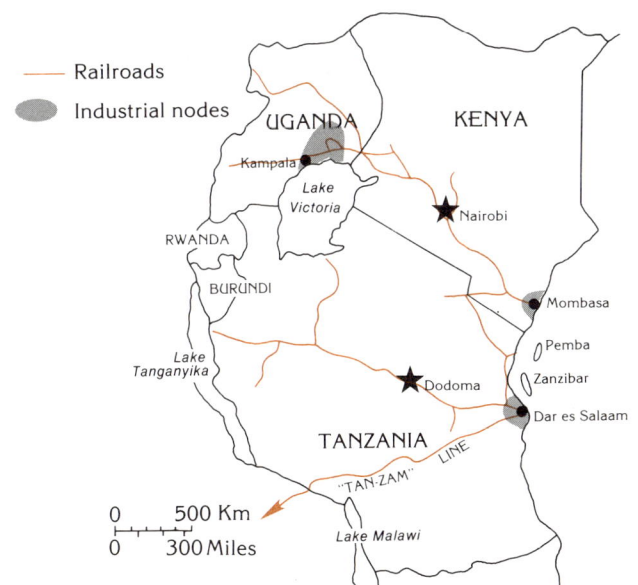

FIGURE 12–10
Transport and Development in East Africa (with Tanzania's New Capital). With an inherited transport infrastructure from colonial investments, but without significant mineral resources, the three larger states of East Africa have augmented their transport systems to further commercialize agriculture and foster rising tourism, particularly in Kenya. Tanzania has shifted its capital from Dar es Salaam to more central Dodoma in an attempt to disperse development investment.

Elephants, Tanzania. Much of the region's spectacular widelife is under serious pressure from both poachers (after hides and ivory) and farmers expanding into former widelife range. Can these developing nations afford to set aside large wildlife refuges? (Courtesy of United Nations)

different cultural and political history than the bulk of mainland Tanzania, having been important Arab trading stations. Similar to the early European trade "forts" on the West African coast, the Arab trade centers were on islands or protected bays for a combination of trade convenience and security from attack. The lucrative trade in slaves and ivory flowed through Zanzibar, enriching the island and providing slave labor for the clove plantations. A British protectorate finally ended slavery in 1897. Zanzibar and Pemba, the island on which most of the world's cloves are grown, became independent in December 1963 as a constitutional monarchy. The African majority, descendants of slaves, overthrew the Sultan and united with Tanganyika a few months later. Zanzibar does retain considerable local autonomy.

Tanzania is making a major effort to further industrialize; most modern industry is located at Dar es Salaam, with secondary nodes at Tanga, Mashi, Arusha, and Zanzibar City. The usual pattern of food processing and other consumer industries is present and new investments from Holland (Phillips Electric) and Japan (Matsushita) are diversifying the economic base.

Tanzania is moving its capital from the old colonial capital and port of Dar es Salaam to the more central location of Dodoma in the now sparsely settled plateau. In this, Tanzania is attempting to refocus national attention and development to the interior. (See Figure 12–10.)

THE SAVANNA TRANSITION ZONE

Angola, Zambia, Malawi, Mozambique, and Malagasy are the five states of this subregion. They are located in the area of climatic transition from tropical rainforests to dryland climates of the southwest and the cooler subtropical climates of the extreme south and southeast coasts of the continent. All three major colonial powers of Africa's past—Portugal, France, and Britain—held lands here. Portugal withdrew from its huge African territories only in the mid-1970's. Zambia and Malawi, then known as Northern Rhodesia and Nyasaland, were unwilling participants in the short-lived Federation of the Rhodesias and Nyasaland until 1963. The Republic of Malagasy, which occupies the entire island of Madagascar (the fourth largest island in the world) off the southeast coast of Africa, became fully independent of France in 1960.

Resource Base   The resource base is extremely varied among the states of the savanna transition. Zambia splits the fabulous Copperbelt with neighboring Zaire, normally supplying about one fifth of international copper exports. The Copperbelt also produces cobalt, lead, and zinc. Malawi, the smallest state of the subregion, has no mineral resources other than some limestone, whereas Angola has oil, diamonds, and iron ore; Mozambique has some coal, iron ore, and bauxite; and Malagasy has relatively underexploited deposits of graphite, chrome, coal, bauxite, and tar sands. The presence or absence of minerals among the countries of the subregions has surprisingly little relationship to their present levels of prosperity.

Population   Malawi, at 49 people per square mile (19 per square kilometer), is the most densely populated unit of the subregion (see Figure 12–11). Angola's 13 people per square mile (5 per square kilometer) make it the least densely populated, while Zambia, Malagasy, and Mozambique fall in the range of 30 to 50 per square mile (12 to 19 per square kilometer). While the population is not uniformly distributed and local densities especially in southern Malawi may reach 300 per square mile (116 per

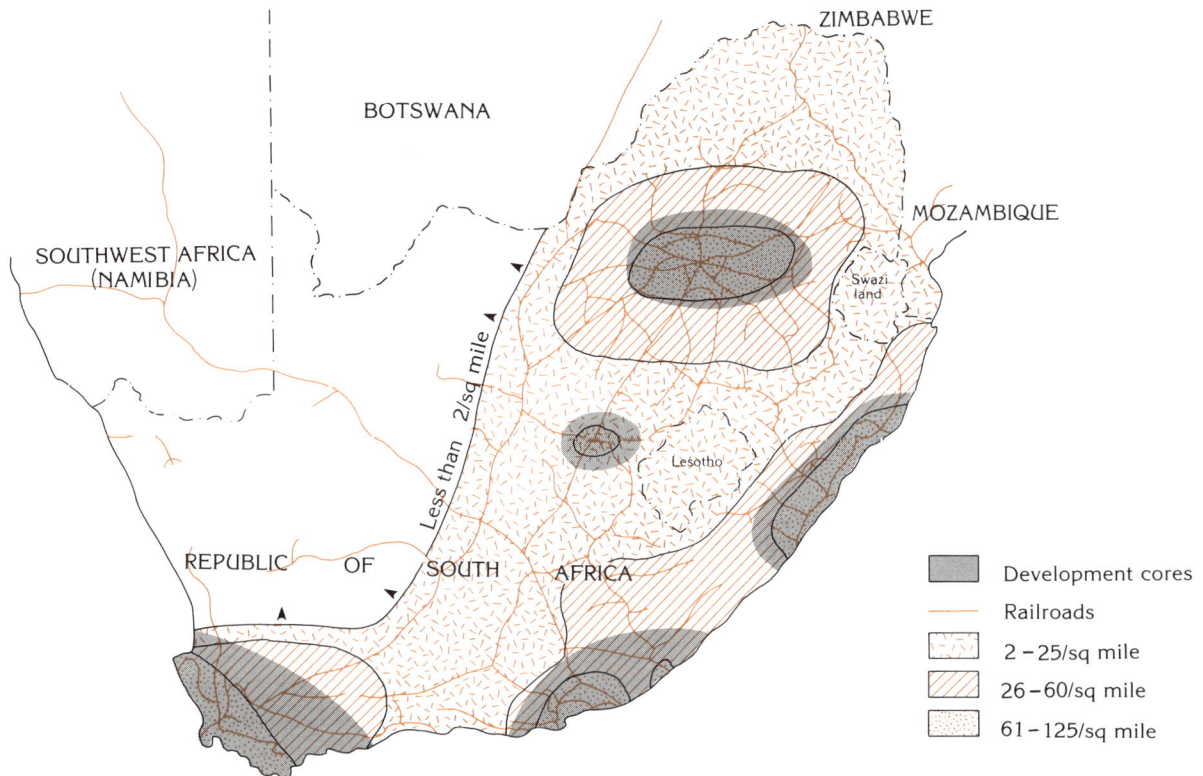

FIGURE 12–11
Southern Africa: Population, Transport, and Development Enclaves. The imprint of colonialism and continuing European culture economies in much of the region, particularly in mining, is reflected in population distribution. South Africa, clearly the region's most advanced economy, has considerable economic and indirect political influence over many of its neighbors through its use of international migrant labor. Former imperial transport systems provide another intertie.

square kilometer), the area is lightly populated, in general, when compared with its agricultural potential.

Madagascar has the most diverse ethnic mixture, due largely to its settlement by Indonesian seafarers who brought with them African brides and slaves. Angola, by far the largest state in the savanna transition (about twice the size of Texas), has three main tribal groups that together comprise more than three quarters of the population. Mozambique has a more complex, and considerably less unified tribal mosaic; many ethnic groups in Mozambique speak different languages and show little inclination to meld into a single culture. The two former Portuguese colonies experienced an abrupt withdrawal of their Portuguese residents at independence.

Angola and Mozambique   The historical relationship of Portugal and its two giant African colonies is a necessary background to understanding the level of economic development, the bitter civil war that forced the Portuguese out, and the present political and economic problems of Angola and Mozambique. In a major world region notoriously short of natural harbors, the Portuguese early

claimed and settled some of the finest harbors south of the equator. Luanda and Lobito in Angola and Maputo (Lourenco Marques) and Biera in Mozambique were all ports of call in Portugal's trade routes to India in the sixteenth century. They are still (except for Luanda) ports of international significance, serving interior mining and agricultural centers from Zaire's Shaba (Katanga) region through to South Africa's Rand, when political considerations do not interrupt logical economic relationships. Portugal's "favorite" between its east and west coast colonies had shifted over time with trade routes and economic policies. The Indian Ocean ports of Mozambique were long of greater importance to Portuguese ships voyaging in the India trade. Once Portuguese learned the secret of the monsoon winds as the Arabs had, probably a thousand years earlier, they recognized the value of Mozambique's ports for awaiting the desired wind direction. The Atlantic ports in Angola were useful as stopovers, but only of secondary importance. With India increasingly dominated by the British, by the eighteenth century, Portugal turned more attention to Brazil. Angola then superseded Mozambique in importance as slaveships began transporting an estimated 3 million Africans across the South Atlantic to Brazil. The slave trade did not end completely until the mid-nineteenth century, although Brazil freed its slaves before Lincoln's Emancipation Proclamation.

Maputo in Mozambique is the closest port to the Witwatersrand-Pretoria-Vereenigeng area, southern Africa's sole major industrial area. Both Mozambique and Angola had seaport termini for international railroads serving southern Africa. Port and transit fees were important parts of the colonies' government revenues (see Figure 12–11). Beira, Maputo, and Lobito are so oriented to international trade of the landlocked interior that neither Portuguese possession developed a transport net for domestic development. For example, the Mozambique ports of Beira and Maputo are linked by rail only by going through Zimbabwe.

Although both Mozambique and Angola have some mineral resources, neither has a mineralized zone to compare with Zaire and Zambia's Copperbelt or South Africa's Rand. Economic development thus rested more on agricultural production. Investment capital was short, so that Portuguese development of its African colonies' agriculture had to be done as inexpensively as possible. Unfortunately, this led to some notorious abuses. A labor code introduced in 1899 required African males, eighteen to fifty-five, to work at least part of the year in occupations acceptable to the Portuguese. If an adult were not in the army, police, or domestic service; had at least fifty cattle of his own; or produced cash crops for export, he could be forced to work on public works projects or accept employment in South Africa. (The Portuguese colony and even independent Mozambique benefited directly from South African payments, government to government, for the use of this labor). The Africans had no defense against being forced into the work program, at what were, literally, slave wages. No wonder that many men of Portuguese Africa eagerly migrated to South Africa for the relatively high pay there. Even today, about 100,000 Mozambiquans work in South Africa at any one time. Additionally, Portuguese policy in Mozambique was to encourage production of cash crops, even though as much as half the adult males in some rural districts would be working elsewhere, "encouraged" by the labor code. In northern Mozambique's coastal plain (Mozambique is 44 percent coastal plain, the highest proportion of any African state over minisize), Africans used to be ordered to plant cotton and sell the crop at fixed, low prices to government warehouses. No matter that so much land was in cotton that insufficient land was left for food crops, so that famines were common in some of southern Africa's best farmland.

The harsh nature of Portuguese colonial policy was for years masked by Portuguese racial attitudes and the well-publicized policy of *assimilado*. In contrast to South Africa, blacks in the Portuguese colonies were not subjected to many of the petty harassments of apartheid. Blacks in Portuguese Africa were served in the fanciest restaurants (if they were "properly" dressed and had the money) and there were no laws forbidding interracial socialization, residence in "white" neighborhoods, or intermarriage. While Portuguese Africa's blacks generally had a standard of living inferior to that of South Africa's more segregated blacks, race relations *appeared* far better. Blacks could attain full citizenship and equality by passing educational, personal wealth, and life-style tests. If an African were living European-style, was literate in Portuguese, and had an "acceptable" income, he or she could apply for assimilado (culturally assimilated) status. This was intended to permit selective upward mobility and to provide a goal to which Africans could aspire. While it is true that assimilados were not segregated nor discriminated against in any official policy or public facility, it is also true that very few Africans had the opportunities to reach an educational and income level that would support a claim to assimilado status. Also, many blacks of superior education with leadership aspirations simply refused to become assimilados. They did not wish to be known as "imitation Portuguese" but rather as Africans proud of their own heritage.

The long period of terroristic guerrilla warfare that finally overthrew Portuguese domination seems to have ended in tragedy. One colonial master of Angola has been exchanged for another, the Soviet Union and its Cuban ally. Angola, which has the potential of becoming one of southern Africa's most diversified and successful economies, must cope with multiple blows to its economy. The 350,000 Portuguese who fled comprised most of the managers, technicians, and bureaucrats without whom no economy can function efficiently. The Angolan economy had been expanding rapidly due to its diversified agricultural exports; fish canning and cement industries; oil, diamond, and iron ore production; and $100 million a year in earnings from the Benguela Railroad between the mineralized areas of Zambia and Zaire and the Angolan port of Lobito. Angola's Communist government cannot control its territory without the assistance of Cuban troops. Angola's oil production is mainly from the tiny **exclave** of Cabinda just north of the Zaire (Congo) River. Cabinda separatists are waging a hit-and-run war for independence. The Benguela railroad has been closed for years, depriving Angola of important foreign exchange earnings, although oil production remains high.

Mozambique appears to be more stable than Angola; like Angola it earns revenue from international traffic via railroads from the landlocked central plateau countries and also from South Africa. The link with South Africa is strong because South Africa sends part of the migrant workers' earnings to Mozambique in the form of gold. The official value of the gold is credited to each worker's account, but the Mozambique government sells the gold on open market at prices far above the official rate and keeps the difference. Thus, South Africa maintains mutually profitable working relationships with black regimes that detest apartheid. Mozambique has perhaps the largest-scale example of a problem common in South Africa's neighbors (and within South Africa itself). If all migrant workers were to suddenly return "home" from South Africa's cities and mines, rural areas in Mozambique would have to support many more people than normal. Soil erosion and environmental degradation could be the result of this potential sudden increase in population density.

Zambia   Zambia is currently trying to decrease its critical dependence on world copper prices. Copper has been the only significant source of foreign exchange and contributes almost half the gross domestic product. Steep fluctuations in copper prices endanger the stability of this economy. The government has embarked on an extensive program of economic diversification. Although Zambia has available unused land and water resources, it spends hard-earned foreign exchange to import food. Food production has risen recently and there are good prospects for eventual exports of corn. The government also operates breweries, flour milling, oil refining, agricultural wholesaling, and even retail businesses. Unfortunately, efficiency is low in some of these enterprises, requiring subsidies rather than generating profits.

In the mid-1970's, Zambia had deliberately shifted its dependence on international railways and foreign ports due to its strong opposition to white minority rule in Zimbabwe and South Africa. In one of their first major aid programs in tropical Africa, China (PRC) built the 1,056-mile (1,700 kilometers) Tanzam Railway between Zambia and the Tanzanian port of Dar es Salaam. Railroad operating difficulties and port congestion at Dar es Salaam forced a reopening of the South African connection when the Benguela Railroad in Angola was closed by civil war and not reopened to international traffic.

Malawi   Malawi's economic development strategy focuses on continuing significant exports of tobacco, tea, and sugar while developing small consumer industries as import-replacements. Malawi has a consistent, if small, budget surplus. The National Rural Development Program, partly supported by funds from Canada, the UK, France, and the European Community (EC), is a major agricultural settlement and productivity scheme, accompanied by an ambitious road-building program. Malawi has served as regional peacemaker, attempting to avoid confrontations while working for the long-term welfare of all people of the south of the continent. Malawi is building a new capital city, Lilongwe, which is more centrally located than the colonial capital, Blantyre, although the former capital continues to grow through its commercial and manufacturing functions.

Malagasy   The Republic of Malagasy has many cultural contrasts with Africa as well as physical separation (the

Copper Refinery in Zambia. A tactic of development is to replace the export of ores with the export of higher-priced refined metals, keeping more of the "value added." This region's mineral riches attract superpower competition for their friendship. (Courtesy of United Nations/Y. Lehmann)

island of Madagascar, a little smaller than Texas, is 250 miles (400 kilometers) offshore from Mozambique). The population of 9 million includes eighteen ethnic groups comprised of various proportions of Asians and Africans. Unlike countries like Malawi, where hominid remains and stone tools have been found dating back more than a million years, Madagascar seems to have been uninhabited until about 2,000 years ago. The central highlands are dominated by groups of more Asian heritage, while the coastal areas' people are more uniformly African in racial heritage. Migrations continued sporadically, bringing more Malaysian and Polynesian peoples to supplement the first arrivals, Indonesians and Africans. More recent arrivals have included Chinese, Indians, and French. The Malagasy language is of Malayo-Polynesian origins and the majority religion is animism with ancestor worship. Although many of Malagasy's people have African blood and the island was an active participant in the slave trade, Malagasy is clearly not African in culture. However, Malagasy is a member of the Organization of African Unity. Although it has only minor trade relationships with any African country, Malagasy recognizes that Africa is the only logical major world region with which it can identify.

Malagasy's economy has grown very slowly since independence from France in 1960. It is relatively isolated from external markets, has an adequate transport-communications infrastructure, and world market prices for its major exports (coffee, vanilla, cloves) have been unstable. Additionally, government policies of direct participation in all sectors of the economy have discouraged foreign investment. The government is pursuing the "Malagasization" of retail trade, formerly controlled by Indian and Chinese residents.

THE SOUTH AFRICAN SUBREGION

Although it would be hard to define "typical" subregions in this large and culturally diverse region, southern Africa is obviously *not* typical. It is the last stand of colonialism, at least in its more obvious, nineteenth century style format. With the exception of Zimbabwe (Rhodesia), the economies of the "independent" states of southern Africa, Botswana, Lesotho, and Swaziland are so closely dependent on the Republic of South Africa that their freedom of political action is less than total. Within the republic, voting is the privilege of adult whites, and whites make up about 17 percent of the population. Directly or indirectly, the majority of that portion of this 17 percent who do vote in South Africa thus controls much of the southern section of the continent.

In the continent south of the equator, independence has flowed southward historically. Just after World War II, South Africa's nearest continental neighbors ruled by blacks were Liberia and Ethiopia, each about 2,000 miles (3,200 kilometers) distant from South Africa and its Southwest Africa (Namibia) mandate. The 1960 independence of the Congo (Zaire) brought black African rule to within approximately 700 miles (1,100 kilometers) of South Africa. The collapse of Portuguese rule in Angola and Mozambique in the mid-70's finally brought fully independent Black African governments to South Africa's borders.

As the Republic of South Africa is clearly the dominant economic and military power of this subregion, there are three logical groupings within the subregion for purposes of discussion. South Africa and its "fifth province," directly-ruled Southwest Africa (Namibia), constitute one unit. Zimbabwe (Rhodesia), in the trauma of transition from minority white rule to majority black rule, is distinctively a separate unit, while the legally independent but economically *dependent* states of Botswana, Lesotho, and Swaziland comprise a third unit.

South Africa and Southwest Africa The Dutch East India Company, whose major interests developed in the Indonesian archipelago, founded Cape Town in 1652. Fresh water, fresh food, a mail drop, and minor repairs were all available—Cape Town was the halfway stop on a lucrative trade route. Also there was a clear potential for a naval base to control the passage from the South Atlantic to the Indian Ocean. It was for this naval power role, as well as the way-station function, that Britain seized the Cape in 1795. The Dutch settlers, already established through four or five generations, resented the British takeover. As slavery had existed on Dutch farms at the Cape since 1658, the African Dutch, or Boers, resented Britain's abolition of slavery throughout its empire in 1807. A strong British military presence, augmented by British migration (emigration from Holland had practically ceased), meant that the Boers had little option but to submit to British law and **acculturation** or leave. They left, beginning in 1836, on the great treks north and east away from British control. The Boers created two independent and landlocked republics, the Transvaal (South African Republic) and the Orange Free State in 1852 and 1854. (See Figure 12–12.)

Relations between the British and the two Republics were never easy. The discovery of diamonds in 1870 at Kimberly, near the Cape Colony's border with the Orange Free State, followed by the gold strikes in the Witwatersrand region of the Transvaal in 1886, attracted scores of thousands of immigrants, mostly from the British Isles. The accompanying investment inflow in transportation,

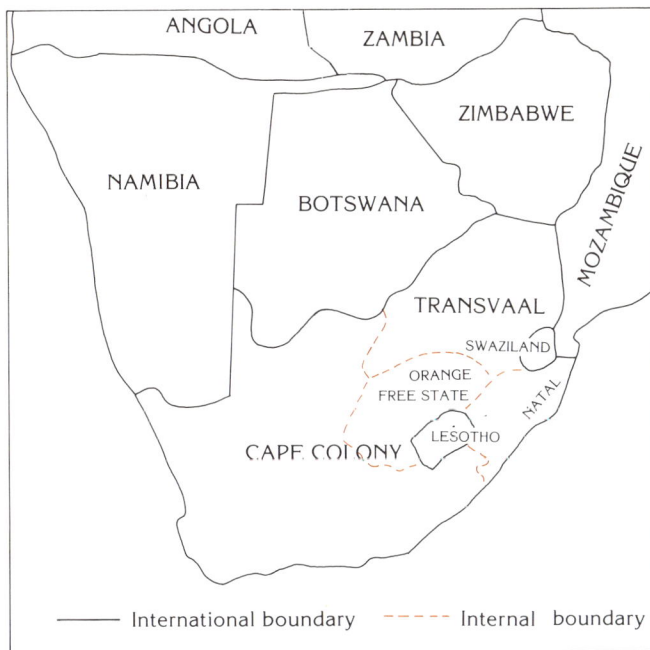

FIGURE 12–12
The Boer Republics and the BLS Countries. South Africa was created from two defeated Boer republics and two British colonies at the conclusion of the Anglo-Boer War. The Boers, a majority within the voting white minority, thus came to power over all South Africa. Three former British protectorates, Botswana, Lesotho, and Swaziland ("BLS" countries), are independent but closely tied to the South African economy.

mining, manufacturing, and urban sectors of the economy seemed more like an invasion to the conservative, agrarian Boers. Frictions between the two cultures led to two Anglo-Boer Wars, in 1880–81, and the more famous rematch in 1899–1902. The second war was a particularly bitter one; a scorched-earth policy and the concept of concentration camps were used by the British during this struggle. The Boer surrender was facilitated by the conciliatory policies of a British Prime Minister who, in effect, proposed a union of the Boer states and British colonies incorporating Boer concepts of race relations. Although the comparatively more liberal British had begun extending the vote to nonwhites in Cape Colony, the new union, inaugurated in 1910, adopted the Boer viewpoint that only whites would vote. It was British policy that only by effectively acknowledging Boer control would a new union loyal to the empire be created. Thus, in the long run the Boers won their war and the fragile beginnings of liberalization and "one person-one vote" in the British Cape and Natal colonies were overwhelmed. This background is essential to an understanding of modern South Africa.

Resource Base The resource base of the Republic can be described as fabulous, but with two critical exceptions—a shortage of water and the absence of petro-

leum. South Africa is in the world's top ten producers of minerals; it leads in gold, gem diamonds, antimony, and vanadium and is one of the top three producers of asbestos, chrome, industrial diamonds, manganese, uranium, and the platinum group of metals. Its reserves of gold ores are estimated to be two thirds of the world's total. South Africa also has extensive deposits of coal, copper, lead, nickel, and zinc. Southwest Africa, or Namibia as it is known to those opposing South African control, is another storehouse of minerals. Namibia is a major producer of diamonds and copper. Lead, zinc, and uranium are also important. Active exploration has so far not discovered significant oil offshore although geological conditions are promising.

Population and Race South Africa's population of 29 million is quite small considering the fact that this country produces a major share of the GNP of the entire region. The average population density is about 55 per square mile (21 per square kilometer) but it is very unevenly distributed (see Figure 12–11) over a land more than twice the size of Texas. Africans comprise 71 percent of the South African population; the largest of many African ethnic groups are the Zulu and Xhosa, each over 5 million. The next largest racial group, the whites or Europeans, forms 17 percent of the total; these are primarily the descendants of Dutch, French, English, and German settlers. "Cape Coloreds" are the result of very early mixing of indigenous peoples and Europeans. Living mostly in the Cape province, they represent 9 percent of the population. Finally there are the Asians, descendants of both Hindu and Moslem Indians brought to Natal in the middle of the nineteenth century to work on sugar plantations.

South Africa's well-publicized problems of race relations identify race as the key question in that nation. The systematic segregation of races acquired legal force and momentum with the triumph of the Afrikaners (Boers), the majority within the white minority. Race became a legal status with far-reaching implications, and people were classified by means of such items as skin-tone color charts. The Nationalist government has since pursued the seemingly impossible goals of **apartheid,** the strict physical separation of the races, and "separate development" economically. The Nationalists took South Africa out of the multiracial British Commonwealth, accepted drastically deteriorated relations with the new Black African states and were deprived of their vote in the UN General Assembly when South Africa refused to comply with UN rulings on the future of Namibia. This quasi-outcast status of South Africa has strongly influenced its economic and military strategy, as the South African leadership sees that country as unfairly victimized by resurgent black national-

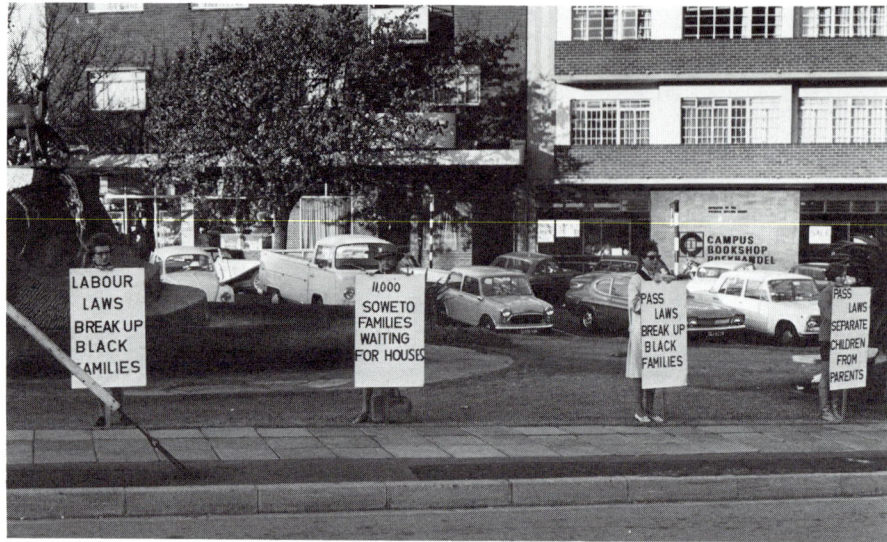

South Africans Protesting Apartheid. These white citizens of South Africa are protesting apartheid regulations. The region's most modernized economy faces the threat of guerrilla warfare, a potential tragedy for all of its citizens. (Courtesy of United Nations)

ism. The South African government notes that black South Africans live on a higher average standard of living than do black Africans generally. While this is certainly true, it is also true that there is a considerable gap between average incomes for blacks and whites in South Africa.

The factor that vastly complicates the drive toward complete apartheid and separate economic development, which may in fact prevent the ultimate apartheid envisioned, is the strong economic interlinkage among South Africans of all races. South Africa's Cape Coloured are generally highly assimilated, culturally, into the modern urban-industrial societies. Unlike the *Bantu,* a term applied to all black South Africans, the Cape Coloured have no stress of **detribalization.** They are not caught between traditional tribal communities and Europeanized urban industrial cultures. They have no tribal homeland to which to return either voluntarily or involuntarily. Mostly Christian, they tend to be skilled workers and lower-echelon managers with living standards between white and black levels.

Asians, whose ancestors were imported as plantation labor, have climbed the economic ladder by dint of hard work combined with frugal living to generate capital for opening small businesses. Many Asians have become quite wealthy. They have also entered some of the professions such as dentistry and medicine. Despite their occasional affluence, Asians are subjected to many of the restrictions of apartheid. Partly because they do not readily assimilate (they maintain Hindu temples or Moslem mosques) the Asians are not completely welcome. Because Asians practically monopolize retail trade at the local level, there is resentment against them and envy of their higher standards of living from many South African blacks.

Agricultural Economy Agriculturally, South Africa is in an enviable position; it is practically self-sufficient in food, in both quantity and variety. Considering its often uneasy relations with the rest of the world, this is an advantage politically-strategically as well as economically. South Africa's range of climates supports a range of crops similar to those of the United States or Australia. Corn, grains, tobacco, sugar, fruit, peanuts, and grapes are all important crops; South African wines have entered world markets with some success, though production is relatively small. Boer farmers have long prided themselves on raising superior livestock, and soil erosion problems induced by overgrazing a generation ago seem to have been solved. South Africa operates the continent's largest fertilizer plant and generally has a very healthy agricultural sector. Wool, sugar, hides, fruit, and meat are among agricultural exports. A chronic problem for many South African farmers is drought: many development schemes, domestic and international, involve water storage and transfer. Namibia, mostly desert or semi-desert, is characterized by stock raising and some subsistence agriculture. Most of Namibia's cultivable land is in the north (on the border with Angola) where most of the Bantu-speaking Africans live. Commercial ranching is controlled by whites. Black African-owned herds are more likely to suffer deadly hoof-and-mouth disease, although the government has provided mass inoculations and technical advice to the tribal herdsmen. Southwest Africa is a major exporter of karakul sheepskins, leather, canned meat, and fish (the cold current offshore supports an important ocean fishery).

Urban-Industrial Development Urban-industrial development is further advanced in South Africa than in any other large region of Africa. The diamond and gold mining industries developing in the late nineteenth century attracted large investments in transportation and other industrial infrastructure. Great cities like Johannesburg grew explosively. Manufacturing was already developing and diversifying when World War II produced many import shortages. Government policy then emphasized a drive toward industrial self-sufficiency, a policy made even more important by the "siege mentality" engendered by general world criticism of South Africa's racial policies. Manufacturing, spurred by this import-replacement strategy, has become the dominant sector of the gross domestic product, but mining and agriculture remain the basic producers for export. Active gold markets greatly benefit South Africa, whose gold mines are experiencing rapid increases in operating costs as shafts go deeper underground, requiring forced-draft cooling (rock temperatures rise sharply as tunnels probe deeper) and higher energy consumption.

Separate Development: The Bantustans   Economic development strategies, racial segregation, environmental problems, and political policies are all intertwined in the creation of the **Bantustans** or tribal homelands. (See Figure 12–13.) The first of the self-governing homelands to be granted independence was the Transkei, with a population of 4 million, in October, 1976. Six other homelands have already or will achieve theoretically independent sta-

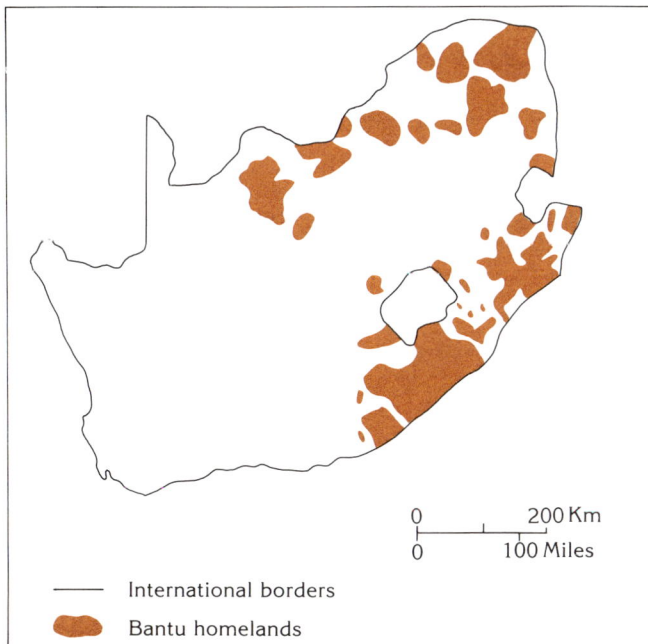

FIGURE 12–13
Bantu Homelands. A territorial outgrowth of apartheid and the buffer zone strategy, the Bantu homelands are regarded as sovereign states by South Africa, but not recognized as such by any other state.

tus, while some others will have self-governance short of independence. Independent Bantustans are intended to produce truly separate economic development for blacks and whites, although there are practical obstacles to this. The technology and capital of "white" South Africa needs the labor and markets of "black" South Africa, and vice versa. South Africa's expanding industrial and mining economy will demand 4 million skilled workers in the early 1980's, much more than half of which will be black.

South Africa's labor needs have long been met by importing long-term migrant workers from Swaziland, Lesotho, Botswana, Mozambique, and Malawi. These workers cannot bring their families during at least their initial contract period. Well paid by the standards of their own country, they are not paid well by developed South Africa standards. They tend to be used in the toughest jobs, especially mining. Since they send substantial amounts of money home to support their families, in addition to direct compensation to their governments, the economies of some of South Africa's neighbors have grown dependent on this international labor migration. The advantage of migrant workers to the South African government is, of course, that they do not (cannot) settle permanently, do not further tip the racial imbalance against the whites, do not consume any measurable social welfare benefits (the aged, handicapped, and minor dependents stay in the sending country) and seldom take any interest in South African politics or civil rights causes. They are effectively isolated from the surrounding society while contributing to its economic growth. This determination by the South African government to use blacks in the labor force while maintaining segregation led to the highly controversial homelands concept.

South Africa has had to reassess its political geographic situation in southern Africa. Its economic interests in its near neighbors, Swaziland, Botswana, and Lesotho, and direct control in Southwest Africa, give it a buffer of sorts in all areas but one; it is in direct contact with revolutionary Mozambique (see Figure 12–12). The "inner buffer" function of the homelands is achieved by placing them in a very difficult choice situation. If the homelands cooperate with outside black nationalist guerrilla forces, they can expect denial of access for their "citizens" to South Africa's economy, as well as more severe retaliation. If they refuse to harbor black insurgents, the homelands may bear the brunt of guerrilla warfare themselves.

South Africa's designation of some homelands as "independent" states is viewed as deceptive by many South African blacks. Many (perhaps a majority) of the people of such "states" as Transkei do not live there permanently; they earn their living in South Africa's factories, mines, and farms. South Africa eventually intends to require passports of homelands residents, officially denying them South African citizenship. As many urban blacks have few, if any, cultural and family ties to their official homelands, their "repatriation" there could amount to exile from the only homes they've known.

The South African administration has encouraged industrial location within the "independent homelands," or at "growth points" on their borders. Few South African industries have selected homeland (or even growth point) locations; the supporting infrastructure of transport, communications, and energy systems tends to encourage urban-suburban South African locations instead. As countries other than South Africa do not recognize the independent status of the homelands, they do not maintain embassies or consulates to aid their own citizens interested in doing business there, practically eliminating foreign investment possibilities in the homelands. South Africa apparently is applying the "independent homelands" technique to Southwest Africa (Namibia), establishing homelands along the Angolan border.

Political Stability   Political stability is, in the short-term view, fairly solid; in the long-term view, it may be shaky. The South African government, which does not permit nonwhites to vote or run for office, is unlikely to be voted out. The South African military is the best equipped in the region and can be expected to act with both high motivation and professional skill in the event of external or internal attack.

To the Afrikaner or Boer majority of South African whites, theirs is the "beloved country," their homeland and the homeland of their ancestors. Virtually all Afrikaners can trace their ancestry in South Africa back to the seventeenth or eighteenth century. This is no recently arrived group of colonists whose hearts, relatives, and passports are in Europe. The Afrikaners have no "home" to go back to, as white settlers in Kenya could return to Britain; they *are* home—they and their people have helped build the country and its society. From their viewpoint, there can be no retreat, no return to a distant homeland.

In the long run, even a determined, united, and well-armed minority may not be able to forestall the evolution of a combination of South Africa's increasingly restive black majority and arms and active guerrilla support from such states as Mozambique, Angola, and Zimbabwe. It would be a tragedy for all races in southern Africa if the region's most advanced industrial economy were to be destroyed or subverted. South African technology and capital has the potential for helping to raise living standards throughout southern Africa if racial tolerance and equity can evolve peacefully.

Economic-Cultural "Capitals"   South Africa contains the only cities that could claim to be economic-cultural capitals in this subregion. Johannesburg is a world city; Cape Town has an historic role as a political center as well as a major cultural and economic center. In South Africa's unique locational decentralization of government functions (reflecting the merger of two British colonies with two Boer Republics), Cape Town is the seat of the legislature, whereas Bloemfontein is the seat of the judicial branch and Pretoria is the administrative capital with most government offices. Durban (Natal) is a possible third South African "regional capital," although this status may be altered by the "inner buffer" strategy, which places much of Durban's hinterland within the homelands.

Botswana, Lesotho, and Swaziland   Botswana, Lesotho, and Swaziland have similar histories as modern states and share a strong economic link with the Republic of South Africa. Each is a ministate in terms of population—Lesotho has 1.5 million; Botswana, about 1 million; and Swaziland, less than three fourths of a million. Together, these three countries have fewer people than metropolitan Houston. The Batswana[1] and Swazi each have a 3 percent growth rate, and the Basotho, 2.1 percent.

The Basotho, under pressure from the Zulu and Matabele, appealed for help and were placed under a British protectorate in 1868. Similarly, the Swazi requested aid against Zulu raiders and were guaranteed independence under British and Transvaalian protection. The Transvaal took over the administration of Swaziland in 1894, with British agreement. The Batswana, their traditional territory under Boer invasion, appealed for British assistance and were granted a protectorate in 1885. All three modern states had claimed larger territories in the mid-to-late nineteenth century and all three were "rescued" from destruction whether at the hands of Boer farmers or unfriendly tribes. In 1909, when the constitution of the Union (now Republic) of South Africa was being written, these protectorates specifically asked *not* to be included within this new state. The British, recognizing the need for some territories in southern Africa not directly under the control of whites, confirmed their separate "protected" status. Lesotho is an enclave within South Africa; Swaziland and Botswana are bordered by South Africa. Lesotho and Swaziland use currency directly convertible to South African rands, and rands freely circulate in their territories. All three states are in a customs union with South Africa—there are no customs or tariff barriers among them. Lesotho, a little smaller than Maryland, sends much of its work force to South Africa for most of the year. At any one time, a quarter of a million Basotho may be absent from the country. Swaziland supplies 30,000 to 40,000 workers to South Africa. Botswana is the most strident of the three in its opposition to South Africa's racial policies but realis-

---

[1]The Batswana are the people of the country Botswana.

tically cooperates with South Africa economically. Lesotho has the narrowest resource base; water is an exportable commodity as it has an annual average rainfall of 28 inches (710 millimeters) and is close to many populated but semiarid regions in South Africa. Unfortunately, this rainfall (in steep terrain that has been farmed and grazed unscientifically) has produced severe erosion. Lesotho's traditional trade routes to the rest of the world have been complicated by the "independence" of Transkei, through which some routes pass. Tensions have arisen with South Africa, but a working relationship is maintained as Lesotho needs the remittances sent back by Basotho workers in the Republic. Also, many South Africans visit Maseru (Lesotho's capital) for a weekend of casino gambling and other activities forbidden at home.

Swaziland is among southern Africa's most prosperous new countries. Although nearly three quarters of the Swazi are still engaged in subsistence agriculture, industrial employment is rising steadily. A serious problem for Swaziland is foreign land ownership; though more than half of the country is communal land in trust for the Swazi nation, as much as 40 percent is held privately by foreigners, most of whom are South Africans. Iron-ore mining, asbestos, and a variety of small-scale consumer industries like plastic packaging supplement the agricultural exports of hides, beef, dairy products, and sugar. Swaziland could be in a very serious situation if revolutionaries from Mozambique were to use it as a base for terrorist activities against South Africa.

Botswana's resources include diamonds, copper, nickel, salt, and coal. The government owns part of the diamond concessions and part of the large copper-nickel complex. Botswana's sparse average population density (3 per square mile [1.3 per square kilometer]) and lack of large urban centers (none over 30,000) reflects the large proportion of its land in the Kalahari Desert. Botswana was distinguished, until 1965, by having its administrative capital located outside its boundaries (at Mafeking) as there simply was no urban center of any size until the new capital at Gaberone was created. Ironically, in a country generally characterized as desert and sparse grazing land, the northern portion is dominated by an immense inland delta of northward-draining rivers. The Okavango Swamps cover 6,500 square miles (16,800 square kilometers). The booming mining economy is expected to expand at about 10 percent a year, strengthening what has been a force for progressive political and economic development in the subregion.

Zimbabwe   Rhodesia, as it was formerly known, was the "last stand" of European colonialism in Southern Africa, if we exempt South Africa itself. A protracted guerrilla war against the white minority government reached major proportions in the late 1970's. Rhodesia had been, for more than a decade, a British colony in rebellion. Eventually a combination of economic pressures and terrorism forced an end to one of the shortest-lived European colonies in Africa.

European penetration of the interior between the flanking Portuguese coastal colonies did not produce any permanent white settlements until quite late in the nineteenth century. Portugal had claimed the interior but had made only sporadic explorations. Empire-builder Cecil Rhodes obtained mineral concessions from local chiefs in 1888; in 1889 the British South Africa Company was chartered to develop this area. The private company's control was terminated in 1923 and Rhodesia's whites were given a choice of joining South Africa or becoming a separate

Maseru Airport, Lesotho. The industrialized world's technology and investments are both necessary in fostering rapid development throughout the region. Here, the impact of both improvements to the transport infrastructure and in public health through disease control are evident. (Courtesy of United Nations/ICAO/G. Fraynl)

colony. The differences between Southern Rhodesia (present Zimbabwe), Northern Rhodesia (present Zambia), and Nyasaland (present Malawi) became apparent then, when Southern Rhodesia's white settlers chose to become a separate colony without assuming responsibility for the other British territories to the north. Northern Rhodesia never had as much as 100,000 whites, and Nyasaland never reached 10,000. At its height, Southern Rhodesia's whites numbered about 275,000, so that the Zambezi River was more than just the boundary between the two Rhodesias—it was the boundary between a colony that whites perceived as "theirs" and the two northern protectorates in which there was implicit recognition of eventual black rule.

Rhodesia in the 60's and 70's was a tragic example of lessons not learned in other parts of Africa where sizeable white minorities had not succeeded in maintaining themselves in power (notably Kenya). Southern Rhodesia's minority even attempted to control the destinies of the two protectorates to its north by forming the short-lived (1953–63) Federation of Rhodesia and Nyasaland. The federation, successful economically in pooling markets and resources, was strongly opposed by Africans in the two protectorates. Southern Rhodesia drafted a constitution in 1961 that initiated voting privileges based on economic (tax-paying) and educational qualifications but looked blatantly racist to most Africans. When Britain insisted that Rhodesia move toward eventual "one-person-one-vote" rule, Rhodesia issued a unilateral declaration of independence (UDI). Britain regarded the UDI as illegal but would not use force to end the rebellion, instead requesting economic pressures on the regime. The economic sanctions were not completely successful, as Mozambique and South Africa, linked by rail to Rhodesia, allowed some Rhodesian trade to flow through their ports (see Figure 12–11). In 1970, a new Land Apportionment Act "divided equally" Rhodesia's land, half (the better half, agriculturally, and that near cities and transport) to the 274,000 Europeans and half to the 6 million Africans. Rhodesian industry boomed in the effort to attain self-sufficiency. It is arguable that sanctions produced positive as well as negative effects on Rhodesia's economy. Import-replacement industries flourished, including food processing, textiles, clothing, transportation equipment, and steel.

Zimbabwe, as it is now known, has an excellent resource base, featuring two thirds of the world's chrome ores, and including coal, asbestos, copper, nickel, gold, and iron ore. There is ample power, most supplied by the giant Kariba Dam on the Zambezi, and the transport infrastructure is well developed. Inflation and the increasing human and financial costs of guerrilla warfare effectively ended the dream of stopping time at the 1900 mark, and a London conference finally inaugurated elections in which all adults, regardless of color, could vote.

Zimbabwe has enormous potential for continuing economic progress and for helping to alleviate the world food crisis. There is considerable room for expansion of agricultural output in this relatively lightly settled (45 per square mile [17 per square kilometer]) country the size of Montana.

Victoria Falls on the Zambezi River. Africa south of the Sahara has some impressive hydro power development and potential, as well as the tourism asset of spectacular scenery. (Courtesy of United Nations)

SUMMARY

A salient characteristic of Africa south of the Sahara is the set of compressional stresses alluded to earlier. Many states in this region have had little more than a century to recover from the effects of the slave trade and only a quarter of a century's existence as independent states. Melding a nation from many different cultural groups, in many instances with a recent colonial history of manipulating tribal differences in "divide-and-conquer" techniques, is being accomplished or attempted in a very compressed time span when compared to the evolution of European nation-states. Boundaries can be expected to be the focus of international tensions. At best these boundaries, many of which cut through logical hinterlands and mining districts, will hinder development and lead to otherwise unnecessary duplication of transport facilities. The great regional disparities in mineral wealth, per capita income, population density, and growth would imply future exaggeration of **developmental differentials.**

TENSIONAL RELATIONSHIPS WITH OTHER REGIONS

Real and potential mineral wealth, strategic geopolitical significance, and relatively light density but expanding population all contribute to a continuing reassessment of the region's significance in world affairs. The termination of European colonies has been followed by a relative dilution of one-time European domination of regional economies and trade relationships. Many states retain close economic relationships with their former colonizing powers, but Western ties to the South African economy are viewed with dismay. The People's Republic of China, the Soviet Union, and the United States have all joined the former colonial powers in seeking influence and trade. Individual states have become adept at playing off superpowers and major powers for gifts, low-interest loans, and favorable trade agreements. The South African problem dominates many African states' international views.

REGIONAL WORLD VIEW

The enormous diversity of the region precludes any general agreement on a world view. While South Africa seeks tacit support from the West, such states as Nigeria and Zaire sense their growing importance in the world's mineral economy and begin to seek corresponding political influence. Inter-African trade, still minor, may expand in the future, but for now, international trade and investment relationships with the industrial world (including Japan) dominate African world views.

case study

GEOGRAPHIC FACTORS FOR UNITY OR DISUNITY IN THE CONGO BASIN

In July of 1960, the Belgian Congo joined the growing list of newly independent states in Africa. Within days of independence, the Republic of the Congo had begun a near-collapse into the terror of chaos. Belgian paratroopers arrived to rescue Europeans caught in the countryside as the Congolese police and army rebelled against their officers. The economy floundered without direction. The southeastern province of the Congo, the Katanga, had declared itself independent and remained so in fact for several years. Belgium, Britain, the United States, and the Soviet Union were all directly interested in the outcome of the Congolese civil war and the independence attempt of Katanga. Trouble rose again in the late 1970's between the central government of Zaire (Congo) and Shaba (Katanga).

The motivations of Katanga independence movements and some contributors to their temporary success are related to the physical, economic, and cultural geography of the Congo basin and to its recent history. Belgium did not seek its one-time colony, eighty times larger than Belgium. The Congo state was a product of conflicting European imperial ambitions and the intrigues of Leopold, King of the Belgians. King Leopold had hired the explorer, Henry Stanley, to sail down the Congo River and thus establish a territorial claim to the entire basin for a private stock company headed by Leopold. The European great powers could agree on the Congo Basin becoming, in effect, the world's largest plantation because it would be a buffer state separating British, French, German, and Portuguese colonial interests. The boundaries drawn in Berlin did not recognize African tribal boundaries.

To control and exploit this vast territory with the handful of Europeans actually there, the Company of the Congo adopted the familiar colonial tool of "divide and rule." The historical animosities of the different linguistic, religious, and cultural groups and tribes were taken advantage of by selecting the most aggressive tribes as "native police," better paid than other Congolese, to enforce the will of the Company. Oppressive enforcement of Company quotas on rubber and ivory collection thus worsened relations among tribal groups in the Congo. Submerging rival tribal loyalties in the interest of a larger state could not occur; the Congo state remained an abstraction, a European idea rather than an African one. The **loyalties set** focused on the tribe and its traditional allies and enemies, rather than upon the state. This factor, aided by a failure of the colonial regime to provide higher education for more than a few Congolese, helped lead to civil war and a Katanga state.

Other contributing factors in the Katanga independence movement were the drainage, transport, and mineral-wealth geography of the Congo. The Congo (Zaire) is unique among the world's largest rivers in having rapids and waterfalls near its mouth. It is as though the Mississippi River cascaded over falls and rapids near New Orleans. The hydroelectric potential is immense, but the barrier to navigation is also huge. In developing the transport system of the basin, the Belgians stitched together a patchwork of navigable sections of the river with short rail links around navigational barriers. Such a system is cheaper to build than an all-rail network or an all-river network (with canals to bypass rapids) but is much more expensive to operate. Each transfer of cargo between different modes of transport (river boat, railroad, ocean steamer) is a labor-intensive bottleneck.

The Shaba (Katanga) province and neighboring Northern Rhodesia (Zambia) shared a rich copper deposit. This area of Shaba around Lubumbushi also produces uranium. A transcontinental east-west railroad had been built to link the Copperbelt with ports on both the Atlantic and Indian oceans. This international transport system was far more efficient than using the Congo's internal river and rail system. Thus, Katanga could (and did) trade with the rest of the world through the then-Portuguese territories without the necessity of dealing with the rest of the Congo. This, in combination with the strong tribal loyalties and almost nonexistent loyalty to a Congo state, aided temporary independence.

REVIEW QUESTIONS

1 How did Europeans outflank Arab control over Trans-Sahara routes and reorient much of Africa's trade?

2 Why are the long-term effects of slaving still apparent in some African societies?

3 How effective has black African nationalism been as a unifying factor in this region?

4   Briefly, describe the nature and effects of compressional stresses.

5   Why were colonial capitals usually also development enclaves?

6   Describe some of the physical handicaps to easy navigation of most African rivers.

7   Why are many West African economies especially vulnerable to world commodity market fluctuations?

8   In what ways has "balkanization" restricted the economic development of much of West Africa?

9   Briefly describe Nigeria's problems of internal unity in terms of physical, economic, and cultural geography.

10 How did colonial policies and practices facilitate disruptive forces within newly independent Zaire (Congo)?

11 How does the persistence of tribalism threaten the integrity of many African states?

12 How did the site and situation of Ethiopia contribute to its persistence as an officially Christian state in a Moslem matrix?

13 Where are the most important zones of mineral wealth in Africa south of the Sahara? Why has at least one become an area of superpower competition?

14 Based on current population growth rates and population-resource ratios, project the region's richest and poorest states in the foreseeable future.

15 How reliable is any attempt at correlating mineral resources and economic development in this region? Why?

16 How does "neo-colonialism" threaten the sovereignty of some states in this region, particularly in foreign policy?

17 Why is it said that the South African Boers "lost the war but won the country"?

18 Why does South Africa receive a surprising amount of unofficial economic cooperation from its black African neighbors?

19 How does South Africa strive for self-sufficiency? What physical assets support this policy?

20 Why is the future of Bantustans considered bleak? Why were they set up in the first place?

1   PHILIP ALLEN and AARON SEGAL, *The Traveler's Africa.* New York: Hopkinson & Blake, 1973.

2   GERALD BENDER, *Angola Under the Portuguese: The Myth and the Reality.* London: Heinemann, 1978.

3   A. BEST and H. DeBLIS, *African Survey.* New York: Wiley, 1977.

4   R. J. HARRISON CHURCH, et al, *Africa and the Islands,* 3rd ed. New York: Wiley, 1971.

5   MONICA COLE, *South Africa.* London: Methuen, 1961.

6   HARM DeBLIS, *Africa South.* Evanston, Ill.: Northwestern University Press, 1962.

7   JAMES DUFFY, *Portugal in Africa.* Cambridge, Mass.: Harvard University Press, 1962.

8   A. T. GROVE, *Africa South of the Sahara.* London: Oxford University Press, 1970.

9   WILLIAM HANCE, *The Geography of Modern Africa.* New York: Columbia University Press, 1975.

10 C. G. KNIGHT and J. NEWMAN, eds., *Contemporary Africa: Geography and Change.* Englewood Cliffs, N.J.: Prentice Hall, 1976.

11 DONALD MORRISON, et al, *Black Africa: A Comparative Handbook.* New York: The Free Press, 1972.

12 CHRISTIAN POTHOLM and RICHARD DALE, eds., *Southern Africa in Perspective.* New York: The Free Press, 1972.

13 WILLI SCHULZ, *A New Geography of Liberia.* London: Longman's, 1973.

KEY TERMS

- cultural hearth
- diffusion
- *Dar al Islam*
- protectorate
- developmental infrastructure
- *Sahel*
- fossil water
- Fertile Crescent
- high-value-added
- infrastructure
- hidden export

- *haj*
- carrying capacity
- overgrazing
- desalination
- entrepôt
- demographic transition
- salination
- food chain
- successor state
- power vacuum
- relict population

13

SOUTHWEST ASIA— NORTH AFRICA

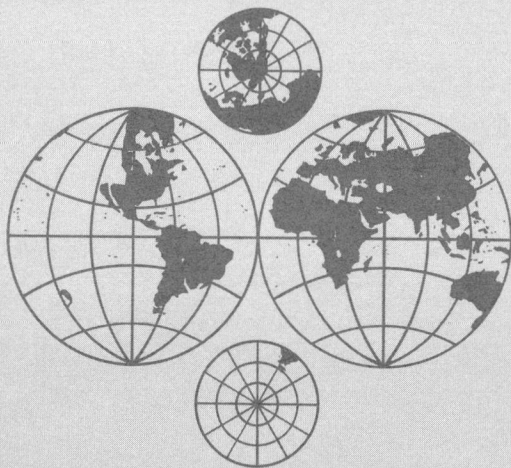

PROLOGUE: THE DRYLANDS CULTURAL HEARTH

Good arguments can be made in support of the idea that civilization arose from multiple origin points that were not in contact with one another originally. For those who believe in a single-source origin of civilization, however, there is no doubt as to the location of that ultimate source. Based on the earliest yet discovered traces of agriculture and urban settlement, the upper reaches of the valleys of the Tigris and Euphrates rivers are generally recognized as the **cultural hearth,** or origin area, of the earliest civilizations. Whether in fact all other early civilizations were the intellectual progeny of the upper Tigris-Euphrates valleys civilizations, this region has had a profound influence on the development of contemporary world civilizations.

The study of the geographic spread of ideas or technology, known as the study of **diffusion,** is an important concept in considering the world significance of this region. It is a cultural hearth, the area of innovation from which diffusion occurred. The upper Tigris-Euphrates valley has been identified as the center of domestication of wheat and cattle. This area may well be the hearth of the basic ideas of agriculture—the deliberate cultivation of certain plants and the raising of animals for food.

The geographic centrality of this region is obvious when looking at the relationship of the three continents of the "old world"—Europe, Asia, and Africa (see Figure 13–1). The core of the region, this cultural hearth lies astride the most probable trade routes among these three continents. The three great monotheistic religions (Judaism, Christianity, and Islam) all spread outward from this hearth. Perceptions of the strategic significance of this area have changed over time, but for most of recorded history it has been considered a key part of the world. Only during the European age of exploration was the importance of this region downgraded in the perceptions of people from other regions. The long struggle of the Christian and Moslem worlds, precisely over the control of that land called holy by three religions, interrupted important trade routes from the Mediterranean Sea eastward to the Orient. This led to Europeans refocusing on such alternatives as maritime exploration of the Atlantic. This resulted in the European discovery of the New World and the development of the circum-Africa route to India. The Mediterranean was no longer the most important and central sea; instead, it became a mere backwater in the new perceptions of the world. The economic centers of the Mediterranean trade (Venice, Genoa, Constantinople, and Alexandria) became relatively less important.

This "Columbus syndrome" was followed by two contemporary historical trends that were linked to each other and to seaward expansionism. European technology and

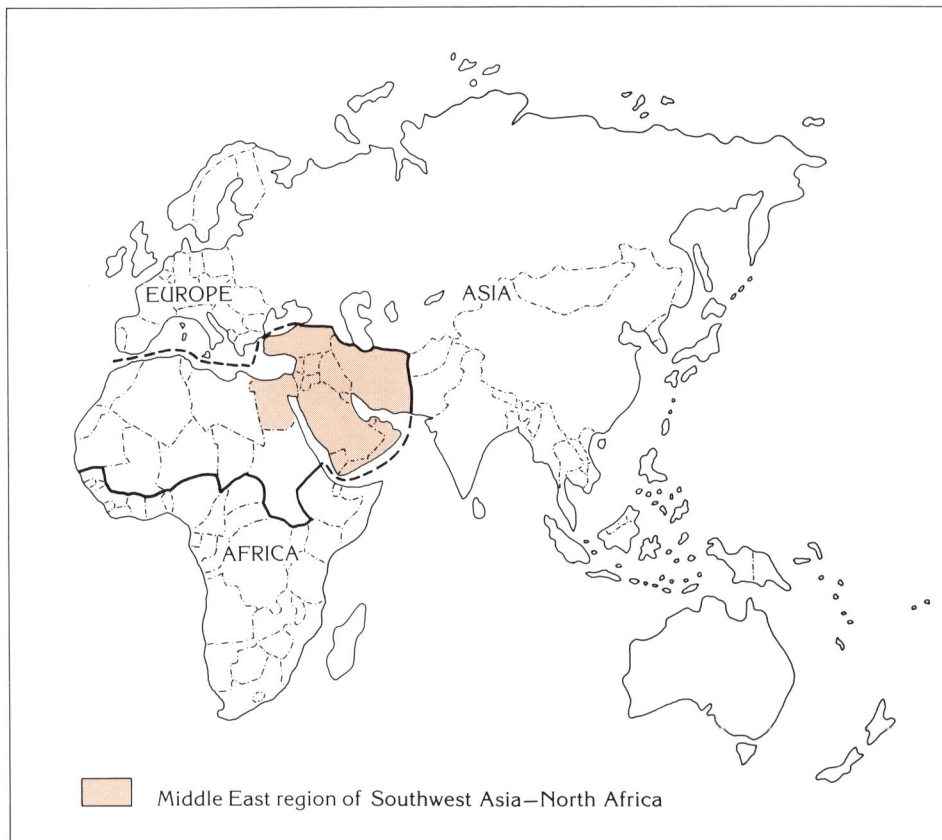

FIGURE 13–1
The Middle East in Relation to Europe, Asia, and Africa. The Middle East is not only a key cultural hearth but is located at the juncture of Europe, Asia, and Africa, serving frequently to interchange and blend ideas and technologies from these continent-scale cultural realms.

sciences surged forward in the Commercial and Industrial revolutions. Ironically, it was the Arab preservation of much of the Greco-Roman world's knowledge of science and geography, together with Arab contributions in these fields and in mathematics, that made it possible for these "revolutions" to be achieved by Europeans as they developed shipbuilding, navigational, and weaponry innovations. The immense wealth once generated by domination of trade routes by the peoples at the core of this region now disappeared with the shifts in trade routes. The *Dar al Islam,* "House of Islam," seemed to stagnate culturally and technologically. Degradation of the regional environment, described later, may have been associated with this decline.

The significance of the region's core in geopolitical terms was reassessed with the opening of the Suez Canal in 1869, once again placing this region in a vital position astride major trade routes. The discovery of the world's largest deposits of oil in what was formerly regarded as resource-poor parts of the world (the Persian Gulf region and North Africa) completed the perceptual rebound of the region to the status of an area critical to the rest of the world.

THE DISTINCTIVENESS OF THE REGION

Few regions have such a high degree of uniformity in the perceptions of people living outside it. The area is commonly thought of as Arab in speech, Moslem in religion, dry in climate, and rich in oil. Each of these general traits applies to some degree and to some parts of the region, yet none applies totally throughout. Nonetheless, it is these factors (among others) on which regional unity is based.

HISTORICAL-CULTURAL CHARACTERISTICS

Until recently there was a prevalent sense here of the past having been far more glorious than the present. The still splendid ruins seemed to dwarf the more meager accomplishments of the present. For several centuries past, relatively little of the area was ruled by fully independent, indigenous governments. Empires, colonies, **protectorates**—all were more common than independent states tial of the Persian Gulf lands provided another motive for colonial control. Since 1920, the growing Arab determination to achieve independence from foreign control has formed a unifying focus of sorts, although the urgency of independence aspirations varied considerably within the region. A resurgent Islam formed another important unifying factor.

ECONOMIC CHARACTERISTICS

There has been relatively little international trade among the countries of this area. Highly developed, industrialized countries tend to have more complex trade relationships, and, in this region, only Israel is clearly a highly developed country. Afghanistan, Jordan, and the two Yemens are definitely underdeveloped, while the rest of the region is in some stage of development. Substantial and varied resource bases exist in Turkey and Iran, while other states in the region tend to have a short list of resources even if

Musicians in Fez, Morocco. This region, which corresponds closely with the historic *Dar al Islam* "House of Islam"—also has other religions and cultures present, but Islamic religion and culture are clearly predominant. (Courtesy of United Nations)

right up until the 1950's. The decaying Turkish Empire was gradually replaced by European colonial or indirect rule by 1920. Arab aspirations to self-rule were used by the British and French to topple the Turkish Empire, but independence was not forthcoming. Instead, League of Nations mandates and European protectorates were extended. French colonial control of North Africa, from Morocco to Tunisia and southward across the Sahara, was matched by British concentration in Egypt, Palestine, Iraq, and the Persian Gulf. British motives included their traditional determination to control the passages between seas and the need to defend the approaches to and the borders of India. By the 1930's, growing realization of the oil poten-

Temple of Abu Simbel, Egypt. Southwest Asia–North Africa contains some of the oldest cultural hearths in the world. The worldwide significance of these ancient cultures was demonstrated by the international effort to relocate these monuments above the rising waters of the Aswan High Dam. (Courtesy of United Nations/UNESCO)

there is oil. The distribution of the two really vital resources of the region, water and oil, is extremely uneven. For obvious reasons, there is a long-established positive correlation between high population density and fresh water resources. Oil, somewhat perversely, tends to be concentrated where people are scarce (see Table 13–1). Egypt, with the second largest national population (after Turkey) in the region, has a proven oil reserve of some 3 billion barrels. Tiny Kuwait, with less than 1.5 million people, has reserves of 71 billion barrels. Those states with enormous ratios of oil wealth to population size make various contributions and subsidies to the large population–low oil resource states. Along with the oil money frequently come attempts to influence the foreign policy of the donee by the donor. The wealth of the regional donors and their development assistance, both to states in the region and elsewhere, results in very high proportions of their gross national product being spent on foreign aid. For example, while the United States spends about one quarter of 1 percent of its GNP on foreign aid, the United Arab Emirates average 10 percent. Saudi Arabia spends 5.8 percent

of its GNP on foreign aid, Qatar spends 7.4 percent and Kuwait, 3.25 percent. Arab oil money goes far beyond the region and tends to be concentrated in building **developmental infrastructure.** Infrastructure development projects being built with Arab oil subsidies, loans, or gifts include: airports in Tunisia and Gambia (West Africa); bridges in Tunisia and Taiwan; hydroelectric dams in Ghana, Mali, and Cameroon; a fertilizer plant in Pakistan; irrigation networks in Bangladesh; port facilities in Algeria, Morocco, and Papua New Guinea, and railroads in the Congo. While there is an expected emphasis on extending aid to less fortunate Moslem brethren, Arab development money is also becoming a major factor in some parts of the developing world that have few Moslems.

PHYSICAL CHARACTERISTICS

Though a dominant physical unifier is the problem of coping with aridity, this region must not be interpreted as being all desert. There is considerable variation in the degree of aridity and certainly in the overall physical land-

TABLE 13–1
Oil production and prospects—North Africa–Southwest Asia region

Selected States	Population	Population Density (square kilometers)	Oil Reserves Total (thousand barrels)	Per Capita	Oil Production Total (thousand metric tons)	Per Capita (metric tons)	World Rank Reserves (percent)	Production (percent)
Projected long-term exporters with high reserves per capita								
United Arab Emirates	240,000	3	31,320,000	130,500	89,200	371.66	5	3
Kuwait	1,200,000	67	66,200,000	55,166	110,000	91.66	10.5	3.5
Qatar	100,000	9	4,000,000	40,000	23,500	235.00	.6	.8
Saudi Arabia	9,520,000	4	165,700,000	17,405	410,000	43.06	27.	12.3
Libya	2,630,000	1	24,300,000	9,239	95,000	36.12	3.9	4.1
Oman	820,000	4	2,500,000	3,048	16,000	19.52	.4	.5
Iraq	12,330,000	28	32,100,000	2,603	115,000	9.32	5	4.3
Iran	35,210,000	21	59,000,000	1,675	255,000	7.24	9.5	8.8
Major producers with lower reserves, and prospect of long-term reduction in exports								
Algeria	18,515,000	8	6,300,000	340	59,000	3.18	1	1.7
Syria	8,150,000	44	2,080,000	266	10,500	1.29	.3	.3
Bahrein	350,000	563	250,000	714	2,700	7.71	.04	.08
Limited producers per capita								
Tunisia	6,216,000	38	2,300,000	370	4,650	.74	.3	.15
Egypt	39,640,000	40	3,200,000	80	27,500	.69	.5	.8
Turkey	43,210,000	55	360,000	8	2,500	.05	.05	.08
(for comparison purposes)								
USA	218,500,000	23	28,500,000	130	485,000	2.21	4.5	14.5
USSR	261,256,000	12	71,000,000	271	572,500	2.19	11.5	19.5
Nigeria	66,630,000	72	18,200,000	271	95,000	1.42	2.9	3.2
World Average Totals	4,208,000,000	31	620,000,000	147.6	3,055,700	.72	100	100

SOURCE: *World Energy Supplies,* New York: United Nations, 1979, 1980.

scape. There are the occasional well-watered river valleys consisting of alluvium deposited by exotic streams (streams with their sources in other, wetter areas) supporting dense populations. The shores of the entire region are ringed by a series of small coastal lowlands often isolated from one another by mountain ranges or the clifflike edges of interior plateaus.

WHAT MAKES THIS REGION DISTINCTIVE?

The spatial association of arid lands and predominantly Islamic population is the most obvious unifier, despite the fact that both arid lands and large Moslem populations are found far beyond the region's bounds. The historical role of this region as a cultural hearth is a significant characteristic if not a unifier. Commonality of cultural background and political interests have led to some regional consciousness and bloc voting in international organizations, generally a positive indicator of major world region status. Lastly, there are clear contrasts with the adjacent world regions.

THE PHYSICAL FRAME

The climate is that of a desert throughout most of the region, and most of it is almost devoid of people, reflecting the limited potential of such climatic areas for supporting people. Consequently, the bulk of the region's population lives in the exceptional zones, where the climate is wetter, milder, and more hospitable. The physical framework has been important in the formation of the region's culture, and its role is prominent as a limiting factor in the traditional scheme of development.

TOPOGRAPHY

The northern fringes of the region consist of a series of folded mountains, essentially extensions of Alpine and Himalayan folding. Sporadic occurrences of older folded mountains are scattered across the central Sahara. Most of the rest of the region consists of ancient, stable continental blocks, sometimes upended into precipitous mountains, sometimes downfaulted into deep, sediment-filled basins. The Great Rift Valley of Africa, drowned by the Red Sea, separates this region into the North African and Southwest Asian parts (see Figure 13–2).

Three riverine valleys, the homes of three ancient civilizations (the Nile, Indus, and Tigris-Euphrates) occupy parts of three larger structural basins. Other structural basins, lacking water, are simply filled with dry sediments and

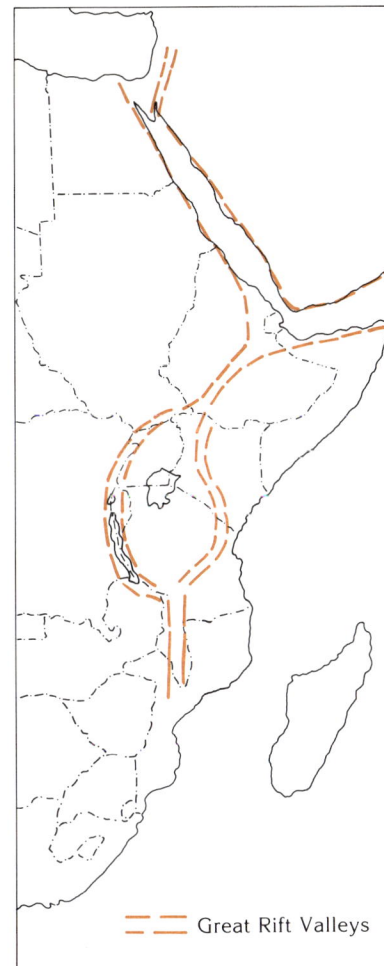

FIGURE 13–2

The Great Rift Valley, East Africa and The Near East. One of the primary topographic features of this region, the Great Rift Valley splits the crust from Mozambique to Tanzania, dividing into two rifts flanking the shallow Lake Victoria. Then the rifts rejoin to cut through the Ethiopian Plateau, forming the trenchlike Red Sea (with a branch forming the Gulf of Aden), splitting again at Sinai to form the Gulfs of Suez and Aqaba, and continuing under the Dead Sea and Jordan Valley.

shifting sands. A series of small coastal lowlands edge the Alpine folds in the Persian Gulf and Mediterranean portions of the region as well as the Red Sea rift. Where such lowlands extend inland, melding with the interior basins, the low-utility desert reaches to the shores. Fault bloc mountains on either side of the rift form the other important mountains. The central Saharan highlands rise to significant heights above the tableland surface, but have little effect on climate.

LAND-SEA RELATIONSHIPS

Most of the great early civilizations would not be characterized as essentially maritime. Nonetheless, the sea played an important role in bringing portions of this area under Roman control, while the Phoenician-Punic Empire that rivaled it was also clearly a maritime culture. The later Islamic empires were more clearly land based.

The sea has had increasing importance in the last two centuries. European powers spread colonial control by sea. Harbors were improved to facilitate trade and military operations. The advent of great regional oil production clearly brings the role of the sea into play, as oil is exported overseas primarily via large tankers. The region is adjacent to, or includes portions of, five major narrows from which ocean commerce can be controlled: The Strait of Gibraltar, the Sicilian Channel, the Suez Canal, the Bab El Mandeb, and the Strait of Hormuz (see Figure 13–3). Each shift in the direction of commerce or the importance of commodities carried has focused on one or more of these narrow passages. The very constriction of sea routes in the area has insured their importance to regional economies.

CLIMATE

There are significant differences in the potential utility of deserts. The northern fringe has a Mediterranean climate with dry, hot summers and cool, moist winters; this zone has a higher degree of utility than the region's deserts, but is never more than a narrow coastal belt. Its eastward extension into Iran is really an orographic (mountain-induced) heightening of precipitation in that country's mountains.

Aspect and shelter often affect frost hazards and precipitation totals sufficiently to make valleys or lowlands more or less usable in accordance with their effect. Higher areas of the North African Atlas or the Turkish and Iranian mountains receive significantly higher precipitation and give rise to streams that provide irrigation water.

Equatorward of the Mediterranean climatic zone is a narrow and fluctuating belt of steppe climate, transitional between desert and water-surplus climates. It reaches its

FIGURE 13–3
Vital Straits, Gibraltar to Hormuz. A series of narrow seas and straits nearly divide the two continental sectors of the region and flank North Africa. The significance of these straits lies in their use as the "oil lifeline" from the Persian Gulf to Europe. The straits potentially increase the vulnerability of the oil lifeline in wartime.

greatest extent in the Middle East. The mountains bordering the rift, where sufficiently high, increase precipitation to steppe conditions in that area. In the southwest corner of the Arabian peninsula, the regime is that of dry winter but with sufficient summer rain to promote sedentary agriculture, even in unirrigated areas.

In the southern extreme of North Africa, there is another transitional zone from desert to steppe to the wetter equatorial climates. Known as the *Sahel,* its rains come in summer. Unreliable and seasonal, these rains depend on the northward shifting intertropical convergence. Whole years go by without rain, while downpours and floods accompany others.

The bulk of the region is true desert, often in its severest form, with very low rainfall of an unpredictable nature, cold nights, scorching days, and searing winds. This is decidedly the prevalent climate. The area is located well within the dominance of the belt of subtropical high pressure. Winds are often offshore, so that little maritime influence is felt here in either its cooling or moisture-bringing aspects.

DRAINAGE PATTERNS

Many of the interior basins have only intermittant streams (they only flow right after a rain), and many streams end in salt lakes or simply disappear into the sands. A few short, swift streams of erratic flow reach the sea in the Mediterranean climatic zone. The Nile has its sources in the Ethiopian Plateau and the East African Highlands. It now rarely reaches the sea in much volume as water is extracted en route by thousands of irrigation projects and by heightened evaporation.

The highlands of the central Sahara produce a radial drainage pattern, out from the highlands and down to the desert sands. In occasional wetter years some of these streams enter systems that flow south to the Gulf of Guinea.

The Tigris and Euphrates receive winter rains and summer snow melt, providing a surprisingly stable flow. They have few permanent tributaries and combine to form the marshy lowlands of the Shatt al Arab in their lower course.

Rivers of sub-Saharan Africa touch on or even enter the North African portion of the region from the south. The Senegal River, fed by tropical rains, is on the southwestern border. The Niger flows north, deep into the Sahara before flowing southward to the Gulf of Guinea. At the juncture of equatorial and desert climates, Lake Chad is an unusual water feature at the region's southern margin.

Underground drainage is of unusual regional significance. Wells that tap underground streams, acquifers fed by different climates in distant areas or **fossil waters** (deep groundwater left over from a time of a much wetter surface) form the only sources of water over vast parts of the area. Their frequency creates a network of settlements that facilitated both transdesert trade and nomadic economies. Two very large areas are almost totally without water, the Libyan Desert and the Rub' al Khali of the Arabian peninsula.

VEGETATION

Wood is scarce, even in mountain areas, when human demands exceed supply and reduce the capability for forest regeneration. The cover of vegetation in the Mediterranean zone is more one of scrub and shrub than forest. It thins perceptibly inland to short steppe grasses and bunch grass in semi-desert reaches. Most of the Sahara has some scattered shrubs, thorn bush, and patches of grass. Only on the leeward sides of mountains and in the many large interior basins does vegetation disappear, leaving a vast empty landscape of shifting sands or barren, rocky windswept surfaces.

THE STRUCTURE OF SUBREGIONS

The groupings of states into subregional units does not imply that they share a uniform culture, political orientation, or even a similar level of economic development. The subregions, like the regions themselves, are practical compromises. Turkey, Cyprus, Iraq, Syria, Lebanon, Jordan, and Israel form the first subregion. The bulk of the Arabian peninsula, including Saudi Arabia, both Yemens, Oman, the United Arab Emirates, Qatar, Bahrain, and Kuwait, forms the second subregion. Egypt and the Sudan are a separate subregion, followed by the North African states of Libya, Tunisia, Algeria, and Morocco. Iran and Afghanistan form another subregion, while the final subregion includes the predominantly Saharan countries of Mauritania, Mali, Niger, and Chad, with the disputed territory of former Spanish Sahara. (See Figure 13–4.)

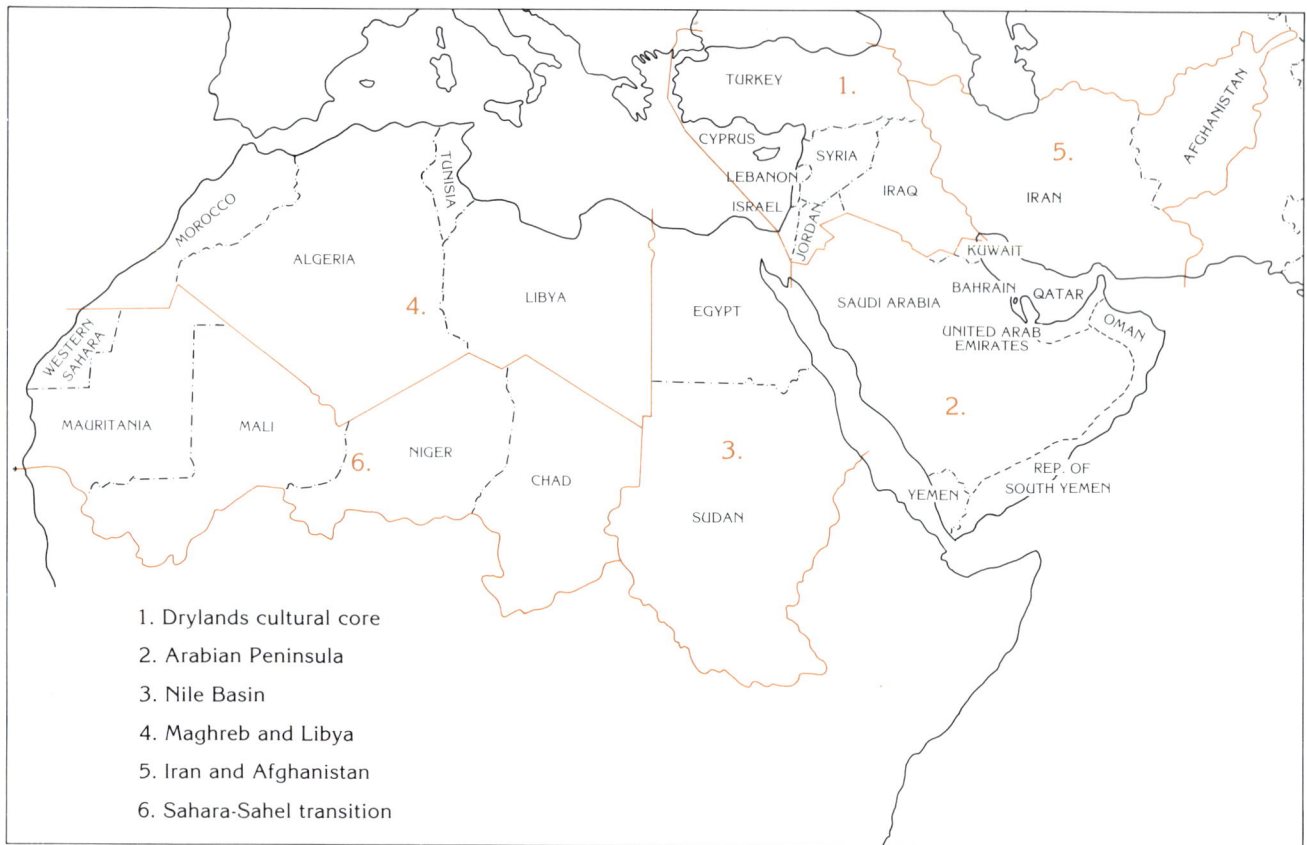

1. Drylands cultural core

2. Arabian Peninsula

3. Nile Basin

4. Maghreb and Libya

5. Iran and Afghanistan

6. Sahara-Sahel transition

FIGURE 13–4
Structure of Subregions and the Fertile Crescent. This large, culturally diverse region is subdivided into six subregions. The time honored, and still significant, concept of the Fertile Crescent is important to the understanding of this area's role as a cultural hearth.

THE DRYLANDS CULTURAL CORE

The antiquity and past importance of this subregion cannot be overstated; its "centrality" is both historical and geographical. A popular name for the region of present day Israel, Lebanon, Syria, and Iraq is the **Fertile Crescent** (see Figure 13–4). *Fertility* in this instance refers to its relative agricultural productivity, due in part to its somewhat wetter climate. It was also fertile, though, in terms of producing civilizations. This region lies near some other early centers of culture—the Nile Valley, Persia, Crete, and Greece. It received stimulating trade contacts from these early important neighbors and in turn sent its new technologies and ideas to them. For thousands of years this area has occupied a focal point in trade routes among European, African, and Asian civilizations.

Damascus, founded about 2500 B.C., is usually credited with being the oldest continuously inhabited city in the world. It was the capital of a powerful empire that stretched from Spain to India during the late seventh and early eighth centuries A.D. Baghdad, Jerusalem, Tyre, and Istanbul (Constantinople) are other ancient cities here.

The oldest city so far uncovered and studied by archaeologists is Catal Huyuk in modern Turkey, a trading, crafts, and administrative center flourishing between 7000 and 6000 B.C. Archaeological excavations in the late 1970's have documented a previously unknown civilization centered in what is now northern Syria. Ebla, the center of a great Semitic empire that controlled lands from the Red Sea north to Turkey and east to Mesopotamia, flourished from 2500 B.C. to 2400 B.C. The extent of its ruins indicate a city of over a quarter of a million people—an astounding figure for such an early period.

By the sixteenth century the area had come under the control of the Ottoman Empire, based in Turkey. When it collapsed through the unfortunate combination of choosing the wrong side in World War I and rising Arab nationalism, the ethnically Turkish core of that empire emerged as the modern state of Turkey and the remainder of this subregion was divided among French and British "mandates." This arrangement cynically betrayed the Arab nationalism that had been made use of in overthrowing the Turkish Empire. The modern history and political problems and aspirations of the subregion are intimately connected with the long period of Turkish domination followed by a brief period of British and French control.

Israel The very existence of the state of Israel has been the center of a storm of opposition. At times, it may have seemed that determination to eradicate Israel was the only unifying force among neighboring Arab states. The Israel-Palestine question shows no sign of being permanently resolved to everyone's satisfaction.

Territorial claims commonly are asserted on the basis of discovery, exploration, settlement, economic development, effective administrative control, and historical (but not necessarily continuous) occupance. Israel's major claim is based on antiquity of settlement and historical claim. This land called Israel has had many rulers. In 70 A.D. the Roman rulers of Palestine (the Roman name for that province) determined to scatter the Jewish occupants of this troublesome area. The *diaspora* or dispersal of the Jews sent them to all corners of the Roman Empire. While some Jews have always lived in Palestine or Israel, from 70 A.D. until after World War II, the majority of the inhabitants of this land were not Jewish. Throughout the centuries following the diaspora, Jews maintained the goal of returning to their ancient homeland. Few practical steps toward this goal were taken until the Zionist Movement of the late nineteenth century. During World War I, the British sought to energize and focus the nationalist ambitions of the Arabs against the Turks, and at the same time tried to influence world public opinion by publicly favoring a "Jewish homeland" in Palestine. The British government did not advocate a Jewish *state* but a more vague "homeland," and it also noted that this homeland should not prejudice the rights of those peoples living there already. (This last clause generally receives less publicity.) Throughout the 1920's, Jewish immigration to Palestine grew slowly. Land, homes, and businesses were purchased, without any coercion, from individuals, for individuals. The Nazi persecutions of the 1930's enlarged the Palestine-bound flow of European Jews.

The period following World War II is extremely controversial. British, Palestinian, Arab, and Zionist viewpoints concerning this time period are widely divergent. The shocking confirmation that Nazi genocidal policies had murdered 6 million Jews (along with millions from other national ethnic or religious groups, including many dissident Germans) swung public opinion in Europe and the Americas towards lifting emigration restrictions on surviving Jews. The British, fearing a bloody confrontation between Arabs and Jews in Palestine, had sought to strictly control Jewish immigration. They knew that the rapidly expanding Jewish population in Palestine, fed by immigration, would create a clear majority over an indigenous Arab population that was not being supplemented by significant in-migration. Jewish immigrants were not about to be denied access to their cherished homeland; the ideal of a Jewish state had taken on a new survivalist appeal after the holocaust. To the Palestinian Arabs, the relaxation of immigration restrictions towards the end of British occupation, plus the unwillingness of many British to zealously and ruthlessly enforce their own rules against the pathetic refugees, was evidence of unwilling Arab involvement in a European problem. The Arab view was that Jewish immigration was the result of catastrophic and regrettable eruption of vicious prejudice in Europe; that Palestinian Arabs were being deliberately pushed aside to compensate European Jews for the tragedy that had befallen them in Europe.

Israel, the size of New Jersey, has a population of about 3 million Jews and over 600,000 non-Jews, mostly Arabs (not counting "occupied territories" on the left bank). Since Israel's independence in 1948, the Jewish population has more than quadrupled. Israel's "law of return" stipulates that any Jew can freely enter Israel as an immigrant; such immigrants have contributed over two thirds of this population increase. The Arab minority (15 percent of the population) has tripled in number since 1948, through high birthrates rather than in-migration. Contributing to Jewish Israelis' sense of insecurity is the fact that Jewish in-migration has slowed considerably since 1973, now barely replacing out-migration, while Arab birthrates remain higher. Among the Jewish population, about half were born in Israel, more than a quarter in Europe and the Americas, and about 22 percent in Asia and Africa. Two major subgroups within the Jewish population are the Sephardim, from other Mid-East and North African states and Balkan or Mediterranean Europe, and the Ashkenazim, or Jews of eastern and central European origin. The Sephardim often had lower educational attainments and in the past alleged economic discrimination by the Ashkenazim. They now form a majority of the Jews (60 percent) in Israel.

Israel's economy is far more advanced and Westernized than those of its neighbors. In contrast to them, Israel has a small portion of its total work force in agriculture (less than 6 percent), while most are engaged in service industries. Israeli agriculture is very modern, with high inputs of capital and technology per land unit. The output is astounding when it is remembered that half of Israel's territory is in the Negev Desert. The major crop exported is citrus, the fourth ranking export in value. Other Israeli agricultural specialties, exported primarily to Europe, are fresh and processed fruits and vegetables, cut flowers, cotton, and peanuts.

The list of natural resources is painfully short for a modern industrial state. Relatively minor deposits of copper, phosphate, sulfur, manganese, and bitumen are

Packing Oranges, Israel. Israel's economy depends on the export of high-quality agricultural specialties as well as high-technology manufactured products and tourism. Here, premium-grade Jaffa oranges are packed for export. (Courtesy of United Nations)

found. The Dead Sea is "mined," by evaporation, for bromide, potash, and salt. Israel's prime resource, however, is its highly skilled, highly energetic, highly motivated population. Israel has had to rely on **high-value-added** industries, a common strategy in resource-poor countries.

Israel's economy reflects a high technological level and a high input of human skills. Polished diamonds are the leading export, though Israel mines no diamonds. Diamond cutting, at least in the Western world, has been a peculiarly Jewish occupation. Many occupations were forbidden to Jews in Medieval and Renaissance Europe, as was ownership of land. Gem cutting was a permitted occupation. Too, in a cultural environment often characterized by hostility and prejudice, it was sensible for one to be able to pocket one's stock of merchandise and flee, carrying in one's brain the necessary "tools" for earning a living—personal skills. The Israeli government actively encouraged diamond cutting and polishing as a classic high-value-added industry in which the transport costs (over whatever distance) remain a tiny fraction of the price of finished goods. Diamonds are mined in Africa, cut in Tel Aviv, and marketed in London, New York, or Amsterdam with no significant cost of transport. Other Israeli industrial exports include textiles and clothing, electronics, chemicals, and fertilizer. Israel's economic growth (a fan-

tastic 10 percent per year for its first quarter century) was fueled by loans and gifts from abroad, as well as the energy and inventiveness of its people. Israel has always had to import large quantities of military equipment, machinery, steel, chemicals, foods, petroleum, and transport equipment. The imbalance between exports and imports, once carried by bond purchases and other capital transfers from Europe and the Americas, has begun to grow rapidly. Tourism, another traditional means of redressing the imbalance of trade, has suffered from regional instability and terrorism.

The economic growth rate has now slowed to about 2 percent a year as Israel copes with serious inflation problems, a decline in tourism, and high military costs. Israel has fought wars in 1948, 1956, 1967, and 1973; the most recent war was especially expensive. The strains of maintaining approximate parity with Arab military machines fueled by oil revenues threaten the survival of Israel as much as do the invasion possibiilties. (See Figure 13–5.)

Israel's transport system is typical of a developed industrial country. Its international airline connects with major European and American cities; its international airport serves over 2 million people a year. Over 6,000 miles (9,650 kilometers) of surfaced roads are supplemented by 500 miles (804 kilometers) of state-owned railways. (In contrast, Sudan, a developing country 123 times the size of Israel, has only 900 miles [1,400 kilometers] of paved roads.)

Israel's internal political stability and economic survival depend on the achievement of peace with both neighboring states and the stateless Palestinians. Heavy Jewish out-migration is a sign of Israel's economic malaise, a small state surrounded by larger, hostile neighbors, few natural resources, a huge military budget, crushing taxes, and rampant inflation. Its main assets include its preferential trade agreement with the European Economic Community and its high level of governmental and individual citizen support from the United States. The unofficial American alliance, however, has been seriously strained by Israeli determination to establish permanent Jewish settlements in its occupied lands. Tensions are not relieved by improving economic and political relationships between the United States and various Moslem countries.

Jordan Unlike Syria, Lebanon, Turkey, or Iraq, Jordan never existed as a nation or state until the breakup of the Turkish Empire. The western part of Jordan is in the great trench partly occupied by the Dead Sea, and the rim of the trench was historically part of the Fertile Crescent. Jordan was part of the former Turkish Empire accorded to Britain, along with Palestine and Iraq. Jordan was created to help sooth Arab nationalists who had expected to

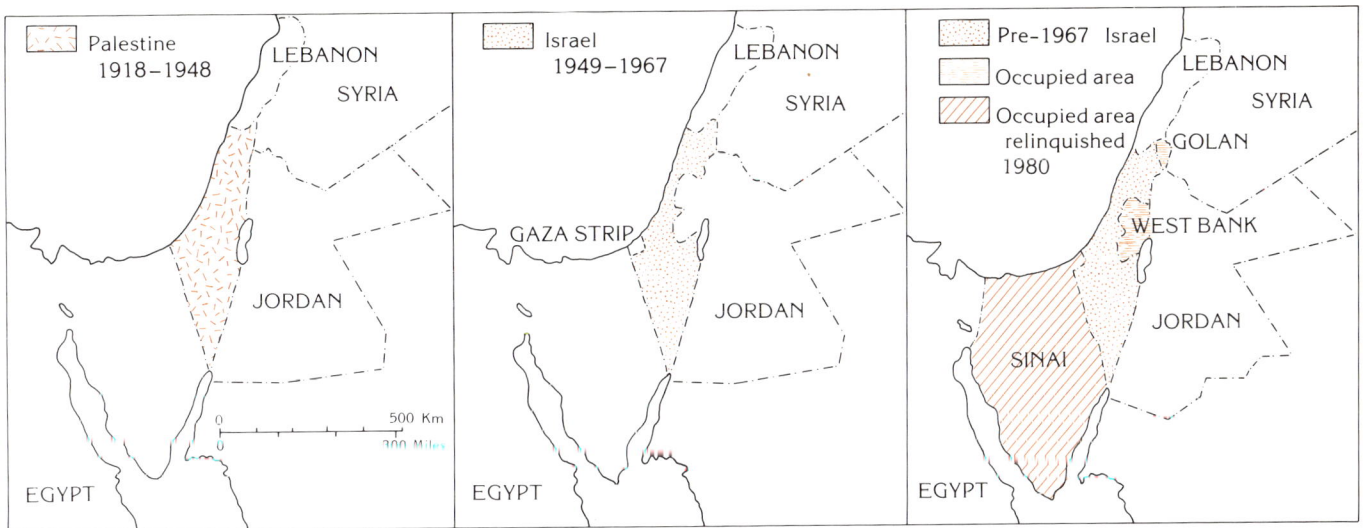

FIGURE 13-5

Israel: Territorial Claims and Occupation. Israel, or Palestine to the Arab world, has fought four wars to acheive and maintain its independence. Israeli-controlled territory expanded as a result of brief, sharp conflicts in 1967 and 1973.

achieve fully independent states. The British mandate ended in independence in 1946. Israel's 1948 War of Independence resulted in some of the west bank territory of Palestine being added (temporarily) to Jordan. Jordan is a country of rocky deserts and wasteland (88 percent of its area). Eleven percent is in agriculture and 1 percent in forest. With few natural resources, tension with Israel, few paved roads, and a generally primitive **infrastructure,** Jordan was assumed to have a bleak future as late as the 1950's. Since then, good planning and heavy injections of aid from the United States have tripled the gross national product. Thousands of acres of irrigated farms have been created in the Jordan Valley. Phosphate is mined for export and potash is extracted from the Dead Sea. A tourist industry has been built from almost nothing to a major supplier of foreign currency. Roads have made such picturesque ruins as Petra accessible and Amman, the capital, has modern luxury hotels.

Jordan (with a population of 3 million), growing at a high rate of 3.2 percent annually, has absorbed about a million Palestinian refugees. The relatively high ratio of Palestinians to Jordanians posed a serious threat to the stability of the state when the heavily armed "resistance" movement disagreed with Jordan's policy of not encouraging raids against Israel from its territory. In 1970, an open conflict resulted in the defeat of the Palestinians. Pro-Western King Hussein is the central figure in Jordon; in some ways he *is* Jordan, and that country could change its present moderate policies radically if he were to be overthrown.

Lebanon Little more than half the area of Israel, Lebanon was once a very bright economic spot in the region. It had a successful economy in a multi-ethnic, multi-religious culture where apparent mutual respect enabled Moslems and Christians to live peacefully and productively. Sadly, Lebanon has suffered a brutal civil war, which has disrupted its economy and may have permanently affected its lucrative service and financial industries that served much of the Middle East. Between 500,000 and 1 million Lebanese fled the country during the 1975–76 civil war; about 40,000 were killed and 200,000 wounded (out of a total population of less than 3.5 million). About 400,000 Palestinian refugees, many in the squalor of "temporary" camps, live in southern Lebanon. Palestinian Freedom Fighters based in Lebanon have been the excuse for frequent Israeli raids into Lebanon in the past. For many years, the internal peace of Lebanon was based on a political agreement recognizing that the population was balanced—half Moslem, half Christian. The Moslem-Christian détente, however, became uneasy when the Moslems felt that they had become a clear majority, due to a higher birthrate. Out of fear of disturbing the delicate Moslem-Christian religious balance, no census has been taken since 1932.

Just under half of all Lebanese work in agriculture; products include the traditional Mediterranean specialties of fruits, wheat, tobacco, and olives. Lebanon was once heavily forested, and its famed cedars were an important item of international trade in the ancient world. Overcutting and soil erosion have all but wiped out the cedars in their homeland. The population grew at a rate of 3.1 percent annually (above the world average) before the civil war. It is 93 percent Arab, with a 6 percent Armenian minority.

Lebanon was one of the world's greatest trading nations. The Lebanese, whose roots go back to the Phoenicians, are still known as shrewd traders. Beirut, the capital, with 1 million population, was well established as the major transshipment and distribution point for the Middle East. Two thirds of Lebanon's GNP was derived from such **"hidden exports"** as banking, commercial services, and tourism. Beirut's international banks handled much of the oil wealth of the Persian Gulf region and served as an important market for foreign exchange and gold. The civil war destroyed much of Beirut's downtown commercial and financial district. With the exception of a few oil refineries and cement plants, Lebanon's other industries were small-scale consumer goods production in and around Beirut.

Recovery is far from impossible. The human talents and knowledge that built the banking industry may be able to restore much of it if tranquility can be restored. The government controls billions of dollars worth of gold and foreign currency reserves to aid in rebuilding. Lebanon may succeed in reestablishing itself as an economic and cultural bridge between Western cultures and the Arab world.

Syria   Syria, like Lebanon, was a French mandate from 1918 to 1946. Its 8 million people are concentrated in the Mediterranean coastal plain, the fertile valleys of the coast ranges, and the Euphrates River Valley. Income per capita ($650) compares with that of Lebanon ($750) and Turkey's ($920); it is lower than that of oil-rich Iraq ($1,700) or high-technology Israel ($3,700). The religious distribution is 87 percent Moslem and 13 percent Christian, while 90 percent are ethnic Arabs. Syria produces some petroleum, but its production will drop sharply in the 1980's as current producing fields are exhausted, though strenuous efforts are underway to find more oil and gas. Syria once collected transit fees from two major oil pipelines crossing its territory. However, the Tapline from Saudi Arabia to the Mediterranean (at Sidon in Lebanon) and the Iraqi pipeline to Tarabulus were both temporarily unused in the late 1970's, depriving Syria of revenues.

The Syrian economy has been one of the fastest growing in the region, in part due to generous grants and loans from neighboring oil-producing states. Syria is a socialist, planned economy in contrast to the free-enterprise, entrepreneurial one of Lebanon. In this water-short, unpredictable rainfall area, major expansion of farmland requires irrigation. Fortunately for Syria, their semiarid northeast contains the upper Euphrates River, one of the largest of this region and a main reason for the designation *Fertile Cresent.* Syria had slipped from net exporter to net importer of food, but the Euphrates Dam, completed in the mid-1970's, should double irrigated land and enable Syria to resume food exports. The dam will also provide electric power for Syria's ambitious industrialization programs.

Syria is urbanizing rapidly; Damascus alone contains more than one quarter of the national population. The transport net is most densely developed in the western part of Syria, connecting the capital with Aleppo, the second city (750,000), and the Mediterranean seaport of Tartus, which is growing rapidly.

Iraq   Mesopotamia, the ancient name of Iraq, is extraordinarily important in the history of both Western and Islamic civilizations. Baghdad, like Damascus, was a "world capital" for a time, the seat of a vast empire stretching from southern Europe to India. Baghdad in the eighth through tenth centuries was a great center of learning in the arts and sciences and a leader in the development of Islamic philosophy and law. Iraq's population of 13 million people has been growing at a rate of 3.7 percent annually, reflecting one of the world's higher birthrates. About three fourths of the Iraqi are Arabs, with a large (20 percent) Kurdish minority in the north and northeast border region; Iraq is 95 percent Moslem.

A more or less constant problem for any Iraqi government is the large Kurdish minority, which has ambitions for a separate state. A 1975 military defeat of insurgent Kurds may have contained the revolt for a while.

Iraq has excellent potential for the expansion of agriculture. It is relatively sparsely populated and has the greatest area in the region with the happy combination of gently sloping land and available water. Agricultural output has lagged behind the impressive birthrate, so that oil revenues have had to be spent for imported foods that Iraq could easily produce itself. The major agricultural potential lies in the largely barren Jezira, between the Tigris and Euphrates, and the floodplains southeast of Baghdad. Water management problems are a far greater obstacle than any lack of water itself.

After nationalization there was a decline in Iraqi oil revenues. The dispute with Western oil companies has since been resolved and Iraq has actively sought Western technology in developing its oil reserves, promising some compensation for nationalized foreign properties. A large proportion of oil revenues seem to be directed toward industrial rather than agricultural development. Iraq has built a new pipeline from its productive northern Kirkuk fields to Dortyol, Turkey, a port on the Mediterranean. This is an alternative to the pipeline through Syria, now unused. Pipelines are also being used to send oil to the new refinery at Basra near the Gulf, and Iraq has built a major deep-sea terminal for oil exports at Al-Fao on the Gulf. At present, cement and textiles are the only modern industries other than oil refining.

Iraq has some difficulties with Syria over the division of Euphrates River water. Relations with Turkey have been good, but relations with Iran, which erupted in war in 1980, focus on the continuing problem of the Kurdish minority in both countries and the territorial counterclaims in the Shatt al Arab border region.

Turkey   With some 42 million, Turkey is the most populous nation in the region. The population growth rate is 2.5 percent, moderate for the region but above the world average. Turks are 90 percent of the population, with a 7 percent Kurd minority. Islam is the religion of 98 percent of the people. Turkey, slightly smaller than Texas and Louisiana combined, has a greater variety of physical environments and crops than other states in the subregion. Major crops are wheat, cotton, tobacco, sugar beets, fruits, and nuts, with tea produced near the Soviet border.

Turkey was the center of the Ottoman Empire, which lasted six centuries and once ruled a vast territory including the Balkans, North Africa, and much of western Asia. The modern republic, founded in 1923, determined to turn its back on imperial traditions and to modernize Turkey quickly. Symbolic of this new focus on a modern nation-state was the move of the national capital from Constantinople (renamed Istanbul) to Ankara in the Ana-

tolian plateau. Constantinople, an ancient and cosmopolitan city, reflected much of the imperial tradition of the Eastern Roman Empire. As a seaport on the most famous of "narrow seas" between the Black Sea and the Mediterranean, Constantinople was a reminder of the internationalist ruler of a polyglot empire. Ankara, inland and in the approximate center of the country, was a symbol of a new, inward-looking republic of a nearly homogeneous ethnic nature.

Turkey is experiencing urbanization at such a rapid rate that squatters' shacks spring up on the margins of cities faster than government agencies can move to supply sanitation systems, roads, or other services. Istanbul, the old capital, is still the largest city (4 million), but Ankara (2.7 million) is growing even more rapidly. Resources include some coal in the north and east, copper, and chromite. Minor oil deposits have been discovered, but the richest potential oil fields are offshore in the Aegean Sea. There, Greek islands lie very close to Turkey's shores, effectively closing off much of the Aegean to Turkish territorial claims. Relations with Greece have never been good. The continuing problem of Cyprus is a major sore-point, and disputes over the potential Aegean oilfields could worsen an already bad situation.

Consumer industries such as textiles and food processing are well developed because Turkey started its drive toward industrialization earlier than its regional counterparts. Government action in starting up industries was important in the rapid growth of Ankara, seated in an undeveloped area with great potential. Private enterprise is now encouraged to promote new industries and new in-

Istanbul, Turkey. Turkey, once an imperial power throughout much of the region, is now a modernizing state of mostly Turkish ethnics, struggling with problems of stability and industrialization. (Courtesy of United Nations)

dustrial locations. Government involvement tends to be in high-capital, heavy industry sectors such as steel, oil, and petrochemicals. The state development bank is an extremely important source of capital; even private industry is stongly influenced by long-range government plans. Turkey has associate membership in the European Common Market, which may force changes in many small, uncompetitive industries in Turkey.

Turkey has had some serious problems in maintaining a strong, stable, yet democratic, government. The choice has seemed to consist of either a strong government or a democratic one.

Cyprus Cyprus, the third largest island in the Mediterranean (after Sicily and Sardinia), has been under foreign domination for most of its history. About twice the size of Delaware, Cyprus lies 44 miles (71 kilometers) south of Turkey. A fertile central plain lies between the southwestern Troomba Mountains and the Kyrenia Range of the north coast. Nicosia, the capital and largest city, is located in this central plain, along with most of the population of 700,-000. The annual growth rate is only 1 percent, reflecting heavy out-migrations occasioned by the long and bitter dispute between Greek and Turkish Cypriots. Although Cyprus is physically much closer to Turkey, Greek ethnics are 78 percent of the population. Turks are the largest minority at 18 percent. Greeks and Turks have shared the island for four centuries. The Turks took Cyprus from Venice in 1571, and ceded the island to Great Britain in 1878 as security for a loan, never repaid. More than a quarter of a century of civil disturbances, climaxing in a campaign of terror, eventually forced the British to grant independence in 1960. The British situation in Cyprus was quite similar to that in Palestine—they recognized that withdrawal and independence would precipitate a civil war among opposed ethnic-religious groups. Cyprus exists under international agreements that give it less than complete sovereignty. Greece, Turkey, and Britain are each guarantors of the island's independence; each may intervene in the interests of the state's security. Sporadic fighting between Greek and Turkish Cypriots has almost precipitated war between Greece and Turkey more than once. Turkish forces occupied almost 40 percent of the island in 1974 when Turkish Cypriots' lives were endangered by civil disturbances. The long guerrilla war and Turkish occupation of part of the island brought about a forced resettlement of both Greek and Turkish Cypriots.

Even under normal conditions, the island's economy had some serious handicaps. About 40 percent of the land is not suitable for agriculture. Chronic water shortages and extreme fragmentation of individual holdings handicap improved production.

THE ARABIAN PENINSULA SUBREGION

A large number of international boundaries here have not been demarcated. When this territorial uncertainty is combined with vast differences in standards of living and strongly polarized international political alignments, the situation has tragic potential for future disputes.

Saudi Arabia, the largest state in this subregion, is approximately the size of the United States east of the Mississippi. However, it has less than 9 million people, and the overall population density is about 7 per square mile (3 per square kilometer). Most population is in scattered clusters along parts of the coasts, in areas of higher elevation, or a few desert oases in north central Saudi Arabia. The southern interior of the peninsula is called the Rub' al Khali or "empty quarter" due to the scarcity of people and the occurrence there of extensive "seas" of sand dunes.

Saudi Arabia is extremely important in the world for two quite unrelated reasons. Saudi Arabia contains two of Islam's holy cities, Mecca and Medina (the third is Jerusalem). Every Moslem is obliged to make a pilgrimage to Mecca at least once in their lifetime if possible. With the great leaps in transportation speed and efficiency, relatively large numbers can now make their *haj* (pilgrimage) to the Prophet Mohammed's birthplace. The November haj now draws over 1.5 million pilgrims, generating considerable revenues for service industries in Mecca, Medina (where the Prophet's tomb is located), and Jidda, the Red Sea port which serves Mecca. Saudi Arabia's other claim to world importance is its vast reserve of petroleum, one quarter of the world's known deposits. With over 173 billion barrels, Saudi Arabia can continue to maintain, even expand, production long after many other producers have "peaked" and are in declining output. Some of Saudi Arabia's oil was exported via the Tapline to the Mediterranean, but almost all is exported from the oil terminal in the Persian Gulf at Ras Tanura (see Figure 13–6). (Arabs would prefer to rename the Persian Gulf *Arabian Gulf.*) The Saudi GDP (gross domestic product) per capita is over $10,000 and rising.

Although Saudi Arabia is investing its oil wealth in economic development and industrial diversification, the bulk of the population is still engaged in agriculture. Forty percent of the country is used for grazing, mostly of very low **carrying capacity** (the capacity for feeding grazing animals without incurring permanent damage to vegetation and landscape). Only 1 percent is suitable for cultivation.

Historically, the Arabian peninsula was first united by the Prophet, but the present kingdom of Saudi Arabia was unified by King Ibn Saud in the period 1902–1932; he pursued a policy of reviving sedentary oasis agriculture.

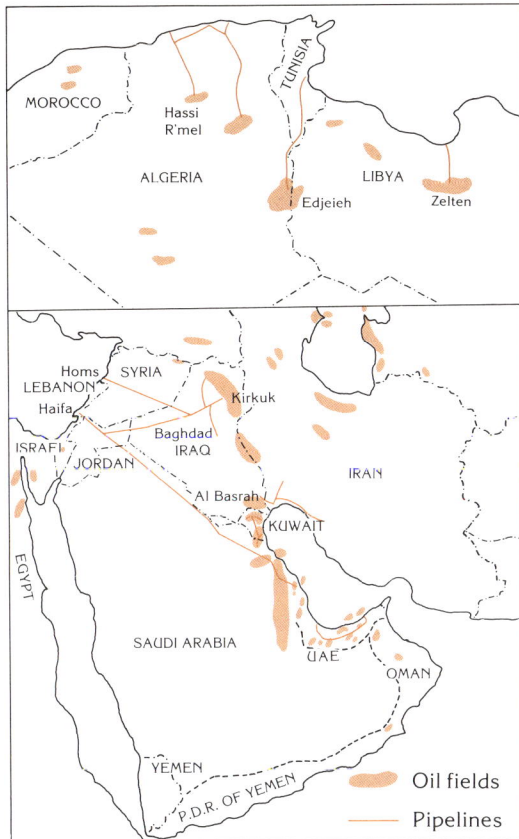

FIGURE 13–6

Oil Fields and Pipelines. The region's oil fields are concentrated in the Persian Gulf (the Arabs would prefer *Arabian Gulf*) and in Libyan and Algerian Sahara, with relatively minor deposits elsewhere. While the gulf fields are quite close to ocean shipping, pipelines have been constructed to convey oil to even more convenient (European) Mediterranean ports. Pipelines are a necessity for the Sahara fields.

His policies of transport development, including a railway from Ad Damman on the Persian Gulf to the capital (Rijadh) and a network of modern roads, enabled the produce of these oases to reach the markets of the gulf oil centers. Crop diversification was encouraged, and problems of poor drainage, salinity, and erratic water supply were tackled by American agricultural missions.

Government investment in agriculture has continued at a high rate. The traditional pastoral nomadism that long dominated the interior has been under political and economic pressure to change. Ibn Saud and his successors have sought to sedantarize nomads for political reasons and to improve their living standards. Expansion of cultivated, irrigated oases often takes good grazing land. Nomads are persuaded to become farmers or oil field workers. At the same time, rising prices for meat and hides have encouraged expansion of flocks among the million or so who still follow the nomadic life. The continuous

availability of water at the pumping stations along the Tapline tends to concentrate herds on nearby grazing lands, thus overgrazing them. **Overgrazing** is also a problem in some formerly remote oases where nomads have switched from draft animals to trucks. Motorized nomadism moves flocks faster and further than ever before. Overgrazing has so eradicated vegetation from some areas, especially near the Tapline, that forage is now trucked in. The changes of deep wells, modern roads, and "truck nomads" are forcing shifts in the traditional economy.

Political and religious conservativism and a strong desire to maintain stability in the critical Persian Gulf dominate Saudi foreign policy. Supplying about a fifth of all American imports of oil, Saudi Arabia has maintained excellent relations with the United States. Saudi policy is to support moderate governments in the area against radical takeovers. The Saudis are in an understandably nervous position in view of their small indigenous population in a country that controls so much wealth and international power in the vital oil industry. To outsiders, there is an almost frantic pace of development of the economy and a strong drive to transform the Saudi Arabian people into a modern, educated people. The responsibilities of wisely spending the incredible oil-generated wealth are a serious, if enviable, burden. An estimated $100 billion (U.S.) in foreign currency reserves is funding both an impressive program of foreign aid and a sizeable program of economic development at home. Saudi Arabia still imports most food requirements; to further increase domestic food production, the Saudis have built many irrigation projects. In addition, steeply rising urban demands for water have led to a 5 million gallon per day **desalination** (removing salt from seawater) plant near Jidda and several smaller plants in other towns. Future industrial development will emphasize petrochemicals and more oil refineries.

The governments of North Yemen (the Yemen Arab Republic) and South Yemen (People's Democratic Republic of Yemen) are agreed on only one point: there should be a united Yemen. There is no mutually agreeable plan for achieving this unification. The two Yemens share relative poverty; a lack of oil or any other valuable mineral is a major reason why North Yemen's per capita income is estimated at about $180 and that of South Yemen at $100. In the past, Yemen was part of a very important series of trade links between Africa and India. Another source of past prosperity was the considerably wetter climate in the high mountains behind the 40-mile (64-kilometer) wide coastal strip of desert. These mountains (up to 12,000 feet [3,700 meters] in elevation) have abundant rainfall and a pleasantly cooler climate than the rest of the peninsula.

North Yemen, with most of the terraced fields of well-watered crops, was formerly self-sufficient in food. Superior quality coffee was once the principal source of foreign exchange. Production has fallen due in part to a severe drought in the early 1970's. North Yemen receives foreign aid from Saudi Arabia, the Soviet Union, and the People's Republic of China (PRC).

South Yemen is much less suitable for agriculture than North Yemen. The capital at Aden, near the Bab al Mandeb, the strategic straits between the Red Sea and the Indian Ocean, was an important trade city and a military base long controlled by the British. After the Suez Canal opened in 1869, Aden became an important coaling station to refuel steamships bound to or from India. As oil replaced coal, a refinery was built at Aden and still supplies the largest source of government income, though the oil refueling function has not fully recovered from the 1967–75 closing of the Suez Canal. What little land is available for cultivation is used, like that of North Yemen, mostly for wheat, sorghum, cattle, sheep, and *qat,* a mildly narcotic leaf which is a natural source of amphetamines. South Yemen depends heavily on foreign aid and various subsidies from the Soviet Union, the PRC, East Germany, and Cuba. Its position on the Bab al Mandeb places military units based there minutes away from the oil lifeline of western Europe. In addition to a general policy of undermining conservative Arab governments everywhere, South Yemen once supported a protracted civil war in the southern province of neighboring Oman, fought brief border wars with Saudi Arabia in 1969 and 1973, and evidently expects to reunite the two Yemens by force.

Oman is far richer than the Yemens, but is not in the same super-rich category as some of its near-neighbors on the Persian Gulf. Per capita income is about $2,300 per year, largely due to the discovery of oil in the 1960's. The fields are relatively small, however, and Oman will run out of oil in this decade unless new fields are discovered or the rate of production slowed. The government is attempting to diversify the economy by exploiting copper reserves and increasing agriculture and fisheries production through new technology. Oman's potential for control of the vital Strait of Hormuz between the Arabian peninsula and Iran means that tanker traffic to or from the Gulf could be easily interrupted, cutting off two thirds of the oil exports of the world.

The seven Arab emirates that make up the United Arab Emerates (UAE) together include less than 1 million people. These people however, enjoy the highest per capita income of any state in the world, over $19,000 per year. For more than a century, 1851–1971, the shieks of the "trucial coast" had a special treaty relationship with Britain that provided military protection and overseeing of foreign relations. Each emirate now retains considerable local autonomy. A major political and cultural problem is the flood of foreigners into the rather lightly populated emirates, attracted by the oil boom. The lack of water will limit development even in these fabulously wealthy states. Abu Dhabi, the largest population group among the seven, plans construction of an oil refinery, a natural gas liquefaction plant, and fertilizer and plastics plants.

Qatar occupies the large peninsula jutting into the Gulf from eastern Saudi Arabia. This Arab state is mainly barren sand and gravel with almost no rainfall; summer temperatures reach 120° (49° C). About the size of Connecticut and Rhode Island combined, the population of about 165,000 is less than half indigenous Qatares; most of the balance are Arabs from throughout the region. Less than one percent of the land is cultivable, but food imports are easily paid for by oil exports (per capita income is $11,500). Qater now has plans for a steel mill, more water desalinating plants, a second petrochemical plant, and a larger fertilizer factory.

Bahrain, a group of small islands off the Gulf coast of Saudi Arabia to the northwest of Qatar, is an oil-producing state of some 305,000 people. Not as wealthy as Qatar or Kuwait, its oil reserves are not expected to last until the end of this century. The per capita income is about $2,500 per year. The population growth rate is an astonishing 3.4 percent, although even that is moderate compared to an 8 percent growth rate for the UAE and 6 percent for Kuwait. These spectacular growth rates include, of course, heavy immigration of people looking for jobs and also wishing to benefit from the generous social welfare programs of the oil-rich states. Bahrain has one of the largest oil refineries in the Middle East at Sitrah, where a major oil-loading terminal can accommodate the largest of supertankers. Facing the familiar problem of diversifying the economy to both keep more of the value added by manufacturing or processing raw materials and to prepare for the eventual end of the oil resource, Bahrain has pursued an imaginative program for diversification. A $72 million aluminum smelter uses natural gas as its fuel. Production is no problem, but marketing all the aluminum has been difficult. A $300 million drydock for ship repair has been completed to further advance Bahrain's role as an **entrepôt** and service center for shipping. Bahrain has also moved to establish itself as a major international banking center to channel Arab money to worldwide investments.

Kuwait's population of more than 1 million occupies an area slightly smaller than New Jersey. Free public education up to the university level gives Kuwait an unusually literate population for a developing country—approximately 80 percent literacy. The per capita GNP of $11,500 is supported by the second largest proven reserve of petro-

Hydroponic Gardening, Kuwait. Kuwait, whose 4 inches of annual precipitation could not produce crops, has invested some oil revenues in hydroponic (soilless) culture of food crops. Tomatoes grown in this fashion, in chemically-enriched water or with water-flushing of roots, have increased yields as much as six times over traditional methods.

leum in the world and by abundant natural gas as well. Kuwait has five oil refineries and has also constructed fertilizer and cement plants. The world's largest water distillation plants are necessary in this state, which has summer temperatures reaching 130° F (54° C) and less than 4 inches (10 centimeters) of average rainfall. With very little arable land but adequate fresh water from desalination and abundant money for experimentation, Kuwait has pioneered large-scale development of *hydroponics,* a technique of growing plants in liquids rather than soil (the roots are suspended in water mixed with nutrients or are periodically flushed with liquid nutrients).

THE NILE BASIN

Egypt and Sudan, the two countries that compose this subregion, are linked by the Nile River. Historically, Egyptian expansion has ebbed and flowed up the Nile Valley.

Egypt Egypt is doubtless the world's greatest oasis; 99 percent of Egyptians live in the Nile Valley and Delta and 99.5 percent of its farmland is irrigated. Only 3.5 percent of this desert nation is settled and cultivated, and almost all of that depends on the life-supporting Nile waters. Population density, agriculture, urbanization, and general economic development all focus on the Nile. The remaining resource base includes iron, phosphates, copper, and enough oil to supply national needs (including some of Egypt's very heavy fertilizer requirements) and still provide a small exportable quantity.

At the turn of this century, Egypt had over 10 million people, a sizeable increase from the 2.5 million estimated a century earlier. Both birth- and death rates were high, as is common in the preindustrial stage of the **demographic transition.** High death rates were largely attributable to disease and malnourishment. Poor sanitation and poor medical care both led to high disease rates, in turn compounded by malnourishment. Famine occurred periodically as fluctuations in the Nile's floods resulted in fluctuations in the amount of land that could be irrigated for crops. The annual flood of the Nile, fed by seasonal rainfall variations in the Ethiopian Highlands (the source of the Blue Nile), surged over the banks of the river, contributing a fresh deposit of fertile silt as well as water. Eroded material from the volcanic rocks of Ethiopia, rich in minerals, helped maintain the highly productive soils despite thousands of years of cultivation. The system of irrigation used was known as basin irrigation—some of the annual flood was impounded in many local basins. With population on the rise, the obvious solution was to increase the area of irrigated land. The British engineers who built the first Aswan Dam did so to stabilize the erratic volume of annual floods. With a major storage reservoir at Aswan, annual variations in the size of the flood could be evened out, reducing the threat of famine. The retention of flood waters in local basins was replaced by continual flow of irrigation water in long-distance canals. Since the completion of that first Aswan Dam, irrigation has been possible on a year-round basis. However, the annual addition of a fresh layer of fertile silt nearly ceased; most of it is now at the bottom of the reservoir. Irrigated soils began to experience problems of **salination** or salt accumulation in their upper layers. The annual floods had formerly dissolved and carried away much of this salt.

The mixed results, positive and negative, of the first Aswan Dam have been compounded by the building of the Aswan High Dam a few miles upstream. The High Dam, built between 1958 and 1970, increased Egypt's land under continual irrigation by 25 percent and enlarged the Sudan's irrigated acreage by 15 percent; it also stopped any downstream movement of silt. In a tropical climate with year-round irrigation, two or even three crops per year are possible. This multiple cropping and the now complete elimination of the annual input of fertile silt have made it necessary for Egypt to become the largest consumer of fertilizer, per cultivated land unit, in the world. The environmental impact of the Aswan High Dam reaches far beyond the Nile Valley. The Mediterranean coasts of the Nile Delta, no longer replenished by silt brought down the Nile, are being eroded by waves and currents. Formerly fresh-water lagoons behind the coastline are being invaded by salt water, killing the fresh-water fish that once thrived there. The coastal region is experiencing some salt-water intrusion into the local water table. Fisheries in the entire eastern Mediterranean are in decline, as mineral nutrients once contributed by the Nile diminish in volume, decreasing in turn the supply of minute plant and animal life on which the **food chain** is based.

Egypt's population growth rate of 2.5 percent per year will double the population in twenty-five years, if continued. Although average birthrates have dropped slightly since World War II, those in rural areas and among poor urbanites remain high. A government agency has made birth control information widely available for fifteen years but with no noticeable effect in the countryside. In each recent year about 1 million more Egyptians are added, together with their needs for housing, education, and eventual employment, and their potential as producers and consumers.

The Egyptians are a fairly homogeneous cultural and racial group; there has been no significant migration into Egypt in many centuries. Over 90 percent are Moslems, with a 7 percent Christian minority. The key to cultural homogeneity is the public consciousness of the splendor of the civilization which arose in the Nile Valley more than 5,000 years ago.

Development Patterns and Development Strategies
Egypt's main emphasis in development is to further expand irrigated land. This is necessary to increase food production for an increasing population while maintaining or increasing exports of cotton and rice. Egypt currently produces only about 75 percent of its food needs. Large-scale cotton production began three quarters of a century ago after the first Aswan Dam increased irrigated acreage. British interests encouraged the growing of long-staple (long-fiber) cotton, a very high-quality raw material for their textile factories. Other major crops are Egyptian clover (for animal fodder and as a soil-enriching crop), corn, wheat, rice, vegetables, and sugar cane. The lush delta area has been experiencing an increase in crop yields. With two or three crops per year, this might seem to offer the hope of upgrading farmers' living standards—until it is remembered that population densities in parts of the delta reach 6,000 per square mile (2,300 per square kilometer). Even with very high productivity, poverty will likely prevail.

Egypt has taken a multifaceted approach to expanding agricultural productivity. The surge in cotton production early in this century helped encourage the formation of large estates; increasing cash incomes for those already large landowners enabled them to purchase more land. At the same time, small farms got smaller because of the inheritance practice of equal shares for each son. The 1952 revolution, which overthrew the notoriously corrupt monarchy, produced a land reform. At that time, 40 percent of the cultivated land was owned by less than 1 percent of the landlords.[1] More than 70 percent of the farmers owned less than 0.5 acre (about 1 hectare). In the reform process, no landlord was allowed to retain more than 200 feddans (a feddan is about 1.04 acres) and no single holding was to be less than 5 feddans. While conditions have definitely improved for many farmers, the plight of landless farmers is still serious. Thus, it is for social as well as economic production reasons that Egypt is striving so hard to bring new lands under irrigation.

Additional irrigated land, besides that supplied by the reservoir behind the Aswan High Dam, is being obtained by three approaches. Areas adjacent to the delta are being irrigated by both Nile water and local ground water. In the northern delta, swamps, lagoons, and saline soils are being reclaimed, expensively, for farmland. In the "new valley" area of southern Egypt (west of the Nile and including the large Kharga oasis) fossil water from the great underground reservoirs of the Nubian sandstone is being tapped by wells up to 900 feet (270 meters) deep. Another approach is to use the present supplies of water more efficiently, allowing more acres to be irrigated without increasing the volume of water supply. Open-ditch irrigation canals are being converted to underground pipes to reduce evaporation. Sprinkler irrigation, more efficient than

[1]Peter Beaumont, Gerald Black, and Malcolm Wagstaff, *The Middle East: A Geographical Study* (London: John Wiley & Sons, 1976), p. 482.

flood irrigation, is being substituted, reducing water consumption per land unit by half.

The Aswan High Dam's enormous hydroelectric generation will be used in part to industrialize the Aswan area with its exploitable minerals (notably iron ore). A village electrification scheme, well underway, will use much of the rest of the energy. Industries planned for villages and small towns include food processing and crafts.

Textiles, using locally grown cotton, are produced for an extremely competitive world market. They are still the major branch of industry, though diversification is proceeding rapidly. Over a million tourists visit Egypt annually, generating another source of income. Millions of Moslems from neighboring countries are attracted to Cairo, the cosmopolitan cultural center that is the largest city of the entire region. Many Westerners, too, are attracted by the warm sunny winters and the fantastic artifacts of one of the world's earliest and greatest civilizations. Suez Canal tolls bring over $500 million a year in government revenues, and a Red Sea-Mediterranean oil pipeline is intended to earn revenues from the many supertankers that cannot use the Suez Canal even after it has been deepened and widened.

Cairo—A World City   With almost 8 million inhabitants at present, and growing faster than many Egyptian planners would like, Cairo is clearly a world city in its cultural leadership, regional influence, and growing international functions. The tragic civil war that has disrupted Beirut's international banking and financial services functions may present an opportunity to Cairo. If Egypt can establish a reputation for political stability and maintain friendly relations with both the West and the oil-rich Arab states, the potential of Cairo will be even further enhanced.

The Sudan   The Sudan is over twice the size of Egypt, yet it has only about 18 million people. The country extends through several physical geographic regions from tropical rainforest to tropical desert. Physically and culturally, the Sudan is two nations; it very nearly became two political states. The semiarid and arid northern two thirds of the Sudan contains 13 million people and all the major cities. The northerners are generally Arabic-speaking Moslems who produce most of the Sudan's exports. The 5 million southerners are largely Negro and Nilotic tribes, animist or Christian in religion, and living in a rural subsistence economy. The southerners mutinied against the Khartoum administration during the transition to independence; a seventeen-year "civil war" followed, though it was more accurately a chronic skirmish. The struggle ended in 1972 when the South was finally granted autonomy on internal concerns.

Bazaar in Cairo. In addition to being Egypt's capital, Cairo ranks as a world city in terms of its cultural importance throughout the region. Cairo is an important center of Islamic study and is attempting to increase its role as an international banking center. (Courtesy of United Nations)

The major export, cotton, is grown mostly in the Gezira, a region between the White and Blue Niles south of the capital, Khartoum. Agriculture can be expanded; only about 75 percent of the potentially productive land is currently cultivated. No commercial minerals have been found, but exploration for oil is active on the Red Sea coast and offshore. The Sudan's transport deficiencies will likely continue to hinder economic development until major investments are made in infrastructure. There is promising potential for hydroelectric power.

One developmental proposal calls for a joint Egyptian-Sudanese canal project through the Sudd region, a swampy area where the sluggish White Nile spreads over a vast area, losing a great volume of water through evaporation. The canal would save annually an estimated 23.5 million cubic yards (18 million cubic meters) of water, which could be used to irrigate more land in both Egypt and Sudan. It would also induce drastic environmental changes in the Sudd.

Now that the North-South conflict has been resolved, apparently to both side's satisfaction, the Sudan has the potential to serve as a link between the Arab world and Black Africa.

THE MAGHREB AND LIBYA SUBREGION

The northwestern corner of Africa, between the sea and the Sahara, is known in the Moslem world as the Jezira al Maghreb, the "Island of the West." In a sense it is an "island" of more densely populated, somewhat better watered lands, surrounded by the Mediterranean and Atlantic to the north and westand the great desert to the south. Desert and sea meet in Libya, where the coastline of the Mediterranean dips southward along the Tunisian coast.

The Maghreb shares some cultural similarities. All three modern states of Tunisia, Algeria, and Morocco were dominated by France from the 1830's through the 1950's. All three states are predominantly Arabic in language, with Berber a second language. Libya, not part of the historic Maghreb, is also Arabic, ethnically and linguistically, with Berber and Black African minorities. The four countries of this subregion vary greatly in natural resource base and and economic development, present and potential.

Libya   Libya, with its vast oil and gas reserves in relation to its relatively small population of 2.75 million, most nearly resembles a western outlier of the Persian Gulf economies. Ninety percent of the people live on less than 10 percent of the land, mostly along the coast and in the great Kufra oasis of the southeastern portion. (See Figure 13–7.) Independent since 1951, Libya was a poor, under-

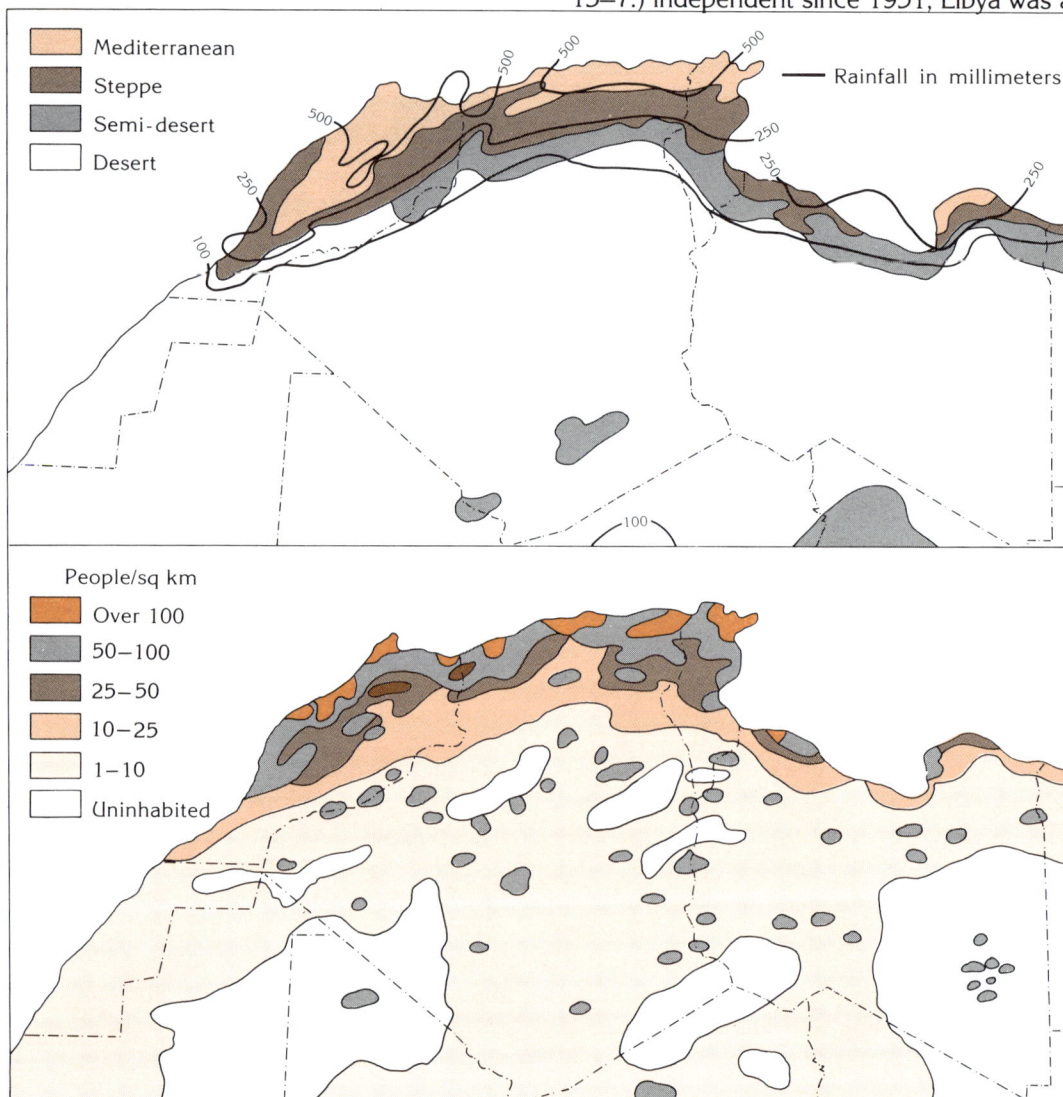

FIGURE 13–7

The Mahgreb: Climate and Population. Islam's "western isle" of relatively better watered lands in the midst of sea and desert shows a close correlation of precipitation and population.

developed state until the discovery of oil in 1959. Production rose quickly until 1970, when the Libyan government decided to cut production substantially to conserve the resource. Libya has an income from oil exports that exceeds its development-investment needs. About the same size as Alaska, Libya is making heavy investments in transportation infrastructure. By law, 15 percent of oil revenues must be set aside in a reserve fund, and 70 percent of the remainder used for economic development. The natural gas resource has only begun to be fully utilized and there are plans for a petrochemical industry fueled by gas.

Oil money is helping to develop the underground water reservoir of the Nubian sandstones. This ancient water reserve, the same one developed in Egypt's "new valley," will support oasis agriculture for several centuries at the maximum planned rate of withdrawal, despite the lack of any natural recharge of the aquifer. The Kufra oasis development is intended to make Libya more self-sufficient in food as well as to expand the food supply to meet demands of one of the world's fastest growing populations (3.7 percent per year).

Tunisia   The Maghreb tends to be less of a petro-economy and more balanced in its agricultural, industrial, and service industry development than Libya. Tunisia's 6.5 million people, living in an area slightly smaller than Florida, have a per capita income of some $800 U.S., roughly comparable to that of Algeria ($900) and Morocco ($650), but not near Libya's affluent $5,100. Tunisia produces, and exports, a variety of Mediterranean-type agricultural products—dates, olives, citrus, figs, grapes, and vegetables. It also produces steel, textiles, clothing, and leather goods in a rather diverse industrial sector. Tunisia's international politics are more conciliatory and positive than some of its neighbors. Tunisia's population increase rate, 2.7 percent, is above the world average but the lowest of the Maghreb.

Algeria   Algeria's large size, equivalent to the entire Midwest of the U.S., supports a population of 17 million, growing at an annual rate of 3 percent. Fifty-six percent of the population is under the age of twenty, giving Algeria a high proportion of dependent youth. The government allocates 12 percent of its total spending on education and has developed an impressive educational system. Ninety-five percent of Algerians live on 12 percent of the land, near the coast; the vast segment of the Sahara held by Algeria has only 0.5 million inhabitants. Algiers, the capital, has over 2 million people and grows rapidly through internal migration. Algeria is that part of the Maghreb controlled longest by France (1830–1962). This long colonial domination and the substantial numbers of French ethnics established there for three or four generations led to their determination to hang on. A bitter revolt resulted that almost precipitated a civil war in France as well.

The highly centralized government of Algeria controls almost every facet of the economy. With much smaller oil reserves, Algerian production is half that of Libya. However, Algeria has the fourth largest proven reserves of natural gas in the world. The Algerians are investing heavily in facilities to liquify gas for export as well as to use it as a feedstock for domestic industries. Algeria has one of North Africa's best developed transport systems, including 2,400 miles (3,900 kilometers) of railroads. Algerians will add to their 4,700 miles (7,600 kilometers) of highway by paving a trans-Saharan highway all the way to the Niger border, enabling it to become a major trading partner with West Africa.

Natural Gas Liquefication Plant, Arzew, Algeria. The region's oil and gas resources, which tend to be concentrated in sparsely settled parts of the region, underwrite elaborate development schemes for those states rich in resources. The liquification of natural gas now enables that resource, once "fired off" as waste, to be economically exported. (Courtesy of United Nations)

Almost one half of all Algerians are employed in agriculture, which contributes less than 10 percent to the GNP. The past agricultural economy was based on the export of inexpensive wine, but there are now surpluses of wine in European markets, and Islam is strongly prohibitionist, eliminating the possibilities of market development in the Moslem world. Algeria has converted the former French estates into huge state farms supporting 5 million people. Algeria exports wheat, olive oil, citrus, and dates, but must also import many basic foods for its rapidly expanding population.

Algeria is considered more moderate than Libya if more activist in supporting revolutionary groups than its immediate neighbors. Algeria's prime foreign relations problem is its dispute with Morocco and Mauritania over the division of Western (former Spanish) Sahara (see Figure 13–8). Algeria wished to become a "two sea" power by obtaining some frontage on the Atlantic through the territory relinquished by Spain in 1976. Moroccan troops promptly took the northern part of Western Sahara, splitting the former colony with Mauritania to the south.

Morocco Morocco's royal government has been more conservative than any other in the area. It actively supports established regimes in Africa against left-wing rebels. Morocco has little oil but is the world's largest exporter of phosphate rock, controlling over 70 percent of known reserves of this important fertilizer and chemical raw material.

There are also substantial deposits of iron ore, manganese, zinc, and cobalt. Some coal, lead, copper, and bauxite round out the region's most diverse mineral base.

Morocco's agricultural economy is a blend of tiny subsistence farms and large modern agribusiness units controlled by a few large landowners. Morocco's population of 19 million grows at a rate of 3 percent per year; it is concentrated in the rich plains of the northwest. Food products—citrus, fresh and canned vegetables and fruits, fish, and seafood—provide about a quarter of the country's foreign exchange.

Economic development is proceeding rapidly. Textiles, clothing, and carpets are major exports. Domestic economic development features expansion of port facili-

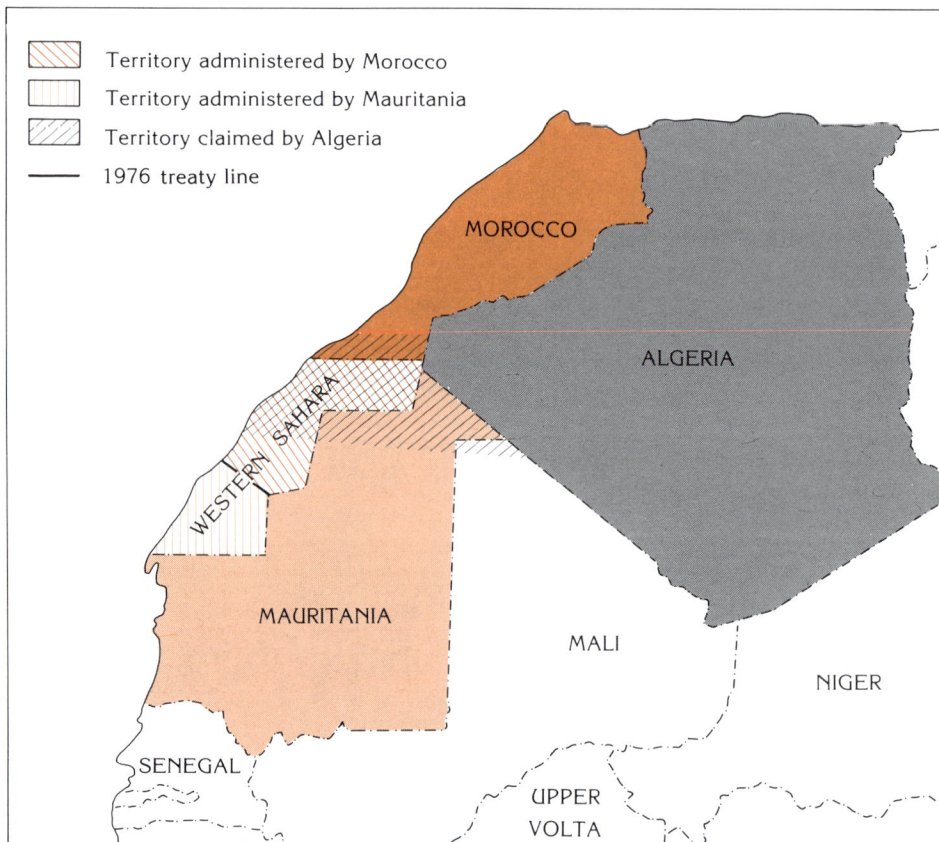

FIGURE 13–8
The Western Sahara Conflict. Following Spain's 1976 withdrawal from former Spanish Sahara, Algeria attempted to acquire territory that would give it frontage on the Atlantic, outflanking its conservative neighbor, Morocco. Morocco invaded the Western Sahara's territory, taking the northern two thirds, and agreeing to Mauritania's occupation of the southern third.

ties and hydroelectric and irrigation projects. A rapidly developing tourist trade emphasizes climate and cultural difference as the primary attractions.

IRAN AND AFGHANISTAN— THE "ARC OF CRISIS"

Few areas anywhere illustrate the basic problems and limitations of the whole concept of regionalization so well. The area is marginal to the larger region of which it is a part, and its people are not Arabs in either language or ethnic heritage, yet they are overwhelmingly Moslem. While Arabic culture has extended its influence into the area to some degree, it represents a thin, discontinuous veneer over an older Persian culture. Iran and Afghanistan are **successor states** to a once large and powerful series of Persian empires, which in turn incorporated Pakistan and parts of Turkey and the states of the Fertile Crescent. Culture and influence once moved from this core to what is now an Arab cultural region.

Never totally a part of Rome, Hindu India, or the Ottoman Empire, it both received and sent cultural impulses to and from those great political units. (See Figure 13–9.) Its position has always been crucial; its role that of contact point (rather than buffer) between and among the great civilizations that arose around it. Once a part of Alexander's empire, its contacts with ancient Greece linked it early to the European world. Subject to invasion from and control by the great Mongol empires of the Middle Ages, it had intimate contacts with both China and India. It remains an area of crucial importance, located between the USSR and the Middle East, between East Europe and the Orient. It is a zone of transition between the Islamic core and the cultures of the Orient.

Diverse in the extreme, yet vaguely homogenous In its Persian heritage, the volatile nature of this area again became all too evident at the close of the 1970's. It is in some ways analogous to an unstable chemical compound derived from diverse elements that shift and change, never permanently amalgamated into a new and lasting substance, yet never quite disappearing or dispersing.

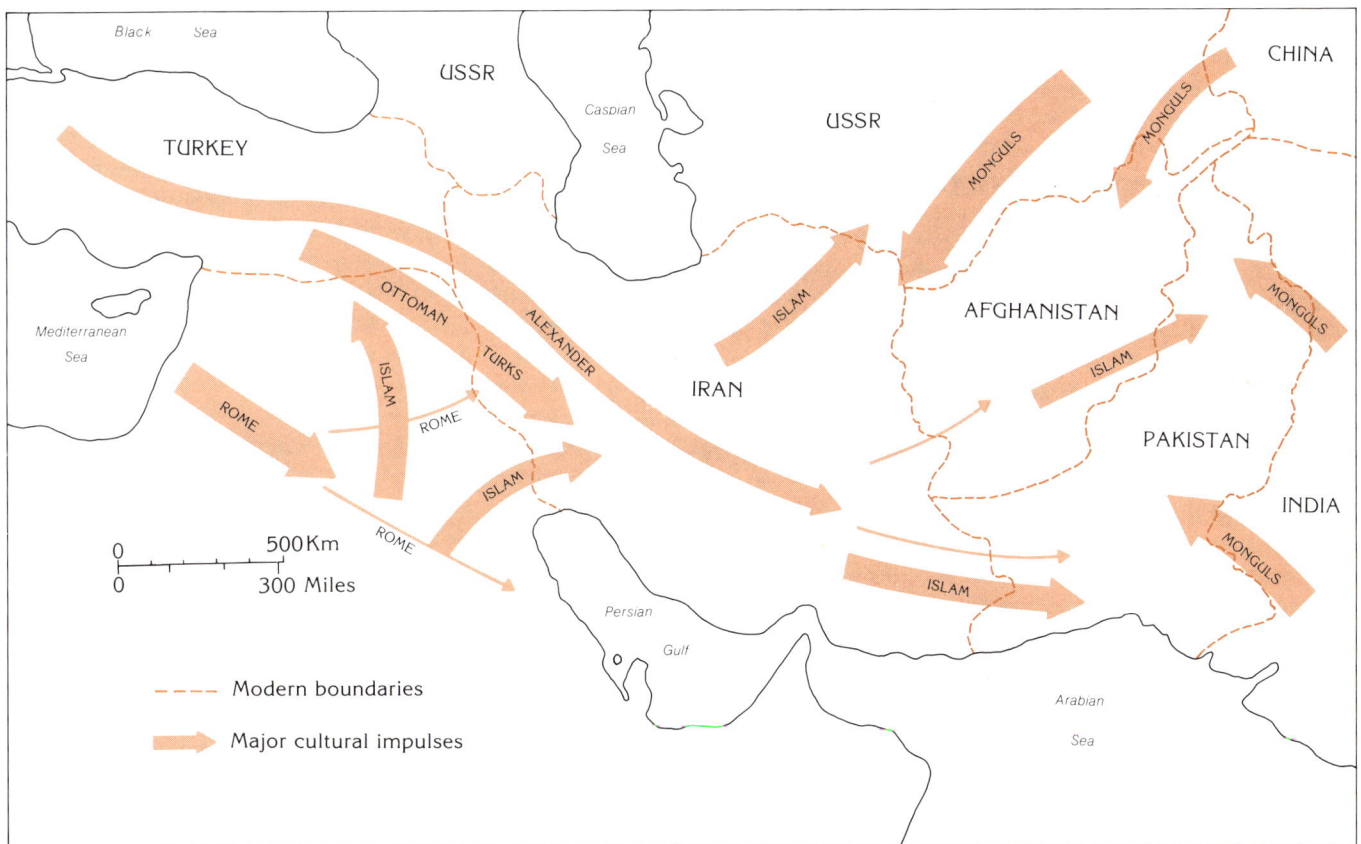

FIGURE 13–9
Cultural Impulses in the Arc of Crisis. The region's "Arc of Crisis" has long been an area of unstable amalgams of cultural inputs, many from relatively distant centers. Frequently, this was a frontier or most distant province of an empire based far away.

Iran Iran's large and varied territory has always had a great developmental potential. It is possessed of reasonably fertile soil over sizeable areas. The mountains, which virtually ring the entire subregion, serve to temper the heat and extract moisture in an area that would otherwise be desert with limited agricultural potential. In consequence, much of the land takes on the characteristics of steppe; some is even Mediterranean in climate. Seasonal winter rains and summer melting of snows provide sufficient water for irrigation of many small oases, collectively providing a sizeable arable area.

Yet the picture of agricultural potential is easily overdrawn. Iran is a populous country and has only a little over 1.0 acre (0.8 hectare) of arable land per person, a limitation that seriously restricted the ability of the government to fulfill promises of land for all farmers. It will seriously affect present plans for the return to a traditional agrarian society as well.

Following classic developmental models, the Shah's "bloodless revolution" (begun in 1963) implemented government purchases of land from landlords for redistribution among a landless peasantry. Former landlords were encouraged (some would say forced) to invest their capital in expanding commercial and industrial enterprises; income from these investments was to compensate for the loss of land rents. The program, and agricultural progress, lagged seriously behind projected targets. Small new farms that resulted lacked both the size and capital necessary to commercial production. Yields of food declined, necessitating importation. Irrigation works, crucial to production and once centrally managed on huge estates, began to degenerate.

Crops-livestock patterns resemble a desert horticulture complementing livestock husbandry and unirrigated grazing land in neighboring districts. Melons, pistachios, almonds, tobacco, apricots, sugar, and tea had the status of basic crops. Wheat, barley and rice are the staple grains of the country. Arable area decreased between 1950 and 1980 at a time of rapid population increase. Grain production doubled from 1961 to 1978, growing faster than the population, which increased by 65 percent during the same period. However, these gains were often made at the expense of other horticultural crops with potentially greater value.

Wheat and barley are often grown without irrigation along the Caspian littoral and in the higher, wetter mountain valleys. Growing industrialization encouraged diversion of irrigated land from food crops to industrial crops like cotton, tobacco, and oil seeds. Net agricultural progress was small. Increased meat demands resulted in overgrazing and consequent erosion on the marginal dryland pastures.

Over half of Iran is a dry interior plateau with no permanent streams. Vast areas of salt wastes in the southeast are as barren as the Rub' al Khali of Saudi Arabia. The only large area of potential farmland is the southwestern coastal plain, the area disputed with Iraq. Peopled largely by Arabs rather than Iranians, it is a continuation of

Shopping Center in Teheran, Iran. As in many developing nations, the contrast between the modernizing cities and still-traditional countryside can set up severe social strains, particularly when powerful conservative elements feel threatened by the pace of modernization and Westernization. (Courtesy of United Nations)

the Mesopotamian plain. Scheduled for huge irrigation schemes (some completed) it was to have redressed the need for food importation. Its future obviously is in doubt.

The greatest single aid to Iranian development is its reserve of oil. With some 60 billion barrels of proven reserves (over double the U.S. reserves) Iran has the potential to remain a major oil power regardless of long years of sustained production. Yet oil is not the only mineral of value; there are commercial deposits of chrome ore, copper, lead, zinc, iron, and manganese and workable deposits of coal. The development of these other mineral reserves was to be accomplished with oil revenues.

The location of the oil resource is also crucial. The largest fields are just north of the Persian Gulf and within the disputed area claimed by Iraq. Routes for export are dependent on Iranian power or the acquiescence of neighboring states.

Despite the fact that Iran was one of the world's earliest exporters of oil (its huge refinery at Abadan, near the Iraq border, was begun by the British in 1909), the impact of oil revenues was not felt until much later. Iran did not achieve a controlling interest in its own fields until 1973.

In addition to using its oil revenues, Iran borrowed heavily from the Export Import Bank and the International Monetary Fund. These massive investments, which frequently involved foreign contracts to design, deliver, and erect entire steel mills, aluminum plants, oil refineries, and auto assembly plants, produced an astounding annual economic growth rate of 11 percent (adjusted for inflation) from the early 1960's through 1973. Per capita income just before the revolution had reached $1,880 per year. The strain on the economy of this very rapid development was obvious by the late 1970's, when agricultural productivity was lagging and inflation was again serious.

Iran had an uneven development in that its influence was felt among relatively small numbers of people and in a few cities and mineral districts. Large segments of the population were relatively poorer as the gap between urban and rural, rich and poor, widened.

Two additional major problems face Iran: population growth and ethnic diversity. Iran has experienced a high population growth rate (3.2 percent) for several decades. Almost half of all Iranians are under the age of fifteen, contributing to the economic strain. The people are concentrated in the north and northwest. With over 70 percent of the national territory in mountains or arid plateaus with few inhabitants, densities are exceptionally high in the populated areas. Almost half the population is urban, an unusually high proportion for a country of Iran's developmental level. As in Latin America, the urban work force contains disproportionate numbers of functionaries, unemployed, underemployed, and service personnel. De-

spite large-scale industrial investment, relatively few workers are employed in the large-scale, capital-intensive new plants. Almost 5 million people jam Teheran, the national capital. Teheran and the Persian Gulf oil-chemical complex are the two major industrial centers.

With continual industrial development, the population problem might be conceivably solved. Its current rapid growth rate is typical of stage 2 of the demographic transition and need not be viewed as of constant duration. However, the ethnic question may prove to be more pressing. Iran's official name, until the declaration of an Islamic Republic on April 1, 1979, was the Empire of Iran. It was indeed an empire by definitions of political geography. Its boundaries included many different ethnic groups, several of which aspired to independence. It is not yet certain to what degree the new government of Iran will be willing to move toward regional autonomy to defuse separatist demands. The Kurds, occupying a historic homeland that includes parts of Iraq and Turkey have been in rebellion repeatedly (see Figure 13–10).

Only two thirds of Iran's population are ethnic Iranians who speak related Indo-European languages like Persian, Baluchi, Bakhtari, and Lur. Language affinity, however, is no guarantee of national affiliation—Kurdish, too, is an Iranian tongue. Some 25 percent of the population speaks a Turkish language. Other ethnic groups with other languages include Arabs in the Tigris-Euphrates lowlands delta area to the southwest, Armenians and Azerbayjanis in the northwest, Jews and Assyrians. This complex ethnic and linguistic mix has the potential for disrupting any central government insensitive to their demands.

Even religion can create problems. Most follow the Shiite sect, while 80 percent of all Moslems belong to the Sunni sect. Shia Islam is the official state religion in Iran. It is a major sect in neighboring Iraq, and is present in many other Islamic countries, adding to the confusion of unclear loyalties. Strong, effective leadership by Shia Moslems in Iran could attract support from groups outside Iran.

Afghanistan Afghanistan is one of those poorly developed corners of the earth that result from decisions made by others. *Remote* and *isolated* are probably the two adjectives most frequently applied to the area. It is at the bottom of the developmental ladder, yet it is not without resources. Afghanistan has had common borders with Iran, China, India, and Russia, yet it has had minimal contact with any of those states. Subjected to repeated invasion, it was normally ruled from some distant seat of empire. As the empire weakened, it would emerge (briefly) as an independent state. Its isolation is certainly not determined by physical factors; it may be in some measure the result of a desire to stay independent—involvement has

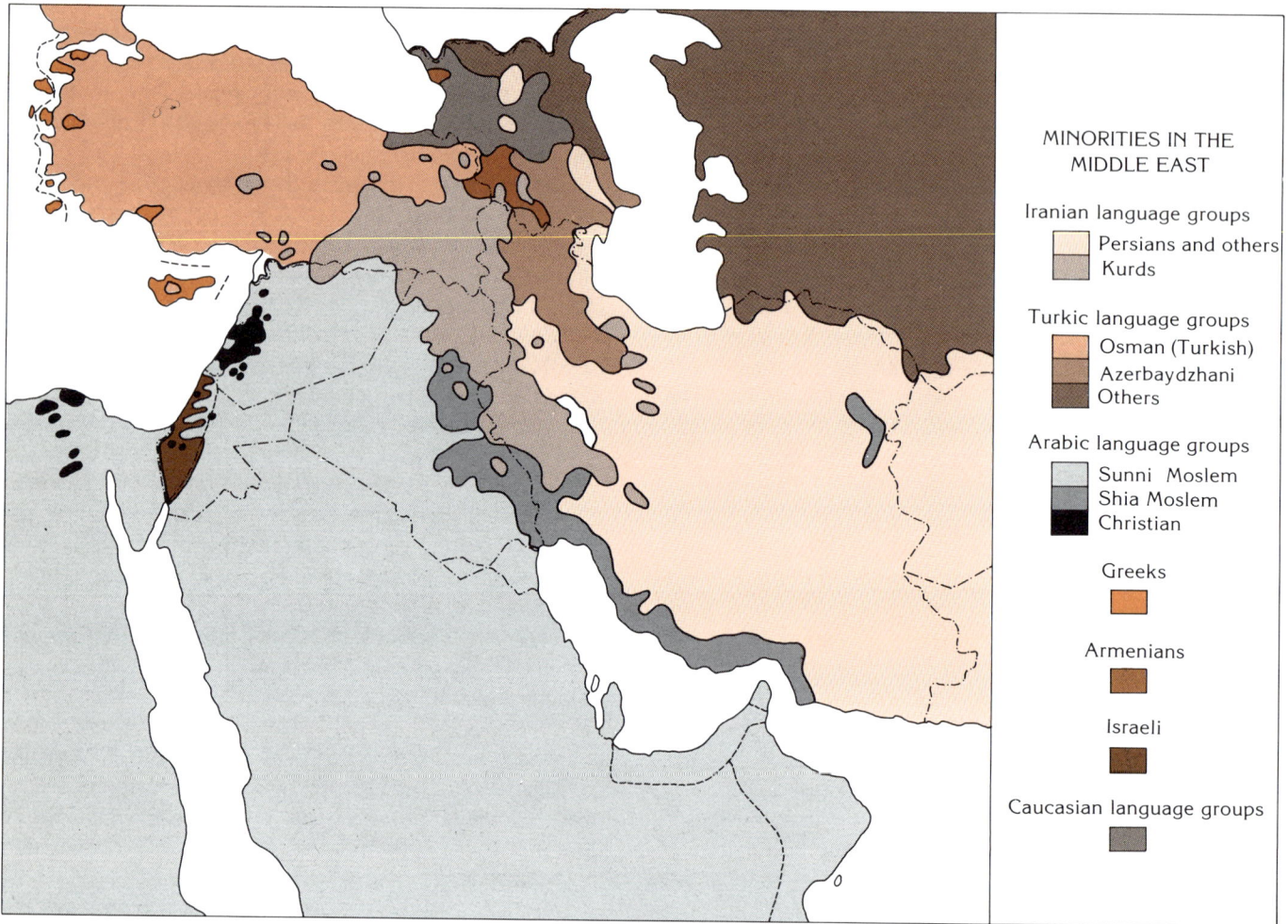

MINORITIES IN THE MIDDLE EAST

Iranian language groups
- Persians and others
- Kurds

Turkic language groups
- Osman (Turkish)
- Azerbaydzhani
- Others

Arabic language groups
- Sunni Moslem
- Shia Moslem
- Christian

Greeks

Armenians

Israeli

Caucasian language groups

FIGURE 13–10

Minority Homelands in the Eastern Sector of the Region. Many of the ethnic minorities of this region would be considered national minorities, that is, minorities that actively aspire to their own state. Such minorities potentially are disruptive of existing states, lending further instability to the arc of crisis.

Sheepherders, Afghanistan. One of the region's poorest and most isolated states, Afghanistan's major exports were sheepskins before its natural gas exports to the USSR drew it toward that country's economic orbit. (Courtesy of United Nations/ H. K. Lall)

historically meant conquest. The current state dates from the eighteenth century, when a native ruler was given protection and recognition by Russia and Britain, who agreed to its existence as a buffer between their colonial spheres.

A landlocked state, its population is scattered among dozens of small but densely populated oases and alluvial fans scattered around the edges of the empty mountain core. Unified control from a central seat has always been difficult. There are no navigable internal waterways, but there are large permanent streams. There are no railroads, but a paved road network is beginning to emerge. The United States has built paved roads linking the country with Pakistan and Iran (see Figure 13–11) while the USSR has paved roads linking Afghanistan to the Soviet frontiers.

Afghanistan's agriculture is considerably more primitive than that of Iran's. The long-term difficulty of access to Afghanistan, the much more restricted range of climates, and the lack of capital investment and modern agricultural technology have all combined to retard development. Cotton, wool, oilseeds, nuts, fruits, and sheep are the major crop and livestock commodities produced. Only about 15 percent of Afghanistan is usable for agriculture; most of this is in narrow valleys in the arid plateaus or on alluvial fans at the foot of the Hindu Kush Mountains. Primary exports are wool, mutton, and lambskins. Some of the wool is woven into carpets for export. Though the

population growth rate is somewhat above the world average, there is no severe shortage of farmland comparable to that of Iran's; much potentially cultivable land is still uncultivated. The country is normally self-sufficient in food. Cotton has been increasing in importance, reflecting higher world market prices.

In contrast to Iran's huge oil reserves, Afghanistan has only 285 million barrels of proven reserves, but little prospecting has been done. Natural gas production is increasing; it is exported by pipeline to the USSR. There are known, commercial-scale deposits of copper, lead, coal, zinc, iron ore, and silver, but exploitation is severely handicapped by the lack of a good transportation system. Even before the revolution of 1979, the Soviet Union was the major trading partner. There is little industry outside Kabul, the capital, other than crafts, and the low per capita income ($125 annually) generates little investment capital. Foreign investment (largely from the USSR) has built textile plants, machine shops, and leather plants in the first steps toward industrialization.

Afghanistan was the scene of a protracted struggle between Russian imperialism, expanding into the **power vacuum** of the underdeveloped areas of central Asia and British imperialism seeking to stabilize the frontiers of India and to dominate historic invasion routes to the subcontinent. Russian power moving south and east toward

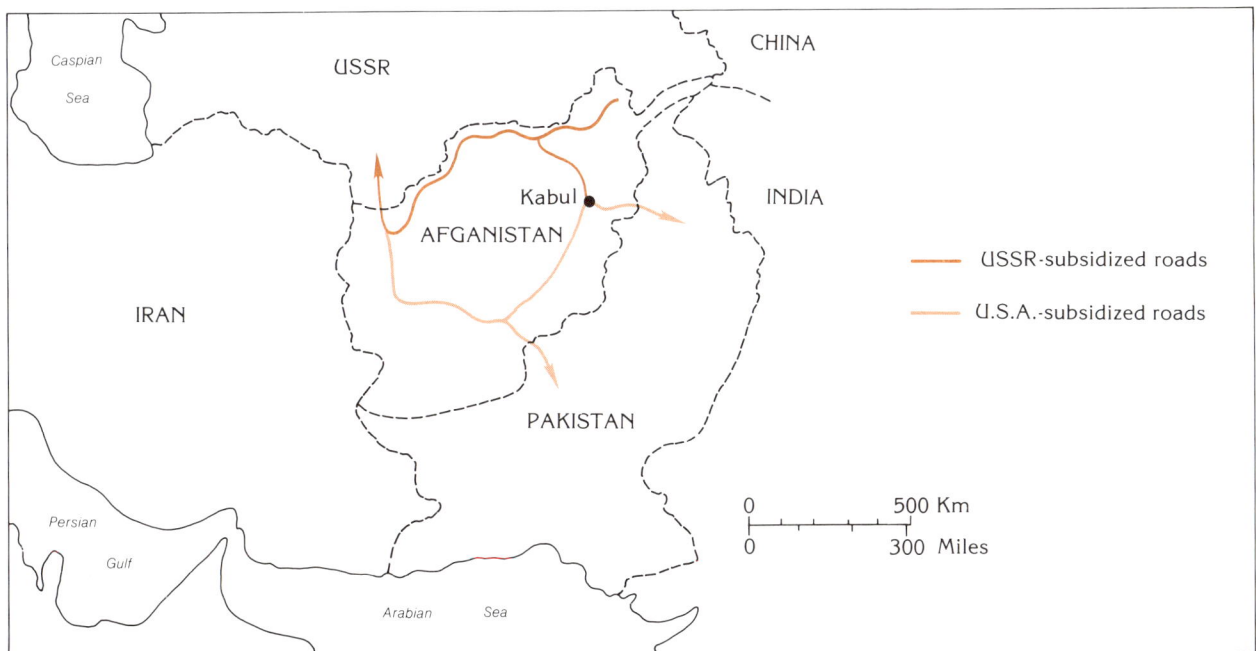

FIGURE 13–11

Afghanistan Road Links. Afghanistan's primitive transport infrastructure features a few modern roads, each built by a contending superpower to link a portion of that strategic state to the Soviet Union or to the western world via Pakistan. In each case, the roads are designed as much for facilitating external purposes as for internal development.

India was countered by British power expanding on the northwest periphery of India. In the 1970's, the Soviet Union, following the historic goals of the tsars, installed a regime friendly to them. A military invasion followed in 1980.

The human legacy of Afghanistan's long tumultuous history of invasion is a multiethnic society of Pushtun, Tajik, Uzbek, Hazarak, Aimaq, and Turkoman groups. Literacy in any language (Dari, an Afghan variant of Persian, and Pushtu are the dominant languages) is only about 10 percent. The Pushtun (Pathan) group is a clear majority (60 percent). Tadzhiks, speaking another Iranian dialect related to Pushtun, constitute 30 percent of the population. The remainder speak one Turkic language or another. The existence of a Tadzhik Peoples' Republic in the USSR has always been thought of as a potential threat to Afghan independence and a springboard for annexation. Soviet investment in the economy in recent years has softened up resistance and gradually increased the contact between the two states, which may climax in outright annexation.

Changing Political Relationships   Political relationships have changed radically in this region since the late 1970's. The exceptionally close, cooperative American-Iranian economic and political relationships collapsed abruptly in the revolution.

Iran's oil wealth had underwritten an impressive military build-up as that country sought to become the dominant power in the gulf following the British withdrawal. Great stresses developed in the formerly rural, conservative and deeply religious society as Western lifestyles and technology became prominent in the rapidly growing cities. The more conservative Moslem clergy saw the too-rapid Westernization as destroying Iran's traditions and deeply held religious convictions. In the long run, the practical problems of an aggressive and militarily expansionist USSR on Iran's borders may make far-off America, tainted with bringing "Westernization," seem relatively less of a threat to Iran's security and indigenous culture.

Afghanistan's strengthening symbiotic economic relationship with the Soviet Union led to Soviet involvement in stabilizing "friendly" regimes in Kabul, much as the British had virtually chosen leaders suitable to themselves in earlier times. It is not yet clear whether Soviet military invasion in 1979–80 will succeed in eliminating guerrilla resistance in the rugged countryside. The guerrilla resistance is supplied by the United States through a now more friendly Pakistan. The Soviet invasion of Afghanistan has tarnished its image among third-world states.

SAHARA-SAHEL SUBREGION

The four states of the Sahara-Sahel subregion were all part of the French empire in North Africa. French remains an official language and, for all except Chad, France remains the most important trading partner. All four states include large areas of the Sahara, the largest desert on earth, but each has a varying proportion of non-desert (or at least semi-desert) territory.

While temperatures of over 150° F (65° C) have been recorded, and there are settlements that have recorded no precipitation for at least a decade and more, the Sahara has been as much a highway (if a difficult one) as a barrier. It is not an easy, or forgiving, environment for the uninitiated, but trans-Saharan contacts have certainly existed for many centuries. North Africa can be imagined as a series of approximately parallel belts of climate-vegetation associations trending east-west across the continent. As noted in the discussion of the Maghreb, the desert makes a transition in the north to semiarid, then Mediterranean climates. To the south of the desert, the transition is again to semiarid, then subhumid climates, but the climatic mechanisms and effects are quite different. Mauritania has very little, Mali and Niger more, and Chad a considerable territory beyond the desert (see Figure 13–12). The climate transition zone on the southern edges of the Sahara produces an area known as the Sahel. While the poleward fringe of the Sahara near the Mediterranean has a winter "wet" season, the summer "wet" (or less dry) season of the Sahel unfortunately is in the high heat season. Evaporation is high and the effectiveness of the sparse precipitation is thus minimized. The volume of rains of the Sahel's "wet" season is also very unpredictable from year to year. This variability in precipitation is the prevalent environmental problem for these four states.

This shifting, unpredictable precipitation pattern over the Sahara-Sahel-savanna transition leads to optimistic, incautious expansion of flocks of domestic animals—cattle, sheep, goats, and camels. In the wetter-than-average years, the flocks prosper and multiply; in drier years, they quickly over-graze the sparse, scattered vegetation cover, contributing to the degradation of the environment; eventually, the animals starve. The collapse of the grazing economy can spell disaster for the human population as well. The only thing predictable about precipitation cycles in the Sahel is that there will be other droughts.

The Sahara-Sahel subregion is a major zone of cultural and racial mixing—Berbers and Arabic people from the desert and various Black African groups from the wetter south. Racial-cultural groups from each side of the Sahara have travelled across and settled on the opposite side of the desert. The four states are large in area and relatively sparsely populated. Mauritania, about four fifths the size of Alaska, has only 1.5 million people. Mali, the next state to the east, has about 6.5 million. Somewhat smaller Niger has 5 million, while Chad has a little over 4 million. These almost empty areas of relatively small economic importance in international trade would appear to

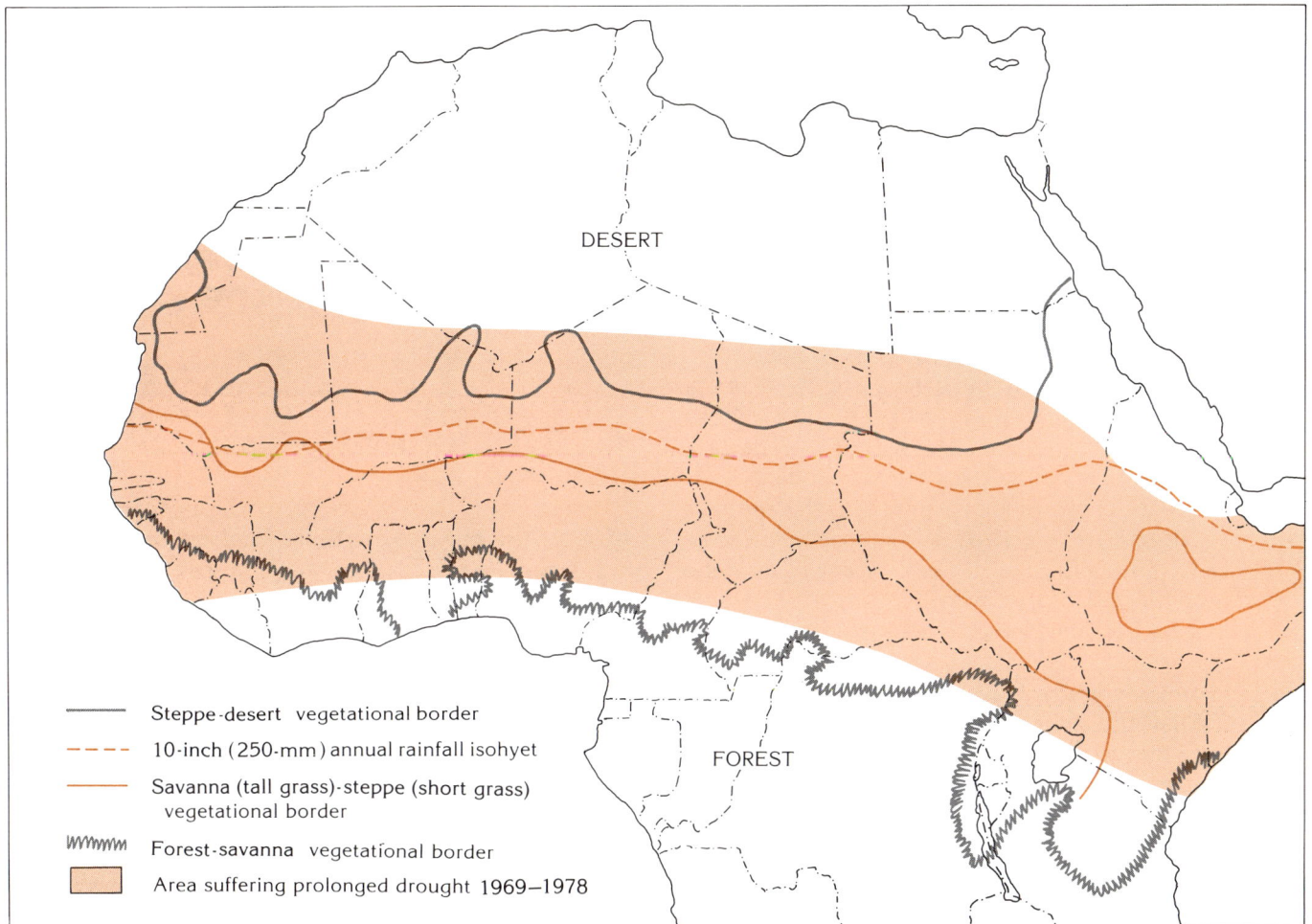

FIGURE 13–12

The Sahel Climate Transition. As in most other climate boundaries, the boundary between arid and semiarid–sub-humid climates on the southern fringe of the Sahara is transitional rather than sharp. In this case, the boundary is further complicated by cyclical precipitation patterns that lead to great fluctuations in the precipitation or vegetational boundaries.

have been almost hopelessly isolated until late in the European colonial expansion. In Mauritania, for example, French control was not completely consolidated until 1934. Surfaced roads are only now being completed across the vast desert, north-south. Enormous areas were devoid of any permanent settlement.

Yet, this part of North Africa and West Africa has a historic importance in the development of cultures. Great Black African empires rose in the Sahel-savanna zone. Ghana, Malinki (Mali), and Songhai flourished from the twelfth to sixteenth centuries, maintaining trade routes to the Mediterranean and the Near East. They were replaced after 1600 by Arab expansion into the Sahara-Sahel. Arab traders ranged from Spain to Nigeria, from western China to Arabia to Mozambique. Isolation is a relative thing.

Extremely isolated **relict populations** of plants and animals, rock carvings and paintings, and fossil remains

all indicate that the Sahara was once a much wetter land. The present desert seems to be the product of some climatic changes that occurred in the past 10,000 years or less. Great rock carvings and paintings depict horse-drawn war chariots, similar to those of the ancient Egyptians, and great flocks of elephants, giraffes, gazelles, and lions and hippopotamuses. Small waterholes isolated by hundreds of miles of desert contain catfish, indicating that there were once permanent streams through the Sahara. Even in Roman times, the Mediterranean fringe of the Sahara had large numbers of elephants, lions, and other animals that were remnant populations of herds that once roamed the Sahara.

Mauritania, named for an ancient Roman province of Africa, has a per capita income of about $400. A narrow belt along the Senegal River, the southwestern border, is productive agricultural land. Livestock grazing occupies much of the Sahel area of Mauritania, while the northern desert is barren except for scattered oases. A major iron ore deposit near the border with the Moroccan-controlled portion of Western (Spanish) Sahara contributes about three fourths of the country's foreign exchange. Mauritania is developing a nearby source of lower-grade ore to replace the present nearly exhausted mine. Copper production fluctuates with world prices as production costs are high. Oil exploration has not yet proven any sizeable reserves. The Atlantic waters offshore include one of the richest fisheries in the world; it is now being exploited through better port facilities and processing plants.

Mali, named for one of the great black kingdoms of the savanna-Sahel, has an even lower per capita GNP than Mauritania. Exports are primarily livestock products—processed meat and hides. There are known deposits of bauxite, iron ore, copper, and phosphate, but the transport system is inadequate to facilitate development at present.

Niger, whose $150 per capita GNP is typical of the eastern three states of this subregion, lost half its livestock in the mid-1970's Sahel drought. Hides and meat are normally exported when herds are large. Other export products are peanuts and cotton. Niger has the fifth largest reserve of uranium in the world.

Chad's territory reaches further into the better watered savanna than its Sahara-Sahel neighbors. It is normally self-sufficient in food except during disastrous droughts, and exports some peanuts and cotton. Fishing in Lake Chad and the rivers feeding it provides large quantities of dried or smoked fish for export. In 1981, Libya temporarily occupied Chad and took control of its government.

In all four states of the subregion, a relatively low population and large area with largely unknown or unexploited minerals presents these people with an uncertain but potentially prosperous future. Stabilizing the water supply could do more than prevent the reoccurrence of the disastrous Sahelian drought of the 1970's; it could enable these states to become regionally significant exporters of meat, fish, peanuts, and other high protein food products to Black Africa, which generally needs an improved diet. There are indications of enough petroleum to at least meet local needs, potentially freeing these countries of dependence on foreign imports. The uranium of Niger and Chad could be a very valuable asset if reliance on nuclear power becomes widespread.

REGIONAL TENSIONS AND RELATIONSHIPS

Almost no other area at any point in history has moved so quickly from background to forefront in international importance. It is not oil alone that is responsible. A look at the world map of regions indicates its pivotal position as the neighbor of Europe, the USSR, South Asia, and Africa south of the Sahara. It spans portions of three continents, and, at its fringes, shares the problems and characteristics of the states and peoples of each of those regions. It is both supplier and market for almost every region of the world—a characteristic it shares with fully developed areas. There should be no doubt that it is a rapidly developing area. Its overall surplus of capital is making this region a major international investor as well as enabling the development of domestic economies. It could become the next fully developed portion of the world.

The single missing ingredient may be peace. The whole region is fraught with potential border disputes; most of the region's states contain potentially disruptive minorities. Governments and leaders have changed rap-

Trans-Sahara Truck Convoys, Mauritania. The Sahara has never functioned as a total barrier to trade and cultural contacts between Africa's Mediterranean coast and its equatorial zones. While never an easy route, it nonetheless was a continuing routeway for the interaction of major world regions. (Courtesy of United Nations)

idly, while internal class differences complicate domestic calm. There is also the question of the reaction of its oil customers, who may feel endangered by the threat of a cutoff of supply or the constant round of price increases.

THE REGIONAL WORLD VIEW

Currently, increases in oil prices fuel new rounds of inflation, which in turn bring another increase in oil prices. Dependent on extraregional sources for food, capital equipment, arms, and many manufactures, the states of the region gain less than might be anticipated from oil price increases.

Any major new oil discoveries could produce a world oil glut with a resulting plummeting of oil prices. New reserves uncovered in the USSR may not enter world markets, but could eliminate the USSR and East Europe as customers for Middle Eastern oil. The newly exploited offshore reserves in Mexico are already being marketed in Europe and the United States. New levels of productive sediments recently discovered under Lake Maracaibo and new finds in the Orinoco River delta and valley are rejuvenating Venezuela's oil industry. Major new fields in China, recent increases in Indonesian production, and the growing production of the North Sea oil fields of Europe all add new productive capacity and new competition for the Persian Gulf and North African producers.

Table 13–2 shows the rapid increase in the importance of this region as an oil producer. It also hints at the shift to oil as an energy source—first accomplished in North America (by 1950), then gradually extending to the rest of the world. It also shows the gradual rise of oil production in yet other world regions—shifts can come rapidly. Although the U.S. and Canada have dropped from over 60 percent of world production to some 17 percent, and Southwest Asia–North Africa has risen from 6 percent to 40 percent, the rest of the world has also increased its share from 32 percent to over 43 percent of total world production.

TABLE 13–2
Percent world oil production by region

	1938	1950	1960	1978
United States and Canada	61.6	51.7	35.6	16.9
Middle America	2.1	2.2	1.6	2.6
South America	13.1	17.5	16.3	5.4
West Europe	0.3	0.6	1.4	4.0
East Europe	2.7	1.1	1.5	0.8
USSR	11.0	7.8	14.5	19.2
East Asia	0.0	0.0	0.7	3.5
South Asia	0.0	0.0	0.1	0.5
Southeast Asia	3.0	2.2	2.2	2.8
Australia-Oceania	0.0	0.0	0.0	0.8
Africa south of the Sahara	0.0	0.1	0.3	3.9
Southwest Asia–North Africa	6.2	16.8	25.8	39.6
Total	100.0	100.0	100.0	100.0

The role of increased conservation through technological efficiency is not yet fully realized. The renewed vitality of coal production in the United States, Canada, and Europe and the role of oil shales, tar sands, and nuclear power all leave the long-term prosperity of this region open to question.

case study
ISRAELI AGRICULTURE

Israeli agriculture is characterized by very high rates of capital investment and technology. In common with most Mediterranean countries, Israel has a positive balance of trade in agricultural products, importing cheaper grains and animal feeds while exporting higher priced, high quality fruits, vegetables, and even some animal products. Israel imports wheat, beef, and animal feed ingredients but manages to supply all or most of the basic foods for its 3.5 million people. Israel's predominantly semiarid and arid land is heavily irrigated (45 percent of cultivated land under irrigation). The capital-intensive irrigation is heavily subsidized by the government; the average price of irrigation water to families is only about one third of the real cost. Because Israel is using just about 100 percent of its land and water resources, any improvements in productivity must be related to high capital and technology inputs. The Israelis have been markedly successful in increasing their efficiency of water use. The volume of water used in agriculture has stabilized over the last decade, whereas irrigated area has increased by 17 percent. In fifteen years, the use-efficiency of irrigation water for citrus rose by 320 percent, vegetables by 190 percent, and fruits by 50 percent. About half of all irrigation water is used for fruit production: citrus, avocado, apples, grapes, dates, olives, peaches, strawberries, melons, and nectarines. Israel also exports large quantities of roses, carnations, gladiolas, and flower bulbs to European markets.

Considering the semiarid nature of most Israeli agricultural land, it is not surprising that the traditional Mediterranean domestic animals (goats and sheep) thrive. It *is* surprising that Israel has a dairy industry that supplies all its domestic market, as dairy cattle are acclimated to cool-summer climates as in northwestern Europe. The European-background culture of many Israelis demands dairy products, and Israel produces these with selective breeding and innovative environmental management of the dairy herds. The quality of Israeli herds is such that breeding stock is exported for additional income. Breeding stocks of goats and sheep are also exported. Israel is self-sufficient in produce, eggs, and potatoes as well as dairy products; it even supplies 85 percent of its beef and 70 percent of its fish needs.

Israeli agricultural technology and planning has been so successful that Israel provides technical assistance to underdeveloped countries by training agriculture development personnel. Some seven thousand planners, technicians, and experts in various fields have received training in Israel. Marketing techniques are emphasized as much as irrigation and selective breeding.

case study
MIDDLE EAST OIL

The present dominance of the Middle East in the world oil markets (60 percent of world proven reserves, 40 percent of world production) is a relatively recent phenomenon. Although oil in commercial quantities was discovered in Iran in 1908, it was only after World War II that this portion of North Africa—Southwest Asia surged forward in world importance. In 1946, the Middle East produced less than one tenth of the world's output. In 1965, the Middle East surpassed the United States as the world's largest producer. As recently as 1973, Canada and Venezuela supplied 40 percent of U.S. imports, compared to 15 percent from the Middle East. By 1980, the Middle East supplied 34 percent of U.S. imports, 60 percent of West Europe's imports, and 75 percent of Japanese imports.

Two physical factors, one geologic and one locational, contribute to the high desirability of Middle East oil. Not only is the area's oil of generally high quality, but the characteristics of underground reservoirs in rock formations permit extremely high rates of production. Average rates of production in barrels per day (B/D) for individual wells are: United States, 17 B/D; United Kingdom, 6,100 B/D; Australia, 1,100 B/D; Saudi Arabia, 10,000 B/D. In addition, the proximity of almost all fields in the Middle East to deep-water ports means that transportation costs are relatively low. The North Africa–Southwest Asia region now contains ten of the top twenty-one oil producers and clearly dominates international trade in oil.

While actual production costs for Middle East oil are enviably low, the sharp price rises beginning in 1973 forced world markets upward, probably instigated recessions in the developed world and had an even more severe impact on oil-importing developing countries, which were virtually bankrupted. OPEC, the Organization of Petroleum Exporting Countries, was formed in 1960 by Saudi Arabia, Iran, Iraq, Venezuela, and Kuwait. Later members are Qatar (1961), Indonesia and Libya (1962), United Arab Emirates (1967), Algeria (1969), Nigeria (1971), and Gabon (1975). Direct government involvement in setting oil prices began in 1971; the official selling prices for premium-grade crude ("Arabian Light") went from $1.34 per barrel in June 1970 to $36.00 per barrel by the end of 1981. The 1970's was also a decade of nationalization of oil fields and production facilities. This coincided with a dramatic shift in dependence on oil as an energy source. In 1950, oil contributed only 10 percent of West Europe's total energy consumption; by 1970, oil's share of a much larger total was 55 percent. Similarly, oil's share in total Japanese energy supply went from 9 percent to 33 percent in the same time frame. Thus, as the world became more dependent on oil and specifically on imported oil, and as Middle East production rocketed up, the industrial nations' multinational oil companies lost control over Middle East oil. Nationalization was accompanied by the formation of an international cartel. The economic and political consequences of these interrelated trends are in the first rank of world problems and will continue to be so for at least another decade.

REVIEW QUESTIONS

1 Why is it assumed that this region includes an important, early cultural hearth?

2 What is meant by the *Columbus Syndrome?* What was its effect on trade routes, and thus the economy, of the eastern end of the Mediterranean?

3 Briefly describe the population distribution pattern of this region.

4 What are the major exceptions to the generalization that this region is a Moslem culture area?

5 In what ways is Israeli agriculture distinguished from that of most of the rest of the region?

6 What are the major in-flows and out-flows of people migrating into or out of Israel? Why does the rising out-flow pose a serious long-term threat to Israel?

7 What cultural factors have facilitated the unofficial Israeli-American alliance? Is there any doubt about the future of this "alliance"?

8 What are the implications of the low spatial correlation of oil and dense populations through the region?

9 What are some of the developmental strategies open to oil-rich, lightly populated Persian Gulf states?

10 Why does Greek control over many small islands close to the Turkish coast pose such a serious problem should oil be discovered in the Aegean Sea?

11 What are Cyprus' prospects for peaceful economic development in view of its recent civil war?

12 How was modern technology affected the nomad's lifestyle?

13 What are the strategic considerations in the acquisition of naval and air bases by the superpowers in the seas and straits around the Arabian peninsula?

14 Briefly describe both the positive and negative results of Egypt's High Aswan Dam. On balance, has it contributed much to the economy?

15 What strategic considerations contributed to Algeria's attempt to acquire part of former Spanish Sahara?

16 What ethnic, linguistic, and cultural factors are involved in demands for provincial autonomy in Iran?

17 What interactions of precipitation variability and pastoralist's decisions has helped to produce tragic environmental degradation in the Sahel?

18 Speculate on the long-term prospects for stability within the region's remaining monarchies.

19 What would the effects be on this region of a major new oil discovery in North America or western Europe?

20 How do Soviet actions in Afghanistan affect the regional patterns of alliances and loyalties to the West?

SUGGESTED READINGS

1 JOHN ANTHONY, *Arab States of the Lower Gulf: People, Politics and Petroleum.* Washington, D.C.: The Middle East Institute, 1975.

2 PETER BEAUMONT, GERALD BLAKE, and J. MALCOLM WAGSTAFF, *The Middle East: A Geographical Study.* New York: Wiley, 1976.

3 M. BRETT, *Northern Africa: Islam and Modernization.* London: Cass, 1973.

4 ROBERT CAMPBELL, *Pakistan: Emerging Democracy.* Princeton, N.J.: Van Nostrand, 1963.

5 J. CLARKE and W. FISHER, eds., *Populations of the Middle East and North Africa.* Cambridge: Heffer, 1972.

6 R. COLLINS and R. TIGNOR, *Egypt and the Sudan.* Englewood Cliffs, N.J.: Prentice Hall, 1967.

7 W. B. FISHER, *The Middle East: A Physical, Social and Regional Geography.* New York: Harper and Row, 1971.

8 GEOFFREY LEWIS, *Modern Turkey.* New York: Praeger, 1974.

9 DAVID LONG, *The Persian Gulf.* Boulder, Colo.: Westview, 1976.

10 STEPHEN LONGRIGG, *The Middle East: A Social Geography.* Chicago: Aldine, 1970.

11 EFRAIM ORNI and ELISHA EFRAT, *Geography of Israel.* New York: Daniel Davey, 1964.

12 R. K. RAMAZANI, *The Northern Tier: Afghanistan, Iran and Turkey.* New York: Van Nostrand, 1970.

KEY TERMS

- ecosystem
- manganese nodule
- overfishing
- food chain
- upwelling
- tragedy of the commons
- "good fairies" hypothesis
- hydrologic cycle
- territorial sea
- continental shelf
- plate tectonics
- social overhead

14

THE LAST FRONTIERS

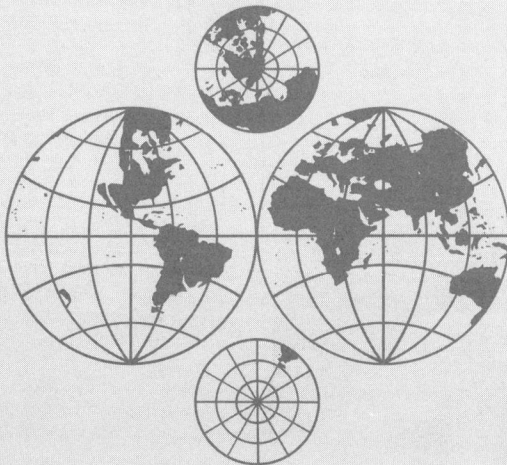

PROLOGUE: THE OCEANS AND POLAR REGIONS: RESOURCE FRONTIERS OF THE CONTEMPORARY WORLD

The frontier is a concept that stirs many positive emotions. One pictures sturdy pioneer families pushing into unknown territory, frequently braving hostile natives, in search of a better life. The frontiers people and their late nineteenth century romantic representative, the cowboy, are heroes and heroines, but they are also symbols of the past. Most historians assert that the American frontier is long past, though some Alaskans would disagree. But there *are* frontiers, in any but the narrowest sense, still in this world. People need not voyage to the planets to find frontiers that offer new opportunities and new challenges. As noted earlier, the tropical and subtropical deserts, the tropical rainforest, and the subpolar regions all exhibit some aspects of the contemporary frontiers. This is apparent in their selective development through new technologies and management techniques. The ultimate frontiers may be in outer space, but those parts of *this* planet that most closely meet the traditional concepts of frontier are the world's oceans and the polar regions.

THE OCEANS AND POLAR REGIONS AS FRONTIERS

The human race has known and used the resources of the seas for many millenia, of course. In the sense of contact with the oceans, their outlines and geographic locations have been known for centuries. However, many areas of knowledge are still being explored. In many ways, we are just crossing the threshold of learning about and using the ocean's resources. Just as thousands of years ago people tended to use the food, energy, and other material resources of the land in a relatively primitive and inefficient fashion, we are using the ocean resources in very limited, unscientific, and wasteful ways. Virtually the entire human race has passed far beyond the hunting and gathering stage in their approach to land resources. We have only just begun to go beyond the simple hunting and gathering of the sea's resources. This is not to say that this initial level of exploitation is not potentially destructive of the environment and some of its biological and mineral resources. There is no doubt that early people exterminated whole species of land animals. As an example, the mammoth was hunted into oblivion in North America. Our relatively slight knowledge of and limited, primitive exploitation of the oceans has a contemporary example of ignorant extermination pending—the plight of the great whales.

Although people have repeatedly probed the fringes of the polar realm for many centuries and the stone age Eskimos have evolved effective survival techniques for that environment, the more typical perception of the polar regions is similar to that of the oceans. They have been viewed as fundamentally hostile, nonsupportive environments, visited only with elaborate cultural modifications and adaptations. Often a specific resource may be *raided,* that is, gathered as quickly as possible with little thought to conservation.

Modern Arctic and especially Antarctic expeditions have featured self-contained life-support systems only relatively less elaborate and comprehensive than those used in moon landings. The human race is still literally on the surface of knowledge and understanding of the oceans and polar regions alike.

PERCEPTUAL HAZARDS OF THE LAST FRONTIERS: THE CASE OF THE GREENLAND VIKINGS

Part of the gap between frontier perception and reality is the problem of adequately interpreting the different physical environment. The natural environment is neither hostile nor friendly—it is simply there. It is impersonal. Disastrous past attempts at extending the settlement and exploitation frontiers must be blamed not on the physical environment but on errors in interpreting the possibilities and limitations of that environment. The trial-and-error nature of attempted extension of the frontier, plus the complex interaction of cultural and physical components of the total environment, can be illustrated by the experience of the Greenland Vikings.

Greenland, mostly covered by the largest ice sheet in the northern hemisphere, may sound like a very unlikely place in which to establish a colony of transplanted Europeans. The Norse had established themselves in Iceland by 863 A.D. Iceland, despite the name, is not nearly as cold or barren as Greenland turned out to be, also despite its name. Iceland lies on the border of the polar climates and the more temperate climates typical of Scandinavia (see Figure 14–1). The North Atlantic Drift, discussed in Chapter 5, circulates enough warm water around the island to raise its temperature above polar levels. The interior of Iceland is cold and infertile, with several small glaciers, but the coast is certainly habitable. Iceland apparently was partially wooded at the time of Norse Viking colonization. Iceland attracted a population of 20,000 to 30,000 people by 1000 A.D. Greenland was a less happy choice of European colonization.

The name *Greenland* might seem like the premier exaggeration of all time. Only small portions of the coast, especially the southwest coast, are free of permanent ice

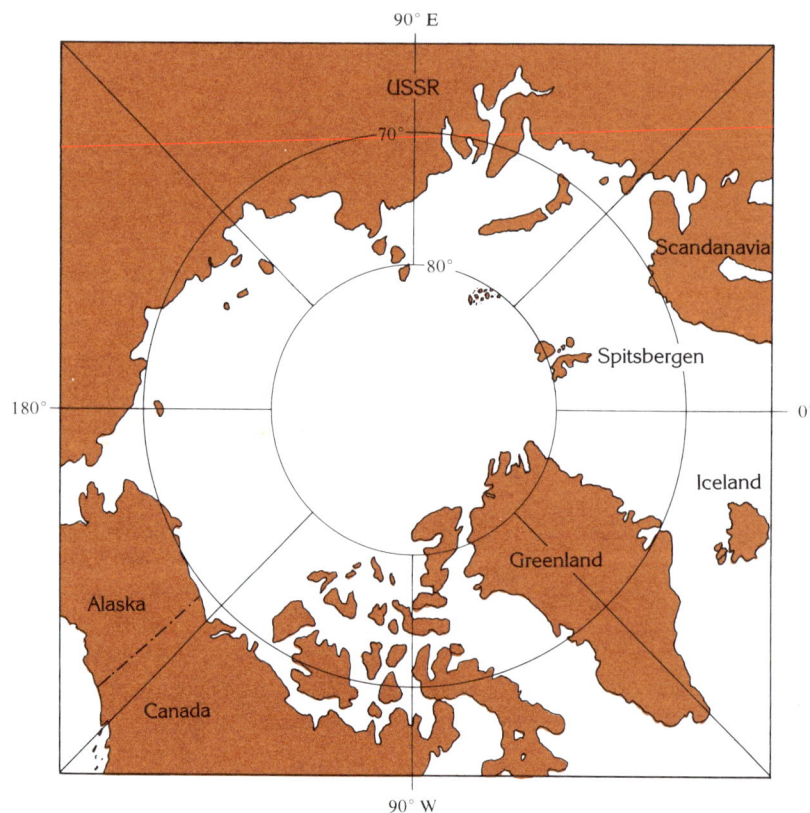

FIGURE 14–1
Iceland, Greenland, and Scandinavia. Greenland was the westernmost long-term permanent colonization of the Scandinavians, who reached it via their more successful Iceland Colony. Settlements on the North American mainland, though, almost certain to have been made, apparently were short-lived.

and snow. Did the discoverer of Greenland, Eric the Red, deliberately falsify his impression of Greenland in order to lure settlers to his colony? After all, it would be in Eric's interest, as leader of his Greenland colonies, to attract as many people as possible to the new lands. *Greenland,* however, was not pure fabrication, although it may have involved wishful exaggeration. In the brief, but long-daylight summer of the tundra, the soggy, rocky coasts would have been carpeted in green. Grasses, sedges, mosses, and many flowering plants could have given the fiords of the southwest coast a deceptively green tinge. Exploration inland would have quickly revealed the permanent ice cap, and settlement would, and did, reveal the fragile nature of this narrow belt of tundra vegetation; but the summer coastline is certainly green.

The Norse Vikings had transferred their culture, including their agriculture and diet, to Iceland quite successfully. Icelandic meadows were just as lush as on many parts of Scandinavia; fish were abundant and the inadequacy of the Icelandic climate for growing grain did not prove a serious handicap. Cattle had been important in Norway, and their importance increased in Iceland. When they settled Greenland, these Norse expected to rely just as heavily on cattle. Dairy products were a very important component of their diet, as remains true today in Scandinavia and Iceland.

Two areas of settlement developed on Greenland. These were called the *east* and *west* settlements, although both were on the southwest coast of Greenland. The west coast has a northward-bound current of relatively warm Atlantic waters, while the icebound east coast is dominated by a southward current of frigid Arctic water. The *east* and *west* settlements referred to their relative location on great fiords along the southwest coast (see Figure 14–2).

Greenland, with no trees beyond a few stunted birches and no metallic ores exploitable by the Vikings, turned out to be a literal dead end for European colonization. It was not a simple case of an overwhelmingly harsh environment whose limitations doomed the colonists. The sites chosen as the east and west settlements were far up the narrow fiords, sheltered by the steep walls of these glacial valleys. Relatively high summer temperatures in these protected valleys allowed the cultivation of some root crops and the growth of pasture grasses. The demands on the very limited capacity of Greenland to produce hay for cattle during the winters were unsupportable in the long run, yet the first Greenland Vikings kept an average of twenty cows per farm. The summers were quite short; water began to freeze in the fiords at the end of August, and the fiords were icebound by October. In the winter season, which lasted 220 days in Greenland, the

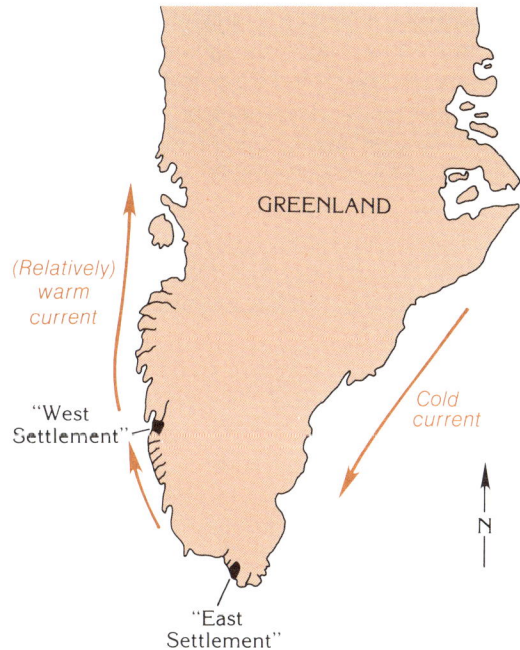

FIGURE 14–2
East and West Settlements, Greenland. Viking colonists on Greenland chose sheltered sites within fiords; both settlements, east and west in relation to one another, were situated on the relatively warmer southwestern coast.

cows were kept in sheds and fed an average of 25 pounds of hay per day; this would amount to over 450 tons of hay per farm per year. Neither the sparse, slow-growing tundra vegetation nor the labor available on these farms could produce and store adequate winter forage. Cows simply demanded too much food to be able to survive many winters there.

There is the possibility that the climate was somewhat warmer in Greenland at the time of the first Viking colonizations. It is equally probable that the climate deteriorated by the thirteenth through the fifteenth and sixteenth centuries, by which time the Norse settlements seem to have been abandoned or ended by the deaths of the last colonists.

Changes in the trade relationship of Greenland and Europe were crucial in the collapse of these colonies, however. Voyages across the stormy ocean to the small Greenland colonies (about 3,000 people in east and west settlements together) were long and risky. The attraction to Greenland had to be the chance of high profits. Greenland's exports at first included small quantities of butter, cheese, and wool woven into fine cloth. The high-profit exports, though, were products of the sea mammals of the coastal waters. Almost indestructable and having some resilience, walrus hide was made into rope hawsers for ships. Walrus tusk was an acceptable substitute for elephant tusk, which was temporarily in short supply in Europe. Indian elephant ivory was difficult to obtain then, as the Crusades had disrupted trade in the eastern Mediterranean. Narwal tusks were more or less a monopoly of Greenland. Narwals have a spiral pattern in their straight, hollow tusks, which coincidentally resembled the horn of the mythical unicorn. Unicorn horn was very rare, naturally, as the beast was nonexistent. Legend had it that powdered unicorn horn was a remedy for various diseases and complaints. Although the Norwegians later developed other walrus fisheries in the North Cape and White Sea areas, Greenland retained its lucrative trade in "unicorn horn." Because they were based at fixed settlements comprised of stone buildings, the Vikings did not travel very far from home and eventually exterminated most of the narwals, walruses, and seals available in their fiords. Also, they most probably ignored the sea mammals as a source of food. Diet is an extremely cultural item. People are highly selective in their food, refusing to consider potential foods, which others may eat, due to cultural and perhaps religious traditions.

The colonies died out, probably literally, due to starvation, because the Vikings misinterpreted the environmental possibilities and had become dangerously dependent on long-distance trade, exchanging animal ivory and furs for food supplements to their declining food productivity in Greenland. The eventual détente between the Christian and Islamic worlds that allowed trade in Indian elephant ivory to resume, the discovery of fossil mammoth ivory in Spitzbergen (a group of islands north of Norway), and the increasing scarcity of sea mammals off the east and west settlements all contributed to the decline of the Greenland trade. When the ships from Norway and the Hanseatic cities of northwestern Europe stopped voyaging to Greenland, the Greenland Vikings found themselves literally marooned. Treeless Greenland could not supply the building material that they assumed they needed for sea-going ships. Whatever craft the Greenlanders had originally were wrecked or rotted by then. With their trade link to Europe broken, their sparsely vegetated pastures hopelessly overgrazed by their flocks of domestic animals, and the local populations of sea mammals virtually exterminated by the hunt for ivory and hides, the Greenlanders faced a totally insufficient food base.

That the physical environment there does not preclude human use is demonstrated by the successful occupance of much of the Arctic by the Eskimos. In context, Eskimo culture was superior to that of the Viking, despite its being on a stone-age level, because it utilized the narrow resource base of the Arctic environment far more efficiently. The maritime Eskimos knew that the sea, not the land, was the basic food resource. They migrated over enormous hunting and fishing territories, never overusing a specific locale's animal and fish life. They fully utilized all nonpoisonous sources of calories that Europeans would reject as food. As an example, they considered seal's eyeballs a delicacy and drank the fermenting contents of a freshly killed seal's stomach with relish, as it was their only source of an alcoholic beverage.

The lesson of the failure of the Greenland Viking colonies, coupled with the persistence of Eskimos in the same severe climate, is that the polar environments must be approached very cautiously. The long trial-and-error

The Arctic Environment. The polar regions are a true frontier, along with the ocean deeps, in that they are viewed as forbidding environments to be visited temporarily to exploit specific resources. The Inuit (Eskimo) and others, on the other hand, have long regarded such seemingly barren landscapes as home. (Courtesy of GeoVisuals/Currier)

experience of the Eskimo in the past must be matched now by thorough research and careful evaluation of this environment, that of the Antarctic, and that of the oceans.

THE OCEANS AS LAST FRONTIERS

The world ocean, covering more than 70 percent of the planet, clearly qualifies as a frontier. There are no permanent settlements in the sea, excepting the small transient populations atop deep-water drilling rigs. Like the polar regions, people are superficially familiar with the oceans. Their outlines have been known for centuries. But we know relatively little of the details of the ocean bottoms, the deep currents as well as surface currents, or how ocean **ecosystems** function.

In the late eighteenth century, Benjamin Franklin first used water temperature and color to determine the location of the Gulf Stream. In the nineteenth century the science of oceanography was firmly established, but it was not until the middle of the twentieth century that scientists could use modern deep-sea sound-echo devices to establish an accurate map of the seabeds. People did not reach the greatest ocean depth, 35,000 feet (11,000 meters) in the "Challenger Deep" of the western Pacific's Mariana Trench, until 1980, twenty-seven years after the highest peak of land, Mount Everest, had been scaled.

UNDERUSED BOUNTY OR OVERUSED SUMP?

Scientists are still exploring and acquiring basic knowledge concerning the mechanisms by which the oceans distribute heat and cold, preventing, along with the atmosphere, a fatal buildup of heat in the tropics where solar energy is concentrated. This "balancing mechanism" also avoids the rapid expansion of polar climates in the zone of minimal solar energy input. In common with perceptions of other frontiers in other times, people tend to hold extreme views of the problems and potentials of the oceans. While some view the sea and seabed as an enormous potential source of expanded food supply and virtually limitless mineral resources, others warn that the sea's food resources are being used at close to the maximum. For some types of biological resources, such as the great whales, we have already overused and even endangered the survival of this resource. The sea is the ultimate recipient of eroded materials from the land masses. For this

reason, the sea has dissolved within it vast quantities of minerals. For the same reason, the sea is the ultimate dump, it is the lowest drainage point, or sump, for every form of pollution. We may be slowly poisoning this vast frontier. Alternatively, we may be on the verge of more fully using its total resource base.

MINERAL RESOURCES OF THE OCEANS

Some minerals are taken directly from seawater. From ancient times, of course, salt (sodium chloride) has been processed from seawater by evaporation. Seawater is a relatively "rich ore" for common salt, as a cubic mile of seawater has 166 million tons of salt dissolved in it. Other minerals in solution are much less concentrated; a cubic mile of ocean contains over 6 million tons of magnesium, which is produced from seawater in the United States. Bromine, at 306,000 tons per cubic mile, is also produced commercially from seawater. However, seawater is a very "lean ore" for most of the metals and other elements it holds in solution. Lead, tin, and copper are all present at 14 tons per cubic mile, nickel is at 2.3 tons, and silver, 1.4 tons per cubic mile. It is not yet possible to economically process such huge quantities of seawater to retrieve them, but the prospect is sometimes alluring. There are, for example, 10 billion tons of gold dissolved in the world's oceans. The problem for would-be "ocean miners" of gold is that these 10 billion tons of gold are dissolved in 330 million cubic miles of water. There are 38 pounds of gold in each cubic mile, or 0.0004 ounce per million gallons of water. To date, only a few dollars worth of gold have ever been extracted from seawater, as the cost of processing is too great to be economically feasible. It seems reasonable to conclude that only relatively highly concentrated materials dissolved in seawater will be mined by processing the water itself.

Far more feasible, economically, are mining possibilities involving submerged placer deposits (streambed-deposited concentrations of minerals), fossil fuels from underwater sedimentary strata, and the mysterious manganese nodules and crusts on the seabed. A more exotic source, possibly as difficult and expensive a source as the water itself, is the concentration of heavy metals in some deep-sea sediments deposited by sediment-laden density currents.

Oil has been pumped from under the relatively shallow seas for almost a hundred years. Advancing technology, in company with advancing prices, has enabled oil companies to drill deeper wells in deeper water. Some

Oil Drilling Platform Being Towed out to Sea, Stravanger, Norway. The evolving technology of seabed and subseabed minerals exploitation will require new concepts of international law. If it becomes possible to exploit minerals beneath the deep seabeds, what state would hold ownership? (Courtesy of United Nations/J. Moss)

experts estimate that there may be as much as 2.5 trillion barrels of oil under the world's continental shelfs that could be recovered.[1] This figure, however, may be far too optimistic in that it includes tar sands and oil shales under water. Recovery of oil from tar sands and oil shales *not* under water has proven expensive and difficult, especially when minimizing environmental damage and pollution is a consideration. Oil is being produced in the North Sea in water depths of more than 1,200 feet (370 meters). Large quantities of natural gas are also being produced from offshore wells (see Figure J). There is a strong probability of more offshore oil and gas in the Arctic basin. Between 20 and 25 percent of oil production is now from underwater wells. (The Case Study considers offshore drilling in more detail.)

Submerged placer deposits are the results of changes in sea level that have submerged former beach and stream deposits. Running water and ocean currents sort material by size in response to gravity and the speed of water motion. The continental glaciers of the Pleistocene period locked up large quantities of water as ice on the continents. Ocean levels fell as much as 300 feet (90 meters), so that many submerged placer deposits at the former mouths of streams are located above or around the 300- to 350-foot depth contours. Tin, diamonds, and gold are currently mined from submerged placers.

Sand and gravel for construction and shells for construction, roadbed material, or as a source of lime are taken from shallow waters now. About $50 million worth of oyster shells alone are taken annually offshore in the United States, primarily in the Gulf of Mexico. Phosphate,

an important fertilizer and chemical raw material, can be taken from the continental shelf and offshore banks. It appears to be plentiful off both Atlantic and Pacific coasts of the United States, Central and South America, off Japan, and near some Pacific Islands.

Sulfur is produced from underwater salt domes, which frequently contain oil and gas, in the U.S. Gulf Coast area. An unusual product of undersea sedimentary rocks is fresh water contained in aquifers that incline under the sea from nearby land and are protected from salt water intrusion by impervious materials. Where there are large populations onshore in arid or semiarid climates, these shallow sea, fresh-water wells could prove a cheaper source of water than desalination.

Manganese nodules, porous, potato-shaped nodules rich in manganese, iron, nickel, copper, and cobalt, are potentially exploitable. Concentrated in the Pacific basin, they are found in all oceans at depths between 9,000 and 18,000 feet (3,000 and 5,000 meters). Large quantities are found on the Blake Plateau, a shallow area off the Carolina coast only 600-3,000 feet (200-900 meters) deep. These nodules seem to be the result of minerals precipitated from seawater, commonly with a core, around which the accretion formed, of a shark's tooth. In addition to the difficulties of dredging in even 600 feet of water, the high silica content may make them economically unusable in current metallurgical technologies.

BIOLOGICAL RESOURCES OF THE OCEANS

The biological resources of the sea include plant as well as animal life. Various kelps are used as food in Japan. Kelp is processed in the United States as an ingredient in

[1] Committee on Resources and Man, National Academy of Sciences and National Research Council, *Resources and Man* (San Francisco: W. H. Freeman and Co., 1969), p. 143.

industrial gums and in gums that provide smooth texture in ice cream. Kelp could be grown on great underwater trellises that would support it near the sunlit surface to speed growth and make harvesting more convenient. Kelp could even be fermented as a source of industrial alcohol.

It is the fisheries of the world that offer more, though varying degrees of, hope in increasing production of high-quality foods for a rising human population. Some biologists are pessimistic about any sizeable increase in food supply from the oceans, warning that "Perhaps the most pervasive myth of the population-food crisis is that mankind will be saved by harvesting the 'immeasurable riches' of the sea."[2] Marine biologists estimate that the total world production of fish, about 60 million metric tons, could be doubled, at most, before disastrous **overfishing** would begin reducing the total catch. Ocean fisheries currently produce only 1 or 2 percent of the total food calorie consumption of the world; doubling the catch obviously would do little to feed an ever-expanding human population. However, those foods supplied by the sea tend to be rich in protein, so that their quality helps compensate for relatively small quantity. Then too, as with other resources, rising prices redefine the resource; fish considered "trash" a few decades ago are now sought out. Consumers acquire a taste for less expensive fish as their favorites begin costing more than beefsteak. As an example, tilefish were once thrown back by American east coast fishermen. Now, tilefish, a very ugly-looking but tasty fish, has won acceptance by consumers and commands a fair price, leading to speculation that the species may be overfished soon.

[2] Paul and Anne Ehrlich, *Population, Resources, Environment: Issues in Human Ecology* (San Francisco: W. H. Freeman & Company, 1970), p. 101.

Problems of Fisheries Exploitation   There are two hazards to ocean fisheries as sources of human food. Overexploitation, catching such large numbers that the species is unable to reproduce fast enough to maintain a population comparable to long-term averages, and pollution, reducing the liveability of the environment, both threaten many fish, shellfish, and sea mammals. Also, it should be remembered that much of the ocean, by volume, is virtually a desert in terms of supporting life. The oceanic **food chain,** like the various food chains of land and fresh water, starts with photosynthesis, the utilization of sunlight in the growth and proliferation of plant life. The base of most oceanic food chains is phytoplankton, tiny photosynthetizing organisms. These flourish in waters rich in mineral nutrients near the surface for maximum sunlight penetration. Shallow coastal waters frequently have life-supporting combinations of sunlight penetrating to the seabed, nutrients supplied by rivers, and the mixing of different currents of ocean water (see Figure 14–3). These currents in the ocean are commonly thought of as primarily horizontal currents, like *rivers in the sea,* a common description of the Gulf Stream. There are "vertical" currents also, with great transfers of water of different temperature, salinity, and turbidity (suspended particles of minerals, clays, organic material, or other debris) taking place. Finally, coral reefs represent entire ecosystems in shallow, tropical water environments. For the same reasons, divers know that wrecks are commonly good hunting grounds for any sealife. Artificial reefs of old tires are sometimes built to attract more fish.

The importance of **upwelling,** the development of vertical currents in the sea bringing mineral nutrients from lower depths up towards the sunlit surface, can be seen in

Fishing Fleet at Paita, Peru. While people have tapped the resources of the sea for thousands of years, evolving technology makes probable both an increased scale and variety of such resource exploitation and an increased risk of serious, if inadvertent, environmental damage. (Courtesy of United Nations/ M. E. Pendl)

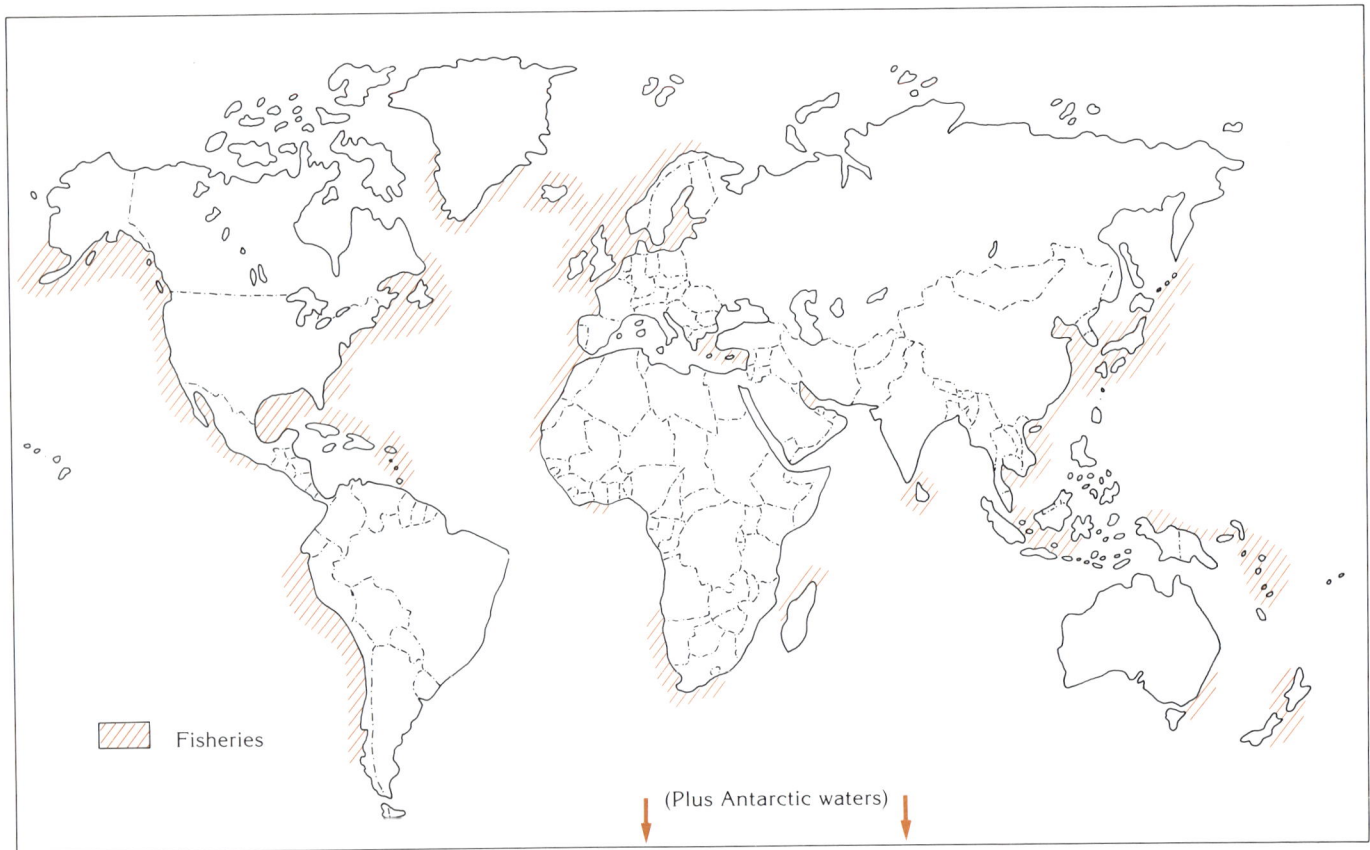

FIGURE 14–3
Major Fisheries of the World. Almost all oceanic food chains depend on photosynthesis in those shallow waters penetrable by sunlight and supplemented by mineral nutrients transferred by drainage from land masses and by ocean currents. Thus, major fisheries tend to be close to shore and more vulnerable to land-origin pollution.

the Antarctic waters, last refuge of the great whales. Biologists observe that the frigid waters of the Antarctic Ocean, fed by the very slowly moving ice sheets, would be nearly sterile without the vertical mixing of some nutrient-laden tropical waters circulating at various depths towards the polar regions. Billions of tiny shrimplike Antarctic krill are the food for those toothless baleen whales, which sieve them from the water. These small crustaceans in turn live off hundreds of billions of diatoms, one-celled algaes encased in crystallike exoskeletons of silica. A typical toothed whale, one that eats fish and squid rather than tiny shrimp, is the humpback, a medium-sized whale. It needs a ton of fish, such as herring, to fill its stomach. The approximately 5 thousand herring in a ton will have each consumed thousands of tiny crystaceans, each of which has consumed over a hundred thousand diatoms.

Overfishing of any species clearly can have ramifications through entire food chains. Modern technology has given fishermen an impressive array of weapons in their war on whole fish species, for the manner of fishing can sometimes come to resemble a war motivated by greed. Those who *are* practical conservationists are too frequently outfished by the less ethical. Echo sounders and sonar devices are used to find the fish. These are supplemented by helicopter spotters in some whaling expeditions. "Factory ships" capable of remaining at sea for months while catching, cleaning, and freezing or canning fish products can range far from their home base, after local fish have been overexploited and greatly diminished in number. Some examples of overexploited fish and fishing grounds include Peruvian anchoveta, California sardines, Atlantic tuna, and North Sea plaice.

The Tragedy of the Commons   Overfishing, including the use of faster ships that literally scoop up everything in their paths, including unwanted species and the immature members of desired species, may take on aspects of selfish competition among nations. The high seas beyond any one nation's control are a form of communal resource.

The commons, a centrally located, community-owned grazing land open to the use of all community members, was a feature of early New England settlement. The commons was useful for the overnight or short-term grazing of animals when farmers did not wish to leave livestock on their own outlying pastures. The concept of the commons may work well among a relatively small, socially homogeneous group with shared values and strong social conscience. The potential for selfish behavior that gives one person a short-term advantage, even if it is recognized that it contributed to long-range disaster, leads to the **tragedy of the commons.** In its original context of communal grazing land, the commons could be abused by individuals placing more than their share of animals to graze there. For example, if a community informally judges that the *carrying capacity* of a commons, that is, the maximum number of animals that can be grazed thereon without permanent destruction of vegetation cover and subsequent soil erosion, is about a hundred per day, than each user should limit use to their proportional share of the environmentally sane maximum. Greedy, selfish individuals will graze more than their fair share. This will result in permanent degradation of the carrying capacity, or at least long-term damage, unless the other users cut back voluntarily on *their* use. Socially responsible users would thus be partially or wholly forced out by selfish users. If all members graze at their proportionate share or higher, the greed of an individual can create disaster. The ocean fisheries are a great commons also. Most fish move freely from territorial waters to international waters, frustrating any one nation's attempt at controlling use of the fisheries to permit a sustained catch. If the fish are there to be caught, a country that does *not* think ahead and attempt to conserve this resource will catch more fish than an environmentally responsible one. "If *we* don't catch them, *they* will" is the prevailing reasoning. There develops an insanely selfish race to grab one's share of the resource before the collective grab destroys that resource. The conservationists suffer all along; everyone suffers in the end. The agonizingly slow development of international controls over whaling is an example of the eventual necessity of international controls over this last great "commons," the sea.

POLLUTION OF THE WORLD OCEAN

The organized looting of rich fisheries by overfishing need not doom most species other than the slowly reproducing sea mammals. While whales bear one offspring, rarely two, after very long gestation periods (up to eighteen months), fin fish and shell fish produce thousands of eggs at a time, and may do so many times a year. Given a chance, many fish populations currently under pressure from relentless fishing could rebound quickly in numbers, given a healthy environment. Most fish produce thousands of eggs at a time because the odds of reaching maturity and reproducing are very low; most fish eat other fish. Pollution of the oceans could retard this rebound from overfishing, though. Most fishing grounds, as noted above, are close to shore, making them especially vulnerable to pollution draining from the land.

The "Good Fairies" Hypothesis   Many countries, industrial regions, and cities around the world appear to believe in what could be characterized as the **"good fairies" hypothesis.** This apparent, if unstated, belief, based on naive ignorance or arrogant assumption that the "tragedy of the commons" applies to pollution as well, is that if unwanted waste and poisonous by-products are dumped into the nearest body of water, they will disappear magically and never bother them again. While any who give serious thought to the problem recognize the fallacy of the "good fairies" hypothesis, the huge size of the world ocean's volume and its remarkable capacity to dilute pollutants and to cope with them by natural means has long deluded people. Relatively small amounts of organic pollution, capable of being readily dispersed and even broken down into nutrients usable by various forms of life in the sea, did seem to be effortlessly and harmlessly disposed of by the natural processes of the sea. It is both the vast increases in the quantity of pollution and the changing nature of the pollutants themselves that threaten to overwhelm the seas, poisoning them at least temporarily if we do not arrange for more intelligent disposal of dangerous chemicals and radioactive materials.

Some inorganic pesticides, for example, are agonizingly slow in breaking down in any environment. Accidental spills of these chemicals or their discard by chemical plants, warehouses, or farmers can produce dramatic "fish-kills" in rivers or lakes. Less dramatic, but inevitable, concentrations of these chemicals in oceans can find their way into the food chain and become progressively more concentrated in the tissues of predators who consume large numbers of smaller creatures, concentrating *their* concentrations of ultimately toxic chemicals. It has been proven, for example, that DDT, a powerful insecticide whose use is now banned, had contaminated the oceans by the late 1960's in sufficient concentrations to induce measurable decreases in the ability of phytoplankton to photosynthesize plant energy. The **hydrologic cycle** (Figure 1–11), shows that the natural and artificial sediment and solution burdens of fresh-water drainage to the world's oceans eventually transfer much of the landmasses' pollutants to the sea. The sea loses water by evaporation, and this water vapor may be precipitated over land again, the resultant seaward drainage transferring more minerals and organic materials to the seas. The only "escape" of water from the seas is through evaporation, which commonly leaves anything other than pure water behind in the ocean. Obviously, if phytoplankton, the base of ocean food chains, is affected by such land-distributed chemicals as DDT, the other forms of life ultimately dependent on phytoplankton will eventually suffer some degree of contamination. The long-term effects of this slow but continual buildup of noxious chemicals are difficult to predict. The individual plant or animal may not be killed outright, but may be weakened so that it falls victim to some disease or predator. Its reproductive capacities may be diminished, so that the overall "population" of the seas may shift toward species or varieties less vulnerable to the specific contaminant. In this manner, reverberations may be noticed up the food chain, as particular types of food or prey become more scarce. Of course, the effects may travel the other way down the food chain if a major predator declines in number, allowing a population explosion among its prey.

POLITICAL CONTROL AND CONTROVERSY

With only two exceptions (the Caspian and Aral seas), all of the world's water bodies large enough to be called "seas" are interlinked and therefore continuous. While some of the waterways connecting the oceans and seas are quite narrow, it is possible for ships to sail into almost any sea without touching land. Sea power has offered im-

mense advantages to those nations that have it. For all of history up until about 125 years ago, water transport has been far more efficient and almost always faster than land transport. Water transport is still cheapest, per weight unit moved a given distance. For many centuries, major portions of the world's economy have depended on the free and unrestricted peaceful use of the oceans as highways. The lack of continued occupance of the sea is directly related to the nonrecognition of any one state's claims to jurisdiction over the "high seas," that is, those sections of the world ocean reasonably far removed from coastlines. The qualification *reasonably* is key to understanding international law concerning the oceans. The rights of transit, control of the so-called **territorial sea,** fishing rights, mining rights, and even the right to prevent pollution—all are more generally accepted custom than universally agreed upon and enforced laws. These customs have evolved over two millenia and are still being redefined, expanded, and altered to suit changing political, technological, and environmental conditions.

The great bulk of the world ocean's surface area has always been recognized by most governments as a great "commons," uncontrolled and uncontrollable by any state. At the same time, governments have recognized varying degrees of national jurisdiction over the seas adjacent to land and to certain classes or types of use of the seas. The territorial sea is that belt of sea and seabed adjacent to the land; full sovereignty extends from land over it as though it were part of the land. Even the right of foreign ships (and now, airplanes) to innocent (peaceful) passage within or over the territorial sea may be restricted in some ways, although custom generally permits it. How far outward from land the territorial sea extends, and precisely

Modern Trawlers off the Grand Banks, Canada–United States. Fishing technology has advanced to the point of threatening some species with near extinction. Competition for the high-quality fish resources of the North American Grand Banks has led to the seaward extension of territorial fishing waters to help control the catch. (Courtesy of United Nations/Y. Nagata)

how this is measured, have never been agreed upon by all states. They are still not uniform. Three nautical miles had become the most common territorial claim by the nineteenth century, and it is the minimum claimed now. Three miles probably became an early standard because this was the approximate distance of effective fire from shore-based cannon in the eighteenth century. Cannon range seemed an eminently practical measure of literally how far a coastal state's power extended out over the sea. Some states that claimed far wider territorial seas were forced to back down by more powerful nations. Generally, it is the nations with sizeable merchant fleets, fishing fleets, and powerful navies that favor narrow territorial seas; they are in the best position to exploit the international "high seas."

The great value of some fisheries, together with recognition that excessive fishing could destroy the resource, led states to extend at least their control of fishing rights, if not total territorial rights, further offshore. Imperial Russia at one time established a 100-mile-wide (160-kilometer-wide) zone to control seal hunting. Developing countries with rich fisheries offshore, such as Peru, now claim (and enforce) 200-mile (320-kilometer) limits. The eight states with 200-mile fishing limits control over 20 percent of the world's total fish catch. By the mid 1970's, the once-predominant 3-mile territorial sea limit was claimed by only twenty-five states, while 12 miles was most popular with fifty-six nations supporting it.

There are really a variety of classes of claims, even within one country's laws. While the territorial sea is the most comprehensive form of claim, countries commonly claim a much wider belt of waters for control of fishing. The taking of shellfish, which spend their adult lives relatively immobile on the seabed, may be reserved to one's citizens no how far offshore on the continental shelf they are found. Most species of finfish are highly mobile, though, freely moving through different state's territorial waters. It is this mobility and the need to conserve the fisheries that may explain the 200-mile limits common in South America. Following World War II, President Truman proclaimed that mineral resources on or under the **continental shelf** (see Figure 14–4) off American coasts were the exclusive property of the United States.

The most recent form of territorial control deals with the problems of pollution control, especially the potential damage of oil spills or oil tanker collisions or wrecks. South Africa requires oil tankers to sail at least twelve miles out from its coasts to minimize pollution in cases of wrecks or from cleaning tanks. The Cape of Good Hope now has heavy tanker traffic from the Persian Gulf to Europe and North America's east coast as the larger tankers cannot use the Suez Canal. Another area of heavy tanker traffic is the Malacca Strait between Indonesia and Malaysia. These two states have extended their territorial waters to the midline of the narrows of the strait and forbidden passage to fully loaded tankers of 200,000 tons or more. Tankers of more than 500,000 tons may not use the strait under any circumstances, whether laden or empty. This forces ships carrying oil from the Middle East to Japan to

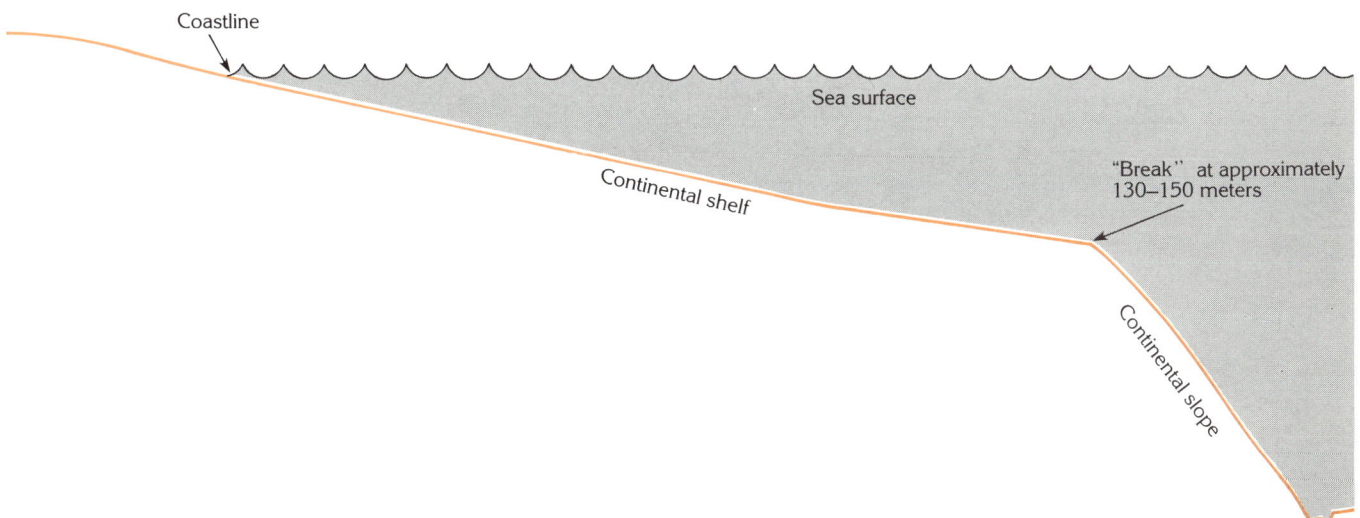

FIGURE 14–4
Continental Shelf and Continental Slope. The relatively shallow waters over the continental shelf and the shelf itself have been regarded in most respects as clearly national territory of the coastal state rather than of international status. Technological advances may advance national claims into deeper waters.

divert to the Lombok Strait between Bali and Lombok (see Figure 14–5). This increases the Gulf-Japan voyage by 950 miles (1,528 kilometers), adding six days to a round trip. Other narrow straits which could be claimed as territorial waters on the Malacca precedent include the Strait of Hormuz, between the Persian Gulf and the Arabian Sea, and the Bab al Mandeb, between the Gulf of Aden and the Red Sea.

The future of political controls over the ocean, the ocean fisheries, and the continental shelves are all unclear. History would indicate that, as the technology of exploiting minerals on and under the continental shelf is improved, the extension of political claims will follow. The 1958 International Convention on the Continental Shelf defined the shelf in potentially expandable terms. The continental shelf is that relatively shallow seabed just offshore that is considered geologically part of the continent. The convention states that the seaward boundary of the shelf, commonly claimed for mineral ownership, is at a depth contour of 200 meters *or* beyond, where "the depth of water permits exploitation of natural resources." In other words, if technology permits drilling or dredging in deeper water, political control would follow. Among the signatories of this Continental Shelf Convention are the United States, the Soviet Union, the United Kingdom, and most of the western European nations, which are all in the lead in developing technologies of underwater minerals exploitation. It is not impossible that the seabeds could some day be completely divided among states for mineral development purposes (if international agreements limiting these rights prove unenforceable).

It is also likely that international agreements on conservation of specific species of marine life, wherever found, in territorial seas or international waters, will limit or prohibit taking some species, as with some of the great whales. This is an extremely important development, as it recognizes the "commons" nature of ocean fisheries. It is likely that international agreements limiting the pollution of the ocean environment will grow out of this cooperation on conserving some endangered species.

The long-term tradition of freedom of innocent passage across the high seas is not likely to be abandoned. The most powerful states have too much at stake in this freedom of the high seas to see it changed.

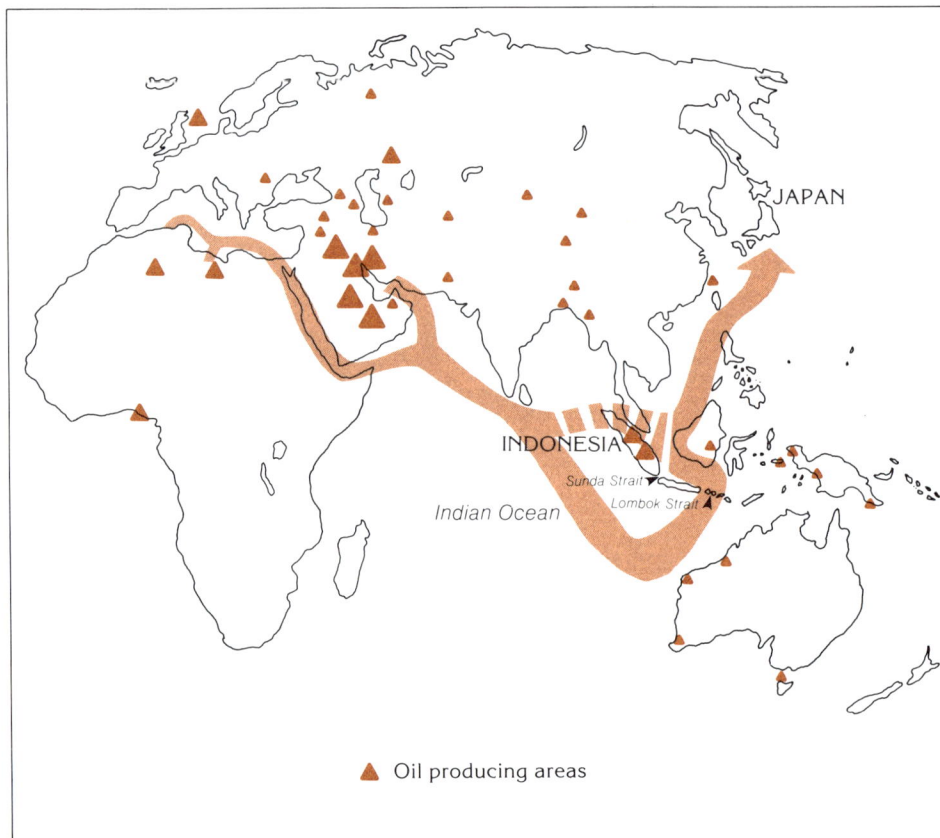

FIGURE 14–5

The Significance of the Lombok Strait in Southwest Asian–East Asian Trade. Because Indonesia and Malaya have closed the Strait of Malacca to large oil tankers to minimize pollution hazards, the Japanese "oil bridge" from the Persian Gulf must detour through the Lombok Strait.

THE "CONSTITUTION OF THE SEAS"

A fundamental problem of regulating the exploitation of minerals on and under the seabed (or even in the seawa-

ter) and of fisheries of various types is that twenty-two states (see Figure 14–6) of the world have no territorial frontage on the "world ocean." Many more do not have the technology and investment capital to exploit the sea's

Soviet Freighter Loading American Grain at Philadelphia. Until this century, most international law concerning the sea focused on the sea as a highway—the right to freely use international waters in peaceful commerce and fishing. The more powerful maritime states, such as the United States and Soviet Union favored as few restrictions as possible on their use of the seas. (Photo by Stansfield)

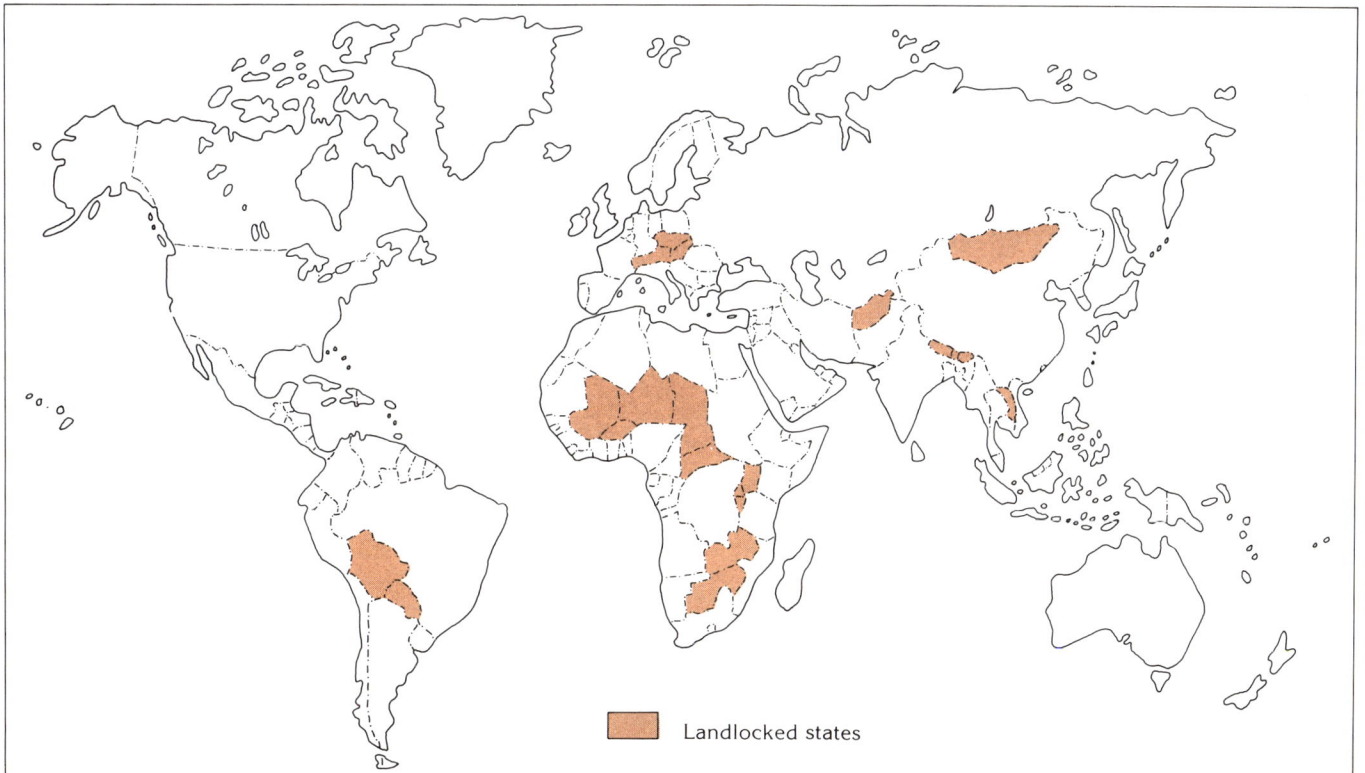

Landlocked states

FIGURE 14–6
States Without Ocean Frontage. Every continent except North America and Australia has some national states that are landlocked and thus have no traditional bases for claims to sharing the mineral and biotic riches of the sea and seabed. A recent international treaty proposal would include all the world's states in sea and seabed resource development.

resources, even though they have ample coastlines. The problem, at least as it is seen by the developing world, is twofold. If we envision the seas as the common heritage of the human race, there are the related problems of regulating exploitation of the "commons," so that this heritage is not recklessly destroyed, and the question of equitable benefit to all, whether their state has an ocean coastline or not and whether they have or lack the technical and economic power to share in exploitation. Such states as Switzerland, Luxembourg, Austria, and Czechoslovakia, landlocked, have the technology level and investment capital to exploit, say, manganese nodules in the Pacific, but have no seaports, much less control over a portion of seabed under territorial waters. Other nations, like Kenya or Ecuador, do not presently possess a technology-capital base to exploit even their own adjacent seabeds, and states like Afghanistan or Uganda have neither a technology-capital base or direct access to the seas.

For many years, the beds and fisheries of lakes shared by two or more states have been entirely divided among the lakeshore states, leaving no unclaimed or international territory. Essentially, it was this "lake" principle that was applied to the division of oil and gas rights under the North Sea (see Figure 14–7). It is highly controversial in terms of "extending" land boundaries out to sea; a difference of a few degrees in the angle at which a land boundary is carried seaward can mean differences of hundreds of square miles in seabed and fisheries claims. The states with large coastlines, and especially states controlling small "ocean islands" (above sea level projections of mostly subsurface mountain chains or plateaus rather than geologic continuations of nearby continental landform systems) would control huge ocean areas. If a "world lake" concept had been applied to the world ocean, no landlocked states would have shared in the exploitation of the seas, and tiny, sparsely inhabited islands like the Falklands (Great Britain) in the South Atlantic and Islas de Juan Fernandez (Chile) in the Southeast Pacific would enable those states to claim vast areas of ocean and oceanbed. Canada's claims to the Pacific would be severely constricted between U.S. claims based on the long Alaska shoreline and the Hawaiian Islands as well as the Washington-Oregon-California coastline.

The obvious inequalities of a "world lake" approach have led to a draft treaty produced by the Third UN Conference on the Law of the Sea in 1980. The treaty must be

FIGURE 14–7
Territorial Oil and Gas Rights in the North Sea. The allocation of oil and gas exploitation rights over the North Sea bed is an example of the so-called Lake Principle that carries land boundaries seaward and leaves no international or unclaimed seabed. Clearly, a minor change in the angle at which land boundaries are continued seaward can have great significance.

ratified by UN members in order to go into effect. Realistically, it must be approved by the governments of the world's leading technological, economic, and military powers if it is to have any chance. The key provisions of this treaty recognize a 200-mile "exclusive economic zone" for each coastal nation, which continues seaward on the continental shelves where applicable. The economic zone includes absolute control over fishing. Beyond the 200-mile–continental-shelf coastal state's jurisdiction, all deep seabed mining is to be shared with a UN-chartered mining company, which will allocate its profits among developing countries. The right of innocent passage by all ships is unrestricted beyond a 12-mile territorial sea outward from coasts, and passage within the 12-mile zone is guaranteed under certain conditions and through important straits.

THE POLAR REGIONS— THE FROZEN SEA AND THE LIFELESS CONTINENT

A bad joke among geographers is that the Arctic and Antarctic regions are "poles apart." There are striking differences between them, but many similarities too. The fundamental difference is, of course, that Antarctica is a continent, larger than Europe and almost twice the size of Australia, while the Arctic is the smallest ocean basin. Antarctica, a little less than 10 percent of the total land area of the planet, is slightly larger than the Arctic basin. In comparison with the "silent continent," the arctic region is a busy place with a relatively large population of people, a rich and varied animal and plant life, and a warmer climate. The Arctic Ocean is a more efficient storer of heat from its brief summer, slowly releasing this heat energy throughout the winter. The Antarctic region is covered by an ice sheet with an average thickness of more than a mile; only tiny fragments of Antarctica's coastline are free from constant ice cover. Antarctica is far colder, with the world's record low of $-126.9°F$ ($-88.3°C$) recorded at the Soviet Antarctica research station "Vostok." The coldest northern hemisphere temperatures are not in the arctic basin at all, but are recorded about 1,500 miles (2,400 kilometers) south of the North Pole in northeastern Siberia. There, Verkhoyansk has experienced $-90°F$ ($-65°C$) in winter, but also has reached average summer temperatures of 60°F (15°C). The Antarctic continent has never, in modern research history, had a month in which the average temperature is above freezing, thus prohibiting most plants from occupying the continent itself. Some nearby islands in the Antarctic Ocean do have "warm" summers,

at least one month with an average temperature above freezing, and these have more variety of plants (see Figure 14–8).

A surprising shared characteristic of the Arctic and the Antarctic is that both have definitely had far warmer climates in the geologic past. There is low quality coal in Antarctica—15 feet (4.5 meters) thick in some places. There is also coal in Spitzbergen, an island group 350 miles (570 kilometers) north of Scandinavia's North Cape. There are traces of oil in and around Antarctica, and there are known and exploited quantities of oil in the Arctic. Both "ends of the earth" have extensive deposits of sedimentary rocks containing plant and animal fossils and imprints. Since the fossil fuels are the product of the decomposition of huge amounts of organic debris from warm, temperate forested environments, coal and oil, along with the fossils, are unmistakable proof of far warmer climates in the Arctic and Antarctic in the distant past.

The generally accepted concept of "wondering continents," or **plate tectonics,** states that the continents and ocean basins are not immovable or permanent entities. There is ample reason for geologists to believe in the inexorable, if slow, migrations, collisions, and founderings or sinkings of huge plates of "solid" crust. All of this evidence, like the mysterious coal of Antarctica and the warm climate fossils of Greenland, tells us that things were not always as they are, and that things will not stay as they are now.

DEFINING THE ARCTIC-ANTARCTIC REGIONS

The Antarctic region would seem to be self-defined. The continent and its nearby islands are so far from, and so different from, the nearest sizeable area of other lands that there is no question of these boundaries. The Arctic is a far different proposition. There, we have the great landmasses of Eurasia and North America protruding above the Arctic Circle. The Canadian archipelago, a few large Soviet island groups, and the world's largest island, Greenland, reach far into the frozen sea. The boundary of the Arctic region is not obvious, nor is it universally agreed upon. To a climatologist, the boundary may be the *isotherm* (a line connecting all places of a given temperature) of 50°F (10°C) for the warmest month, or the area with an average annual temperature of 32°F (0°C) or less. To a plant geographer, the Arctic is north of the tree line, that region too cold for trees but either in permanent ice and snow or having a short summer in which grass, sedge, mosses, and lichens may grow. These plants and temper-

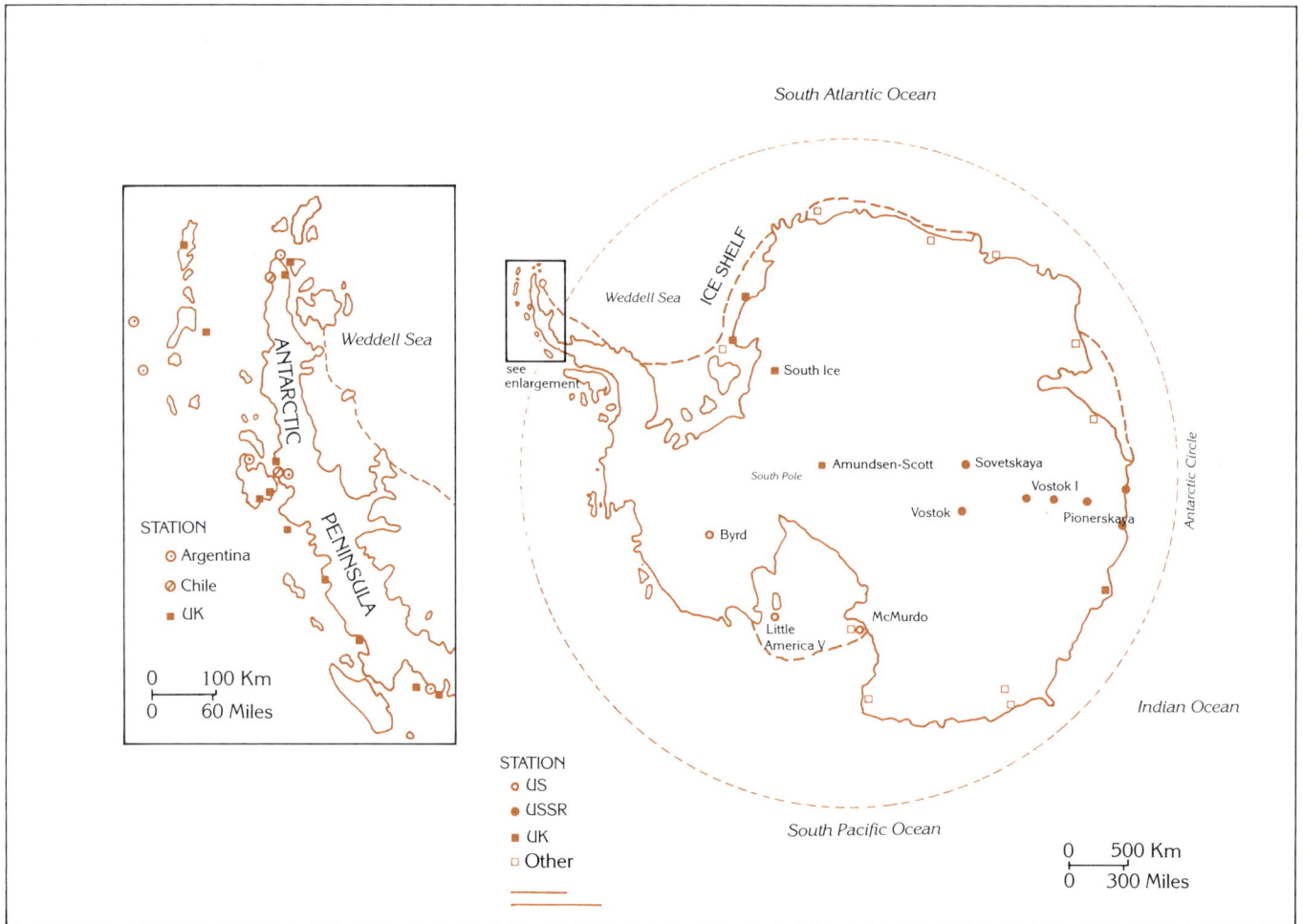

FIGURE 14—8

Antarctica: Climate and Locations. Because it is a continent rather than a small ocean basin, as in the Arctic, Antarctica records the world's lowest, and consistently lowest, temperatures. Only the edges of the Palmer Peninsula and offshore islands ever record above-freezing conditions.

ature definitions coincide, roughly (see Figure 14–9). The plant boundary is much more erratic and complicated than the temperature definition, though, as plants are also sensitive to other factors of the environment and to climate variables not measured by monthly average temperatures. The Arctic region, by either definition, has areas that reach summer temperatures of 70°F (21°C) to 80°F (26°C) in interior locations. The coasts have a lower temperature range from winter to summer. Flowering plants blossom in Peary Land, the northernmost land in the world; the Arctic seems to have abundant life compared with the Silent Continent. Antarctica has life only on its coasts, where the moderating influence of the sea and the only land *not* covered by permanent ice combine to support a sparse array of mosses, lichens, and three species of flowering plants. These exist on the Palmer Peninsula, that northward thrust of land reaching within 600 miles

(970 kilometers) of the southern tip of South America. Here on the Palmer Peninsula, in a latitude comparable to central Norway, there are also Antarctica's greatest concentration of native land animals. They are mites, ticks, flies, and lice. These insects live on the vegetation cover, such as it is, or are there because of the seasonal population of penguins. Penguins and seals spend part of their lives on the ice shelves and rocky ledges of the coast. Nothing else, beyond a very few bacteria, survives naturally in Antarctica.

In contrast, the Arctic flora contains some nine hundred kinds of flowers, thousands of lichens, and about five hundred varieties of mosses. The animal species of the continents surrounding the Arctic basin tend to have extended, via highly specialized and adapted varieties, into the Arctic environment or at least into its fringe. Birds, dogs, foxes, wolves, wolverines, reindeer, caribou, bears,

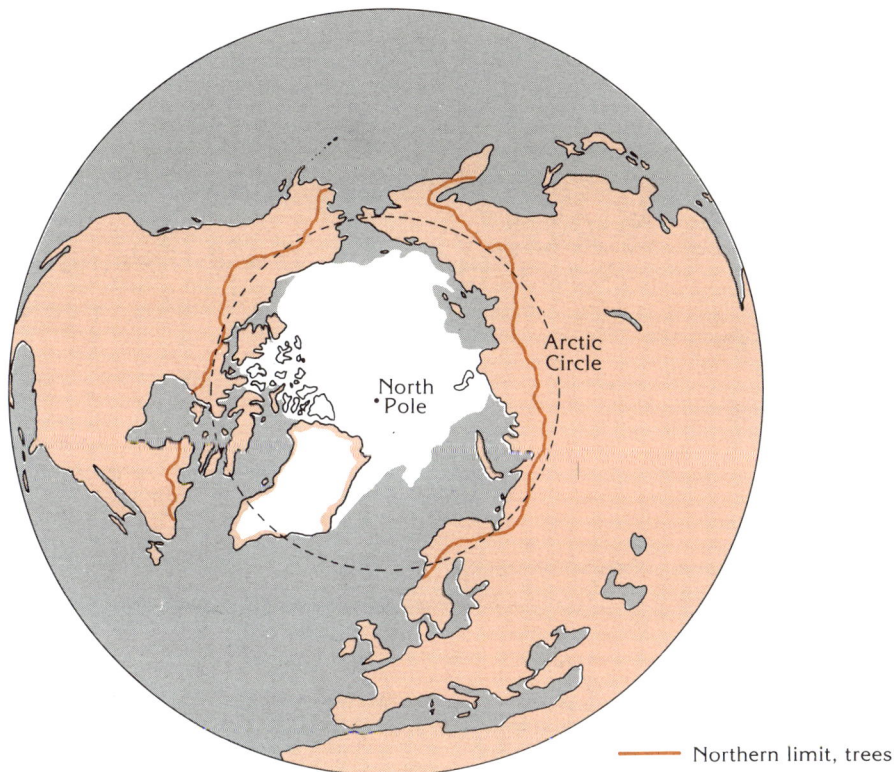

——— Northern limit, trees

FIGURE 14—9
Arctic: Climate and Vegetation Boundaries. In contrast to the almost lifeless Antarctic continent, the somewhat warmer Arctic has a rich variety, if generally low density, of plant and animal life. The Arctic region is usually bounded by temperature or vegetation characteristics.

ground squirrels, ducks—the list of Arctic animals is seemingly endless compared with the insects, migratory seabirds, and sea mammals and penguins of the Antarctic. The long list of Arctic inhabitants is based, of course, on the superior quality and variety of Arctic plant life. The Antarctic coast has only about 1,000 square miles (260 hectares) of ice-free land out of 5.5 million square miles (1.4 million hectares). In this tiny area, the air temperature goes above freezing for about twenty days in an average year. Antarctica contains a little more than 90 percent of the world's ice, 7 million cubic miles of ice. Antarctica is the highest in average elevation—6,000 feet (1,800 meters) above sea level—of all the continents. The ice reaches to depths of over 10,000 feet (3,000 meters), depressing the continent itself under such an enormous weight that the land mass has sunk further into the semiplastic mantle of the earth. If all this ice should melt, the sea level around the world would rise by over 200 feet (60 meters), drowning most of the world's great cities and Antarctica itself would slowly rebound an estimated 1,800 feet (550 meters). Like the Arctic, but more so, the Antarctic is a desert in terms of precipitation. The "white continent" receives an average of 5 inches (13 centimeters) of

The Arctic Farming Fringe, Finnish Lapland. This Lapp family farm is on the Arctic frontier—food and income are derived from reindeer, sheep, cattle, and salmon fishing. The Scandinavians, Canadians, Soviets, and Americans are all experimenting with suitable plants and animals to extend their Arctic farming frontiers. (Courtesy of United Nations)

snow per year. The strong persistent winds spreading out over the heart of the continent move this small amount of snow about so much that it seems like much more. The air over Antarctica is so cold that it can hold very little water vapor. The Arctic region receives less than 10 inches (250 millimeters) of precipitation a year, except for the southern portions of Baffin Island and Greenland. People do not perceive the polar regions as having so little precipitation because what comes down stays around for a very long time—there is so little heat around to evaporate water or sublimate ice and snow that water (ice or snow) seems to be everywhere.

THE ERA OF DISCOVERY AND EXPLORATION

In these last frontiers, the era of discovery and exploration is still with us. The North Pole was not visited by people (people at least who knew that it was the North Pole and could write about it) until 1909. The Antarctic Circle was first crossed by Captain James Cook in 1774 and the Antarctic mainland was first sighted in 1820 by Americans Benjamin Pendleton and Nat Palmer. Norwegian Roald Amundsen reached the South Pole in 1911. For much of the human race's certain knowledge of the rim of the Arctic Ocean and the existence of Antarctica, exploration was a very slow and erratic effort. There is no certain knowledge of how far north any explorer reached until the tenth century discovery of Greenland by Eric the Red.

In true European discovery fashion, the major motivation for Arctic exploration was commercial—the drive to find the "Northwest Passage" around the North American continent and finally get to the fabled orient. A series of explorers reconnoitered the approaches to the high Arctic, culminating in the tragedy of the Franklin expeditions of 1844–47. This was a major effort to finally discover that Northwest Passage, mounted by the British navy, reasoning that steamships could go further faster then any previous efforts. No one survived the nearly three-year ordeal in the Arctic, but no fewer than forty relief expeditions were mounted to try to rescue them; in the process, people learned more about the Arctic in a decade than in the preceding two centuries.

Just as the 1960's were characterized by a major nationalistic effort to achieve firsts in the exploration of space, culminating in the American landing on the moon, the turn of the century witnessed a frantic race to reach the poles. Knowledge of the polar environment and its special problems had expanded rapidly since the Franklin expedition's failure. By 1909, Robert Peary and his black associate, Matthew Henson, had twenty years of Arctic ex-

ploration experience and made the final last push. Norwegian Roald Amundsen distinguished himself in polar exploration by both finding the long-sought Northwest Passage of the Arctic, in 1906, and being the first to reach the South Pole five years later.

ANTARCTICA: INTERNATIONAL LAND OR COLONY?

The conflicting claims to territory in the Antarctic are closely related to the history of its discovery and exploration. These claims are in temporary legal limbo, but potentially they could cause another territorial race not dissimilar to the scramble for America four centuries ago.

Many of the early discoveries were as much accidental as anything else. They were made by sailors venturing far into Antarctic waters in search of seals and whales. Captain James Cook's venture into Antarctic waters and his discovery of South Georgia, an island at 55° S in the Atlantic, showed a sea rich in whales and seals. An abundance of whales was good news back in North America and Europe, where whale oil was necessary in lubrication and in lighting. Drake's first oil well was almost a century in the future. Reports that the Antarctic seas were rich in whales was like the discovery of another east Texas–scale petroleum reserve would be to contemporary Americans. Energetic pursuit of whales had greatly reduced their numbers in more traditional hunting grounds. The small, rather barren-looking islands north of Antarctica made handy reprovisioning and repair stops for the whalers and sealers of the early nineteenth century—one reason why such desolate, remote islands were claimed, settled, and defended by European states. American and British naval expeditions began to chart the coast of the newly discovered continent in the 1830's and 40's. Other states prominent in Antarctic explorations in the nineteenth and early twentieth centuries were France, Belgium, Russia, Sweden, Germany, and Norway. Japan sent an expedition in 1911, apparently to bolster claims to whaling rights. Australia joined the ranks of major exploring nations in 1911, and became very active in the 1930's. New Zealand, a logical staging point for Antarctic exploration, has become very active since World War II.

The original motivations for much of Antarctic exploration—the phenomenal wealth of the fisheries near the continent—are becoming even more attractive today. These waters are the last refuge for some of the great whales; if these huge mammals survive, it will be there at the "bottom" of the planet. However, it is on the Silent Continent itself, and perhaps beneath its continental shelf, that economic reasons for fixing permanent boundaries of national claims may wait. Antarctica's coal has been known at least since the Scott expedition of the first decade of this century. Quantities seem to be great, but quality is usually quoted as being low. There are definite signs of oil, but so far little knowledge of quantities possible. Other minerals present include gold, tin, silver, molybdenum, antimony, and platinum. Obviously, production costs would be higher, given the same geologic circumstances, than almost any other place on earth. But, just as obviously, there are no local rulers to contend with, nor any **social overhead** of placating local populations with welfare and development handouts.

In more normal environments, a territorial claim is made initially by exploration and/or conquest. So far, so good. Many nations, as noted above, could assert a claim by right of discovery and detailed, scientific exploration. However, such tentative claims to land by right of discovery and exploration have, in the past, been backed up by effective settlement on a permanent basis, by some degree of economic development, and by a permanent presence of civil authority and perhaps military garrisons. Antarc-

tica's "population" is not a population in the same sense of Sweden's or North Dakota's. No one has been born there; no one has died there of old age after long occupancy. No one person has ever lived out the bulk of his or her life there. Antarctica's population is more like that of nuclear submarines—a relatively long-term tour of duty under onerous conditions for a small group of specially selected people, most of whom hold military rank. The transient population of Antarctica at any one time may be 1,000 or less. Its "peak population" during the summer of the International Geophysical Year of 1957–58 was about 10,000; a dozen nations participated. There are fifteen permanently manned research stations in the Antarctic at present: two British, five U.S., one joint U.S.–New Zealand, one New Zealand, one French, one Australian, and four Soviet. Chile has, on occasion, maintained a small research base on the coast. Most national claims (see Figure 14–10) are based on a combination of discovery of a particular stretch of coastline, exploration of the interior, and some permanent or long-term establishment of a research station.

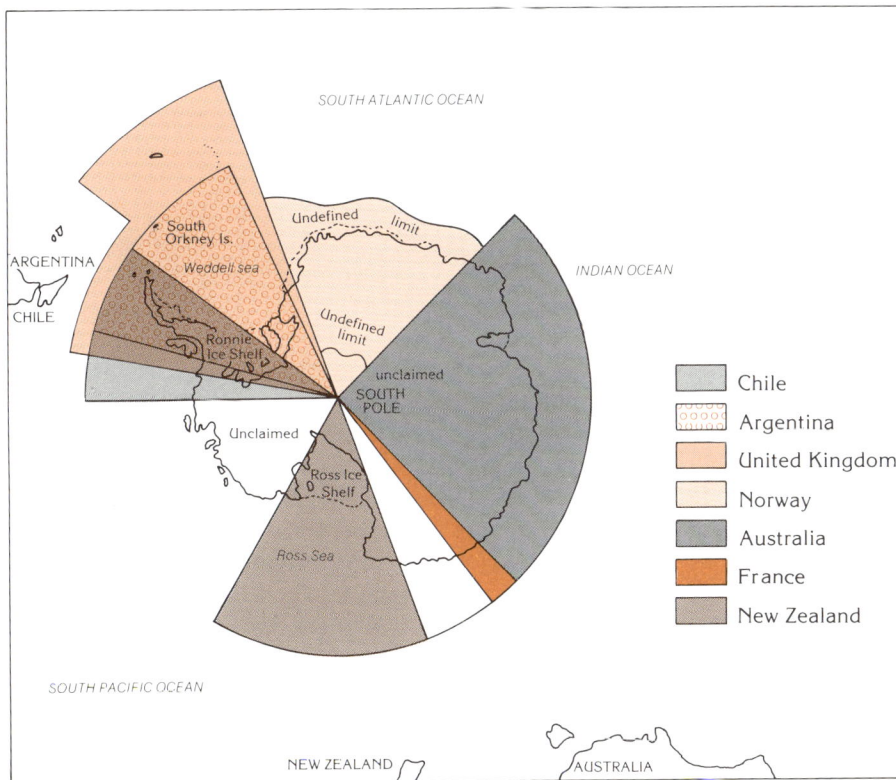

FIGURE 14–10

Antarctica: National Claims. By international treaty, national claims to Antarctica are temporarily not recognized. The claims shown precede this treaty and are based on historical, exploration, or scientific research station operation bases. The United States could legitimately claim much of the continent on the basis of both original discovery and active research stations. The Soviet Union also maintains permanent research stations.

The present territorial claims of nations in Antarctica are in a legal limbo. The United States, which has a good case for claiming much of the continent by right of discovery, explorations, and "permanent" occupance, has decided not to make any formal claim but reserves the right to do so in the future. Great Britain made a formal claim to the "seal islands" offshore in 1908, adding chunks of mainland where no one seemed to object. The French promptly entered a claim to keep Britain from swallowing the whole continent. Argentina and Chile then entered claims mostly on the grounds that they were physically closer than anyone else. Australia and New Zealand made claims on the grounds of preventing the continent, relatively close to them, from being closed to their scientists and possible military bases. Norway laid claim on the basis of frequent visits of Norwegian whalers and sealers. The United States, Soviet Union, Japan, Belgium, Sweden, and Germany, along with South Africa, have some basis for claims but are not advancing them at the moment. The American "non-claim" dates back to 1924 when Secretary of State Charles Evans Hughes gave an opinion that discovery, not followed by any permanent settlement, could not support a valid claim to territory. Settlement in traditional terms certainly remains out of the question, but permanent research stations exist, and permanent mineral exploitation sites are not improbable in the future. The Treaty of Antarctica, signed by Argentina, Australia, Belgium, Chile, France, Great Britain, Japan, New Zealand, Norway, South Africa, the United States, and the Soviet Union, demilitarizes the continent and sets aside all problems of land claims for thirty years. It was ratified in 1961, so that 1991 (or before, if the treaty is broken) may witness a land grab of monumental proportions if mineral explorations yield promising finds, which is quite likely.

One of the most inventive, not to say humorous, forms of territorial claims to Antarctica was made by Hitler's government in 1938–39. Germany had some historic basis for claims going back to 1911. The 1938–39 expedition in the *Schwabenland,* a ship equipped for launching seaplanes, attempted to do what has never been done, before, or since—actually mark claims on the ice. Pointed metal shafts with stabilizing fins like giant arrows were dropped from seaplanes. The shafts usually penetrated about three inches, remaining upright, and displaying a stamped swastika on the fin. No one paid any attention to this ingenious way of claiming and staking out territory, and Hitler went on to more consequential claims in Europe. An interesting potential claim, more recently asserted indirectly by Argentina as its territorial heir, is that of Spain. Ferdinand Magellan, discoverer of the strait bearing his name, thought that Tierra del Fuego, "lands of fire," to the south of his strait might be the tip of a southern continent, but he did not further explore southward. This 1520 "discovery" (Francis Drake proved that Tierra del Fuego was not part of any continent fifty-seven years later) was accompanied by a general claim. Argentina and Chile assert that they are successor states to the Spanish crown's territorial claims to "all land to the south" and that claim extends beyond Tierra del Fuego to all of Antarctica. Historians note, however, that *no* nation bothered to enter a claim to Antarctica for eighty-eight years after the discovery of that continent in 1820.

STRATEGIC SIGNIFICANCE OF THE POLAR REGIONS

The polar regions were once blank spots on globes that could be largely ignored, except for providing a challenge to daring explorers and interesting material for anthropologists in the form of the much-studied Eskimo. While the ocean fisheries resources of both the Arctic and Antarctic were known and valued, the environment seemed to have little interest beyond that, economically or politically. That earlier judgement has changed radically. Almost 90 percent of the world's population lives on the continents surrounding the Arctic Ocean; the two superpowers face each other across this ocean—the shortest routes for delivery of intercontinental ballistic missiles to and from the United States and the Soviet Union go across the polar region. The voyage of nuclear submarines beneath the polar ice pack, pioneered by an American sub, forever changes the strategic significance of the Arctic. Jet aircraft regularly fly over the North Pole, the shortest route from East Asia to West Europe. The major finds of oil and gas around the periphery of the Arctic basin are matched only by prospector's hopes for more. The Soviet Union, Canada, Norway, and the United States are all developing new technologies and techniques for polar construction, mining, road building, agriculture, grazing, and environmental protection.

The thirty-year moratorium on territorial claims in the Antarctic is a postponement, not an elimination, of a land scramble. Those nations with the larger, permanently occupied, numerous scientific research bases will be in the strongest position to make claims—they will already occupy at least part of their claims. The expense of maintaining these bases will favor the major powers.

Main research themes include weather, glaciology, and geology. An imaginative suggestion for using the numbing cold and almost total lack of bacteria in Antarctica is to use it as a literal deep freeze. Surplus food can be stored almost indefinitely without any deterioration, due to both low temperature and low humidity. Bread, cheese, oranges, and chocolate from the 1912–13 Scott expedition are still edible today. Some diners have complained of a certain lack of taste in the oranges, but there has been no spoilage at all.

CONCLUSIONS: ETHICAL EXPLOITATION AS A LONG-TERM MANAGEMENT GOAL

The human race's use of the resources of these "last frontiers" poses familiar questions within a continuing controversy. What right do people have to the biological and mineral resources of the planet? What are the limits to exploitation? What are the long-range goals of conservation?

THE CRISIS SYNDROME

Cyclical awareness of environmental concerns and the necessity of conservation, resulting in a series of popular conservationist movements, has been related to the perception of crises. Conservation becomes a mass crusade when the public becomes aware of serious problems, usually in resource exploitation. Conservation programs and policies, in other words, tend to be *reactive* to perceived threats of the destruction of a particular resource or environmental mileau. Pioneering America geographer George Perkins Marsh, writing in the 1860's of the adverse effects of rapid clearing of woodlands, helped foster an environmental awareness that led to the creation of national forests. In the 1930's, another conservation crusade was launched in response to the "dust bowl" and its dramatic evidence of human mismanagement of land and water resources. Again, in the late 1960's, crisis rhetoric urged a comprehensive conservation program to minimize the negative impact of high-technology industrial societies on the world resource base and the total environment.

While there is no doubt that protection of the environment and conservation of resources is an absolute must for the future of the human race on this planet, there is a wide spectrum of philosophies of conservation. At one extreme are the preservationists, the purists of the movement, who would prefer to preserve intact pristine natural environments with as few traces of human occupance and use as possible. In the most extreme view, people are to tiptoe timidly through nature as lightly as possible. Their critics call them "tree worshipers" and some much less complimentary names; to the preservationists, too many others are "rape and run" types, eager to exploit, heedless of consequences, entranced by quick profits.

USE WITHOUT ABUSE

The middle of the road view, perhaps the majority view, is that the human race is part of nature, neither passive observers of a perfect, untouched environment, nor reckless users and abusers of it. The Judeo-Christian ethic apparent, if not always recognized as such, in the Western approach to the natural world and its resources features the concept of responsible stewardship. Use is implicit, but so is conscious recognition of responsibility to future generations of people and the protection of life-forms against wanton destruction or oblivion.

Fortunately, there is evidence that the protection of the environment and the conservation of species is a popularly accepted goal. Informed stewardship of the earth and its life-forms requires a thorough understanding of ecological relationships of the physical and cultural environments. It is not enough, for example, to restrain the slaughter of the great baleen whales if serious depredations on their krill food supply are allowed or if pollution of the seas diminishes their reproductive abilities.

Ethical exploitation as a long-term management goal is based on the following assumptions:

1. Human beings will continue to depend on the total resource base of the earth (even if minor-scale importation of extraterrestrial materials becomes feasible);

2. There are, in addition to ethical, philosophical, and aesthetic reasons, practical considerations compelling avoidance of irreversable destruction of any resource, including biological resources;

3. No form of life (excepting only virulent bacteria or viruses) should ever be allowed to become extinct, if only in recognition of their potential value to people;

4. Clearly, we cannot permit the poisoning of the environment, by any form of industrial, chemical, or radiation pollution, that may have immediate or long-range effects on the human habitability of any part of the earth.

With these principles in mind, the strategies of long-term management for ethical exploitation should include

1. Inventory of the resource-base quantity, quality, and distribution;

2. Identification of shortfalls and potential shortfalls, followed by research programs aimed at "stretching" finite resources through more efficient use or the development of substitutes or synthetics; and conservation of biological resources through more efficient use, ecological studies to identify acceptable harvest

rates, and possible "farming" of the biological resource under controlled environments, selective breeding, improved diets, and protection against predators and disease;

3. Comprehensive study of effects of all varieties of pollution on the environment and its life-forms, including people. A *holistic* approach to the problems of environmental management and ethical resource exploitation is the only one capable of providing answers to these complex and interrelated challenges.

GEOGRAPHY AND PROBLEMS OF RESOURCE MANAGEMENT

Geographers ideally are equipped to deal with complex issues to which there are no simple answers. By training,

geographers study inherently complex issues involving many-faceted interrelationships between the human and physical worlds. In the evolution of an ethical management philosophy for the world's oceanic resources, the Antarctic continent and Arctic areas, and even those resources of the settled world, geographers can expect to play an important role. A challenge to the United States will be the exercise of positive leadership in a world in which industrialization is seen as a very desirable goal among preindustrial societies. It is not uncommon for states in the early stages of industrialization to regard concern for the environment as a luxury of advanced societies (whose environmental resources have previously been ruthlessly exploited and polluted). The "tragedy of the commons" must be averted before the human race's common heritage and home is pillaged.

Processing Whales in the Azores. While only Japan and the Soviet Union now operate large "factory ships" in whaling, many small whales are still taken in local waters by small ships. This whale processing plant is in the Portuguese Azores. (Courtesy of Creamer)

case study
OFFSHORE OIL AND GAS

In the late nineteenth century, offshore wells were drilled by both the United States (off southern California) and Russia (in the Caspian Sea). These first offshore wells were drilled in relatively shallow water and in the immediate vicinity of producing fields onshore. Despite the fact that offshore drilling is always more difficult and significantly more expensive than onshore operations, offshore drilling is increasing because the potential rewards are greater. A background paper recently prepared by a major oil company explains "There is a better chance of finding large fields capable of significant production in the undrilled offshore basins than in the mature, well-drilled onshore producing areas."[3] Total offshore production runs an estimated 13 million barrels per day, which makes it about one fifth of total world production. Most of the reserves of Europe, Asia, and Australia are offshore. Almost every major oil-producing region has some offshore production (see Figure 14–3). Offshore reserves form an estimated 240 billion barrels, 37 percent of the world total. There are currently about seven hundred rigs drilling underwater.

As in the case in onshore drilling for oil and natural gas, the trend has been towards drilling offshore in progressively more remote areas and in progressively more difficult physical circumstances. Offshore drilling is handicapped by an additional set of problems beyond the geological ones usually encountered. Tides, high waves and strong winds, storms including hurricanes, ice flows, fog, icebergs, and locations astride busy shipping lanes are all added hazards of some offshore drilling sites.

Recent steep rises in oil prices have supported matching escalations in capital expended to explore and bring into production offshore fields. The new drilling operations water depth records (not counting the depth of the well into the seabed) have gone from 1,500 feet (460 meters) (in the Santa Barbara Channel off California) in 1970 to 4,800 feet (1,500 meters) off Newfoundland by 1979. Drilling ships currently are designed to operate in as much as 6,000 feet of water (1,800 meters). There are three types of mobile rigs for drilling exploratory wells. The jackup rig, equipped with elevator legs, can be towed into position and its legs lowered to the bottom with the platform then jacked up to a safe height. These rigs have a maximum water depth usage of 300 feet (90 meters).

Semi-submersible rigs are moored by huge anchors of up to 20 tons each; about one hundred are in use. Drill ships have a hole through the hull through which drilling takes place. Unlike semi-submersibles, most do not depend solely on anchors but maintain position above the well by propellers (thrusters) in a "dynamically positioned," computer-controlled system. An advantage of this dynamic positioning is that the rig can be moved out of the way faster if an iceberg threatens it, which is common in the Labrador Sea.

The hazards of spills have been well publicized, often featuring the Santa Barbara Channel "blowout" (uncontrolled flow due to sudden increase in pressure combined with equipment failure or human error). In an average year, about 80,000 metric tons of oil enter the sea from offshore drilling and producing operations; this is estimated at about 2 percent of the total oil entering the oceans from all sources. The average rate of blowouts has been 1 in 250 wells; obviously, as more wells are drilled, the probability of blowouts increases. Better technologies of detecting pressure changes and automatically shutting valves to avoid blowouts are partly offset in effectiveness by the extreme depths and generally hazardous working conditions of many new wells. The worst blowout so far occurred in the Bay of Campeche, offshore Mexico, when a well blew out in June 1979 and was not successfully capped until March 1980; 450,000 tons of oil entered the sea, coating beaches along Texas's Padre Island and instigating a major study of its ecological impact. Preliminary findings are that permanent damage to the environment may be minimal, as was discovered by a survey of the effects of the Santa Barbara Channel spill of 1969. These findings are substantiated by a study of Lake Maracaibo, Venezuela, where shallow-water offshore production has taken place for decades without any detectable accumulations of petroleum-derived hydrocarbons in commercially caught fish.

---

[3] Exxon Corporation, "The Offshore Search for Oil and Gas," 4th edition, 1980, p. 2.

The rapid advances in offshore drilling technology, with new depth records every year, emphasizes the importance of updating international law regarding the mineral resources of the ocean depths. Offshore drilling definitely will increase in importance to the world economy and as a potential hazard, if only temporary, to sea life.

REVIEW QUESTIONS

1　In what ways does our exploitation of ocean resources resemble a "frontier" stage?

2　Criticize the view that the experience of the Greenland Vikings substantiates an environmental determinist view.

3　What minerals are presently produced from seawater? What minerals are most likely to be added to this list in future?

4　What are the environmental degradation potentials of greatly expanded exploitation of seabed oil and gas fields?

5　Why may greatly expanded production from ocean fisheries be difficult to sustain?

6　Why are most rich fisheries located in shallow water near land masses?

7　Describe the role of ocean currents, both horizontal and vertical, in supporting the ocean food chain.

8　What is the nature of the "tragedy of the commons"?

9　How does the hydrologic cycle function to make the world's oceans a final "dump" for some pollutants?

10　Why do technological advances in both fishing and mining industries tend to result in extension of territorial waters or some other type of national control?

11　Why do many of the world's countries wish to replace or modify the "lake" principle of assigning territorial control over seabeds?

12　Why are the plant and animal populations of the Arctic more varied and abundant than those of Antarctica?

13　Why do some of the mineral resources of the Arctic and Antarctic regions indicate either drastic changes in the regions' relative locations or in the earth's climate in the past?

14　What are the political and economic motives that may produce an Antarctic "land rush" as countries attempt to assert sovereignty there?

15　What geographic factors, in combination with technological advances in weaponry, have converted the Arctic basin into a highly strategic area?

SUGGESTED READINGS

1　LEWIS ALEXANDER, *Offshore Geography of Northwestern Europe.* Chicago: Rand McNally, The AAG Monograph Series, #3, 1963.

2　LEWIS ALEXANDER, ed., *The Law of the Sea.* Columbus: University of Ohio Press, 1967.

3 SAMUEL BOGGS, *International Boundaries: A Study of Boundary Functions and Problems.* New York: AMS Press, 1966 (reprinted from the Columbia University Press—1940 edition).

4 CENTRAL INTELLIGENCE AGENCY, *Polar Regions Atlas.* Washington, D.C.: National Foreign Assessment Center, CIA.

5 J. F. LOVERING and J. R. V. PRESCOTT, *Last of Lands—Antarctica.* Melbourne: Melbourne University Press, 1979.

6 MYRES McDOUGAL and WILLIAM BURKE, *The Public Order of the Oceans: A Contemporary International Law of the Sea.* New Haven, Conn.: Yale University Press, 1962.

7 J. R. V. PRESCOTT, *The Political Geography of the Oceans.* New York: John Wiley & Sons, 1975.

GLOSSARY

Aboriginal people The earliest settlers of a part of the earth, or at least those inhabitants, usually of a low level of development, in place at the time of "discovery" by more advanced cultures.

Acculturation The adoption, or modification to some degree, by people of one culture, of behavior patterns, language, religion, technology, or life style of another culture. Commonly, material culture is more willingly adopted than are ideologies, religions, or languages, but these too may be wholly or partly absorbed by another culture.

Advance capital (See **march capital.**)

Agribusiness The name given to large-scale, highly mechanized farming in the United States, commonly controlled by corporations.

Agricultural-industrial complex In Bulgaria, a planned regional development with interdependent agricultural and industrial aspects.

Agricultural Revolution The major advance in stabilizing the human food supply by selecting, planting, and cultivating crops and selectively breeding and herding animals.

Animal roulette A term, critical of the phenomenon, describing the practice of deliberately (sometimes accidentally) introducing exotic, nonnative species into a different environment where the animal may have no natural enemies.

Antipodes concept The antipodes are the exact opposite, as in location on the opposite side of the earth; the most distant possible location or, by extension, the most directly opposite to a given philosophy.

Apartheid The official policy of "separate development" of racial groups, including residential segregation, of the government of South Africa.

Arable land Land that is capable of being cultivated.

Assimilado In Portuguese colonial Africa, the status of "assimilated" to Portuguese culture attainable by Africans; citizenship by aspiration to the ruler's culture.

Assimilation pressures "Melting pot" pressures on a minority to minimize or even abandon their distinctive cultural traits, including their religious practices, their dress, and their food preferences.

Atolls Low-profile islands of coral taking a roughly broken-circle form enclosing a lagoon. Thought to be associated with volcanic subsidence (Darwin's Theory).

Autarcky The achievement of self-sufficiency in production of all raw materials and manufactures. Theoretically, the state in autarcky would be invulnerable to interruptions or dislocations in international trade.

"Balkanization" The political fragmentation of an area into many small units based on a mosaic of ethnic, linguistic, historical, and/or religious associations.

Bantustan In South Africa, a theoretically independent state composed of a "tribal homeland" imbedded within South Africa. No state other than South Africa recognizes their independent status.

Barrier-and-channel effect The tendency for drainage features (rivers), topographic valleys, or other phenomena in the physical environment to guide or route traffic and traffic arteries.

553

Basement complex In geology, the crystalline (igneous) rock of the crust underlying later veneers of sediments or recent volcanics.

Beneficiate In mining, the process of enriching an ore by concentrating the economic mineral. This then enables longer-distance shipment of ores. By extension, the enrichment of a material or activity to make it more viable.

Buffer In political geography, a political unit that functions, by design or accident, to separate two potential belligerents; intended to reduce tensions.

Caliche A crust of mineral salts in soil, left behind by evaporation of water.

Capital intensive Industry characterized by very high investment in plant and equipment per employee, for example, oil refining.

Carrying capacity A measure of the capability of pasture to "carry" or support livestock without suffering any permanent damage or deterioration. By extension, a measure of the ability of any areal resource base to "carry" any human use without deterioration.

Caste A class grouping in the Hindu religion and society based on occupation. Caste reflects social status and has broad economic implications in India.

Causal relationship A cause-and-effect relationship, often implied, but not necessarily proven, by a spatial correlation.

Central place hierarchy Christaller's theory that larger-sized central places, with more complete arrays of goods and services, will be spaced at correspondingly further distances apart than smaller, less sophisticated central places.

Central places Those places in which goods and services are made available to surrounding hinterland populations. They are central to their trade area and are part of a hierarchy of such places.

Central place theory Developed by geographer Walter Christaller to explain the spatial patterns of service centers or "central places" in a homogeneous agricultural plain. His theory seeks to explain the spacing of different levels in a hierarchy or rank-order of service centers.

Centrifugal force In industrial location, a force that favors movement outward from the center of production, for example, a declining significance of raw material costs in a coal-field-oriented steel mill.

Centripetal force In location, a force that favors concentration at the established center of production, for example, cheaper transport to distant markets.

Changing interactions The phenomena of, and study of, the changing interrelationships—economic, political, cultural, strategic—among world regions, and within them as well.

Chernozem A Russian term, now in general use, for "black earth"—humus- and mineral-rich prairie soils capable of supporting heavy crop yields when supplied with adequate moisture.

Circulation In political geography, the set of factors such as transport and communications facilities, which facilitate strong interdependence among parts of a national unit; strong circulation favors unity.

Client state A state in a subordinate, dependent relationship with a more powerful state.

Closed city A city to which further migration is restricted by government; common in Communist societies.

Collective farms Communist area farms theoretically owned by members but actually owned and managed by the government. Workers are paid in proportion to the economic success (or failure) of the farm.

Collectivization In Communist states, the process of forming collective farms, usually replacing private farms.

Colony A territory directly under the control of another state. Colonies were usually founded or conquered by that state, which then retained virtually full control of both domestic and foreign affairs.

Comecon (CMEA) The Communist counterpart of West Europe's European Economic Community. The Soviet Union encouraged the establishment of the Council for Mutual Economic Assistance, or Comecon, in 1949. Full members are the USSR, Poland, East Germany, Czechoslovakia, Hungary, Romania, and Bulgaria. Yugoslavia is an associate member.

Commercialization The process of moving from a subsistence economy toward an exchange, cash-based economy with implied individual specialization of production.

Commercial Revolution The five centuries in Europe prior to the Industrial Revolution in which the techniques, technology, and systems of long-distance trade and finance were established, providing the groundwork for industrialization.

Commune Communal living centers, in mainland China in the 1950s designed to destroy old traditions and group people together for more efficiency in use of space and production. Their form has changed, and their role has been reassessed.

Complementarity That situation in which two or more areas produce different goods, resulting in flows (movement) for the purpose of exchange. Farm production and factory production are complementary, assuring movement in both directions.

Compressional stress The societal and individual stresses resulting from the very rapid sequence of fundamental changes as a preindustrial society evolves towards a high-technology, urban-industrial one and as tribalism is submerged in a growing nationalism.

Continental drift The imperceptably slow movement of continents, or parts of continents associated with plate tectonics. (See **tectonic plates.**)

Continentality In climate, the set of climatic influences of large land masses, heating and cooling faster than sea surfaces, leading to more extreme temperatures in land mass interiors than over or adjacent to seas.

Core The heartland of a state, an area that is the center of political and economic power and from which flow political direction and economic development. It is usually relatively densely settled.

Correlation A geographic association of two or more factors. It may suggest a cause-and-effect relationship between them, but this relationship must be investigated cautiously.

Corridor functions A set of transport services associated with a heavily used routeway, often related to physical factors such as mountain passes or river valleys.

Cottage industry Any complete production or phase of a manufacturing or processing sequence, such as assembly, that is carried out in the worker's residence rather than in a factory.

"Creaming" of resources The practice, implicit or explicit, of first skimming off the richest, most readily exploited, most accessible part of the total resource.

Culture The total complex of learned and inherited life style, including material items such as technology, architecture, and clothing and such abstracts and behavior patterns as language, law, and religion.

Cultural amalgam A blending of diverse cultural elements into a new compound or blend.

Cultural assimilation The process of absorption of one cultural group, such as an ethnic or religious minority becoming culturally part of the majority, indistinguishable from it in most respects.

Cultural crossroads A part of the world, as in East Europe, that has experienced many diverse cultural contacts, invasions, and currents.

Cultural divide The boundary zone between peoples of different cultures.

Cultural hearth The center of origin of a culture or an item of culture; the origin area of an idea or technology that subsequently diffused to other areas and peoples.

Cultural shatterbelt (See **shatterbelt.**)

Cyclical industry An industry in which the pattern of demand fluctuates considerably through time, perhaps on a repeating cycle of rising, then falling, markets.

Dar al Islam The "House of Islam" or traditional extent of Islamic religion and culture—the Arabian peninsula, North Africa, the Near East, Turkey, Iraq, and Iran.

Decentralization The policy and/or process of spatially dispersing any function or activity from a former concentration.

Demographic transition A model of population growth (birth- and death rates) that characterizes a society moving through and completing the Industrial Revolution and associated health-care revolution.

Density A description of the relationship between the number of any phenomenon and the size of the area in which it is distributed. A large number in a small area is a high density.

Desalination The desalting of sea water to produce potable water, or the flushing out of salt concentrates from long-term irrigated soils.

Desertification The process of human-induced microclimatic changes that expand the desert at the expense of its sub-humid margins. Environmental mismanagement, such as destruction of forests and overgrazing, contributes to desertification of formerly productive lands.

Detribalization The movement of tribal members into an urban industrial society to the point of losing touch with the remaining tribal groups and discontinuing traditional practices. Incomplete acculturation into the modern society may mean a cultural limbo status for a time.

Developing area An optimistic term for a state or region that has not yet attained full development or industrialization. Continuing advance is implied but may not always occur.

Development A general level of technology, economic sophistication, and standard of living; an index of economic achievement.

Developmental differential A strong and obvious difference in development level, whether within or between states.

Developmental gap The ominous trend in which rich, industrial countries grow richer faster than poor countries become less poor. The gap between rich and poor is growing wider rather than narrower.

Developmental infrastructure The complex of transport, communications, energy development and transmission, and basic production facilities that must be established for development to proceed.

Developmental strategy The conscious plan for directing economic development based on selective investment and exploitation to speed overall development.

Development enclave A zone of relatively modern industrialization within predominantly underdeveloped countries.

Diaspora The deliberate dispersal of the Jewish population of Palestine under the Romans, following the destruction of Jerusalem in 70 A.D.

Diffusion The outward spread, not necessarily in proportion to distance and time, of an idea, an innovation, or a piece of material culture. There are both physical and cultural barriers to the spread and adoption of new ideas or material culture.

Distributional pattern The spatial incidence of any variable forms a distributional pattern, which may provide clues to causal relationships when compared to the distributional pattern of other phenomena.

Dynamic adaption An on-going and active attitude of selective but enthusiastic adaption of new ideas and technology. Adaption, as opposed to adoption, refers to partial incorporation of new technology, application within a different context, or some significant modification rather than total acceptance.

Economic heartland The most important, concentrated area of agricultural, mining and/or industrial production within a state; most probably, the most heavily populated region.

Economic hinterland The surrounding or even distant area that has a close economic relationship with the city or region whose hinterland it constitutes; commonly, a raw materials supply and/or market zone.

Economic maturity In Rostow's stages of economic growth, the stage by which all major sectors of the economy have been modernized through application of the principles of the industrial revolution.

Ecumene Originally described the (known) inhabited world; now used more specifically to delimit the area populated by more than two people per square mile.

Ecumene triangle In the USSR, the triangle that approximates the most populated, most productive, most industrialized part of the country; the triangle is, in general terms, Leningrad to Novosibirsk to Odessa to Leningrad.

Ejido A Mexican land reform settlement in which land is managed collectively and in which education and technology

Enclave A piece of foreign-controlled territory within a state's boundaries.

are used to upgrade the level of production. Farms, however, are individually owned.

Entrepôt A transport center and exchange point, almost always a seaport, that serves as a trading center for another area, sometimes across international boundaries.

Environmental degradation The deterioration in the quality of the environment that occurs through erosion, pollution, and general mismanagement or rapacious management.

Environmental determinism The belief that human cultures are strongly influenced and molded by forces of the physical environment, primarily climate.

Environmentalism The appreciation for, and concern for, the conservation and protection of the total physical environment; not to be confused with environmental determinism.

Estancias Literally, "estates," essentially the same as *haciendas.*

Ethnocentrism The tendency for any nationality or ethnic group to view the world as it relates to them; implicitly or explicitly, there is an assumption that one's own homeland is the center of the world.

European Economic Community Founded in 1958 by France, West Germany, Netherlands, Belgium, Luxembourg, and Italy, the community's members have no tariffs or restrictions on interchanges of goods, raw materials, capital or labor. The United Kingdom, Eire, Denmark, and Greece have joined since.

Exclaves Pieces of one's territory physically separate and surrounded by the territory of another state. An exclave of one state would be an enclave within another state.

Exotic stream A permanent stream flowing through an area whose climate does not support permanent streams. The "exotic" (out of place) stream exists due to sources in a more humid climate.

Expatriate worker A national of one country who lives and works in another country on a fairly long-term basis, but who retains citizenship in, and will eventually return to, his or her "home" country.

Fall line In the eastern United States, the physiographic boundary between the Piedmont of the Appalachians and the Coastal Plain, marked by falls or rapids where streams leave the resistant rock of the Piedmont for the softer sediments of the Coastal Plain.

Farm city Soviet experiment designed to increase the efficiency of both farm units and services to farm workers. The cities have proven to be relatively inefficient, and no new ones are planned.

Fertile Crescent The traditional term identifying the region of the Near East from present-day Israel, Lebanon, and Syria's better-watered Mediterranean-type climate to the great oasis of the Tigris-Euphrates valleys. The contrast to less favored deserts and rugged mountains elsewhere led to the designation *fertile.*

Finite resource (See **fund resource.**)

Flow resource A resource that, with prudent management, will continue as a resource forever. Forests, hydro power, and fisheries could (and should) be managed as flow or renewable resources.

Food chain The system of predator-prey relationships among lifeforms within an ecosystem. Almost all food chains are based on plants consumed by animals that are in turn eaten by other animals, who themselves might be preyed upon.

Foreign trade zone A legally designated area within which imported materials may be processed, stored, and re-exported without payment of tariffs or other taxes on import-export.

Formal region There is no dominant center implied in a formal region, which may be uniform concerning a specific criterion or at least exhibit an acceptable degree of uniformity.

Forward capital A capital chosen for its advance, peripheral location to facilitate further conquest or enhance external contacts.

Forward port A port on the outer edge of a landmass, commonly on a peninsula or at the mouth of an estuary, serving primarily passenger traffic anxious to transfer to faster land transport.

Fossil fuel A source of thermal energy resulting from the fossilization of organic material flourishing in past geologic eras: coal, lignite, natural gas, or petroleum.

Fossil water Water from underground reserves that is the result of more humid conditions in past eras. The contemporary climate is not capable of producing or recharging this underground supply, which is a fossil of different conditions in the past.

Friction of space The cost and/or inconvenience of overcoming distance. Decreases in time-distance or cost reduce friction of space.

Frontier mentality The attitude, alleged to be common among frontier pioneers, that resources are virtually limitless and thus need not be conserved.

Functional region Sometimes called a nodal region, this region has a functional relationship with a node or center; a seaport's hinterland would be a type of functional region.

Fund resource Unlike a flow resource, a resource that is finite. There are fixed amounts of these resources available (even if all of them have not been discovered yet), and when these "funds" are used up, there are no more—they are not renewable.

General farming Unspecialized agriculture with a wide variety of crops and livestock produced on every unit.

Geographic context (See **Geographic perspective, Spatial correlation.**)

Geographic explanation Explanation of a distributional pattern or phenomena considering a wide range of potential influences from the physical and cultural sets of geographic or spatial phenomena.

Geographic perspective The viewpoint that seeks to place any phenomenon or pattern within a geographic context, that is, seeking spatial relationships.

Geography The science of distributions. Geography is concerned with spatial variations in any physical or cultural phenomena.

Geothermal power Energy generated by using the internal heat of the planet. Geothermal energy is tapped on a very limited scale as suitable geological conditions are highly localized and corrosion problems from dissolved minerals are a serious handicap.

Global interaction As a large-scale phenomenon, a characteristic of the modern world with its global interchanges of raw materials, technology, people, energy, capital, manufactured goods, information, and culture.

Great Leap Forward The ill-considered plan for accelerated economic development in the People's Republic of China during the 1950's. A feature was the "backyard iron furnace," which produced little metal of usable quality but distracted labor from vital agricultural production.

Green belt A buffer-zone of open space used to separate different functional areas in planned communities; first used in Howard's *Garden Cities*.

Green Revolution A description of the recent, rapid strides in agricultural science in selective plant breeding, cultivation, and fertilization techniques that significantly increase food crop yields per land unit.

Green rush The feverish migration into a newly accessible, potential agricultural area; the farm frontier version of a gold rush.

Gross national product (GNP) A popular measure of level of industrialization and economic development. It is the total monetary value of all goods and services produced per year, commonly expressed per capita.

Growth pole In developing nations, a city or economic region selected for planned investment and growth, which, it is hoped, will stimulate general regional growth by attracting other economic activities.

Haj The pilgrimage of a Moslem to the holy city of Mecca. Every Moslem is to make this pilgrimage at least once in a lifetime if at all possible.

Hardpan formation The development of a crust or concretion of minerals within soil. This hardpan hinders drainage and the development of root systems and generally lowers the agricultural utility of soil.

Hearth The source area (in agriculture, culture and so on) of any innovation; the area of origin from which an idea, technique, artifact, crop, or good is diffused to other areas.

Hidden export The providing of a service rather than the exporting of tangible goods for earning foreign exchange. Tourism, insurance and financial services, transport services, rental of facilities, and ship's crews could all represent hidden exports.

High value added A product or industry in which the total value of the finished goods is much higher than that of its constituant raw materials.

Hinge function A function resulting from a location between two complementary or unlike physical areas or between two different cultural areas. These locations with hinge functions are centers of trade and interchange.

Hinterland The area tributary to, in an economic relationship, a particular center, as in a seaport's service area, handling imports and exports for its hinterland.

Hydroponics The science of growing plants with their root systems immersed in, or flushed by, nutrient-laden water rather than in soil.

Iconography In political geography, the set of shared beliefs, heroes, myths, sense of destiny, and interpretation of history that is a basis for national unity (an icon is a symbol of belief and faith).

Import replacement The strategy of fostering domestic production of consumer goods to reduce imports in a developing economy.

Indigenisimo In Latin America, the resurgence of interest in, and pride in, native Amerindian culture and ancestry.

Industrial Revolution The eighteenth century (and continuing) period of rapid advance in use of inanimate power, more complex machinery, and the factory system, to revolutionize the scale and efficiency of industry, transport, and communications, agriculture and mining. It must be emphasized that the antecedents of this "revolution" developed over centuries in many parts of the world.

Infant mortality rate A statistical measure of children, other than the stillborn, who do not survive to their first birthday. This rate is often used as a key indicator of development level as modern industrial societies generally have low rates.

Infrastructure (economic) The transportation networks (roads, rails, and so on), capital equipment, housing stock, and other physical structures that are found within an area; the internal collection of structures, facilities and phenomena with capital value in any economy.

Innovation The creation of a new idea or technique, new technology or modification, extension or new application of existing concepts; the spread of the innovation over space is diffusion.

Integrated economy One in which primary, secondary, and tertiary sectors of the economy are at approximately the same level of development and interrelated within the domestic economy.

Intensive agriculture The intensive use of land for production. Large amounts of labor (and capital equipment, fertilizer, and so on) are applied per land unit. Productivity is very high, but so is investment of time and energy.

Interior drainage A phenomenon, common in deserts, in which drainage systems do not reach the sea due to low precipitation and high evaporation; streams end in salt lakes or disappear in valleys with no outlets.

Intertropical convergence Sometimes called the equatorial low, the zone in which air circulating equatorward from each hemisphere's Subtropical high pressure converges and then rises vertically, producing heavy precipitation.

Intervening opportunity In economic geography, some location intermediate between a source and market destination that offers the same economic opportunity (resource, market, etc.) and therefore is more desirable due to lower transport cost.

Irredenta Literally, an "unredeemed territory"; claimed by a state on the basis of its cultural, ethnic, or linguistic makeup, but still controlled by another state.

Kombinat In Soviet economic planning, the "pairing" of two distant industrial complexes based on complementary raw materials. Iron ore is carried from one area to a coal-based "partner," and coal carried on the return trip.

Labor intensive That in which labor costs are an unusually high component of the total production cost of the finished product or service. Education is an example.

Land tenure Forms of land control and ownership. Various forms of land tenure include freehold (private ownership by the farmer), tenancy, plantations, rented lands, and the like.

Laterite A soil condition, common in the tropics, in which water-soluble minerals are leached out by abundant water, leaving mostly iron and aluminum oxides, which, exposed to the atmosphere by erosion, can form an almost impenetrable layer.

Laterization The leaching process that leaves only a residue of iron and aluminum oxides in tropical soils.

Latifundium An estate owned by landlords, often absentee, who hire day labor; characteristic of the Mediterranean, Middle East, and much of Latin America.

Leaching A natural process in which plant nutrients are rinsed from the top layers of the soil to deeper levels, making it difficult for roots of crop plants to reach a food supply. It occurs in all areas where precipitation exceeds the potential for evaporation, and it results in infertile (or less fertile) soils.

Leisureopolis A leisure- and recreation-oriented linear strip of urbanization in which development is aligned with, and based on, a natural recreation amenity such as a shoreline.

Location strategy The practical application of geographic analysis; the system of identifying the point of best potential for an economic enterprise, maximizing profit, and minimizing costs.

Loess Fine-grained materials transported and deposited by wind. Frequently of glacial origin, this windborne material can become the basis of exceptionally productive soil.

Loyalties set The hierarchial order of one's loyalties to groups or associations, including tribes, ethnic groups, homeland regions, and political units.

Machine tool A machine that makes other machines; metal fabricating and shaping machinery; capital equipment. A machine tool industry is at the apex of industrial development.

Magnetic anomaly An apparent concentration of metallic ores indicating the desirability of further exploration, detected by ground exploration or satellite scan.

Mainland-rimland The basic cultural region division in Middle America, proposed by geographers John Augelli and Robert West.

March (advance) capital A capital deliberately located in a position close to an advancing or contested frontier rather than in a more central, secure location; a capital located for close communication with military forces.

Marche area An advancing frontier in a hostile territory; the heavily militarized zone along the advancing frontier.

Maritime orientation The psychological, as well as economic and cultural, emphasis on seaborne opportunities and contacts.

Megalopolis The term assigned by geographer Jean Gottmann to an urbanizing region in which two or more great cities are growing toward one another along interconnecting transport routes.

Megalopolitan Characteristic of, or potentially resembling the original, northeastern U.S. seaboard Megalopolis.

Ministates Independent political units of relatively very minor territorial scale, as in Andorra, San Marino, or Monaco.

Mirror-image colony Similar in some aspects of physical geography and having a relatively small aboriginal population, a colony that was seen as a potential replica of the "parent" society.

Mixed economy One in which there are some elements of both socialist (government ownership of the means of production) and free-enterprise types of control.

Model An abstract simplification of reality designed to eliminate peripheral or unrelated phenomena in order to focus study on basic factors and relationships.

Monsoon The seasonal reversal of winds, onshore in summer, offshore in winter, associated with the presence of temperature-induced pressure systems over land and water surfaces. Its most dramatic effects are over southern and eastern Asia. The term commonly applies specifically to the onshore, summer monsoon.

Monsoonal The effects of, or having some characteristics of, the monsoon phenomenon.

Moraines Ridges, hills or veneers of glacially deposited materials, characteristically of unsorted debris at right angles to stream drainage.

Nation A cultural unit, a group of people tied and identified by their cultural distinctiveness. A nation may or may not constitute a state as well.

Nationalism The cultural complex of loyalties based on commonalities of interest and experience. Loyalty must be to the larger political unit rather than to tribal or subregional authorities.

National minority An ethnic, linguistic, or cultural minority controlled by another state, but with ambitions for political independence.

Nation-state A happy coincidence, territorially, of a nation (a culturally distinctive group) and a state. The national territory may still have some unassimilated minorities, however.

Neocolonial Relating to the policies of industrial states to dominate the economies of independent states that were colonies and thus limit the freedom of action of these former colonies.

NEP The "new economic policy" of Lenin; a temporary return to limited individual ownership and enterprise that occurred during the early years of Communist control in the USSR.

Network A transportation framework composed of interconnected nodes (settlements) and links (routes).

New town In planners' definitions, a community with a complete set of urban functions (residential, recreational, retailing, administrative, manufacturing, and so on) that was totally designed and planned prior to construction. Nothing was left to chance or was unplanned.

Nonalignment The political stance of states refusing to be identified as consistent supporters or allies of either of the contending superpowers seeking global influence.

Ocean island An island that is relatively remote from all continents and is geologically not part of a continental mountain system but rather results from tectonic and/or coral activity.

Ocean trench A huge, arclike deep trench in the ocean floor just off a continent-fringing island arc, associated with tectonic plates in collision.

"Oil bridge" The term applied to the continuous shuttle of oil tankers between the Persian Gulf and Japan.

Oriental intensive agriculture East Asian-culture area's characteristic heavy inputs of labor and organic fertilizer to produce multiple crops intercultivated with wet rice.

Orientation bias The general direcitonal trend (or preference) for movement; the directional flow that is average or dominant.

Orographic precipitation Precipitation induced by an air mass being forced to rise over a mountain barrier, decreasing its temperature and so bringing it, sometimes, to dew point, condensation, and precipitation.

Outport A port closer to the margins of the land mass, specializing in handling passenger vessels or out-sized ships such as supertankers. In Newfoundland, tiny fishing ports scattered around the coast.

Overcapacity Physical means of production, as in steel mills, that are, at least temporarily, surplus to demand.

Overdeveloped economy One that is heavily dependent on imported industrial resources, even imported foods, and is out of balance with the local resource base.

Overgrazing The practice or phenomenon of allowing too many domestic animals to graze a specific area, resulting in permanent damage to the vegetation and soil of that area.

Overpopulation Usually defined as a situation in which a country or region is consistently unable to adequately feed all of its people. Rather than being a specific ratio of people to area, the precise definition varies, depending on level of economic development.

Pacific ring of fire The general area of tectonic (earthquake) activity and vulcanism around the edge of the Pacific basin that is associated with plate tectonics.

Paramos In Latin America, that part of vertical zonation agriculture that is too cool for crops but used for grazing.

Pattern Some degree of regularity in a spatial distribution. Pattern is repeated (or repeatable) and predictable to a degree.

Pax Britannica The historical period, approximately 1815 to 1914, during which Britain's paramount power acted to restrain major wars among great powers (but there were many lesser wars).

Perception The problem of different people selectively observing and interpreting different items in the same environment or section of reality. Their varying cultural backgrounds may thus lead to very different conclusions and assumptions about a landscape.

Permafrost The permanently frozen subsoil of arctic environments that hinders drainage and complicates construction of buildings and roads.

Physiologic density The density of human population relative to cultivated area rather than to total area.

Pidgin language A makeshift language composed of vocabulary and structure borrowed from several different languages; specifically, the makeshift language developed in Papua New Guinea and related or nearby territories.

Planned economy A centrally planned economy with either absolute government control or majority involvement.

Plant obsolescence The process of a plant (building, machinery, and associated facilities for production) becoming less economic to operate in competition with newer plants using the latest technology.

Plebescite A poll of the citizenry on a possible change in political affiliation to another state.

Population explosion The term describing the unprecedented sharp, sustained increase in world population growth rates over the past three centuries, related primarily to declining death rates.

Population pressure The perception that a country or region has difficulty in adequately feeding the human population. There is no *density* figure that defines this pressure; rather, it is related to economic development and resource utilization as much as to physical density.

Population pyramid A graph used to display the age and sex characteristics of a population. A "normal" population graph has an approximately pyramidal shape, for there are large numbers of youth compared to the elderly.

Power vacuum A situation, temporary in nature, in which a particular area has no political or military power beyond its territory, and there is no involvement of outside powers.

Primate city A city that occupies the pinnacle of the urban hierarchy in a country or major region. It has the greatest array of specialized goods and services and has, in some senses, a nationwide hinterland.

Private plot In Communist states, a small land unit from which a farmer can sell produce of any kind on free markets and keep the proceeds, which he cannot do in collective production. Much of Communist states' fresh fruits, vegetables, and eggs are from such limited "private" production plots.

Protectionist tariff An import tax imposed specifically to give market advantages to domestic sources.

Protectorate A political unit that has less sovereignty than does a true state but more than does a colony. Typically, foreign policy and defense are controlled by the "protector," but domestic policy is only generally guided and not administered from outside.

Push-pull mechanisms Negative and positive location factors. A "push" mechanism favors an activity moving out to a more attractive location; a "pull" is a positive reason attracting an activity to it.

Quaternary employment In the traditional threefold division of economic activity, primary is obtaining raw materials, secondary is manufacturing, and tertiary is all services. Jean Gottmann's quaternary category segregates services, largely intangible, performed by highly specialized, highly educated or trained people.

Rationalization of holdings The trading of one compact plot for the many scattered strips of land that may be in one ownership due to relics of feudal land systems, inheritance, and dowry. (It is much more efficient, hence more rational, to farm one large unit rather than many small scattered ones.)

Region An areal unit smaller than the globe, defined by criteria selected for degree of relative homogeneity (for example, a climate region) or a region involving some degree of functional interaction (such as a port hinterland or a metropolitan commuting region).

Regional approach (See **Regional geography.**)

Regional capital In large areal units, such as Canada or the United States, a city that functions as an economic administrative and cultural "capital" even if it is not also a provincial or state political capital; examples include Atlanta and Los Angeles.

Regional geography The study of all factors of the total environment—cultural and physical—that have significance to the understanding of that subdivision of the earth's surface. The focus is on an area and all geographic variables interrelated there.

Regional growth pole (See *growth pole.*)

Regional interdependence A strong degree of economic mutual benefit tying together various parts of a region.

Relict population A small survivor of a formerly more dense population, as of a small remnant population of a once widespread plant or animal species.

Reorientation A perceptible, sometimes dramatic shift in economic and/or cultural directional relationships.

Rump state The small residual left from the defeat or collapse of a once much larger political unit, as in the end of an empire.

Russification In the Soviet Union, as in tsarist Russia, the policy of encouraging, or forcing, the cultural assimilation of non-Russian ethnics into the majority culture.

Sahel In North Africa, the climatic and vegetational transition southward from the Sahara to the better-watered savanna and rainforest areas. Precipitation is highly erratic year to year, and overgrazing combined with drought has led to human catastrophes.

Salination The process in which soluble minerals become poisonously concentrated in the top layer of desert soils by surface evaporation of irrigation water. It can be avoided or slowed by "flushing" and drainage systems.

Satellite Although theoretically sovereign, a state that in fact has foreign policy and general policy guidelines, at least for some domestic affairs, imposed from without. The term is popularly applied to East European Communist countries dominated by the USSR.

Selva The tropical rainforest of broadleaf evergreens, with a closed canopy at the top, or a series of partial canopies.

Sensible temperature The perceived temperature affecting people; a result of temperature, humidity, and wind-speed factors.

Settlement nuclei Nodes of greater density of settlement within a less dense matrix.

Shatter zone or shatterbelt The territory, commonly fragmented politically, that lies between more powerful, expansionist cultures. Frequently a politically unstable area. East Europe and Southeast Asia are examples.

Siberian River Reversal The huge water-engineering project, partially complete, to partially "reverse" the northward flow of Siberian rivers (Ob, Yenesei, Lena) in order to increase irrigation in Soviet Central Asia, generate power, and increase navigability.

Silvaculture Growing trees as a long-term crop through selective breeding, planting, and culling of poor specimens or unwanted, competing species.

Site The most local and immediate scale of location. It is the narrowest definition of location and refers to the specifics of immediate surroundings.

Situation A broader definition of *location;* location relative to a larger region or country or the world.

Slash-and-burn (shifting cultivation) The land-use system evolved in areas of marginally fertile soils, commonly in wet tropics, in which the farmers clear, plant, harvest, and then move onto a fresh patch of land after a season or two, using the land in a long-term rotation rather than planting the same land year after year.

Sovereignty The concept of totally independent right and power to govern a territory and pursue foreign policy without interference from outside interests.

Soviet model The economic development model in which producer goods, such as steel mills and truck factories, receive priority over consumer goods. It could also be called the "heavy-industry-first" model.

Spatial correlation An obvious relationship between two or more variables through space. The presence or absence of one variable is related, apparently but not necessarily, to the presence or absence of another variable.

Spatial interactions Interchanges of materials, people, culture, or other economic and political forces, not necessarily tangible, across space or territory.

State An independent, sovereign unit with an established territory and a permanent population.

State farm Associated with Communist economies; large, state-owned farms whose labor is paid wages in proportion to hours spent at work at a job category assigned a particular hourly rate, much as in a factory. State farms often have production of seed, experimentation, and breeding as their major functions.

Stream capture The "capture" by a headward-eroding stream of part of the headwaters of another stream system by providing a steeper gradient.

Subregion A smaller division of a region, again defined by selection of a degree of similarity or a specific economic or cultural relationship.

Suburbia The lower density fringes of a central urban place; "suburbia" contains more people than do central cities in the United States, and many urban functions are carried out in suburbia.

Successor state A new state that arises from the re-forming of political units following the collapse of an empire or very large state.

Sun Belt tourism Tourism, whether domestic or international, that is motivated by a warmer, sunnier climate and related amenities rather than cultural considerations.

Superpowers The largest, most powerful states; those exerting most power in international affairs and having the greatest military and economic forces.

Systematic geography That which focuses on the spatial patterns of a specific physical, economic, or cultural factor. Agricultural or transportation geography represent systematic organization of spatial patterns.

Taiga A Russian term for the slow-growing boreal forest, the transition from mid-latitude forest to tundra.

Takeoff In Rostow's stages of economic growth, the stage of high reinvestment in expanding enterprises, coupled with proliferation of the principles of scientific research and mass production in major sectors of the economy.

Tectonic activity "Mountain-building" or crustal deformation activity, as in earthquakes; associated with tectonic plate movement.

Tectonic plate A huge plate of crustal material, of which there are an unknown number, that is in motion and colliding with other plates, resulting in "drifting continents," vulcanism, and earthquakes.

Tierra caliente In Middle and South America, the "hot land" or tropical zone at the lowest elevation in vertical zonation.

Tierra fria The "cold land" at higher elevations in vertically-zoned agricultural lands; typical crops include potatoes.

Tierra templada The "temperate land" in vertical zonation; crops would include grains and mid-latitude fruits and vegetables.

Time-place utility Part of the set of variables that determine whether a particular material is of economic use. Uranium would have lacked time-place utility to pre-Columbian Indians.

Transport infrastructure The physical facilities for modern transport that support economic development. Examples include port facilities, airports, roads, and railroads.

Tribute territories In imperial systems, such as that of the ancient Chinese empire, territories enjoying some degree of autonomy so long as they acknowledged the "overlord" by sending tribute.

Use-pressure The burden of large numbers of users or visitors who inevitably, if unwittingly, deteriorate a facility or landscape by sheer numbers.

Value added A measure of the difference in cost of raw materials and price of the finished goods. The value added is a result of the skill of labor and the use of capital equipment.

Vertical zonation The altitude-induced changes in climate (temperature) that enable cultivation of different crops at different altitudes.

Village autarky Autarky is the state, or goal, of independence from "outside" materials or products. Village autarky or self-sufficiency, was Ghandi's goal for India.

Virgin Lands program An effort, between 1954 and 1959, to increase Soviet cropland by about 20 percent. The Virgin Lands, mostly in Kazakhstan, were too dry to have been cultivated before. The program was not a success.

Vital rates The two rates, birth and death, that are used in conjunction with migration data to depict changes in, and prospects for, a population.

Von Thünen model A model, postulated by nineteenth century German scholar von Thünen, to analyze the interaction of accessibility to market and land value and land use. His theory is still generally valid, with modern modifications.

White Australia policy The unofficial term for Australia's preference for immigrants from Europe rather than Asia; the policy, never totally exclusionary, has been relaxed somewhat.

World city A city of international significance, politically, economically, and/or culturally. Tokyo and Paris are examples.

World language A language that is widespread in use due to its commercial, scientific, and academic utility. They are commonly multinational in use (for example, French, English, and Spanish).

INDEX